Where to Fish
2004-2005

89th EDITION

THOMAS HARMSWORTH PUBLISHING
COMPANY

89th Edition published 2004 by
Thomas Harmsworth Publishing Company
Old Rectory Offices
Stoke Abbott
Beaminster
Dorset DT8 3JT
United Kingdom

This hardback edition
© 2004 Thomas Harmsworth Publishing Company
ISBN 0-948807-54-7
ISSN 1362-3842
Internet address: www.where-to-fish.com

Advertisements in this book have been inserted in the form in which they have been received from the advertisers. Care has been exercised in the acceptance of them, but the publisher accepts no responsibility for any loss through advertisers' malpractice. Advertisements have been accepted on the understanding that they do not contravene the Trades Descriptions Act 1968, the Sex Discrimination Act 1975, the Wildfowl and Countryside Act 1981 or any other Act of Parliament.

The publisher regrets that it can accept no responsibility for any errors or omissions within this publication, or for any expenses or loss thereby caused.

A few words included in this directory may be asserted to be proprietary names. The presence or absence of such names should not be considered to affect the legal status of any such names or trade marks.

British Library Cataloguing-in-Publication Data
A catalogue record of this book is available from the British
Library
ISBN 0 948807-54-7

Printed in Great Britain by
Antony Rowe Ltd, Chippenham, Wiltshire.

CONTENTS

FISHING IN THE BRITISH ISLES

FISHING ABROAD

Abbreviations: The following abbreviations are used throughout the book: S, salmon; T, trout; MT, migratory trout, NT, non-migratory trout; C, char; FF or FW, freshwater (ie coarse fish); RD, River Division (or its equivalent); s, season; m, month (National Rivers Authority list only); f, fortnight; w, week; d, day; t, ticket; ns, nearest railway station; m means mile or miles, except when it is used in conjunction with t, ie, mt, when it means monthly ticket. Likewise, st means season ticket, wt weekly ticket, dt daily ticket, and so on.

FISHERY AGENTS

ENGLAND

F P D Savills, 20 Grosvenor Hill, Berkeley Square, London, W1K 3HQ (tel: +44 (0)20 7499 8644; fax: +44 (0)20 7495 3773; web: www.fpdsavills.co.uk).

Knight Frank LLP, 20 Hanover Square, London W1S 1HZ (tel: +44 (0)20 7629 8171; fax: +44 (0)20 7491 0854; e-mail: farms.estates@knightfrank.com; web: www.knightfrank.com).

Sale & Partners, 18-20 Glendale Road, Wooler, Northumberland NE71 6DW (tel: +44 (0)1668 281611; fax: +44 (0)1668 281113; web: www.saleandpartners.co.uk; e-mail: cam@saleandpartners.co.uk). Tweed salmon fishing *(see advt)*.

Strutt and Parker, 37 Davies Street, London, W1S 2SP (tel: +44 (0)20 7629 7282; fax: +44 (0)20 7499 1657; web: www.fishshootstalk.com). Fishing Agency: contact Peter Baxendale (tel: +44 (0)20 7318 5188; e-mail: peter.baxendale@struttandparker.co.uk).

WALES

Knight Frank LLP, 22 Broad Street, Hereford HR4 9AP (tel: +44 (0)1432 273087; fax: +44 (0)1432 275935; web: www.knightfrank.com; e-mail: hereford@knightfrank.com).

Chester-Master Ltd, Dolgarreg, North Road, Builth Wells, Powys LD2 3DD. Salmon fishing on Wye, Usk and tributaries. By the day or week (tel: +44 (0)1982-553248; fax: +44 (0)1982 553154; e-mail: builth.wells@chester-master.co.uk).

SCOTLAND

Bell-Ingram, Durn, Isla Rd, Perth PH2 7HF (tel: +44 (0)1738-621121; fax: +44 (0)1738 630904; web: www.bellingram.co.uk). Deveron, Cassley, Dee, etc.

CKD Galbraith, Lynedoch House, Barossa Place, Perth PH1 5EP (tel: +44 (0)1738 451600; fax: +44 (0)1738 451900; web: www.sportinglets.co.uk). Agents for fishing on a wide range of estates throughout Scotland.

Knight Frank LLP, 2 North Charlotte Street, Edinburgh EH2 4HR (tel: +44 (0)131 225 8171; fax: +44 (0)131 225 4151; web: www.knightfrank.com; e-mail: edres@knightfrank.com).

Tweed Salmon Fishings (J H Leeming), Stichill House, Kelso, Roxburghshire TD5 7TB (tel: +44 (0)1573 470280; fax: +44 (0)1573 470259; web: www.tweedsalmonfishing.co.uk (also www.leeming.co.uk); e-mail: info@leeming.co.uk). **FISHING LINKS: FishSalmon,** Stichill House, Kelso, Roxburghshire TD5 7TB. Call centre (tel: +44 (0)1573 470612; fax: +44 (0)1573 470259; web: www.fishsalmon.co.uk; e-mail: info@fishsalmon.co.uk). Scottish rivers. **FishTweed,** c/o FishSalmon, Stichill House, Kelso, Roxburghshire TD5 7TB. Call centre (tel: +44 (0)1573 470612; fax: +44 (0)1573 470259; web: www.fishtweed.co.uk; e-mail: info@fishtweed.co.uk). *TweedLine (calls cost £1/min):* Weekly report/prospects (tel: +44 (0)9065 583 410); Daily river levels (tel: +44 (0)9065 583 411); Next 30-day rod availability fax-back (tel: +44 (0)9065 583 412 - from fax machine). River Tweed. **FishDee,** c/o FishSalmon, Stichill House, Kelso, Roxburghshire TD5 7TB. Call centre (tel: +44 (0)1573 470612; fax: +44 (0)1573 470259; web: www.fishdee.co.uk; e-mail: info@fishdee.co.uk). *DeeLine (calls cost £1/min):* Weekly report/prospects (tel: +44 (0)9065 500 410); Daily river levels (tel: +44 (0)9065 500 411); Next 30-day rod availability fax-back (tel: +44 (0)9065 500 412 - from fax machine). River Dee. **FishTay,** c/o FishSalmon, Stichill House, Kelso, Roxburghshire TD5 7TB. Call centre (tel: +44 (0)1573 470612; fax: +44 (0)1573 470259; web: www.fishtay.co.uk; e-mail: info@fishtay.co.uk). *TayLine (calls cost £1/min):* Weekly report/prospects (tel: +44 (0)9065 546 810); Daily river levels (tel: +44 (0)9065 546 811); next 30-day rod availability fax-back (tel: +44 (0)9065 546 812 - from fax machine). River Tay.

Strutt and Parker, 37 Davies Street, London, W1K 2SP (tel: +44 (0)20 7629 7282; fax: +44 (0)20 7499 1657; web: www.fishshootstalk.com). Fishing Agency: contact Peter Baxendale (tel: +44 (0)20 7318 5188; e-mail: peter.baxendale@struttandparker.co.uk).

Thurso Fisheries Ltd, Thurso East, Thurso, Caithness KW14 8HP (tel: +44 (0)1847 8963134; fax: +44 (0)1847 896295; web: www.thursofisheries.co.uk; e-mail: info@thursofisheries.co.uk). River Thurso.

FISHING HOLIDAY AGENTS

Angling Club Lax-á ehf, Vatnsendablettur 181, 203 Kópavogur, Iceland (tel: +354 557 6100; fax: +354 557 6108; web: www.lax-a.is; e-mail: arnibald@lax-a.is). Plan and sell tours on 30 first-class salmon and trout rivers in Iceland, Argentina, Greenland, Scotland and Ireland; fishing on the top salmon, trout and char rivers in Iceland. Each client has a tailor-made tour, including licenses, full board and lodging, guide and transfers; guest-houses, hotel and car rental also available.

Arthur Oglesby's World Fishing Holidays, 9 Oatlands Drive, Harrogate, N Yorks HG2 8JT (tel/fax: +44 (0)1423 883565; web: www.worldfishingholidays.com; e-mail: grace@oglesby.co.uk).

Chris Hill, 119 Montagu Street, Newtown, TAS 7008, Australia (tel: +61 (0)3 62 282264; fax: +61 (0)3 62 284441; web: www.fishingtasmania.com; e-mail: Chris@fishingtasmania.com). 3 to 7 day packages, trout fly fishing in Western Lakes and Central Highland lakes.

FishQuest! Global Angling Adventures, Fieldstone Marina, 3375-B Highway 76 West, Hiawassee, Georgia 30546, USA (tel: +1 706 896 1403; Toll Free: +1 888 891 3474; fax: +1 706 896 1467; web: www.fishquest.com; e-mail: questhook@aol.com). Freshwater and saltwater fishing expeditions throughout Alaska, Canada, USA, Mexico, Central America, Peru, Amazon, Caribbean, Venezuela, Argentina & Chile, Australia & New Zealand and Africa to the client's specificaation. Other web sites: www.peacock-bass.com, ques-tackle.com and payara-fishing.com).

Half Stone Sporting Agency (Roddy Rae), 6 Hescane Park, Cheriton Bishop, Exeter EX6 6JP (tel/fax: +44 (0)1647 24643; web: www.flyfishing-uk.co.uk; e-mail: roddyrae@flyfishing-uk.co.uk). Trips organised to suit and you can discuss your requirements right up to the minute you leave. Destinations include Alaska, America, Australia, Bahamas. Cuba, Iceland, Trophy Browns and New Zealand &c. *(For tuition, see Devon FlyFishing.)*

Mike Hopley, P.O. Box 4273, Soldotna, AK 99669, USA (tel: +1 907 262 7773 (Summer); +1 360 371 8973 (Winter); fax: +1 907 262 7765; web: www.alaskancharters.com; e-mail: rufishn@alaska.net). Personalised guided Alaskan fishing, with accommodation, featuring Kenai River salmon, and saltwater halibut.

Marlin Lodge, Benguerua Island, Bazaruto Archipelago, Mozambique (web: www.marlinlodge.co.za). Big game fishing for sailfish and marlin, wahoo, barracuda, yellow fin, skipjack and other species; excellent accommodation available, located along beach of Flamingo Bay. Bookings can be made through **Mozambique Tourism, P O Box 2042, Rivonia, Gauteng 2128, South Africa** (tel: +27 11 803 9296/+27 11 234 0599; fax: +27 11 803 9299; web: www.mozambiquetourism.co.zo; e-mail: travel@mozambiquetourism.co.za).

Roxton Bailey Robinson Worldwide, 25 High Street, Hungerford, Berkshire RG17 0NF (tel: +44 (0)1488 689701; fax: +44 (0)1488 689730; web: www.rbrww.com; e-mail: fishing@rbrww.com). Salmon fishing in Russia, Norway, Iceland, Alaska, Scotland and Ireland. Trout fishing in UK, USA, Argentina, Chile, New Zealand and elsewhere. Freshwater fishing in Africa, Alaska, America West, Argentina, Brazil, Canada, England, Ireland, Iceland, New Zealand, Russia and Scotland.Saltwater and deep sea fishing in Africa, Australia, Bahamas, Cuba, Mexico, Seychelles, Belise, Venezuela, Guatemala and Dubai.

Talking Travel - Africa, P O Box 2079, Link Hills 3652, Kwa-Zulu Natal, South Africa (tel: +27 (0)31 763 3904; mob: +27 (0)72 602 6729; web: www.talkingtravel.co.za; www.africa-uncovered.com; e-mail: safaris@talkingtravel.co.za). Deep-sea and fly fishing off the coasts of Mozambique, Tanzania, Kenya, Madagascar and South Africa, as well as river trout in South Africa; Nile perch in Uganda and tiger fishing on the Zambezi and Lake Kariba, Zimababwe. They cater for the experienced and/or learner fisherman; individuals or groups, and with or without professional guides. Talking Travel - Africa, a subsidiary of Integrated Conservation Africa (Pty), is able to combine fishing with safaris.

BERKSHIRE TROUT FARM

The largest restocking farm in UK
(Established 1907)

BROWN, RAINBOW, TROUT

Hand selected pink fleshed for restocking rivers, lakes, reservoirs, etc.

Delivered by lorry or land-rover to waterside

Hungerford, Berks RG17 0UN

Tel: 01488 682520   **Fax: 01488 685002**

Top End Sportfishing Safaris, Postal address: PMB 239, Winnellie, NT 0822, Australia (tel: +61 8 8978 3664; fax: +61 8 8978 3666; web: www.octa4.net.au/tess; e-mail: info@topendsportfishing.com.au). Location: Lot 354, Snake Bay, Melville Island. Fully government accredited Safari Operator.

Viv's Sportfishing & Wilderness Fishing Safaris, P O Box 95, Howard Springs, NT 0835, Australia (tel: +61 8 8983 2044; fax: +61 8 8983 2786; web: www.vivsbarra.com.au; e-mail: vbss@octa4.net.au). Northern Territory Mothership (TSMY 'Swordfish') and Inland Fishing Tour specialists.

Wildside, Netherknock, Bentpath, nr Langholm, Dumfriesshire DG13 0PB (tel: +44 (0)13873 70288) 78 Grove St, Wantage, Oxon. OX12 7BG (tel: +44 (0)1235 227 228; e-mail: king@legend.co.uk). Wildside is a cooperative venture, run by *Esk & Borders Instruction and Guide Service* (Tony King), in conjunction with *Westlake Fly Fishing* (Ian Hockley) that offers salmon and sea-trout fishing in Scotland, Ireland, USA and Norway, as well as accompanied and guided trips to Indian Ocean (Kenya), Tasmania, New Zealand and South America. *(For tuition &c., see Esk & Borders Instruction and Guide Service and Westlake Fly Fishing).*

BRITISH FISH FARMS

Anna Valley Trout Farm Ltd (William G. Hawkings-Byass) Salisbury Road, Abbots Ann, Andover, Hants SP11 7ND (tel: +44 (0)1264 710382; fax: +44 (0)1264 710909; web: www.annavalleytroutfarm.co.uk; e-mail: enquiries@annavalleytroutfarm.co.uk).

Berkshire Trout Farm, Hungerford, Berkshire, RG17 0UN (tel: +44 (0)1488-682520; fax: +44 (0)1488 685002). Brown and rainbow trout.

Bibury Trout Farm, Bibury, near Cirencester, Gloucestershire GL7 5NL. Rainbow and brown trout bred on Coln (tel: +44 (0)1285 740212/740215; fax: +44 (0)1285 740392). Catch Your Own fishery on R Coln.

Brookleas Fish Farm (T. Lobb) Ludbridge Mill, East Hendred, Wantage, Oxon OX12 8LN (tel/fax: +44 (0)1235 820 500; web: www.trouttrader.co.uk; e-mail: office@hamper.com)

Cerne Valley Trout Farm (C. J. Tottle) Golden Springs Farm, Waddock Cross, Dorset DT2 8QY (tel: +44 (0)1929 463 295).

Corgary Trout Farm (H J Johnston) Castlederg, Co Tyrone BT81 7YF (tel: +44 (0)1662 671209).

Danebridge Fisheries Ltd (D C Chadwick) Danebridge, Wincle, nr Macclesfield, Cheshire SK11 0QE (tel: +44 (0)1260 227293).

Exe Valley Fishery Ltd, Exbridge, Dulverton, Somerset, TA22 9AY (tel: +44 (0)1398 323328; fax: +44 (0)1398 324079; web: www.exevalleyfishery.co.uk; e-mail: enquiries@exevalleyfishery.co.uk). Rainbow trout available.

Hook Springs Trout Farm (Major A E Hill) Hooke, Beaminster, Dorset DT8 3NZ (tel: +44 (0)1308 862553).

Holbury Lakes Trout Fishery, The Fishery Manager, Holbury Lane, Lockerley, Romsey,

Hants SO51 0JR (tel: (day) 01794 341619, (eve) 01264 810633; web: www.holbury-lakes.co.uk).

Kilnsey Park Trout Farm (Anthony & Vanessa Roberts) Kilnsey, Skipton, North Yorkshire BD23 5PS (tel: +44 (0)1756 752150; fax: +44 (0)1756 752224; web: www.kilnsey-park.co.uk; e-mail: info@kilnseypark.co.uk).

Larkwood Trout Fishery (A E G Woods & I D McGregor) Icklingham Road, West Stow, Bury ST Edmunds, Suffolk IP28 6EZ (tel: +44 (0)1284 728612).

Lechlade Trout Fisheries (T Small) Burford Road, Lechlade, Glos. GL7 3QQ (tel: +44 (0)1367 253266).

Loch Leven Fisheries, Kinross Estates Office, Kinross KY13 7UF. Trout (tel: +44 (0)1577 863407; fax: +44 (0)1577 863180).

Nidderdale Trout (R W Scott) Throstle Nest Farm, Summerbridge, Harrogate, N Yorks HG3 4JS (tel: +44 (0)1423 780449).

Trent Fish Farm Ltd, The Old Mill, Mercaston, Ashbourne, Derbyshire DE6 3BL (tel: +44 (0)1335 361411).

Upper Mills Trout Farm, Glyn Ceiriog, nr Llangollen LL20 7HB (tel: +44 (0)1691 718225; fax: +44 (0)1691 718188; web: www.trout-farm.co.uk; e-mail: janet@trout-farm.co.uk).

West Acre Trout Farm, King's Lynn, Norfolk PE32 1TS (tel: +44 (0)1760 755240; fax: +44 (0)1760 755466). Brown and rainbow trout for immediate delivery.

Further information about **British Fish Farms** can be had from **British Trout Association,** Executive Officer, 8/9 Lambton Place, London, W11 2SH (tel: +44 (0)20 7221 6065; fax: +44 (0)20 7221 6049; web: www.britishtrout.co.uk; e-mail: bta@trout.sagehost.co.uk).

FISHING SCHOOLS AND COURSES

The Arundell Arms Fly Fishing School, Lifton, Devon PL16 0AA (tel: +44 (0)1566 784666; fax: +44 (0)1566 784494). A full range of residential courses from beginners' to advanced. Private tuition also offered.

Game Angling Instructors Association, Ian Moutter, 23 High Street, Coldstream, Berwickshire TD12 4AP (tel: (h) 01890 883931; (o) 0131 557 8333; web: www.gameanglinginstructors.co.uk). The Association has approximately 350 members both in the UK and abroad (which includes STANIC, SGAIC and APGAI qualified instructors) skilled to give a range of tuition from simple casting lessons to full residential courses. The web-site gives a full list of member, or they can be contacted through the Secretary.

School of Casting, Salmon & Trout Fishing, Michael Waller and Margaret Cockburn, Station House, Clovenfords, Galashiels, Selkirkshire TD1 3LT (tel/fax: +44 (0)1896 850293; e-mail: fishingschool@onetel.net.uk). Brown trout, sea trout and salmon on River Tweed and other waters in area. Private & group instruction in all aspects of fly fishing.

Seafield Lodge Hotel, Alasdair Buchanan, Woodside Ave, Grantown on Spey, Moray PH26 3JN (tel: +44 (0)1479 872152; fax: +44 (0)1479 872340). Access to seven miles of Association water.

Register of Experienced Fly Fishing Instructors and Schools (REFFIS). Most members of REFFIS offer fishing, as well as instruction. For full list of members, contact REFFIS Chairman, Richard Slocock, Lawrence's Farm, Tolpuddle, Dorchester, Dorset DT2 7HF (tel: +44 (0)1305 848460; web: www.reffis.co.uk; e-mail: sally.slocock@virgin.net).

Blackwater Fly Fishing Instruction & Guide Service (Doug Lock) Ghillie Cottage, Kilbarry Stud, Fermoy, Co Cork, Ireland (tel: +353 2 532720; fax: +353 2 533000; web: www.speycast-ireland.com; e-mail: flyfish@eircom.net). Spey casting tuition and salmon fishing 'off the reel', on Munster Blackwater River; REFFIS and Orvis approved. Doug is a member of the fly dressers guild and devisor of the Kilbarry Stud Fly.

Caithness & Sutherland Angling Services, Lesley Crawford, Askival, Caithness KW14 7RE (tel/fax: +44 (0)1847 811470; e-mail: lesley@crawford40.freeserve.co.uk). Tuition and guiding on many Caithness and Sutherland wild brown trout lochs, plus various renowned salmon and sea trout rivers.

Castalot Fly fishing services (Bob Waters) Flowtide, 16 Anslem Ave, Bury St Edmunds, Suffolk IP30 0LG (tel: 01284 724887) offer fly-fishing tuition and courses for trout on both still-water and stream.

Clonanav Fly Fishing Centre, Andrew Ryan, Ballymacarbry, Clonmel, Co Waterford, Eire (tel: +353 52 36141; fax: +353 52 36294; web: www.flyfishingireland.com).

Devon FlyFishing School, The (est. 1987), (Roddy Rae), 7 Herons Brook, Okehampton, Devon EX20. 1UW (tel: +44 (0)1837 54731; web: www.flyfishing-uk.co.uk; e-mail: roddyrae@flyfishing-uk.co.uk)). Brown trout, sea trout and salmon fishing, let by day, week, or season. Private beats on Exe, Taw, Mole and Torridge. Guided trips to New Zealand and Australia.

DreamStreams Ltd (Pat O'Reilly APGAI & Sue Parker, STANIC) Swyn Esgair, Drefach-Felindre, Llandysul SA44 5XG (tel/fax: +44 (0)1559 371879; web: www.first-nature.com/dreanstreams; e-mail: pat@first-nature.com). Flyfishing courses and casting instruction in the Teifi Valley, West Wales. Weekend courses during the season from April to October, specialising in wild brown trout fishing in springtime, sea trout (sewin) fishing in summer, and salmon fishing in autumn. Private fishing beat on the River Teifi. Also free fishing and conservation lessons for young people during the school summer holidays, in conjunction with Llandysul Angling Association.

Esk & Borders Instruction and Guide Service, Tony E King, Netherknock, Bentpath, nr Langholm, Dumfriesshire, Scotland, DG13 0PB, (tel: +44 (0)13873 70288; web: www.fly-fishing.fsbusiness.co.uk; e-mail: king@legend.co.uk). Packages for salmon, sea trout, trout, grayling and night fishing for sea trout, for all anglers from beginner to expert. Also offer saltwater fly fishing and fly fishing for pike. *(For Fishing Abroad, see Wildside.)*

Fishing Breaks Ltd, Simon Cooper, Walton House, 23 Compton Terrace, London N1 2UN (tel: +44 (0)20 7359 8818; fax: +44 (0)20 7359 4540; web: www.fishingbreaks.co.uk; e-mail: info@fishingbreaks.co.uk). Leading chalkstream fishing agents in S England (R Test, Itchen, Dever, Wallop Brook, Avon, Nadder, Kennet & Wylye); fly-fishing school at Nether Wallop Mill, Stockbridge, Hants.

Highland Angling Services (Robert Brighton) 12 Fyrish Crescent, Evanton, Rossshire, Scotland IV16 9YS (tel: +44 (0)1349 830159; mob: 0831 394694; web: talk.to/has; e-mail: has@cali.co.uk). Highland loch fishing, with tackle and transport. Hotel and self-catering accommodation available.

Ian Moutter, 23 High St, Coldstream, Berwickshire TD12 4AP (tel: +44 (0)131 557 8333; fax: +44 (0)131 556 3707; e-mail: casting@ianmoutter.co.uk). Instruction on river and stillwater fisheries in the Scottish borders and Cornwall, specialising in salmon and sea trout.

John Pennington, 24 Upper Burnside Drive, Thurso, Caithness, KW14 7XB, (tel: +44 (0)1847 894641; web: www.btinternet.com/~john_pennington/contact.htm; e-mail: john_pennington@btopenworld.com). Fishing and guiding on Halladale River.

Lenches Lakes and Fishery (Terry Beale) Hill Barn Orchard, Church Lench, Evesham, Worcs. WR11 4UB (tel: +44 (0)1386 871035 (office); 01822 613899 (home). Individual or group instruction on all aspects of fly-fishing; specialties include Nymph, Dry Fly Fishing and Fly Dressing; various casting techniques. Accommodation available.

Norfolk Flyfishing (Tim Gaunt-Baker), Oaktree Farmhouse, Church Road, Wretton, Kings Lynn, Norfolk PE33 9QR (tel: +44 (0)1366 500426; e-mail:gauntbaker@hotmail.com). Tuition in all aspects of game angling: dry fly to stillwater, salt water; fly fishing for the Massive Pike of the Norfolk Fens. Courses are held for beginners, juniors, ladies and experienced fishermen.

Sally Pizzi, Tumbleweed Cottage, Curry Mallet, nr Taunton, Somerset TA3 6SR (tel: +44 (0)1823 480710). Individual or group stillwater fly fishing available on an hourly basis; beginners are especially welcome during the school holidays. Accommodation can be arranged

Simon J Ward, Guide and Instructor, 20 Primrose Way, Locks Heath, Southampton, Hants. SO31 6WX (tel: +44 (0)1489 579295; e-mail: simward@lineone.net). Chalk streams in southern England. Tuition: casting clinics (1.5hrs) to full courses (1-4 days); fly tying lessons on request; custom fly dressing service.

Test Valley School of Fly Fishing, Jerry Wakeford, 44 Butler's Close, Lockerley, Romsey, Hants SO51 0LY (tel: +44 (0)1794 341990; web: www.learnflyfishing.co.uk; e-mail: info@learnflyfishing.co.uk).

Wessex Fly Fishing School, Richard Slocock, Lawrence's Farm, Southover, Tolpuddle, Dorchester, Dorset DT2 7HF (tel: +44 (0)1305 848460; web: goflyfishing.co.uk; e-mail:

sally.slocock@virgin.net). Lakes, pools, chalk-stream fishing for trout on Rivers Piddle and Frome; catch and release river fishing for wild brown trout a particular feature; lake and river tuition from highly experienced instructors (all types of fly fishing and fly casting taught, including Spey casting). B&B and self-catering accommodation available.

Westlake Fly Fishing, Ian Hockley, 78 Grove Street, Wantage, Oxon OX12 7BG, (tel: +44 (0)1235 227228; fax: +44 (0)1235 227227). *(For Fishing Abroad, see Wildside.)*

Under instruction on the Tamar. *Photo: Melanie Healy*

DISABLED FACILITIES

LIST OF WHEELYBOAT LOCATIONS

On 1 March 2004 the *Handicapped Anglers Trust* changed its name to *The Wheelyboat Trust*. Originally established for the benefit of disabled anglers, the Trust has been providing its wheelchair-accessible Wheelyboats to numerous waters countrywide since 1985; this year will see the 100th boat come off the production line. The Trust long since identified that the Wheelyboat fulfils a far greater role than just an angling boat and the change of name will surely more accurately relate to the principal objectives of the Trust, and better reflect its broader remit.

# indicates *Mk II* Wheelyboat

NORTH EAST

Northumberland	**Leaplish Waterside Park** ...... Kielder Water	Trout fishing	01434 240365
Northumberland	**Kielder Water** .... Falstone	Trout fishing & .... pleasure boating	01660 40398
South Humberside	**Elsham Hall Country Park** .... Brigg	Trout fishing	01652 688698
Yorkshire	**Bellflask Fishery** .... Ripon	Trout fishing	01677 470716
Yorkshire	**Farmire Fishery** .... Knaresborough	Trout fishing	01423 866417
Yorkshire	**Harewood House Lake** .... Leeds	Pleasure boating	01132 181006
Yorkshire	**Walton Hall Trout Fishery** .... Walton	Trout fishing	01924 242990

MIDLANDS

Cheshire	**Westlow Mere** .... Congleton	Trout fishing	01260 270012
Derbyshire	**Carsington Water** .... Ashbourne	Trout fishing	01629 540769 01629 540478 www.stwater.co.uk
Derbyshire	**Press Manor Fishery** .... Chesterfield	Trout fishing	01629 760996
Hertfordshire	**Rib Valley Lake** .... Ware	Trout fishing	01920 484913
Leicestershire	**Eyebrook Reservoir** .... Caldecott	Trout fishing	01536 770264 www.eyebrook.com
Leicestershire	**Thornton Reservoir #** .... Leicester	Trout fishing	01530 230807
Lincolnshire	**Toft Newton Reservoir** .... Lincoln	Trout fishing	01673 878453
Shropshire	**Swan Hill** .... Ellesmere	Fishing & pleasure .... boating	01691 624448
Warwickshire	**Packington Trout Fisheries** .... Meriden	Trout fishing	01676 522754
Worcestershire	**Upton Warren Sailing Lake** ... Droitwich	Fishing & pleasure .... boating	01527 861426

The Wheelyboat's stability has made such craft redundant for the disabled. *Photo: Al Mogridge.*

EAST ANGLIA

Norfolk	**Fritton Lake & Country Park**	. Coarse fishing	01493 488288
Norfolk	**Eels Foot Inn**	Coarse fishing &	01493 730342
	Rollesby Broad	pleasure boating	
	. . . .	www.broads-authority.gov.uk	

SOUTH EAST

East Sussex	**Arlington Reservoir #**	Trout fishing	01323 870810
	Eastbourne	www.southeastwater.co.uk	
East Sussex	**Powdermill Reservoir**	Trout fishing	01424 870498
	Sedlescombe	www.hastingsflyfishers.co.uk	
Essex	**Hanningfield Reservoir**	Trout fishing	01245 212034
	South Hanningfield	www.eswater.co.uk	
Kent	**Bewl Water**	Trout fishing	01892 890352
	Lamberhurst		
Kent	**Bough Beech Reservoir**	Coarse fishing	01732 851544
	Sevenoaks		
Kent	*Maidstone Ex-Services AC*	Coarse fishing	01622 813737
	Gravelly Ways, Yalding	*(Membership enquiries)*	
London	**PHAB Holly Lodge**	Pleasure boating	020 8948 3209
	Richmond Park	for residents	

SOUTH WEST

Avon	**Blagdon Lake**	Trout fishing	01275 332339
	Blagdon		
Cornwall	**Stithians Reservoir**	Trout fishing	01209 860301
	Redruth	www.swlakestrust.org.uk	
Devon	**Exeter Canal**	Pleasure boating	01395 272644
	Exmouth	for residents	
Gloucestershire	**Friday Island**	Pleasure boating	01285 770226
	Cirencester	for residents	
Somerset	**Clatworthy Reservoir**	Trout fishing	01984 624658
	Taunton	www.wessexwater.co.uk/recreation	
Somerset	**Sutton Bingham Reservoir**	Trout & coarse fishing .	01935 872389
	Yeovil		
Somerset	**Wimbleball Reservoir**	Trout fishing	01398 371372
	Brompton Regis	www.swlakestrust.org.uk	
Wiltshire	**Coate Water**	Trout & coarse	01793 522837
	Swindon	fishing	01793 433165

NORTH WEST

Cumbria	**Esthwaite Water**	Trout fishing	01539 436541
	Ambleside		
Cumbria	**The Lough**	Trout fishing	01228 576552
	Carlisle		
Lancashire	**Stocks Reservoir**	Trout fishing	01200 446602
	Slaidburn		

WALES

Anglesey	**Llyn Alaw**	Trout fishing	01407 730762
	Holyhead		
Ceredigion	**Teglan Fishery**	Coarse fishing	01570 471115
	Lampeter		
Conwy	**Llyn Brenig**	Trout fishing	01490 420463

	Cerrigydrudion		
Dyfed	**Llys-y-Fran Reservoir**	Trout fishing	01437 532694
	Haverfordwest		
Gwent	**Llandegfedd Reservoir**	Trout fishing	01291 673722
	Pontypool		
Gwynedd	**Maes y Clawdd**	Trout fishing	01678 530239
	Bala		
Monmouthshire	**Wentwood Reservoir**	Trout fishing	01895 444707
	Caldicott	www.wentwood-reservoir.co.uk	

SCOTLAND

Caithness	**St John's Loch**	Trout fishing	01847 896956
	Dunnet.		01847 851270
Clackmannanshire	**Gartmoran Country Park**	Trout fishing	01259 214319
	Alloa		
Fife	**Lochore Meadows Country Prk**	Trout & coarse	01592 414300
	Lochore	fishing	
Highland	**Loch Achonachie**	Fishing	01349 862455
	Dingwall		(George Cameron)
Lanarkshire	**Newmill Trout Fisheries**	Trout fishing	01555 870730
	Cleghorn		
North Lanarkshire	**Hillend Reservoir #**	Trout fishing	01236 843611
	Caldercruix		
Perthshire	**Butterstone Loch**	Trout fishing	01350 724238
	Dunkeld		
Perthshire	**Kenmore Hotel**	Salmon & trout fishing	01887 830765
	Loch Tay.		(Paul Fishlock)
Skye	**Storr Lochs**	Trout fishing	01478 612612
	Portree		
Stirling	**Lake of Menteith**	Trout fishing .	01877 385648/385664
	Port of Menteith.	www.menteith-fisheries.co.uk	

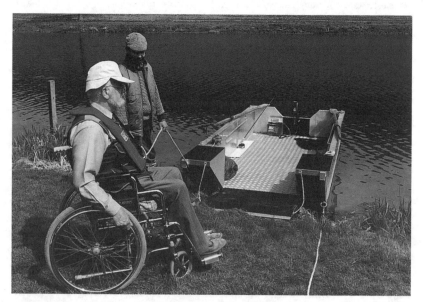

The Wheelyboat's stability ensures the safety of wheelchair users.

Stirling	**Invertrossachs Estate** .... Trout fishing 01786 832212
	Stirling 07788 721457
West Lothian	**Cobbinshaw Loch #** .... Trout fishing 01501 785208
	West Calder 07880 601935
West Lothian	**Linlithgow Loch** .... Trout fishing 07831 288921
	Linlithgow

NORTHERN IRELAND

Co Antrim	**Tildarg Fishery** .... Trout fishing 01960 340604
	Ballyclare 01960 322216
Co Fermanagh	**Belleisle Estates** .... Trout fishing 028 6638 7231
	Lisbellaw .... www.belleisle-estate.com
Co Fermanagh	**Coolyermer Lough** .... Trout fishing 028 6634 1676
	Letterbreen .... www.flyfishery.com
Co Tyrone	**Parklake Fishery** .... Trout fishing 02887 727327
	Dungannon

IRELAND

| Co Cavan | **Belturbet Angling Assoc** ...... Trout fishing ...... +353 4995 22359 |
| | Belturbet .... +353 4995 22657 |

For further information on *The Wheelyboat Trust*, contact Andy Beadsley (Director), North Lodge, Burton Park, Petworth, West Sussex, GU28 0JT (tel/fax: 01798 342222; website: www.wheelyboats.org; e-mail: wheelyboats@tiscali.co.uk). *The Wheelyboat Trust* is a registered charity.

FISHING IN ENGLAND and WALES

Environment Agency structure, close seasons, licence duties etc.

The Environment Agency is the leading public body for protecting and enhancing the enviroment in England and Wales. The Agency works to maintain, improve, and develop fisheries, by monitoring, rescuing, stocking and habitat improvements; to improve water quality, habitat and river flows; to protect fisheries, the Agency enforces statutory fishing legislation and bye-law regulations generally. The Agency also provides help to anglers through the supply of information, restoration and promotion of fisheries, and the protection of wildlife.

The Agency is also responsible for the issue of compulsory rod licences. In England and Wales anyone aged 12 years or older who fishes for salmon, trout, freshwater fish or eels must hold an Environment Agency rod licence. In addition, permission to fish, if necessary, must be gained from the owners or tenants of the fishing rights. Failure to produce a valid Agency rod licence when fishing is a criminal offence. Rod licence income helps the Agency to perform its necessary fishery duties.

Rod licences are available from post offices in England and Wales. They are also obtainable from some larger fisheries, or by post from Environment Agency National Rod Licence Administration Centre, PO Box 432, Richard Fairclough House, Knutsford Rd, Warrington WA4 1HH or over the internet (www.environment-agency.gov.uk/fish). Concessionary rates are available for persons aged 12 to 16, and aged 65 years and over, or in receipt of incapacity benefit or severe disability allowance. War pensioners in receipt of an unemployment supplement are also entitled to the concession. Full season and concessionary junior rod licences can be purchased by telephone 7 days a week from 8.00am to 8.00pm on 0870 1662662. Please note that from this number only full annual licences can be purchased. 8-day or 1-day licences must be purchased from Post Offices. Licence charges for 2004/2005 are as follows:

Salmon and Migratory Trout - Full Season £62.00 (concessionary rate £31.00), 8 consecutive days £19.50, single day £6.50.

Non-migratory Trout and Coarse - Full Season £23.00 (ordinary concessionary rate £11.50; junior £5.00), 8 consecutive days £8.00, Single day £3.00.

Where local rules and regulations permit, up to 4 rods may be used at a time when fishing for coarse fish and eels. One rod licence will be required for a maximum of 2 rods and rods must be fished no more than 3 metres apart. A maximum of 2 rods can be used on stillwaters for salmon and trout but only one rod may be used when fishing for salmon, trout and migratory trout on rivers, streams, drains and canals.

Anglers are reminded that the expression 'immature' in relation to salmon means that the fish is less than 12in long; taking immature salmon is prohibited throughout England and Wales. In relation to other fish the expression 'immature' means that the fish is of a length less than that prescribed by bye-law. Unless otherwise stated, it may be assumed that the length is measured from the tip of the snout to the fork of the tail.

The word 'salmon' means all fish of the salmon species. The word 'trout' means all fish of the salmon species commonly known as trout. The expression 'migratory trout' means trout that migrate to and from the sea. The expression 'freshwater (ie coarse) fish' means any fish living in fresh water except salmon, trout, all kinds of fish which migrate to and from tidal water, eels and their fry.

National Salmon bye-laws: In April 1999 Ministers confirmed new Agency fisheries byelaws to protect stocks of early-run salmon. The bye-laws are designed to increase the stock of early-run salmon by reducing the number killed by both anglers and nets. The national bye-laws relating to rods are as follows: Any angler catching a salmon before 16 June must return it with minimum injury. Angling for salmon before 16 June can only be with artificial fly or artificial lure. N.B. More stringent existing local regulations will remain in force, such as fly only at certain times on several rivers including the Usk, Wye, Dee.

NOTE: In the following lists the telephone numbers are those at which to contact officers

Environment Agency Regions

North West
North East
Midlands
Welsh
Anglian
Thames
South West
Southern

NORTH WEST

NORTH EAST

MIDLANDS

ANGLIAN

WELSH

THAMES

SOUTH WEST

SOUTHERN

during office hours. For the reporting of pollution, flooding, fish in distress, risks to wildlife, illegal dumping of hazardous waste, and poaching, an emergency hotline exists on a 24 hour free service: 0800 807060. Environment Agency general enquiries may be made through: 08459 333111.

> **Abbreviations:** The following abbreviations are used throughout the book: S, salmon; T, trout; MT, migratory trout; NT, non-migratory trout; C, char; FF or FW, freshwater (ie coarse fish); s, season; m, month; (following list only); f, fortnight; w, week; d, day; t, ticket; ns, nearest railway station; c&r, catch and release. In the lists of fishing stations the abbreviation m means mile or miles, except when it is used in conjunction with t, ie, mt, when it means monthly ticket (it may also refer to metres, where the context is obvious). Likewise, st means season ticket, wt weekly ticket, dt daily ticket, and so on.

Environment Agency

For general enquiries, you should call the Environment Agency's new national customer contact service. Everyone there is able to answer fisheries questions, or will know someone who can. The number is 08708 506506. The service is available from early morning to early evening. Alternatively, anglers can e-mail: enquiries@environment-agency.gov.uk.

There is a 24-hour emergency hot-line for reporting all **environmental incidents** (incl damage or danger to the natural environment; pollution; poaching; fish in distress and risks to wildlife; illegal dumping and flood incidents) relating to air, land and water: **0800 807060**. Additional information can be obtained from the Agency's website: www.environment-agency.gov.uk/fish.

> There is a River Level Information Line for four of the Regions, as follows: North East: 0906 619 7722; North West: 0906 619 7733; Midlands: 0906 619 7744; Welsh: 0906 619 7755.
> A salmon counter information line on 0906 619 7723 (Premium line) provides monthly information on North East rivers. These are charged at 60p per minute on these 0906 numbers.

Regions of the Environment Agency.

SOUTHERN REGION, Guildbourne House, Chatsworth Road, Worthing, Sussex BN11 1LD (tel: 01903 832000; fax: 01903 821832. Web: www.environment-agency.gov.uk/fish).

Principal Fisheries Officer (Southern Region): Dr Cristina Vina-Herbon.

Main rivers controlled: Darent, Cray, Medway, Stour, Eastern Rother, RM Canal, Adur, Arun, Ouse, Cuckmere, all rivers in Pevensey Levels, Test, Itchen, Hamble, Meon, Beaulieu, Lymington, Fletch, Keyhaven, Eastern Yar, Medina, and the tributaries of all these rivers.

Area offices.
Kent: Orchard House, Endeavour Park, London Rd, Addington, West Malling, Kent ME19 5SH (tel: 01732 875587; fax: 01732 875057).
Fisheries and Recreational Technical Team Leader: Jan Whitmore.
Main rivers controlled: Medway, Darent, Eastern, Rother, Royal Military Canal, Stour, Cray and all associated tributaries.

Sussex: Saxon House, Little High Street, Worthing BN11 1DH (tel: 01903 215835; fax: 01903 215884).
Fisheries and Recreational Technical Team Leader: Jan Whitmore.
Main rivers controlled: Rother (western), Arun, Adur, Ouse, Cuckmere and Pevensey Levels; all inland waters in Sussex and coastal waters to 6 naut.m from Hastings to Chichester.

Pollution, flooding and illegal fishing reporting: emergency hotline: 0800 807060.

Hampshire/Isle of Wight: Hampshire/Isle of Wight Fisheries Technical Specialist, Colvedene Court, Wessex Way, Colden Common, Winchester, Hampshire SO21 1WP (tel: 01962 713267; fax: 01962 841573).
Main rivers controlled: Test, Itchen, Meon, Wallington, Lymington, Hamble, Beaulieu, Keyhaven, Eastern Yar, Medina (most of Hants and Isle of Wight). Note: Hants Avon controlled by Suoth West Region (Blandford office).

Pollution, flooding and illegal fishing reporting: 24 hour emergencies number - Freephone: 0800 807060.

SOUTH WEST REGION, Headquarters: Manley House, Kestrel Way, Exeter, Devon, EX2 7LQ (tel: 01392 444000; fax: 01392 444238).

Principal Officer: Martin Williams (fax: 01392 352371; e-mail: martin.williams@environ-ment-agency.gov.uk).

Regional General Manager: Richard Cresswell.

Cornwall Area: Sir John Moore House, Victoria Square, Bodmin, Cornwall PL31 1EB (tel: 01208 78301; fax: 01208 78321).
Fisheries, Recreation & Biodiversity Team Leader: Simon Toms.
Main rivers controlled: Camel, Fowey, Looe, Lynher, Plym, Tamar, Tavy, Yealm and tributaries, including Bude Canal.

Devon Area: Exminster House, Miller Way, Exminster, Devon EX6 8AS (tel: 01392 444000; fax: 01392 442109).
Fisheries, Recreation & Biodiversity Team Leader: Nigel Reader.
Main rivers controlled: Avon, Axe, Dart, Erme, Exe, Lyn, Otter, Taw, Teign, Torridge and tributaries, including Exeter and Tiverton Canal.

North Wessex Area: Rivers House, East Quay, Bridgwater, Somerset TA6 4YS (tel: 01278 457333; fax: 01278 452985).
Customer Services Manager: Dr A Hicklin.
Fisheries Technical Specialist: Dr R Merry.
Main rivers controlled: Axe, Bristol Avon, Brue, Parrett and their tributaries, including Tone, Huntspill, King's Sedgemoor Drain and Bridgwater and Taunton Canal. West Somerset rivers flowing into the Bristol Channel.

South Wessex Area: Rivers House, Sunrise Business Park, Higher Shaftesbury Rd, Blandford Forum, Dorset DT11 8ST (tel: 01258 456080; fax: 01258 455998).
Fisheries, Recreation & Biodiversity Team Leader: Judith Crompton
Fisheries and Recreational Technical Team Leader: Andy Strevens.
Main rivers controlled: Hampshire Avon and Stour, Frome, Piddle, Brit and Char. (All rivers entering the sea between Lyme Regis and Christchurch).

Rod Seasons:

Devon and Cornwall Areas
Salmon: Avon: 15 April to 30 November (E). Erme: 15 March to 31 October. Axe, Otter, Sid: 15 March to 31 October. Camel: 1 April to 15 December. Dart: 1 February to 30 September. Exe: 14 February to 30 September *(contact Agency for details of a temporary season extension)*. Fowey, Looe: 1 April to 15 December. Tamar, Tavy, Lynher: 1 March to 14 October. Plym: 1 April to 15 December. Yealm: 1 April to 15 December. Taw, Torridge: 1 March to 30 September. Lyn: 1 February to 31 October. Teign: 1 February to 30 September. Lim: 1 March to 30 September. **Migratory trout:** Avon: 15 April to 30 September. Erme: 15 March to 30 September. Axe, Otter, Sid: 15 April to 31 October. Camel, Gannel, Menalhyl, Valency: 1 April to 30 September. Dart: 15 March to 30 September. Exe: 15 March to 30 September. Fowey, Looe, Seaton, Tresillian: 1 April to 30 September. Tamar, Lynher, Plym, Tavy, Yealm: 3 March to 30 September. Taw, Torridge, Lyn: 15 March to 30 September. Teign: 15 March to 30 September. Lim: 16 April to 31 October. **Brown trout:** Camel, Fowey: 1 April to 30 September. Other rivers and streams in Devon and Cornwall areas: 15 March

to 30 September. All rivers in North and South Wessex Areas: 1 April to 15 October. All other waters: 17 March to 14 October. **Rainbow Trout:** all rivers, 1 April to 15 October. **Coarse fish and eels:** Rivers, streams, drains, Kennet and Avon Canal, Bridgwater and Taunton Canal: 16 June to 14 March. Enclosed waters, no close season.

North and South Wessex Areas
Salmon: Frome and Piddle - 1 March to 31 August. Other rivers - 1 February to 31 August. **Migratory Trout:** 15 April to 31 October. **Trout:** Rivers 1 April to 15 October. Reservoirs, lakes and ponds 17 March to 14 October.

NORTH WEST REGION, Richard Fairclough House, Knutsford Road, Warrington WA4 1HG (tel: 01925 653999; fax: 01925 415961).

Regional Director: Robert Runcie
North Area Manager (Cumbria): Kim Nicholson

Central Area Manager (Lancashire): Bernadette Carr

South Area Manager (Cheshire, Greater Manchester, Merseyside): Annette Pinner

Pollution and illegal fishing reporting: tel 24-hour emergency hotline: 0800 807060.

North Area (North):
Fisheries and Recreational Technical Team Leader: Keith Kendal (tel: 01768 866666).
North Area (South):
Fisheries and Recreational Technical Team Leader: Jeremy Westgarth (tel: 01768 866666).
Main rivers controlled: Esk, Liddel, Lyne, Irthing, Petteril, Wampool, Caldew, Ellen, Derwent, Eamont, Eden, Cocker, Ehen, Irt, Esk, Brathay, Duddon, Crake, Rothay, Leven, Kent, and their tributaries. Lakes Derwentwater, Thirlmere, Ullswater, Haweswater, Bassenthwaite, Windermere, Wastwater, Coniston Water, Esthwaite Water, Grasmere, Rydal Water.

Central Area
Fisheries and Recreational Technical Team Leader: Stephen Whittam (tel: 01772 339882).
Main rivers controlled: Ribble, Hodder, Lune, Wyre, Calder, Crossens, Yarrow, Douglas, Alt, Keer and their tributaries.

South Area
Fisheries and Recreational Technical Team Leader: Michael Turner (tel: 01925 840000).
Main rivers controlled: Roch, Irwell, Tame, Etherow, Mersey, Goyt, Bollin, Dean, Weaver, Dane, Gowey, and their tributaries.

Close seasons: Salmon: 1 November to 31 January, except R. Eden and all rivers lakes and waters, tributary to or connected with R Eden - 15 October to 14 January. **Sea Trout:** 31 Oct to 31 Mar, except Border Esk and all waters tributary to or connected with it - 16 Oct to 30 April. **Brown Trout:** Non-migratory (other than rainbow trout) with rod and line, 1 Oct to 14 Mar. **Rainbow Trout:** 1 Oct - 14 Mar; in reservoirs, lakes and ponds, none. **Char:** 1 Oct to 14 March, except in Coniston Water, 1 Nov to 30 Apr; in Windermere, 1 Oct to 30 Apr, except if using artificial lure from a moving boat: from 15 Mar. **Coarse Fish:** 15 March to 15 June (no close season for coarse fish in enclosed waters). **Eels:** in non-tidal parts of rivers and streams, and rivers canalised for navigation purposes, 15 Mar to 15 June. No close season in tidal waters; nor in waters with no salmon and/or trout (other than with rod and line).

NORTH EAST REGION, Rivers House, 21 Park Square South, Leeds LS1 2QG (tel: 0113 244 0191; fax: 0113 246 1889). @SINGLE = **Fisheries Development Manager:** Steve Chambers (tel: 0113 231 2465; fax 0113 231 2375; web: www.environment-agency.gov.uk).

Northumbria Area, Tyneside House, Skinnerburn Rd, Newcastle Business Park, Newcastle upon Tyne, NE4 7AR (tel: 0191 203 4000; fax: 0191 203 4004).
Fisheries and Recreational Technical Team Leader: Jim Heslop (tel: 0191 2034068).
Main rivers controlled: Aln, Coquet, Fant, Wansbeck, Blyth, Tyne, Wear.

Close seasons: S: 1 Nov to 31 Jan. **MT:** 1 Nov to 2 Apr. **NT:** 1 Oct to 21 Mar, excluding Kielder Water, Broomlee Lough, Craglough Loch, Greenlee Lough, Derwent Reservoir, and East and West Hallington where the close season is 1 Nov to 30 Apr. **FF:** 13 Mar to 15 June.

Dales Area, Coverdale House, Amy Johnson Way, Clifton Moor, Yorks YO30 4UZ (tel: 01904 692296; fax: 01904 692297).
Fisheries and Recreational Technical Team Leader: Jihn Shannon (tel: 01904 692296).
Main rivers controlled: Tees, Swale, Ure, Esk, Derwent, Wharfe, Nidd, Ouse.

Close seasons: for River Tees and tributaries northward as per Northumbria Area. For Staithes Beck, River Esk and tributaries of the Ouse and Humber, as per Ridings Area.

Ridings Area: Phoenix House, Global Avenue, Leeds LS11 8PG (tel: 0113 244 0191; fax: 0113 213 4609).
Fisheries and Recreational Technical Team Leader: Pat O'Brian (tel: 0113 2134868).
Main rivers controlled: Aire, Calder, Rother, Don, Dearne and River Hull.

Close seasons: Salmon: 1 Nov to 5 April. **Migratory Trout:** 1 Nov to 2 April. **Non-Migratory Trout:** 1 October to 24 March. **FF:** 15 March to 15 June.

All anglers are required to make a return of any Salmon or Migratory Trout caught. The use of gaffs is prohibited throughout the Region at all times. The use of Crayfish as a bait is also prohibited throughout the Region at all times, and other bait restrictions apply during freshwater fish close season. Copies of the simplified or full bye-laws can be obtained from the Regional office or the Regional website.

ANGLIAN REGION, Kingfisher House, Goldhay Way, Orton Goldhay, Peterborough PE2 5ZR (tel: 01733 371811).

Northern Area: Waterside House, Waterside North, Lincoln, LN2 5HA (tel: 01522 513100). (Enquiries tel: 01522 513100).
Team Leader - Fisheries, Recreation & Biodiversity: Caroline Tero (tel: 01522 785829); main area of work: habitat restoration, fish movement permits, planning/land drainage consent consultation, advisory.
Team Leader - Ecological Appraisal, Chris Reeds (tel: 01536 385109).
Area Environment Manager, David Hawley.
Main rivers controlled: Nene, Welland, Witham, Ancholme (as well as smaller rivers between the last two).

Central Area: Bromholme Lane, Brampton, Huntingdon, Cambs. PE18 8NE (tel: 01480 483990). (Enquiries tel: 01480 414581).
Team Leader - Fisheries, Recreation & Biodiversity: Roger Handford (tel: 01480 483990).
Team Leader - Ecological Appraisal Team: Terry Clough (tel: 01480 483841); main area of work: all fisheries and biological monitoring, e.g. fisheries surveys, invertebrates surveys, plant surveys, fish rescues.
Main rivers controlled: Ouse and all its tributaries.

Eastern Area: Cobham Rd, Ipswich, Suffolk IP3 9JE (tel: 01473 727712; fax: 01473 724205). (Enquiries tel: 01473 727712).
Area Environment Manager (Essex): Team Leader - Fisheries, Recreation & Biodiversity: Amanda Elliott (tel: 01473 706734).
Team Leader - Ecological Appraisal Team: Ros Wright (tel: 01473 706351).
Area Environment Manager, Dr Charles Beardall (e-mail: charles.beardall@environment-agency.gov.uk).

Main rivers controlled: all rivers flowing eastwards between The Wash and River Thames.
Close Seasons: S and MT: 29 September to last day of February. T: 30 October to 31 March. Rainbow T: no close season on enclosed waters, otherwise 30 October to 31 March. **FF:** 15 March to 15 June on rivers, streams, drains, all waters in Broads area, and some SSSIs.

Emergency hotline: **0800 807060.**

MIDLANDS REGION, Sapphire East, 550 Streetsbrook Road, Solihull B91 1QT (tel: 0121 711 2324; fax: 0121 711 3990).

Principal Officer: Tim Pickering.

Lower Severn Area
Fisheries and Recreational Technical Team Leader: Al Watson, Riversmeet House, Newtown Industrial Estate, Northway Lane, Tewkesbury, Glos GL20 8JG (tel: 01684 850951; fax: 01684 293599).
Main rivers controlled: Severn, Warwickshire Avon and all other tributary streams in the Severn south of Worcester and all other canals and pools. The Agency also owns or rents water on the Avon and Severn.

Upper Severn Area
FFisheries and Recreational Technical Team Leader: Mike Exeter, Hafren House, Welshpool Rd, Shelton, Shrewsbury SY3 8BB (tel: 01743 272828; fax: 01743 272138; e-mail: mike.exeter@environment-agency.gov.uk).
Main rivers controlled: Severn and tributaries north of Worcester, Teme, Vyrnwy, Tanat, Banwy, Tern, Roden, Mease, Perry and all other canals and pools.

Trent Area
Lower Trent Area
Fisheries and Recreation Team Leader: Penny Thorpe, Trentside Offices, Scarrington Rd, West Bridgford, Nottingham NG2 5FA (tel: 0115 945 5722; fax: 0115 846 3643).
Main rivers controlled: Trent, east of Dove confluence, Soar, Derbyshire Derwent and their tributaries, all canals and pools.

Upper Trent Area
Fisheries and Recreation Team Leader: Phil Wormald, Sentinel House, Wellington Crescent, Fradley Park, Lichfield, Staffs WS13 8RR (tel: 01543 444141).
Main rivers controlled: Trent west of Dove confluence, Tame, Dove, Manifold, Churnet and their tributaries, Blithe, Penk, Sow, Anker, Blythe and all other canals and pools.
Close seasons: Brown trout: 8 October to 17 March inclusive. Rainbow trout: 8 October to 17 March inclusive in all rivers, streams, drains and canals. In reservoirs, lakes and pools there is no national close season, although owners/managers may wish to impose their own. Salmon: 8 October to 31 January inclusive. Catch and release method restrictions apply from 1 February to 15 June inclusive, when all salmon caught must be returned alive to water. Freshwater fish: 15 March to 15 June inclusive in all rivers, streams, drains and on specified stillwater and canal SSSIs. On stillwaters and canals (excluding specified SSSIs) there is no national close season, although owners/managers may wish to impose their own. Eels: There is no national close season, but hook and bait restrictions apply in all rivers, streams and drains, from 15 March to 15 June inclusive.
Pollution reports: Please report any pollution or dead fish to the following Freephone number: 0800 807060.

THAMES REGION, Kings Meadow House, Kings Meadow Road, Reading, RG1 8DQ (tel: 0118 953 5000; fax: 0118 950 0388).

Principal Officer - Fisheries: Philip Bolton (tel: 01189 535653; e-mail: philip.bolton@environment-agency.gov.uk)

Team Leader - Fisheries & Biodiversity (West): Chris Robinson; Lambourne House, Howbery Park, Wallingford, Oxon OX10 4BD (tel: 01491 828353).
Main rivers controlled: River Thames (source to Hurley); Rivers Churn, Coln, Windrush, Evenlode, Cherwell, Ray, Cole, Ock, Thame, Wye, Oxford Canal; Kennet, Kennet and Avon Canal, Lambourne, Pang, Leach, Enborne.

Team Leader - Fisheries & Biodiversity (North East): M Carter; 2 Bishops Square, Business Park, St Albans West, Hatfield, Herts AN10 9EX (tel: 01707 632 315).
Main rivers controlled: Rivers Lee, Stort, Rib, Ash (Herts), Mimram, Beane and tributaries, Roding, Rom, Beam, Ingrebourne and tributaries, Colne, Colnebrook, Ver, Misbourne, Gade

Chess and tributaries. Grand Union Canal, Slough Arm, Paddington Arm. Brent, Crane and Duke of Northumberlands River.

Team Leader - Fisheries & Biodiversity (South East): J Sutton; Swift House, Frimley Business Park, Camberley, Surrey, GU16 7SQ (tel: 01276 454 425).
Main rivers controlled: Rivers Thames (Wargrave to Yantlet), Loddon, Blackwater, Wey, Mole, Wandle and 5 London tributaries. Canals: Basingstoke.
River Pollution, Fish Mortality and Disease: Reports by Members of the Public: phone FREEFONE RIVER POLLUTION. This number covers the whole of the Thames Region catchment 24 hours a day, 7 days a week; or phone 0800 807060.

Seasons: Salmon and Trout (excluding rainbow trout): 1 April to 30 September; enclosed waters: 1 April to 29 October. **Rainbow trout:** 1 April to 30 September (does not apply to enclosed waters). **Freshwater fish:** 16 June to 14 March.

Lock & Weir fishing permit is available for limited lock and weir fishing at 18 sites; apply to Kings Meadow House.

Please report salmon or sea trout captures to Reading Office: tel: 0118 953 5511.

ENVIRONMENT AGENCY, WALES, Ty Cambria, 29 Newport Road, Cardiff CF24 0TP (tel: 02920 770088; fax: 02920 798555; web: www.environment-agency.wales.gov.uk).

In the interests of furthering salmon conservation, the Agency is urging anglers to practise catch and release of all rod-caught salmon.

Strategy & Policy Manager, Fisheries, Conservation & Recreation: Mr Michael Evans.

AREAS OF THE AGENCY
Northern Area: Ffordd Penlan, Parc Menai, Bangor, Gwynedd LL5 2EF (tel: 01248 670770).
Fisheries and Recreational Technical Team Leader: R Brassington (fax: 01248 670561).
Special Enforcement Team Leader: Dave Lee.

Main rivers controlled: Dee (Welsh) Clwyd, Elwy, Alwen, Alyn, Ceiriog, Ceirw, Lliw, Tryweryn, Twrch, Bala Lake and their feeders. Also waters in an area bounded by watersheds of rivers (including their tributaries and all lakes) running into the sea between the eastern boundary of the Division's area at Old Gwyrch, Denbighshire, and the southern extremity at Upper Borth, Cardiganshire: Dulas, Conway, Lledr, Llugwy (with Lakes Elsi, Crafnant, Cowlyd, Eigiau, Conway, Melynllyn, Dulyn), Aber, Ogwen (with Lakes Anafon, Ogwen, Idwal, Ffynnon, Loer), all waters in Anglesey, Seiont, Gwyrfai, Llyfni (with Lakes Padarn, Cwellyn, Gader, Nantlle), Erch, Soch, Rhydhir, Afon Wen, Dwyfawr, Dwyfach (with Lake Cwmystradlyn), Glaslyn, Dwyryd, Prysor (with Lakes Dinas, Gwynant, Llagi Adar, Trawsfynydd, Gamallt, Morwynion, Cwmorthin), Glyn, Eisingrug (with Lakes Techwyn Isaf, Techwyn Uchaf, Artro, Mawddach, Eden, Wnion (with Lakes Cwm Bychan, Bodlyn, Gwernan, Gregennen), Dysynny, Dovey, Dulas, Twmyn (with Lake Tal-y-Llyn).

South West Area: Maes Newydd, Llandarcy, Neath, Port Talbot SA10 6JQ (tel: 01792 325500; fax: 01792 325511).
Fisheries and Recreational Technical Team Leader: Dave Mee.
Special Enforcement Team Leader: Selby le Roux.

Senior Special Enforcement Officer: Steve Williams

Main rivers controlled: Neath, Afan, Kenfig, Ogmore, Ewenny, Llynfi, Tawe, Afan, Kenfig, Gwendraeth Fawr, Gwendraeth Fach and Loughor. Towy, Teifi, Taf, Eastern and Western Cleddau, Gwaun, Nevern, Aeron, Clarach, Rheidol, Ystwyth, Wyre, and the tributaries of these rivers.

South East Area: Rivers House, St Mellons Business Park, Cardiff CF3 0LT (tel: 02920 770088; fax: 02920 362920; e-mail: simon.bonwick@environment-agency.gov.uk).
Fisheries and Recreational Technical Team Leader: Bill Purvis.

Senior Enforcement Officer: Steve Barker.

Main rivers controlled: Thaw, Ely, Taff, Rhymney, Usk and tributaries, including Cilienni, Honddu, Yscir, Bran, Cray, Senni, Tarrell, Cynrig, Crawnon, Rhiangoll, Gwryne-fawr, Grwynefechan, Olway, Afon Lwyd and Ebbw and tributary Sirhowy. Wye and all rivers and brooks of the Wye watershed including Monnow, Trothy, Lugg, Arrow, Ithon and Irfon. Information on river levels for angling on the rivers Usk and Wye can be obtained on the Agency's rivercall number: 0906 619 7744.

24-hour pollution, flooding, fish in distress, risks to wildlife, illegal dumping of hazardous waste, and poaching emergency freephone: 0800 807060.

Arthur Oglesby, a legend in his day, fishes Kenya water. *Photo: Grace Oglesby.*

ENGLISH FISHING STATIONS

Main catchments are given in alphabetical order, fishing stations listed in mouth to source order, first main river, then tributaries. Where national borders are crossed - e.g. Wye and Border Esk - allocation has been arbitrary. Some small streams have been grouped in counties rather than catchments.

Environment Agency rod licences are now required almost everywhere in England and Wales for all freshwater fishing. Details appear on pages 16-24. A list of fishing clubs appears at the end of each national section. 'Free fishing' means only that a riparian owner is reputed to allow fishing without making a charge. It does not imply a right and such information should be checked locally before an attempt to fish is made. All charges shown are exclusive of VAT unless otherwise stated. Reduced charges to juniors, the disabled, pensioners, and in some instances to ladies, are now quite commonplace. In many instances, they are specified. Where they are not, they may nevertheless be in force. If in doubt, ask when booking.

ADUR

(For close seasons, licences, etc, see Southern Region Environment Agency, p18).

Rises SW of Horsham and flows into the English Channel at Shoreham. Sea trout, trout, and very good coarse fishing, with match weights in excess of 70lb.

Shoreham (W Sussex). Bass, codling, flats, eels, mullet from harbour and shore. Passies Perfect Tackle, Passies Ponds, Church Farm, Coombes, Lancing BN15 0RS (tel: 07710 756257; www.coombes.co.uk), has 2 coarse lakes, with carp, chub, roach, etc. Dt £7, conc.

Upper Beeding (W Sussex). Chub, bream, perch, rudd, roach, dace, eels and pike. Central Assn of London & Provincial Angling Clubs (CALPAC) fishes 3,000 yds of prolific tidal stretch; dt £5, conc, from bailiff on bank; no night fishing; open 15 Jun-15 Mar.

Bramber and **Steyning** (W Sussex). Bream, roach, chub, dace, pike and carp. Pulborough AS has 3m from Bramber Bridge upstream to Streatham Old Railway Bridge. On tidal water, low water best; dt £5, conc from Bramber Newsagency. River also has run of sea trout.

Henfield (W Sussex). Henfield & Dist AS has fishing rights on 12m of Mid and Upper Adur, from Streatham Bridge to Wineham, also west arm from Locks Estate to Partridge Green, with sea trout, brown trout, very large pike, carp, perch, large shoals of bream, eels, and other coarse species, and coarse fishing in lakes and ponds, with large carp; no dt, membership: apply to Hon Sec or Prime Angling. Worthing & Dist PS has two stretches of Adur fishing in vicinity, with bream, carp, chub, pike, perch, gudgeon, roach, rudd, tench; Patching Pond, 4m west of Worthing; Laybrook Fishery, 2m from Ashington; dt £7, conc, from Worthing and Littlehampton tackle shops. Society is affiliated with Sussex Anglers Consultative Association. Tackle shop: Prime Angling, 74 Brighton Rd, Worthing BN11 2EN (tel: 01903 527050); for Worthing & DPS tickets: Squires Fisheries, 25 Southwick Square, Brighton BN4 4FP (tel: 01273 592903).

ALDE

(For licences, etc, see Anglian Region Environment Agency, p21)

A small Suffolk stream, rising near Saxmundham and flowing into the North Sea at Orford Haven, 6½m NE of Felixstowe. Sea fish.

Aldeburgh (Suffolk). Bass, codling, flatfish, etc, can be taken in estuary from jetty and boat; cod and whiting from beach; October and November best months. Hotels: Brudenell, White Lion, Wentworth, East Suffolk (*see also Suffolk, Sea Fishing Stations*).

Snape (Suffolk). River tidal. Mullet, bass, eels below sluice. Fishing free. Other free fishing at Thorpness Mere, nr Leiston. Tackle shop: Saxmundham Angling Centre, Bakery Yard, rear of Market Place, Saxmundham IP17 1AH (tel: 01728 603443): day tickets, details of local lake fishing for carp, tench, perch, bream, rudd and pike, and details of local fishing clubs. Hotels: White Hart, Bell.

ALN

(For close seasons, etc, see North East Region Environment Agency, p20)

Short Northumberland river, flowing into North Sea at Alnmouth. Trout and sea trout, occasional salmon; usually a late run river.

Alnwick (Northumberland). Aln AA water (owned by the Duke of Northumberland), 5 to 7 miles of trout, sea trout and occasional salmon; stocked yearly with brown trout, av 1¼lb; no fishing between old road bridge and foot bridge at Lesbury; salmon: st £70, trout £50; mt £45; wt £40, dt £20 (jun £5 trout only), conc, from R L Jobson & Son, Tower Showrooms NE66 1SX (tel: 01665 602135) during business hours. Coquet and Till within easy reach. Hotels: White Swan, Bondgate Within; Plough, Bondgate Without; and Schooner, Alnmouth.

ANCHOLME

(For close seasons, etc, see Anglian Region Environment Agency, p21)

This river, in South Humberside and Lincolnshire, with its tributaries drains about 240 square miles of country. Falls into the Humber at **South Ferriby**, where there is a sluice and tidal lock. The lower part is embanked for about 19 miles. The fishing rights are leased to Scunthorpe & District Angling Association; temporary membership day permits are obtainable from their bailiffs on the bankside. The river is abundantly stocked with coarse fish, especially roach and bream, and recently perch. Winter shoals found mainly at **Brigg**. Other choice sections at **Broughton, Snitterby, Horkstow** areas. Fishing accesses: South Ferriby Sluice, 4m from Barton upon Humber: **Saxby Bridge**, 6m from Barton upon Humber: Broughton, Castlethorpe, Cadney and Hibaldstow Bridges near Brigg through which town river passes; Brandy Wharf, Snitterby, Bishop Bridge, 6m from Market Rasen. Improvement work recently completed at Scabcroft, Broughton and Brigg. Disabled fishing stands at Brigg and at Hibaldstow Bridge. The Assn also has both banks of River Rase from Harlem Lock to Carr Lane where it runs into Ancholme at Bishop Bridge. At Barton upon Humber are **Barton Broads** mixed coarse fishery, 6½ acres, Malt Kiln Lane. For tickets, *see Goole;* **Pasture House Fishery**, 12 acres; silver fishery on banks of Humber; dt £5 from Mr & Mrs Smith, Barton upon Humber DN18 5RB (tel: 01652 636369). Tackle Shop: Barton Kingfisher Bait & Tackle, 102 High St, Barton upon Humber DN18 5PU (tel: 01652 636868); Chapmans Tackle, 27 Beechway, Scunthorpe DN16 2HF (tel: 01724 862585); Guns & Tackle, 251 Ashby High Str, Scunthorpe DN16 2SQ (tel: 01724 865445).

ARUN

(For close seasons, etc, see Southern Region Environment Agency, p18).

Rises on NW border of Sussex, flows past Horsham and enters English Channel at Littlehampton. Noted coarse-fish river, largely controlled by clubs. Some sea trout; May to October.

Littlehampton (Sussex). *See under Sea Fishing Stations.* HQ of Littlehampton & Dist AC is at Arun View Hotel, right by river. Billingshurst AS has R Arun fishing at Pallingham, and three lakes. Worthing & Dist PS has Patching Pond, 4m W of Worthing; coarse. Dt £7, conc, from Arun Angling Centre, Units 5/7 True Blue Precinct, Wick, Littlehampton BN17 7JN (tel: 01903 718546); and other Littlehampton and Worthing tackle shops **Arundel** (W Sussex). River tidal and

---

Keep the banks clean

Several clubs have stopped issuing tickets to visitors because of the state of the banks after they have left. Spend a few moments clearing up.

mainly mud-bottomed. Roach and dace run large; bream, perch, pike, chub and occasional sea trout. Bass and mullet taken in fair numbers June, July, August between Ford railway bridge and Arundel, where fishing is free. Leger best method when tide running; trotting down successful in slack water. **Back Arun Fishery**, Station Approach; 10 acres mixed fishery; dt £6 on site. Tackle shop: Tropicana, 5 & 6 Pier Rd, Littlehampton BN17 5BA (tel: 01903 715190). Hotels: Norfolk Arms; Howards.

Chalk Springs Fishery, Park Bottom, Arundel, West Sussex, BN18 0AA (tel: 01903 883742; web: www.chalksprings. com); four lakes, clear water, stocked with brown and rainbow trout of 2-20lb; dt £36 (5 fish), £32 (4 fish); part-day £26.50, £20.00; refreshments, lodge on lakes, tuition, tackle for sale.

Amberley (W Sussex). Chub, bream, roach, dace, rudd, eel, perch, pike. Worthing & Dist PS control stretch in the area of Houghton Bridge; dt £7, conc, from Post Horses, Aladdins Cave Antiques, London Rd, Ashington (tel: 01903 893232); Houghton Bridge Tea Gardens, Amberley BN18 9LP (tel: 01798 831558), and Worthing tackle shops. Western Rother AC has two stretches on the Arun: ½m from **Greatham** north, on west bank, and 1½m from Stopham Bridge north, on west bank. The Central Association of London & Provincial Angling Clubs hold both banks downstream of Houghton Bridge to South Stoke, tidal water. Railway station 2 mins walk from fishery. Dt £5 from bailiff on bank, £4 conc in advance. No night fishing on CALPAC water. This area to Stopham involved in Sussex RD improvement scheme.

Pulborough (W Sussex). Pike, bream to 7lbs, roach to 2½lbs, chub, dace, perch, rudd, large carp. Central Association of London & Provincial ACs leases tidal stretch at Swan Meadow. Station is 7 mins walk from fishery. Dt £5, conc, from bailiffs. No night fishing on CAL-PAC water. Pulborough AS has fishing on the tidal Arun from Pulborough to Greatham Bridge, approx 3m, 1m on **Rother**, 3m on **Adur**; also eleven lakes, incl **Duncans Lake**, Pulborough (good for young anglers) and **Goose Green** (6 small lakes) near **Ashington**; coarse fish; members only: st £62, conc, from Hon Sec; Carringdale Angling Centre, Bury

Gate RH20 1NN (tel: 01798 830007). RMC has 1½m stretch; st (2 rods) £22, conc £12. *(For RMC Angling see Chertsey)*. At **Wisborough Green** Crawley AS has water; dt. At **Horsham** is Newells Pond Carp fishery, two lakes of 4.2 acres each; st only, from Tim Cotton, Newells Pond House, Newells Lane, Lower Beeding RH13 6LN (tel: 01403 891424). Horsham & DAA has **R Arun** around Horsham and near Pulborough (both closed during the traditional close season); no dt, members only; st £42; the assn also has Roosthole, Birchenbridge (disabled swim), Island, and Sun Oak Ponds, and Foxhole, most open all year: apply Hon Sec. Worthing & Dist PS has 1m of western arm of **R Adur** nr Horsham: coarse; well weeded in summer, but good fish taken between weed beds. Club also has **Laybrook Lakes**, Pulborough; dt £7, conc, from Post Horses, Aladdins Cave Antiques, London Rd, Ashington (tel: 01903 893232); Houghton Bridge Tea Gardens, Amberley BN 18 9LP (tel: 01798 831558), and Worthing tackle shops. **Whitevane Pond Fishery**, Mrs Teresa Yeates, Forest Grange, Off Forest/Pease Pottage Rd, Horsham (tel: 01403 791163): 10 acre lake with large carp to 39lb 12oz; dt £15 2 rods, 24 hr £25. **Furnace Lakes**, Slinfold (tel: 01403 791163), 4m from Horsham: 6 acre lake with carp to 30lbs, large rudd, bream, etc, and 2½ acre lake, mirror and common carp, roach, skimmer bream, etc; dt £10 2 rods, £15 3 rods, 24 hr £20, conc. Also Specimen Lake; carp to 38lb; and Roman Lake: catfish to 56lb, carp to 47lb; dt £15 2 rods, £25 24-hour, no conc.

Rudgwick (W Sussex). Roach, bream, chub, perch, pike, carp, large eels. Southern Anglers fish ½m non-tidal river at Bucks Green, u/s of road bridge; tickets for members guests; also exchange tickets with four other clubs for several Sussex and Hampshire waters. Rudgwick AS fishes from Slinfold to Gibbons Mill. Hazelcopse, Baynards, nr Rudgwick RH12 3AF (tel: 01403 822878): 2 lakes of 3½ acres, with salmon, rainbow and brown trout; dt £27 4 fish, £17 2 fish, c&r after limit. Tackle shops: Tropicana, 6 Pier Rd, Littlehampton BN17 5BA (tel: 01903 715190); Prime Angling, 74 Brighton Rd, Worthing BN11 2EN (tel: 01903 527050).

Tributaries of the Arun.

WESTERN ROTHER:
Petworth (W Sussex). Pike, perch, roach, dace, chub, few trout and sea trout. Leconfield Estate operate a commercial fishery, and let trout rods on their section of the Rother; contact Smiths Gore, Estate Office, Petworth GU28 0DU (tel: 01798 342502). Petworth AC has 5½m in all, members only, but 2-week holiday ticket from Hon Sec; also stretch downstream from Coultershaw Mill to Shopham Bridge, and 1m (N bank only) from Shopham Bridge; then both banks for 1m from Fittleworth Bridge; st £75 from Hon Sec; Club also has Petworth House Lower Pond; coarse. Contact Richard Etherington, Smiths Gore, Exchange House, Petworth GU28 0BF (tel: 01798 343111), for 1½m stocked fly fishing on Rother for browns, 3 miles from Petworth. **Burton Mill Pond** holds good pike, perch, roach, rudd, carp, tench. **Duncton Mill**; 8 acre Trout farm and fishery, on chalk spring fed lakes; brown, brook, tiger and rainbow trout, average bags 3 fish, 7½lb total; all facilities, incl tuition and rod hire (tel: 01798 342048). Pulborough AS has **Moor Farm Lakes**; coarse; apply Hon Sec; no dt.

Selham (W Sussex). Pitshill Fly Fishing Waters: 1½m part double bank downstream from Lods Bridge.

Midhurst (W Sussex). Western Rother AC has six stretches of river and four lakes, including **Cooks Pond** at Milland, and **Minsted Pit**; coarse fish incl dace, roach, rudd, bream, tench, perch, carp, pike, eels. Tickets for Rother £4, Rotherfield Pond £6 conc, from Backshall's Garage, Dodsley Lane, Easebourne, Midhurst GU29 9BB; membership from Treasurer.

Chithurst (W Sussex). Petersfield & Dist AC is affiliated to the Hants & Sussex Anglers Alliance who have fishing on the Arun, **Rother**, and eleven stillwaters. Fishing is predominately coarse with most species; permits for Heath Lake, Petersfield, 22 acres (with carp to 27lb) from local tackle shop; dt on bank from bailiff; enquiries to Hon Sec. Tackle shop: Rods & Reels, 418 Havant Rd, Farlington PO6 1NF (tel: 02392 789090).

AVON (Bristol)

(For close seasons, licences, etc, see South West Region Environment Agency, p19).

Coarse fishing now excellent in places. Large chub, barbel, pike, bream, roach. Trout in weir pools, including exceptional specimens occasionally, and in some tributaries. Much of Avon controlled by Bristol, Bath & Wiltshire Anglers (BB&WAA), a merger of eleven clubs known as "the Amalgamation". Fishing includes many stretches of Bristol Avon, Somerset Frome, Bristol Frome, stretches on Brue, and coarse lakes. Membership costs £30 (concessions for ladies, juniors and pensioners), obtainable from tackle shops in the main Avon centres or Hon Sec. Dt waters.

Bristol. On Avon and Frome and in Somerset. Some free fishing on Environment Agency licence from Netham Weir u/s to Hanham, towpath only. Good sport with trout on **Blagdon Lake, Chew Valley** and **Barrow Reservoirs** *(see Somerset streams, lakes and reservoirs)*. Among coarse fishing lakes in area are **Bowood** (2m W of Calne, dt at waterside); **Longleat** *(see Warminster)*; **Bitterwell Lake** (N of Bristol) excellent bream, roach, rudd, common, mirror and crucian carp, perch; tuck shop; tackle sold; dt on bank, £4 per rod (£2 second rod), £2 conc and after 4pm, from Mrs C W Reid, The Chalet, Bitterwell Lake, Ram Hill, Coalpit Heath, Bristol BS17 2UF (tel: 01454 778960); bank fishing only; disabled: by notice. **Henleaze Lake** (north of Bristol, no dt; information at gate on how to apply. **Abbots Pool**, Abbots Leigh, is run by North Somerset Council, PO Box 146, Town Hall, Weston-super-Mare, BS23 1LH (tel: 01934 888888). Tackle shops: Veals Fishing Tackle, 61 Old Market St, Bristol BS2 0EJ (tel: 0117 9260790); Fish & Field, 60 Broad St, Chipping Sodbury BS17 6AG (tel: 01454 314034); Scott Tackle, 42 Soundwell Road, Staple Hill BS16 4QP (tel: 0117 956 7371); S Shipp, 7 Victoria St, Staple Hill Bristol BS16 5JP (tel: 0117 956 6985); Avon Angling Centre, 348 Whitewell Road, Bristol BS5 7BW (tel: 0117 951 7250); Bristol Angling Centre, 12 Doncaster Road, Southmead, Bristol BS10 5PL (tel: 0117 950 8723).

Keynsham (Avon). Chub, perch, eels, roach and dace. Free fishing on Environment Agency licence at R **Chew** confluence, end of recreation ground, left bank; also R Chew in Keynsham Park. Bathampton AA has one mile of single bank on R Chew at Compton Dando, nr Keynsham; trout, coarse fish; members only; st £22, conc, from Keynsham Pet & Garden Centre, 5 Bath Hill, Keynsham, Bristol BS31 1EB (tel: 0117 9862366); or Veals Fishing Tackle, 61 Old Market St, Bristol BS2 0EJ (tel: 0117 9260790). Bristol & West Federation has fishing here (**The Crane**). The waters start at the junction of the lock canal behind the Marina and stretch continously u/s to the **Swineford Brook**, opposite the Swan Inn, about 3½m, the water being divided into 4 match sections; also **Jack Whites** and **The Chequers**; dt £4, conc from local tackleists. All these waters are fished by arrangement with the Bristol & Bath Federation of Anglers. Tackle shop: Keynsham Pet & Garden Centre *(above)*; Avon Angling Centre, 348 Whitewell Road, Bristol BS5 7BW (tel: 0117 951 7250). Hotels: The Grange Hotel; Manor Lodge; The Old Chapel, Compton Dando.

Saltford (Avon). Bathampton AA has 2½m on Avon. Newbridge (famous for big bream bags, fish to 9lb) to Kelston (nr Bath), including Newton St Loe and Saltford; most coarse fish, including carp and tench, few large trout. St £20, conc, from local tackle shops and Hon Sec. BB&WAA has stretch at Swineford.

Bath (Avon). Coarse fish; barbel present from here to Limpley Stoke; few large trout. Also good base for Rivers Chew and Frome, with reasonable trout fishing. Some free Avon fishing at Pulteney Weir d/s to Newbridge, along towpath; Bathampton Weir u/s to car park, most of footpath. Bath AA are part of BB&WAA, and has water at **Kensington Meadows**; **Windsor Bridge** (a short section of left bank d/s of bridge); **Lambridge** (300 metres from the d/s end of the rugby ground to the old tip field; **Grosvenor** (from the Grosvenor footbridge d/s on the right bank for ¾m to just behind the Safeway supermarket, plus 1 field d/s on left bank from the bridge, approx ¼m. Good trout fishing in tributary streams, all preserved. **Kennet and Avon Canal** to Winsley Hill preserved by Bathampton AA; assn also fishes on Newton Park (mainly carp), Hunstrete (3 lakes totalling 10 acres) and Lydes Farm (now re-opened), also Box Brook nr Bathford on A4 (fly only for brown trout), and River Chew at Compton Dando. Contact Hon Sec. National Trust has coarse Bath Lake (the lower of the 3 lakes at Prior Park Landscape Garden; enquire Avon & Tributaries AA; members only. Tackle shop: Mr Patrick Hemming, Fishing Dept, I M Crudgington Ltd, 37 Broad Str, BA1 5LP (tel: 01225 464928), has information and tickets for Bathampton AA waters; membership £22, conc; Bacon's Tackle, 83 Lower Bristol Rd BA2 3BQ (tel: 01225 448850). Hotels: Bailbrook Lodge; Eagle House.

Bathampton (Avon). All-round fishing (barbel, roach, chub, pike, bream). BB&WAA has water at **Bathmpton Weir Pool**, **Bathampton Manor Waters**; the rights extend from the weir d/s a short distance; also the Amalg's **Bathford Candy's** waters extend 2 fields u/s from the tollbridge for approx 1½m; membership £30, conc £10, dt £4. Bathampton AA has water here, and at **Kelston**, **Newton St Loe**, **Newbridge**, **Saltford**, and on **Kennet and Avon Canal**, **Hunstrete**, **Newton Park** (possibly the most prolific carp fishery in the area) and Lydes Farm, and **Box Brook**; members only; st £22, conc, from Hon Sec and tackle shops in Bristol, Bath, Keynsham, and Chippenham. Hotels: Cranleigh; Eagle House.

Claverton (Avon). Bathampton AA has 2m; very good chub, and barbel; other coarse fish. St £25, conc, contact Hon Sec; local tackle shops. BB&WAA has 2m stretch from Midford Brook, d/s to the railway embankment, passing under Dundas Aqueduct, including Midford Brook from the B3108 road bridge to the main river; membership £30, conc £10, dt £4. Hotel: Limpley Stoke Hotel.

Warleigh (Avon). Bathampton AA has four meadows here: (as Claverton above). BB&WAA has fishing u/s and d/s of the Dundas Aqueduct.

Limpley Stoke (Wilts). Good all-round fishing; large carp, with tench, chub, roach bream and trout; fly-fishing on **River Frome** at Freshford and **Midford Brook** at Midford; preserved by Avon & Tributaries AA. BB&WAA has fishing at **Haydens Field** and the **Cabbage Patch**; from the mouth of Midford Brook, u/s for approx ½m; and Midford Brook itself, u/s to the B3108 road bridge. Amalg also has Avoncliffe to Limpley Stoke, divided into 3 match zones. Bathampton AA holds **Kennet and Avon Canal** from

Limpley Stoke to confluence with Avon at Bath (5½m): dt from Hon Sec, tackle shops. Hotel: Limpley Stoke Hotel.

Midford (Avon). **Midford Brook**; trout only; preserved and stocked by the Avon & Tributaries AA.

Freshford (Avon). BB&WAA has water on Avon; from behind the sewerage works, nr Freshford railway station for 1¼m d/s to the bungalows at Limpley Stoke; dt £4. **Frome**: trout, coarse fish, stocked and preserved by Avon & Tributaries AA; from Avon up to Farleigh Hungerford. Limited dt for members' guests; assn also has part of Avon, Freshford to Avoncliffe, fly only water on **Midford, Wellow** and **Cam Brooks**. BB&WAA also has water on Wellow Brook (Stoney Littleton) and **Cam Brook** (Dunkerton); trout and coarse; dt £4.

Bradford-on-Avon (Wilts). Coarse fish, including pike, few trout. **Kennet and Avon Canal**; coarse fish.

Melksham (Wilts). Coarse fish, few trout. Avon AC has 5m of river and 4m of canal; dt £3 from tackle shops. BB&WAA has **Lacock** (National Trust) stretch, 1½m u/s from bridge; excellent barbel; membership £30, conc £10; dt £4; Amal also has 2m at **Queenfield Farm**; 3 fields left and d/s; 2 fields right and u/s to Mead Farm waters; tickets from Lacock sub-PO, 12 High Str, SN15 2LQ (tel: 01249 730305). Leech Pool Farm has coarse fishing at **Broughton Gifford**. Tackle shop: Melksham Angling Centre, Melksham House, Melksham SN12 6ES (tel: 01225 793546).

Chippenham (Wilts). Chub, barbel, bream, perch, roach, carp, pike. Chippenham AA has water, details from Hon Sec; st £22, wt £8, dt £4 from Premier Angling, who also have dt for **Sword Lake**, coarse, and **Sabre Lake**, coarse with carp; these lakes are also fished by BB&WAA. The Amalgamation also has about 1½m of river between here and **Lacock**. Calne AA has **River Marden**, st £20, dt £3, from Pre-

mier Angling *(below)*. **Devizes AA waters**: 15m of **Kennet** and **Avon Canal**, 1m of Avon at Beanacre, Melksham, various coarse, dt £3.50, conc. Avon AC has Avon from Beanacre to Whaddon, st £14, dt £3. These and others from Premier Angling, 19 New Road, Chippenham SN15 1HT (tel: 01249 659210); T K Tackle, 123a London Rd, Calne SN11 0AQ (tel: 01249 812003); House of Angling, 59/60 Commercial Rd, Swindon SN1 5NX (tel: 01793 693460). Mill Farm Trout Lakes, Worton, nr Devizes SN10 5UW (tel: 01380 813138), 2 dt lakes, 3½ acres each; Bill Coleman. Ivy House Lakes, nr Swindon SN15 4JU, all species, carp to 20lbs; dt £5 1 rod, £6 2 rods, conc; P and J Warner (tel: 01666 510368).

Christian Malford (Wilts). Several fields controlled by BB&WAA here; at Upper Christian Malford, the fishing extends for approx 2m u/s under M4 bridge to just below weir. At Lower Christian Malford, Amalg has 1½m from car park d/s. BB&WAA also at **Hungerdown Meadows, Sutton Benger**; waters extend for field above M4 bridge and 2 fields below, to just above Weir, approx ¾m total. Calne AA has two meadows on church side. Tickets from T K Tackle, 123a London Rd, Calne SN11 0AQ (tel: 01249 812003). Somerfords FA has water upstream from Seagry to Kingsmead Mill (part of it, from Dauntsey road bridge, is trout water) and 2m above Kingsmead Mill on left bank and 1m on right bank. Good chub and perch. Assn also has water on **Frome**; dt for trout and coarse fishing issued. Golden Valley FC has water at Seagry.

Malmesbury (Wilts). BB&WAA has approx 1½m d/s from bridge (**Daniel Well**); membership £30, conc £10, dt £4. At **Cowbridge Farm** BB&WAA has approx 1½m total to just above Malmesbury bypass bridge. Amalgamation also has fishing on **Burton Hill Lake**; members only.

Lower Moor Fishery, Oaksey, Malmesbury, Wiltshire SN16 9TW (tel: 01666 860232; fax: 01666 860765): 34 acres of excellent trout fishing on Mallard Lake, any kind of fly fishing, stocked rainbow and brown; dt £22 or £14 (4 and 2 fish limits); Juv £11 (2 fish); fine fly hatch, exceptional mayfly and damsel; open end of Mar to New Years Day.

Tributaries of the Avon (Bristol)

FROME (Bristol). Rises near Chipping Sodbury and joins Avon estuary near Bristol. Small tributaries upstream provide ideal conditions for trout. Fishing on **Mells River, Whatley** and **Nunney Brooks.** Coarse species are barbel, bream, carp, eel, perch, roach, tench, chub and grayling. At **Stapleton,** BB&WAA has water from bridge d/s on left bank to Wickham Hill Bridge, and then on both banks down to the weir; dt £4 from tackle shops.

Frampton Cotterell (Glos). Most of lower Frome controlled by Bristol, Bath and Wiltshire Anglers.

Yate (Glos). Frome Vale AC has water from Moorend Weir to viaduct. Dodington Park Lake, 6m; carp, perch; preserved.

CHEW: From Confluence to Compton Dando, coarse fish; thereafter, trout.

Keynsham (Avon). Keynsham AA has fishing *(see Avon).*

Malmesbury (Wilts). Free fishing on Environment Agency licence at Sherston Avon u/s of Cascade at Silk Mills; Tetbury Avon u/s Station Yard Weir, Fire Station, left bank. Club also has long stretch of **Woodbridge Brook.**

Chewton Keynsham (Avon). Approx 1m of water, d/s to Rock Mill Cottages held by BB&WAA; dt £4. Stretch in Keynsham Park free to licence holders.

Compton Dando (Avon). Mainly trout, grayling and dace. Keynsham AA also has water from Keynsham Mill to Compton Dando; all coarse fishing; apply Keynsham Pet & Garden Centre, 5 Bath Hill, Keynsham, Bristol BS31 1EB (tel: 0117 9862366).

Pensford (Avon). Trout and coarse fish. Lakes: **Hunstrete Complex Lakes,** nr Keynsham; three lakes with carp, tench, bream, roach, perch; Bathampton AA; members only; additional special dt must be obtained before fishing from local tackle shops; st £22, conc from Hon Sec and tackle shops; disabled platforms. Hotel: The Grange Hotel.

Stanton Drew, Chew Magna, Chew Stoke (Avon). Trout dominant; some roach and dace; no spinning; dt from local inns and Bristol tackle shops from June 15 to Sept 30 (Mon-Fri only). BB&WAA has ¾m right bank u/s from Bonds Bridge to the brook at the top of the upper meadow; dt £4. *(For Chew Reservoirs, see Somerset (lakes and streams)).*

BOYD BROOK: Trout in upper reaches, coarse fish; Golden Valley FC has stretch above and below Bitton.

CAM BROOK: Trout. Avon & Tributaries AA has water (members only). Cameley Trout Lakes are at Temple Cloud. St and dt, apply to J Harris, Hillcrest Farm, Cameley, Temple Cloud, Bristol BS39 5AQ (tel: 01761 452423); tickets available in car park.

BYE (BOX) BROOK: Wild brown trout, grayling. Bathampton AA has water from Shockerwick to **Box**, 2m; fly only; members only, additional special dt must be obtained before fishing from Bath or Bristol tackle shops; st £35 and specialist information only from: A Wallace, 53 Edgeworth Rd, Kingsway, Bath BA2 2LT (tel: 01225 422491; e-mail: adrian.wallace@tinyworld.co.uk). By Brook Fly FC and Two Mills Flyfishers has water for members. Manor House Hotel, Castle Combe, has ½m of good trout fishing in grounds. Hotels: Bailbrook Lodge. Tackle shop: Melksham Angling Centre, Melksham House, Melksham SN12 6ES (tel: 01225 793546); Steve's, 3 Station Road, Warminster BA12 9BR (tel: 01985 214934).

FROME: Coarse fish, trout.

Frome (Som). Frome & Dist AA has twelve miles above and below town, and coarse fishing lake at Marston, 3m from Frome. Regular matches. Membership £13 pa, conc, dt £3, conc. Information from Hon Sec. Witham Friary Lake coarse fishing open all year, Witham Hall Farm, Witham Friary, nr Frome (tel: 01373 836239). Tackle shops: Haines Angling, 47 Vallis Way, Frome BA11 1BA (tel: 01373 466406). Hotel: George, Market Place.

Woolverton (Avon). Trout, coarse fish.

MARDEN: Coarse fish, trout.

Calne (Wilts). Trout, barbel, chub, rudd, carp, golden orfe, tench, pike, perch, roach, dace, bream; fly fishing 1 Apr-15 Jun; 6m held by Calne AA: st £20 & dt £3 from T K Tackle. Assn also fish section of R Avon at Christian Malford, and Spye Park Lake. Disabled stages available, jun coaching and matches. **Bowood Lake**, large pike (to 33lb), perch, carp, tench, roach; details from Bowood Estate, Calne, Wilts SN11 0LZ (tel: 01249 812102), who issue st £141-£70.50; waiting list; North end of lake private. *Note: access to lake only at Pillars Lodge entrance on Calne - Melksham road.* Tickets for Sabre Lake, nr Calne, and other local waters, from T K Tackle, 123a London Rd, Calne SN11 0AQ (tel: 01249 812003).

AVON (Hampshire)

(For close seasons, licences, etc, see South West Region Environment Agency p19)

In years gone by the most famous mixed fishery in England. In its upper reaches, the Avon is a typical chalk stream, populated by free-rising trout and grayling.

Christchurch (Dorset). Avon and Stour. Excellent sea and coarse fishing in Christchurch Harbour, which is leased to Christchurch AC. Bass, mullet, flounders and (higher up) dace, roach, bream and eels. Other Club waters include several stretches of Dorset Stour from Christchurch Harbour to Wimborne, lakes and gravel pits with large carp and pike. Membership £110 per annum. Dt for these waters and the Royalty Fishery on the Avon can be obtained from Davis Fishing Tackle Shop; June 16 to Mar 14 inclusive. The Royalty Fishery price structure ranges between £20 per day for salmon, sea trout and coarse fishing, to £6 single rod for coarse fishing, with concessions. Davis will supply brochure on request and sae. Top Weir Compound, Parlour and Bridge Pool (best sea trout pool), permits from Davis Fishing Tackle. No advance bookings on Main River. All salmon to be returned. Permits for fishings on Stour and in Christchurch Harbour also obtainable from Davis Fishing Tackle *(see also Stour, Dorset)* and Pro Fishing Tackle. For other salmon and sea trout fishing apply early to Davis Fishing Tackle. Small coarse fisheries in vicinity: Gold Oak Farm, Hare Lane, nr Cranborne BH21 5QT (tel: 01725 517275): seven lakes with carp and tench, dt £7, £5 half day, evng £3, conc; Beeches Brook Fishery, Forest Rd, Burley (tel: 01425 402373); Turf Croft Farm Fishery, Forest Rd, Burley, nr Ringwood BH24 4DF (tel: 01425 403743); **Hordle Lakes**, Golden Hill, Ashley Lane, **New Milton** (tel: 01590 672300): coarse fishery on seven lakes. Dt on site. Good sea fishing at Mudeford; boats. Tackle shops: Mr G K Pepler, Davis Fishing Tackle Shop, 75 Bargates, Christchurch BH23 1QE (tel: 01202 485169). Hotel: Belvedere Guest House, 3 Twynham Avenue BH23 1QU.

Winkton (Dorset). Mr G K Pepler, Davis Fishing Tackle Shop, 75 Bargates, Christchurch BH23 1QE (tel: 01202 485169) now sole agents for coarse fishing on this fishery. Season is June 16 to Mar 14; good roach, large chub and barbel, pike; also dace, perch. Dt £7. Salmon fishing is offered, March 15 to June 15 only. Hotel: Fishermans Haunt.

Ringwood (Hants). Ringwood & Dist AC has fishing on rivers as follows: **Avon**; Breamore, 1½m (barbel, chub), Fordingbridge (trout), Ibsley, 2m (S and specimen coarse fish), side streams at Ibsley, Ringwood, 2m (coarse fish), Fordingbridge Park, ¼m (coarse fish); **Stour**; twelve stretches totalling more than 12m (coarse fish); also nine still waters totalling over 120 acres. Dt for much of the water from tackle shops. Dt £7.50 from Ringwood Tackle for ¾m both banks above Ringwood; 1¼m E. bank below and several coarse fishing lakes, dt £7.50. **High Town**, Ringwood: 23 acre pit containing most coarse species. Tickets from Ringwood and Christchurch tackle shops. Other dt waters: river at Lifelands Fishery; Martins Farm Carp Lake, W Ball, Woodlands, **Wimborne** BH21 8LY (tel: 01202 822335) dt £8; Hurst Pond. Tackle shops: Ringwood Tackle, 5 The Bridges, West Str, Ringwood BH24 1EA (tel: 01425 475155); Davis Fishing Tackle Shop, 75 Bargates, Christchurch BH23 1QE (tel: 01202 485169). Hotels: Crown, Star Inn, Fish Inn, White Hart.

Fordingbridge (Hants). Trout, grayling, perch, pike and roach. Park Recreation Ground has fishing, dt from Council grounds staff, Sept to Mar. Burgate Manor Farm Fishery let to Wimborne AC, who also have 1m of Avon, and 10 coarse lakes. Mostly members only with guests. St £75 + £8 joining fee from Wessex Angling Centre, 321 Wimborne Rd, Oakdale, Poole BH15 3DH (tel: 01202 668244). Two excellent stillwater fisheries in the vicinity. **Damerham** and **Lapsley's Fishery** (ex Allens Farm). Hotel: Ashburn.

Breamore (Hants). Bat and Ball Hotel has 2m of salmon, trout and coarse fish on dt basis.

Salisbury (Wilts). Avon, Bourne, Ebble, Nadder and Wylye; trout, grayling, coarse fish; preserved. Salisbury & Dist AC has water on Avon at the following locations: **Charford** (1m located 7m S of city); 3m of water within city limits (although in the countryside); **Durnford** (3m of chalk stream; 20 beats); **West Amesbury** (2m of double/single bank; stocked brown trout; late grayling; Ratfyn Farm and Countess Water (1m of double bank and ¾m single bank); at **Fordingbridge** there is club water behind the Game Conservancy; coarse fish, occasional salmon; at **Durrington** there is a joint venture between the Club and Parish Council, offering a chance to cast a fly at a trout before fishing on the Club's pre-mium waters. The club also has coarse fishing on **Petersfinger Lakes**, 2m E of City; **Steeple Langford Lakes** (two), 10m W; **Wellow Lakes** (two), 12m E, towards Southampton; membership circa £130 (game), conc; coarse £62; limited dt for waters within city boundary from Reids Tackle or John Eadie (*both below*). Club also issues permits for Charlton fishing, from Post Office, Downton Cross Roads. All details from Secretary. The Piscatorial Society has Avon fishing nr **Amesbury**, members only. Other local clubs: Tisbury AC has **Wardour Castle Lake** and **Dinton Lake** with bream, carp, roach, tench, perch; and 3m of R Nadder, with dace, roach, chub, perch etc; membership £25, conc, guest dt £4 from Hon Treasurer. Downton AA has 2½m of Avon with specimen chub, roach, barbel, etc. Membership for both these at Reids Tackle (*below*). London AA has **Britford Fishery**; 5m of Avon, Old River and Navigation; excellent coarse fishing, good sport with trout, some salmon; members only: st £39, conc, dt £5 from LAA. Dt also on bank. **Avon Springs Fisheries**, Recreation Rd, Durrington

Deep wading is a frequent but dangerous necessity; here practised in the Hampshire Avon at Braemore. *Photo: Environment Agency, South Wessex Area.*

SP4 8HH (tel: 01980 653557; web: www.fishingfly.co.uk): two spring fed lakes beside R Avon, of three and five acres, stocked with brown and rainbow trout from 2lbs to double figures. Best rainbow 2002, 15lbs 4oz; best brown, 17lbs, 9oz. Prices are as follows. Lakes: st £960, £330 for 10 tickets. Full dt £40, 4 fish limit; half-day £30, 3 fish; evening £20, 2 fish; juv £22. River: dt £40, 2 fish limit. Accom, nr fishery: Parkhouse Motel; Plume and Feathers, Shrewton. Waldens Farm Fishery, Waldens Estate, **West Grimstead** SP5 3RJ (tel: 01722 710480), has coarse fishing on 5 lakes, total 7.5 acres. St £70, dt £6 (payable on bank), conc. Has match lake with 27 pegs for hire to clubs. Tackle shops: John

Eadie, 20 Catherine Str, SP1 2DA (tel: 01722 328535); Reids Tackle, Kingsway House, Warminster Rd, Wilton SP2 0AT (tel: 01722 743192). Hotels: Old Mill House, Warminster Rd, South Newton SP2 0QD (tel: 01722 742458) (special terms for Salisbury & Dist AC members; hotel can arrange fishing); White Hart; Red Lion; Grasmere; Harnham; Lamb, Hinton; Bell, South Newton.

Netheravon (Wilts). Trout, grayling; preserved. The 6m from **Enford** to **Bulford** is The Services Dry Fly FA (Salisbury Plain) water; strictly members only (restricted to serving or retired service personnel and MOD employees), dt from Hon Sec.

AVON (Hampshire) tributaries

BOURNE: Enters near Salisbury. Trout, grayling, coarse fish. Fishing stations: **Porton** and **Salisbury** (Wilts). Salisbury & Dist AC has premium water at **Hurdcott**; ¼m of clear brook style fishing: fine trout and grayling; apply Hon Sec; waiting list; club also has ¾m u/s; members only.

EBBLE: Joins Avon below Salisbury; good trout fishing, but mostly private.

WYLYE: Trout, grayling.

Wilton (Wilts). 6 miles preserved by Wilton Fly Fishing Club, full-time keeper, club room, wild brown trout (stocked with fry and fingerlings), grayling; closed membership; no dt. Wyle Fly FC has stretches at **Steeple Langford, Quidhampton**, and elsewhere; members and their guests only. Fishing Breaks Ltd, Walton House, 23 Compton Terrace, London N1 2UN (tel: 020 7359 8818; web: www.fishingbreaks.com) has day rods on R Wylye.

Stapleford (Wilts). Salisbury & Dist AC has fishing here (3m W of Salisbury); ¾m fine dry fly; excellent autumn and winter grayling; members only.

Warminster (Wilts). **Longleat** Estate: excellent coarse fishing in three lakes in Longleat Park; Bottom and Middle, mixed fishing, Top Lake, specimen carp. Tickets are issued by Bailiff, Nick Robbins Longleat Estate, Warminster BA12 7NW (tel: 01985 844496; mobile: 078896 25999); dt £6, 24 hr £12 2 rods, £15 3 rods; the Estate also has **Shearwater**

Lake, mixed coarse, 37 acres, off A350 at Crockerton (same prices). The Sutton Veny Estate, Eastleigh Farm, Bishopstrow, Warminster BA12 7BE (tel: 01985 212325), lets rods, part rods and quarter-rods on 4m of Wylye, chalk stream dry fly and upstream nymph only, brown trout Autumn nymph fishing for grayling; upper beats are for wild fish; c&r only.

NADDER: Tributary of Wylye. Trout, grayling, roach, dace, chub. Mostly preserved by landowners. Fishing stations: **Wilton, Tisbury**. Tisbury AC has 3m, guest tickets from Hon Sec. Salisbury & Dist AC has a short stretch at Barford St Martin; also at Bulbridge, on the Earl of Pembroke's estate; also Nadder Meadows, a newly acquired stretch on a 5-year lease: dry fly for trout and grayling. The Club also has 2m of coarse fishing 10 mins from Salisbury, with views of Cathedral and water meadows; membership circa £130, conc; limited dt from Reids Tackle or John Eadie (*below*). Tisbury AC also has Old Wardour and Dinton Lakes; carp, roach, pike, tench; st £25, conc. Fishing Breaks Ltd, Walton House, 23 Compton Terrace, London N1 2UN (tel: 020 7359 8818; web: www.fishingbreaks.com) has day rods. Tackle shop: Reids Tackle, Kingsway House, Warminster Rd, Wilton SP2 0AT (tel: 01722 743192); John Eadie Ltd, 5 Union Str, Andover SP10 1PA (tel: 01264 351469). Hotel: South Western; Tisbury AC HQ.

AXE

(For close seasons, licences, etc, see South West Region Environment Agency, p19)

Rises in Dorset and flows south to the English Channel at Axemouth. Trout, sea trout and salmon. Fishing difficult to come by, but one or two hotels can provide facilities.

Seaton (Devon). Trout, salmon. Some sea trout fishing from L Burrough, Lower Abbey Farm, Axminster EX13 8TS (tel: 01297 32314). Axe estuary fishable (for bass, mullet, flounders, etc). Salmon, sea trout, rainbow and wild brown trout fishing on 1m at **Colyton**: dt from Mrs E Pady, Higher Cownhayne Farm, Colyton, EX24 6HD (tel: 01297 552267). Hotel: Pole Arms.

Axminster (Devon). Axe, Yarty; trout and salmon. Trouting good especially in April and May. At **Uplyme**, Amherst Lodge, Dorset DT7 3XH (tel: 01297 442 773): day ticket fishery with six fly fishing lakes; brown and rainbow; dt £15 c&r, 2 fish £15 to 6 fish £35; tuition from bailiff. Hotels: Cavalier, Bear Inn, Colyton.

Crewkerne (Som). Stoke-sub-Hamdon AA has trout fishing from Bow Mills to Creedy Bridge on **Parrett**; members only. Joining fee £12, conc; dt £4 **Bearley Lake**; wt river £2.50. Yeovil AA has trout and coarse fishing on **Yeo** and tributaries; st £11 for Yeovil section; £12 Ilchester section from tackle shops. Trout fishing in **Sutton Bingham Reservoir**, near Yeovil; enquiries to Fishing Lodge BA22 9QH (tel: 01935 872389). At North Perrott is Pitt Farm (tel: 01460 72856); coarse fishing; dt £5. Tackle shops: Yeovil & Dist Angling Centre, 27/29 Forest Hill, Yeovil BA20 2PH (tel: 01935 476777); Stax Angling Centre, South Str, Montacute TA15 6XH (tel: 01935 822645).

BLACKWATER

(For close seasons, licences, etc, see Anglian Region Environment Agency, p21)

Rises in NW of county, flows by Braintree to Maldon and empties into North Sea through large estuary. Coarse fish include pike, chub, rudd and some carp.

Maldon (Essex). Maldon AS has river and pond fishing in Maldon area; three stretches totalling 1½ of **R Blackwater**. All coarse; carp over 30lb, tench, roach, rudd, bream, dace, gudgeon, perch, pike; membership £62, conc; dt £8 (evng £4) for Chelmer from bailiff on bank or tackle shop. RMC Angling **Chigborough** gravel pits of 8½ acres at **Drapers Farm**. Coarse fish: tench, bream, crucian, etc. Group Water. St (2 rods) £30, conc £18. *(For RMC Angling see Chertsey).* Tackle shop: East Essex Angling Centre, 48 The Street, Heybridge, Maldon CM9 4NB (tel: 01621 840414). Hotels: Swan, White Hart, King's Head.

Chigboro Fisheries, Heybridge, Maldon, Essex CM9 4RE (tel: 01621 857368). 4 lakes: Home Water 16 acre lake with brown and rainbow trout of average weight 2lb 11oz, fly only. Lake record, 19¼lb: 4 boats; Rook Hall, 6 acres; Priory Pool, 1 acre; plus big trout water. St, design your own, min 5 tickets; Dt £18 (2 fish), or £28.00 (4 fish), 2 fish + c&r, £25; tuition available. Coarse fishing: four lakes, 20 acres total, large carp and other species, incl catfish to 46lb. St £80; dt £6; £10 24 hrs. Corporate days welcome.

Witham (Essex). Blackwater and **Brain**. Coarse fish. Kelvedon & DAA has 7½m from here to **Braintree**, and also below Witham towards Maldon; members only; sub £60, conc, from tackle shops, including Angling Essentials, 14 Church St, Witham CM8 2JL (tel: 01376 512255). **Witham Lake**, 5½ acres, **Olivers Lake**, 3 acres; **Bovingdon Mere**, **Hatfield Peverel**; 4 acre lake coarse fishery: Colchester APS waters.

Kelvedon (Essex). Kelvedon & DAA has numerous stretches as well as water on Suffolk **Stour**; Essex **Colne**; still waters; **Tiptree Reservoir**; three 2-acre pits at **Layer Marney** near Tiptree, Colchester; **Hunts Farm Reservoir**, near Maldon; **Shemming's Pond** near Kelvedon: all good mixed fisheries; two 6-acre **Silver End Pits** near Witham; **Seabrook's Reservoir**, at Little Leighs nr **Chelmsford**, and **Martin's Pits** (one small pit only) in Tiptree (all good carp waters); all members only; sub £60 (conc) from tackle shops in Chelmsford, Witham, Tiptree and Colchester. Tackle shop: Angling Essentials, 14 Church St. Witham CM8 2JL (tel: 01376 512255).

Coggeshall (Essex). Coarse fish. Colchester APS fish Houchins Reservoirs, *(see Colchester)*.

Braintree (Essex). Braintree and Bocking AS owns most of water on main river, both banks, from Shalford to Bradwell Village and on **Pant**. Well stocked with roach, perch, rudd, dace, and chub. St £20, Juv £6.50, OAP £5 from subscription Sec. *For Gosfield and Sparrows Lakes see Essex (Streams and Lakes).* Tackle shop: Bill's Tackle, 95-97 High St, Braintree CM7 1JS (tel: 01376 552767). Hotels: Horne, White Horse.

Chelmer and CAN: Coarse fish:

Chelmsford (Essex). River stocked: roach, dace, bream, tench, carp, pike, perch, chub. Public fishing in town parks. Chelmsford AA has fishing as follows: Boreham Mere, Boreham; Blunts Mere, Cants Mere and Wick Mere, **Ulting**; Broads Mere and Tuftnell Mere, **Great Waltham**; all mixed fisheries, with carp, bream, tench, rudd, roach, barbel, chub; all members only; st £55 + £7 entry, conc. Instruction is offered, and matches are organised. Contact Hon Sec. Newland

Hall Fisheries, **Roxwell**, Chelmsford CM1 4LH (tel: 01245 231463), have Brook, Moat, Park and Osiers Lakes, total of approx 10 acres. The fishing is for carp, roach, tench, etc, with high match weights. Platforms for disabled. Dt available. RMC Angling gravel pit at **Boreham** offers good mixed fishing, incl carp to over 20lb on a small secluded Special Venue lake. St £30, conc £18. *(For RMC Angling, see Chertsey).* Marconi AS has **Boreham Pits** 2, 3, 4 (carp, tench, bream, pike etc) and **Boreham Quarry** (carp & pike); also 5m **R Wid**; club Hylands Reservoir, 2 acres; mixed coarse; members only; st £60; apply Marconi Social Club, Behive Lane, Chelmsford. Blasford Hill Fisheries, Little Waltham, nr Chelmsford CM3 3PL (tel: 01245 362772): lakes stocked with carp, tench, roach, and other species. Dt £5, conc, on bank. Tackle shops: Ronnie Crowe Ltd, 63 Maldon Rd, Gt Baddow, Chelmsford CM2 7DN (tel: 01245 471246), who has permits for local clubs. Hotels: County; White Hart, Witham.

BLYTH (Northumberland)

(For close seasons, licences, etc, see North East Region Environment Agency, p20)

Rises near Throckington and flows 20m to North Sea at Blyth. Trout and grayling with coarse fish (especially roach) in lower reaches. Stretches from Stannington A1 Bridge to Bedlington controlled by Bedlington and Blagdon AA, members only, no tickets.

BRUE

(For close seasons, licences, etc, see South West Region Environment Agency, p19).

Rises in Mendips and flows to Bristol Channel at Burnham. Coarse fish throughout. From West Lydford to Glastonbury, a number of weirs provide deep water in which coarse fish predominate. A good late season river, contains numbers of most coarse species.

Highbridge (Som). Roach, bream, etc. North Somerset AA fishes Rivers **Kenn**, **Apex Pit**, between Highbridge and Burnham, (match record 55lb 11oz), Newtown Pond, Highbridge (carp to 20lb), Walrow Ponds, North Drain; st £20; wt £10; dt £3, conc (all assn waters); from local tackle shops. Weston-super-Mare AA has **River Axe** fishing, Old R Axe, South Drain. Bridgwater AA has **Huntspill River**, **Kings Sedgemoor Drain**, North and South Drains. **Emerald Pool Fishery**, off Puriton Rd, Highbridge TA9 3NL (tel: 01278 794707), purpose-made lake stocked with large carp, tench, perch, bream, etc; dt and refreshments on site. **Lands End Fisheries**, Heath House,

Wedmore BS28 4UQ (tel: 07977 545882), three lakes with various carp species and others; dt £5, conc. Permits for these and local fishings, and club information from tackle shops Veals Fishing Tackle, 1A Church Str, Highbridge TA9 3AE (tel: 01278 786934). Highbridge AA is part of N. Somerset AA. Further information from Hon Sec. BB&WAA has 3 fields u/s of Black Bull Bridge on R Brue (right bank), plus 2 fields u/s on left bank, and 2 fields d/s on right bank; as well as Pawlett Ponds and other lakes; st £30, conc £10, dt £4. Hotels: Highbridge; The George (clubs accommodated) is recommended locally, for visiting anglers.

Bason Bridge (Som). Area around milk factory noted for carp; fish run up to 35lb or so. Also roach, chub, tench, perch and pike. BB&WAA has 150 metres on right bank d/s from bridge to old station house: dt £4. Contact Veals Fishing Tackle, 1A Church Str, Highbridge TA9 3AE (tel: 01278 786934).

Mark (Som). Carp, pike, perch, roach, chub, tench. North Somerset AA has 2½m on river and 3 to 4m on North Drain; dt and wt from Hon Sec (see Highbridge). Inn: Pack Horse.

Glastonbury (Som). Roach, bream, chub, etc, throughout the River Brue. Glaston Manor AA has approx 12m of water from Lydford to **Westhay**; membership and st from tackle shops. At **Tealham Moor**, BB&WAA has 2m from North Drain Pumping Station u/s; dt £4 from tackle shops. Tackle shops: Street Angling Centre, 160 High Str, Street BA16 0NH (tel: 01458 447830); Thatchers Pet & Tackle, 18 Queen St, Wells BA5 3DP (tel: 01749 673513).

BUDE RIVER AND CANAL

(For close seasons, licences, etc, see South West Region Environment Agency, p19)

Bude Canal AA has 1¼ miles of wider than average canal with good banks and full variety of coarse fish; dt on bank.

Bude (Cornwall). Bass from beaches, breakwater and rocks; bass and mullet in estuary of Bude River; details from Hon Sec Bude & Dist SAA. Bude AA has fishing on a total of 6½m of banks of **Tamar** and **Claw** from near Bude to half way to Launceston; wild brown trout and some dace in downstream beats; membership £5, wt £5, dt £3; membership enquiries (with 50p if map req.) to Hon Sec,

Bude AA. **Tamar Lake** and **Crowdy** (trout reservoir) controlled by South West Lakes Trust *(see Cornwall lakes, etc)*. **Bude Canal** (roach, bream, eels, dace, perch, carp to 25lb and tench) 1m from town centre towards Marhamchurch leased by Bude Canal AA; dt £4, conc; on bank. Tackle shop: Bude Angling Supplies, 6 Queen St, Bude EX23 8BB (tel: 01288 353396).

BURE

(see Norfolk and Suffolk Broads)

CAMEL

(For close seasons, licences etc, see South West Region Environment Agency, p19)

A spate river, rising on Bodmin Moor near Davidstow, flowing about 30m to enter the Atlantic between Pentire and Stepper Points. Salmon, sea trout and small brown trout. Grilse from June, with the main runs in October, November and December. Sea trout from June to Aug. Best brown trout fishing in tributary **De Lank**. Salmon fishing in upper reaches dependent on heavy rainfall. There is a voluntary restriction in operation covering the whole river. No fishing in April; in Sept all sea trout to be returned, and a limit of 2 salmon per day and 4 per week, and 4 sea trout per day; also no selling of fish and no maggots. A salmon broodstock scheme operates Nov/Dec when rod-caught salmon can be donated to a designated hatchery. Salmon season ends 15 Dec.

Wadebridge (Cornwall). Trout, sea trout, salmon; good mullet, bass and flounder fishing in tidal reaches; estuary is now a bass nursery area, restrictions apply; shore fishing allowed. Approx 6m held by Wadebridge & Dist AA at Pencarrow, Grogley, Wenford, and **River Allen** above Sladesbridge, 5½m. Membership of Wadebridge & Dist, via long waiting list; dt on all waters except Grogley, £15 to £25 (depending on season), wt £60 to 30 Sept only; thereafter, 1 Oct to 30 Nov, daily limit of 4 dt at £25, conc; and sea-

fishing boat bookings, from Camel Valley Sportfishing, 5 Polmorla Rd, Wadebridge PL27 7NB (tel: 01208 816403). B&B St Anne's Cottage (tel: 01208 77413); Halfway House, St Jidgey (tel: 01208 812524). *(For sea fishing see Padstow.)*

Bodmin (Cornwall); between Camel and Fowey; Bodmin AA issues visitor permits (ten per day) on some 12 miles of the best water; details from Hon Sec; wt £40, dt £15 from May 1-Nov 30; no permits in Dec; st, wt and dt from Hon Sec; concessions for jun and OAP; free maps from Hon Sec, on receipt of sae. Liskeard & DAC has stretch of Camel; apply to local tackle shops *(see Liskeard)*. Mr T Jackson, Butterwell, Nanstallon, Bodmin, PL30 5LQ (tel: 01208 831515) has 1½m salmon and sea trout fishing, occasional day permits with preference given to residents, fly only, June-Aug; self-catering cottage and limited B&B. **Fenwick Trout Fishery**, Old Coach Rd, Dunmere, Bodmin PL31 2RD (tel: 01208 78296) features two acre lake stocked with rainbow trout, record 13lbs 3oz, and 570 yards of salmon fishing on R Camel. Dt £22 4 fish; £14 2 fish; £15 salmon river bank permit. Lakeview Country Club, **Lanivet** (tel: 01208 831808) has 3 coarse fishing lakes, 6 acres, stocked; specimen carp, bream,

tench. Dt £5, conc. **Temple Trout Fishery**, Temple Rd, Temple PL30 4HW (tel: 01208 821730); 2 gravel pits totalling 7 acres, stocked with brown, rainbow, golden and blue trout; range of dt (at fishery); apply at fishery for membership of Temple Steelheads FFC. **Innis Moore Trout Fishery**, 7 acres. Contact tackle shop: Roger's Tackle Shop, Stan Mays Store, Higher Bore St, Bodmin PL31 1DZ (tel: 01208 78006) (closed Wednesday), who also issue tickets for Fowey (Lostwithiel AA and Liskeard AA waters), Camel (Bodmin AA waters), Wadebridge AA on Camel. Also prime private beat on Camel: contact Bill Pope, 3 Tresarrett Manor Farm, Blisland PL30 4QQ (tel: 01208 850338).

CHESHIRE (Lakes/Reservoirs)

APPLETON RESERVOIR, nr Warrington. Trout fishery controlled by Warrington AA; members only; under negotiation as we go to press: membership is by annual subscription plus joining fee, with generous concessions. This is one of the larger fishing clubs of Great Britain, controlling approximately sixty fisheries on rivers, lakes, reservoirs, canals and pools; contact Hon Sec.

ARNFIELD RESERVOIR, Tintwistle, nr Manchester. United Utilities trout fishery controlled by Arnfield FFC; game fish; contact Hon Sec.

BLACKSHAW MOOR LAKES, Leek. 4 acre coarse fishery; carp, tench, bream, roach. Prince Albert AS water, members only.

BOSLEY RESERVOIR. Fishing station: **Bosley.** Roach (good), bream, pike, perch, carp. Prince Albert AS water, members only.

BOTTOMS RESERVOIR. Macclesfield, Cheshire. Prince Albert AS. Dt £5, conc £2, issued from Barlows of Bond Street, 47 Bond St, Macclesfield SK11 6QS (tel: 01625 619935).

CAPESTHORNE POOLS, Siddington. Large carp, tench, bream, roach, rudd and

pike. All pools now controlled by Stoke-on-Trent AS; no dt; season 1 June to 14 March; contact Hon Sec.

DOVE MERE, SAND MERE, Allostock, Knutsford. Prince Albert AS waters, members only. Heavily stocked, including large carp. St £85; waiting list.

GREAT BUDWORTH MERE (or MARBURY MERE). Nr. Northwich, 50-acre lake holding good bream, pike, etc; Northwich AA; apply to Hon Sec. **Pickmere** and **Petty Pool** are assn waters nearby.

HORSECOPPICE RESERVOIR, Macclesfield. Trout fishing leased to Dystelegh Fly FC; members only, no permits.

LANGLEY BOTTOMS and **Lamaload Reservoirs.** Nr Macclesfield. Langley Bottoms (dt £5 from Barlows) now coarse fishing, Prince Albert AS. Lamaload, Good fly fishing for trout. Prince Albert AS. Limited dt £12 from Barlows of Bond Street, 47 Bond St, Macclesfield SK11 6QS (tel: 01625 619935).

LEADBEATERS RESERVOIR. Controlled by Prince Albert AS; members only. Tackle shop: Barlows of Bond Street, 47 Bond St, Macclesfield SK11 6QS (tel: 01625 619935).

Fishing available?

If you own, manage, or know of first-class fishing available to the public which should be considered for inclusion in **Where to Fish** *please apply to the publishers (address in the front of the book) for a form for submission, on completion, to the Editor. (Inclusion is at the sole discretion of the Editor). No charge is made for editorial inclusion.*

LYMM DAM, Lymm, beside A56. 15 acre lake, good all year round fishing with big carp (a lot in excess of 20lb) and pike, bream (to 10lb 3oz). Lymm AC water, many pegs, bookable for matches to a maximum of 30 pegs; contact Hon Sec for this and seven other dt waters; membership £42 plus £16 entry, conc; dt £2.50 on bank, conc.

OULTON MILL POOL. Fishing station: Tarporley. Well stocked with good carp, bream, tench and pike. Dt from Mill Office.

RIDGEGATE RESERVOIR, Macclesfield, brown and rainbow. Macclesfield FC, dt £12, from Hon Sec; some river and stream fishing for members only.

ROMAN LAKES LEISURE PARK, Marple, nr Stockport SK6 7HB (tel: 0161 4272039; web: www.romanlakes.co.uk). Roach, perch, tench, bream to 8lb, carp to 30lbs, pike to 20lbs. Dt £5 per rod, juv £3.50, with concessions, at site (day permits only).

ROSSMERE LAKE. 6 acres. Fishing station: **Wilmslow.** Heavily stocked. 80 match pegs. Prince Albert AS, members only.

TEGGSNOSE RESERVOIR, Macclesfield. Now coarse, with carp to 20lb, bream 5lb plus, tench, roach, perch; Macclesfield Waltonian AC. Dt only from Barlows of Bond Street, 47 Bond St, Macclesfield SK11 6QS (tel: 01625 619935).

THORNEYCROFT HALL LAKES, Gawsworth. Prince Albert AS water, members only. Carp, tench, roach, pike.

GAWSWORTH FISHERY, Wall Pool Lodge, off Church Lane, Gawsworth, SK11 9RQ (tel: 01260 223442); 3 lake complex with coarse fishing, open all year round, dawn to dusk; dt on bank, £6 one rod, conc for OAP and juv matches and night fishing by arrangement; barbless hooks; also 60 peg match canal on Serpentine.

COLNE (Essex)

(For close seasons, licences, etc, see Anglian Region Environment Agency, p21)

Rises in north of county and flows to North Sea via Colchester. Improving as coarse fishery.

These youngsters, members of the Bollington & Royal Oak Angling Society, consider their tactics.

Colchester (Essex). Colchester APS controls one short stretch, with roach, chub, perch, pike, bream, dace; no tickets. The society's other waters, with excellent catfish, carp and pike fishing, include **Layer Pit**; pike, perch, bream, roach, rudd, tench, carp; **Houchins Reservoirs**, Coggeshall, coarse, large catfish; **Snake Pit**, large carp and catfist, pike, tench; **Inworth Grange**, Tiptree (mainly carp); five stretches on Suffolk **Stour**; **Hatfield Peverell Lakes**; Witham Lake; **Olivers Lake** at Witham; **Preston Lake**, 20 acre mixed coarse fishery, and Bovingdon Lakes, good carp. Members only on all waters except Oliver's Lake, dt and membership from Angling Essentials *(below)*: st £60, conc to jun, OAP, disabled. Just south of Clochester is National Trust 2½ acre Mill Pond, Paxman's AC water, members only (tel: 01206 798457). Colchester Piscatorial Society has water on Langham Ponds, 5m of Stour and 2m of Colne; st £35 members only. ½m of Colne fished by Kelvedon & DAA. Colchester tackle shops: K D Radcliffe Ltd, 150 High Str, CO1 1PG (tel: 01206 572758); Carp Unlimited, Unit 16, Peartree Business Centre, Stanway, Colchester CO3 5JN (tel: 01206 760775); W E Wass, 73 London Road, Copford, Colchester CO6 1LG (tel: 01206 212478). Witham tackle shop: Angling Essentials, 14 Church St. Witham CM8 2JL (tel: 01376 512255). Hotels: George, Red Lion.

Aldham (Essex). Colnes AS has water at Fordham and Aldham, three stretches of Stour near Bures, three reservoirs, one lake and two ponds, and Blackwater stretch; most species; improved access for disabled; members only; contact Hon Sec or Sudbury tackle shops.

Halstead (Essex). Halstead and Hedingham AC waters are: stretch of R Colne; several miles of **R Pant**; Sparrows Pond, **Gosfield**, with coarse fishing incl carp, tench, bream etc; **Halstead Reservoir**, with carp, tench, rudd; **Stebbing Reservoir**, with carp, bream, perch; Gosfield Sandpits, with tench, bream, perch, etc. Membership £23, conc, from Bill's Tackle, 95-97 High St, Braintree CM7 1JS (tel: 01376 552767); no dt. For **Rayne Lodge Fishery**, Rayne Rd, Braintree CM7 2QT (tel: 01376 345719), carp, roach, rudd, bream, tench: dt at the lakes, £7, juv £5.

COQUET

(For close seasons, licences, etc, see North East Region Environment Agency, p20)

Rises in Cheviots and enters North Sea near Warkworth. Salmon, sea trout and trout. Sport still very good. Facilities for visitors. Good run of spring salmon.

Warkworth (Northumberland). Trout, sea trout; salmon from Feb onwards to late summer and autumn. Duke of Northumberland leases large part of his water to Northumbrian Anglers Federation; st £85 salmon, £60 trout; conc for OAP; visitor all-fish all-waters (excl tidal) wt £70; dt £25. Applications to Head Bailiff, Thirston Mill, Felton, Morpeth NE65 9EH (tel: 01670 787663; www.northumbria-nanglersfed.co.uk), or tackle dealers for trout permits only; additional permit for tidal section £65. Permits for 2m beat, situated 1m d/s from Weldon Bridge, Longframlington, £22 or £16 (salmon, brown, sea trout), from The Weldon Gun Room, Weldon Bridge, Longframlington, NE65 8AY (tel: 01665 570011).

Acklington (Northumberland). Trout, sea trout and salmon. Northumbrian AF water on Coquet and tributary, Thirston Burn.

Felton (Northumberland). Salmon, sea trout (spring and autumn), trout; river permit from water bailiff, Head Bailiff, Thirston Mill, Felton, Morpeth NE65 9EH (tel: 01670 787663; www.northumbriananglersfed.co.uk). EA licence from Post Office, Main St, NE65 9PN (tel: 01670 787239).

Weldon Bridge (Northumberland). Nearest station: Morpeth, 9½m. Trout (sea trout and salmon, late summer and autumn). Anglers Arms Hotel, Weldon Bridge, Long Framlington NE65 8AX, has fishing, maximum 3 rods, on 1m north bank. Free for residents, otherwise £10 dt (tel: 01665 570655).

Rothbury (Northumberland). A late salmon run and excellent sea trout fishing in June and Oct. Brown trout, including fish to 3lb. Northumbrian AF has 4m of Coquet *(see Warkworth)*. **Fontburn Reservoir**, Ewesley, nr Rothbury, trout fishery of 87 acres with wild browns, and stocked browns, rainbows, fly only; record rain-

bow, 26lb 8oz; brown 9lb 4oz; dt water (tel: 01669 621368); licences from machine on site (£1 coins needed). Hotels: Queens Head, Rothbury; Newcastle House, Rothbury; Three Wheat Head, Thropton; Whitton Farm House.
Holystone (Northumberland). Salmon (late), trout; mostly private. Holystone Burn, trout; Grasslees Burn, trout. Inn: Salmon, where particulars may be had.
Harbottle (Northumberland). Good trout and some late salmon fishing on Coquet and Alwin. Upper Coquetdale AC has extensive parts of upper river; members only.

CORNWALL (streams, lakes, etc)

(For close seasons, licences, etc, see South West Region Environment Agency p19)

ARGAL RESERVOIR, nr Penryn. South West Lakes Trust coarse fishery of 65 acres, with carp to 35lbs, large perch, pike to 35lb, bream, tench, eels. St £125 (day and night), £85 st (day), 24-hour £8.75, dt £4.75, conc £3.75; open all year, 24 hr day. Permit from self-service kiosk.

BOSCATHNOE RESERVOIR, Penzance; 4 acre, stocked South West Lakes Trust coarse fishery, with bream, roach, tench, crucian carp, gudgeon, eels; st £125 (day and night), £85 st (day), 24-hour £8.75, dt £4.75, conc £3.75, from Newtown Angling Centre, Newtown, Germoe, Penzance TR20 9AE (tel: 01736 763721), or Heamoor PO, Golval (tel: 01736 365265); or H Symons, Ironmonger, Market Place, St Ives TR26 1RZ (tel: 01736 796200).

BUSSOW RESERVOIR St Ives. South West Lakes Trust coarse fishery, with bream, roach, tench, carp, eels, rudd, perch, etc. Open all year, 24 hour day; St £125 (day and night), £85 st (day), 24-hour £8.75, dt £4.75, conc £3.75 from Newtown Angling Centre, Newtown, Germoe, Penzance TR20 9AE (tel: 01736 763721); or H Symons (below). Other coarse fisheries near St Ives: **Nance Lakes**, with carp, roach, rudd, bream; **Woonsmith**, with carp, roach, tench, rudd, bream, etc, and trout; **Sharkeys Pit**, Hayle: carp, roach, rudd, gudgeon, eels; permits from H Symons, Ironmonger, Market Place, St Ives TR26 1RZ (tel: 01736 796200).

STITHIANS RESERVOIR, Redruth. 247 acres. South West Lakes Trust brown and rainbow trout fishery; fly only. Season Mar 15-Oct 31. Full st £200, dt £12, conc £10.50. Limited boats, bookable 24 hrs in advance. Permits from Watersports Centre, Stithians (tel: 01209 860301).

PORTH RESERVOIR, Newquay. 40 acres, South West Lakes Trust fishery, bream, rudd, tench, roach, perch, eels, and carp. Open all year, 24 hour day; St £125 (day and night), £85 st (day); 24-hour £8.75, dt £4.75, conc £3.75 from self-service unit at car park.

CROWDY RESERVOIR, Camelford. 115 acre South West Lakes Trust wild trout fishery. Fly, spinning and bait fishing zoned. Season Mar 15-Oct 12. Free to valid EA licence holders.

SIBLYBACK LAKE, Liskeard. 140 acres. Fly only, premier South West Lakes Trust fishery, with stocked rainbow trout. Season Mar 23-Oct 31. Dt £17.50 from self-service kiosk; st £400, conc; Watersports Centre, Siblyback, Common Moor, Liskeard. Ranger (tel: 01579 342366). Boats (bookable in advance) and bank fishing.

COLLIFORD LAKE, Liskeard. 900 acres. South West Lakes Trust fly fishery, with natural brown trout only. Full st £130, dt £9.75, conc. No boats. Open 15 Mar-12 Oct. Permits from Colliford Tavern, Colliford Lake, St Neot, Liskeard PL14 6PZ (tel: 01208 821335).

CONSTANTINE BROOK. Fishing station; **Constantine**, ns Penryn WR, 6m. Trout. Constantine joins estuary of **Helford River**. Sea fishing off Helford Mouth *(see Falmouth)*. Ashton, near **Helston, Wheal Grey Pool**; stocked coarse fishery with large carp.

DRIFT RESERVOIR. Near **Penzance** (3m); sixty-five acres in quiet valley. Wild brown and stocked rainbow trout (fly only). Limit, 3 rainbows/day, 3 wild browns. Wt £30, dt £10, eveng £7, from West Cornwall Angling, Alexandra Road, Penzance (tel: 01736 362363), Newtown Angling Centre, Newtown, Germoe, Penzance TR20 9AE (tel: 01736 763721); honesty box in boathouse. 2m from Penzance, **Tin Dene Fishery**: 2 pools with carp to 25lbs, roach, rudd, etc, trout; dt £3, conc; Mr John Laity, Bostrase, Millpool, Goldsithney TR20 9JG (tel: 01736 763486). Also St **Buryan Lake** carp pool.

HAYLE. Fishing stations: **Relubbus,**

Hayle Causeway and **Gwinear**. Trout and sea trout. Bass and mullet fishing from the Estuary; some bass on Gwithian Rocks. South West Lakes Trust has mainly coarse and fly fishing in the area. Marazion AC has three coarse pools in St Erth, nr Hayle, tickets, dt £5 (conc) from The County Angler, 39 Cross St, Camborne TR14 8ES (tel: 01209 718490); Newtown Angling Centre, Newtown, Germoe, Penzance TR20 9AE (tel: 01736 763721). Tackle shop: Angoves Sports, 40 Fore St, Copperhouse, Hayle TR27 4DY (tel: 01736 752238).

WEST LOOE RIVER. A small spate river running through Herodsfoot to the Looe estuary. Good runs of sea trout, which fish well in summer. Liskeard & District AC has water. Tickets from Tremar Tropicals, 11 Market St, Liskeard PL14 3JH (tel: 01579 343177); chandlers at The Quay, East Looe; or Lashbrooks Tackle Shop, Bodmin. **East Looe River** also fishes well for sea trout, but local knowledge is required. 6m west of Looe on B3359 near Lanreath, are Shilla Mill Lakes and Lodges: 2 coarse lakes, one specimen carp lake; fishing is for guests, no day permits; contact Mr & Mrs J Pearce, Lanreath, Looe PL13 2PE (tel: 01503 220886). Hotels: Punch Bowl, Lanreath; Kylmiaven, Looe. Looe: good sea fishing. Boats available, tackle and tickets from East Looe Chandlers on the quay in E Looe.

LYNHER. A noted salmon and sea trout river with a reputation for early fish. Rises on Bodmin Moor, as do Fowey and Camel, and runs to Tamar estuary via Saint Germans. Smaller than Fowey but more natural, there being no big reservoirs in catchment to modify spates. Good runs of sea trout (end Mar to end May), smaller sea trout and grilse from June, and good summer night fishing for sea trout. Season ends 14 Oct, end of season has good salmon fishing, given some rain.

Callington (Cornwall). Liskeard & District AC has several good beats on Lynher, also on **Fowey** and **Inny River** (tributary of Tamar), all providing salmon and sea trout. For sea trout only, club has beats on **Seaton** and **West Looe Rivers**. Visitor tickets from Tremar Tropicals, 11 Market St, Liskeard PL14 3JH (tel: 01579 343177); East Looe Chandlers on the quay in E Looe; or Lashbrooks Tackle Shop, Bodmin; membership applications (limited to 250) from Trevor Sobey, Trevartha Farm, Pengover, nr Liskeard PL14 3NJ (tel: 01579 343382); **Siblyback** and **Colliford** lakes are near; memb £60 + £15 joining fee, wt £50, dt £15, conc.

LUXULYAN RIVER. Fishing station: **Par**. Polluted, but tributary **Redmoor River** has good head of trout. Sand-eels at Par Sands, mackerel from the bay, pollack by Gribben Head and near harbour, and bass between harbour and Shorthorne Beach. Boats for hire at Par and Polkerris. Hotels: Royal, Par; Carlyon Bay, St Austell.

MELANHYL. Newquay. Brown trout and occasional sea trout. Contact. Sec, St Mawgan AC or The Merrymoor Inn, Mawgan Porth for tickets.

OLD MILL RESERVOIR, Dartmouth. 4 acre South West Lakes Trust coarse fishery with carp, roach, rudd, bream, tench, eels. Open all year, 24 hour day. Season ticket only, on application to South West Lakes Trust, Higher Coombepark, Lewdowne, Okehampton, Devon EX20 4QT (tel: 01837 871565).

PETHERICK WATER. Fishing station: **Padstow**. Small trout. Estuary now a bass nursery area, prohibiting fishing for bass. Other species scarce.

RETALLACK WATERS, St Columb, TR9 6DE (tel: 01637 881160): 20 acres of water, with separate coarse and specimen lakes; carp and pike to 25lb, roach, rudd, tench, eels; dt water, tackle and bait from 'The Tackle Cabin' on site; open seven days a week. **Meadowside Fisheries**, Winnards Perch, St Columb Major TR9 6DH (tel: 01637 880544; web: www. meadowsidefisheries.co.uk); two lakes with carp and mixed coarse fish; fishery is incorporated within the Cornish Birds of Prey Centre; dt £4.50 1 rod, £5.50 2 rods, conc: Maggie Early.

ST ALLEN RIVER, Truro. St Allen and

Keep the banks clean

Several clubs have stopped issuing tickets to visitors because of the state of the banks after they have left. Spend a few moments clearing up. This includes lengths of broken nylon. If discarded, serious injuries can be caused to wild birds and to livestock.

Kenwyn Rivers at Truro; **Tresillian** River (3m from Truro on St Austell road); **Kennel** or **Perranarworthal** River (5m from Truro); a few sea trout run into **Lower Tresillian** River. Gwarnick Mill Fly Fishing Lake, St Allen, Truro TR4 9QU (tel: 01872 540487); lake of 1½ acres fed by St Allen River, with rainbow trout av 2lb; dt £21 for 4 fish, £17 for 3 fish, £12 for 2 fish. Truro tackle shops: City Angling Centre, Palace Yard, Pydar Str, TR1 2AZ (tel: 01872 275340); Wsb Tackle, Unit 3a Goonhavern Ind Est, TR4 9QL (tel: 01872 571752). Hotel: The Morgans, Perranporth *(see also Sea Fishing Stations)*.

SEATON RIVER. Rises near Liskeard, runs through Hessenford to the sea across the beach at Seaton. It fishes well for sea trout from May onwards, with occasional browns. Liskeard & Dist AC has lower stretch, which is the only fishable part of river. Tickets from Tremar Tropicals, 11 Market St, Liskeard PL14 3JH (tel: 01579 343177); East Looe Chandlers on the quay in E Looe; or Lashbrooks Tackle Shop, Bodmin.

TAMAR LAKE (UPPER), Bude. 81 acres, South West Lakes Trust coarse fishery with carp, bream, tench, roach, rudd, eels. St £125 (day and night), £85 st (day) from SWLT; 24-hour £8.75, dt £4.75, conc £3.75, from self-service kiosk on site. Tamar Lake (Lower) now closed, other than to South West Lakes AA; apply to Trust office.

TIDDY. Fishing station: **St Germans.** Sea trout to Tideford, trout elsewhere.

VALENCY. Fishing station: **Boscastle.** Valency is 4m long; holds small trout and few sea trout. Hotels: Wellington, in Boscastle (Environment Agency licences); Eliot Arms, Tregadillet 15m. Sea fishing good for bass, mackerel, pollack, etc.

WHITEACRES COUNTRY PARK, White Cross, **Newquay,** TR8 4LW (tel: 01726 860220). Eleven stocked coarse fishing lakes in 100 acres. Carp to 25lb, tench 7lb, catfish to 45lb, large bream and roach. Night fishing, matches and competitions.

CUCKMERE

(For close seasons, licences, etc, see Southern Region Environment Agency, p18).

Formed by two tributaries, which join at Hellingly, and enters sea at Cuckmere Haven, west of Beachy Head. Mainly coarse fish, roach, bream, chub, carp, perch, dace and pike.

Alfriston (E Sussex). Fishing controlled by the Southdown AA, membership from The Polegate Angling Centre or any Eastbourne tackle shop. Dt £5 for several club fisheries. Below Alfriston Lock the river is salt and tidal, being open to mouth at Cuckmere Haven. In summer grey mullet are plentiful near Exceat Bridge (Eastbourne-Seaford road); also bass and occasionally sea trout. Cuckmere, tidal to ½m upstream from Alfriston. At **Berwick,** Langley AC has coarse fishing on Batbrooks Pond; club also fishes **Langney Haven, Hurst Haven, Kentland Fleet.** Tickets from Tony's Tackle, 211 Seaside, Eastbourne BN22 7NP (tel: 01323 731388); Polegate Angling Centre, 101 Station Road, Polegate BN26 6EB (tel: 01323 486379).

Hailsham (E Sussex). Cuckmere 2m. Southdown AA (formed 1997 from merger of Hailsham AA and Compleat Anglers FC) has extensive fishing on Cuckmere between Alfreston and Horsebridge (Hailsham); **Wallers Haven; Pevensey Haven,** and other waters. Membership £50, conc, dt £5 for accompanied guests on some fisheries from Hon Sec or tackle shops: Polegate Angling Centre, 101 Station Road, Polegate BN26 6EB (tel: 01323 486379); Tony's Tackle, 211 Seaside, Eastbourne BN22 7NP (tel: 01323 731388).

CUMBRIA (lakes)

(See English Lake District)

CUMBRIA (streams)

(For close seasons, licences, etc, see NW Region Environment Agency, p20, unless otherwise stated).

ANNAS. Fishing station: **Bootle.** Small trout; good sea trout and salmon; late.

Millom AA has fishing, also water on **Esk, Lickle, Irt, Duddon, Devoke Water, Black Beck** and **Lazy.** St £100 + £20 entrance from Hon Sec, Millom & Dist AA. Dt £12 from Millom TI; Broughton TI; Haverigg PO; Waberthwaite PO. Environment Agency licences from Waberthwaithe P O, Haverigg P O, Millom P O.

BLACK BECK. Fishing station: **Green Road.** This stream rises on Thwaites Fell, and in 7½m reaches Duddon Estuary. Millom AA has water, entrance, Race Grove, The Green, nr Millom. Tickets from secretary.

CALDER. Empties into Irish Sea some 150 yards from mouth of Ehen. Salmon, sea trout, a few brown trout. Sea trout run large; 10lb and more. Best June onwards: good salmon fishing, July-Oct.

EHEN. Outflow of Ennerdale Water. Flows into Irish Sea on west coast of Cumberland. Salmon, sea trout (June to Oct) and brown trout. Egremont & Dist AA has good salmon, sea trout and brown trout fishing for 7m both banks, from **Egremont** to Sellafield; st £30, wt £30, no dt, conc; May 1-Oct 31 apply Hon Sec. Good fishing in upper reaches held by Wath Brow and Ennerdale AA; st and wt: from Farren Family Store, 50 Main Str, Cleator CA23 3BX (tel: 01946 810038). Hotels: Royal Oak, Beckermet; Sea Cote (St Bees).

ELLEN. Rises on Great Lingy Hill and flows into the Solway Firth at Maryport. Salmon and sea trout runs increasing; best late July onwards. Good brown trout fishing (Mar-June best).

Aspatria (Cumbria). Trout; sea trout, and salmon from July. Hotels: Grapes, Sun.

ESK. Rises near Scawfell and flows into Irish Sea near Ravenglass. Good runs of salmon, sea trout, July onwards.

Ravenglass (Cumbria). Salmon, sea trout. Rivers Mite and Irt here join Esk estuary *(see also Irt).* Millom AA has south bank on Esk at Ravenglass, in three stretches. Membership, wt and dt from Sec. May and June are best for trout; Sept, Oct for salmon.

Eskdale (Cumbria). Trout, sea trout, salmon; various private owners. Millom &

Dist AA fishes Dalegarth Estate water, two beats at Gill Force and Beckfoot; good fly fishing, and worming; also stretch at Brantrake, with sea trout from June, salmon from July, Sept-Oct best months. Contact Hon Sec. Inexpensive fishing on **Wastwater** and **Burnmoor Tarn.** Good sea fishing for bass within five miles.

IRT. Outflow of Wastwater, joining Esk in tidal water. **Bleng** is main tributary. Runs of salmon and sea trout July onwards, some heavy fish taken. Gosforth Angler's Club has National Trust stretch; no boats, weekly permits obtainable: apply Hon Sec.

Holmrook (Cumbria). Salmon, sea trout, brown trout. Short free stretch in village. Millom AA holds two stretches, approx 1,200 yds, Holme Bridge and Drigg Village; tickets from Holmrook Garage; Waberthwaithe and Haverigg POs.

Netherwastdale (Cumbria). On **Wastwater Lake;** trout, permits *(see English Lake District).* Greendale Tarn and Low Tarn feed Wastwater. Sport is good in May and June.

MITE. Flows south for short course from slopes near Eskdale to join estuary of Irt and Esk at **Ravenglass.** A late river. Sea trout, good brown trout, occasional small salmon later on, but few opportunities for visitors.

POAKA BECK. Barrow AA water; no dt with membership by member sponsorship.

WAMPOOL. Fishing stations: **Wigton** and **Curthwaite.** Wampool, under the name of Chalk Beck, rises on Broad Moor. Sea trout in lower reaches mostly free.

WAVER. Trout stream, flowing into the Solway Firth. Some water free, but most subject to agreement by farmers and landowners. Waver has run of sea trout and herling, particularly in its lower reaches.

CRUMMOCK BECK (tributary of Waver). Flows into Holm Dub, tributary of Waver. Free, but difficult to fish.

Leegate (Cumbria). Waver, 1m E.

WHICHAM BECK. Fishing Station: **Sile Croft.** After a course of 6m runs into Haverigg Pool, which joins Duddon estuary at Haverigg.

DARENT

(For close seasons, licences, etc, see Southern Region Environment Agency, p18).

Rises by Westerham and enters Thames estuary at Dartford. Water retention has been improved by weirs. Modest trout fishing in upper reaches, coarse fishing downstream, roach, dace, chub.

Dartford (Kent). Dartford & Dist A & PS has lakes along river valley which hold coarse fish, (Brooklands, see Kent) plus stretches of **Medway**, **Beult** and **Lesser Tiese**, members only, waiting list; the Society also has **Sutton at Hone** Lakes: carp, tench, roach, bream, rudd, pike, perch; also **Horton Kirby Lakes**: carp, tench, roach, bream, rudd, crucian carp, pike, perch; st £50 (ladies £25), conc; dt from bailiff on bank; members only. RMC Angling has three lakes at Sutton at Hone. 2 small lakes (1 & 3) are Special Venue lakes with carp, tench and other species. St £40, conc £25. Lake 2 (4 acres) is a Syndicate Venue with a large head of 30lb mirror and common carp to 45lb. Ticket £275 (2 rods) covers Lakes 1 & 3 also; waiting list. (For RMC see Chertsey). Darenth Fishing Complex (tel: 01322 290150): two syndicate lakes, Toplake, and Big Lake, which contain carp over 55lbs; and five day/night ticket lakes, including **Tree**, and **Long Lake**, with good head of small carp, and other coarse fish, incl occasional catfish to 65lbs. Also 3 stocked beginners' ponds fish 1lb-4lb; also 60 peg match lake & specemin carp lake, fish to 30lb. Lamorbey AS fishes 3 acre lake at Lamorbey Park, **Sidcup**; 28 swims, tench, rudd, crucian carp; dt on part of water. Access for disabled. Tackle shops: Dartford Angling Centre, 84 Lowfield St, Dartford DA1 1HS (tel: 01322 228532); Tackle Box, 251 Watling St, Dartford DA2 6EG (tel: 01322 292400); Danson Angling, 159 Blendon Road, Bexley DA5 1BT (tel: 0208 298 9090).

Shoreham (Kent). Trout, chub, roach, dace. Darent Valley Trout Fishers have good 2½m stretch of water between Shoreham and Eynsford; strictly members only (waiting list).

Sevenoaks (Kent). River preserved. Holmesdale ACS has the following waters, for members and guests only: **Chipstead Lakes**, with bream, roach, perch, rudd, carp, pike; **Longford Lake**; similar variety of coarse species; **Montreal Park Lake** nr **Riverhead**, Sevenoaks; mainly junior water; joining fee £20, annual subscription £50, conc, from Hon Sec; and from tackle shops: Biggin Hill Angling Centre, 216-218 Main Road, Biggin Hill, Westerham TN16 3BD (tel: 01959 570265); A & I Tackle, 33-35 High St, Green Street Green, Orpington BR6 6BG (tel: 01689 862302); Manklows Kit & Tackle, 44 Seal Road, Sevenoaks TN14 5AR (tel: 01732 454952). Manklows will supply useful general information about local fishing.

Tributary of the Darent

CRAY: Coarse fish.

Crayford (Kent). Thameside Works AS, (members of Rother Fisheries Association) has fishing for bream, roach, perch, rudd, pike, carp, tench; members only. They also have a lake at Northfleet, Cobham and Shorne Country Park lakes. Coarse fish. Dt for Shorne only, £3.50, £1.50 jun from bailiff. Membership from R Graham, 186 Waterdales, Northfleet DA11 8JW (tel: 01474 351456); (sae please). **Ruxley Pits, Orpington**, coarse fish; Orpington & Dist AA has five lakes, 40 acres in a Nature Reserve, all coarse fish, pike to 28lbs, large tench. Members and guests only; no dt. Tackle shop: A & I Tackle, 33-35 High St, Green Street Green, Orpington BR6 6BG (tel: 01689 862302). Other Assn waters: R Medway and Eden nr Tonbridge; R Teise at Yalding.

DART

(For close seasons, licences, etc, see, South West Region Environment Agency p19)

The East and the West Dart rise two miles apart on Dartmoor. East Dart runs to Postbridge and thence to Dartmeet, where it unites with West Dart which flows through Two Bridges. The West Dart above Dartmeet (with the exception of the right bank from Huccaby Bridge to Dartmeet), and the East Dart above Dartmeet (with the exception of the left bank from Wallabrook Junction to Dartmeet), belong to Duchy of Cornwall. The river has runs of salmon and peal (sea trout). Best months for salmon are May to Sept in the lower reaches and also higher up, depending on water. For peal May to Sept are favoured in the main river, and tidal water of Totnes Weir Pool in May and June. Wild brown trout are mainly small.

Dartmouth (Devon). In river, fishing for ray, bass (shore only), whiting, mackerel, garfish, mullet, and pouting. Coastline for dogfish, bull huss, bass, wrasse, whiting, dab, plaice, turbot, brill and conger. Boats effective in river and sea. Skerries Bank, inshore and offshore wrecks popular venues. Flatfish most prolific off Skerries Bank. Dartmouth Angling & Boating A, clubhouse open every Mon, Wed, Fri and Sat (7pm-11pm); st £6, conc. Salmon, peal and trout fishing in Dart on Dart AA water (see Totnes, Buckfastleigh) and a trout reservoir. Lake fishing on **Slapton Ley** and **Old Mill Reservoir**; pike, rudd, etc *(see Devonshire, small streams and lakes)*. Tackle shops: Sport 'n' Fish, 16 Fairfax Place Dartmouth TQ6 9AB (tel: 01803 833509); Brixham Bait & Tackle, 10 The Quay, Brixham TQ5 8AW (tel: 01803 853390); Devon Angling Centre, Unit 4/5, Orchard Way, Chillington, Kingsbridge TQ7 2LB (tel: 01548 580888). Hotels: contact Tourist Information Centre (tel: 01803 834224).

Totnes (Devon). Salmon, peal, trout. Dart AA controls Dart from Staverton Weir to Austins Bridge, left bank only; Totnes Weir salmon av 10lb; peal 3lb in May-June and about 1lb thereafter. 4lb and 5lb peal not rare. School peal run from late June to mid-Aug. Nearly all peal caught after dark in normal conditions; Aug usually best. Fly only for peal and trout. Newhouse Fishery, Moreleigh, Totnes TQ9 7JS (tel: 01548 821426), has 4 acre trout lake open all year. Dt £21 5 fish, £18 4 fish; also 4 pools on R Avon dt £15 brown trout, £30 salmon, sea trout. New Barn Angling Centre, Totnes Rd, Paignton TQ4 7PT, has 6 coarse lakes (tel: 01803 553602); dt £6 1 rod. Hotels: Seymour, Royal Seven Stars and Cott Inn (at Darlington). Sea Trout Inn, TQ9 6PA (tel: 01803 762274), is close to the river at Staverton, and exclusively sells tickets on behalf of Dart AA; dt £10 brown trout, £20 sea trout (2 fish limit), £20 salmon; £20 for Totnes Weirpool.

Buckfastleigh (Devon). Salmon, peal, trout. SWW Plc has fishery, ¼m Dart, Austins Bridge to Nursery Pool; salmon, sea trout. St £45, 16 rods. Holne Chase Hotel, Poundsgate, near Ashburton, TQ13 7NS (tel: 01364 631471), has about 1m right bank upstream from bridge, with seven pools; fishing for hotel guests only, £25 per rod day; ghillies and tuition if required. Hotel can arrange fishing on the Moor with Duchy permit, and a further 9m through the Dart AA between Holne and Totnes; 4 miles let to visitors from Buckfastleigh to Totnes. Tickets from Sea Trout Inn, Staverton TQ9 6PA (tel: 01803 762274), dt £20 salmon, £20 sea

Fishing the West Dart requires skilful casting. *Photo: Hugh Clark, FRPS.*

trout (2 fish limit), £10 brown trout, conc. Permits also from Watercress Farm, Kerwells, Chudleigh, Newton Abbot TQ13 0DW for fishing near Ashburton.

Princetown (Devon). Permits for salmon and trout fishing on main river, **East** and **West Dart**, **Wallabrook**, **Swincombe** and **Cherrybrook** from most tackle shops in S Devon; also the Prince Hall Hotel, Two Bridges Hotel, both Princetown; Huccabys News, 33a Fore St, Buckfastleigh TQ11 0AA (tel: 01364 643206); and Princetown Post Office. Salmon best May-Sept. Charges: S and MT, st £139, wt £77, dt £22.60; T, st £56.60, wt

£16.50, dt £5.15. Prince Hall Hotel, nr Two Bridges, Dartmoor PL20 6SA (tel: 01822 890403), has fine riverside location; hotel stocks flies and Duchy licences, and will advise on local fishing, tuition, ghillie service, etc; supplies EA licences.

Hexworthy (Devon); Salmon, sea trout (peal), brown trout. Forest Inn Hotel, Hexworthy PL20 6SD (tel: 01364 631211); dt, wt or st, at hotel, for Duchy of Cornwall water on presentation of EA licence. Ghillie, instruction offered. Good centre for E and W Dart and Cherrybrook.

DEBEN

(For close seasons, licences, etc see Anglian Region Environment Agency, p20)

Short Suffolk river (about 30 miles long) rising near Debenham and flowing to North Sea near Felixstowe. Coarse fishing.

Woodbridge (Suffolk). Tidal. Roach, pike, tench, perch above town. Club: Woodbridge & Dist AC, who also has Loam Pond, Sutton, Holton Pit and Braxhall Decoy; st £30, dt £5, conc, from Saxmundham Angling Centre; Anglia Photographics & Sport *(below)*. Framlingham & Dist AC (tel: 01473 623228) has half mile one bank River Deben at Wickham Market; also **Hayward's Reservoirs** at **Wickham Market**, **Youngman's Reservoirs** at Charsfield, and one other still water fishery, at **Parham** near **Framlin-**

gham; coarse fishing, members only, st £35, conc; apply Stuart Clay Traps, Melton IP12 1DG (tel: 01394 385567). Tackle Shop: Saxmundham Angling Centre, Bakery Yard, rear of Market Place, Saxmundham IP17 1AH (tel: 01728 603443); Anglia Photographics & Sport, 63 The Thoroughfare, Halesworth IP19 8AR (tel: 01986 873333). Hotels: Bull, Crown.

Wickham Market (Suffolk). Roach, perch, pike. Woodbridge AC has river and Wickham Market Reservoir.

DERWENT (Cumbria)

(For close seasons, licences, etc, see South West Region Environment Agency p19)

Rises on north side of Scafell and flows through Borrowdale, Derwentwater and Bassenthwaite Lakes to the Solway Firth at Workington. Salmon and trout practically throughout length. A late river. Best months for salmon, July to October. Trout fishing on some stretches excellent. River also holds pike and perch.

Cockermouth to **Workington** (Cumbria). Salmon, sea trout, brown trout. Trout and salmon fishing may occasionally be permitted on dt; enquiries to fishery Manager, Cockermouth Castle (tel: 01900 826320); permit charges under review. Permits for **Cocker** and **Derwent** also (limited); waters through town can be fished on permit from Tourist Information Office, Town Hall, Market St, CA13 9NP (tel: 01900 822634), by residents and visitors staying locally on weekly basis. Cockermouth AA has water on Cocker (members only) but issues dt for **Cogra Moss**. **Mockerkin Tarn**, stocked with carp. Fishing within reach on Bas-

senthwaite, Loweswater, Crummock and Buttermere. Nr Cockermouth are Gilcrux Springs Trout Farm, Gilcrux, Wigton, CA7 2QD (tel: 01697 322488), with brown, American brook, rainbow, and tiger trout; also Ellerbeck Farm and Fishery, Brigham CA13 0SY (tel: 01900 825268), coarse fishing on day permit £5; ticket on bank. Tackle shops: Graham's Gun and Sports, 9-15 South William St, Workington CA14 2ED (tel: 01900 605093); Complete Angler, 4 King St, Whitehaven CA28 7LA (tel: 01946 695322). Hotels: Trout, Globe; Cockermouth Pheasant, Bassenthwaite Lake; Sun, Bassenthwaite.

Bassenthwaite (Cumbria). Derwent, 1m N; trout, salmon; private. Lakes: Bassenthwaite; pike, perch, trout, occasional salmon *(see English Lake District - Bassenthwaite)*. Hotels: Swan; Pheasant; Armathwaite Hall, Keswick CA12 4RE (tel: 01768 776551).

Keswick (Cumbria). For rivers Derwent and Greta. Salmon, trout (average ½lb), pike, perch, eels; mid August onwards for salmon. Portinscale to ½m above Bassenthwaite Lake, Keswick AA water; assn stocks Rivers Derwent and Greta with 500 12" browns each year; fly only for trout; visitors salmon wt £125, dt £25; trout permit, 2 fish limit, includes Derwentwater, wt £40, dt £8 (reductions for juniors on all fishing) from Keswick P O, CA12 5JJ (tel: 017687 72269); visitors st by application to Sec; tickets issued for Derwent cover Greta also; for full details of water controlled by Keswick AA, write to secretary, enclosing sae, or contact main post office. Tackle shop: Field & Stream, 79 Main Str, CA12 5DS (tel: 017687 74396). Hotels: Hazeldene, Queen's Royal Oak, Lake, George, County King's Arms. The Derwentwater Hotel.

Borrowdale (Cumbria). Trout, salmon; gin-clear as a rule and best fished after dark. Lakes: Derwentwater; trout, perch, pike; small charge for fishing. Watendlath Tarn 2m S; Scafell; Blea Tarn, 4m S; trout. Hotels: Scafell; Borrowdale; Hilton Keswick Lodore, CA12 5UX (tel: 017687 77285), can arrange fishing.

Tributaries of the Derwent (Cumbria)

COCKER: Salmon, sea trout, trout. July to October best for migratory fish. Mostly private.

Scalehill (Cumbria). Cockermouth. 7m Cocker: Salmon, sea trout, trout. Privately let by National Trust lakes. Hotel: Scale Hill.

Cogra Moss. 40 acre trout reservoir 8m S of Cockermouth. Browns and rainbows. Contact Cockermouth AA.

NEWLANDS BECK: not worth fishing.

GRETA: Trout (av ¼lb); salmon.

Threlkeld (Cumbria). Keswick AA has fishing here *(tickets see Keswick)*. Best months for salmon Sept and Oct; mostly spinning and worm fishing; fly only for brown trout; apply Hon Sec; st see Derwent. Glenderamackin Beck; trout; fishable throughout length, but very narrow and fish few and far between.

DEVONSHIRE (streams and lakes)

(For close seasons, licences, etc, see SW Region Environment Agency, p19)

AVON. Rises on Dartmoor and flows 22m SE, entering English Channel near Thurlestone via long, twisting estuary. Tide flows to Aveton Gifford. Trout (3 or 4lb), sea trout, salmon.

Thurlestone (Devon). Near mouth of Avon estuary. Capital bass fishing off Bantham Sands at mouth.

Aveton Gifford (Devon). Sea trout (end of May onwards), some salmon; good dry-fly trout water (3 to the lb). Banks heavily wooded; good wading. Mt, ft, wt, from post office at Loddiswell.

Loddiswell. Brown trout, salmon, sea trout; Avon FA has a total of 14½m; no day tickets; capital bass and pollack in Kingsbridge estuary. Hotels: King's Arms; Buttville; Torcross (for Slapton Ley).

Brent (Devon). Salmon, trout, sea trout. Red Brook, 2m N; trout. Black Brook, 2m S; trout. Hotel: Anchor.

Avon Dam (8m NE of Totnes). South West Lakes Trust, brown trout fishery, zoned worm, spinning and fly fishing free to Environment Agency licence holders. No boats. Season March 15-Oct 12. Reservoir is about 1½m beyond **Shipley Bridge**, car parking on site.

BELLBROOK VALLEY TROUT FISHERY, Oakford, Tiverton EX16 9EX (tel: 01398 351292). Set in picturesque Devon valley. Four specimen lakes, min stock 3lb, and three normal fishing lakes; specimen fishing, dt £39 4 fish, £34 3 fish, £22 2 fish; various other permits obtainable. Record rainbow 2000, 25lb 12oz. Tuition by arrangement. Corporate party days. Accommodation at fishery farmhouse.

BLAKEWELL FISHERY, Muddiford, Blakewell Lane, nr Barnstaple EX31 4ET. Brown and rb. trout av. 2¼ lb. Various day permits from £22, 5 fish, to £16, 2 fish, from fishery. Tackle hire and tuition on site. This establishment also runs a commercial fish farm; Richard or

John Nickell (tel: 01271 344533).

BURRATOR RESERVOIR, Yelverton. 150 acres, South West Lakes Trust. Zoned fly fishing and spinning for brown and rainbow trout. Open Mar 15-Sept 30. Dt £9.75, st £130 (conc), from Yelverton Garage, 1 Moorland Villas, Tavistock PL20 6DT (tel: 01822 853339).

CRAFTHOLE, nr Torpoint. A popular little South West Lakes Trust fishery of 2 acres, dammed, stocked with carp and tench. Season permit, with limited day permits £5 each; dt from The Liscawn Inn PL11 3BD (tel: 01503 230863). For st contact South West Lakes Trust, Higher Coombepark, Lewdowne Okehampton Devon EX20 4QT (tel: 01837 871565).

DARRACOTT, Torrington. 3 acre coarse fishery run by South West Lakes Trust, with carp, tench, bream, roach, rudd, perch, eel. Open all year, 24 hour day. St £125 (day and night), £85 st (day), 24-hour £8.75, dt £4.75, conc £3.75 from N Laws, Summerlands Tackle, 16-20 Nelson Road, Westward Ho! EX39 1LF (tel: 01237 471291); or Whiskers Pet Centre, 20 South St, Torrington EX38 8AA (tel: 01805 622859).

ERME. Rises on Dartmoor and flows 14m S to Bigbury Bay. Trout.

FERNWORTHY RESERVOIR, near **Chagford,** on Dartmoor. South West Lakes Trust. 76 acres, natural and stocked brown trout fishing, largest 4lb 2oz. Open April 1-Oct 12. Dt £9.75, conc. Self-service unit by Boathouse.

JENNETS RESERVOIR, Bideford. 8 acres, South West Lakes Trust coarse fishery, with carp principally, to 23lb, as well as tench, bream, roach, perch, eels. Open all year, 6.30am to 10.00pm. Dt £4.75, conc £3.75 from N Laws, Summerlands Tackle, 16-20 Nelson Rd, Westward Ho! EX39 1LF (tel: 01237 471291); also from Bideford TIC, The Quay EX39 2QQ (tel: 01237 477676).

KENNICK RESERVOIR, Christow. A South West Lakes Trust Dartmoor fishery, with stocked rainbow trout. Boats bookable in advance (tel: 01647 277587); Allenard Wheely Boat for disabled. Permits from self-service kiosk, £17.50 per day, full season £400, conc. Open 23 Mar-31 Oct.

MELBURY RESERVOIR, Bideford. 12 acre South West Lakes Trust reservoir, open all year, 6.30am to 10.30pm. Carp, bream, roach, perch, eels. St £120 (day and night), £80 st (day), dt £4.75, conc

£3.75 from N Laws, Summerlands Tackle, 16-20 Nelson Rd, Westward Ho! EX39 1LF (tel: 01237 471291).

MELDON RESERVOIR (3m SE of Okehampton). 54 acres, natural brown. Spinning, bait and fly fishing, South West Lakes Trust fishery, free to Environment Agency licence holders. Season Mar 15-Oct 12.

LYN, near Lynmouth (Devon). This beautiful river has good run of salmon, July onwards. Also sea trout and brown trout; latter small. Environment Agency **Watersmeet** and **Glenthorne** fisheries: limits, 2 salmon, 6 sea trout, 8 trout. Restricted season and methods. Salmon and sea trout: tickets from Tourist Information Centre, Town Hall, Lynton EX35 6BT (tel: 01598 752225); Lynmouth PO. Season March 1-Sept 30. Other contacts for East Lyn fishing are Rising Sun Hotel, Harbourside, Lynmouth EX35 6EQ; Doone Valley Riding Stables, Brendon. *(See also Sea Fishing Stations).*

PLYM. Devon salmon and sea trout river which rises above Lee Moor and flows south-west to Plymouth, skirts the east of the town to enter the Sound on the south side.

Plymouth (Devon). Good runs of sea trout on Plym and Tavy. Salmon run late on Plym, Oct to 15 Dec. Plymouth & Dist Freshwater AA has R Plym from Plymbridge upstream for about 3m, and Tavy, north of Tavistock; annual subscription £95 from Hon Sec, dt (Mon-Fri only) from Snobee or DK Sports *(below).* Length above Bickleigh Bridge, controlled by Tavy, Walkham and Plym FC; club issues tickets (salmon, sea trout, brown trout) for its water, here and on Tavy, Meavy and Walkham; salmon st £125, dt £17.50, brown trout st £45, mt £22, from Osborne & Cragg (DK Sports) *(below);* Tavistock Trout Fishery, Parkwood Road, Tavistock PL19 9JW (tel: 01822 615441) 5 trout fly lakes; dt £18.50 to £37 (4 fish); Yelverton Garage, 1 Moorland Villas, Tavistock PL20 6DT (tel: 01822 853339), tickets for Burrator Reservoir and Plym, Tavy and Meavy. *(see Tamar - Tavy).* Sea fishing excellent. Tackle shops: Snowbee (UK) Ltd, Drakes Court, Langage Business Park PL7 5JY (tel: 01752 334933); Osborne & Cragg (DK Sports), 37 Breton Side, Plymouth PL4 0BB (tel: 01752 223141); Tackle & Bait Shop, 93 Victoria Rd PL5 1RX (tel: 01752 361294).

MEAVY. Tributary of the Plym, on which Burrator Reservoir blocks salmon migration. Joins main river at Shaugh Bridge. Fishing governed by overspill when Burrator is full. Fishing stations: **Shaugh** and Clearbrook. National Trust water fished by Plymouth & Dist FAA; members only (conservation area).

OAREWATER, Brendon. Trout.

ROADFORD FISHERY, nr Okehampton. South West Lakes Trust fishery, with wild and stocked brown trout. More than 700 acres, c&r policy, barbless hooks. Dt £14.00, conc, from Angling and Watersports Centre, Lower Goodacre, Broadwoodwidger, PL16 0JL. Boats available. Open 23 Mar-12 Oct. Enquiries, ranger (tel: 01409 211514).

SID, Sidmouth. Trout.

SLADE RESERVOIRS, Ilfracombe. South West Lakes Trust fisheries. **Lower Slade,** coarse fishing for pike, carp, tench, bream, roach, rudd, gudgeon and perch. St £125 (day and night), £85 st (day), 24-hour £8.75, dt £4.75, conc £3.75 from Variety Sports, 23 Broad St, Ilfracombe EX34 9EE (tel: 01271 862039).

SLAPTON LEY, Dartmouth 7m. Pike, rudd, roach, eel and perch. Part of National Nature Reserve, boats only, bank fishing prohibited; for day tickets only, £15-£26, for one, two or three anglers and depending on length of stay, apply Field Centre, Slapton, Kingsbridge, TQ7 2QP (tel: 01548 580685); life-jackets on site, compulsory for anglers under 18 years of age. Also in vicinity, Coombe Water Fishery, Coombe Lane, **Kingsbridge** TQ7 4AB (tel: 01548 852038), with carp, tench, bream, roach; dt on site. Tackle shops: Sport 'n' Fish, 16 Fairfax Place Dartmouth TQ6 9AB (tel: 01803 833509); Anchor Sports Cabin, Unit 7 Anchor Centre, Bridge St, Kingsbridge TQ7 1SD (tel: 01548 856891); Devon Angling Centre, Unit 4/5, Orchard Way, Chillington, Kingsbridge TQ7 2LB (tel: 01548 580888). Hotels: The Torcross and (in Slapton) the Tower Inn. Many guest houses.

SQUABMOOR RESERVOIR. E Bud-

leigh. South West Lakes Trust has water. Bait fishing for coarse fish, with carp to 25lbs, tench, bream, roach, rudd, eels; st £125 (day and night), £85 st (day), 24-hour £8.75, dt £4.75, conc £3.75 from Exmouth Tackle and Sports, 20 The Strand, Exmouth EX8 1AF (tel: 01395 274918). **Hogsbrook Lakes**, 2½ acres, at Woodbury Salterton is dt coarse fishery nearby. Carp, tench, bream, roach and rudd; dt £4.50; night fishing by appointment only; alcohol ban: contact bailiff, Russett Cottage, Woodbury Salterton, Exeter EX5 1EW (tel: 01395 233340).

STAFFORD MOOR FISHERY, Winkleigh EX19 8PP (tel: 01805 804360); six lakes of thirty acres total; all coarse; pleasure, match and specimen; tackle and bait available; rod hire and tuition; single permit £6, conc.

TRENCHFORD RESERVOIR (8m NE of Newton Abbot). South West Lakes Trust pike fishery of 45 acres, pike to 30lb. Open all year. £85 st (day) from SWLT; 24-hour £8.75, dt £4.75, conc £3.75 from self service kiosk at Kennick. Kennick ranger tel: 01647 277587.

VENFORD RESERVOIR, Ashburton. Wild brown trout. Spinning and bubble-float fishing, free to licence-holders. Season: March 15-Oct 12. Contact South West Lakes Trust, for more details.

WISTLANDPOUND RESERVOIR, South Molton. South West Lakes Trust natural brown trout and stocked rainbow fishery. Fly only, open Mar 15-Oct 31. Dt £12, conc £10.50, from Post Office, Challacombe EX31 4TT (tel: 01598 763229); Variety Sports, 23 Broad St, Ilfracombe EX34 9EE (tel: 01271 862039).

YEALM. Rises on southern heights of Dartmoor and flows 12m south and west to English Channel, which it enters by a long estuary. Trout, sea trout, occasional late salmon. Fishing private. Estuary is now a bass nursery, bass fishing prohibited.

Newton Ferrers (Devon). On estuary. One of finest deep-sea fishing stations in south-west. Hotel: River Yealm has its own harbour frontage and jetty.

DORSET (streams)

(For close seasons licences, etc, see South West Region Environment Agency, p19)

BRIT and **ASKER**. Fishing station: **Bridport**. Trout. Rivers mostly private or over-grown. Also **Radipole Lakes**; dt for

latter: coarse fish; tickets from Weymouth tackle shops. Dt £6 for **Osmington Mills Lake** (carp and tench) on site only (tel: 01305 832311). Trout fishing at **Watermill Lake**, well stocked with rainbows. Mangerton Mill, Bridport, DT6 3SG (tel: 01308 485224); fly only; dt £5 to £15.

CHAR. Fishing station: **Charmouth**. Char is some 7m long; trout, private. General sea fishing. Hotels: Queen's Arms, Hammons Mead.

CORFE. Rises 1m W of Corfe Castle and runs into Poole Harbour 5m down. Coarse fishing sometimes permitted by landowners. Dt can be obtained for Arfleet Lake at Corfe Castle.

DURHAM (reservoirs)

DERWENT. Edmundbyers. 1,000 acre Northumbria Water trout water. Hotel: Lord Crewe Arms. *Reservoir also partly in Northumberland.*

SMIDDY SHAW, and **WASKERLEY**. Good trouting, preserved by North West Durham AA; limited dt £10, 2 fish, Waskerley only; tickets from fishing lodge near dam wall; wild brown, stocked rainbow; Smiddy Shaw, members only. Season March 22-Oct 31. Nearest towns: **Wolsingham**, **Consett** and **Stanhope**. Hotel: Royal Derwent at Allensford.

EDEN

(For close season licences, etc, see North West Region Environment Agency, p20)

Rises south of Kirkby Stephen and empties into Solway Firth 5m NW of Carlisle. Salmon, sea trout, brown trout and grayling. Still some spring fish, but now more a back-end river. Sea trout in lower and middle reaches and tributaries from June onwards. Trouting best in middle and upper reaches, fish run to good average size for north. Chub in parts.

Carlisle (Cumbria). Salmon in spring and autumn, sea trout and herling in May to July, brown trout fair, good grayling. Carlisle AA has 7m on Eden, permits from tackle shops; visitors salmon st £100, wt £50, dt £10-£20; trout £17, wt £7, dt £2. Tackle shops: McHardy's Fishing Tackle, South Henry Str, CA1 1SF (tel: 01228 523988); Eddie's Fishing Tackle, 70 Shaddongate, CA2 5UG (tel: 01228 810744). Hotels: Crown and Mitre; Central; Hilltop; many guesthouses.

Wetheral (Cumbria). Salmon and sea trout preserved for 3m, both banks from Warwick Bridge upstream, by the Yorkshire Fly-fishers' Club here and at Great Cozzrby; Cairn Beck, 2m, Irthing, 3m N. Scotby Beck, 2m W at Scotby. Hotel: Crown.

Lazonby (Cumbria). Salmon, trout and grayling. 1m of west bank Lazonby Parish Council fishing; permits from Post Office (in Co-op) CA10 1BG (tel: 01768 898210), Midland Hotel CA10 1BG (tel: 01768 898901), or Joiners Arms CA10 1BL (tel: 01768 898728); dt £12 game, wt £36; dt £10, wt £30 coarse. Tackle shop: Charles R Sykes, 4 Great Dockray, Penrith CA11 7BL (tel: 01768 862418); Norris's, 21 Victoria Road, Penrith CA11 8HP (tel: 01768 864211).

Langwathby (Cumbria). Salmon, trout; preserved by Yorkshire FFC.

Culgaith (Cumbria). Trout; preserved by Yorkshire FFC from Culgaith to below Langwathby apart from vicinity of Watersmeet. Winderwath, left bank is Penrith AA water, members only; membership £140, conc half price, juv £5; apply Hon Sec. Hotels: Black Swan, Culgaith.

Temple Sowerby (Cumbria). Salmon, trout, grayling; preserved (with some miles of Eamont) by Yorkshire FFC; members only. Penrith AA (with 35m of fishing in all) has Powis House Water above Bolton Village; water upstream of Oustenstand Island. Membership £140, conc half price, juv £5; dt £10 from Charles R Sykes, 4 Great Dockray, Penrith CA11 7BL (tel: 01768 862418); The Punch Bowl Inn, Askham, Penrith (tel: 01931 712443); Langwathby PO & Stores, Langwathby, Penwith (tel: 01768 881342); Pooley Bridge PO (tel: 017684 86266). (*See Penrith.*) King's Arms Hotel has trout fishing for guests on 1½m of Eden; licences and tickets at hotel; trout average 1lb.

Kirkby Thore (Cumbria). Salmon, trout and grayling. Penrith AA preserves 2m brown trout fishing on main river and Kirkby Thore Beck near Long Marton. Membership £140, conc half price, juv £5; dt £10 from Charles R Sykes, 4 Great Dockray, Penrith CA11 7BL (tel: 01768 862418); The Punch Bowl Inn, Askham, Penrith (tel: 01931 712443); Langwathby

PO & Stores, Langwathby, Penwith (tel: 01768 881342); Pooley Bridge PO (tel: 017684 86266).

Appleby (Cumbria). Eden trout are very free risers, averaging about ¾lb with better fish to 3 and even 4lb. Appleby AA has 14m of R Eden, excellent fly fishing water, and offers dt £8 for stretch ¾m above Jubilee Bridge (fly section and bait section), or £15 for stretch between Bolton Bridge and Ouenstands Bridge (all fly fishing). Membership £70 + £20 entry non-resident, £35 resident, conc, from H Pigney and Son (*below*). Tufton Arms, Market Square CA16 6XA (tel: 017683 51593) has tickets for guests on Appleby AA water; Tufton Arms has salmon and trout flies; good quality rods for sale; tuition and courses from John Pape; also late availability sporting agency. Tackle and permits from H Pigney & Son, Chapel St, Appleby CA16 6QR (tel: 017683 51240).

Kirkby Stephen (Cumbria). Kirkby Stephen & Dist AA has about 15m on main river and becks, fly only. (*See Belah and Scandal Tributaries*). Visitor st £95, joining fee £40, conc, from Hon Sec; also for wt £40, dt £15. Fly fishing ponds at Bessy Beck Trout Fishery, Newbiggin-on-Lune CA17 4LY (tel: 015396 23303), booking advisable; 8am to dusk all year. Hotels: Kings Arms; Black Bull, White Lion, Croglin Castle.

Tributaries of the Eden

PETTERIL joins Eden at Carlisle. Good trout fishing. Penrith AA has 4m middle to upper reaches; members only. Lower half mostly private.

Plumpton (Cumbria). Trout.

IRTHING. Rises on Grey Fell Common and joins Eden east of Carlisle. Salmon, trout, grayling and few sea trout.

Brampton (Cumbria). Irthing; 1m N; Gelt, 1m S; trout, grayling, chub. Brampton AS preserves 8-10m; st £22-£24, wt £15, dt £6 and Environment Agency licence from Brampton Post Office, Front Str, CA8 1NN (tel: 016977 2301); trout average ½ to ¾lb, best after April. Hotels: White Lion; Scotch Arms; Howard Arms.

Gilsland (Cumbria). Haltwhistle & Dist AA fishes 7m of double bank, brown trout only; visitors welcome, dt £20, wt £50, from: Greggs Sports, Market Square, Haltwhistle NE49 0BG (tel: 01434 320255).

EAMONT flows from Ullswater Lake. Penrith AA has approx 6m of this water; membership £140, conc half price, juv £5; dt £10 from Charles R Sykes, 4 Great Dockray, Penrith CA11 7BL (tel: 01768 862418); The Punch Bowl Inn, Askham, Penrith (tel: 01931 712443); Pooley Bridge PO (tel: 017684 86266). Lake Ullswater good trout fishing; free, but Environment Agency licence required.

Penrith (Cumbria). Eamont, 1m S; trout. Upper portion (trout and salmon) preserved by Penrith AA (fly fishing only for visitors) from Pooley Bridge on both banks to below Stainton; also on **Eden**, **Lowther** and on becks. Visitors weekly ticket covering a variety of fishings, £40, dt £10, from Sykes (*see below*); the Punchbowl Hotel, Askham, Penrith. Trout fishing at **Blencarn Lake**, 15 acres, from Mr and Mrs J K Stamper, Blencarn Hall CA10 1TX (tel: 01768 88284). Dt £18-£12, 4 and 2 fish, fly only; facilities, piers for disabled. Yorkshire Flyfishers preserve left bank of Eamont from Brougham Castle down to Barrack Bank and then on left bank only to below Udford; members only. Other water on Eamont private. Tackle shops: Charles R Sykes, 4 Great Dockray, Penrith CA11 7BL (tel: 01768 862418); John Norris, 21 Victoria Road, Penrith CA11 8HP (tel: 01768

Check before you go

While every effort has been made to ensure that the information given in **Where to Fish** *is correct, the position is continually changing, and anglers are urged, in their own interests, to make preliminary enquiries before travelling to selected venues. This is especially important with reference to prices quoted. Inevitably the rate of inflation is affecting stability in this quarter. Anglers' attention is also drawn to the fact that the hotels mentioned under the various fishing stations do not necessarily have water of their own. Any amendments or further data for inclusion in subsequent editions, and any comments, will be welcome.*

864211).
Haweswater, 10m SE; currently, no permit is required *(see Westmorland lakes)*. Hotels: Crown; George; Edenhall, near Langwathby. Tackle shop: Charles R Sykes, 4 Great Dockray, Penrith CA11 7BL (tel: 01768 862418).
Pooley Bridge (Cumbria). Eamont; trout. Penrith AA water. Membership £140, conc half price, juv £5; dt £10 from Charles R Sykes, 4 Great Dockray, Penrith CA11 7BL (tel: 01768 862418); The Punch Bowl Inn, Askham, Penrith (tel: 01931 712443); Langwathby PO & Stores, Langwathby, Penwith (tel: 01768 881342); Pooley Bridge PO (tel: 017684 86266).
Patterdale (Cumbria). The becks Goldrill, Grizedale, Deepdale and Hartsop; free. Aira Force below NT property (3m) free. N Hawes and Riggindale Becks, permits N West Water. Blea Tarn and Smallwater, N West Water. **Ullswater**. Trout numerous, average three to pound. Evening rise during May and June yields heavy baskets; six brace of trout in evening quite common; day fishing also good; and heavier fish begin to move about middle of May; free; numerous boats. Angle Tarn, permits. Greenside Reservoir, Red Tarn, Grizedale Tarn,

free. Hotels: Ullswater, Patterdale; White Lion, Brotherswater; Glenridding (boats).
LOWTHER (tributary of Eamont). No fishing for salmon, spawning river only. Sport with trout remains good (av ¾lb). Penrith AA holds substantial stretches of good fly water on river; other assn water on Eden and Eamont. Membership £140, conc half price, juv £5; dt £10 from Charles R Sykes, 4 Great Dockray, Penrith CA11 7BL (tel: 01768 862418); The Punch Bowl Inn, Askham, Penrith (tel: 01931 712443); Langwathby PO & Stores, Langwathby, Penwith (tel: 01768 881342); Pooley Bridge PO (tel: 017684 86266).
LYVENNET. Good trout stream; runs in a few miles below Temple Sowerby. Leave from farmers in some parts. 1m preserved for Yorkshire Flyfishers' Club.
BELAH. Flows from Pennine fells to join Eden 2m below Kirkby Stephen. Lower reaches, from Brough Sowerby, rented by Kirkby Stephen & Dist AA; members only.
SCANDAL BECK, Smardale (Cumbria) and **Crosby Garrett** (Cumbria). Kirkby Stephen & Dist AA has water. *(See Kirkby Stephen under Eden.)*

ENGLISH LAKE DISTRICT

(For close seasons, licences, etc, see North West Region Environment Agency, p20)

See also web: www.lakedistrictfishing.net (updated fortnightly)

BASSENTHWAITE, 5m Cockermouth; 8m Keswick. Long famous for its pike, also perch and some brown trout. Hotels: Pheasant Inn; Swan; Armathwaite Hall, Keswick CA12 4RE (tel: 01768 776551).
BIGLAND WATERS, Bigland Hall Estate, Backbarrow LA12 8PB (tel: 015395 31728). 13 acre coarse fishery and 16 acre fly only trout lake (barbless hooks only). Trout dt £18 4 fish, £12 for 6 hours 2 fish; coarse dt £5, conc; contact the Fisheries Manager.
BLEA TARN. About 2m above Watendlath Tarn; perch; some trout.
BLELHAM TARN. Ns **Windermere**. Pike, perch, roach, eels, brown trout. National Trust water now controlled by WADAA, open all year. Assn also controls fishing bank nr boathouse and rocks at northern end of tarn. Livebaiting prohibited; boats not allowed. Limited permits £5 (2 per day) from Hawkeshead

Tourist Information Centre, Main Car Park, Hawkeshead LA22 0NT (Tel: 015394 36525).
BORRANS RESERVOIR South Lakeland. Managed by North Tyneside M.B.C., Educational Dept, High Borrans, Outdoor Pursuit Centre, Windermere.
BROTHERSWATER. Good trout and pike. National Trust, fishing free; west shore only; no boats.
BUTTERMERE. National Trust lake. Char, trout, pike, perch. Permits (st £50, wt £20, dt £5) which also cover Crummock and Loweswater, from Mr or Mrs Parker, Dalegarth Guest House, Buttermere, Cockermouth CA13 9XA (tel: 017687 70233); rowing boats for hire.
CLEABARROW TARN, Windermere. WADAA fishery, 2 acres, 20 pegs. No close season. Well stocked, carp (20lb), tench (5lb), bream (7lb), roach, rudd, golden rudd, gudgeon. Fishery is weedy,

strong tackle recommended; members only; apply Hon Sec.

CODALE TARN, 4m from **Grasmere**. Perch, some trout; free. Hotels: *(see Grasmere)*.

CONISTON. Trout, char, perch, pike. Free, licence needed. Boats from Coniston Boating Centre, Lake Rd, Coniston LA21 8EW (tel: 015394 41366). Licences from Sun Hotel LA21 8HQ (tel: 015394 41248) for local club, Coniston & Torver DAA, which has fishing on Yew Tree Tarn; fly only, dt £8, juv £4, conc. Hotels: Sun, Black Bull, Crown, Ship Inn.

CRUMMOCK WATER. National Trust lake. Pike, trout, char, perch; salmon and sea trout from Cocker sometimes caught by trolling. Fishes best June and July; st £50, wt £20, dt £5, covering also Buttermere and Loweswater from Mr & Mrs M V McKenzie, Woodhouse, Buttermere CA13 9XA (tel: 017687 70208). Rowing boats for hire, £6 p/hr; £15 half-day, £20 per day; best periods for Crummock, Buttermere and Loweswater are: trout, late May and early June (good mayfly hatch); char, July and August (special technique required: trolling 60 to 90 feet down). Accom at Woodhouse, also self-catering.

DERWENTWATER. Keswick. Trout very good size, are best fished from a boat in mayfly season. National Trust and Keswick AA water. Good sized perch and pike, salmon present but rarely taken; wt £20, dt £5 (which includes all KAA waters) from Keswick PO; TIC, Moot Hall, Main Str, Keswick CA12 5NJ (tel: 017687 72645); Field & Stream *(see Keswick);* Youdale Newsagents, Main Str, Keswick; Boats may be hired from Nicoll End, and Keswick landings. Many hotels and guest houses.

DEVOKE WATER near **Ravenglass** (5m E). Moorland tarn offering sport with fair sized trout. Millom AA holds rights. Membership and dt obtainable from Hon Sec; Haverigg PO; Bridge Garage, Holmrook; TI Millom and also Broughton; Waberthwaite PO.

DRUNKEN DUCK TARNS, Ambleside. Brown trout to 4½lb, rainbow to 6lb; dt £12 (reductions for ½ day and evenings), from Drunken Duck Hotel, Barngates LA22 0NG (tel: 015394 36347).

DUBBS TROUT FISHERY, Windermere. A quiet upland reservoir, controlled by WADAA, open 15th March to 31st Dec inclusive. Stocked rainbow and brown trout; fly only, 2 fish limit; dt £11 from

Ings Filling Station (A591); Tourist Information Centres; local fishing tackle shops.

EASEDALE TARN, 3m from **Grasmere**. Coarse only. Free fishing; no boats. Managed by National Trust, The Hollens, Grasmere, Cumbria LA22 9QZ (tel: 015394 35599).

ENNERDALE, ns **Whitehaven**. Trout, char; controlled by Ennerdale Lake Fisheries formed by Egremont Anglers, Wath Brow; st £15 and wt £10 (no dt) from J & L O'Neil, Wath Brow Stores & PO, 121/2 Ennerdale Road, Wath Brow, Cleator Moor, Cumbria CA25 5LP; enquiries from permit secretary *(see clubs list)*.

ESTHWAITE WATER (nr **Hawkshead**, Cumbria). 280 acres stocked trout fishing. Rainbows to 16lb 3oz, browns to 10lb 12oz. spinning, worming or fly; also specimen pike. Boats with electric o/b, also boat for disabled. Dt from Esthwaite Water Trout Fishery, The Boathouse, Ridding Wood, Hawkshead LA22 0QF (tel: 015394 36541); accommodation plentiful; for Hawkshead Anglers membership contact Hon Sec; st £103.

FISHER TARN, ns **Kendal**, 3m. Kendal's water supply. Trout. Fisher Tarn Anglers: Hon Sec, Mr Colin Stamper, 58 Valley Drive LA9 7AG (tel: 01539 727813); dt £12 from tackle shop: Kendal Sports Shop, 30 Stramongate, Kendal LA9 4BN (tel: 01539 721554).

GHYLL HEAD TROUT FISHERY, Windermere. 11 acre WADAA stocked fishery, fly only. Open 15th March - 31st Dec. Rainbow and brown trout, 2 fish limit; all tagged fish must be returned to the water. Dt £11 from Newby Bridge Motors on A590; Tourist Information Centres, local tackle shops.

GRASMERE, ns **Windermere**. Summer fishing, pike over 20lb regularly caught, perch, eels, roach, trout; National Trust WADAA water, open all year. Live-baiting with fish is strictly prohibited, dead baiting and lure fishing are the most productive methods. Find underwater dropoffs for the best sport. Boat fishing can be good, boats from boathouse at northern end of lake. Dt £5 (Juv/OAP £2.50), wt £10.00 (Juv/OAP £5.00); st £30.00 (Juv/OAP £15.00); permit also allows fishing on Rydal Water, River Rothay, River Brathay, High Arnside Tarn, Moss Eccles Tarn, School Knott Tarn & Hayswater; also the assn's Winderemere fishery at Graythwaite; coarse anglers should join the assn as coarse members £30; boat on Grasmere; check bait restrictions (15 Mar to 15 June incl only saltwater deadbaits allowed). Permits from: Tourist Information Centre, Grasmere (tel: 015394 35245), local fishing tackle shops, Barney's News Box, Grasmere (7.00 am. - 5.30 p.m.).

GREAT RUNDALE TARN, ns **Long Marton,** 5m. Seamore Tarn and Little Rundale Tarn are in the vicinity. Small trout.

HARLOCK RESERVOIR, South Lakeland. Trout water managed by Barrow AA; brown trout; dt with member from Hon Sec.

HAWESWATER, ns **Penrith** or **Shap.** A good head of wild brown trout, char, gwyniad and perch. Bank fishing, fly only, free to all holders of Environment Agency licence. No maggot or loose feeding.

HAYESWATER RESERVOIR, Patterdale. WADAA water, 34 acres, 9m north of Ambleside, open 15th March - 30th Sept. Wild brown trout, fly only; dt £5 (Juv/OAP £2.50), wt £10.00 (Juv/OAP £5.00), st £30.00 (Juv/OAP £15.00). This permit also allows fishing on Grasmere, Rydal Water, High Arnside Tarn, Moss Eccles Tarn, School Knott Tarn & Rivers Rothay and Brathay; and the assn's Windermere fishery at Graythwaite. Permits from: Tourist Information Centres (nearest at Glenridding), local fishing tackle shops.

HIGH ARNSIDE TARN, Ambleside; SCHOOL KNOTT TARN, Windermere; MOSS ECCLES TARN, Hawkeshead. Three small National Trust fly fisheries, stocked by WADAA, open 15 March-30 Sept; dt £5, juv/OAP, £2.50, wt £10-£5, st £30-£15, from TICs, local tackle shops; Tower Bank Arms, Sawrey (tel: 015394 36334) has Moss Eccles tickets.

HIGH NEWTON TROUT FISHERY, High Newton. WADAA trout fishery, 10.8 acres, open 15th March - 31st Dec, rainbow and brown trout dt £11.00. The reservoir is very well stocked throughout the year with rainbow trout. A large number of specimen tagged rainbows are introduced at the start of each season. These are sport fish and must be returned if captured. The tagged fish are in addition to normal stockings which will continue as usual. All anglers must use barbless hooks (squashed barbs) and the use of buoyant lures or boobys on sunken lines

Open day on Esthwaite Water. *Photo: David Coleman.*

is prohibited. Permits from Newby Bridge service station; tackle shops or TICs.

HOLEHIRD TARN, Windermere, 3 acre WADAA water, open all year round. Carp (20lb), crucian carp (1lb), tench (5lb), roach (2lb), bream (8lb), rudd (2lb), chub (5lb), gudgeon. Dt £5.00 (Juv £2.50). The number of anglers permitted at Holehird is limited to ten at any one time, consequently a peaceful day is usually guaranteed. Four day permits are sold per day and only from Troutbeck Filling Station, A591. Permits may be obtained in advance of fishing from the filling station or by sending a cheque made out to WADAA with s.a.e to Mr. C. J. Sodo, Ecclerigg Court, Ecclerigg, Windermere, Cumbria LA23 1LQ. Fishing is permitted from one hour before sunrise to one hour after sunset. Overnight parking or night fishing is strictly prohibited.

KENTMERE FISHERY, nr Windermere (tel: 01768 88263, evenings only). Two lakes, of 20 and 4 acres with brown and rainbow trout, and 400 yds of Kent River, with sea trout and two salmon pools. Dt £20, 4 fish limit (2 brown, 2 rainbow), half-day or evening £15; permits from Woofs Newsagents, 22 Main Str, Staveley LA8 9LN (tel: 01539 821253).

KILLINGTON RESERVOIR, ns **Oxenholme,** 3m. Trout, pike, perch. Leased to Kent AA, st £50, dt £9, Juv dt £4 from Kendal tackle shops, including Carlson Tackle Shop, 64/66 Kirkland, Kendal LA9 5AP (tel/fax: 01539 724867; web: www.carlsons.co.uk) or Keeper, Water Keeper's Lodge at reservoir; conc st to jun.

LOUGHRIGG TARN, nr **Ambleside.** Pike, perch, roach, rudd, dace, eels, and brown trout; no boats allowed; wt & dt: apply to M A Murphy, Tarn Foot Farm, Skelwith Bridge, Loughrigg, nr Ambleside (tel: 015394 32596).

LONGLANDS LAKE. Cleator, West Cumbria. Wath Brow and Ennerdale Anglers, stocked monthly; dt from Farren Family Store, 50 Main Str, Cleator CA23 3BX (tel: 01946 810038); or L & J O'Neil, Wath Brow Stores & PO, 121/2 Ennerdale Road, Wath Brow, Cleator Moor, Cumbria CA25 5LP (tel: 01946 810377).

LOWESWATER. National Trust lake. Pike, perch, trout (av 1½-2lb but hard to catch; fly only up to June 16); no fishing from Oct 31-Mar 15. For dt £5, wt £20, st £50, apply to Mr and Mrs Leck, Water

End Farm, Loweswater CA13 0SU (tel: 01946 861465).

MEADLEY RESERVOIR. Cleator Moor, West Cumbria. Brown trout and rainbow. Permits from J & L O'Neil, Wath Brow Stores & PO, 121/2 Ennerdale Road, Wath Brow, Cleator Moor, Cumbria CA25 5LP.

MOCKERKIN, near Loweswater. Tarn stocked with carp by Haigh AA, Whitehaven.

PENNINGTON RESERVOIR, South Lakeland. Brown and rainbow trout fishing, Barrow AA. Dt £12 with member from Hon Sec.

RATHERHEATH TARN, Kendal. 5 acre WADAA coarse fishery, open all year. Carp (20lb), tench (5lb), roach (2lb), bream (7lb), rudd, crucian carp, perch, gudgeon; dt £5 (Juv £2.50) from: Plantation Bridge Filling Station, A591 (Open 7.00 am. - 9.00 p.m.), Tourist Information Centres, local tackle shops, including Carlson Tackle Shop, 64/66 Kirkland, Kendal LA9 5AP (tel/fax: 01539 724867; web: www.carlsons.co.uk). A special platform for disabled anglers stands just inside the entrance gate ten metres from the car park. Fishing is permitted from one hour before sunrise to one hour after sunset. Overnight parking or night fishing is strictly prohibited.

RYDAL WATER, Ambleside. WADAA water, open 16th June - 14th March. Pike, perch, eels, roach, trout. Rydal Water offers similar fishing to Grasmere and is a popular pike fishery producing fish to the mid-twenty pound mark. Parking is at White Moss Common or Rydal Village. Most pike are caught near underwater features around the islands and off the various points. Boat fishing is not permitted. The Association wants to conserve pike stocks in all fisheries so please use adequate tackle and have unhooking gear at hand; dt £5 (Juv/OAP £2.50), wt £10.00-£5, st £30.00-£15.00). NB. This permit also allows fishing on Grasmere, River Rothay, River Brathay, High Arneside Tarn, Moss Eccles Tarn, School Knott Tarn & Hayswater, and the assn's Windermere fishery at Graythwaite. Permits from: Tourist Information Centres, local tackle shops, Barney's News Box, Grasmere (7.00 a.m. - 6 p.m.). Coarse anglers should join the assn as coarse members £30.

SKELSMERGH, ns **Kendal,** 3m. Now privately owned, with large tench and perch regularly caught. St available; dt £5 on bank or phone C Taylor, Garnett Folds, LA8 9AS (tel: 01539 823284).

SPRINKLING TARN. Right up Stye Head Pass. Trout. Good on a favourable day until July.

STYE HEAD TARN. Same information as Sprinkling Tarn.

THIRLMERE. Perch, pike, trout. Free fishing to Environment Agency licence holders. No maggots, live baits or loose-feeding; no fishing SW corner. For further information contact Edward Holt, Land Agent, Northern Estates Office, The Old Sawmill, Thirlmere, Keswick CA12 4TQ (tel: 017687 72334).

ULLSWATER, ns **Penrith**. Covers 2,200 acres; dt £5; pike, perch, brown trout; rowing boats and powered boats on water. Hotel: Inn on the Lake, Lake Ullswater, Glenridding, Penrith CA11 0PE (tel: 017684 82444), has private fishing for guests only. Permits and tackle from Ullswater filling station.

WATENDLATH TARN. Keswick 3m. Brown and rainbow trout fishery, fly only, stocked weekly; boats. Open all year, dt, half-day, evenings; for this National Trust trout fishery apply to Mrs Richardson, Fold Head Farm, Watendlath CA12 5UW (tel: 017687 77255). Apply to Stan Edmondson for Watendlath Trout Fishery, Borrowdale, Keswick CA12 5UY (tel: 017687 77293); Mr Edmondson also has day tickets for 1m fishing on **River Cocker**.

WINDERMERE, nr **Windermere**. Largest English lake, 10½m long and nearly 1m wide. Good pike and perch, also eels, char and trout (trout best March-June), and roach (pike: only permitted baits are lures, spinners, flies and saltwater deadbaits). Fishing free, apart from Environment Agency licence. EA will prosecute anglers using live baits or freshwater deadbaits; this applies to several named lakes in the area (check first). Big fish taken by trolling. Boats from Bowness Bay, Waterhead Bay and Fell Foot National Trust Park. Local association, Windermere, Ambleside & Dist AA, has special corporate membership arrangement with sixty hotels, which give residents two rods per day on WADAA fisheries. Assn waters include 4m of Windermere Lake shore at Graythwaite Estates, near south-west end of lake; also **Grasmere, Rydal Water**, Rivers **Rothay, Brathay**, six tarns, Ghyll head and Dubbs Trout Fisheries, High Newton Reservoir, Grange-over-Sands. Details are elsewhere in text. **Ratherheath** and **Cleabarrow** Tarns are now coarse fisheries, dt £5, from local tackle shops: Carlson Tackle Shop, 64/66 Kirkland, Kendal LA9 5AP (tel/fax: 01539 724867; web: www.carlsons.co.uk); and Tourist Information Centres. Hotels: Lonsdale, Lake Rd; Cragwood Country House; Applegarth; Oakthorpe. Ambleside: Skelwith Bridge; Langdale Chase; Fisherbeck. All these offer free fishing on WADAA waters.

YEW TREE TARN, near **Coniston**. Rainbow and brown trout, fly only, no boats; Coniston & Torver DAA National Trust water; apply Lake District National Park Information Centre, Ruskin Avenue, Coniston LA21 8EH (tel: 015394 41533).

ESK (Border)

(Esk in England is under North West Region Environment Agency; close seasons, licences, etc, see p20. For statutory close season in Scotland, see Fishing in Scotland; no licence needed).

Rises in Dumfriesshire and flows into the Solway Firth but is classed as an English river. The Border Esk and main tributary, Liddle Water, are primarily sea trout and salmon waters from above Langholm and from Newcastleton to the mouth. Heavy runs of sea trout and herling from June to September. Salmon run from July onwards but September and October are the best months. Chub and dace in lower reaches provide good sport in winter.

Canonbie (Dumfries and Galloway). Salmon, sea trout; Buccleuch Sporting Ltd, Esk & Liddle Fishery Office, Ewesbank, Langholm DG13 0ND issue permits by appointment or post. Fly fishing: spinning and worming allowed only when river level exceeds markers provided; no Sunday fishing. St £49 to £382, wt £11 to £128, dt £8 to £40. Children ½ price: Canonbie and Lower Liddle wt and dt from Cross Keys Hotel (below); Head Bailiff, Iain Bell at Estate Office (tel: 013873 71416) for st and information. Six private beats are let on weekly basis to parties of three rods, directly by Buccleuch Sporting Ltd. Liddle tickets from Holm Hardware, Douglas Square, Newcastleton (tel: 013873 75257); also contact Stevenson and Johnstone, Bank of Scotland Buildings, Langholm, Dumfriesshire DG13 0AD for all tickets. No rod licence needed. Hotels: Cross Keys in Canonbie (tel: 013873 71205) who supply wt and dt; Eskdale Hotel at Langholm supply Langholm wt and dt.

Langholm (Dumfries and Galloway). Salmon, sea trout. Certain stretches of Esk and its tributary the Liddle, are under the control of Buccleuch Sporting Ltd (*see above*). Netherby Estate, Longtown,

issues permits for salmon and sea trout fishing at **Netherby**, through Edwin Thompson, Bute House, Rosehill, Carlisle CA1 2RW (tel: 01228 548385); Sunday fishing and night fishing allowed on Netherby waters; restrictions on spinning and worm fishing; full particulars from secretary. **Black Esk Reservoir**: bank fishing; fly and spinner only. Salmon and sea trout fishing on **River White Esk**, 6m, both banks, with a number of named pools, 12m from Langholm. Salmon and sea trout run from late July. Hotels: Eskdale, Douglas or Cross Keys (Canonbie).

Westerkirk (Dumfries and Galloway). Salmon, sea trout, herling, trout.

Tributaries of the Border Esk

LIDDLE: Salmon, sea trout, herling, brown trout.

Newcastleton (Roxburgh). Salmon, sea trout, herling, brown trout. Buccleuch Sporting Ltd have much water. Tickets for 5m stretch. (*See Canonbie*). Bailey Mill Farm Holidays and Trekking Centre, Bailey TD9 0TR (tel: 016977 48617), offer fishing holidays on 7m of Liddle, with accommodation, also 12m of Esk nr **Longtown**. Oak Bank Fisheries, Longtown, have trout and carp fishing. Tickets from local tackle shops.

LYNE: Lyne rises on Bewcastle Fells and

joins Esk ½m above Metal Bridge. Salmon, sea trout, herling, trout.

SARK: Trout stream about 10m long, forming for a short distance boundary between England and Scotland, and emptying into Solway at **Gretna**.

KIRTLE WATER: Stream which empties into the Solway at Kirtlefoot. Sea trout, herling, trout. Rigg and Kirtleside farm, Rigg.

Kirtlebridge (Dumfries and Galloway). Sea trout and trout; short free length. Winterhope Burn. Penoben Burn. Annan, 3m SW. Well-stocked reservoir 3m off,

Dalegarth Guest House, Cockermouth, supplied this shot of the magnificent Buttermere. *Photo: M Parker.*

Middlebie Dam, fishable by permit; trouting very good.

Kirkpatrick (Dumfries and Galloway). Trout.

ESK (Yorkshire)

(For close seasons, licences, etc, see North East Region Environment Agency, p20)

Rises on Westerdale Moor and runs into sea at Whitby. Salmon, sea trout, trout and grayling. Good runs of sea trout, river has twice held British record, 1994 was highest ever total. The River Esk Action Committee, representing riparian owners and anglers, is dedicated to the furtherance and improvement of this once great salmon river. In partnership with the National Park and Environment Agency, it is carrying out an annual programme of habitat improvement and restocking, using own hatchery. For further information, please contact Egton Estate Office (tel: 01947 895466/7).

Whitby (Yorks). Salmon, sea trout, trout, grayling, eels; largely preserved by the Esk FA from Ruswarp to Sleights. Visitors' tickets from Mr Sims, Millbeck, The Carrs, Ruswarp, Whitby YO21 1RL (tel 01947 603855 or 601610). No maggot fishing is allowed; fishing from Iburndale Beck down to Ruswarp Dam; below weir, sea fish only; st, dt. Tackle shop: Whitby Angling Supplies, 65/67 Haggersgate, Whitby YO21 3PP (tel: 01947 603855). Hotels: Wheatsheaf; Horseshoe.

RUSWARP (Yorks). Salmon, sea trout, trout, grayling, eels; preserved for 2m by Esk Fishery Association. Tickets from Mr Sims, Millbeck, The Carrs, Ruswarp, Whitby YO21 1RL (tel 01947 603855 or 601610).

Sleights (Yorks). Salmon, sea trout, trout, grayling, eels; preserved by Esk Fishery Association. Tickets for water up to Sleights from Mr Sims, Millbeck, The Carrs, Ruswarp, Whitby YO21 1RL (tel 01947 603855 or 601610).

Goathland (Yorks). Murk Esk; trout. Goathland FC water.

Grosmont (Yorks). Trout, salmon; preserved by the Esk FA above to Glaisdale, and below to Whitby.

Egton Bridge (N Yorks). Salmon, sea trout; some water preserved by the Esk FA.

Other water (1¼m both banks) owned by Egton Estate, Estate Office, Egton Bridge, nr Whitby YO21 1UY (tel: 01947 895466/7); tickets issued throughout season (6 Apr to 31 Oct), 3 rods per day. Trout fishing in **Scaling Dam** (worm and fly). Hotels: Horse Shoe; Wheatsheaf Inn; Postgate.

Glaisdale (N Yorks). Salmon, sea trout, trout; preserved below by the Esk FA *(see Whitby).* Esk FA bailiff, D J Swales, Rosedene, Priory Park, Grosmont, Whitby YO22 5QQ (tel: 01947 895488); members only; waiting list. Hotel: Mitre.

Danby (N Yorks). Salmon, sea trout, brown trout, grayling, preserved by landowners & Danby AC. Danby AC has about 8m of water stocked each year with approx 800 11" brown trout; also water between Castleton and Lealholm; st (limited) £15, dt £4, (£6 Oct), conc, from Duke of Wellington (Danby); Post Offices, Castleton and Danby. Restrictions on method according to date. Accommodation, licences, tickets, at Duke of Wellington. Tackle shops: Angling Supplies, 65 Haggersgate, Whitby YO21 3PP (tel: 01947 603855); Keith's Sports, 31 Milton St, Saltburn-by-Sea TS12 1DN (tel: 01287 624296).

Tributaries of the Esk (Yorkshire)

MURK ESK: Salmon and trout. Tributaries are: Little Beck, Brocka Beck, Eller Beck, Little Eller Beck. Fishing station: Grosmont.

COMMONDALE BROOK: **Commondale** (Yorks). Trout: preserved by the owners.

ESSEX (streams, lakes and reservoirs)

(For close seasons, licences, etc, see Anglian Region Environment Agency, p21)

ARDLEIGH RESERVOIR, nr **Colchester**. Off the A 137. Coarse fishing only, all year, excellent bream and pike. Rowing boats; electrical outboards only. St £125, dt £5, Juv £3, on site. Boats, min 2 persons, £25. Enq to Fishery Manager, Ardleigh Reservoir, nr Colchester, Essex CO7 7PT (tel: 01206 230642).

CONNAUGHT WATERS, **Chingford**. Roach, bream, carp; free.

EPPING FOREST PONDS. Fishing permitted in most ponds except where prohibited by notices, namely Alexandra Lake, Eagle Pond, Shoulder of Mutton Pond; no boats; no night fishing. Charges apply to the following: Ornamental Water, Perch Pond, Hollow Pond, Connaught Water (best access for disabled), Highams Park Lake, Wake Valley Pond, pay bailiff on site. The remaining are free. Further information from Forest Information Centre (tel: 020 8508 0028) or Superintendent of Epping Forest, The Warren, Loughton, Essex IG10 4RW (tel: 020 8532 1010). Tackle shop: Keswall Woodford, 618 Chigwell Road, Woodford Green IG8 8AA (tel: 020 8504 1929).

FISHERS GREEN, Waltham Abbey. Pike, carp to over 40lb, tench, bream, roach, barbel to 14lb 12oz, chub to over 7lb, perch, eels. An RMC Angling Special Venue fishery of 68 and 65 acre gravel pits, 3,900m of R Lea, 3,160 of **Lea Relief Channel**. St 2-rods £50 (£65 incl night), conc £30 (£35). *(For RMC Angling, see Chertsey.)*

GOSFIELD LAKE, Halstead (Essex). 45 acres; well-stocked with carp, perch, roach, tench, pike. Inquire C W Turp, Gosfield Lake, Church Road, Gosfield CO9 1UD (tel: 01787 475043); dt (7.30 am - 7.30 pm) £6, conc to jun, obtainable from the shop.

GREEN OAKS FLY FISHERY, Potash Rd, **Billericay** CM11 1HE (tel: 01277 657357). 2½ acre lake stocked weekly, open 8am till dusk all year round. Best brown 12lb 8oz, rainbow 15lb 4oz. Instruction, refreshments and flies for sale on site.

HANNINGFIELD RESERVOIR. Near **Chelmsford.** Excellent brown and rainbow trout fishery, average weight 2lb, good numbers of fish to 24lb 10oz. Regular stocking. Bank and boat fishing, incl boats for disabled. Enquiries to Fisheries Manager, Fishing Lodge, Giffords Lane, South Hanningford CM3 8HX (tel: 01245 212034) shop (tel: 01245 212031) office. web: www.eswater.co.uk.

HATFIELD FOREST LAKE. Near Hatfield Broad Oak and Bishop's Stortford: National Trust property, 10 acre coarse lake set in ancient woodland; st, dt (tel: 01279 870678).

HOOKS MARSH. 40 acre RMC Angling Group Water gravel pit nr **Waltham Abbey.** Bream, tench, roach, perch and pike. St (4 rods) £30, conc £18. *(For RMC Angling, see Chertsey).*

LAYER PITS. 6m S of **Colchester**; controlled by Colchester APS; coarse fish; members only.

NAZEING MEADS, Meadgate Lane, Nazeing, Essex. Four gravel pits totalling 125 acres. Carp are main species (up to 40lb), with large bream (13lb 2oz), roach, tench, eels and pike (to 30lb). Winter ticket £50, st (day only) £55 st (day & night £97), conc. Enquiries to Lee Valley Information Service, Hayes Hill Farm, Stubbins Hall Lane, Waltham Abbey EN9 2EG (tel: 01992 702200).

STAMBRIDGE FISHERIES, Stambridge Road, **Great Stambridge**, Essex SS4 2AR (tel: 01702 258274): three lakes, of sixteen, twenty and forty swims each, and carp to 10lbs or 25lbs, depending on water. Mirror, common, leather and wild, also crucian carp; roach, rudd, golden rudd, bronze and silver bream, and other species. No pike or zander. Dt from £5 per rod on bank or from barn; night fishing by pre-booking; bait and tackle on site; all facilities.

STANFORD-LE-HOPE. Two RMC Angling gravel pits, 13 acres, one Special Venue (Lake 1; st 2-rods £40, conc £25) and the other Group Venue water (Lake 2; st £30, conc £18). Large carp, crucian, perch, pike, roach, tench. Tackle shop: Stanford Tackle, 12 Wharf Road, SS17 0DH (tel: 01375 676739). *(For RMC Angling, see Chertsey).*

MARDYKE: Fishing stations: **Purfleet** and **Ockendon.** Rises by East Horndon and flows 12m to Thames at Purfleet. There are some club lengths. Moor Hall & Belhus AS has two members only coarse fisheries at South Ockendon, st on application to Sec.

PANT. Bocking. Upper part of R Blackwater *(see Blackwater in main list).*

ONGAR. Coarse fish; good chub, roach, dace and perch.

PASSINGFORD BRIDGE. Roach, chub, pike; bream, carp, tench. Barkingside & Dist AS has 1½m downstream; bailiff on water; dt from bailiffs on bank for ¾m u/s of bridge. Woodford AS has 1½m north of bridge; Elm Park AS has water; dt from bailiff. **Romford.**

SOUTH WEALD LAKES. Thorndon is a fishing run by Essex County Council; usual freshwater fish, esp. carp; dt on bank: Weald Office, Weald Country Park, South Weald, Brentwood, Essex CM14

5QS (tel:01277 216297).
WANSTEAD & WOODFORD LAKES AND PONDS. Eagle Pond, Snaresbrook (roach, perch, carp); **Knighton Wood Pond, Woodford; Hollow Pond, Whipps Cross**; all free.
OTHER TICKET WATERS. Priory Lakes, Priory Park, **Southend**; Eastwood Pit, **Rayleigh**; Essex Carp Fishery (crucian carp, bream) at Mollands Lane, **South Ockendon**; Old Hall Lake, **Herongate**; Moor Hall Farm Fishery, **Aveley**; Raphael Park Lake, **Romford**; Danbury Park Lakes, near **Chelmsford**; Harwood Hall at Corbets Tey, and Parklands Lake, both near **Upminster**; Warren Pond, **Chingford**; carp, bream. Tickets mostly from bailiffs on site. Essex tackle shops: Pro Master Angling Centre, Fullwell Parade, Fullwell Ave, Ilford IG5 0RF (tel: 020 8551 4033; web: www.promasterangling.co.uk); Hornchurch Angling Centre, 226 Hornchurch Rd, Havering, Hornchurch RM11 1QJ (tel: 01708 620608); County Angling, 19 Suttons Lane, Hornchurch RM12 6RD (tel: 01708 477834).
For Walthamstow reservoirs, see under London.

EXE

(For close seasons, licences, etc, see South West Region Environment Agency p19)

Rises in Somerset on Exmoor and runs south through Devon to Exmouth. Salmon and trout, with grayling and coarse fish in lower reaches. At several points on upper reaches trout fishing (moorland) and salmon fishing may be had by hotel guests.

Exeter (Devon). Bream, carp, dace, gudgeon, pike, perch, roach, rudd, tench and eels. **Exeter Ship** and **Tiverton Grand Western** Canals contain bream, carp, pike, perch, rudd, roach, tench, eels and dace. Hotels on canal banks: Double Locks, Turf. Exeter & DAA (amalgamation of local clubs) has coarse fishing rights on R Exe, on **Culm** and **Creedy**, from City Basin to Turf Basin on Exeter Ship Canal, and on ponds at Kingsteignton, Sampford Peveril, Feneck; also at Kia Ora pond. St, visitors wt, dt. For fishing on Tiverton Canal contact Tiverton & DAC (tel: 01884 242275) or tackle shops. At Exwick right bank visitors may fish for ½m, and from Exwick Mills d/s 400 yds below Exwick Rd Bridge; Exeter & DAA water. Environment Agency has 3m of salmon fishing on lower Exe in Cowley and Countess Wear areas; dt £4, st £59.25, fly or spinning, from 14 Feb to Sept 30, from Civic Centre (tel: 01392 265193). Apply Exeter AC, Smythen Str; dt £3.50, wt £14, st £28, conc, for Exeter & Dist AA waters and other from tackle shops. South View Farm Fishery, Shillingford St George, Exeter EX2 9UP (tel: 01392 832278): 6 acres of coarse fishing on three lakes, with various species of carp to 29lb, tench, rudd and other coarse; £5 dt on bank, facilities on site. One permit a day for salmon fishing (weekdays only) from Exeter Angling Centre, Smythen Str, EX1 1BN (tel: 01392 436404/435591).

Brampford Speke (Devon). Salmon, trout, dace, roach, chub; preserved. Pynes Water, from here down to Cowley Weir (2½m) fished by local syndicate. Exeter & Dist AA water towards Stoke Canon (see Culm).
Silverton (Devon). Trout, chub, roach, dace, pike, perch; preserved. Exeter & Dist AA has coarse fishing on Culm here (see Exeter and Culm).
Tiverton (Devon). Exe, Lowman and Little Dart; trout, salmon. **Grand Western Canal**; bream, pike, perch, roach, tench. Tiverton & DAC has river, canal and lake fishing in vicinity. Canal dt from tackle shops, other waters, members only. Exe preserved for 2m both above and below town (trout and grayling) by Tiverton FFC, fly only; residential qualification, but guest tickets; st for residents only. River walk in Tiverton, ½m, free trout fishing to juv. Tackle shop: Exe Valley Angling, 19 Westexe South, EX16 5DQ (tel: 01884 242275). Hotels: Bark House at Oakford Bridge; Fisherman's Cot, Bickleigh (beat on Exe).
Dulverton (Som). Salmon, trout, grayling. Usually good run of salmon (May onwards and autumn) to Dulverton and beyond, depending on water conditions. Trout fishing good on Exe and **Barle** (four to lb). Some free fishing for guests at Lion Hotel, Bank Square, Dulverton TA22 9BU (tel: 01398 323444). Royal Oak, Winsford, TA24 7JE (tel: 01643 851455), has a mile of river, free fishing

for guests. **Exe Valley Fishery**, Exebridge, Dulverton TA22 9AY (tel: 01398 323328); one large and two small lakes stocked with rainbows averaging 2lb+, dt £5.50 (plus £3.50 per kilo caught) on site throughout year, 5 fish limit. At **Broford**, 5m double bank of Little Exe, with wild brown trout, fly only; dt £10, from tackle shop: Lance Nicholson, Gloster House,

High Str, Dulverton TA22 9HB (tel: 01398 323409). Hotels: Lion Hotel; The Anchor Inn, (Jeff White) Exebridge, Dulverton, TA22 9AZ (tel: 01398 323433; e-mail: anchor_inn@btopenworld.com) which also has fishing rights along garden bank (about 100m); salmon, trout and grayling; dt on site from shop.

Tributaries of the Exe

CREEDY: Trout, coarse fish. Also B&B and restaurant facilities.

Cowley Bridge (Exeter). Coarse fish. Exeter & Dist AA has rights, left bank only (*see Exeter*).

Crediton (Devon). Trout. Yeo 3m; trout. Crediton FFC has over 5m, mainly double bank, on Rivers **Creedy**, **Culvery** and **Yeo**, also 1½m on R Taw. Five day visitor tickets £20. Contact Hon Sec.

CULM: Trout, coarse fish, few grayling.

Stoke Canon, **Rewe** and **Silverton** (Devon). Dace, chub, roach, perch and occasional grayling. Exeter & Dist AA

has water.

Hemyock (Devon). Trout, small and few. Lower water preserved and stocked by Hemyock-Culmstock syndicate.

Clayhidon (Devon). Upper Culm FA preserves about 4m in this district (see Hemyock). No Sunday fishing. Hotel: Half Moon.

Killerton (Devon). National Trust controls coarse fishing on Killerton Estate; tickets from tackle shops for Exeter AA water.

BARLE. Runs through beautifully wooded valley and holds salmon (av 7-10lb) and trout (av 8-10 in).

FAL

(For close seasons, licences, etc, see South West Region Environment Agency, p19)

Rises near Roche and flows about 23 miles, due south, past Grampound and Tregony to the English Channel at Falmouth.

Falmouth (Cornwall). Trout fishing in **Argal Reservoir**, coarse fishing in **College Reservoir**: large pike and carp. Trout in some of the small streams flow-

ing into creeks around Falmouth.

Tregony (Cornwall). Trout, 2m off runs Polglaze Brook, 4m long; trout.

FOWEY

(For close seasons, licences, etc, see South West Region Environment Agency p19)

Rises on Bodmin Moor, runs down a steep valley at Golitha and enters sea by a long estuary at Fowey. Cornwall's foremost sea trout river, with good salmon fishing also. Run of big sea trout and some salmon in April and May and runs continue throughout the year. Peal (small sea trout) come in numbers in July and August when there is also a run of grilse. Salmon fishing continues to mid-December, and a run of big winter fish (up to 20lb) can be expected late in the season.

Fowey (Cornwall). Capital sea fishing *(see Sea Fishing section)*.

Lostwithiel (Cornwall). Sea trout, salmon, brown trout. Lostwithiel FC has approx 4m double bank fishing on two pools; season tickets £55, conc, may be purchased from Treasurer, R Lashbrook, Roger's Tackle Shop, Stan Mays Store, Higher Bore St, Bodmin PL31 1DZ (tel: 01208 78006) (closed Wednesday).

Respryn Bridge (Cornwall). Most water above the bridge is in the hands of Lanhydrock AA, NT Cornwall Regional Office,

Lanhydrock Park, PL30 4DE; st £55 (waiting list), wt £30, dt £15, conc; artificial bait only; free fishing on section between Respryn Bridge and footbridge. Hotels: Royal Talbot, King's Arms, Earl of Chatham, Royal Oak, Globe, Trevone Guest House and Restormel Lodge.

Liskeard (Cornwall). Liskeard & Dist AC has several beats on Fowey, also **Lynher**, and on minor rivers, West Looe, Seaton and Inny; visitor tickets: st £60 + £15 joining fee, wt £55, dt £20 from Tremar Tropicals, 11 Market St, Liskeard PL14

3JH (tel: 01579 343177); East Looe Chandlers on the quay in E Looe; or Lashbrooks Tackle Shop, Bodmin. Membership (limited to 250): apply Trevor

Sobey, Trevartha Farm, Pengover, nr Liskeard PL14 3NJ. Memb £60 + joining fee £15, wt £55, dt £20, conc.

FROME AND PIDDLE (Dorset)

(For close seasons, licences, etc, see South West Region Environment Agency, p19)

Frome rises above Hooke in West Dorset and flows into the English Channel at Poole Harbour near Wareham. Piddle rises in a mill pond 1 mile north of Piddletrenthide and enters Poole Harbour near mouth of Frome near Wareham. Both are chalk streams and closely preserved but sport may sometimes be had. Some very good sea trout have been caught in the Frome, which also receives a run of heavy salmon. Trout in both rivers plentiful and good. Bass run up to where the river enters Poole Harbour. Piddle carries very small stock of heavy salmon. River is in fine condition due to successful efforts of River Piddle Protection Association.

Wareham (Dorset). On Frome and Piddle; salmon, sea trout, trout, grayling, pike, roach and dace. Free coarse fishing on towpath side of R Frome, from Wareham South Bridge downstream. EA licence required. Salmon and trout preserved. Mr Bowerman, Morden Estate Office, Charborough Park, Wareham BH 7EN, sometimes has season and other rods available as follows: salmon, Frome and Piddle; trout, Piddle and Bere Stream, and River Stour, coarse fishing. Environment Agency lets 14 rods for the season (on the basis of two per day) for fishery on Piddle; salmon, sea trout; £233.82 (incl VAT): details from Area Conservation Officer (tel: 01258 456080). South Drain nr Poole Harbour is Wareham & Dist AS water. Club has local waters, membership £40, £10 jun. Tackle shop and bait: Purbeck Angling, 28 South Str, BH20 4LU (tel: 01929 550770). Hotels: Red Lion and Black Bear.

Wool (Dorset). Frome: Salmon, sea trout. Spring salmon scarce, summer and autumn fish more plentiful. Season and other rods on 1¼m Woolbridge beat sometimes available from Mr Bowerman, Morden Estate Office, Charborough Park, Wareham BH20 7EN (tel: 01258 857204). Dorchester & Dist AS uses the Woolbridge beat for coarse fishing only from 1 November to 28 February. Contact Hon Sec. Nr **Tincleton**, **Pallington Lakes**: now club water; no tickets. At Tolpuddle, and 7m from Dorchester, **Wessex Fly Fishing** and **Wessex Chalk Streams Ltd** Lawrences Farm, DT2 7HF (tel: 01305 848460): 12 chalk stream beats on Rivers Frome and Piddle, lakes and pools; tuition (Reffis member); c&r on rivers, 10 fish limit, barbless hooks;

lake dt £26, 6-hour £22, 4-hour (after 2pm) £18; rivers, from £19 to £65, depending on season and beat; tackle shop on site, also self-catering accom and B&B.

Dorchester (Dorset). Frome: brown trout and grayling; Dorchester FC has 6½m water in vicinity of Dorchester; u/s dry fly or nymph fishing; limited dt £30, from J Aplin *(see below)*. Rest of river preserved by landowners. Dt and licences from tackle shop. Dorchester & Dist AS has coarse fishing for 3.8m stretch of **Stour**. Contact Hon Sec. St £40, conc (no dt). Revels Coarse Fishery at Cosmore, DT2 7TW (tel: 01300 345301); dt avail afternoon £4, conc; 24 hours £6.50; party and match bookings welcome; separate specimen lake. At **Kingcombe**, Higher Kingcombe Farm. 8 ponds - coarse fishing; Paul Crocker (tel: 01300 320537); st £75, £3 full day, £2 evenings, £5 night. Dorchester & Dist AS has exclusive use of No 6 Lake; apply Hon Sec; no dt, st £40. The Society also has West Knighton Lake. **Rawlsbury Waters**, 4 small trout lakes (tel: 01258 817446). **Flowers Farm Lakes**, Hilfield, Dorchester, Dorset DT2 7BA (tel/fax: 01300 341351); trout fishery of 5 lakes, brown and rainbow; dt £22, half-day £16, evng £12.50; full day limit 4 fish; half day 3 fish; evng 2 fish; open all year. At Common Farm, Hermitage, DT2 7BB (tel: 01963 210556) is Hermitage Fishing Lakes; 3 trout lakes (rainbow and brown) and 1 coarse (carp); dt £15 (4 fish), half-day £12 (3 fish), envg £9 (2 fish). Tickets for Luckfield Lake Fishery, 1½ acres, Broadmayne, with carp, and for R Frome fishing, from Tackle shop: John Aplin, Specialist Angling Supplies, 1 Athelstan Road, Dor-

Pallington Lakes in Dorset, an interesting configuration: an example of the fast growing supply of coarse fisheries with, in this case, mirror carp to 30lb 12oz.

chester DT1 1NR (tel: 01305 266500).   Hotel: King's Arms.

GIPPING (Orwell)

(For close seasons, licences, etc, see Anglian Region Environment Agency, p21)

Rises between Stowmarket and Bury St Edmunds, and flows into the North Sea by an estuary near Ipswich. Coarse fish.

Ipswich (Suffolk). Most coarse fish. From Yarmouth Rd Bridge to Norwich Railway Bridge, 1m, dt on bank or tackle shops; 2m stretch from Railway Bridge to Sproughton Bridge; Gipping APS water; members only; Town section, st or dt on bank or tackle shops; Gipping APS controls 10m between Needham Market and Ipswich; members only; and has section of river from Bramford to Ipswich; members only; also other fishings, which include several coarse lakes in vicinity. **Alton Water**, 350 acre coarse fish reservoir at Anglian Water Services Ltd, Holbrook Rd, Stutton, Ipswich, IP9 2RY (tel: 01473 589105), under control of AW, with bream to 7lb and pike to 25lb, plus roach and perch. St £25, dt £3, conc, on site or from local tackle shops. Tackle shops: Viscount Fishing Tackle, 207 Clapgate Lane IP3 0RF (tel: 01473 728179); G R Markham, 717 Woodbridge Rd IP4 4NB (tel: 01473 727841); Bosmere Tackle, 57 High Str, Needham Market IP6 8AL (tel: 01449 721808).

Stowmarket (Suffolk). Permits to fish Green Meadow stretch from Bosmere Tackle, *see below.* Stowmarket & Dist AA has short stretch of **Rattle**; members only. Gipping Valley AC fishes river here, and at **Needham Market** and **Claydon**; also **Needham Lake**, 10 acres: most coarse fish stocked; Gipping APS has Alderson Lake at Needham Market; and Causeway Lake at Baylham; Barham Pit (B Pit); members only. Membership from Bosmere Tackle, 57 High Str, Needham Market IP6 8AL (tel: 01449 721808).

GLOUCESTERSHIRE (streams)

BIDEFORD BROOK. Fishing station: **Awre**. Rises in Abbot's Wood and flows

7m to Severn estuary; coarse fish; preserved. **Blackpool Brook** enters at Awre; Forest of Dean AC; members only.

CONE. fishing station: **Woolaston**. Cone rises by Hewelsfield, and is 5m long. Eels and flounders.

FROME. Rises near Cheltenham and flows into Severn estuary. Coarse fish; a few trout higher up. Fishing stations: **Stonehouse** (Glos), coarse fish, and **Stroud** (Glos), a few trout and coarse fish. Several brooks in vicinity. Pike and coarse fishing in Stroudwater Canal. Stroud AA controls 2m Thames at Lechlade and 1m at Newbridge.

NAILSWORTH BROOK (tributary of Frome). Fishing stations: **Nailsworth** (Glos) and **Woodchester** (Glos). Brook reported polluted in parts. Lakes: Longfords Lake, pike, carp. Woodchester Park lakes: pike, perch, roach, tench, brown and rainbow trout; NT water now preserved by Priory Angling Club.

HOPE BROOK. Fishing station: **Westbury-on-Severn**, ns Grange Court, 1½m. Hope Brook rises 2m above Longhope, runs 5m to Westbury and Severn estuary (1m). Coarse fish, mostly preserved. Inn: Red Lion.

LITTLE AVON: Small Gloucestershire stream flowing into Severn estuary.

Berkeley (Glos). Coarse fish, trout, Waterley Brook. Fishing below Charfield preserved. Close by station rises Billow Brook, which runs thence 3m to estuary. Clubs have water on **Gloucester and Berkeley Canal**; 16m Sharpness to Gloucester.

LYD. Chub, roach, perch. Fishing station: **Lydney**. Lydney AA holds stretch from railway station to Tufts Junction; dt on bank or tackle shop below. Club also has **Lydney Lake** (carp, roach and perch), **Lydney Canal** and a dam. Tackle Shop: Peter James Sports, 17 Newerne St, Lydney GL15 5RA (tel: 01594 842515).

GREATER MANCHESTER RESERVOIRS

These are trout fisheries, unless otherwise stated.

BUCKLEY WOOD RESERVOIR, Rochdale. Rochdale Waltonian Anglers; dt water (*see club list*).

CASTLESHAW (LOWER) RESERVOIR, Oldham. Trout. Controlled by Oldham United Anglers; for dt contact

Hon Sec. **GORTON (LOWER) RESERVOIR.** Coarse permits on bank, suitable for disabled anglers. Contact Manchester City Council (*below*).

GORTON (UPPER) RESERVOIR, 'Lawrence Scott Arm'. Coarse fishing permits on bank. Further details from Manchester City Council, Leisure Dept, Debdale Centre, Debdale Park, 1073 Hyde Road, Gorton, Manchester M18 7LJ (tel: 0161 223 5182).

HOLLINGWORTH LAKE, Littleborough. Fishing for roach, perch, pike, tench, carp, bream. Contact Chief Warden, Visitors' Centre, Hollingworth Lake Country Park, Rakewood Rd, Littleborough, Lancs OL15 0AQ (tel: 01706 373421). Tickets from Visitors' Centre, or from ranger on bank.

KITCLIFFE RESERVOIR, Rochdale. Trout. Controlled by Oldham FFC. For dt contact Hon Sec.

LITTLE SEA RESERVOIR, Oldham. Medlock AC; contact Nick Naum, 23 Winchester Avenue, Chadderton, Oldham OL9 0RH (tel 0161 6787626).

LUDWORTH RESERVOIR, Stockport. Crossland's AC. Dt for members guests only.

OGDEN RESERVOIR, Rossendale. Rainbows with head of browns. For information contact Hon Sec Haslingden & Dist FFC; dt from Wensleys Butchers, 2 The Parade, Broadway, Helmshore BB4 4HD (tel: 01706 214681).

RUMWORTH LODGE, Bolton. Royal Ashton AC, D T Dobson, 1 Parkway, Westhoughton. Dt water.

WALKERWOOD TROUT FISHERY, Brushes Road, **Stalybridge,** SK15 3QP (tel: 07721 619399; web: www.walkerwood.free-online.co.uk). Fly only, all browns to be returned. Best brown 11lb, best rainbow 18lb 8oz. Dt £17, conc, 4 fish, at Car Park. A range of season tickets on offer.

WATERGROVE RESERVOIR, Rochdale. Dt from warden on site at the sailboard club, or from Hollingworth Lake.

HAMPSHIRE (Streams, lakes and canal)

(For close seasons, licences, etc, see Southern Region Environment Agency, p18).

BASINGSTOKE CANAL. Fishing stations: **Greywell, North Warnborough, Odiham, Winchfield, Crookham, Fleet, Farnborough, Aldershot, Ash Vale, Woking, West Byfleet,** where canal joins R Wey. Pike, carp, roach, good tench, perch, bream (to 8lb); fishing from towpath only; dt for 32m of the canal from Greywell Tunnel to R Wey from bailiffs on bank (head bailiff Garry Goddard (tel: 01252 677060); The Basingstoke Canal Centre, Mytchett Lake Rd, Mytchett, Surrey GU16 6DD (tel: 01252 370073); and tackle shops. Raison Brothers, 2 Park Road, Farnborough GU14 6JG (tel: 01252 543470); Equinox, 81 High St, Odiham RG29 1LB (tel: 01256 702548); Goldsworth Angling Centre, 73-75 Goldsworth Rd, Woking GU21 1LJ (tel: 01483 776667). Further enquiries about Basingstoke Canal to BCAA Treasurer; also contact The Creel (*below*); dt £3, juv £1.75, OAP/disabled £1.75. Farnborough AS also has rights on **Whitewater** at **Heckfield, Loddon** at **Winnersh, Shawfields Lake,** 3 acres, mixed, Hollybush Lakes at **Farnborough,** and gravel pits. **Willow Park Fisheries,** Youngs Drive, Ash, nr Aldershot GU12 6RE (tel: 01252 325867) three lakes totalling over 13 acres stocked with carp (to 31lb), tench and other coarse fish; 120 pegs; bait and refreshments on site; dt on site £10 1 rod, £14 2 rods, and £23 for 24-hours, concession for jun; disabled facilities. Four RMC Angling lakes at **Frimley** (Group Water). Carp, crucian carp, bream, perch, tench, perch, rudd, eel and pike. Large specimens recorded. St £40, conc £25 two rods. *(For RMC Angling, see Chertsey.)* Tackle shops: Tackle Up, 151 Fleet Road, Fleet GU51 3PD (01252 614066); M J Borra, The Creel, 36 Station Road, Aldershot, Hants GU11 1HT (tel: 01252 320871); Raison Brothers, 2 Park Road, Farnborough GU14 6JG (tel: 01252 543470); Equinox, 81 High St, Odiham RG29 1LB (tel: 01256 702548); Goldsworth Angling Centre, 73-75 Goldsworth Rd, Woking GU21 1LJ (tel: 01483 776667).

BEAULIEU. The Beaulieu River is approx 14 miles long. Tickets for tidal stretch, Bailey's Hard to Needs Ore (bass, mullet), st £18, dt £3, from Harbour Master, Buckler's Hard SO42 7XB(tel: 01590 616200) or Resident Land Agent, John Montagu Building, Beaulieu (tel: 01590 612345); access from Bailey's Hard and Buckler's Hard. Coarse fishing on **Hat-**

chet Pond (Forestry Commission); bream, carp, tench and pike; tickets from Forestry Commission, The Queen's House, Lyndhurst SO43 7NH (tel: 02380 283141), campsite offices during camping season and local tackle shops (st £60 2 rods, wt £15, dt £5, VAT incl, jun conc, barbless hooks only). Children may fish free on Janesmoor Pond. Hotel: Montagu Arms.

DAMERHAM TROUT LAKES, The Lake House, Damerham Fisheries, **Fordingbridge**, SP6 3HW (tel: 01725 518446); six lakes, and river for st holders; r and b trout; open March to October. Season rods only, full, half, quarter, guest, prices on application.

FLEET POND. Fishing station: **Fleet**. Cove AS water. No tickets. Tackle shop: Tackle Up, 151 Fleet Road, Fleet GU51 3PD (01252 614066).

HAMBLE. Sea trout and trout. **Bishop's Waltham.** Fishing mostly private.

HOLBURY TROUT LAKES, Lockerley, Near **Romsey**, Hants SO51 0JR (tel: 01794 341619): fishery of four lakes, stocked with rainbow and blue trout (average caught 3lb, largest 13lb 9oz), and ⅔m of River Dun, both banks, stocked brown trout. Dry fly and nymph only on river, wet and dry fly on lakes. No c&r. Various tickets, incl full dt for lakes and river £44 (w/e only) limit 6 fish; lakes only dt £35 limit 4 fish; half day £20. Full facilities on site, and tuition if required.

LYMINGTON RIVER. Fishing station: Lymington. Sea trout (2-11lb), brown trout (¾ to 1lb). Sea trout best June to Sept. Fishing improved by Brockenhurst Manor FFC; private. Mixed fishery at **Sway Lakes**, Barrows Lane, Sway Lymington SO41 6DD (tel: 01590 682010); carp to over 33lbs; dt on bank. Tackle and bait from Loni's Angling Centre, 258 Barrack Road, Christchurch BH23 2BJ (tel: 01202 484518).

MEON. Trout; sea trout in lower reaches. Fishing station: **East Meon**; Portsmouth & Dist AS (members of Hants & Sussex Alliance) holds some thirty waters around **Portsmouth** and across Hampshire and W Sussex, which include coarse fishing on Arun, Rother, Ember, Hamble, and Wallington; dt on some waters; club also has **Hilsea Moats**, Eastern and Western, coarse; dt on both £6; also Funtley Pond, 3m W of Fareham; membership £75 per annum, conc: enquiries to Hon Sec, or local tackle shops. Other fisheries in vicinity: at Staunton Country Park, Havant PO9 5HB (tel: 023 9245 3405): a 3 acre lake with carp, bream roach, dt from Park Office (10am-5pm). Meon Springs Fly Fishery, Whitewool Farm, East Meon, Petersfield GU32 1HW (tel: 01730 823249): 3 acres lakes, rainbows, between East and West Meon; tickets from bailiff: dt £38 4 fish, £31.50 3 fish, £25 2 fish, £18 c&r. Chiphall Lake Trout Fishery, 5 acres: Northfields Farm, Wickham. Wintershill Lake, Wintershill Farmhouse, Durley, SO32 2AH (tel: 01489 860200): trout fishing on 3½ acres; for full season, half season, 4-day and day rods contact Lake Bailiff (tel: 023 8060 1421). Tackle shops: Rovers Tackle Shop, 178A West St, Fareham PO16 0EQ (tel: 01329 220354); Allan's Marine, 143 Twyford Ave, Stamshaw, Portsmouth PO2 8HU (tel: 02392 671833).

SANDLEHEATH. Six lakes and three chalk stream beats at **Rockbourne Trout Fishery**, Sandleheath, Fordingbridge, Hampshire SP6 1QG. Excellent fishing for rainbow trout in lakes and brown trout in streams, fly only, various period terms from dt £45 (5 fish), £36 (4 fish), £20 evng (2 fish). Blocks of tickets at discount, conc; also fish tickets min 10 fish at £10/fish (no max). Tuition, tackle hire, licensed cafeteria (tel: 01725 518603).

WAGGONERS' WELLS, near **Haslemere**. Three lakes; National Trust waters, now managed by Greyshott AC. Coarse fishing; carp, roach, tench, gudgeon, a few trout; dt from Greyshott Tackle, 1 Crossway Road, Greyshott, Hindhead GU26 6HJ (tel: 01428 606122), or bailiff on bank. Hotel: Punchbowl Hotel, Hindhead.

WARBURN. Dace, trout, salmon; preserved; leave sometimes from landowners; joins sea at **Key Haven**.

HERTS AND GREATER LONDON (reservoirs and lakes)

(see also London Reservoirs)

ALDENHAM (Herts). **Aldenham Country Park Reservoir**. Managed by Herts CC. Coarse fishing, incl. tench, pike to 37lb, carp to 39lb, plus very good roach and bream. No night fishing. Dt £4 (jun, OAP £2.00), punt £6-£4. Dis free. From bailiff on site or from Park Manager, Park Office, Dagger Lane, Elstree WD6 3AT (tel: 020 8953 9602; bailiff's mobile tel: 020 8953 4978).

Shepperton (Middx); **Ashmere Fisheries**, Felix Lane, Shepperton TW17 8NN: four lakes, total 20 acres, stocked with rainbow trout; boats; annual membership only; apply Mrs Jean Howman (tel: 01932 225445). Dt £5, 2 rods, carp to 35lb, large head of pike (British record tench here) for **Sheepwalk Lakes** from Ashford Angling Centre, 357 Staines Rd West, Ashford Common, Middlesex TW15 1RP (tel: 01784 240013). RMC has 2 lakes of 9 and 7 acres (Group Water); coarse with carp to over 36lb; st £26, conc £15. *(For RMC Angling, see Chertsey.)*

STANSTEAD ABBOTS. RMC Angling coarse fisheries consisting of 3 gravel pits. The 30-acre Special Venues lake is noted for carp to 40lb 3oz with good bream and tench. St 2-rods £50, conc £30. The remaining 2 lakes and part of the main river are Group Water fishings: excellent small carp, roach, perch, bream, tench. St £30, conc £18. RMC also have a Syndicate Venue at Armwell: 2 small lakes heavily stocked with carp of all sizes; st £150. *(For RMC Angling, see Chertsey.)*

TRING (Herts). Four large reservoirs: **Marsworth, Startops End** and **Wilstone** (2m from Tring) main feeders for Grand Union Canal. Good fishing for specimen hunters. Bream over 16lb, former British record tench 12½lb, pike to 30lb, many large roach, specimen catfish. Sunday fishing now permitted. St £80 2 rods; £100 3 rods; £120 4 rods (including night fishing), conc; dt £4, conc £3, evening £3. Tickets obtainable on bank from bailiff, B C Double, Reservoir House, Watery Lane, Marsworth HP23 4LY (tel: 01442 822379). The fourth reservoir is a private trout fishery. The Tring Anglers have exclusive fishing rights on the Grand Union canal from Tring station to Cooks Wharf (the latter venue being members only) along with the Wendover Arms and several miles of the Aylesbury Arms of the canal. Also the **R Thame** at Chearsley, Shabbington Island and Ickford; **R Ivel** at Shefford, plus an excellent members only bream and tench lake fishery near Soulbury. The Club has a comprehensive water-sharing scheme with Barnet & Dist AC. Tring Anglers st £38, dt £3 where applicable, conc half price. Tackle shop: Chiltern Tackle, 33 Western Rd, Tring HP23 4BQ (tel: 01442 825257).

HULL

(For close seasons, licences, etc, see North East Region Environment Agency, p20)

Tidal river between Hempholme and Hull is free of any permit charge and is popularly fished by an increasing number of coarse anglers. Upstream of Beverley first-class sport may be had with roach, dace, pike, chub, bream, etc. West Beck is an excellent but preserved trout fishery of chalk-stream character.

Hull (North Humberside). Drains giving good coarse fishing. Free fishing on E.A. licence from North Frodingham to Hull. Hull & Dist AA has water on **Derwent** at **Breighton, Wressle**; on the **Rye** at **Butterwick** and **Swinton**; and on the **Trent** at **Carlton**; also the **Brandsburton Ponds** (open all the year), Tilery Lake, the Broomfleet, Motorway, and other ponds, 9m of **Market Weighton Canal**, 17m from Hull, mixed coarse fishery, 1m of **R Foulness**, north bank; membership is unrestricted; Stone Creek and Patrington Haven hold flounders; good sea fishing. Rush Lyvars Lake, Preston Road, coarse fishery at **Hedon**, dt water (tel: 01482 898970). **Pickering Park Lake** owned by City Council, fine pike; coarse dt £3.40, juv/OAP £1.70 from ranger on bank (tel:

01482 614966). At Aldbrough on Sea, Lambwath Lakes, 5 pond complex of 120 pegs, good match fishing for carp, tench, orfe and bream; D Heslop, 999 Sutton Rd, Hull HU8 0HU. Tackle shops: Fishing Basket, 470 Beverley Rd HU5 1NE (tel: 01482 445284); G W Hutchinson & Co, 31 Anlaby Rd HU1 2PG (tel: 01482 223869).

Beverley (East Yorkshire). Tidal River Hull and drains give good coarse fishing; from Hull Bridge upstream through **Arram, Aike Wilfholme, Baswicke** and **Hempholme** to Frodingham Beck: North East Region Environment Agency, for enquiries; weedy June to Nov; some of best winter fishing from The Ship Yard to Weel. **Beverley Beck**, canalised stream, 1m long, 60 pegs, good access for disabled. Stocked with most coarse species, but mainly roach to 2lb, bream 7lb, tench and chub, perch, pike to 30lb; dt £3, conc, from Total Petrol Station, Waterside Rd, Beverley or on bank. Further information: Paul Caygill (mob: 07976 779983). Dt £4 for 2 coarse ponds in Lakeminster Park, Hull Rd, HU17 0PN (tel: 01482 882655). **Leven Canal** (6m): coarse fish; fine tench. Tackle shop: Beverley Angling Centre, 8 Maple Drive HU17 9QJ (tel: 01482 869948). Hotel: Beverley Arms.

Brandesburton (East Yorkshire). River Hull 3m W, excellent coarse fishing in gravel pits *(see Hull);* at **Leven Park Lake,** 6m N of Beverley coarse lake; mixed coarse with 2 log cabins for weekly hire with own pegs; dt £5, conc (tel: 019645 44510).

Wansford (East Yorkshire). Free left bank below Lock Dow to Brigham. **Driffield Canal Fishery,** from Town Lock, Driffield along B1249 to Snake Holme Lock, ½m west of Wansford. Trout, both bait and fly. **West Beck** preserved by Golden Hill AS and West Beck PS; members only.

Tributaries of the Hull

FOSTON BECK (or KELK or FRODINGHAM BECK):
North Frodingham, Foston-on-the-Wolds and **Lowthorpe** (East Yorkshire). Rises in Yorkshire wolds; true chalk stream containing brown trout averaging well over the pound. Preserved.

DRIFFIELD BECK:
Driffield (East Yorkshire). Provides chalk stream fishing for trout and grayling of high order. Driffield AA. Kellythorpe Trout Lake now in private hands. For **Pickering Trout Lake,** Newbridge Rd, Pickering, N Yorks YO18 8JJ (tel: 01751 474219).

ISLE OF MAN

The geographical nature of the Isle of Man tends to dictate the type of river, fish and hence fishing one may encounter when angling in the Island. Being a relatively mountainous place, rivers and streams are small, fast flowing and very clear. Excellent sport can be had in the numerous small trout streams, which hold fine stocks of native brown trout.

There are very few preserved stretches of river in the Island and a well chosen word with the land owner is often all that is required to enable an angler to fish in peace. Approx one half mile of the River Douglas through the Nunnery Estate is exclusively reserved for the Manx Game FC and small sections of the Rivers Dhoo and Glass can only be fished under permit from the Douglas & District Angling Club; contact Hon Sec. *(see Clubs)*

Natural and artificial baits are allowed on the Island's rivers, ponds and streams; however, other than in Eairy Dam, live bait, ground bait or organic matter must not be used in any reservoir. In addition, rubber worms or similar artificial bait are not allowed, including any substance with which artificial bait may be impregnated to attract fish by sense of smell. Further details of all freshwater angling can be obtained from the Freshwater Fisheries Officer, Cornaa, Maughold (tel: 01624 812224).

Anglers must abide by the regulations wherever they fish. These include: (1) Not to use or carry a gaff or tailer. (2) Not to use a line that exceeds 10lb breaking strain. (3) Not use more than one hook on a line unless (a) Pennel or Stewart tackles are being used for bait fishing; (b) a 'point with two droppers' is being used for fly fishing only; (c) a spinner is being used for spinning only. (4) Not use a spinner except (a) in a reservoir where the spinner does not exceed 10gms in weight and does not exceed 65mms in length, inclusive of hook and dressing or (b) in a river where the spinner does not exceed 15gms in weight and does not exceed 100mms in length, inclusive of hook and dressing. (5) Not to use a hook larger than No 6 Redditch scale, unless the hook is comprised in an artificial fly. (6) Return all foul hooked fish to the water. (7) Return to the water unharmed any freshwater fish hooked which is less than 18 cm in length overall. (8) Wading in the reservoirs is prohibited. (9) A landing net must be used when fishing at a reservoir at all times, and when fishing for migratory fish in rivers. (10) Fishing for salmon or sea trout from the foreshore, in any estuary or at sea is not permitted.

The river fishing season commences on 1 Apr, and finishes on the 30 Sept for trout, with an extension to the end of Oct in respect of angling for salmon and sea trout only. The reservoir season begins on 10 Mar and continues until 31 Oct.

An *'Other Waters'* fishing licence is required to fish any river or pond, and a separate licence is required should you wish to fish the reservoirs. Anglers fishing the rivers during the month of October *must* hold an *'Other Waters'* season licence.

There is a daily bag limit for the rivers of 6 fish, of which no more than 2 may be salmon or sea trout, and catch and release must not be continued after the 6th (final) fish is caught and killed. There is also a bag limit for the reservoirs of 4 trout per day and anglers must not continue to fish after catching and killing the maximum number of fish. Full details of all the Regulations can be obtained from the Department of Agriculture Fisheries and Forestry.

Fishing Licences

Fishing licences are obligatory by law and 2004 costs are as follows; **Reservoirs:** st £95 (juv £32), wt £32 (juv £11), dt £11 (juv £6). **Other Waters:** st £32 (juv £11), wt £11 (juv £6), dt £6 (juv £3.50).

Whilst these prices are very reasonable, they are not to be ignored. It is an offence not to be in possession of a valid fishing licence whilst fishing. Failure to produce a valid licence on demand to an authorised officer could result in prosecution and confiscation of fishing tackle. Warranted Fisheries Officers and River Watchers patrol all the fisheries on a regular basis.

Licences are obtainable from: Department of Agriculture Fisheries and Forestry, Rose House, 51-59 Circular Road, Douglas (tel: 01624 685835; web: www.gov.im/tourism); from Department of Tourism and Leisure, Information Bureau, Sea Terminal, Douglas IM1 2RG (tel: 01624 686766); from Onchan Commissioners, and from several tackle shops and from most Post Office.

No licence is required for sea fishing, which from pier, rocks or boat is excellent, especially for Pollack (locally called callig), mackerel, cod and codling, whiting and plaice. Chief bait for ground fish is mackerel, but lugworm, sand eels and shellfish are also used. Jigging with white and coloured feathers and artificial sand eel for Pollack, mackerel and cod is successful.

'Could be a tench?' A member of Framlingham & District Angling Club fishes Moat Hall water, near Framlingham, Suffolk. *Photo: M Temple.*

Good centres for most species are Peel, Port Erin, Port St Mary and Ramsey.

The Department of Tourism & Leisure in Douglas issues useful booklets on sea and river fishing (tel: 01624 686766); additional information can also be obtained from their web-site: www.gov.im/tourism.

At this time there are eight reservoirs open for trout fishing **West Baldwin** lies near the centre of the Island, a large water, about a mile long and 500ft above sea level. Good access as road runs along the western side, where shallower water is to be found; fly fish or spin. The **Clypse** and **Kerrowdhoo** lie one beyond the other, about 1½ miles north of Onchan - both are fly fishing only. **Ballure** is a small reservoir nestling about 300ft in the hills, just south of Ramsey where anglers may fly fish or spin. **Cringle** reservoir is in the south of the Island; at approx 750ft it can be breezy but the mangificent views down to Langness Lighthouse make it well worth while; the western side has the deeper water but all round the underwater contours mean a variety of depths; fly fish or spin. **Sulby Reservoir** is a huge upland (c700ft) water, close to the A14 Sulby-Snaefell road; shallower water along the western edge from the car park; fly fish or spin; the dam and area to the west is well signed *no fishing* zone. **Block Eairy** reservoir stands at 750ft above sea level and fishing involves a steep hill walk just west of Sulby Valley; fly-fish or spin. **Eairy Dam** is not a water supply and therefore the restrictions on the use of live organic bait do not apply; it lies to the east of the old mining village of Foxdale, about 500ft above sea level. All reservoirs hold an excellent stock of wild brown trout and have ample parking close by (apart from Block Eairy), though facilities for disabled anglers are limited.

Reservoirs are stocked on weekly basis throughout the season with Rainbow Trout reared at the Government's fish hatchery at Cornaa. All the Island's fish are raised here and visitors can visit the site to see the rearing pools and feed the fish. Opening hours are 10am - 4pm on each Wednesday during the Easter and Summer school holidays. A preliminary phone call is appreciated in the event of bad weather (tel: 01624 812224).

There are two private fisheries on the island. They are: Riverside Fishery, Patrick Road, St Johns; managed by Ken Jervis (tel: 01624 801715). Limited morning tickets may be available on this 3 acre fishery; fly only and all fish are to be kept. Also Kennislough, Lower Ballaclucas Farm, Trolloby Lane, Top Crosby Road, Marown; managed by John Stringer (tel: 01624 851887). ¾ acre lake, stocked with large rainbow trout in double figures; tuition available. Either category of fishing licence is valid for fishing these private commercial fisheries.

Salmon and sea trout are both native to the island and Manx rivers hold surprisingly good stocks of migratory fish. Given enough water, there should be sea trout in the major streams by June, with salmon arriving later in the year, usually by late September. The main streams frequented by migratory fish are the Sulby River in the northern half of the island, the Neb, which flows into the sea at Peel on the West coast and the Douglas River. Sea trout can also be found in some of the larger pools in the smaller streams. The principal rivers are as follows:

Sulby River. Starts at Sulby Reservoir and runs into the sea at Ramsey. The top section from the dam to around Sulby Bridge is a rocky, fast flowing mountain stream with alternating pools and runs. Downstream the character changes into a wider and slower running water with long deep stretches and much bankside vegetation; salmon (from Aug), sea trout.

Laxey River. 5m long; trout; rises below Snaefell and runs into the sea at Laxey. The bottom mile is difficult through the village; however, Laxey Glen is much easier; above here to Glen Roy there is 1m of very rough fishing. Fishing station: **Laxey**.

River Dhoo. Flows across the central valley to Douglas; private fishing to Braddan Bridge, above which it is slow flowing through agricultural land (somewhat polluted). **River Douglas** is formed by junction of Dhoo and Glass, half a mile above the town of **Douglas**.

River Glass. Starts at West Baldwin Reservoir and flows down to Douglas; private fishing up to the Tromode area; above here, ask permission to fish an increasingly wild stream and its little tributary, the Baldwin River. Glass largely rented by Douglas & Dist AC. Manx Game FC has fishing on these rivers; residents only, no guest tickets.

River Neb. Flows from the **Little London** area, through **Glen Helen**, where there are a number of deep pools to **St John's**; here **Foxdale River**, 6m long, joins on left bank; finally enters the sea at **Peel**. Trout; salmon from Sept; first class river for migratory fish.

Brown Trout Fishing: There are numerous smaller streams on the Island, many of which hold good stocks of wild brown trout. Access to the upper reaches of some of these streams may be restricted by the overgrown nature of the banks, however the lower sections are more easily reached. Many anglers chose to spin rather than fly fish due to the dense cover, however excellent results will come to the practised fly fisherman. These include **Colby Stream:** rises near Earystane Plantation and running through Colby Glen to the sea at Kentraugh; private fishing in the lower reaches. **Cornaa River:** starts below North Barrule and runs through Ballaglass Glen to the sea at Port Cornaa; mainly brown trout in the pools in the Glen, although migratory fish may found in the lower sections. **Glen Maye Burn:** the stream flows down through Glen Rushen and enters the sea at Glen Maye, passing through an impressive gorge; sea trout may be found in the section below the waterfall and good stocks of brown trout throughout. **Santon Burn:** this stream starts in Foxdale and flows in to the sea east of Ballasalla; upper sections are narrow and overgrown, and flow through an impressive gorge with good pools in the bottom mile. **Silver Burn:** starts in the St Marks area on the slopes of South Barrule and flows through open meadows to the sea at Castletown; best sport downstream for about 1 mile to Castletown.

Island Tackle Shops: Hobbytime, 8 Castle St, **Douglas** (tel: 01624 621562; fax: 01624 661721); The Roland Westcott Tackle Company, 1 The Shops, Ballaquayle Rd, **Douglas** IM2 5DF (tel: 01624 629599); The Ramsey Warehouse, 37 Parliament St, **Ramsey** IM8 1AT (tel: 01624 813092); The Tackle Box, Strand Rd, **Port Erin** IM9 6HE (tel: 01624 836343); and Raymond Caley, M J Caley Post Office & Stores, Sulby Glen, nr **Ramsey** IM7 2HR (tel: 01624 897205).

For further information please contact: Department of Agriculture Fisheries and Forestry, Rose House, 51-59 Circular Road, Douglas, Isle of Man IM1 1AZ (tel: 01624 685835); Manx Game Fishing Club *(see Clubs)*. *(For sea fishing on the Island, see under Sea Fishing Stations.)*

ISLE OF WIGHT

(For close seasons, licences, etc, see Southern Region Environment Agency, p 18).

Freshwater fishing on the Island is better than is generally appreciated. The **Yar** from St Helens, Bembridge, to Alverstone holds fair numbers of roach, dace and rudd, with perch, carp and bream to 7lb in some stretches. Isle of Wight Freshwater AA has coarse fishing for dace, roach, carp, bream, perch, tench, pike and others at Yarbridge and Alverstone on Yar, dt on bank for Alverstone only; **Gunville Pond**, Newport: pike to 21lb, common and mirror carp to 21lb, tench, bream, perch, roach, rudd; **Merstone Fishery**, 3 coarse lakes: carp to 20lb, bream to 9lb, perch, tench, roach, rudd, **Somerton Reservoir**, Cowes: 2 acres; common and mirror carp to 15lb, roach, rudd, perch; dt from Scotties Tackle Shop *(below)*. IWFAA membership £30 (plus £5 joining), conc; for further information, contact Hon Sec. Hale Manor Lakes are both 1 acre, carp and mixed coarse. Hale Manor, Arreton PO30 3AR (tel: 01983 865204). Nettlecombe Farm, **Whitewell** (tel: 01983 730783): 3 ponds of varying depth and at different levels. Stocked carp, roach, perch. Ideal for children. Gilees Pond, Stag Lane, Newport: carp, rudd, roach, bream. Dt £2 from Scotties, *below*. Tackle shops: The Sports Shop, 9 Union Str, **Ryde** PO33 2DU (tel: 01983 563836); N R Young, The Sports Shop, 70 Regent Str, **Shanklin** PO37 7AJ (tel: 01983 862454); 'Scotties', 22 Fitzroy St, **Sandown** PO36 8HZ (tel: 01983 404555). Light sea fishing, for which freshwater tackle may be employed, at Whippingham (River Medina), Fishbourne (Wootton Creek) and in Bembridge Harbour; mullet, bass, flatfish, etc.

ITCHEN

(For close seasons licences, etc, see Southern Region Environment Agency, p18).

Rises some miles north-west of Petersfield and flows via Winchester into Southampton Water at Southampton. Famous Hampshire chalk stream. Trout fishing excellent, but strictly preserved for most part. Some salmon and sea trout lower down, but also preserved. Principal tributaries are **Arle** and **Candover Brook**; both strictly preserved.

Southampton (Hants). Itchen and Test estuaries. Pout, whiting and eels in Southampton Water; and whiting, bass, grey mullet from the piers and quays. Free coarse fishing from public footpath between Woodmill and Mansbridge. **Lower Itchen Fishery**, Gaters Mill, Mansbridge Road, West End SO18 3HW, offers salmon, brown trout, sea trout, grayling and night sea trout fishing on season basis, and some dt; corporate fishing days; contact Embley Ridge, Gardeners Lane, Romsey, Hants (tel: 02380 814389; mobile: 07885 175540). **Leominstead Trout Fishery**, Emery Down, **Lyndhurst** SO43 7GA has 8 acres of trout and coarse fishing, trout dt £25, 2 fish limit, £28 3 fish, £35 5 fish; coarse: (tel: 023 8028 2610). **Mopley Farm Cadland Fishery**, c/o The Ruffs, Blackfield SO45 1YX (tel: 023 8089 1617); several coarse ponds with specialist carp fishing, mirror, common, ghost to 26lbs plus; access for disabled; various permits, incl dt on bank £5.00, conc, night permit £7.50. For **Holbury Manor Pond**, with tench, carp, pike, roach, rudd contact Gang Warily Recreation and Community Centre, Newlands Rd, Fawley SO45 1GA (tel: 023 8089 3603); st £20, wt £5, no dt, conc. **Gang Warily Pond** is for under 15's only; st £3 from Gang Warily reception; st, wt, dt from Jubilee Hall, Fawley Square, SO45 1DD (tel: 023 8089 3603). Tackle shop: Bells Sports, 9 New Rd, Hythe, Southampton SO45 6BP (tel: 023 808 42065).

Eastleigh (Hants) Trout, salmon and grayling; preserved. Eastleigh & Dist AC has various coarse and limited game fishing, incl 3 stretches of river, Upper and Lower

Itchen Navigation, and 12 lakes. Dt £6 for one of these, Lakeside Park, Eastleigh, on site at cafe and from tackle shops. Bishopstoke FC has water, which affords excellent sport. Water holds large trout. Salmon run right up to Brambridge. Some sea trout also come up; private. Junior st from Borough Council for Bishopstoke Riverside Rd stretch. Tackle shop: Eastleigh Angling Centre, 325 Market Str, SO50 5QE (tel: 023 806 53540).

Bishopstoke (Hants), ns Eastleigh. Salmon, trout and grayling; preserved by Bishopstoke FC and other owners.

Winchester (Hants). Trout and grayling. Free fishing on NRA licence between the city weirs, and the left bank of the **Itchen Navigation**, between Blackbridge and St Catherine's Lock. The Rod Box, London Road, King's Worthy, Winchester SO23 7QN (tel: 01962 883600), offers dry fly fishing on st and dt basis and other rods on celebrated private stretches of the **Test** and on the **Itchen, Arle** and **Anton,** and can arrange fishing on lakes; charges on request. Tackle shop: The Rod Box (*above*).

Itchen Abbas (Hants). Trout; preserved by riparian owners. **Avington Trout Fishery** (tel: 01962 779 312), three lakes plus stretch of R Itchen carrier, provide excellent trout fishing. Open all year, stocked daily; limit 1 or 2 brace; dt British rainbow record broken there several times. Tackle Shop: The Rod Box, London Road, King's Worthy, Winchester SO23 7QN (tel: 01962 883600). Many hotels.

Arlesford (Hants). **Candover Brook, Alre, Itchen;** trout; preserved by riparian owners. Grange Lakes, Alresford Pond; coarse fish; preserved.

KENT (lakes and streams)

BEWL WATER: The Fishing Lodge, **Lamberhurst,** Tunbridge Wells TN3 8JH (tel: 01892 890352); 770 acre SW fly-only trout fishery; st (full) £540, 8 fish daily; (Mon-Fri) £430; dt £17.60 (8 fish); evenings, £13.20, 4 fish, conc (please phone); motor and pulling boats, £22.20 and £13 (2 anglers each); evenings: £15.80 and £9; courses of instruction, wheelyboat for disabled on water; season: March 21-Nov 21. Bewl Bridge Flyfishers' Club offers various advantages to members; enquiries to Hon Sec.

BROOKLANDS LAKES, 20 acres, almost

in centre of Dartford. Dartford & Dist APS, variety of coarse fish, carp to 32lb, tench, bream, roach, pike to 28lb; dt £5 1 rod, £7 2 rods, £9 3 rods, conc, from bailiff on bank. Tackle shop: Dartford Angling Centre, 84 Lowfield St, Dartford DA1 1HS (tel: 01322 228532).

BOUGH BEECH RESERVOIR. Near **Tonbridge;** 226 acres, st for pike and coarse; apply to Mr K Crow, Honeycroft Farm, Three Elm Lane, Golden Green, Tonbridge TN11 0BS (tel: 01732 8515440).

BURNHAM RESERVOIR (3m north of

Maidstone). Coarse fishery of 12 acres; carp to 35lbs, 100lb bags of bream, good roach and chub. No day tickets, but membership offered. £64 pa, joining fee £15, conc. Contact Medway Victory Angling and Medway Preservation Society.

CHIDDINGSTONE CASTLE LAKE Good coarse fishing, especially carp. No night fishing. Dt £10 from Caretaker at lakeside. One onlooker only per fisherman at £3.50, adults only. Apply to the Administrator, Chiddingstone Castle, near **Edenbridge**. TN8 7AD. (tel: 01892 870347).

LONGFORD LAKE. Sevenoaks. Private water of Holmesdale AS, who also have junior water Montreal Park Lakes; fishing for members and guests only, membership from Hon Sec; from Manklows Kit & Tackle, 44 Seal Road, Sevenoaks TN14 5AR (tel: 01732 454952); A & I Tackle, 33-35 High St, Green Str Green, Orpington BR6 6BG (tel: 01689 862302).

LULLINGSTONE LAKE, near **Eynsford**. Trout. Kingfisher APS; no tickets.

MID KENT FISHERIES, Chilham Water Mill, Ashford Rd, **Chilham** CT4 8EE (tel: 01227 730668); coarse fishing on 17 lakes, from 26 to 3 acres, well stocked with all species; catches include British record carp 61lbs 7oz, bream to 15lbs, perch, rudd, tench 13lbs, catfish 45lbs and pike to 36lbs. Also available 2 rivers, Royal Military Canal and 104 peg match fishing lake; membership £195 to £85, dt £5; st brown trout on river £375. Company also has **Thanington** (Milton Complex); carp, bream, tench, pike. New Mid Kent Fisheries water *(see Maidstone)*.

MOTE PARK LAKE. Maidstone *(see Medway)*. Coarse fishery of 26 acres; large carp, roach, tench, bream; dt £5; contact Medway Victory Angling & Medway Preservation Society.

PETT POOLS. Fishing stations: **Winchelsea**, 2m; Rye, 4m. 25 acres, coarse fish; Clive Vale AC has fishing; carp, rudd to 2lb, tench, bream, perch, eels and pike; st £35, conc, dt £5; tickets from Clive Vale AC.

ROMNEY MARSH. Much good fishing on marsh, especially in main drains to Rother; best in summer (large bream shoals); water on low side in winter. Clubs with water here are: Ashford & Dist APS; Cinque Ports AS; Clive Vale AC (who fish **Jury's Gap Sewer; Clive Vale** reservoirs (carp); Rye & Dist AS; Tenterden & Dist APS; Lydd AC; Linesmen AC (also waters on **Medway, Beult** and **Stour**; details: Hon Sec). Tackle shops; Marsh Tackle, 17 Littlestone Road, New Romney TN28 8LN (tel: 01797 366130); Point Tackle Shop, Allendale, Dungeness TN29 9ND (tel: 01797 322049), and Hastings tackle shops: Steve's Tackle, 38 White Rock, Hastings TN34 1JL (tel: 01424 433404; web: www.stevestackle.co.uk); Angling Centre, 33/35 The Bourne TN34 3AY (tel: 01424 432178).

ROYAL MILITARY CANAL. Summer fishing only; level partially lowered in winter for drainage. Stations: **Hythe** and **Ashford**. Cinque Ports AS has 7m from Seabrook outfall to Giggers Green; carp, bream, roach, rudd, tench, eels, perch; pike; most sections have dt from bailiff or tackle shops. West Hythe Ballast Pit is members and dt water. Rother FA fishes 3m from Appledore Dam to Iden Lock; dt from bailiff on bank. Sperringbrook Sewer, nr Appledore, is CALPAC water, and may be fished from Mock Hill Farm to Arrow Head Bridge; dt £5 on bank.

SCHOOL POOL. At Oare, 1½m N of **Faversham**. Controlled by Faversham AC; large pool containing carp (30lb plus), tench, bream, roach, rudd and pike; dt £5 1 rod, £10 2 rods, in advance only, from Mr and Mrs Kennett, 14 Millfield, Faversham ME13 8BY (tel: 01795 534516). Faversham AC also has Bysingwood Lake and Bracher Pools, Faversham, mixed fisheries with carp, tench, roach, etc; members only. **Twin Lakes**, Uplees Rd, nr Oare, Faversham: dt £6, conc, for carp to 28lb, tench, roach, perch to 5lb from tackle shop: Ashford Tackle, 52 St Marys Rd, Faversham ME13 8EH (tel: 01795 530160).

LANCASHIRE AND CUMBRIA (Westmorland) streams

(For close seasons, licences, etc, see North West Region Environment Agency, p20 unless otherwise stated)

BELA. Cumbrian trout stream, flowing from Lily Mere to estuary of Kent at Milnthorpe. Much of its course is through low-lying country with heavy water. Size of fish better than in some northern streams; many dry-fly reaches. Salmon

and sea trout below Beetham Mills private. One of the earliest of northern streams; fishing starts March 3.

Milnthorpe (Cumbria). Trout. Preserved by Milnthorpe AA and confined to members and guests. Association also preserves St Sunday's Beck from Deepthwaite Bridge and Peasey Beck from Farleton Beck downwards and thence, from confluence of these streams, to Beetham Mills, which is as far as salmon run. Fishing below mills private. Sport very good in March, April, May and Aug. Licences and tackle from Kendal Sports, 28-30 Stramongate, Kendal LA9 4BN (tel: 01539 721554). Hotels at Milnthorpe: Cross Keys, Bull's Head, Coach and Horses; Wheatsheaf at Beetham.

Oxenholme (Cumbria). Bela, 2m E. Beehive Beck, 1m E. Old Hutton Beck, 3m SE. **Killington Reservoir**; large area of water, 3m E. Pike, perch and some big trout. Now privately fished. *(See Kendal).*

CONDOR. Fishing station: Galgate. Brown trout and sea trout.

DUDDON. Fishing station: **Broughton-in-Furness**. Sea trout, salmon. Millom & Dist AA has rights to 366 yds of north bank from Duddon Bridge downstream, and Hall Dunnerdale stretch. Assn also has water on **Esk, Lickle** (which joins Duddon on left bank, close to Broughton-in-Furness), **Annas, Irt, Lazy, Devoke Water** (salmon, sea trout, trout); **Black Beck**; also **Baystone Bank Reservoir**, Copeland, and Broughton Tower Ponds; membership and day tickets for Assn waters from Hon Sec; Bridge Garage, Holmrook; Waberthwaite PO; Haverigg PO, Millom PO; Broughton PO. Hon Sec supplies maps of ticket waters £2.

Ulpha (Cumbria). Good sea trout and salmon, few brown trout. All river below down to Ulpha Bridge private. **Devoke Water** (large trout) may also be fished from here. Millom AA has rights, wt and dt, limit 4 fish. Applications for membership to Hon Sec. Below this point Duddon runs into estuary. Hotel: Old King's Head.

KENT. Fast-flowing salmon and trout stream running into Morecambe Bay. Excellent for salmon and sea trout following spates from June onwards. Good brown trout fishing all season.

Kendal (Cumbria). Salmon, sea trout, brown trout. A few spring salmon with main run and sea trout moving up about June; plentiful Aug onwards given water.

South of the town to Basinghyll Bridge (mainly both banks) held by Kent AA, the bottom gorge of which is fly only (National Trust - Sizergh Estate); wt £60-£20; dt £15-£7 (not Sept/Oct), which cover u/s waters also to Burneside; tickets from Carlson *(see below)*. Kendal & Dist AC fishes ponds at Old Hutton, and nr Grange-over-Sands. **Killington Reservoir** (ns Oxenholme), is property of British Waterways; pike, perch, roach and brown and rainbow trout; fishing rights leased to Kent AA, st £50, dt £9. Tackle shops: Carlson Tackle Shop, 64/66 Kirkland, Kendal LA9 5AP (tel/fax: 01539 724867; web: www.carlsons.co.uk); Kendal Sports, 30 Stramongate, Kendal LA9 4BN (tel: 01539 721554), who issue permits. Hotels: Kendal Arms; Stonecross Manor.

Staveley (Cumbria). Trout, salmon and sea trout in Sept and Oct. Staveley & Dist AA has 4m of local Kent and Gowan fishing. Tickets from Woofs Newsagents, 22 Main Str, Staveley LA8 9LN (tel: 01539 821253). Hotels: Eagle and Child, Duke William.

MINT (tributary of Kent). Best fished from Kendal. Joins Kent about 1m above town; holds good head of small trout. Kent AA has lowest water *(see Kendal)*.

SPRINT (tributary of Kent). Joins Kent at Burneside. Burneside AA (see Burnside) has about 1m of fishing from junction with Kent. Kent AA has ½m (L bank only). Salmon and sea trout from Aug; brown trout small; banks much wooded.

KEER. Rises 4m above Borwick, runs into Morecambe Bay 3m below **Carnforth**. Good sea trout and brown trout (no coarse fish). Carnforth AA has water; wt and dt on application to Hon Sec. **Wych Elm Fly Fishery**, Milnthorpe Rd, Holme, Carnforth LA6 1PX (tel: 01524 781449): 2 acre lake with rainbow, brook, brown, golden and tiger trout; dt £21, 4 fish, £17 3 fish, £12 sport, half-dt £12.50 2 fish, £7 sport, evng & 3-hour £8 1 fish, £6 sport.

LEVEN: Drains Windermere, and is joined by River Crake (from Coniston Water) at Greenodd, near Ulverston, before flowing into Morecambe Bay. Salmon, sea trout, trout.

Ulverston (Cumbria). Salmon, sea trout, trout. Ulverston AA has fishing **Knottallow Tarn**, brown trout, fly only; dt £10 from Hon Sec and Rods & Sods, The Ghyll, Ulverston; and coarse on **Ulverston Canal**, 1¼m long, specimen tench, carp, etc; restocked; dt on bank. Match permits from AA Sec. Assn also has Sandhall Ponds, specimen carp, members only; disabled bridge access and pegs. Hotels: Armadale, Queen's, King's, Bay Horse, Lonsdale House.

Lake Side (Cumbria). Salmon, trout, pike, perch, trout. Some free fishing; other sections of the shore private; inquire locally.

TORVER BECK (tributary of Coniston lake), Torver (Cumbria). Lakes: Coniston, 1m E; pike, perch and trout, Goat's Water, 3m NE. Beacon Tarn, 5m S. Hotel: Church House Inn.

CRAKE (tributary of Leven):

Greenodd (Cumbria). Crake; salmon, sea trout, trout. Ulverston AA offers £4 dt on bank for **Ulverston Canal** fishing: coarse fish. **Rusland Pool River**, tributary of Leven.

Coniston (Cumbria). Yewdale Beck, Torver Beck, 2½m S. Duddon, 8m west; salmon, sea trout. Millom & Dist AA has water at **Duddon Bridge** and **Hall Dunnerdale**. Membership and tickets, *see Devoke Water*. Coniston Lake: pike, perch, char, trout and eels. Char fishing very good from May to October. Lake free to holders of E.A. licence. For boats and tackle, *see Coniston, English Lake District*. River Crake flows from S end of Coniston Lake; salmon, sea trout. Esthwaite Lake, 4m east; stocked trout fishery *(see Hawkshead)*.

GRIZEDALE BECK (tributary of Leven):

Hawkshead (Cumbria). Forestry Commission, small brown trout, low population at present; contact Forestry Commission (tel: 01229 860010).

RIVERS ROTHAY & BRATHAY, Ambleside. WADAA fisheries. Open, brown trout, migratory trout and salmon close seasons are as for NW Region EA fishery bye-laws. These rivers are the main feeders to Windermere and offer small

river fishing for brown trout, sea-trout and the very occasional salmon. They are best fished when above normal level using worm or fly. Maggots, cheese and offal baits are prohibited. The Association does not control all the fishing on these rivers and anglers should ascertain where angling is permitted. The large pool near the head of Windermere contains pike and perch as well as trout. Autumn fishing is usually best when lake trout and sea trout take up residence in the river prior to spawning. At this time of year very large trout can be caught. Dt £5.00 (Juv/OAP £2.50), wt £10-£5, st £30-£15, from Tourist Information Centre, local fishing tackle shops. NB. This permit also allows fishing on Grasmere, Rydal Water, High Arnside Tarn, Moss Eccles Tarn, School Knott Tarn & Hayswater; and the assn's Windermere fishery at Graythwaite.

TROUTBECK (trib of L Windermere).

Scandal Beck, Ambleside; trout, preserved.

WINSTER. Parallel with Windermere for 6m. Joins the sea by **Grange-over-Sands.** Sea trout, brown trout, eels. Kendal & Dist AC has R Winster fishing at **Meathop,** nr Grange-over-Sands, stocked with coarse fish. Other club waters nearby include Witherslack Hall Tarn, roach, perch, eels, pike; membership open. Wigan & Dist AA has 2m of river, trout and sea trout (no dt); 26m of Leeds and Liverpool Canal from Johnsons Lock Chorley to Saracens Head Scarisbrick. Assn also fishes eighteen stillwaters in vicinity of **Wigan, Chorley** and **Hindley,** and two canals, all coarse fishing with dt £2-£3, conc; also stretches of Rivers **Ribble** at **Elston, Wyre** at St **Michaels, Douglas** at **Wigan,** coarse fishing; no rivers dt, members only; st £20, juv £2, OAP £6: contact Membership Sec.

LANCASHIRE (lakes and reservoirs)

(see North West Region Environment Agency, p20, unless otherwise stated).

ANGLEZARKE RESERVOIR, Wigan. Coarse fishing. Southport & DAA issues dt. Open 15 Jun to 15 Mar.

BARROW-IN-FURNESS RESERVOIRS. Barrow AA has trout fishing in five reservoirs; also Cavendish Dock for brown trout; dt with member; apply Hon Sec. Furness FA (Game section) issues day tickets for stocked waters. Coarse section fishes 5 waters, 3m from Barrow-

in-Furness, Ormsgill Reservoir.

BARNSFOLD WATERS. 7m NE of Preston. Two trout lakes, 22 acres, fly only; st and dt £19 to £8; boats £5 to £12: J F Casson, Barnsfold Waters, Barns Lane, Goosnargh, Preston PR3 2NJ (Tel: 01995 61583); tackle shop on premises.

BLACKMOSS RESERVOIRS, Pendle. Brown trout dt £12.50 for this Blackmoss FFA water from Anglers All *(see Colne)*;

Pendle Inn, Barley (tel: 01282 614808); for further information contact Hon Sec; water consists of 2 reservoirs: Upper and Lower.

BUCKLEY WOOD RESERVOIR, Rochdale. Leased by NWW to Rochdale Walton AS; dt water. Inquire Hon Sec *(see also Mersey and Rochdale).*

BROWNHILL RESERVOIR. Between Colne and **Foulridge.** Feeder for Leeds and Liverpool Canal. Holds brown trout; preserved by Colne AA, tickets for members' guests only.

CANT CLOUGH RESERVOIR, Burnley. Fished by Mitre AC; dt £10 2 fish; fly only; brown trout only; season 15 Mar to 30 Sept: apply Anglers All, The Old Forge, 6 Raglan St, Colne BB8 0ET (tel: 01282 860515).

CHURN CLOUGH RESERVOIR, Pendle. Now re-let to Colne Water AC (see Laneshaw Reservoir for tickets).

CLOWBRIDGE RESERVOIR, Rossendale. Coarse dt on site at Rossendale Valley Water Park Shop. United Utilities reservoir.

COLDWELL (LOWER) RESERVOIR, Pendle. Nelson AA. Trout day ticket from Coldwell Inn Activity Centre. Dt £15; 3 fish limit; rainbow; fly only.

DEAN CLOUGH RESERVOIR, Hyndburn. Brown and Rainbow trout, fly only, Lancashire FFA water, dt £13, 2 fish limit, from Hyndburn Angling Centre, 71 Abbey Str, Accrington BB5 1EH (tel: 01254 397612).

DILWORTH (UPPER) RESERVOIR, Ribble Valley. Trout; Ribchester & Dist AA has water; dt from Happy Shopper, Higher Rd, Longridge.

DINGLE RESERVOIR, Blackburn. Dingle Fly Fishing Club; enquire locally.

EARNSDALE RESERVOIR, Darwen. Brown and rainbow trout. Darwen AA has rights on reservoir; good fly water, dt £12, 2 fish, from Sunnyhurst PO, Harwood St, Darwen BB3 1PD (tel: 01254 702957).

ENTWISTLE RESERVOIR, Blackburn. Entwistle Flyfishers. Dt £14.

GRIMSARGH RESERVOIR, Preston. Red Scar AA; dt £5, conc, from Carters, Preston.

GRIZEDALE LEA RESERVOIR. 9 m south of Lancaster. Rainbow trout, 1 Apr-30 Nov; Kirkham & Dist FFC water, fly only, limit 3. Membership £165 plus £165 joining fee. Dt (limited), from Hon Sec, or from A Helme, The Veterinary Surgery, 13-17 Freckleton St, Kirkham, Preston PR4 2SN; or from A F Hodgson, 5 Hillside Ave, Kirkham, Preston PR4 2YR; or G Steel, 114 Highcross Ave, Poulton-le-Fylde FY6 8XB.

HAGGS RESERVOIRS. Hynburn Road, **Accrington.** Roach, carp, chub, tench, Accrington New Anglers water; members only. Water has disabled platform.

HEAPY RESERVOIRS. Chorley. Reservoirs 1,2,3 and 6: roach, carp, perch, bream, tench. Wigan & Dist AA water. Dt on all except no. 6. St £20, juv £2, OAP £6. Map books £1.50 + sae from Membership Sec or from bailiffs.

BIRKACRE RESERVOIR, Chorley. Wigan & Dist AA water. Dt £2, membership £20, juv £2, conc, from bailiff, or contact Hon Sec.

HODDLESDEN, Blackburn. Trout, Darwen Loyal Anglers.

LANESHAW RESERVOIR, Pendle. Brown and rainbow trout, fly only, barbless hooks. Dt £12 (2 fish), evng £7 (1 fish) from J&F Clark (newsagents), 68 Keighley Road, Colne BB8 0JN (tel: 01282 865809); Anglers All, The Old Forge, 6 Raglan St, Colne BB8 0ET (tel: 01282 860515).

MITCHELS HOUSE RESERVOIRS, Higher Baxenden: formerly Accrington & Dist FC waters; currently vacant; wild browns, rainbows.

OGDEN RESERVOIR, Rossendale. Haslingden & Dist Fly FC; Trout fishing dt £14.50, 3 fish limit; also has **Holden Wood Reservoir,** Grane, Haslingden (no dt): contact Hon Sec.

PARSONAGE RESERVOIR, Hyndburn. Trout fishing, Bowland Game FA; contact Hon Sec for dt, £12.

PENNINGTON FLASH, Leigh. Good coarse fishing. Pennington Flash AA issues st and d £1 on bank, conc; inquiries to Hon Sec.

UPPER RIVINGTON RESERVOIR. Closed 1 Apr to 15 Jun; Pike Fishing Syndicate; members only; pike; no keep nets; no barbed hooks; no gravel bait &c.

LOWER RIVINGTON RESERVOIR. Coarse fishing. Dt £20, conc. Permits available from Great House Information Centre.

UPPER RODDLESWORTH RESERVOIR. 25 acres in West Pennine Moors, managed by Horwich & Dist FFC; stocked with rainbows to 12lbs, and wild brown population; dt; from The Black Dog Inn, Belmont; Royal Arms Hotel,

Tockholes.

LOWER RODDLESWORTH and RAKE BROOK RESERVOIRS, Chorley.
Coarse fisheries with pike to 30lbs, managed by Withnell AC. Dt £4, conc; from Brinscall Post Office, School Lane, Brinscall PR6 8QP (tel: 01254 830225). For further information contact Hon Sec.

STOCKS RESERVOIR. Slaidburn. 350 acre trout fishery, stocked weekly with brown, blues and rainbow trout to 22½lb, also indigenous stock of wild browns. Fly only, there is a close season. 20 boats with motors; and bank fishing, tackle on site, Wheelyboat for disabled; st, dt and sporting tickets; 4 and 2 fish limit; juv free with paying adult; tickets from Mr Ben Dobson, Stocks Fly Fishery, Catlow Rd, Slaidburn BB7 3AQ (tel: 01200 446602); telephone for boat before coming; Paul Bebb (English international) offers ghillie and guiding service. Tackle shop: Anglers All, The Old Forge, 6 Raglan St, Colne BB8 0ET (tel: 01282 860515).

SWINDEN RESERVOIR, **Burnley**, ten minutes drive from town centre. Trout fishing, Burnley AS; dt £12, 2 fish from Roggerham Gate Inn, Todmorden Road, Brierclisse, Burnley BB10 3PQ (tel: 01282 422039) below reservoir; all browns to be returned.

WALVERDEN RESERVOIR, **Pendle**. Coarse fishing for perch, tench, pike, eels, carp, roach; dt and st from bailiffs on site; further information from Parks, Cemeteries & Outdoor Recreation, Marsden Hall Farm, Walton Lane, Nelson BB9 8BW (tel: 01282 661600).

WORTHINGTON RESERVOIRS. **Wigan**. 3 reservoirs of 5, 7 and 3 acres, all coarse with roach, perch, carp, bream, barbel. Now Dream Agling Tackle water, 63 Preston Road, Standish, Wigan WN6 0JH (tel: 01257 472707); dt £3 coarse, £5 carp; dt on bank or from shop. Tackle shops: Wigan Angling Centre, 15 Orrell Rd, Orrell, Wigan WN5 8EY (tel: 01942 226427). **Orrell Water Park**, Lodge Rd, Orrell; 2 lakes; dt on bank; on site is Lake View Tackle, 38 Lodge Rd, Orrell, Wigan WN5 7AT (tel: 01695 625634); and many others in Chorley, Westhoughton, Blackburn, Leyland, and Preston.

LEE or LEA

(For close seasons, licences, etc, see Thames Region Environment Agency, p22).

Walton's river; flows through Bedfordshire and Hertfordshire then along boundary between Essex and Middlesex to join Thames near Blackwall; 46m long. Urban development and canalization have largely removed its charm, but still holds good quantities of barbel, and large bream, carp, pike, chub, perch. Very little free fishing, but permits are obtainable from bailiffs on most stretches and fishing is allowed from Cheshunt to Bow throughout the 'old close season.'

Tottenham (London). **Bow** to **Ponders End** controlled by Lee Anglers' Consortium (LAC) *(see clubs)*. St £25, dt £3, conc. Good access points are at Lea Bridge Rd, Hackney Marshes, Carpenters Rd, Dace Rd. Dt from bailiffs. **Picketts Lock** and **Stonebridge Lock**, where there are permanent platforms on the Tottenham Marshes bank, are fisheries used for matches, with roach, carp and bream. TW reservoirs close to Tottenham Hale (roach, perch, carp, bream, pike; or stocked with brown and rainbow trout) *(see under London)*. Bailiff on bank for assistance, Tom Rowley *(see clubs)*. Other LAC water: at Edmonton, north of A406, there are permanent platforms on the **Lee Park Way** (opposite the tow path) where roach and bream show well from May onwards. Above and below Picketts Lock for bream and roach; and

below Ponders End Lock, roach shoal and skimmers up against locks and under bridges in winter; skimmers and good bream are caught opposite Ford factory and down opposite the trees on golf course. Tackle shop: Don's of Edmonton, 239 Fore Str, Edmonton N18 2TZ (tel: 020 8807 5219); J&B's Fishing Tackle, 594 Hertford Rd, Edmonton N9 8AH (tel: 020 8805 6050; web: www.jbfishing.co.uk).

Enfield Lock (Middx). Plenty of roach, perch, bream, tench, double figure carp and pike; dt; controlled by LAC *(see Tottenham)* from Enfield Lock to **Ponders End**. Access from Ordnance Rd for Enfield Lock to Rammey Marsh Lock. Also small section of R Lee Channel (near Rifles PH) for chub and barbel. Access for Ponders End up to Enfield from Wharf Rd, Ponders End. Bream, skim-

Fishing from a float tube on Rib Valley Lake.

mers, roach and carp from near bridges, locks, opposite the Navigation Inn and new footbridge from behind 'Makros' (off Mollison Ave). The 'canopy' area up to the Turkey Brook noted for large shoals of bream, but proving hard to catch.

Waltham Abbey (Herts): **Lee Relief Channel**, now called Walton's Walk, from David Stoker Sluices to Highbridge St, Waltham Abbey: 1½m of bank, mixed coarse fishing, with chub, tench, bream, carp, pike, and occasional bags of roach. This fishery is run by Lee Valley Information Service, Hayes Hill Farm, Stubbins Hall Lane, Waltham Abbey EN9 2EG (tel: 01992 702200); apply to LVRPA. From **Waltham Cross** to **Rammey Marsh Lock**; roach, tench, carp and skimmers; controlled by LAC; car park in High Bridge Str gives access to upper section. Parking at bottom of Lee Rd provides access down, under M25 to Rammey Marsh Lock. This stretch is known for its large tench, carp and winter pike. There is mixed coarse fishing on 2 4-acre lakes, Claver Hambury Lakes; dt £7; club bookings available; tickets from Simpsons of Turnford, Nunsbury Drive, Turnford EN10 6AQ (tel: 01992 468799).

Cheshunt (Herts). Good chub, roach, tench, bream fishing, controlled by LAC. (*See Tottenham*). Lee Navigation to Cheshunt:

from **Aquaduct Lock** downstream, the R Lee becomes a canal. Access from Hertford Rd(off A10) to Cadmore Lane and Windmill Lane for the Cheshunt to Waltham Common Lock section. Nr Aqueduct Lock Hertford AC share 4 pits, Slipe Lane Pits; coarse, members only: st £21, apply Hon Sec. Kings Arms and Cheshunt AS run Brookfield Lake, with carp, tench, bream, perch; dt £3 one rod, £5, two rods, from Simpsons *below;* other society waters include local rivers, lakes and gravel pits; matches, outings, newsletter organised, new members welcome.

North Met Pit, gravel pit of 58 acres, various coarse species incl large carp (to 44lbs), pike (to 30lbs), tench (to 10lbs 2oz); LVRPA water (*see Waltham Abbey*). Also **Bowyers Water**, 35 acre gravel pit, with carp (to 41lbs 8oz) and pike; day & night st £132, conc; contact LVRPA (*see Waltham Abbey*). Near Dobbs Weir is 9-acre lake **Essex Netherhall**, large carp and tench; limited to 30 permit holders; st (incl night fishing), £300, dt £10 to £15 from Simpsons. Tackle shop: Simpsons of Turnford, Nunsbury Drive, Turnford EN10 6AQ (tel: 01992 468799).

Wormley (Herts). **Slipe Lane Pits**, four gravel pits of 25 acres with large tench, bream (to 10lbs 4oz), carp (to 34lbs), pike (to 27lbs 3oz). St (day only) £30, conc.

Run by LVRPA (*see Waltham Abbey*).
Broxbourne (Herts). **Carthagena Fishery**, consisting of Weir Pool, 2 lakes (one with carp to 32lbs); ¾m of Old R Lee, 1m of Lee Navigation, bream, tench, carp, chub, roach, rudd; st only for Weir Pool, river and stream, £60, juv, OAP £40; dt for carp lake £10; Carthagena Lake, syndicate only: from Jerry Hammond, Carthagena Lock (tel: 01992 463656); towpath from Nazeing New Rd to Dobbs Lock, dt £3-£1.50, from bailiff on bank. **Old Mill and Lee Navigation Fishery**, Mill Lane, Weirpool, Lee Navigation, with roach, chub, pike, perch; dt £3, conc; run by LVRPA (*see Waltham Abbey*). Day tickets from bailiff on bank.

Hoddesdon (Herts), ns Rye House or Broxbourne. On Lee, Stort and New River Lee. **Admiral's Walk Lake**, 25 acre gravel pit at Conker lane, pike (to 29lb 8oz), tench, bream, roach, carp; dt £35, conc; **Dobbs Weir Fishery**, coarse fish (carp to 26lbs 5oz; rainbow to 4lbs 4oz; British record chub 8lb 13oz); dt £3 on bank, conc; both fisheries run by LVRPA (*see Waltham Abbey*).

Rye House (Herts). Roach, chub, dace, bream, pike, perch, tench. Rye House Bridge to October Hole is London AA water; additional fisheries at Wormley on canal, and Kings Weir Canal and Old River; barbel, dace, chub, roach. Members only: st £39, conc; dt £3.50 from LAA. West Ham AC controls east bank and LAC, west bank, at Fieldes Weir; dt from bailiff.

St Margaret's (Herts). River Lee. River fishing from towpath; LAC (*see Tottenham*).

Ware (Herts). River Lee Navigation, controlled by LAC. Deep flowing section through Ware town, weedy in summer, with roach, perch and chub. Above the lock there are permanent platforms, nos. 120 backwards to Hertford. Roach, perch and chub. Below the Ware town road

bridge, pegs 46 to 70: roach, perch and skimmers. Hardmead Lock to Amwell Section. Slow flowing with good specimen carp, bream and chub for the specialist angler; also LAC water (*see Tottenham*). Ware AC have members only carp ponds. Membership £40, conc; apply Hon Sec. Rib Valley Fishing Lake, Westmill Farm, Ware SG14 3HJ (tel: 01920 484913; web: ribvalleyfishinglakes.com) 13 acres, 3 lakes, fly or coarse; rainbow trout from 2lbs dt £26, 4 fish, plus other ticket options from bailiff; wheelyboat on trout lake.

Hertford (Herts). For **Lee**, **Mimram**, **Beane**, **Rib** and **New River**. Abbey Cross AS have water; members only; st £75: apply Hon Sec. Hertford town (Folly Bridge) downstream to Marina: fast, deep flowing section, with summer streamer weed. Good specimen fish area for chub, bream, carp and barbel. Downstream of Hertford Marina, there is Dicker Mill canalised section and The Meads below Hertford Lock; good for carp, roach, perch and bream; permanent platforms join up with Ware: LAC water. London AA has stretch from Town Mill gate to junction with Lee Navigation (¾m); members only: st £39, conc, dt £3.50 from LAA. For Hertford AC contact Hon Sec. For Ware AC Hon Sec; both clubs have local fishing. Hotels: Salisbury Arms, Dimsdale Arms, White Hart, Station.

Hatfield (Herts). Hatfield & Dist AS has rights on river from Mill Green to Essendon (about 2½m); including seven-acre Broadwater (large carp and bream); members only.

Luton (Beds). Tring Reservoirs (10m); Grand Union Canal (10m); Great Ouse (20m). Club: Leighton Buzzard AC waters. Tackle shop: Tavistock Angling, 95 Tavistock St, Bedford MK40 2RR (tel: 01234 267145).

Tributaries of the Lee

STORT: Preserved from source to Bishops Stortford.

Roydon (Essex). Roach, dace, perch, pike, chub, bream, carp, rudd, gudgeon, eels, bleak, pope. Globe AS fishes Stort and backwaters here, with the species listed; members only. Ware AC has water between Hunsdon Mill Lock and Parndon Mill Lock; members only; st £41.50; con-

tact Hon Sec. Global Enterprises Ltd, Roydon Mill Park, Roydon, Essex CM19 5EJ (tel: 01279 792777) has 2m free fishing for guests camping or caravanning. This includes well stocked weir pool; also residents-only 40 acre water-ski lake with carp to 30lbs, pike to 25lbs, and bream to 10lbs; dt £5 per rod. Two RMC Angling gravel pits of 16 acres plus 160 mtrs R

This 12lb Koi was captured in the early evening at Lavender Hall Fisheries.

Stort at **Ryemeads**, offering large pike, chub, dace, tench, bream and roach; the Stort is shallow but fishes well for chub and roach, particularly in winter. Group Water: st 2 rods: £30, conc £18. *(For RMC Angling, see Chertsey.)*

Harlow (Essex). Coarse fishing at Netteswell Pond, Oakwood South Pond and on south bank of Stort Navigation between Burnt Mill Lock and Harlow Lock, all managed under agreement between Harlow Council and Stort Valley AC; species are carp, roach, rudd, bream, tench, perch, pike, etc. More details from either club Secretary (tel: 01279 437888); or bailiff 01279 864874). Enquiries to Harlow District Council, Parks and Landscapes Service, Mead Park Depot, River Way, Harlow CM20 2SE (tel: 01279 446998). Boxmoor & Dist AS has stretch of Stort Navigation, as does Harlow DC. *See Boxmoor.* London AA has water at **Spellbrook** and **Thorley**; membership £39, conc; club also has water at **Pole Hole Fishery**, nr Eastwick; enquiries to Hon Sec. Tackle shop: Harlow Angling Centre, 5 Long House, Bush Fair, CM18 6NR (tel: 01279 444249), who also issue tickets for Hollyfield Carp Fishery, Newlands Hall and Nets Well Pond.

Sawbridgeworth (Herts). Good head of all coarse fish with many large roach; fishes best Sept onwards. Sawbridgeworth AS has from confluence at Spellbrook to confluence of Little Hallingbury Brook, left hand bank; pike fishing (after 1Oct). Visiting parties welcome; apply Hon Sec for reservation. Mixed lake fishery ½m from

---

POLLUTION

Anglers are united in deploring pollution. To combat it, urgent action may be called for at any time, from anyone of us. If numbers of fish are found dead, dying, or seriously distressed, take samples of both fish and water, and contact the officer responsible for pollution at the appropriate Environment Agency office. For hot-line, see Environment Agency section at front of book.

Sawbridgeworth Station, on Little Hallingbury Rd. Members only, £3 per rod.

Bishop's Stortford (Herts). Navigational stretch opened by British Waterways; Bishop's Stortford & Dist AS has coarse fishing to Spellbrook Lock (tickets), a length at Harlow, Cam at Clayhithe, lakes, 10 acre gravel pit. Hotels: Foxley, George.

ASH. Fishing stations: Widford (Herts)

and **Hadham** (Essex); a few trout, pike, etc; preserved.

RIB: Trout, coarse fish. For Rib Valley Fishing Lake *(see Ware).*

BEANE: This once-excellent trout stream has been largely ruined by abstraction. Some stretches still hold good fish, however. No public fishing except at Hartham Common, Herts.

MIMRAM: Trout, preserved.

LINCOLNSHIRE (small streams)

(For close seasons, licences, etc, see Anglian Region Environment Agency, p21)

GREAT EAU or WITHERN. Rises above Aby and flows some 12m to sea at Saltfleet; coarse fish; much free water; fishes best in autumn.

Saltfleet (Lincs), ns Saltfleet, 3m. Grayfleet, South Eau, and Mar Dyke; coarse fish; some free water. At Saltfleetby St Peters is pond on which fishing is permitted by dt, purchased from shop near pond; no Sunday fishing. Sea trout in Haven in Sept; also flounders.

Louth (Lincs). Great Eau private above bridge on main Louth-**Mablethorpe** road, including Calceby Brook, Aby and South Ormesby Park; free below to licence holders as far as Gayton lugs, thence ½m private to members of Mablethorpe, Sutton-on-Sea Dist AC (also another ¾m stretch). Louth Crown & Woolpack AC has small coarse pond at Charles St, good tench, membership £15, conc. **Theddlethorpe** (Mablethorpe Dist AC), and free below Cloves Bridge. Altogether 10m free fishing to licence holders; coarse fish, including good roach, bream, perch, pike, rainbow trout (few and mostly small) and grayling. **Lud** generally free below Louth to Alvingham. Coarse fishing in ponds at **Louth, North** and **South Somercotes, Fulstow,**

Saltfleetby, Legbourne, West Ashby, Hogsthorpe, Chapel St Leonards, Skegness, Wainfleet, Authorpe, Addlethorpe, Alford, Farlesthorpe, Spilsby, all on dt on bank. Sutton Brick Pits, Alfred Rd, **Sutton-on-Sea**; dt at adjacent houses. Hatton Lake; dt £3.50, coarse (tel: 01673 858682). **Louth Canal** from **Alvingham** to sea outlet at **Tetney** controlled by Witham & Dist JAF; coarse fish. Tackle shops: Castaline, 18/20 Upgate, Louth LN11 9ET (tel: 01507 602149); Belas, 54-56 High Str, Mablethorpe LN12 1AD (tel: 01507 473328). Hotels: Kings Head, Lincolnshire Poacher, both Louth.

STEEPING. Rises 5m above **Spilsby** (1m off on left bank), runs thence to **Wainfleet** and joins the sea 4m below near **Skegness**; coarse fish; Wainfleet AC controls Steeping and **Wainfleet Relief Channel**; st £10, dt £2.50, conc: Storr's Fishing Tackle, 37/38 High St, Wainfleet, Skegness PE24 4BJ (tel: 01754 880378). Tickets for Swan Lake; Holland's Pond on bank. Spilsby AA has **Ereby Canal**; good bream, tench, perch, etc; members only; confined to 13m radius; st and dt from Hon Sec. Hotels: Wool Pack; Angel Inn.

LINCOLNSHIRE (small lakes and ponds)

Ashby Park Fisheries, Horncastle LN9 5PP (tel: 01507 527966): 7 lakes, mixed coarse fishing with carp to 24lb 8oz, bream to 9¾lb, and most other species, incl eels to 5¾lb. Dt £5 and bait on site.

Belleau Bridge Lake, Belleau Bridge Farm, **Alford** LN13 0BP. 6 acre coarse fishery, dt from Mr Harrop (tel: 01507 480225).

Brickyard Fishery, South Rd, **South Somercotes,** Louth LN11 7PY (tel: 01507 358331). 4 acre coarse fishing

water, dt £5 on site.

Charles Street Pond, Louth. 1 acre lake with crucian carp and tench. St only, from local tackle shops, open all year.

Goltho Lake, Goltho, Wragby LN8 5JD (tel: 01673 858358/858907). Lincoln, 10m. 2 acre mixed coarse fishery, dt £3 on site.

Grange Farm Leisure, Mablethorpe LN12 1NE. 4 coarse lakes, 1 trout and 1 carp lake. Dt only, sold on site. Also tackle and bait shop, and cafe (tel: 01507

472814); sells EA permits.

Grimsthorpe Lake, Grimsthorpe & Drummond Castle Trust (tel: 01778 591205). 36 acres, mixed coarse fishing; dt £6.50.

Haverholme Park Lake, nr Sleaford; contact Mr Dave Gash (tel: 01526 833553); carp average 7-8lbs, roach, bream, perch; dt £5 on bank.

Lake Helen, Mill Lane, Sutterton PE20 2EN. Mixed coarse fishery of 2¾ acres; contact H Greeves (tel: 01205 460681).

Hill View Lakes, Skegness Rd, **Hogsthorpe**, Chapel St Leonards PE24 5NR (tel: 01754 872979); three lakes, two mixed coarse, one carp; dt from cafe; barbless hooks only.

Hollands Park, Wedland Lane, **Thorpe St Peter** PE24 4PW (tel: 01754 880576). Coarse fishing lakes, dt £3.50 for carp lake; others £3 on site.

Hatton Trout Lake, Hatton, nr Wragby LN8 5QE (tel: 01673 858682); coarse; dt on site, £4.

Lakeside Leisure Ltd, Chapel St Leo-

nards, PE24 5TU (tel: 01754 872631). Four mixed coarse lakes, two with 10 species, the others 20 and 24 species respectively, dt on site, £4, £6.20 double; tackle on site.

Oham Lakes, Alford, LN13 0JP. 3 acre coarse fishery, with tackle shop and other facilities on site. Contact D Higham, Maltby le Marsh, Alford LN13 0JP (tel: 01507 450623).

Bainton Fisheries, Lolham Level Crossing, West Deeping. 7 gravel pits between Peterborough and Stamford in the Welland Valley. Excellent summer tench venue, with good carp; also rudd, bream, chub, perch, eels, pike, catfish; st and syndicate members only from Ian Wakeford (tel: 01572 756368; web: www.predator-fishing.co.uk). Permits £100 p/a to £35 p/a.

Rossways Water, 189 London Rd, **Wyberton** PE21 7HG (tel: 01205 361643); two lakes mixed coarse fishing, carp to 30lb, large bream and tench; dt £4, subject to

This young man comes from Norton, Gloucestershire. His smile says it all!

availability; barbless hooks only; caravans to let on site.

Skegness Water Leisure Park, Walls Lane, Ingoldmells, Skegness PE25 1JF (tel: 01754 769019); 7 acre lake with tench, perch, bream, golden orfe, and carp; dt from manager's office.

Starmers Pit, Tritton Rd, **Lincoln** (tel: 01522 534174) Lincoln & Dist AA water; 7 acre lake, mixed coarse fishery with large pike, eels, carp, bream and tench. Dt £3.50, conc £2.50, on site; details of membership £22, conc, from Hon Sec; also information on **Boultham Park Lake**.

Sycamore Lakes, Skegness Rd, **Burgh-le-Marsh**, PE24 5LN (tel: 01754 811411); 5 acre mixed coarse fishery of four lakes, with carp to 28lb, tench, rudd, roach, perch, orfe; Woodland Lake stocked with smaller fish, ideal for matches; dt £4.50, conc, at lakeside; tackle and bait shop, lakeside cafe, accom on site.

Tattershall Leisure Park, Sleaford Rd LN4 4LR (tel: 01526 343193); 7 lakes, mixed coarse fishing, dt on site, £4.

Toft Newton Fishery, Toft-next-Newton, **Market Rasen** LN8 3NE (tel: 01673 878453); 40 acre reservoir, bank and boat fly only fishing, stocked twice weekly, rainbow and brown trout; season varies, usually mid-Jan to mid-Dec; dt £20, 8 fish, £17, 6 fish, £15, 4 fish, £8, 2 fish; boat £10, £5.00 ½ day; Wheelyboat and facilities; tackle hire and tuition on site.

Thorpe le Vale Fishery, Ludford, Louth LN8 6AR (tel: 01472 398978); 5 acre trout fishery, brown & rainbow; fly only; dt £9.50 (2 fish), £14 (4 fish); open all year.

Vickers Pond. Saltfleetby Fisheries, Main Road, Saltfleetby, Louth LN11 7SS (tel: 01507 338272). 3 ponds with tench, bream, carp and grass carp. Dt on site (small tackle and bait shop). No groundbait, and carp not to be kept in nets.

Willow Lakes, Foston, nr **Grantham**. 7 lakes: 1 specimen with carp to 24lb, 6 mixed coarse, dt £5, conc, on site; contact Mr Chilton, Willow Lodge, Newark Rd, Foston, Grantham NG32 2LF (tel: 01400 282190).

Woodlands Fisheries, Ashby Rd, **Spilsby** PE23 5DW (tel: 01790 754252); three coarse lakes (with 2 on stream for 2004) with mixed species, best carp 18lb 8oz, tench over 5lb, roach 2lb, best mixed bag 2001 104lb; dt £4.50, £2 for second rod, conc; tackle and refreshments on site.

LONDON (Thames Water Reservoirs)

Most of the waters referred to below are in the area termed Greater London. All are easily accessible from Central London. A number are rented by angling clubs and reserved for members, but at others fishing is offered to the general public at modest charges on season or day ticket basis.

It seems appropriate to mention here two important angling bodies: first, the **London Anglers' Association**, which has water on many miles on rivers, streams and lakes (125 fisheries in all). The Association now has about 5,000 full members through 160 affiliated clubs. It has offices at Izaak Walton House, 2A Hervey Park Road, Walthamstow, London E17 6LJ (tel: 020 8520 7477). For a brochure and application form please send a stamped addressed envelope to the above address. Annual membership (associate membership) senior £39.00, husband & wife £58.00, senior citizen permit £22, jun associate membership £21.

The **Central Association of London and Provincial Angling Clubs** (CALPAC) has about 120 affiliated clubs and fisheries on rivers, canals and lakes in the South of England. Day tickets issued for many fisheries; £5. Full details from Hon Sec.

Among tackle shops in Central London are: Hardy Bros, of 61 Pall Mall SW1Y 5JA (tel: 020 7839 5515); Farlows of Pall Mall, 9 Pall Mall, SW1Y 5LX (tel: 020 7839 2423) *(see advt on spine)*. Tackle dealers in the suburbs are too numerous to list. Tackle shops in Metropolitan area listed under individual centres.

Thames Water Reservoirs where fishing rights are let to clubs include the following:
Cheshunt (North) to Kings Arms A.C.
Reservoirs open to the public for game fishing (stocked with rainbow or brown trout).
Walthamstow Nos 4 & 5 are stocked with brown and rainbow trout. Bank fishing, fly only on **5**.
East Warwick, fly only, let to syndicate.

Reservoirs open to the public for coarse fishing.

Salmon are less plentiful on the River Lune since the 1966 outbreak of disease, but there is still good fishing to be had. *Photo: Arthur Oglesby.*

West Warwick Reservoir, Walthamstow Nos 1, 2 & 3, High and **Low Maynard, Coppermill Stream**. Dt on all except West Warwick and Lockwood, st only. Best catches to date include carp 34lb, pike 29lb, bream 13lb, perch 4lb 10oz, plus large roach, barbel, chub and dace.

LUNE

(For close seasons, licences, etc, see North West Region Environment Agency, p20)

Rises on Ravenstonedale Common (Westmorland) and flows through beautiful valley into Irish Sea near Lancaster. Excellent sport with salmon, sea trout and brown. August to October best for salmon and sea trout.

Lancaster (Lancs). Salmon, sea trout, trout, coarse fish. Environment Agency has Halton and Skerton Fisheries. Salmon, 16 Jun to 31 Oct, sea trout, 1 Apr to 30 Sept. Brown trout 15 Mar to 30 Sept. Coarse fishing 16 Jun to 14 Mar, all weekdays only. Salmon, c&r only, on EA waters. Evening permits for sea trout on both beats at Halton, £9.00, from Anne Curwen, Greenup Cottage, Hornby Rd, Caton, LA2 9JB (tel: 01524 770078). Mrs Curwen also sells permits for Lancaster & Dist AA, Caton fishing. Lansil Sports and Social Club LA1 3PE (tel: 01524 39269) has 1½m both banks just above tidal stretch, with additional coarse fishing for usual species plus specimen bream (12lb+); salmon st £55 + £25 joining fee, other fishing, £25, conc. Littledale Fishery, nr Caton, mixed coarse; tickets from Morecambe Angling Centre, Thornton Rd LA4 5PB (tel: 01524 832332). Lonsdale AC fishes Upper Swantley; mixed fishery; open but restricted membership. Tackle shops: Stephen J Fawcett, Gunsmiths, Fishing Tackle & Countrywear, 7 Great John Str, LA1 1NQ (tel: 01524 32033), who supply licences and specialist information on Lune, Greta, Wyre and Wenning; Gerry's of Morecambe, 5-7 Parliament St, Morecambe LA3 1RH (tel: 01524 422146); Morecambe Angling Centre (*above*); Carlsons Tackle Shop, 64/66 Kirkland, Kendal LA9 5AP (tel/fax: 01539 724867; web: www.carlsons.co.uk).

Caton (Lancs). Lancaster & Dist AA has fishing over 1½m both banks for which dt is available. Twenty year waiting list for membership. Permits £10 to £20 depending on season, weekdays only, from Anne Curwen, Greenup Cottage, Hornby Rd, Caton, LA2 9JB (tel: 01524 770078). No dt Saturdays and Sundays, though Sunday fishing is allowed to members. Fly only when water level 1ft 6in or below; worm prohibited in October, except at water level of 3 ft. No maggot, shrimp, prawn or grub fishing. No boat fishing, no dogs. Prince Albert AS also have water, and at **Killington**, members only. Bank House Fly Fishery (Mrs Jan Dobson), Low Mill, Caton LA2 9HX, has 2 acres stocked brown, rainbow, tiger and blue trout fishing. Dt £22.50 (4 fish) and half-dt £15.50 (2 fish); fishing lodge, with all facilities, piers for disabled.

Hornby (Lancs). Salmon, sea trout, trout. Lancaster AA has Claughton stretch (*see Caton*). No dt. From Wenning Foot (North) for ¾m, Southport Fly Fishers, members only.

Kirkby Lonsdale (Cumbria). Salmon, sea trout, trout. Trout and sea trout fishing is very good; average 1½lb; sea trout up to 8lb. Kirkby Lonsdale AA has approx 4m of water, upstream and downstream of town; limited 5 day visitors permit (except Oct) from Tourist Information Centre, 24 Main St, LA6 2AE (tel: 015242 71437). Clitheroe AA has water commencing 10yds from Stanley Bridge d/s, on left bank past water board pipe bridge; dt for members' guests only. Below Kirkby Lonsdale & Dist AA water, Lancaster & Dist AA has water. Lancashire FFA has fishing here and at Tebay. Entrance fee £250, annual subscription £270, half sub for youths 16-21. Redwell Carp and Coarse Lakes: four lakes of stocked fishing, dt £7 (1 rod), £10 (2 rods), conc; contact Ken & Diane Hall, Kirkby Lonsdale Rd, Arkholme LA6 1BQ (tel: 015242 21979). Hotels: Red Dragon; King's Arms; Sun; Snooty Fox; Orange Tree. Pheasant Hotel at Casterton, 1m upstream, is convenient for assn waters. Salmon (best August, September); sea trout (June onwards), trout.

Barbon (Cumbria). Lune, 1m W Barbon Beck. Barbon is good centre for Kirkby Lonsdale AA water. Hotel: Barbon Inn.

Sedbergh (Cumbria). Sedbergh AA has approx 3m on Lune and tributaries, 16m **Rawthey**, from source to Lune, 4m **Dee** and 2m **Clough**. Brown trout stocked annually; salmon and sea trout from July. Visitors st £200 from Visitors Hon Sec; dt £10, wt £50 & conc, from "Three Peaks Outdoors" Ltd, 25 Main Str, LA10 5BN (tel: 015396 20446). Mr Metcalfe, Holme Open Farm, Sedbergh LA10 5ET (tel: 015396 20654) has stretch of R Rawthey; tickets at the farm. Hotels: The Bull, The Dalesman.

Tebay (Cumbria). Salmon and sea trout (August onwards best), trout (average 3 to lb). Tebay AA has 17m of good water; wt £30, OAP £25, OAP £45; juv £5; limited dt from Cross Keys Inn, Tebay CA10 3UY (tel: 015396 24240); occasional season permits, from Secretary. Hotel: Cross Keys.

Tributaries of the Lune

RAWTHEY. Trout, with sea trout and occasional salmon late in season. Sedbergh AA has virtually whole of river from its source at Fell End down to Lune, and tributaries Dee 2m, and Clough, 1m; visitor's dt available.

WENNING. Sea trout (good), brown trout, few salmon (late). Best latter part of season. Fishing station:

High Bentham (Yorks). Bentham AA has about 3½m of water; fast stream, good sport; visitors' tickets: st, wt, dt (jun ½) from Hon Sec. Prince Albert AS has stretches of Wenning at Hornby Castle and

Robert Hall Estate. Barnoldswick AC have two stretches of Wenning, upstream from Farrars Viaduct, downstream from Clintsfield Viaduct. **Bentham Trout Farm** and Fishery is at Low Mill, Bentham LA2 7DA (tel: 015242 61305); dt £12, 4 fish limit, to £6, 2 fish, conc. Hotels: The Coach House, Black Bull. Punch Bowl Hotel also has ¾m private trout and sea trout fishing and issues dt. Clapham accom: Flying Horseshoe Hotel; New Inn, Arbutus House.

GRETA. Trout (4 to 1b) and late run of salmon and sea trout. Nearest towns: **Ingleton** and **Burton-in-Lonsdale** (Yorks). Trout. Hotel: Punch Bowl, Burton-in-Lonsdale (licences).

MEDWAY

(For close seasons, licences, etc, see Southern Region Environment Agency, p19).

Kentish river joining estuary of Thames at Sheerness through estuary of its own. Coarse fish (abundant bream, record barbel, 1993) with few trout in upper reaches.

Maidstone (Kent). Free on EA licence from Maidstone to East Farleigh, North Bank, except new mooring area. Maidstone Victory Angling and Medway PS have first class fishing from Yalding down to Maidstone, **R Rother** and **R Beult** fishing, and various stillwaters. Membership from Hon Sec and local tackle shops. Free fishing for residents on Brookland Lake (visitors dt £1), Snodland Council (tel: 01634 240228). Mallards Way Lake, details from Len Valley A & PS. Sittingbourne AC has 4 coarse lakes in vicinity, membership from Hon Sec (www.sittingbourneangling.clansites.co.uk). New Mid Kent Fisheries water: Larkfield, nr Maidstone; 4 Lakes from 46 acres to 20 acres: carp, tench, bream, pike; members only: £135 p/a: Contact fishery at Chilham Water Mill, Ashford Rd, Chilham CT4 8EE (tel: 01227 730668); Bluebell FC has 2 small ponds; good carp; apply Maidstone Angling Centre; also for dt £5, conc, for Mote Park. RMC has 30 acre lake here, tench, perch, rudd, carp; st (4 rods) £30, conc £18. *(For RMC Angling see Chertsey).* Tackle shops: Maidstone Angling Centre, 15 Perryfield Str, ME14 2SY (tel: 01622 677326); Nicks Tackle, 10 Knightrider Str, ME15 6LP (tel: 01622 673899); Mid Kent Tackle, 146 Milton Str, ME16 8LL (tel: 01622 200274). Medway Bait and Tackle, 64B St Johns Road, Gillingham ME7 5NB (tel: 01634 856948). Inns: Medway; West Kent; Rose and Crown; Queen's Head.

East Farleigh (Kent). Free fishing as described under Maidstone; thence mostly Maidstone Victory Angling and Medway Preservation Soc water; weekday dt from Maidstone tackle shops. Inn: Victory.

Wateringbury (Kent). Large carp and tench, chub, bream, roach. Maidstone Victory Angling and Medway Pres Soc has most of towpath bank here and at **Teston**, incl Teston Bridge Picnic site; dt. Medway Wharf Marina, Bow Bridge ME18 5ED, has fishing for boat and caravan owners using their services; dt £5; (tel: 01622 813927). Barking AS has a meadow; members only but open to visiting clubs. Inn: King's Head.

Yalding (Kent). Chub, bream, perch, rudd, dace, roach, eels, and pike. Free fishing on E.A. licence u/s from Yalding Sluice 200m, south bank. Maidstone Victory Angling and Medway Preservation Soc has towpath bank downstream of Railway Inn, also Medway at **Nettlestead, Teston, Barming** and Unicumes Lane, weekday tickets from tackle shops; on bank for Teston fishing. Yalding AS has water; dt (weekdays only). Orpington & Dist AA has water on **R Teise** here, members only. Central Assn of London and Prov AC has one meadow at junction of Medway and **Beult**; members only, membership open. Other CALPAC stretch, 1,200 yds Yalding Medway, dt £5, conc, from bailiff on bank. No night fishing on CALPAC water. Inns: Railway (tackle, but no accommodation); George; Anchor (boats).

Tonbridge (Kent). Tonbridge & Dist A & FPS has 9m of Medway, 1½m of Eden and 8 pits of 4 to 30 acres, the 2 large ones are dt water; dt £3/rod, also for parts of Medway; contact Sec for details; vacancies for membership; £30 + £10 joining fee, concessions for OAP, ladies and juniors. Paddock Wood AC has water at **Gedges Lake**, coarse fishing (tel: 01892 832730); members only; st £38 + £30 joining, conc. **Mousehole Lake**, 3 acre now coarse fishery, on B2015 at Nettleshead Green; dt on site all year. Orpington & Dist AA fishes Medway and Eden, near

Tonbridge; members only. Tackle shops: Tonbridge Rod and Line, 17a Priory Rd,TA9 2AQ (tel: 01732 352450); Medway Tackle, 103 Shipbourne Rd, TN10 3EJ (tel: 01732 360690).

Tunbridge Wells (Kent). Royal Tunbridge Wells AS has coarse fishery at **Ashurst** and **Fordcombe**, trout waters, stock in spring, on **Medway** from Hartfield to Ashurst, and coarse fishing from Ashurst to Poundsbridge (4m), also on **Teise** below Finchcock's Bridge to Hope Mill, **Goudhurst**. Grayling and barbel in places. Fishing on three ponds also; membership limited; annual subscription £70, joining fee £15, concessions for married couples and jun; Society also has Cole-brook Park, 1m north of Tunbridge Wells; members and guests only. Crowborough AA have several ponds and lakes local to **Crowborough**, with large pike, carp, tench, bream; st £40, conc. Tackle shop: Friendly Fisherman, 25 Camden Rd, TN1 2PS (tel: 01892 528677); M A Wickham, 4 Middle Row, E Grinstead RH19 3AX (tel: 01342 315073).

Ashurst (Kent). Coarse fish, some trout, grayling, barbel to 17lb. Royal Tunbridge Wells AS has water *(see above)*. Limited tickets for members' guests only.

Fordcombe (Kent). Trout, coarse fish, barbel to 16¼lb, large carp. Royal Tunbridge Wells AS has water, limited tickets for members' guests.

Tributaries of the Medway

BEULT: Excellent coarse fishing; lower reaches noted for chub, bream and tench; trout higher. Gravesend Kingfisher A & PA (stretches at **Smarden**, **Hunton**, **Headcorn** and **Staplehurst**; members only); London AA has water at **Hunton** and **Linton**; members only; membership £39, conc. Dartford AA has fishing. CALPAC has 400 yds at Medway junction, members only. No dt.

EDEN: Coarse fish.

Penshurst (Kent). On Eden and Medway; coarse fish. Penshurst AS has rights from Ensfield Bridge to Pounds Bridge and from The Point on Medway to weir on Eden; members only. No dt.

Edenbridge (Kent). Coarse fish. 8m controlled by Edenbridge AS (members only, no dt) also a mile at Penshurst. Short stretches rented by Holland AS, also Crawley AS. Edenbridge AS also has good carp lake and a new lottery-funded mixed coarse lake; members only: apply Hon Sec; membership £50 plus £15 joining fee. Tackle Shop: M A Wickham, 4 Middle Row, E Grinstead RH19 3AX (tel: 01342 315073); Biggin Hill Angling Centre, 216-218 Main Road, Biggin Hill, Westerham TN16 3BD (tel: 01959 570265).

TEISE: Joins Medway at Yalding. Trout, coarse fish.

Laddingford (Kent). London AA has water for members only at Mileham Farm, Hunton Bridge and Reed Court Farm; good for roach, tench and carp; plenty of pike but most are small; membership £39, conc.

Goudhurst (Kent). Teise Anglers' and Owners' Association holds 8m of water from Goudhurst to Marden; brown, natural browns and rainbow trout; mainly fly only, and winter grayling and coarse fishing. Members only (fee on application); juniors welcomed. Assn also has stocked farm reservoir for trout fishing at Marden. Apply to Hon Sec. Season: April 3 to Oct 31; winter Nov 1 to March 14.

Lamberhurst (Kent). Royal Tunbridge Wells AS has trout and coarse fishing water d/s of the Chequers Hotel for approx 4½m; members and guests only.

MERSEY

(For close seasons, licences, etc, see North West Region Environment Agency, p20)

Forms Liverpool Channel and seaport. Main river, having been polluted for 100 years and of no account for fishing except in higher reaches has, thanks to Environment Agency initiatives with industry, seen salmon return to the river basin. Tributaries contain trout.

Liverpool (Merseyside). Liverpool & Dist AA has stretch on **Leeds & Liverpool Canal**. Northern AA has stretches on Macclesfield Canal and **R Weaver** at **Vale Royal**; dt £2.50 on rivers, £2 canals, conc. For **Shropshire Union Canal**, see *English Canal Fishing*. Taskers, and Johnsons, have information on all Liverpool park lakes: Sefton, Walton, Greenbank, Stanley, Calderstones and Newsham: dt waters from banks; parks lakes free. Tackle shops: Johnson's Angling Centre, 469 Rice Lane, L9 8AP (tel: 0151 525 5574); Taskers Sports & Angling, 25-29 Utting Avenue, Liverpool 4L4 7UN (tel: 0151 260 6015); Hoppy's, 14 Sefton Str, Litherland L21 7LB (tel: 0151 928 5435).

Wirral (Cheshire). Assn of Wirral Angling Clubs comprises thirteen clubs, and actively promotes lake and pond fishing on Wirral. Club coarse fishing waters include Birkenhead Park Upper (matches only) and Lower Lakes; Central Park Lake, Wallasey; Arrow Country Park Lake. Annual and monthly permits from bailiffs and tackle shops. Caldy Anglers have Caldy Ponds, Wirral, also 43m canal fishing; members only.

St Helens (Merseyside). Two NNW coarse fisheries in vicinity: **Leg O'Mutton Dam**, controlled by St Helens AA; and **Paddock Dam**, Holme Rd, Eccleston, with bream, roach, tench, perch, carp, pike; controlled by St Helens Ramblers AS. Good carp, roach, chub, tench and dace in **St Helen's Canal** (Church Street length); and Blackbrook Canal, both St Helens AA waters; club also has The Brook, the outfall of Carr Mill Dam; also Carr Mill Dam itself; club also has The Dig Pit and Taylor Park Lake (for this, apply at boathouse). Lymm AC offer dt on Sankey St Helens Canal at Warring-ton; dt £2.50, conc, on bank. Wigan Angling Centre, 15 Orrell Rd, Orrell, Wigan WN5 8EY (tel: 01942 226427) supply licences for **Carr Mill Dam**, 10 acres; no dt. St Helens Tackle shop: Star Angling, 101 Duke Str, WA10 2JG (tel: 01744 738605).

Stockport (Cheshire). Stockport & Dist AF has **River Goyt**, Marple to Stockport; members only; apply: Hazel Grove Angling Centre, 2 Fiveways Parade, Hazel Grove SK7 6DG (tel: 01625 858643); Stockport Angling Centre, 28 Sandy Lane, Reddish, Stockport SK5 7NZ (tel: 0161 429 6777).

Whaley Bridge (Derbyshire). River here known as **Goyt**; no longer polluted; dt (not Sundays), for one bank only. **Cote Lodge Reservoir**, High Peak. Trout water, Old Glossop AC, dt obtainable: contact Hon Sec. **Errwood Reservoir**, High Peak, is the headwater of the Goyt in an area of outstanding natural beauty; 80 acres, trout water stocked monthly; Errwood FFC; dt £12 (3 fish, catch or release) from tackle shops in Whaley Bridge, Macclesfield and elsewhere. **Peak Forest Canal** starts here; coarse, sport patchy. Lock pools at **Marple** stocked with carp and tench. Canal to Ashton Junction being opened and dredged.

Tributaries of the Mersey

NEWTON BROOK (tributary of Sankey Brook):
BOLLIN:
Heatley (Cheshire). Occasional trout, roach, dace, pike. Lymm AC has several lengths of Bollin at Reddish and Little Heatley, near Lymm, part double bank, mostly single; club also controls a large number of fisheries on Severn, Vyrnwy, Dane, Sankey St Helens Canal, and many lakes and ponds about the north of Cheshire with trout and coarse fishing; some of these are dt waters, membership costs £42 per annum, joining fee £16, conc, apply to N Jupp, Secretary.
Ashley (Cheshire). Bollin, 1m N; trout, roach, dace, pike; Bollin and Birkin AA; private.
BIRKIN (tributary of Bollin):
Knutsford (Cheshire). Birkin, 4m; Bollin and Birkin AA has water; private. **Tabley Mere**, 3m, is let to Lymm AC; no permits. Toft Hall Pool, 1½m S; occasional permits. **Tatton Mere**, Knutsford, coarse fishing; dt on bank. **Redesmere** and **Capesthorne Lakes** (6m S of Wilmslow on A34 road); Stoke-on-Trent AS waters; members only; society also has **Fanshawe Pool**; carp, tench, rudd, also members only. Capesthorne Hall stock pond: very good carp fishing, dt on bank, or from Keith Whalley, Bailiff, East Lodge, Capesthorne Hall, Macclesfield SK11 9JY. Tackle shop: Trev's Tackle, 13-17 the Paddock, Handforth SK9 3HG (tel: 01625 528831).
IRWELL:
Manchester. Some river waters have been leased to clubs. At **Poynton**, 10m out, Stockport & Dist FA has pool; st only. 18m from Manchester, at Northwich, is coarse fishing in Weaver (*see Weaver*). Bolton & Dist AA has **Manchester, Bolton & Bury Canal**, from Hall Lane to Blue Wall length, 6 reservoirs, and other fisheries; no day tickets, but st from tackle shops in district. Warrington AA has a twenty mile stretch of **Bridgewater**

Canal as well as water on Dee, **Ribble**, **Severn** and tributaries and **Dane**, reservoirs, meres, etc; apply Hon Sec. Victoria AC controls **Turks Head Reservoir**, members only. Chorlton Water Park, Maitland Ave, Chorlton M21 2ND (tel: 0161 881 5639): dt and st fishing for large carp to 25lb and pike to 26lb, roach, bream, perch; st & dt. Tackle shops: Swinton Angling Centre, 57 Worsley Road, Swinton, Manchester M27 1NQ (tel: 0161 794 2784); Trafford Angling Supplies, 34 Moss Rd, Stretford M32 0AY (tel: 0161 8641211). **Bolton** tackle shop: Bolton Angling Centre, 185 St Helens Rd, Bolton BL3 3PS (tel: 01204 658989).

ROCH:

Bury (G. Manchester). Bury & Dist AS and has stretches of R Irwell, several small ponds and reservoirs including **Elton**; mostly coarse fishing. Bury AS members £15 + £5 joining fee, concessions. Trout fishing at Entwistle (Entwistle FFC) and Dingle (Dingle FFC). **Haggs Reservoir**, Hyndburn Rd, Accrington, Accrington New Anglers water.

Rochdale (G. Manchester). Rochdale Walton AS. **Buckley Wood**, 1m N (coarse and trout), also Healey Dell Lodge, dt only on application to Hon Sec. Rochdale & Dist AS has trout and coarse fishing at Castleton (dt; visitors must be accompanied by member). Todmorden AS has coarse fishing on **Rochdale Canal**, from Lock 37 (Summit West) to Lock 51 (Castleton, Manchester Road); st £30 + £10 entry fee, conc, from tackle shops. Tackle shops: Towers of Rochdale, 52 Whitworth Rd, OL12 0EZ (tel: 01706 646171); Kay's, 18 St Mary's Gate OL16 1DZ (tel: 01706 647211); Rochdale Angling Centre, 161 Yorkshire Str, OL12 0DR (tel: 01706 527604), who issues tickets for Todmorden AS and Bury AC. *For Rochdale Canal see also Calder (Yorks) - Hebden.*

TAME:

Ashton-under-Lyne (G. Manchester). NWW reservoir **Walker Wood**, 2m NE; trout.

MIDLANDS (reservoirs and lakes)

BARKER'S LAKE, Ringstead, 25 acres stocked with carp to 25lb, bream to 6lb, tench, good pike in winter; part of Ringstead Island complex, with Brightwell's Lake, backwater and main R Nene. Wellingborough Nene AC water.

BODDINGTON RESERVOIR, Byfield (Northants). 65 acres; carp from 4lbs to 8lbs, plus roach, tench, perch and pike; dt (weekdays) £5 on bank (£6 w/e), conc, evng £3, no night fishing; 24 hour information line: 0113 281 6895; or contact Fisheries and Environmental Manager, British Waterways, South East Waterways, Ground Floor, Witan Gate House, 500-600 Witan Gate, Central Milton Keynes MK9 1BW (tel: 01908 302556); contact on the bank: Head Bailiff (tel: 07740 534 891); match booking welcome; record match weight over 200lbs.

BLENHEIM LAKE. Woodstock, Oxon. Excellent tench, perch, roach, bream in summer; pike in winter to 40lb. Boat fishing only for visitors. Apply to The Estate Office, Blenheim Palace, Woodstock, Oxon 0X20 1PS for details of current charges (tel: 01993 811432). Tackle shop: Predator Angling Centre, 6 The Kidlington Centre, Kidlington OX5 2DL (tel: 01865 372066); who also sell dt £6 for Manor Lake, **Kirtlington**: tench carp roach, perch, bream.

CARSINGTON WATER, nr Ashbourne, Derbyshire. Owned by Severn Trent Water Ltd, Carsington Water, Visitor Centre, Ashbourne, Derbys DE6 1ST (tel: 01629 540696); opened as predominately a brown trout fishery in 1994; season 27 Mar-7 Oct; up to 11,000 fish stocked during 2001; day and part-day tickets for bank and boats, plus concessionary for bank only; dt £14, evng £11; rowing boats £10 p/day, £7 p/evng; petrol boat £20 p/day, £13 p/evng. Wheelyboat £15 p/day, must be pre-booked. Contact Watersports Centre (tel: 01629 540478) for day-to-day bookings. Facilities, licences and catering on site. Enquiries to the Fishery Office *(above)*.

CASTLE ASHBY LAKES. Northampton 7m; coarse fishing in three lakes, all mixed coarse, leased to Mr M A Hewlett, Castle Ashby Fisheries, 176 Birchfield Rd East, Abington, NN3 2HG (tel: 01604 712346); dt waters, from bailiff on bank. **Menagerie Pond** (specimen carp fishery); membership £160; details from Estate Office, Castle Ashby, Northampton NN7 1LJ (tel: 01604 696232).

CLAYDON LAKES. Buckingham, 6m.

Upper and Middle Lakes at Middle Claydon, near Winslow, are Leighton Buzzard AC water; Danubian catfish, pike-perch, large bream, big carp; members only; st £32.

CLATTERCOTE RESERVOIR, Banbury (Oxon). 20 acres, principally carp to 23lb, chub, roach, perch, tench to 7lb, bream, crucian carp to 3lb; dt £5, night fishing by arrangement with bailiff (tel: 07740 534892); match bookings welcome: record match weight 220lb; 24 hour information line: 0113 281 6895.

CLUMBER PARK LAKE (100 acres). National Trust property, 4½m from **Worksop** (tel: 01909 476653); coarse fish (including pike); 16 June to 14 March, 7am to dusk; st £50, dt £4 (jun and dis £2.00) from bailiff on bank.

COSGROVE LEISURE PARK Milton Keynes, 2m (Bucks). Coarse fishing on 10 lakes from 2 to 25 acres, and Rivers Tove and Great Ouse. 2 lakes; members and campers only. Contact Manager, Cosgrove Leisure Park, Milton Keynes MK19 7JP (tel: 01908 563360). Tackle and bait shop on site, food and refreshments, camping, caravan site. Tackle shop: Milton Keynes Angling Centre, St Giles House, Victoria Road, Bletchley, Milton Keynes MK2 2QH (tel: 01908 374400)

CRANFLEET CANAL. Roach, perch, gudgeon. Trent Lock held by Long Eaton Victoria AS, also Erewash Canal, Long Eaton Lock to Trent Lock; membership £18, concessions.

DENTON RESERVOIR. Denton (Lincs). Excellent mixed coarse fishing with large carp; held by Grantham AA; st £16, conc, from Hon Sec, bailiffs and tackle shops. No day tickets.

DRAYCOTE WATER FISHERIES, near Rugby (Warks). 600 acre reservoir owned by Severn Trent Water Ltd. Brown and rainbow trout. 50,000 rainbows stocked twice-weekly over Mar-Oct; dt £17, 8 fish limit; evngs £12, 5 fish limit; OAP, jun, dis, £12 (5 fish). Rowing boats £13, motor boats £21, evening £14; disabled facilities, catering and courses; optional c&r. Information from Keith Causer, Fishing Lodge (tel: 01788 812018).

DRAYTON RESERVOIR, Daventry. 20 acres, principally carp to 26lbs, also roach, perch and tench; average catches, 100lb plus, with 200lb per day often recorded, match record 405lbs; dt £5 Mon-Fri, £6 w/ends from patrolling bailiff, £3

A 22lb mirror carp taken from Whelford Pools, Fairford, Glos. *Photo: Ros Godden.*

conc; match bookings welcome, 120 pegs; no night fishing; contact Fisheries and Environmental Manager, British Waterways, South East Waterways, Ground Floor, Witan Gate House, 500-600 Witan Gate, Central Milton Keynes MK9 1BW (tel: 01908 302556); contact on the bank: Head Bailiff (tel: 07889 532563); 24 hour BW information line (tel: 01132 816895) updated weekly.

DUKERIES LAKES, Worksop. Welbeck Estate fisheries controlled by Welbeck Estate Office (tel: 01909 500211); members only. Clumber Lakes; National Trust: dt on bank; mixed coarse; 16 June to 14 March (tel: 01909 476592). Worksop & DAA, has rights on **Sandhill Lake**, (80 pegs), with bream, tench, roach, rudd, carp, perch; **Woodsetts Quarry Pond,** dt £3 on the bank.

EYEBROOK RESERVOIR. Caldecott (Leicestershire), off A6003 Uppingham to Corby Rd, south of Caldecott village, follow AA signs. 400 acres of excellent trout fishing. Well-stocked water, mostly rainbows, a few browns; now stocking with blue trout (7000 in 2004). Fly only, good bank and boat fishing. Season 25 Mar-31 Oct. Season and day tickets and E.A. licences obtainable from new, purpose-built fishing lodge with disabled access. All bookings and inquiries to Eyebrook Trout Fishery, The Fishing Lodge, Eyebrook Reservoir, Great Easton Road, Caldecott, Leics LE16 8RP (tel: 01536 770264, web: www.eyebrook. com). St £375, dt £15, evng £10, 3-day £109, conc. Boats £15/day motor; rowing boats £9; 2 wheelyboats. Hotels: Falcon, High Str East, Uppingham; Vaults, Uppingham, 5m N; Corby Hilton, Corby. B&B at Mrs J Wainwright, Homestead House, Ashley Rd, Medbourne, Market Harborough LE16 8DL (tel: 01858 565724).

FOREMARK RESERVOIR. Nr **Repton,** Derbys DE65 6EG. 230 acres, owned by Severn Trent Water Ltd. Season last Thursday in Mar-14 Dec; open all winter w/e bank fishing only. 25,000 rainbows stocked throughout season. Dt £15, 8 fish, afternoon £12 four fish, evening £8, 2 fish. Conc, £11, 5 fish; sporting ticket £10. Rowing boats £11.50 to £5. Motor boats £21 to £10. Disabled facilities, catering and courses. Enquiries and permits on site from Colin Lawrenson, Fishing Lodge (tel: 01283 703202).

GRAFHAM WATER. St Neots (Hunts).

3m off A1 at Buckden: 1,560-acre reservoir stocked with brown and rainbow trout; pike Oct/Nov. Managed by Anglian Water Services from the lodge at Mander Car Park, West Perry PE28 0BX (tel: 01480 810531; fax: 01480 812488). Records include b trout 19lb 12oz, r 13lb 3oz. St £160 to £649; dt £17, 8 fish limit, conc; c&r option. Beginners dt £5, 1 fish. Motor boats £10 to £22. It is advisable to book these in advance. New fishing lodge on site with tackle shop, restaurant, access for disabled.

GRIMSBURY RESERVOIR. Banbury (Oxon). Coarse fishery leased to Banbury & DAA; dt £5 for non members, concessions for juniors, from local tackle shops (*see Banbury*).

HARLESTHORPE DAM. Clowne, Derbys. Coarse fish, with pike to 22lb, carp to 32lb. St £110, dt £5 (£6 for 2 rods), £4 after 3 pm, on site. Enquiries to owner Carol Sibbring (tel: 01246 810231).

LADYBOWER RESERVOIR, Ashopton Rd **Bamford,** S33 0AZ (Derbyshire). Season 1 mar-15 Oct. St £294, midweek st £252. Dt £12.20, afternoon £8.60, conc dt £8.20; rowing boats £11.20, petrol motor £22; disabled facilities. Limited permits from warden for fly fishing on R Derwent below Ladybower Dam. All prices include VAT. Enquiries to Alan Pernell, Fishery Office (tel: 01433 651254).

NASEBY RESERVOIR, Northants. 85 acres. Carp to 19lb, tench to 5lb, rudd. Leased by BW to Naseby Water AC.

NANPANTAN RESERVOIR. 2m S of **Loughborough.** 8-acre coarse fishery.

OGSTON RESERVOIR, near **Chesterfield,** Derbyshire. 203-acre trout fishery owned by Severn-Trent Water Plc, and fished by Derbyshire County AC, day tickets are obtainable from Clay Cross Tackle; membership £220, annual subscription £170.

PACKINGTON FISHERIES, Meriden (Warks). Excellent trout fishing on 4 lakes (total 50 acres); st from £220, dt £24 5 fish, £16 2 fish. Good fishing on **Somers** fishery for carp, tench, roach, bream and rudd; 11 lakes (wheelyboat on 2 lake, must be booked in advance) and 1m of Blythe; dt £6, conc. Apply Packington Fisheries, Somers Lodge, Somers Lane, Meriden, nr Coventry CV7 7PL (tel: 01676 523833). Cafe, toilets and tackle shop on site.

PATSHULL PARK FISHERIES, Nr Pattingham, **Wolverhampton** WV6 7HY (tel: 01902 700774; web: www.patshullpark.co.uk). 75 acre lake, well stocked with b and r trout; fly only. St £290, incl 25 fish and boat hire, dt £20 for 5 fish; and other variations. Boats £8 for 2. Permits from Fishing Lodge. Regular fly fishing contests held. Pike fishing is allowed during winter months. Small stocked coarse pool.

PITSFORD WATER, Northampton 5m. 750 acres, managed by Anglian Water Services. Rainbow and brown trout, around 30,000 fish released during season. Good fly hatches all season. Dt (6 fish/c&r) £16, conc. Morning/evening £11 (4 fish). Beginners £5. Boats £20 to £10. Pike fishing from 16 June on selected dates. Access for disabled. Permits and tackle from Pitsford Lodge, Brixworth Rd, Holcot NN6 9SJ (tel: 01604 781350).

RAVENSTHORPE RESERVOIR, Northampton 8m. 100 acres, the home of modern reservoir trout fishing, established 1891; managed by Anglian Water Services. Brown and rainbow trout. Rod average 2002, 4.5 fish. 2 fish limit, c&r. Dt £18, conc, mornings/evenings: £12 (1 fish c&r). Beginners £5. Boats £18 to £6. Apply to Ravensthorpe Fishing Lodge, Ravensthorpe Reservoir, Teeton Road, Raversthorpe NN6 8LA (tel: 01604 770875). Accom, White Swan Inn, Holcot; Poplars Hotel, Moulton.

RUTLAND WATER, Leics. Stamford & A1 5m, **Oakham** 3m; managed by Anglian Water Services; Normanton Fishing Lodge, Rutland Water South Shore, Edith Weston, Oakham, LE15 8HD (tel: 01780 686441). 3,100 acres, 17m of fishing bank, largest stocked trout fishery in Britain. Browns to 15 lbs and rainbows to 14 lbs, 100,000 plus released per season. Pike fishing in late Oct-early Nov. 65 motor boats; including single manned. Competition facilities. St £160 to £649; dt £17, 8 fish limit, conc; catch-and-release option; boat hire £120 to £22, incl for disabled. Full restaurant facilities, access for disabled and tackle shop on site.

SHUSTOKE RESERVOIR. Shustoke; **Coleshill** 3m. Leased to Shustoke FF by STW. dt on site from 12 Apr.

SULBY RESERVOIR. 1m **Welford**, 14m

Northampton. Coarse fishing; exclusive syndicate fishery of 100 anglers, with specimen carp to around 35lb; limited st only; contact MEM Fisheries Management Ltd, Bufton House, Walcote, Lutterworth, Leics LE17 4JS (tel: 01858 571117).

STAUNTON HAROLD RESERVOIR, near **Melbourne**, Derbys. Severn-Trent W coarse fishery, 209 acres, leased to Swadlincote AC; dt £5 on bank. Tackle shop, Melbourne Tackle and Gun, 64 Church St, Melbourne DE73 1EJ (tel: 01332 862091); issues dt for 20-acre Melbourne Pool, specimen tench, bream, carp.

SYWELL RESERVOIR. Northampton 6m. Now a County Park. Tench to 10lb, pike (over 20lb), perch, roach and carp (tel: 01904 479797).

THORNTON RESERVOIR. Cambrian Fisheries, Fishing Lodge, Reservoir Rd, Thornton, **Leicester** LE67 1AR (tel: 01530 230807). STW reservoir, 76 acres. Open 1 Feb-17 Nov. Trout, annual stocking of 15,000, fly only. St range from £500 to £130; dt £16.75 to £7, according to limit, which varies from 6 fish to 2 fish. Boats £6.50 and £4.50. Tickets on site; also tuition; tackle available.

TITTESWORTH RESERVOIR, near **Leek**, (Staffs): 184 acre trout water now leased by STW to Tittesworth Fly Fishers Ltd; st £295 (18 fish/week), dt £17 (6 fish) and boats: advance bookings from Fishing Lodge, Meerbrook ST13 8SN (tel: 01538 300389) at reservoir; concessions to jun, OAP and regd disabled.

TRIMPLEY RESERVOIR, near **Bewdley**, Worcs. Trout, fly only, from 1 March-June 30; Jul 1-Oct 15, mixed fishery; then coarse fishing until Feb 28; st £110 weekday, £75 weekend; mixed £40; coarse £15. There is a £15 joining fee. Dt for guests of members only. Write for details to sec, Trimpley AA. Tackle shop: Mal Storey Angling Centre, 129 Sutton Road, Kidderminster DY11 6QR (tel: 01562 745221).

WELFORD RESERVOIR, near **Welford,** Northants, 20-acre coarse fishery. Many specimen bream, pike, carp, tench, perch and roach; st £30 to fish 2 rods, (jun half price) from BW or bailiff W Williams, Welford Grange Farm, Welford, Northants.

Part of the angler's library and tackle. *Photo: Arthur Oglesby*

NENE

(For close seasons, licences, etc, see Anglian Region Environment Agency, p21)

Rises in West Northamptonshire and flows to Wash. Good, all-round coarse fishery slow-running for most part. Roach and bream predominate, the bream in particular running to a good average size; also carp, chub, perch, pike.

Wisbech (Cambs). Centre of intricate system of rivers and drains, including the Nene-Ouse Navigation Link; all waters well stocked with pike, bream, roach, perch and some good tench. Fenland Assn of Anglers is centred in Wisbech. King's Lynn AA sub hires sections of **Pophams Eau**, and **Middle Level Main Drain** (12 miles of fishing); assn st £30, conc, wt £12, dt £3.50; **Great Ouse Relief Channel** provides 11m of good fishing from Denver Sluice to King's Lynn. Tackle shops: Brian Lakey, 12 Hill Str, PE13 1BA (tel: 01945 585278); March Angling Centre, 88A High St, March PE15 9LQ (tel: 01354 658747). Hotels: Rose and Crown, Marmion House.

Peterborough. Excellent centre for roach, bream, chub, tench, carp, rudd, eels and pike. Peterborough AC now controls most of the N bank of the Nene from **Wansford** to the Dog in a Doublet and some fishings on the S bank in the same area. Dt **Ferry Meadows Lakes**, £3, book

£17.50 from bailiffs. Whittlesey AA has local fishing on fenland dykes: **Bevilles Loam** from Ponders Bridge to Goosetree Corner; and **Whittlesey Dyke** from Ashline Sluice to Floods Ferry; st £12, dt £3, juv £1, from bailiff or from Sec, or local tackle shops. Wansford AC waters now members only. Deeping St James AC has Nene fishing at Wansford and Stibbington. At **Wansford** A1 road bridge, Stamford Welland AAA have ½m of south bank, downstream. First-class sport in fen drains and brick pits, but many pits being filled in. Eldernall Carp Lake, Coates, Whittlesay; £5 dt on bank for carp, tench, roach, etc; barbless hooks only, no groundbait, hemp; licences, st, wt and dt from all tackle shops (*below*) and local coarse fisheries **Gerards Pit** at **Maxey**, **Werrington Lakes**, **Tallington Lakes**. Sibson Fisheries, New Lane, Stibbington, PE8 6LW, have coarse lake with large carp, tench, bream; dt usually in advance (tel: 01780 782621). At Northey Park is a mixed fishery (tel: 07889 711555). At Turves is **Kingsland Reservoir**: 2 carp lakes, one silverfish (tel: 01733 840312). At Eastrea are **Decoy Lakes**: specimen coarse fish; tackle shop (tel: 01733 202230). Tackle shops: Webbs Fishing Tackle, 196 Newark Ave, PE1 4NP (tel: 01733 566466); information and permits on various local waters; Sheltons of Peterborough Ltd, 67A South Str, Stanground PE2 8EX (tel: 01733 565287), all local handbooks available; Wade, Peterborough. Hotel: Newark.

Elton (Northants). Leicester & Dist Amal Soc of Anglers has a stretch here; members only; apply Hon Sec; st £12. Coventry & Dist AA has 70 pegs at Fotheringhay. Good head of carp, tench, roach and chub. Full bk £17, conc, dt £2.50.

Warmington (Northants). Warmington AC has 2 to 3 miles from d/s of Fotheringhay to u/s of Elton, members only; £12 pa, no dt. Water let to clubs for matches, of up to 50 pegs. Bluebell Lakes, Tansor, Oundle PE8 5HN (tel: 01832 226042): fishery consists of Kingfisher, Swan, Sandmartin, Wood Pool and Bluebell Lakes, 1½m stretch of Nene, and Willow Creek, a backwater of 750 yds. Good coarse fishing with large carp, chub, bream, tench and pike. Membership and dt sold at fishery. Deeping St James AC fishes two stretches of Nene and coarse lake at **Stibbington**.

Oundle (Northants). Roach, bream, carp, tench, dace, etc. Oundle AA has water on both banks; limited st £10, dt £2; conc. Oundle AA also has local Nene fishing. Coventry & Dist AA has 70 peg stretch from road bridge u/s right hand bank with good head of bream, roach, chub, pike and dace. Book £17, dt £2.50 on bank. Wellingborough Nene AC has 3m at Barnwell, just upstream of Oundle and 2 acre gravel pit (tench, pike, perch and rudd); members only. **Elinor Trout Fishery**, Aldwinkle, 50 acre lake stocked weekly with browns and rainbows, fly only; dt £17 (6 fish), evening £12 (3 fish), boats £8 or £5; conc; full st £370, bank; enquiries to E Foster, Lowick Rd, Aldwinkle, Kettering NN14 3EE (tel: 01832 720786); coarse lake also on site, with tench, bream and roach. Tackle shop: Alans Angling Mart, 86 Rockingham Rd, Corby, Northants NN17 1AE (tel: 01536 202900) (Oundle AA tickets). Hotels: Talbot; Ship; Chequered Skipper, Ashton

(Oundle HQ).

Thrapston (Northants). Kettering Thrapston & Dist AA has **Aldwinkle Pits** and three coarse lakes at Thrapston; dt £3 from bailiff on banks or tackle shops. Earls Barton AC controls ½m R Nene at Ringstead, nr Thrapston; 1m at Cogenhoe; and 1½m at **Earls Barton**; also Hardwater Lake, Earls Barton; members only, membership £20, conc. Tackle shop: Motastore & Cycle Centre, 75 High Str, NN14 4JJ (tel: 01832 732312); issues KTDAA st and dt.

Rushden, **Higham Ferrers** and **Irchester** (Northants). Coarse fish. With new sewage works completed, fishing now showing marked improvement. Rushden & Higham Ferrers Irchester AA have water at **Turvey** and **Sharnbrook** on Ouse: barbel, chub, bream, pike, perch; members only; st £15, £7 juv, frozen until 2005, from Turvey PO, Bedford; tackle shops. Information, tackle and Rushden club cards (membership £15, conc) from Baits and Bits (*below*); Bob Webster & Sons (*below*). Shefford & DAA has 2 lakes, one of 56 acres; mixed coarse; members only; apply Hon Sec; also 1400 metres Great Ouse on same site; members and guests; st £40, conc, for all waters. Excellent trout fishery at **Ringstead Grange**, Ringstead, Kettering NN14 4DT (tel: 01933 622960); 36 acres, well-stocked with large fish. Record brown 10lb 6oz, record rainbow, 14lb 4oz; dt £16, limit 6 fish, conc £11; evngs £10, 3 fish; boat for one or two £8 extra, evening £5, from bailiff on site. Tackle shop: Baits and Bits, 26 Church St, Rushden NN10 9YT (tel: 01933 353007); Bob Webster & Sons, 37 High St, Irthlingbourgh NN9 5TE (tel: 01933 650110). Hotels: Rilton; Westward, both Rushden.

Wellingborough (Northants). Wellingborough Nene AC from one meadow above Hardwater Crossing to Ditchford Weir, plus nine other Nene stretches; other club waters: **Great Ouse** at **Harrold; Barker's Lake**, pond, and backwaters at Barnwell, Ringstead, Denford and Ditchford; also 2 small carp ponds at Grendon; these fisheries contain many large carp, chub, bream, pike, etc; membership £25, conc, from Hon Sec. Kettering, Thrapston & Dist AA has Nene fishing between Denford and Pilton, also **Islip Lake**, mixed coarse fishing, and **Aldwinkle Pits** nr Thrapston; dt £3 from bailiff or tackle shops. Northampton Nene AC has from Doddington up to paper mills, excluding Earls Barton AC water (1m) and water at **Billing** (*see Castle Asby, Billing and Northampton*). Earls Barton AC has The Dam; 2 acres; coarse; members only. Tackle shops: Ron's Tackle, 2 Church Way NN8 4HJ (tel: 01933 226913); Aquaflow, Victoria Rd, (tel: 01933 270463).

Castle Ashby (Northants). Pike, perch, bream, tench, roach; preserved for most part by Northampton Nene AC, which issues dt; bailiff on bank. Lakes on **Castle Ashby Estate** (1¼m S); pike, bream, tench, perch, roach; dt from bailiff at waterside or estate office (tel: 01604 712346). (*See also Midlands Reservoirs*). Hotel: Falcon.

Billing (Northants). Pike, roach, perch, bream, tench, chub: preserved by Northampton Nene AC which issues dt for 1½m on bank of river opposite Ecton Pits. Good coarse fishing at Billing Aquadrome (tel: 01604 408181 or 01933

679985); seven lakes open all year (river: from June 16 to Oct 16), st £40, wt £15, dt £5; all on site. At Earls Barton, Hardwater Lake, large mixed coarse gravel pit; Earls Barton AC; members only; membership £20, conc; apply Hon Sec or tackle shop: M F Perkins, The Square, Earls Barton NN6 0NT (tel: 01604 810274).

Northampton (Northants). Pike, perch, bream, chub, roach, carp, etc; Northampton Nene AC controls north bank from Weston Mill to Clifford Hill Lock; water on Nene at Kislingbury. Castle AA fishing includes north bank Nene by Carlsberg Brewery, Barnes Meadow (north bank), Midsummer Meadow, Becket's Park, Wappham Lake, Green Farm, Sixfields Reservoir, Sharman Lake, and lakes at Canons Ashby (dt £6); membership £35, conc; dt £5 for lakes, £3 for river or canal. Northampton good centre for lake and reservoir fishing. **Heyford Fishery**, Weedon Rd, Nether Heyford, NN7 3LG (tel: 01327 340002): a purpose-built match fishery, 1,200m long, 133 pegs, with annual stocking of 800lbs of carp, roach, bream, and other coarse species; also specimen carp lake and juniors lake; dt £5, conc, on bank. Northampton Britannia AC controls 2m local canal fishing, members only; cards from local tackle shops: Gilders, 250/2 Wellingborough Rd, NN1 4EJ (tel: 01604 636723); The Sportsmans Lodge, 44 Kingsthorpe Rd, Kingsthorpe Hollow NN2 6EZ (tel: 01604 713399).

Weedon (Northants). Pike, perch, bream, roach. **Grand Union Canal**. Northampton Nene AC has rights from A5 bridge Dogford above Weedon to Yardley Gobion (16m); dt from bailiff; available for match bookings; club also has Ransome Road Gravel Pits and Weedon Road Pit; dt from bailiff; also Blue Lagoon and Meadow Lake: dt on bank. At **Fawsley Park** are two lakes with pike, roach, rudd, etc; dt from club. Nene and Ouse licences needed for canal. **Hollowell Reservoir**, 140 acres, pike to 35lb, large roach and rudd; st, dt, available; The Fishery Warden, c/o Pitsford Water, Holcot, NN6 9SJ (tel: 01604 781350).

Tributaries of the Nene

OLD RIVER NENE:
March (Cambs). Pike, perch, bream, rudd, roach, tench. Fen drains. **Old River Nene**

mostly free to licence-holders. **Reed Fen** (south bank) is now private fishing. **Twenty Foot** controlled by March & Dist

AA (tickets). **Popham's Eau,** and **Middle Level** are King's Lynn waters. **Forty Foot** is now leased by Chatteris WMC; dt on bank. **Mortens Leam,** 5m from March, 7m of river fishing from Rings End to Whittlesey; wide variety of coarse fish; dt on bank. Cambridge FPAS has Block Fen Lakes; coarse; dt on bank. Tackle shop: March Angling Centre, 88A High St, March PE15 9LQ (tel: 01354 658747). Hotels: Griffen; Station.

Ramsey (Hunts). Pike, perch, bream, etc. Ramsey AC has fishing on **Forty Foot Drain,** and **Old River Nene** at Ramsey St Mary's and Benwick: roach, bream, perch, tench, pike, zander and eels; dt waters. Yaxley Farcet Holme & Dist AA have fishing on one bank from Horsey Toll to Ashline Sluice; also Yaxley Lode to North West Cut; also Monks Lode to New Look Cut; also Raveley Drain; contact Hon Sec. Tackle shop: The Ramsey Warehouse, 37 Parliament Str (tel: 01624 813092); F Wade & Son, 247 High St, Old Fletton, Peterborough PE2 9EH (tel: 01733 565159); H R Wade & Sons, 74/78 Great Whyte, Ramsey PE26 1HU (tel: 01487 813537); bait and Ramsey AC tickets etc.

WILLOW BROOK: Trout, coarse fish; preserved.

King's Cliffe (Northants). Willow Brook. Welland, 3m NW.

ISE:

Kettering (Northants). **Cransley Reservoir** (syndicate only); roach, perch and tench. For water on **Nene** at **Thrapston,** apply Kettering, Thrapston & Dist AA. Tackle and licences from Alans Angling Mart, 86 Rockingham Rd, Corby, Northants NN17 1AE (tel: 01536 202900).

Geddington (Northants). Preserved to Warkton.

STRECK:

Crick (Northants). Streck, 2m S. Dunsland Reservoirs (pike, perch, etc) 3m SW; private.

Daventry (Northants). Long Buckby AA has 6m single bank of Grand Union Canal from southern end of Braunston Tunnel to Whilton Marina, and from Norton Locks to A5; mixed coarse; dt £3 on bank, conc. **Daventry Reservoir,** Daventry Country Park, Northern Way, Daventry NN11 5JB (tel: 01327 877193). Coarse fishery, good pike fishing in winter, bream in late summer and autumn; dt on bank. **Drayton Reservoir** *(see Midlands reservoirs and lakes)*. Hellidon Lakes Hotel, Hellidon NN11 6GG has fishing (tel: 01327 262550).

NORFOLK AND SUFFOLK BROADS

(Rivers Bure, Waveney and Yare)

(For close seasons, licences, etc, see Anglian Region Environment Agency, p21)

Rivers Bure, Waveney and Yare, their tributaries and Broads are among the finest coarse fisheries in England. They contain pike, perch, roach, dace and large chub. Some banks of tidal water which may be fished free. For details, contact Environment Agency Fisheries (tel: 01603 662800). Some Broads are preserved and can be fished on payment. Rivers and most Broads very busy with boating traffic in summer, so early morning and late evening fishing advised. Best sport in autumn and winter at Wroxham or in the boatyards. Boats are essential for the most part.

BURE

Strong current from Yarmouth to little above Acle; upper reaches gentle and ideal for float fishing. The river contains a good head of coarse fish. Excellent roach, bream and pike etc, at Thurne Mouth, St Benets, Horning, Wroxham. Several Broads are connected and can be fished as well as tributaries Thurne and Ant.

Stokesby (Norfolk). Bream, roach, pike, perch. Strong tides and sometimes brackish; legering best; free.

Acle (Norfolk). Bream, roach, pike, perch. Tides often strong. River traffic heavy in summer. Acle and Burgh Marshes free fishing on E.A. licence. Inns: East Norwich Inn; Travel Lodge, A47 By Pass,

Acle.

South Walsham and **Upton**: 4¾m R bank from South Walsham Broad to Bure confluence and d/s past Upton Dyke is EA water free to licence-holders.

St Benets Abbey, bream and roach. North bank from Ant d/s, Norwich & DAA; dt for St Benets Abbey and Cold Harbour from A T Thrower & Son, Ludham PO NR29 5QQ; also Ludham Bridge Stores. Accommodation at Holly Farm, and Olde Post Office.

Horning (Norfolk); ns Wroxham, 3½m. Good coarse fishing; free to licence holders; boat almost essential; roach, rudd, bream, perch, pike, tench; river very busy in summer, hence early morning and late evening fishing gives best results. At **Woodbastwick** opposite Horning Ferry public house Environment Agency has 100m of right bank, tidal; free to licence-holders. Broads: **Ranworth** (tickets for Inner Ranworth from store on Staithe); **Decoy** (club water), **Salhouse** (dt issued); and **Wroxham**, small charge, upstream. Tackle shop: Horning Fishing Tackle and Chandlery, 106 Lower Str, NR12 8PF (tel: 01692 631401). Several boat yards. Hotels: Swan, Kepplegate and Petersfield House Hotel.

Wroxham (Norfolk). Roach, rudd, bream, pike, perch, tench; good pike and bream in winter; boats only. Much river traffic, summer. Broads: **Wroxham Broad, Bridge Broad, Salhouse Broad**, mainly boats. Tackle shop: Wroxham Angling

Centre, Station Rd NR12 8UR (tel: 01603 782453). Hotels: Broads; Hotel Wroxham.

Coltishall (Norfolk). Boats in vicinity. Hotels: King's Head; Risings; Norfolk Mead.

Buxton Lamas (Norfolk). All banks now private.

Abbots Hall (Norfolk). Ingworth. Brown trout, stocked 4 times during season. 1m both banks, dry fly, or upstream nymph only, open to Salmon and Trout Assn members only. Applications to Simon Dodsworth, c/o The National Trust East Anglia Regional Office, Blickling, Norfolk NR11 6NF (tel: 01263 733471). Tackle shop: Angling Direct, 277 Aylsham Road, Norwich NR3 2RE (tel: 0800 085 8169).

Bure Valley Lakes, nr **Aylsham** NR11 6NW (tel: 0126 358 7666); two coarse lakes: one specimen carp lake, fish to 33lbs, roach and tench.

Blickling (Norfolk). Dt for **Blickling Lake** (20 acres), from bailiff at 1 Park Gates, Blickling NR11 6NJ; £5, conc; no night fishing; tickets on bank in summer; pike season Oct 1 to Mar 14.

Tributaries of the Bure

THURNE: Slow-flowing, typical Broadland river; tidal below Potter Heigham. Coarse fish, good bream, pike and roach. Environment Agency free fishing at **Potter Heigham, Martham, Thurne Marshes**. In the spring of 2003 the Environment Agency built new stages along river (Potter Heigham) especially for disabled.

Thurne Mouth (Norfolk). Good roach, bream, rudd, perch and eels. Hedera House (tel: 01692 670242), has ½m of river, with fishing for guests at self-catering chalets; contact Miss C Delf.

Potter Heigham (Norfolk). Popular centre; good roach and bream; fair-sized eels. Bure. 3m, S. Broads: **Womack**, 1½m; **Hickling Broad** and **Heigham Sound** (tench, bream, roach, perch). Approx 3½m left bank, Martham to Repps and 4½m right bank Martham to Coldharbour free to licence-holders. Access points at Ferry Rd, Martham; Potter Heigham Bridge and Repp's Staithe. Boats from Whispering Reeds Boatyard, Staithe Rd, Hickling, Norwich NR12 0YW (tel: 01692 598314; web: www.whispering

reeds.net). Tackle shop: Lathams of Potter Heigham, Bridge St, NR29 5JE (tel: 01692 670080). Hotels: Broads Haven, Broadland House.

Martham (Norfolk). Rudd, tench, bream, roach, perch, pike; fishing platforms upstream of Martham Ferry; free fishing; **Heigham Sound** 1m free on EA licence. Martham & Dist AC fishes **Martham Pits**, Staithe Rd, 3½ acres good coarse fishing, with tench to 6lbs, bream over 7lbs, carp over 20lbs, good stock of silver fish; good sized rudd, perch and crucian carp over 3lb; 6 boats; dt £4 from Budgens, 88 Repps Road, Martham, NR29 4QZ (tel: 01493 740190). Membership £30 p/a (waiting list), conc; boats all the year round: Whispering Reeds Boatyard, Staithe Rd, Hickling, Norwich NR12 0YW (tel: 01692 598314; web: www.whisperingreeds.net). Tackle shop: Lathams of Potter Heigham, Bridge St, NR29 5JE (tel: 01692 670080).

ANT:

Ludham. Roach, bream, eels, perch, pike. 2¼m of the river, upstream and downstream of Ludham Bridge, free to licence-holders.

Irstead and **Neatishead** (Norfolk). Good bream, perch, rudd, pike; also tench and roach. Fishing free.

Stalham (Norfolk). River clear, slow-running and weedy in summer; roach, rudd, bream, perch, pike and few tench. Broads: **Barton**, 1m; bream, roach, eels, perch and big pike; rod licence needed; can only be fished from a boat. Boats from Cox's Boatyard Ltd, Staithe Rd, Barton Turf, Norwich NR12 8AZ (tel: 01692 536206). **Hickling**, 3m by road; good pike, bream, etc. Sutton Broad overgrown. Tackle shop: Broadland Angling and Pet Centre, 24-26 High Str, Norwich NR12 9AN (tel: 01692 580959). Hotel: Sutton Staithe Hotel and Kingfisher. Barton Angler Country Inn, Neatishead NR12 8XP, and can arrange fishing through Wroxham Angling Centre, Station Rd NR12 8UR (tel: 01603 782453).

Wayford Bridge (Norfolk). Upper Ant; head of navigation; fishing free to licence-holders; roach, rudd, perch, pike, tench, bream; boat advisable; river is narrow and fairly busy at times in summer; weedy and clear. Bait and tackle from Stalham. Good fishing also above the head of Ant Navigation in Dilham and North Walsham Canal, navigable to rowing boats as far as Honing Lock. Caravan site and food at Wood Farm Inn.

North Walsham (Norfolk). Several coarse fisheries in locality. Gimmingham Lakes, with carp to 30lbs, Roughton, with carp, tench bream, roach, and perch; Felmington, with roach, perch, tench, carp; dt for all of these, and other local tickets and information from tackle shop: Angling Direct, 277 Aylsham Road, Norwich NR3 2RE (tel: 0800 085 8169). Inns; Ockley House; Toll Barn.

SAW MILL LAKE: Fishing station: **Gunton** (Norfolk) near Cromer; 16 acre lake in Gunton Park, 3m; coarse fish; dt from machine on bank. At Felbrigg Hall, just north, National Trust have 4 acre coarse lake (tel: 01263 837444). Tackle shop: Marine Sports, 21 New St, Cromer NR27 9MP (tel: 01263 513676).

Horning (Norfolk). **Salhouse Broad**; too much traffic in summer, but good fishing in early mornings and from Oct to March. Dt issued. **Ranworth Broad** (tickets for Inner Ranworth from store on Staithe). **Malthouse Broad**; free. **Decoy Broad**; now open only to clubs. Tackle shop: Horning Fishing Tackle and Chandlery, 106 Lower Str, NR12 8PF (tel: 01692 631401). Licences from Post Office.

Ormesby, Rollesby and **Filby**. Fishing by boat only, from Filby and Eels Foot Inn. These Broads are connected and undisturbed by motor cruisers and yachts, but electric outboards may be used. Fishing good everywhere. Excellent pike in winter. Wt £27.50. **Little Ormesby Broad**, free fishing by boat only.

Salhouse (Norfolk). Salhouse Broad, 1m NE; few pike in winter.

Broads connected with the Bure

Wroxham Broad, 1m N; *(see Wroxham);* Information and boat-hire from Wroxham Angling Centre, Station Rd NR12 8UR (tel: 01603 782453). **Decoy** or **Woodbastwick Broad**, 2m NE; fishing on payment. **Ranworth Broad**, 3m E; good for bream. These three are controlled by Norwich & DAA. **South Walsham Broad**, 5m E; public access; boat necessary; good bream and pike fishing.

Wroxham (Norfolk). **Wroxham Broad**, boat fishing, and part bank fishing by yacht club. **Salhouse Broad**, right bank, 2m SE; mainly boat fishing, but bank fishing after a long walk. Charges may be made on bank or through boat hire. Tackle shop: Wroxham Angling Centre, Station Rd NR12 8UR (tel: 01603 782453).

Broads connected with the Thurne and Ant

Potter Heigham (Norfolk). **Heigham Sounds**; fine fishing in summer; pike fishing, roach and bream in winter (free). Pike fishing on Horsey (no live-baiting). Womack Water dredged and cleared of weed, and may be fished from quay below. *(For hotels, boats, etc, see entry under Thurne.)*

Hickling (Norfolk). **Horsey, Barton** and **Hickling Broads**, bream, roach, pike, perch. All free except Horsey; dt from keepers. Licences from Post Office and stores; boats for hire.

Martham (Norfolk). R Thurne. Bream.

WAVENEY

Flows along Norfolk-Suffolk border. Fishing from tidal limit at Ellingham. Between Geldeston Lock and St Olaves, the tidal river gives some wonderful sport with bream in summer, winter roach and pike at Beccles Quay.

Lowestoft (Suffolk). Oulton Broad and Waveney, which connects with Broad; bream, perch, roach, pike, etc; boats at Broad. Flounders and smelts in harbour. Good sea fishing in Oct, Nov and Dec from boats and beach for whiting, cod and flatfish. Several Broads within easy reach. Much of **River Hundred** is Kessingland AC water. **Oulton Broad** (Suffolk). Broad gives good sport with eels to 5lb, bream, roach, perch, etc, but crowded with boats in summer. Bank fishing from Nicholas Everitt Park. EA 2m of free fishing at Puddingmoor Lane, **Barsham**; and 170 yds at **Worlingham**; boat fishing best on tidal river. Good perch and pike (best Oct-March); roach (good all season, best Jan, Feb, Mar), bream (moderate, best June-Nov); dace. **North Cove**; 400 yards with bream to 7lb, big pike, st from Post Office. **Oulton Dyke** (north side only); bream (excellent Aug, Sept, Oct); perch, roach, eels. Club: Oulton Broad Piscatorial Society. Tackle shops: Ted Bean, 175 London Rd NR32 1HG (tel: 01502 565832). Hotels: Wherry; George Borrow; Broadlands.

Haddiscoe (Norfolk). **New Cut**: good coarse fishing; free. **Fritton Lake**, Countryworld, Fritton, Gt Yarmouth NR31 9HA (tel: 01493 488288): 163 acres; well known for bream in summer, and pike in winter, also perch, roach, rudd, tench, eel, carp; open all year; dt, boats for hire, Wheelyboat for disabled; holiday cottages to let, with fishing included.

Worlingham (Suffolk). 170 yds of Suffolk bank free fishing via Marsh Lane.

Beccles (Suffolk). Good roach, bream, pike, etc; best early or late in summer but especially good Oct onwards, when river traffic eases off. Free fishing from Beccles Quay. 400 yds stretch at **Aldeby** is George Prior AC water. **Aldeby Pits** coarse fishery is 5m from Beccles, on Waveney. Tackle shop *(see below)* is helpful, and issue st and dt for waters belonging to Beccles, Bungay Cherry Tree AC, and Harleston and Wortwell clubs, on river and lakes; charges range from st £17 to £5; dt from £5 to 50p. Tackle shop: Angling (Direct) Suffolk, Unit 4C1, Ellough Industrial Estate NR34

7TF (tel: 01502 713379). Hotels: King's Head; Waveney House; Ship House.

Geldeston (Norfolk). Good pike, roach, perch, bream, etc; free. Inns: Wherry (licences) and Geldeston Lock. Tackle shop in Beccles (3m).

Barsham (Suffolk). 2m free fishing on Suffolk bank from Puddingmoor Lane.

Bungay (Suffolk). Good roach, chub, bream, perch, pike and tench; fishes best at back end. Bungay Cherry Tree AC has from Earsham to Geldeston, 2m between Wainford and Ellingham, mostly roach, and **Ditchingham Club Pits**, which has disabled platforms. Members only on all waters except **Broome Pits**, dt £2.50 on bank (tel: 01986 895188); St £30, juv £10, conc, holiday 14-day permits £12.50 from local tackle shops. Contact Hon Sec. Tickets also (including dt for visitors) from Outney Meadow Caravan Park NR35 1HG (tel: 01986 892338), who also offer fishing on private stretch of river. Suffolk County AAA has Bungay Common stretch.

Homersfield (Suffolk). Pike, perch, roach (large), dace, tench. 300 yds of free fishing. Hotel: Black Swan, Homersfield IP20 0ET.

Harleston (Norfolk). Waveney, 1m S; coarse fish. Harleston, Wortwell & Dist AC has fishing on Weybread Pits, 6 lakes stocked with most coarse species. Weybread Fishery, Mill Lane, Weybread IP21 5TP has dt (booking only) (tel: 01379 588141) has mixed coarse fish. Waveney Valley Lakes (tel: 01986 788676), tickets on bank. Waveney Angling, 5 London Road, Harleston IP20 9BH (tel: 01379 854886); Angling (Direct) Suffolk, Unit 4C1, Ellough Industrial Estate NR34 7TF (tel: 01502 713379).

Eye (Suffolk). **Dove Brook**; large dace. Fishing in Waveney at Hoxne, 3m.

Diss (Norfolk). **Waveney** and **Dove**. Diss & Dist AC has good quality stocked water on Waveney at Scole, Billingford, Hoxne, Brockdish, 6m total, best end Sept onwards; Dove at Oakley, d/s of bridge, roach, rudd, bream, pike, tench; **Diss Mere**, 5 acres, mirror carp, tench, roach and crucian carp; no dt; st £18, 2-week ticket half st price, conc £9, for all fisheries from Pegg Angling Supplies, Wills

Yard, Chapel St, Diss IP22 4AN (tel: 01379 640430). Hotel: Saracens Head.

YARE

Rises few miles from East Dereham and flows through Norwich to Yarmouth. Tidal, still one of the best Broads rivers for roach and bream, the main species; specially good for roach in middle reaches, bream in lower.

Great Yarmouth (Norfolk). Broads and rivers. Rivers Yare, Bure and Waveney fall into **Breydon Water** (Bure joined in upper reaches by Thurne and Ant). In all, some 200 miles of rivers well suited to boat and bank angling are within easy reach; some Broads are landlocked, strictly reserved for angling and free from river traffic; others connected to rivers, but mostly best fished from boat. Many Broads easily accessible; also rivers **Bure, Thurne, Ant** and **Waveney**. Trout in Bure. Also good sea fishing. Tackle shops: Pownall and Son, 74 Regent Rd NR30 2AJ (tel: 01493 842873); Greensted Tackle, 73 High Str, Gorleston-on-Sea NR31 6RQ (tel: 01493 602474); Dyble & Williamson, Crown Cott, Hemsby Rd, Scratby, Great Yarmouth NR29 3PQ (tel: 01493 731305).

Reedham (Norfolk). Strong tide; legering best; roach, perch, bream, eels; free at Langley on E.A. licence. Hotel: Ship.

Cantley (Norfolk). Roach, bream, perch; bream and perch plentiful; fishing free to licence-holders; mostly by leger. Inn: Red House.

Buckenham (Norfolk). Carp, bream, roach, perch; pike; Great Yarmouth AA has fishing here and at Claxton, Rockland and Langley, 2,900 yds left bank and 5,200 right bank; mouth of Hassingham Dyke is good spot; dt £3 from Beauchamp Arms. Lakes Strumpshaw Broad, 1m NW. Rockland Broad, 1½m SW on other bank of river; free.

Brundall (Norfolk). Roach, bream, perch in Yare. Several reaches between Coldham Hall and Surlingham Ferry can be fished by boat. Surlingham Broad belongs to National Trust; fishing only fair in sum-

mer; water shallow and weedy; pike in winter.

Norwich (Norfolk). Free fishing at Earlham Bridge to Cringleford Bridge, 2m of left bank, with dace, roach, chub, bream, pike. **Wensum** above city holds fine roach, perch, dace, chub and pike. Good roach and bream fishing at **Rockland Broad**; 7m from Norwich; but poor access to banks. 10m from Norwich, Haveringland Hall Park, Cawston NR10 4PN, has excellent coarse fishing lake, open all year on permit, dt £5 2-rods, from manager's office (tel: 01603 87 1302). Norwich & DAA has water on **Bure, Thurne,** and **Ant, Ranworth Broad** and **Woodbastwick Decoy** (fishing by boat only on last two waters); dt (Coldharbour and St Benets) from Hon Sec and tackle shops. Anglian Water coarse fishery: **Taverham Mill Lake,** Taverham, Norwich NR8 6TA (tel: 01603 861014); lake, with carp, roach, pike, bream, etc; and stretch of R Wensum with barbel, chub, roach, dace; tackle shop, self-catering accom on site. St and dt for lake, st only on river; free to lodge residents on both. Nr **Attleborough** is Manor Lake, part of Rockland Manor, Scoulton Rd, Rocklands NR17 1UW (tel: 01953 483226); crucian, mirror, common and ghost carp (to 25lb), tench, rudd, perch; st £90; tickets from Rockland Manor. Tackle shops: Gallyons Country Clothing and Fishing Tackle, 7 Bedford Str, NR2 1AN (tel: 01603 622845); Brundall Angling Centre, Riverside House, Brundall, NR13 5PY (tel: 01603 715289), large mail order tackle shop, with large fishing tackle discount warehouse; has fishing dinghies on Yare. Hotel: Maid's Head.

Tributaries of the Yare

CHET:

Loddon (Norfolk). Free coarse fishing in Chet at Loddon Staithe: roach, bream. This water now navigable and fishes best in autumn and winter when traffic finishes. Hotels: Swan, and Angel Inn, Loddon; Hardley Floods preserved. White Horse, Chedgrave.

WENSUM: Coarse fish (good chub and barbel).

Norwich (Norfolk). Tidal. Riverside Rd, Oak Str and Hellesdon Mill controlled by City Amenities Dept; chub, barbel &c. Free fishing at Fye Bridge Steps, Cow Tower, Bishop Bridge, Yacht Station and d/s of Foundry Bridge to apprx 100yds d/s of Carrow Bridge.

Costessey (Norfolk). Chub, roach, dace, bream and pike. Norwich & DAA have 600 yds u/s of Costessey Mill; membership from local tackle shops or Hon Sec; assn also has Wensum Fisheries; 3 lakes. At **Taverham**, 5 RMC Group Water gravel pits known as the **Ringland Lakes**, large carp, pike, roach, bream, and 480m R Wensum. St (2 rods only) £30, conc £18. *(For RMC Angling see Chertsey).* **Costessey Lakes**, 100 acres AW coarse fishery, carp to 39lb, st and dt from Taverham Mill Fishery Tackle Shop, Taverham, Norwich NR8 6TA (tel: 01603 861014). **Shallowbrook Lakes**, Norwich Rd, New Costessey NR5 0LA: 4 lakes totalling 11 acres, coarse fish, st £100, dt £6; contact Martin Green (tel: 01603 747667 or 01603 744680).

Drayton (Norfolk). Free fishing at Drayton Green Lane for half mile, with roach, chub, bream, dace and pike.

Attlebridge (Norfolk). Good trout fishing here, some miles of water being preserved. Tud, 4m S; private. **Reepham Fishery**, Beck Farm, Norwich Road, Reepham NR10 4NR (tel: 01603 870829; web: www.reephamfishery.co.uk); 3½ acre spring-fed lake, with carp to 28lb, tench to 6lb, roach, rudd. Dt £6, conc, from bailiff on bank; crucian carp to 4lb, also koi, chubb, golden orfe. Disabled swims, facilities on site. Open 6.30 to dusk (9pm latest). At Clay Lane, **Swannington** is Natures Haven Fishing Lakes, 10m NW of Norwich (tel: 01603 260303; e-mail: natures.haven@farmline.com); 76 pegs; carp, tench, bream, roach, perch, rudd. Dt £5, conc, on bank.

Lenwade (Norfolk). Fishing in three old gravel pits set in 25 acres, administered by the trustees of two Great Witchingham charities. There is a lake with carp to 30lbs, plus mixed coarse fishing. Permits £5 day, £9 night (conc. jun, OAP) from bailiff.

Swanton Morley (Norfolk). Dereham & Dist AC has water, *see Lyng, below.* **Swanton Morley Fishery**, bream roach, rudd, tench, perch, pike, carp (tel: 01362 692975); dt £5 on bank. Permits and information from F W Myhill & Sons, 7 Church St, East Dereham NR19 1DJ (tel: 01362 692975). Accom with free fishing on R Wensum: J Carrick, Park Farm, Swanton Morley NR20 4JU (tel: 01362 637457). Fishing and shooting parties welcome at Wensum Valley Golf Club, Beech Avenue, Taverham, Norwich NR8 6HP (tel: 01603 261012).

Hellesdon (Norfolk). Roach, chub, dace, carp, pike. Free fishing from Mill Pool to New Mills.

Lyng (Norfolk). Fine roach, dace and some trout. Dereham & Dist AC has Wensum here, and at **Swanton Morley**, (2 stretches); chub, pike, roach, dace, etc; **Lyng Pit**; carp, tench, bream, pike, roach; **Billingford Pit**, tench, bream, carp, roach; six pits at Swanton Morley with pike, bream, tench, roach and carp, perch, chub; membership £40, conc, from Myhills (*below*), or from Hon Sec. Near East Dereham, Salmon and Trout Assn has **Roosting Hill Fishery**, Beetley, North Elmham; two rainbow lakes (6 and 2 acres); S&TA members syndicate only; dt for S&TA members; 1 May to end Oct; contact R G Bunning (tel: 01362 860352). Mr Rogers, Lakeside Country Club, Lyng, Norwich NR9 5RS (tel: 01603 870400; web: www.lakeside-countryclub.co.uk), has 35 acres of coarse lakes, the largest of 26 acres for Kingfisher Lakes FC only; carp, bream, pike; accom and catering on site. Tackle Shop: F W Myhill & Son, 7 Church St, Dereham NR19 1DJ (tel: 01362 692975). Other tackle shop: Churchills of Dereham, 26 Norwich St, Dereham NR19 1BX (tel: 01362 696926). Accom, Park

---

Check before you go

While every effort has been made to ensure that the information given in **Where to Fish** *is correct, the position is continually changing, and anglers are urged, in their own interests, to make preliminary enquiries before travelling to selected venues. This is especially important with reference to prices quoted. Inevitably the rate of inflation is affecting stability in this quarter. Anglers' attention is also drawn to the fact that the hotels mentioned under the various fishing stations do not necessarily have water of their own. Any amendments or further data for inclusion in subsequent editions, and any comments, will be welcome.*

Farm, Swanton Morley.

North Elmham (Norfolk). Fishing in Wensum for pike, roach, perch, dace and few trout. Fakenham AC has Railway Lake, 1 acre, mixed coarse; dt £5.

Fakenham (Norfolk). Salmon and Trout Assn members have Bintry Mill Trout Fishery on Wensum; browns; 2m mostly double bank; dt for Assn members only; dry fly and nymph only; contact C T Lawton (tel: 01603 872393). Trout, dace, roach, perch, gudgeon, eels. Fakenham AC has 2m, dt water, also **Willsmore Lake**, Hayes Lane, with carp, bream, tench, etc; 6 tickets daily on lake, £8, Mon-Sat from Dave's Fishing Tackle, Millars Walk NR21 9AP (tel: 01328 862543). Nr **Beeston** (8m south) is **Bridge Farm Fisheries**; carp, tench, roach, rudd, golden rudd, golden orfe, koi carp; dt, conc, at lakeside).

TASS or **TAES:**

Swainsthorpe (Norfolk). Yare, 3m N. **Taswood Lakes**, Mill Rd, Flordon NR15 1LX (tel: 01508 470919); good carp and other coarse fish. Dt £6 (coarse), night £12.00 by appointment.

BASS:

Wymondham (Norfolk). Yare, 4m N at Barford and 6m N at Marlingford; roach. Club: Wymondham AC: season tickets £5 from Hon Sec. Tackle shop: F W Myhill & Son Ltd, 36 Fairland St, NR18 0AW (tel: 01953 602272). Hotel: Abbey.

BLACKWATER: Trout; preserved.

Booton (Norfolk). Booton Clay Pit, with carp to 30lb, bream to 10lb and large roach, tench, etc; stocked by Cawston Angling Club. 24 hour dt £6 from bailiff on bank. Under 16, 50p. For further details contact S Brownsell, 27 Holman Close, Aylsham NR11 6DD (tel: 01263 732263).

Broads connected with the Yare

Buckenham (Norfolk). **Rockland Broad**, 1½m SW; good roach fishing and pike fishing in winter; free; boat required; slipway available; also free fishing at Rockland Staithe (winter best).

Brundall (Norfolk). Belongs to National Trust; shallow water grown up in summer, but good for pike in winter. C Bettell, 96 Berryfields, Brundall NR13 5QQ, runs guided pike fishing trips on the

To enjoy a day's fishing one does not have to fish! This is Herons Mead, Orby, Skegness.

Broads. Tackle shop: Brundall Angling Centre, Riverside, Brundall NR13 5PS

(tel: 01603 715289).

NORFOLK (small streams)

(For close seasons, licences, etc, see Anglian Regional Environment Agency, p21)

BABINGLEY RIVER. Fishing station: **Castle Rising.** Reduced water levels; little fishing and limited access.

GLAVEN. Rises 3m E of **Holt** and joins sea at **Cley**, 6m down. 1m at Cley. Fishing now held privately. No permits. There are several small coarse lakes in this area. **Letheringsett, Booton** at **Cawston, Selbrigg** at **Hemstead**; dt on bank.

NAR. Rises above **Narborough** to enter the Wash at **King's Lynn**. Chalk stream brown trout fishing; private. 1m both banks below Narborough Mill, stocked, fish 11" upwards, dry fly and upstream nymph fishing only, reserved for Salmon and Trout Assn syndicate members; S&TA members can apply for dt £20 (3 fish). At Narborough, trout (3) and coarse lakes (2) plus trout stream; dt £8 trout, plus £1.95 per lb, coarse dt £7.50 for Meadow Lake, £6 Millers Lake. Enq to Narborough Trout and Coarse Lakes, Main Rd, Narborough, nr King's Lynn PE32 1TE (tel: 01760 338005).

TASS. Rises N of **Wacton**, 11m S of **Norwich**, to enter Yare on outskirts of city.

OTTER

(For close seasons, licences, etc, see South West Region Environment Agency, p19)

Noted Devonshire trout stream flowing into English Channel immediately east of Exe. Mullet in estuary and some sea trout, with brown trout of good average size for West Country higher up, where hotels have some excellent dry-fly water.

Budleigh Salterton (Devon). Tidal. Free fishing from river mouth to Clamour Bridge (about 1½m, both banks) to visitors staying in East Budleigh or Budleigh Salterton. Sea trout, brown trout, grey mullet plentiful but difficult to catch. Fishing on both banks from Clamour Bridge to Newton Poppleford. Sea fishing; bass, flatfish, etc, from extensive beach. *(see Sea Fishing Stations under Sidmouth).*

Ottery St Mary (Devon). Some good trout water in vicinity.

Honiton (Devon). Deer Park Hotel, Buckerell Village EX14 3PG (tel: 01404 41266), has 3m (both banks) of wild brown trout fishing; trout up to 2lb, average 1lb; dt £30, £25 after 4pm, at hotel; hotel also has 2 acre lake; 3 lakes with rainbow trout at Otter Falls, Rawbridge, nr Honiton. Otter Inn, **Warton**, has trout fishing on 100 yds of Otter. Coarse fishing on 3 acre lake at Fishponds House Hotel, Dunkeswell, EX14 4SH (tel: 01404 891358); carp, rudd, tench, and roach; day and season tickets sold at hotel. Hollies Trout Farm and Fisheries, Sheldon EX14 0SQ (tel: 01404 841428), trout pond of 1½ acres, spring fed; open all year.

OUSE (Great)

(For close seasons, licences, etc, see Anglian Region Environment Agency, p21)

Rises in Buckinghamshire and flows north-east through Northamptonshire, Bedfordshire, Cambridgeshire, Huntingdonshire and Norfolk, entering the North Sea by The Wash. Coarse fishing throughout. Slow, winding river for most part. Roach and dace are to be found in quantity, together with barbel and bream. Between Newport Pagnell and Bedford there are large chub and barbel.

King's Lynn (Norfolk). Coarse fish of all kinds except barbel. King's Lynn AA has water on the Ouse from Modney Court to Denver Sluice east bank; Denver Sluice to Danby's Drove, west bank; on the Wissey, from Dereham Belt to R Ouse; on the **Relief Channel Drain**, King's Lynn to Denver Sluice; on the **Middle Level** Drain from St Germans to Three Holes, 8m; Ten Mile Bank, and pits; senior st £30, junior £5, conc £15, wt £12, dt £3.50, from bailiffs. Gatton Water, Hillington, nr Sandringham: coarse fishing in 8 acre lake for visiting campers, and caravans; contact Mr Donaldson (tel: 01485 600643). Woodlakes Holiday Park,

A 13lb zander from Roswell Pits, Ely, captured by a young master. *Photo: Brian Tedds.*

Holme Rd, Stow Bridge, PE34 3PX (tel: 01553 810414), 8m south of King's Lynn, coarse fishing on five lakes, the largest 12 and 10 acres; carp to 30lbs, pike, roach, tench, bream, rudd, perch, etc; dt £8 mid-week, £10 w/e and bank holidays, conc for juv, OAP; contact Robin Hall. Swaffham AC has Bradmoor lakes, Narborough, stocked with carp, bream, etc; st £28, conc from Kev's Tackle. Tackle shops: Anglers Corner, 22 Windsor Rd PE30 5PL (tel: 01553 775852); Geoff's Tackle Box, 38 Tower St, King's Lynn PE30 1EJ (tel: 01553 761293); Kev's Tackle, 2 Mangate St, Swaffam PE37 7QN (tel: 01760 720188). Hotel: Park View.

Downham Market (Norfolk). Coarse fish, sea trout; tidal. Cut Off Channel if King's Lynn water, 12m from Wretton Fen Rdto Denver Sluice. Tackle shop: Howlett Cycles and Fishing, 53 High St, PE38 9HF (tel: 01366 386067).

Hilgay (Norfolk). King's Lynn AA water on Ouse and **Wissey** *(see King's Lynn)*. London AA has water on Ouse; dt from bailiffs.

Littleport (Cambs). Ouse and **Lark**; coarse fish, except barbel, good pike and bream, with roach, perch, zander; Littleport AC has fishing on Ouse: old Littleport A10 Bridge u/s to Sandhills Bridge, both banks, except Boat Haven on west bank; bream to 7lb, roach, rudd, perch, eels, pike, zander, carp; permits £3 from bailiff on bank; club books from tackle shop in village; full membership £12, conc. London AA controls 14m of water from Littleport Bridge to Southery (Norfolk), both banks; dt from bailiffs; night permit available, also 24-hour ticket. Ely Beet Sports and Social Club, Lynn Rd, Ely CB6 1DD (tel: 01353 662029) has fishing on both banks of Ouse at confluence; contact Paul Verdon (tel: 01353 610143); dt £4 on bank. Tackle shop: Coleby's Tackle, 15 Granby Str, CB6 1NE (tel: 01353 860419); Benwick Sports Angling Centre, 29 Main St, Little Downham CB6 2ST (tel: 01353 698936).

Ely (Cambs). Free fishing in Ely town centre. Coopers AC have ½m downstream of railway bridge; dt on bank; bookings from Hon Sec; Ely Beet S&SC AC have 4½m from Foremill Wash to Sandhill Bridge at Littleport (dt on bank; bookings from Paul Verdon (tel: 01353 610143)); also Roswell Pits, Ely; Littleport AC have ¾m from Sandhill Bridge downstream; dt on bank: bookings from Paul Frost (tel: 01353 860353). Tackle shop: Coleby's Tackle, 15 Granby Str, CB6 1NE (tel: 01353 860419); Benwick Sports Angling Centre, 29 Main St, Little

Downham CB6 2ST (tel: 01353 698936).
Earith (Hunts). Histon & Dist AC has apprx 1m opposite village, members only; st. **Old West River**. Earith Bridge to Pope's Corner (Cambs); partly hired by Cambridge Albion AS; good coarse fishing; **Old Bedford River** from Earith to Welches Dam controlled by Cambridge Albion AS; members only but dt on bank. Ploughman's Pit (good carp, bream, pike. The Hundred Foot (Earith to Sutton Gault), rented by Cambridge FPAS, tidal; practically all coarse fish, except barbel; **Borrow Pit** nr Ely, coarse fish, dt £3 (£4 on bank), in advance, from Hon Sec or local inns for Cambridge FPAS water.
Over and Swavesey (Cambs). Bream, perch, chub, rudd, tench, pike, dace and zander. Sea trout runs up to the locks; fish over 12lb taken. Occasional salmon.
Holywell Ferry (Hunts). Hotel: Ferry Boat. Pike, bream, roach, rudd, chub, etc; free; boats; good fishing, especially roach.
St Ives (Hunts). All coarse fish, bream, dace, perch, chub, gudgeon in quantity; also carp, barbel, rudd and tench. Ample bank fishing, but boats for hire. St Ives & DFPAS has 3m water; st £14, dt £2, conc. Adjoining water at Bluntisham, plus lake at Hemmingford Grey, nr St Ives (dt £3 to be purchased before from address shown on notice boards) held by London AA. Histon & Dist AS has Holywell stretch. Tackle shop: St Ives Angling Centre, 8 Crown St, PE27 5EB (tel: 01480 301903). Hotels: Golden Lion, Slepe Hall.
Godmanchester (Hunts). Good bream, roach, chub and chance of carp. Godmanchester A & FPS has about 10m; tickets from Hon Sec or tackle shop; st £10, dt £3.50. London AA has Portholme Meadow, Berry Lane Meadows and 1¼m Old West River at Stretham (members only). Boats from Huntingdon; no free fishing. Tackle shop: Stanjay Sports, 7 Old Court Hall, Godmanchester PE29 2HS (tel: 01480 453303), who manage **Woolpack Fishery**, Cow Lane, 60 acres of well stocked coarse fishing; gold ticket £180 all lakes; lakes 1, 2, 3 & 8 white st £60 (24 hours), green ticket dawn till dusk £30, conc; dt £4. Stanjay also has Cromwell Lake, 2½ acres, 36 match pegs (bookable) st £70, dt from shop £5; large coarse fish water. Hotels: Black Bull, Exhibition, Bridge and George.
Huntingdon (Cambs). Chub, bream, roach

and tench; good when boat traffic declines. Huntingdon A&FPS has water from Town Bridge to Hartford Church; platforms for disabled; permits, st £12, conc, dt £3, juv st £6, from tackle shops. London AA (*see Clubs*) has **Portholme Meadow**, **Alconbury Brook** (Huntingdon), **West Meadow**, **Lea Brook** (Godmanchester) and **Willow Tree Island** (at Offord); **Brampton Mill Pool** and millstream, and also lake and river at **Brampton**; members only; membership £36, conc. Brampton AS has two stretches of Ouse, 4 brooks and 2 lakes; mainly st (£15) but dt on river and one lake. Biggleswade, Hitchin AA has 1m at Brampton; members only. Tackle shops: Sports & Fashions, 51 High Str, PE18 6AQ (tel: 01480 454541); Stanjay Sports, 7 Old Court Hall, Godmanchester PE29 2HS (tel: 01480 453303); Ouse Valley Angling, 25/31 Huntingdon St, St Neots PE19 1BG (tel: 01480 386088).
Offord Cluny (Hunts). Stocked by Environment Agency. Chub, roach, bream, tench, carp, barbel, catfish. Offord and Buckden AS has 3m of Great Ouse between St Neots and Huntingdon, incl two weir pools; membership £16, dt £3, conc, from bank by car park; from Stanjay, Godmanchester; from The Swan PH, Offord Cluny. Several sections are free of boat traffic at all times. Coach-party enquiries to E Blowfield, 4 Monks Cottages, Hunts End, St Neots PE19 5ST (tel: 01480-810166).
St Neots (Hunts). St Neots & Dist A&FPS has several stretches and are expanding their fishings; Wilden Reservoir (members only); good tench, chub to 7lbs, bream, roach and big carp; st £20, conc, from tackle shops; dt for most of R Ouse fishing (not Wray House), from bailiffs. Luton AC has 3 stretches at Black Cat, Wyboston Lakes and Eaton Ford; also at Wyboston Lakes (2 coarse lakes, one dt); dt £4 on bank, conc. Letchworth Garden City AA has water at **Little Paxton**, dt £4, membership £50, conc. Milton Keynes AA has, under sharing arrangements with Letchworth Garden City AA, approx 1m of R Ouse at **Little Paxton** nr **St Neots** and 1.5m of Great Ouse at **Felmersham** in Beds (for further information contact Milton Keynes sec, Trevor Johnson (*see Clubs*)). London AA has water at **Tempsford** and **Blunham** (*see Ivel*). Tackle shops: Ouse Valley Angling, 25/31 Huntingdon St, St Neots PE19

1BG (tel: 01480 386088). Hotels: The Oak Motel, Crosshall Rd.

Biggleswade (Beds). Ouse, Ivel; Biggleswade, Hitchin AA has 7m on mid Ouse, starting at Tempsford, and 15 acre **Gingerbread Lake** at Eaton Socon with large carp, tench, rudd, bream, with access also to the river here; st £35, conc, from Hon Sec and local tackle shops; club also has Links Pool nearby; mixed coarse; members only. Under sharing arrangements with RMC Angling, Milton Keynes AA has access to 1m of R Ouse at **Harrold** in Beds and 1m of R Ivel near **Biggleswade**, Beds (for further information contact Milton Keynes sec, Trevor Johnson *(see Clubs)).* Blue Lagoon and Green Lagoon, **Arlesey** (4m S); large coarse lake, Letchworth Garden City AA; dt on Green Lagoon only £6, membership £50, conc. Tackle Shop: Sportsman's Lodge, 147 Harrowden Road, Bedford MK42 0RU (tel: 01234 269724).

Bedford (Beds). Approx 4m water in town centre and above, free to E.A. rod licence-holders. Council controls three lakes at Priory Country Park, dt £2.60 on bank. Bedford AC has fishing and issues limited dt at £6, obtainable from Tavistock Angling or Hon Sec, along with tickets for seven other local fishing clubs. Shefford & DAA has Willington Lake; mixed coarse (carp to over 40lb); members only; assn also fishes Great Ouse here. Vauxhall AC controls **Radwell** complex, 6m of Ouse (both banks in many places), and seven gravel pits of total 100 acres at Sharnbrook; ¾m R Ouse at **Felmersham**; club also has 600 yds at **Kempston**, and ½m at **Willington**; also 8 acre coarse lake, **Woburn Sands**; and holds stretch of **R Ivel** close to Sandy (Girtford Bridge); members only plus guests; st £34, conc; membership details from Membership Sec. Kempston AC, now amalgamated with Vauxhall AC, has 2½m at Kempston Mill on the Ouse; dt from Tavistock Angling or on bank. Luton AC has 40-peg stretch at Biddenham Baulks; members only; apply Hon Sec or tackle shops; club also has ¾m left bank at Lavendon Mill; members only; also 5 acre reservoir at Steppingley, near Ampthill; mixed coarse; members only. Blunham & Dist AC has stretches at Gt Barford, 1,000 yds; Willington, 2,000 yds; and Oakley, 1,500 yds, good mixed coarse fishing with roach, chub, bream, barbel, etc; members only, £35, £12 conc.

Ampthill AFPS fish **Ampthill Reservoir**, and **Marston Pits**; membership £32. Hotels: Embankment, Swan. Tackle shops: Tavistock Angling, 95 Tavistock Str, MK40 2RR (tel: 01234 267145); Sportsman's Lodge, 147 Harrowden Road, Bedford MK42 0RU (tel: 01234 269724).

Felmersham (7m N of Bedford). Vauxhall AC fishes ¾m here and ¼m at **Willington**, membership £34, conc. Shefford & DAA has ½m here, noted for barbel; members only. Letchworth Garden City AA has left bank d/s of road bridge; no dt, membership £50, conc.

Sharnbrook (Beds). Vauxhall AC has water. Shefford & DAA has ¾m; members only. RMC Angling has (Group Water) **Harrold Fishery** (1,500m Ouse, 1,200m Ivel at Lower Caldecott), with carp, chub, roach, dace, pike, catfish, barbel. St £22, conc £12 (one permit covers Ouse and Ivel). *(For RMC Angling see Chertsey).*

Newton Blossomville (Bucks). Coarse fish (large barbel). Northampton Nene AC has water; strictly limited; members only from Hon Sec or local tackle shops.

Newport Pagnell (Bucks). Good barbel, roach, bream, chub, perch. Stretch fishes well in winter. RMC Angling has 3m of river above town at Tyringham Estate, offering large barbel to 15lb 4oz, chub, bream, roach and dace. Group Water: st £22, conc £12, *(For RMC Angling, see Chertsey.)* Newport Pagnell FA leases Newport Pagnell Lakes from AW. Hotel: Bull Inn (club HQ). Milton Keynes AA has 6/7m of bank on R Ouzel from Bletchley, through Milton Keynes to Newport Pagnell and 6.5m of tow path on Grand Union Canal in **Milton Keynes** (for further information see Hon Sec below).

Stony Stratford (Bucks). Deanshanger & Stony Stratford AA has 6m of Ouse; bream, roach, perch, chub and pike, plus Grand Union Canal at **Castlethorpe**, st £15, dt £3 on bank, or £3 from Sportsmans Lodge, 26 Church St, Wolverton, Milton Keynes, Bucks MK12 5JN (tel: 01908 313158). Milton Keynes AA has approx 6m of bank on Great Ouse between **Stony Stratford and Newport Pagnell**; 2m of bank on R Tove at **Castlethorpe**; approx 10 lakes totalling 270 acres in Milton Keynes (Furzeton, Caldecotte, Tear Drops (3), Lodge Lake, Willen Lakes (2), Bradwell Lake, Jubilee Pit). Finally access to **Emberton Park** at

Olney (just outside Milton Keynes) which includes ¾m of the Great Ouse and 6 lakes totalling 100 acres (incl. Heron, Glebe and Willow lakes). For further information contact Milton Keynes sec, Trevor Johnson (*see Clubs*).

Cosgrove Lodge lakes at Cosgrove (Northants): noted for roach, tench, bream, pike; dt on water. Hotels: Cock; Bull.

Buckingham (Bucks). Chub, roach, perch, dace, bream, pike. Buckingham & Dist AA has several miles of fishing on Ouse and tributary Padbury Brook, plus two stillwaters in area. Good quality coarse fishing throughout, with increased water flows of winter months bringing out best in the river. Assn records include carp 39lb 4oz, pike 27lb 4oz, bream, chub and tench over 7lb; adult membership £32, dt £4, conc (disabled via membership sec; proof must be provided): from Jakeman Sport, 5 Bourbon St, Aylesbury; J & K Angling, Sheep St, Bicester; Tingewick P O; Londis, 41 Nelson St, Buckingham. Mounthill Angling Syndicate has 2m between Beachampton and Deanshanger, mostly double bank, with large perch, pike, roach, dace, bream, barbel; membership limited, contact P Welling, 1 South Park Gardens, Berkhamsted, HP4 1JA. Leighton Buzzard AA, Claydon Lakes, 6m; no dt. At Stowe Landscape Garden National Trust has 3 coarse lakes; dt accompanied by NTAC member; contact Asst Head Gardener (tel: 01280 822850). At **Mursley**, Church Hill Fishery, Swanbourne Rd, MK17 0JA: 3 lakes of 15 acres stocked with r and b trout; dt £30, half-day £20, 4 and 2 fish (tel: 0129672 0524). Pimlico Farm Pools, Tusmore, Bicester OX27 7SL (tel: 01869 810306): 3 lakes with carp, perch, roach, rudd, tench; 50 pegs, open dawn till dusk; disabled access, matches, self-catering accom.

Tributaries of the Ouse (Great)

WISSEY:

Hilgay (Norfolk). King's Lynn AA have 2m of both banks down to Ouse. St £15, wt £12, dt £3.50, conc. London AA issues dt for Five Mile House Farm; dt £3.50 on bank; also 24-hour ticket; good for zander.

LITTLE OUSE: Good bream and roach.

Brandon (Suffolk). The above species, plus dace, perch, pike (good), a few chub and zander. Brandon & Dist AC has 2 ponds and ¾m river at Recreation Park; no dt, membership £15 annually with concessions, from Recreation Centre. Hotel: The Ram.

Thetford (Norfolk). Little Ouse and Thet. Roach, rudd, tench, chub and pike; and dace to specimen size. Fishing free for 7 miles through town centre out to Santon Downham.

LARK: Trout and coarse fish.

Mildenhall (Suffolk). Brown trout, carp, rudd, roach, tench, bream, pike, dace, gudgeon, chub. Mildenhall AC has several stretches excellent coarse fishing on Lark at Mildenhall, u/s and d/d at Isleham Lock, and West Row Drains, around West Row village; for £10 st, contact Hon Sec (tel: 01638 718205). Lark APS has fly fishing for browns between Lackford and Barton Mills; coarse fishing on various stretches from Barton Mills to West Row Fen; fly only trout; membership £125 (st only); coarse st £20, conc £10 (under 12's free) from Hon Sec; dt £4 from Barton Mills PO or £5 on bank; disabled facilities at Barton Mills (ten platforms), where there is also a lake, and Mildenhall (three platforms). Tackle shops: Tackle Up, 49a St Johns St, Bury St Edmunds IP33 1SP (tel: 01284 755022); Hooked, 127 All Saints Rd, Newmarket CB8 8ES (tel: 01638 661594); Matthews Garden Centre, 18 High St, Lakenheath, Brandon IP27 9JS (tel: 01842 860284). Hotels: White Hart, High St; Riverside, Mill St.

Bury St Edmunds (Suffolk). Coarse fish. Bury St Edmunds AA has L Ouse, stretches on Blackbourne, Stour and Glem; and 5 lakes: at Barrow; Thetford; Little Whelnetham; Great Whelnetham; Glemsford: coarse; st £45, conc: contact John Easdown (see clubs). Tackle shop: Tackle Up, 49a St Johns Str, Bury St Edmunds IP33 1SP (tel: 01284 755022); which has information on a variety of coarse fisheries in area, incl Weybread Fishery, with large carp, roach etc; Marsh Farm Lakes, Saxmundham; Barway Lake, nr Ely; Cross Drove Fishery, Hockwold-cum-Wilton; Swangey Lakes, Gt Ellingham.

CAM or **RHEE**: Excellent fishery, with good roach and pike. Best catches between Baitsbite Lock and Clayhithe Bridge.

Waterbeach (Cambs). Letchworth Garden

City AA has 1200 yards right bank d/s of Clayhithe Bridge; dt £4 on bank. Contact Hon Sec. Cambridge FPAS has Reach, Burwell and Wicken Lodes.

Cambridge. R Cam can fish well, with roach, chub, dace, and many other species. Fishing disallowed on college property. University Sports and Social Club controls R Cam at Cantelupe Farm; permits from club. Cam from near Pike and Eel Pub, Chesterton, d/s through Baitsbite Lock to Clayhith Bridge, Cambridge FPAS; st £20, conc, dt £3 in advance, from Hon Sec local tackle shops; also lakes; inquire Hon Sec for permits. Waterbeach AC controls Cam, Baitside Lock area, also at **Upware**, Humphreys Wash and Wests Wash. Club also has rights on **Swaffham Bulbeck Lode**, and Atkin and Leland Waters, Landbeach which is for members only; st £20, £5; club also has Magpie Lake here; mainly carp for match and dt. Cambridge Izaak Walton Soc has ¾m at Dernford Farm, Stapleford (**Granta**); brown trout, chub, dace, perch. Members only; contact Hon Sec. Cambridge Albion AS controls Cam at Wicken; Dimmocks Cote to Upware; and d/s towards Fish & Duck Pub; st £25, dt £4, on bank or from tackle shops; the Old West River at Stretton Bridge, and **Old Bedford River** from **Earith** to Welches Dam, a good pike water. Histon & Dist AS controls **Old West River** from Hermitage Lock to old pump engine, and two other stretches; should be fished early in day, owing to boat traffic; st £18, conc, dt £3 in advance, a surcharge on bank; club also fishes lake complex at **Milton**, excellent carp; dt £5, st £33; and Counterwash Drain from Earith to Manea on both banks, tench, roach, rudd, pike, etc. Cambridge Albion AS has Peacock Lake at **Cottenham**; mixed coarse; dt on bank or tackle shops £5. **R Ouse** nr **Over** controlled by Over and Swavesey AS. St £15, conc, from Cooper (*see below*). Agrevo ASC controls **Drayton Fen**, 80 acres, with good carp, tench, pike, also Holywell and Swavesey Lakes and Gt Ouse; inquire Coopers (*below*). London AA has water for members only at **Swaffham Prior** and **Upware**; members only; membership £39, conc. Tackle shop: Farrington, 2/4 Ferry Lane, CB4 1NT (tel: 01223 461361); Cooper & Sons, 1 Carlton Terrace, Carlton Way, CB4 2DA (tel: 01223 365987).

Barrington. Cambridge Izaak Walton Soc

has ¾m here; chub, dace, pike; members only; contact Hon Sec.

OLD WEST RIVER: Good stock of coarse fish. **Milton Lake**. Large carp and other coarse fish.

IVEL: Dace, roach, barbel, bream, chub and perch.

Tempsford (Beds). Ouse and Ivel. Biggleswade, Hitchin AA has water on both rivers; members only; st £35; family £45, conc. London AA has several miles on Ouse here and at Blunham; members only; membership £39, conc.

Blunham (Beds). Ouse (1m W). Blunham & Dist AC controls 1,000 yds local fishing; also Gt Ouse at Oakley, Willington and Gt Barford; Halls Pit, nr Sandy; Barford Lake, Gt Barford; Willington Gravel Pits; members only, £32, £10 conc. Below Blunham Bridge to Ouse held by Biggleswade, Hitchin AA; club also has right bank of Ivel from Langford Mill to Broom Mill; no dt; club also has right bank u/s of Langford Mill. Shefford AC has left bank, at **Shefford**, shared with The Tring Anglers. Members only. Nearest tackle shops, Bedford.

Lower Caldecote (Beds). RMC Angling has ¾m stretch at Manor Farm, Group Water, with dace, chub etc; st £22, conc £12. (*For RMC Angling, see Chertsey.*)

Langford (Beds). Letchworth Garden City AA has fishing opposite garden centre; no dt, membership £50, conc; Assn fishes most of Ivel through its membership of the Ivel Protection Association.

Henlow (Beds). Letchworth Garden City AA fishes Poppy Hill Complex in Henlow: 4 lakes and river at Henlow Village, entry via Park Lane. Shefford & DAA fishes Airman Pit, 1m west; mixed coarse, mainly carp and catfish; members only; apply Hon Sec.

HIZ (tributary of Ivel). Ivel Protection Assn has a stretch; also Letchworth Garden City AA; members only.

OUZEL: Coarse fish.

Leighton Buzzard (Beds). Luton AC has 12m **Grand Union Canal** from Pitstone, through Leighton Buzzard to Stoke Hammond; towpath; dt £4, conc, from bank; mixed coarse. Leighton Buzzard AC by agreement with Luton AC has 3m of Canal. Also **Claydon Lakes**, **Tiddenfoot**, and Rackle Hills Pits and other pits; concessions to jun & OAP. Berkhamsted AS controls Bridigo Pond, Linslade, nr Leighton Buzzard; mixed carp and coarse fishery; also Steat Farm, Cublington, carp fishery, both members only. RMC Angling has 2 small lakes, including **Jones Pit**, famous for catfish; stocked also with carp. Group Water: st (2 rods) £40, conc £25. (*For RMC Angling, see Chertsey*).

RELIEF CHANNEL: not strictly a tributary but included here because of its traditional status as an excellent coarse fishery in its own right, now re-established as such, after a difficult period with zander, by an intensive programme of investigation and re-stocking by AWA. Now rented to Wisbech & Dist AA which issues dt.

TOVE: Coarse fish.

OUSE (Sussex)

(For close seasons, licences, etc, see Southern Region Environment Agency, p18).

Rises few miles south-east of Horsham and flows for 33 miles to enter English Channel at Newhaven. Tidal for 12 miles from mouth to point 4m upstream of Lewes. Coarse fish and trout, but notable for run of big sea trout.

Lewes and **Barcombe Mills** (E Sussex). Sea trout (good), barbel, perch, bream, roach, dace, chub, carp and pike. Ouse APS has west bank from Hamsey to Barcombe Mills (about 4m) and certain stretches of non tidal water above the mills. Sea trout from May to Oct, but June to October best, given rain; permits; contact John Goodrick, Applegarth, School Lane, Barcombe BN8 5DT (tel: 01273 400380). Barcombe Mills Pool and side streams reserved for sea-trout fishing and open to permit holders at £5 per rod per day bookable in advance. Decoy Wood Fisheries, 1 Decoy Cottages, Laugthon Rd, Ringmer BN8 6DJ (tel: 01273 814344): coarse fishing in 4 acre lake; good stock of carp, rudd, roach, tench, perch, the odd pike; book 24 hours in advance. Tackle shop: Uckfield Angling Centre, 212A High St, Uckfield TN22 1RD (tel: 01825 760300). Hotels: Shelleys; White Hart; Crown (all Lewes); for Barcombe Mills: Anchor Inn.

Isfield (E Sussex). Coarse fish, trout and sea trout. Isfield & Dist AC has sections of Ouse at Isfield and Barcombe Mills; also has stretches of **Uck** at **Uckfield**, and lakes around **E Grinstead**, **Uckfield**, **Horsted Keynes** and elsewhere, twenty four fisheries in all. Large carp, tench, bream, perch, eels and pike; st £65 plus £15 joining fee, conc, from Memb Sec (sae); no dt. Hotels: Laughing Fish, Isfield. (Tackle see Lewes).

Haywards Heath (W Sussex). Coarse fish and trout. Haywards Heath & Dist AS has 11½m both banks of **Ouse** from **Linfield** down to **Newick**, and several lakes, including **Balcombe Lake**, **Slaugham Mill Pond**, **Valebridge Mill Pond**; fishing coarse mainly, trout in river, and is for members only; membership open to approved applicants, with concessions; a few river dt £6 from Sporting Chance. Tackle shops: Sporting Chance, Unit 2, 29 Boltro Rd, RH16 1BP (tel: 01444 454095); Burgess Hill Angling Centre, 143 Lower Church Rd, Burgess Hill RH15 9AA (tel: 01444 232287) for Hassocks AS and Henfield & DAS.

UCK: mainly coarse fishing below Uckfield with occasional sea trout. Joins Ouse at Isfield.

Isfield (E Sussex). Coarse fish and trout. Isfield & Dist AC has water from here to **Uckfield** (members only), with excellent coarse fishing and trout to 3lb.

Check before you go

*While every effort has been made to ensure that the information given in **Where to Fish** is correct, the position is continually changing, and anglers are urged, in their own interests, to make preliminary enquiries before travelling to selected venues. This is especially important with reference to prices quoted. Inevitably the rate of inflation is affecting stability in this quarter. Anglers' attention is also drawn to the fact that the hotels mentioned under the various fishing stations do not necessarily have water of their own. Any amendments or further data for inclusion in subsequent editions, and any comments, will be welcome.*

OUSE (Yorkshire)

(For close seasons, licences, etc, see North East Region Environment Agency, p20)

Forms with Trent the estuary of the Humber. Coarse fish, with some trout. Dunsforth, Beningbrough and Poppleton reaches noted for barbel and chub. Large bream present but difficult to catch. Most water held by Leeds and York clubs. Tributaries give excellent trout and coarse fishing.

Goole (E Yorkshire). Don enters Ouse here. Several different clubs have amalgamated for fishing the **Aire & Calder Canal** from Goole to Crowcroft Bridge nr Pollington; information from R S Tackle and Guns; as for West Cowick Pond, and Big Hole Pond at Rawcliffe. Carlton AC has dt £3 for several fishings around Selby and Goole, including West Haddlesey Lake, available from Hon Sec; Hon Treasurer, Harry Park (tel: 01405 860791); Field Sports *(below)*. Selby AC offers dt £2.50 (yearbook £10) on bank at Selby Canal between Brayton and Burn Bridges, with roach, chub, carp, dace and other species; club also Burn Bridge to Paperhouse Bridge. Local fisheries too numerous to list, but three of note are: Moorfields Carp Fisheries, Goole ED14 8BQ; dt £5 (tel: 07710 817150); Kilpin Fish Pond, Howden DM14 7TJ (tel: 01430 430196) dt £5, mixed coarse. Selby tackle shops: Selby Angling Centre, 69 Brook Str, YO8 4AL (tel: 01757 703471); Field Sports, 24/26 New St, Selby, N Yorks YO8 0PT (tel: 01757 709607); R S Tackle and Guns, Unit 1, Carlisle St, Goole DN14 5DS (tel: 01405 720292).

Acaster (N Yorks). Coarse fishing. Castleford Anglers fish on 150 yds below old salmon hut. Dt £1. Fish include barbel; above dam, trout and coarse fish. Accommodation: Manor Guest House.

Naburn (N Yorks). Below dam, right bank to old salmon hut, York Amalgamated. Left bank, tickets £3 from lock keeper.

York (N Yorks). Coarse fish; some free fishing on public waters. On left bank nearly all free except 8m from Rawcliffe Ings and Clifton Ings up to Aldwark. York & DAA has fishing on **Ouse, Derwent, Nidd** and several still waters; st £28, conc, dt £4 from local tackle shops for lower Nidd; ½m on Derwent, each fishery members only. Tackle shops: Anglers Corner, 41 Huby Court, Walmgate York YO1 9UD (tel: 01904 629773).

Poppleton and **Newton** (N Yorks). Good barbel, pike, etc. York Amalgamation has extensive stretches; including National Trust water at Beningbrough Hall; coarse: barbel, bream, eel, gudgeon, roach, ruffe; dt from York tackle shops; Newton on Ouse AC also fishes this water; dt from Blacksmith's Arms, Newton on Ouse YO30 2BN (tel: 01347 848249).

Lower Dunsforth. From Lower Dunsforth to Aldwark Bridge (about 4m right bank) fishing is largely in the hands of Leeds & Dist ASA. Dt from Angler Inn, Lower Dunsforth YO26 9SA (tel: 01423 322537). Leeds & Dist ASA also has good length at **Hunterslodge** on opposite side below Aldwark bridge (left bank); and a futher length at Linton-on-Ouse adjoining bottom of Hunterslodge to canal mouth. Tickets as above.

Tributaries of the Ouse (Yorkshire)

DON. Rises on Wike Head and flows through Sheffield and Doncaster to the estuary of the Ouse; after 150 years of pollution from the Sheffield steel industry, this river is once more fishable. The Environment Agency has stocked over past twelve years, and 30lb nets of roach have been caught. Hemp and tares are best summer baits, maggots and casters in winter.

Doncaster (S Yorks). Doncaster & Dist AA has much widespread coarse fishing, including water on the canalised Don and **South Yorkshire Navigation Canal** at Sprotborough, 4m d/s to Doncaster Prison; 5m of **Idle** from Newington to Idle Stop; 10m of the **Torne**; the 6m of **New Junction Canal** from Barnby Dun to the **Aire & Calder** junction; also BW **Southfield Reservoirs, Cowick,** 110 acres total, 40lb bags of roach and bream. Dt £2.50 on banks at many of these fisheries. **Thrybergh Reservoir,** 34 acres, near **Rotherham**; Rotherham MBC trout fishery; permits on site; Rotherham MBC also has **Fitzwilliam Canal,** Rotherham 1m, dt. BW Castleford Anglers have **Woodnook Reservoir**; st from Assn HQ and tackle shops. Barnby Dun Social AC have st £5, dt £2 on bank at S Yorkshire Navigation Canal between **Barnby Dun** and Kirk Sandall, with chub, roach, perch, bream, gudgeon (tel: 01302 886024 for match bookings). **Hayfield Fishing Lakes**, Hayfield Lane, Auckley, DN9 3NP (tel: 01302 864555); 2 lakes with 157 pegs, mainly carp, roach, rudd, tench, gudgeon, etc; dt £5, conc. Tackle shops: Doncaster Angling Centre, 207 Carr House Rd DN4 5DR (tel: 01302 363629). R & R Sports, 40 High Str, Bawtry DN10 6JE (tel: 01302 711130); has dt for a variety of coarse fishings in area, incl Chesterfield Canal, R Idle, Warping Drain.

Sheffield (S Yorks). **Damflask Coarse Fishery** (YW reservoir), 5m W; contact Yorkshire Water Services, Catchment & Recreation Manager, Western House, Western Way, Halifax Rd, Bradford BD6 2LZ (tel: 01274 372742); mt and dt on site; bream in summer and autumn, specimen pike in winter; roach perch and chub through year; numbers of specimen fish is increasing. **Underbank**, corporation reservoir, coarse fishing and a few large trout. Tickets from attendant's office. Further information under *'Yorkshire Lakes'*. Sheffield & Dist AA has water on Rivers **Trent**, trout fishing at Thurgoland on **Don**, and **Chesterfield Canal** from A631 to Trent junction; dt £3 issued for most waters. **Stainforth and Keadby Canal** controlled by joint committee including Rotherham, Doncaster, and British Railways clubs; dt on bank. At **Staveley** Urban District Council have five acre lake stocked annually with coarse fish; dt and st; also **Foxtone Dam**; dt. Chapeltown & Dist AA fish **Westwood** and **Howbrook Reservoirs**, and ponds, various coarse species; st £10, dt £3, from G & S Hamstead, Tackle Shop, 14 the Guardian Centre, Rotherham S65 1DD (tel: 01709 365454), or bailiffs. Tackle shops: Kerfoot Fishing Tackle, 6 Southey Green Rd S5 8GW (tel: 0114 2313265); Bennetts of Sheffield, Stanley St, Sheffield, S3 8JP (tel: 0114 275 6756); Gunnies, 279 Buchanan Rd S5 8AU (tel: 0114 232 1437); Chesterfield Angling, 34 Chester St, Chesterfield S40 1DW (tel: 01246 208710).

Oughtibridge (S Yorks). Sheffield 6m; free fishing, mainly roach, trout, dace, chub, barbel, with some grayling, perch. Mainly shallow, some pools and disused weirpools.

DEARNE (tributary of Don):

Barnsley (S Yorks). Dearne; Free fishing on length within Hoyle Mill Country Park. Mainly free, between here and **Darfield**, and through common near Wombwell. Stocked at **Haigh**, where Wakefield AC has water. Club also has lakes near **Wakefield**, fishing on R Calder, and Calder & Hebble Navigation. Membership from Wakefield tackle shops. Darfield Colliery AC has Netherwood Country Park Lake, Bradberry Balk Lane, Wombwell; dt (OAP/jun conc) on bank; st/books from Hon Sec. Barnsley MBC owns Cannon Hall Lake, Barkhouse Lane, Cawthorne (tickets from machine); and Dearne Valley Park Lake, Hoyle Mill (free fishing on selected sections of river and lake bank). Information from B Hearne, Countryside Officer, Barnsley MBC, Planning Services, Central Offices, Kendray St, S70 2TN (tel: 01226 772566). Barnsley & Dist AAS fish **Brampton Canal**; dt £2.50, conc (full book £20); **Worsbrough Country Park** fishing, Worsbrough Bridge; Assn also has Sally Walshes Dam, 13 acres, 6m s of town at Emsworth; dt on bank; excellent coarse carp fishery. **Worsbrough Canal**, Drop AC (tel: 01226 750659). **Barnsley Canal**, fishing on north bank only, Brian McGraw Jnr (tel: 01226 247131). Barnsley & Dist AAS also has **Smithies Fishing Lake**, Smithies Lane; dt on bank or contact Hon Sec. Tackle shops: Tackle Box, 11 Doncaster Rd S70 1TH (tel: 01226 247131); Wombwell Angling Centre, 25 Barnsley Rd, Wombwell, S73 8HT (tel: 01226 750659).

Claycross (Derby). Lakes: Williamthorpe Ponds, 2m NE. Wingerworth Hall Lakes (two), 2½m NW. Great Dam, 3½m NW.

ROTHER (tributary of Don):

Killamarsh (Derby). Short Brook. Lakes: Woodhall Moor Dams, 2m E. Barlborough Hall Lake, 3m SE. Pebley Dam, 3m SE. Harthill Reservoir, 3m E. Woodhall Pond, 3m E.

AIRE: Issues from ground at Aire Head, half a mile south of Malham village. Its upper reaches contain quality trout and grayling, which give place to coarse fish between Steeton and Keighley. Keighley AC has stretch at Marley and several more at Keighley and Skipton, with trout, chub, roach, pike, plus other fishing on ponds and 3m Leeds & Liverpool Canal; st £22, dt £2, conc. Tackle shops in

Keighley. *(For Malham Tarn-see Ribble-Settle).*

Beale (W Yorks). Bradford No 1 AA has 3m left bank above and below bridge, and a further 1½m u/s; coarse, mainly roach; members only.

Leeds (W Yorks). Contains roach, bream, chub, trout, perch. Adel Beck and Dam (private). **Roundhay Park Lakes**, 4m NE. Leeds & Dist ASA have fishing; dt £2 from local tackle shops. Larger lake (Waterloo) contains trout, pike, perch, roach, tench, carp, etc; no fishing on small lake; trout under 10ins to be returned immediately; 3-fish limit. Assn has extensive fishing on Ouse and tributaries, canals and lakes, dt for many waters; full details from Hon Sec. Also trout at Pool and Arthington *(see Ouse (Yorks) - Wharfe).* Castleford & Dist SA fish Fairburn Ings and Fairburn Cut; dt £1 on site. At **Swinsty** and **Fewston** is Washburn Valley Game Fishery and **Thruscross Reservoir** (wild browns, c&r), 5m W of **Harrogate**, YWS reservoirs (see Damflask Coarse Fishery), containing rainbow trout, also wild brown; visitors' dt (4 fish; 2 fish evng) can be had from machine at Swinsty Moor car park; st from Fishing Warden at Reservoir Lodge, Fewston, Harrogate HG2 1SV (tel: 01943 880658); st £300 (limit 100 trout per season), dt £10 '(4 fish), conc, fly only. Tackle shops: Kirkgate Anglers, 95 Kirkgate, LS2 7DJ (tel: 0113 243 4880); Bob's Tackle Shop, 1A Chapel Lane, Garforth LS25 1AG (tel: 0113 286 7112); Headingly Angling Centre, 58 North Lane, Headingly LS6 3HU (tel: 0113 278 4445), agents for Leeds & Dist ASA, and four other local clubs.

Bradford (W Yorks). Aire, 7m N. Stockton AA have small stretch at Middleham; members only; apply Hon Sec. Bradford City AA has extensive rights here and on water on the canals at Apperley Bridge and near Skipton; on **Wharfe, Ure** and **Swale**, reservoirs and lakes. Assn fishes Saltaires length of **Leeds and Liverpool Canal**. Bradford No 1 AA has water on **Wharfe** at **Addingham**, Denton, **Aire** near **Skipton**, **Swale** at **Gatenby, Ure** at Middleham, **Nidd** at Ramsgill and Nun Monkton, **Derwent**, also **R Calder** at Elland, and reservoirs; Association also has 1000 yards of River Ouse at Nun Monkton; membership £30, entrance £20, conc. Tackle shops: Westgate Anglers, 63 Westgate BD1 2RD (tel: 01274 729570);

Wibsey Angling Centre, 208 High St, Wibsey, Bradford BD6 1QP (tel: 01274 604542); Richmonds, 71 Park Rd, Bradford BD5 0SG (tel: 01274 721042).

Bingley, Saltaire (W Yorks). Trout, coarse fish; Bingley AC has 1m through Bingley coarse fish; restocked annually with trout; 2m of Leeds and Liverpool Canal, with large carp and others; st £25 and dt £2, from tackle shop. Club has good trout fishing on **Sunnydale Reservoir**, Eastmorton; trout and coarse fish, dt £3.50; also two dams and beck. Trout waters are for members only. Bradford No 1 AA has two lengths, left bank, along Bingley Cricket and Football Fields, d/s; members only. Trout and coarse preserve in **Myrtle Park**; water restocked; dt £2, conc; dt £2 for **Leeds & Liverpool Canal**; Saltaire AA (HQ Ring of Bells, Bradford Rd, Shipley) has 4m stretch of Aire, mixed fishery, dt water, best match bag 2003, 30lbs chub; and **Tong Park Dam**, brown and rainbow trout, dt £4 from Wibsey Angling Centre, 208 High St, Wibsey, Bradford BD6 1QP (tel: 01274 604542). From Bankfield Hotel downstream to Baildon Bridge (both banks, except Roberts Park) is also Saltaire AA water.

Keighley (W Yorks). Trout, grayling, coarse fish, chub plentiful. Sport improved after restocking. Keighley AC shares 14m; trout to 5 lbs; best May-June and Sept. Club also shares fishing on the **Leeds-Liverpool Canal**; Calden Canal; **Huddersfield Narrow Canal**; Lancaster Canal; Llangollen Canal; Macclesfield Canal; **Shropshire Union Canal**; and has fishing on **Whitefields Reservoir**, stocked with carp, tench, roach and perch, and, for members only; **Roberts Pond** (large tench, carp, pike). Dt for R Aire and canal. *(See also Yorkshire lakes, reservoirs, etc).* Tackle shops: K L Tackle, 127 North Str, BD21 3AB (tel: 01535 667574); Willis Walker, 109 Cavendish Str, Keighley BD21 3DG (tel: 01535 602928).

Cononley (W Yorks). Trout, perch, chub, roach, dace, bream, grayling; dt after June 1, for Bradford City AA water, dt £4 from Post Office, 2/4 King Str, BD20 8LH, or tackle shops from 16 June.

Skipton (N Yorks). Trout, grayling, pike, chub, roach, perch, dace and bream. At Skipton, Skipton AA has three miles of fishing, mainly both banks; st £53 (entrance fee £17), dt £5, from Hon Sec or tackle shops; association also has rights on **Embsay Reservoir** (trout) (wt £28, dt £9), **Whinnygill Reservoirs** (trout and coarse fish) dt £5. The club shares water with Bradford City AA from Carleton to Snaygill. Near Skipton at **Kilnsey Park** BD23 5PS, are two trout lakes of 3 acres (tel: 01756 752150); dt £16, juv £10. Bradford No 1 AA has **Bradley, Broughton** and **Sandbeds** fisheries, left bank; members only. Hotels: Highfield, Devonshire.

Bell Busk (N Yorks). Trout; preserved by owners. Lakes: **Conniston House**; trout. **Eshton Tarn**, 2m NE; pike. **Malham Tarn**, 8m N; trout and perch; tickets *(see Ribble-Settle)*.

CALDER (tributary of Aire): Good coarse fishing from Brighouse to Sowerby Bridge. River Calder and Calder Canal run side by side for 2½m at Wakefield Rd, Sowerby Bridge, Halifax (7 access roads and ample parking facilities) making access the same for both. Grayling to 1½lb, brown and rainbow trout in river.

Halifax (W Yorks). Calder 2m S. Clubs: Halifax & Dist AC (dams); Ryburn & Halifax AS (formerly Dean Clough & Ryburn AS) has 4m good coarse fishing on Calder, Sowerby Bridge to Luddenden Foot; 3m of **Calder and Hebble Navigation**; and some good brown trout fishing at Sowerby Bridge; st £16, conc, dt £3, from Jewsons (see *below*), and other local tackle shops. Other societies: Brighouse AA has stocked coarse fishery with barbel; st £15 plus joining fee £5, conc; dt for canal £2, conc from tackle shops below; Friendly AC, The Friendly Inn, Ovenden Road. Ripponden Flyfishers have good trout fishing in **Ryburn Reservoir**, Ripponden. Brighouse AA and Bradford No 1 AA controls 14m on Calder above and below **Brighouse**; heavily restocked and now provides sport with good-quality trout to 4lb, roach and chub; st £30 + £20 joining fee from Jewson; dt. Brighouse AA also has water on canal from Brighouse to Salter Hebble; also Brookfoot Lake; 3 acres, mixed coarse, plus specemin carp; dt £2.50, conc, from tackle shops. Hebden Bridge AC has canal fishing and brown trout fishing in area. Tackle shops: A J Jewson, 28 Horton St, Halifax HX1 1PU (tel: 01422 354146); Calder Angling Supplies, 39a Rastrick Common, Brighouse HD6 3DW (01484 711063). Hotels: Imperial Crown; Calder & Hebble Inn; Black Horse Inn, Brighouse.

Hebden (W Yorks). At **Todmorden** (Yorks, postal address Lancs), Todmorden AS has mixed coarse fishing which includes the **Rochdale Canal** (Locks 13-51) within the Todmorden boundary; **New Mill Dam; Walsden Printing Co Lodges; R Calder; Portsmouth Reservoir; Cliviger Fishponds; Queen St Mill**; also (at Littleborough) **Grove Fishery, Croft Head** and **Lower Townhouse Fishery**, and **Whiteley Knowl Reservoir**. All members only except: Cliviger Fishponds; Grove Fishery and Croft Head and Lower Townhouse. Annual membership £30 + £10 entry, conc (from local tackle shops, incl Macks, 33a Parliament St, Burnley BB11 3JU (tel: 01282 427386). Ryburn & Halifax AS (formerly Dean Clough & Ryburn AS) have 4m Calder fishing from Luddeden Foot to Salterhebble Locks, trout, coarse; 3m of **Calder and Hebble Canal**, from Sowerby Bridge Marina to Salterhebble Lock (200 pegs); 2m of **River Hebden**, from Hardcastle Crags to Hebden Bridge (trout only); **Swamp Dam**, from Finkle St, Luddeden Foot; no boats on Society waters; match availability; st £15, dt £3, conc; tickets from surrounding tackle shops. **Calder and Hebble Navigation**: from Salterhebble Top Lock, through Brighouse, Lower Hopton Bridge, Thornhill, to upstream of Ganny Lock, the following clubs have water: Bradford No. 1, Thornhill C & BC. Ryburn & Halifax AS has Dead Arm to Salterhebble Locks; Mackintosh AC has The Quays Travel Lodge, Halifax water, 200 metres; Brighouse AA has Calder and Hebble Canal, from Salterhebble Locks to Brighouse; Hebden Bridge AC has Rochdale Canal from end of Tods Waters to Sowerby Bridge Marina; also part of Calder. Unity AC has fishing on R Calder; Milby Cut, **Boroughbridge**; Dyehouse Dam, Oakenshaw; all waters contain coarse fish, roach, rudd, bream, tench, perch, etc, members only on most, but dt for good coarse fishing on **Leeds and Liverpool Canal**, £3, conc. Membership £11, conc. Tackle shops: A J Jewson, 28 Horton St, Halifax HX1 1PU (tel: 01422 354146); Chris Roberts Fishing Angling, 22 Chapel Hill, Huddersfield HD1 3EB (tel: 01484 545032); Wibsey Angling Centre, 208 High St, Wibsey, Bradford BD6 1QP (tel: 01274 604542); Unity AC membership. Hotel: Queen.

COLNE (tributary of Calder):

Huddersfield (W Yorks). Holme Valley PA fishes **R Calder** from Battyeford to Mirfield, Magdale Dam and pond at Holmfirth; dt on river, and pond from tackle shops. Facilities for the disabled. **Hill Top, Sparth,** and **Longwood Compensation Reservoirs, Huddersfield Narrow Canal,** all Slaithwaite & Dist AC waters, dt obtainable. Tickets from Chris Roberts Fishing Tackle, *(below)* Marsden Post Office; Holme Valley Sports, 76 Huddersfield Road, Holmfirth HD7 1AZ. Hotel: Huddersfield and many others.

Slaithwaite (W Yorks). Slaithwaite & Dist AC has fly only trout fishery from Marsden to Slaithwaite, no fishing in village centre, then east stretch from Linthwaithe Steps, all members only, no dt; **Narrow Canal,** Slaithwaite to Bargate and three other stretches, three reservoirs, dams and ponds; trout, coarse fish; st £25, conc, enquiries to Hon Sec. Tackle shop: Chris Roberts, 22 Chapel Hill, Huddersfield HD1 3EB (tel: 01484 545032).

HOLME (tributary of Colne);

Holmfirth (W Yorks). River has wild brown trout, as well as usual coarse species. Holme Valley PA has water from Holmfirth to steps Mill, Honley, except 50 yard stretch by old Robinson Mill Dam, and Honley Village Trust land. Assn also controls stretch of R Calder; Magdale Dam, members only, and Cinderhills Pond; all waters coarse fishing, with roach, tench, perch, etc; dt on pond and on Calder, from Sec or Holmfirth Information Centre. Membership £19 plus joining, conc. Slaithwaite & Dist AC fishes most of stretch from Holmebridge to Bottoms Dam, river is extremely shallow and overhung, with many small wild trout. Members only. **Holmstyes Reservoir;** trout (Huddersfield 8m) preserved by Huddersfield AA; st £38; waiting list. **Boshaw Reservoir** (Huddersfield 8m); preserved as above. Tackle shop: Chris Roberts, 22 Chapel Hill, Huddersfield HD1 3EB (tel: 01484 545032).

DERWENT: Rises in high moors and flows almost to coast near Scarborough where it turns south and enters estuary of Ouse. Its upper reaches, most easily reached from Scarborough, are trout and grayling waters *(see Ayton).* Lower down coarse fish predominate, barbel included.

Wressle (East Yorkshire). Coarse fish free, some access.

Breighton (East Yorkshire); ns Wressle 1m. Bubwith 1m. Chub, dace, pike, etc; fishing free.

Bubwith (East Yorkshire). Coarse fish; Howden & Dist AC: 4m controlled by Mike Redman, 2 Meadowfield, Breighton Rd, Bubwith YO8 7DZ (tel: 01757

Todmorden Angling Society holds a junior match at Cliviger Fishponds, West Yorkshire.

288891).

Ellerton; roach, perch, dace, bream, chub, eels and pike; flatfish lower down.

East Cottingwith (N Yorks); ns High Field, 4m. Coarse fish (pike and chub very good). York AA controls East Cottingwith Water (2m). York & DAA has 10m of good coarse fishing on **Pocklington Canal**; dt from local tackle shops. At **Thorganby**, on other side of Derwent, Ferry Boat Inn has day tickets for approximately 1½m of river. Very good pike fishing.

Pocklington (N Yorks). **Pocklington Canal**; Well stocked with bream, roach, perch, pike, etc. York & DAA water.

Ellerton Landing (N Yorks). Hotel: White Swan, Bubwith.

Kexby (N Yorks). Pike, chub, etc. York, and Leeds Amalgamated, societies have water; members only.

Stamford Bridge (N Yorks). Excellent for roach, pike, chub, dace. York & DAA has fishing on good length; on right bank down to Kexby; on left bank 2 fields below car park; also pits; dt £4 at cafes in Stamford Bridge.

Howsham (N Yorks). Coarse fishing. York & DAA has water on Derwent and Barton Hill Beck, from Kirkham Abbey to Howsham, members only; Bradford No 1 AA has left bank at Howsham Wood; members only.

Kirkham Abbey (N Yorks). Coarse fish, some trout. Leeds and York Amalgamations have water; members only. Malton & Norton AC has water; book £10; members only.

Castle Howard (N Yorks). **Castle Howard Great Lake** contains specimen coarse fish, including pike, perch, tench, bream, roach; bank fishing only. However due to over-fishing in the North Sea, cormorants have seriously reduced lake stocks. For further details, see *'Yorkshire Lakes.'*

Huttons Ambo (Yorks). Roach, pike, dace, eels, gudgeon, grayling, perch and few trout. South bank, 1m down and 1m up, held by Malton and Norton AC, no dt; membership £15 pa. North bank held by Huttons Ambo AC for 2m down and 2m up; membership, for people resident within 10m Malton, £5 pa. Dt £2.50 from village post office (open Sundays). Bream and roach heavily stocked.

Malton (Yorks). Coarse fish, mainly roach. Malton and Norton AC. Waters extend to 1m below Huttons Ambo. Membership discretionary, issued by Hon Sec, and C

Swift *(below)*. Good deal of free water on Derwent and Rye. Tackle shops: C Swift, 25 Castlegate YO17 0DP (tel: 01653 694580); tickets for Malton & Norton AC waters. Hotel: Green Man.

Yedingham (Yorks). Coarse fish. Providence Inn, Station Rd, YO17 8SL (tel: 01944 728231) has private stretch; enquire of landlord.

Ganton (Yorks). Chub, pike, dace, grayling; dt for 1m each way from Hay Bridge, from Mr and Mrs Seller, Bogg Hall Farm YO12 4PB (tel: 01944 710391), at first house across railway crossing at Ganton; dt £2. Ruston Beck, 2m W. Dt waters at **Seamer** (Malton Rd), from house by stream.

Hackness (Yorks). Derwent AC, controls 10m of trout (brown and rainbow) and grayling fishing down to **East Ayton**; members only.

FOSS BECK (tributary of Derwent). Fishing station: **Fangfoss** (Yorks); fishing private.

SPITTLE BECK (tributary of Derwent)

Barton Hill (Yorks). Derwent, 2m E. Whitecarr Beck, 4m SE. Loppington Beck, 4m SE. Swallowpits Beck, 5m SE at Scrayingham. York & DAA have trout water **Barton Hill Beck**, members only.

RYE (tributary of Derwent): Trout, grayling, other coarse fish.

Ryton (Yorks).

PICKERING BECK (tributary of Rye) and **Costa Beck** (chalk stream). Trout, grayling.

Pickering (Yorks). About 1m of free fishing in town; private above, preserved below (3m) by Pickering FA; fly only; membership limited to 120. Water also on **Costa Beck** and **Oxfold Becks**, trout and grayling, and Duchy of Lancaster water, **Newbridge**; two trout lakes; dt for members' guests only. Club HQ: Bay Horse Hotel. One 2-acre lake is 9m from Pickering, wild and stocked brown trout fishing: Hazelhead Lake, Newgate Foot Farmhouse, Saltersgate, Pickering YO18 7NR (tel: 01751 460215); open 1 Apr to 31 Oct; dt £15 (4 fish), 4hr £10 (2 fish). Pickering Trout Lake, Newbridge Rd, Pickering YO18 8JJ (tel: 01751 474219): open 1 Mar to 31 Oct, dt from £5 coarse, £16.50 fly; tackle shop and flies on site. Hotels: White Swan, Black Swan, Forest and Vale.

SEVEN (tributary of Rye): Trout, grayling; some coarse fish.

Newsham Bridge (Yorks). York & DAA

has water (one field) on Seven and Rye; no dt.

Marton (Yorks). Private from mill to Marton; below Marton some free water; grayling, pike, chub, dace and a few trout. Tackle shop in Malton, 12m.

Sinnington (Yorks). Seven AC has 2½m downstream from the main road; brown, rainbow trout, some grayling; members only, long waiting list. Coarse fishing mainly below large weir and bottom farm.

WATH BECK (tributary of Rye):

Slingsby (Yorks). Trout; preserved. Rye, NE.

DOVE-IN-FARNDALE (tributary of Rye):

Kirby Moorside (N Yorks). Dove-in-Farndale, 1m E; trout; private. Dt for stretches downstream of Kirby Moorside from some of the farms. Hodge Beck, in Sleightholme Dale, 1m W, trout only. Hotel: King's Head.

THORNTON BECK (tributary of Derwent):

Thornton-le-Dale (N Yorks). Trout and grayling; preserved. Pickering Beck, 3m W. Derwent, 3m S. Hotels: The Hall; The Buck; all Thornton-le-Dale.

WHARFE: Rises on Cam Fell and flows 60m south-east to join Ouse near Cawood. Trout in upper reaches, with coarse fish downstream.

Ryther (N Yorks); ns Ulleskelf, 3m. Castleford & Dist ASA has water; mainly coarse fish. Hotel: Ryther Arms.

Ulleskelf (N Yorks). Coarse fish; preserved by Leeds & Dist ASA; dt £3 from the Ulleskelf Arms, Church Fenton Lane, LS24 9DW (tel: 01937 531508).

Tadcaster (N Yorks). Trout, chub and dace, good head of barbel perch and bream; preserved by Tadcaster Angling and Preservation Association on both banks downstream from road bridge, ¾m east bank, and 1½m west bank Grimston Park; st £15 for locals only; dt £3, conc. Tickets from Hon Sec; The Bay Horse; Newsagent.

Boston Spa (W Yorks). Trout, grayling other coarse fish (chub, barbel and pike good; bream introduced). Most rights held by Boston Spa AC; dt £3 from Super Shop Newsagents, High Street; also Kirkgate Anglers, Leeds; club stocks water with trout and grayling. Limit two trout, one grayling, or vice-versa; trout 12". May best month for trout and August and September for barbel and chub.

Wetherby (W Yorks). Wetherby & Dist AC water (stocked with trout and coarse fish) extends from Collingham Beck to Wetherby Weir, south bank (about 350 yards in Collingham Wood, south bank is private); club also has four fields between golf course and playing fields, north bank; this water is open for visitors on st (above weir), and dt; members only below and on weir, but visitors may fish if accompanied by a member; same charge as above; no legitimate bait or lure barred; trout limit 11"; dt from: Wetherby Service Station, Deighton Rd, LS22 4TS (tel: 01937 587966); and Collingham & Lincoln News, Main Str, Collingham, Wetherby LS22 5AS(tel: 01937 572232).

Collingham (W Yorks). Wetherby AC has water here; trout and coarse fish including barbel, grayling and good dace.

Pool (W Yorks). Grayling, trout, dace, chub; preserved by the Leeds & Dist ASA which has 5m of fishing from River **Washburn** to Castley Beck on left bank; no wading 25 March to 15 June; 3 trout/grayling limit. Dt £3 from Leeds and Otley tackle shops. Members of Leeds AA, small private club, may fish Harewood Estate preserves, 3m right bank, 2m left bank.

Otley (W Yorks). Otley AC hold 2m left bank and 2½m right bank below Otley Bridge, and two lengths above the bridge. Fishing for members only, no dt. Dt £3 for Leeds & Dist ASA **Knotford Lagoon**, near Otley; large carp and other coarse fish; stocked; also some rainbow trout; no wading. Bradford No 1 AA has second Knotford Lagoon. At Yeadon (6m) Airboro' & Dist AA has **Yeadon Tarn**, Cemetery Rd; Good catches of roach, perch, carp, bream, tench. Dt £4 from newsagent in same road, and tackle shop in Otley: Angling and Country Sports, 36 Cross Green, Pool Road, Otley LS21 1HD (tel: 01943 462770).

Burley and **Askwith** (W Yorks). Trout, grayling, chub, dace. Bradford clubs have rights for members only.

Addingham (W Yorks). Bradford No 1 AA has four lengths on left and right bank, and Steven Bank Fishery, no dt obtainable. Bradford No 1 AA has some left bank at Denton, members only. Addingham AA has river from High Mill caravan site to Farfield Cottages on left bank, and right bank from Stephen Bank to Kexgill Beck, with trout (stocked twice a year with browns 1¼ to 2½lbs) and grayling; dt £12, conc from Addingham

PO; membership limited to 50, hence waiting list; apply Hon Sec. Tackle shops at Keighley and Harrogate.

Ilkley (W Yorks). Ilkley & Dist AA have water from Old Bridge to Stepping Stones, both banks, with trout, grayling, dace and chub. Dt £10.00 (April 15-Sept 30 inc) from Tourist Information Centre, Station Rd, Ilkley, LS29 8HA (tel: 01943 602319). Membership £70 + £38 joining, jun £25 (no joining fee), OAP £35, some vacancies. Club also has two coarse ponds. Contact Hon Sec. Addingham AA has river between Addingham and Bolton Abbey, brown trout and grayling only. Hotels: Riverside, Craiglands, Cow and Calf.

Bolton Abbey (N Yorks). Trout and grayling. 5 miles stretch (both banks) on R Wharfe, fly only. Bailiffed, concentrating on wild trout fishery, light stocking only. Trout April 1-Sept 30. Grayling only 1 Oct to 31 Dec. All grayling to be returned. St £275, wt £85, dt £18; c&r; 2 fish limit (not less than 10"). Fishing not recommended on Sundays and Bank holidays. Contact River Keeper (tel: 07752 887556) or Estate Office, Bolton Abbey, Skipton BD23 6EX (tel: 01756 718000; web: www.boltonabbey.com). Hotels: Devonshire Arms, Bolton Abbey; Devonshire Fell, Burnsall.

Burnsall (N Yorks). Brown trout (av ½lb-1lb; many large fish), grayling; preserved by Appletreewick, Barden and Burnsall AC from Linton Stepping Stones, below Grassington, to Barden Bridge, some 7m mostly double bank fishing. Joining fee £200, st £495; dt £20 for trout, 1 June to 30 Sept (excluding June and Sept weekends); wt £90, conc, fly only; limit three brace; grayling dt £10 Nov-Jan (fly only); waters re-stocked regularly with trout from ½ to 1lb and over. Club also has **Lower Barden Reservoir** (rainbow); no tickets. Tickets from Red Lion Hotel, and Devonshire Fell Hotel, Burnsall BD23 6BT (tel: 01756 729000). Half price juvenile tickets are available for those under 18 years, and those under 15 must be accompanied by an adult.

Grassington (N Yorks). Trout (av ¾lb), grayling (av ¾lb); preserved by Linton, Threshfield and Grassington AC for 2½m both banks (also in Captain Beck and Linton and Threshfield Becks until August 31); wt £55, dt £16 for fly-fishing only; long waiting list for membership; no night or Sunday fishing; no canoeing;

trout season: April 1 to Sept 30 inclusive; grayling only from Oct 1 to Feb 28; st £20, dt £5; fly only during Oct; fly only tickets £16, excl Sunday, from Dales Book Centre, 33 Main Str, BD23 5AA (tel: 01756 753373); or Black Horse Hotel, Grassington. Saltaire AA also has left bank at **Linton**, no dt. Fishing best in May. **Eller Beck**, **Hebden Beck**, 2m E. Lakes: **Blea Beck** dams 4m NE. Hotels: Black Horse (Saltaire AA HQ), and others.

Kilnsey (N Yorks). Brown trout. Preserved by Kilnsey AC (National Trust, Upper Wharfedale) of 65 members, from Chapel House Farm u/s to Beckamonds; artificial fly only, limit three brace over 10"; dt £25 between 9am and 10am (number limited, and none on Sundays or Bank Holidays) from Keeper, Ken Slaymaker, Tennant Arms Hotel, Kilnsey, via Skipton BD23 5PS (tel: 01756 752301). Hotels: Tennant Arms, Falcon.

Buckden (N Yorks). Trout. Bradford City AA has 2m; dt £5 from Dalesgarth Holiday Cott. Other fishing for guests at Buck Inn BD23 5JA; dt issued.

SKIRFARE (tributary of Wharfe); lower reaches well stocked with brown trout, average 1lb.

Arncliffe (N Yorks). Some Skirfare Fishing preserved by Kilnsey AC, dt water *(see Kilnsey)*. 2½m on upper reaches of Skirfare, unstocked; open to guests at Falcon Inn, BD23 5QE *(see advt)*; dt water, no Sunday fishing.

FOSS (tributary of Ouse): Trout.

Earswick (N Yorks). Free fishing on right bank. Owners are Joseph Rowntree Trust.

Strensall (N Yorks). Foss Navigation Cut, 1m NE. **Whitecar Beck**, 1m NE. York & DAA has coarse fishing here and at **Towthorpe**; members only.

NIDD: About 1½m from Pateley Bridge the river flows from the outlets of its Gouthwaite compensation reservoir, meandering through Nidderdale. Brown trout and grayling; with coarse fish from Birstwith downstream in increasing numbers. Nidderdale AC waters.

Nun Monkton (N Yorks). Coarse fish. Bradford No 1 AA has 1m good coarse fishing here on left bank, both banks at **Ramsgill** and left bank at **Summerbridge**, for members only. Also 2½m right bank at **Cowthorpe**.

Kirk Hammerton (N Yorks). Coarse fish. Following on Harrogate AA water *(see Goldsborough)* almost all fishing downstream to where Nidd joins the Ouse controlled by Leeds and York Amalgamations. York & DAA holds York side of river from Skip Bridge on Boroughbridge Rdupstream for about 1m to the railway bridge and also for about 1m above Hammerton Mill dam. Tickets from York tackle shops; and Aykroyd, Skip Bridge Filling Station, Green Hammerton.

Goldsborough (N Yorks). Trout, grayling and mixed coarse fishing, including pike and barbel. Left hand bank at Goldsborough, Knaresborough Piscatorials. From Little Ribston downstream through Walshford Bridge to first meadow below Cattall Bridge belongs to Harrogate AA. Association also has both banks of **Crimple Beck** from confluence with Nidd above Walshford Bridge up to Spofforth. Waiting list for membership. Dt issued by Hon Sec to members' guests only. Water otherwise strictly preserved.

Knaresborough (N Yorks). Trout, grayling and coarse fish, including barbel. Practically all fishing in vicinity controlled by Knaresborough AC and Knaresborough Piscatorials. Former issues st £25 and dt £5 for good stretch upstream from Little Ribston village. Club also owns fly only trout lake in Knaresborough area, members only. Full membership £180 plus £200 entry fee. Knaresborough Piscatorials fish 8 miles of Nidd, plus various stretches of Ure and Swale, mostly in area of Knaresborough, Skipton. Trout, chub, barbel, roach, bream, perch, rudd, dace, pike, may be caught in club waters. Fees, £80 pa, conc. York Amal has good stretches here. Tickets from M H & C Johnson, 2 Briggate HG5 8BH (tel: 01423 863065). Free fishing on Nidd, rt bank, 1m: downstream limit - A59 road bridge (access at side of Yorkshire Lass Pub House); upstream limit - top of 'Horseshoe' Field above private single track ve-

hicular bridge. Dropping Well Estate, High Bridge, Knaresborough has 1m dt fishing. **Farmire Trout Fishery**, 3 acre lake in 12 acre site, at Farmire House, Stang Lane, Farnham, Knaresborough HG5 9JW (tel: 01423 866417), has b and r trout fishing; dt £20 4 fish, £15 2 fish; barbless hooks, c&r after bag limit; secure parking; heated cabin; facilities.

Ripley, Nidd Bridge (N Yorks). Trout, grayling and coarse fish. Knaresborough AC holds left bank u/s to Hampsthwaite, fly only, members only.

Birstwith (N Yorks). Trout and grayling above Birstwith Dam upstream to upper reaches of Nidd. Below Dam there are also coarse fish. Knaresborough AC has right and left bank downstream from Hampsthwaite Bridge. Members and their guests only.

Darley (N Yorks). Trout and grayling water, preserved by Harrogate Fly Fishers. No tickets.

Pateley Bridge (N Yorks). Trout and grayling. From Gouthwaite, 1½m above Pateley Bridge down to below **Summerbridge**, 11m total, owned and rented by Nidderdale AC, who hold nearly all water, both banks, except short pieces here and there which are private; half is dt water; also Scar House Reservoir; permits: wt £30, dt £8-£6; jnr wt £15, dt £5-£3, for three lengths of river and Scar House, at Royal Oak (*below*); or local post offices in Lofthouse, Pateley Bridge, Glasshouses and Summerbridge; anglers must obtain tickets before fishing. Disabled platforms on one length of dt water. Royal Oak Hotel, Dacre Banks, Harrogate HG3 4EN (tel: 01423 780200), offers two-day fishing breaks, with en-suite B&B, packed lunches, evening meals, and trout fishing on R Nidd and Scar House Reservoir; £99 per head. Hotels: Roslyn, Grassfield, all Pateley

The grayling is a fish of the north, a lover of cold, pure water. Here the angler fishes the Nidd in winter. *Photo: Grace Oglesby.*

Bridge and The Sportman, Wath, Pateley Bridge.

Gouthwaite (N Yorks). River enters **Gouthwaite Reservoir**, privately owned and fished; no permits. Below reservoir Nidd private on left bank downstream; other bank Nidderdale AC water.

CRIMPLE (tributary of Nidd). This river is now private fishing.

Harrogate (N Yorks). Trout and coarse fishing, within easy reach of town in Nidd, Wharfe and Ure, and stillwaters. Tickets, tuition and guiding services from Orvis Co (*see below*). Harrogate & Claro CAA have 1½m Nidd right bank d/s from Killinghall Road Bridge. Harrogate Flyfishers preserve excellent trout and grayling water at Darley. Coarse river fishing on the R Ure at Newby Hall, **Skelton-on-Ure**. St £40, dt £5; dt available from the Estate Office, Newby Hall, Skelton-on-Ure, Ripon HG4 5AE (tel: 01423 322583 (after 9am); web: www.newbyhall.com) or from Village Store, Skelton or from Water Bailiff (Bishop Monkton side only). Tackle shops: Linsley Bros, 55 Tower Str HG1 1HS (tel: 01423 505677); Orvis, 17 Parliament St, Harrogate HG1 2QU (tel: 01423 561354). Hotels: Crown, Majestic, Old Swan, St George, Cairn, Prospect.

KYLE: Coarse fish.

Tollerton (N Yorks). Coarse fishing free down to Alne. Ouse at Aldwark, 4m W, and Linton Lock, 3m S and 7m NE, at Stillington.

URE (or **YORE**): Noted for grayling, but also holds good trout. Coarse fish from Middleham downstream.

Boroughbridge (N Yorks). Fine coarse fishing (especially chub, barbel, pike and roach; bream breeding); few trout and grayling; Boroughbridge & Dist AC, issues dt £2 (weekdays only, from June 1-Feb 27) sold at Post Office and Horsefair Grocers. Bradford No 1 AA has Langthorpe stretch, left bank, and Roecliffe, right bank. Unity AC has water here; roach, chub, perch, pike; no dt, st £11, conc, from Wibsey Angling Centre, 208 High St, Wibsey, Bradford BD6 1QP (tel: 01274 604542). Harrogate & Claro AC have ¾m left bank d/s of road bridge; dt £5 from Three Horse Shoes, Main Street. Hotel: Boroughbridge Social Club.

Ripon (N Yorks). Trout, dace, pike, perch, chub (nets to 100lb), bream, barbel, roach; preserved for 6m both banks by Ripon Piscatorial Assn; Assn also has **Ripon Canal,**(roach, bream, carp, perch); Racecourse Lake, (carp to 30lb, gudgeon, rudd); and 2m on **R Laver** (brown trout, grayling; fly only; worm from 30 Sept); visitors dt £5.50, wt £17, st £49.50; dt and wt from Ripon Angling Supplies. Ripon AC has 1½m both banks **R Skell** at Ripon and 1m on Ure, 2m u/s of Ripon. Members and guests only, no dt. Waiting list for membership. Lakes: Queen Mary's Ponds; coarse fish; Bradford No 1 AA. Roger's Pond, coarse dt £5 from Angling Centre. **Leighton Reservoir**, Swinton Estate Office, Masham, Ripon HG4 4JH (tel: 01765 689224); 100 acre trout fishery, dt £15, evng £8, conc, from fishing hut. Tackle shop: Ripon Angling Supplies, 58/9 North Str, HG4 1EN (tel: 01765 604666).

Tanfield (N Yorks). Trout, grayling; preserved for about 5m, mostly both banks, by Tanfield AC. Guests must be accompanied by member. Full time bailiff employed. Long waiting list. Two trout fisheries at West Tanfield: Bellflask, brown and rainbow, dt £20, 4 fish; run as fishery and nature reserve, barbless hooks; contact Brian Moreland (tel: 01677 470716). Tanfield Lodge Lake, West Tanfield, Ripon (tel: 01677 470385); brown and rainbow, 11½ acres, disabled access; open 15 Mar to 13 Oct; dt £10, 4 fish, £5 evening, juv, 2 fish.

Masham (N Yorks). Trout (stocked), grayling. 6½m west bank belongs to Swinton Estate; limited st; details from Estate Office, Swinton, Masham; well stocked 2½m stretch of Swinton water fished by Masham AC; brown trout and grayling; waiting list: st £140 + £30 joining fee; jun conc; grayling membership Oct-end Feb, £50; apply to A R Proud, River Keeper, 38 Park St, Masham HG4 4HN (tel: 01765 689361). Yorkshire Flyfishers hold Clifton Castle water (about 2m) above Masham; no tickets; tackle, information, and large selection of flies, from A Plumpton, Hairdresser, Silver St. Hotel: King's Head. **Leighton Reservoir** near here (*see Yorkshire Lakes*).

Cover Bridge (N Yorks). Trout, grayling. East Witton Estate issue dt on **R Cover** from Hullo Bridge to Cover Bridge. Mostly both banks, fly only; dt £4, juv £2 from Cover Bridge Inn, East Witton, Leyburn DL8 4SQ (tel: 01969 623250).

Middleham (N Yorks). Trout, chub, grayling. Bradford No 1 AA has right bank here, left bank at **Langthorpe**, and right bank at **Roecliffe**, members only. Fishing may be had in Leeds & Dist ASA waters at Middleham Deeps and 1m downstream from Middleham Bridge, left bank. Excellent barbel, chub, grayling, a few large trout, and the odd salmon; year book holders only. Cover Bridge Inn *(above)* has £4 dt for trout and grayling fishing on **R Cover**.

Redmire (N Yorks). Trout, grayling; preserved. Restocked; fly only. All fishing now by st only (£150); numbers limited; apply Estate Office, Leyburn DL8 5EW. Trout best April, May and June; grayling Oct and Nov. Hotels: King's Arms, Redmire; White Swan, Middleham; Rose and Crown, Bainbridge; Wensleydale Heifer, West Wittom.

Aysgarth (N Yorks). Trout, grayling. Bradford City AA has approx 2m from footbridge, both banks, 3¾m both banks at **Worton Bridge**; Palmer Flatt Hotel has short stretch. Wensleydale AA water extends from 2m west of Hawes to Worton Bridge, plus ¾m beyond on north bank only; st £30, wt £14, dt £8, conc; grayling only st £8, dt £4; tickets from The Rose & Crown, Bainbridge; The Crown Inn, Askrigg and The Victoria Arms, Worton. HQ: Rose & Crown Hotel, Bainbridge, Leyburn DL8 3EE (tel: 01969 650225).

Askrigg (N Yorks). Trout, grayling; preserved by Wensleydale AA, *(see above)*; tickets from The Rose & Crown, Bainbridge; The Crown Inn, Askrigg and The Victoria Arms, Worton. Hotel: King's Arms.

Bainbridge (N Yorks); Wensleydale AA water includes 6m on Ure, both banks of **R Bain**, upstream from the Ure; half-way to Semer Water, and the west bank all the way; the south-east shore of the lake and the feeder streams on Raydaleside; for tickets, *see above*. Hotel: Rose & Crown Hotel *(above)*.

Hawes (N Yorks). Brown trout, grayling; Hawes and High Abbotside AA has upper reaches of river, including tributaries. The fishing is pleasant, peaceful and not crowded. Sunday fishing, no ground bait, platforms for disabled. Visitors welcome: st £50, wt £25, dt £10, conc, from Hon Sec, "Three Peaks Ltd", Riverside House, Bridge End, Hawes DL8 3NH (tel: 01969 667443); The Gift Shop; Board Hotel, Main St; or Caravan Club site, all in Hawes. Below Hawes Wensleydale AA

has several miles of excellent water. Disabled anglers may fish Widdale Beck at Apperset, near Hawes. Hotel: White Hart.

SWALE: Good chub and barbel water. Trouting best in upper reaches, water improving.

Helperby (N Yorks). Coarse fish; right bank from Swing Bridge to Myton Plantation controlled by Leeds & Dist ASA; (car parking £1 at Oak Tree pub in village). Bradford No 1 AA has water above and below Thornton Bridge; members only; also Raskels Lake, 6 acres, 45 pegs, mixed coarse, especially tench. Helperby & Brafferton AC have left bank from footbridge d/s for ¾m, also **Fawdington Fishery**, from ½m above Thornton Bridge, approx 1½m u/s to Fawdington Beck mouth. Chub, barbel, dace, pike, roach, perch; dt £3, conc, for both these waters, 16 Jun-14 March, from Post Office; Oak Tree Inn, Helperby (tel: 01423 360268); B&B also offered at farm.

Topcliffe (N Yorks). Noted coarse fishing centre; especially good for chub and barbel. Thirsk AC has Skipton and Baldersby fishing, dt from D Stratton, 11 Saxty Way, Sowerby, Thirsk (tel: 01845 524610). Bradford No 1 AA has 900 yds at **Catton**, and further water at Topcliffe, members only. Assn of Teeside & Dist ACs has 1½m at **Sand Hutton**; members only. **Cod Beck**; trout; preserved by Bradford City AA; members only.

Pickhill (N Yorks). Coarse fish; trout. Bradford No 1 AA fishes 1,800 yards at Scarborough farm, right bank. Members only.

Maunby (N Yorks). Bradford No 1 AA has two lengths left bank, members only.

Gatenby (N Yorks). Bradford No 1 AA has three stretches of right bank here. Members only.

Morton-on-Swale (N Yorks). Trout grayling, pike, chub, dace, barbel; fishing good. Northallerton AC has 2½m left bank downstream from A684 road bridge.

Great Langton (N Yorks). Trout, grayling, coarse fish; Kirkby Fleetham AC has both banks for 2m downstream from Langton Bridge, linking up with Northallerton AC's water at Bramper Farm; fly only; no tickets; membership limited, with preference given to local residents.

Catterick (N Yorks). Good mixed fishing; trout, grayling, dace, chub, barbel, few roach and pike. Trout from 8oz to 1lb; fast takers. Richmond & Dist AS has 14m of water on both banks, Richmond being the centre. Ferryhill AC also has 1½m trout and coarse fishing above and below village, good barbel, chub, grayling, no dt. Hotels: Farmers' Arms; Angel Inn.

Richmond (N Yorks). Richmond & Dist AS preserves 14 miles above and below town centre, stocked with trout, plus most coarse species; st £27, wt £15, dt £5, conc; from tackle shop: Richmond Angling Centre, 8 Temple Square, Graven Gate, Richmond DL10 4ED (tel: 01748 822989).

Reeth (N Yorks). Swale; trout. Black Bull Hotel has water for residents; dt.

Muker (N Yorks). Trout; strictly preserved. Muker Beck; trout; Thwaite Beck, 1m W; trout; free. Summer Lodge Beck, 5m E; trout; preserved.

Keld (N Yorks). Trout; plentiful but small; preserved.

GUN BECK (tributary of Swale):

Husthwaite (N Yorks). Centre for good trout fishing on **Husthwaite Beck**; dt from York tackle shops.

Coxwold (N Yorks). Hole Beck and Gun Beck preserved.

BEDALE BECK (tributary of Swale):

Leeming (N Yorks). Swale, 2m NE; preserved by Black Ox AC from A1 road to confluence with Swale, excepting only two small fields above Leeming Bridge. Trout and coarse fish; st £12 from R M Wright, 5 Lascelles Lane, Northallerton DL6 1EP.

COD BECK (tributary of Swale); good trout water.

Thirsk (N Yorks). Good local fishing for barbel and chub. Thirsk AC has water on Swale and Cod Beck; dt from D Stratton, 11 Saxty Way, Sowerby, Thirsk (tel: 01845 524610). York & DAA have 5½ acre lake at **Sand Hutton**; also Park View and Claxton Ponds, 20m SE, all members only. Hotels: Royal Oak, Three Tuns.

Sessay (N Yorks). Cod Beck, 2m W; Thirsk AC, Swale, 2m SW; Bradford club now has fishing on P J Till's farm (The Heights). The Oaks Fishery, David and Rachel Kay, The Oaks, Sessay, nr Thirsk YO7 3BG (tel: 01845 501321): 7 lakes with carp and other coarse species; disabled access; dt £6, conc. Inn: Railway, Dalton; Horsebreakers Arms, Sessay.

Brawith (N Yorks). Trout; preserved.

Topcliffe (N Yorks). Bradford City AA has water here, and on **Cod Beck**.

WISKE (tributary of Swale).

Otterington (N Yorks). Cod Beck, 2m E. Broad Beck. Sorrow Beck, 4m E.

Northallerton (N Yorks). Dace, chub, pike; preserved: fishing good. Northallerton AC has fishing on several miles of water on the Swale at Morton Bridge. 1m northwest is Parklands Fishery, 3 acres, stocked with carp, tench, roach, rudd, perch &c; dt on bank £5, conc. Tackle shop: Northallerton Angling Centre, 4a Zetland Str, DL6 1NA (tel: 01609 779140) *(see also Morton-on-Swale).*

PARRETT

(For close seasons, licences, etc, see South West Region Environment Agency, p19)

Rises in hills on border of Somerset and Dorset, and flows into Bristol Channel near Bridgwater. Roach, bream and dace predominate. Thorney-Middle Chinnock stretch and some of tributaries hold trout. Occasional salmon and sea trout run through into Tone.

Bridgwater (Som). River tidal here. Docks now a Marina. Bridgwater AA fisheries are as follows: **King's Sedgemoor Drain** from ¾m above Greylake Bridge, where 18ft Rhyne enters Cary River to A38 Road bridge at Dunball. Good roach, rudd, pike, tench, bream, carp and perch. **North Drain** (jointly held with North

Somerset AA), **South Drain** (jointly held with Glaston Manor AA); **Huntspill River; Bridgwater and Taunton Canal**, and the docks; **Dunwear, Screech Owl**, and **Combwich Ponds**, (carp, bream, roach, rudd, tench, perch). Assn also has access to Somerset Levels Association of Clubs (SLAC) waters on Rivers **Parrett**

Fishing Available?

If you own, manage, or know of first-class fishing available to the public which should be considered for inclusion in **Where to Fish** *please apply to the Publishers (address in the front of the book) for a form for submission, on completion, to the Editor. (Inclusion is at the sole discretion of the Editor). No charge is made for editorial inclusion.*

and **Isle**; st £27, wt £17, dt £5, from tackle shops in area or Hon Sec, with concessions for jun, OAP; permits cover all waters; pocket maps from Hon Sec. Day/night coarse fishing at Avalon Fisheries, 25 acres, large tench and carp (tel: 01278 456429). Pawlett Ponds, River Rd, **Pawlett**, 5 lakes, BB&WAA water, with carp, bream, tench, large roach, perch etc; dt £5 from Brickyard Farmhouse (*below*). Tackle shop: Somerset Angling, 74 Bath Rd TA6 4PL (tel: 01278 431777). Accommodation with special facilities for anglers: Brickyard Farmhouse, River Rd, Pawlett, TA6 4SE (tel: 01278 685709); Crossways Inn, West Huntspill (tel: 01278 783756).

Langport (Som). Parrett; pike to 30lbs, large perch, carp, bream, roach, hybrids, tench, chub, rudd, eels. Langport & Dist AA has rights to 6½m; Assn is member of Somerset Levels Association of Clubs (SLAC); st holders may fish SLAC waters on Parrett and Isle. Assn also owns 2¼ acre **Coombe Lake**, stocked with carp, bream and others; st £12, wt £5 and dt £3, conc, obtainable from Fosters Newsagents, Bow St; Yeovil & Dist Angling Centre, 27/29 Forest Hill, Yeovil BA20 2PH (tel: 01935 476777). Stoke-sub-Hamdon AA has stretches at **West Chinnock** to **Thorney Lakes**: st £12 from Stax (*below*). Thorney Lakes & Caravan Park, Muchelney, Langport TA10 0DW (tel: 01458 250811, Ann & Richard England), has coarse fishing, with carp to 25lb, and other species, dt £5 on bank, conc; both lakes closed at night. **Viaduct Fishery**, Cary Valley, Somerton TA11 6LJ (tel: 01458 274022); 6 coarse lakes; includes tackle shop, bait, tuition; 140 pegs; dt £5, conc, from fishery's tackle shop. Tackle shop: Stax Angling Centre, South Str, Montacute TA15 6XH (tel: 01935 822645). Accommodation: Langport Arms Hotel; Dolphin Hotel.

Crewkerne (Som). Trout, coarse fish. Seven miles above and below Stoke-sub-Hamdon controlled by Stoke-sub-Hamdon AA (part of South Somerset AF); trout fishing (with restocking) from Bow Mills to Hurdle Pool; 1 Apr to 31 Oct (trout av ¾lb); members only; coarse fishing, 12 different species including 3 types of carp, from Hurdle Pool to Thorney Mill; st £10, dt £2.50, conc jun & OAP, from local tackle shops, incl Planet Video and Angling, 19 High St, Chard TA20 1QF (tel: 01460 64000); Stax Ang-

ling Centre, South Str, Montacute TA15 6XH (tel: 01935 822645).

TONE: Trout and coarse fish above Taunton; below, most species of coarse. Weedy in summer below **Taunton** but provides first-class coarse fishing in winter. Fast stretch at Taunton to Bathpool, Creech, Ham, Knapp and Newbridge.

Taunton (Som). Good coarse fishing free on town stretch. Taunton AA has water on **Bridgwater Canal** at Taunton; **West Sedgemoor Drain** from Pincombe Bridge, Stathe; **R Tone** fast stretch at Taunton, Creech and Ham; Ponds at Walton, Norton and Wych Lodge (3 acres). Assn also has Maunsel Ponds, 5m NE of Taunton; 3 ponds situated in the grounds of Maunsel House; well stocked with roach, rudd, tench, carp, perch. St £27, wt £12, dt £5, conc, from tackle shops (*below*). Enterprise Angling have tickets £3.50 for British Telecom pond, nr Taunton, carp, roach, skimmers; no night fishing. Tackle shops: Topp Tackle, 63 Station Rd, TA1 1PA (tel: 01823 282518); Enterprise Angling, 42 East Reach, Taunton TA1 3BA (tel: 01823 282623). Hotels: Castle (which advises visiting anglers on local facilities).

HILLFARRANCE BROOK (a Tone tributary, from Hillfarrance to confluence with Tone). Trout, grayling. Axe contains trout and sea trout in lower stretches; no tickets.

Wellington (Som). Trout, roach, dace; trout average ½lb. Wellington AA has water from Fox Bros' works 2m up stream, and ¾m below, brown trout, grayling, roach, dace; members only. Thereafter preserved by owners. **Langford Lakes**, Langford Budville, Wellington, TA21 0RS (tel: 01823 400476): four stocked coarse fishing ponds on conifer plantation, with mixed, carp to 25lbs, tench and bream fishing; barbless hooks only; no keepnets, natural bait only; £5 2 rods, £4 1 rod. Tackle, tickets and licences from Wellington Country Sports, 24 High Str, TA21 8RA (tel: 01823 662120).

Wiveliscombe (Som). Tone, Milverton Brook and Norton Brook; trout; banks bushed.

NORTON BROOK (tributary of Tone):

Bishops Lydeard (Som). Trout; banks overgrown.

MILVERTON BROOK (tributary of Tone).

Milverton (Som). Trout; private; banks

bushed.

YEO: Coarse fish, some trout.

Long Load (Som). Good coarse fishing on Long Load Drain. Controlled by the 4 clubs of the South Somerset AF (recently in abeyance).

Ilchester (Som). Mainly roach, dace, good chub fishing. St and wt for 6m stretch u/s and d/s of Ilchester, plus Long Load Drain, from Yeovil & Dist Angling Centre (*see Yeovil*); Stax Angling Centre, South Str, Montacute TA15 6XH (tel: 01935 822645). Ilchester & Dist AA (part of South Somerset AF) has 6m fishing above and below Ilchester on **Yeo** and **Cam**; st £12, conc. At **Martock** are **Ash Lakes**. Coarse fishing on three ponds; dt £5 on bank. Contact Ash Lakes, Ash, Martock TA12 6NZ (tel: 01935 823459).

Yeovil (Som). Roach, dace, chub. Yeovil and Sherborne AA (part of South Somerset AF) have water downstream of **Sherborne Lake**, **Sutton Bingham Stream** from Filter Station to Yeovil Junction and R Wriggle from Yetminster to R Yeo; trout. St £10, conc from tackleists below; also have tickets for local river and still-water fisheries. Lyons Gate Caravan Park, Cerne Abbas, DT2 7AZ (tel: 01300 345260) has four good coarse lakes with carp to 30lb, roach, tench; dt £5. At Stoford is Old Mill Fishery, Tucking Mill Farm BA22 9TX (tel: 01935 414771); over 21 species of coarse fish in four

lakes and river; dt £5, evng £2. Mudford AC (part of South Somerset AF) has 3m of river from Mudford to Chilton Cantelo; st £8 from tackle shop. Tackle shops: Yeovil & Dist Angling Centre, 27/29 Forest Hill, Yeovil BA20 2PH (tel: 01935 476777); Stax Angling Centre, South Str, Montacute TA15 6XH (tel: 01935 822645). Hotels: Mermaid; Manor; The Choughs.

ISLE: Prolific chub water; also roach, dace, etc. First E1/2 mile from junction with Parrett held by Somerset Levels Association of Clubs (SLAC) of Anglers.

Isle Brewers (Som). Roach, chub, dace, some trout from Fivehead Rdto Hambridge; Newton Abbot FA has R Ilse at Hambridge, and many coarse lakes and ponds. *See Newton Abbot.*

Ilminster (Som). Roach, chub, dace. Chard & DAC has 1½m of water from Hortbridge, Ilminster, to Winterhay; members only, conc, from Planet Video and Angling (*see below*). Ilminster AA has 5m from Ilminster to Isle Brewers; st £16, conc, from tackle shop (*see below*).

Chard (Som). Chard Reservoir; carp, bream, roach, tench, eels and perch; dt £6 from Planet Video (*below*); Chard & DAC has Perry Street Pond; 11/ acres; mixed coarse; st £15 from tackle shop. Tackle shop: Planet Video and Angling, 19 High St, Chard TA20 1QF (tel: 01460 64000).

RIBBLE

(For close seasons, licences, etc, see North West Region Environment Agency, p20)

Rises in the Pennines and flows 69 miles into the Irish Sea between St Anne's and Southport. Good coarse fishing lower down, between Great Mitton and Preston. Also coarse fishing in Church Deeps. Best salmon, sea trout, brown trout and grayling fishing is between Settle and Great Mitton. Tributary Hodder has good salmon, sea trout and brown trout fishing throughout length but much affected by water abstraction. Upper waters impounded in Stocks Reservoir. Its main tributary, the Loud, also provides good trout and sea trout fishing.

Preston (Lancs). Coarse fish, few salmon and sea trout. 2m Preston Federated Anglers water through town; st £12, dt £2.00, including other waters on **Ribble** and **Wyre**, and **Rufford Canal**. Ribble & Wyre FA has a broken 3-4 miles of Wyre; members only; st £18, which entitles anglers to fish 1m of Ribble and Heapy Reservoirs at Chorley and 21m of Leeds & Liverpool Canal from Johnsons Hill Locks (Blackburn) to Red Lion Bridge at Scarisbrick (Southport); also Fan Lodge at Bickershaw (Wigan), and other Wigan fisheries. **Twin Lakes Trout Fishery**,

Croston PR26 9AA (tel: 01772 601093): 12 acres, stocked mainly fly only (1 lake any method, with restrictions) rainbow, blue and brown trout, best rainbow 19lbs 6ozs; dt £21 (4 fish), ½ day £13.50 (2 fish), boats from £6, double. Other local fishing: Greenhalgh Lodge Fishery, Greenhalgh Lane, nr Kirkham PR4 3HL (tel: 01253 836348); carp; dt £6.50, conc. Hudson's Farm, Rawcliffe Rd, St Michaels PR3 0UH (tel: 01995 679654): mixed coarse fishery of 2 ponds and 2 lakes: large carp, bream, tench; dt £5, up to 3 rods, £3 conc; from farm. R

Crossens, 1m from Southport, fished by Southport & Dist AA. Tackle shops: Catch 22 Fishing Tackle, Birkdale Trad Est, Liverpool Rd, Southport PR8 4PZ (tel: 01704 568450). Tackle shop in Preston: Carters Fishing Tackle, 85/88 Church Str, PR1 3BS (tel: 01772 253476), has information on much Lancashire fishing.

Longridge (Lancs). Ribble, 3m SE. Hodder, 5m NE. Salmon, sea trout and trout. Loud 2m N. Most of right bank preserved by Loud & Hodder AA; visitors' tickets issued if accompanied by member. Prince Albert AS, Macclesfield, own several miles above M6 bridge. Warrington AA has 1½m stretch at **Hurst Green**; members only.

Ribchester (Lancs). Lancashire FFA have 1m here, and water at **Gisburn** and at **Walton-le-Dale**; also **Hodder** at **Newton and Chaigley, Lune** at Kirkby Lonsdale and Tebay; **Irt** at Santon Bridge, all with salmon, sea trout, some browns. Membership £270 p/a + £250 joining fee; juv. Tickets only to members' guests. Other local body is Ribchester & Dist AC; dt £4; barbel, chub, dace, gudgeon, pike, eels and roach. Tickets for Ribchester Village Front from Spar, Church Str (after 7.00am) or White Bull (during opening hrs); dt coarse only from 15 June to 15 March.

Mitton (Lancs); ns Whalley, 2m. Salmon, sea trout, trout and coarse fish. Environment Agency controls left bank d/s from Mitton Bridge; Salmon fishing open Feb 1-Oct 31; brown trout Mar 15-Sept 30; coarse, June 16-Mar 14; permits from Old Stone House Eating Establishment Ltd, Mitton Rd, Mitton, Clitheroe BB7 9PQ (tel: 01254 826544). Mid-Ribble AS has over 2.6m right bank of **R Hodder** above and below Lower Hodder bridge, nr Stonyhurst, down to Hodder Foot, also right bank Ribble from Hodder Foot to Starling Brook (½m below Dinckley Bridge), and left bank of Ribble at **Long Preston**. Waters stocked annually with trout, good returns for migratory fish, also coarse fishing; members only, limited guest tickets; membership £415, guest dt £10. Details from Hon Sec.

Clitheroe (Lancs). Trout, salmon, sea trout. Clitheroe AA Ltd fishes 3m of Ribble, mostly double bank, and 1m of **Lune**, at **Kirkby Lonsdale**; members only, no dt. The Inn at Whitewell, in the Forest of Bowland, offers fishing to guests at £10-

£50 per day depending on season; salmon best towards end of season (*see Whitewell*). By the A59 between Clitheroe and Accrington, Pendle View Coarse Fishery A59 By-Pass BB7 9DH, dt £5 1 rod on bank; phone (tel: 01254 822208) for details. Blackburn & Dist AA have several miles on Ribble and other fisheries on **Lune, Wenning, Aire, Gilpin** and reservoirs. Ribble Valley Borough Council, issues st £31 to residents (£41 non residents), conc, for water at Brungerley and below Edisford Bridge. Wt £20 for visitors, also dt £8.75 for Edisford alone, all from T I Centre, 12-14 Market Place, Clitheroe BB7 2DA (tel: 01200 425566). Two rods on Hodder for residents of Red Pump Hotel, Bashall Eaves; dt issued. Tackle shop: Ken Varey's Outdoor World, 4 Newmarket St, Clitheroe BB7 2JW (tel: 01200 423267). Hotels: Inn at Whitewell; Old Post House; Calf's Head, Gibbon Bridge; Parkers Arms.

Sawley (N Yorks). On Ribble. Salmon, sea trout, trout and grayling. Trout and salmon fishing good. Several miles preserved by Yorkshire FFC (visitors' tickets through members only). Inn: Spread Eagle.

Gisburn (N Yorks). Trout, salmon. Lancashire FFA have water at Ribchester and Gisburn, and at Walton le Dale. Fly fishing for members only. Hotels: Stirk House.

Long Preston (N Yorks). Ribble, 1m W. Trout, grayling, odd salmon, coarse fish. Left bank is preserve of Padiham & Dist AS. Members only. Staincliffe AC also have water, members plus 5 tickets for their guests. Hotels: Boar's Head; Maypole.

Settle (N Yorks). Settle AA has 7½m of good trout and grayling fishing in Ribble between Langcliffe, Settle and vicinity of Long Preston; wt £50, dt £15 at Royal Oak Hotel (tel: 01729 822561), during licensing hours; fly only; limit 1½ brace; water stocked yearly. **Malham Tarn**, National Trust water, is 6m from Settle and holds large wild trout, fly only; c&r policy; dt water (boats only) (*see Yorkshire lakes, reservoirs, etc*). Further north are Manchester AA's waters. Licences from post offices. Other hotels at Settle: Falcon Manor and Golden Lion.

Horton in Ribblesdale (N Yorks). Trout; preserved from source to Helwith Bridge, including all tributaries, by Manchester AA; assn also has **Newhouses Tarn** (fly only); stocked b and r trout; no tickets.

Tributaries of the Ribble

HODDER: Good salmon and trout water.

Higher Hodder Bridge (Lancs and Yorks). Salmon, sea trout, trout, grayling and coarse fish.

Chipping (Lancs). Hodder, 1½m E. Salmon, sea trout and grayling. Loud, 1m SE. Trout and sea trout. About ½m of Hodder below Doeford Bridge on right bank and several miles of **River Loud** are preserved by Loud & Hodder AA; tickets if accompanied by member. Hotel: Derby Arms.

Whitewell (Lancs). Salmon, sea trout, trout, grayling. The Inn at Whitewell, Forest of Bowland BB7 3AT (tel: 01200 448222; fax: 01200 448298), has six rods for residents only on 7m of Whitewell FA water (both banks); dt £10-£50 depending on season; salmon runs best towards end of season; also supplies dt for Stocks Reservoir. The Red Pump Hotel, Bashall Eaves, has two rods 8m further down the river.

Newton (Lancs); Lancashire FFA have water downstream from Newton to Dunsop Bridge.

Slaidburn (Lancs); ns Clitheroe, 8½m. Hodder; salmon, sea trout and trout. Tickets for several miles of Hodder from The Jam Pot Cafe, Slaidburn. **Stocks Reservoir** in vicinity: excellent trout fishery; for dt contact Stocks Fly Fishery, The Board House, Catlow Road, Slaidburn (tel: 01200 446602). Hotel: Bounty.

CALDER: Coarse fishing. Some club water.

Elland (Yorks). Bradford No 1 AA fishery extends u/s of Elland Road Bridge for approx 1,800 yds. Members only.

Whalley (Lancs). West Calder. Ribble, 2m W; salmon, sea trout and coarse fish. Hodder, 2m W; salmon, sea trout and trout. St Helens AA have ¾m of River Calder at Whittams Farm, Billington; st £18, conc; apply Hon Sec.

Barrowford (Lancs). Pendle Water; trout. Colne Water and Pendle join near Bar-

rowford to form Calder. **Leeds and Liverpool Canal** from Barnoldswick to East Marton (10m), and 3½m at Keighley leased to Marsden Star AS; dt water.

Burnley (Lancs). **Hapton Lodges Reservoir** at Hapton now coarse; Blythe AC. Marsden Star AS fishes Gawthorpe Hall Pool at Padiham, members only, tench, carp, perch fishing. At **Lowerhouse Lodge**; carp, bream, roach, perch, tench, pike; Pendleburnley & Dist AS water; dt £5 on bank, conc £3. Tackle shop: Macks Fishing Tackle, 33a Parliament Str, BB11 3JU (tel: 01282 427386).

COLNE (tributary of Calder). Free now of pollution; holds some trout and coarse fish.

Colne (Lancs). Colne; trout. Water held by Colne Water AS. **Leeds and Liverpool Canal** held by Marsden Star AS (10m from Barnoldswick to Bank Newton, and 3½m Howden to Morton); pike, trout, tench, bream, roach, rudd, carp and perch; st and dt for waters held by both clubs. Marsden Star AS also fishes Gawthorpe Hall Pond, Padiham, members only. Barrowfield AA fishes Knotts Lane Ponds at Colne; coarse fish; members only. Pendle Leisure Services, supplies tickets for **Foulridge Lower Reservoir**, roach, bream, pike, tench, carp. Dt also on bank; also **Ball Grove Lake**. For more information, contact Jackson's (*below*). Tackle shops: Anglers All, The Old Forge, 6 Raglan St, Colne BB8 0ET (tel: 01282 860515); Jackson's Fishing Tackle, 27 Albion Str, Earby, Yorks BB18 6QA (tel: 01282 843333; web: www.jackfish.net); Boyces, 44 Manchester Road, Nelson BB9 7EJ (tel: 01282 614412).

Foulridge (Lancs). Four British Waterways reservoirs: **Lower Foulridge** (or **Burwains**), **Upper Foulridge**, **Slipperhill**, **White Moor**. Let to clubs: coarse fishing, dt on bank at Lower Foulridge from Pendle Leisure Services.

ROTHER

(For close seasons, licences, etc, see Southern Region Environment Agency, p18).

Rises near Rotherfield and reaches the sea at Rye Bay. Mostly coarse fish, with trout in upper reaches and tributaries but runs of sea trout increasing. Mullet and bass in estuary.

Rye (E Sussex). Near mouth of Rother; coarse fish. Free fishing from roadside

bank between Iden and Scots Float, nr Rye. Clive Vale AC has 1m of **Tilling-**

ham River above Rye and **Rother** at Wittersham to Iden Bridge; south bank footpath for 2 fields on **Royal Military Canal** at Winchelsea; st £35, conc from Hon Sec or local tackle shops. Romney Marsh is close by. Several clubs have water, including Rother FA which has 12m of Rother and Royal Military Canal; dt on bank £3. Clive Vale AC has **Saunders Gravel Pits**, Rye Harbour; carp to 25lb, tench, roach, rundd, eels etc. Members only, st £28, conc.

Wittersham (Kent). Roach, chub, bream, perch, pike, tench, bleak, eels, and other species. Rother FA has 7m of Rother, accessible at Robertsbridge, Salehurst, Udiam, Bodiam, Newenden, Potmans Heath and Blackwall Bridge at Wittersham, also 3m of Royal Military Canal from Iden Lock to Appledore; membership open to clubs, not individuals; mostly members only, but £3 dt on canal and Blackwall Bridge, £1.50 juv, from bailiff on bank; clubs can book matches on both: contact G Parry, Tackle & Gun Shop, Tenterden. Clive Vale AC have 2 good stretches at Blackwall Bridge and Otter Channel junction; st £35, conc, from Hon Sec or Hastings tackle shops. Hastings, Bexhill & Dist FAA has **Rother and Hexden Channel** between Rolvenden and Wittersham; st £38, with concessions.

Newenden (E Sussex). Large bream, chub and roach; Rother Fishery Assn has fishing rights, terms described under *Wittersham*. Maidstone Victory Angling & Medway PS fish Rother here and at **Blackwall** and **Salehurst**. Membership on application.

Bodiam (E Sussex). Trout (small), coarse fish. Maidstone Victory Angling & Medway PS fish Rother here. Hastings, Bexhill & Dist FAA has 500 yds fishing on south bank with prime chub and dace, membership £38, conc. Edenbridge AA has 2 sections d/s of Bodiam Castle. Members only, no dt. Contact Hon Sec. Hotels: Castle, Justins.

Etchingham (E Sussex). Burwash AC has National Trust water on **River Dudwell** (tributary of the Rother); trout; members only. Hastings, Bexhill & Dist FAA has **Wishing Tree Reservoir**, a lake and ponds, dt £6 on bank, conc. CALPAC control **Speringbrook Sewer**, Snargate, nr **Appledore**, fen-like fishing of about 2,000 yds, with chub, roach, bream, dace, perch, pike; members only. No night fishing on CALPAC water. At **Burwash** is **Lakedown Trout Fisheries**, 4 lakes, 5 acres each, b and r trout from 1½lb to 16lb; for tickets contact Lakedown Trout Fisheries, 2 Oakenwood Cottages, Witherenden Hill, Etchingham TN19 7JP (tel: 01435 883449).

Stonegate (E Sussex). Wadhurst AS has trout water; dt to members' guests only. Hotel: Bridge.

Tenterden (Kent). Tackle & Gun has tickets for a large number of local fisheries. These include Rother FA (*see Wittersham*), Tenterden AC (incl various ponds, Dowels Sewer, Hexden Channel, Rother at Potmans Heath); Northiam AC (carp lakes and several miles of Rother); Rye AC (R Tillingham and R Brede, good coarse fishing); Headcorn AC (carp ponds in Biddenden area); also tickets for **Hawkhurst Fishery** (tel: 01580 753813), 11 lakes, with trout and coarse fishing; Tenterden Trout Waters, Combe Farm, Tenterden TN30 6XA (tel: 01580 763201): 3 lakes of 5 acres total, stocked with brown and rainbows, for fly fishing; day £25, conc, and half-day permits £15 from 8.30 am to dusk. Tackle shop: Tackle & Gun. 3 Eastwell Parade, High St, TN30 6AH (tel: 01580 764851)

BREDE: Rother tributary; chub to 5lb, bream to 7lb, roach, rudd, tench, pike to 25lb and mullet in summer; also run of sea trout. Barbel recently introduced; a few small trout in upper reaches; approx 6 miles controlled by Clive Vale AC; members only, st £35, conc, from Hon Sec or local tackle shops. Fishing stations **Rye, Winchelsea**.

POLLUTION

Anglers are united in deploring pollution. To combat it, urgent action may be called for at any time, from any one of us. If numbers of fish are found dead, dying, or seriously distressed, take samples of both fish and water, and contact the officer responsible for pollution at the appropriate Environment Agency. (Emergency Hotline for reporting all environmental incidents relating to air, land and water: Tel. 0800 80 70 60).

SEVERN

(For close seasons, licences, etc, see Midlands Region Environment Agency, p22)

Longest river in England. Rises in Wales (N Powys) and flows 180m into Bristol Channel. Fair salmon river, with commercial fisheries near mouth; spring salmon in January/April and May. Average size good. Some trout and grayling in upper reaches, but river noted chiefly for coarse fishing, especially for chub in the upper reaches and barbel in the middle river. Shad run up river in May and are taken on rod and line, principally at Tewkesbury Weir.

Sharpness (Glos). Coarse fishing in the **Gloucester and Berkeley Canal** from Severn Bridge to Hempstead Bridge, Gloucester (about 16m); bank licence from any bridge house.

Gloucester (Glos). Gloucester United AA controls several miles of Severn from Hawbridge u/s and d/s, and Stank Lane; dt £2, from bailiffs; Assn also has water from **Lower Lode** to **Deerhurst**; on gravel pit at **Saul** (Gardners Pool). BW dt on bank or from tackle shops for **Gloucester Sharpness Canal**). Red Lion Inn, Wainlode Hill, Norton GL2 9LW (tel: 01452 730251), has Severn fishing with facilities for disabled; tickets from hotel; all freshwater and some game fish; dt £4 at Inn and site shop. **Witcombe Reservoirs**: three lakes of 12, 9, and 5 acres, fly only; Troutmaster water, stocked rainbow trout of 2lbs av; st £650-£280, dt £35-£15, depending on limit; boats bookable in advance: Mrs M Hicks Beach, Witcombe Farm, Great Witcombe GL3 4TR (tel: 01452 863591). Staunton Court, Ledbury Rd, Staunton GL19 3QS (tel: 01452 840230; web: www.stauntoncourtfishing.com), has stocked coarse fishing on Match Lake, Dovecote Lake and Pleck Pool, with carp to 27lbs, roach to 2lbs, rudd, tench to 8lbs, etc; £5 dt and tackle shop on site (fresh bait and equipment). Tackle shops: Allsports, 126/128 Eastgate Str, GL1 1QT (tel: 01452 522756); Gloucester Rod & Gun Room, 67 Alvin Str, GL1 3EH (tel: 01452 410444); Tredworth Tackle, 78 High Str, Tredworth GL1 4SR (tel: 01452 523009); Ian Coley 442/444 High St, Cheltenham GL50 3JA (tel: 01242 522443). Hotels: New County, Fleece, New Inn.

Tewkesbury (Glos). Salmon, twait and coarse fish. Avon: coarse fish. Below weir shoals of big bream. Birmingham AA has 38 stretches on Severn including those at Bushley, Ripple, Ukinghall Pool, Severn Stoke, Deerhurst, Apperley (2 pools at Apperley, also). Tewkesbury Popular AA has 80 pegs on Severn from mouth of Avon to Lower Load, with bream, chub, barbel, eels, gudgeon, pike and bleak, and salmon, and **Avon** from Healings Mill to Abbey Mill, Ham side; bream, roach, chub, skimmer, bleak, gudgeon; membership £15, conc, from Robert Danter at Tewkesbury Fishing Tackle *(below)*; salmon permits issued each year. Gloucester United AA have water at Drirhurst and Lower Lode. Dt from tackle shops and Hon Sec. Tackle shop: Tewkesbury Fishing Tackle Shop, 31 Barton Str,GL20 5PR (tel: 01684 293234); Cheltenham Angling Centre, 442 High St, Cheltenham GL50 3JA (tel: 01242 582270). Hotels: Abbey; Malvern View; many others.

Ripple (Worcs). Bream, pike, perch, chub, dace, roach. Environment Agency fishery, 1900 yds free to licence holders, is on left bank, at M50 viaduct.

Upton upon Severn (Worcs). Chub, barbel, bream, roach, dace, perch and pike. Environment Agency has 1200 yds of west bank above old railway embankment, free to licence holders, mainly bream, barbel and roach fishing. Upton upon Severn AA has 10 pegs at Hanley Rd, 42 pegs at Upper Ham. Free parking. Dt £2 from G Shinn, tackle shop, 21/23 Old Str, WR8 0HN (tel: 01684 592102). Birmingham AA has 4 meadows, dt £4 from tackle shops. Hotels: King's Head, Swan, Star.

Worcester (Worcs). Barbel, bream, chub, roach. Free fishing behind cricket ground. Worcester & Dist United AA has stretches at Kempsey below Worcester, 350m l bank; Pixham Ferry, 800m r bank; West Diglis, 900m r bank; East Diglis, 350m l bank; Pitchcroft, 800m l bank. Assn also has stretches of **Avon**, and 2,500m l bank **Teme** at Knightwick. Dt through Hon Sec or through tackle shop *(see below)*; dt £4 Mon-Fri on bank for 6 pegs at Bevere Lock (tel: 01905 640275), Birmingham AA has stretches at Severn Stoke, Hallow, Kempsey, Grimley, rights on Worcester and Birmingham Canal from King's Norton to Blackpole (near Worcester); bream, roach, perch, pike. Tackle shop: Alan's Fishing Tackle, 26

Malvern Road, Worcester WR2 4LG (tel: 01905 422107) has tickets for Evesbatch Fisheries, two lakes with carp and roach.

Lincombe and **Holt** (Worcs). Wharf Inn, Holt Fleet WR6 6NN (tel: 01905 620289) has section at Holt Fleet, 19 pegs with barbel and bream; disabled access, dt £4 from inn; also 2 carp pools, 6 acres. Holt Fleet Restaurant (tel: 01905 620286) has 550m r bank with barbel and chub; dt £4 on bank; 25 pegs. Dt £4.50 for Lincombe Lock DY13 9PP, 180m l bank, from keeper on site (tel: 01299 822887).

Stourport-on-Severn (Worcs). At confluence of Severn and Stour: barbel, chub and large roach; also **Staffordshire and Worcestershire Canal**: coarse fish. Lyttelton AA has 80 pegs right bank u/s of Stourport. Tickets from Marks only. Birmingham AA has ½m both banks; also Ribbesford, Lickhill and Newhalls; dt £4 from tackle shops. Tackle shop: Watercraft Tackle, 81 Barracks Rd, DY13 9QB (tel: 01299 877784); Marks Fishing Tackle, 11 Raven Str, Stourport-on-Severn DY13 8UU (tel: 01299 871735), where Lyttelton AA tickets are sold. 1¼m both banks downstream of **Cilcewydd Bridge** is Environment Agency fishery, free to licence holders.

Bewdley (Worcs). Chub, roach, dace, barbel. Telford AA has 2,000m l bank from Buildwas village to Dale End Park, information from Hon Sec; dt £3, conc, on bank or tackle shop, Rod & Gun. Ye Olde New Inn, Pound Green, Arley DY12 3LT (tel: 01299 401 271) water. Kidderminster AA has 120 pegs, 2½m water, above and below town (Bewdley); 34 pegs at **Winnalls** below Stourport; membership cards £24, conc. Birmingham AA has six stretches in vicinity, incl Lyth Farm and Ladyham; dt £4. Cards for both Assns from Stan Lewis, (*see below*). Stan Lewis runs riverside guest-house with B&B and clubroom, and issues tickets for 1½m Severn at Bewdley (with record roach) and 9 local pools under his own supervision, with excellent roach, chub, and pike to 26lbs 8 ozs. Tackle shops; Rod & Gun, 3-5 High Str, Dawley, Telford TF4 2ET (tel: 01952 503550); Stan Lewis, 2 Severn Side South, Bewdley DY12 2DX (tel: 01299 403358); Marks Fishing Tackle, 11 Raven Str, Stourport-on-Severn DY13 8UU (tel: 01299 871735). Hotels: George; Horn & Trumpet.

Upper Arley (Worcs). Salmon, trout, grayling, chub, dace, pike, etc. Dowles Brook,

3m S. Birmingham AA has stretches at **Arley Stanley, Arley Kinlet, Arley, Aveley** and **Trimpley**; dt £4 from tackle shops. Hotels: Valentia, Harbour and Unicorn (last two issue dt).

Hampton Loade (Salop). Birmingham AA has extensive fishing here, on both banks, and at **Alveley**; dt £4 from tackle shops.

Bridgnorth (Salop). Barbel, roach. Ship Inn (tel: 01746 861219) has 270m west bank, at £3.50 on bank. Birmingham AA has stretches at **Knowle Sands, Danery, Quatford** and **Eardington; Willey Park Pools** at **Broseley** (5m) and pools at **Ticklerton** are also on club card; rainbow, brown and some American brook trout; dt £4 from tackle shops. At Quatt 4m SE National Trust have Dudmaston Pools; Kniver Freeliners AC water; coarse fish; members only (tel: 07790 565871); also Birmingham AA's 1½mm of bank running through the estate; salmon & coarse; dt £4 from tackle shops. **Boldings Pools**, Astley Abbotts, Bridgnorth WV16 4SS: twelve lakes with carp and tench and other coarse species, dt £5, conc (tel: 01746 763255). **Shatterford Lakes**, Bridgnorth Rd, Shatterford DY12 1TW (tel: 01299 861597): four trout lakes; prices according to lake; conc; also three coarse lakes with carp, catfish, roach, perch etc; dt £8 3 rods; most lakes accessible to disabled. Small tackle shop at fishery. Townsend Fishery (tel: 01746 780551); 5 coarse pools and one specimen lake; large carp, catfish and other coarse species, tickets on bank. Kingsnordley Fisheries, **Kingsnordley**, Bridgnorth WV15 6EU (tel: 01746 780247): 12 day ticket pools, with bream, barbel, tench, roach, chub, and large carp; dt £4 on bank, specimen pool £6, extra rods £1 each (specimen pool £2). Astbury Falls Fish Farm WV16 6AT (tel: 01746 766797), has £15 half dt (5 hours) 2 trout; £20 full day, 3 trout; also coarse dt £5, for large carp. Tackle shop: Mal Storey Angling Centre, 129 Sutton Road, Kidderminster DY11 6QR (tel: 01562 745221). Hotels: Severn Arms; Falcon; Croft; Kings Head.

Coalport (Salop). Chub, barbel, pike, etc, fewer roach and dace than are found farther downstream. Some free water. Rowley Regis & Dist AS has stretch on right bank; no tickets. Telford AA has Sweeneycliffe House fishery, 700m l bank; also right bank upstream to Tile Museum, about 800m; dt £3 on bank, or from Rod

& Gun, 3-5 High Str, Dawley, Telford TF4 2ET (tel: 01952 503550).

Ironbridge (Salop). Barbel, chub, roach, perch, etc. Environment Agency has 600 yds of fishing on left bank free to licence-holders (tel: 01743 272828), for information. Dawley AS has right bank d/s from power station fence to Free Bridge, also pools at **Telford, Broseley** and **Dawley**; dt £4, conc, on all waters from bailiffs. Queens Arms AC (tel: 01952 592602) has 3 stretches, total 51 pegs u/s and d/s of Free Bridge; dt from bailiff on bank. Little Dawley Pools, Telford AA water: three pools with carp, roach, bream, tench, crucians, ide; dt on bank or from Rod & Gun. Assn also has left bank from bend below rowing club steps u/s to railway bridge; and from fence above private gardens to top of the island opp power station (about 1200m); also 3 meadows opp Buildwas church (1200m); dt on bank. Tackle shops: Rod & Gun, 3-5 High Str, Dawley, Telford TF4 2ET (tel: 01952 503550); WAC Tackle, St Georges (tel: 01952 610497). Hotel: Tontine.

Atcham (Salop). Barbel, chub. Environment Agency has 2,895m r bank. Macclesfield Prince Albert AS has members only fisheries here, at **Bicton, Melverley, Longnor, Royal Hill, The Isle, Welshpool, Newton**, and elsewhere, a total of twenty nine Severn beats. Also fishings on the rivers **Gam, Vyrnwy** and **Banwy**, members only.

Shrewsbury (Salop). Town waters, 1800m both banks, dt £2.50 from tackle shops, or double on the banks; waters managed by Shrewsbury Angling Management Committee; all enq to Sundorne Fishing Tackle; good winter fishing for barbel, chub, roach. The Old Swan, SY4 1EB (tel: 01743 850750), 4m west of town at Montford Bridge, has 1m; barbel, eels and good pike. Old LMS AC has fine stretch at **Emstry**, with fords and runs; dt from local tackle shops. St Helens Ramblers AS have two stretch at Shrewsbury, permits only. Birmingham AA has stretches at **Underdale**, Shrewsbury, **Pool Quay** and **Buttington Bridge**, west of the town; dt £4 and permits from Sundorne Fishing Tackle. Warrington AA has water at Atcham and Rossall (nr Montford Bridge) with large chub and barbel; members only. At Atcham National Trust has Attingham Park; part coarse only, part salmon and coarse; Lymm AC water; membership and dt; membership apply

Hon Sec; dt from Cross Houses Garage, nr Shrewsbury (tel: 01743 761235). Wolverhampton AA has ¾m at Montford Bridge; dt £2.50 from bailiff on bank. Tackle shops: Kingfisher Angling Centre, 9 New St, SY3 8JN (tel: 01743 240602); Sundorne Fishing Tackle, 1 Sundorne Avenue SY1 4JW (tel: 01743 361804).

Melverley (Salop). Chub, dace. Environment Agency has two meadows on left bank, about 500 yds, free to licence holders (tel: 01743 272828, for details). Chester AA has 800yds immediately d/s of Environment Agency stretch.

Llandrinio (Montgomery). Chub, dace, trout, barbel, salmon; leave from farmers. Lymm AC has water on Severn and Vyrnwy, members only. Canal; coarse fish, tickets *(see Welshpool)*. **Maerdy Brook**, 2m SW. Arddleen Brook, excellent trout, dace and chub. Hotel: Golden Lion.

Welshpool (Powys). Salmon, trout, coarse fish (inc grayling). Trout small in streams, few but big in river. Welshpool & Dist AC (now in Montgomeryshire AA) which has 6m of coarse and game fishing in **Severn, Camlad, Vyrnwy, Banwy**; also 6m of **Montgomery Canal** (coarse fishing). The Welshpool river stretch is at **Lower Leighton**, 750m and 1,500m. Club also has 2 pools at Groes, 3m east, mixed coarse; dt from tackle shops in Welshpool. Black Pools trout fishery, fly only, is 1m from Welshpool on Llanfair Rd. Bank and boat fishing (dt £9 and £4) on Marton Pool, Marton, 5m SE; good coarse fishing; apply to Site Manager, Marton Pool Caravan Park. Warrington AA has Hope Farm stretch, Welshpool. For **Glyndwr Fishery**, Dolanog, Welshpool, contact Howard Thresher, 18 Cromwell's Meadow, Crediton, Devon EX17 1JZ (tel: 01363 777783). Hotels: Westwood Park; Bear, Newton; Black Lion, Llanfair Caereinion.

Forden (Powys). Montgomery, 3m. Trout, salmon, chub, dace, etc. Birmingham AA has 3m; dt £4 from tackle shops. Camlad; trout, grayling, chub; Montgomeryshire AA has water on river; tickets from tackle shops.

Montgomery (Powys). Severn, 2m; trout, salmon, grayling, chub, pike and perch. **Camlad**, 2m N; good trout, grayling, chub. Montgomeryshire AA has water; tickets. Warrington AA has waters at Caerhowell Hall, **Dolwen, Fron** and **Llanidloes**. Also **Vyrnwy, Dee**, canals and

Fishing lodges are rather better equipped than they once were. This one stands at The Lenches Lakes, Worcestershire.

pools. Tackle shops in Welshpool and Newtown.

Abermule (Powys). **Severn** and **Mule**; salmon, trout, grayling, coarse fish; mostly private but dt for some lengths. Water not always fishable in summer. Montgomeryshire AA has Mule from Abermule village u/s for 4 miles both banks; dt from Hon Sec or tackle shops; st £22, conc, wt £10, dt £3. Warrington AA has stretch; Lymm AC has 1,000 yds, members only, trout and grayling.

Newtown (Powys). Salmon, trout, grayling, pike, chub, dace; 3m, mainly right bank, beginning at municipal car park, with bream; information from Severnside and Newtown AC. Environment Agency has free fishery of 500yds north bank beside sewage farm at **Penarth**, with chub and dace (tel: 01743 272828 for details). Newtown & Dist FC control **Fachwen Pool** (now a coarse fishery with all types of fish and carp up to 30lb); dt from Newtown & Dist AC; Assn also controls the river upstream from the park for 2m, which incl **Vaynor Estate** and **Penstrowed**; st £22 and dt £5 from Newtown Angling. Severnside AC has extensive Severn fishing at Newtown, Penstrowydd, Vaynor, Glan Hafren Hall, Do-

lerw Park and pools. Prince Albert AS has stretch here. Penllwyn Lodges (tel: 01686 640269) offers self-catering log cabins with fishing in 1m of canal plus small lake; tench, chub, carp. Tackle shop has dt for canal at **Abermule**. Tackle shop: Newtown Angling, 3 Severnside Centre, Short Bridge Str, SY16 1AA (tel: 01686 624044). Hotels: Elephant and Castle, Maesmawr Hall, Dolforwyn Hall.

Caersws (Powys). Maesmawr Hall Hotel, SY17 5SF sell dt. Trout, coarse fish, some salmon. Caersws AA has 6m double bank in vicinity of Caersws and Llandinam with good brown trout and grayling; fly, spinning and worm. St £65, dt £10, conc, (also covers Llandinam fishery) from Spar shop; Llandinam PO; Maesmawr Hall Hotel. For trout fishing at **Caersws** and at **Clewedog Dam**, apply to Kingfisher Angling Centre, 9 New St, Shrewsbury SY3 8JN (tel: 01743 240602) for dt and information. Hotels: Maesmawr Hall; Buck; Red Lion; Unicorn.

Llandinam (Powys). Trout and grayling fishing on both banks. Caersws AA controls Dinam Fishery, fly only, st £70, dt £10, conc; from Llandinam PO and Stores SY17 5BY (tel: 01686 688226), or *see*

Caersws. Hotel: The Lion.

Llanidloes (Montgomery). Trout, salmon, pike, chub, dace, grayling. Llanidloes AA has about 20m fishing on upper **Severn**, **Afon Clywedog** and other tributaries. St and dt from Hon Sec. Warrington AA has Dolwen Bridge to Llanidloes. Upper Penrhyddlan, 1,125m r bank, grayling fishing, dt on bank (tel: 01686 412584 for information). Environment Agency has 805m on right bank beginning at sewage works, which is free fishing to licence holders, mostly chub, dace, with grayling (tel: 01743 272828 for details). Warrington AA, has water downstream. At **Trefeglwys** (4m N) is caravan park with fishing (trout and coarse) on **Trannon**. Best months for trout April-July. **Llyn Ebyr**, 30 acre coarse lake with perch, pike; tickets £3 per rod + £1 for boat from J Williams, Llyn Ebyr (tel: 01686 430236). Hotels: Lloyds, Unicorn, Queen's Head, Angel, Temperance, Royal Oak, Red Lion.

Tributaries of the Severn.

LEADON: Trout, coarse fish (some barbel introduced).

Ledbury (Hereford). Ledbury AA has trout water, no dt. Castlemorton Lake; coarse fishing; free, but licence necessary. Three Counties Fisheries have 25 peg carp pool here, with roach, tench and rudd. Management also runs 2 pools at Redbank Farm; coarse: carp, roach, rudd, tench, bream; also Pixley Pool, carp only; and near Ross-on-Wye Biddlestone Pool; carp, tench and bream; dt on banks, except Pixley for which contact Field Cottage, Ryton, nr Dymock, Glos GL18 2DH (tel: 01531 890455). Hotel: Royal Oak, The Southend.

AVON: The principal tributary of the lower Severn. Roach, chub, dace and perch dominate higher reaches; bream, barbel and pike, the latter patchily distributed.

Tewkesbury (Glos). Confluence of Avon and Severn, connected also by 'Mill Avon'. Weirs and weir-pool fishing, including twaite shad during the spawning run. Cheltenham AC controls 2m of Avon at Corpus Christi by **Strensham** village. Good coarse fishing, chub, roach, bream, perch, pike included. Membership £11, dt £2, conc, (Mon to Sun only) from Hon Sec, Cheltenham tackle shops or the Bell Inn, Eckington WR10 3AN. Mythe Pool, Tewkesbury: 10 acre coarse lake with bream, roach; tickets from Alan's Fishing Tackle, 26 Malvern Road, Worcester WR2 4LG (tel: 01905 422107). Birmingham AA also has water at Birdsmeadow and Mythe Court; dt £4 from tackle shops.

Twyning (Glos). Chub, dace, roach, pike, perch, bream. Birmingham AA has ½m stretch; dt £4 from tackle shops.

Eckington (Worcs). Most species of coarse fish, principally bream, big head of roach. Hotel: Bell Inn WR10 3AN (tel: 01386 750205), ¼m from river, is HQ of Eckington AC, which controls over 4m, 200 pegs of lower Avon, with many coarse species. Permits obtainable; st £11.

Pershore (Worcs). Roach bream. Worcester & Dist United AA has 900m at Burlington, and 1,000m at Pensham. Information from Assn (tel: 01886 888 459); dt from Alan's Fishing Tackle, 26 Malvern Road, Worcester WR2 4LG (tel: 01905 422107). Birmingham AA has water here, both banks and at Pensham, Birlingham, **Nafford, Eckington, Bredon, Twyning, Bredons Hardwick** and at Mythe Farm and Wood End; dt £4 from tackle shops. Some free water in recreation ground. Hotel: Angel.

Evesham (Worcs). Pike, perch, bream, roach, dace, gudgeon, chub, bleak. Evesham AA has 60 pegs in town, and 26 pegs behind football club, dt £2.80 from bailiff on bank. Club has free fishing for jun and disabled at Workman Gardens, Waterside. Dt on bank for Crown Corp Meadows, 60 pegs. At **Hampton Ferry**: E W Huxley & Son, Hampton Ferry Fishery WR11 4BP (tel: 01386 442458), has 104 pegs. Dt £3 (incl car park) from bailiffs or Raphael's Restaurant. Anchor Meadows, **Harvington**: 500m right bank with barbel and chub, dt on bank, or The Bungalow, Anchor Meadows (tel: 01386 48065). Birmingham AA has fisheries at Swifts, **Wood Norton, Chadbury, Charlton, Cropthorne, Fladbury, Lower Moor** and **Wick**; dt £4 from tackle shops. Manor Farm Leisure (caravan holidays), Anchor Lane, Harvington WR11 8PA (tel: 01386 870039), has ¾m coarse fishing on Avon. Bait Box *(below)* has 1m north bank of Avon at **Wilmots Waters**; 30 pegs (parking behind); dt £4, conc, from shop. Waterside and Workman Gardens, reserved for disabled and juv anglers. Twyford Farm, Evesham, has ½m right bank, chub, roach; tickets on bank. Licences from post office. **The Lenches Lakes**, Hill Barn Orchard, Evesham Rd, Church Lench, Evesham WR11 4UB (Mrs Marlene Badger)(tel: 01386 871035): stocked rainbow trout fly fishing on two lakes of 3½ acres each; fish av 2lbs-2½lbs, record 11lbs 6ozs; dt £35, half-day £20, evening £15, membership £25, conc members only; tackle sold on site. Tackle shop: Bait Box, 122 High Str, WR11 4EJ (tel: 01386 442955). Alcester tackle shop: Alcester Sports and Tackle, 3A High St, Alcester B49 5AE (tel: 01789 762200).

Stratford-upon-Avon (Warwick). Royal Leamington Spa AA has Lido and Recreation Ground fishing, dt £3 on bank; River Avon and College Pool at Wasperton, members only. Local club, Stratford-upon-Avon AA has 200 pegs on R Avon at Luddington and Manor Farm, and **R Stour** at Preston-on-Stour and Wimpstone, with good variety of coarse fish in both; membership £24, dt £3, conc from Stuart's Angling Centre before fishing; club also has 50 pegs on Stratford Canal at Wilmcote; dt on bank; also 7 meadows on Avon at Stratford (60 pegs); and 30 pegs on Hampton Lucy Brook; dt on bank or from Stuart's, which also issues tickets for ADAC water: 27 pegs Luddington Village Hall; 100 pegs South Stratford Canal; membership £24, dt £3 before fishing, conc. Lifford AC has North Stratford Canal, Lifford Lane to Brandwood Tunnel, 60 pegs. Birmingham AA has stretches at **Avon Meadows**, **Welford**, **Barton**, **Bidford**, **Marlcliff**, **Cleeve Prior** and **Salford Priors**; dt £4 from tackle shops; good chub and dace. Alveston Village Assn AC has 47 pegs on Avon at **Alveston**, with chub, bream, roach, carp, barbel dt £3, conc, from Hon Sec. At **Moreton in Marsh**, Lemington Lakes: five small pools with carp, rudd, roach, tench, bream, dt £6 water (tel: 01608 650872). Tackle shop: Stuart's Angling Centre, 17 Evesham Rd CV37 9AA (tel: 01789 293950). Hotels: Welcombe, Falcon, Arden and many others.

Leamington (Warwick). Bream, chub, dace, roach, pike, perch. Avon at **Wasperton** and **Stratford** Lido and Recreation Ground preserved by Royal Leamington Spa AA. Assn, also has 12½m in Grand Union Canal, Offchurch to Napton, coarse fish (good carp and tench in June, July, Aug); R **Leam**, **Offchurch** to outfall of Avon; dt £2, conc, for most of these at Stratford; annual membership £19, conc, from The Tackle Cellar (*below*). Tackle shop: Baileys Fishing Tackle, 30 Emscote Rd, Warwick CV34 4PP (tel: 01926 490636).

Rugby (Warwick). Chub, roach fishing. Environment Agency has free fishery at Avon Mill, ½m north bank beside B4112 road (for details, tel: 01684 850951). Avon Ho AC have water on Oxford Canal nr Barby; club also has 3 pools at Kings Newnham and stretch of upper Avon; membership from Banks and Burr (*below*). Knightley AC fishes 4m of Grand Union Canal, from Crick Tunnel to **Yelvertoft**; large carp, eels, bream, and good stocks of smaller fish; st £11 from Knightley Arms, conc; dt on bank, or from Yelvertoft PO. **Foxholes Fisheries, Crick**, Northants NN6 7US (tel: 01788 823967; web: www.foxholesfisheries.co.uk): 4 pools fishable on season ticket, £50-£120; and 1 dt pool, £5, or £10 two rods; pre-pay self-vend system; all species stocked; one lake is specialist water with carp to 35lbs: contact Roger Chaplin. **Spring Pools** are three pools close to Rugby at Newton; all species, dt on bank, or tel: 0799 0710666. **Clifton Lakes** on A5 offer 8 pools and 1 lake plus length of R Avon; dt on bank. **Newbold Quarry**, old established water for good tench and roach fishing, run by The Avon Mill AC; contact Avon Mill Pub or Banks & Burr. Draycote Water close by Dunchurch, dt from lodge on site. For tickets for **Coombe Pool**, 85 acres nr Coventry; bream, carp tel: 02476 453720. Tackle shops: Banks & Burr, 25/27 Claremont Road, CV21 3NA (tel: 01788 576782); Rugby Tackle Mail Order, 155A Bilton Rd, Rugby CV22 7DS (tel: 01788 570645). Hotels: Grosvenor; Three Horseshoes, both Rugby; Post House, Crick.

ARROW joined by the **Alne** at Alcester; flows into Avon at Salford Priors: Coarse fish, some trout.

Salford Priors (Worcs). Arrow and Avon; coarse fish. Birmingham AA has ¾m; dt £4 from tackle shops.

Wixford (Warwick). Pike, perch, roach, dace, chub and bream; dt £3 for about 1m of water on Ragley Park Estate from Fish Inn, Wixford B49 6DA (tel: 01789 778593), or from bailiff on bank. Lakes: Ragley Park, 1m NW. B&B next door to inn.

Redditch (Worcs). Redditch & Dist FA are local federation, who fish **Arrow Valley Lake**, with carp to 25lb, large roach and other coarse fish; dt £5.50 on site, Avon at Wick nr **Pershore** and **Birmingham - Stratford Canal**. Tackle shops: Powells Fishing Tackle, 28 Mount Pleasant, Redditch B97 4JB (tel: 01527 62669); Corn Stores, 360 Evesham Rd, Crabbs Cross B97 5JB (tel: 01527 541982). Hotels: Royal, Southcrest.

Alvechurch (Worcs). Barnt Green FC has rights on **Upper and Lower Bittell Reservoirs**, **Arrow Pools** and **Canal feeder**. **Lower Bittell** and **Mill Shrub** trout (fly only), remainder coarse fish. Fishing for members and their guests.

STOUR (tributary of Avon): Coarse fish, trout, mostly preserved.

Shipston (Warwick). Shipston-on-Stour AC has water; members only. Birmingham AA has Stour fishing at Milcote; dt £4 from tackle shops. Hotel: George.

LEAM (tributary of Avon): Coarse fish.

Eathorpe (Warwick). Red Lion waters, **Hunningham**, from Red Lion (tel: 01926 632715). Warwick DC (tel: 01926 450000) has 750m at Pump Room Gardens, Leamington Spa; dt on bank; and Leamington Mill Gardens, 350m l bank; both with roach, perch.

HAM BROOK (tributary of Leam): Coarse fish.

Fenny Compton (Warwick): Good pike, bream, tench, roach in **Oxford Canal**. **Claydon**.

SOWE (tributary of Avon): few fish.

Coventry (W Midlands). Excellent trout and coarse fishing on **Packington Estate**. **Meriden**. More than five miles of river fishing and 160 acres of lakes. Rainbow and brown trout; also coarse fishery 2m off. *(For details see Midlands (reservoirs and lakes)).* Coventry & Dist AA has extensive fishing on rivers, canals and reservoirs and coarse fishing in **Trent** and **Soar** at Thrumpton, **Ouse** at Turvey, **Nene**; day tickets for some of this fishing may be had from tackle shops in Coventry area or Hon Sec. Canal waters include stretches on **Coventry Canal** and **Oxford Canal**. Dt £5 from bailiffs for Assn's **Napton Reservoirs**, noted bream (to 6lb), carp (to 31lb), tench and roach water, also pike to 22lb. 6m from town. Full Coventry book £17, dt £5, conc. **Hopsford Hall Fishery**, Shilton Lane, nr Withybrook. Carp to 20lb and other coarse species. Good access for disabled.

Dt £5, conc, from bailiff on bank. Royal Leamington Spa AA control **Jubilee Pools**, at Ryton-on-Dunsmore; for membership, *see Leamington*. **Lavender Hall Premier Fisheries**, Lavender Hall Lane, Berkswell CV7 7BN (tel: 01676 530299): five well stocked lakes with carp, tench, bream, roach, etc; dt from lodge. **Coombe Pool**, 85 acres nr Coventry CV3 2AB; bream, carp (tel: 02476 453720), dt from Visitor Centre or on bank £3.50. **Flecknoe Farm Fisheries**, 5 acres; carp (tel: 01788 899022/899017); mostly carp; dt £5 on bank. Tackle shops: Rugby Tackle Mail Order, 155A Bilton Rd, Rugby CV22 7DS (tel: 01788 570645); Lanes Fishing Tackle, 31 London Road, Coventry CV1 2JP (tel: 024 7622 3316) (assn cards). Hotel: Brandon Hall Hotel, Brandon.

TEME: Trout and coarse fish, with a few salmon; grayling. Very large barbel, strong tackle recommended. Trout in upper reaches.

Worcester (Worcs). Barbel, chub. Worcester & Dist UAA has 1,200m l bank at Knightwick; dt for both from Reynolds Tackle, Worcester. Birmingham AA has water at Cotheridge, 4m west of Worcester; dt £4 from tackle shops. The Talbot at Knightwick WR6 5PH (tel: 018868 21235) has fishing on both banks; dt £7.

Leigh (Worcs). Trout, chub, dace, grayling, pike, perch, salmon. Bransford AS and local clubs rent Leigh to Powick; members only. Birmingham AA has water here (Leigh and Brockamin); dt £4 from tackle shops.

Broadwas (Worcs). Trout, grayling, chub, dace. Birmingham AA has stretch of left bank here and at Eardiston, 1¼m; dt £4 from tackle shops.

Knightwick (Worcs). Salmon, trout, barbel, roach, dace, chub. Permits for one mile with large barbel and chub, from Stan Lewis, 2 Severn Side South, Bewdley DY12 2DX (tel: 01299 403358); dt £3.

Tenbury (Worcs). Barbel, chub. Peacock Waters (tel: 01584 881411) has 900m l bank; st only £100. Tickets (campers only) for Little Hereford, 500m right bank d/s of bridge, A Jones, Westbrook Farm, Little Hereford, Ludlow SY8 4AU (tel: 01584 711280). Tenbury FA has approx 4m of Teme above and 1m of **Ledwyche Brook**, trout, salmon and grayling, and barbel, chub, pike etc; membership £90; £20 salmon dt, dt £15 game, £10 coarse; from Hon Sec (tel:

01584 810345/695). St Michaels Pools, New House Farm, St Michaels, Tenbury WR15 8TW (tel: 01568 750245): dt £25, conc; brown and rainbow trout, fly only. Hotels: Crow; Royal Oak; B&B at Deepcroft Farmhouse.

Ludlow (Salop). Birmingham AA has water from Eastham Bridge to Eardiston, incorporating Lindridge and Puddleford; dt £4 from Ludlow Tackle. **Delbury Hall Trout Fishery**, Diddlebury SY7 9DH (tel: 07779 465937); dt £20, 2 fish limit; 2 trout lakes; 5 acres; fly only. Dt for **Hyde Pool** at Wooferton (coarse); **Lower Bromden Pools**, Wheathill (5 pools: coarse) from Ludlow Tackle. Tickets for **Little Hereford Carp Pool** from 'Haynall-Villa' SY8 4BG (tel: 01584 711589); 1 acre; carp; dt £3. Tackle shop: Ludlow Tackle, Old Service Station, Bromfield Rd SY8 1DW (tel: 01584 875886) supplies river reports, directions and information on venues in the area. Hotels: The Feathers, Angel, Bull, Bull Ring Tavern, Charlton Arms, and Exchange.

Knighton (Powys). Mainly trout; preserved except for 1m free to licence-holders. For brown and rainbow trout, fly fishing pool nr **Llangunllo**, G Morgan, Gefnsuran, Llangunllo LD7 1SL (tel: 01547 550219); reserved for residents only; farmhouse accom on site. Hotels: Norton Arms.

ONNY: Good trout, chub, etc.

Plowden (Salop). Trout, chub; private water. Plowden Club has 4m trout fishing at Plowden Estate, members and guests only, no dt; occasional membership, £120 plus joining fee; contact S J Finnegan, The Old School, Brimfield SY8 4NZ.

SALWARPE: Trout, coarse fish. Birmingham AA has 1,300 yds at **Claines**; dt £4 from tackle shops.

Droitwich (Worcs). Trout above, coarse fish below. Severn 6m W. Droitwich & District AS has water at **Holt Fleet**. Noted chub waters. Society also has **Heriotts Pool** (large carp). Two sections of Droitwich Canal at Porters Mill: 36 pegs, stocked with carp, chub, bream, roach and rudd: dt £2.50 on bank. **Astwood Fishery**, Stoke Prior, Bromsgrove (tel: 01905 770092) 2 acre pool and 2 1-acre pools with carp to 30lb and bream to 8lb, tench; dt £5 on bank.

Bromsgrove (Worcs). Tardebigge Reservoir now syndicate water. Upper and Lower Bittel Reservoirs owned by Barnt Green FC; members only *(see also*

Arrow-Alvechurch). Hewell Grange Lake; st only via Colin Pace, Hewell Grange Prison. (See also Worcester and Birmingham Canal). Upton Warren Lake, 18 acres with carp, bream, roach etc; dt on bank for 12 pegs (majority for members only); contact Outdoor Education Centre, Upton Warren B61 7ER (tel: 01527 861426); boat and several pegs for disabled. Tackle shops; Ensign Fishing Tackle, 3 Stoke Rd, B60 3EQ (tel: 01527 833322).

STOUR: Once heavily polluted, but fish now returning in some areas, principally lower river.

Stourbridge (Worcs). **Staffordshire and Worcestershire Canal;** coarse fish. Tackle shop: Club 2000 Fishing Tackle, 86 Wynall Lane, DY9 9AQ (tel: 01384 892892).

Dudley (W Midlands). Lakes: Pensnett Grove Pool, Middle Pool, Fenns Pool, 3m SW *(see Brierley Hill)*. Himley Park Lakes (tel: 01902 324093); 16 acres good coarse fishing with carp and tench, dt on bank; swims accessible to disabled. Plenty of fishing in canals within 6m radius. Lodge Farm Reservoir; Dudley Corporation. At Parkes Hall, **Coseley**, 2½m away, is good pool for which dt can be had; coarse fish (Dudley Corporation). Tackle from Hingley All Sports & Hobbies, 164 Lower High St, Stourbridge DY8 1TR (tel: 01384 395438).

SMESTOW (tributary of Stour): Polluted.

Wolverhampton (W Midlands). Smestow, 2m W; polluted. Some fishing in **Penk** at Penkridge. Most local water on Severn held by Birmingham AA; dt £4 from tackle shops. Patshull Park, nr Pattingham WV6 7HR (tel: 01902 700774) trout and coarse, dt at lodge; John Price, Pool Hall, Lower Penn WV4 4XN (tel: 01902 763031), carp and other coarse, dt from car park shop. Lakes at Himley Park have dt. Swan Pool, **West Bromwich** (tel: 0121 553 0220): 20 acres with carp and pike, tickets on bank. **Staffordshire Worcester Canal** is Wolverhamton AA water; dt £2.50 on bank. Tickets from local tackle shops.

TERN: Coarse fish, some trout.

Telford (Salop). Tickets from tackleist TAC, Church Str, St Georges TF2 9JU (tel: 01952 610497), for Telford AA and other local clubs, including a good stretch at Ironbridge for barbel; also pools, flashes and lakes, including **Holmer Lake,** noted for roach (to 3lb) and bream (to 10lb); club also has Apley Pool, Wellington, good quantities of carp; Little Apley Pool opp Blessed Robert Johnson School, Wellington, very suitable for disabled; also Middle Pool, Oakengates; carp, bream, tench, roach, pike; also Priorslee Flash at St George's; Randlay Pool and Blue Pool, Telford Town Park: dt for each on bank £3. Assn also has Madebrook Pools, created for the disabled, adjacent to Stirchley Leisure Centre; 15 anglers; for all Assn contest bookings: contact Mrs Ellen Rogers (tel: 01952 410789). Uppington Estate Waters: tickets for stretch in Wroxeter; from Estate Office, Uppington Estate, Uppington TF6 5HL (tel: 01952 740223); Uppington Estate fishing between Cressage Bridge and the Rocks at Eyton on Severn has been let to Prince Albert AS. Mr John Beddoes, The Farmhouse, Eyton-on-Severn, Wroxeter SY5 6PW (tel: 01952 510223) has 1m single bank at Eyton. Baylis Pool TF11 9PG, 10 acres with carp, bream; dt £4 coarse; £7 carp; on bank (tel: 01952 460530). 10 minutes from Junction 6 of M54 are **Swann Pool** (4 pegs, dt £5) and **Malthouse Pool** (25 pegs, dt £4); apply in advance to Rod & Gun, 3-5 High Str, Dawley, Telford TF4 2ET (tel: 01952 503550).

Crudgington (Salop). A few trout and coarse fish.

Hodnet (Salop). Tern. 1m E; a few trout and coarse fish. Strine Brook, 2m E. Lakes: Rose Hill Ponds, 4m NE. **Hawkstone Park Lake**, 3½m; excellent tench and carp water (40lb bags not uncommon) and large roach, rudd, pike and eels; private preserve of Wem AC, membership closed.

Market Drayton (Shrops/Staffs). Trout and coarse fish. Environment Agency has free fishery of 1,200 yds on right bank, mainly d/s of Walkmill Bridge, around sewage works; details from EA. For stocked section, Tern Fisheries Ltd, Broomhall Grange, M Drayton TF9 2PA (tel: 01630 653222); dt £16, 6 fish, ½ day £10, 3 fish, eve £6, 2 fish. At **Great Sowdley**, 7m SE, are canal reservoirs; perch, pike, roach, tench, carp. Market Drayton AC fishes Shropshire Union Canal at Knighton, Bridges 45-47, dt on bank. Fenton & Dist AS has **White Farm Pools** at Ashley.

MEESE (tributary of Tern); Trout, coarse fish.

Newport (Salop). Meese, 1m N; trout; pri-

vate. Lakes: Chetwynd Park Pond, 1m N. Minton's, Limekiln and Wildmoor Pools, 3m S. Moss Pool, 1½m NE. Park AC has good coarse fishing water on Shropshire Union Canal, with carp to 20lb, bream to 5lb, perch to 4lb: dt £3 on bank. Telford AA has ½m of disused Newport & Shrewsbury Canal (SSSI) in town centre; dt £2 on bank. Tackle shop: Newport Tackle, 91A High Str, TF10 7AY (tel: 01952 820334). Hotels: Bridge Inn.

REA: Trout, grayling; preserved.

Minsterley (Salop). Trout, grayling, Minsterley Brook. Habberley Brook, 3m SE. Lake: Marton Pool, 7m SW.

SHELL BROOK (tributary of Roden):

Ellesmere (Salop). Shell Brook, 2m NW; preserved. Halghton Brook, 4m N. Roden, 6m SE. Lakes: **Ellesmere Meres**, noted for bream (12lb plus). Ellesmere AC (most waters are st for locals only £35) has **Whitemere** and **Blakemere** (dt £5 for bank fishing only); Sunday fishing is allowed; boats on most assn waters for members only; club members may fish 4m stretch of **Shropshire Union Canal**; coarse fish; also dt water. Hotels: Black Lion, Bridgewater, Red Lion; tickets (*see also Shropshire lakes*).

PERRY: Trout, preserved.

Ruyton-Eleven-Towns (Salop). 300m stretch on 1 bank with chub and pike; dt from Bridge Inn.

VYRNWY; Provides sport with trout, grayling, coarse fish and salmon.

Llanymynech (Salop). Trout, salmon, grayling, roach, perch, pike, eels, chub, barbel, etc. Oswestry AC has water here, members only, £10 st, conc. For Lord Bradford's water at Lower House Farm inquire of agent, Llanymynech. Other hotels: Bradford Arms, Cross Keys, Dolphin. Good trout fishing at **Lake Vyrnwy** (*see lakes in Welsh section*).

Llansantffraid (Powys). Warrington AA has water here on Vyrnwy and **R Cain**, on Vrynwy at **Four Crosses**, and **Cross Keys**.

Meiford (Powys). Montgomeryshire AA has 750m 1 bank at Great Dufford Farm, 12 miles away, with barbel and chub; st £22 from Hon Sec; dt £3 from Welshpool tackle shops.

MORDA (tributary of Vyrnwy): mostly trout, but some coarse fish in lower reaches.

Oswestry (Salop). Most river fishing preserved. Vownog Fishing Lake, **Porthywaen** SY10 8LX, well stocked with r trout (tel: 01691 828474). Trewalyn Fly Lakes, Deythaur, Llansantffraid (tel: 01691 828147): trout fishing; Prince Albert AC; members only. Tickets from Shropshire County Council; West Lake Trout Fishery, 2½ acres, stocked r and b trout fishing, fly only; dt £20; 2 acre coarse lake, dt £5. Trench Farm, Redhall Lane, Penley LL13 0NA (tel: 01978 710098); carp fishing on three pools, dt £6, conc; coarse, carp to 38lb. Five coarse fishing ponds: Middle Sontley Farm, Wrexham LL13 0YP (tel: 01978 840088); dt £6 on bank; mirror carp to 27lb, common carp to 22lb, tench and bream to 8lb; night fishing £6, phone first. Tackle shops: Guns and Ammo, G & A Building, 95 Beatrice St, Oswestry SY11 1HL (tel: 01691 653761).

TANAT (tributary of Vyrnwy): Trout (good average size), chub and grayling.

Llan-y-Blodwel (Salop). Horseshoe Inn has 1½m (dt £3), 3 rods per day, fly only, and Green Inn, Llangedwyn, has short stretch; dt issued (3 rods only); fly only.

Llanrhaiadr-y-Mochnant (Powys); trout; free. Tanat, 1m; trout, grayling, chub, etc; 6m from Llangedwyn to Llangynog strictly preserved; no dt.

CAIN (tributary of Vyrnwy): Trout, coarse fish.

Llansantffraid (Powys). Trout. Warrington AA has two stretches.

BANWY (tributary of Vyrnwy): Trout, grayling, chub, pike, dace and chance of salmon here and there.

Llanfair-Caereinion (Powys). Montgomeryshire AA has right bank downstream from town bridge to boundary fence; mainly trout, some chub and dace; dt £3 from tackle shops. At **Cyffronydd** Warrington AA has 610 yds; 700 yds right bank at **Neuadd Bridge**. Caereinion Hotel: Wynnstay Arms.

SHROPSHIRE LAKES

ELLESMERE LAKES. Fishing station: **Ellesmere**. Excellent coarse fishing in Ellesmere (noted for bream), **Crosemere**, **Newton Mere**, **Blakemere**, **Whitemere** (bream of 12lb 4oz taken); controlled by Ellesmere AC who issue dt £5 for **Blakemere**. Local members only for **Hardwick Pool** (1m) noted tench water; dt from Pretty Things, Ellesmere, or local garage.

WALCOT LAKES. Lydbury North, 3m NE of Clun. Two extensive lakes, Walcot East controlled by Birmingham AA; tench, pike and other coarse fish; dt £4 from tackle shops.

SOMERSET (streams, lakes and reservoirs)

(For close seasons, licences, etc, see South West Region Environment Agency, p19)

AXE. Rises on Mendips and flows 25m NW to Bristol Channel near Weston-super-Mare. A few trout in upper reaches and tributaries, but essentially a coarse fish river, containing a mixture of the usual species, with roach now predominating.

Weston-super-Mare and Bleadon (Som). Weston-super-Mare & Dist AA fishes Old R Axe, Hobbs Boat to Cowbridge, and Lympsham to Crab Hole; South Drain, Gold Corner to Edington Junction; North Drain, pumping station to Blakeway Bridge; R Brue, at Manor of Mark; assn waters contain roach, bream, carp, perch, rudd, pike, eels; no night fishing; active junior section; st £22, conc, wt £10 and dt £4 from Hon Sec. North Somerset AA has water on **Brue** near **Highbridge**, **Old River Kenn (Blind Yeo)**, **Congresbury Yeo**, and **North Drain**, Newtown and Apex Lakes, and Walrow Pond (jointly with Bridgwater AA), together with some smaller rivers; membership £20, conc. Clevedon & Dist Freshwater AC fish Old River Kenn and R Kenn (Blind Yeo) at **Clevedon**, also Congresbury Yeo in Congresbury. Mainly bream, roach, tench, pike, a few trout; dt £3 from tackle shops. Somerset Levels Association of Clubs (SLAC) have **Parrett** from Thorney to Yeo, and below Langport. Two coarse fisheries near Clevedon: Plantations Lakes, Middle Lane, Kingston Seymour, 2½ acres, stocked with 12 species, carp to 22lbs, tea room on site; dt; Bullock Farm Fishing Lakes, Kingston Seymour BS21 6XA (tel: 01934 835020; fax: 01934 835927; web: www.bullockfarm.co.uk), four lakes with 88 swims, stocked with large variety of species. Dt at lakeside. Tackle shops: Veals Fishing Tackle, 1A Church Str, Highbridge TA9 3AE (tel: 01278 786934); Redmans Angling Centre, 8e

Church Road Upper BS23 2DT (tel: 01934 419996); Chris's Angling, 12 Regent St, Burnham-on-Sea TA8 1AX (tel: 01278 794442).

BRICKYARD PONDS: Pawlett. BB&WAA tench fishery; st or dt from Hon Sec or tackle shops *(see Bristol).*

BRISTOL RESERVOIRS:
Chew Valley, Blagdon and **Barrow** reservoirs provide some of the best lake trout fishing in Europe, with a total annual catch of over 50,000 fish of high average size. Season and day tickets obtainable. All fishing is fly only. Limits are four brace per day, two brace per evening bank permit. For all waters, st £555, apply to: Bristol Water Plc, Recreations Department, Woodford Lodge, Chew Stoke, Bristol BS40 8XH (tel: 01275 332339; e-mail: bob.handford@bristolwater. co.uk). Details as follows:

Barrow Reservoirs - Barrow Gurney; 3 lakes, open April to November; brown and rainbow trout; bank fishing only; dt £11 and part dt £8.50 from self-service kiosk. St also available; conc for juniors, OAPs and registered disabled; tackle hire & tuition can be arranged. Contact Woodford Lodge, Chew Stoke, Bristol BS40 8XH (tel: 01275 332339).

Blagdon Lake - Blagdon; Open April to November; noted brown and rainbow trout water. Bank dt and part dt from self-service kiosk. Rowing boats from Blagdon Lodge office (advance booking recommended). Dt £15.50 obtainable on all waters; disabled boat anglers catered for. Concessions for jun (under 17), OAP and registered disabled. Tackle shop, tackle hire and tuition arranged; Contact Woodford Lodge, Chew Stoke, Bristol BS40 8XH (tel: 01275 332339).

Chew Valley Lake - Chew Stoke. Open April to November; noted brown and rainbow trout water where fish run large. Bank dt and part dt from self-service kiosk. Motor boats from Woodford Lodge office (advance booking recommended). St £455 and dt £13.50 tickets are obtainable on all waters; disabled boat anglers catered for. Concessions for jun (under 17), OAP and registered disabled. Tackle shop and restaurant at Woodford Lodge. Tackle hire and tuition arranged. Pike fishing from Woodford Lodge, Chew Stoke, Bristol BS40 8XH (tel: 01275 332339).

Cheddar Reservoir, Cheddar. Coarse fishery managed by Cheddar AC; st £40, dt

£5, conc; permits and tickets from Broadway House Caravan Park, Axbridge Rd BS27 3DB (tel: 01934 742610), on main Cheddar to Axbridge road, opposite reservoir; no tickets available at the water: Bristol Angling Centre, 12 Doncaster Rd, Southmead, Bristol BS10 5PL (tel: 0117 950 8723); Veals Fishing Tackle, 1A Church Str, Highbridge TA9 3AE (tel: 01278 786934); Thatcher's Pet & Tackle, 18 Queen St, Wells (tel: 01749 673513).

WESSEX WATER RESERVOIRS: Wessex Water, Claverton Down Road, Claverton Down, Bath BA2 7WW. Brochure enquiries (tel: 008457 300600). St from above address; dt from dispensing units at reservoirs. Season ticket covering a specific reservoir: £320 (4 days/week). Dt £14, conc £12, evng £8, block ticket. Boat £12 (2 anglers max). Limits: 4 fish on st, 5 fish on dt, 2 fish on evening ticket; various conc. **Clatworthy Reservoir**. 12m from **Taunton** in Brendon Hills; 130 acres brown and rainbow trout; fly only; 2¼m bank fishing. Season: 17 Mar to 18 Oct; permits from Fishing Lodge; wheelyboat for disabled; st, dt, block available, conc. For further info, contact ranger (tel: 01984 624658).

Durleigh Reservoir. 2m W of **Bridgwater**. 80 acres; coarse fishing, carp, roach, bream, pike. Biggest recently, pike 27lb, carp 18lb, bream 7lb. Dt £5, evngs £2.50 (for more information, tel: 01278 424786).

Hawkridge Reservoir. 7m W of Bridgwater. 32 acres. Brown and rainbow trout; fly only. Season Mar 17-Oct 15; st, dt, block available, conc. Boat or bank (tel: 01278 671840).

Otterhead Lakes. About 1m from **Churchingford** nr Taunton. Two lakes of 2¾ and 2 acres; brown and rainbow trout; fly only; no boats. Season Mar 18-Oct 11; controlled by Wessex Water; very overgrown; leased to local club.

Sutton Bingham Reservoir. 4m S of **Yeovil**. 142 acres. Brown and rainbow trout; average 1¼lb; fly only, bank or boat; Wheelyboat available for disabled. Season Mar 17 to Oct 15; dt £12 from ranger. Sutton Bingham Fishing Lodge, 1 Abbotts Mill (tel: 01935 872389), conc; st available.

CHARGOT WATER, Luxborough. 3 ponds. Trout; fly only.

DONIFORD STREAM (Swill River at Doniford) and **WASHFORD RIVER**,

Taunton. Trout; preserved.
HORNER WATER. On National Trust Holnicote Estate, Selworthy TA24 8TJ; upstream from Packhorse Bridge, Horner, to Pool Bridge, approx 2½m; fly fishing, small wild trout; dt £1 (4 fish limit) from Horner Tea Garden (tel: 01643 862380) or Estate Office (tel: 01643 862452).
WIMBLEBALL LAKE, Dulverton. 374 acres. South West Lakes Trust, fly only, well-known stocked rainbow trout fishery. Season Mar 24-Oct 31, boats bookable in advance. Dt £17.50, boats £11.00,

(Wheelyboat for disabled), conc, from self-service kiosk at Hill Farm Barn. Ranger tel: 01398 371372. Tackle shop: Lance Nicholson, Gloster House, High Str, Dulverton TA22 9HB (tel: 01398 323409). Hotel: Exton House; B&B at lake: Gillian Payne, Lower Holworthy Farm, Brompton Regis, Dulverton TA22 9NY (tel: 01398 371244). There is a campsite at lake.
YEO. Fishing station: **Congresbury**. Tidal, good fly water for trout; a few coarse fish.

STOUR (Dorset)

(For close seasons, licences, etc, see South West Region Environment Agency, p19)

Rises in Wiltshire Downs and flows through Dorset, joining Hampshire Avon at its mouth at Christchurch. Noted coarse fishery throughout year (large barbel, chub, roach, dace, bream and pike).

Christchurch (Dorset). Avon and Stour. Pike, perch, chub, roach, tench, dace. Christchurch AC has many miles of Stour, Avon, plus numerous gravel pits, lakes and ponds. Limited dt for lower Stour and harbour, and Lifelands stretch of Hants Avon, Ringwood, from Davis *(address below)*. Club membership, £110 pa, conc, juv and OAP. **Hordle Lakes**, 1m from New Milton; 5 lakes of total 5 acres, coarse fishing. Dt £2-£6 from Davis *(see below)*. Coarse fishing can be

had on Royalty Fishery waters *(see Avon)*, and Winkton Fishery. Sea fishing from Mudeford in Christchurch Bay is fair. Tackle shops: Davis Fishing Tackle Shop, 75 Bargates, Christchurch BH23 1QE (tel: 01202 485169). Hotel: King's Arms, Christchurch.
Throop (Dorset). Throop fisheries; 5½m of top quality coarse fishing; now Ringwood AC water; dt £7.50 from Christchurch tackleists.

STOUR (Dorset) - Tributaries

Wimborne (Dorset). Good chub, roach, bream, barbel, dace and pike. Some trout in Stour, also in R Allen. Small runs of salmon and sea trout. Salisbury & Dist AC has 2 adjoining stretches; apply Hon Sec. Red Spinner AS has water at Barford and Eyebridge; about 5m in all; members only. Wimborne & Dist AC has approx 10m of Stour in Wimborne, Longham to Child Okeford; 10 coarse lakes (from Wareham to Ringwood) and 5 trout lakes (from High Ansty to Winterbourne Zelston); 10m of Stour (from Gains Cross to Longham) and 1m stretch of Avon at Fordingbridge; mainly members + guests only; membership £75 pa, plus £8 joining fee; guest wt £25, dt £6; contact Hon Sec. Some guest tickets obtainable from Wessex Angling Centre *(below)*, and from Minster Sports. Environment Agency own **Little Canford Ponds**, Wimborne, coarse fishery with good access for disabled; leaflet from Conservation Officer at Rivers House, Sunrise

Business Park, Blandford Forum DT11 8ST (tel: 01258 456080); but as we go to press the fishing is up for sale. National Trust have single bank of River Allen at Kingston Lacy; dt from Estate Office (tel: 01202 882493). Tackle shops: Minster Sports, 8 West St, Wimborne BH21 1JP (tel: 01202 882240); Wessex Angling Centre 321 Wimborne Rd, Oakdale, Poole BH15 3DH (tel: 01202 668244). Hotels: King's Head, Three Lions, Greyhound.
Sturminster Marshall (Dorset). Southampton PS has about 2m here. Coarse, a few trout; contact Minster Sports, 8 West St, Wimborne BH21 1JP (tel: 01202 882240) and local tackle shops.
Shapwick (Dorset). Coarse fish. Southampton PS has several miles of fishing here; dt, conc, from Minster Sports, 8 West St, Wimborne BH21 1JP (tel: 01202 882240).
Blandford Forum (Dorset). Roach, chub, dace, perch, bream, carp, grayling, eels,

and pike; good all year. Some tench. Durweston AC has Stour from Durweston Bridge u/s to Enford Bottom; st £30, conc, dt £3, river. Contact Hon Sec. Dorchester & Dist AS has 600 yards south bank and 1100 yards north bank near **Shillingstone** (Child Okeford); also water at **Little Hanford** (Chesil Farm), and Hanford Farm; enquire Hon Sec; no dt; membership £40, conc. Blandford & Dist AC has Stour fishing from Durweston Bridge d/s to Charlton Marshall. Membership £27.50, conc; dt £4, conc, from John Candy, Todber Manor Fisheries Shop, Todber, nr Marnhull DT10 1JB (tel: 01258 820384); and tackle shop: Arthur Conyers, 3 West Str, Blandford DT11 7AW (tel: 01258 452307).

Sturminster Newton (Dorset). Chub, roach, dace, pike, perch, tench, bream; fishing very good. Dorchester & Dist AS has Factory Farm, near **Marnhull**, u/s from Red Bridge (both banks) and d/s (north bank only); apply Hon Sec; no dt; st £40, conc. Sturminster and Hinton AA has 7m above and below town; 2 lakes at Stoke Wake, with tench; lake at Okeford Fitzpaine, mixed fishery, members only, st £17.50; for wt £10 and dt £4 apply to Todber Manor Fisheries Shop, Todber, nr Marnhull DT10 1JB (tel: 01258 820384); or Kevs Autos, Sturminster Newton. Hotel: White Hart.

Stalbridge (Dorset). Chub, roach, tench, dace, pike. Stalbridge AS has 2m of Stour, 2m on **Lydden** and 3 lakes at **Buckland Newton**; dt £5, conc from C C Moores, Church Hill, Stalbridge.

Gillingham (Dorset). Trout and coarse fish. Dorchester & Dist AS has fishing at Marnhull: Contact Hon Sec. St £40, conc (no dt). Gillingham & Dist AA has 7m fishing from Gillingham to Marnhull. **Turner's Paddock Lake**, Stourton (dt £5), and **Mappowder Lakes**, (dt £4) from tackle shops or club treasurer; **Loddon Lakes**, members only. Turners Paddock; dt £5 (weekdays only). St £22, conc. Tackle shops: Todber Manor Fisheries Shop, Todber, nr Marnhull DT10 1JB (tel: 01258 820384); Stalbridge Angling, High St, Stalbridge DT10 2TJ (tel: 01963 362291). Hotel: Royal.

Stourton (Wilts). **Stourhead New Lake** on Stourhead (Western) Estate at Stourton, near Mere: now a fly fishing syndicate water; rods from April to September; contact Malcolm Bullen (tel: 01747 840624). National Trust have leased to Gillingham & DAA Stourhead's Turners Paddock Lake; coarse; members, & dt from Todber Manor Fisheries (tel: 01258 820384).

MOORS:

Verwood (Dorset). Trout in parts, otherwise mainly roach; Ringwood club has water.

STOUR (Kent)

(For close seasons, licences etc, see Thames Region Environment Agency, p22).

Rises in two arms north-west and south-east of Ashford, where they join. From junction river flows about 30m north-east and east to sea beyond Sandwich. Below Canterbury, good roach fishing with fish to 2lb common, bream to 6lb and pike over 20lb. Trout fishing restricted to club members in upper reaches.

Sandwich (Kent). River fast-flowing from Minster to Sandwich (Vigo Sluice); good fishing for bream and roach; few perch and tench; sea trout and grey mullet. Free fishing from quay and from Ropewalk; bream, rudd, roach. Private fishing from Richborough Road, upstream. Sandwich & Dist AA has Reed Pond and Swallowbrook Water; and North and South Streams, **Lydden. Stonar Lake** (stocked, carp and rudd) is Canterbury & DAA water; members only. Tackle shop: Sandwich Bait & Tackle, South East Water Gardens, Dover Rd CT13 0DG (tel: 01304 613752). Hotel: Bell.

Grove Ferry. Stour and Little Stour. Betteshanger Colliery Welfare AS has 6m on Stour from **Plucks' Gutter** to **Stonar**. Roach, bream and mullet (Red Lion stretch, June-Aug). Society also has stretch at **Minster**. Tickets from Hon Sec, Red Lion or bailiff on bank.

Canterbury (Kent). Trout, tench, bream, roach, rudd, pike, etc. Free within city boundary for residents, except for municipal gardens stretch. Canterbury & Dist AA hold water from city boundary d/s to Plucks Gutter, 9m both banks; brown trout stocked, run of sea trout; dt £5 on stretch from Grove Ferry bridge to Plucks Gutter, from bailiff on bank; Assn also has Stour and Trenley Lakes, fine coarse fishing, and **Fordwich Lake**, trout pool, members only; Assn also has new water at **Littlebourne Lakes** (3 lakes); carp, tench and perch; all lakes members only; membership £49 to £24.50, + joining fee £24.50 to £12.25. For more information, contact Hon Sec. At Calcott Hill, Sturry, are **Longshaw Farm Fishing Lakes**; carp, tench, perch, roach; dt £6 (tel: 01227 710263). **Tyler Hill Coarse Fishery** (tel: 01227 764048) is open all year; for prices please phone; mixed coarse. Tackle shop: Stour Angling Centre, 53 Sturry Rd, CT1 1BU (tel: 01227 478421); Sandwich Bait & Tackle, South East Water Gardens, Dover Rd, Sandwich CT13 0DG (tel: 01304 613752). Hotels: County; Falstaff; George and Dragon.

Ashford (Kent). Ashford AS holds **River Stour** between **Ashford** and **Wye** (members only). Cinque Ports AS controls 4½m of Royal Military Canal from Seabrook Outfall, Hythe, to Giggers Green, Ashford; st £15 (+ entrance fee £7.50, conc), dt £2, conc 50p, from bailiff. Ashford Working Men's Club has a pit; good tench, carp, rudd; members only; no dt. At **Bethersden** is Chequer Tree Trout & Coarse Fishery, Chequer Tree Lane TN26 3JR (tel: 01233 820078; web: www.chequertreefishery.co.uk); dt £20 (3 trout) to £7 (coarse), conc; licences, tuition, tackle hire and camping facilities on site; no boats; carp to 22lb. Mid Kent Fisheries, Chilham Water Mill, Ashford Rd, Chil-

ham CT4 8EE (tel: 01227 730668) have 18 acre Conningbrook; carp, pike, perch. Tackle shops: Ashford Tackle Shop, Umit 115, Ellingham Way Ind Est, TN23 6LZ (tel: 01233 630914); Dens Tackle, 73 Dymchurch Rd, Hythe CT21 6JN (tel: 01303 267053); Micks Tackle, 1 Thirlestane Dymchurch Rd, Hythe CT21 6LB (tel: 01303 266334). Hotels: County, Kent Arms.

LITTLE STOUR: Same fish as main river but overgrown in places. Most fishing now private.

WANTSUM. Tench, bream, perch, roach, gudgeon, chub, dace, eels and some pike. Wantsum AA controls 120 peg stretch (90 pegs of which available for dt) from 'Chambers Wall' area of St Nicholas-at-Wade and continues to the north where it meets the sea wall; dt £3, juv £0.50 from bailiff on bank. On R Stour, at Pucks Gutter, the club controls 32 pegs on south bank d/s from 'Dog & Duck'; roach, bream, perch, gudgeon and chub; dt £3, juv £0.50 from bailiff on bank. The club also controls a lake complex in East Kent area (members only); memberships available to fish all year round (where permitted); st £35 plus £17.50 joining fee, jnr £20 plus £10 joining fee, conc £22.50 plus £11.25 joining fee; for futher information contact Hon Sec *(See clubs)*. Tackle shop: Kingfisheries, 34 King Str, Margate CT9 1DA (tel: 01843 223866).

STOUR (Suffolk)

(For close seasons, licences etc, see Thames Region Environment Agency, p22).

Coarse fish river forming border between Suffolk and Essex. Enters sea at Harwich via large estuary. Some sea trout in semi-tidal waters below Flatford. Environment Agency are regularly stocking the river with barbel.

Harwich (Essex). Harwich AC has several coarse fisheries in area: Dock River; Bradfield Hall Lakes; The Dykes, Harwich, with roach, rudd, pike, perch, carp, eels, bream; members only; weekly membership sold at Marvens DIY, 691 Main Road, Dovercourt, Harwich CO12 4LZ (tel: 01255 502901).

Manningtree (Essex). Tidal; roach, dace, perch, pike and occasional sea trout (fish of 9lb caught). Lawford AC has stretch at **Cattlewade** (A137 bridge); dt on bank. Dt from bailiff, Mr Tripp, for Elm Park and Hornchurch Dist AS stretch between club notices at **Flatford Mill**; contact bailiff at The Granary, Flatford, East Bergholt, Colchester CO7 6UL (tel: 01206

298111). Hotel: White Hart.

Nayland (Suffolk). Bream, chub, dace, perch, pike, roach, tench. Colchester APS has water here and at **Wiston, Boxted, Langham** and **Stratford St Mary**. New membership £60, to Box 1286, Colchester CO2 8PG; no dt. Colnes AS has stretches at **Little Horkesley**.

Bures (Essex). Colnes AC has stretch. London AA controls a good deal of water at **Bures Lake** and river; also **Main Meadow, Bures Mill Pool** and **Secretaries Farm Fisheries**; members only, but some waters open to associates at Bures.

Henny Bridge (Essex). Great Cornard AC fishes from Henny Bridge to Henny Weir; book a month in advance, dt £1.50. London AA has fisheries at Shalford Meadow; also Edgars Farm and Lamarsh Broad Meadow; members only; membership £39, conc.

Sudbury (Suffolk). Bream, roach, chub, dace, tench, carp, perch, pike, gudgeon. Sudbury & Dist AC has 7 stretches of Stour (dt £5 conc from Sudbury Angling); **Doneylands Lake**, Colchester; **Stantons Farm Reservoir**; membership £33, conc from Sudbury Angling Centre; also for Colchester APS water, **Snake Pit Lake** and (Sudbury & DAC) **Rushbrook Farm Lake**. Information from Tackle Up. Hadleigh & Dist AS have various stretches on Stour, R Brett and 6 local stillwaters; restricted membership £31,

conc, guest tickets offered on rivers; contact Hon Sec. Long Melford & DAA has water from Clare to Sudbury, with coarse species incl large chub, bream, roach, pike to 37lbs; and Suffolk Glem; membership from tackle shops or Hon Sec. Tackle shops: Sudbury Angling, 14 North Str, Sudbury CO10 1RD (tel: 01787 312118); Tackle Up, 49a St Johns Str, Bury St Edmunds IP33 1SP (tel: 01284 755022).

Cavendish and **Clare** (Suffolk). London AA controls water here. At **Glemsford**, the Assn has 3 lakes near the river on the Essex/Suffolk border; members only; membership £39, conc.

SURREY (lakes)

BURY HILL FISHERIES. Nr Dorking. Well known coarse fishery of four lakes, the largest of which is 12½ acres. Particularly known for its tench, roach, carp, bream, pike and zander fishing, all of which run to specimen size; also good stocks of rudd, perch and crucian carp; open all year, bank and boat fishing; tuition courses, full facilities include sit down cafe, all of which are suitable for disabled anglers; dt £11, one rod, second rod £5.50 extra; boat: £5.50 per person; evening £5.50 per rod; concessions to jun, OAP; match bookings and corporate days organised; further details from Fishery Manager, Estate Office, Old Bury Hill, Surrey RH4 3JU (tel: 01306 883621; web: www.buryhillfisheries.com).

FRENSHAM PONDS. Farnham (4m). 60 acres and 30 acres. Farnham AS has rights on Great Pond, and Little Pond, leased from NT; coarse fishing; members of Farnham AS only.

FRIMLEY, nr Camberley. 4 RMC Angling lakes totalling 47 acres stocked with carp to 40lb and all other coarse species. Group Water: st (2 rods) £40, conc £25. *(For RMC Angling, see Chertsey.)*

RIPLEY. **Papercourt** fishery, Sendmarsh. Large carp to over 30lb, pike, bream, tench to 11lb, chub, perch, eels, roach. An RMC Angling Group Water fishery. St £30, conc £18. *(For RMC Angling, see Chertsey.)*

YATELEY COMPLEX, Yateley. This RMC complex consists of 14 lakes and a stretch of R Blackwater. Syndicate Venue: **North** and **Car Park** lakes between them hold carp to 50lbs; £400 pa

2-rods summer/autumn, 3-rods winter; waiting list. Night tickets allow fishing on all the Yateley lakes (except North and Car Park lakes); St £200 4-rods, £160 3-rods, £120 2-rods. **South Lake** and **Sandhurst Lake**, both heavily stocked with carp to 30lb; dt only £6 or 24-hour £10 from Yateley Angling Centre, 16 The Parade GU46 7UN (tel: 01252 861955 (agent RMC)). **Pads Lake** is of 4 acres; famous carp water and up to 10 anglers can book the lake for the day: contact RMC Angling. *(For RMC Angling, see Chertsey.)*

SWAN VALLEY, Pond Farm Lane, **Yateley**. Four lakes with carp to 38lbs, tench to 8lbs, pike to 27lbs; dt £5-£10, night £8-£10, 24 hours £15-£20, from Academy Angling Centre, 80 High St, Sandhurst GU47 8ED (tel: 01252 871452). Tackle shop: Yateley Angling Centre, 16 The Parade GU46 7UN (tel: 01252 861955).

TRILAKES, Yateley Road, **Sandhurst**, Berks GU47 8JQ (tel: 01252 873191): mixed fishery; well stocked with tench, very large carp (common, mirror, crucian, ghost), bream, roach, perch, pike, eels; open 9.30am to 6.30pm or sunset if earlier; open all year; purchase dt on entry, £8; car park, cafe, access for disabled. Tackle shop: Yateley Angling Centre, 16 The Parade GU46 7UN (tel: 01252 861955).

VIRGINIA WATER. Virginia Water, Johnson Pond and Obelisk Pond, Windsor Great Park fishable by season ticket only; coarse fish; st £55 (incl VAT). Early application advised in writing, to

Crown Estate Office, The Great Park, Windsor, Berks SL4 2HT (tel: 01753 860222)(sae).

WILLOW PARK FISHERIES, Youngs Drive, Ash, nr Aldershot GU12 6RE (tel: 01252 325867). Three lakes of 13 acres, mixed fishery stocked with a variety of species: carp (to 31lb), tench and other coarse fish; 120 pegs; bait and refreshments on site; dt on site £10 1 rod, £14 2 rods, and £23 for 24-hours, concession

for jun; disabled facilities.

WINKWORTH LAKES. Winkworth, nr Godalming. National Trust property. Trout fishery (fly fishing and boats only) managed by Godalming AS; st £195, plus entry fee of £90; details from Hon Sec; club also has Birtley House, one lake at Bramley; trout; fly only; apply Hon Sec.

WIREMILL POOL, nr **Lingfield.** Coarse fish include tench up to 6lb, bream up to 7lb, roach up to 3lb, carp up to 6lb.

SUSSEX (lakes and streams)

ARDINGLY RESERVOIR. Ardingly, nr Haywards Heath. 198 acre coarse fishery with excellent pike, fish to 30lbs, also good stocks of bream, roach, tench etc; coarse season 1st June-31st May; pike season 1 Oct-1 May. (Only very experienced specialist pike anglers allowed, 18+). Enq to The Lodge, Ardingly Reservoir, Ardingly, W Sussex RH17 6SQ (tel: 01444 892591).

ARLINGTON RESERVOIR, South East Water, Fishing Lodge, Berwick, Polegate BN26 6TF (tel: 01323 870810). Excellent rainbow trout fishery. Dt and members tickets from self-service lodge on site (tackle for sale/hire); special membership rates on request. Boats and engines for hire (best to book). Disabled boat and platform.

BARCOMBE RESERVOIR, nr Lewes, BN8 5BY. 40 acres, South East Water, fly fishing for rainbow trout only. Information from Fishing Lodge (tel: 01273 814819); dt from self-service lodge.

BUXTED. Uckfield. Oast Farm, Lephams Bridge, TN22 4AU (tel: 01825 733446; web: www.oastfarm.co.uk): coarse pond, with carp, roach, tench; dt at farm shop: Mr Greenland. Boringwheel Trout Fishery, Cackle St, TN22 3DU **Nutley** (tel: 01825 712629); brown and rainbow; dt from fishery. Tackle shop: Uckfield Angling Centre, 212A High St, Uckfield TN22 1RD (tel: 01825 760300).

CHICHESTER CANAL. Chichester (W Sussex). Chichester Canal Trading has 2½m from Chichester to Donnington Bridge, with roach, rudd, perch, carp, tench, bream, pike, eels, chub and dace; no fish to be removed; st £40, wt £8.50, dt £3.50, conc, from bailiffs on bank. Southern Anglers have 1¾m south from A27 road, with tench, carp, roach, perch, pike; 24 hr fishing; annual subscription £40, conc. Chichester & DAA have free

canal fishing. Mixed fishery at Lakeside Village, Vinnetrow Road, PO20 1QH (tel: 01243 787715); 12 lakes; carp, perch, pike, rudd, roach, bream, tench; dt £5 from office, or £8 on bank (24hrs); conc; no boats. Tackle shops: Southern Angling Specialists, 2 Stockbridge Place, Stockbridge Rd, PO19 2QH (tel: 01243 531669); Shore Line Angling, 7 Shore Rd, East Wittering, PO20 8DY (tel: 01243 673353). Selsey tackle shop: Raycrafts, 119 High Str, Selsey PO20 0QB (tel: 01243 606039), sells canal angling tickets.

LAKE VIEW FISHERIES. 1m SE of Crawley. 8 acre estate lake; carp to 25lb, tench, crucians, perch to 4lb; dt from bailiff or Jack Frost Tackle, Reynolds Place, West Green, Crawley RH11 7HB (tel: 01293 421351/521186; web: www.jfon line.co.uk).

DARWELL WATER. At Mountfield, **Robertsbridge** TN32 5DR (tel: 01580 881407; mobile 0771 3093 606), coarse fish; 180 acres; leased from Southern Water; dt £10 (3 rods) pike; other £7 (3 rods); boats £8 day extra, to be booked 48 hrs in advance from bailiff. Take care over approach route down small lanes.

FRAMFIELD PARK FISHERY, Brookhouse Rd, Framfield, nr Uckfield TN22 5QJ (tel: 01825 890948). Three coarse fishing lakes totalling over 17 acres. Good match weights, with large tench, bream and carp. Shop on site. Bailiff will give instruction free to juniors.

POWDERMILL WATER. Sedlescombe. 52 acres, brown and rainbow trout to 20lb; dt £16.50 6 fish, conc. Boats available. For membership, contact Hon Sec, Hastings Flyfishers Club Ltd. Bookings: tel: 01424 870498 between 9.30 and 10.30am.

MILTON MOUNT LAKE. Three Bridges (W Sussex). Crawley AS water (st £50);

carp; members only (guest dt available); Club also has **Standford Brook** (trout; fly only) in Tilgate Forest; Campbells Lake, carp to 30lb+, tench to 11lb, bream, pike to 28lb, roach &c; New Pond, Pease Pottage (carp and crucian carp, tench); the Mill Pond, Gossops Green; Buchan Park lakes, nr **Crawley**, carp, pike etc; dt £6 on some waters, from Jack Frost Tackle, Reynolds Place, West Green, Crawley RH11 7HB (tel: 01293 421351/521186; web: www.jfonline. co.uk).

CLIVE VALE RESERVOIRS. Harold Road: mixed coarse fishery, Clive Vale AC; st £35, junior £17; dt £4.50, junior £2.50.

ECCLESBOURNE RESERVOIR. Hastings. Good carp, tench, roach, bream pike and rudd. Now privately fished: no tickets. Tackle shops: Steve's Tackle, 38 White Rock, Hastings TN34 1JL (tel: 01424 433404; web: www.steves tackle.co.uk); A R Tackle, 8 Castle St, Hastings TN34 3DY (tel: 01424 422094); Hastings Angling Centre, 33-35 The Bourne, Hastings Old Town (tel: 01424 432178).

PEVENSEY LEVELS. Marshland drained by various streams into **Pevensey Haven** and **Wallers Haven**; good coarse fishing on large streams (pike, roach, rudd, perch, bream, carp and tench), most of best waters rented by clubs. Fishing stations: **Eastbourne, Hailsham, Pevensey**. Southdown AA has major stretches of Pevensey Haven between Pevensey and Rickney, also Railland's Ditch and Chilley Stream (tench, bream, rudd, perch, carp and eels); both banks of Wallers Haven (renowned pike, tench and bream); water on **R Cuckmere** on both banks between Horsebridge and Alfriston, Abbots Wood and three other small lakes at Arlington, stocked with large carp, and other species. Tickets, st £50 + £10 joining fee, no dt, from Hon Sec at Polegate Angling Centre, 101 Station Road, Polegate BN26 6EB (tel: 01323 486379); or from Anglers Den, 6 North Rd, Pevensey Bay.

SCARLETTS LAKE. 3 acres, between E Grinstead and **Tunbridge Wells**. Good coarse fishing, roach to 3lb 15oz, carp incl (free st offered to any angler beating record carp, 29lb 8oz) dt £6.50, conc, at lakeside; st £70 from lakeside or Jackson, Scarletts Lake, Furnace Lane, Cowden, Edenbridge, Kent TN8 7JT (tel: 01342 850414).

WEIR WOOD RESERVOIR. Forest Row (Priory Road) (W Sussex), 1½m; **East Grinstead**; 280 acres. Now wholly coarse: yearly £200 day and night, dt £8 1

Some say that if you can't get to an Irish Blackwater, this kind of fishing takes some beating! Here the anglers fish at Boringwheel Trout Fishery, Nutley.

A 1½lb brown trout is carefully returned to the water. *Photo: Press Manor Fisheries, Chesterfield*

rod, £10 2 rods; boat £10/day (24 hour notice), honesty box; enquiries to Peter Knight, Stone Cottage, Ridgeway Road, Dorking RH4 3EY (tel: 01306 882708).

Tackle shop: Mike Wickams Fishing Tackle, 4 Middle Row, E Grinstead RH19 3AY (tel: 01342 315073).

TAMAR

(For close seasons, licences etc, see South West Region Environment Agency, p19)

Rises in Cornwall and follows boundary between Devon and Cornwall for good part of course, emptying finally into Plymouth Sound. Holds salmon, sea trout, brown trout to the pound not uncommon.

Milton Abbot (Devon). Endsleigh Fishing Club has 12m, salmon and sea trout; dt £15-£45. Average salmon catch 230; 90% taken on fly. Good car access to pools; tuition on site. Apply to Melanie Healy, 52 Strode Rd, Fulham, London SW6 6BN (tel: 020 7610 1982).

Lifton (Devon). Tamar, **Lyd**, **Thrushel**, **Carey**, **Wolf** and **Ottery**; trout, sea trout (late June to end Sept), salmon (May, to mid-October). Hotel: Arundell Arms, Lifton, Devon PL16 0AA (tel: 01566 784666; fax: 01566 784494; web: www.arundellarms.com), has 20m of excellent water in lovely surroundings; 23 individual beats, also 3-acre trout lake, brown and rainbow trout to 9lb. Licences and tackle at hotel, fly fishing courses (beginners and semi-advanced) by two resident instructors. Dt (when there are vacancies) for S

s & st £22-£25, according to date; lake trout £25, brown trout £22. *(See advt).*

Launceston (Cornwall). Salmon, sea trout, trout. Permits can be obtained for seven miles of Tamar, also **Ottery**, **Kensey**, **Inney** and **Carey** from Launceston AA; dt, which has about 16m of fishing in all. Lakes and ponds: **Stone Lake**, 4½ acres coarse fishing. **Tredidon Barton Lakes** PL15 8SJ, dt £5; mixed coarse, carp to 20lb (tel: 0156686 288). **Alder Quarry Pond**, Lewdown, Okehampton EX20 4PJ (tel: 01566 783444), 4½ acres, coarse, dt water. **Dutson Water**, coarse fishing dt £5 from Holmleigh Garden Centre.

ne of the most famous sporting hotels in England, the Arundell Arms has 20 miles of its own fishing on the Tamar, Lyd, Carey, Wolf and Thrushel. Delicate dry fly fishing for wild brown trout, exciting mid-summer, night seatrout fishing, salmon from mid-May and a beat of your own on some of the most beautiful moorland-fed rivers in Devon.

We also run courses for beginners and give advanced tuition on river and lake fishing.

An all-round sporting hotel that is warm and comfortable and noted for friendliness, good food and good wine.

- *AA 3 rosetted restaurant.*
- *Skilled instruction and advice.*
- *2 and 4 day beginners' courses*
- *Stocked 3 acre lake.*
- *Shooting, hunting, riding, golf.*

Details from Anne Voss-Bark

THE ARUNDELL ARMS

Lifton, Devon PL16 0AA
Tel: 01566 784666 Fax: 01566 784494
e-mail: reservations@arundellarms.com

Tackle shop: Homeleigh Garden Centre, Dutson, Launceston PL15 9SP (tel: 01566 773147). Hotels: White Hart; Eagle House; Race Horse Inn, North Hill.
Bridgerule (Devon). **Tamar Lakes** here: South West Lakes Trust waters for which tickets are issued, *(See Cornwall lakes).*

13 lakes (total 34 acres) coarse fishing lakes, with various carp species, orfe, tench, and others; contact J Ray, Clawford Vineyard, Holsworthy EX22 6PN (tel: 01409 254177); B&B on site. Hotel: Court Barn, Clawton, Holsworthy.

Tributaries of the Tamar

TAVY: A moorland spate river, rises in Cranmere Pool on Dartmoor and flows about 17m before entering Tamar estuary at Bere Ferrers. Excellent salmon and sea-trout river.
Tavistock (Devon). Tavy, Walkham and Plym FC; limited membership; salmon, sea trout and brown trout permits for visitors on main river, **Meavy**, **Plym** and **Walkham**; spinning allowed but no natural baits; salmon and sea trout st £125, dt £17.50; brown trout st £40, mt £20, wt £15, dt £5, from Tavistock Trout Fishery *(below)*; Yelverton Garage, 1 Moorland Villas PL20 6DT (tel: 01822 853339).
Tavistock Trout Fishery, Parkwood Rd, Mount Tavy PL19 9JW (tel: 01822 615441): 1m from A386 towards Oakhampton, nr Trout 'n' Tipple Hotel (tel: 01822 61886); fishing on five lakes beside R Tavy; dt 7 days a week; rods for hire £5, plus permit; well stocked children's fishing lake; fly tackle shop. Other Hotel: Bedford (salmon and trout fishing on Tamar and Tavy).
Mary Tavy (Devon). Brown trout; late run of salmon and sea trout. Fishing mostly privately owned. Plymouth & Dist Freshwater AA has rights at **Peter Tavy** (members only, st £95 from Hon Sec.
Yelverton (Devon). Good centre for Tavy, Walkham and Plym FC waters. Salmon, sea trout. Ticket suppliers listed under Tavistock. **Coombe Fisheries**, Miltoncombe: two 1 acre lakes with rudd, roach, tench, bream, ghost carp in top lake; various carp in bottom lake. Open all year, dawn till dusk, barbless hooks only; contact S Horn, New Venn Farm, Lamerton, Tavistock PL19 8RR (tel: 01822 616624).
WALKHAM (tributary of Tavy): rises north-west of Princetown, and joins the Tavy below Tavistock. Upper reaches rocky and overhung, but downstream from Horrabridge there are many fishable pools. Peal run from July onwards.
INNY: Trout, sea trout.
LYD: Trout, sea trout, some salmon.
Lifton (Devon). Arundell Arms *(see advt)* has fishing for salmon, sea trout and brown trout, also on main river and other tributaries.

TAW

(For close seasons, licences etc, see South West Region Environment Agency, p19)

Rises on Dartmoor and flows 50m to Barnstaple Bay, where it forms estuary. Salmon with sea trout (peal) from May onwards. Excellent brown trout always available and good coarse fishing in places nearby: links with local fisheries.

Barnstaple (Devon). Bass and mullet in estuary. Salmon, sea trout, peal, trout, roach and dace. Salmon best March, April, May; peal July, August. Barnstaple & Dist AA has water immediately below New Bridge; and on **Yeo** (trout and sea trout); and on ponds; members only; membership/st £30 from Hon Sec; and from local tackle shop. Riverton House and Lakes, **Swimbridge**, EX32 0QX (tel: 01271 830009), has coarse fishing on two 2 acre lakes with large carp, bream, tench, roach, perch, rudd; night fishing by prior arrangement: dt £5, half day £3.50; self-catering cottages and B&B on site. At

Braunton, coarse fishing at Little Comfort Farm, EX33 2NJ (tel: 01271 812414; web: www.littlecomfortfarm.co.uk) with carp over 16lbs; dt on site £6-£3; self catering cottages; apply Mr & Mrs Milsom. C L and Mrs Hartnoll, Little Bray House, **Brayford** EX32 7QG (tel: 01598 710295); who also have about 1m (both banks) of Bray; small trout only; dt £2. For other trout fishing see tributary Yeo. East and West Lyns, Badgeworthy Water and Heddon are accessible, as well as fishing on Wistlandpound and Slade Reservoirs. Tackle shop: The Kingfisher, 22 Castle Str, EX31 1DR (tel: 01271

344919) supplies local tickets and information.

Chapelton (Devon). Salmon, peal, trout, dace. Taw private down to New Bridge.

Umberleigh (Devon). Salmon, peal, trout; preserved. Rising Sun, EX37 9DU (tel: 01769 560447; web: www.risingsuninn. com) rents rods to give access to almost 4m of water (eight beats) for residents; fly only after April 30; sunday fishing is allowed; salmon best March, April, May, August and September; sea trout June, July, August and September; brochure, giving charges, etc, on request; dt £45. Other hotel: Northcote Manor, Burrington.

South Molton (Devon). Oaktree Fishery, Bottreaux Mill, EX36 3PU (tel: 01398 341568), has three well-stocked lakes: two match, one specimen, large carp, tench, roach, open all year; dt £5, £6 two rods, conc, at fishery.

Eggesford, Chulmleigh (Devon). Fox & Hounds Country Hotel, EX18 7JZ (tel: 01769 580345), has 7m of private salmon, sea trout and brown trout fishing on Taw (4 beats); spinning March to Apr; fly only from Apr 1; no fishing in Feb; dt £30; visiting ghillie, tuition; limited

tackle on sale; 3 day fishing packages: full details from hotel.

Coldridge (Devon). Taw Fishing Club has water from Brushford Bridge to Hawkridge Bridge; very good trout fishing; complimentary for members' guests only; st £60 + joining fee £60; limited to 30. Also Crediton FFC has access: contact Hon Sec.

Chenson (Devon). Chenson Fishery, salmon from 1 Mar, sea trout from Apr, trout; st only; contact Jon Needham, Chennestone Cottage, Chenson, Chulmleigh EX18 7LF (tel: 01363 83411).

North Tawton (Devon). Trout. K Dunn, The Barton EX20 2BB (tel: 01837 82129) also issues dt for about 1m.

YEO (Barnstaple): Sea and brown trout. Barnstaple & Dist AA has water on Yeo, st from Barnstaple tackle shop. *(See Barnstaple).*

BRAY (tributary of Mole):

South Molton (Devon). South Molton AC has right bank from Brayly Bridge u/s to Newton Bridge, with salmon, trout and peal, fly only; members only. Tackle shop: Sports Centre, 130 East St, South Molton, EX36 3BU (tel: 01769 572080). Hotels: The George; The Tiverton.

TEES

(For close seasons, licences etc, see North East Region Environment Agency, p20)

Rises below Cross Fell in Pennines, flows eastward between Durham and Yorkshire and empties into North Sea near Middlesbrough. The Tees Barrage was completed in June 1995, and has already created a much cleaner river, upstream. Fish are being caught throughout all previously tidal stretches, from the new Princess of Wales Bridge to Thornaby and above. Well stocked from Middleton-in-Teesdale down to Croft.

Middlesbrough (Cleveland). NWA reservoirs **Lockwood** and **Scaling Dam** in vicinity. Stocked with trout; dt on site. Middlesbrough AA have R Tees at Over Dinsdale, Thornaby and Preston Park, **Stockton**; trout, salmon and usual coarse fish, 8 stretches of **R Swale** at Ainderby, Gatenby, Maunby, Skipton, Kirby Wiske, Danotty Hall, Holme and Baldersby, Marske Reservoir (stocked with carp) and ponds, all good coarse fishing. Local tackle shops: Anglers Choice, 53 Clive Rd, Middlesbrough TS5 6BH (tel: 01642 850428), who has st £27 (+ £10 entry), conc, for Middlesbrough AA waters; Cleveland Angling Centre, 2 Westbury St, Thornaby, Stockton on Tees TS17 6PG (tel: 01642 677000).

Stockton (Cleveland). Trout; grayling, coarse fish on one of best stretches of

river. Stockton AA has over 10m at **Gainford, Winston, Middleton-one-Row,** nr Darlington, **Aislaby,** nr Yarm, and on **Swale,** nr **Ainderby** (Morton-on-Swale) and above Great Langton, lower reaches of Tees and Swale fishings. Free stretches in the Stockton town area; fish well for silver fish (roach, perch and bream). Lower Tees AC has good stretch from Bowesfield Lane upstream to Thornaby; bream; tickets from Tackle Box, who also sell tickets for **Charlton's Pond,** Billingham (carp to 20lb, tench and bream to 6lb; 6 acres). **Hartlepool Reservoir** is coarse fishery run by Hartlepool & Dist AC; contact Hon Sec; members only; st £35, conc. Tackle shop: Flynn's Fishing Tackle, 12 Varo Terrace, Stockton TS18 1JY (tel: 01642 676473); Tackle Box, 46 Station Rd, Billingham TS23 1AB (tel:

01642 532034). Stockton Tees permits are sold at Anglers Choice, 53 Clive Rd, Middlesbrough TS5 6BH (tel: 01642 850428).

Eaglescliffe, (Cleveland). Yorkshire bank in Yarm free fishing. **Leven** joins just below Yarm. Trout and coarse fish. Middlesbrough AA to above falls; Thornaby AA and Yarm AA together up to Hutton Rudby; excellent brown trout fishing; occasional sea trout.

Yarm (Cleveland). Tidal good coarse fishing; chub, dace, roach, occasional trout. Some free fishing inside of loop surrounding town, ½m, on E.A. licence. Mixed fishery, deep, slow moving water. Yarm AA, strong team club with 15m of Tees fishing at Low Middleton, Yarm, Over Dinsdale, Sockburn and Piercebridge; members of Assn. of Teeside & Dist Angling Clubs, with 10m water; £38 + entry fee.

Neasham (Durham). Free fishing for 300 yards behind Fox and Hounds pub (mixed fishery).

Sockburn (Durham). Chub, dace, roach. Approx 3m controlled by Assn of Teesside & Dist Angling Clubs, which consists of Thornaby AA, Yarm AA, Darlington Brown Trout Anglers and Stockton Anglers; no dt.

Croft (Durham). Fair head of trout, grayling and coarse fish. Free fishing for 200 yds upstream of road bridge. Several miles controlled by Thornaby Anglers, members only, application forms from W P Adams (*see Darlington*).

Darlington (Durham). Trout, grayling, coarse fish; occasional salmon. Council water free to residents. Darlington AC fish 10½m between Croft, Darlington and High Coniscliffe, and 1m of **Clow Beck**, 3m S of Darlington; north bank; strictly for members only. Darlington Brown Trout AA has water at Middleton One Row, also on **Swale**; dt for members' guests only. Stockton AA has water at **Winston**, Gainford and Winston. Hartlepool & Dist AC fishes 1¼m single bank; excellent pike; members only; st £35; contact Hon Sec. Tackle shops: W P Adams Fishing Tackle & Guns, 42 Duke Str, DL3 7AJ (tel: 01325 468069) (has permits for several small coarse ponds in vicinity, and for R Tees fishing); Darlington Angling Centre, 341 North Rd, DL1 3BL (tel: 01325 481818).

Piercebridge (Durham). Trout, grayling, dace, chub, gudgeon; st for Raby Estates

water, £65 trout, £45 coarse; Estate Office, Staindrop, Darlington DL2 3NF (tel: 01833 660207). Otherwise preserved. Hotel: George.

Gainford (Durham). Trout, grayling, coarse fish. Up to Winston, most of the water held by Stockton AA; no tickets. Alwent Beck, 1m W; trout; private. Langton Beck, 2m N.

Barnard Castle (Durham). Trout, grayling. Free fishing on south bank d/s from stone bridge to Thorngate footbridge. Taking of salmon prohibited. M Hutchinson, Thorngate Mill, has fishing offered. At **Eggleston** Bishop Aukland AC has 3½m of Teise; members only; salmon and sea trout may be taken. Barnard Castle FFC has water from Tees Viaduct to Baxton Gill, near **Cotherstone**, private club water; stretch above Abbey Bridge to beyond Tees Viaduct on south bank, and from Lendings caravan park to Tees Viaduct on south bank. Barnard Castle AC has from a point below Abbey Bridge to Tees Viaduct on north bank; private club water, but some dt to visitors staying locally. Darlington FFC has 2½m above and below Abbey Bridge, 1m below Barnard Castle. Water holds trout and grayling; members only; club also has 2m one bank of River Greta; 2 beats; members only. Grassholme (dt £16 8 fish, conc), Selset and Balderhead (dt £7 8 fish), Blackton (dt £17 8 fish, conc) and Hury (dt £6; coarse) reservoirs, 5m NW; dt obtainable for all from Grassholme fishing lodge (tel: 01833 641121, 7am to 3pm; web: www.nwl.co.uk/leisure); Northumbrian Water Ltd waters (NW) (*see Tees Valley Reservoirs*). **Langlands Lake** fly fishing, Langlands Farm, **Barningham**, Richmond DL11 7ED (tel: 01833 621317), rainbow trout, dt £9, joint father and son dt £12. All local permits from F E Wilkinson Guns, 40 Horsemarket, Barnard Castle DL12 8NA (tel: 01833 631118). Hotel: King's Head, Market Place.

Mickleton (Durham). Trout. Strathmore Estate water, st £65, wt £40, dt £12, conc, st for salmon/trout £125, for S bank between Cronkley Bridge and County Bridge in Middleton in Teesdale; J Raine & Son, 25 Market Place DL12 0QA (tel: 01833 640406). Hotel: Teesdale, Middleton.

Middleton in Teesdale (Durham). Trout (plentiful but small), a few late salmon. Several miles open to dt on Raby Estate water (tel: 01833 640209, office hours); dt from J Raine & Son 25 Market Place, Middleton-in-Teesdale, or Estate Office. Tickets available for Strathmore Estate water, on south bank between Cronkley Bridge and County Bridge from tackle shop; fly only, dt £12 (trout), wt £40, st £65; £125 (salmon & trout). Tackle shops: F E Wilkinson Gun Shop, 40 Horsemarket, Barnard Castle DL12 8NA (tel: 01833 631118).

GRETA: Trout.

Bowes (Durham). All private fishing.

TEIGN

(For close seasons, licences etc, see South West Region Environment Agency, p19)

Rises from two sources high on Dartmoor, which form the North and South Teign, joining west of Chagford while still small streams. Between Chagford and Steps Bridge river runs through a wooded gorge, which is best fished around Fingle bridge. Upper Teign contains trout, sea trout and salmon. Principal tributary is Bovey. Salmon, sea trout (peal) and brown trout. Teign usually fishes best for salmon from late May to September. River flows to sea through an estuary beginning below Newton Abbot

Newton Abbot (Devon). Salmon, sea trout, trout; preserved by Lower Teign FA from Sowton Weir to Teignbridge (stretch from New Bridge to Preston Footbridge members only); three separate beats; dt (3 per beat) £20, valid for 24 hrs from sunrise; spinning by day, at night fly only; Assn also has 3m on Bovey, members only *(see Bovey)*. Newton Abbot FA has six lakes at **Rackerhayes**; 1 for juniors only; full members only on **Island Pond** and parts of **Dores Pond**; four at **Kingsteignton**, five ponds at **Coombe-in-**

Teignhead (good dt water); one full members water at **Bovey Tracey**; newly acquired pond beside Stover Canal, and extra waters in Somerset. Fisheries contain carp to 36lbs, pike to 20lbs, large tench to 11lb, roach, rudd, perch, bream; dt £5, conc, on some of these waters; senior full membership £50, conc; coarse fish, including carp. **Watercress Farm**, Chudleigh TQ13 0DW, 4 acres trout fishing (tel: 01626 852168). **Trago Mills** has 600 yds coarse fishing, dt £3, OAP, jun £2; G Mole (tel: 01626 821111). Decoy

This angler on a shallow stretch of the Teign in Devonshire requires no lessons in casting. *Photo: Roddy Rae.*

Lake, small coarse lake open all year, stocked. Tackle shop: Tackle Trader, 2 Wharf Road, TQ12 2DA (tel: 01626 331613).

Chudleigh (Devon). Salmon, sea trout, trout; Lower Teign FA has water (*see Newton Abbot*). 2½ acre coarse lake at Finlake Woodland Village; dt water in winter; residents only in summer 31 Mar to 31 Oct. Newton Abbot FA has Wapperwell Pond here; dt, seniors only.

Chagford (Devon). Salmon, sea trout, brown trout; Upper Teign FA preserves about 14m in all, on left and right bank, fly only before June 1 on some parts and whole season elsewhere; size limit 8". Full annual sub £150, trout membership £55, juv conc; apply Hon Sec. Brown trout st £40, wt £17.50, dt £5; salmon and sea trout dt £15; from PO Drewsteignton and James Bowden & Son, The Square, Chagford TQ13 8AH (tel: 01647 433271); also limited sea trout dt on 2 short stretches, Chagford Weir, £7. Limited temporary members salmon and sea trout dt £15, from Fingle Bridge Inn, Drewsteignton, Exeter EX6 6PW (tel: 01647 281287); seasons; salmon: 1 Feb to 30 Sept; sea and browns: 15 Mar to 30 Sept. Devon and UK Fly Fishing School offers salmon and sea trout fishing and instruction; 7 Herons Brook, Okehampton, EX20 1UW (tel: 01837 54731; web: www.flyfishing-uk.co.uk). Fernworthy Reservoir, 3½m.

Tributary of the Teign.

BOVEY: Salmon, sea trout, trout.

Bovey (Devon). On Bovey and Teign. Fishing above Bovey preserved by landowners and below by Lower Teign FA; no tickets. Lakes: Tottiford (coarse) and Kennick Reservoirs (stocked rainbows), South West Lakes Trust waters; (*see Devon lakes, streams, etc*). Hotels: Manor House, one mile from North Bovey (water on Bovey and Bowden, and salmon and trout fisheries on Teign); Glebe House, North Bovey.

TEST

(For close seasons, licences etc, see Southern Region Environment Agency, p18).

Rises from springs in the chalk near Overton, above Whitchurch and flows via Stockbridge and Romsey to enter Southampton Water. Brown and rainbow trout, salmon run as far as Romsey. The Test and Itchen Association represents virtually all riparian owners and many who wish to fish these rivers and their tributaries. The secretary maintains a register of rods to let *(see clubs list)*. Roxton Bailey Robinson let beats on a daily, weekly and seasonal basis: 25 High St, Hungerford, RG17 0NF (tel: 01488 683222).

Romsey (Hants). Trout and grayling fishing good; salmon fishing good below the town, all preserved by the different landowners. Test Valley Angling Club has various lakes and river stretches in vicinity, and also water from Eastleigh across to Romsey, covering Marchwood and Totton. Subscriptions are £75 + £15 joining fee, £30 + £5 joining jun, £50 + £10 joining fee OAP; contact Hon Sec. **Broadlands Estates** has salmon fishing on 3 beats of ¾m each; sea trout (up to 100 each year, av 2½lb); and trout fishing on three ¾m beats of Test and on 3m carrier stream. Average season salmon catch, 25 fish, average weight 7½ lb; salmon rods and ½ rods, a named day per week for two for £1090 and a named day for two per fortnight for £545. Trout fishing st for one rod (1 day per week) is £1,480 and £740 (1 day per fortnight), 2 brace + c&r, dry fly and upstream nymph. Trout fishing in carrier stream, st £1,200, 2 people. There is also an excellent 2½ acre pleasure fishery with large carp, roach, bream, tench; enquiries: Estate Of-

---

Keep the banks clean

Several Clubs have stopped issuing tickets to visitors because the state of the banks after they have left. Spend a few moments clearing up.

fice, Broadlands, Romsey SO51 9ZE (tel: 01794 518885); fisheries Manager, John Dennis (tel: 023 8073 9438). Dt for residents from Council Offices, Duttons Road, for Romsey Memorial Park; limited to two rods daily; salmon, few small trout, grayling, coarse fish. For Tanyard beat, opp Broadlands, contact Brian Lown (tel: 01784 452410; mob: 07801 227095); syndicates of four only. Good trout fishing at **Two Lakes**, near Romsey *(see Hampshire, streams, lakes, etc)*.

Stockbridge (Hants). Greyhound Hotel has water stocked with brown and rainbow trout; Dry fly and nymph only; fish average 3lb; dt £90 outside mayfly season,

otherwise £110; 2 fish limit; instruction can be arranged. Early booking advisable as rods are limited; special fishing/accommodation package can be arranged: Tom Renshaw (tel: 01264 810833). Tackle from Orvis, Bridge House, High Str, SO20 6HB (tel: 01264 810017).

Awbridge (Hants). Fishing Breaks Ltd, Walton House, 23 Compton Terrace, London N1 2UN (tel: 020 7359 8818; web: www.fishingbreaks.com) has rods here; also on **R Itchen**, **Avon** above Amesbury, and **R Dever, Wallop Brook, R Nadder, R Wylye, R Kennet, R Piddle** and **R Frome**; dt £125 on Arle.

Fullerton Bridge (Hants). Trout (av 2lb 8oz). Season mid-April to end of Sept.

Tributaries of the Test

WALLOP BROOK:

Nether Wallop (Hants). Fishing Breaks Ltd, Walton House, 23 Compton Terrace, London N1 2UN (tel: 020 7359 8818; web: www.fishing breaks.com) has day rods.

ANTON: Trout, grayling.

Andover (Hants). Anton joins Test at Testcombe Bridge. Trout and grayling; all preserved. Andover AC owns Foxcotte Lake at **Charlton**, 50 to 60 pegs approx. Usual coarse species; also has access to Broadlands Lake at **Romsey** and **Basingstoke Canal**; dt from tackle shop John Eadie Ltd, 5 Union Str, Andover SP10 1PA (tel: 01264 351469) or Charlton PO. **Dever Springs Trout Fishery**, Barton Stacey SO21 3NP: 2 lakes, 7 acres and river (contact tel: 01264 720592). Tackle shop: John Eadie Ltd, 5 Union Str, Andover SP10 1PA (tel: 01264 351469). Hotels: Star and Garter, White Hart, Junction, George, Anton Arms, Globe

Central.

PILL HILL BROOK: Trout, grayling.

Amport and Monxton (Hants). Trout and grayling. Nearly as long as Anton, but pure chalk-stream. Monxton Mill reach greatly improved and contains full head of locally bred brown trout averaging 14oz, with occasional heavier fish. Fishing preserved by landowners. Dry-fly only.

DEVER: Trout, grayling. Dever joins Test at Newton Stacey.

Bullington. Fishing Breaks Ltd, Walton House, 23 Compton Terrace, London N1 2UN (tel: 020 7359 8818; web: www. fishingbreaks.com) has rods here. For trout fishing on 1,000 yds at head of river, and three lakes, D Henning, Chapel Cottage, Old Lane, Ashford Hill RG19 8BG. Day and season rods offered.

BOURNE:

St Mary Bourne (Hants). Bourne joins Test above Longparish.

THAMES

(For close seasons, licences, etc, see Thames Region Environment Agency, p22).

Second longest river in England. Tidal reaches much recovered from pollution and fish returning in considerable numbers. The river is now considered the cleanest metropolitan estuary in the world. Salmon and sea trout in river, together with dace, roach, flounder, bream, perch, carp and smelt; rainbow trout are caught quite regularly in the freshwater tideway. River worth fishing from Southwark Bridge upstream. Downstream of this point, estuarine species such as eel, flounder, bass and even whiting may be caught. Above Teddington Lock boat traffic largely spoils sport in summer, except in weir pools, but fishing can be good early and late. River fishes well from October to March. Holds good stock of coarse fish, with excellent bream and barbel in some stretches. Perch seem to be making a welcome return to the river throughout its length. However, the tremendous dace fishing of recent years has declined. Bream, roach and perch now dominate the lower river, above Teddington, with chub becoming more numerous the further up the river one goes. Among famous tributaries are Kennet, which comes in at Reading and is one of best mixed fisheries in England. Trout and coarse fish run large. Higher up, Coln, Evenlode and Windrush are noted trout streams, but for most part are very strictly preserved and fishing difficult to obtain. Fishing on Thames open up to City Stone at Staines. Above, permission often necessary and lock-keepers and local tackle shops should be consulted. Thames Environment Agency issues annual permits on eighteen locks and weirs, and these are entered below, in the appropriate section of the text. The Thames Angling Preservation Society, founded in 1838, has restocked seven tributaries - now keeps close watch on water quality and fish stocks in whole Thames basin. It is not a fishing club, but a fishery preservation society supported by anglers, membership details from secretary, A E Hodges, The Pines, 32 Tile Kiln Lane, Bexley, Kent DA5 2BB. London Anglers Association (LAA, Izaak Walton use, 2A Hervey Park Road, London E17 6LJ) still has Eton Wick.

London Docklands. Redevelopment has led to increased angling facilities at **Shadwell, Millwall, Royal Docks** and **Southwark,** each locality with its own angling society.

Isleworth to **London Bridge** (G London). Tidal. Dace, flounder, eel, roach, perch, with some carp and bream. Juvenile bass common at seaward end of this stretch; free from towpath or boats and foreshore throughout Central London 2 hrs each side of low tide. Fly-fishing for dace on shallows when tide is down. Reach down past Chiswick Eyot can be good for roach, dace; towpath only; free. Tackle shop: Hounslow Angling Centre, 265 Bath Road, Hounslow TW3 3DA (tel: 020 8570 6156).

Richmond (G London). Tidal below Teddington Lock, non-tidal above. Down to Isleworth is fishing for roach, dace, bream, perch, eel, the odd chub; free from towpath or boats. Barnes and Mortlake APS are local club, with water on Grand Union Canal at Brentford from Thames Lock to Clitheroe Lock (dt on bank), and **'Clockhouse Pool'** at Bedfont Country Park. In Richmond Park **Pen Ponds** hold pike, carp (leather, mirror, common, ghost), tench and perch; open 16 Jun to 14 Mar; st £17, conc £9 (I.D. required); apply in person to Park Superintendent at The Royal Parks Agency, Holly Lodge, Richmond Park, Richmond, TW10 5HS (tel: 020 8948 3209; fax: 020 8332 2730; e-mail: richmond@royalparks.gsi.gov. uk); or obtain by writing an application form with proof of rod licence ownership (enclose sae). Tickets on bank day and night for coarse fishing in Potoma Lake, Gunnersbury Park. Near Epsom CAL-PAC has Stew Ponds on the Epsom Common; mixed coarse; dt on bank £5. Tackle shop: Ron's Fishing Tackle Shop, 465 Upper Richmond Rd West, East Sheen SW14 7PU (tel: 020 8876 4897); Surbiton Angling Centre, 177 Hook Rd, Surbiton KT6 5AR (tel: 020 8391 4110).

Twickenham (G London). Coarse fishing; free from boats and towpath. Deeps hold barbel, roach, bream, eel, carp. Corporation allow fishing from Radnor, Orleans and Terrace Gardens. Syon Park Trout Fishery, Brentford, managed by Albury Estate Fisheries, Estate Office, Albury, Guildford GU5 9AF (tel: 01483 202323). Tackle shop: Guns and Tackle, 81 High Str, Whitton TW2 7LD (tel: 0208 898 3129). Hotels: Bird's Nest, White Swan.

Teddington (G London). Thames holds dace, roach, bream, eel, perch; free fishing from towpath. **Molesey Lock** is fishable on special Environment Agency annual permit, which covers 18 locks and weirs; contact Kings Meadow House, Kings Meadow Rd, Reading, Berks RG1 8DQ (tel: 0118 953 5000). Hotels: Anglers', Clarence, Railway.

Kingston (G London). Canbury Gardens is very popular stretch and has yielded large carp, bream, perch and roach.

Hampton Court (G London). Thames, Mole; coarse fish. Hampton Court Palace Gardens, Surrey KT8 9AU (tel: 020 8781 9500): contact Ticketing Office, The Barrack Block at palace; postal applications only. **Long Water** and **Rick Pond,** also **Bushy Park: Diana Pond, Heron Pond** and **Leg of Mutton Pond;** coarse fish; st (conc) waters (prices subject to annual review); no night fishing. Tackle shop: Fishing Unlimited, 70 Bridge Road, East Molesey KT8 9HF (tel: 020 8941 6633).

Hampton (G London). Hampton Deeps hold bream, pike, perch and sometimes a good trout; free fishing from towpath and boats.

Sunbury (Surrey). Excellent for all-round angling; free. Fine weir and weir shallows fishable (tel: 019327 82089); barbel, chub, dace, bream and occasional trout and salmon may be taken. Hotel: Magpie.

Walton-on-Thames (Surrey). Bream, perch, dace, chub, carp and pike; perch and pike in backwater. Tackle shop: The Tackle Exchange, 97A Terrace Rd, KT12 2SG (tel: 01932 242377).

Shepperton (Surrey). Pike, barbel, perch, bream and carp; free; boats for hire. Shepperton Lock is Environment Agency fishery; contact Kings Meadow House, Kings Meadow Rd, Reading, Berks RG1 8DQ (tel: 0118 953 5000) for permit details. Sheepwalk Lakes: 2 lakes, 7 acres, with carp to 30lbs, tench to 9lbs, bream to 11lbs, good pike fishing; access for disabled; dt £5 for two rods, from Ashford Angling Centre (*see Chertsey*). Two RMC Angling gravel pits, 16 acres, coarse fishing for carp, roach, chub, pike, eels, etc. St £30, conc £18. *(For RMC Angling, see Chertsey.)* Hotel: Anchor.

Weybridge (Surrey). There is local free fishing in Thames and **R Mole**. Members of Weybridge AC and other clubs have fishing on 6 sections of **Wey Navigation** Canal between Town Lock and Walsham Lock and have formed Wey Navigation Angling Amalgamation; Club is also member of the Basingstoke Canal AA with access to 30m of canal from New Hall to Basingstoke; dt £4 from bailiff. Weybridge AC also fishes 1,000 yards d/s and 1,000 yards u/s of Wey Bridge on R Wey; dt £2 from tackle Shop: Weybridge Guns & Tackle, 137 Oatlands Drive, Weybridge KT13 9LB (tel: 01932 842675). Hotels: Ship, Thames St; Lincoln Arms, Thames Street; Oatlands Park; Blue Anchor.

Chertsey (Surrey). Pike, perch, chub, roach, bream, occasional trout; free fishing from boats and towpath. Between Chertsey Weir and Penton Hook, Staines, good nets of bream caught all year, also perch. Chertsey Bridge is very popular for piking, with fish to 25lbs. RMC Angling (*see below*) have 4½ acre gravel pit and 1,000m of River Bourne. Excellent tench, bream, carp, roach and pike in pit, chub, roach, dace and perch in river. Group Water. St (2 rods) £30, conc £18. Club: Addlestone AA, which has water at **New Haw**, **Wey** and **Bourne** and a gravel pit at Laleham; dt to members' guests only. RMC Angling have a stretch of Wey at **Addlestone**, 800m total, with pike, barbel, chub to over 6lb, carp, roach, bream, dace, perch. Group Water. St £22, conc £12. **RMC Angling** (*see Miscellaneous Fisheries in Clubs List*) run many

fisheries throughout southern England, and they may be contacted at RMC Angling, Coldharbour Lane, Thorpe, Surrey TW20 8RA (tel: 01932 583630; web: www.rmcangling.co.uk). A £1000 4-rod Gold Card allows anglers to fish all RMC waters. RMC also manage 'Special Venues.' A Special Venues Permit enables anglers to fish all Group Waters and all Special Venues: £150 4-rods (conc £80), £125 3-rods (conc £65), £100 2-rods (conc £55). For 'Group Waters' anglers may purchase a Group Water Permit which enables the angler to fish all Group Waters (including night fishing Theale): £110 4-rods (conc £60), £90 3-rods (conc £50), £70 2-rods (conc £40). Free fishing on Shortwood Common, Ashford: 3 acre lake with carp to 20lbs, tench, etc. Ashford Lakes: three lakes of 1 acre each, with large carp, tench, bream, good head of roach and pike. Disabled access. Dt £5 per rod, from tackle shop: Ashford Angling Centre, 357 Staines Rd, West, Ashford Common, Middlesex TW15 1RP (tel: 01784 240013).

Staines (Surrey). Good coarse fishing; free from boats and towpath. Environment Agency fisheries at Penton Hook Lock, and Bell Weir Lock, **Egham**; contact Kings Meadow House, Kings Meadow Rd, Reading, Berks RG1 8DQ (tel: 0118 953 5000) for permit details. Club: Staines AS, stretch opposite Runnymede; members only. National Trust has 1m of bank; st, dt (on bank) available; contact warden's office (tel: 01784 432891). One mile free water in **R Colne** at Staines, with good roach, dace, chub, barbel and perch. At **Twynersh** are 5 lakes, mixed fish, dt on site. RMC has **Longfield Long Lake** here, tench, bream, carp; st (2 rods) £40, conc £25. Also **Longfield Road Lake** st £200 (4 rods), £160 (3 rods), £120 (2 rods). RMC also have **Fox Pool**, well known for its carp; st £250 (4 rods), £200 (3 rods), £150 (2 rods). *(For RMC Angling, see Chertsey.)* Tackle shop: Davies Angling, 47/49 Church Str, TW18 4EN (tel: 01784 461831).

Wraysbury (Berks). RMC Angling **Kingsmead Island Lake**: a Syndicate Venue lake of 50 acres with carp to 40lbs and other coarse species. St 4-rods £160, 3-rods £120, 2-rods £100. **Kingsmead Lake One** is a Group Water coarse lake of 30 acres; carp to over 30lb, other coarse fish; st (2 rods) £60, conc £40. RMC Angling also has Syndicate Water fishing at **Horton** nr Wraysbury, including **Horton Church Lake Syndicate**, 14 acres with carp to 40lb; st £450, waiting list; **Horton Boat Pool**, 6 acres: catfish to 52lb, and other coarse fish; st 4-rod £200, 3-rod £160, 2-rod £120. RMC also has **Crayfish Pool**, Park Lane, a 2 acre lake; carp over 39lb; st £250, waiting list. **Wraysbury 1**, home of former British Record carp of 56lb 6oz, is a Syndicate Venue water; st 4-rods £200, 3-rods £160, 2-rods £120. **Wraysbury 2** is a Group Water fishery, best suited to the specialist; tench, bream, pike, carp to over 30lb; st (2 rods) £30, conc £18. *(For RMC Angling, see Chertsey.)* Berkshire Fisheries Assoc. has Slough Arm of G Union Canal from **Cowley** to Slough Basin, approx 5m, excellent fishery in summer, very little boat traffic. Specimen tench and other species, and good pike fishing in winter; dt from bailiff.

Windsor (Berks). Chub, barbel, bream, roach, dace, perch, pike. Fishing from south bank below Windsor Bridge and north bank to Eton-Windsor road bridge, by EA licence only. Dt issued for club waters near Maidenhead; enq tackle shops. Salt Hill AC has Clewer Meadow, Windsor, dt on bank. Old Windsor AC has **Romney Island** and **Meadow** fishing to east of Windsor; all river species; junior trophies and tuition available; st £30, conc, dt £4, conc, at Romney on bank; from Windsor Angling Centre *(see below)*; or Maidenhead Bait & Tackle, 11-13 Station Parade, Station Hill, Cookham SL6 9BR (tel: 01628 530500; fax: 01628 530505). Free public fishing on right bank from Victoria Bridge u/s to railway bridge; water known as Home Park. Royal Berkshire Fishery, North St, Winkfield (tel: 01344 891101): 3 small lakes with coarse fish; dt on bank. Fishing can be had in Windsor Great Park ponds and Virginia Water *(see Surrey lakes)*. Tackle shops: Windsor Angling Centre, 153 St Leonard's Rd, SL4 3DW (tel: 01753 867210); Stows Angling Centre, 8 Upton Lea Parade, Wexham Rd, Slough SL2 5JU (tel: 01753 521612; web: www.stows.co.uk).

Boveney (Bucks). Coarse fish. Backwater good for pike, and weir pool for trout and barbel. Towpath free. London AA Eton Wick fishery here. Hotels: Clarence, Royal Windsor.

Bray (Berks). Weir pool good for coarse fish and a few trout, and free from boat or punt. Bray Mill tail from 1m above lock to lock cut private. Towpath free. Environment Agency fishery at Bray Lock; contact Kings Meadow House, Kings Meadow Rd, Reading, Berks RG1 8DQ (tel: 0118 953 5000) for permit details.

Maidenhead (Berks). Roach, pike, perch, barbel, dace, chance of trout. Some free fishing right bank, Maidenhead Bridge to Boulter's Lock. Hurley Lock, Environment Agency fishery; contact Kings Meadow House, Kings Meadow Rd, Reading, Berks RG1 8DQ (tel: 0118 953 5000) for permit details. Thames Valley AA has Left bank u/s from Boveney Lock to gardens at Dorney Reach; permits from Hon Sec; dt for clubs stretch from My Lady Ferry to gardens at Maidenhead from bailiff. Tackle shop: Kings Fishing Tackle, 18 Ray Str, SL6 8PW (tel: 01628 629283).

Cookham (Berks). Cookham & Dist AC has right bank u/s of Cookham road bridge to Bourne End Railway Bridge; chub, bream, barbel, roach, dace, perch, carp; membership £10; dt £2 purchased before fishing from tackle shop. Free fishing on **Odney Island**. London AA has water at Spade Oak Ferry; members only; membership £39, conc. Tackle shop: Maidenhead Bait & Tackle, 11-13 Station Parade, Station Hill, Cookham, SL6 9BR (tel: 01628 530500). Hotels: Ferry, Royal Exchange, King's Arms, Bell and Dragon, Crown.

Bourne End (Bucks). Wide, open water with some shallow stretches, good for fly fishing. London AA has water here. Stretch also open to associates. Marlow AC has Spade Oak Pit near Little Marlow; mixed coarse; members only; apply Hon Sec.

Marlow (Bucks). Usual coarse fish, including barbel. Free fishing d/s from Marlow Lock ½ end of Riverside Drive, ½m stretch. Marlow AC has water from Riverswood Drive to opp first islands and left bank u/s from Marlow Bridge opp Temple Island, and pits; club also has at stretch at Medmenham and a backwater; members only. Tickets from Kings Fishing Tackle, 18 Ray St, Maidenhead SL6 8PW (tel: 01628 629283). At West Wycombe Park, 5m north, National Trust brown and rainbow trout lake is synicate-managed; for st (subject to availability) contact Estate Office (not NT) (tel: 01494 524411).

Hurley (Berks). Hurley Lock, Environment

Agency fishery; contact Kings Meadow House, Kings Meadow Rd, Reading, Berks RG1 8DQ (tel: 0118 953 5000) for permit details.

Henley (Oxon). Pike, chubb, roach, perch, tench, bream, eels. Free fishing u/s from Promenade to Cold Bath Ditch. Environment Agency fishery at Marsh Lock; contact Kings Meadow House, Kings Meadow Rd, Reading, Berks RG1 8DQ (tel: 0118 953 5000) for permit details. Oxon and Bucks bank water controlled by society for members only. Also from end of Henley Promenade upstream to Marsh Lock, bridges and meadows upstream from Marsh Lock. Tackle shop: Swiss Farm International Camping, Marlow Rd, RG9 2HX (tel: 01491 573419). Boats: Hobbs.

Wargrave (Berks). Thames and Loddon; good coarse fishing.

Sonning (Berks). Much fishing from **Shiplake** to Sonning Bridge on Oxfordshire bank controlled by Shiplake and Binfield Heath AS; members only. Guests at White Hart can fish private stretch of ½m on Berkshire bank towards Shiplake. Reading & Dist AA has Sonning Eye fishery (lake and river); members only. Environment Agency fishery at Shiplake Lock; contact Kings Meadow House, Kings Meadow Rd, Reading, Berks RG1 8DQ (tel: 0118 953 5000) for permit details.

Reading (Berks). Most coarse fish. Reading Borough Council controls length from opposite Caversham Court Gazebo to 1½m u/s of Caversham Bridge. The fishing from Thames-side Promenade to Scours Lane is controlled by Thames Water. There is some free water on the **Kennet** from Horseshoe Bridge to County Weir (adjacent to Inner Distribution Road). Reading & Dist AA, comprising about forty affiliated clubs, control twenty eight miles of river and canal, plus fourteen lakes in Berkshire and Oxfordshire. Subscription £37, with concessions. Supplementary permits on six specimen waters, £35-£70; £6 dt offered for Wylies Lake and 20 other venues, stocked, with coarse and specimen fishing in Reading vicinity; dt available from tackle shops (all other Reading & Dist AA waters are members only plus guests). Farnborough AS has good trout and coarse fishing on **Whitewater** at Heckfield (8m), also 2m fly only stretch; trout membership on application to Hon

Sec; coarse st £44, joining fee £17.50, dt £6. At Bradfield, **Pang Valley trout lake** (tel: 0118 932 3422), approx 6 acres, stocked with rainbow trout; dt £25, 4 fish limit, £15 2 fish, on bank. RMC Angling has coarse fisheries on permit at **St Patrick's Stream**, **Twyford** and **Theale** (2 lakes, total 52 acres); coarse; st (2 rods) £30, conc £18. Twyford, managed by BBONT, has 34-acre lake and 900 yard section of R Loddon; coarse Group Water; st £30, conc £18. *(For RMC Angling, see Chertsey).* At Theale is **Haywards Farm Fishery**, Station Rd, RG7 4AS (tel: 01189 323422); 2 lakes totalling 18 acres; rainbows and browns; 1 Mar to 30 Nov; dt on site £25 (4 fish) half day £15 (2 fish). Tackle shops: Reading Angling Centre, 69 North'land Avenue RG2 7PS (tel: 0118 987 2216); Thames Valley Angling, 258 Kentwood Hill, Reading RG31 6DR (tel: 0118 942 8249); Tadley Angling, Padworth Common Rd, Padworth RG7 4NR (tel: 0118 970 1533). Hotels: Thameside; Thames House; Pennyfarthings, Swallowfield.

Tilehurst (Berks). Purley (now free fishing water); Reading & DAA have Mapledurham on the Oxfordshire bank. Free fishing from towpath to Caversham *(see restrictions under Reading).* Tackle shop: Thames Valley Angling, 258 Kentwood Hill, Tilehurst, Reading RG31 6DR (tel: 0118 942 8249); tickets for Reading FC. Hotel: Roebuck Hotel.

Goring (Oxon). Pike, bream, roach, chub, perch and (in weir pool especially) barbel and a few trout. Fishing can be had from towpath above and below lock.

Pangbourne and **Whitchurch** (Berks). Thames and **Pang**. Trout, perch, pike, roach, bream, chub, dace. River fishes well in winter; free fishing 1½m above and below Whitchurch Bridge; good coarse fishing; boats for hire. Weir pool private. Pang holds trout, especially near Tidmarsh, but is strictly preserved; trout at its mouth. Pangbourne and Whitchurch AS is affiliated with Reading & Dist AA, and fishes in a number of localities, including 3m of R Kennet with good chub, barbel, roach and dace; st £37 from Hon Sec.

Moulsford (Berks). All coarse fish. London AA has water here; members only. Hotel: Beetle.

South Stoke (Oxon). London AA controls the water from footbridge above railway bridge down to Beetle and Wedge ferry;

members only, membership £39, conc.

Wallingford (Oxon). Reading & Dist AA has Severals Farm fishing: two sections, above and below Bensons Lock. Jolly Anglers have several miles u/s and d/s of Wallingford; roach, dace, chub, barbel, perch, bream, pike, carp and eels; dt £5 available on the bank (for below town road bridges only; members only above). Tackle shops: Rides on Air, 45 St Mary's Str, OX10 0ER (tel: 01491 836289); Wallingford Sports Shop, 71 High Str, OX10 0BW (tel: 01491 837043).

Cleeve (Oxon). Usual coarse fish. London AA: for Gatehampton Farm details; ¾m fishing good for bream; some perch, roach, chub; members only; membership £39, conc (open to associates).

Benson (Oxon). Usual coarse fish. Benson

& DAC has water for ¾m u/s from the Marina in Benson; st £6, dt £3 from Benson Marina and bailiffs on bank; some Sundays reserved for matches. Benson Lock is Environment Agency lock and weir fishery; contact Kings Meadow House, Kings Meadow Rd, Reading, Berks RG1 8DQ (tel: 0118 953 5000) for permit details.

Shillingford (Oxon). Wallingford AA has water upstream; dt from Hon Sec. Shillingford Bridge Hotel, Shillingford Hill, Wallingford OX10 8LZ (tel: 01865 858567), has good pike fishing with trout, tench, dace, etc, on ¼m (both banks) reserved for guests and members of High Wycombe AC.

Little Wittenham (Oxon). Thame comes in here.

Two fine brown trout from the river Nidd, North Yorkshire, the upper reaches of which are renowned for spirited brown trout and grayling. *Photo: Arthur Oglesby.*

Clifton Hampden (Oxon). Oxford & Dist AA has water here, d/s from the scenic bridge for nine fields. Bream, chub and roach, also large barbel; dt on part of this water from tackle shops only, night fishing by arrangement. Clifton Lock is Environment Agency fishery; contact Kings Meadow House, Kings Meadow Rd, Reading, Berks RG1 8DQ (tel: 0118 953 5000) for permit details. Inn: The Barley Mow.

Appleford (Berks). London AA controls from just above the railway bridge down to beginning of Clifton Hampden cutting; right bank only; members only; membership £39, conc.

Culham (Oxon). Sutton Courtenay AC has pits; no day tickets.

Abingdon (Oxon). Bream, chub, pike and barbel good. Free fishing for residents. Tickets from Town Clerk's office for the 1½m controlled by Council, from Nuneham railway bridge to notice-board 200 yds u/s from Culham footbridge; details from Old Abbey House, Abbey Close, Abingdon OX14 3JD (tel: 01235 522642); fishery includes weir, but must be fished from bank. Abingdon & Oxford Anglers Alliance has much local fishing. The Alliance trout section has lake at **Standlake**, Oxon, st £48, entrance fee £25; members and their guests only: contact Hon Sec. Alliance also has water at Bablock Hythe.

Sandford-on-Thames (Oxon). Pike, bream, roach, perch, etc. Abingdon A & RA have water. Environment Agency lock and weir fishery at Sandford Lock; contact Kings Meadow House, Kings Meadow Rd, Reading, Berks RG1 8DQ (tel: 0118 953 5000) for permit details.

Iffley (Oxon). Thames (or Isis). From Botley Road Bridge d/s to Folly Bridge is Oxford & DAS water; large shoals of roach, perch and chub; dt from tackle shops. Inn: Isis Tavern.

Oxford (Oxon). Thames (Isis), **Cherwell** and **Oxford Canal**. All coarse fish. Milton Keynes has access to 1m of R Thames at **Oxford**. N Oxford AS has water on Thames, at **Gostow** and **Carrot's Ham**, Cherwell, canal, and carp and tench fishing in **Dukes Lake**. Their best water is **Seacourt Stream** at Carrot's Ham, with many species. Club offers dt on water between Godstow and Seacourt Overspill, and Seacourt Stream from Overspill to A420; st £20, conc, dt £3.50 from tackle shops. **Donnington** and **Iffley**

water held by Oxford & Dist AA. Good roach fishing, also chub. Heavy boat traffic here. Assn is an affiliation of clubs local to Oxford. It has excellent coarse fishing on Thames at **Medley**, **Kennington**, **Newbridge**, and elsewhere, with dt £3.50 from tackle shops only. (4½m W of Oxford, **Farmoor Reservoirs**, Cumnor Rd, Farmoor OX2 9NS. No.1 leased by Farmoor Flyfishers; members only. Reservoir No.2, Cumnor Rd, is 240 acre trout fishery, stocked with brown and rainbow, fly only from boat or bank; dt and st from gatehouse; facilities for disabled; tel: 01865 863033 for advance bookings. Tackle shops: Fat Phil's Angling Centre, 334 Abingdon Rd, OX1 4TQ (tel: 01865 201020). Hotels: Swan, Islip.

Eynsham (Oxon). Good coarse fishing; large bream. Oxford Angling & Pres Soc has water *(see Oxford)*. Eynsham Lock fishing open to holders of Environment Agency lock permits; contact Kings Meadow House, Kings Meadow Rd, Reading, Berks RG1 8DQ (tel: 0118 953 5000) for permit details. Hotels: Ye Talbot Inn, Railway, Red Lion.

Bablock Hythe (Oxon). Ferryman Inn, Bablock Hythe, Northmoor OX29 5AT (tel: 01865 880028), issues dt for Reading & Dist AC water adjacent; and for Hardwicke Fishing Lakes (2m) and Farmoor (5m); trout. Special rates for anglers.

Newbridge (Oxon). Near Witney. Good coarse fishing (bream increasing), few trout in the **Windrush**. Shifford Lock is one of Environment Agency's fisheries (long walk necessary); contact Kings Meadow House, Kings Meadow Rd, Reading, Berks RG1 8DQ (tel: 0118 953 5000) for permit details. Newland AC has water from **Shifford** to within 600 yds of Newbridge; and Heyford Lakes, Standlake, with specimen fish; st, dt for lakes only from State Fishing *(below)*. Hotels: Rose Revived (¾m water on Thames and Windrush; good coarse fish, some trout) and May Bush (½m water on Thames). Rose Revived Hotel, Newbridge OX8 7QD (tel: 01865 300221); for customers only. Witney AS have Thames fishing here, R Windrush, trout only, and coarse pit; members only, £25 per annum, conc. Stroud AA have 1m of Thames; dt available. Tackle shop: State Fishing Tackle, 19 Fettiplace Rd, Witney OX28 5AP (tel: 01993 702587), who can give further information.

Radcot (Oxon). Bream, chub, barbel, roach,

perch, pike, occasional trout. Swan Hotel, OX18 2SX (tel: 01367 810220), has ½m, dt available. Radcot AC has 5m, st only, £17.50, conc; apply Hon Sec, Swan Hotel, or Turner's Tackle. Clanfield AC also has left bank, Old Man's Bridge to Rushey Lock, st only, £12, 3m fishing; membership apply Hon Sec. Four Environment Agency lock fisheries, at Rushey; Radcot; Grafton Lock; and Buscot Lock; contact Kings Meadow House, Kings Meadow Rd, Reading, Berks RG1 8DQ (tel: 0118 953 5000) for permit details. Permits for stretch from **Buscot** to Grafton Lock, season cards for Radcot AC and Clanfield AC, from Turner's Tackle and Bait, 4A Station Rd, Faringdon, SN7 7BN (tel: 01367 241044). National Trust has dt for Little Lake, Buscot Park; coarse; contact Steve Cole, Cotswold Angling (tel: 01793 721173).

Lechlade (Glos). For Thames, Coln and Leach. Phoenix AA controls 2m of Thames at Lechlade upstream from Trout Inn to Murdoch Ditch. Permits for weir pool only, from Trout Inn, GL7 3HA (tel: 01367 252313); dt £5. For Highworth AC water between Lechlade and Buscot (western beat), contact D M Bryant (tel: 01793 644173). For South Cerney AC water (eastern beat) contact M Vines of South Cerney AC; dt water. Tackle shop: Turner's Tackle and Bait, 4A Station Rd, Faringdon, SN7 7BN (tel: 01367 241044).

Cricklade (Wilts). Thames known here as Isis. Isis AC has No 1 Lake at **South Cerney** (Glos), carp to 30lb; membership £34.50, dt £3 from tackle shops; dt allows angling on stretch of Avon at Sutton Benger. South Cerney AC has several lakes in Cotswold area, membership £35, conc, from House of Angling, 59/60 Commercial Rd, Swindon SN1 5NX (tel: 01793 693460).

Tributaries of the Thames

MOLE: Coarse fish.

Esher (Surrey). Pike, roach, perch the odd big chub. Feltham Piscatorials have 'The Ledges'. Epsom AS has ½m at Wayne Flete and ½m on Wey at **Weybridge**; apply Hon Sec. Tackle shop: Weybridge Guns & Tackle, 137 Oatlands Drive, Weybridge KT13 9LB (tel: 01932 842675).

Cobham (Surrey). Central Association of London and Provincial Angling Clubs (CALPAC) has 1½m of Mole here, various coarse species; and Manor Pond, holding pike, carp, roach, tench and bream; members only. Further CALPAC stretch, 1½ miles at **Hersham**: chub, perch, roach, dace, eels, pike, dt £5, conc, sold on bank. Cobham Court AC have water adjacent and above: large chub, pike, very big perch and eels. Some rainbows stocked.

Leatherhead (Surrey). Leatherhead & Dist AS have waters above A246 road bridge. Sunmead AS has water at Norbury Park, Leatherhead, with chub, roach, dace, perch, together with carp and pike to double figures; dt £5 on bank. Tackle shops: S C Fuller, 32 South St, Dorking RH4 2HQ (tel: 01306 882177).

Dorking (Surrey). Coarse fish. Dorking and Dist AS has about 4m of Mole and three lakes; large stocks of carp, tench, bream, roach and barbel. Members only. Contact A Fuller, Fullers Tackle *(below)*. **Furze Farm Fishery**, Knowle Lane, nr Cranleigh; 3½ acre mixed fishery; dt £8 (1 rod) £10 (2 rods) on bankside; contact P Knight, Stone Cottage, Ridgeway Rd, Dorking RH4 3EY (tel: 01306 882708). Tackle shop: S C Fuller, 32 South St, Dorking RH4 2HQ (tel: 01306 882177). Hotels: White Horse; Pilgrim.

Brockham (Surrey). Chub, roach, carp and bream. Brockham AS water.

Betchworth (Surrey). Chub dominate below weir, anything can, and does appear above weir. Carshalton & Dist AS has water; members only.

Sidlow (Surrey). Roach dominate, together with perch, carp, chub. Horley PS fish much of this water.

WEY: Coarse fish, trout higher up.

Weybridge (Surrey). Wey Amalgamation have water here *(see Thames)*, tickets from bailiff.

Woking (Surrey). Roach, chub, pike, etc. Woking & Dist AS has rights on 23 miles of river bank and two ponds (perch, carp and tench) at Send; dt for members' guests only. New members welcome; details from Hon Sec. Tackle shop: Weybridge Guns & Tackle, 137 Oatlands Drive, Weybridge KT13 9LB (tel: 01932 842675).

Wisley (Surrey); ns Ripley. Ponds: Wisley Mere, Hut Pond, and several other ponds on Ripley Common and Ockham Common; carp, pike, perch, roach.

Guildford (Surrey). Guildford AS has about 9½m R Wey; lakes at Broad Str, and Whitmoor Common (carp to 19lb in Britton Pond). At Shamley Green **Willinghurst Fisheries,** Shamley Green GU5 0SU (tel: 01483 275048): 11 lakes, all coarse; dt £8 (1 rod), £12 (2 rods), conc; barbless hooks; night fishing by appointment only. **Albury Estate Fisheries,** Estate Office, Albury, Guildford GU5 9AF (tel: 01483 202323); 8 lakes, totalling 16 acres, of brown and rainbow trout fishing; 3 dt waters: **Powdermills** (5lbs av), **Weston** (2½lbs) and **Vale End** (2½lbs); one syndicated: **Park** (2lbs av); dt waters £45-£20 per day. Limit 4 fish. Instruction, if required. **Brittens Pond,** Salt Box Lane, Jacobs Well; big carp, perch, roach, etc. Dt £4. Tackle shops: Peter Cockwill Game Angling, Stream Cottage, The Street, Albury GU5 9AG (tel: 01483 205196). Accommodation: Drummond Arms, Albury.

Shalford (Surrey). Wey; bream, roach, pike, etc. **Tillingbourne;** trout; preserved. Inns: Parrot, Victoria, Sea Horse, Percy Arms, Chilworth.

Godalming (Surrey). Godalming AS has Wey from old A3 bridge, just above Stag Inn, Eashing, to Guildford Rowing Club in Guildford (about 8m); coarse fish incl barbel; some grayling and trout on upper reaches. Society also has **Broadwater Lake** (10 acres) which holds carp, roach, tench and perch; **Busbridge Lake** (4 acres), coarse; **Johnsons Lake** at Enton (21 acres), coarse; and **Bramley Park Lake** (3 acres), coarse; **Marsh Farm, Milford,** adjacent to Johnsons Lake; 2 7-acre lakes; mixed coarse; no carp. No waiting list: entry fee £65, st £50, conc. Peper Harow Flyfishers have 2m of Wey and three ponds (brown and rainbow trout); rods limited; st only. **Wintershall Waters,** Bramley, is 3 acre trout fishery; st only (tel: 01483 275019). Tackle shop: Guildford Angling Centre, 92/94 Haydon Place GU1 4LR (tel: 01483 506333). Hotels: The Manor Inn.

Frensham (Surrey). Farnham AS has Frensham Trout Fishery; **Frensham, Great** and **Little Ponds,** roach, perch, carp, etc; open membership for coarse fishing; st from M J Borra, The Creel, 36 Station

Angling is reputed to be the largest participatory sport in the country. Here a day on Fringe Lake, Rickmansworth, would appear to bear that out.

Road, Aldershot, Hants GU11 1HT (tel: 01252 320871).

Haslemere (Surrey). Coarse fish. At St Patricks Lane, **Liss**, is coarse fishing on 2 lakes, plus 5 ponds at **Rake** for matches only.

Farnham (Surrey). Farnham AS offers extensive local fishing, for members only. Club coarse fishing waters include 1m R Wey at **Dockenfield** and **Elstead; Frensham Ponds;** Badshot Lea Ponds; Lodge Pond; Stockbridge Pond at **Tilford, Loddon** at **Winnersh,** lakes at **Yateley,** incl specimen water; **R Whitewater** nr Riseley, small stream with chub, perch and roach; no day tickets; st £58, joining fee £25, conc; apply Membership Sec for details. Note: all waters heavily fished early in season.

COLNE: Coarse fish, some trout.

Wraysbury (Berks). Blenheim AS has Colne Brook from Wraysbury Station Rd to Hythe End Bridge; coarse fish and occasional trout. Also **Cargill Lake** and **Watts Pool,** members only; joining fee £10, conc, st £65, conc. Twickenham PS and Staines AC have gravel pits; no tickets.

West Drayton (G London). Trout, pike, perch, bream, dace, roach, tench, chub. Grand Union Canal is near. **Lizard Fisheries,** Trout Rd, West Drayton (tel: 07931 255897): all species of carp to 35lbs; dt from pay and display machine on site; £8, one rod dawn to dusk (£10 2 rods); contact Dave Brett.

Uxbridge (G London). Pike, perch, roach, dace and bream. Fishing free on Uxbridge Moor. London AA holds long stretches of **Grand Union Canal,** on which dt is issued. National Trust **Osterley Park Lake** holds bream, tench, pike, roach, carp; limited st £23, conc; no night fishing; enquiries to Head Gardener, Osterley Park, Jersey Rd, Isleworth, Middx TW7 4RB (tel: 020 8232 5050). **Farlows Pit, Iver,** holds roach, tench, carp, bream, pike; limited number of st.

Denham (Bucks). Colne; coarse fish. Blenheim AS has 6½m of **Grand Union Canal** from Denham Lock 87 to Rickmansworth Lock 81; bream, roach, carp, perch, chub, pike. St £40, conc. Dt £3, conc, on bank from bailiff on stretches lock 81-83, and lock 85-87. Tackle shops: Harefield Tackle, 2-4 High St, Harefield, Uxbridge UB9 6BU (tel: 01895 822900); Fishermans Cabin, 795 Field End Rd, South Ruislip HA4 0QL (tel: 0208 422 9546).

Harefield (G London). **Savay Lake,** Moorhall Road: 52 acre gravel pit stocked with specimen fish; st from P Broxup, Fishery Manager, 309 Shirland Road, London W9 3JL (tel: 020 8969 6980). **Bowmans Lakes,** London Colney, **St Albans:** three lakes, two of which have 60 and 100 pegs, with large bream, large carp and pike; tickets: enquiries to Ben Tucker, 8 Pleasant Place, Uxbridge Road, Rickmansworth, Herts WD3 9XZ (tel: 01895 824455). London AA has **Moor Mill Pits:** four gravel pits; and fishing on **River Ver,** a small river suitable to stalking dace, chub, roach; Pits contain carp over 40lb, tench, crucian and roach; membership £39, conc; dt on bank.

Rickmansworth (Herts). Trout, chub, dace, roach, pike, perch. Blenheim AS has 6½m of **Grand Union Canal** between Denham Lock 87 and Rickmansworth Lock 81 (good roach and bream); dt £3 from bailiff on Pounds Lock 81-83 and Lock 85-87. Limited st from Harefield Tackle. (Note: no dt on section between Springwell Lock No 83 and Black Jacks Lock No 85; members only); st £65 (weekdays only £40 Locks 83-85), conc; dt £3, conc and from tackle shops. Watford Piscators have 4m of canal; also two stretches of **R Gade,** with barbel, large roach, shoals of bream and chub, good perch; three stretches of R Colne; and six coarse lakes, incl Tolpits, Castles, Stanleys, Thurlows, and Rouseburn Lakes, Cassiobury Park; club also has 12 to 16 jun section; all waters members only, except two sections of canal, dt £2.50; membership £95, conc. Kings Langley AS has 2m of canal at Hunton Bridge, also short stretch of R Gade. Information from Tackle Carrier (*below*). **Chess;** trout, preserved. **Gaywoods Fishery** (formerly known as Kings Langley Fishery), Home Park Link Rd, **Kings Langley** WD4 8DZ (tel: 07778 030939 or 01923 269578): 4 acre dug-out pond with carp to 24lbs, tench, roach, perch, etc; dt £8, two rods, juv £6. Tingrith Coarse Fishery, **Tingrith** (tel: 01525 714012): three pools with carp, tench, bream etc; dt £8 (1 rod). Tackle shops: Harefield Tackle, 2-4 High St, Harefield UB9 6BU (tel: 01895 822900); Fishermans Cabin, 795 Field End Rd, South Ruislip HA4 0QL (tel: 0208 422 9546); Tackle Carrier, 155-7 St Albans Rd, Watford WD24 5BD (tel: 01923 232393).

Watford (Herts). Boxmoor & Dist AS has stretch of river here, members only; st £45 + joining fee £30 + key deposit; apply to Hon Sec. **Gade** at Cassiobury is free fishing for approx 1m. Ticket waters: Elstree and Tring reservoirs and Grand Union Canal. London AA issues dt for canal from Hunton Bridge to Tring. Free fishing in Gade in Cassiobury Park. Watford Piscators have fishing in Rivers Gade and Colne, lakes, and dt water on Grand Union Canal (*see Rickmansworth*). Tackle shop: Tackle Carrier, 155-7 St Albans Rd, Watford WD24 5BD (tel: 01923 232393). Hotels: Maldon, Clarendon, Rose and Crown.

CHESS: Brown and rainbow trout - one of few British streams where rainbows spawn naturally. There is free public fishing at Scotts Bridge Playing Fields, Rickmansworth.

Chorleywood (Bucks). Chess; trout.

GADE: coarse fish.

Boxmoor (Herts). Boxmoor & Dist AS has private water at Westbrook Mere, Bourne End, with large carp, bream, tench, pike, roach, rudd and perch; club also has Upper Ouse at **Stoney Stratford**, Colne at Watford, and Stort Navigation at Harlow, all mixed fishing, matches throughout year; membership £45, plus £30 joining fee; apply Hon Sec; Assn also has **Durrants Hill** in Apsley, Hemel Hempstead. Harlow District Council, Parks and Landscapes Service, Mead Park Depot, River Way, Harlow CM20 2SE (tel: 01279 446425) also has parts of Stort Navigation; inquiries to Harlow DC. **Boxmoor Trout Fishery**, 3 acres of converted water cress farm. St £360 to £260 on flexible basis; inquiries to R Hands, 23 Sebright Rd, Boxmoor, Hemel Hempstead HP1 1QY (tel: 01442 393381).

Berkhamsted (Herts). Visitors can fish London AA water on Grand Union Canal; coarse fish, dt £3.50, juv £1.50 from bailiff. No free water. Hotels: King's Arms (Trust House), Crown, Swan.

LODDON: coarse fish, barbel improving, trout scarce.

Twyford (Berks). St Patrick's stream (fine barbel), held by RMC Angling. St £28, conc £15. (*For RMC Angling, see Chertsey*).

Arborfield Cross (Berks). Farnham AS has a stretch at Sindlesham Mill, Winnersh; coarse fish, barbel in faster stretches (*see Wey - Farnham*). Cove AS also has water near here at **Shinfield** and on **Hart** and **Whitewater**; members only (*see also Fleet*). Farnborough AS has 2½m R Loddon at **Winnersh**, 4m R Whitewater at Heckfield, Basingstoke Canal and Shawfields Lake and Hollybush Pits; fine mixed coarse fishing, fly fishing, membership on application. Felix Farm Trout Fishery, Howe Lane, **Binfield**, RG42 5QL (tel: 01189 345527); 10 acres, stocked with brown and rainbows between 2-10 lb; dt £25, 5 fish, ½ day £22, 3 fish, evening £17, 2 fish; boats for hire: contact Peter Pearmain at fishery for more details.

KENNET: One of England's finest mixed coarse fisheries; upper reaches noted for trout and grayling.

Theale (Berks), Water west of point 1m upstream of Bridge House (Wide Mead Lock) strictly preserved; few trout and coarse fish. Englefield Lake, 2m; pike, and fine tench and carp (private). Reading & Dist AA has much water on lower **Kennet** at Theale, Rushey Meadow, Calcot, Lower and Upper Benyons, Ufton, Pad-

worth Mill and elsewhere, the **Holybrook** and backwaters, together with 9 local gravel pits, 120 acres; dt (£6) on a few venues from tackle shops. Blenheim AS fishes Kennet and Holybrook at Southcote. Barbel, roach, dace, chub, perch. Members only, £65 pa, £10 joining fee, conc. At **Burghfield**, four RMC Angling lakes, including **Burghfield Match Lake**, Special Venue water of 2 acres with big carp and other species; st 2-rods £40, conc £25; **Burghfield Blue Pool**, 3 acre Special Venue lake; mirror carp to 28lb and other coarse fish; st £40, conc £25. RMC also have Group Water to include 2 lakes (one of 94 acres) and 1m R Kennet; mixed fishing with carp to over 40lb. Lake st £40, conc £25; river st £30, conc £18. *(For RMC Angling, see Chertsey.)*

Aldermaston (Berks). Coarse fish and few trout. Old Mill, Aldermaston RG7 4LB (tel: 0118 9712365), issues permits for about ½m of water with four weirs, and small lake with carp to 30lbs; dt £10 at door, £12 in bank. CALPAC has 750 yard stretch of Kennet at **Padworth**, with large barbel, tench, bream, pike, etc; members only, membership £35 + £10 joining fee, conc. London AA has 2m of narrow winding stream, **Fisherman's Brook**, a tributary of the R Kennet; chub, dace, roach; members only; membership £39, conc.

Thatcham (Berks). Fishing between Reading and Thatcham controlled chiefly by Reading & Dist AA. Members only on river and Hambridge Lake, but dt £6, conc, on site for Wylies Lake, Thatcham. Details from Hon Sec *(see clubs list).* Thatcham AA has water on canal, R Kennet plus lakes; members only, £35 per annum + £10 joining; contact Hon Sec or tackle shop below. Tackle shops: Thatcham Angling Centre, Unit 4, 156 Sagecroft Road, Thatcham RG18 3BQ (tel: 01635 871450); Crown Mead Angling Centre, 10 Crown Mead, Bath Rd, That-

cham RG18 3JW (tel: 01635 863092).
Newbury (Berks). On Rivers Kennet and **Lambourn** and **Kennet and Avon Canal**; trout and coarse fishing. Newbury & Dist AA, Thatcham AA and Reading & Dist AA, Civil Service AS hold water in this area. Kintbury AC owns canal and river fishing; st £12. For these and other local clubs contact Field and Stream *(below).* CALPAC has Kennet fishery at Bulls Lock, with large barbel and other coarse species. Some brown and rainbow trout have been caught; members only. Tackle shop: Field and Stream, 109 Bartholomew Str, RG14 5DT (tel: 01635 43186).

Hungerford (Berks). Kennet and **Dunn**; trout, grayling; preserved. **Hungerford Canal** fishing in hands of Hungerford Canal AA (3m) (tickets from Thatcham Angling Centre - see Thatcham). CALPAC has fishery at **Sulhampstead**, 750 yds of river, followed by 700 yds of canal, with large barbel and other coarse species. No night fishing; dt £5, conc, from Canal Cottage or on bank. Reading & Dist AA has water (Froxfield). Accommodation at Red Lion, Three Swans, Bear, Lamb Hotel (Canal AA HQ).

Lockinge (Oxon). Lockinge Fishery, John Haigh, The Walled Garden, Ardington, Wantage OX12 8PN (tel: 01235 831500); stocked trout fishing on lakes and streams, running through Ardington and Lockinge, nr Wantage; av brown and rainbow, 2lb; st £697; season rods only, max 4 fish per wk.

Marlborough (Wilts). Trout at Axford, Marlborough & District AA has fishing rights in **Kennet and Avon Canal** from Milkhouse Water to Little Bedwyn; members only; st £30 + £5 entry, conc. Wroughton AC fish **Wroughton Reservoir**, Overtown Hill, Wroughton, Swindon; members only. BB&WAA has **Tockenham Reservoir**, near Swindon; members only, st £30 from House of Angling *(below).* Tackle shop: Cotswold

---

Check before you go

Angling, Omar Grange, Hyde Road, Swindon SN2 7SE (tel: 01793 721173); Swindon Angling Centre, 5 Sheppard Street, Swindon SN1 5DB (tel: 01793 619909); House of Angling, 59/60 Commercial Rd, Swindon SN1 5NX (tel: 01793 693460). Hotels: Aylesbury Arms, Savernake, Castle and Ball, Crown (Marlborough AA HQ).

THAME: Coarse fish.

Dorchester (Oxon). Thames and Thame. Coarse fish; good chub and dace, and carp quite numerous. Dorchester AA has water; dt from Hon Sec or Fleur-de-Lys. Oxford & Abingdon AA has a lake here.

Thame (Oxon). The Tring Anglers have water at Ickford, the Shabbington Island, and **Chearsley**, members and guests tickets. St £38, dt £3, conc half price. Tackle shops: Rides on Air, 45 St Mary's Str, Wallingford OX10 0ER (tel: 01491 836289); Wallingford Sports Shop, 71 High Str, Wallingford OX10 0BW (tel: 01491 837043).

Eythrope (Bucks). Roach, bream, perch, chub, good dace. Aylesbury Dist and Izaak Walton AA has water (4m from Aylesbury), members and friends only. Blenheim AS has water at Shabbington and backwaters; roach, dace, chub, perch. Members only, annual sub £65, £10 entrance, usual conc.

CHERWELL: Coarse fish.

Islip (Oxon). Cherwell and Ray; good chub, roach, perch and pike fishing may be had in the Cherwell. The Bicester & DAA has ½ acre carp pool, 2m Bicester; st £8 from tackle shops. Oxford & Dist AA (which includes Bicester & DAA) has Cherwell at Enslow, Kirtlington and Northbrook; wt from tackle shops. Tackle shops: J & K Tackle, 62/64 Sheep St, Bicester OX26 7LG (tel: 01869 242589). Inns: Red Lion, Swan.

Heyford (Oxon). Oxford & Dist AA has South Oxford Canal from Enslow Bridge to Heyford Wharf; dt £2.50 from Oxford tackle shops.

Banbury (Oxon). Banbury & DAA has much local water on R Cherwell; and canal fishing, incl stretches at Cropedy, Nell Bridge, Clifton, Somerton, Heyford and Bletchington, also **Clattercote** and **Grimsbury Reservoirs**; also **Spital Farm**, Grimsbury; also **Slinket Lake**, Aynho; dt £5, conc, for reservoirs only from tackle shops. **Farnborough Hall Lake** is leased to Banbury & DAA. Coarse fishing at Butler Hill Farm, Gt

Rollright, OX7 5SJ, tickets on bank; carp to 25lbs, large rudd, chub, bream; tickets at fishery. Rye Hill, Milcombe, and **Chacombe Fishery**, carp, bream, tench, etc, dt at fishery. **Cheyney Manor Fishery**, Manor House, **Barford St Michael** OX15 0RJ; The moat contains carp, and fishpond has rudd, roach, tench, perch; tickets from bailiff (tel: 01869 338207). Castle AA fishes two lakes, 6 acres, at **Canons Ashby**: carp to 22lb, bream and roach. **The Goldfish Bowl**, Boulderdyke Farm, off Chapel Close, Clifton, nr Deddington OX15 0PF (tel: 01869 338539): carp lake, 18 pegs, disabled access. **Nellbridge Coarse Fishery**, Aynho OX17 3NY (tel: 01295 811227): 3 lakes stocked with tench, roach, carp, perch, bream, pike, rudd; dt £5 (2 rods); disabled access; 100 pegs plus, open dawn till dusk. Tackle shops: Castaway, 86 Warwick Rd OX16 7AJ (tel: 01295 254274); Banbury Gunsmiths, 47A Broad St, OX16 8BT (tel: 01295 265819); K & M Fishing Tackle, 23 West Rd, Chipping Norton OX7 5EU (tel: 01608 645435).

EVENLODE: Trout, coarse fish (roach and dace especially).

Long Hanborough (Oxon). Red Spinner AS rents 9m of the Evenlode from **Fawler** to **Cassington**; trout (re-stocked annually), dace, roach, chub, pike; members only. Good fishing on **Blenheim Park Lakes**. Excellent tench, perch and roach, with pike in winter. Boat fishing only. *(See Midlands lakes, reservoirs, etc)*. **Salford Trout Lakes**; 5 and 3½ acres stocked with rainbow and brown trout; dt £24 (4 fish limit), ½ day and evening, £16; st £240 also offered; contact fishery office or E A Colston, Rectory Farm, Salford, Chipping Norton OX7 5YZ (tel: 01608 643209).

WINDRUSH: Trout, grayling, coarse fish (dace up to 1lb and 2lb roach not rare).

Witney (Oxon). Large trout; preserved below; leave must be obtained from the Proprietors; good hatch of mayfly. Witney AS (HQ Eagle Vaults) has water. No dt and membership £25 pa restricted to county as a rule, but outside applications considered; apply Hon Sec. Club now has water on gravel pits at **Stanton Harcourt** (carp, tench, etc). Vauxhall AC has stretch here; members only; also lake at Stanton Harcourt; good carp. Newland AC has Windrush from Witney d/s, and Heyford Lakes Fishery, dt £5. **Richworth Linear Fisheries** have seven pools near

Stanton Harcourt on B4449 road. Fishery records incl pike to 30lbs, carp to 42lbs. Lakes include **Hunts Corner Lake, Hunts Corner Pond, Harwicke Lake, Smiths Pool, Manor Farm Lake, St Johns Pool, Oxlease** and **The Float Lake**; dt on banks; bailiff (tel: 07885 327708). The fisheries also have **Guy Lakes (Gaunts, Unity, Yeomans)** and **River Windrush**; members only; contact Fishery Manager, 10A Rackstaw Grove, Old Farm Park, Milton Keynes MK7 8PZ (tel: 01908 645135; web: www.linearfisheries.co.uk). Tackle shop: States Fishing Tackle, 19 Fettiplace Rd, Witney, Oxon OX28 5AP (tel: 01993 702587).

Minster Lovell (Oxon). Cotswold Flyfishers have 10m at **Swinbrook** and **Stanton Harcourt**; trout (restocked yearly), fly only; membership limited; no dt. Witney AA has water on Windrush at **Worsham** (1m above village; trout re-stocked yearly) and on Thames at **Newbridge** and **Standlake**; trout, grayling, coarse fish; fishing much improved. **Linch Hill Leisure Park**, Stanton Harcourt OX29 5BB; Stoneacres Lake mixed coarse fishing; dt £18 (24 hrs); apply for dt rates, conc, (tel: 01865 882215). Tackle shop: States Tackle *(see Witney above)*. Hotel: Old Swan Inn.

Burford (Oxon). Burford AC holds approx 1m, with brown and rainbow trout to 5lbs, grayling, large roach, perch, chub, dace, gudgeon, and pike to 9lbs; all grayling to be returned; st £20, conc, from Hon Sec; dt £5 from Highway Hotel, Burford OX8 4RG (tel: 01993 822136). Club is affiliated with Oxford & Dist AA. Tackle shop: K & M Fishing Tackle, 23 West Rd, Chipping Norton OX7 5EU (tel: 01608 645435). Hotels include Cotswold; Gateway; Lamb; Highway.

COLN: notable dry fly fishing for trout of good average size; grayling.

Fairford (Glos). Trout; excellent; April 1 to Sept 30; grayling Oct-Mar; dry fly only upstream; not stocked; tickets can be had for 1½m from Bull Hotel, Market Place, GL7 4AA (tel: 01285 712535); Catch/return; trout of 1-1½lb plentiful; dt £27, half day £20 (reduction for residents). **Whelford Pools Fishery**, Welford Rd, Fairford GL7 4DT (tel: 01285 713649); dt waters, 3 lakes joined by 2 channels; 4 acres in total; carp to 29lb, tench to 12lb; dt £8 (£15 24 hrs), conc; on site or bankside; syndicate lake, waiting list.

Bibury (Glos). Coln: trout. Swan Hotel GL7 5NW (tel: 01285 740695) has 300 yds facing hotel, day tickets from hotel: dry fly only, 3 rods on offer.

TORRIDGE

(For close seasons, licences, etc, see South West Region Environment Agency p19)

Rises on Cornwall Devonshire border, but is also fed from Dartmoor via a tributary, the River Okement. It flows into Bideford/Barnstaple Estuary. Salmon, sea trout, peal and brown trout.

Bideford (Devon). River for 2m on east side, and two reservoirs, at **Gammaton**, stocked with brown and rainbow trout, leased by Torridge Fly Fishing Club; st £100 from Hon Sec, written application only; dt £12.50 from Summerlands Tackle, 16-20 Nelson Road, Westward Ho! Bideford EX39 1LF (tel: 01237 471291). **Weare Giffard**, 1m right bank, salmon, sea trout, brown trout; dt £27 (salmon and sea trout), residents £22; browns £18 (£14) from Half Moon Inn, Sheepwash, Beaworthy, N Devon EX21 5NE (tel: 01409 231376). Hotels: Royal, New Inn, Tanton's.

Torrington (Devon). Salmon, sea trout, brown trout. Fishing lodge and day rods on **Beaford** stretch; contact Group Capt P Norton-Smith, Little Warham, Beaford, Winkleigh EX19 8AB (tel: 01805 603317). The Clinton Arms, Frithelstock, nr Torrington EX38 8JH (tel: 01805 623279) has 1½m both banks; dt £20 per rod, max 3 rods. Coarse fishing at **Darracott Reservoir**, Torrington; 3 acres is South West Lakes Trust water, open all the year, 24 hr day; st £125 (day and night), £85 st (day), 24-hour £8.75, dt £4.75, conc £3.75 from Summerlands Tackle, 16-20 Nelson Rd, Westward Ho! EX39 1LF (tel: 01237 471291); *see above*. Tackle shops and SWLT tickets: The Kingfisher, 22 Castle St, Barnstaple EX31 1DR (tel:01271 344919); Whiskers Pet Centre, 20 South St, Torrington, EX38 8AA (tel: 01805 622859).

Shebbear (Devon). Devil's Stone Inn, EX21 5RU (tel: 01409 281210), can arrange with local farmers for 2½m of salmon, sea trout and brown trout fishing on

Torridge; fly and spinning; excellent dry-fly trout water. Nearest beat 1m.

Sheepwash (Devon). Half Moon Inn, Sheepwash, Beaworthy, N Devon EX21 5NE (tel: 01409 231376), has 12m of private salmon, sea trout and brown trout fishing on Torridge. Season 1 Mar to 30 Sept, spinning allowed in Mar, otherwise fly only. Fishing available for non-residents but guests have priority; must be booked in advance; dt for non-residents £27 salmon and sea trout, residents £22; £18 (£14) brown trout. Brochure on request. Tackle shop at hotel, also tackle for hire, and rod licences available.

Hatherleigh (Devon). Torridge, Lew, Okement; salmon, sea trout, brown trout. 4 coarse lakes at **Halwill**, 'Anglers Eldorado'; specimen fish: carp, golden tench, golden orfe, golden rudd, koi, grass carp, all on £4 dt per rod, conc: Mr Zyg Gregorek, The Gables, Winsford, Halwill Junction EX21 5XT (tel: 01409 221559), who also offers fishing and fishing holidays as follows: Anglers Paradise: luxury accom and 12 lakes, with coarse fish incl carp to 30lbs, unusual species such as golden orfe, golden rudd, golden tench, for residents only; Anglers Eldorado, four coarse lakes on dt; Anglers Shangri-La, three lakes of up to 240 pegs for match fishing; Anglers Utopia, three villas, purpose built for disabled, with lake fishing; tackle shop on site. Hotel: New Inn, Meeth (½m on Torridge; dts for salmon and trout).

Tributaries of the Torridge

LEW: Sea trout, trout.

OKEMENT:

Okehampton (Devon). Fishing presently suspended on this stretch of Okement, to allow stocks to grow. **Highampton Trout Fishery** is accessible from Oakhampton. Tackle shop: C P Angling, 3 The Arcade, Fore Str, EX20 1EX (tel: 01837 53911).

WALDON: Principal tributary of Upper Torridge.

Mill Leat Fishery, Thornbury, Holsworthy EX22 7AY (tel: 01409 261426), offers dt £5 on ½m stretch with brown trout, and 3 acre stillwater, with rainbows; self-catering accom at same address.

A grilse in the net on the Little Warham Fishery on the Torridge. *Photo: Capt P Norton-Smith.*

TRENT

(For close seasons, licences, etc, see Midlands Region Environment Agency, p22)

Largest river system in England. Rising in Staffordshire, Trent drains much of Derbyshire, Nottinghamshire and Lincolnshire, and empties into Humber. A hundred years ago, one of England's principal fisheries; now recovering its status following massive effort at water quality improvement. The tidal water, in particular, now fishing excellently. Some famous trout-holding tributaries, notably Dove, Wye and Derwent.

Gainsborough (Lincoln). Pike, perch, roach, carp, barbel, chub. There are a few fish to 3m below Gainsborough. Tidal. Scunthorpe AA has 1m at South Clifton, east bank; dt on bank; also 1m at Girton, plus ½m at Besthorpe; dt on bank. Lincoln & Dist AA has water south of Gainsborough at North Clifton and Laughterton. Membership £22, dt £3.50 from bailiff, D Ellerker, Mill Hill House, North Clifton NG23 7AZ. Good local carp fishery: Daiwa Gull Pool, nr Scunthorpe; two lakes of 10 and 34 acres, with carp to 34lbs, catfish 32½lbs; syndicate only; contact N J Fickling, 27 Lodge Lane, Upton, Gainsborough DN21 5NW. Tackle shop: The Tackle shop, 9 Kings Str, DN21 1JS (tel: 01427 613002).

Marton (Lincoln). Tidal water. Free fishing at Littleborough. Excellent catches of roach.

Torksey (Lincoln). Chub, roach. Lincoln & Dist has fishing east bank at Laughterton and North Clifton; dt £3.50, conc (annual membership £22, conc £13) from bailiff D Ellerker, Mill Hill House, North Clifton NG23 7AZ. White Swan AC has 15 pegs of natural bank and 15 pegs off platforms, between Lincoln and Gainsborough; dt £2.50 on bank. B&B at White Swan Hotel, 400yds from bank. Scunthorpe & Dist AA (tel: 01652 655849) has Dunham Bridge. Worksop & DAA fishes 25 pegs of Torksey Arm, and 4 pegs on opp bank below lock up to White Swan fishery, with chub, roach, bream, skimmer; dt £3 on bank (bailiff, Ken Bradshaw, tel: 01427 717492).

Dunham (Notts). Rotherham & Dist AA offers dt for its fishing on right bank, u/s and d/s of Dunham.

High Marnham (Notts). Worksop & DAA has water above the Mansfield stretch at **Normanton-on-Trent** (35 pegs); dt on bank, £3. Sheffield & Dist AA also has 40 pegs on left bank at Normanton, dt £3, before commencement of fishing.

Sutton-on-Trent (Notts). Tidal water. Pike, roach, dace, chub. Lincoln & Dist AA has fishing at **North Clifton** and

Laughterton. Dt £3.50, conc £2.50 (annual membership £22, conc £13) from bailiff, D Ellerker, Mill Hill House, North Clifton NG23 7AZ. Scunthorpe & Dist AA has **South Clifton** fishing; dt on bank.

Collingham (Notts). Club water. Trent 2m W; pike, carp, barbel, roach, dace, chub, perch, bream. Collingham AA has 4m from Cromwell Weir to Besthorpe parish boundary; dt £3 from bailiff on bank. All round coarse fishing. Worksop & DAA waters are from immediately above the weir to just below Winthorpe Lake (185 pegs); also 40 pegs above lake to Winthorpe rail crossing; also waters on opp bank at Ness Farm (40 pegs): report to farm for dt for this stretch; also Footits Marsh (30 pegs); otherwise dt on bank, £3. Hotels: Royal Oak, King's Head, Grey Horse.

Muskham (Notts). Nottingham Piscatorial Society preserves from Fir Tree Corner (Kelham boundary) to Crankley Point, both sides, including gravel pits; members only.

Averham, Kelham (Notts). Very good coarse fishing. Preserved by Nottingham Piscatorial Society for members only; roach, dace, chub (excellent fly water) - from weirs at Staythorpe to South Muskham boundary on both sides of the river.

Newark-on-Trent (Notts). Roach, dace, pike, chub, bream, barbel, gudgeon, perch, eels. Newark & Dist Piscatorial Federation has Trent at Rolleston, East Stoke, Winthrope, Kelham Hall; tidal Trent at Girton and Cottam, and **Newark Dyke** at three sections; dt £3 on some waters; Federation also has water at Winthorpe Lake. Nottingham AA fishes from Farndon Ferry to Newark Dyke; dt from bailiff on bank. Other dt stretches: Worksop & DAA controls from Cromwell Lock and Winthorpe Lake to Winthorpe Crossing, 225 pegs; Ness Farm, 40 pegs; Footits Marsh 25 pegs; dt on bank £3, conc. Holme Marsh fishing: 185 pegs both banks, dt on bank, and 40 pegs at Winthorpe Crossing, contact Secretary D

Brown. Newark & Dist PF controls water from Crankly Point to Winthorpe Crossing. Dt £4 on bank. Trent Lane, **Collingham**, Collingham AA water; tickets on bank. Tackle shop: Newark Angling Centre, 29 Albert St, Newark NG24 4BJ (tel: 01636 686212).

Farndon (Notts). South bank let to Nottingham AA; dt £3 issued.

Rolleston (Notts). Newark & Dist PF have fishing here, members only. Greet, trout; preserved. Nottingham AA has water at **Farndon Ferry** (opp Rolleston); dt from bailiff; matches can be arranged in advance. Sheffield & Dist AA has left bank at **Normanton**, dt £3 on bank.

Fiskerton (Notts). Good roach, chub and barbel fishing. Nottingham Piscatorial Society water from Greet mouth (Fiskerton) to Farndon, (excluding members field and car park); good roach, barbel and chub; dt £3 from Fiskerton PO; Nottingham tackle shops; no permits on bank. Barnsley & Dist AAS have one mile of left bank; dt £2.50 from PO shop; conc, st. The Greet enters Trent at Fiskerton; preserved.

Hoveringham (Notts). Dt £3 on bank for Nottingham AA stretch from old Star and Garter 1¾m u/s. Midland AS has stretch to Caythorpe, barbel, roach, chub, bream, gudgeon, etc; 146 pegs, dt £2.50, conc, on bank, matches bookable, apply Hon Sec.

Gunthorpe (Notts). Good coarse fishing; roach, dace, chub. Nottingham & Dist FAS has north bank water u/s and d/s of Gunthorpe; dt £3 on bank. Good pub near water, The Anchor.

Burton Joyce (Notts). Chub, roach (mainly), dace. Nottingham & Dist FAS has good north bank stretch for which dt (£3) issued (matches arranged, booked in advance after Nov 1 for following season); tickets from bailiff; Stoke Ferry Boat Inn.

Shelford (Notts). Stoke Weir to Gunthorpe Bridge, Nottingham AA water; dt £3 on bank.

Radcliffe-on-Trent (Notts). Roach, chub, dace and gudgeon, with perch, pike and tench in Lily Ponds. North Bank from Stoke Weir down to **Gunthorpe**, Nottingham & DFAS; dt £2. From Stoke Weir up to Radcliffe Ferry, including Lily Ponds, Nottingham & Dist FAS; dt £3. Fedn also holds from Radcliffe Ferry upstream (members only) and water below Radcliffe railway bridge *(see Burton Joyce);* u/s southbank to rowing course at

Holme Pierrepont.

Colwick (Notts). Colwick Country Park, Mile End Rd, Colwick, NG4 2DW (tel: 0115 987 0785), is operated by Nottingham City Council; and includes a 65 acre trout fishery, and coarse waters on River Trent (with 40 bookable match pegs), and lake; permits and information from Fishing Lodge, at above address. Nottingham AA has fishing rights for 1 field from Viaduct downstream; dt £3 on bank; access through Industrial Estate u/s of viaduct. For other local fishing information, contact Colwick Flyfishers, Kevin Saxton, 35 Ivy Grove, Carlton, Nottingham NG4 1RG (web: www.boat86.freeserve.co.uk).

Nottingham (Notts). Good mixed fishing. Several miles in city free. Nottingham AA (tel: 0115 9199500) has Beeston, south bank. **Colwick**, viaduct d/s 600 yds; **East Bridgford**, 180 yds below weir (members only); d/s for 1,350 yds; dt £3 from bailiff. Nottingham PS has fishing at **Rolleston** and **Fiskerton**; dt from tackle shops only; largely members only. Long Eaton Victoria AS has 30 pegs below Colwick sluices, left bank; dt £2. Nottingham & DFAS have dt at Clifton Bridge; other clubs with Trent fishing near town are Nottingham Waltonians (right bank north of Clifton), Nottingham AA, (several stretches on both banks, south of town). Nottingham & DFAS comprises upwards of 68 clubs, with water at **Burton Joyce, Thrumpton, Gunthorpe, Carlton, Hazelford, Clifton Grove,** and **Holme Pierrepont.** Midland AS (tel: 0115 9634487) has 14 pegs at Hoveringham and Caythorpe; dt £2.50, conc, on bank. Parkside AC has **Grantham Canal,** and **Castle Marina,** both near Nottingham; dt £2 on bank on all waters except Marina, members only. Lake in **Wollaton Park** may be fished by dt from Parks Superintendent, Wollaton Park. **Sutton Lake** (not to be confused with Sutton Lake, Shropshire): 17 acre trout fly water, fished by Derbyshire County AC; also 20 acre coarse lake and 20 acre trout lake, plus 2m of Trent, both on 100 acre site alongside river; members only. Long Eaton Victoria AS has left bank below sluice at Colwick; dt £2 on bank. National Watersports Centre, Holme Pierrepont (tel: 0115 9821212), offer angling on 62 acre coarse lake with roach, perch, dt on bank. Tackle shops: Netherfield, 75 Victoria Road, Nether-

Section 2 of the River Trent at Thrumpton: Coventry & District Angling Association water.

field, Nottingham, NG4 2NN (tel: 0115 987 0525); Junction Tackle, 210 Tamworth Rd, Long Eaton NG10 3GS (tel: 0115 973 6326); and many others.

Beeston (Notts). Chub, roach, dace, bleak, gudgeon; preserved by Nottingham AA; dt for stretch from N Bank Lock from bailiff; assn also has water on **Beeston Canal**; assn also has 250 acre Attenborough ravel Pits, mostly members only (st £34); mixed coarse. Tackle shop: Supertackle, 192 Station Rd NG9 2AY (tel: 0115 922 9669). Hotels: Brackley House; Hylands.

Thrumpton and Long Eaton (Notts). Roach, bream, dace, chub, perch, barbel. Long Eaton Victoria AS has 2 meadows d/s of Cranfleet Lock. Full membership £18, conc. Coventry & Dist AA also has water here with large barbel and carp, dt £3.50 for Ferry Farm on bank, and for sections above weir. Soldiers & Sailors AC have Trent Lock, dt on bank; contact Mr Walker (tel: 0115 9721478). **Erewash Canal**. Roach, gudgeon, bream, carp, perch, chub. Nottingham AA has canal at Sandiacre; dt £3 on bank. Long Eaton Victoria AS has **Soar**, at Kegworth, dt £2 on bank, Ratcliffe, members only; canal fishing, on Cranfleet Canal (Trent Lock),

Erewash Canal, (Long Eaton Lock to Trent Lock), also ponds in Long Eaton, members only. Long Eaton & Dist AF has 120 pegs on **Erewash Canal** from Long Eaton to Sandiacre Lock; dt £2; apply bailiff (tel: 0115 9720348) or tackle shops. Tackle shops: Junction Tackle, 210 Tamworth Rd, Long Eaton NG10 3GS (tel: 0115 973 6326). Hotels: Elms; Europa; Sleep Inn.

Sawley (Notts). Above moorings, Olympic AC offer day tickets, purchased in advance. Pride of Derby AA has fishing on both banks above and below M1 motorway bridge, from Marina down to R Derwent, and 1m at Willington on Repton bank; also 5 lakes (including Redhouse Lake) and ponds of 60 acres total (including Ully Gully); st £40, wt £18, conc from Hon Sec.

Barrow-upon-Trent (Derbys). **Manor House Fishery**: 20 pegs designed for disabled anglers, most with vehicle access, open Monday to Sunday; excellent chub, roach, barbel and perch. Details of fishery, contact Barry Poxon, Chairman, Practical Angling for the Disabled AC; also for dt (which are not issued on bank) but may be issued to non-disabled anglers; membership applicants must be in receipt of DLA, mobility allowance or war pensions equivalent; disabled toilets. The fishing is available for matches hire.

Burton-upon-Trent (Staffs). Free fishing for Burton residents either side of St Peters Bridge (Stapenhill Pleasure Gardens and Waterside); no dt. Burton-upon-Trent Mutual AA have fishing which includes **Dove** at **Tutbury** to confluence with Trent; Trent at **Walton** and The Meadows in town; Trent at Cuttlebrook; gravel pit at **Kings Bromley**; Branstone Water Park; and other waters; members only. Warrington AA has **Claymills** river fishery. **Hartshorne Dams**, 2 coarse lakes, are 2 min off A50 at Woodville; dt Mr David Burchell, Manor Farm, Hartshorne DE11 7ER (tel: 01283 215769). Pride of Derby AA has 12m of **Trent and Mersey Canal** in vicinity; also water on Dove at Scropton; st £40, wt £18, conc from Hon Sec. Willsley Lake, Moira, has dt for carp to 30lbs, good stocks of bream, etc. Tickets for canals, various stretches on the R Trent and eight local trout and coarse venues from tackle shops. 5m east of town, National have three ponds: perch, roach, rudd; at Calke Abbey, Ticknall; Wheel Inn AC water, members only (tel: 01283 226176). Tackle shop: Burton Angling Supplies, 31 Borough Rd DE14 2DA (tel: 01283 548540). Hotels: Queen's, Station and Midland.

Alrewas (Staffs). Chub, dace, roach. Prince Albert AS has fishing on both banks, north of Alrewas, below Alrewas AC water on right bank. Birmingham AA has water here, **Wychnor**, **Kings Bromley** and at **Yoxall**; dt £4 from tackle shops. **Trent and Mersey Canal**, dt from keeper. All three clubs, members only. Catton Park Fishing: 1,500m, and 10 acre pool with carp and roach; dt on bank (tel: 01283 716876). Midland Game & Coarse Fisheries, P Jackson, Fisherwick Wood Lane, Lichfield, Staffs WS13 8QQ (tel: 01543 433606); seven lakes between Lichfield and Alrewas, all year-round fishing.

Rugeley (Staffs). Usual species. Armitage to Rugeley, and Wolseley Bridge to Colwich are all BW direct managed. Bridge 69 to Wolseley Bridge is Hednesford AC water on **Trent and Mersey Canal** from Armitage to Wolseley Bridge. From here to Colwich held by British Waterways; dt from them; roach, pike, perch. **Blithfield Reservoir**, 4m NE; trout; Blithfield Anglers Ltd allows fishing on season permit only; visiting anglers may buy a visitor permit (£54) limited to 2 in a boat for the day, engine included. Inquiries to Fishery Office, **Blithfield Reservoir**, Abbots Bromley, Rugeley, Staffs WS15 3DU (tel: 01283 840284).

Stone (Staffs). Stone & Dist AS fishes 750m Trent left bank here. Hanley AS has a stretch of double bank between Sandon and Burston. Crown AC has pools at Eccleshall and Market Drayton, as well as Shropshire Union Canal; dt.

Stoke-on-Trent (Staffs). Fenton & Dist AS has fishing on **R Dove** (barbel, chub and grayling); **R Churnet**, trout and coarse; **Stoke Overflow**, with large carp; **Knypersley Reservoir**; **Trent & Mersey Canal** fishing (Stoke-on-Trent to Barlaston); **Sutton Brook**, Hilton, and 2 pools at **Cheadle**; st £25, conc, for Trent & Mersey Canal stretch, as for **Smith Pool** and **Longton Park Lake**, from Dolphin Discount (*below*), and other tackle shops. At **Newcastle-under-Lyme**: Cudmore Fishery, six pools with carp, barbel, bream, tench, chub, incl specimen pool; tickets from the Lodge, Pleck Lane, Whitmore ST5 5HW (tel: 01782 680919). Tackle shops: Pickerings, 38 Moorland Road, Biddulph, Stoke on Trent ST8 6EW (tel: 01782 814941); Abbey Pet Stores, 1493 Leek Road, Abbey Hulton ST2 8DA (tel: 01782 534667); Dolphin Discount Tackle Shop and Warehouse, Old Whieldon Road, Stoke ST4 4HW (tel: 01782 849390); Mellors Tackle, 30/32 Brunswick St, Hanley ST1 1DR (tel: 01782 266742); and many others.

Trentham (Staffs). Village about 3m from Stoke-on-Trent on main road London to Manchester. Lake of 80 acres at Trentham Gardens Coarse Fishery, Stone Rd, Trentham ST4 8AX; bream, carp, roach, rudd, pike and perch; st £150 from Estates Office Reception (tel: 01782 657519).

Weston-on-Trent (Staffs). Coarse fishing in **Trent and Mersey Canal**; chub, roach, bream, perch.

Tributaries of the Trent

IDLE: Excellent coarse fishing in parts, with bream, roach, chub, predominating.

Misterton (Notts). Gate Inn AC (tel: 01427 891106) has 1,500m at Haxey Gate, dt £2 from HQ, Gate Inn, Haxey Rd, Misterton DN10 4BA (tel: 01427 890746). No fishing on right bank from Misterton to West Stockwith, or on right bank from Langholme parish boundary to West Stockwith.

Misson (Notts). Doncaster & Dist AA has 100 pegs on stretch from Newington to Misson. Good roach, bream, perch, pike; st £16, conc, and dt £2.50 from tackle dealers.

Bawtry (Notts). Chub, roach main species. Environment Agency has 500 yds of left bank free to licence holders (tel: 0115 9455722). Doncaster & Dist AA has Newington stretch; dt £2.50 on bank. Tackle shop: R & R Sports, 40 High Str, DN10 6JE (tel: 01302 711130).

Retford (Notts). Poulter, 4m S. Meden, 4m S. Maun, 4m S. Idle above Retford private. Derbyshire County AC has 6½m, Lound to East Retford, with chub, roach, dace, bream, barbel, pike; members only, but river tickets only for £15. Club also controls 2m coarse fishing on R Trent at Willington, 5m on Derwent, and trout fishing on Dove, Manifold, Ogston Reservoir and various trout lakes in Derbyshire and Nottinghamshire, in separate membership categories and fees; contact Hon Sec. For Idle permits (st £15) contact by post Ron Trevis, The Homestead, Sutton Lane, Sutton Scarsdale, Chesterfield S44 5UP. Club also fishes Sutton Lake (17 acres), and Tiln Lake; both fly only for browns and rainbows; members only; st £170. Worksop & DAA controls a stretch of the **Chesterfield Canal** from Drakeholes Tunnel to West Retford bridge, 10½m, famous for chub and roach, match weights up to 50lb; limited membership; dt £2.50 on bank, conc. Retford & Dist AA fishes 5½m **Chesterfield Canal** at Retford, and **Carlton**, also 2m **R Till**, **Saxilby**, various coarse species. **Woodside Lake**, Lound, further Retford AA coarse fishery, with bream, tench, roach. Dt on bank, £3.00, membership £10, conc. **Daneshill Lakes**, 30 acres with carp and pike, tickets on bank or from local newsagents. Information from Daneshill Lakes, Lound Low Rd, Ranskill, nr Retford (tel: 01909 770917). **Hallcroft Coarse Fisheries**, Hallcroft Rd, Retford DN 22 7RA (tel: 01777 710448): four lakes total 16 acres with bream, roach, carp, tench, perch, chub, and river fishing; dt £4.50 at cafeteria. Tackle shops: Retford Angling Centre, 10

Northfield Way, Hallcroft, Retford DN22 7LJ (tel: 01777 706168); Worldwide Angling Supplies, Hallcroft Fisheries, Retford DN22 7RA (tel: 01777 704569).

TORNE and NEW IDLE. Doncaster & Dist AA has 5m from Epworth Road Bridge to Pilfrey Bridge and water on **Stainforth and Keadby Canal**; dt £2.50 from Doncaster and Bawtry tackle shops. Scunthorpe & Dist AA has water on the Three Rivers from Pilfrey Bridge to the half way point to the outflow at Keadby; known for its tench, pike and bream; dt on bank.

Althorpe (S Humberside). **Stainforth & Keadby Canal**; coarse fish; about 14m of water above and down to Trent; good fishing; rights held by Sheffield, Rotherham, Doncaster, Scunthorpe and British Rail associations. Other fishing stations for canal are **Thorne** and **Crowle**. **Lindholme Lakes**, Sandtoft, Doncaster DN9 1LF (tel: 01427 872905), mixed fishery on 5 lakes: 2 general coarse lakes and a 14 acre carp syndicate lake, and a carp lake; dt £12 (first 2 fish) then c&r, 4 fish £15, 4 fish £18; £5 (coarse), conc.

Crowle (S Humberside). Excellent centre for coarse fishing. **Stainforth and Keadby Canal**, and **Torne** are ½m from Crowle Central Station; Doncaster & Dist AA; roach, tench, bream, perch, carp, pike. Three Drains on A18; Sheffield & Dist AA; roach, perch, tench, carp; licences, association books and dt from hotels or Hon Sec (enclose s/a envelope). Tackle shops: many in Doncaster and Scunthorpe. Hotels: South Yorkshire, Crowle; Friendship Inn, Keadby. Tackle shops in Doncaster (17m) or Scunthorpe (10m).

RYTON (tributary of Idle); Coarse fish.

Worksop (Notts). On Ryton and **Chesterfield Canal**; coarse fish. Worksop & DAA has 10½m of canal from W Retford Bridge to Drakeholes Tunnel. **Clumber Park Lake** (National Trust 100 acre lake), where dt and st can be had from Estate Office, Clumber Park S80 3AZ (tel: 01909 476592); 7am to dusk; st £50, dt £4, both conc; dt on bank. **Woodsetts Quarry Pond**, 8 acres; Steetley Pond, Oakshires; and **Sandhill Lake**; coarse fish; dt £2.50-£3 on all water. Grafton AA fishes 4m of Chesterfield Canal (from Bracebridge Lock to Shireoaks Bridge) in and around town; predominantly large bream, chub, rudd, ruffe, carp, skimmer bream, gudgeon, plenty of roach; st £12, conc, (limited); dt £2 on bank from bailiff. For **Langold Lakes**, 14 acres with bream and carp, north of Worksop, contact Site Office (tel: 01909 730189) or Bassetlaw Leisure Centre, Eastgate, Worksop S80 1QS (tel: 01909 480164). Tackle shops: Angling Supplies, 49 Retford Rd S80 2PU (tel: 01909 482974); Ken Ward Sports, 6 Carlton Rd S80 1PH (tel: 01909 472904); Gateford Angling Supplies, 155 Gateford Rd S80 1UD (tel: 01909 531115).

MAUN (tributary of Idle): Improving fish stocks: chub, dace, roach. Little formal access; apply to local landowners.

Mansfield (Notts). Field Mill Dam; coarse fish, dt. Vicar Water, Clipstone; coarse fish, dt. **Kings Mill Reservoir**, Sutton Rd: Nottingham AA water, with carp, roach, bream, dt £3 on bank. Mansfield & Dist AA has Bleasby Gravel Pits; st £20, conc; from Hon Sec and tackle shops; these pits are shared with Midland AS (members only). Permits for local coarse ponds also from Mansfield Angling, 20 Byron Street, Shirebrook, Mansfield NG18 5PR (tel: 01623 633790).

Sutton-in-Ashfield (Notts). Lakes: Lawn, Dam. King's Mill Reservoir, 1m NE; tickets on bank. **Hardwick Lakes**, Hardwick Hall, are 6m W; National Trust water, all coarse ponds; Carr Ponds is members only club water (tel: 01246 850242); Great Pond, and Millers Pond, are st, dt waters (tel: 01246 851787); Rowe Ponds (5) club members only (01773 717648). Tackle shop: Horace Burrows, 91 Outram Str, NG17 4AQ (tel: 01623 557816). Hotels: Nag's Head, Denman's Head.

DEVON: Coarse fish.

Bottesford (Notts). Smite, 3m NW at Orston. Car Dyke, 5m NW. Bottesford AA preserves 5m of **Grantham Canal** at Bottesford, Muston Bridge and Woolsthorpe-by-Belvoir; st and dt from Hon Sec and from bailiffs on bank. Good coarse fishing, with pike over 27lb. Other Assn waters are **River Witham** at Westborough, members only; **River Devon** at Cotham Grange, right bank d/s of Wensor Bridge to Pack Bridge, 1½m, members only. Tackle shop: Arbon & Watts Ltd, 96 Westgate, Grantham NG31 6LE (tel: 01476 400014).

Belvoir Castle (Leics). Between Melton Mowbray and Grantham, **Belvoir Lakes** and **Knipton Reservoir** (coarse fish); open all year; st £60, ½ st £40, dt £6 on

bank, conc £4.50, from Estate Office, Belvoir Castle, Grantham NG32 1PD (tel: 01476 870262; fax: 01476 870443), also from Knipton Shop. For **AJS Fisheries**, Birch Cottage, Hungerton Hall, Hungerton, Grantham NG32 1AJ; contact the Fishery Manager (tel: 01476 870647). **Nottingham and Grantham Canal**: Bottesford & DAA has water. Other stations on canal are **Long Clawson**, **Harby**, **Hose** and **Stathern**.

GREET: Trout; coarse fish; preserved.

Southwell (Notts). River private. Trent, 3m SE at Fiskerton. At Oxton, 5m SW, Nottingham Fly Fishers' Club has a trout lake at Gibsmere; strictly members only, long waiting list. Greet FC, too, has trout fishing. Derbyshire County AC has Coneygre and Widgeon Lakes; brown and rainbow; fly only; pike also in winter; members only; st £170.

West Hallam (Derby). Lakes: **Mapperley Reservoir**, 2m N, **Shipley Park Lakes**, **Loscoe Dam** and stretch of Erewash Canal all NCB waters; st £20, conc, from Hon Sec; Dt £2 from park rangers for some waters (max 2 rods).

SOAR: Very popular coarse fishery with anglers in the Leicester area. Environment Agency fishery at **Thurmaston**,

A nice bag of fine winter grayling taken on trotted redworm, caught from a small tributary
of the Derbyshire Derwent. But grayling are found in fast-flowing clean rivers in most parts
of Great Britain, south of the Scottish Highlands. *Photo: Bruno Broughton,* who also
caught the fish.

nearly 1,000 yds right bank free to licence holders, west of A46 road.

Radcliffe (Derby); Good coarse fishing. Long Eaton & Dist AF administrate between Kegworth and Radcliffe Flood Locks, and 1m Trent, Trent Lock, south bank; dt from tackle dealers. Soldiers & Sailors AC have Trent Lock fishing, and Barkers Pond, Long Eaton; mixed coarse; dt £2 on bank; contact W Walker, 41 Hawthorne Ave, Long Eaton NG10 3NG (tel: 0115 9721478).

Kegworth (Derby). Roach, dace, bream, tench, chub, perch. Two meadows u/s of Kegworth Bridge held by Long Eaton Victoria AS; dt and st. Nottingham AA has from Kingston Dyke one field u/s to boatyard (members only). Long Eaton AF has good 2m stretch from Kegworth to Ratcliffe, 90 pegs; coarse; dt £2 from Anchor Inn, Station Rd, (tel: 01509 672722); tackle shops at Long Eaton and Borrowash. Soar AS has water here. Kegworth AS has approx 400 mtrs.

Normanton-on-Soar (Leics), Good coarse fishing. Loughborough Soar AS water.

Loughborough (Leics). Loughborough Soar AS has fishing near here with large carp, chub, bream, roach, perch, plus dace and barbel on two stretches; dt in advance from Soar Valley Tackle (*below*), or on bank; for information contact Hon Sec. **Proctor's Pleasure Park**, Barrow-on-Soar LE12 8QF (tel: 0150 9412434): lake and river fishing, mainly carp, bream, tench, perch; dt £3 (3x£1 coins) from machine on site; lake open during close season. **Charnwood Water**: 11 acre lake with carp, pike; council fishery; dt £2.60 per rod, conc from Soar Valley Tackle. Tackle shops: Soar Valley Tackle, 7 Woodbrook Rd LE11 3QB (tel: 01509 231817). Hotels: King's Head.

Quorn (Leics). Roach, bream. Quorn AS has rights on stretches of river and 1m of canal. River fishes best in autumn and winter.

Barrow-upon-Soar (Leics). About 3m river and canal fishing; good roach and bream; recently restocked. Fishes best autumn and winter. Loughborough Soar AS has water. (*See Loughborough*), also Quorn AC. Proctor's Park has about 1m fishing (*see Loughborough*). Leicester & DAA has 2m; one bank; dt £3 on bank; st £12 from Hon Sec or local tackle shops; assn also has stillwater at Walton on the Wolds, well-stocked with carp, roach, skimmers; dt only, in advance from local tackle shop in Syston: Match Catch, 14 The Green, Syston LE7 1HQ (tel: 0116 2600850).

Leicester (Leics). Coarse fish. 6,000m between Leicester and Barrow on Soar, towpath side, held by Leicester & DAA; also **Nene** at Ironbridge, and canals; membership £12; dt £3 on bank. Wreake AC has 4,500 1 bank **Wreake** at **Brooksby**. Wigston AC: Soar and canal; dt and st. **Leicester Canal**; some good coarse fish but boat traffic ruins summer sport. Very high quality stillwater fishing in twelve lakes totalling 22 acres in **Mallory Park** (tel: 0116 2774131), 8m from Leicester; st £230, conc, (covering all twelve lakes). The Pool, Groby, 5m NW; bream, tench, roach, pike; dt from house at pool. Broome AS (the largest club in Leicestershire with over 600 members) fishes 1 lake on Watermead Park, **Birstall**; good tench and bream fishing; also 5 coarse lakes at Asfordby; 2 lakes at **Frolesworth** with carp to 20lbs, and mixed coarse; 2 acre lake at **Syston** with large carp, and good head of small fish, and stretches of **Soar**; membership £40 p/a + £10 joining fee, conc, from Hon Sec. Tackle shops: The Angling Man, 228 Melton Rd, LE4 7PG (tel: 0116 266 5579); Match Catch, 14 The Green, Syston LE7 1HQ (tel: 0116 2600850); Angling Corner, 3 Denton St LE3 6DD (tel: 0116 223 0008). Hotels: Grand, Royal, Hermitage (Oadby).

Narborough (Leics). Hinckley & Dist AA has water here containing trout and grayling; permits from permits sec. Broome AS has a stretch here and at **Wanlip**, roach, perch, chub, barbel; members only.

WREAKE (tributary of Soar): An attractive coarse fishery on which Wreake AC and Asfordby & Melton AC have extensive coarse fishing rights between Thrussington and Melton Mowbray; all members only.

Asfordby (Leics). Roach, perch, dace, pike, chub. Asfordby SOA has water on Wreake and pits at **Frisby** (1m); members only, no dt. Broome AS also has water at Frisby (5 lakes); members only.

Melton Mowbray (Leics). Local club: Asfordby and Melton Society of Anglers have Hoby, Frisby, Ashfordby and Sysonby; members only. **Kala Lakes**, Hoby Rd, Ashfordby, has carp to double figures, dt £5, conc, on bank. **Eye Kettleby Lakes**, off Leicester Rd, three lakes with large carp, etc, dt £4-£5 on bank, or contact Arbon & Watts (*below*). Disabled swims at both these fisheries. Tackle shop: Arbon & Watts, 39 Sherrard St LE13 1XH (tel: 01664 855030).

DERWENT: Noted trout and grayling water in upper reaches; downstream coarse fish come into their own. Derbyshire County AC have several stretches (9 miles) upstream and downstream of Derby.

Sawley (Derby). Coarse fish. Pride of Derby AA has rights, also on **Trent** between Swarkestone and Willington; one mile of **R Dove** at **Scropton** and 12m of Trent and Mersey Canal between Shardlow and Burton upon Trent; and several ponds (including Grimleys Ponds); members only, st £40, wt £18, conc from Hon Sec. Long Eaton & Dist AF has 750 yards south bank of Trent at Sawley; accessible by ferry boat weekends only; very good fishing, dt £2. Soldiers & Sailors AC has Derwent fishing nearby at **Draycott**, members only; contact W Walker (tel: 0115 9721478).

Borrowash (Derby). Coarse fish. Earl of Harrington AC waters (*see Derby*). Derbyshire County AC has 6½m stretch, mainly double bank, Borrowash to Sawley with barbel, chub, roach, bream, carp, tench, perch and pike; st £25, contact Ron Trevis, The Homestead, Sutton Lane, Sutton Scarsdale, Chesterfield S44 5UP (post only). Nottingham & Dist FAS has fishing rights at Riverside Farm Estates, on Derwent, mill streams and lake. Strictly members only.

Spondon (Derby). Coarse fish; preserved by Earl of Harrington AC. Chaddesden Brook, 1m NW, and Locko Park, 2m N. Private.

Derby (Derby). Coarse fish, Earl of Harrington AC has Derwent from Borrowash Road Bridge u/s to Darley Park, st £18, dt £2 in advance from tackle shops below, conc (from Hon Sec); and from Borrowash u/s to Railway Bridge. Derby City Council issues dt, ½ conc, for Derwent from Darley Abbey to Derby Railway Station. Council issues tickets for coarse fishing at **Alvaston Lake**, **Markeaton Park Lake**, **Allestree Park Lake** and **Derwent** in **Darley Abbey Park**: DCC, Derby City Parks, 15 Stores St, Derby DE21 4BD (tel: 01332 367800); dt £3.20/rod, conc, from ranger on bank. Locko Park Lake and Chaddesden Brook private. Other clubs: Pride of Derby AA

(*see Sawley*); Derby RIFC (water on Derwent, **Trent**, **Dove**, **Ecclesbourne**; canals). Earl of Harrington AC (Derwent, 1m of **Big Shrine** at Borrowash, dt); Derbyshire County AC has fishing on Derwent at Allestree, 1½m; fly fishing for trout and grayling; also coarse; the club also has Hoon Hay Farm Lake, 6 acres; fly only for browns and rainbows; members only; st £170; also Willington Fisheries: 2m of River Trent, a 20 acre coarse lake and 20 acre trout lake, both members only. Fenton & DAS has Colley Croft Lake near Etwall. At Kedleston Hall, National Trust has 2 coarse lakes; good winter fishing; carp, pike, tench; contact Head Warden (tel: 01332 842338). Tackle shops: Angling Centre Derby, 33 Nightingale Road, DE2 8BG (tel: 01332 380605); Derwent Tackle, 2 Station Road, Borrowash, Derby DE72 3LG (tel: 01332 662379); Melbourne Tackle & Gun, 64 Church Street, Melbourne, Derby DE73 1EJ (tel: 01332 862091).

Duffield (Derby). Coarse fish, trout and grayling. Derbyshire Angling Federation has 3m from Milford Bridge to Little Eaton, trout and coarse fish, also R Ecclesbourne from Duffield to Derwent confluence; st £28, conc, from Belper Tackle, 37 Bridge St, Belper DE56 1AY (tel: 01773 822525).

Belper (Derby). Chub, roach, bream, perch, barbel, pike, occasional grayling, trout; Belper & DAC: 6m covered by st, £25, conc, incl 2½ acre **Wyver Lane Pond**, large carp etc; 2m covered by dt £3, conc, from Belper Tackle, 37 Bridge St, Belper DE56 1AY (tel: 01773 822525), which also issues dt (£5) (conc £4) for **Possey Lodge**; carp, tench, roach etc.

Ambergate (Derby). Few trout, pike, coarse fish. Derbyshire County AC has water; coarse; members only; st £170. Alderwasley Ponds, 2m NW. **Butterley Reservoir** and **Codnor Park Reservoir**; roach, bream, tench, carp, pike; Ripley & Dist AA waters, st £18, dt £2 from Hon Sec, bailiffs and tackle shops. Hotel: Hurt Arms.

Whatstandwell (Derby). Mostly grayling, brown and rainbow trout, with chub, barbel, some dace and odd perch. Derwent Hotel, Derby Rd, Whatstandwell, Matlock DE4 5HG (tel: 01773 856616), has ¼m fishing; rather overhung with trees, but plenty of fish and good wading in low water; car park on bank. £2.50 dt for visitors, free fishing to hotel guests. Derbyshire County AC has 2m of Derwent. At **Hartington**, Charles Cotton Hotel SK17 0AL (tel: 01298 84229) has 1m double bank, dt £15, 4 fish limit, fly only.

Cromford (Derby). Trout; fly only; preserved below road bridge (both banks), as far as and including Homesford Meadows, by Cromford Fly Fishers; members only, no tickets; waiting list. Above bridge, Derbyshire County AC water, 1m; fly only in trout season; coarse in winter; members only; st £170. Hotel: Greyhound.

Matlock (Derby). Trout (some rainbows), grayling and coarse fish. Matlock AC issue wt and dt; water at Matlock and Matlock Bath; trout and coarse; about 1m. Derbyshire County AC has water, 500 metres; fly only in trout season; grayling in winter; members only; st £170. **Press Manor Fishery**, Birkin Lane, **Wingerworth**, nr Chesterfield, off Matlock-Chesterfield A632 Road (web: www.pressmanorfishery.inuk.com), has three lakes as follows: 5 acre trout lake with stocked rainbow, brown, brook and tiger trout, qualified instruction on site. Dt £15 for 3 rainbows then c&r, evening £12 (2 rainbows then c&r). Float tubing allowed; facilities and 2 disabled platforms; wheelyboat; 3 acre mixed coarse lake, roach, bream, etc, dt £4, eve £2.50, on bank, specimen carp lake, large mirror and common, dt £6; 26-hour ticket £12. Permits from cabin or tackle shops. Contact Mr Maher, Bentley Cottage, Matlock Green, Matlock DE4 3BX (tel: 01629 760996, or mobile 07976 306073). Nearest fly tackle shop: The Fly Fishing Shop, 3a Hebden Court, Matlock St, Bakewell DE45 1EE (tel: 01629 813531).

Rowsley (Derby). Haddon Estate, Bakewell DE45 1LA (tel (the agent): 01629 812855) owns River Wye from Rowsley to just north of Bakewell, together with Rivers Lathkill and **Bradford** for most of their length. Wye has pure wild rainbows, and is one of the few rivers in which they breed; and fine head of natural browns. Dt £30 low season (evng £19), £60 high season: fly only; grayling fishing is open in the winter; for information contact Head River Keeper, Warren Slaney; dt are also obtainable from the Peacock Hotel, Rowsley, DE4 2EB (tel: 01629 733518) to residents and non-residents; high season dt £60, low season £30. Darley Dale FFC has 3m both banks, and 200 yards of Wye; members only; st £410; dt

for guests with members; apply Hon Sec. Warrington AA has fishing at Darley Abbey.

Baslow (Derby); nr Bakewell, 4m. The Cavendish Hotel, DE45 1SP (tel: 01246 582311), originally the famous Peacock, has unique sporting rights over Derwent, unavailable any other way; 6 rods on the **Chatsworth Fishery**, from Old Bridge at Baslow to Smelting Mill Brook at Rowsley (brown and rainbow trout, grayling). For **Monsal Dale Fishery** on R Wye, from boundary of Chatsworth Estate below Cressbrook Mill to New Bridge at Ashford Marble Works (brown and rainbow trout) (courtesy of Chatsworth Estate), contact Stephen Moores (Keeper), Rose Cottage, Monsal Dale SK17 8SZ (tel: 01629 640159). For annual membership of Chatsworth Fishery and Monsal Dale Fisheries apply to Estate Office, Edensor, Bakewell DE45 1PJ (tel: 01246 565300).

Hathersage (Derby). Trout, grayling; preserved by the Derwent FFC; also at Bamford and Grindleford (members only).

Bamford (Derby). Trout, grayling. Derwent FFC has water below Bamford Mill; and from Bamford Mill to Yorkshire Bridge; members only. Peak Forest AC has **River Noe** upstream from Derwent confluence to Edale; fly fishing for brown and rainbow trout and grayling; also Bradwell Brook and Castleton Brook, Hope, trout and grayling; members only; subscriptions £250; contact Hon Sec.

Ladybower. Centre for **Ladybower and Derwent Reservoirs;** trout; fly only *(see Midlands reservoirs and lakes).* Hotels: Ladybower Inn, Yorkshire Bridge Inn, Ye Derwent Hotel, Bamford (1m), Anglers' Rest (1m), Rising Sun, Bamford (2m).

AMBER (tributary of Derwent): trout, coarse fish.

Alfreton (Derby). St £30, dt £4 from Ripley AC for reservoir at **Butterley**: pike, perch, roach, tench, bream, and carp; dt also from keepers. Sheffield Trout Anglers have water on Amber at Wingfield. Tackle shop: Alfreton Angling Centre, 11 Park St DE55 7JE (tel: 01773 832611). Hotels: George, Castle. Also fair fishing in Derwent at Ambergate, 5m SW.

WYE (tributary of Derwent): One of few rivers in which rainbow trout breed. Also holds good brown trout.

Bakewell (Derby). Trout. Fishing preserved by Haddon Hall Estate. Details are to be found under **Rowsley**, above.

Monsal Dale (Derby). The Chatsworth Estate has excellent trout fishing on ¾m double bank. 4 rods per day only. Apply for day tickets at £25, to River Keeper, Rose Cottage, Monsal Dale, Buxton SK17 8SZ (tel: 01629 640159; web: www.chatsworth.org).

Buxton (Derby). River private. Brown and rainbow trout fishing in **Lightwood** and **Stanley Moor reservoirs**. Tackle shop: Peak Aquatics, Staden Lane, Buxton SK17 1AS (tel: 01298 24438).

DOVE. Dovedale waters, where Izaak Walton and Charles Cotton fished, are preserved, no tickets. Good sport with trout and grayling elsewhere. In lower reaches, where Churnet enters Dove, angling is improving. Stretches below Uttoxeter, Doveridge, Marchington, Sudbury, etc, also improving: barbel, chub, grayling, pike present. Very limited opportunities for day tickets.

Uttoxeter (Staffs). Trout, grayling. Uttoxer AA preserves good deal of water between Rocester and Uttoxeter; no permits. Leek and Moorlands FC has water here (also **Crakemarsh Pool**). Membership £26 + £12 joining fee, conc; 3,000m l bank. Fenton & Dist AS has water on Dove.

Rocester (Staffs). Salmon, trout, grayling. ¼m single bank, dt £10, contact Mr Appleby (tel: 01889 590347). **Churnet**; fishing improving; private.

Ashbourne (Derby). Several miles of **R Henmore** and **Bentley Brook**, both tributaries stocked with trout and grayling, and two small lakes controlled by Ashbourne Fly Fishers' Club; st only; no dt. National Trust has South Peak Estate, including Dovedale; fly only; Leek & Dist FFC water; anglers must obtain info about procedures to guard against infection by Signal Crayfish (tel: 01889 882583). In **Dovedale** 3m of good trout and grayling fishing can be had by guests at Izaak Walton Hotel, Dovedale DE6 2AY (tel: 01335 350555). Yeaveley Estate nr Ashbourne DE6 2DT (tel: 01335 330247; web: www.yeaveley-estate.co.uk), has fly fishing for rainbow and brown trout on 1½ acre lake, open all year; membership available, dt £22, 3 fish, then c&r, all browns to be returned; tuition by appointment, flies for sale. Derbyshire County AC has Bishop's Pool, near Ashbourne; members only; st

£170; also River Dove at Church Mayfield; trout, fly only; coarse in winter. Hotel in Ashbourne; Green Man; hotel at Mayfield, 2m SW (Staffs); Royal Oak.

Hartington (Derby). Trout. Derbyshire County AC has 2m and 25 weirs double bank at Wolfscote Dale; fly for wild and stocked browns and grayling; members only; st £170. Charles Cotton Hotel has about 250 yds of the River Dove; residents only. Proprietor will give data about stretches permitted by farmers.

CHURNET (tributary of Dove): Mixed fishery: trout, grayling, coarse.

Leek (Staffs). Trout, coarse fish; preserved above Leek town by landowners. Fishing improving. Leek and Moorlands FC has coarse fishing on Leek Arm of Caldon **Caldon Canal**; **Deep Hayes Country Park**, Longsdon; **Heron Marsh Pool**, Rudyard; **Crakemarsh Pool**, nr Uttoxeter; also **R Dove** and **R Churnet**; tickets for Deep Hayes Country Park from Leek Pets and Fishing Centre (*see below*), otherwise members only; membership £26 + £12 joining fee, conc. Stoke-on-Trent AS has Horsebridge Pool, 1m from town at Horsebridge; members only; apply Hon Sec. **Turners Pool**, Swythamley, nr Rushton Spencer SK11 0SL; coarse fish, dt £6: contact Mr Wilshaw (tel: 01260 227225). **Rudyard Lake** is 3m NW, 170 acre reservoir; very good bream, with roach, perch, and pike to 30lb; dt price depends on season; punts on half and full day from water bailiff (tel: 01538 306280); match lengths pegged. Basford Coarse Fishery, Turners Croft, **Basford** ST13 7ET (tel: 01538 360616); carp and other coarse fish, dt £5, conc, at poolside. **Tittesworth Reservoir**: 189-acre Severn-Trent W trout fishery. *(See Midlands reservoirs and lakes).* Tackle shops: Leek Pet and Fishing Centre, 33 St Edward St ST13 5DN (tel: 01538 398958).

MANIFOLD (tributary of Dove): Offers visitors few opportunities.

Longnor (Staffs). Buxton, 7m; trout. Dove, 1m E; trout, grayling. Crewe and Harpur Arms stretch, Derbyshire County AC; members only; Part of Hoo Brook and Manifold is National Trust property; trout restocked; anglers must obtain info about procedures to guard against infection by Signal Crayfish (tel: 01889 882583).

MEASE. Coarse fish. Fishing stations are: **Measham** (Leics); **Snarestone** (Leics); and **Ashby-de-la-Zouch** (Leics); **Nether-**

seal (Derby); **Edingale** and **Harlaston** (Staffs); Birmingham AA has water at last three; dt £4 from tackle shops. Hotels: Queen's Head, Royal.

SEAL BROOK (tributary of Mease): a small watercourse with few fish.

Over Seal (Leics). Lakes: Ashby Wolds Reservoir, 1m N.

TAME: After a long history of pollution, much recovered under the care of the Severn-Trent W. Fish now present in many stretches. Further improvement scheduled.

Tamworth (Staffs). Tributary Anker holds roach, pike and perch. Town waters are all let to clubs, tickets from Tamworth Tackle. 500m double bank in castle grounds may be fished through Dosthill Cosmopolitan AC, 69 High St, Dosthill, Tamworth B77 1LG (tel: 01827 280024); chub, barbel, roach, dace, perch; dt £1.50 on bank. Mease; roach, chub, dace; Haunton, **Harleston**; dt from W T Ward and Harleston Mill. Local clubs: Lamb AC; Fazeley Victory AC; Birch Coppice AC; Tamworth WMC, Polesworth AC; which fishes Coventry and Birmingham Canals; some tickets on offer. Tackle shops: Tamworth Fishing Tackle, 23 Lichfield St B79 7QE (tel: 01827 66701); Hambry's Fishing Tackle, The Square, Polesworth.

Kingsbury (Warwicks). Kingsbury Water Park, Bodymoor Heath Lane, Sutton Coldfield, B76 0DY (tel: 01827 872660): nr Tamworth, 2m from Junction 9 of M42; 13 fishing lakes, with specimen carp to 32lb, tench to 8lb, large bream, roach, perch and pike; some pegs suitable for disabled; a variety of season and day permits offered, from a family st at £130, to dt £1.90, conc; car park fee £2.50; contact Information Centre at above address.

Sutton Coldfield (W Midlands). Lakes at Visitors Centre, Sutton Park, Park Rd, Sutton Coldfield B74 2YT (tel 0121 3556370): Bracebridge Pool, Blackroot Pool, Powell's Pool, Keepers; fishing includes carp to 30lb, bream, roach, pike, and other species; st £23.50 (for all Birmingham waters), dt £2.70 (£1.40 jun) on bank. Penns Carp Fishery, Penns Hall, Wylde Green; dt from tackle shop, or on bank. Local club: Sutton Coldfield AS has fishing on rivers and lakes. Tackle shop: Fosters of Birmingham, 214 Kingstanding Rd, B'ham B44 8JP (tel: 0121 344 3333). Hotel: Penns Hall, beside fishery.

ANKER (tributary of Tame): coarse fish;

best sport in winter.

Polesworth (Warwick). Coventry & Dist AA has 2m plus Alvecote Pools; good head of tench and chub in river, large carp and bream in pools. Dt £2.50 on bank. Book £17 from Hon Sec. Assn also has 7m on canal; dt from Assn, bailiffs and tackle shops.

SENCE (tributary of Anker): small stream, but good trout and grayling in places, as well as chub, roach and dace.

BOSWORTH BROOK (tributary of Sence): Trout; preserved.

Market Bosworth (Leics). Bosworth Brook, 1m North; trout; preserved by owner of Bosworth Hall. Sence, 3m W. Tweed, 3m SW. Lakes: The Duckery, Bosworth Park, 1m S; pike, etc. Gabriel Pool, 3m NE.

BOURNE BROOK (tributary of Bourne). Fishing station: Plough Inn, **Shustoke**, Warwicks. Trout fishing in Avon Division STW Shustoke Reservoir.

BLYTH (tributary of Tame): Coarse fish. Centres: **Coleshill** (Warwicks). Chub, perch, pike, roach. **Hampton-in-Arden** (Warwicks). Chub, dace, roach. **Solihull** (Warwicks). Earlswood Lakes, 6m SW; ticket for three coarse lakes on bank from bailiff. **Olton Mere** coarse fishing; apply to sec, Olton Mere Club.

REA (tributary of Tame): Urban river with poor access. Poor habitat and water quality result in poor fish stocks.

Birmingham (W Midlands). Birmingham AA, formed from a number of local clubs, controls extensive water on river, canal and lake throughout the Midlands and into Wales. The club-card gives details of all fishing rights, which include numerous fisheries on **Severn and tributaries, Trent and tributaries, Wye and tributaries,** canals, lakes and ponds. A detailed guide with excellent maps is issued from Assn HQ (*see clubs list*); members only st £23 (for those members of affiliated clubs; st £26 for associate members (for individuals who do not belong to any affiliated club (or who are concessionary); conc member £13; joint membership £31 (1 male + 1 female) (from Hon Sec only); family membership £40 (from Hon Sec only); under 10's £1; night permits (on certain venues) from Hon Sec only £5; day tickets £4 are not available on banks, and must be purchased from club agents (usually tackle shops). White Swan Piscatorials own or rent waters on the **Severn, Avon, Teme, Mease, Tern,**

Rea, Lugg, Ithon, Herefordshire Arrow and numerous pools; st £32 + £32 entrance fee; limited; day permits to members' guests only. Reservoir at **Edgbaston** fishable on permit. **Park Lakes**: coarse fishing on 14 lakes and pools in city; dt from park keepers. Special st for pensioners. Tackle shops: William Powell, 35-37 Carrs Lane, City Centre B4 7SX (tel: 0121 643 0689); Fosters of Birmingham, 214 Kingstanding Rd, B'ham B44 8JP (tel: 0121 344 3333); and many others. Many hotels.

Lifford (Birmingham). Lifford Reservoir. Good coarse fishing. Dt from park keeper.

FORD BROOK (tributary of Tame). Fishing stations : **Pelsall** and **Walsall** (W Midlands). Brook polluted. Lake: Hatherton Lake; pike. Swan AC leases **Sneyd Pool**, Bloxwich, Essington Wyrley Canal, coarse fishing; dt £2.50 on bank; match booking. Walsall & Dist AS has **Hatherton Canal**. **Park Lime Pits**; carp, bream, roach, perch, pike; dt and st for small charge. **Aboretum Lake**; bream, tench, roach, perch, pike; dt.

SOWE: Coarse fish, some trout.

Stafford (Staffs). Upstream of town; perch, pike, dace, roach, chub. Downstream; perch, roach, bream, chub, occasional trout. Free for about ½m upstream of town on left bank only; remainder preserved by Izaak Walton (Stafford) AA. This association has fisheries on the Sowe, the **Penk, Trent & Mersey Canal, Shropshire Union Canal** and **Hopton Pools**, carp, tench and other coarse fish; apply Hon Sec for annual membership, wt and dt and Holts. Tackle shop: Holts Fishing Tackle, 122 Marston Rd, ST16 3BX (tel: 01785 251073). Hotels: Swan, Station, Vine, Royal Oak, Garth, Tillington Hall.

Eccleshall (Staffs); Trout; preserved. Stoke-on-Trent AS has Ellenhall Pools (Ellenhall Park Farm); no night fishing; members only; apply Hon Sec.

PENK (tributary of Sowe):

Penkridge (Staffs). Coarse fish. **Staffordshire and Worcestershire Canal.** Stafford AA has water *(see Stafford); Radford Bridge (Staffs). Izaak Walton (Stafford) AA has water here d/s from Roseford Bridge at Acton Trussell to Milford Aquaduct; dt from Holts Fishing Tackle, Stafford. **Gailey Upper Reservoir,** Cannock, 34 acres, trout fishery managed by Tern Fisheries, Broomhall Grange, Market Drayton; stocked rainbows, browns, blue trout; open all year, pike fishing Nov-Mar; also fly fishing for pike all year; dt £28 (7 fish), 8-hours £23 (5),.5-hours £18 (4), conc; apply to Gailey Fishing, Gailey Lea Lane, Penkridge, Staffs ST19 5PT (tel: 01785 715848).

TYNE

(For close seasons, licences, etc, see North East Region Environment Agency p20)

Formed by junction of North and South Tyne at Hexham, and empties into North Sea at Tynemouth (Northumberland). Since recovery from pollution this river is considered by some to be the best salmon river in England; trout fishing fair. Pike are increasing in lower reaches (below Hexham) and dace in the North and South Tyne.

Newcastle upon Tyne (North'land). **Whittle Dene Reservoirs**, nr Stamfordham, 17 acres; coarse fishery; dt £6 from fishing lodge at reservoir (tel: 01207 255250). Swallow George Hotel, **Chollerford**, NE46 4EW (tel: 01434 681611), has fishing; dt at hotel. Westwater Angling Ltd has water on Whittle Dene Reservoir; members only, st £485, conc; contact Hon Sec. Free fishing at Killingworth Pond, N Tyneside. **Killingworth Lake** is dt coarse fishery. Felling Flyfishing Club has reasonably priced fishing on the following: **North Tyne**, approx 5½m through Bellingham; 4m of **R Rede**, through West Woodburn, incl Ingram pool, salmon and sea trout; 2½m of Co-

quet, d/s from Weldon Bridge; 1.5m of **R Till**, on Fenton Estate nr Milfield; 2½m of **R Wear** between Durham City and Franklin, under-fished stretch, with browns and grayling. Contact either Brian Tindle, Membership Sec (tel: 0191 4151977); or Bagnall & Kirkwood (*see below*). Tackle shops: St Antonys Angling Centre, 1200 Walker Rd, NE6 3JN (tel: 0191 276 4774); Bagnall & Kirkwood, 28 Grey St, Newcastle upon Tyne NE1 6AE (tel: 0191 2325873). Whitley Bay tackle shop: W Temple, 43 Ocean View NE26 1AL (tel: 0191 252 6017).

Ryton (Tyne and Wear). Salmon, trout, coarse fish. Federation water. Ferryhill AC have 1½m stretch, which can be reached via Heddon on the Wall; contact Hon Sec.

Wylam (North'land). Federation water. Salmon; trout, coarse fish.

Prudhoe (North'land). Trout, coarse fish; salmon; water here and at **Ovingham** and **Wylam** preserved by the Northumbrian AF; also Coquet at Warkworth, Felton and Rothbury; st £85 salmon, sea trout, brown trout, conc, from Head Bailiff, Thirston Mill, Felton NE65 9EH (tel: 01670 787663; www.northumbrian anglersfed.co.uk); £60 trout, from most Newcastle tackle shops and Tyne Valley Flooring, Bank Top, Station Road, Prudhoe NE42 5PR.

Mickley (North'land). Trout, coarse fish, salmon; Federation water *(See Prudhoe)*. Lakes: Whittle Dene Reservoirs, 5m N.

Corbridge (North'land). Trout and dace; trout plentiful but small with runs of sea trout and salmon. Corbridge Riverside Sports Club has 3m on south bank; membership restricted to persons living locally; dt to members' guests only.

Hexham (North'land). Trout (av ¾lb), coarse fish; salmon improving. Tynedale Council, Prospect House, Hexham NE46 3NH (tel: 01434 652200), owns ½m on south bank off Tyne Green from Hexham bridge upstream. St £32.10, dt £5.60, conc for residents, OAP, etc, from TIC, Wentworth Car Park NE46 1QE. All other salmon water preserved. Langley Dam, 8m west of Hexham: 14 acre lake stocked weekly with r trout. Fly only. Dt £17, 5 fish; £10, 3 fish. NWW Derwent Reservoir, 10m east, 1,000 acres; dt for brown and rainbow trout, £16 (8 fish), conc £14; Dam and north bank fly only, south bank fly and multibait (tel: 01207 255250). Club: Hexham AA has water; no tickets. Westwater Angling Ltd has water at Hallington Reservoir and Whittle Dene Reservoir ns Hexham; members only, st £485, conc; contact Hon Sec. Accom (B&B), run by local fisherman: Susan Forte, 10 Alexandra Terrace, NE46 3JQ (tel: 01434 601954). Tackle shop: ARE Angling Centre, 10B Hencotes, Hexham NE46 2EJ (tel: 01434 605952); Top-Tackle, Anick Rd, (tel: 01434 606991).

Tributaries of the Tyne

DERWENT: Stocked brown trout, average about 1lb, with fish to 3lb, some grayling.

Swalwell (Durham). Derwent Haugh to Lintzford is now pollution free, held by Axwell Park and Derwent Valley AA; dt for b and r trout, fly only until June 1, then limited worm. Enquiries to PO Box 12, Blaydon NE1 25TQ.

Shotley Bridge (Durham). Derwent, 1m W; trout and grayling. Derwent AA preserves about 14m of river from Lintzford to **Derwent Reservoir** *(see Durham reservoirs)* and one bank above reservoir to Baybridge; worming allowed after July 1, except one bank above reservoir to Bay Bridge, fly only. Open membership; dt from Royal Derwent Hotel, Allensford, Durham DH8 9BB (tel: 01207 592000). Licences from Post Office, Shotley Bridge. Hotels: Crown; Cross Swords.

NORTH TYNE: trout water, with one or two salmon.

Chollerford (North'land). Trout, coarse fish. The George Hotel, Chollerford NE46 4EW (tel: 01434 681611), has ¾m bank fishing upstream of bridge for residents and non-residents. Trout average ½lb; dt £12.

Bellingham (North'land). Trout, salmon sea trout; best July-Oct. Felling Flyfishing Club has approx 5½m from Low Carriteth u/s of Bellingham to Tail of the Eels pool d/s several excellent named pools. Best salmon to date 23lbs, best sea trout 12lbs, and brown to 3½lbs. Contact Brian Tindle, Membership Sec (tel: 0191 4151977); members only; st £300. Ferryhill AC have 1300 yds d/s from Burn, dt £5/£10 depending on season (wt £25/£40) from Country Store in town centre; also from Brown Rigg Holiday Park. Riverdale Hall Hotel, NE48 2JT (tel: 01434 220254), has 3m salmon and trout fishing for residents, on Tyne (3 beats) and Rede. Licences; Bellingham Hardware, Park Side Place. Hotels: Rose and Crown, Cheviot, Black Bull, Riverdale Hall.

Falstone (North'land). Forest Enterprise offers dt £3, wt £15, st £25, for stretch between **Butteryhaugh** and **Deadwater**; the permit also covers Akenshaw, Lewis, and Kielder, and is sold at Kielder Castle Forest Centre (tel: 01434 250209); who also issue tickets for River Rede. Falstone FC issues permits for 2m of North Tyne, £10 per day, £20 between Sept-Oct, £75 per season, from Blackcock Inn NE48 1AA (tel: 01434 240200), or from A

Banks, 5 Hawkhope Rd, Falstone NE48 1BD (tel: 01434 240158).

Kielder (North'land). Major NW reservoir of 2,700 acres. Stocked with browns and rainbows, also contains a good head of wild brown trout; 'Silver Explorer' season ticket, covering other NW waters £569 (24 fish p/w; max 8 p/d), conc £489; dt £16 (8 fish), conc; boats for hire £18; fly, trolling and worm; tickets on site (tel: 01434 250312). Hotels: Riverdale Hall, Bellingham; Percy Arms, Otterburn.

REDE: Trout and pike, with few autumn salmon.

Otterburn (North'land). Otterburn Tower Hotel, NE19 1NS (tel: 01830 520620), has 3½m on Rede, south of Mill Bridge; trout dt £20. **Sweethope Lake**, Lough House, Sweethope, **Harle** NE19 2PN (tel: 01830 540349): trout fishing for natural b, stocked r; sessions are from 9am to 1pm, 1pm to 5pm, 5pm to 9pm (£12 each, 3 fish); £24 for 8hrs (6 fish) or £16 for 3 fish; £15 all day c&r; boats £5 per session; worm fishing Oct to Dec; holiday cottages on site. Hotel, Percy Arms.

SOUTH TYNE: A spate river, usually fishes well by September. One or two clubs issue tickets for trout and salmon fishing.

Fourstones (North'land). Trout and salmon. Newbrough and Fourstones AA has 2½m of north bank only; no visitors' tickets.

Haydon Bridge (North'land). Trout and late salmon. South Tyne AA preserves 5m of water; enquiries to Clarke Newsagents, Church St NE47 6JG (tel: 01434 684303); visitor wt.

Haltwhistle (North'land), Brown trout, sea trout, salmon. Haltwhistle & Dist AA has visitors wt £50, dt £20, conc, for 7m around Haltwhistle; Bellister Estate National Trust water is 1½m of double and single bank fishing; members only (apply Hon Sec); for visitor tickets apply: Greggs Sports, Market Square NE49 0BG (tel: 01434 320255). 3m NE of Haltwhistle is National Trust Crag Lough, syndicate managed; browns and rainbows; members only, apply Barry Jones (tel: 0191 2512260). Hotels: Manor House, Wallace Arms.

Alston (Cumbria). Salmon, sea trout, trout. Alston & Dist AA has 10m of water from Lambley Viaduct to Alston Weir; to 31 Jul dt £8, wt £25; 1 Aug to 31 Oct dt £19, wt £55, conc, from Sandra Harrison, News and Essentials CA9 3SE; Alston Post Office CA9 3HP; or from Hon Sec or Hon Treasurer; visitor st £90. Hotel: Kirkside Inn, Knarsdale (issues wt & dt).

EAST ALLEN: not much fished.

WANSBECK

(For close seasons, licences, etc, see North East Region Environment Agency p20)

Northumberland trout stream which fishes well under favourable conditions of water, but opportunities for visitors are few.

Morpeth (North'land). Brown trout; preserved by Wansbeck AA for 5m; members only. Water in town free to licence holders. **Fontburn Reservoir**, NW fishery of 87 acres, with stocked rainbow (to 26lb 8oz) and wild brown trout (to 9lb 4oz) and blues; dt £16, £14 conc on site (£1 coins needed), 8 fish limit, fly only c&r; permits from lodge (tel: 01669 621368). Tackle shop: Amble Angling Centre, 4 Newburgh St, Amble, Morpeth NE65 0AQ (tel: 01665 711200) Hotels: Waterford Lodge, Queen's Head, Angler's Arms, Weldon Bridge.

Tributary of the Wansbeck

BROOKER BURN:
Longhirst (North'land). Wansbeck, 2m S; trout. Lyne, 2m N.

WAVENEY

(see Norfolk and Suffolk Broads)

WEAR

(For close seasons, licences, etc, see North East Region Environment Agency p20)

Rises on Kilhope Moors in extreme west of Co Durham and enters North Sea at Wearmouth. After history of pollution, river now contains salmon, sea trout, grayling, brown trout, dace, chub, roach and barbel, perch and bream. Tributaries Browney and Rookhope are improving, with Browney sustaining a run of sea trout. Bedburn preserved.

Chester-le-Street (Durham). Sea trout, brown trout (stocked by club) excellent coarse fish. Chester-le-Street AC has 10m good water with the above species plus salmon, dace, chub, barbel, eels, roach; st £57, conc, dt £1.25 available. Hartlepool & Dist AC fishes 1m single bank; mambers only, st £35; contact Hon Sec. Dunelm City AC fishes Chester Moor and Frankland stretches; contact G Hedley (tel: 0191 386 4603).

Durham (Durham). Trout, sea trout. Free fishing on EA licence from Ice Rink to Sewage Works, also Ice Rink to Kepier Farm Boundary. Last stretch to Orchard Wall is strictly private. Durham City AC has more than 2½m on river, and stillwater fisheries stocked with coarse fish; st £47, conc; dt for guests of members only; enquiries to Hon Secretary. National Trust has ¾m single bank at Moorhouse Woods just north of city; tenanted; ring regional office (tel: 01670 774691). Grange AC has stretch of river at Kepier Woods, migratory fish, good head of brown trout, grayling, chub, dace, large pike; and Brasside Pond; dt water. Bear Park, Cornsay and New Branspeth Assns all have water on **Browney**, 4m W of Durham; limited dt; restocking. Ferryhill & Dist AC have Wear fishing, also Browney, both banks to Wear junction, and R Gaunless, 1½m from West Auckland, with brown trout; with 2000 yards of excellent Wear salmon and sea trout pools and specimen coarse fish (Brockbank stretch). The Club also has access to Association waters in the Croxdale area; apply Hon Sec for dt waters availability. 9m SE, Hartlepool & Dist AC have 4½ acre Tilery Lake at Wingate; and Kenny's Pond at Hutton Henry (2 acres), both mixed coarse; members only; contact Hon Sec. Near Stanley are **Beamish Lakes**, a trout fishery; fly or worm (tel: 07930 803336), dt on site. Tackle shop: Bagnall & Kirkwood, 28 Grey St, Newcastle upon Tyne NE1 6AE (tel: 0191 2325873). Tackle shop: Turners Fishing Tackle, 25 Front St, Sacriston, Durham DH7 6JS (tel: 0191 371 1804).

Willington (Durham). Willington & Dist AC has fishing at Sunnybrow to Page Bank; dt £6 trout, £10 salmon/sea trout (£15 Oct); coarse ponds £5, conc; from

Bonds Tackle Shop, 81 High St, Willington, Bishop Aukland DL15 0PE (tel: 01388 746273); and Lee's Fishing Tackle, 73 High St DL15 0PF (tel: 01388 747571), who also sell Ferryhill AC.

Bishop Auckland (Durham). Sea trout, brown trout, grayling, salmon. Bishop Auckland & Dist AC controls some 20m of water on Wear, between Witton le Wear and Croxdale; members only. Also Witton Castle Lakes, trout stillwater; dt at lodge; membership £121 details from Hon Sec; club also has the Angling and Conservation Centre at Witton Park; specemin carp fishery and mixed coarse; dt and st at Centre. Ferryhill & Dist AC has fishing at **Croxdale, Tudhoe, Witworth Estates; Byers Green** and **Old Durham** fisheries, also **Newfield** and **Page Bank**. Club waters also include Rivers **Browney, Tees, Swale, Skern, Gaunless** and various coarse fishing ponds. Some dt waters; membership £35, plus £10 entrance fee, conc. Hotel: Manor House, West Auckland.

Witton le Wear (Durham). Bishop Auckland AC *(see above)*.

Wolsingham (Durham). Trout, sea trout (good). Wolsingham AA has water; members only (limited st £29 + £10 joining, for visitors). Long waiting list. No dt. At Hagbridge, **Eastgate** (about 8m W), Northumbrian Environment Agency has leased stretch to Weardale FFC; st £15 from Hon Sec, dt £6 from The Paper Shop, Front Str, in Stanhope. North-West Durham AA has trout fishing on **Hisehope, Waskerley** and **Smiddy Shaw Reservoirs**; contact Hon Sec. **Tunstall Reservoir** is a NWL fishery, leased to Weardale FFC; st £70 (from Austin Lowery, tel: 01388 811768); dt £15 from The Paper Shop, Front Str, in Wolsingham.

Frosterley (Durham). Trout, sea trout. About 1½m water belongs to Frosterley AC; members only, who must reside in area.

Stanhope (Durham). Trout, sea trout and salmon. About 2m water (both banks) belongs to Stanhope AA; members only, limited membership £25, when available; sea trout June onwards. Weardale Flyfishers has 2m u/s from Stanhope; dt £6 from newsagent. For **Eastgate** fishing:

Miss Bell (tel: 01388 528414). Tackle shop: Fisher Communications, 4 Market Place DL13 2UJ (tel: 01388 528464). Hotels: Packhorse; Bonny Moorhen.

Upper Weardale (Durham). Trout, sea trout (Sept and Oct). Upper Weardale AA has 6m in total of Wear and tributaries from Westgate to Cowshill; st £35, wt

£12 (not available Sept/Oct), dt £6 (Sept/Oct £8), conc, from The Post Office, St John's Chapel (tel: 01388 537214); water re-stocked 3 times per season with 12in brown trout. Hotels: Cowshill, Cowshill (tel 01388 537236); Golden Lion, St John's Chapel (tel: 01388 537231).

Tributary of the Wear

BROWNEY: now free of pollution; trout and sea trout.

Langley Park (Durham). Langley Park AA lease river here. Assn also has R Wear at Durham, trout and coarse, and coarse ponds.

Burn Hill (Durham). Waskerley, Tunstall Hisehope and **Smiddy Shaw Reservoirs** close together on moors between Stanhope and Consett. *(See above and under Durham Reservoirs).*

WEAVER

(For close seasons, licences, etc, see North West Region Environment Agency, p20)

Rises south-west of Cheshire and flows into Mersey estuary. Most species of coarse fish, trout in the upper reaches. British Waterways have a cooperative scheme, the Weaver Waiters, which invites fishing clubs to partake in the management of the River Weaver Navigation between Saltisford and Weston, and represents a long-term strategy of improvement and development of the lower reaches of the river. Contact Regional Manager for further details (See English Canal Fishing).

Northwich (Cheshire). Good coarse fishing held by Northwich AA. Water on **Weaver, Dane, Trent and Mersey Canal** (about 17m); **Billinge Green Pools; Great Budworth Mere; Petty Pool Mere** (limited access); **Pickmere Lake**; comprehensive st (all waters); st £35 from tackle shop; no dt; exceptional concessions to OAP and regd disabled, from Box 18, Northwich; no tickets sold on bank. Lymm AC has carp complex (specimen fish) at Belmont Estate, 4m north; members only. Tackle shop: Vale Royal Angling Centre, 84 Station Rd, CW9 5RB (tel: 01606 46060). Hotels: Moulton Crow Inn, Moulton; Mayfield Guest House, London Rd.

Winsford (Cheshire). Roach, bream, perch, carp. Winsford & Dist AA have stretch from New Bridge upstream to Church Minshull, several pools around Winsford and R Dane at Middlewhich, with barbel and perch; st £22, conc, dt £3 on bank for Dane, Mon-Fri and Weaver, Newbridge to Bottom Flash. Lymm AC has 7 acre lake at Marton; mixed coarse, many specimen; members only. Crewe LMR Sports AS has Sandhole Pool (coarse fish) and good tench water at **Warmingham** (½m).

Crewe (Cheshire). Weaver 2½m W. No fishing in Crewe, but Crewe LMR Sports

and Social Centre, Goddard Str, CW1 3HL (tel: 01270 214886) has 3m of Weaver near Nantwich (4m away) on Batherton Estate; **Sandhole Pool** (1m), and **Doddington Hall Pool** (5m), rights on **Shropshire Union Canal** and stretches of **Severn, Weaver** and **Dane**; as well as good bream, tench and pike fishing on **Hortons Flash**; guest tickets are not issued for any of these waters; dt on bank for Macclesfield Canal; coarse fish *(see also Congleton).* Tackle shop: Crewe Angling Centre, 87 Victoria Street, CW1 2JH (tel: 01270 253891).

Nantwich (Cheshire). Trout, grayling, dace, roach, chub, Nantwich AS controls nearly all Weaver near Nantwich; st only; water starts on Reaseheath Estate and stretches SE of town for 7m mainly on both banks, broken at Batherton Mill. Society also has stretch on **Severn** at Trewern. Other clubs with water near Nantwich are Pioneer AA, Amalgamated Anglers and LMR Sports (all Crewe) and Wyche Anglers; Winsford and Dist AA control **Weaver**, from Newbridge to Church Minshull; flashes; pools; st from Hon Sec. Winsford Club's pools contain fine tench, carp, bream and pike. **Shropshire Union Canal** controlled by BW: dt from bank ranger; st from tackle shop. Other waters within 10m of Nantwich are: Big Mere, Osmere, Blakemere (boats), Combermere (boats). Egerton Lake, Egerton Fruit Farm, Cholmodely; carp water of 50 pegs, dt £5, from bailiff; information from Secretary, Caldy Anglers. Tackle shop: Stapeley Angling Centre, Stapeley Water Gardens, London Rd, CW5 7LH (tel: 01270 611500). Hotels: Lamb, Crown, Three Pigeons.

Audlem (Cheshire). Adderley Brook. Birchall Brook, 2m NE. Lake: Woolfall Pool, 2m NE. Hotels: Lamb, Crown. *(for club water see Nantwich).*

Wrenbury (Cheshire). Nantwich AS has water in area; no tickets. Marbury Brook. Sale Brook, 2m S. Baddiley Brook, 2m N. Hotel: Combermere Arms, Burleydam, Whitchurch.

Tributaries of the Weaver

DANE: Trout in upper reaches, but difficult to come by. Coarse fishing, with odd trout and grayling lower down.

Northwich (Cheshire). Chub, dace and roach. Northwich AA have fishing, dt offered.

Davenham (Cheshire). Trout, barbel, roach. Davenham AC have fishing, members only, Davenham to Leftwich.

Middlewich (Cheshire). Dace, roach, chub. Winsford & Dist AA have fishing from Croxton Lane to King St, dt water, also right bank d/s to Bulls Wood; dt available. Middlewich Joint Anglers have Trent and Mersey Canal and Shropshire Canal stretches, and pool and river fishing, which includes **R Dane**, left bank u/s from Byley Bridge, approx 2m; right bank u/s approx ½m, both banks between Byley and Ravenscroft Bridge, and from Wheelock confluence on left bank d/s; also **R Wheelock**, right bank u/s from R Dane confluence, and left bank d/s to Bullswood, Bostock, approx 4m. Chub, dace, roach, gudgeon, barbel, and other species. Also **Tetton** and **Sparrow Grove** lakes: coarse; st £30, conc; dt £5 at some waters, on bank. Tackle shop: Dave's of Middlewich, Lewin St, CW10 9AS (tel: 01606 833853). Hotel: Boars Head.

Swettenham (Cheshire). Prince Albert AS has much of R Dane; here, and at Allgreave, Congleton, Byley, and Wincle, members only.

Congleton (Cheshire). Dace, roach, chub, gudgeon and occasional grayling and perch. 5m of prolific water in and around Congleton controlled by Congleton AS, plus excellent carp and coarse fishing in **Goodwins Pool**; disabled pegs; society also has Macclesfield Canal, and Trent & Mersey Canal at The Romping Donkey; coarse; membership £25 + £5 joining fee, conc; dt £3 from Terry's *(below)*. From Radnor Bridge towards Holmes Chapel partly controlled by Prince Albert AA,

Grove and Whitnall AA and Warrington AA. St for Prince Albert AA stretch at **Somerfordbooths** from secretary or tackle shops; Assn also has water on Severn. Eaton Flyfishers have fly only water from Eaton to North Road; members and guests only. **Moreton Coarse Fisheries**, New Rd, Astbury, nr Congleton CW12 4RY (tel: 01260 272839): fishing on 3 lakes, dt £6 (extra rod £1), conc (except w/e), from manager in office; carp to 28lb, large bream and tench; barbless hooks only, bays for disabled. **Westlow Mere Trout Fisheries**, Giantswood Lane CW12 2JJ (tel: 01260 270012); dt £17, 6 fish, £14, 3 fish, conc, dawn to dusk £9 c&r, half day £7 c&r, evng £6 summer only c&r; boat £6/day. **Macclesfield Canal**: Warrington AA; roach, perch, tench, bream, pike; recently dredged; st only. Lymm AC has stretches of Dane at Sproston near Holmes Chapel, members only. Astbury Meadow Garden Centre, Newcastle Rd, has coarse fishery on site. Stoke AA has **Astbury Mere**, with large pike, carp, roach, bream, perch; members only. Tackle shop: Terrys of Congleton, 47A Lawton St CW12 1RU (tel: 01260 273770), has club memberships for Congleton AS, Mow Cop Anglers, Biddulph Anglers.

Bosley nr **Macclesfield** (Cheshire). Roach, chub, carp, bream, pike; private. Lake: **Bosley Reservoir**; Prince Albert AS water, members only.

Macclesfield (Cheshire). Extensive fishing controlled by Prince Albert AS, a nationally famous club with many rivers, lakes and reservoirs in the NW of England and in Wales. These include many stretches on the R Dane, the **Severn**, the **Ribble**, **Wye**, **Wenning**, **Wharfe**, **Towy**, **Teifi**, **Cothi**, **Banwy**, **Twymyn**, **Trent**, **Dove**, **Winster**, **Vyrnwy**, **Lledr**, **Dulas**, **Dysinni**, **Dee**, **Dovey**, **Mawddach** and **Lune**; **Marbury Mere**, Whitchurch, **Isle Lake**, Shrewsbury, **Langley Bottoms** and **La-**

maload **Reservoirs,** Macclesfield and others. Long waiting list for membership. Dt issued for a few of their waters. **Dane-bridge Fisheries,** SK11 0QE, has small (2 acre) trout lake at Wincle, fish to 16lb, sporting ticket £8 (5 hours), dt £20 (3 fish), £12 (2 fish, 5 hours); instruction can be arranged (tel: 01260 227293). **Marton Heath Trout Pools,** Pikelow Farm, School Lane, Marton SK11 9HD (tel: 01260 224231); seven acres of stocked trout fishing, rainbow and brown; tuition; barbless hooks only; coarse pool on site well stocked with common, mirror and crucian carp, roach, etc; tackle available; sells EA licences. Macclesfield Waltonian AS has **Teggsnose Reservoir,** coarse fish, carp to 20lb; dt £5 from Barlows *(below).* Other clubs: Macclesfield FC (12m on Dane and **Clough,** preserved; no tickets). **Macclesfield Canal;** good

carp, pike, roach, etc. Prince Albert AS has approx 6m, from Buxton Rd Bridge to Robin Hood Bridge. Dt from Barlows *(below).* **Redesmere** and **Capesthorne;** roach, bream, tench, perch, pike, mirror and crucian carp; dt as guest of member from bailiff. East Lodge, Capesthorne *(see Cheshire lakes, meres, etc).* Other waters in area: **South Park Pool;** carp, roach, perch, pike; dt from pavilion. **Knypersley Reservoir;** dt from bailiff. No night fishing. Tackle shop: Barlows of Bond Street, 47 Bond St, Macclesfield SK11 6QS (tel: 01625 619935).

WHEELOCK (tributary of Dane):

Sandbach (Cheshire). Clubs with fishing in vicinity are Northwich AA, Winsford & Dist AA, Middlewich Joint Anglers. Congleton AS has ½m here of Trent & Mersey Canal; dt from Terry's *(see Congleton).*

WELLAND

(For close seasons, licences, etc, see Anglian Region Environment Agency, p21)

Rises near Market Harborough and flows through Lincolnshire Fens to The Wash. Coarse fishing very good, much of it controlled by clubs. Upstream of Market Deeping river is renowned for large winter catches of chub and roach. Downstream, river is much wider, with regular banks and excellent access, and slow flowing with bream, roach, tench and eels, also a popular match and pike venue. Fen Drains hold roach, bream, tench and pike, North and South Drove Drains improving, especially in winter.

Spalding (Lincs). Welland, from Spalding to The Deepings, provides 12m of good fishing for pike, perch, chub, roach, dace, bream and tench; controlled by Spalding AC to Crowland. Dt on bank. **Lincoln-shire Drains;** good coarse fishing. At South Holland Drain, Foreman's Bridge Caravan Park, Sutton Rd, Sutton St James PE12 0HU (tel: 01945 440346), has permits for Holbeach & Dist AC water in **South Holland** and **Little Holland Main Drains;** £3 dt, £10 wt; disabled pegs. Spalding FC preserves Counter, North, South Drains; pike, perch, roach, carp, rudd, bream, tench; also **River Glen** from Guthram Gowt to Surfleet village bridge and **New River** from Spalding to Crowland. **Coronation Channel** also fishable. Deeping St James controls **Vernatts Drain** through East Midlands Anglers Fedn; dt on bank £3.

Cowbit (Lincs). Pike, perch, dace. Spalding FC water *(see Spalding).*

Crowland (Lincs). Pike, perch, dace. Nene, 2m SE at Black Horse Mills. New River from Spalding to Crowland preserved by Spalding FC; pike, roach, perch, dace,

rudd, bream, tench.

Deeping St James (Lincs). Chub, dace, roach, bream, rudd, pike. Deeping St James AC controls much water in vicinity, including Several Fishery, above town at junction of old river; Welland at Market Deeping and **Tallington;** Nene fishing; the **Bourne Eau; R Glen.** All mixed fisheries, dt obtainable. Tackle shop: P D's Tackle, 721 Lincoln Rd, Peterborough PE1 3HD (tel: 01733 344899).

Market Deeping (Lincs). Several Fishery controlled by Deeping St James AC. It extends 6½m from Market Deeping to Kennulph's Stone, on Deeping high bank. Also a new double bank fishing from Wards Farm to Four Mile Bar, along about 5m. Notice boards erected. Dt £3.50 on most club waters, from bailiffs. Tackle shop: P D's Tackle, 721 Lincoln Rd, Peterborough PE1 3HD (tel: 01733 344899). Accom at Broughtons B&B, 44 Halfleet.

Stamford (Lincs). Chub, dace, roach, pike, perch; fishing free to licence holders on N bank between Town and Broadeng

Bridges; approx 1¼m. Elsewhere preserved by Stamford Welland AAA; approx 18m of water, stretching from Barrowden to confluence of R Gwash and w bank of **Gwash**, eight stretches in all; chub to 5lb, bream to 7lb; st £15, jun £3, OAP free, from Hon Sec or tackle shop. **Burghley Park Lake**, 1m SE (bream and tench, some rudd), Monday to Saturdays; dt £5 to fish island side of Burghley Lake from Burghley Estate Office, 61 St Martins, Stamford, PE9 2LQ (tel: 01780 752075). Tackle shop: Allen's Tackle Box, 13A Foundry Rd, PE9 2PY (tel: 01780 754541).

Ketton (Leics). Oakham AS has water here and on **River Chater**; members only; coarse fish.

Rockingham (Northants). 400 acre Eyebrook Reservoir is only 2m distant, just south of Caldecott; good trout fishing *(see Midlands reservoirs and lakes)*. At **Corby**, District Council (tel: 01536 402551) runs coarse fishery on Corby Boating Lake, with specimen carp. Hotels: Elizabeth; Hilton, Corby.

Market Harborough (Leics). **Saddington Reservoir**; contact Jim Mason (tel: 0116 2887229) is Saddington AA water. Enquiries to Hon Sec. Broughton and Dunton AC has members only lake at Liere. Permits for 2m stretch of Foxton Canal at Tungsten, with good roach fishing, from local tackle shop. Wellingborough Nene AC have 5m of Grand Union Canal between Foxton Locks and Theddingworth; apply Hon Sec. 1½ acre coarse lake with carp, roach, tench and other coarse fish, in grounds of Welham Lodge, Market Harborough; dt £5 on bank, conc £3; Tina (tel: 01858 433067). **CJ's Fishery**; 3 lakes; carp and match; 4m NW; dt on bank. **Mill Farm Fisheries**, Gilmorton, nr Lutterworth; 2 lakes totalling 6 acres; carp, tench (tel: 01455 552392); also **Holly Farm Fisheries**, Ashby Magna; 3 lakes, carp (tel: 01455 202391); tickets on site. Tackle shop: Oadby Angling, 89 London Rd, Oadby, Leicester LE2 5DN (tel: 01162 710789); Rugby Tackle Mail Order, 155A Bilton Rd, Rugby CV22 7DS (tel: 01788 570645). Hotels: Angel, Grove.

Tributaries of the Welland

GLEN: River free from Surfleet village to reservoir, coarse fish; trout above Bourne.

Surfleet (Lincs). Glen free below village. Preserved above by Spalding FC.

Pinchbeck (Lincs). Permits issued by Welland and Nene RD. River Welland, 2m SE at Spalding; also Coronation Channel.

Counter Drain (Lincs). Counter Drain; coarse fish; Spalding FC.

Bourne (Lincs). Glen holds trout upstream.

GWASH: Fair trout and grayling stream. Private fishing. Stamford Welland AAA have confluence with Welland to Newstead road bridge, west bank.

CHATER:

Ketton (Leics). Roach and dace. Stamford Welland AAA has stretch from junction with Welland to Ketton road bridge, both banks.

EYE BROOK: Good head of roach, dace and chub; trout upstream.

WITHAM

(For close seasons, licences, etc, see Anglian Region Environment Agency, p21)

Rises south of Grantham and flows northward to Lincoln, then south-eastward to Boston, where it enters the Wash. Above Grantham noted mainly for trout and grayling, mainly private. Between Grantham and Lincoln it is a good mixed coarse fishery, with chub, dace and barbel, mainly private clubs. Winter areas include Kirkstead and Tattershall Bridge sections. From Lincoln to Boston it is entirely embanked with excellent roach and bream fishing. The fishing rights for the majority of this length are leased to the Witham & District Joint Anglers' Federation. Members of the following affiliated associations have free fishing: Grimsby ASA; Boston AA; Lincoln & Dist AA; Worksop AA; Newark PF. Otherwise, temporary members, day-permits from their bailiffs on the bankside or local tackle shops. Main fishing accesses are **Washingborough, Bardney, Southrey, Stixwold, Kirkstead Bridge** to **Tattershall Bridge** (road alongside), **Chapel Hill, Langrick Bridge** and **Boston. Woodhall Spa** is another good centre for Witham angling, with several hotels catering for anglers, including Kings Arms.

Boston (Lincs). Angling facilities excep-   tionally good; at least 100 miles of good coarse fishing (pike, perch, dace, tench, roach and bream) in Witham; Witham & Dist JAF holds 26m between Lincoln and Boston, also tributaries. Boston & Dist AA waters: **South Forty Foot Drain**, **Sibsey Trader** (carp to 20lb), **Bargate Drain** (Horncastle Rd), **River Glen** at Guthrum and Tongue End, the **Bourne Eau**, and **East and West Fen Catchwaters**. Disabled pegs on Trader Drain. St £13, conc, dt £3. Free fishing on Hob Hole Drain, Kelsey Drain and West Fen System, on each of which Boston DAA have the match rights (tel Mrs Mallett on 01205 871815). Tackle shops: Vanguard Fishing Tackle, 25 Wide Bargate PE21 6SR (tel: 01205 369994); Boston Angling Centre, 11 Horncastle Rd PE21 9BN (tel: 01205 353436). Accom at Fairfield Guest House, 101 London Rd; Kings Arms, Horncastle Rd.

Lincoln (Lincs). Good coarse fishing. Witham fishes best from Aug to Oct with bream predominant. Witham & Dist JAF has Witham from Stamp End Lock to Boston West on right bank, with exception of a few short stretches, Witham left bank, Lincoln 1,500 yds d/s of Stamp End Lock to Bardney, with exception of 1,200 yds in Willingham Fen, Witham at Stixwould to Kirkstead Bridge; **Sincil Drain/South Delph** between Stamp End Lock and point 630 yds u/s of Bardney Lock; **North Delph**, **Branston Delph**, **Sandhill Beck**, **Timberland Delph**, **Billinghay Skerth**. Dt £3 from bailiffs on bank. Lincoln & Dist AA has excellent coarse fishing on **Trent**; 5m **Upper River Witham**, Lincoln to R Brant confluence; **Till** at Lincoln, **Saxilby** and **Sturton by Stow**; drains, dykes, **Boultham Park**, and **Starmers Pit** (good bream, eels, pike, carp and others species); Witham & Dist JAF waters. Membership books £22 from tackle shops, concessions to jun,

OAP; dt on banks. 11m **Fossdyke Canal** between Torksey and Lincoln, mainly roach and bream; also Witham & Dist JAF managed. **North Hykeham**; **Richmond Lakes**, 40 acres, coarse; dt £1.50, on bank. Tackle shops: South End Angling, 447 High Str, LN5 8HZ (tel: 01522 528627); G Harrison & Son, 55 Croft Str, LN2 5AZ (tel: 01522 569555); Boundary Pet Stores, 6 Bunkers Hill LN2 4QP (tel: 01522 520772); Newport Tackle Shop, 85 Newport LN1 3DW (tel: 01522 525861); Feed'n'Weed, 22 Birchwood Centre LN6 0QQ (tel: 01522 695528). Hotels: Barbican; Brickmakers Arms; Branston Hall; Red Lion, many others.

Grantham (Lincs). Grantham AA has good coarse fishing on Witham, **Grantham Canal**, and **Denton Reservoir**; dt £3 for canal only; on bank; membership from Arbon & Watts *(below)*; membership £16, conc £8. Assn is a member of the federation of Midlands clubs, which includes Boston, Oakham, Newark, Asfordby and Deeping St James clubs, and has been established to protect fisheries in area and leases waters on **Bourne Eau** and the **Glen**; membership: apply Hon Sec. Assn also has **Queen Elizabeth Pond**, Queen Elizabeth Park for disabled and OAP's only; tench, crucian, rudd. 3m from Grantham is National Trust Towthorpe Hollow Ponds; carp and tench; no ground bait; apply property manager (tel: 01476 592900). **Woodland Waters,** Willoughby Rd, Ancaster, Grantham NG32 3RT (tel: 01400 230888), has match lake, with large head of tench, and specimen lake, with carp over 30lbs; dt £5 (£8 carp), conc; holiday camping on site. Tackle shops: Arbon & Watts Ltd, 96 Westgate, Grantham NG31 6LE (tel: 01476 400014), has many local permits, and sole supplier for Grantham AA.

Tributaries of the Witham

SOUTH FORTY FOOT DRAIN:
Good coarse fishing. From Boston to Little Hale Drove, Boston & Dist AA. Matches booked through Hon Sec. Centres are **Boston, Wyberton, Hubberts Bridge, Swineshead, Donington.**

RIVER BAIN:
Tattershall (Lincs). Good stretch of river with large chub, occasional barbel, also good bream, perch, and pike to 25lbs.

Horncastle (Lincs). Rivers Bain and War-

ing; trout, roach; preserved. Some good chub water, free fishing. Tupholme Brook 7m NW. Horncastle AA has Bell Yard Pit and about 1½m on Horncastle Canal; club book £18, conc, from Hon Sec. **Revesby Reservoir**, 35 acres, coarse fish; contains big pike, roach, tench, bream, perch, eels; apply to Estate Office, Revesby, Boston PE22 7NH (tel: 01507 568395). Other water on site, the Wong, 4 acres, syndicate water with carp.

Tickets for local fishing from tackle shop: Synchro Sports, 9 Market Place LN9 5HB (tel: 01507 523366). Hotels: Bull, Red Lion, Rodney.

FOSSDYKE NAVIGATION: Fossdyke held by Witham & Dist JAF. Centres: **Lincoln, Saxilby** and **Torksey.** Good coarse fishing, especially noted for bream. Match bookings to Glynn Williams (tel: 01909 474940).

HOBHOLE DRAIN, EAST AND WEST FEN DRAINS: All canalised lengths of river forming part of the fen drainage system. Hold good stock of coarse fish (bream, roach, perch, pike, tench); area includes following waters: **Maud Foster, Sibsey Trader, East Fen Catchwater** drains, **West Fen, Kelsey** and **Bellwater** drains. St and dt from Boston tackle shops; match pegs £3. Hobhole and West Fen drains may be fished free on EA licence only. St covers also fishing on **Witham,**

SLEA: Rises west of Sleaford and enters Witham at Chapel Hill. Trout in upper reaches. Coarse fish, particularly roach, elsewhere. Private fishing throughout length. Hotel: Carr Arms.

WYE

(For close seasons, licences, etc, see Welsh Region Environment Agency, p23).

Most famous of English salmon rivers. Rises on south side of Plynlimon near source of Severn and enters estuary of Severn 2m south of Chepstow. Most of rod fishing in private hands, but there are several hotels and one or two associations with rights on river. Sea trout fishing is of no account, but coarse fishing in middle and lower reaches exceptionally good. No free fishing. Licences may be obtained from local post offices and sub-post offices and have usually to be produced when obtaining tickets or other permits to fish. Good brown trout fishing in Upper Wye and tributaries, very little trout fishing in Middle Wye. Roger Stokes, Springfield, Peterchurch HR2 0RT (tel: 01981 550540) is responsible for letting 2m double bank on Lower Wyesham which has excellent fly water; ghillie available; let by season £1000 per rod one day per week; reputedly one of best Wye fishings.

Redbrook (Gwent). Chub, dace, pike, perch, salmon. Contact the Post Office, Redbrook. For Whitebrook fishing, V Cullimore, Tump Farm, Whitebrook, Gwent. At **Fairoak Fishery**, The Cot, St Arvans, Chepstow, Monmouth NP16 6HQ (tel: 01291 689711), fly only fishing for trout on three waters; various tickets on site, incl £30 5 fish, £17 2 fish; lodge on site, with good facilities for anglers, incl disabled; expert tuition, with a purpose built novice pool; Troutmaster water.

Monmouth (Monmouthshire). Wye holds salmon, pike, trout, grayling, chub, dace; preserved. Town water is fishable on day, week and annual permit, coarse and salmon, from Council Offices, Monmouth NP5 3DY (tel: 01600 715662). Monmouth Dist AS own or rent 7m of three rivers: Wye, coarse fishing during salmon close season, on both banks from Wye Bridge downstream; **Monnow**, with trout, grayling, chub, dace, carp, 3m of single or double bank trout fly fishing; **Troddi** at Dingestow, over 5m of single or double bank trout fishing, all methods; contact Hon Sec. Skenfrith AS also has local water, members only, details from Hon Sec. **Trothy**, trout; preserved.

Symonds Yat (Hereford). Salmon, trout and coarse fishing all preserved. 1½m both banks between **Goodrich** and Symonds Yat controlled by Newport AA. Good S water; members only.

Kerne Bridge (Hereford). Chub, dace, pike, perch, salmon, trout; preserved. Castle Brook, Garron, 2m; trout. Luke Brook, 2m. Lammerch Brook, 5m.

Ross (Hereford). Salmon, trout, barbel, bleak, carp, bream, roach, large pike, chub and good dace. Ross-on-Wye AC has fishing on Town Water, Weir End and Benhall, approx 5m; membership £30 plus joining fee, wt £15, dt £4, conc, for town water on bank or from G B Sports (*below*); club also has waters outside salmon season at Sallack, 5m u/s. Ebbw Vale Welfare AC has 2½m at **Foy**, with chub, dace, roach, barbel; members only, membership open to application. Hotels: Royal, Radcliffe Guest House. Ross-on-Wye AC will be pleased to help visitors; send sae if writing. **Foy Bridge Fishery**, Lyndor HR9 7JW (tel: 01989 563833) has 250 metres double bank, spinning and fly fishing; boat for hire. Wye Lea County Manor, **Bridstow**, HR9 6PZ (tel: 01989 562880), has 1m single bank from Backney to Wye Lea; salmon (4 rods); mixed coarse; ghillie; boat. Licences and tackle from G&B Sports, 10 Broad St, Ross HR9 7EA (tel: 01989 563723).

Hereford (Hereford). Salmon, trout, grayling, other coarse fish incl big chub, and more recently barbel. Hereford & Dist AA holds 11½m bank on Wye and 8m **Lugg**, 2m intended as rainbow and brown trout fishery, with dt; dt £20 salmon, £15 trout (2 fish) or £25 (4 fish); in addition, three stillwater fisheries, one trout and two coarse fish; members only; three types of membership offered; salmon members may fish some 18 named pools, fishable at various heights; membership applications to Hon Sec. 40 pegs at Luggs Mouth to Shipley, Holme Lacy nr Hereford; contact Monte Bishop, 12 Old Eign Hill, HR1 1TU (tel: 01432 342665); permits from Mordiford PO. Letton Court, Hereford HR3 6DJ, has salmon fishing on 1½m of Wye, dt £20-£25; also coarse fishing on 1½m of river and two lakes with chub, tench, carp, pike, dt £5; Brian Powell (tel: 01531 890455). 3m from Kington is **Bollingham Pools**; brown and rainbow trout, fly only; contact R F Pennington, Bollingham Pools, nr Eardisley HR5 3LE (tel: 01497 831665). Birmingham AA has water on Lugg at Dinmore and Moreton; dt £4 from tackle shops. Longworth Mill, **Lugwardine** HF1 4DF (tel: 01432 850226), has fishing on Wye, and a short stretch on the Lugg. For Byford fishing on Garnons Estate, Bridge Sollars, who sometimes have salmon dt; in advance only, also coarse dt; phone bailiff, Phil Jordan (tel: 01981 590270 before 9pm); and Red Lion, Bredwardine. Local tackle shop: Woody's Angling Centre, 67 Whitecross Road, Hereford HR4 0DQ (tel: 01432 344644). Hotels: City Arms; Green Dragon; Farm Hand; Firkin; Booth Hall. Red House Farm, Eaton Bishop, caters for anglers.

Bredwardine (Hereford). Red Lion Hotel HR3 6BU (tel: 01981 500303), has tickets for 8m, salmon, trout, coarse fishing.

Hay-on-Wye (Hereford). Salmon, trout, pike, perch, chub. Hay-on-Wye Fishermans Assn has local fishing, with trout, grayling and coarse, not salmon. EA licences from post office. Permits (£25 to £3) for Hay Town Council water from J&P Gamon, Paddles and Pedals/Hay-on-Wye Newsagents, 15 Castle St, HR3 5DF (open 6.30am to 5.30 pm) (tel: 01497 820604). Swan at Hay Hotel, Church St HR3 5DQ (tel: 01497 821188), has permits for fishing on Wye, £25 non-residents, £15 residents. **Llangorse Lake** can be fished from here. Tackle shop: Sportfish, Winforton, nr Hay-on-Wye HR3 6EB (tel: 01544 327111); F W Golesworthy & Sons, 17 Broad St, HR3 5DF (tel: 01497 820491). Hotel: Rose and Crown.

Glasbury-on-Wye (Powys). Salmon, trout, chub, dace, grayling, pike. Fishing in Wye and Llynfi preserved. Llangorse lake is accessible.

Builth Wells (Powys). Salmon (best April, May, June and Oct); good head of grayling, wild brown trout declining. Groe Park & Irfon AC has 2m on Wye incl ½m double bank, 1m on Irfon, incl ½m double bank, with 9 salmon catches on Wye and 4 late season catches on **Irfon**. Fly fishing only during trout season on Irfon and 2 sections of Wye. Club stocks heavily with brown trout. 3-day salmon permit £25, trout £18, trout dt £9, juv £3, coarse dt between 1 Oct-end Feb £5, from The Park Hotel; T D Niblett & Co, 43 High St (tel: 01982 553624); or M Morgan, The Beeches, 10 Cae Llewellyn, Cilmery, Builth Wells (tel: 01982 552759); no keep nets for grayling on club waters, prawn and shrimp for salmon banned; club also owns Llyn Alarch, 1½ acres, nr Builth, stocked rainbows; platforms for disabled anglers; 4 fish limit, dt £16, conc, from Mrs Morgan (*above*). A few country memberships available, salmon £64, trout £32, contact Hon Sec. **Elan Estate Reservoirs** accessible *(see Rhayader)*. Cueiddon, Duhonw, Baili and Edw preserved. Tackle shop: Rods & Reels, 10a Broad St, Castle Courtyard, Builth Wells. Hotels: Park Hotel; Lion; Caer Beris Manor Hotel.

Newbridge-on-Wye (Powys). Salmon, trout, grayling, chub, dace, pike, roach; preserved, Ithon; trout; preserved.

Rhayader (Powys). Wye; trout (av ½lb; Wye record, 10½lb, caught at Rhayader Bridge), salmon. Rhayader AA has 4m on **Wye**, 3m on R **Marteg** to St Harmon, 1½m on R **Elan**, and 16-acre **Llyngwyn** at Nant Glas, rainbow trout to 6lbs; fly only. River dt £5, lake dt £12.50, st £95, conc, from John and Les Price, Nant-y-Mynach Farm, Nantmel, Llandrindod Wells, LD1 6EW (tel: 01597 810491), or Mrs Daisy Powell, newsagent, West Street, Rhayader (tel: 01597 810451). Brown trout fishing in **Elan Valley**,

(Caban Coch, Garreg Ddu, Pen-y-Garreg and Craig Goch), all fly only, st £65, dt £8, conc, from Visitors' Centre below Caban Coch dam (10am-6pm), and Mrs Powell *(above)*. Dt £5 for local Wye stretch. **Llngwyn Fishery**; dt £12.50, st £95, conc, from Nant-y-Mynach Farm *(above)*; tickets also from Newsagents; all waters fly only; 6 fish limit per day; minimum size 10in. **Claerwen Reservoir** (650 acres), controlled by WW. Elan Valley Hotel, LD6 5HN (tel: 01597 810448; web: www.elanvalleyhotel.co.uk), caters

for anglers, and has various fishing permits. Mr and Mrs C Easton, Glanrhos, Llanwrthwl, Llandridod Wells LD1 6NT (tel: 01597 810277), have accom for anglers, and ¾m west bank of Wye north of Llanwrthwl Bridge, 7 pools, with plentiful trout and grayling, salmon late season, fly only; dt £6, longer term permits available at discounted rates by arrangement. Hotels: Crown Inn, North St; Lamb & Flag, North St; Bear, East St; Elan Valley Hotel, Elan Valley, nr Rhayader.

Tributaries of the Wye

TROTHY: Trout, some assn water.

Dingestow (Gwent). Trout; preserved. Glamorgan AC, Cardiff, has 6m fishing; inquiries to the Hon Sec. Monmouth & Dist AS has 4m, mostly double bank. Trout and eels, excellent mayfly; st £20, dt £6.

MONNOW: Good trout and grayling stream. The Gamefishers Club has water on **Lugg**, **Rea**, **Monnow** and several brooks; trout and grayling; day permits to members' guests only; contact Hon Sec. Monmouth & Dist AS has 3m of Monnow, *see Monmouth.*

Skenfrith (Hereford). Trout, chub, dace.

Pandy (Gwent). Trout, grayling; preserved. Honddu: trout; preserved. Hotel: Pandy

Inn.

HONDDU (tributary of Monnow): Trout.

Llanfihangel Crucorney (Gwent). Permits for trout fishing here may be purchased at local post office.

LUGG: Trout and grayling, with coarse fish in some stretches.

Mordiford (Hereford). Trout, grayling, etc. Leominster AC has water; Birmingham AA also has good stretch here, also water at Tidnor, Lugg Mill, Bodenh+am, Dinmore, Marden and Moreton; dt £4 from tackle shops. The Moon Inn, HR1 4LW (tel: 01432 870236) is HQ of fishing club, and has permits for water at Holme Lacey. Tickets for Sufton Estate fishing,

This Chesterfield Angler plays a brown trout. *Photo: Press Manor Fishery.*

both banks between Mordiford Bridge and Wye junction, also for Leominster AC, from Post Office & Stores, Mordiford HR1 4LN (tel: 01432 870235).

Longworth (Hereford). Longworth Mill, Lugwardine HR1 4DF (tel: 01432 850226) has trout and coarse fishing on **Wye**; advance booking recommended.

Lugwardine (Hereford). 8½m preserved by Hereford & District AA; dt for right bank d/s starting some 150 yds below the Worcester Rd.

Leominster (Hereford). Trout, grayling, pike, perch, dace. Above town Lugg preserved by landowners. White Swan Piscatorials also have water; otherwise preserved by landowners. **Pinsley Brook**; trout, grayling; landowners sometimes give permission. Mr T Brooke, Nicholson Farm, Docklow HR6 0SL (tel: 01568 760346), has coarse pools at Docklow: dt £6, and holiday cottages to let. Hotels: Royal Oak (where fishing can be arranged for guests); Talbot.

Kingsland (Hereford). Lugg. Arrow, and Pinsley Brook; trout, grayling. Fishing generally preserved by landowners. 2m from Kingsland is River Arrow at Eardisland. Accommodation: Angel and Mortimer Cross.

Presteigne (Powys). Lugg, Arrow and Teme afford excellent trout and grayling fishing, generally dry fly; preserved. The Gamefishers Club has Lugg here, as well as Honddu near Pontrilas; Rea, Cradley Brook and Leigh Brook near Worcester; and Severn tributaries Tanat and Cound Brook near Shrewsbury; all brown trout waters, fly only, members only: apply Hon Sec. Near Presteigne, holiday flat and B&B in Georgian farmhouse, with fly fishing for trout on 4-acre Hindwell Lake; stocked annually with 300-400 rainbows and browns; boat on water. Details from Mrs A Goodwin, Hindwell Farm, Walton, Presteigne LD8 2NU (tel: 01544 350252).

FROME (tributary of Lugg). Trout, preserved.

Ashperton (Hereford). Frome, 2½m Leddon, 2½m. Devereux Park Lakes, 4m.

ARROW (tributary of Lugg): Trout, grayling, dace; but few opportunities for visitors.

Pembridge (Hereford). Trout, grayling, dace; preserved by landowners. White Swan Piscatorials have a stretch at Ivington. No tickets. Inn: New Inn.

Kington (Hereford). Trout; preserved. Inns:

Swan, Royal Oak.

LLYNFI: Trout, grayling, etc; preserved.

Glasbury-on-Wye (Hereford). Lynfi enters Wye here. Trout, grayling, chub. Fishing good, but mostly preserved.

Talgarth (Powys). Llynfi. Dulais brook. Rhiangoll; trout. Treffrwd, 2m. **Llangorse Lake** (pike, perch) can be fished from here (4m); boats for hire. Hotel: Castle. Visitors' tickets from local association.

IRFON: limited salmon, trout few unless stocked; good grayling.

Llangammarch Wells (Powys). Lake Country House Hotel, LD4 4BS (tel: 01591 620202) has about 5m of Irfon and nearby streams (**Garth Dulas, Chwefri**, etc), and some rods for salmon fishing on Wye negotiated each year and charged accordingly. Also 2½ acre trout lake in grounds, brown and rainbow; fish to 3½lb. Lake and rivers restocked annually; fly only, wading sometimes essential. Wt and dt offered: salmon dt £25, trout and grayling £20. Limit 2 brace from lake, £3.00 per lb caught. Seasons on Irfon: trout 3 Mar-30 Sept; salmon 26 Jan-25 Oct; grayling 16 Jun-14 Mar. Lake open all year.

Llanwrtyd Wells (Powys). Trout. 3m of Association water. Lakes.

ITHON: Trout, chub, few salmon. Good hotel and assn water.

Llandrindod Wells (Powys). Trout, grayling, chub, some eels and salmon. Llandrindod Wells AA controls 5m of trout fishing close to town, mainly between Disserth and Llanyre Bridges. Limit 2 brace per day. Sunday fishing; no spinning for trout allowed, 9" size limit; waders essential; open to visitors on st £27, wt £20, dt £6.50, conc, from Wayfarers, Ddole Rd Enterprise Park LD1 6DF (tel: 01597 825100), who supply tackle. Accom with private fishing at Disserth Caravan and Camping Park, LD1 6NL (tel: 01597 860277). Hotel: The Bell, Llanyre; Llanerch Inn.

Penybont (Powys). Trout, chub, grayling, dace, eels, pike. Hotel: Severn Arms LD1 5UA (tel: 01597 851224/344), has 6m of trout fishing on Ithon, free to residents, otherwise dt £6; fish run to 3lb average. Licences at post office in village. Tackle from Wayfarers at Llandrindod Wells.

Llanbadarn Fynydd (Powys). Upper Ithon. New Inn, LD1 6YA (tel: 01597 840378), has 3½m trout fishing; free to guests (fly only); dt for visitors; also access to Esgair trout lake; dt from inn.

WYRE

(For close seasons, licences, etc, see North West Region Environment Agency, p20).

From Churchtown downstream coarse fish and brown trout. Above Churchtown limited amount of salmon, sea trout and brown trout fishing.

Fleetwood (Lancs). Sport in estuary improving as water quality improves; flatfish mostly.

St Michael's (Lancs). Mainly brown trout and coarse fish. Ribble and Wyre FA have fishing at St Michaels, some sea trout. Hotel: Grapes.

Churchtown (Lancs). Salmon, sea trout, trout and coarse fish. Warrington AA has fishing here.

Garstang (Lancs). Salmon, sea trout, trout and coarse fish. Garstang AA preserves 3m both banks. Fly only. No dt, members only. Hotels: Royal Oak, Eagle and Child, Crown.

Scorton (Lancs). Salmon, sea trout, trout, coarse fish. Wyresdale Anglers have 7m water; no tickets.

YARE

(See Norfolk and Suffolk Broads)

YORKSHIRE (lakes, reservoirs, canals and streams)

(For close seasons, licences, etc, see North East Region Environment Agency p20)

BRANDESBURTON PONDS. Several ponds offering varied sport to leisure anglers and specialists. Hull & District AAA, membership from local tackle shop or Secretary. No dt.

BURTON CONSTABLE LAKES. 25 acres, at caravan park in grounds of Burton Constable Hall; excellent coarse fishing for roach, bream, perch, tench, carp and pike; st £50, wt £15, dt £5 (£6 2 rods) from Warden, Old Lodges, Sproatley, nr Hull HU11 4LN (tel: 01964 562508); or on bank; season 1 Mar-31 Oct.

CASTLE HOWARD GREAT LAKE. Near **Malton.** 78 acres, formerly noted for specimen pike over 40lb, perch, tench to 10lb, bream to 14lb, roach, and eels to 8lb+. However due to over-fishing in the North Sea, cormorants have significantly reduced lake stocks. It is not intended to re-stock, nor to close the fishing which, for the time being will be free to customers of the touring park.

CHELKER, SILSDEN, LEESHAW and WINTERBURN RESERVOIRS. Trout; 25 year waiting list for the local club. No tickets. Near Silsden and Ilkley.

DAMFLASK and UNDERBANK RESERVOIRS. YW Services Ltd. Damflask Coarse Fisheries (tel: 01274 372742), 5m from Sheffield. Underbank, 10m from Stocksbridge now let to Hadfield Anglers; dt on bank. Both coarse fisheries, bank fishing only. Disabled access at high water (with caution). Damflask

day and monthly tickets sold from machines at reservoirs. Further enquiries to Yorkshire Water, PO Box 500, Western House, Western Way, Halifax Rd, Bradford BD6 2LZ (tel: 01274 691111).

DOE PARK RESERVOIR, Denholme. 20 acres. Coarse fish; let to Bradford City AA; dt £5, Mon-Fri incl, 7 am (8.30 weekends) until 1 hour after sunset.

EMBSAY, and WHINNYGILL RESERVOIRS. Let by YW to Skipton AA; both open all year round (2 fish limit); st £53 + £17 entrance fee, conc; dt £9 (Embsay, trout), £5 (Whinnygill, trout, roach, bream and perch); £5 winter coarse fishing; assn also has fishing on R Aire, dt £5; tickets obtainable from Paper Shop, Embsay, and Earby tackle shops.

FEWSTON, SWINSTY and THRUSCROSS (wild browns only) **RESERVOIRS.** YWS Ltd trout fishery, 153 acres each, fly only, spinning (Swinsty only Oct-Nov), barbless hooks. Regular stocking, 1lb 6oz av, 3lb rainbows. Dt (limit 4/2 fish), from machine at Fishing Office at Swinsty Moor Plantation (tel answer machine: 01943 880658). Area for disabled bank anglers only, at Swinsty Lagoon where worm or fly may be used. Av catches 3 fish per rod. Near **Harrogate** and **Otley.**

HORNSEA MERE. Hornsea HU18 1AX. Yorkshire's largest inland water (350 acres). Very good pike, carp, bream, rudd, perch, roach, tench. Hornsea Mere

Marine Co (tel: 01964 533277); dt £2, junior £1, punts £7 day + £2 per person fishing (limited boat and bank fishing).

LEIGHTON RESERVOIR. Masham, N Yorks. 105 acre water-supply reservoir on the Swinton Estate stocked with rainbow trout (some very large) and browns; for season and day ticket fishing; barbless hooks; dt £14, (4 fish), evening £8, (2 fish), conc £10 (3 fish), from fishing hut in car park; catch and return allowed after limit reached. Swinton Estate Office, Swinton, Masham, Ripon, N Yorks HG4 4JR. Phone 01765 689224 for further details.

LEVEN CANAL. Beverley 6m. 3m of good coarse fishing.

LINDHOLME LAKE FISHERIES, Sandtoft. 4 acre fly only trout lake; 13 acre mixed coarse lake; 3 acre match lake, and 4½ acre mixed pool; day tickets £18, 4 fish, to £12, 2 fish, trout; £5 coarse, at fishery. Enquiries to Lindholme Leisure Lakes Ltd, Don Farm House, West Carr, Epworth, Doncaster DN9 1LF (tel: 01427 872 905).

MALHAM TARN. 6m from **Settle.** A Nature Reserve owned by the National Trust; boat fishing only, for trout with fly; barbless hooks only; c&r only; no keepnets; no bank fishing; fish may run large; dt £10 boat, £10/rod, conc; weekends, £16 boat, £12 rod, no conc; no outboard motors allowed; bookings and detailed information from Warden or Secretary (tel: 01729 830331); phone bookings recommended. Seasons May 1 to Sept 30; accommodation locally.

MARKET WEIGHTON CANAL. Fishing stations: **Newport** and **Broomfleet.** 6m long; bream, perch, roach, pike. Match fishing leased from Environment Agency. Dt sold locally.

MORE HALL RESERVOIR. Sheffield 7m. YW Services Ltd water now leased to Moor Hall FF; trout, fly only; contact 01709 531159; dt available; barbless hooks.

SCOUT DIKE, Penistone. 16m from Sheffield. YW water now leased to Barnsley TA (tel: 01484 866231). Trout.

SHIPTON LAKE. Shipton-by-Beningbrough. Tench, perch, roach, pike. Bradford City AA, members only.

STAINFORTH AND KEADBY CANAL. Controlled by joint committee including following clubs: Rotherham, Doncaster, Scunthorpe AA and British Railways. Usual Coarse fish.

THORNTON STEWARD RESERVOIR, Bedale. 35 acre Felling FFC *(see below)* trout fishery known as **Thornton Steward Game Fishery,** 4m E of Leyburn; fly only, barbless hooks; regularly stocked with rainbows, 1lb 6oz to 4lb; also contains wild brown; open all year to members; 4 or 2 fish limit; no boats; dt £15, conc, from PO Fingall; ticket information from Joan Hainsworth, Hargill House, Finghall, Leyburn DL8 5ND (tel: 01677 450245).

TILERY LAKE, Faxfleet, nr Goole; 60 acres of water with carp to 30lb, bream, pike and roach; controlled by Hull AA, st from Hon Sec or tackle shops in Hull and Goole locality; no night fishing without special permit, from Night Permit Sec.

ULLEY COUNTRY PARK, nr Sheffield. Rotherham MBC. 33 acre coarse fishery with bream, roach, perch, pike, rudd. Disabled platform; no closed season at present; st £44, conc; dt £3, conc, from ticket machine at fishery; tackle shop on site; enquiries to Ulley C P, Pleasley Road, Ulley S26 3XL (tel: 01709 365332).

WORSBROUGH RESERVOIR, Barnsley. Coarse fish, all species, open all year. Barnsley & Dist AAS has rights; season book £20, conc £10; dt £2.50 from bailiffs walking the bank; keep nets, bloodworm, hempseed also now allowed.

NORTHUMBERLAND, Co DURHAM, and CLEVELAND RESERVOIRS. These groups of reservoirs, managed or leased by Northumbrian Water, include both stocked and wild trout fishing. **Fontburn; Grassholme** (140 acres); **Cow Green** (12 fish); **Scaling** (105 acres); **Blackton** (66 acres); **Hury** (125 acres coarse fishery: roach); **Derwent; Hanningfield** (8 fish), managed by Essex and Suffolk Water. For **Kielder** *(see North Tyne)*. Prices are as follows: 'Silver Explorer' season ticket, covering other NW waters £569 (24 fish p/w; max 8 p/d (unless indicated)), conc £489; dt £16 (8 fish), conc; Cow Green: 'Twelve fish' permit dt £8, conc £7; available from fishing lodges, or self-service, or local post offices. Bank fishing only, except Kielder and Fontburn. For information: Kielder: (tel: 01434 250312); Fontburn: (tel: 01669 621368); Grassholme, Blackton and Hury (tel: 01833 641121); Scaling Dam: (tel: 01287 644032); Hanningfield (tel: 01245 212034; web: www.eswater. co.uk), Derwent: (tel: 01207 255250). **Lockwood Beck,** 60 acres; stocked weekly with 2-14lb rainbows, open 8 am till sunset; tuition, bank and boat fishing: dt £19, 4 fish, plus c&r; evngs £13, 2 fish; boat £12, £8 evngs: The Fishing Lodge, Lockwood Beck, Lingdale, Saltburn by the Sea, TS12 3LQ (tel: 01287 660501).

ENGLISH CANAL FISHING

B ritish Waterways own over 1,200 miles of canal, and 89 operational supply reservoirs. The large majority of these fisheries are licensed to fishing clubs, but the BW retains direct control of fishing on a number of canal sections, and several reservoirs (shown below) or in the appropriate geographical section of the book, with season or day tickets easily obtainable.

Up to 100,000 anglers over the age of 12 fish British Waterways fisheries regularly. They form an important part of the coarse fishing on offer in England and Wales. Roach, perch, bream, gudgeon, eels, pike, dace, chub, and other coarse fish are to be found. Carp to 48lb have been reported from the Grand Union Canal, and in some lightly boated sections, a good head of tench, larger bream and crucian carp are present. Stocking levels are extremely good and surpass the EIFAC designated standard. The fishing is governed, as elsewhere, by water quality and natural food supply. Facilities for anglers in wheelchairs have been introduced in places; competitions can be arranged on directly controlled waters on application to the Regional Fisheries Manager. The North West Region has introduced various schemes, which include the **Waterways Anglers Together**, by which a number of fishing clubs share the leasing of 43m of Shropshire Union Canal, 40m of Llangollen Canal, 45m of Leeds and Liverpool Canal, 55m of Lancaster Canal, and a further 30m on eight additional waterways: members of participating clubs are able to fish anywhere on the 250m of fisheries included in the scheme as often as they like at no extra charge (a whole year at less than half the day ticket charge); participating clubs pay an Annual Registration Fee, £365 (irrespective of size); valid permits then obtainable for each and every member (0.99p per member). The **Waterway Wanderers Permit** is valid on the same waters; the latter offer st £15 adult (£10 conc), dt £2 (£1.50 conc) and a monthly permit £10 (adult) (£7.50 conc); available for participating clubs and covers all fishing under the scheme. Monthly and day permits are available but should be obtained in advance; night fishing available by special permit only. Finally, as a permit is required to fish anywhere on the canals (even from a boat), there is a **Welcome to the Waterways** permit, £10 (adult) (£7.50 conc), available for one month only to cover holidays and administered by BW; waters included in this scheme are those stretches of following canals controlled by BW; Ashton, Caldon, Huddersfield Narrow, Leeds and Liverpool, Llangollen, Macclesfield, Manchester Bolton & Bury, Lancaster, Montgomery, Shropshire Union, Peak Forest, Trent & Mersey Canals (except Preston Brook to Middlewich, and Whielden Road Bridge to Stoke Bottom Lock); also it should be noted that the Weaver Navigation and reservoirs are not included; all income from these monthly permits are used in restocking the waterways. For all permits and further information for the above, contact John Harding, 34 Nantwich Rd, Tarporley CW6 9UW (tel: 01829 732748) or the Regional Fisheries Manager. Before fishing anywhere in England or Wales, it is necessary to have an Enviroment Agency Rod Licence, obtainable from most Post Offices. **Anglers should take special care to avoid overhead power lines on all canals. Do not assemble tackle near power-lines and do not carry assembled tackle from peg to peg.**

There are four administrative areas of waterways fisheries, three of which are administered by **British Waterways: North West and Wales & Border Counties Region, Navigation Road, Northwich, Cheshire CW8 1BH** (tel: 01606 723800, fax: 01606 871471); **Central Shires and West Midlands Region, Peel's Wharf, Lichfield Street, Fazeley, Tamworth,**

Check before you go

While every effort has been made to ensure that the information given in **Where to Fish** *is correct, the position is continually changing, and anglers are urged, in their own interests, to make preliminary enquiries before travelling to selected venues. This is especially important with reference to prices quoted. Inevitably the rate of inflation is affecting stability in this quarter. Anglers' attention is also drawn to the fact that the hotels mentioned under the various fishing stations do not necessarily have water of their own. Any amendments or further data for inclusion in subsequent editions, and any comments, will be welcome.*

Staffordshire B78 3QZ (tel: 01827 252000; fax: 01827 288071); **South East Region, Ground Floor, Witan Gate House, 500-600 Witan Gate, Central Milton Keynes MK9 1BW** (tel: 01908 302500), which covers the regions of the South East, South West, London and Scotland. The fourth region, the **North East Region**, is now administered by a specialist Rural Asset Management Company, **Smith-Woolley, Collingham, Newark, Notts. NG23 7LG** (tel: 01636 892456; fax: 01636 893045; e-mail: mjones@smith-woolley.co.uk) who retain a database of all club waters in the region, and whose involvement mirrors that of the other Fishery Officers (as above). This region was recently split into East Midlands Region (head office: Newark) and Yorkshire Region (head office: Leeds), and now encompasses Huddersfield Narrow and parts of the Leeds & Liverpool canal (previously part of the North West Region). Their southern boundary is King's Lock (Leicester) on the Grand Union South.

Some of the fishing clubs mentioned below are, for reasons of space, not in the club lists of this edition. The Regional Fisheries Manager at the appropriate office will supply addresses and other information.

SOUTH EAST REGION:

Grand Union Canal; Osterley Lock to Hayes (not let). Hayes to West Drayton, Central Assn of London & Prov AC. West Drayton to Denham, London AA. Denham to Batchworth, Blenheim AS. Sabeys Pool and part of R Chess, West Hampstead AS. Batchworth to Lot Mead Lock, Sceptre AC. Lot Mead to Cassionbury Park, Watford Piscators, and to Hunton Bridge, Kings Langley AS. Hunton Bridge to Tring, London AA. Tring to Cheddington, Tring Anglers. Cheddington to Stoke Hammond. Luton AC. From Stoke Hammond to Great Linford, Milton Keynes AA. Great Linford to Wolverton Bridge, North Bucks Div. SE Midlands, CIU Ltd. Old Wolverton to R Ouse Aqueduct, Galleon AC. 400m Canal and Broadwater at Cosgrove, Mr & Mrs M Palmer, Lock House, Cosgrove. Cosgrove to Castlethorpe, Deanshanger & Old Stratford AA. Castlethorpe to Yardley Gobion, Britannia AC. Yardley Gobion to Dodford, Northampton Nene AC. Brockhall to Watling Street Bridge, Daventry AC. Norton Junction to southern

Canals are often narrow and sheltered waters, making less dramatic venue than rivers. Not so the Aire & Calder canal near Selby. *Photo: L Rogers.*

end of Braunston Tunnel, AM-PRO UK Ltd AC.

Grand Union: Arms and Branches:

Wendover Arm; Main Line to Tringford Pumping Station, Tring Anglers. **Aylesbury Arm**; Main Line to Red House Lock, Tring A. Red House Lock nr Aston Clinton to u/s of Aylesbury Basin, Aylesbury & Dist AF. To the Basin Terminus, Aylesbury Canal Society. **Northampton Arm**; Main Line to Milton Malsor, Britannia AC. Milton Malsor Bridge 3 to Lock 17, Castle AA. Bridges 13 to 17, Castle AA. Gayton Marina, Gayton AC. **Leicester Branch**; Norton Junction to A5 road bridge, Towcester & Dist AA. A5 road bridge to Watford Staircase locks, Am-Pro Long Buckby AC. North end of Crick Tunnel to Bridge 20, Knightley AC. Bridges 20 to 22 at Yelverton, (not let). Bridges 27 to 29, Finedon AC. Bridges 29 to 31, (not let). Bridges 31 to 33, Team Gilders, Northants. Bridges 36 to 38, Lutterworth & Dist AC. Bridges 38 to 42, White Hart Match Group. Bridges 37 to 39, (not let). Bridges 41 to 45, Brixworth AC. North Kilworth to southern end of Bosworth Tunnel, White Hart Match Group. Bridges 47 to 51, White Hart MG. Bridges 51 to 60, Wellingborough Nene AC. **Welford Arm**, Lock to footbridge, White Hart Floor AC. The whole of the **Slough Arm** is let to Gerrards Cross & Uxbridge Dist AS (contact Mr Turton, 50 Lancaster Rd, Uxbridge UB8 1AR). **Market Harborough Arm**; Junction, Foxton Boats Ltd. Foxton to Mkt Harborough, Tungstone FC, Desbo-rough and Rothwell AC, Mkt Harborough AC. Foxton to Leicester, Wigston AS.

Oxford Canal (North); Bridges 101 to 97, Braunston AC. Bridges 97 to 85, Willoughby, Braunston Turn and Braunston Tunnel, Braunston AC. Willoughby Wharf Bridge to Bridge 83, (not let). Bridges 80 to 77, Avon Ho AC. Bridge 76 to Hillmorton Top Lock, Avon Ho AC. Hillmorton Bottom Lock to Bridge 9, (not let).

Oxford Canal (South); Dukes Cut, Wolvercote Pool, Hythe Bridge Street to Kidlington Green Lock, North Oxford AS. Kidlington Green Lock to Bullers Bridge, N. Oxford AS. Bullers Bridge to Langford Lane, Kidlington AS. Langford Lane to Bridge 221, Banbury & DAA. Bridge 221 to end of moorings at Thrupp, Thrupp Canal Cruising Club. Thrupp to Bridge 216, Banbury & DAA. Bridges 216 to Lower Heyford, plus River Cherwell at Enslow, Kirtlington, and Northbrook, Oxford & Dist AA. Lower Heyford to Aynho, Banbury & Dist AA. Aynho to Banbury, Banbury & DAA. Banbury to Cropredy, Banbury & Dist AA. Cropredy Lock to Bridge 148, Browning Castle. Bridge 148 to Claydon, Sphinx C. Claydon to Fenny Compton, Ford (Leamington) AC. Fenny Compton Marina to Bridge 136, Cowroast Marina AC. Folly Bridge to Napton Junction, Leamington Liberal AC. Napton Junction to Bridge 103, and Bridges 101 to 102, Coventry & Dist AA. Bridge 102 to Bridge 103, (not let).

LONDON REGION:

Grand Union: Arms and Branches:

Paddington Arm; Bulls Bridge Junction to Lock Bridge at Paddington, London AA. **Paddington Basin**; Westminster AC.

Regents Canal; Little Venice to Islington, (not let). Islington to Mile End, London AA. Mile End Lock to Commercial Rd, (not let). **Hertford Union Canal**; Junction with Regents Canal nr Victoria Park to Lee Navigation at Old Ford, (not let). **Slough Arm**; Whole of Arm from junction with Main Line at Cowley to Slough, Gerrards Cross & Uxbridge AC.

River Lee Navigation; Limehouse Basin to Blackwell Tunnel, (not let). Bow Lock stretch, Lee Anglers Consortium. Cheshunt, off-side bank plus Cadmore Lane Gravel Pit, Metrop Police AS. West bank Old R Lee, Kings Weir, W E Newton, Slipe Lane, Wormley. Carthegena Lock, Mr P Brill, Carthagena Lock, Broxbourne, Herts. Above Kings Weir to below Aqueduct Lock, London AA. Dodds Wier, L.V.R.P.A. Weir Pool at Feildes Weir, and Feildes Weir Lock to Rye House Station Bridge, plus stretch ½m u/s of Ryehouse Bridge, Lee Anglers Consortium. Ryehouse Bridge for 1020 metres, London AA. Offside Bank between Hardemeade and Stanstead Locks, Ware AC. The backwaters of the River Lee, the **Bow Back Rivers** are all under the control of the Lee Anglers Consortium (contact D F H Meadhurst, P O Box 19426, London E4 8UZ (tel: 020 8524 7270)

River Stort Navigation; From junction with Lee Navigation to Lower Lock, Lee Anglers Cosortium. From Road Bridge 6 to Railway Bridge 7, Roydon, Two Bridges AS. To Hunsdon Mill Lock, Globe AS. Stort and Stort Navigation at Burnt Mill, Harlow FA. Burnt Mill Lock to Parndon Lock, Stort Valley AA. Spellbrook Backwater, O J Smith, Spellbrook Lane East, Bishops Stortford. Bishops Stortford and to Spellbrook Lock, Bishops Stortford & Dist AS. Further stretch to Sawbridgeworth AS.

SOUTH WEST REGION:

Kennet and Avon Canal; Eight stretches from Bear Wharf, Reading, to Kennet Junction, Reading & Dist AA, with the exception of stretch nr Sulhampstead Lock, Central Assn of London & Prov AC. Woolhampton Lock to Heales Lock and stretch nr Oxlease Swing Bridge to Heales Lock, Glendale AC. Heales Lock to Midgham Bridge, Reading & Dist AA. Junction with Kennet at Northcroft, Two stretches at Midgham Lock, Reed Thatcham AA. Thatcham to Widmead Lock, Thatcham AA. Bulls Lock to Ham Lock, Newbury AA. Ham Mill (offside bank) I Fidler, Ham Mill, London Road, Newbury. Whitehouse Turnover Bridge to Greenham Lock, Twickenham PS. Greenham Lock to Greenham Island, Newbury, and Northcroft to Guyers Bridge, Newbury AA. Two sections at Kintbury (560 yds), Civil Service AS. Ladies Bridge nr Wilcote to Milkhouse Water Bridge, Pewsey and District AA. Ladies Bridge to Semington Bridge, Devizes AA. Semington Bridge to Whaddon Bridge, Avon Dist AA. Whaddon Bridge to Avoncliffe Aqueduct, Airsprung AC. Avoncliffe Aqueduct to Limpley Stoke Bridge, (not let). Limpley Stoke Bridge to R Avon confluence, Bathampton AA.

Bridgwater and Taunton Canal; Bridgwater to Durston, Bridgwater AA. Durston to Taunton, Taunton AA.

Gloucester and Sharpness & Stroudwater Canals; Hempsted Bridge, Gloucester, to Sharpness, leased to Gloucester Canal Angling on the towpath side. Frontage of Borrow Silos (150 yds), Babcock AC. Tanker Bay Area, MEB AC. Offside bank at Two Mile Bend, nr Gloucester, and Rea Bridge to north of Sellars Bridge, Gloucester United AA. Stroudwater Canal; Walk Bridge to 'Feeders', Frampton & Dist AA, also from Ryalls Farm to 'Stone' nr Frampton. Walk Bridge to Whitminster, Whitbread AC.

River Severn Navigation; Island bank at Upper Lode Lock Syndicate, Diglis, BW directly controlled. Belvere Lock, Lock Island, left bank 350 yds d/s. East bank at Diglis, Anglers Stay AC. Bevere Lock, Mrs M E Smith, Bevere Lock, Grimley. Holt Lock u/s and d/s, A S Portman, Holt Lock, Holt Heath, nr Worcester. Salmon rights, Lincomb Lock, P Gough, Courtnay House, Feiashill Road, Trysull WV5 7HT. Coarse rights, M Charles, Lincomb Lock, Stourport. West bank, Sabrina AC.

CENTRAL SHIRES/WEST MIDLANDS:

Ashby Canal; Stretches leased by Shackerstone & Dist AC, Measham AC, Barvek AC, Swadlincote AA.

Birmingham and Fazeley Canal; Tyburn to Curdworth Tunnel, Dams and Lock AC, BRS (Midlands) AC, Stirrup Cup AC. Curdworth Tunnel to Whittington is Birmingham AA, Horseshoes AC, Lamb AC Suffield Lodge AC, Barford AA.

Birmingham Canal Navigation (BCN), Wyreley and Essington Canal; Cannock Extension; Chase Social AC. **BCN Rushall and Daw End Branch Canal;** leased to Pelshall Social AC, Trident AC, Fletchers Tackle AC, Hawkins AC, WMTS AC. **BCN Soho Loop,** Fisherman of England AC.

Coventry Canal; Plough AS, Birchmoor AC, Amington AC, Tamworth Progressive AC, Weddington Social Club AS, Dordon AC. Huddlesford Junction to Fradley Junction, Lamb AC, Lichfield Marina AC, Pirelli AC, Drayton Manor AC, Belgrave AS.

Grand Union Canal, Main Line; North Napton Junction, through Calcutt Bottom Lock to Junction Bridge, Warwick, Royal Leamington Spa AA. Junction Bridge to Ugly Bridge, Gaydon AC. **Saltisford Arm;** Saltisford Canal (Trading) Ltd. Shrewley Tunnel to Rowington, Tunnel Barn AC. Rowington to Chessets Wood and Small Arm at Kingswood Junction, Massey Ferguson Recreation C. Knowle,

Civil Service AC. Knowle Top Lock to Birmingham; Wild Manufacturing AC, Lode Mill AC, Commercial Cleaners AC, Label Innovations AC.

Staffordshire and Worcester Canal, southern section; York Street Stourport to Botterham Lock, Birmingham AA. Botterham Lock to Dimmingsdale Lock, Wolverhampton AA. **Stratford-upon-Avon Canal**; leased by Redditch FA, Studley AC. **South Stratford Canal**; Stratford AA, White Swan AC. **Worcester and Birmingham Canal**; Diglis Basin to Blackpole Bridge, Worcester UA. Blackpole Bridge to Kings Norton Tunnel, Birmingham AA. In the northern section, there are stretches held by Lilleshall & Dist AS, Chubb AS, Goodyear AS, Bridgenorth AC, Four Ashes FC. Roseford Bridge to Milford Aqueduct, Izaac Walton (Staffs) AA. Milford Aqueduct to Great Haywood Junction, Potteries AS.

Trent and Mersey Canal; Derwent Mouth to Weston-upon-Trent, Pride of Derby AA. Weston-upon-Trent, Derby Railway AC. Weston-on-Trent to Clay Mills, Pride of Derby AA. Clay Mills Bridge to Wychnor Lock, Burton Mutual AA. Findern Crossing Pond, Derby RAC. Wychnor Lock - south west, Alrewas AC. Section to Woodend Turn, Woodside Ca-

ravan Park AC. Wolseley Bridge to Colwich Lock, Norton Lido AC. Bridge 58 to Bridge 62, Bass AC. Bridge 66 to Bridge 68, Peartree WMC AC. Hoo Mill Lock to Bridge 77, Izaac Walton AA. Bridge 77 to Bridge 79, Creda House AC. Weston Lock to Bridge 81, Saracens Head AC. Bridge 82 to Sandon Lock, Gorms Mills Juniors AC. Aston Lock to Bridge 91, Wedgewood AS. Bridge 91 to Meaford Lock, Stones AC. Meaford Lock to Trentham Lock, Fenton AS. Middlewich Junction to Preston Brook Tunnel, Trent and Mersey AA. Booth Top Lock to Middlewich Junction, Cheshire AA. Bridge 159 to Booth Lane Top Lock, Middlewich JA. Bridge 149, Hassall Green to Middlewich Junction, Cheshire AA. Bridge 138, Rode Heath to Bridge 149, Hassall Green, Waterway Wanderers. Lawton Lock 52, to Bridge 138, Rode Heath, Waterway Wanderers. Bridge 135 to Lock 50, Royal Doulton AC. Bottom Lock 46 to Bridge 135, Church Lawton, Alsager A. Harecastle Tunnel North to Bottom Lock 46, and Bridge 129 to Harecastle Tunnel (South), Waterway Wanderers. Bridges 126, Longport to 129, Tunstall, red Lion Anglers. Whieldon Road Bridge to Stoke Summit Lock, Stoke City & Dist AA. Trentham Lock to Stoke Basin, Fenton & Dist AC.

NORTH WEST REGION:

Ashton Canal; Junction with Rochdale to Fairfield Bottom Lock, Waterway Wanderers/WAT. Fairfield Bottom Lock to Fairfield Top Lock, Water Sports Adventure Centre. Fairfield Top Lock to Whitelands Road Bridge, Waterway Wanderers/WAT.

Huddersfield Narrow Canal; water tends to acidity, but contains trout. Ward Lane, Diggle to Lock 24 Saddleworth, Saddleworth & Dist AS. Lock 24 to Milton Mill Bridge, Mossley, Diggle AC. Milton Mill Bridge, Mossley to Scout Tunnel, Border Anglers & Naturalists. Scout Tunnel to Grove Road Bridge 95, Cairo Anglers (PFF Group Section). Grove Road Bridge 95 to Mottram Road Bridge 99, Croft AS. Mottram Road Bridge 99 to Caroline St Stalybridge *(not available for letting)*. Caroline St Stalybridge to Lock 1, Waterway Wanderers/WAT.

Lancaster Canal; Stocks Bridge, Preston to Aldcliffe Rd Bridge No 96, Waterway Wanderers/WAT. Aldcliffe Rd Bridge

No 96 to Nelson St Bridge No 101, Lancaster Pike & Coarse Angling Synd. Nelson St Bridge No 101 to Stainton, Waterway Wanderers/WAT. Stainton to Canal End *(not available for letting)*.

Leeds and Liverpool Canal; Liverpool to Halshall Warehouse Bridge 25, Liverpool & Dist AA. Halshall Warehouse Bridge 25 to Moss Lane Bridge No 80, Wigan & Dist AA. Moss Lane Bridge No 80 to Johnson's Hillock Bottom Lock *(not available for letting)*. Johnson's Hillock Bottom Lock to Top Lock Bridge 82, Waterway Wanderers. Top Lock Bridge 82 to Engine Bridge 84, Darwen Loyals AC. Engine Bridge 84 to Long Ings Bridge No 153, Waterway Wanderers/WAT. Long Ings Bridge No 153 to Greenberfield Locks *(not available for letting)*. **Leigh Branch**: Poolstock Lock to Dover Bridge, Pearson & Knowles AC. Dover Bridge No 4 to Plank Lane Swing Bridge No 8, Ashton Centre, Northern AA. Plank Lane Swing Bridge to Leigh

Wharf, Leigh & Dist AA.

Manchester, Bolton and Bury Canal; Elton Reservoir to Ladyshore Road Bridge, Manchester Bolton & Bury Canal AA. Ladyshore Road Bridge to Canal End at Paper Mill, Tongue AC. Canal End at Paper Mill to Hall Lane, (not available for letting). Hall Lane to Nob End, Bolton & Dist AA. Nob End to Ringley Lock, Prestolee, Manchester Bolton & Bury Canal AA. Ringley Lock, Prestolee to Park House Bridge Road, (not available for letting). Park House Bridge Road to Lumns Lane Track Agecroft, Salford AC.

Peak Forest Canal; Dukinfield Junction to

Canal Terminus, Whaley Bridge, Waterway Wanderers/WAT.

Rochdale Canal; Junction Calder & Hebble to Callis Lock, 13 Hebden Bridge, Hebden Bridge AS. Callis Lock, 13 Hebden Bridge to East Summit Lock 36 Warland, Todmorden AS. East Summit Lock 36 Warland to Manchester Road Bridge, Castleton, Todmorden AS. Manchester Road Bridge, Castleton to Lock 55 Slattocks, Castleton AS. Lock 55 Slattocks to Lock 92 Castlefields, M/C, Waterway Wanderers/WAT.

St Helens Canal; Carr Mill End to Old Double Locks, St Helens AA.

WALES & BORDER COUNTIES:

Caldon Canal; very good water quality. Eturia to Bedford St Double Lock, *(not available for letting)*. Bedford Street Lock 2 to Planet Lock 3, Cauldon AC. Planet Lock 3 to Caldon Road Bridge No 6, Waterway Wanderers/WAT. Caldon Road Bridge No 6 to Lichfield Bridge No 8, Cauldon AC. Lichfield Bridge No 8 to Stockton Brook Bridge No 25, Waterway Wanderers. Stanley Rd Bridge No 25 to Stanley Road Bridge No 26, *(not available for letting)*. Stanley Road Bridge No 26 to Hazlehurst Junction, Waterway Wanderers. Hazlehurst Junction to Hazlehurst Bottom Lock, *(not available for letting)*. Hazlehurst Bottom Lock to Woods Lock Bridge No 45, Waterway Wanderers. Woods Lock Bridge No 45 to Willow Cottage Bridge No 47, Waterway Wanderers. Willow Cottage Bridge No 47 to Oak Meadow Ford Lock Bridge 48, Waterway Wanderers/WAT. Oak Meadow Ford Lock Bridge 48 approx 600m d/s past Bridge 48, Embreys Bakeries AC. Approx 600m d/s past Bridge 48 to Bridge No 49, *(not let by BW)*. Bridge 49 to Flint Mill Bridge 51, Potteries AS. Bridge 51 to Bridge No 55, Waterway Wanderers. Bridge No 55 to Canal Terminus, Froghall Wharf. **Leek Branch;** Hazlehurst Junction to Horse Bridge No 6, Waterway Wanderers. Horse Bridge No 6 to Canal End nr Leek, Leek & Moorlands AC.

Llangollen Canal; Hurleston Locks to Hampton Bank Bridge No 50, Waterway Wanderers. Hampton Bank Bridge No 50 to Bridge No 51, Fernwood FC. Bridge No 51 to Little Mill Bridge No 55, Waterway Wanderers. Little Mill Bridge No 55 to Red Bridge No 58, *(not available for*

letting). Red Bridge No 58 to White Bridge No 59, Ellesmere, *(not available for letting)*. White Bridge No 59, Ellesmere to Prices Bridge No 68, Waterway Wanderers. Prices Bridge No 68 to Nicholas Bridge No 2, *(not available for letting)*. Nicholas Bridge No 2 to Kings Bridge 49A, Waterway Wanderers. **River Prees**, junction with main line to Whixall Marina, Whixall Marina AC. River Dee, Berwyn Point A to R Dee, Berwyn Point B, Waterlog AC.

Macclesfield Canal; Marple Junction Bridge No 1 to Buxton Road Bridge No 37, Not let by BW to Northern AA. Buxton Road Bridge No 37 to Congleton Bridge No 61, Not let by BW to Prince Albert AS. Congleton Bridge No 61 to Townfield Bridge No 66, Waterway Wanderers. Townfield Bridge No 66 to Buxton Rd Bridge No 68, Congleton AS. Buxton Rd Bridge No 68 to Porters Farm Bridge No 72, Warrington AA. Porters Farm Bridge No 72 to Lamberts Lane Bridge No 77, Warrington AA. Lamberts Lane Bridge 77 to Henshall's Bridge No 80, Victoria & Biddulph AS. Henshall's Bridge No 80 to Simpsons Bridge No 85, Warrington AA. Simpsons Bridge No 85 to Rowndes No 2 Bridge No 86, Middleport AC. Rowndes No 2 Bridge No 86 to Hall Green Stop Lock No 93, Warrington AA. Hall Green Stop Lock No 93 to Hardingswood Junction, Kidsgrove & Dist AA.

Middlewich Branch Canal; Barbridge Junction to Cholmondeston Lock, Waterway Wanderers. Cholmondeston Lock to Railway Bridge No 5A, Venetian Marine AC. Railway Bridge No 5A to Bridge No 22 Clive, Waterway Wanderers. Bridge

No 22 Clive Green to Bridge No 32, Middlewich Junction, Middlewich Joint Anglers.

Monmouth and Brecon Canal; Bridge No 45 Cwmbran to Birdspool Bridge No 70, Waterway Wanderers/WAT. Birdspool Bridge No 70 to Saron's Bridge No 74, Pontypool AA. Saron's Bridge No 74 to Tod's Bridge 95a, Waterway Wanderers/WAT. Tod's Bridge 95a to Llanfoist, Beacon Park Boats (tel: 01873 858277). Llanfoist to Dan-y-Graig Bridge No 107, Waterway Wanderers/WAT. Dan-y-Graig Bridge No 107 to Dark Bridge No 109, Gilwern Wood Anglers. Dark Bridge No 109 to Ashford Tunnel, Waterway Wanderers/WAT. Ashford Tunnel to Turn Bridge No 162 Brynich, Brecon Coarse AC. Turn Bridge No 162 Brynich to Theatre Basin Brecon, Waterway Wanderers/WAT. **River Usk**; at Llanfrynach and Brynich, private fishing.

Montgomery Canal; Frankton Junction to Rednal Basin, Waterway Wanderers/WAT. Rednal Basin to Redwith, Waterway Wanderers/WAT. Redwith to Dam 600m E of Bridge 92, *(not available for letting)*. Dam 600m E of Bridge 92 to Bridge 92, Llanymynech, Waterway Wanderers. Bridge 92, Llanymynech, to Burgedin Locks, Waterway Wanderers. Burgedin Locks to Bridge 106, incl Wern Clay Pits, Churchstoke AC. Red Bridge No 106 to End of Moors Street 112, Waterway Wanderers/WAT. End of Moors Street 112 to Buttington (Rhallt) 115, Not let by BW to Montgomery AA. Buttington (Rhallt) 115 to Recreation Ground Bridge 119a, Waterway Wanderers/WAT. Recreation Ground Bridge 119a to Belan Locks, Not let by BW to Montgomery AA. Belan Locks to Berriew, Waterway Wanderers/WAT. Berriew to Bridge 131, Waterway Wanderers/WAT. Bridge 131 to Bridge 133, Waterway Wanderers/WAT. Bridge 133 to Bridge 134, *not let*. Bridge 134 to Tan-y-Fron Bridge 136, Penllwyn Lodges AC. Tan-y-Fron Bridge 136 to Freestone Bridge No 153, Waterway Wanderers/WAT. **River Severn** at Penarth Weir Point A to Point B, Potteries AS.

Shropshire Union Canal. Audlem Bottom

Lock to Ellesmere Port Bridge No 147, Waterway Wanderers/WAT. Ellesmere Port Bridge No 147 to Junction with Ship Canal, *(not available for letting)*. Coole Lane Bridge 82 to Austins Bridge 83, Wynbunbury AA. Junction Dee Branch/R Dee, Elver Fishing.

Trent and Mersey Canal; Trentham Lock to Winkles Works/Stoke Basin, Fenton & Dist AS. Whieldon Road Bridge to Stoke Flight Bottom Lock, Dolphin Boats AC. Stoke Flight Bottom Lock to Stoke Summit Lock No 40, Waterway Wanderers. Stoke Summit Lock 40 to Bridge 126 Longport, Middleport AC. Bridge 120 Forge Lane Etruria to Bridge 126 Longport, Middleport AC. Bridge 126, Longport to Bridge 128 Longport, Waterway Wanderers. Bridge 128 Longport to Bridge 128A Tunstall, Red Lion Anglers. Bridge 128A to Bridge 129 Tunstall, Waterway Wanderers/WAT. Bridge 129 Tunstall to A500 link, Chatterley, Embreys Bakeries AC. A500 link, Chatterley to Harecastle Tunnel (South), Waterway Wanderers. Harecastle Tunnel (North) to Lawton Lock 50, Waterway Wanderers. Lawton Lock 50 to Lawton Lock 52, *(not available for letting)*. Lawton Lock 52 to Bridge 145 Pierpoint Top Lock, Waterway Wanderers/WAT. Bridge 145 Pierpoint Top Lock to Bridge 147 Hassall Green, Congleton AS. Bridge No 147 Hassall Green to Rookery Bridge 159, Waterway Wanderers/WAT. Rookery Bridge 159. Rookery Bridge 159 to Booth Lane Top Lock, Middlewich Joint Anglers. Booth Lane Top Lock to Middlewich Junction, Cheshire Match Group. Middlewich Junction to Preston Brook Tunnel, Trent & Mersey Canal AA.

River Weaver; Eaton Bank Pool, not let. Witton Pool, not let. Saltersford, Warrington AA. Frodsham Cut and R Weaver Sutton, Warrington AA. Sutton Pool, Warrington AA. R Weaver Frodsham, *vacant*.

Weaver Navigation; Winsford Town Bridge to Newbridge, Winsford & Dist AA. Newbridge to Bostock Works, Meadow Bank Sports & Social Club. Newbridge to Saltersford, Northwich AA.

NORTH EAST REGION:

Chesterfield Canal; River Trent to Drakeholes Low Wharf, Sheffield & Dist

AA. Clayworth Church Lane Bridge to Retsford Bridge, Worksop & Dist AAA.

West Retford Lock & Thunder Bridge & Old Barracks (Ranby) to Chequer House Bridge, Retford & Dist AA. Chequer House to Bracebridge Lock, Worksop United AA. Bracebridge Lock to Shireoaks Low Locks, Grafton AA. Norwood Tunnels to Thorpe Top Trebble Locks, Wales & Kiveton Prrk Colliery AC. Bottom Lock (Cinder Hill) to Top Lock (Shireoaks Low Locks), Station Hotel AC. River Trent (Torksey) to Lift Br (Brayford Pool, Lincoln), Witham & Dist Joint AF. R Trent to Drakesholes Low Wharf, Sheffield & Dist AA. **River Trent:** u/s Gunthorpe (lft bank), Ashfield AC. u/s Gunthorpe Weir (rt bank), Nottingham AA. d/s Gunthorpe Weir, Nottingham Fed. Stoke Weir (Lock Island), Ashfield AA. Hazleford Lock (lft bank, u/s of weir), not available (private letting). Lenton Wharf adj. to Clifton Bridge, Nottingham Fed. Hazleford Backwater (rt bank, d/s weir), King Fisher AC. Cromwell Weir (rt bank, d/s), Collingham AA. Cromwell Lock (d/s - lock side), Ashfield AC. Fossdyke Arm (Torksey), Worksop & Dist AA. North Leverton (lft bank), no info. Marton (rt bank), no info. Newark Dyke (various sections), Newark & Dist Piscatorials. Lincoln to Kirkstead, Witham & Dist Joint AF. Langrick Bridge (d/s), EA Dring Farms Ltd.

Beeston & Erewash Canal; Beeston Lock to Lenton Chain, Nottingham AA. Lenton Chain to Meadow Lock, Nottingham FA. Shipley Lock to Langley Mill Lock, NCB 5 Area FC. Shipley Lock to Barkers Lock, Cotmanhay AC. Barkers Lock to A6096 Road Br, Awsworth & Cossall AC. Stanton Lock to A6096 Station Road Br, Nottingham FA. Pasture Lock to Stanton Lock, Draycott AC. B5010 Road Br (Sandiacre) to Pasture Lock, Nottingham AA. Sandiacre Lock to B5010 Bridge, West End AC. Long Eaton Lock to Sandiacre Lock, Long Eaton Fed. Trent Lock to Long Eaton Lock, Long Eaton Victoria AS, also **Cranfleet Canal. Grantham Canal;** Bridge 2 to Bridge 7, Nottingham AA. Kinoulton (Wilds Br 26) to Mackley's Bridge, not let. Bridge 33 to Smite Aqueduct, Friars Well Estate. Smite Aqueduct to Bridge 37, not let. Bridge 37 to bridge 39, Nottingham AA. Irish Jacks Br to Wild's Br, Parkside FC. Bridge 40 to Bridge 42, not let. Irish Jacks Br 27 to Kinoulton Br 28, not let. Kinoulton to Hickling, not let. Bridge 44 to Bridge 48,

not let. Bridge 51 to Bridge 53, Barnstone AC. Bridge 53 to Bridge 54, Ropsley AC. Codnor Park Fishery at Sawley. Bridge 7 to Cotgrave Road, Nottingham AA. Cotgrave Road to Hollygate Lane, Nottingham AA. **River Soar Navigation;** North Lock to Pillings Flood Lock, Leicester & Dist AS.

Calder & Hebble Navigations: Stainland Road to Brighouse Gas works, Brighouse AA. Salterhebble Top Lock to Chain Bridge, Ryburn AS. Battyeford Cut & right bank River Calder, Ail Bank AC. A6026 to Stopway road bridge, Nestle AC. R Calder to u/s Elland, Bradford No 1 AA. R Calder at Copley, Ryburn AS. R Calder (rt bank - Batteford Flood Gates to 250m d/s, Holme Valley PA. Kirkless Cut (R Calder), Kirkless & Brighouse, Bradford No 1 AA. Kirkless Park Brook to Wood Lane Bridge, Holme Valley PA. Mirfield Cut, Old Bank AC. R Calder to u/s Granny Lock, Unity AC. Thornhill Flood Lock to Forge Lane, Earlsheaton Charity Anglers. D/s Dewsbury Cut to Figure of 3 Locks & Dewsbury Cut, Thornhill AC. Figure of 3 Locks to Broad Cut Road Br, Wakefield AC. Horbury Road Br to Br 31, Wakefield AC. Left bank R Calder d/s Broad Cut to Thorne's Cut, Wakefield AC. Thorne's Cut to A636 Road Bridge, not let. Weir at Horbury Junct to Railway Bridge, no info. R Calder (Castleford, Bradford No 1 AA. R Calder d/s Woodnook Lock, Castleford AC. Greenwood Cut, Gas AC.

Aire & Calder Navigations: Wakefield Branch: Kings Road, Woodnook, Walton AC. Godman St to Woodlesford Lock, Leeds & Dist ASA. Woodlesford Lock to Woodlesford Br (A642), Wortley AC. Woodlesford Br to Fleet Br, Allerton Bywater Colliery AC. R Aire (Ferry Br), Leeds & Dist ASA. Off-side adj Great Heck Basin, South Yorkshire Boat Club. Whitley Lock to Heck Br, Castleford & Dist AS. Whitley Old Br to Pipe Br, not let. Whitley Old Br to M62 Motorway, Bradford No 1 AA. Ferrybridge Flood Lock to Mill Br, not let.

Huddersfield Broad Canal; Broadreach Lock to Harrison's Br & R Calder (Broadreach), not let. Heck Br to works (Goole), Booth Ferry JAC. Aspley Basin to Lock 1, Nigel Hurst Fishing Tackle (Gas AC). Forge Lane to Double Locks, not let. Altofts Lock to Kings Road Lock, not let. **Huddersfield Narrow East;** Huddersfield to Lock No 2E, WAT. Lock

2E to 3E (not available). Lock 3E to 8E, WAT. Lock 8E to 9E, Hayle Ing. WMC & Inst (Ang. Sect). Lock 9E to 11E Milnsbrudge (not available). Lock 11E to 17E Linthwaite, Slaithwaite & Dist AC. Lock 17E Linthwaite to 21E Slaithwaite, Slaithwaite & Dist AC. Lock 21E Slaithwaite to 23E Slaithwaite, not available. Lock 23E Slaithwaite to 24E, WAT. Lock 24E Slaithwaite to 26E, Scholes AC. Lock 26E to West Slaithwaite Road Bridge, WAT. West Slaithwaite Road Bridge to Lock 34E Marsden, Slaithwaite & Dist AC. Lock 34E Marsden to 150m above Lock 42E, WAT (restriction 6pm - 8am only). 150m above Lock 42E to Standege Tunnel, not available. **Pocklington Canal**; Pocklington to Derwent junction, East Cottingwith, York & Dist AA. **Ripon Canal**; terminal to R Ure junction, Ripon Piscatorials. **RiversGreat Ouse, Ure** and **Milby Cut**; Lock Island (Naburn) and Naburn (above weir & lock, no info. Milby Cut to Milby Lock; Harrogate & Claro Conservative AA. Also on Ure and Milby Cut at Boroughbridge, Unity AC. **Selby Canal**; wide commercial waterway. Selby Basin to Bawtry Road bridge, Wheatsheaf AC. Bawtry Bridge to Brayton Bridge, Wheatsheaf AC. Brayton Bridge to Burn Bridge, Selby & Dist AA. Burn Bridge to Paperhouse Bridge, Selby & Dist AA. Paperhouse Bridge to Tankards bridge, no info.

Grand Union: Arms and Branches: Grand Union Canal (North); Pillings Flood Lock to Loughborough Lock, Quorn AS. Loughborough Lock to Kegworth Old Lock, Loughborough Soar AS. Lock Island at Kegworth Weir, Quorn AS. Kegworth Flood Lock to Ratcliffe Lock, Long Eaton & Dist AF. Bridge 84 to North Lock, Leicester, Wigston AS.

Leeds & Liverpool Canal (East); Greenberfield Locks to Bank Newton Top Lock, not available. Bank Newton Top Lock to Cowling Swing Br. No 191, WAT. Cowling Swing Br. No 191 to Brunthwaite Swing Br. No 192, Keighley AC. Brunthwaite Swing Br. No 191 to Lodge Hill Br. No 194, WAT. Lodge Hill Br. No 194 to Granby Swing Br 197A, Marsden Star AS. Granby Swing Br 197A to Dowley Gap Top Lock, WAT. Dowley Gap Top Lock to Dowley Gap Bottom Lock, not available. Dowley Gap Bottom Lock to Dock Swing Br. 209, Saltaire AA. Dock Swing Br. 209 to Field Locks

Thackley, WAT. Field Locks Thackley to Idle Swing Br 212, Unity AC. Idle Swing Br 212 to Thornhill Br. 214B, Idle & Thackley AA. Thornhill Br. 214B to Calveley Lodge Swing Br. 216, WAT. Calveley Lodge Swing Br. 216 to Horseforth Road Br 216A, Listerhills Old Boys AA. Horseforth Road Br 216A to Rodley Swing Br No 217, Rodley Boat AC. Rodley Swing Br No 217 to Ross Mill Swing Br 219, WAT. Rodley Swing Br No 217 to Moss Swing Br 218, Leeds & Dist ASA. Newley Lock to Redcote Br. No 224, WAT. Redcote Br. No 224 to Spring Garden Lock No 6, Leeds & Dist AA. Spring Garden Lock No 6 to Bridge 225H, WAT. Bridge 225H to Office Lock Leeds, not available.

Sheffield & South Yorkshire Navigation (Stainforth and Keadby Canal); Keadby Lock to Mauds Bridge, Stainforth & Keadby Joint AC. Bramwith Lock to Barnby Dun Swing Bridge, Northfield Bridge to aqueduct on New Junction Canal, and on past Sykehouse Lock, Doncaster & Dist AA.

Sheffield & South Yorkshire Navigation; wide commercial section. Lock 5 to Lock 7, Tinsley Wire AC. Tinsley & Dist ACA have the following sections: Lock 12 (R Don) to Jordans Lock; Jordans Lock to Holmes Lock and Lock 12 to Lock 8. Swingbridge to Rawmarsh Road Br; Rawmarsh Road Br to Rotherham Lock; Holmes Lock to Ickles Lock; Sprotborough to Mexborough Top Lock, Rotherham & Dist UAF and Kilnhurst Br to Eastwood Top Lock, all controlled by Rotherham & Dist UAF. Overflow Weir (Eastwood) through Lock to swingbridge, E Herringthorpe AC. Kilnhurst & Swinton, Kilnhurst & Dist AC. Mexborough Top Lock to Railway Br, Kilnhurst & Dist AC. **New Junction Canal**: Barnby Dun & Aire & Calder, Doncaster & Dist AA. Long Sandall to Sprotborough, Doncaster & Dist AA. Kirk Sandal (Old Br) to Long Sandall (railway br), Pilkington AC. Barnby Dun Br to Old Br Kirk Sandall, Barnby Dun Bridge SC. Dunston Hill Br to Stainforth Br, Stainforth AA. **Sheffield & Tinsley Canal:** Broughton Lane to Lock 3, Outokumpu Stainless Sports & SC. Broughton Lane & Locks 3 & 5, Tinsley Canal, Forgemasters Sports & SC. Broughton Lane to Coleridge Road, Albert Inn. Between bridges at Coleridge Road and Darnall Road, Fox House Social Club AS. Darnall Road Br to Shirland Road Br, no let. Shirland Rd to Staniforth Rd, no info. Bacon Lane to Bernard Road, no info. By-Pass Br to

Ickles Lock, no info. Stainforth Road to Bacon Lane, no info. Bernard Road to Cadman Street, no info.

RESERVOIRS AND LAKES in ENGLISH CANAL SYSTEM:

Butterly Reservoir, . Ripley & Dist AC.

Caldon Canal Reservoirs. Stanley, dt on site. **Rudyard,** dt on site. **Knypersley,** not let by BW to Cheshire AA.

Calf Heath Reservoir, nr Wolverhampton. Good coarse fishery with carp, tench, big bream. Leased to Blackford Progressive AS.

Combs Reservoir, Peak Forest Canal; *(vacant).*

Earlswood Lakes. BW direct managed fishery. Three Lakes totalling 85 acres. Engine Pool, commercial carp fishery; Windmill Pool, stocked with roach, perch, bream, pike; Terry's Pool, roach, bream. Dt on bank from bailiff. Match booking enquiries (tel: 01827 252066).

Elton Reservoir, Greater Manchester, *(vacant).*

Ferry Bridge Ponds(& R Aire), **Aire & Calder.** Leeds & Dist ASA.

Gailey Lower Reservoir, nr Wolverhampton. 64 acre coarse fishery. Management under review, fishing temporarily closed.

Gayton Pool, Gayton, nr Northampton. Carp fishery; Gayton AC members only.

Halton Reservoir, Wendover. Coarse fishery leased from BW by Prestwood & Dist AC; contact Hon Sec.

Harthill, nr Worksop. Coarse fishing leased by Handsworth AC.

Himley Hall Lake, Himley. Trout, coarse fish. Enquiries to Dudley Corporation.

Huddersfield Narrow Canal Reservoirs. Brunclough, Saddleworth & Dist AS; **Tunnel End,** vacant; **Redbrook,** vacant; **March Haigh,** vacant; **Black Moss,** vacant; **Swellands,** vacant; **Slaithwaithe,** Slaithwaite & Dist AC; **Sparth,** Slaithwaite & Dist AC. **Diggle,** Pennine Shooting & Sports AS.

Lifford Reservoir. Birmingham Parks. Dt from park keeper.

Lodge Farm Reservoir, Dudley. Coarse fishery. Enquiries to Dudley Corporation.

Leeds & Liverpool Canal Reservoirs. Barrowford Reservoir, *(vacant).*

Lower Foulridge Reservoir, Borough of Pendle Council, Town Hall Pendle BB8 0AQ (tel: 01282 865500 xtn 401).

Rishton Reservoir, *(not available for letting).*

Slipperhill Reservoir, *(not available for letting).*

Upper Foulridge Reservoir, *(not available for letting).*

Whitemoor Reservoir, *(not available for letting).*

Saddington Reservoir, Grand Union Canal, North. Saddinton AC.

Stockton Reservoir. Excellent coarse fishery, tickets on the bank. Match booking enquiries (tel: 01827 252066).

Sneyd Pool, Walsall. Excellent carp and tench fishing, leased by Swan AC. Dt on bank.

Southfield Reservoir, Aire & Calder. Doncaster AA.

Stanley Reservoir, Stoke-on-Trent. Coarse fishery leased by Stoke-on-Trent AS.

Sulby Reservoir, Northants. Specimen carp to 36lb, numerous 20lb fish. Limited dt. Unique platforms designed exclusively for carp fishing. Contact Southern Region. Annual permits only.

Tardebigge Reservoir, Bromsgrove, specimen carp fisherey, Tardebigge AC.

Trench Pool, Telford. 16 acres, coarse fishing. Avenue AC. Dt on bank.

Upper and Lower Bittell Reservoirs (nr **Bromsgrove**). Rights owned by Barnt Green FC, who stock Lower Bittell and adjacent Arrow Pools with trout; other pools hold coarse fish, including pike and bream. Tickets for coarse fishing to members' personal guests only *(see also Arrow tributary of Warwickshire Avon).*

Welford Reservoir, Northants. Bream, tench and pike to 20lb plus.

Wormleighton Reservoir, nr Banbury. Tench to 9lb. Contact Mr Roe (tel: 01926 853533).

Wern Clay Pits, Montgomery. Leased by Mid-Wales Glass AC.

Winterburn Reservoir, Leeds & Liverpool Reservoir East. Not available.

Woodnook Lock Reservoir, Calder & Hebble. Castleford AC.

ENGLISH SEA FISHING STATIONS

In the following list the principal stations are arranged in order from north-east to south-west and then to north-west. Sea fishing can, of course, be had at many other places, but most of those mentioned cater especially for the sea angler. Clubs secretaries and tackle shops are usually willing to help visiting anglers either personally or by post on receipt of a stamped and addressed envelope. Details of accommodation, etc, can generally be had from the local authority amenities officer or information bureau of the town concerned. Those fishing the Devon and Cornwall estuaries should be aware of prohibitions on the taking of bass in some areas.

Seaham (Co Durham). Cod, whiting, flounder (winter); coalfish, flounder, plaice, dab, mackerel, cod (summer). Excellent fishing from North Pier, open only to members of Seaham AC, Clifford House, South Terrace, SR7 7HN (tel: 0191 581 0321). Club has 500 members, and well equipped HQ; promotes annual competitions and active junior section. Membership £12, conc. Further information from John McKenna, Competition Sec. There is disabled access on both piers, and promenade. Tackle shop: Rigs Angling Supplies, 72 Church Str, SR7 7HE (tel: 0191 581 7915).

Sunderland (Co Durham). Fishing from river, pier, beaches and rocks, for codling (best Oct-Apr), whiting (best Sept-Feb), coalfish, flounders, eels, throughout year. Roker Pier provides good sport with cod and flatfish. North Pier is free of charge to anglers, good access for disabled. Several small-boat owners at North Dock will arrange fishing parties, but there are also good beaches. R Wear banks at entrance good for flounders throughout year. Bait can be dug in Whitburn Bay and bought from tackle shops. Clubs: Sunderland Sea AA, membership £10 per year; Ryhope Sea AA (both affiliated to Assn of Wearside Angling Clubs). Tackle shop: Rutherfords, 125 Roker Ave, SR6 0HL (tel: 0191 565 4183). Hotels: Parkview.

Saltburn (Cleveland). Flatfish, coalfish, codling, whiting, mackerel, gurnard, some bass in summer and haddock late autumn. Float-fishing from pier in summer gives good sport; good codling fishing Oct to March. Tackle Shop: Keith'S Sports, 31 Milton Str, TS12 1DN (tel: 01287 624296). Tourist Information: 3 Station Building, TS12 1AQ (tel: 01287 622422).

Redcar (Cleveland). Five miles of fishing off rock and sand. Principal fish caught: Jan-April, codling; April-June, flatfish; summer months, coalfish (billet), whiting, mackerel, gurnard. Larger codling arrive latter part of August and remain all winter. South Gare breakwater (4m away); good fishing, but hard on tackle, spinning for mackerel successful. Good fishing from beach two hours before and after low tide. Competitions throughout year. Tackle shops: Redcar Angling Centre, 159 High St, Redcar, TS10 3AH (tel: 01642 474006).

Whitby (N Yorks). A popular centre for boat fishing on hard ground and wrecks, with charter boats travelling up to 60 miles from Whitby. Cod taken from boats, British record cod, 58lb 6oz caught here, as well as catches of haddock, coalfish, whiting, flatfish, sea bream, catfish, ling, mackerel, etc. Boat festival in July. West Pier: fishing only from lower part of pier extension. Mainly sandy bottom, but weeds and rock towards end. Billet, codling, flatfish, mackerel and whiting in season. East Pier: mainly on rocky bottom, weed off pier extension. More and bigger codling off this pier. Beach fishing from the sands either to Sandsend or Saltwick: billet, codling, flatfish, whiting, mackerel, a few bass. Small area at end of New Quay Rd for children only. No fishing allowed in harbour entrance. Best baits are lugworm, mussel, peeler crab. Local assn: Whitby Sea Anglers, meets in winter only, at Pier Inn, Pier Rd. Boats to accommodate 8 to 12 persons on hire at quays: Achates (tel: 01947 605536); Chieftain (tel: 01947 820320), and others. Tackle shop: Rods & Reels, 67 Church Str, YO22 4AS (tel: 01947 825079).

Scarborough (N Yorks). Sea fishing good from boat or harbour piers most of year. Autumn whiting very good in bay. West Pier fishes on sandy bottom, East Pier on rock, with better chances of bigger codling. Marine Drive good all year round cod fishing. Codling most plentiful Aug onwards. Winter codling fishing from

First or Second Points to south of Scarborough and the Marine Drive. Mackerel, June-Sept, float or spinning. Various boats take out parties; large bags of cod in 12hr sessions sometimes taken. Many over 20lb, ling also, 20lb plus from wrecks. Festival in Sept. Charter boats for hire, taking 8-12 anglers. Charge: approx £3 per person per hour; longish trips to fish reefs and wrecks now popular. Tackle shops: GB Angling, 119 Victoria Rd, YO11 1SP (tel: 01723 365000); Scarborough Angling Centre, 7 Market Way, YO11 1HR (tel: 01723 381111). Harbour Master: Harbour Dept, West Pier, YO11 1PD (tel: 01723 373530).

Filey (Yorks). Cod, coalfish, ling, mackerel, flatfish, bass, pollack. Famous Filey Brigg, ridge of rocks from which baits can be cast into deep water, is fishable in most weathers and tides. Ledgering with crab and mussel baits (summer), worm and mussel (winter) can produce good catches of cod, coalfish and wrasse. Use of a sliding float with mussel, and mackerel bait is effective technique for coalfish, pollack and mackerel (Jul-Sept). At Reighton Sands, ledgering with mussel, rag, lug and mackerel baits can produce flounders, some dabs, and occasional plaice or bass. Preferred method for bass is spinning. Local bait digging prohibited, good supplies from local tackle shop. Launching site for small privately owned boats. Local clubs: Filey Brigg AS organises fishing festival every year (first week of Sept), with 6 boating and 8 shore events. Filey Boat AC. Good flyfishing for coalfish (billet) from Brigg. Tourist Information: John Str, YO14 9DW (tel: 01723 518000).

Bridlington (N Humberside). South Pier may be fished free all year and North Pier in winter only. Sport in summer only fair - small whiting, billet, flatfish mainly - but good codling from Dec-March. Launches and cobles sail daily from Harbour at 0730, 0930, 1330, 1800 during summer. They operate from 3 to 60 mile radius around **Flamborough Head**, or wrecks. Catches include cod, haddock, plaice, ling and skate. Rock fishing from shore at Thornwick Bay. Bait: lugworm may be dug in South Bay and small sand eels caught by raking and digging on edge of tide. Sea angling festival Sept. Boats: many boats available; inquire tackle shop. Tackle shop: Linford's, 12 Hilderthorpe Rd, YO15 2BB (tel: 01262

678045). Hotels: Windsor, Londesborough and others.

Hornsea (N Humberside). Tope, skate, flounders, occasional bass from shore; cod, haddock, plaice, dabs, tope, skate from boats. May to Oct. Whiting, dabs, codling, Oct to May. Tackle shop: East Coast Fishing Tackle, 18 Willows Drive, HU18 1DA (tel: 01964 535064).

Grimsby (NE Lincs). Sea fishing along Humber bank free, and along foreshore to Tetney Lock; plaice, codling, dabs, flounders, eels. West Pier: st from Dock Office. Good centre for fens and broads. Clubs: Humber SAC, Cromwell Social Club (SA section). Tackle shops: Fred's Fishing Tackle, 413 Weelsby Str, DN32 8BJ (tel: 01472 352922); Humberside Angling Centre, 63 Pasture Str, DN32 9AB (tel: 01472 250400); Sparkes Bros Fishing Tackle, 43a Cromwell Avenue DN31 2DR (tel: 01472 342613); Dave's New & Used Fishing Tackle, 78 Durban Rd, DN32 8BA (tel: 01472 313260). Many hotels and B&B.

Mablethorpe (Lincs). Good sea fishing from Mablethorpe to Sutton-on-Sea. Beach all sand; mainly flatfish, but some bass, skate, mackerel, tope from boats. Cod in winter. Sept-Dec best. Boat fishing limited by surf and open beach. Good flounders in Saltfleet Haven; also sea trout in Sept. Local club: Mablethorpe, Sutton-on-Sea & Dist AC (water on Great Eau for members only). Tackle shop: Bela's, 54-56 High Str, LN12 1AD (tel: 01507 473328). Hotels at Mablethorpe, Trusthorpe, Sutton-on-Sea.

Skegness (Lincs). Beach fishing for cod, dab and whiting in winter; silver eels, dabs and bass in summer; whiting and dab in Sept and Oct. Chapel Point (producing many cod over 4lbs), Huttoft Bank and Ingoldmells the best beaches in winter, 3 hrs before high tide until 2 hours after. Lugworm best bait. No charter boats operate in Lincolnshire. Club: Skegness SAC. Tackle and bait from Skegness Fishing Tackle, 155 Roman Bank PE25 1RY (tel: 01754 611172); Vanguard Fishing Tackle, Midland Bldgs, Skegness Rd, Ingoldmells, PE25 1NP (tel: 01754 874950).

Salthouse, near **Sheringham** (Norfolk). Sea here is deep quite close in shore, and fishing considered good. Good flatfish, Oct-Jan. Occasional bass and mackerel in summer.

Sheringham (Norfolk). Flatfish all year;

cod autumn and winter, mackerel June-
Sept. Beaches good all year, best months
April and May. Best sport west of lifeboat
shed towards Weybourne or extreme east
towards Cromer. Centre beaches too
crowded in season. Bait can be ordered
from tackle shops. Boat fishing best well
off shore. Tope to 40lb and thornbacks to
20lb; plenty of mackerel. Blakeney: good
launching ramps. Tackle shop: Brights
The Outdoor Man, 8 Wyndham Str, NR26
8BA (tel: 01263 825858). Tourist Information: New Rd, NR1 2DH (tel: 01263
822874).

Cromer (Norfolk). Good all-year fishing;
winter months: codling, whiting and
dabs; summer: bass, flounder, dabs, mullet and mackerel. Around the third breakwater east of the pier the water is deeper,
last three hours of flood tide best time.
Occasional mackerel from end of pier.
Boat fishing in calm weather (beach-
launching). Fresh lugworm baits from
tackle shop: Marine Sports Shop, 21 New
St, Cromer, NR27 9HP (tel: 01263
513676) open Sundays during holidays.
Hotels: Cliftonville; Red Lion; Western
House, recommended for anglers.

Great Yarmouth, (Norfolk). All styles of
sea fishing catered for, including two
piers, several miles of perfect shore line
for beach angler, two miles of well-
wharved river from harbour's mouth to
Haven Bridge, and boat angling. To north
are Caister, Scratby, Hemsby, Winterton,
Horsey, Sea Palling, Weybourne etc, and
to south, Gorleston-on-Sea and Corton.
The riverside at Gorleston from the lifeboat shed leading to the harbour entrance,
and Gorleston Pier are popular venues.
Sport very similar in all these places;
Sept-Jan, whiting, dabs, flounders, eels,
cod from latter end of Oct. From Apr-
Sept, Winterton known for good bass
fishing. Most successful baits are lugworm, herring or mackerel; lug, peeler
crab and squid for bass, flatfish etc, Apr-
Sept. Boats: Bishops (tel: 01493 664739);
Dybles: (*below*). Tackle shops: Gorleston
Tackle Centre, 7/8 Pier Walk (tel: 01493
662448); Dyble & Williamson, Crown
Cott, Hemsby Rd, Scratby, NR29 3PQ
(tel: 01493 731305).

Gorleston-on-Sea (Norfolk). Whiting, cod,
dabs and flounders from beaches and in
estuary (best Oct to March); good bass
May to Sept. Sport good in these periods
from boats, pier or at Harbour Bend in
river and on beaches. Baits: lugworm,

crab and ragworm. Freshwater fishing
(coarse fish) within easy reach on rivers
and broads. Boats: Bishop Boat Services,
48 Warren Rd, NR31 6JT (tel: 01493
664739). Tackle shops: Gorleston Tackle
Centre, 7/8 Pier Walk (tel: 01493
662448); Greensted Tackle Centre, 72-73
High Str, NR31 6RQ (tel: 01493 602474).

Lowestoft (Suffolk). Noted centre for cod,
autumn-May. Also whiting, flatfish, pollack and coalfish, with bass, tope, ray
from charter boats and mullet in warmer
months. Lugworm best bait. Good sloping beaches to north and south. Hopton,
Pakefield, Kessingland are best. North
best on flood, south on ebb. Club: Lowestoft SAS. Baits from tackle shop: Sam
Hook (Lowestoft) Ltd, 132 Bevan Str
East, NR32 2AQ (tel: 01502 565821).
Further information from Tourist Information: Royal Plain NR33 0AP (tel:
01502 523000)

Southwold (Suffolk); ns Halesworth. Good
codling, whiting, bass, plaice, flounder,
dab, pollack, mackerel, mullet fishing
from beach, October to March. Bass main
species in summer from harbour or shore;
soles and silver eels also provide sport
May to Sept. Reydon Lake is local freshwater fishery. Licences from Purdy's
Newsagents, 37 High Str, IP18 6AB (tel:
01502 724250). Tackle shop: Southwold
Angling Centre, 9 Station Rd, IP18 6AX
(tel: 01502 722085). Hotels: Swan,
Crown.

Felixstowe (Suffolk). Fishing in autumn
and winter for cod and whiting. Excellent
bass fishing in recent years, with fish well
into double figures from sea front and
Rivers Orwell and Deben; garfish by day
and sole at night, and with eels in the
estuaries, May-Sept; flounders from Oct-
Jan from the Orwell towards Ipswich.
Skate fishing good in May, June and July,
especially in harbour. Other species:
pouting, plaice, tope. Good sport from
boats, good fishing in evenings from
Manor Terrace to Landguard Point, Sept
onwards. Pier closed, pending restoration. Wrecking trips obtainable locally.
Felixstowe SAS organises matches,
beach festivals, and cater for the needs of
boat anglers, with a compound of 50 dinghies adjacent to club HQ. Tackle shop:
Castaway Tackle, 20 Undercliffe Rd
West, IP11 2AW (tel: 01394 278316).

Harwich and **Dovercourt** (Essex). Bass
(from Halfpenny Pier), mullet, eels, garfish, flatfish, sting-ray, thornback, soles

(all May to Sept), whiting, pouting, codling (Sept to March). Best fishing from boats, but Stone Breakwater, Dovercourt is good (covered by water in high tide). Several good boat marks in estuary of Stour and Orwell and in harbour approaches. Best baits: lug, king rag, soft and peeler crabs. Club: Harwich AC (freshwater). Tourist Information: Clacton-on-Sea, Harwich, CO12 3HL (tel: 01255 506139).

Walton (Essex). Cod, skate, mullet and dab are species most commonly caught, best fishing is from pier, Frinton Wall and Frinton Sea Front. Cod fishing begins about second week in Sept and runs to end of March. Club: Walton-on-Naze Sea AC. Boats may be chartered in Walton: Terry Woodrow 2 Florence Rd, CO14 8HP (tel: 01255 675664). Tackle shop: J Metcalfe, 15 Newgate Str, CO14 8DT (tel: 01255 675680). Hotels: Walton Tavern; Queens; Regency.

Clacton (Essex). Mainly autumn and winter fishing for whiting and cod. Summer fishing from beach, pier and boats for dabs, plaice, bass, eels, thornback, dogfish, tope, sting ray to 50lb. Matches arranged by Clacton Sea AC. Tackle shop: Brian Dean Fishing Tackle, 43 Pallister Rd, CO15 1PG (tel: 01255 425992) baits, permits and information. Hotels: Frandon, Kingscliff, many others, from Tourist Information: 2 Pier Ave, CO15 1QR (tel: 01255 423400).

Southend-on-Sea (Essex). Mullet, bass, mackerel, scad, garfish, plaice and flounders are the main catches from the pier during the summer, with cod, codling and large flounders in the winter. Boats operate from various moorings. Thornback, stingray, smoothhound, bass, tope, plaice and cod can be caught. Pier: st day £45.50, night £40.50; dt £3.30, conc. Application form from Southend Council, Directorate of Leisure Services, Civic Centre, Victoria Ave, SS1 3PY (tel: 01702 215620). Off season shore fishing in vicinity, with all year round facilities at the Thorpe Bay and Westcliff bastions, also the river Crouch. Numerous open, pier, shore and boat events organised. Tackle shops: Southend Angling Centre, 5/6 Pier Approach, SS1 2EH (tel: 01702 603303) has a variety of local freshwater fishing permits on sale; Jetty Anglers, 47 Eastern Esplanade, SS1 2ES (tel: 01702 301777); Essex Angling Centre, 109 Leigh Rd, Leigh-on-Sea, SS9 1JH (tel:

01702 711231).

Sheerness (Kent). Popular marks around Sheerness are Bartons Point; New Sea Wall, Garison; East Church Gap; cod and whiting plentiful from beaches in autumn. Tackle shop: Island Bait & Tackle Shop, 68 Halfway Rd, ME12 3AT (tel: 01795 668506); fresh baits always obtainable.

Whitstable and **Tankerton** (Kent). Good fishing in spring and summer on shore between Swale and Whitstable. Dabs, plaice, bass, skate, flounders, eels, etc. Lugworm and white ragworm are to be found in shallow areas. Peeler crabs are plentiful in Swale estuary. Cod in winter from Tankerton beach. Boats for hire. Freshwater fishing on Seasalter Marshes, near Whitstable; roach, rudd, tench, pike, eels. Tackle shop: Tight Lines Bait & Tackle, 98 Tankerton Rd, Whitstable CT5 2AH (tel: 01227 281677). Tourist Information: 7 Oxford Str, Whitstable, CT5 1DB (tel: 01227 275482).

Herne Bay (Kent). Excellent spring fishing for flounders, bass and eels, bags of up to 20lb may be expected on peeler crab bait, which can be collected locally or bought at tackle shops in April and May. In June, bass move into the shallow warm water of the estuary. These may be caught with the last of the peeler crab, ragworm, and by spinning. In July and August bass are plentiful, black bream, lesser spotted dog, smoothound and stingray may be caught with ragworm on beaches between Bishopstone and Reculver. Local record stingray, over 40lb. Whiting in autumn and winter on main beaches: just after dark is the best time to fish for them. Excellent facilities for anglers with own dinghies to launch and recover from new slipway. Local information on best marks, etc, from tackle shops. Club: Herne Bay AA, (HQ) 59/60 Central Parade, CT6 5JG (tel: 01227 362127). Tackle, bait and licences: Ron Edwards Fishing Tackle, 50 High Str, CT6 5LH (tel: 01227 372517). Hotels: Victoria, Adelaide and Beauville Guest Houses, all Central Parade.

Margate (Kent). Noted for mixed catches. Plentiful bass often taken from shore and boat on paternoster or spinning. Stone pier good flatfish and whiting in winter. Bass from rocks at low water. April and May mixed bags of bass and eels. Most popular rock marks are at Foreness, Botany Bay, Kingsgate, Dumpton Gap.

Skate at Minnis Bay, Birchington. Also dogfish and thornback ray from boats. Tackle shop: Kingfisheries, 34 King Str, CT9 1DA (tel: 01843 223866).

Broadstairs (Kent). Bass, plaice, flounders eels, from beaches or stone jetty. Best in winter months. Lugworm usual bait, dug in Pegwell Bay. Tackle shop, see Margate. Tourist Information: 6b High Str, CT10 1LH (tel: 01843 583334).

Ramsgate (Kent). Good sport along 2m of shore, harbour piers (free fishing), and Eastern and Western Chines. East Pier gives ample scope, best in winter. Beaches crowded in summer, so night fishing best. In spring and summer good bass fishing (from shore), also soles, flounders, dabs and thornbacks. In autumn and winter; whiting. Pegwell Bay, Foreness and Dumpton Gap are good boat marks for mackerel, bass. Three boats operate at Harbour. Goodwin Sands produce skate, bass, dogfish, spurdog, tope and plaice. The Elbow and Hole in the Wall, also marks for boat fishing. Lugworm may be dug in Pegwell Bay. Licences, baits, fishing trips and freshwater angling information from tackle shops. Charter boat for wreck fishing: A Booth, 6 St Augustines Park, CT11 0DE (tel: 01843 595042). Tackle shop: Fisherman's Corner, 6 Kent Place, CT11 8LT (tel: 01843 582174). Hotels in Thanet too many to list.

Sandwich (Kent). Bass at the mouth of the haven; sea trout and mullet run up the river; flounders, grey mullet, plaice, dabs, codling and pouting more seaward. Entry to Sandwich Bay by toll road, 9am to 5pm. For winter cod fishing, deep water off yacht club end of bay is best. Local club: Sandwich & Dist AS. Tackle shop: Sandwich Bait & Tackle, South East Water Gardens, Dover Rd, CT13 0DG (tel: 01304 613752). Hotels: Bell; Haven Guest House *(for freshwater fishing see Stour (Kent))*.

Deal and **Walmer** (Kent). Excellent sea fishing throughout the year from beaches and Deal Pier, open 8 am to 10 pm, all night Friday and Saturday. Winter cod fishing, from Sandown Castle, Deal Castle, Walmer Castle. Charter boats take anglers to the Goodwin Sands and the prolific waters of the Downs. Cod, skate and whiting in winter; plaice, bass, dabs, sole, mackerel, eels, flounders, dogfish and garfish throughout summer. Strong tidal currents. Tables from local tackle

shops. Deal & Walmer Inshore Fishermen's Assn supplies list of boats: David Chamberlain (tel: 01304 362744). Clubs: Deal & Walmer AA; Deal 1919 AC. Tackle shops: The Foc'sle 33 Beach Str, CT14 6HY (tel: 01304 374013); Channel Angling, Deal Pier, Beach Str, CT14 6HZ (tel: 01304 373104). Tourist Information: High Str, Deal CT14 6BB (tel: 01304 369576) for information on boats.

Dover (Kent). Excellent boat and beach fishing in the area; cod taken from wrecks and sand banks; good fishing for bass, codling, whiting and flatfish. Good beach fishing from Shakespeare Beach. Prince of Wales Pier suitable for all anglers, incl junior and handicapped. Admiralty Pier controlled by Dover Sea AA: open 8 am to 4pm, and 6am to 9pm Fri and Sat. £3 dt, conc. Access to Sandwich Bay is by toll road, £4. Boat trip: Dover Motor Boat Co (tel: 01304 206809) to fish Southern Breakwater departs 9 am from Dump Head, Wellington Dock, £4 + £3.50 fishing charge. Tackle shops: Bill's Bait & Tackle, 121 Snargate Str, CT17 9DA (tel: 01304 204542); Brazils, 162 Snargate Str, CT17 9BZ (tel: 01304 201457). Hotels: Ardmore, Beaufort; many others.

Folkestone (Kent). Good boat, beach and pier fishing. Conger, cod, bass, bream, flatfish, whiting, pouting and pollack, with mackerel in mid-summer. Pier open to anglers, £4 per day, £1.50 conc. Cod caught from boats on the Varne Bank all through the year, but from the shore, Oct-Feb only. Beach fishing best dusk onwards for bass and conger. The Warren produces good catches of cod in winter and bass in summer. Good sport from pier. Some good offshore marks. Popular rock spots are Rotunda Beach, Mermaid Point, Sandgate Riviera. For tickets, boats and bait apply: Folkestone Angling, 12 Tontine Str, CT20 1JU (tel: 01303 253881). Hotels: Burlington, Windsor and others.

Sandgate (Kent). Very good fishing from beach and boats. There is a ridge of rock extending for over a mile 20 yds out from low-water mark. Bass good July-October; codling, whiting, pouting, conger March-May, August-Nov; good plaice taken May-June, especially from boats. Best months for boat fishing, Sept-Nov. Tackle at Folkestone. Hotel: Channel View Guest House.

Hythe (Kent). Fishing from boat and shore for bass, codling, pouting, whiting, conger and flats. Princes Parade, Seabrook, is popular for cod fishing, between Sept and Jan, lugworm is the best bait. Open storm beach, giving pouting, whiting, bass, mackerel, sole, dab and flounder in summer and cod (up to 25lb), whiting and pouting in winter. Clubs: Seabrook Sea AS; Castaways Sea AS; The Fountain SAC. Tackle shops: Dens Tackle, 73 Dymchurch Rd, CT21 6JN (tel: 01303 267053); Micks Tackle, 1 Thirstane Rd, CT21 6LB (tel: 01303 266334). Hotels: Fern Lodge; Romney Bay House, New Romney.

Dungeness (Kent). Cod fishing around the lighthouse, with whiting, and dab in winter; pout, bass, dab, eels and sole in summer. Best baits in winter are black or yellowtail lugworm. Denge Marsh is a top venue for sole, marks are at Diamond and towards Galloways, ragworm and lugworm for bait. Best months: May to Oct for boat fishing; Oct to Feb for shore fishing. Tackle shop: The Point Tackle Shop, Allendale, TN29 9ND (tel: 01797 320049).

Hastings (Sussex). Sea fishing from pier and boats. Tope, bass, conger, plaice, codling, whiting, etc. Boats from local fishing clubs. Hastings and St Leonards SAA has its own boats on beach opposite headquarters; club boundary, Beachy Head to R Rother at Rye. Winching facilities. Annual International Festivals: boat in June/July; shore in October/Nov. Bait, tackle: Steve's Tackle Shop, 38 White Rock, TN34 1JL (tel: 01424 433404); Hastings Angling Centre, 33/35 The Bourne, TN34 3AY (tel: 01424 432178).

St Leonards (Sussex). Good sea fishing all the year round from boats and beach for flatfish, bass, mackerel, conger, tope, whiting, cod, bull huss, turbot. Tackle shops, see Hastings.

Bexhill (Sussex). Boat and shore fishing. Cod, conger, whiting (Sept to end Dec). Dabs, plaice, mackerel, tope (July-Sept). Bass, best months May, June and July. Club: Bexhill AC (Hon Sec will help visitors, enclose sae). Freshwater fishing in Pevensey Sluice, Pevensey Haven and dykes; coarse fish. Hastings, Bexhill & DFAA have 3 miles of Wallers Haven, one bank, coarse, members only. Tackle shop: Hook Line & Sinker, 54 Sackville Rd, TN39 3JE (tel: 01424 733211). Hotel: Jarvis Cooden Beach; Lilburn.

Eastbourne (Sussex). Boat, pier and shore fishing. Dabs, huss, pouting and conger (all year), cod in winter and skate (May to Dec). Best for plaice and bream from April to Oct. Also soles, whiting, flounders, mullet. Good bass and mullet in warmer months. Notable tope centre, many around 40lb; June and July best. Some of the best beach fishing for bass around Beachy Head (up to 17lb). Pollack from rocks. Flatfish off Langney Point and from landing stages of pier. Best marks for beach fishing are on east side of pier. West side can be rocky in places. Club: Eastbourne AA, Club House, Royal Parade, BN22 7AA (tel: 01323 723442). Membership £36; full-time boatman. Boats available to members, £42pa. Tackle shops: Anglers Den, 6 North Rd, Pevensey Bay, BN24 6AY (tel: 01323 460441).

Seaford (Sussex). Beach and boat fishing. Bass, cod, codling, conger, flats, huss, mackerel and few ling and pollack. Good night fishing off beach. Catches of tope few miles offshore. Seaford AC has freshwater fishing on five local waters, members only; apply tackle shop. Tackle shop: Peacehaven Angler, 135a South Coast Rd, Peacehaven, BN10 8PA (tel: 01273 586000).

Newhaven (Sussex). Centre for deep sea fishing. Beach fishing for bass excellent May-Oct, mackerel and garfish. Flounders from Tide Mills Beach. Good cod fishing from beaches between Seaford Head and Newhaven's East Pier, late Oct to early March. Breakwater gives good all-round sport, with bass, and cod all running large. Boat fishing excellent for cod in winter, large Channel whiting also give good sport. Monkfish off Beachy Head late August and Sept. Club: Newhaven Deep Sea AC, Denton Island, BN9 9BA (tel: 01273 517330). Tackle shop: The Newhaven Angler, 107 Fort Rd, BN9 9DA (tel: 01273 512186). Tourist Information: 20 Council Offices, Fort Rd, BN9 9QF (tel: 01273 515712). Hotel: Sheffield.

Brighton and Hove (Sussex). Very good bass fishing from boats, trolling with variety of plug baits, Apr-Oct. Charter boats operate from Shoreham, Newhaven and Brighton Marina, for deep sea and wreck fishing. In spring and summer boat fishing produces bream, bass, conger, tope, plaice and dabs; shore fishing: mackerel off marina wall, bass at night or l/w surf, mullet. Winter boat fishing for large cod, whiting, bull huss; shore for whiting, flounders and cod. Most dealers supply bait. Hove Deep Sea AC members launch boats from beach, and generally fish inshore marks. Membership £35 pa plus £30 joining, allows free use of boats, equipment, car park. Active social club (tel: 01273 413000 for details). Marina arms for mackerel, garfish, pollack, occasional bass, fishing fee, £2.50 per rod per day. Tackle shop: Brighton Angler, 1/2 Madeira Drive, BN2 1PS (tel: 01273 671398).

Shoreham and **Southwick** (Sussex). Boat and harbour fishing. Bass (July and August); grey mullet, skate and huss (June to Sept); cod and whiting (Sept to Dec); dabs, plaice, pouting, black bream, mackerel and flounders (May onwards). Mullet fishing in River Adur near Lancing College very good July-August; light paternoster tackle and red ragworm recommended. Baits: white rag, red rag and lugworms may be dug from beach and mud banks of river. Mussels and other baits can also be obtained. Tackle shop: Squires Fisheries, 25 Southwick Square, Southwick, Brighton, BN4 4FP (tel: 01273 592903)

Worthing (Sussex). Beach and pier fishing. Flounder, bass, whiting, codling, plaice, mullet, eels. Mixed catches from boats. River Adur, east of Worthing, noted for flounders, mullet and eels. Bait digging in Adur restricted to between toll bridge and harbour. Local association: Worthing Sea AA (HQ: Worthing Pier). Boats from harbours at Shoreham and Littlehampton. Popular one day pier festival held in early September. Tackle shops: Prime Angling, 74 Brighton Rd, Worthing, BN11 2EN (tel: 01903 527050).

Littlehampton (Sussex). Noted for black bream, which are taken in large numbers during May and early June, but wide variety, including skate, smoothhound (spring), whiting and cod (winter best) and plaice. Mid channel wrecking for cod, pollack, ling and conger (spring onwards). Well known marks are Kingmere Rocks for black bream, West Ditch for smoothhound, Hooe Bank for conger. A large fleet of boats caters for sea anglers, and there is good fishing from beaches and in harbour. Boats list from Harbour Master, Harbour Office, Pier Rd, BN17 5LR (tel: 01903 721215). Tackle shop: Tropicana, 6 Pier Rd, BN17 5BA (tel: 01903 715190); Arun Angling Centre,

True Blue Precinct, Wick Str, BN17 7JN (tel: 01903 718546).

Bognor Regis (Sussex). Good sea fishing at several marks off Bognor. Tope, bass, pollack, mackerel, whiting, wrasse. From May to July bream are plentiful. The conger, skate and sole fishing is very good. Grey mullet abound in the shallow water between Felpham and Littlehampton Harbour. Good cod fishing between September and November. Bass weighing 5-10lb and more caught from pier and shore. Good shore fishing for bass, mackerel, cod, smooth hounds off East and West Beaches at **Selsey**. Club: Selsey Angling & Tope Club. Tackle shops: Bognor Regis Angling Centre, 24 West Str, PO21 1XE (tel: 01243 866663); Raycrafts Angling Centre, 119 High St, Selsey, PO20 0QB (tel: 01243 606039), who has tickets for Chichester Canal fishing.

Hayling Island (Hants). From the South Beach of Hayling Island good fishing can be had with a rod and line for bass, plaice, flounders, dabs, whiting, etc, according to season. Fishing from boats in Hayling Bay for tope, skate, bass, mackerel, etc, is popular and a much favoured area is in the vicinity of the Church Rocks and in Chichester Harbour. Portsmouth AS has coarse lake in area. Tackle shop: Paige's Fishing Tackle, 36 Station Rd, Hayling Island, PO11 0EH (tel: 02392 463500) (open Sundays).

Southsea (Hants). Over 4m of beach from Eastney to Portsmouth Harbour provide good sport all year. Bass fishing especially good from spring to September. Flatfish and rays numerous, large mackerel shoals in midsummer. Best sport from boats. Boom defence line from Southsea to IoW, although navigational hazard, is probably one of the best bass fishing marks on the South Coast. Vicinity of forts yields good bags of pollack, bass, black bream, skate, etc. Tope fishing good during summer. Portsmouth, Langstone and Chichester within easy reach and provide good sheltered water in rough weather. Boats can be hired from Portsmouth boatmen; large charter boat fleet in Langstone harbour. Club: Southsea SAC. Club: Southsea Sea Angling Club. Tackle shops: A & S Fishing Tackle, 147 Winter Rd, Southsea, PO4 8DR (tel: 023 92739116); Allan's Marine, 143 Twyford Ave, Portsmouth, PO2 8HU (tel: 023 92671833).

Southampton (Hants). Fishing in South-

A typical beach competition scene. This one at Blackpool Sands, three miles west of Dartmouth. *Photo: Brian Comer*

ampton Water really estuary fishing; thus not so varied as at some coastal stations. However, flounders abound (float and/or baited spoon fishing recommended), and whiting, pouting, silver eels, conger, bass, grey mullet, soles, dogfish, thornback, skate, stingray, plaice, dabs, scad, shad, mackerel have all been caught. At the entrance to Southampton Water, in Stokes Bay and the Solent generally, excellent tope fishing may be had. Angling from Hythe Pier, and from Netley and Hamble shores, but best fishing from boats. Southampton Water is rarely unfishable. Good sport in power station outflow. Tackle shops: Eastleigh Angling Centre, 325 Market St, Eastleigh SO50 5QE (tel: 023 80653540); South Coast Tackle, 179 High St, Lee-on-the-Solent, PO13 9BX (tel: 023 92550209).

Lymington (Hants). Sting-ray, smoothound, bass, eels in summer; cod, whiting, flounder, rockling, in winter. Hurst Castle and Shingle Bank good fishing all year round for bass, cod, garfish, mackerel, rays; Lymington and Pennington sea walls for flounders, eels, bass, mullet. Lymington and Dist SFC fishes areas from Eastern boundary of Emsworth to western side of Lyme Regis, including Solent and all round Isle of Wight. Charter skippers operate from Lymington and Keyhaven. Around

Needles area, good fishing for black bream, tope, smoothound and bass in summer months; large cod, Oct-Feb. Tackle shop: Forest Sports & Tackle, 23b High St, Milford on Sea, Lymington, Hants SO41 0QF (tel: 01590 643366).

Mudeford (Dorset). Christchurch Harbour at Stanpit is good for bass and grey mullet. All-round sea fishing in Christchurch and Poole Bay, the vicinity of the Ledge Rocks and farther afield on the Dolphin Banks. Fishing is free below Royalty Fishery boundary (a line of yellow buoys across harbour). Tope, dogfish, conger, bream, pout, pollack, whiting and good sport spinning for mackerel and bass. Plaice off Southbourne; flounders, dabs, skate and sole off beaches at Highcliffe, Barton and Southbourne; flatfish, bass, whiting, etc, from quay, beach, groyne or shore at Hengistbury Head; large tope, stingray, skate and occasional thresher shark off The Dolphins. Fairly good cod fishing in winter, Needles-Christchurch Ledge, Pout Hole and Avon Beach (off Hengistbury Head). Whole squid favourite bait, but large baited spoons and jigs also successful. Good sole from Taddiford and Highcliffe Castle (best after dark). Groyne at Hengistbury good for bass in summer; sand eels by day and squid by night. Best months for general sport, mid-June to mid- or late Sept. Most local fishermen now take parties out mackerel fishing in summer. Flounders, eels, bass and mullet taken inside the harbour. Boats from R A Stride, The Watch House, Coastguards Way, Mudeford. Tackle shop: Pro-Angling Centre, 258 Barrack Rd, Christchurch, BH23 2BJ (tel: 01202 484518); Davis Fishing Tackle, 75 Bargates, Christchurch, BH23 1QE (tel: 01202 485169). Hotels: Avonmouth, Waterford Lodge, The Pines Guest House.

Bournemouth (Dorset). Fishing good at times from the pier yielding bass, grey mullet, plaice, dabs, etc. Excellent catches of plaice, dabs, codling, silver whiting, mackerel (spinning), tope up to 40lb, conger, skate, from boats. Shore fishing, when sea is suitable, for bass and other usual sea fish. Bait supplies fairly good. Club: Christchurch & Dist FC. Tackle shops: Christchurch Angling Centre, 7 Castle Parade, Bournemouth, BH7 6SH (tel: 01202 480520); Bournemouth Fishing Lodge, 904 Wimborne Rd, Moordown, BH9 2DN (01202 514345). *(For freshwater fishing, see Avon (Wiltshire) and Stour (Dorset)).* Accommodation: Royalty View Guesthouse.

Poole (Dorset). Boat, beach and quay fishing in vast natural harbour. Great variety of fish, but now noted for deep-sea boat angling and bass fishing. Conger, tope, bream, etc, are caught within three miles of the shore. Bass, plaice, flounders, etc, caught inside the harbour at Sandbanks and Hamworthy Park in their seasons. Local tackle shops should be consulted for up-to-the-minute information. For boat fishing facilities contact Poole Sea Angling Centre. Sea Fishing (Poole) Ltd, Fisherman's Dock, The Quay, BH15 1HJ (tel: 01202 679666), also cater for bass and deep-sea angling. Baits favoured locally: mackerel, squid, sand eel and ragworm. Tackle shop: Poole Sea Angling Centre, 5 High Str, BH15 1AB (tel: 01202 676597).

Swanage (Dorset). Double high tide in Swanage and Poole Harbour. Species taken from pier and beach incl bass, mullet, pollack, mackerel, flounder, wrasse and pouting. Beach here too crowded for daytime fishing, but boat fishing is very good, with skate, conger, bream, huss, dogfish, pollack, large wrasse, tope and other species. Good cod fishing in winter, a few miles offshore, and boats are on hire at Poole and Weymouth. In summer,

boats operate from Swanage Angling Centre, just off quay. Local knowledge is essential, as tides and races are very dangerous for small boats. Several open angling competitions are held each year. Tourist Information is at The White House, Shore Rd, Swanage, BH19 1LB (tel: 01929 422885). Tackle and boat hire from tackle shop: Swanage Angling Centre, 6 High St, BH19 2NT (tel: 01929 424989). Many hotels.

Weymouth (Dorset). Centre for the famous Chesil Beach, Shambles Bank, Portland and Lulworth Ledges. The steeply sloping Chesil Beach provides year-round sport for many species, but autumn and winter best for mackerel, codling, whiting, bream and dogfish; and summertime best for garfish, triggerfish and various visiting Mediterranean species; beach fishes best at night; fairly heavy tackle required. Good conger fishing at the Chesil Cove end, Ringstead Bay, Redcliffe and round the piers. Piers yield good sport all year round. Good bass from Greenhill beach in heavy surf, with variety of flatfish at most times. Ferrybridge and the Fleet noted for bass, mullet and flounders. Boat fishing: In the area around Portland Bill some blonde and thornback rays, skate give good sport, while the notable Shambles Bank continues to yield turbot and skate, etc. Lulworth Ledges have a large variety of fish including tope, blue shark, conger, skate, dogfish, black bream, pollack, whiting, etc. Best baits are lugworm, ragworm, soft crab, mackerel and squid. No boats from Chesil Bank, but 20 boatmen operate from Weymouth throughout year. Angling Society booklet from Weymouth Publicity Office, Weymouth Corporation and Hon Sec. Tackle shop: Denning Tackle & Guns, 114 Portland Rd, Wyke Regis, DT4 9AD (tel: 01305 783145).

Portland (Dorset). Good bass fishing in harbour; live prawns for bait. Mullet, mackerel, whiting and conger are plentiful. No longer charter boats from fishermen at Castletown (for the harbour). Shore fishing from Church Ope Cove, The Bill and on the beach. Near the breakwater is a good spot.

Bridport (Dorset). Beach fishing yields bass, pouting, flatfish, thornback rays and conger, with whiting and cod in winter and large numbers of mackerel in summer. From boats: black bream, conger, pollock, whiting, pout, dogfish, bull huss, rays, cod and wrasse; West Bay is the angling centre. Burton Bradstock, Cogden, West Bexington and Abbotsbury are popular venues on Chesil Beach. Eype and Seatown favoured to west. Bait: lugworm, ragworm, squid, mackerel favoured. For boat hire from West Bay for offshore wreck fishing trips inquire at tackle shops. Club: West Bay Sea AC, has thriving junior section with special competitions, etc. Tackle shops: West Bay Water Sports, 10a West Bay, DT6 4EL (tel: 01308 421800); The Tackle Shop, West Bay, DT6 4EN (tel: 01308 428226). Hotel: The George, West Bay.

Lyme Regis (Dorset). Bass may be caught from the shore. Best baits are live sand eel, fresh mackerel, (sometimes obtainable from motorboats in harbour), or ragworm from tackle shop. Mackerel may be caught from May to October. Pollack plentiful in spring months. Conger and skate can be caught from boats about 2m from shore. Deep sea day and half day trips from Charter boats bookable. Self-drive motor boats are on hire at the Cobb Harbour, also tackle, mackerel lines free of charge, salted bait available. Information from Harbour Master, The Cobb, Lyme Regis, DT7 3JJ (tel: 01297 442137). Tackle shop: Chris Payne, The Tackle Box, 20 Marine Parade DT7 3JF (tel: 01297 443373).

Seaton (Devon). Boat fishing. Pollack, pouting, conger, wrasse (March to Sept), bass (virtually all year, but best Sept-Nov), bream, mackerel, dabs, skate, plaice, dogfish. Axe estuary good for bass, mullet and sea trout: dt water. Local Club: Seaton SAC; Beer & Dist Sea AC, c/o V Bartlett, 9 Underleys, Beer, Devon EX12 3LX (tel: 01297 20287). Tackle shop: Royal Clarence Sports, Harbour Rd, Seaton, EX12 2LX; (tel: 01297 22276). Tourist Information: Harbour Rd, EX12 2TB (tel: 01297 21660). Hotel: Seaton Heights.

Sidmouth (Devon). Sea fishing in Sidmouth Bay. Mackerel (May to Oct), pollack (excellent sport spring and summer east and west of town), bass (to 13lb in surf at Jacob's Ladder beach during summer), wrasse, large winter whiting (July-Oct on rocky bottom), skate to 105lb and conger to 44lb have been taken; bull huss to 19lb, and tope. Also plaice, dabs, flounders and occasional turbot. Club: Sidmouth SAC, Esplanade, EX10 8BG (tel: 01395 512286). At **Budleigh Salter-**

ton, a few grey mullet in river, but fairly uncatchable; beach best fished at night for flat-fish. Tackle Shop: Sidmouth Tackle and Pet Supplies, Shopping Centre, High Str, EX10 8LD (tel: 01395 512626).

Exmouth (Devon). Main species caught here in summer are pollack, wrasse, pout, whiting, garfish and mackerel. Favourite baits are lugworm, ragworm, peeler crab and sand eel. Pollack are caught on artificial sand eels. Popular places are: car park near Beach Hotel, docks area, estuary beaches, where flounders are caught, mid Sept to Jan. Deep Sea and wreck fishing trips can be booked in the area, with chances of conger eel &c. Tackle shop: Exmouth Tackle, 20 The Strand, EX8 1AF (tel: 01395 274918).

Dawlish (Devon). Dabs and whiting in bay off Parson and Clerk Rock and between Smugglers' Gap and Sprey Point. Mackerel good in summer. Conger eels and dogfish about ¾m from shore between Parson and Clerk Rock and Shell Cove. Good fishing sometimes off breakwater by station and from wall of Boat Cove. Boats from Boat Cove. Tackle shop; see Teignmouth.

Teignmouth (Devon). Sea fishing ideal (especially for light spool casting with sand-eels for bass). Bass, pollack, flounders in estuary. Mackerel, dabs and whiting in the bay. Good flounder fishing from the shore. Deep sea, wreck and offshore trips are possible. The town has an annual sea fishing flounder festival. Club: Teignmouth SAS (HQ: River Beach). Tackle shops: Fairweather News, 52 Northumberland Place, TQ14 8DE (tel: 01626 773380) (bait for sea angling, information); The Rock Shop, Northumberland Place. Boats and bait obtainable on river beach. Details of accommodation from Tourist Information Centre, The Den. It should be noted that the estuary is a bass nursery area between May and October.

Torcross; nr **Kingsbridge** (Devon). Hotel: Torcross Apartment Hotel, offering both self-catering facilities and high-class catering beside the Slapton Ley nature reserve and coarse fishery. Slapton Sands; ns Kingsbridge. The sea fishing is very good, especially the bass fishing. Hotel can make arrangements. *(For coarse fishing see Slapton Ley)*. Tackle shop: Devon Angling Centre, Unit 4/5 Orchard Meadow, Orchard Way, Chillington, Kingsbridge, TQ7 2LB (tel:

01548 580888).

Torquay (Devon). Excellent centre for sea fishing, most species found. Base for famous Skerries Bank and Torbay wrecks; conger, cod, pollack, turbot, flatfish, whiting, etc. Hope's Nose peninsula provides best venue for shore angler, with bass and plaice mainly sought. Other species caught are dabs, wrasse, mullet, flounder, gurnard. Babbacombe Pier good for mackerel. Bass and pollack off the rocks. Natural bait hard to come by, but tackle dealers can supply. Local association: Torbay & Babbacombe ASA. Tackle shops: Quay Stores, 23 Victoria Parade, TQ1 2BD (tel: 01803 292080). *(For freshwater fishing, including Torquay Corporation reservoirs, see Teign and Dart).*

Paignton (Devon). Summer and autumn best. Bass, mackerel and garfish can be taken from beaches between Preston and Broadsands and from harbour, promenade and pier respectively. Mullet also present, but very shy. Fishing from rock marks, too. Club: Paignton Sea AA, who have information service and social centre for anglers at HQ: Ravenswood, 26 Cliff Rd, The Harbour (open 7.30 pm onwards); annual membership £8. Tackle shops: The Sportsman, 7 Dartmouth Rd, TQ4 5AB (tel: 01803 558142); Venture Sports, 371 Torquay Rd, TQ3 2BT (tel: 01803 523023). Coarse fishing 2½m away at New Barn Angling Centre, TQ4 7PT (tel: 01803 553602), a series of lakes and pools, dt water.

Brixham (Devon). Boat fishing in bay for plaice, dabs, mackerel. Good pollack off East and West Cod rocks of Berry Head. Neap tides best; baits: worms or prawn. Farther out is Mudstone Ridge, a deep area, strong tide run, but good general fishing with big conger. Local boats take visitors out to deep water marks (wreck fishing) or to Skerries Bank, off Dartmouth, for turbot, plaice, etc; advance bookings (at harbour) advisable. Shore fishing: bass, pollack, wrasse, conger, mackerel from Fishcombe Point, Shoalstone and the long Breakwater. Grey mullet abound in the harbour area (bait, bread or whiting flesh). Bass from St Mary's Beach (best after dark) and south side of Berry Head (bottom of cliffs) for flat fishing. Sharkham Point good for mackerel and bass (float with mackerel, strip bait or prawn for bass). Mansands Point good for bass and pollack (float). Night fishing from Elbury or Broadsands beach for bass, flatfish or conger (use thigh boots). Club: Brixham SAA. Tackle shop: Brixham Bait & Tackle, 10 The Quay, TQ5 8AW (tel: 01803 853390). Quayside Hotel has boats.

Dartmouth (Devon). River holds large conger, record around 60lb; thornback ray to 17lb: best bait, prawn; also dabs, flounder, mullet, pollack, pouting. Baits, squid, ragworm, peeler crab, prawns. Shore angling is best from late Sept. Good marks are Warfleet Creek, mullet; rocks at castle, with garfish, mackerel, scad, wrasse, bass and other species caught; Leonards Cove, bass, mullet, wrasse, pollack in summer, whiting and codling in winter; Combe Rocks, boat fishing for wrasse, pollack, dogfish, bass, garfish, mackerel, rock pouting, ling, conger; Western Black Stone, best at night for bass: Homestone Ledge and Mewstone are boat locations. Charter boats available. Association Club House is at 5 Oxford St. Tackle shop: Sport 'n' Fish, 16 Fairfax Place, Dartmouth, TQ6 9AB (tel: 01803 833509). Hotels: Castle, Dart Marina. *(For freshwater fishing, see Dart).*

Salcombe (Devon). Mackerel June to Sept and turbot, dabs, flounders, plaice, skate and rays rest of year. Entire estuary is a bass nursery area, and it is illegal to land boat caught bass. Plenty of natural bait. Beaches crowded in summer, but fishable in winter. Wreck fishing for conger, bream, etc. June-Oct. Turbot numerous. Boats: Whitestrand Boat Hire, Whitestrand Quay, TQ1 1XX (tel: 01548 843818); Tuckers Boat Hire, Victoria Quay, TQ8 8DA (tel: 01548 842840); both sell tackle and bait; Salcombe Boat Hire (tel: 01548 844475). Club: Salcombe & Dist SAA (HQ: Kings Arms); annual membership £6 (conc); annual festival, four weeks from mid August; special prizes and trophies for visitors throughout season.

Newton Ferrers (Devon). Noted station on Yealm Estuary. All-year bottom fishing; bass, flounders, pollack (from rocks), with mullet, conger, mackerel and flat fish from boats; shark June-Oct. Good base for trips to Eddystone. Boats available. Abundant bait in estuary. Hotels: River Yealm, Family, Anglers, Yachtsmen.

Plymouth (Devon). One of finest stations in country for off-shore deep water fishing at such marks as East & West Rutts, Hands Deep and, of course, famous Eddystone Reef. Specimen pollack, conger, ling, whiting, pouting, cod, bream and mackerel plentiful. Fishing vessels for charter are Decca and Sounder equipped - fast exploring numerous wrecks within easy steaming of port; outstanding specimens taken. Inshore fishing for same species off Stoke Point, The Mewstone, Penlee, Rame and The Ledges. Sheltered boat and shore fishing in deep water harbour and extensive estuary network - at its best in autumn for bass, pollack, flounders, thornback and mullet. Shore fishing from rocks at Hilsea, Stoke, Gara Point, Rame Head, Penlee and Queeners for bass, pollack and wrasse, etc. Beach (surf) fishing at Whitsands and sand bar estuaries of Yealm, Erme and Avon rivers for bass, flounder and ray. All angling associations in city - British Conger Club (affiliated with ninety seven sea angling clubs), Plymouth Federation Sea AC and Plymouth SAC - now under one roof, on waterfront, at Mountbatten Water Sports Centre. Visiting anglers cordially welcomed. Tackle shops: Tackle & Bait Shop, 97 Victoria Rd, PL5 1RX (tel: 01752 361294); Clive's Tackle & Bait, 182 Exeter Str, PL4 0NQ (tel: 01752 228940). Charter boats are all moored on Sea Angling Centre Marina, Vauxhall Quay. Plymouth Angling Boatman's Assn (tel: 01752 666576).

Looe (Cornwall). Important centre for all-round sport. Bass, pollack and mullet from 'Banjo Pier' breakwater, October to March. Excellent bass fishing in Looe River when fish are running, and mullet. Good rock fishing from White Rock, Hannafore, and westwards to Talland Bay, where pollack, bass, conger and wrasse can be taken. Eastwards, flatfish from beaches at Millendreath, Downderry and Whitsand Bay. Bass, flounders, eels, pollack and mullet from river at quayside and upriver. Excellent sport from boats on deep-sea marks; porbeagle, mako, blue and some thresher shark taken, and wide variety of other fish. Clubs: Looe is HQ of Shark AC of Gt Britain (tel/fax: 01503 262642) and is official weighing-in station for British Conger Club. Local club: Looe Sea AA. Deep sea boats and information from Looe Chandlery, Millpool Boatyard, West Looe, PL13 2AE (tel: 01503 264355); MarineCo, The Fish Quay, East Looe, PL13 1AQ (tel: 01503 265444). Boat charges are £35 per head; £12 inshore. Looe Information Bureau is at The Guildhall, Fore St, PL13 1AA (tel: 01503 262072).

Polperro (Cornwall). Few boats, shore fishing weedy. Bass, whiting, pollack, mackerel are most likely catches. Tackle shops: see Looe. Hotels: Claremont, Noughts & Crosses, Ship, Three Pilchards; also farm accommodation.

Fowey (Cornwall). Excellent sport with bass (June to Oct) in estuary and local bays from Udder to Cannis. Pollack numerous and heavy (20lb and more). Good bream, cod, conger, dogfish, ling, mullet, mackerel, wrasse, whiting and flatfish (big flounders and turbot). Bass, mullet and flounders taken from river. Par Beach to west also good for bass. Rock fishing at Polruan, Gribben Head and Pencarrow. Sand-eel, rag and lugworm obtainable. Clubs: Polruan Sea AC, 9 Greenbank, Polruan. Boats: Fowey Diving Services, 21 and 27 Station Rd, PL23 1DF (tel: 01726 833920; web: www.foweyboathire.freeserve.co.uk), has boats for 2 to 7 anglers, for day, half-day, or weekly hire. Tourist Information: 5 South Str, PL23 1AR (tel: 01726 833616). Fowey Fishing Tackle, 19 Station Rd, Caffa Mill (tel: 07866 798245).

Mevagissey (Cornwall). Excellent sea fishing, boat and shore, especially in summer. Shark boats are based here (local club affiliated to the Shark AC of Great Britain). Mevagissey Shark Angling Centre will make arrangements for shark and deep-sea trips. £25 per day, £13 half day. Shore fishing quite productive, especially bass from beach. Good night fishing at Pendower and Carne beaches, near Veryan, in Gerrans Bay area; best on falling tide and at low water, best bait squid and lug worm. Rock fishing productive at Blackhead near St Austell, dogfish, pollack, wrasse, gurnard, garfish, plaice, flounder. Good pollack off Dodman Point and from marks out to sea. Bass in large numbers again owing to bass nursery in Foy estuary. Excellent sport with large mackerel at Gwinges and close to Dodman from late Aug. Sport from the pier can be very good at times, especially with mullet; weights in excess of 2oz must use a shock leader. Club: Mevagissey SAC (HQ: The Ship Inn, Pentewan, St Austell; visitors welcome); annual sub £6. Tackle shop: Mevagissey Shark Angling Centre,

West Wharf, St Austell, PL26 6UJ (tel: 01726 843430).

Gorran Haven (Cornwall). Same marks fished as at Mevagissey. Rock fishing in area. Bass from sand beach. The Gorran Haven fishermen offer some facilities for visitors wishing a day's fishing. Excellent pollack fishing from boat with rubber sand-eel off Dodman Point.

Falmouth (Cornwall). Excellent estuary, harbour (pier, shore and boat) and offshore fishing, especially over Manacles Rocks. Noted for big bass and pollack, latter taken off wreck and rock marks. Pendennis Point for wrasse and pollack; St Anthonys Head for wrasse, black bream at night in autumn. Porthallow for coalfish and conger; Lizard for wrasse, mackerel, and conger at night. Bait in estuary or from tackle shops. For boats, inquire at Tackle Box. Tackle shop: Tackle Box, Swanpoll Str, TR11 3HU (tel: 01326 315849). Details of hotel accom from Tourist Information: 28 Killigrew Str, TR11 3PN (tel: 01326 312300). *(For freshwater fishing, see River Fal)*.

Porthleven (Cornwall). Bass are to be taken from the rocks in Mount's Bay. Best bass fishing from Loe Bar, 1½m E. Good pollack and mackerel fishing outside the rocks. Nearly all fishing is done from the Mount's Bay type of boat in deep water. For charter boats, contact Harbourmaster. Tackle shop (Easter to end-October) Porthleven Angling Centre, Mount Pleasant Rd, TR13 9JS (tel: 01326 561885). Hotel: Tye Rock.

Penzance (Cornwall). Excellent boat, pier, rock and shore fishing for pollack, mackerel, mullet and bass. Long Rock beach recommended, best Jun-Nov; bass, ray, flatfish. Marazion beaches offer flatfish and ray. Pier at Lamorna, turbot, gurnard and dogfish. Breakwater at Sennen, the same. Boat trips can be arranged with Newtown Angling. Shark fishing also possible. Best months: June-Nov. Club: Mount's Bay AS (HQ: Bath Inn, Penzance). Annual fishing festival, five weeks, Aug-Sept. Tackle shop: Newtown Angling Centre, Newton Germoe, TR20 9AE (tel: 01736 763721).

Mousehole, via **Penzance** (Cornwall). Good station for fishing Mount's Bay. Excellent mackerel, bream, pollack, conger, whiting, bass close to harbour according to season. Sheltered from west. Rock fishing in rough weather. Bell Rock

between Newlyn and Mousehole has produced record catches. Between Mousehole and Lamorna, Penza Point, Kemyell Point and Carn Dhu are marks. Best grounds: Longships and Runnel Stone. Good results with sharks. Hotels: Old Coastguard.

Isles of Scilly. From shores and small boats around islands, wrasse, pollack, mackerel, conger and plaice; farther off in deep sea, particularly on The Powl, south-west of St Agnes, big catches made of cod, ling, conger, pollack, etc. Mullet pay periodical visits inshore, but usually caught by net; bass rare in these waters. Some shark fishing July and August, all tackle provided. Peninnis Head and Deep Point on St Mary's are good rock marks for pollack, wrasse and mackerel. Boating can be dangerous, so experience essential. Accommodation limited, early bookings advisable between May and Sept. Tackle shop: Sports Mode, The Parade, TR21 0LP (tel: 01720 422293). Other information from Tourist Information: Hugh Str, St Mary's, TR21 0LL (tel: 01720 422536). For boats inquire of Sports Mode.

St Ives (Cornwall). Bass, flounder, turbot, plaice, mackerel and garfish plentiful in St Ives area. Surf fishing from shore, especially from island, Aire Point, Cape Cornwall, Portheras, Besigrau, Man's Head, Clodgy Point; Godrevy Point offers mackerel, pollack and wrasse, which are also found at Navax Point. Chapel Porth good for ray and turbot. Boat fishing gives sport with mackerel (summer months) and large pollack (off reef from Godrevy Island). For boats contact Harbourmaster (tel: 01736 795081). Bass, tope, mullet, flatfish and occasional sea trout taken in Hayle river estuary. Trout fishing on Drift Reservoir, Penzance and St Erth Stream (4m). Tackle shop: Symons of Market Place, TR26 1RZ (tel: 01736 796200) sells tackle and bait, also local coarse permits. Hotels: Dunmar; Demelza; St Margarets, and many others.

Newquay (Cornwall). Boat, beach; rock and estuary fishing. Mackerel (April to Oct); school bass (June-Sept); larger fish July onwards, including winter; pollack (May-Nov); flatfish, wrasse (May-Sept). Mullet good from June-Sept. Beach fishing at Perranporth, Holywell Bay, Crantock and Watergate Bay: ray, turbot and plaice. Off-peak times only. Shark and deep sea fishing possible. For boats, contact Boatmans Assn, Kiosk 4, South Quay (tel: 01637 876352, evng: 873585); Anchor Sea Angling Centre South Quay TR7 1HR (tel: 01637 877613). Trout fishing in Porth Reservoir. Tackle Shop: Atlantic Angling, 9b Cliff Rd, TR7 2NE (tel: 01637 850777). Numerous hotels.

Padstow (Cornwall). Trevose Head, Park Head and Stepper Point are good marks in summer for float fishing and spinning for mackerel, pollack, garfish, bass, wrasse, rays, dog fish, plaice, turbot, occ. tope, and in winter for whiting, codling, dogfish, conger. Carneweather Point nr Polzeath is recommended for all-year-round fishing with cod in winter, but beware of dangerous ocean swells. The beaches at Trevone, Harlyn, Mother Ivys, Boobys, Constantine, Treyarnon, Porthcothan, Mawgan Porth, provide surf casting for bass, plaice, turbot, rays. The estuary has good flounder fishing in winter. Club: Grenville Fishing Club, Social Club, St Dennis; or contact tackle shop: Padstow Angling Centre, Strand House, South Quay, Padstow, PL28 8BL (tel: 01841 532762). Hotel: Treyarnon Bay.

Bude (Cornwall). Codling, flatfish, mackerel, whiting and dogfish from breakwater and Crackington Haven. Northcott Mouth Crooklets, Maer, for skate and flatfish. Widemouth Bay is good venue. Rays may be taken from shore in late summer and autumn. Rock fishing is to be had from Upton, Wanson and Millock. Several boats work from Port Isaac in summer. Club: Bude & Dist SAC, annual subscription, £3.50. Tackle shop: Bude Angling Supplies, 6 Queen Str, Bude, EX23 8BB (tel: 01288 353396).

Hartland (Devon); ns Barnstaple, 24m. Good all-round sea fishing, especially for bass at times with india-rubber sand-eel, prawn or limpet from beach or rocks according to tide (bass up to 11½lb have been caught); whiting, mullet, conger and pouting also taken. Tackle shop: Summerlands Tackle (see Westward Ho!). Hotels: Hartland Quay, New Inn, King's Arms.

Lundy (Bristol Channel). Good mackerel, conger, pollack and wrasse inshore. Ray, plaice, dabs, tope and bass at East Bank. 1¼ to 2½m E. Good anchorage at Lundy, but no harbour. Boats occasionally on hire for 8 persons fishing. For accommodation write to The Agent, Lundy, Bristol Channel, N Devon EX39 2LY.

Clovelly (Devon); W of Bideford. Whiting, cod, conger, bull huss, dogfish and the occasional plaice caught all the year round; ray in spring, bass and mackerel in summer. Few inshore boats; fishing from the breakwater forbidden from 9 am to 6 pm in summer. Hotels: New Inn; Red Lion.

Bideford (Devon). Bass (from the bridge, in summer) flounders, mullet higher up the river. Tackle Shop: Summerlands Tackle, 16-20 Nelson Rd, Westward Ho, EX39 1LH (tel: 01237 471291).

Westward Ho (Devon). Extensive beach and rocks from which bass, dogfish, smooth-hounds, bull huss, tope and mackerel may be taken in summer; codling to 10lbs in winter. Tackle Shop: Summerlands Tackle, 16-20 Nelson Rd, Westward Ho, EX39 1LH (tel: 01237 471291). Baits, and advice offered to anglers. **Appledore**, north of Bideford in Torridge estuary, in summer has good bass fishing from rocks. Cod and whiting in winter. Lugworm beds at Appledore and Instow. Few boats.

Ilfracombe (Devon). From pier: conger, pollack, whiting, dabs. Capstone Point, bass, wrasse. Capstone Rocks, similar species; Watermouth Cove, mixed bag: pollack, coalfish, wrasse, bass, a few flatfish. From boat, conger, skate, ray; mackerel Jun-Sept. Cod Dec-Feb. Bait: mackerel, squid, sand eel. Club: Ilfra-

combe and District AA, c/o Variety
Sports. Reservoir trout fishing *(see freshwater section)*. Tackle and bait from Variety Sports, 23 Broad Str, EX34 9EE (tel:
01271 862039). Details of accom from
Tourist Information Centre: The Promenade EX34 9BX (tel: 01271 863001).
Lynmouth (Devon). Good harbour and boat
fishing. Grey mullet and bass from harbour arm. Drift fishing for pollack and
mackerel. Tope, skate and conger in Lynmouth Bay and off Sand Ridge, 1m. Best
months: June to Oct. Tackle shop: Churchill House, Church Hill, Lynton EX35
6HY (tel: 01598 752557). Several hotels
in Lynton and Lynmouth; details from
Lynton Tourist Office, Town Hall, Lynton, EX35 6BT (tel: 01598 752225)
(tickets for Lyn). *(For freshwater fishing
see Lyn)*.
Minehead (Som). Beach, boat and rock
fishing, principally for tope, skate, ling,
thornback ray, conger, cod, bass and flatfish (Dunster to Porlock good for bass
from beaches). Dogfish in bay. Mackerel
in summer. Harbour and promenade walls
provide sport with mullet, codling and
some bass. Boats: through the tackle shop
named below, all year round. Bait from
sands at low water. Club: Minehead &
Dist SAC. Tackle shops: Minehead
Sports, 55 The Avenue, TA24 5BB (tel:
01643 703423); Westcoast Tackle Supply, Fisherman's Corner, Quay Str, TA24
5UL (tel: 01643 705745).
Watchet (Som). Watchet and Dist Sea Angling Society fishes all the year round,
covering coast from St Audries Bay to
Porlock Wier. Monthly competitions
from piers and shore. Codling, bass, whiting, conger and skate, according to season. Good boat fishing. New members
welcomed by AS. Tackle shop: Westcoast
Angling Centre, 53 Swain Str, TA23 0AG
(tel: 01984 634807).
Weston-super-Mare (Avon). Record list of
the Weston-super-Mare Sea AA includes
conger at 25lb, sole at 2lb 8oz, bass 13lb,
skate 16lb 8oz, cod at 22lb, silver eel at
4lb, whiting and flounder at 2lb. Best
venues 2 hours either side of low tide are
Brean Down, conger, skate; Weston
Beach, whiting, flatfish; Knightstone, the
same. Woodspring is fishable throughout
year, best at autumn. For baits, beds of
lugworms are to be found along the low
water mark of the town beach and off
Kewstoke Rocks. Also from Tackle shop:
Weston Angling Centre, 25A Locking
Rd, Weston-s-Mare, BS23 3BY (tel:
01934 631140).
Southport (Merseyside). Dabs and
flounders, with whiting and codling in
winter, chief fish caught here; also skate,
mullet, dogfish, sole, plaice, conger, gurnard and some bass. Shore flat and sandy,
and fishing mainly from pier. Local
clubs: Southport SAC. Good coarse fishing on River Crossens run by Southport &
DAS. Tackle shops: Tight Lines Angling
Centre, 2 Hampton Rd, PR8 6SS (tel:
01704 541014); Catch 22 Fishing Tackle,
Birkdale Trdg Est, Liverpool Rd, PR8
4PZ (tel: 01704 568450). At **Liverpool**,
Mersey is cleaner nowadays, and cod,
bass and whiting are taken at Alexander
Dock.
Blackpool (Lancs). Seven miles of beach,
and fishing from North Pier, but boat
fishing is the best option, although fewer
boats are now operating. Tickets for certain parts of Wyre from tackle shops.
Coarse fishing in Stanley Park Lake; dt
£3.50. Tackle shop: Blackpool Angling
Centre, 326 Church Str, Blackpool, FY1
3QH (tel: 01253 290961); Bait & Tackle,
52a St Annes Rd, FY4 2AS (tel: 01253
470004). Many hotels.
Morecambe and **Heysham** (Lancs). Beach
and stone jetty fishing throughout year.
Beaches yield plaice, flounders, dabs,
bass and eels from June to October, and
dabs, codling, whiting and flounders in
winter. Estuary catches up to 100
flounders to 2lb weight at Arnside. Stone
Jetty has been extended, angling free;
good catches of plaice, flounders, codling, whiting. At Heysham Harbour and
North Wall whiting, cod, flounders, dabs,
pouting, conger and mullet can be taken.
Storm Groynes is producing good flatfish. Tackle shops: Morecambe Angling
Centre, Thornton Rd, Morecambe, LA4
5PB (tel: 01524 832332).
Fleetwood (Lancs). Plaice, whiting, skate,
codling, tope, etc, from boats and shore.
Club: Fleetwood & District AC. Tackle
shop: Blackpool Angling Centre, 326
Church Str, Blackpool, FY1 3QH (tel:
01253 290961).
Barrow-in-Furness (Cumbria). Boat and
shore fishing for tope, bass, cod, plaice,
whiting, thornback skate. Good marks include Foulney Island, Roa Island, Piel Island, Scarth Hole and Black Tower
(Walney Island) and Roanhead. Good
beach areas are Priory Point to Canal
Foot, bait may be dug here, also, and

Greenodd from sea wall alongside A590 and from car park. Tackle shop: Angling and Hiking Centre, 275 Rawlinson Str, L14 1DH (tel: 01229 829661).

ISLE OF WIGHT

The Island provides a wealth of shore and boat fishing, and sheltered conditions can always be found, Bass are the main quarry for beach anglers, but pollack, conger, mackerel, pouting, thornback rays, flatfish and wrasse, with occasional tope, are also taken. Black bream, skate and shark are caught by boat anglers as well as the species already mentioned. Cod run regularly to 20lb in autumn. Due to strong tides on the north coast and lack of harbours on the south coast, the visiting angler would be best advised to arrange boat trips with one of the local charter skippers working out of Yarmouth or Bembridge. Strong tides also mean heavy leads and sometimes, wire line. There are a large number of fishing clubs on the island. T I centres provide information about them.

Alum Bay. This necessitates a steep descent from the car park down the steps provided. From March to October there is a chair lift in operation. Fishes well after dark for large conger, bass, rays and sole, especially when rough. From the old pier remains to the white cliffs is the main area, although the rocks to the east, towards Totland, make a good station from which to spin for bass in the tide race, or to light leger with squid or mackerel. Deep water at all states of tide.

Atherfield. A number of record fish have been taken from this stretch. The beach is of shingle with scattered rock, easily reached via path alongside holiday camp. Bass, rays, pout, etc after dark, to mackerel, squid and cuttle baits. Crab bait produces smooth hounds. Ragworm fished over the drying ledge to the left of this mark produces large wrasse and bass, day or night. Large cod in late autumn.

Bembridge. Species to be caught include bass, pout, conger, ling, bream, dogfish, turbot, brill, pollack, skate and ray. The shore from Whitecliff to Bembridge is mainly rock formation with stretches of shingle and is good ground for bass and conger although not fished a great deal. Bass, mullet, eels, among the rocks. Here, the beach turns to fine flat sand and flatfish and bass are taken. Bembridge Harbour is a wide inlet with St Helens on the opposite bank. Shark fishing, July-August, drifting from St Catherines Light to Nab Tower. Boats and bait obtainable on shore. A sand gully near the 'Crab and Lobster' can be fished from the rocks. Fine bream may be taken from boats on Bembridge Ledge, early May to June, plenty of mackerel, also. A good number of fish are taken in the harbour: flounders, eels, bass. Many large mullet can be seen but are seldom fished for. Very strong tide in narrowest part of entrance. Kin-

grag and lugworm are good baits for ledgering and small mud ragworm on light float tackle is successful. Baited spoon or wander tackle works well for flounder and plaice. Sea wall at St Helens is a convenient place to park and fish over the top of the tide. Club: Bembridge AC, holds 12 competitions p.a., open to non-members. The Club has 50 moorings to let to members.

Bonchurch. Bass, conger, wrasse and pout from beach. Good fishing in gulleys between the extensive rocks at flood tide, after dark, especially after a south westerly gale.

Brooke. A shallow water mark that fishes well when the sea is coloured. Expect conger, bass, pout, plus cod in late autumn. One good spot is to be found in front of easy cliff path, 200 yds to left of point.

Chale. Best beach for rays on island, reached by steep cliff path. Specimen small eyed rays are taken on frozen sand eel, day or night, from Mar-Sept, when sea is coloured after a storm. Some bass and conger, plus mackerel in summer.

Colwell Bay. A shallow sandy beach with easy access. Bass, sole, wrasse after dark, when crowds have gone home.

Totland Bay. Next to Colwell Bay, deeper water. More chance of bass, especially when rough. It's possible to fish straight from a car on the sea wall. Fishing is good beside the disused pier.

Compton Bay. 1m west of Brooke. Long flat sandy beach with patches of flat rock. Occasional bass when the sea is rough. Avoid the rocks under the cliff at the west end, where there is a danger of major cliff falls.

Cowes. The River Medina runs from Newport to Cowes Harbour and offers flounder fishing throughout the year with the best sport from the late summer to autumn. The shoals move about the river with the tide and location is often a matter of local knowledge. As a general guide the fish may be expected further upstream on the stronger spring tides. Weights average up to a pound. Bass also move into the river and have been taken to 4lbs, often on flounder tackle. Rowing boats may be launched from the Folly Inn on the East bank, reached by turning off the main Newport to East Cowes road. Kingston power station about a mile down from Folly is a good boat mark for school bass, plaice, sole. Mullet and silver eels may be caught anywhere. Ragworm is usually used in preference to lugworm.

Cowes Harbour. Bass, flounder, plaice and sole may be taken by the boat angler from either side of the fairway above and below the floating bridge and during the summer there are many large mullet within the harbour. Inside the breakwater to the east, flounder and plaice are taken on the bottom from along the edge of the hovercraft channel to inshore towards the East Cowes Esplanade. Flounder and plaice are also taken from the mud-flats outside the East Cowes breakwater.

West Cowes Esplanade to **Gurnard**. Float fishing and spinning from the slipways and jetties for bass and mullet. Along the Princes Green to Egypt Light, bass and conger can be found and in late summer bass often venture close in under the walls in search of prawns and may be taken by trailing a worm over the balustrade and walking it quietly along. At Egypt Light, the shingle slopes steeply so long casting is unnecessary, and tope have occasionally been landed here as well as bass to 8lb, and cod to 20lb in late autumn. The sandy patches among the rocks may yield sole and plaice in season. Car parking here.

Freshwater Bay. Pouting, bass, small pollack and few conger. Fish from middle of beach when rough. Survey at low tide, then fish after dark. Very easy access.

Newport. Nearest sea fishing in River Medina; flounders, school bass, mullet, plaice, eels. Tackle/ boat hire from Scotties, branch at 11 Lugley Str, PO30 9HD (tel: 01983 522115).

Newtown. Bass and flounders in Newtown River. Clamerkin reach is best, using light gear and ragworm. Limited access, as large area is nature reserve.

Ventnor to **St Catherines**. Series of rocky ledges and gullies, best surveyed at low

water. Bass, conger, pout, wrasse etc after dark and some mullet during calm days.

Yarmouth. Flounder and mullet and school bass in harbour. Bass, rays and mackerel from pier in summer. Notable cod venue in late autumn but strong tides prevail.

Ryde. A very shallow, sandy beech, popular with holiday makers. Bass, small pollock, plaice, flounders, eels, bream and grey mullet from pier. Conger, dogfish, dabs, skate, mackerel from deep water marks, and plaice, flounder, bass and sole fishing inshore. Cod up to 24lb taken in autumn. Sheltered resort giving ideal fishing conditions all year. All beaches fishable. King rag and lugworm plentiful. Boats can be hired along shore.

Sandown. Fishing from end of pier (daytime only) produces plaice, rays, bass and bream on sandy ground. Float fishing produces mackerel, scad, small pollack and mullet. Local club: Sandown and Lake AS, organising frequent open competitions. Visitors welcome. Membership £12 annually (£6 juveniles) dt £1.50 from pier. Boat hire and tackle; Scotties, 22 Fitzroy Str, PO36 8HZ (tel: 01983 404555).

Seaview. From St Helens to Seaview the coast is a mixture of rocks and sand and shingle. Priory Bay is reached by boat and provides very good mackerel and bass fishing. Plaice may be taken to 3lb from early April, with lugworm. During the summer months bream can also be taken from this spot. From June onwards, bass and mackerel are shoaling and large catches from boats are common. Cod are also taken late in the year.

Shanklin. Pier has been demolished. Various other venues exist which fish well for specific species, such as sting ray, but require very detailed directions re access, times to fish, etc. Contact Scotties of Newport for such details, and to obtain a wide variety of suitable baits.

Totland. Bass off shingle bank from boat. Bass, conger from shore. Fishing also from pier. Boats from Fair Deal Amusements, The Pier. Hotels: Chalet, Sentry Mead.

Ventnor. The western end of the beach is good for bass, skate, pout and conger and harbour and the sea wall in front of the canoe lake is a good bass spot. Club: Ventnor AC (associate members welcome). Tackle and bait: J Chiverton 70 High Str, PO38 1LU (tel: 01983 856481). Beach fishing *(see also Bonchurch).*

Wootton. School bass and flounders.
Yarmouth. Bass, small pollack; pier fishing.

CHANNEL ISLANDS

Wide variety of sport from beaches, rocky headlands and boats. Many specimen fish landed from deep-sea marks. Shark fishing growing in popularity. Boats easy to come by.

Guernsey. No fewer than 52 different species are recorded in Bailiwick of Guernsey rod-caught record list. Guernsey is 15 miles from the Hurd Deep, near major shipping lanes, and hundreds of wrecks yield high catches. Inshore, many headlands offer first-class spinning, and a flat, sandy, west coast gives good surf-casting for bass and a few flatfish. Several Guernsey fish accepted as new British records. The most common species are bass, bream, conger, dogfish, garfish, mackerel, mullet, plaice, pollack and wrasse. Anglers may fish anywhere from the shore except for marinas, the fishermans quay, and the land reclamation to the south of St Sampson's Harbour. Bottom fishing is productive in spring, late autumn and winter; spinning in summer. Long casting is no advantage, on westerly rocks. Baits: ragworm is found in the rocky bays on west coast, Grand Havre, Bordeaux North, to Beaucette Marina, Bellgreve Bay; lugworm in sandy bays, especially, Grand Havre, Cobo and Vazon. Crabs, prawns and white rag can also be obtained. In north east, Fort Doyle is one of the best marks; south east, Soldiers Bay. South west cliffs are fishable but dangerous. There are over ten different fishing competitions between June and December. Local clubs: Guernsey SAC; Guernsey Freshwater AC; Guernsey Mullet Club; Castaways AC, and others; the central point for these clubs is The Sea Anglers Representative Committee, c/o Pinewood, Jerbourg Rd, St Martins (tel: 01481 237755). Tackle shops: Western Tackle Supplies, Rue de la Hougue, Castel, GY5 7EB (tel: 01481 256080); Mick's Fishing Supplies, Unit 6, Les Canus Rd, GY2 4UJ (tel: 01481 700390); Tackle and Accessories Centre, Rue de l'Eglise, Castel GY99 9ZZ (tel: 01481 251844). Baits, rod hire; Boatworks Plus, St Peter Port, GY1 1AU (tel: 01481 726071). For further information about Guernsey fisheries contact States of Guernsey Department of Fisheries, Raymond Falla House, PO Box 459, Longue Rue, St Martins, Guernsey GY1 6AF (tel: 01481 235741). Tourist Information publishes official sea angling guide, £1, widely obtainable.

Jersey. Winter fishing yields pollack, ray and other flatfish, conger, a few bass, cod fishing can be good. Spring: garfish, early mackerel off such points as Sorel and La Moye; grey mullet, occasional porbeagle and blue shark and other species. Summer is good for all forms of fishing, by boat on offshore reefs, which is 80% of charter angling. Excellent fishing for bream commences in May and continues to Oct, fish up to 5lb. Rays (incl blonde rays, over 30lb) are caught in good quantities on inshore sandbanks, as well as brill and turbot, especially early and late season. In autumn, whitebait concentrates at places such as Belle Hougue bring in large mackerel and bass, and flatfish move into shallow waters in the Islands bays. Venues: St Helier's harbour heads; Noirmont Point; St Brelade's Bay; La Corbiere; L'Etacq; Plemont; Greve de Lecq; Bonne Nuit Bay harbour; Bouley Bay harbour; Rozel Bay harbour; St Catherine's breakwater; St Aubin's Bay. Charter boats: 'Anna II', from La Collette Marina, contact Tony Heart, Flat 2, 7 Coma Villa, Clarendon Rd, JE2 3YW (tel: 01534 888552; mob: 07797 725301); 'Theseus', D Nuth (tel: 01534 858046; mob: 07797 728316). Local club: Jersey SFC. Jersey Freshwater AA, has coarse and trout dt: R A Mallet (tel: 01534 723882). Tackle shops: Iron Stores Marine, 15/16 Commercial Buildings, JE1 3UD (tel: 01534 877755); JFS Sport, 7 Beresford Str, JE2 4WN (tel: 01534 874875); St Ouens Motor Works, La Grande Route de St Ouen JE3 2HY (tel: 01534 481870); all St Helier.

ISLE OF MAN

The Island's coastline is extremely varied. The long, flat, surf beaches of the North contrast sharply with the sheer faces of the South. Similarly, its fishing methods and species of fish are equally diverse. Despite the Island's location, coastline and clean waters, saltwater angling from both shore and boat remains unexploited and largely undiscovered. Information is obtainable from Isle of Man Tourist and Leisure Department, Information Bureau, Sea Terminal, Douglas, IM1 2RG (tel: 01624 686766).

Castletown. Conger, pollack, cod, wrasse, tope, flatfish from beach and boat; best months, June to Oct. Big skate from boats 600 yds off Langness; best Aug–Sept. Boats for hire locally. Tackle shop, see Port Erin.

Douglas. Plaice, sole (British record lemon sole), coalfish, pollack, flounder from Victoria Pier; best months, May to Oct, coalfish, wrasse, cod, plaice, dabs, sole from boats in Douglas Bay. Rock fishing off Douglas Head; float or spinner (good for pollack). Cod, wrasse, red gurnard, plaice, Little Ness Head to Douglas Head; skate from boats 2m out, and large tope, conger, cod, etc. Club: Douglas (IOM) & District AC, annual membership fee £12 (£4 discount before 28 Feb), jun £3 (membership includes trout fishing rights in **R Glass**); contact Hon Sec for further information and applications for membership *(see English Clubs)*. Tackle shops: Hobbytime, 8 Castle St, Douglas (tel: 01624 621562; fax: 01624 661721); The Roland Westcott Tackle Company, 1 The Shops, Ballaquayle Rd, Douglas IM2 5DF (tel: 01624 629599). Hotels: Chesterfield, Devonian.

Kirk Michael. Beach fishing from here to Point of Ayre is excellent for bass, flatfish, dogfish. Tackle shop, see Ramsey. Hotel: Lyngarth.

Laxey. Plaice, dabs and bass from March to Oct from beach. Cod, mackerel, flat-fish, offshore from boats at Garwick Bay. Tackle shop *(see Douglas)*. Hotel: Bridge Inn.

Peel. Breakwater: cod, coalfish, dogfish plentiful all year round; mackerel, dog-fish, coalfish, plaice, flounder, dabs (July to Oct). Beach: similar. Rock fishing: from Castle rocks and headlands plenty of pollack. Sand eel best bait all season. Limited lugworm on beach. Boat fishing, but hire limited: cod and haddock in winter. In spring and summer spur dogfish common. Rock fishing off St Patrick's Isle for mackerel, wrasse, coalfish; float and spinner. Local club; Peel Angling Club. Hotel: Fernleigh

Port Erin. Good sport from pier and breakwater for pollack, mackerel, wrasse, grey mullet, coalfish, angler fish and conger. The bay yields flatfish and mackerel, with cod in the colder months. Tackle shop: The Tackle Box, Strand Rd, Port Erin, IM9 6HE (tel: 01624 836343). Hotels: Balmoral; Falcons Nest.

Port St Mary. Probably best centre on island. Pollack, coalfish, wrasse from rocks, pier, boats (most of year). Flatfish and mackerel offshore and pier during herring season. Tope, skate, cod, conger, ling from boats. Several competitions. Inquiries to Hon Sec, Southern AC. Visitors welcome. Tackle shop *(see Douglas)*. Hotels: Bay View; Shore.

Ramsey. No fishing from pier. Dogfish, codling, whiting, flounder, dab, coalfish, plaice, mackerel, rockling; from Ramsey beach to Point of Ayre, plus bass (Aug–Sept), tope, bull huss. Pollack also taken by spinning with artificial sand-eel. For help with bait and boats, contact officials of Ramsey AC (tel: 01624 812279, after 6pm); annual membership fee £10, conc 50p. Tackle shop: The Ramsey Warehouse, 37 Parliament Str, IM8 1AT (tel: 01624 813092). Hotels: Hillcrest House, Sulby Glen.

FISHING CLUBS & ASSOCIATIONS IN ENGLAND

The English fishing clubs and associations listed below are by no means the total number of those existing. Club secretaries retire or change address, often after a comparatively short term of office, making it all too probable that the address list is out of date by the time it is issued. This regrettable fact also applies to the club lists in the others national sections of the book. Please advise the publishers (address at the front of the book) of any changed details for the next edition. The names and addresses of countless more fishing clubs and associations may be obtained from the various regional offices of the Environment Agency, from British Waterways, and from such federated bodies as the British Conger Club, *(see below)*.

NATIONAL BODIES

Anglers' Conservation Assn
6 Rainbow Street
Leominster
Herefordshire HR6 8DQ
Tel: 01568 620447
Angling Trades Assn
Federation House
Stoneleigh Park
Warwickshire CV8 2RF
Tel: 02476 414999
Fax: 02476 414990
Web: www.sports-life.com
e-mail: info@sportslife.org.uk
Atlantic Salmon Trust
Director: J B D Read
Moulin
Pitlochry
Perthshire PH16 5JQ
Tel: 01796 473439
Fax: 01796 473554
Web: www.atlanticsalmontrust.org
e-mail: salmontrust@aol.com
Assn of Stillwater Game Fishery
Managers
Packington Fisheries
Meriden, Coventry
West Midlands CV7 7HR
Tel/Fax: 01676 522754
British Conger Club
Mrs Diana Byrne
2 Drake Court
264 Citadel Road
Plymouth, Devon PL1 2PY
Tel: 01752 223815
(Affiliated with ninety eight sea angling clubs)
British Record (rod-caught) Fish
Committee
Secretary: David Rowe
Level 5, Hamlyn House
Mardle Way

Buckfastleigh
Devon TQ11 0NS
Tel: 01364 644643
Fax: 01364 644486
Web: www.nfsa.org.uk
e-mail: ho@nfsa.org.uk
British Trout Assn
8/9 Lambton Place
London, W11 2SH
Tel: 0207 221 6065
Fax: 0207 221 6049
Web: www.britishtrout.co.uk
e-mail: office@britishtrout.co.uk
British Waterways HQ
(for regional fishing enquiries see canals section)
Willow Grange
Church Road, Watford
Hertfordshire WD17 4QA
Tel: 01923 226422.
Fax: 01923 201400.
Confederation of English Flyfishers
(recognised authority on competitive fly-fishing in England)
Hon Sec: Peter Godfrey
1 Bridge Terrace
Bedlington
Northumberland NE22 7JT
Tel: 01670 823839
Web: www.ceff.co.uk
Countryside Alliance
Simon Hart
367 Kennington Road
London SE11 4PT
Tel: 0207 840 9200
Fax: 0207 793 8899
Web: www.countryside-alliance.org
Freshwater Biological Assn
The Director
The Ferry House
Far Sawrey, Ambleside

Cumbria LA22 0LP
Tel: 015394 42468
Fax: 015394 46914
Web: www.fba.org.uk
e-mail: chiefexec@fba.org.uk
Game Angling Instructors Assn
Hon Sec: Ian Moutter
23 High Street
Coldstream
Berwickshire TD12 4AP
Tel: 01890 883931
Web: www.gameanglinginstructors.
co.uk
Grayling Society
R Cullum-Kenyon
Rockvale Cottage
Redlap
Dartmouth
Devon TQ6 0JR
Tel: 01803 835204
e-mail: cullumkenyon@btopenworld.
com
Web: www.graylingsociety.org
International Fly Fishing Assn
Ian Campbell, Secretary & Treasurer
Cruachan
16 Marindin Park
Glenfarg
Perth & Kinross
PH2 9NQ
Tel: 01577 830582
e-mail: iffa@glenfarg.com
**Marine Biological Assn of the
United Kingdom**
The Secretary
The Laboratory
Citadel Hill
Plymouth PLI 2PB
Tel: 01752 633100
Fax: 01752 633102
Web: www.mba.ac.uk
e-mail: sec@mba.ac.uk
National Federation of Anglers
Halliday House
Egginton Junction
nr Hilton
Derbyshire DE65 6GU
Tel: 01283 734735
Fax: 01283 734799
Web: www.nfadirect.com
e-mail: office@nfahq.freeserve.co.uk

National Federation of Sea Anglers
NFSA Development Officer, D Rowe
NFSA Office
Hamlyn House
Mardle Way
Buckfastleigh
Devon TQ11 0NS
Tel: 01364 644643
Web: www.nfsa.org.uk
**Register of Experienced Fly Fishing
Instructors & Schools (REFFIS)**
Chairman: Richard Slocock
Lawrences Farm
Tolpuddle
Dorchester
Dorset DT2 7HF
Tel: 01305 848460
Web: www.reffis.co.uk
Ribble Fisheries Assn
*(amalgamation of 18 local clubs and
owners)*
Keith B Spencer (Chairman/Secretary)
36 Heap street
Burnley BB10 1RL
Tel: 01282 706042
Salmon & Trout Assn
Paul Knight, Director
Fishmongers' Hall
London Bridge
London EC4R 9EL
Tel: 020 7283 5838
Fax: 020 7626 5137
Web: www.salmon-trout.org
e-mail: hq@salmon-trout.org
Shark Angling Club of Great Britain
Linda Reynolds
The Quay
East Looe
Cornwall PL13 IDX
Tel/Fax: 01503 262642
Wheelyboat Trust (The)
Director: Andy Beadsley
North Lodge
Burton Park
Petworth
West Sussex GU28 0JT
Tel/Fax: 01798 342222
Wild Trout Trust (The)
92-104 Carnwath Road
London SW6 3HW
Web: www.wildtrout.org
e-mail: ronnie@wildtrout.org

CLUBS

Abbey Cross Angling Club
P Monery
Ambleside

Albury Walk
Cheshunt
Herts. EN8 8XQ

Abingdon & Oxford Anglers Alliance
(alliance of Abingdon & Dist ARA, Clifton Hampden & Dist PS and Oxford APS)
R Bateman
16 The Gap
Marcham
Oxon OX13 6NJ
Tel: 01865 391809

Accrington New Anglers
Brian Stevens
15 Windsor Avenue
Church
nr Accrington
Lancashire BB5 6LN
Tel: 01254 871370

Addingham Angling Assn
H D Sunderland
West Most Cottage, Balgreggan Cottages
Sandhead
Stranraer DG9 9LH
Tel: 01776 830316
Web: www.ilkley21.freeserve.co.uk

Aln Angling Assn
Alan Lawson
White House Cotts
Alnwick
Northumberland NE66 2LN
Tel/fax: 01665 579272

Alston & District Angling Assn
John Pullin
Nether Leys
Wardway
Alston
Cumbria CA9 3AP
Tel: 01434 381260
or
Martin Ould, Treasurer
Little Gill Cottage
Ashgill
Alston CA9 3HB
Tel: 01434 381270
Web: www.rsissons.freeserve.co.uk

Altrincham & District Angling Club
John Deas
111 Hoylake Rd
Sale
Cheshire M33 2XJ
Tel: 0161 969 7475

Alveston Village Angling Club
Mark Pitcher
62 Avon Crescent
Stratford upon Avon CV37 7EZ
Tel: 01789 268110

Ampthill Angling & Fish Preservation Society
Dick Ward
15 Kingfisher Road
Flitwick
Beds MK45 1RA
Tel: 01525 751850

Appletreewick Barden & Burnsall Angling Club
J R Harding
86 Drakesfield Road
London
SW17 8RR

Arnfield Fly Fishing Club
(not available as we go to press)

Avon Angling Club
Percy Edwards
56 Addison Road
Melksham
Wilts SN12 8DR
Tel: 01225 705036

Avon Fishing Assn (Devon)
(not available as we go to press)

Avon & Tributaries Angling Assn
Andrew Donaldson
104 Berkeley Road
Bishopston
Bristol BS7 8HG
Tel: 0117 9442518

Aylsham & District Angling Club
K Sutton
17 Town Lane
Aylsham
Norfolk NR11 6HH
Tel: 01263 732433

Banbury & District Angling Assn
Brian Syde: Treasurer
17 Timms Road
Banbury
Oxon OX16 9DL
Tel: 01295 270796

Barnsley & District Amalgamated Anglers' Society
Tony Eaton
60 Walton Street
Gawber, Barnsley

Fishing Clubs

When you appoint a new Hon. Secretary, do not forget to give us details of the change. Write to the Publishers (address in the front of the book). Thank you!

Yorks S75 2PD
Tel: 01226 203090
**Barnstaple & District Angling
Assn**
S Toms
Upcott Farm
Brayford
N Devon EX32 7QA
Tel: 01598 710857
Barnt Green Fishing Club
Hon Sec
c/o The Keeper
Keeper's Cottage
Cofton Church Lane
Barnt Green
Worcs B45
Barrow Angling Assn
Brian Pickthall
Sandside
Kirkby-in-Furness
Cumbria LA17 7UA
Tel: 01229 889552
Basingstoke Canal Angling Assn
Jeff Bunch
2 Wentworth Close
Ash Vale
Aldershot GU12 5NB
Tel: 01252 326421
Web: www.basingstokecanalaa.co.uk
or
Hon Treasurer: David Wright
2c Marlborough Gardens
Oakley
Basingstoke
Hants RG23 7AH
Tel: 01256 780666
Bathampton Angling Assn
D Crookes
25 Otago Terrace
Larkhall
Bath, Avon BA1 6SX
Tel: 01225 427164
Web: www.bathampton.org
Bedford Angling Club
Mrs M E Appleton
18 Moriston Road
Bedford
Beds MK41 7UG
Tel: 01234 354708
**Bedlington & Blagdon
Angling Assn**
S Symons
8 Moorland Drive
Bedlington
Northumberland NE22 7HB
Tel: 01670 822011
Belper & District Angling Club
Paul Spencer
35 Field Lane

Belper
Derbys
Tel: 01773 825197
Bembridge (IOW) Angling Club
Peter Knight
North Quay
St Helens
Isle of Wight
Tel: 01983 875030 (club)
Tel: 07966 538319 (Hon Sec)
Benson & District Angling Club
Chairman: D Cook
24 The Cedars
Benson
Wallingford
Oxon OX10 6LL
Tel: 01491 834540
**Berkhamsted & District Angling
Society**
P Welling
1 South Park Gardens
Berkhamsted
Herts HP4 1JA
Tel: 01442 875106
Bewl Bridge Flyfishers Club
John Hancock
Trodgers Way
Little Trodgers Lane
Mayfield
TN20 6PN
Tel: 01435 872171
Bicester & District Angling Assn
(now part of Oxford & District AA)
Biggleswade, Hitchin Angling Assn Ltd
John Lincoln
25 Grosvenor Gardens
Biggleswade
Tel: 01767 316693
Billingshurst Angling Society
Peter Stockwood
School House
Billingshurst
W Sussex RH14 9RX
Tel: 01403 782160
Birmingham Anglers' Assn Ltd
John Williams
106 Icknield Port Road
Rotton Park
Birmingham B16 0AA
Tel: 0121 454 9111
Web: www.baa.uk.com
e-mail: baajnw@btinternet.com
(9.30am to 1.30pm Monday to Friday)
Bishop Auckland Angling Club
John Winter
7 Royal Grove
Crook
Co Durham DL15 9ER
Tel: 01388 762538

Bishop Auckland & District Angling Club Ltd
J Winter
7 Royal Grove
Crook
Co Durham DL15 9ER
Tel: 01388 762538

Blackmoss Fishing Assn
John Dateson
23 Grove Street
Barrowford
Lancs BB9 8PW
Tel: 01282 697500

Blandford & District Angling Club
Peter Brundish
10 Windmill Road
Blandford
Dorset DT11 7HG
Tel: 01258 453545

Blenheim Angling Society
F W Lancaster
Briarwood, Burtons Lane
Chalfont St Giles
Bucks HP8 4BB
Tel: 01494 764977
Web: http://homepage.ntlworld.com/gordonstorey/blenheim/

Blunham Angling Club
Graham Palmer
5 Brockwell
Oakley
Beds MK43 7TD
Tel: 01234 823959

Bodmin Anglers' Assn
R Burrows
26 Meadow Place
Bodmin
Cornwall PL31 1JD
Tel: 01208 75513

Bognor Regis & Dist Freshwater Angling Club
Steven Tubb
15 Norman Way
Middleton-on-Sea
Bognor Regis
W Sussex PO22 7TW
Tel: 01243 585775
Web: www.brdfac.co.uk

Bolton & District Angling Assn
Terence A McKee
1 Lever Edge Lane
Great Lever
Bolton, Lancs BL3 3BU
Tel: 01204 393726

Boroughbridge & District Angling Club
c/o M Burgess
No 1 Bungalow
Littlethorpe Rd
Ripon

N Yorks HG4 1TZ
Tel: 01765 690715

Boston & District Angling Assn
(Affiliated local clubs: Lincolnshire Disabled Anglers, Coach & Horses AC, Wainfleet AC, Don's Saturday Club, Fishtoft AC, Horncastle AC, Lincs/Fenland Pike Club, Lindis AC, Louth & Dist AC, Napoleon AC, Orchard Park AC, RAF Coningsby AC, Riverside Tackle AC, Sibsey AC, Stickney AC, Unicorn AC)
Mrs Barbara Clifton
1 Kings Crescent
Boston
Lincs PE21 0AP
Tel: 01205 353302

Boston Spa Angling Club
A Waddington
The Cottage
17 The Village
Thorp Arch
Wetherby, Yorks.
LS23 7AR
Tel: 01937 842664

Bottesford & District Angling Assn
Brian Cross
12 The Square
Bottesford
Notts NG13 0EY
Tel: 01949 843164

Bowland Game Fishing Assn
John Ellithorn
3 Felton Way
Much Hoole
Preston PR4 4GD
Tel: 01772 613740

Boxmoor & District Angling Society
Mike Heylin
41 Crofts Path
Leverstock Green
Hemel Hempstead
Herts HP3 8HB
Tel: 01442 230925
Web: www.bdas.org

Bradford No 1 Angling Assn
Memb. Sec: J Sparks
12 Fairway Walk
Wibsey
Bradford BD7 4JW
Tel: 01274 578382
or
Hon Sec. H M Foster
8 Micklethwaite Drive
Queensbury
Bradford BD13 2JZ
Tel: 01274 881851

Bradford City Angling Assn
M Briggs

4 Brownhill Close
Birkinshaw BD11 2AS
Tel: 01274 684906
Brampton (Cambs) Angling Society
Kevin Medlock
1 Stanch Hill Rd
Sawtry, Huntingdon
Cambs PE28 5XG
Tel: 01487 830984
Brampton Angling Society
Bill Walton
6 Irthing Park
Brampton
Cumbria CA8 1EB
Tel: 016977 3698
Brandon & District Angling Club
Paul Macloughlin
43 The Paddocks
Brandon
Suffolk IP27 0DY
01842 812979
Bridgwater Angling Assn
M Pople
14 Edward Street
Bridgwater
Somerset TA6 5EU
Tel: 01278 422397
Brighouse Angling Assn
D W Noble
2 Penuel Place
Halifax
West Yorks HX3 9LB
Tel: 01422 383798
Web: www.bhaa.co.uk
Bristol, Bath & Wiltshire
Amalgamated Anglers (BB&WAA)
Jeff Parker
16 Lansdown View
Kingswood,
Bristol BS15 4AW
Tel: 0117 9672977
Bristol & West of England Federation
of Anglers
B Lloyd
386 Speedwell Road
By Kingswood
Bristol BS15 1ES
Tel: 0117 9676030
Brixham Sea Anglers' Society
Mike Bailey
5 Deep Dene Close
Brixham, Devon TQ5 0DZ

Tel: 01803 853252
Broome Angling Society
A Smith
10 Lords Avenue
Benskins Croft
Leicester LE4 2HX
Tel: 0116 2357210
Web: www.broomeanglingsociety.com
Brunswick Brothers Angling Society
Terry Taylor
40 St Andrews Road
Cranbrook
Ilford IG1 3PF
Tel: 020 8554 4600
Buckingham & District Angling
Assn
Mrs J Begley
2 The Dene
Steeple Claydon
Buckingham MK18 2PB
Tel: 01296 738637
Bude Canal Angling Assn
Brian Powell
B R Auto Spares
The Strand
Bude
Cornwall EX23 8RA
Tel: 01288 352755
Bungay Cherry Tree Angling Club
I Gosling
37 St Mary's Terrace
Flixton Road
Bungay
Suffolk NR35 1DW
Tel: 01986 892982
Burford Angling Club
Stephen Mattingley
c/o The Highway Hotel
117 High Street
Burford
Oxon OX8 4RG
Tel: 01993 822136
Burnley Angling Society
Hon Sec: Andrew Barron
via Roggerham Gate Inn
Todmorden Road
Brierclisse
Burnley BB10 3PQ
Tel: 01282 422039
Burrator Fly Fishers Assn
Richard Adney
192 Lipson Road

Fishing Clubs

When you appoint a new Hon. Secretary, do not forget to give us details of the change. Write to the
Publishers (address in the front of the book). Thank you!

Plymouth PL4 7NX
Tel: 01752 216788

Burton-on-Trent Mutual Angling Assn
D J Clark
7 Denton Rise
Burton-on-Trent
Staffordshire DE13 0QB
Tel: 01283 544734
Web: www.burtonmutual.co.uk

Burwash Angling Club
J Deeley
Red Tiles
Straight Mile
Etchingham TN19 7BA
Tel: 01580 819298

Bury St Edmunds Angling Assn
John Easdown
11 Fiske Close
Bury St Edmunds
Suffolk IP32 7LX
Tel: 01284 753602

Caersws Angling Assn
c/o 1 Bronierion Cottages
Llandinam
Powys SY17 5DF
Web: www.caersws-aa.co.uk

Caldy Anglers
Mary Day
50 Glenwood Drive
Irby CH61 4UH
Tel: 0151 648 4664

Calne Angling Assn
Miss J M Knowler
123A London Road
Calne
Wiltshire SN11 0AQ
Tel: 01249 812003

Cambridge Albion Angling Society
R Gentle
34 Ramsden Square
Cambridge CB4 2BL
Tel: 01223 426711

Cambridge Fish Preservation and Angling Society
G Tweed
27A Villa Road
Impington
Cambridge
Cambs CB4 9NZ
Tel: 01223 234616
Web: www.cambridge-fpas.co.uk

Cambridge Izaak Walton Society
Richard Cloke
16 Tamar Close
St Ives
Huntingdon PE27 3JE
Tel: 01480 464588

Canterbury & District Angling Assn
R D Barton
Riversdale
14 Mill Road
Sturry, Canterbury
Kent CT2 0AF
Tel: 01227 710830

Carlisle Angling Assn
G Proud
39 Borland Avenue
Carlisle CA1 2SY
Tel: 01228 401151

Carnforth Angling Assn
(not available as we go to press)

Castaways Angling Club
Huntly Lodge
Bordel Lane
Vale
Guernsey GY3 5DB
Tel: 01481 242309

Castle Angling Assn
Ray Gregory
38 Manor Park
Nether Heyford NN7 3NN
Tel: 01327 341 443
Web: www.castleaa.com

Central Assn of London & Provincial Angling Clubs (CALPAC)
Mrs D Wheeler
314 Old Lodge Lane
Purley, Surrey CR8 4AQ
Tel: 020 8660 2766
Web: www.calpac.info\

Chard & District Angling Assn
Alan Gage
31 Caraway Close
Chard
Som TA20 1HP
Tel: 01460 64055

Cheddar Angling Club
Trevor Harvey
Mulberry House
Barrows Road
Cheddar
Somerset BS27 3AY
Tel: 01934 743959

Chelmsford Angling Assn
Membership Secretary
61 Readers Court
Great Baddow
Chelmsford
Essex CM2 8EX
Tel: 01245 474246

Chester-le-Street & District Angling Club
G Curry
62 Newcastle Road
Chester-le-Street

Co Durham DH3 3UF
Tel: 0191 388 7072
Chichester & District Angling Society
Mrs C Luffman
28 Wellington Road
Bognor Regis
W Sussex PO21 2RR
Tel: 01243 829899
Chichester Canal Trading Ltd
John Cooper
Jaspers
Coney Road
East Wittering
Chichester
W Sussex PO20 8DA
Tel: 01243 671051
Chippenham Angling Club
J Duffield
95 Malmesbury Road
Chippenham
Wilts SN15 1PY
Tel: 01249 655575
or
Club HQ
Liberal Club
Gladstone Road
Chippenham
Christchurch Angling Club
John Cheetham
19b Willow Way
Christchurch
Hants BH23 1JJ
Tel: 01202 490014
Clanfield Angling Club
Doug Foreshew
117 Farmers Close
Witney
Oxon, OX28 1NR
Tel: 01993 200371
**Clevedon & District Freshwater
Angling Club**
A Law
3 Sunny Vale
Riverside Park
Clevedon
North Somerset BS21 7XB
Tel: 01275 544814
(see North Somerset AA)
Clitheroe Angling Assn
R S Eaves
3 Park Terrace
The Green
Wrea Green
Preston PR4 2WN
Tel: 01772 685779
Clive Vale Angling Club
Brian Christopher
40 Marine Court
St Leonards-on-Sea

E Sussex TN38 0DN
Tel: 01424 438987
Cockermouth Angling Assn
Ken Simpson
Tranby
Moor Road
Great Broughton
Cockermouth CA13 0XB
Tel: 01900 815523
Colchester Angling Preservation Society
Jean Masters
11 Enville Court
Highwoods
Colchester
Essex CO4 9NF
Tel: 01206 835187
Colchester Piscatorial Society
R J Moore
66 The Willows
Colchester
Essex CO2 8PX
Tel: 01206 766650
Collingham Angling Assn
June Wilson
93 Breamer Road
Collingham
nr Newark
Notts NG23 7PN
Tel: 01636 892700
Colnes Angling Society
Paul Emson
16 Station Road
Earls Colne
Colne Engaine
Colchester, Essex CO6 2ES
Tel: 01787 223331
Colwick Flyfishers
Kevin Saxton
35 Ivy Grove
Carlton
Nottingham NG4 1RG
Web: www.boat86.freeserve.co.uk
Congleton Angling Society
Neil Jellis
83 Derwent Close
Alsager
Stoke-on-Trent ST7 2 EL
Tel: 07754 797296
Coniston & Torver District Angling Assn
Bill Gibson
4 Barratt Croft
Coniston
Cumbria LA21 8DT
Tel: 015394 41887
Coopers Angling Club
John Dickens
2 Witchford Rd
Ely
Cambs CB6 3DP

Tel: 01353 663398
Cotterstock Angling Assn
Mrs Margaret Wing
Manor Farm Cottage
Cotterstock
Peterborough PE8 5HD
Tel: 01832 226340
Coventry & District Angling
Assn
John Hyde
1 Oak Tree Avenue
Green Lane
Coventry CV3 6DG
Tel: 024 764 18893
Crediton Fly Fishing Club
c/o 18 Cromwells Meadow
Crediton
Devon EX17 1JZ
Tel: 01363 777783
Web: www.fly-fishing-club.co.uk
Danby Angling Club
Roger Payne
30 West Lane, Danby
Whitby
N Yorks Y021 2LY
Tel: 01287 660607
Darfield Colliery Angling Club
15 Wilson St
Wombwell
nr Barnsley S73 8LR
Tel: 01226 211209
Darley Dale Fly Fishers Club
Jim Scully
86 Main Road
Gedling
Notts NG4 3HG
Tel: 0115 962 1590
Web: www.ddffc.net
Darlington Anglers Club
John Leighton
44 Low Coniscliffe
Darlington DL2 2JY
Tel: 01325 287307
Darlington Brown Trout Angling
Assn
E Willans
35 Chandos Street
Darlington
Tel: 07960 999441
Darlington Fly Fishers Club
J E D Brown
1 Baydale Farm Cottages
Coniscliffe Road
Darlington DL3 8TA
Tel: 01325 487999
Dart Angling Assn
D H Pakes
Holly How
Plymouth Road

South Brent
Devon TQ10 9HU
Dartford & District Angling
& Preservation Society
A J Curnick
Lake House
2 Walnut Tree Avenue
Wilmington
Kent DA1 1LJ
Tel: 01322 270397
Dartmouth Angling & Boating
Assn
Mrs Joan Porter
6 Church Close
Dartmouth
Devon TQ6 9DH
Tel: 01803 835830
Darwen Anglers' Assn
F W Kendall
45 Holden Fold
Darwen
Lancashire BB3 3AU
Tel: 01254 775501
Darwen Loyal Anglers
(not available as we go to press)
Dawley Angling Society
Mike Tuff
18 New Road
Dawley, Telford
Shropshire TF4 3LJ
Tel: 01952 590348
Deal & Walmer Angling
Assn
Mrs Pettit
Toby Jug
South Toll House
Beach Street
Deal CT14 6HZ
Tel: 01304 369917
Deal & Walmer Inshore
Fishermen's Assn
President; D Chamberlain
34 The Strand
Walmer, Deal
CT14 7DX
Tel: 01304 362744
Dean Clough & Ryburn AS
(see Ryburn & Halifax Angling Society)
Deanshanger & Stratford Angling
Assn
T Valentine
34 Mallets Close
Stony Stratford
Milton Keynes MK11 1DQ
Tel: 01908 565446
Deeping St James Angling Club
K W Allum
5 Conway Avenue
Walton

Peterborough PE4 6JD
Tel: 01733 577241

Derbyshire Angling Federation
Steve Clifton
8 Damside
Belper
Derbys DE56 1HZ
Tel: 01773 821582

Derbyshire County Angling Club
David T Holmes
12 Bakers Hill
Heage
Belper
Derbys DE56 2EL
Tel: 01773 856562
Web: www.derbyshirecountyac.org.uk

Dereham & District Angling Club
D Appleby
6 Rump Close
Swanton Morley
Norfolk NR20 4NH
Tel: 01362 637591

Dingle Fly Fishing Club
(enquire locally)

Doncaster & District Angling Assn
Jim J Taylor
Caretakers Bungalow
Sprotborough
Doncaster DN5 7SB
Tel: 01302 787506
Web: www.doncaster-and-district-angling-association.co.uk

Dorchester & District Angling Society
John Smith
11 Kings Road
Dorchester
Dorset DT1 1NH
Tel: 01305 268674

Dorchester Fishing Club
John Grindle
36 Cowleaze
Martinstown
Dorchester, Dorset DT2 9TD
Tel: 01305 889682
Web: www.grhe.co.uk

Dorking & District Angling Soc
c/o Andrew Fuller
28/32 South St
Dorking RH4 2HQ
Tel: 01306 882177
Web: www.dorkingas.co.uk

Durham City Angling Club
G Hedley
3 Hawthorn Crescent
Gilesgate Moor
Durham DH1 1ED
Tel: 0191 386 4603

Durweston Angling Assn
V T R Bell
Endcote
Durweston
Blandford, Dorset DT11 0QE
Tel: 01258 451317

Earl Manvers Angling Assn
G R Dennis
11 First Avenue
Carlton
Nottingham NG4 1PH
Tel: 0115 987 9994

Earls Barton Angling Club
R Line
9 New Street
Earls Barton
Northampton NN6 0NN
Tel: 01604 812059

East Hastings Sea Angling Club
The Stade
Hastings
East Sussex TN34 3PZ
Tel: 01424 430230

Eastbourne Angling Assn
The Club House
Royal Parade
Eastbourne
East Sussex BN22 7AA
Tel: 01323 723442

Eastleigh & District Angling Club
Hon Sec: Philip Clift
15 Goldfinch Lane
Lee on Solent
Hants PO13 8LN
Tel: 023 9235 9369
Web: www.eadac.org.uk
e-mail: phil.clift@ntlworld.com

Edenbridge Angling Society
H Fennell
22 Church Lane
Copthorne
W Sussex, RH10 3PT
Tel: 01342 713519

Egremont & District Angling Assn
Permit Sec: Neil Thompson
The Hatchery
Little Mill
Egremont
Cumbria CA22 2PR
Tel: 01946 823778

Ellesmere Angling Club
Kevan Busby
7 Penda's Park
Penley
Wrexham LL13 0NN
Tel: 01948 830695
or
Comrades Club
8 Victoria Street

Ellesmere SY12 0AB
Tel: 01691 622419

**Elm Park & Hornchurch District
Angling Society**
c/o Romside Social Club
Brooklands Lane
Romford
Essex RM7 7EA

**Ely Beet Sports & Social Club
Angling Club**
Paul Verdon
Lynn Rd
Ely
Cambs. CB6 1DD
Tel: 01353 662029

Ennerdale Lake Fisheries
Sam Laird
5 Churchill Drive
Moresby Parks
Whitehaven
Cumbria CA28 8UZ
Tel: 01946 694820

Entwhistle Flyfishers
I A Rigby
10 Wayoh Croft
Edgeworth
Bolton BL7 0DF
Tel: 01204 852049

Errwood Fly Fishing Club
T Speake: President
92 Grange Road
Bramhall
Stockport SK7 3QB
Tel: 0161 4397268

**Evesham & District Angling
Assn**
Howard Norledge
50 Coronation Street
Evesham
Worcs WR11 3DB
Tel: 01386 47776

Exeter & District Angling Assn
Rowley Palmer
4 Diamond Road
City Industrial
Exeter EX2 8DN
Tel: 01392 668935

Fakenham Angling Club
G Twite
16 Back Street
Hempton, Fakenham
Norfolk NR21 7LR

Farnborough & District Angling Society
K J Hankin
8 Fairview Road
Ash
Aldershot
Hants GU12 6AT
Tel: 01252 313082

Farnham Angling Society
M J Borra
The Creel
36 Station Road
Aldershot
Hants GU11 1HT
Tel: 01252 320871
Web: www.farnhamanglingsociety.co.uk

Faversham Angling Club
Nick Prior
1C St Nicholas Road
Faversham
Kent ME13 7PG
Tel: 01795 590824

Felixstowe Sea Angling Assn
End Manor Terrace
Felixstowe
Suffolk IP11 8EL
Web: www.fsas.org.uk
or
Hon Sec: R Leonard
5 Kersey Road
Felixstowe
Suffolk IP11 2UL
Tel: 01394 211779

Fenton & District Angling Society
Clifford Yates
5 Gatley Grove
Meir Park
Stoke-on-Trent
Staffs ST3 7SH
Tel: 01782 396913
Web: www.fentondas.co.uk

Ferryhill & District Angling Club
Hon Sec: B Hignett
74 Grasmere Road
Garden Farm Estate
Chester-le-Street
Co Durham DH2 3EU
Tel: 0191 388 3557

Filey Boat Angling Club
Terry Holmes
10 Queen Terrace
Filey
N Yorks YO14 9LR
Tel: 01723 514953

Filey Brigg Angling Society
Janine Robinson
168 West Road
Filey
N Yorks YO14 9NF
01723 514315

Flyfishers' Club
Commander T H Boycott OBE RN
69 Brook Street
London W1K 4ER
Tel: 020 7629 5958
(Private members club, no fishery)

Framlingham & District Angling Club
(not available as we go to press)
Friendly Angling Club
The Friendly Inn
Ovenden Road
Halifax
W Yorks HX3 5QG
Tel: 01422 365287
Frome & District Angling Assn
Garry Collinson
94 Nunney Road
Frome
Somerset BA11 4LD
Tel: 01373 465214
Gamefishers Club
Bob Jones
7 Durley Road
South Yardley
Birmingham B25 8EE
Tel: 0121 603 8017
**Gillingham & District
Angling Assn**
Simon Hebditch
30 Meadowcroft
New Road
Gillingham
Dorset
Tel: 01747 825931
Gipping Angling Preservation Society
Richard Young
126 Valley Road
Ipswich
Suffolk IP2 0PW
Tel: 01473 222240
Godalming Angling Society
M R Richardson
87 Summers Road
Farncombe, Godalming
Surrey GU7 3BE
Tel: 01483 422791
Web: godalminganglingsociety.co.uk
Goole & District Angling Assn
L Rogers
39 Clifton Gardens
Goole
E Yorks DN14 6AR
Tel: 01405 769096
Gosforth Angler's Club
G Thomas
11 Fell View Park
Gosforth
Seascale
Cumbria CA20 1HY
Tel: 019467 25367
Grafton Angling Assn
G D Williams
9 Edward Street
Worksop
Notts S80 1QP

Grantham Angling Assn
*(a member of East Midlands Angling
Federation that includes Boston, Oak-
ham, Newark, Ashfordby, Deeping St
James)*
S Shields
1 Hornsby Road
Grantham
Lincs NG31 7XD
Tel: 01476 576281
**Great Yarmouth & Norfolk County
Angling Assn**
K Ford
2 Parana Road
Sprowston
Norwich NR7 8BG
Tel: 01603 483923
Groe Park & Irfon Angling Club
J L Burton
Angle House
Pentrosfa Crescent
Llandrindod Wells, Powys LD1 5NW
Tel: 01597 822404 (day)
Tel: 01597 823119
Guernsey Mullet Club
M Weysom
6 La Cachette
Clos des Caches
St Martin
Guernsey GY4 6PL
Tel: 01481 237678
Hadleigh & District Angling Society
R T Catterall
Victory Cottage
Church Walk
Hadleigh
Ipswich IP7 5ED
Tel: 01473 822028
**Haltwhistle & District Angling
Assn**
Chris Wilson
Melkridge House, Melkridge
Haltwhistle
Northumberland NE49 0LT
Tel: 01434 320942
**Harleston, Wortwell & District Angling
Club**
Geoff Doggett
68 Pilgrims Way
Harleston
Norfolk IP20 9QE
Tel: 01379 853464
Hartlepool & Dist Angling Club
A Wilkinson
52 Brigandine Close
Seaton Carew
Hartlepool TS25 1ET
Tel: 01429 866880

Harwich Angling Club
John Pettitt
211 Main Road
Dovercourt
Harwich
Essex CO12 3PJ
Tel: 01255 508625
Web: www.harwichac.co.uk

Haslingden & District Fly Fishing Club
W Monk
6 Ryde Close
Haslingden
Rossendale BB4 6QR
Tel: 01706 211724

**Hastings & St Leonards Angling
Assn**
Marine Parade
Hastings
East Sussex TN34 3AG
Tel: 01424 431923

**Hastings, Bexhill & District Freshwater
Angling Assn**
Alan Carter
156 Ninfield Road
Bexhill-on-Sea TN39 5BD
Tel: 01424 223234

Hastings Flyfishers' Club Ltd
Capt D E Tack
Ogwen
23 Wealden Way, Little Common
nr Bexhill-on-Sea
E. Sussex TN39 4NZ
Tel: 01424 843957
Web: www.hastingsflyfishers.co.uk

**Hawes & High Abbotside Angling
Assn**
G Phillips
Holmlands, Appersett
Hawes
North Yorks DL8 3LN
Tel: 01969 667362

Hawkshead Anglers
David Barry
Esthwaite View Caravan Park
Hawkshead, Ambleside
Cumbria LA22 0QA
Tel: 015394 36506
(Limited to 100 members; 20 juniors)

Hay-on-Wye Fishermen's Assn
not available as we go to press

**Haywards Heath & District Angling
Society**
Peter Parr
61 Meadow Lane
Lindfield
West Sussex RH16 2RL
Tel: 01444 482009
Web: www.hhdas.co.uk

Hebden Bridge Angling Club
C Neil Pickles
17 Underbank Avenue
Hebden Bridge
West Yorks HX7 6PP
Tel: 01422 843309

Helperby & Brafferton Angling Club
F Marrison
Gardener's Cottage
Helperby, York
North Yorks YO6 2PQ
Tel: 01423 360632

Hereford & District Angling Assn
P O Box 35
Hereford

Herne Bay Angling Assn
Honorary Secretary
c/o HQ, 59 Central Parade
Herne Bay
Kent CT6 5JG
Tel: 01227 362127
Web: www.hbaa.co.uk

Hertford Angling Club
Chris Bite
12 Stafford Drive
Broxbourne
Herts EN10 7JT
Tel: 01992 467585

Histon & District Angling Society
Colin Dodd
122 Rampton Road
Willingham
Cambs CB4 5JF
Tel: 01954 260365

**Holmesdale Angling & Conservation
Society**
Mrs J Sivyer
28 Brigstock Road
Belvedere
Kent DA17 6DP
Tel: 01322 437766
Web: www. holmesdale.acs.btinternet.
co.uk

Holme Valley Piscatorial Assn
P Budd
39 Derwent Road
Honley, Holmfirth
Yorkshire HD9 6EL
Tel: 01484 662058

Horncastle Angling Assn
Lorraine Hassall
21 Low Toynton Road
Horncastle
Lincs LN9 9LL
Tel: 01507 527420

Horsham & District Angling Assn
PO Box 22
Horsham
West Sussex RH12 5YT

Web: www.hdaa.supanet.com
or
G Hillman (address as above)
Tel: 01403 271855
Horwick & District Fly Fishing Club
Patricia Unsworth
4 Old Swan Close
Egerton
Bolton, Lancs BL7 9UW
Tel: 01204 591905
Hull & District Angling Assn
W Brame
P O Box 188
Hull HU9 1AN
**Huntingdon Angling & Fish
Preservation Society**
Miss Anne M Wallis
8 Clayton's Way
Huntingdon
Cambs PE29 1UT
Tel: 01480 458935
Huttons Ambo Angling Club
Paul Thompson
Firby Hall
Firby
Yorks YO6 7LH
**Idle & Thackley Angling
Assn**
Charles Taylor Hardaker
24 Park Avenue
Thackley
Bradford
West Yorks BD10 0RJ
Tel: 01274 615016
Web: www.idleandthackaa.supanet.com
Ilkley & Dist Angling Assn
B Moore
6 North Croft Grove
Ilkley LS29 9BB
Tel: 01943 604653
Isfield and Dist Angling Club
Mrs M Walter
3 Dene Path
Manor Park
Uckfield
East Sussex TN22 1LY
Tel: 01825 762385
**Isle of Man Fly Fishing
Assn**
Ray Caley: President
Caley's Stores
Sulby
Isle of Man IM7 2HR
Tel: 01624 897205
**Isle of Wight Freshwater Angling
Assn**
R J Kirby
125 Furrlongs
Newport

Isle of Wight PO30 2BD
Tel: 01983 529617
Web: www.isleofwight-fishing-uk.co.uk
Jolly Anglers
Jeremy Denton
6 Trenchard Close
Wallingford
Oxon. OX10 9BA
Tel: 01491 834769
Keighley Angling Club
Treasurer/Secretary
D Freeman
62 Eel Holme
View Street
Beechcliffe
Keighley
West Yorks BD20 6AY
Tel: 01535 663695
Kelvedon & District Angling Assn
Brian Pike
11 Keene Way
Galleywood
Chelmsford CM2 8NT
Tel: 01245 262545
Web: www.kdaa.co.uk
Kempston Angling Club
(now merged with Vauxhall AC)
K Green
24 The Elms
Kempston
Beds MK42 7JW
Tel: 01234 854165
Kent (Westmorland) Angling Assn
C T Preston
Yewtree House
Underbarrow
Kendal LA8 8AY
Web: www.kentangling.co.uk
Keswick Angling Assn
Mike Tinnion
50 Latrigg Close
Keswick
Cumbria CA12 4LG
Tel: 017687 72127
**Kettering, Thrapston & District
Angling Assn**
Mike Cardy
17 Thurston Drive
Kettering
Northants NN15 6GN
Tel: 01536 518178
**Kidderminster & District Angling
Assn**
M Millinchip
246 Marlpool Lane
Kidderminster
Worcs DY11 5DD
Tel: 01562 753471

Kilnsey Angling Club
Edward Wood
Moorside House
Union Lane
Ogden
Halifax, W Yorks HX2 8XP
Tel: 01422 244720

King's Lynn Angling Assn
Mick R Grief
67 Peckover Way
South Woonton
King's Lynn
Norfolk PE30 3UE
Tel: 01553 671545

Kirkby Lonsdale & District Angling Assn
David Halton
77 Fairgarth Drive
Kirkby Lonsdale
Carnforth LA6 2FB
Tel: 015242 71069

Kirkby Fleetham Angling Club
M L Smith
26 Eden Grove
Newton Aycliffe
Co Durham DL5 7JG
Tel: 01325 312843

Kirkby Stephen & District Angling Assn
Anthony Kilvington
Market Square
Kirky Stephen
Cumbria CA17 4QT
Tel: 017683 71495

Kirkham & District Fly Fishers' Club
D Wardman
65 Longhouse Lane
Poulton-le-Fylde
Lancashire FY6 8DE
Tel: 01253 883993

Knaresborough Piscatorials
M Craven
77 Kingsley Road
Harrogate
N Yorks HG1 4RD
Tel: 0780 1429797
or
Memb Sec: M Johnson
2 Briggate
Knaresborough
N Yorks HG5 8BH
Tel: 01423 863065

Knightley Angling Club
c/o The Knightley Arms
49 High street
Yelvertoft
NN6 6LF
Tel: 01788 822401

Lamorbey Angling Society
Membership Officer

PO Box 56
Sidcup
DA15 9ZQ

Lancashire Fly-Fishing Assn
J P Shorrock
Plane Tree House
Lomas Lane
Balladen
Rossendale
BB4 6HH

Langport & District Angling Assn
Dennis Barlow
'Florissant'
Northfield
Somerton
Somerset TA11 6SJ
Tel: 01458 272119
Web: www.langportaa.com

Lanhydrock Angling Assn
B Muelaner
The National Trust Estate Office
Lanhydrock Park
Bodmin
Cornwall PL30 4DE
Tel: 01208 265211

Lark Angling Preservation Society
E T West
8 Arrowhead Drive
Lakenheath
Brandon
Suffolk IP27 9JN
Tel: 01842 861369

Lee & Heys Angling Club
Nigel Bunn
4 Hey Crescent
Lees
Oldham
Lancs OL4 3LJ
Tel: 0161 626 9183

Lee Anglers' Consortium
Memb Sec: Dennis Meadhurst CPFA
P O Box 19426
London
E4 8UZ
Tel: 020 8524 7270
Hertford to Feildes Weir: Bailiff
Dave Anderson: 07931 521917
Cheshunt to Bow Lock: Bailiff
Tom Rowley: 07931 521916

Leeds & District Amalgamated Anglers Assn
Graham Park
75 Stoney Rock Lane
Beckett Street
Leeds
West Yorks LS9 7TB
Tel/fax: 0113 248 2373

Leek & Moorlands Angling Club
Roy Birch-Machin
53 Novi Lane
Leek
Staffs ST13 6NX
Tel: 01538 371128

Leicester & District Amalgamated Society of Anglers
Dave Tasker
2Curlew Close
Syston
Leicester LE7 1XA
Tel: 0116 2607525

Leigh & District Angling Assn
A Gornall
Tel (mob): 0788 990 6080

Leighton Buzzard Angling Club
Brian Smalley
102 Heath Rd
Leighton Buzzard
Beds LU7 3AD
Tel: 01525 379099

Letchworth Garden City Angling Assn
Memb Sec: Malcolm Theakstone
36a Broadwater Avenue
Letchworth
Herts SG6 3HF
Tel: 01462 620448
Web: www.letchworthangling.org.uk

Lewisham Piscatorials Assn
D J Head
75 Riverview Park
Catford
London SE6 4PL
Tel: 020 8690 4603

Lifford Angling Club
P Taylor
e-mail: Petetaylor@connectfree.co.uk

Lincoln & District Angling Assn
Colin W Parker
4 Pottergate Close
Waddington
Lincoln LN5 9LY
Tel: 01522 720777

Liskeard & District Angling Club
W H Eliot
64 Portbyhan Road
West Looe
Cornwall PL13 2QN
Tel: 01503 264173

Littleport Angling Club
David Yardy
168 High Barns
Ely
Cambs CB7 4RP
Tel: 01353 669323

Liverpool & District Angling Assn
Chairman: Jo Farrell
10 Windermere Drive
Maghull
Liverpool
Merseyside L31 9BQ
Tel: 07764 926643

Llandrindod Wells Angling Assn
B D Price
The Cedars
Llanyre
Llandrindod Wells
Powys LD1 6DY
Tel: 01597 823539

London Anglers' Assn
A E Hodges, FIFM
Izaak Walton House
2A Hervey Park Road
Walthamstow
London E17 6LJ
Tel/Fax: 020 8520 7477
Web: www.londonanglers.net
e-mail: admin@londonanglers.net

Long Buckby Angling Club
M Hill
33 South Close
Long Buckby
Northants NN6 7PX
Tel: 01327 843091

Long Eaton & District Angling Federation
D Neale
16 Staunton Close
Castle Donington
Derby DE74 2XA
Tel: 01332 814122

Long Eaton Victoria Angling Society
D L Kent
2 Edge Hill Court
Fields Farm
Long Eaton
Notts, NG10 1PQ
Tel: 0115 849 2854

Long Melford & District Angling Assn
N Mealham
6 Springfield Terrace
East Street
Sudbury
Suffolk CO10 2TS
Tel: 01787 377139

Lonsdale Angling Club
G Parkinson
30 Chequers Avenue
Lancaster LA1 4HZ

Looe Angling Club
The Quay
E Looe
Cornwall PL13 1DX
Tel: 01503 263337

Lostwithiel Fishing Assn
R Lashbrook
Roger's Tackle Shop, Stan May's Store
Higher Bore Str
Bodmin PL31 1DZ
Tel: 01208 78006

Loughborough Soar Angling Society
Stan Sharpe
25 Rupert Brooke Road
Loughborough
Leicester LE11 4NJ
Tel: 07702 305132

Lowestoft Sea Angling Society
57 Lorne Park Road
Lowestoft
Suffolk NR33 0RB
Tel: 01502 581943

Luton Angling Club
Chairman: D W Edwards
4 Stratton Gardens
Luton
Beds LU2 7DS
Tel: 01582 728114
Web: www.lutonac.org

Lydney Angling Club
(not available as we go to press)

Lymington & District Sea Fishing Club
Mrs G Moody
'Gina-Mia'
Hundred Lane, Portmore
Lymington
Hants SO41 5RG
Tel: 01590 674962

Lymm Angling Club
Neil Jupp
P O Box 350
Warrington WA2 9FB
Tel: 01925 411774
Web: www.lymmanglers.net

Macclesfield Flyfishers' Club
John Harrison
20 Ryles Park Road
Macclesfield SK11 8AH
Tel: 01625 263312

Macclesfield Waltonian Angling Society
Michael E Bowyer
7 Ullswater
Macclesfield
Cheshire SK11 7YN
Tel: 01625 434806
Web: www.waltonians.co.uk

Maidstone Victory Angling & Medway Preservation Society
J Perkins
33 Hackney Road
Maidstone
Kent ME16 8LN
Tel: 01622 202686

Maldon Angling Society
David Spalding
Rustling Oaks
Field View Drive
Little Totham
Essex CM9 8ND
Tel: 01621 892197
Web: www.maldonas.co.uk

Malton & Norton Angling Club
S Peel
19 Leahurst Close
Norton, Malton
Yorks YO17 9DF
Tel: 01653 692824

Mansfield & District Angling Assn
John Smith
16 Holmwood Road
Rainworth
Mansfield NG21 0HT

Manx Game Fishing Club
P O Box 95
2A Lord Street
Douglas
Isle of Man

Marazion Angling Club
Newtown Angling Centre
Newtown
Germoe
Penzance TR20 9AE
Tel: 01736 763721
e-mail internettackle@hotmail.com

Marconi Angling Society
Andrew Allen
58 Roxwell Avenue
Chelmsford
Essex CM1 2NX
Tel: 01245 260807

Marlborough & District Angling Assn
Malcolm Ellis
Failte Elcot Close
Marlborough SN8 2BB
Tel: 01672 512922
Web: www.marlboroughangling.co.uk

Marlow Angling Club
Carol Wise
4 Beaconsfield Cottages
Cores End Road
Bourne End, Bucks SL8 5HW
Tel: 01628 532588
Web: www.communigate.co.uk/bucks/

marlowanglingclub

Marsden Star Angling Society
Jeff Hartley
3 Duerden Street
Nelson
Lancs BB9 9BJ
Tel 01282 603362

Martham & District Angling Club
Kevin Poole
9 Pine Close
Martham
Gt Yarmouth
Norfolk NR29 4SG
Tel: 01493 748307

Medway Victory Angling & Medway Preservation Society
John Perkins
33 Hackney Rd
Maidstone
Kent ME16 8LN
Tel: 01622 202686

Medlock Bridge Angling Club
N Naum
23 Winchester Avenue
Chadderton
Oldham
Lancs, OL9 0RH
Tel: 01616 787626

Middlesbrough Angling Club
R Thompson
25 Endsleigh Drive
Acklam, Middlesbrough
Cleveland TS5 4RG
Tel: 01642 863067

Middlewich Joint Anglers
Colin Wyatt
12 Darlington Street
Middlewich
Cheshire CW10 9AJ
Tel: 01606 832257

Midland Angling Society
J Bradbury
19 Ethel Avenue
Hucknall
Notts NG15 8DB
Tel: 0115 9634487

Mid-Ribble Angling Society
J W Whitham
Pendleside
58 Lingmoor Drive
Burnley BB12 8UY
Tel: 01282-411340
Web: www.midribble.co.uk

Mildenhall Angling Club
M Hampshire
63 Downing Close
Mildenhall
Suffolk IP28 7PB
Tel: 01638 718205

Millom & District Angling Assn
D J Dixon
1 Churchill Drive
Millom
Cumbria LA18 5DD
Tel: 01229 774241

Milton Keynes Angling Assn
Trevor Johnson
52 Jenkinson Road
Towcester
NN12 6AW
Tel: 01908 270000
Web: www.mkaa.co.uk

Montgomeryshire Angling Assn
Bernie Jones
13 Maesowen
Welshpool
Powys SY21 7QY
Tel: 01938 554971

Moor Hall & Belhus Angling Society
Dave Dix
1 Arne Close
Stanford-le-Hope
Essex SS17 8QP
Tel: 01375 360999

National Coal Board No5 Area FC
Michael Webster
27 Ashforth Avenue
Marlpool, Heanor
Derbyshire DE75 7NH
Tel: 01773 719745

Newark & District Piscatorial Federation
J N Garland
58 Riverside Road
Newark
Notts NG24 4RJ
Tel: 01636 702962

Newhaven Deep Sea Angling Club
Denton Island
Newhaven
East Sussex BN9 9BA
Tel: 01273 517330

Newport Pagnell Fishing Assn
R D Dorrill
7 Bury Street
Newport Pagnell
Milton Keynes MK16 0DS
Tel: 01908 610639

Newton Abbot Fishing Assn
Adam Bojar
19 Kiln Road
Bovey Tracey
Newton Abbot
Devon TQ13 9YJ
Tel: 01626 834032
Web: www.newtonfishing.com

Nidderdale Angling Club
T Harpham
P O Box 7
Pateley Bridge, nr Harrogate
North Yorks HG3 5XB
Web: www.nidderdaleac.co.uk

Norfolk & Suffolk Flyfishers Club
Chairman: Derek Armes
100 Cozens Hardy Road
Norwich NR7 8QQ
Tel: 01603 423169

Northallerton Angling Club
Dick Wright
5 Lascelles Lane
Northallerton
North Yorks DL6 1EP
Tel: 01609 776850

Northampton Britannia Angling Club
G H Richmond
34 Ilex Close
Hardingstone
Northampton NN4 6DS
Tel: 01604 760021

Northampton Nene Angling Club
Maggie Petch
38 Grangewood
East Hunsbury
Northampton NN4 0QN
Tel: 01604 705205
e-mail: petch4fish@aol.com
Web: www.northamptonneneangling club.co.uk

Northern Anglers' Assn
Gerry Wilson
11 Guildford Avenue
Chorley
Lancs PR6 8TG
Tel: 01257 249372

North Oxford Angling Society
Andrew Crisp
4 Grove Street
Summertown
Oxford OX2 7JT
Tel: 01865 553800

North Somerset Assn of Anglers
(Embracing Highbridge & Clevedon clubs)
R Newton
64 Clevedon Road
Tickenham

Clevedon
Somerset BS21 6RD
Tel: 01275 856107

Northumbrian Anglers' Federation
Alan Bagnall
Thirston Mill
West Thirston
Felton
Morpeth
Northumberland NE65 9EH
Tel: 01670 787663
Web: www.northumbriananglersfed. co.uk

North West Durham Angling Assn
L F Owens
Aarhus
View Lane
Stanley
Co Durham DH9 0DX
Tel: 07759 140895

Northwich Angling Assn
62 Station Road
Northwich
Cheshire CW9 5RB
Tel: 01606 350751

Norwich & District Anglers Assn
C Wigg
3 Coppice Avenue
Norwich NR6 5RB
Tel: 01603 423625

Nottingham Anglers' Assn
David Turner
3a Beckhampton Road
Bestwood Park
Nottingham NG5 5SP
Tel: 0115 9199500
Web: www.nottinghamanglers.co.uk

Nottingham & District Federation of Angling Societies
William Belshaw
17 Spring Green
Clifton Estate
Nottingham NG11 9EF

Nottingham Piscatorial Society
Ernest Jolly
Chesil Bank
Shaw Street
Mansfield
Notts NG18 2NP
Tel: 01623 470124

Offord & Buckden Angling Society
John Astell

Fishing Clubs

When you appoint a new Hon. Secretary, do not forget to give us details of the change. Write to the Publishers (address in the front of the book). Thank you!

154 Eastrea Road
Whittlesey
Cambs PE7 2AJ
Tel: 01733 350919
Oldham Fly Fishers Club
N Lambert
39 Elmpark Way
Rochdale
OL12 7JQ
Oldham United Anglers
J K Lees
10 Packwood Chase
Chadderton
Oldham OL9 0PG
Tel: 0161 624 5176
Old Windsor Angling Club
Alan Beaven
88 St Andrews Way
Slough
Berks SL1 5LJ
Tel: 01628 602537
Oundle Angling Assn
Roger Lee
41 New Road
Oundle
Peterborough PE8 4LE
Tel: 01832 274010
Ouse Angling Preservation Society
Permit Sec: Andrew Woolley
14 The Martlets
Mill Lane
South Chailey
E Sussex BN8 4QG
Tel: 01273 891312
Web: www.oaps.freeuk.com
Over & Swavesey District Anglers
Society
D Cook
75 Willingham Road
Over
Cambs CB4 5PE
Tel: 01954 230076
Oxford & District Anglers Assn
Hon Sec: J D Rayner
Cotmore House
Rycote Lane
Thame OX9 2JB
Tel: 01844 216866
Web: www.odaa.net
Padstow Sea Angling Club
Social Club
Padstow
Cornwall
Paignton Sea Anglers' Assn
Hpn Sec: Tony Deaks
Clubhouse "Ravenswood"
26 Cliff Rd
Paignton
Devon TQ4 6DH

Tel: 01803 553118
Web: www.daba.eclipse.co.uk/
Park Angling Club
M Kelly
14 Sycamore Close
Wellington
Telford
Salop TF1 3NH
Tel: 01952 244272
Parkside Fishing Club
D Fallows
27 Woodstock Avenue
Radford
Nottingham NG7 5QP
Tel: 01159 787350
**Peak Forest Angling Club
(Derbyshire)**
Colin Jones
1 Willow Croft
Hope Road
Bamford
Hope Valley
Derbys S33 0AL
Tel: 01433 659909
Pennington Flash Angling Assn
Ken Buxton
22 Hope Carr Lane
Leigh WN7 3XA
Tel: 01942 517610
Penrith Angling Assn
Andrew Dixon
3 Newtown Cottages
Skirwith
Penrith, Cumbria CA10 1RJ
Tel: 01768 88294
Peterborough Angling Club
Lindsay Horseman
21 Carron Drive
Werrington
Peterborough PE4 6NX
Tel: 01733 575606
Petersfield & District Angling Club
(member of Hants & Sussex Alliance)
Graham Hodges
6 Beechwood Court
Liss
Hants GU33 7TZ
Tel: 01730 894863
Petworth Angling Club
Steve Jupp
172 Hawthorn Road
Bognor Regis
W Sussex PO21 2UY
Tel: 01243 821950
Pewsey & District Angling Club
D Underwood
51 Swan Meadow
Pewsey
Wilts SN9 5HP

Tel: 01672 562541
Plymouth & District Freshwater Angling Assn
D L Owen
39 Burnett Road
Crownhill
Plymouth PL6 5BH
Tel: 01752 705033
Portsmouth & District Angling Society
(part of Hants and Sussex Alliance)
Dave Coombs
122 Stebbington Avenue
North End
Portsmouth PO2 0JL
Tel: 02392 792461
Practical Angling for the Disabled Angling Club (PAD Angling Club)
Barry Poxon
Park Cottage, The Park
London Rd
Shardlow
Derby DE72 2GP
Tel: 01332 799086
e-mail (bailiff): angler@cwcom.net
Pride of Derby Angling Assn Ltd
Alan Miller
16 Mercia Drive
Willington
Derby DE65 6DA
Tel: 01283 702701
Web: www.prideofderby.co.uk
Prince Albert Angling Society
Hon Sec: J A Turner
15 Pexhill Drive
Macclesfield
Cheshire SK10 3LP
Tel: 01625 422010
or
Memb Sec: C Swindells
37 Sherwood Road
Macclesfield
Cheshire SK11 7RR
Priory Angling Club
Brian Ponting
157 St Mary's Road
Tetbury GL8 8BY
Tel: 01666 503605
Pulborough Angling Society
Mick Booth
5 South Lane
Houghton
Arundel
W Sussex BN18 9LN
Tel: 01798 831525
Web: www.pulboroughas.com
Radcot Angling Club
Paul Tinson
9 Thorpesfield

Alvescot
Oxfordshire OX18 2QF
Tel: 01993 841645
Ramsey Angling Club (Cambs)
Match Sec: Keith Rayment
27 Princes Street
Ramsey
Cambs PE26 1JW
Tel: 01487 814077
Ramsey Angling Club (I.O.M.)
Chairman: Chris Culshaw
Parkhill
Coburg Road
Ramsey
Isle of Man IM8 3EH
Tel: 01624 812279
Reading & District Angling Assn
A C Hughes
217 Beech Lane
Earley
Reading RG6 5UP
Tel 0118 9867 430
Web: www.rdaa.co.uk
Red Scar Angling Assn
Sid Morley
2 Maple Grove
Grimsargh
Preston PR2 5LP
Tel: 01772 653123
Red Spinner Angling Society
R Keys
226 Churchgate Road
Cheshunt
Herts. EN8 9EQ
Tel: 01992 622131
Retford & District Angling Assn
H Wells
31 Ainsdale Green
Ordsall
Retford, Notts DN22 7NQ
Tel: 01777 702227
Rhayader & District Angling Assn
David Davis
Galedrhyd
Elan Valley
nr Rhayader
Powys LD6 5HD
Tel: 01597 811306
Ribble & Wyre Fisheries Assn
S A Gray
18 Lord Street
Wigan
Lancs WN1 2BN
Tel: 01942 321008
Ribbledale Angling Assn
Fred Higham
99 Waddington Road
Clitheroe BB7 2HN
Tel: 01200 423314

Web: www.ribblesdaleangling.co.uk
Ribchester & District Angling Club
D Harwood
The Fold
15 Smithy Row
Hurst Green
Clitheroe BB7 9QA
Tel: 01254 826252
or
HQ: Ribchester Sports & Social Club
Church St
Ribchester
Lancs.
Richmond (Yorks) & District Angling Society
P Bennett
1 Theakston Lane
Richmond
N Yorks DL10 4LL
Tel: 01748 824894.
Ringwood & District Angling Club
Peter Hutchinson
Cornerways Cottage
Gorley Road, Poulner
Ringwood, Hants BH24 3RB
Tel: 01425 476415
Web: www.ringwoodfishing.co.uk
Ripon Angling Club
Roger Trees
43 College Road
Ripon
N Yorks HG4 2HE
Tel: 01765 602277
Ripon Fly Fishers
C J Clarke
6 Church Close
Sharow
Ripon
N Yorks HG4 5BL
Tel: 01765 601677
Ripon Piscatorial Assn
Colin Mackay
20a Skell Villas
Wellington Street
Ripon
North Yorks HG4 1PH
Tel: 01765 601142
Rochdale Walton Angling Society
Adrian Clarkson: Treasurer
39 Vicarage Road North
Rochdale
Lancs, OL11 2TF
Tel: 01706 656452
Rochford Angling Club
L Dorey
231 Kents Hill Road
Benfleet
Essex SS7 5PS
Tel: 01268 752610

Ross-on-Wye Angling Club
Terry Gibson
10 Redwood Close
Ross-on-Wye
Herefordshire HR9 5UD
Tel: 01989 567775
Rother Angling Club
C Boxall
Innisfree
Ashfield Road
Midhurst
West Sussex GU29 9JX
Tel: 01730 813885
Rother Fishery Assn
Vince Gould
1 All Saints Road
Hawkhurst
Kent
Tel: 01580 754898
Royal Leamington Spa Angling Assn
Match Sec: Pauline Haynes
2 Cassandra Grove
Heathcote
Warwick CV34 6XD
Tel: 01926 424491
Web: www.leamingtonangling.co.uk
Rudgwick Angling Society
Peter Connett
11 Greenfields Road
Horsham
West Sussex RH12 4JL
Tel: 01403 217678
Rushden & Higham Ferrers Irchester Angling Assn
John Boswell
49 Washbrook Road
Rushden
Northants NN10 9UY
Tel: 01933 313039
Royal Tunbridge Wells Angling Society
Ronald Mott
1 Lucas Close
East Grinstead RH19 3YG
Tel: 01342 324718
Web: www.beehive.courier.co.uk/ang
ling grtwas
Ryburn & Halifax Angling Society (prev. Dean Clough & Ryburn AS)
T Hooson
4 Chester Terrace
Boothtown
Halifax
West Yorks HX3 6LT
Tel: 01422 345447 (day)
Tel: 01422 344223 (evenings)
Saddleworth & District Angling Club
Chairman: J Stanford

2 Wharmton View
Greenfield
Oldham OL3 7JU
Tel: 01457 875200
St Helens Angling Assn
Les Bramilow
4 Bassenthwaite Avenue
St Helens
Merseyside WA11 7AB
Tel: 01744 601287
St Helens Ramblers Angling Society
Alec Twiss
71 Sherdley Road
St Helens
WA9 5AD
Tel: 01744 611670
**St Ives & District Fish Preservation
& Angling Society**
H Pace
48 Fairfields
St Ives
Cambs PE27 5QF
Tel: 01480 469254
St Mawgan Angling Club
Chairman: T J Trevenna
Lanvean House
St Mawgan, Newquay
Cornwall TR8 4EY
Tel: 01637 860316
**St Neots & District Angling & Fish
Preservation Society**
Mrs D Linger
Skewbridge Cottage
Great PaxtoSt Neots
Huntingdon
Cambs PE19 4RA
**Salcombe & District Sea Anglers'
Assn**
Kings Arms
Salcombe
Devon TQ8 8BU
Tel: 01548 842202
Salisbury & District Angling Club
Secretary
29a Castle Street
Salisbury
Wilts SP1 1TT
Tel: 01722 321164
Web: www.salisburydistrictac.co.uk
**Sandwich & District Angling
Assn**
J Heyburn
15 Fords Hill
Cliffsend
Ramsgate
Kent CT12 5EL
Tel: 01843 590510
Sawbridgeworth Angling Society
A Vidler

11 The Orchards
Sawbridgeworth
Herts CM21 9BB
Tel: 01279 724444
Saxmundham Angling Club
Barbara Wilson
15 Walpole Road
Bramfield
Halesworth
Suffolk IP19 9AB
Tel: 01986 784317
**Scunthorpe & District Angling
Assn**
M Storey
12 Mill Close
Scawby Brook
Brigg
North Lincs
DN20 9LL
Tel (mob): 077 177 48523
Sedbergh Angling Assn
Lee Dandy
Ellerthwaite
Buckbank Lane
Sedbergh
Cumbria LA10 5LL
Tel: 015396 21500
or
Hon Visitors Sec: C S Dandy
Brookfield
Cautley Rd
Sedbergh
Cumbria LA10 5LG
Tel: 015396 20092
Selsey Angling & Tope Club
Mike Bell: President
19 Littlefield Close
Selsey
West Sussex PO20 0DZ
Tel: 01243 607998
Services Dry Fly Fishing Assn
Major C D Taylor
c/o HQ 43 (WX) BDE
Picton Barracks
Bulford Camp
Salisbury SP4 9NY
Tel: 01980 672161
Seven Angling Club
Mrs B J Stansfield
Sun Seven
Sinnington
Yorks YO62 6RZ
Severnside Angling Club
Steven Potts
902 Falcon Court
Newtown SY16 1LQ
Tel: 01686 624871
**Sheffield & District Anglers'
Assn**

Irving Street
Sheffield
South Yorks S9 4RF
Tel: 0114 244 6700
Shefford & District Angling Assn
J Leath
3 Ivel Close
Shefford
Beds SG17 5JX
Tel: 01462 812323
Skenfrith Angling Society
Andy Holloway
2 Mount Pleasant
St Weonards
Hereford HR2 8PH
Tel: 01981 580387
Skipton Angling Assn
M L Mawson
6 Lytham Close
Skipton
N Yorks BD23 2LF
Tel: 01756 794022
Slaithwaite & District Angling Club
D Rushforth
122 Longwood Gate
Longwood
Huddersfield
HD3 4US
Tel: 01484 651028
South Cerney Angling Club
M Vines
Fishermans Rest
Broadway Lane
South Cerney
Cirencester GL7 5UH
Southdown Angling Assn
(amalgamation of Compleat Angler FC and Hailsham AA)
Geoff Begley
Polegate Angling Centre
101 Station Road
Polegate
E Sussex BN26 6EB
Tel: 01323 486379
Web: www.southdown-angling.org
Southern Anglers
Mrs Mary Hamilton
22 Fern Close
Petersfield
Hants
Tel: 01730 301354
Southsea Sea Angling Club
c/o 42 Granada Road
Southsea
Hants PO4 0RG
Tel: 023 92825508
South Somerset Anglers Federation
(Amal of Yeovil & Sherborne AC, Mud-
ford AC, Ilchester AC, Stoke-sub-Ham-
don AC)
Chairman: Keith Hodder
53 Sycamore Drive
Yeovil
Som BA20 2NQ
Tel: 01935 427046
Stalbridge Angling Society
T Seamark
20 The Meads
Milborne Port
Somerset
Tel: 01963 250856
Stamford Welland Amalgamated Anglers Assn
G J Money
7 Florence Way
Market Deeping
Lincs PE6 8PG
Tel: 01778 380245
Stanhope Angling Assn
David Reay
Bondisle Way
Stanhope
Bishop Auckland
Co Durham DL13 2YU
Tel: 01388 526267
Stockport & District Anglers Federation
Carl Kay
18 Pickmere Terrace
Dukinfield
Cheshire SK14 2BX
Tel: 0161 355 1058
Stockton Angling Assn
S R Targett
19 Tofts Close
Low Worsall
Yarm
TS15 9QA
Tel: 01642 781825
Web: www.stocktonanglingassociation.
co.uk
Stoke-on-Trent Angling Society
A Perkins
Muirhearlich
Fowlers Lane
Light Oaks
Stoke on Trent, ST2 7NB
Tel: 01782 541500
Web: www.sotangling.com
Stoke-sub-Hamdon & District Angling Society
D Goad
2 Windsor Lane
Stoke-sub-Hamdon
Somerset
Stort Valley Angling Society
Bob Groom

28 Park Mead
Harlow
Essex CM20 1RJ
Tel: 01279 437888
**Stratford-on-Avon Angling
Assn**
Chris Green
40 Lodge Road
Stratford-on-Avon
Warwickshire
Tel: 01789 552012
**Sturminster & Hinton Angling
Assn**
Teresa Goddard
11 Friars Moor
Sturminster Newton
Dorset DT10 1BH
Tel: 01258 472069
Web: www.s-haa.co.uk
**Sunderland Sea Angling
Assn**
Tom Parkin
c/o 125 Roker Avenue
Roker
Sunderland SR6 0HL
Tel: 0191 565 4183
Sunmead Angling Society
(now part of CCAC)
P Tanner
24 Ryebrook Road
Leatherhead
Surrey KT22 7QG
Tel: 01372 379199
Sutton Coldfield Angling Society
Gary Poulton
7 Wheatmoor Rise
Sutton Coldfield
West Midlands B75 6AW
Tel: 0121 378 2152
Swan Angling Club
J Stanhope
4 High Road
Lane Head
Willenhall
West Midlands WV12 4JQ
Tel: 01902 630110
Swanage & District Angling Club
Peveril Slipway
Swanage
Dorset
Taunton Angling Assn
Jon Helyer
24 Priorswood Road
Taunton
Somerset TA2 7PW
Tel: 01823 257559
Web: www.taunton-angling.co.uk
(Tone, Taunton Canal, Drains)

Taunton Fly-Fishing Club
Michael Wollen
Graylings
Frog Lane
Coombe St Nicholas
Chard TA20 3NX
Tel: 01460 65977
Tavy, Walkham & Plym Fishing Club
Roger Round
7 Buena Vista Close
Glenholt
Plymouth PL6 7JH
Tel: 01752 701945
Taw Fishing Club
J D V Michie
Hillside Farm
Bratton Clovelly
Okehampton
Devon EX20 4JD
Tel: 01837 871156
Tebay Angling Assn
Caroline Rudd
7 Highfield
Tebay
via Penrith
Cumbria CA10 3TJ
Tel: 015396 24574
Teignmouth Sea Angling Society
Nigel Drew
c/o Civil Solutions Ltd
Old Newton Road
Heathfield
Devon TQ12 6RW
Tel: 01626 202480
Teise Anglers' and Owners' Assn
C J Turpin
Weald Barn House
Weirton Hill
Boughton Monchelsea
Kent ME17 4JS
Telford Angling Assn
Stan Harris
1 Grange Close
Stirchley
Telford
Salop TF3 1EX
Tel: 01952 590605
Temple Steelheads Fly Fishing Club
Temple Trout Fishery
Temple Rd
Temple PL30 4HW
Tel: 01208 821730
Web: www.templetroutfishery.freeserve.
co.uk
Tenbury Fishing Assn
Mrs L M Rickett
The Post House
Berrington Road
Tenbury Wells

Worcs WR15 8EN
Tel: 01584 810695

Test & Itchen Assn Ltd
Jim Glasspool
West Haye
Itchen Abbas
Winchester SO21 1AX
Tel: 01962 779245

Test Valley Angling Club
(amalg. with Southampton Piscatorial Soc)
Mrs Pat Hogben
1A Rumbridge Street
Totton
Southampton
Hants SO40 9DQ
Tel: 02380 863068
Web: www.wellmann.freeserve.co.uk

Tewkesbury Popular Angling Assn
Robert Danter
31 Barton Street
Tewkesbury
Glos GL20 5PR
Tel: 01684 293234

Thameside Works Angling Society
Jeff Buxton
52 Poplicans Road
Cuxton
Rochester, Kent ME2 1EJ
Tel: 01634 739179

Thames Valley Angling Assn
(amal of 9 Thames Valley clubs)
Jeff Woodhouse
Conifers
Ash Road
High Wycombe
Bucks HP12 40W
Tel: 01494 523988

Thetford & Breckland Angling Club
S J Armes
Springfield the Street
Great Hockham
Thetford
Norfolk IP24 1NH
Tel: 01953 498686

Thirsk Angling Club
Colin Weaver
2 Garden Cottages
South Crescent
Sowerby
Thirsk YO7 1RA
Tel: 01845 524633

Thornaby Angling Assn
Graham Jeavons
38 Briardene Court
Bishopsgarth
Stockton-on-Tees
Co Durham TS19 8UX
Tel: 01642 585770

Tisbury Angling Club
Treasurer:
E J Stevens
Knapp Cottage
Fovant
Salisbury SP3 5JW
Tel: 01722 714245
or
Subscript Sec: B Broom
28 The Hollows
Wilton
Salisbury SP2 0JD
Tel: 01722 743255

Tiverton & District Angling Club
Eric Priest
Crantock
Blundells Road
Tiverton EX16 4NA
Tel: 01884 243454

Todmorden Angling Society
R Barber
12 Grisedale Drive
Burnley
Lancs BB12 8AR
Tel: 01282 702344
Web: www.todmorden-angling.fsnet.co.uk
or
HQ
Hollins Inn
Walsden
Todmorden
West Yorks

Tonbridge & District Angling and Fish Preservation Society
Alex Heggie
POBox 131
Tonbridge TN11 8WB
Tel: 01732 832352
Web: www.tonbridge-angling.co.uk

Torbay & Babbacombe Assn of Sea Anglers
Mrs C Wilden
100 St Marychurch Road
Torquay
Devon TQ1 3HL
Tel: 01803 325748

The Tring Anglers
Memb Sec: Neil Williams
35 Tring Rd
Wilstone
Tring, Herts HP23 4PE
Tel: 01442 823579
Web: www.tringanglers.org.uk
e-mail. info@tringanglers.org.uk

Ulverston Angling Assn
David Anderson
4 Hoad Terrace
Ulverston

Cumbria LA12 7DJ
Tel: 01229 586221
Unity Angling Club
E K Mann
19 Busfield Street
Bradford
Yorks BD4 7QX
Tel: 01274 720072
Upper Teign Fishing Assn
R Rae
6 Hescane Park
Cheriton Bishop
Exeter EX6 6JP
Tel: 01647 24643
Upper Thames Fisheries Consultative
R Knowles
360 Banbury Road
Oxford OX2 7PP
Tel: 01865 552451
Upper Weardale Angling Assn
H C Lee
7 Westfall
Wearhead
Co Durham DL13 1JD
Tel: 01388 537482
Uttoxeter Angling Assn
I E Davies
Three Oaks
Hollington Lane
Stramshall
Uttoxeter
Staffs ST14 5AJ
Vauxhall Angling Club
R W Poulton
Apt 4, Charlewood House
Church Road
Apsley Heath MK17 8TA
Tel: 01908 281621
Web: http://ourworld.compuserve.com/
homepages/vauxac
or
Memb Sec: R Morris
27 Humberstone Close
Luton
Beds LU4 9ST
Tel: 01582 571738
Victoria & Biddulph Angling Society
A Armstrong
12 Lagonda Close
Knypersley
Stoke on Trent
Staffs ST8 6PZ
Tel: 01782 518212
Wadebridge & District Angling Assn
Jon Evans
Polgeel Cottage
Polbrock
Wadebridge PL30 3AN

Tel: 01208 812447
Wainfleet Angling Club
c/o Storr's Fishing Tackle
37/38 High St
Wainfleet
Skegness PE24 4BJ
Tel: 01754 880378
Walkham, Tavy & Plym Fishing Club
Roger Round
7 Buena Vista Close
Glenholt
Plymouth
Tel: 01752 701945
Wansford, Yarwell, Nassington & District Angling Club
S Longfoot
2 Dovecote Close
Yarwell
Peterborough PE8 6PT
Tel: 01780 782627
Wantsum Angling Assn
Hon Sec: Mark Ellcock
P O Box 314
Margate
Kent CT7 9BQ
Tel: 01843 841360
Mob: 07966 262338
e-mail: mark.ellcock@lineone.net
Ware Angling Club
Dennis Bridgeman
30 Musley Lane
Ware SG12 7EW
Tel: 01920 461054
Wareham & District Angling Society
Dave Cave
9 Shore Gardens
Upton
Poole
Dorset BH16 5DX
Tel: 01202 624182
Warmington Angling Club
R Bosworth
2 Buntings Lane
Warmington
Peterborough PE8 6TT
Tel: 01832 280360
Warrington Anglers' Assn
Frank Lithgoe
PO Box 71
Warrington
Cheshire WA1 1LR
Tel: 01928 716238
Web: www.warrington-anglers.org.uk
Waterbeach Angling Club
Mrs Day
10 Northfields Lode
Cambridge CB5 9EU
Tel: 01223 812050

Web: www.waterbeachac.co.uk
Wath Brow & Ennerdale Angling Assn
(see Ennerdale Lake Fisheries)
Sam Laird: Treasurer
Tel: 01946 694820
Watford Piscators
Press & Public Relations Officer
Peter Hadwin
54 Hagden Lane
Watford WD18 0HE
Web: www.watfordpiscators.co.uk
or
A J Huntley
37 Oaklands Avenue
Oxhey,
Watford WD1 4LN
Tel: 01923 242959
Weardale Fly Fishers Club
S W Bisset
Prospect Cottage
6 East End
Stanhope
Bishop Aukland DL13 2XS
Tel: 01388 528616
Wellingborough & District Nene Angling Club
R Blenkharn
66 Redland Drive
Kingsthorpe
Northampton NN2 8TU
Tel: 01604 847106
Wellington Angling Assn
M Cave
60 Sylvan Road
Wellington
Somerset TA21 8EH
Tel: 01823 661671
Wensleydale Angling Assn
Chairman: L Mason Scarr
Cravenholme
Bainbridge
Leyburn
N Yorks DL8 3EG
Tel: 01969 650488
West Bay Sea Angling Club
Richard Daw
Flat 2
30 East Street
Bridport
Dorset DT6 3LF
Tel: 01308 421272
Weston-super-Mare & District Angling Assn
Rob Stark
Weston Angling Centre
25a Locking Road
Weston-super-Mare
Somerset BS23 3BY

Tel: 01934 631140
Westwater Angling Ltd
G H Corry
3 Crossways
East Boldon
Tyne & Wear NE36 0LP
Tel: 01434 681405
Weybridge Angling Club
Howard Whiting
79 Gaston Way
Shepperton
TW17 8EZ
Tel: 01932 242978
Membership from:
Weybridge Guns & Tackle
137 Oatlands Drive
Oatlands Village, Weybridge
Surrey KT13 9LB
Tel: 01932 842675
Wey Navigation Angling Amalgamation
Secretary
c/o Village Hall
Byfleet
Surrey
Weymouth Angling Society
Dave Pay
Angling Centre
Commercial Road
Weymouth, Dorset
Tel: 01305 785032
White Swan Angling Club
N Barratt
Three Trees
Newark Road
Torksey Lock
Lincoln LN1 2EJ
Tel: 01427 718342
Whittlesey Angling Assn
J Warren
55 Bellmans Road
Whittlesey
Cambs PE7 1TY
Tel: 01733 203800
Wigan & District Angling Assn
Memb Sec: K Hogg
95 Holme Terrace
Wigan W1N 2HF
Tel: 01942 492376
or
J Pigeon
6 St Andrew's Drive
Springfield
Wigan WN6 7RQ
Tel: 01942 206807
Wimborne & District Angling Club
Graham Pipet
12 Seatown Close
Canford Heath
Poole

Dorset BH17 8BJ
Tel: 01202 382123

Windermere, Ambleside & District Angling Assn (WADAA)
Hon Sec: J Newton
18 Templand Park
Allithwaite
Grange-over-Sands LA11 7QS
Tel: 015395 38869

Winsford & District Angling Assn
Ken Hilditch
Field View
Clive Lane
Winsford CW7 3NU

Wirral Angling Clubs (Assn of)
Chairman: Malcolm Gillies
17 Rockville Street
Rock Ferry
Birkenhead
Tel: 0151 645 3396
or
Hon Sec: S Ross
18 Orchard Grange
Moreton
Birkenhead CH46 6DZ

Witby Sea Anglers Assn
D Johnson: Treasurer
14 Runswick Avenue
Whitby
Yorks YO21 3UB
Tel: 01947 604025

Witham & District Joint Anglers Federation
Stewart Oxborough
6 Ormsby Close
Cleethorpes
South Humberside DN35 9PE
Tel: 01472 508639

Withnell Angling Club
P O Box 41
Chorley
Lancs PR6 8JZ

Wolverhampton Angling Assn
Bill Turner
37 Prole Street
Park Village
Wolverhampton WV10 9AD
Tel: 01902 457906

Woodbridge & District Angling Club
D Ward
c/o Saxmundham Angling Centre
Bakery Yard, rear of Market Place
Saxmundham IP17 1AH
Tel: 01728 603443

Worcester & District United Angling Assn
John Wells
Poplar Cottage
Poplar Road
Worcester
Worcs
Tel: 01886 888459

Worksop & District Anglers Assn
D Brown
4 Dove Close
Worksop
Notts S81 7LG
Tel: 01909 486350

Worthing & District Piscatorial Society
Bill Scholes
23 The Lawns
Sompting
Lancing BN15 0DT
Tel: 01903 764818
Web: www.worthingpiscatorials.homestead.com
e-mail: bill@wscholes.freeserve.co.uk

Wroxham & District Anglers Assn
R Westgate
31 The Paddocks
Old Catton
Norwich
Norfolk NR6 7HF
Tel: 01603 401062
e-mail: wroxham.angling@virgin.net

Yarm Angling Assn
Mike Dresser
c/o 4 Blenavon Court
Yarm
Teesside TS15 9AN
Tel: 01642 786444

Yaxley Farcet Holme and Dist Angling Assn
Paul Marriott
72 Portchester Close
Park Farm
Peterborough PE2 8UP
Tel: 01733 893804

Yeldington Piscatorial Society
Hon. Secretary
Rectory Cottage
Stoke Abbott
Beaminster DT8 3JT

York Angling Assn
S Skelton
23 Paddock Close
Wilberfoss
York YO4 5LX
Tel: 01759 388138

York & District Amalgamation of Anglers
Bob Hutchinson
16 Manor Park Close
York YO30 5UZ
Tel: 01904 651346
Web: www.communigate.co.uk/york/ydaa

MISCELLANEOUS

Anglian Water Services
  Recreation Department: Wing WTW
  Morcott Road
  Wing
  Oakham LE15 8SA
  Tel: 01572 653021
  e-mail: fishing@anglianwater.co.uk
RMC Angling
  Adrian Ellis
  Coldharbour Lane
  Thorpe
  Surrey TW20 8RA
  Tel: 01932 583630

  Web: www.rmcangling.co.uk
South West Lakes Angling Assn
  (former South West Water fishings)
  Higher Coombepark
  Lewdown
  Oakhampton
  Devon EX20 4QT
  Tel: 01837 871565
  Web: swlakestrust.org.uk
  e-mail: info@swlakestrust.org.uk
  37 871565
  Web: swlakestrust.org.uk
  e-mail: info@swlakestrust.org.uk

WELSH FISHING STATIONS

In the pages that follow, the catchment areas of Wales, are given in alphabetical order, being interspersed with the streams and the lakes under headings such as 'Powys (streams)'; 'Gwynedd (lakes)', etc. The rivers of each catchment area are arranged in the manner described under the heading 'English Fishing Stations', on *p.25* and the other notes given there apply equally to Wales. The whole of the Wye and the Severn, it should be remembered, are included in the section on England, while the whole of the Dee is listed among the Welsh rivers.

Note: *Sea trout are commonly referred to as 'sewin' in Wales although some associations define sewin as immature sea trout returning to the river for the first time.*

AERON

(For close seasons, licences, etc, see Welsh Region Environment Agency, p23)

Rises in Llyn Eiddwen, 7m north-west of Tregaron, and flows about 17m to sea at Aberaeron. Excellent run of sewin from June onwards with smaller salmon run. Brown trout plentiful but small. Spate river fishes well on a retreating flood.

Aberaeron (Dyfed). Salmon, sea trout and brown trout. Aberaeron Town AC has a 2½m stretch on R Aeron; 3m on **Arth**, a stream to the north, which holds fine brown trout and has an excellent run of sea trout; and 3 stretches on **Teifi**, north of Lampeter. A further 1½m of private fishing available upstream of club waters; Llanerchaeron Estate, National Trust; contact Property Office (tel: 01545 570200); tickets from Aeron Sports; st £40, wt £20, dt £10. Tackle shop: Aeron Sports & Fishing Tackle, Bridge St, Aberaeron SA46 0AP (tel: 01545 571209).

ANGLESEY (streams)

(For close seasons, licences, etc, see Welsh Region Environment Agency, p23)

ALAW. Llanfachraeth (Anglesey). Rises above Cors y Bol bog and flows some 7m to sea beyond Llanfachraeth, opposite Holyhead. Fishes well (trout) for first three months of season and again in September when good run of small sea trout expected; usually too low in summer. Permission of farmers.

BRAINT. Llangeinwen (Anglesey). Small stream which flows almost whole width of the island, parallel with Menai Straits, to sea at Aber Menai, beyond Llangeinwen. Trout, some sea trout, but usually fishable only first three months of season. Permission of farmers.

CEFNI. Llangefni (Anglesey). Rises above Llangwyllog, flows through Llyn Frogwy, on to Llangefni and Cefni Reservoir, and then to sea in 6m. Lower reaches canalised. Only fair-sized river in island. Brown trout and chance of late salmon or sea trout. Permission of farmers.

CEINT. Pentraeth (Anglesey). Small stream entering sea at Red Wharf Bay; some trout; permission of farmers; summer conditions difficult.

FFRAW or GWNA. Bodorgan (Anglesey). Under the name of Gwna rises 4m above Bodorgan and waters Llyn Coron just below village. Stream then takes name of Ffraw and runs to sea at Aberffraw in 2m. Little more than brook. One or two pools fishable early on, but overgrown June onwards. Trout, some sea trout.

WYGYR. Cemaes (Anglesey). Small stream falling into sea at Cemaes Bay. Trout; restocked. Good sea fishing in bay. Hotels: Harbour, Cemaes Bay, Gwynedd LL67 0NN (tel: 01407 710273); Cefn Glas Inn, Llanfechell, Amlwch, Gwynedd LL68 0PT (tel: 01407 710526).

ANGLESEY (lakes)

Bodafon Lake. Llanallgo (Anglesey). Rudd and tench; contact Trescawen Estate, Anglesey, Gwynedd.

Cefni Reservoir. Llangefni (Anglesey), 172 acres: brown and rainbow trout, fly only; good wading; boats. Leased by Welsh Water plc to Cefni AA. Permits from D G Evans (Treasurer), Wenllys, Capel Coch, Llangefni LL77 7UR (tel: 01248 470306); dt and wt from Peter

Rowe, Jewellers, above Mon Properties, Glanhwfa Rd, Llangefni and Anglesey Bait Centre, Gallows Point, Beaumaris. St adults £110, sen citizens £85, student (18-21) £55, juniors £22, dt £12, wt £40. Hotels: Bull Hotel; Nant yr Odyn Country, Turnpike Nant LL77 7YE; Tre Ysgawen Hall, Capel Coch LL77 7UR.

Cwn Reservoir. Holyhead (Anglesey). Coarse fishing on 2 acre reservoir; carp, rudd, bream, roach and tench; open all year round.

Holyhead (Anglesey). Ynys Mon AA has 20 pegs at **Breakwater Park** (3 pegs for wheelchair anglers) dt £4 (half-price juniors).

Llyn Alaw. Llantrisant (Anglesey). Situated in open lowland countryside this productive 777 acre reservoir offers fly fishing, spinning and worming, for brown and rainbow trout; season 20 Mar - 17 Oct for brown; last Saturday in Mar - 24 Oct for rainbow; dt £13.50, concessions £12.50, evening £11.50, junior (2 fish) £7, st £405 (concession £354), from Visitor Centre at reservoir (dt and evening from machine in car park); boats (rowing or with engine) for hire; boat for disabled at no extra charge; worms, flies, weights, spinners and a wide variety of other tackle for sale at Visitor Centre; further information from Llyn Alaw Visitor Centre, Llyn Alaw Reservoir, Llantrisant, Holyhead, Anglesey LL65 4TW (tel: 01407 730762). Accommodation: caravans and camping at Bodnolwyn Wen Farm, Llantrisant, Holyhead, Anglesey LL65 4TW (tel: 01407 730298); B&B at Lastra Farm Hotel, Amlwch, LL68 9TF (tel: 01407 830906); and caravans and camping, plus meals, at The Ring (Public House), Rhosgoch, Anglesey LL66 0AB (tel: 01407 830720).

Llyn Bryntirion. Dwyran (Anglesey). Carp, tench, roach and perch fishing on 3 ponds (3 acres of water); all year; no barbed hooks or keepnets; only one rod per angler; dt from J Naylor, Bryntirion Working Farm, Dwyran, Anglesey LL61 6BQ (tel: 01248 430232).

Llyn Coron. Bodorgan (Anglesey). Brown trout and sea trout. Controlled by syndicate (max 40 members), joining fee plus £150 per season; dt £10 (4 fish limit); evening ticket (after 4 pm) £8 (2 fish); contact bailiff, Mr Cliff Girling, Windy Ridge, Llanfaelog, LL63 5TA (tel: 01407 810801). Permits also available at fishing lodge on lakeside. Holiday cottages are available.

Llyn Dewi. Llandeusant (Anglesey). Coarse fishing on 1 acre lake; carp, roach and rudd; open all year. Ynys Mon AA has water; also for **Nant Anog Lake** 40 pegs, 5 for wheelchair anglers; recently stocked with chubb.

Llanerchymedd (Anglesey). Coarse and game fishing on ½ acre lake; rudd and brown trout; fishing is only available for guests at Llwydiarth Fawr (guest house); contact R & M L Hughes, Llwydiarth Fawr, Llanerchymedd, Anglesey LL71 8DF (tel: 01248 470321). Ynys Mon AA has 40 pegs on Llyn Nant Anog at Carmel; dt £5 (half-price juniors). Also 14 pegs on Llyn Tacan at Carna Farm, Llanfair-yn-Neubwll; dt £5 (half-price juniors).

Llyn Maelog. Rhosneigr (Anglesey). Roach, perch, rudd, bream, eels, pike. Permission to fish from various landowners. Dt £5, conc, for 450 yards of right hand bank (looking at lake from the road) of Ynys Mon AA water from Wayside Shop, LLanfaelog, Rhosneigr. Hotels: Maelog Lake and Glan Neigr.

Llyn y Gors. Llandegfan (Anglesey). 10 acres coarse fishery, four lakes. Mixed lake with carp, tench, roach, rudd and perch ; carp lake with carp to 30lb; pike and catfish; match lake and children's lake. Permits, large tackle shop and bait on site. Self-catering cottages, tents and tourers. Further information from tackle shop, Llyn y Gors, Llandegfan, Menai Bridge, Anglesey, LL59 5PN (tel: 01248 713410; web: www.llynygors.co.uk).

Llyn Edna Trout Fishery. Llanerchymedd (Anglesey). Llyn Edna is 5 acre, man-made lake; stocked with rainbow and blue trout. Tickets from the lodge at the water. Contact Neil Johnson, Medora House, Llanddeusant, LL65 4AD (tel: 01407 730930 (evngs)). Accommodation in self-catering cottages: contact Andrew Gannon, Parc Newydd, Carmel, nr Llanerchymedd LL71 7BT (tel: 01248 470700) which also has 2 coarse fishing lakes.

Ty Hen Carp Lake. Rhosneigr (Anglesey). 1½ acres of natural spring water (Ph 7.8, nitrate 0.01) for specimen carp, tench, roach and rudd; st £40 at office; caravan residents only; no dt; all fish to be returned to water; barbless hooks; no keepnets: contact Bernard Summerfield, Ty Hen Farm, Station Road, Rhosneigr, Anglesey LL64 5QZ (tel: 01407 810331;

web: www.tyhen.com).

Tyddyn Sargent. Benllech (Anglesey). Coarse fishing on 1¾ acre lake; common carp, ghost carp, crucian carp, perch, roach, rudd, tench and bream; barbless hooks only. Accommodation and tickets: contact K Twist, Tyddyn Sargent, Tynygongl, nr Benllech, Anglesey LL74 8NT (tel: 01248 853024).

CLEDDAU (Eastern and Western)

(For close seasons, licences, etc, see Welsh Region Environment Agency, p23)

East Cleddau rises on the east side of Prescelly Mountains and flows 15m south-west, partly along old Carmarthenshire border, to north branch of Milford Haven. West Cleddau rises in the hills and valleys south-west of Mathry and flows east towards Castle Morris. It is joined by streams such as the Afon Cleddau and Nant-y-Bugail and then flows south-east to Wolf's Castle. Here it is joined by the Afon Anghof and Afon Glan Rhyd. It then flows south to Haverfordwest and on to join the E Cleddau in a creek in the Haven. Fishing for sewin and trout is mainly in June, July and August; for salmon in August.

WESTERN CLEDDAU: Salmon, sewin and trout.

Haverfordwest (Pembrokeshire). Pembrokeshire AA has 15m stretch along A40, Haverfordwest to Fishguard, (Wolf's Castle); salmon, sea trout, brown trout; visitors: wt £60 (8 consecutive days), dt £15, juv (under 12) £5; members: st £60 + £15 joining fee; wheelchair anglers half price: permits from County Sports, 3 Old Bridge Rd, Haverfordwest, Pembs SA61 2EZ (tel: 01437 763740). The club also has a sea trout stocking programme in place. Pembrokeshire AA have a purpose-built disabled fishing facility at Treffgarne, which includes concreted surface, safety barrier and parking for 3 cars; also a picnic table with wheelchair access . Accommodation: The Rising Sun Inn, Caravan and Camp Site, St David's Road, Haverfordwest, SA62 6EA (tel: 01437 765171). United Utilities manages 2 reservoirs in the area on behalf of Welsh Water plc. **Llys-y-Fran Reservoir** (212 acres), rainbow trout reared in cages within the reservoir and brown trout. Season Mar - 31 Oct; limited winter fishing only until mid Dec; catch limit 6 fish (half-day 4 fish); size limit 10"; boats; permits and tackle from Llys-y-Fran Visitor Centre Shop (below). **Rosebush Reservoir** (33 acres) brown trout fishery in Prescelly Hills. Now operated by local syndicate but bank and boat rods from Llys-y-Fran Reservoir; advanced booking advisable. For further information contact J Waddington, Visitor Centre, Llys-y-Fran Reservoir, Clarbeston Road, nr Haverfordwest, Pembs SA63 4RR (tel: 01437 532732/532694). **Hayscastle Trout Fishery**, 3 acre, stocked trout lake; fly only. Booking advisable; permits from Hayscastle Trout Fishery, Upper Hayscastle Farm, Hayscastle, Dyfed SA62 5PU (tel: 01348 840393). Riparian owners may give permission elsewhere. Sewin fishing good June to August. Tackle shop: County Sports, 3 Old Bridge, Haverfordwest SA61 2EZ (tel: 01437 763740); tickets Pembrokeshire AA, Llangwarren Trout Lake, E & W Cleddau. Hotels: Mariners, Mariners Square SA61 2DU.

EASTERN CLEDDAU. Trout in all rivers and tributaries in E Cleddau area; stocks mostly small fish under 7½". Trout, sewin and salmon in Syfynwy, a tributary of E Cleddau. Picton Waters AA has 3m; right bank from Gelly Bridge downstream to Holgan Farm and several stretches on left bank from Penlan Farm to Llawhaden Bridge; limited st; wt details on application; contact Hon Sec *(see Clubs)*.

Llanycefn (Pembrokeshire). Fishing in E Cleddau controlled largely by individual syndicates as far as the ford at Llandissilio; day tickets are sold by T & P J Murphy, Llangwm Farm, Llanycefn, Clynderwen, SA66 7LN (tel/fax: 01437 563604). U/s seek farmers permission; d/s fishing is expensive and it is necessary to join syndicates. Glancleddau Farm, Felinfach and Landre Egremont have holiday caravan parks where visitors enjoy some of the best fishing in the area. Rod licences from Post Office, Felinfach, Cardigan, Dyfed SA43 8AE (tel: 01570 470321).

CLWYD

(For close seasons, licences, etc, see Welsh Region Environment Agency, p23)

A celebrated sea trout and salmon river which has its source in the high ground to the north of Corwen and runs down through Ruthin, passes Denbigh, St Asaph and Rhuddlan and finally enters the Irish Sea at Rhyl. Best fished for sea trout from June onwards as these fish tend to run during latter part of the month. The native brown trout population is composed of small fish, though stocking of larger specimens is undertaken annually by most of the angling clubs. There are no coarse fish species in this area.

Rhyl (Wrexham). Salmon, sea trout, brown trout. No permits needed for stretch from sea to railway bridge, however, no holding pools, therefore salmon and sea trout tend to run straight through; for salmon, trout and eels, rod licence needed; close season 17 Oct-1 March. Rhyl & Dist AA is one of the oldest fishing clubs in the Vale of Clwyd; the majority of its waters are rented, but the club is fortunate in owning the fishing rights on 2 substantial stretches on the **R Elwy** known as Maes Elwy and Pont y Ddol; it rents 2 further stretches **Pentre Isaf** and **Bron Heulog**; all beats on the **R Clwyd** (Bryn Clwyd, Wern Ddu and Bryn Polyn, and Bodfair) are rented. About 10m fishing in total; all stretches contain pools which give good fishing, holding salmon, sea trout and trout. Members only, limited membership. St £85 + joining fee; apply to Hon Sec. Waiting list; conc for juv. **Tan-y-Mynydd Lakes**; rainbow, brown and brook trout from 1½ to 15lb; 5 purpose-built trout lakes, total 4 acres; contact Bryn and Neil Roberts, **Tan-Y-Mynydd Trout Fishery**, (Tan-y-Mynydd Trout & Leisure), Moelfre, Abergele, Clwyd LL22 9RF (tel: 01745 826722); prices between 1 fish (4 hrs) £11 to 4 fish (8 hrs) £21; sporting tickets 4 hrs £8, 6 hrs £11; restaurant and bar available; also self-catering cottages.

St Asaph (Denbighshire). Salmon, sea trout and brown trout. St Asaph AA has excellent and various fishing: 6 beats on Clwyd; 3 beats on **Elwy**, 4m in St Asaph area; a beat on **Aled**, 1½m double bank at **Llansannan**; st £80 (conc, family tickets) + £30 joining fee (no joining fee for juniors); day permits for Elwy; and dt £10 on all waters, from Foxon's Tackle, Lower Denbigh Rd, LL17 0ED (tel: 01745 583583), which, in addition to a comprehensive range of tackle, sells various permits (St Asaph AA; Denbigh & Clwyd AC), and offers expert advice on all aspects of fishing both game and coarse. Hotel: Oriel House.

Denbigh (Wrexham). Clwyd, 2m E; salmon, sea trout, brown trout. Denbigh & Clwyd AC has extensive water on Clwyd, **Ystrad**, **Elwy**, **Wheeler**, and also on small stocked trout lake; members only; tickets from Hon Sec. **Llyn Brenig** and **Alwen Reservoir**, 11m SW; trout. **Llyn Aled**, 11m SW; coarse. Permits for Llyn Brenig, Alwen Reservoir and Llyn Aled; from Llyn Brenig Visitor Centre, Cerrigydrudion, Corwen, Conwy LL21 9TT (tel: 01490 420463); boat for disabled on Llyn Brenig. St Asaph AA has fishing on **Lake Prion** at Denbigh; brown and rainbow trout; dt £10 available at Foxon's (see above). Hotel: Fron Haul.

Ruthin (Wrexham). Trout, salmon, sea trout. Denbigh & Clwyd AC has water on Clwyd and on **River Clywedog**; dt £10 from Foxon's Tackle, Lower Denbigh Rd, LL17 0ED (tel: 01745 583583). Hotel: Ruthin Castle.

Tributaries of the Clwyd

ELWY: Brown trout, sea trout (June onwards), salmon. No coarse fish.

St Asaph (Wrexham). St Asaph AA has Gypsy Lane Waters: dt £10 from Foxon's Tackle, Lower Denbigh Rd, LL17 0ED (tel: 01745 583583). Capenhurst AC has water; salmon, sea trout and trout; members only (£50 p/year).

Bodelwyddan (Denbighshire). Bodelwyddan Game Anglers controls three stretches on the Elwy, 1m of which is double bank; also some lake fishing; tickets available; contact Hon Sec *(see Clubs)*; also Foxon's Tackle, Lower Denbigh Rd, LL17 0ED (tel: 01745 583583).

Llansannan (Wrexham). St Asaph AA has 1½m double bank on **Aled**. At Llannefydd are **Dolwen** and **Plas Uchaf Reservoirs**, well stocked with brown and rainbow trout; fly, spinning and worming; 6 fish limit; season mid-Mar to end-Oct; permits from Spar shop in

Bodelwyddan, St Asaph; and Foxon's Tackle, Lower Denbigh Rd, St Asaph LL17 0ED (tel: 01745 583583); contact Llyn Brenig Visitor Centre, Cerrigydrudion, Corwen, Conwy LL21 9TT (tel: 01490 420463); booking advised as rods limited to 16. Concession OAP and jun.
WHEELER: Trout.
Afonwen (Wrexham). Denbigh & Clwyd AC has 2m; fly only.
CLYWEDOG: Salmon and sea trout (very late), trout. All water strictly preserved.

Ruthin (Wrexham). Denbigh & Clwyd AC has stretch from confluence with Clwyd to Rhewl; and has water in Bontuchel and Llanrhaeadr areas; dt £10 from Foxon's Tackle, Lower Denbigh Rd, LL17 0ED (tel: 01745 583583). Capenhurst AC has stretch at Bontuchel; salmon, sea trout and trout; members only (£50/year); members children (under 18) may fish free of charge, but must be accompanied by adult.

CONWY

(For close seasons, licences, etc, see Welsh Region Environment Agency, p23)

Rises on Migneint, in the County of Conwy and flows between the old Caernarvonshire and Denbighshire boundaries for much of its course, emptying into the Irish Sea near Conwy. The upper part of its valley is noted for its beauty. Spate river with salmon runs throughout season (best from mid-August); grilse early July; sea trout runs from June to the end of season.

Conwy (Gwynedd). Tidal; sea fishing only. Codling, dabs, plaice, bass and mullet above and below suspension bridge; boats for hire. Salmon and sea trout; Prince Albert AS has Belmont fishery, at Meenan Abbey. **Llyn Gwern Engan**, a small lake on Sychnant Pass Common; rudd, tench, carp, gudgeon; also free fishing, contact Snowdonia National Park Committee, Penrhydeudraeth, Gwynedd LL48 6LF (tel: 01766 770274). **Llyn Nant-y-Cerrig**, Brynymaen, 1½ acres; carp, bream, tench, perch; tickets at lakeside or local tackle shops; for further information contact Llandullas AC (Jan Hills), c/o Goleugell, Eglwysbach, Colwyn Bay, Clwyd LL28 5UH (tel: 01492 650314). **Clobryn Pool**, Clobryn Rd, Colwyn Bay; tench, crucian carp, roach, rudd, perch. **Glas Coed Pools**, Bodelwyddan, set in grounds of Bodelwyddan Castle, carp, tench, roach, rudd; no dt. **Trefant Pool**; stocked with tench, carp, roach, rudd and perch; dt £4 from Foxon's Tackle, Lower Denbigh Rd, LL17 0ED (tel: 01745 583583). Permits for Llyn Nant-y-Cerrig, Clobryn Pool, Glas Coed Pools and Trefant Pool from tackle shops. Tackle shop: Paddy's Bait & Tackle, Unit 4 Happy Valley Road, Llandudno LL30 2LP (tel: 01492 877678).

Dolgarrog (Gwynedd). Salmon, sea trout and brown trout; deep tidal pools. Dolgarrog FC has 1½m of tidal water. Club also has brown trout fishing on **Llyn Coedty, Llyn Eigiau, Llyn Melynllyn** and **Llyn Dulyn**, (no boats on these lakes); permits from Hon Sec; Talybont Garage. **Llyn Cowlyd** (5m W Llanwrst), trout reservoir belongs to Welsh Water plc; st £10.

Llanrwst (Gwynedd). Salmon and good sea trout; brown trout poor. Llanrwst AC has various beats on R Conwy at Llanrwst and Trefriw; some sections members only; limited wt and dt from Hon Sec; Sunday fishing allowed. Permits from Forestry Commission, Gwydyr Uchaf, for left bank of **Machno** from junction with Conwy and portion of right bank; dt from P Haveland, Manchester House, Penmachno, Betws-y-Coed LL24 0UD (tel: 01690 760337). Hotels: Maenan Abbey Hotel (has salmon and trout); and Eagles

---

Check before you go

*While every effort has been made to ensure that the information given in **Where to Fish** is correct, the position is continually changing, and anglers are urged, in their own interests, to make enquiries before travelling to selected venues. This is especially important with reference to prices quoted. Anglers attention is also drawn to the fact that hotels mentioned under the various fishing stations do not necessarily have water of their own. Any amendments or further data for inclusion in subsequent editions, and any comments, will be welcome.*

Hotel, Bridge St, Llanrwst LL26 0LG.

Betws-y-Coed (Conwy). Salmon, sea trout, brown trout. Betws-y-Coed AC has 4½m of salmon, sea trout and brown trout fishing on Conwy and **Llugwy**; on the Conwy, from the Waterloo Bridge (left bank) downstream to the confluence of the **Llugwy**. The club also three trout lakes: **Elsi Lake**, stocked with some American brook trout, brown trout and rainbows; **Llyn Goddionduon** (brown trout); **Llyn Bychan** (brown trout). St £135 (£65 for partially disabled), juv st £20, from Hon Sec; dt from £18 (river), and £12.50 (lake) from Hon Sec or Pendyffryn Stores (Newsagents), Pendyffryn, Betws-y-Coed LL24 0AN (tel: 01690 710436). Gwydyr Hotel has 12m of salmon and sea trout fishing; season 20 Mar - 17 Oct; priority tickets for resident-s; dt subject to availability. For further information contact Owen Wainwright, Gwydyr Hotel, Betws-y-Coed LL24 0AB (tel: 01690 710777). Other hotels: Waterloo; Glan Aber; Church Hill Hotel; B&B Tyn-y-Bryn.

Ysbyty Ifan (Conwy). Brown trout. Methyr Tydfil AA has water; contact Hon Sec. National Trust has stretch at Ysbyty Ifan and Dinas Water on upper Conwy; fly, worm and spinning; permits from National Trust, Ysbyty Estate Office, Betws y Coed LL24 0HF (tel: 01690 710636); and Robin O Ellis, Bron Ryffydd, Padog, Betws-y-Coed, Conwy LL24 0HF (tel: 01690 710567). For holiday cottages contact The National Trust Holiday Booking Office, PO Box 536, Melksham, Wiltshire SN12 8SX (tel: 0870 4584422 (brochures 0870 4584411)).

Tributaries of the Conwy

ROE: Trout.

Rowen (Gwynedd). **Conwy Water Gardens & Aquatic Centre & Coarse Fishery**, Glyn Isa, Rowen, nr Conwy LL32 8PT (tel: 01492 650063) has 3 lakes stocked with carp, bream, tench, golden orfe, roach, rudd, barbel and chub. Dt and half-dt available from shop. Bank: 7.30 am to dusk, Wed-Sun, all year (closed Mondays & Tuesdays except Bank Holidays). Dt £6.50, half-dt £4.50, under-12's free; good access for disabled. Accommodation: self-contained cottages (fishing free).

DULYN: Brown trout.

Dolgarrog FC has fishing; dt £10, contact Hon Sec.

PORTH-LLWYD: Brown trout; Dolgarrog FC has fishing; dt £10 contact Hon. Sec.

DDU: Brown trout.

Pont Dolgarrog (Gwynedd). Trout. Ddu enters Conwy ½m below village; drains Llyn Cowlyd. **Llyn Cowlyd**, brown trout and Arctic char; fly only; £10 dt from Welsh Water plc. Dolgarrog FC has fishing on **Afon Ddu**; dt £10, contact Hon. Sec.

CRAFNANT: Trout.

Trefriw (Gwynedd). Trout fishing on Llyn Crafnant, one of the most beautiful lakes in Wales, 63 acres, stocked rainbow trout supplementing wild brown trout. Sunday fishing. Day tickets, rod licences, boats, cafe, self-catering accommodation, toilets, car parking and information from Mr or Mrs J Collins, Lakeside Café, Llyn Crafnant, Trefriw LL27 0JZ (tel: 01492 640818). Hotel: Princes Arms; and Fairy Falls.

LLUGWY: Salmon, sea trout, brown trout.

Betws-y-Coed (Conwy). Betws-y-Coed AC has a stretch, both banks, from Swallow Falls downstream to the confluence of Conwy on right bank and to railway bridge on left bank. Permits from Hon Sec or Pendyffryn Stores (Newsagents), Pendyffryn, Betws-y-Coed LL24 0AN (tel: 01690 710436).

LLEDR: Trout, sewin, salmon.

Dolwyddelan (Gwynedd). Dolwyddelan FA fishing on River Lledr both above and below the village, and at Pont y Pant; salmon, brown trout and sea trout; good late season salmon runs; sea trout from 1st July. Wt (Mon-Fri) and dt for visitors, although wt only for visitors resident in village. Permits and tackle, including locally tied flies, from Post Office, Dolwyddelan, Gwynedd LL25 0NJ (tel: 01690 750201). Prince Albert AS has two stretches, at Bertheos and Hendre; enquire Hon Sec. Hotel: Elen's Castle Hotel, Dolwyddelan.

MACHNO: Trout.

Penmachno (Conwy). National Trust has water on Machno; dt available; fly or worm depending on season; no salmon fishing above Conwy Falls; brown trout only; permits from National Trust, Ysbyty Estate Office, Betws y Coed LL24 0HF (tel: 01690 710636); and Robin O Ellis, Bron Ryffydd, Padog, Betws-y-

Coed, Conwy LL24 0HF (tel: 01690   710567).

DEE (Welsh)

(For close seasons, licences, etc, see Welsh Region Environment Agency, p23)

Usually has a spring run of fish up to 30lb. Grilse enter in June and there is a run of grilse and summer fish until the end of the season as a rule. In spring most fish are taken from Bangor to Corwen. Trout from Bangor upstream and grayling above Llangollen. Coarse fish predominate downstream of Bangor. River holds good bream, roach, dace, perch and pike.

Holywell (Flintshire). **Forest Hill Trout Farm**, Mostyn, nr Holywell, CH8 9EQ (tel: 01745 560151): fishing on 3 lakes fed by spring water, stocked with home reared rainbow and brown trout; fly and bait. Tea, coffee, facilities for disabled. **Seven Springs Trout Farm and Fisheries**, Caerwys, nr Mold, Flintshire CH7 5EZ (tel: 01352 720511); 3 pools over 1 acre, containing rainbow and brown trout; fly and bait; tackle hire and tuition; anglers room, toilet and gutting room; tickets at fisheries (bookings taken). Coarse fishing at **Gyrn Castle Fishery**, Llanasa, Holywell, Flintshire CH8 9BQ; 2 lakes: 3 acres and 1 acre; well stocked with carp, rudd and tench; heaviest carp to date - 30 lbs; barbless hooks only. Fishermen's hut with tea and coffee-making facilities. Closed May; open 1 Nov to 1 Jan Sunday to Thursday only. Dt £15 (large lake £18), accompanied juv £7; only 12 permits per day allowed. Disabled access; permits from Mr Partington, Gyrn Castle Estate, South Lodge, Glan-yr-Afon (tel: 01745 561672). **Flour Mill Pool** is a 4 acre fishery situated in Greenfield Valley Heritage Park (Admin Centre), Basingwerk House, Greenfield Valley, Holywell, Flintshire CH8 7QB (tel: 01352 714172); crucian carp, tench, perch, bream, ghost, common and mirror carp, gudgeon, roach; permits from Admin Centre; st £15, dt £5, conc.

Connah's Quay (Wrexham). Connah's Quay & Dist AC water. Club has coarse fishing at **Wepre Pool**, **Warren Pool** (Broughton) and **Shropshire Union Canal** from Ellesmere Port via Chester to Nantwich; st and dt from Deeside Fishing Tackle, 28 Chester Rd East, Shotton, Deeside CH5 1QA (tel: 01244 813674).

Chester (Cheshire). Coarse fish. Little permit-free fishing. No licence for coarse fishing in tidal waters. Most fishing on River Dee controlled by Chester AA. Assn also has fishing on **River Severn**; no day tickets; st £12 (OAP and jun £6) for trout and coarse fishing only from

Hon Sec or Chester area tackle shops. Free fishing from Mon to Fri, on Eaton Estate from public footpath that adjoins river. **River Gowy**, which runs into Mersey, passing by Mickle Trafford about 3m from Chester; Warrington AA has water. **Meadow Fishery**, Mickle Trafford CH2 4EB (tel: 01244 300236), rainbow trout; 5 acres; st and dt. Tackle shops: Henry Monk (Gunmakers) Ltd, 8 Queen Str, CH1 3LG (tel: 01244 320988); Jones Fishing Tackle & Pet Foods, 39 Vernon Rd, CH1 4JJ (tel: 01244 390596); Chester Tackle Locker, 140 Tarvin Rd, CH3 5EE (tel: 01244 345069).

Holt (Wrexham). Salmon, trout, pike, bream. Dee AA rent approx 10m of Dee from Chester AA in the Farndon and Sutton Green area. Maps can be obtained from Hon Sec, price 50p plus SAE. Assn issues salmon permits (limited) for Sutton Green stretch; separate trout and coarse fish permits; permits from local tackle shops and B W Roberts, 23 Alpraham Crescent, Upton, Chester (tel: 01244 381193). All waters in the Chester area and downstream to Queensferry controlled by the Chester AA; match permits and membership cards from B W Roberts (Hon Sec); no day tickets issued for these waters. Instruction for juniors and competitive events for all members. Warrington AA has Shocklach Water and stretch at Almere; members only, but visiting anglers accommodated, providing they supply date of visit in advance. Lavister AC has 1m stretch (left bank) upstream from Almere Ferry; bream, dace, roach, perch, pike; members only st £10, apply Hon Sec. Waters on the **Grosvenor Estates** at Churton and Aldford downstream to Chester; free freelance fishing but matches must be booked with the Eaton Estate Office, Eccleston, Chester CH4 9ET (tel: 01244 684400). Tackle shops: Jones Fishing Tackle & Pet Foods, 39 Vernon Rd, Chester CH1 4JJ (tel: 01244 390596); Chester Tackle Locker, 140 Tarvin Road, Chester CH3 5EE (tel: 01244 345069).

Bangor-on-Dee (Wrexham). Salmon, trout, coarse fish. Bangor-on-Dee Salmon AA has 2 stretches; one downstream from town, the other near Shocklach; member only but membership available; permits from Warrington AA has water on Worthenbury Brook. Tackle shops: Deggy's Fishing Tackle, 2 Ruabon Road, Wrexham, Clwyd LL13 7NU (tel: 01978 351815). Hotel: The Buck Hotel.

Overton (Wrexham). Bryn-y-Pys AA has 7m on R Dee between Overton Bridge and Bangor-on-Dee; rainbow and brown trout, grayling and coarse fish; st £36, £26 (OAP) and £10 (junior); entrance fee £10. Dt £10 (trout season) and £4, from Deggy's Fishing Tackle, 2 Ruabon Road, Wrexham, Clwyd LL13 7NU (tel: 01978 351815). Boat Inn, Erbistock, has salmon and trout beat. **Trench Farm** has 3 pools (3 acres) with carp to 35lb, tench, rudd, roach and crucian carp; day tickets only £6, conc (under 16's must be accompanied by adult); contact Mr or Mrs M A Huntbach, Trench Farm, Redhall Lane, Penley, Wrexham LL13 0NA (tel: 01978 710098).

Cefn Mawr (Wrexham). Trout, salmon, coarse fish (including pike and excellent grayling fishing); world fly-fishing championships have been held on this water; and site of Commonwealth Fly Fishing championships 2002. Maelor AA has 6m, with good autumn salmon fishing on 2 beats, coarse fishing, stocked brown trout, and very good winter grayling; st £120 salmon, st trout £40, dt £8, 4 fish per day limit; contact Chairman (tel: 01978 820608) or Derek's *(below);* coarse fishing good September onwards. Newbridge AA has Wynnstay Estate Waters from Newbridge Old Bridge downstream on wooded bank, approx 3m; salmon, trout, grayling, dace and pike fishing; members only, except for salmon rods on top beat; members to reside within local radius of 5m; salmon permits from Hon Sec, membership £35 per annum; salmon rods £60, one named day throughout season for non-members. Tackle shop: Derek's Fishing Tackle, London House, Well St

LL14 3AE (tel: 01978 821841). Hotel: Wynnstay Arms, Ruabon; Greenbank Guesthouse, Victoria Sq, Llangollen LL20 8EU (tel: 01978 861835).

Llangollen (Denbighshire). Salmon, sea trout, brown trout, grayling. Llangollen AA has 14m of bank fishing in and around the town. All waters have good access and parking provided. Downstream from Horseshoe Falls, all methods for salmon and trout; above Horseshoe Falls, all methods for salmon, fly only for trout and grayling. Trout water stocked with 5,500 trout per season, averaging 12" with larger fish up to 3lbs. Both trout and grayling fishing excellent and near best on River Dee. Salmon fishing good from May to end of season, average catch for club is 65 fish. Wt £40 (S) and £25 (T), dt £15 (S) and £6 (T). No waiting list for trout membership. Permits from Watkin & Williams Hardware, 4 Berwyn St, LL20 8ND (tel: 01978 860652). Half day closing Sunday 8am to 10am, 2pm to 6pm. **Abbey Fishery**, a trout farm 1½m from Llangollen; 2 bait ponds, 1 fly pond and ½m on Eglwseg River, a tributary of the Dee. Accommodation in log cabins. Contact Nia Parry-Roberts, Penvale Lodges, Abbey Fishery, Llangollen, Denbighshire LL20 8DD (tel: 01978 860266). Hand Hotel, Bridge St, Llangollen, Denbighshire LL20 8PL (tel: 01978 860303), has own stretch of water below the bridge on right bank; fishing on hotel stretch of river for hotel residents only. Liverpool & Dist AA has salmon and trout fishing at Chain Bridge; st and dt.

Glyndyfrdwy (Denbighshire). Salmon, trout and grayling. Corwen & Dist AC has 1½m (mainly single bank) on Berwyn Arms Water; 5 named salmon pools; fly only; salmon, trout and grayling; contact Membership Sec (tel: 01824 710609). Midland Flyfishers has 3m of trout fishing on the Dee from Groeslwyd to Glyndyfrdwy; dt £6; D Jones, Llanon, Twynedd (tel: 01490 430363); Watkin & Williams Hardware, 4 Berwyn St, LL20 8ND (tel: 01978 860652); Berwyn Arms Hotel, Glyndyfrdwy, Corwen LL21 9EY

Fishing available?

If you own, manage, or know of first-class fishing available to the public which should be considered for inclusion in **Where to Fish***, please apply to the publishers (address in the front of the book) for a form for submission, on completion, to the editor. (Inclusion is at the sole discretion of the editor). There is no charge for inclusion.*

(tel: 01490 430210).

Corwen (Wrexham). Corwen & Dist AC has **Rhug Estate** Trust, approx 3½m mostly double bank, trout and grayling, fly only except winter grayling; ¼m stretch at **Cynwyd** including large holding pool, salmon, trout and grayling; ¾m stretch at **Carrog**, 3 named pools and runs, salmon, trout and grayling; 1½m stretch at Glyndyfrdwy; 2 stretches, 1m (double bank) and ¾m (double bank), between Cynwyd and Llandrillo, salmon, trout and grayling; and Chain Pool at Bonwn; five stretches varying in length, mostly in Corwen area; salmon trout and grayling; club also has several miles of water on **Rivers Alwen** and **Ceirw** at Bettws Gwerfil Goch and Maerdy; salmon and sea trout, mid to late season; and good trout early and late; no dt; members only; joining fee £25-£50; various categories of ticket £25-130; apply to Membership Sec (tel: 01824 710609). Capenhurst AC has stretch at Carrog; salmon, sea trout, trout and grayling; members only (£50 p/year). **Gwyddelwern Pool**, Corwen, ¾ acre lake, stocked with coarse fish (large carp and tench); permits from D M Lewis, Maes-y-Llyn, Gwyddelwern, Corwen, Wrexham LL21 9DG (tel: 01490 412761). Rod licences from Corwen Post Office. Hotels: Owain Glyndwr, Central, both Corwen; and Berwyn Arms, Glyndyfrdwy.

Cynwyd (Wrexham). Trout, grayling, salmon. Corwen & Dist AC has stretch on Dee from Glascoed to Cynwyd Bridge; plus 1¾m double bank (salmon, trout and grayling) above Cynwyd Bridge; and trout fishing on **Cynwyd Reservoir**; Sunday fishing, fly only; members only; st available, contact membership secretary. Crown Inn, Llanfihangel, has free fishing for guests.

Llandrillo (Wrexham). Salmon, trout, grayling, perch and pike. Strictly preserved by executors of Duke of Westminster's Pale Estate. Corwen & DAC has water at Cilan Bridge, 1m single bank below and 1½m single bank above bridge, including 1m double bank; members only; st at various prices, apply

membership secretary.

Llandderfel (Gwynedd). Salmon, trout, grayling. Pale Hall Country House Hotel, Llandderfel, nr Bala, Gwynedd LL23 7PS (tel: 01678 530285), has prime salmon and trout fishing during game season; permits free for hotel residents. Excellent grayling fishing provides ideal winter sport with specimens reaching 3lbs. Fishing is based on 6m of **River Dee** with access to brown trout in mountain lake.

Bala (Gwynedd). Salmon, trout, pike and grayling. Bala & Dist AA has water, including from confluence with Tryweryn to outlet Bala Lake and fishing on Bala Lake (members only); also **Rivers Tryweryn** (both banks between weir and Tryweryn Bridge; both banks above and below Bont Tyn-Ddol); **Lliw** (upper and lower reaches near Craig y Tan (2m both banks); **Llafar** (left bank d/stream from road bridge; both banks u/stream from road bridge); **Lynn Tryweryn** (trout, fly only); flyfishing only during game fishing season; st £45 (residents), £55 (non-residents), wt £20 (residents), £35 (non-residents), dt water (Bala outflow only), conc; available from Derwen Stores, 6 Stryd Fawr, LL23 7AG (tel: 01678 521084); Post Office, High Str, Bala (tel: 01678 521084); Tourist Information Centre, Penllyn Pensarn Rd, Bala, Gwynedd LL23 7YE (tel: 01678 521021). **Bala Lake** or **Llyn Tegid**; trout, roach, perch, pike, grayling, eel; owned by Snowdonia National Park Authority; permits from tackle shops and Lake Warden, Warden's Office, 24 Ffordd Pensarn, Bala LL23 7SR (tel: 01678 520626). Hotels and accommodation: White Lion Royal; Plas Coch.

Llanuwchllyn (Gwynedd). Trout and grayling. Prince Albert AS has trout and grayling fishing on nine stretches of Dee, here and elsewhere and Twrch; members only; waiting list. Dolhendre Uchaf Caravan Park, Llanuwchllyn, Bala LL23 7TD (tel: 01678 540629), has private fishing for owners of caravans on site only, on the River Lliw (trout and coarse fish, including the unique gwyniad).

Tributaries of the Dee

ALYN: Trout. Drains hills to west of Clwydian Range, runs past Mold towards Wrexham and finally opens into lower part of Dee on Cheshire Plains near Farndon at Almere.

Rossett (Wrexham). Trout. Rossett & Griffin FF has wild brown trout fishing on 2½m stretch (both banks) on well maintained and stocked section of R Alyn between Rossett and Gresford, nr Wrexham; members only; fly only; bag limit; st £44 and £5 (juniors); permits from Hon Sec. Warrington AA have water lower down and stretch on Dee, at Almere. Tackle shop: David Gibson, 13 Pepper Row, Pepper Str, Chester CH1 1EA (tel: 01244 316132). Hotel: Trevor Arms Hotel.

Rossett and **Gresford** (Wrexham). Trout. Rossett & Griffin FFC has one stretch 3½m of Alyn; members only; dt available; apply Hon Sec.

Wrexham (Wrexham). Wrexham & Dist AA has water on Alyn; trout fishing, fly only. Permits issued to guests of members only. Dee Valley Water plc, Packsaddle, Wrexham Rd, Rhostyllen, Wrexham, Clwyd LL14 4DS (tel: 01978 846946), manage 3 local reservoirs: **Ty Mawr Reservoir** (20 acres), **Penycae Upper Reservoir** (7 acres) and **Penycae Lower Reservoir** (5 acres). The fishing is quiet and secluded with very clear water; possible to locate and stalk individual fish (stocked up to 6 lbs). Brown and rainbow trout; fly fishing only. St £260, dt £20-£13 (Penycae) and £18-£12 (Ty Mawr). At least 12 hrs notice must be given in order to reserve a rod. Number of rods limited. Contact the bailiff (tel: 01978 840116). Ponciau AS has **Ponciau Pool**, 2½m from Wrexham; roach, bream, tench, carp; members only. Rhostyllen AC (affiliated to Dee AA and Chester AA) has coarse fishing at pool near Sontley; club also has access to extensive game and coarse fisheries on **Dee**, **Severn** and **Shropshire Union Canal**. Tackle shops: Deggy's Fishing Tackle, 2 Ruabon Road, Wrexham, Clwyd LL13 7NU (tel: 01978 351815); Derek's Cycles & Fishing Tackle, Wells Str, Cefn Mawr, Wrexham LL14 3AE (tel: 01978 821841). Hotel: Trevor Arms Hotel, Marford, Wrexham.

Llay (Wrexham). Llay AA has good coarse fishing on **Llay Reservoir** (tench, carp, rudd, perch, pike); and **Cymau Pool** (carp, rudd, tench, perch, roach, crucian carp and gudgeon) at Caergwrle; members only; st £10 (jun £5 and OAP £5) from Hon Sec, local shops or bailiff on bank; no dt; residents have preference. Hotels: Crown Inn; and Mount Pleasant.

Hope (Wrexham). Wrexham & Dist AA has trout fishing from Llong railway bridge to Pont y Delyn; fly only; permits issued to members' guests only. Brown and rainbow trout fishing at **Tree Tops Fly Fishery**; eight lakes stocked with rainbow and brown trout. Rods to hire and basic tuition by arrangement. Cafe, tackle shop and accommodation. For further details contact Joy or Peter Price, Tree Tops Fly Fishery, Llanfynydd, nr Wrexham, Flintshire LL11 5HR (tel: 01352 770648).

Mold (Wrexham). Mold FF has stretch on Alyn; and fishing on **New Lake**, Rhydymwyn; all fisheries stocked with brown and rainbow trout; they also have trout fishing on **Pistyll Pool** at Nercwys, 1½ acres (stocked brown and rainbow trout); members only; day tickets if accompanied by member, conc for juv. **Pen-y-Ffrith Fly Fishery**, Llandegla Rd, Llanarmon-yn-Ial, Mold, CH7 4QX (tel: 01824 780501); 3 spring fed lakes stocked regularly with rainbows from 2lbs to 20lbs, some brown and blue trout; 8 hours fishing, 4 fish limit, 4 hrs 2 fish; also c&r; tackle shop on site, book in at lodge. Buckley AA has **Trap Pool**, a good mixed fishery; permits from Lionel's Tackle Shop, Pentre Lane, Buckley, Flintshire CH7 3PA (tel: 01244 543191). Coarse fishing at **Gweryd**

Lakes, Gweryd Lodge, Plas Lane, Lla-narmon-yn-Ial, nr Mold, Denbighshire CH7 4QJ (tel: 01824 780230). 12½ acre lake with specimen carp; 1¾ acre lake with silver fish, crucian carp, perch and tench, etc. Dt £5, £6 Fri/Sun, conc. Accom on site.

Cilcain (Flintshire). Cilcain FFA has four trout reservoirs nearby; stocked with rainbow trout; fly only; dt £12, 2 brace limit. Permits from the village Post Office. **Nant-y-Gain Fishery**, 2 pools stocked with brown and rainbow trout, fly only. Access and facilities for disabled anglers. Tickets and refreshments available on site. Contact Glyn or Judy Jones, Nant-y-Gain Fishery, Cilcain, Flintshire CH7 5PE (tel: 01352 740936).

Nannerch (Wrexham). **Sarn Mill Fly and Coarse Fisheries**, Denbigh Road, Nannerch, nr Mold CH7 5RH (tel: 01352 720854), 4 pools; 2 pools fly only, stocked with wild browns and rainbow trout; 2 pools coarse fishing, roach, rudd, tench and carp; open all year; disabled access. **Wal Goch Fly Fishing**; 2 lakes (2½ and ½ acre); brown and rainbow trout; open all year; fly only; max 20 rods; floodlights, catch-and-release, trickle stocked; monthly £50 competition for biggest fish; contact Philip Robinson, Wal Goch Fly Fishing, Wal Goch Farm, CH7 5RP (tel: 01352 741378).

CEIRIOG: Trout.

Chirk (Wrexham). Ceiriog Fly Fishers have 8m, both banks, from Dee Junction to Chirk, and from Chirk Aquaduct to Pontfadog Village; good fishing, trout and grayling; fly only; keepered and stocked with browns. No tickets; strictly members and guests only. St £150 from to Hon Sec, conc. **Chirk Trout Fishery**, LL14 5BL (tel: 01691 772420); two small lakes for fly only now, plus a children's lake; stocked with rainbow, brown, and American brook trout; dt available. Hotel: The Hand Hotel, Chirk; Golden Pheasant, Pontfadog, Llwyn Mawr.

Glyn Ceiriog (Wrexham). Glyn Ceiriog FC has trout fishing on **River Teirw** at Pandy, nr Glyn Ceiriog.

Llanarmon Dyffryn Ceiriog (Wrexham). Ceiriog, 2½m, brown trout. The West Arms Hotel, Llanarmon D C, Llangollen LL20 7LD (tel: 01691 600665), has 1½m (both banks) trout fishing; shallow clear water with some deep pools; free to hotel residents; dt for non-residents; limit 2 rods per day; fly only. Hand Hotel, Lla-

narmon Dyffryn Ceiriog, Pwllheli LL53 6AB (tel: 01691 600666) arranges trout and coarse fishing for guests.

ALWEN: Flows out of large reservoir (trout, perch) on Denbigh Moors and enters Dee near Corwen. Very good trout fishing and some salmon.

Cerrig-y-Drudion (Conwy). Cerrig-y-Drudion AA has river fishing on Alwen and on **R Ceirw**, parallel with A5 road. Crown Inn, Llanfihangel Glyn Myfyr, has fishing on ¼m of bank for small wild brown trout; fly and worm; permits (free to hotel residents). Dwr Cymru Welsh Water plc manage three reservoirs north of town. **Llyn Brenig**, 919-acre reservoir amid heather moorland and forest; fly only, brown and rainbow trout. Llyn Brenig was the venue for 1990 World Fly Fishing Championship and regular Home Fly Fishing Internationals; st £440, dt £14.50, evening £12.50, boats £19 w/ends, weekdays £17 per day; Wheely-boat £5 (wheelchair users only); season: Mar-Nov; concessions OAP & jun; block bookings offered. **Alwen Reservoir** (368 acre), moorland reservoir stocked with rainbow and brown trout, although also natural population of brown trout and perch; dt £11; fly fishing, spinning and worming permitted; catch limit 6 trout; season Mar-Nov; **Llyn Aled Reservoir** (110 acres), holds large numbers of roach, perch and pike and is a good match venue; occasional wild brown trout; no close season for coarse fish; concessions OAP and jun; tickets and further information from Llyn Brenig Visitor Centre, Cerrigdrudion, Corwen, Conwy LL21 9TT (tel: 01490 420463); where there is also a café and well-stocked tackle shop. Fly fishing at **Dragonfly Fisheries**, on the A5, Cerrig-y-Drudion, Corwen, Clwyd LL21 9SW (tel: 01490 420530); blue trout (2001 Welsh record at 10¾lb), rainbow and brown trout; stocked daily with fish from 3lb min to 28lb; dt £21, plus variants, conc; min 4 hours £12.50 (1 fish), £15 (2 fish); 6 hours £15 (1 fish), £17.50 (2 fish). Periods can be fully fished out.

TRYWERYN: Joins Dee below Lake Bala. Good trout fishing.

Bala (Gwynedd). Bala AA has 2 stretches on Tryweryn, **Llyn Celyn** and mountain lake **Cwm Prysor**; also Dee outflow; Dee below sluice gates; Dee at Llandderfel. Tickets from Hon Sec, tackle shop (below) or Tourist Information, Penllyn

Pensarn Rd, LL23 7YE (tel: 01678   Tegid Str LL23 7UR (tel: 01678 520382).
521021). Tackle shop: Spaner-a-Hanner,

DYFI (DOVEY)

(For close seasons, licences, etc, see Welsh Region Environment Agency, p23)

Rises on east side of Aran Fawddwy and flows 30m south and south-west to Cardigan Bay at Aberdovey. Has long estuary and provides splendid sport with sewin (sea trout) and salmon. Many large sea trout taken. Salmon run in from July to October; sea trout from May on. Best months: July, August, September. Small tributaries hold some little trout, and permission can generally be obtained from owners.

Aberdyfi (Gwynedd). At estuary mouth; surf and estuary fishing. Free trout fishing in Happy Valley on permission of farmers; stream; trout small.

Machynlleth (Powys). Sea trout and salmon. The New Dovey Fishery Association controls 15m (both banks) of river between Llyfnant stream and Nant Ty-Mawr and left bank, from opposite Llyfnant mouth to Abergwybedyn brook. Season rods available when vacancies occur (long waiting list - contact Hon Sec). Upper reaches st £150 from Hon Sec; limited visitors wt £160 from Mrs L Humphreys, Post Office, Cemmaes Rd, Machynlleth, Powys SY20 8JZ (tel: 01650 511422); and Hon Sec (tel/fax: 01654 702721); dt £14.50 for upper reaches, juv dt £3.50 (when accompanied by adult); no Sunday fishing. Prince Albert AS has fishing on single bank Dulas North, tributary of Dyfi ½m upstream. Corris Caravan Park SY20 9HD has fishing for caravan owners only (tel: 01654 761220). Permission from farmers for **Pennal Stream**; rapid water; trout small. Tackle shop: Greenstiles, 4 Maengwyn Str, SY20 8AE (tel: 01654 703543). Hotels: Wynnstay Arms, White Lion.

Llanbrynmair (Powys). On **River Twy-**myn, a tributary of **Dyfi**; sewin, salmon. Llanbrynmair & Dist AC has water on Twymyn from village to confluence with Dyfi (apart from one stretch held by Prince Albert AS); and wild brown trout fishing on **Lakes Gwyddior** and **Coch-Hwyad**, both lakes 25 acres with a boat on each; best months Jul-Oct; dt water, conc available from Mrs D R Lewis, Bryn-Llugwy Llanbrynmair, Powys SY19 7AA. Prince Albert AS control 3m of Twymyn (members only), and Dyfi at **Aberangell** and **Dinas Mawddwy**; enquiries to Hon Sec.

Dinas Mawddwy (Gwynedd). Sewin, salmon, trout; fishing good. Brigands Inn, Mallwyd, Dinas Mawddwy SY20 9HJ (tel: 01650 531208), has some of the best pools on upper reaches and stretch on Cleifion; dt and wt available. The Dolbrodmaeth Inn, Dinas Mawddwy, Machynlleth, Powys SY20 9LP (tel: 01650 531333), has ½m stretch on Dyfi in grounds of hotel; sewin, salmon, trout; tickets available. Dolgellau AA issues tickets for 12m of Rivers Mawddach and Wnion, and Lake Cynwch (all in vicinity of Dolgellau). Prince Albert AS has 2½m stretch of Dyfi at Gwastad Coed, Gwerhefin; members only.

DWYRYD

(For close seasons, licences, etc, see Welsh Region Environment Agency, p23)

Rises in small, nameless pool 3m above Tanygrisiau and flows into Cardigan Bay through estuary north of Harlech. A classic spate river with deep pools which hold good numbers of fish following a spate. Sea trout enter the river towards the end of May: these tend to be large fish with the 1-3lbs following in June. Fresh sea trout still enter the river in October. The first run of salmon appear in July with increasing numbers in August, September and October.

Maentwrog (Gwynedd). Dwyryd Anglers Ltd has fishing at **Tan-y-Bwlch Fishery** on River Dwyryd (north bank only), 1¾m downstream from Maentwrog Bridge; st £55 (limited), wt £30 (any 7 consecutive days) and dt £8; concessions for juniors and OAPs; permits from Gareth Price, Tackle Shop, Hafan, Fford Peniel, Ffesti-niog, Gwynedd (tel: 01766 762451); Dwyryd Anglers Ltd also has 3½m (double bank) of private water on Dwyryd; a very limited number of season rods may become available, contact G. Price for information.

Blaenau Ffestiniog (Gwynedd). Principal trout lakes controlled by Cambrian AA as follows: **Dubach**, well stocked with brown trout; **Manod**, fishing rather rough due to rocky shore conditions, holds plenty of fish; **Morwynion**, most easily accessible, average weight 12ozs; **Cwmorthin**, well stocked with brown trout 8-9ozs. Other Cambrian AA lakes: **Dubach-y-Bont**, fish to 2½lbs no rarity, **Barlwyd, Cwm Foel** and **Cwm Corsiog**. St £35, wt £16, dt £4. **Tanygrisiau**

Reservoir (2m NW), 95 acres, stocked with brown and rainbow trout; controlled by local syndicate. Spinning and bait fishing allowed. Permits for Cambrian AA waters and for Tanygrisiau from F W Roberts, Fishing Tackle, 32 Church Str, Blaenau Ffestiniog, Gwynedd LL41 3HD (tel: 01766 830607). Hotels: Pengwern Arms, Ffestiniog.

Tributaries of the Dwyryd

PRYSOR:
Trawsfynydd (Gwynedd). Prysor AA controls 5m on **Prysor River**, which provides good fishing towards the end of the season when late trout run upstream; season 1 Apr-30 Sep; also 3m on upper **Eden**: salmon and sea trout July onwards; Assn also manages **Trawsfynydd Lake**, 1200 acres; brown and rainbow trout (average 1½lb), perch and rudd; season: rainbow trout 1 Feb-31 Dec; brown trout 1 Mar-30 Sept; coarse fish 1 Feb-31 Dec; fly fishing, bottom fishing and spinning; boats with motors for daily hire; fly only from boats. St £195, wt £50 and dt £11;

boats with motors per day at w/end £36 (pair) and midweek £30 (pair); conc for OAP; fly only from boats; regular trout stocking. Membership and permit enquiries to Hon Sec. Tickets J & J Newsagents, Manchester House, Trawsfynydd (tel: 01766 540234). Hotels: Cross Foxes and White Lion, Trawsfynydd; Grapes and Oakely Arms, Maentwrog; Abbey Arms and Pengwern Arms, Ffestiniog. Accommodation at Old Mill Farmhouse, Fron Oleu Farm LL41 4UN (tel/fax: 01766 540397) and Bryncelynog Farms, Trawsfynydd and in self-catering chalets at Trawsfynydd Holiday Village.

DYSYNNI

(For close seasons, licences, etc, see Welsh Region Environment Agency, p23)

Rises in Llyn Cau, on steep southern side of Cader Idris, then falls rather rapidly via Dol-y-Cau. Falls into Talyllyn Valley about half a mile above well known Talyllyn Lake. Emerging from lake, flows westwards as typical upland stream to Abergynolwyn where, joined by the Gwernol, it turns north through narrow valley until it enters upper end of broad Dysynni Valley. At Peniarth it becomes deep and sluggish and finally enters Cardigan Bay 1½m north of Tywyn. Trout along whole length and tributaries, and sea trout (sewin) and salmon travel beyond Talyllyn Lake and up to Dolgoch on Afon Fathew. In lower reaches good sport may be had, early and late in season, with trout and sewin; August generally best. Also excellent grey mullet and bass in estuary.

Tywyn (Gwynedd). Salmon, sewin, trout, eels, with grey mullet in tidal parts and excellent bass fishing at mouth and from adjacent beaches. Rod licence only needed for fishing on estuary. Tywyn Post Office issues permits for several beats on River Dysynni and EA rod licences and permits for Peniarth. **Penowern Water**, ½m left bank from confluence with Afon Fathew; private waters; contact Richard Jones, Ysgubor-

lau, Bryncrug LL36 9RY. **Peniarth Estate** has 3½m of double bank, either side of the Dysynni Bridge; st, wt, dt available; contact the Estate Office, Peniarth, Llanegryn LL36 9UD (tel: 01654 710101); permits for 1 beat and north bank of Afon Fathew from Tywyn Post Office; tickets from Siop-y-Bont, Brycrug; Middle Peniarth Estate beat is private. Ystumaner AA water near Abergynolwyn, 6m from Tywyn, st £35,

---

Keep the banks clean

Several clubs have stopped issuing tickets to visitors because of the state of the banks after they have left. Spend a few moments clearing up. This includes lengths of broken nylon. If discarded, serious injuries can be caused to wild birds and to livestock.

dt £7, from Railway Inn, Abergynolwyn. Prince Albert AA has Upper Peniarth Estate beat; members only. Peniarth Estate also has caravan park, 3m from Tywyn. Tackle shop: Barry's Fishing Tackle, 6 College Green, Tywyn LL36 9BS (tel: 01654 710357).

Abergynolwyn (Gwynedd). Salmon, sea trout, brown trout. Ystumaner AA has 3m on Dysynni; stocking at intervals during seasons; bag limit 4 trout, 2 salmon, 2 sea trout; membership for local residents only; visitors permits: st £25, wt £12, dt £5 (conc for jun), from Railway Inn, Abergynolwyn. Hotel: Tyn-y-Cornel *(see below)*.

Talyllyn (Gwynedd). Salmon, sea trout, brown trout. Tyn-y-Cornel Hotel and Ta-

lyllyn Fishery, Talyllyn, Tywyn, Gwynedd LL36 9AJ (tel: 01654 782282); issues permits for **River Dysynni**, 3½m of mostly double bank fishing; **Talyllyn Lake**, 220 acres; and **Llyn Bugeilyn**, 45 acres. Salmon, sea trout, first rate brown trout fishing; tackle shop, ghillies, fishing tuition, boat hire (with engine) and tackle hire; boat hire priority given to hotel residents but day tickets usually available; Talyllyn: dt £17, half-dt £12; boat permit additional full day £20, part day £14; Dysynni: £8.50 (lower river: Peniarth Estate beat); £5 (middle/upper river: Ystumaner AA water). Llyn Bugeilyn, £10; + £10 for boat. Hotel also sells permits for Ystumaner AA plus EA licences; tackle shop on site at Fishery.

GLASLYN

(For close seasons, licences, etc, see Welsh Region Environment Agency, p23)

Rises in Llyn Glaslyn, 3m south-west of Pen-y-Gwyrd, and flows through three lakes to Beddgelert then along Pass of Aberglaslyn to lower reaches and Porthmadog, where it enters the sea. Noted sea trout river and efforts are being made to increase salmon run. Best trout fishing in upper reaches, mountain lakes and tributaries. Best spots for salmon and sewin are: Glaslyn Hotel Bridge; Verlas; and above the pass. A fast-flowing river: steep access to best pools.

Porthmadog (Gwynedd). Glaslyn AA has most of 14m both banks of R Glaslyn between Porthmadog and Beddgelert, and far bank of **Dinas Lake**; trout, sea trout and salmon; average catches over past 5 years, 530 sea trout, 35 salmon, 16 grilse. No prawn fishing; no ground bait; no boat fishing. St £65, wt £30 and dt £15; conc for OAPs, dis and juv. Tickets from The Fisherman, *(below)*; K Owen, Llyndu Farm, Nantgwynant, Beddgelert, Gwynedd LL55 4NL; Penrhyn Guns *(below)*; P O Beddgelert. **Llyn Cwmystradllyn**, Caernarfon Rd, wild brown trout fishery and rainbows, 95 acres, 6 bag limit; dt £10. **Llyn Glan Morfa Mawr**, 5 acre lake, rainbow trout, Morfa Bychan LL49, 9YH: contact Justin Roberts (tel: 01766 513333); rainbow (av 2lb - any method) 8 bag limit, dt £14; father & son ticket (4 fish each) £16, from Fishery. Camping field adjacent. **Bron Eifion Trout Fisheries**, Criccieth, Gwynedd, fly-only lake and bait lake; 6 fish limit. Permits from The Fisherman, Central Buildings, High St, Porthmadog, Gwynedd LL49 9LR (tel: 01766 512464), open 7 days a week, fresh bait sold; Penrhyn Guns, 7 High St, Penrhyndeudraeth LL48 6BN (tel: 01766

770339), who also sell permits for Artro & Talsarlau FS waters; st £40, dt £8, conc (coarse fishiong lake dt £6). For Bron Eifion and Glan Morfa Mawr, Companions Pets & Tackle Shop, 48a High St LL52 0EY (tel: 01766 522805; web: www.ang lingwales.co.uk). Hotels: Royal Sportsman, High St; Madog Hotel, Tremadog; Owens Hotel, 71 High Str, LL49 9EU has tackle room and freezers for keeping fish (tel: 01766 512098).

Beddgelert (Gwynedd). Sea trout and salmon. Best for sea trout mid-May to early Sept; salmon May-Oct. Glaslyn AA has Glaslyn from Beddgelert to Porthmadog; and **Llyn Dinas**, 2m NE, sea trout and salmon. Permits - Mon to Fri; left bank (only) on Llyn Dinas, no boats, one day; concessions jun & OAP; permits from Beddgelert Post Office, Beddgelert, Caernarfon, Gwynedd LL55 4UY (tel: 01766 890201). National Trust has fishing here, **Nantgwynant**; apply North West Wales Area Office (tel: 01690 713300). National Trust also water at **Aberglaslyn**; Glaslyn AA fishing; dt available; apply Hon Sec. Many good hotels, guest houses, and B&B.

GWYNEDD (rivers and streams)

(For close seasons, licences, etc, see Welsh Region Environment Agency, p23)

ABER. Aber, nr Llanfairfechan (Gwynedd). Aber rises in Llyn Anafon, runs to Aber and sea in 2m. Trout (average 7-8 in). Now a Nature Reserve. No fishing.

ARTRO. Rises in Llyn Cwm Bychan, 6m E of Harlech, and enters sea 1m below Llanbedr. Good bass fishing in tidal waters. Noted for night fishing for sea trout. Good fly pools below village and above Dol-y-Bebin.

Llanbedr (Gwynedd). Artro and Talsarnau FA has salmon and sea trout fishing on Artro. Assn also has water on **River Nantcol**, brown trout; **Cooke's Dam**, rainbow trout; **Llyn Tecwyn Uchaf** (brown trout) and **Llyn Tecwyn Isaf** (stocked with carp, roach, rudd, tench, perch) at Talsarnau; **River Glyn** at Talsarnau, sea trout and salmon; and **Llyn Fedw** at Harlech, brown trout. St £40, wt £20, dt £8. Concessions for OAP and junior. Permits from The Old Bakery, Newsagent & General Stores, Llanbedr LL45 2LE (tel: 01341 241380); Post Office, Talsarnau; and tackle shops in Penrhyndeudraeth. Hotels: Victoria; Ty-Mawr.

DARON. Aberdaron (Gwynedd). Daron and Cyll-y-Felin run down two valleys and join at Aberdaron; restocked and hold good sized trout. Sea fishing for mackerel, pollack, lobster, crab, etc., from rocks or boat. Tackle and bait and licences from GW & AG Jones, Eleri Stores, Aberdaron LL53 8BG (tel: 01758 760233).

DWYFOR. Best part of river lies 1m W of Criccieth, where there is length of 12m unobstructed and good for fly fishing. Salmon fishing has greatly improved owing to restrictions on netting. Sewin very good; late June to Oct; night fishing best.

Criccieth (Gwynedd). Sea trout and salmon. Criccieth, Llanystumdwy & Dist AA controls about 10m both banks. Assn also has about 2m on **Dwyfach**; shorter river than Dwyfor (about 10m) and rather heavily wooded; st £100, wt £50, 72-hrs £30, dt £15, from Companions Pets & Tackle Shop, 48a High St LL52 0EY (tel: 01766 522805; web: www.ang ling-wales.co.uk). Rod licences from Post Office. Companions Pets also sells tickets for **Eisteddefa Fisheries**, 2 new fishings, one coarse lake and one carp; with a trout lake now open; tickets also on bank. Good sea fishing in this area. Hotels:

Glyn y Coed; Lion; Marinewise; George; Caerwylan.

ERCH. Pwllheli (Gwynedd). Pwllheli & Dist AA has brown trout, sea trout and salmon fishing on **Rivers Erch** and **Rhydhir**; Assn also has brown and rainbow trout fishing on **Llyn Cwmystradllyn**; approx 10m NW; 95-acre lake holding wild and stocked brown trout; an upland fishery, situated in the heart of the rugged foothills of Snowdonia; bag limit 6 trout per day; st £53, wt £25, dt £10 (includes two rivers); concessions for juniors and OAPs; permits from D & E Hughes, Walsall Stores, 24 Penlan St, LL53 5DE (tel: 01758 613291); Companions Pets & Tackle Shop, 48a High St LL52 0EY (tel: 01766 522805; web: www.anglingwales.co.uk). The Fisherman, Central Bldgs High St, Porthmadog, Gwynedd, LL49 9BT (tel: 01766 512464), who also sell permits for rivers Dwyfor and Glaslyn.

GEIRCH. Nefyn (Gwynedd). Geirch, 2m W, 5m long; good sea fishing at Morfa Nefyn.

GWYRFAI. Issues from Llyn Cwellyn, near Snowdon, and flows into Menai Strait through Betws Garmon and Llanwnda. Salmon, sea trout, trout.

Betws Garmon (Gwynedd). Seiont, Gwyrfai and Llyfni AS controls much of Gwyrfai; salmon, sea trout and brown trout; wt £70, dt £15; the society provides top quality self-catering accommodation in Old Corn Mill, on banks of Llyfni at Pantllyfni; contact Hon Sec for details (tel: 01248 670666); society permits and accommodation from Cwellyn Arms Hotel, Rhyd-ddu, LL54 6TL (tel: 01766 890321; web: www.snowdoninn.co.uk). **Bont-newydd Fishery**, salmon, sea and brown trout; dt from G J M Wills, Bryn Mafon, Caethro, Caernarfon LL55 2TE (tel: 01286 673379 - after 6pm) or his Bangor office, Treborth Leisure; tel: 01248 364399.

Rhyd-Ddu (Gwynedd). Seiont, Gwyrfai and Llyfni AS offers boat fishing on **Lynn Nantlle**, salmon and sea trout fishing; **Llyn Cwm Dwythwch**, Llanbers, and **Llyn Cwm Silyn**, Nantlle all have excellent wild brown trout; **Llyn Cwellyn**, brown trout, char, salmon and sea trout; **Llyn-y-Dywarchen**, regularly restocked with rainbow and brown trout, fly only, bag limit 4; wt £70, dt £15 (Llyn Cwellyn £10 and Llyn-y-Dywarchen £10); permits from Cwellyn Arms, Rhydddu LL54 6TL (tel/fax: 01766 890321; web: www.snowdoninn.co.uk); boat packages available, enquiries to Hon Sec (tel: 01248 670666).

LLYFNI. Penygroes (Gwynedd). Rises in Drws-y-Coed, 4m E of town and runs through Nantlle Lake; salmon, sea trout (good), trout. Seiont, Gwyrfai and Llyfni AS controls most of river; wt £70, dt £15; permits from A D Griffiths, Newsagent, Snowdon St; society also has fishing on **Llyn Nantlle**; boat bookings (only) for salmon and trout; apply to Hon Sec (tel: 01248 670666); the society provides top quality self-catering accommodation in Old Corn Mill, on banks of Lllyfni at Pantllyfni; contact Hon Sec for details; accommodation and boat bookings: Cwellyn Arms, Rhyd Ddu (tel: 01766 890321).

SOCH. Llangian (Gwynedd). Trout and rudd; an early stream; dry fly useful; weeds troublesome later; some sewin, late; plenty of sea fishing, bass, pollack, whiting, flatfish, at Abersoch, from which this stream can be fished. Hotels: Rhydolion (Soch runs on boundary of farm, equipment available); Coed-y-Llyn, Sarn Bach Rd, Abersoch.

YSGETHIN. River rises in **Llyn Bodlyn**. Brown trout, Arctic char.

GWYNEDD (lakes)

(For close seasons, licences, etc, see Welsh Region Environment Agency, p23)

Bala Lake or **Llyn Tegid. Bala** (Gwynedd). Owned by Snowdonia National Park Authority, Penrhydeudraeth. Permits from Lake Warden, Warden's Office, 24 Ffordd Pensarn, Bala LL23 7SR (tel: 01678 520626). Salmon may sometimes be taken and trout early in season. Pike, perch, roach, grayling, eels. Bala is largest natural lake in Wales, 4m long, ¾m wide. Here, too, is found that rare and interesting fish called the gwyniad, a land-locked whitefish. Coarse fishermen will find all their wants more than provided for; pike up to 25lb; perch and good roach. Rod licence required.

Llyn Celyn. Bala (Gwynedd). Situated in the Snowdonia National Park at the foot of the Arenig Mountains; rainbow trout are stocked to supplement wild brown trout. Reservoir managed under licence by Bala & Dist AA. Sunday fishing.

Cwm Bychan Lake. Llanbedr (Gwynedd). Trout and sewin; good fishing. For permission to fish, apply to Farm Manager, Cwm Bychan Farm, Cwm Bychan. For **Gloywlyn Lake** apply Cwmrafon Farm. **Llyn Perfeddau**, trout, good fishing; free.

Maentwrog (Gwynedd). **Y-Garnedd**, 1m N (trout) and **Hafod-y-Llyn**, 1m NW (pike, coarse fish) are both private. Cambrian AA lakes in area: **Morwynion, Cwmorthin, Manod, Barlwyd, Dubach, Dubach-y-Bont, Cwm Foel, Cwm Corsiog**. Permits from F W Roberts, 32 Church St, Blaenau Ffestiniog, Gwynedd LL41 3HD (tel: 01766 830607).

Talsarnau (Gwynedd). Artro and Talsarnau FA has water on **Llyn Tecwyn Uchaf** and **Llyn Tecwyn Isaf**, brown trout; and on **River Glyn**, sea trout and salmon; st £45, wt £20, dt £6; permits from Post Office. Hotels: Ship Aground; Motel.

LLWCHWR (or LOUGHOR)

(For close seasons, licences, etc, see Welsh Region Environment Agency, p23)

Rises some 3m east of Llandybie on Taircarn Mountain and flows 15m south-west through Ammanford and Pontardulais to Burry Inlet, north of Gower Peninsula. Fishing very good for sewin, and some brown trout and salmon (Apr-July; Aug-Oct best). Salmon and sewin runs reported to be increasing. Most fishing controlled by clubs, from whom tickets are

---

Fishing available?

If you own, manage, or know of first-class fishing available to the public which should be considered for inclusion in **Where to Fish** *please apply to the publishers (address in the front of the book) for a form for submission, on completion, to the Editor. (Inclusion is at the sole discretion of the Editor). No charge is made for editorial inclusion.*

available.

Llanelli (Carmarthenshire). Carmarthenshire County Council controls fishing on **Upper and Lower Lliedi Reservoirs**; with game fishing only on Upper Lliedi; boat hire is available for members of Llanelli AA at £6 per day; the bottom Lliedi Reservoir is now a coarse fishery of 32 acres. The council also has fishing at **Furnace Pond** and **Old Castle Pond** (carp, bream and pike), and **Cwmoernant Reservoirs, Carmarthen**. Within Council's jurisdiction is **Gwellian Pool**, nr Kidwelly, with trout, sewin and salmon; st and dt from Tourism and Leisure Office, Tyr-Nant, Trostre Bus Park, Llanelli, SA14 9UT (tel: 01554 747500). Tackle shop: Anglers Corner, 80 Station Rd, SA15 1AN (tel: 01554 773981).

Llangennech (Carmarthenshire). Llangennech AC has 4m on **River Gwendraeth Fach** between Llandyfaelog and Llangendeirne Bridge near Kidwelly; and 2m on **River Morlais**, a tributary of R Loughor, from the road bridge at Llangennech upstream. Season 3 Mar-17 Oct. Mainly brown trout with good runs of sea trout in both rivers. Waters stocked with average 12" brown trout at intervals during the season. Bag limit 4 fish. St £25 plus £15 joining fee, conc for juv, OAPs and disabled. Season members only, application

forms from Hon Sec (tel: 01554 821637); or Anglers Corner, 80 Station Rd, Llanelli SA15 1AN (tel: 01554 773981). Club offers fresh water and some sea fishing competitions; and, during the close season, runs fly-tying classes.

Pontardulais (Glamorgan). Trout and a run of sea trout; some salmon. Pontardulais & Dist AA has 6m good fishing; concessions for OAP and jun. **White Springs Lakes**, Holiday Complex, Garnswllt Rd, Pontardulais, Swansea SA4 8QG (tel: 01792 885699); 6 coarse lakes with large carp, tench, golden orfe, etc; 1 specimen carp lake; night-fishing and tents allowed; lakeside parking; tickets on site in shop, also maggots, ground bait, tackle and rods for sale; licensed lodge; accommodation in holiday apartments. Tackle shop: Tackle Broker, 100 St Teilo Str,, Pontarddulais SA4 8SS (tel: 01792 885519).

Ammanford (Dyfed). Ammanford & Dist AA has water on middle and upper reaches of Llwchwr and tributaries. Boat for club members at **Llys-y-Fran Reservoir**, much improved sea trout run, biggest fish 16½lb. Permits for these and other local waters from Tightlines Direct, 72-74 Wind St, Ammanford, Carmarthenshire SA18 3DR (tel: 01269 592380).

Tributaries of the Llwchwr

AMMAN. Trout, sewin, few salmon. Very fast running; fishes well in spate.

Ammanford (Dyfed). Ammanford & Dist AA has water on **Llwchwr**, 5m; **Amman**, 3m; **Lash**, 3m; **Marlais**, 3m; ½m; **Gwili**, 1½m; sea trout run from May onwards; concessions for juniors, youths and ladies; instruction, fly-tying classes and competitions; club boat based on Usk

Reservoir, £5 to members; permits from Tightlines Direct, 72-74 Wind St, Ammanford, Carmarthenshire SA18 3DR (tel: 01269 592380); and Hon Sec. Hotel: Glynhir Mansion.

MARLAIS BROOK. Llandybie (Dyfed). Sewin, July onwards. **Llwchwr**, 3m. **Gwendraeth Fawr**, 5m W. **Llyn Lechowen**, 5m W.

MAWDDACH

(For close seasons, licences, etc, see Welsh Region Environment Agency, p23)

Rises in hills between Bala and Trawsfynydd Lakes and flows 10m south to confluence with Wnion, 2m below Dolgellau, and thence through long estuary to sea at Barmouth. One of the best rivers in Wales for salmon and sea trout fishing, also brown trout, and is all preserved, although permits can be had for some stretches. Successful stocking with locally hatched salmon and sea trout. Salmon and sea trout may be taken up to Pistyll Mawddach.

Barmouth (Gwynedd). Rivers Mawddach and **Wnion**; lower reaches of Wnion have excellent night fly fishing for sewin and sea trout, in various named pools. Dolgellau AA has fishing on both rivers; permits, *see Dolgellau*. Run of sea trout and

salmon is from beginning of June to end of season. Trout fishing on **Cregennan Lakes**, Emlyn Lloyd, Fridd Boedel Farm, Arthog, nr Fairbourne (tel: 01341 250426/250468); 2 natural lakes owned by the National Trust, situated on northern slopes of Cader Idris overlooking beautiful Mawddach Estuary; 27 acre lake with island, wild brown trout only, fly, spin or worm; dt £8 and evening £6; 13 acre lake, regularly stocked with rainbows, plus a good head of wild brown trout, fly only; dt £15 and evening £8; boat for hire but booking advisable. Permits from Fish Tales, Bridge St, Dolgellau OL40 1AU (tel: 01341 421080); or at Fridd Boedel Farm *(see above)*. **Penmaenpool** (Gwynedd). Salmon, sea trout. Dolgellau AA waters; salmon and sea trout fishing on lower beats of Mawddach. National Trust has Dolmelynllyn Estate; dt water; spin, worm or fly depending on season; fishing normally available only to residents of Hotel Tyn-y-Groes (tel: 01341 440275) and Dolmelynllyn Hotel (tel: 01341 440273).

Ganllwyd (Gwynedd). Salmon, sea trout. Dolgellau AA has left bank of upper beat from Ganllwyd to Tyn-y-Groes Pool. Tickets from Fish Tales, Bridge St, Dolgellau OL40 1AU (tel: 01341 421080); Plas Dolmelynllyn Hall *(see below) (see Dolgellau)*. Hotels: Tyn-y-Groes, Ganllwyd, (1½m salmon and sea trout fishing on river); Plas Dolmelynllyn Hall, Ganllwyd, LL40 2HP (tel: 01341 440273) has 1½m salmon and sea trout fishing on Mawddach right bank, priority given to guests.

Tributaries of Mawddach.

WNION: Salmon, sewin, sea trout. The Rivers Mawddach and Wnion are well known for the excellent salmon and sea trout fishing. Dry weather only effects the upper reaches of the two rivers, as lower beats cover tidal waters.

Dolgellau (Gwynedd). Salmon and sea trout. Wnion runs by Dolgellau and joins Mawddach 2m below town. Best months for salmon and sea trout: May-Oct. Sewin fishing: Jul-Oct. The Dolgellau AA owns 13m of salmon and sea trout fishing on Mawddach and Wnion, two rivers with some of the best catches in Wales, situated in and around Dolgellau. Both stocked with salmon and sea trout each year from the local Mawddach Hatchery. Excellent evening and night fishing for sea trout on lower beats of Wnion. Assn also has wild brown trout and rainbow

A 3lb brown trout; Glyndwr Fishery Beat 5, River Vyrnwy. *Photo: Howard Thresher.*

trout fishing on **Llyn Cynwch,** near well-known Precipice Walk. Permits from W D Pugh & Sons Ltd (petrol station), Bala Road, LL40 2YE; Mile-End Garage (next to the Little Chef); Llion James, Newsagent, Eldon Square; Beachcaster Fishing Tackle *(below)*. St £62, wt £40, rivers dt £16, juv st £19 (allows fishing on the two rivers and Llyn Cynwch), lake dt £10; also from Fish Tales. Tackle shops: Fish Tales, Bridge St (tel: 01341

421080); Beachcaster Fishing Tackle, Glasfryn High St, Barmouth LL42 1DS (tel: 01341 281537). Hotels: Fronolau Farm Hotel, Tabor, Dolgellau LL40 2PS (tel: 01341 422361); Dolmelyn Hall Hotel (both Dolgellau AA tickets); Plas Dolmelynllyn Hall (with private fishing, *see Ganllwyd*); Tynygroes Hotel, Ganllwyd; George III Hotel, Penmaenpool, Dolgellau.

OGWEN

(For close seasons, licences, etc, see Welsh Region Environment Agency, p23)

Rises in Ogwen Lake, halfway between Bethesda and Capel Curig, with tributaries running in from Ffynnon Lloer and Bochlwyd Lakes, and runs from lake to outlet at Menai Straits, near Bangor, about 10m in all. Excellent trout fishing; leased by Ogwen Valley AA from Penrhyn Estate. Trout, sea trout (sewin) and salmon. Autumn good for salmon.

Bangor (Gwynedd). **Ogwen,** 2m E; salmon, sewin, trout. Sea trout run starts about mid-June. Salmon best Aug-Oct. Parts of river leased by Ogwen Valley AA; visitors permits, wt £30, dt £12, conc for juv. Tackle shop: Bangor Angling Supply Stores, 21 The High St, Bangor, Gwynedd LL57 1NP (tel: 01248 355518). Hotels: Waverly; British; Castle; Railway.

Bethesda (Gwynedd). Ogwen Valley AA has approx 5m of River Ogwen and tributaries near Bethesda; sea trout and salmon from July onwards. Assn also has brown trout fishing on four lakes: **Ogwen, Idwal, Ffynon Lloer** and **Bochlwyd.** Lake Ogwen stocked annually. Wt £30 and dt £12. Concessions for juniors. Permits from W Edwin (Grocer), opp Victoria Hotel, High St; Ogwen Bank Caravan Park; or Ogwen Falls Cafe, nr Ogwen Cottage, Ogwen Lake; Lorne House (Newsagent), 82 High Str.

POWYS (lakes)

Gludy Lake, Cradoc, **Brecon,** LD3 9PA (tel: 01874 610427). Fly fishing for brown and rainbow trout to 14lbs, with boats, electric outboards, full self-catering lodge sleeps up to nine; dt for exclusive use of whole lake (up to 6 anglers) £220, (various prices for other combinations: apply Lake House).

Llyn Clywedog. Llanidloes (Powys). NW 3m; 615 acres; Llanidloes & Dist AA; small part of reservoir used by sailing club; western half is fishery area; well stocked with brown and rainbow trout averaging 1¾lb; fly only; boat hire; fishing and boat permits from Mrs Gough, Traveller Rest Restaurant, Longbridge Str, Llanidloes SY18 6EE (tel: 01686 412329); rod licence required is supplied by Mrs Gough. **Dol-llys Farm** has free fishing for their caravan users; contact O S Evans, Dol-llys Farm, Llanidloes, Powys SY18 6JA (tel: 01686 412694). Hotels: Mount Inn; Unicorn; Lloyds; Trewythen Arms.

Llangorse Lake. Llangorse (Powys). Holds good pike, good bream, perch,

roach, eels. Fishing from boats only; can be hired. Permit needed to launch privately owned boats. Caravans for hire from Apr-Oct; some tackle from lakeside shop; permits and boats from Ray Davies, Lakeside Caravan and Camping Park, Llangorse Lake, Brecon, Powys LD3 7TR (tel: 01874 658226). Llynfi runs from lake to Wye at Glasbury and holds a few trout; overgrown in places; requires short rod. Hotel: Red Lion.

Talybont Reservoir. Brecon (Powys). Reservoir in Brecon Beacons National Park, 318 acres, good wild brown trout fishery; season 20 Mar - 17 Oct; fly only; catch limit 6 fish; size limit 9 inches; permits from Garwnant Centre, off A470 Rd above Llwynonn Reservoir: Garwnant Visitor Centre, Cwmtaf CF48 2HT (tel: 01685 723060); further information from C Hatch, Area Manager, United Utilities Operational Services Ltd., Sluvad Treatment Works, Llandegfedd Reservoir, New Inn, Pontypool, Monmouthshire NP4 0TA (tel: 01495 769281).

Lake Vyrnwy (Powys). Lake (1,100 acres)

stocked with rainbow and brown trout, also a strong wild brown population; annual catch 3000 to 3500 averaging ¾lb; by fly and from boat only; dt and half-dt from hotel only; ghillies and instructors can be arranged together with hire of rods; disabled fishing from bank by special arrangement; apply to Lake Vyrnwy Hotel, Lake Vyrnwy, via Oswestry, Montgomeryshire SY10 0LY (tel: 01691 870692; web: www.lakevyrnwy.com). Ceiriog FF also has fishing; members and guests only.

SEIONT

(For close seasons, licences, etc, see Welsh Region Environment Agency, p23)

Rises in two tarns in Cwm-glas, under crest of Snowdon, and runs to Llanberis, 3m, where it enters the Llanberis Lakes, Llyn Peris and Llyn Padarn. Flows thence into Menai Straits at Caernarfon. Attractive river with long flats, nice runs and excellent pools holding salmon (May onwards), sea trout (June onwards), and brown trout. Trout rather small, but in faster water can give good account of themselves.

Caernarfon (Gwynedd). Salmon, sea trout, trout. Seiont, Gwyrfai and Llyfni AS has 40m of salmon, sea trout and brown trout fishing on **Rivers Seiont, Gwyrfai** and **Llyfni**; assn also has boat and bank fishing on **Llyn Padarn**, brown trout, char, salmon, sea trout; **Llyn Cwellyn**, brown trout, char, salmon, sea trout; **Llyn-y-Dwarchen**, 35 acres, rainbow trout and brown trout, fly only; season ticket on application only; wt £60, dt £15 (£8 Llyn Padarn and Llyn Cwellyn; £10 Llyn-y-Dywarchen), from Post Bach Newsagent, 55 Pool St; A D Griffiths, Newsagent, Penygroes; North Wales Angling Centre, Pool St LL55 2AF (tel: 01286 677099); Garth Maelog, 51 High St, Llanberis, LL55 4EU (tel: 01286 870840), which stocks tackle; Cwellyn Arms, Rhyd-Ddu (tel: 01766 890321) who also provide accommodation and boat bookings; maps and information from Hon Sec (see clubs). Seiont Manor Hotel, Llanrug, Caernarfon, Gwynedd LL55 2AQ (tel: 01286 673366), offers free fishing for guests on all club waters. Accommodation: Lake View Hotel, Tan-y-Pant LL55 4EL (tel: 01286 870422).

Llanberis (Gwynedd). Brown trout, Arctic char, salmon, sea trout. Seiont, Gwyrfai

Fishing the white water on the Clywedog near Ruthin. *Photo: A T Howdon.*

and Llyfai AS has bank and boat fishing on almost the whole of **Llyn Padarn**; dt £8 from Garth Maelog *(below)*; Beran Garage, Deinolen. Special boat permits allow fishing on Lakes Padarn, Cwellyn, Dywarchen, and Nantlle, by booking only (tel: 01248 670666). Permits, rods and tackle from Garth Maelog, 51 High St, LL55 4EU (tel: 01286 870840). Hotels: Lakeview, LL55 4EL (tel: 01286 870422); Dolbadarn, High St, Caernarvon, LL55 4SU (tel/fax: 01286 870277).

SOUTH EAST WALES

(For close seasons, licences, etc, see Welsh Region Environment Agency, p23)

AFAN. **Aberavon** (West Glamorgan). Small trout stream (with sewin on lower reaches) on which Afan Valley AC has water from Aberavon to Cymmer. Assn has improved sport; 3 salmon caught in 1991 season; tremendous runs of sewin in last few years; regular stocking. Fly only in March; worming allowed rest of season; spinning June-Sept at certain water levels. **River Nedd** 4m away; trout, sewin. Tackle shop: Afan Angling Centre, 7 Riverside, Aberafan Centre, Port Talbot SA13 1EJ (tel: 01639 883123) (club dt and jun st). Hotels: The Twelve Knights; Aberavon Hotel.

CADOXTON STREAM. **Cadoxton** (South Glamorgan). Cadoxton Stream rises 6½m from Cardiff and enters the sea 2m below Cadoxton. Small trout; permission from farmers (Glamorgan RD).

Eglwys Nunydd Reservoir. **Margam** (West Glamorgan). Corus (Port Talbot) reservoir. Excellent trout fishing, brown, tiger, blue and rainbow. Season: 3 Mar - 31 Oct. Very high stocking levels. Special terms for working and retired employees, and families. 4 boats for members. Fishing lodge for anglers. No new licences available for 2004 due to restorative work. Apply Corus Sports Club, British Steel plc, Groes, Margam, Port Talbot (tel: 01639 871111 extn 3368) during day.

NEATH. Rises in the Brecon Beacons and flows 27m to sea. Salmon, sewin, brown trout. Tributaries of the Neath are **Dulais** and **Pyrddin**.

Neath (West Glamorgan). Neath and Dulais AA has fishing on **River Neath** from Rehola to the estuary except for a short private beat; both banks; trout, sea trout and salmon. Assn also has both banks on **River Dulais** above Aberdulais Falls to the treatment works at Crynant. St £45, wt £50. Dt £20; from Rock & Fountain, on B4242 between Aberdulais and Resolven. Limit of 100 members out of area. Concessions for juniors and OAPs. Skewen Coarse AC has fishing on: **Ten-nant Canal**, Aberdulais to Jersey Marine (all species); **Neath Canal**, Tonna to Briton Ferry (all species except pike); **Square Pond** at Briton Ferry (carp, roach, rudd, tench, bream, perch, eels, grass carp); and **Lower Reservoir** at Briton Ferry (carp, roach, rudd, perch, trout, bream); 2 rods only on all waters except Square Pond where 3 rods allowed; permits available from Membership Secretary (tel: 01639 639657); Tackle and Bait, 149 Windsor Road, Neath SA11 1NU (tel: 01639 634148); and Mainwarings, 44 Vivian Road, Sketty, Swansea SA2 0UH (tel: 01792 202245); Afan Angling Centre, 7 Riverside, Aberafen Centre, Port Talbot SA13 1EJ (tel: 01639 883123). Hotel: Castle.

Glynneath (West Glamorgan). Glynneath & Dist AA has salmon, sea trout and brown trout waters on Neath and its tributaries, **Pyrddin**, **Nedd Fach**, **Mellte**, **Hepste** and **Sychryd**. Fly, worm and spinning from June only. Junior (under 12s) competition in June. Joining fee £15 for full and OAP's; st £30, OAP & 12-18 yrs £15; under 12's £7.50; wt £15; OAP & 12-18's £7.50, under 12's £5; dts £8, £4 and £2.50 respectively. Coarse fishing on canal, between Tonna and Neath, also from Assn. Membership and joining fee from Hon Sec; daily and weekly permits from Hon Sec; Dave Pitman's Hair-Stylist, 3 Heathfield Buildings, Glynneath (tel: 01639 720127), which also sells a large selection of fishing tackle; Tackle and Bait; Old White Horse Inn, Pontnedd-fechan. Pyrddin AS (10m from Neath) has water; trout, salmon, sea trout; permits from Hon Sec. In headwaters of the Neath is Ystradfellte Reservoir. Tackle shop: Tackle and Bait, 149 Windsor Road, Neath SA11 1NU (tel: 01639 634148).

OGMORE.

Porthcawl (Mid Glamorgan). Porthcawl AA has coarse fishing on **Wilderness Lake** and **Pwll-y-Waem Lake**; carp, bream, tench, roach, perch and eels; conc for juv; permits from Porthcawl Angling *(below);* and tackle shop Ewenny Angling, 11B Ewenny Rd, Bridgend CF31 3HN (tel: 01656 662691). Ewenny Angling has application forms for Glamorgan AC; (for river details - web: www.ogmoreriver.com); Porthcawl Angling Centre, 10 Dock Str, CF36 3BL (tel: 01656 772404). Hotel: Brentwood; Ewenny Guesthouse.

Bridgend (Mid Glamorgan). Ogmore AA has 15m of Ogmore and tributaries **Ewenny, Llynfi** and **Garw**; salmon, sea trout and brown trout; membership is restricted but weekly tickets are available from secretary; concessions for juniors; competitions for juniors; and fly-tying and casting lessons. Garw Valley AA has water on Ogmore and Garw. Membership restricted to residents but weekly tickets £20 for visitors, conc for juniors and OAPs; Contact Hon Sec. Tackle shops: Ewenny Angling, 11B Ewenny Rd, Bridgend CF31 3HN (tel: 01656 662691; web: www.ewennyangling.co.uk); Keens, Marine and Angling Superstore, 117-119 Bridgend Rd, Aberkenfig, Bridgend, Mid Glamorgan CF32 9AP (tel: 01656 722448). (For river details - web: www.ogmoreriver.com). Hotel: Heronstone.

Maesteg (Mid Glamorgan). **River Llynfi**, a tributary of Ogmore; trout and sea trout. Llynfi Valley AA has 8m (Maesteg to Tondu); trout, sea trout and salmon. Fly-fishing-only stretch and no spinning until 1 Jul; members only; st £30 + £25 joining fee from Hon Sec. (For river details - web: www.ogmoreriver.com).

RHYMNEY. Rhymney (Mid Glam). About 30m long, rises above town. Excellent grayling, chub, roach and dace fishing run by Caerphilly AC; further information from Green's Fishing Tackle. Rhymney & Dist AS has rights on Butetown Pond, Rhymney, and Bryn Brith Pond, **Pontlottyn**; also **Cwm-Darren Lake**; Rhos-las, nr **Dowlias**; with fishing on **Wye** between Oct and Feb at Boughwood, near Lyswen. All well stocked with coarse fish of usual species; pike in Rhos-las, all fish to be returned to water; dt on all waters except canal. Matches run most Saturdays for juniors and Sundays for seniors Jun-Aug, plus aggregate awards. New members st £12, conc, dt £3, from Hon Sec; Cal White, 39 The Square, Pontlottyn, Mid Glamorgan CF81 9PD (tel: 01685 841245), who also

sell tickets for some Merthyr Tydfil AC water, and provide information on Rhymney Carp Syndicate waters. Other tackle shops: Greens Fishing Tackle, Pontllanfraith, Blackwood NP12 2BU (tel: 01495 221881); and Tiles and Tackle, 27 Castle St, Tredegar, Monmouthshire NP2 3DG (tel: 01495 717001).

TAWE. Lower tidal reach now impounded by a barrage. Salmon and sewin runs have increased in recent years and they can be caught from Abercraf to Morriston. Upper reaches noted for scenery. Fishing controlled by clubs in all but tidal reaches.

Swansea (West Glamorgan). Swansea Amateur AA has salmon and sea trout fishing on the upper reaches of **Cothi** and a section of **Towy** at Llanwrda. Assn is a private company with a limited membership with a limited allocation of tickets for members' guests. Llangyfelach & DAA has 6m of River **Llan** from Loughor Estuary; stocked annually with browns; salmon & sea trout in first 3 miles; st £25, dt £10, conc; assn also has 1m River **Lliw**; salmon, sewin; tickets for both from Country Stores, Gowerton and Mainwarings. Swansea AC has coarse fishing at Gower on **Fairwood Lake**, pike, bream, carp, perch, tench, roach, rudd, eels; also **Gelli Hir**, Tir Mynydd Road, Three Crosses; 3 lakes; carp to 20lb, good head of tench to 7lb; dt from Mainwaring's or Country Stores, Gowerton. City and County of Swansea has coarse fishing on 3 lakes. **Singleton Boating Lake**, Singleton Park, 2 acres; carp, tench, rudd, perch, crucian carp, eels; angling permitted when boats not in use; **Clyne Valley Pond**, small, very deep lake; perch, rudd, eels, trout; **Pluck Pond**, Lower Swansea Valley, 1 acre; perch, rudd. Brynmill & Dist AC have coarse fishing at **Fendrod Lake**, 15 acres, 82 pegs, with fairly good head of fish from carp up to 20lb and bream up to 8lb, with an extra bonus of attractive surroundings; and at Half Round Ponds, two ponds of one acre each, with rudd, perch, tench; permits £3.50, juveniles/OAP/disabled £2.40 on bank; from Mainwaring's (below); or from Leisure Services Dept, The Guildhall, Swansea SA1 4PE (tel: 01792 635411). **Shimano Felindre Trout Fishery**; rainbow, brown and golden trout; fly only. Tackle for sale and hire; casting lessons. Contact Jud Hamblin, Manager, Shimano Felindre Trout

Fishery, Blaen-Nant Ddu, Felindre, Swansea SA5 7ND (tel: 01792 796584). Riverside Caravan Park has stretch on Tawe; touring caravan park with all facilities; for further information contact Riverside Caravan Park, Ynysforgan Farm, Morriston, Swansea SA6 6QL (tel: 01792 775587). Tackle shops: Mainwaring's Angling Centre, 44 Vivian Road, Sketty, Swansea SA2 0UH (tel: 01792 202245; web: www.mainwaring s.co.uk), has permits for a number of lake and river fisheries within range of Swansea, both coarse and game; Hook, Line & Sinker, James Court, Swansea Enterprise Zone, Winchwen SA1 7DA (tel: 01792 701190); Siop-y-Pentref, Ynystawe, Swansea SA6 5AY (tel: 01792 842533): full and day permits on sale.

Pontardawe (West Glamorgan). Pontardawe and Swansea AS has stretch on R Tawe from **Ynysmeudwy** to **Morriston**; brown trout, sea trout and salmon; new adult members £65 (£50 renewal), OAP's £15, seriously disabled £15, 11-17's £10, under 11's £3; tickets available by post from secretary or from Mainwaring's *(see below)*; Hook Line & Sinker at Llansam-

let *(see Swansea)*; Siop-y-Pentref, Ynystawe, Swansea SA6 5AY (tel: 01792 842533), or H R Jones (Ironmongers) at Clydach. Tackle shop: Mainwaring's Angling Centre, 44 Vivian Road, Sketty, Swansea SA2 0UH (tel: 01792 202245; web: www.mainwarings.co.uk).

Ystradgynlais (West Glamorgan). Tawe & Tributaries AA has 25m on **Tawe** and tributaries **Twrch**, **Gwys**, **Llynfell**, **Giedd**, **Lech**, **Gurlais** and **Cwn Du**, above Pontardawe; salmon, sea trout, brown trout and eels; trout stocked regularly up to 3lbs. Assn runs its own brown trout hatchery and rearing pond complex (during 1997, stocked waters with over 15,000 brown trout measuring from 9-18in). Membership restricted to local residents but permits available to non members. St £63 and dt £18. Concessions for juniors and OAPs. Junior river competition held annually. Fly-tying and casting tuition during close season. Permits from J G Davies Fieldsports, Station Road, Ystradgynlais SA9 1NT (tel: 01639 843194). Hotels: Copper Beech; Abercrave Inn; and Gwyn Arms Public House, Craig y Nos, Swansea Valley.

SOUTH WEST WALES (lakes)

Lake Berwyn. Tregaron (Ceredigion), 4m SE. Liming has taken place and as a result it holds excellent brown trout up to 1-2lbs. Stocked periodically. Tregaron AA hold fishing rights; Assn also has wild brown trout fishing on R Teifi, and Teifi Pools, three remote mountain lakes with plenty of wild browns; st £105, river only £57.50, Teifi Pools only £57.50, Lllyn Berwyn only £57.50; wt (all waters) £42.50; dt (river & Berwyn) £10, Teifi Pool £10. Concessions for OAP's, juveniles; permits: Medical Hall, Tregaron; Post Office, Pontrhydfendigaid; Post Office, Llanddewi Brefi; Post Office, Llanfair Clydogau; Alan Williams, Lampeter Angling, 57 Bridge Str, Lampeter SA48 7AB (tel: 01570 422985 (evngs: 01570 434313)). Tackle shop: Flymail Tackle Shop, 3 Terrace Road, Aberystwyth SY23 1NY (tel: 0808 100 2251).

Devil's Bridge (Ceredigion). Aberystwyth AA has the Penrhyncoch lakes in the hills between Devil's Bridge and Nant-y-Moch Reservoir (**Llyn Craig-y-Pistyll, Llyn Rhosgoch, Llyn Syfydrin, Llyn Blaenmelindwr** and **Llyn Pendam**); the Trisant Lakes 2m SW of Devil's Bridge,

(**Llyn Frongoch and Llyn Rhosrhydd**); and part ownership of **Llyn Oerfa** and **Llyn Glandwgan**. Some are stocked, others self-stocking. Several contain trout up to 3lb. Fly only on Rhosgoch, Frongoch and Rhosrhydd; spinning and fly only on Craig-y-Pistyll. Permits: Aeron Sports & Fishing Tackle, Kings Halls, Terrace Road, Aberystwyth SY1 2ED (tel: 01970 624830), st £120, dt £20, conc; Discount Tackle, 3 Terrace Road, Aberystwyth SY23 1NY (tel: 01970 611200), who also sell Tregaron AC tickets. Hotel: Hafod Arms SY23 3JL.

Nant-y-Moch and **Dinas Reservoirs. Ponterwyd** (Ceredigion). These waters are set in the hills 12m E of Aberystwyth. Dinas, 38 acres, stocked weekly with brown and rainbow trout; fly, spinning and worming. Nant-y-Moch, 600 acres, native and stocked brown trout, fly only. **Cwm Rheidol Dam**, native and stocked brown trout, salmon and sea trout; fly spinning and worming; permits from the Power Station gate, Capel Bangor; further information from the Power Station, Mr Peter Bevan, at Cwm Rheidol (tel: 01970 880667).

Pembroke (Pembrokeshire). Pembroke Town Mill Pool; mullet, bass, flatfish; also trout and sewin higher up. At **Stackpole**, 3m south, National Trust has 74 acres Bosherston Lily Ponds; coarse; fishing from numbered pegs (1-74) only; st £40, conc, dt £6 (in advance) £7 at lakeside; contact warden (tel: 01646 661359); Hotel: Milton Manor.

Talybont (Ceredigion). Talybont AA has exclusive rights on **Llyn Conach, Llyn Dwfn, Llyn Nantycagal** and **Llyn Penrhaeadr**. Lakes some 7-9m into hills from village; 3 lakes stocked with brown trout; native wild brown in Penrhaeadr.

Fly only on all lakes except Nantycagal. Boat hire on all lakes for holders of season tickets; st £45, dt £10 (bank only). Permits from Spar Store, Talybont; Mrs Hubbard, Compton Gift Shop, High St, Borth, Ceredigion SY24 5JD (information and tackle also available); Flymail Tackle Shop, 3 Terrace Road, Aberystwyth SY23 1NY (tel: 0808 100 2251).

Teifi Lakes. Pontrhydfendigaid (Ceredigion). Lakes at headwaters of Teifi. Permits from Post Office, Pontrhydfendigaid.

SOUTH WEST WALES (rivers and streams)

(For close seasons, licences, etc, see Welsh Region Environment Agency, p23)

ALUN. St David's (Pembrokeshire). 6m long; 4m suitable for fishing, mostly on private property with owners permission; trout good quality but small. Boat trips and limited fishing tackle from Robert O Evans, Ystwyth Stores High St, St Davids SA62 6SD (tel: 01437 720399). Rod licences from Post Office, 13 New St.

BRAWDY BROOK. Brawdy (Pembrokeshire). Small trout. Brook, 7m long, is mostly on private property. Licences can be purchased at Post Office, 13 New Dew Str, St David's.

CARNE. Loveston (Pembrokeshire). Carne rises 1½m W of Templeton, runs 3m to Loveston, and 1m down is joined on left bank by **Langden Brook**. Little or no rod fishing interest; fishing wiped out in 1993 with agricultural pollution; although an important spawning area for salmon and sea trout. Possible sea trout late in season, if adequate flows and no pollution. From confluence of Carne and Langden Brook into Cresswell, fishing controlled by Cresselly Estate, c/o Owen & Owen, 140 Main St, Pembroke, SA71 4HN (tel: 01646 621500). Coarse fishing reservoir at **Roadside Farm**; common, crucian and mirror carp, bream and roach; well stocked; tranquil surroundings and ample parking; day, week and year permits; contact D A Crowley, Roadside Farm, Templeton, Narberth, Dyfed SA67 8DA (tel: 01834 891283). Carp fishing at West Atherton near Narberth. Tackle shop: Bay Fishing Tackle, Norland House, High Str, Saundersfoot, Pembs SA69 9EJ (tel: 01834 813115); Whitland AA tickets.

CAREW BROOK. Carew (Pembrokeshire). This river, which rises by Redberth, is 4m long, joining sea water at Carew which is an inlet from Milford Haven. Although there is an element of rod fishing effort put into this river and its tributaries, the controlling interest is the farmer and the catchment is prone to agricultural pollution. The river does support a very small number of sea trout which only seem to appear in the close season.

CLARACH. Good numbers of sea trout can be found in the river late July onwards.

Aberystwyth (Ceredigion). Enters sea 1m N of Aberystwyth. Holds trout, sewin and occasional salmon; preserved. Permission from farmers. Tackle shop: Aeron Sports & Fishing Tackle, Kings Halls, Terrace Road, Aberystwyth SY1 2ED (tel: 01970 624830); Flymail Fishing Flies, from 3 Terrace Rd, Aberystwyth, SY23 1NY (tel: 0808 100 2251).

GWAUN. Fishguard (Pembrokeshire). This 8-9m trout stream rises on lower

---

Fishing available?

*If you own, manage, or know of first-class fishing available to the public which should be considered for inclusion in **Where to Fish** please apply to the publishers (address in the front of the book) for a form for submission, on completion, to the Editor. (Inclusion is at the sole discretion of the Editor). No charge is made for editorial inclusion.*

The perfect starting point, the tackle shop: not only a mine of information, but an all-important supplier of tickets and tackle

slopes of Prescelly Mountains, and runs through a beautiful wooded valley. Trout not large but provide excellent sport with fly, and sewin also caught in season. A few salmon. Tackle shop: Goodwick Marine Services, 1 Wern Road, Goodwick SA64 0AA (tel: 01348 873955). Hotel: Glanmoy Country House.

GWENDRAETH FACH. Kidwelly (Carmarthenshire). Carmarthen & Dist AC has 2m fishing about 2m north of town, both banks; very good trout fishing; occasional sea trout; st only £140, conc; contact The Fishfinder, 51 King St, Carmarthen SA31 1BH (tel: 01267 220226). Llangennech AC has 4m stretch from Pont Antwn to Llangendeirne Bridge, brown trout and sea trout. **Gwendraeth Fawr** runs 1m E from Kidwelly; trouting fair. Hotel: White Lion; Pen-y-Bac Farm (river fishing for trout, sewin and salmon; tuition and equipment).

LLANDILO BROOK. Maenclochog (Pembrokeshire). Small trout. Electrofishing surveys show very few fish of takeable size. No angling clubs. Seek permission from farmers to fish.

LLETHI. Llanarth (Ceredigion). Llethi Gido rises 3m above Llanarth, and 2m down is joined on left bank by brook 4m

long. Llethi runs to Llanina and sea. One mile NE runs Drowy to sea, 4m long. Small trout. **Llanarth Coarse Fishery** (tel: 01545 580598), ¾m south of Llanarth, 2 acre pool, heavily stocked with carp; mixed silver fish pond, open 7 days a week; dt £5, conc. **Nine Oaks Trout and Coarse Fishery**: Mr John Steels, Oakford, nr Aberaeron, SA47 0RW (tel: 01545 580482); fly and coarse fishing, 2m inland between Newquay and Aberaeron; rainbow and brown trout in four pools; carp to 25lbs, tench and bream in coarse fishing lake. Tackle hire, beginners tuition and accommodation. Trout dt £18, 4 fish, £10 evening, 2 fish, £5 coarse.

MARLAIS. Narberth (Pembrokeshire). Gwaithnoak, 2m. Eastern Cleddau, 2m. Taf, 5m. Small trout. NW of Narberth is Glandwr Fishery, Pontygafel Farm, Glandwr, Pembs SA34 0YD (tel: 01437 765732), rainbow, brown, blue trout.

MULLOCK BROOK. St Ishmael's (Pembrokeshire). Small trout, 6m long, joining the sea at Dale Road.

NEVERN: Nevern (Pembrokeshire). River rises near Crymych and flows to sea at Newport; fast-flowing, densely wooded, deep holding pools. Nevern AA has salmon, sea trout and brown trout fishing; 6m on **Nevern**, nr Newport; st apply Hon Sec, juveniles £10; wt £36 and dt £18, available from Trewern Arms, Nevern SA42 0NB (tel: 01239 820395); Y Siop Lyfrau (Bookshop), Newport; The Reel Thing, Lower Guildhall Market, Cardigan, Ceredigion, SA43 1HJ (mobile: 07985 739183); concessions for juniors; coaching for beginners and juniors (fly only); there are also club outings and fly-tying lessons. Hotels: Trewern Arms; Cnapan, Newport; Salutation Inn, Felindre Farchog. Guest House, Llys Meddyg, East St, Newport.

PERIS. **Llanon** (Ceredigion). Peris is 6m long. Llanon, 4m long, runs ½m. Small trout. Hotel: Plas Morfa.

RHEIDOL. **Aberystwyth** (Ceredigion). Salmon, sea trout. Hydro-electric scheme governs flow. River almost entirely Aberystwyth AA water. Assn also has 2m stretch on **River Ystwyth**; and trout fishing on 9 lakes. Permits from Aeron Sports & Fishing Tackle, Kings Halls, Terrace Road, Aberystwyth SY1 2ED (tel: 01970 624830); st £120, dt£20, conc. Assn has 2 caravans (6-berth) to let at **Frongoch Lake**, approx £120 per week; includes week's fishing on the whole fishery and exclusive use boat for 4 days of the week. Coarse fishing at **Capel Bangor Golf Club**; 2½ acre pond; carp, roach and tench. Permits from W Evans, Capel Bangor Golf Club, Capel Bangor, Aberystwyth SY23 3LL (tel: 01970 880741). Hotels: Conrah; Chancery; Bay.

WYRE. **Llanrhystyd** (Ceredigion). Trout (small), some salmon and sometimes good for sewin. Fishing controlled by a number of riparian owners.

YSTWYTH. A natural, gravel bed spate river. Brown trout stocked in spring; large sea trout run in first spate in June, several runs of smaller sea trout July to Sept. Salmon usually run Mid Aug to early Oct.

Aberystwyth (Ceredigion). Llanilar AA has most of river, approx 15m both banks, from Aberystwyth to Pontrhydygroes; some brown trout in Llanilar area. Best sea trout fishing is by fly at night, spinning in high water and with quill minnow as water clears; fly is also effective during the day when there is a touch of colour in the water; st £48, wt £28, dt £12, conc, from Hon Sec; Aeron Sports & Fishing Tackle; Llanilar Garage; Blaenplwyf Post Office, nr Aberystwyth SY23 1DS (tel: 01970 612499); and Royal Oak, Llanfarian SY23 4BS. Mr and Mrs Tovey, Fron Farm, **Bont-newydd**, SY23 4JG (tel: 01974 251392), have 3 lakes with rainbow, brown trout, atlantic salmon, and one coarse fishing lake; tuition (free) by appointment. **Trawscoed Estate Fishery** has over 3m stretch on the central reaches of R Ystwyth, sea trout from June onwards; **Birchgrove Reservoir** situated in Forestry Commission woodlands, 1½ acres, carp fishing; and **Maesllyn Lake**, 5 acres, stocked with rainbow and brown trout, boat available; for further information contact Estate Manager, Mr Lewis, Trawscoed Estate, Aberystwyth (tel: 01974 831267); accommodation can be arranged; permits and rod licences are available at the Post Office. Tackle Shop: Aeron Sports & Fishing Tackle, Kings Halls, Terrace Road, Aberystwyth SY1 2ED (tel: 01970 624830).

TÂF

(For close seasons, licences, etc, see Welsh Region Environment Agency, p23)

Rises on Prescelly Mountains and flows about 25 miles south-east to Carmarthen Bay at mouth of Towy. Has good runs of sewin and salmon most years. Brown trout fishing good upstream of Whitland.

St Clears (Carmarthen). Good salmon and sewin; brown trout fair. April, May, Sept best for salmon. Sewin mid-June onwards. Carmarthen & Dist AC have water on Tâf and stretch on **Dewi Fawr**. St Clears & District AA has 5m on Tâf, from St Clears to Llanddowror; salmon, sea trout and brown trout. Assn also has salmon, sea trout and brown trout fishing on **R Ginning**, 3m; **R Dewi Fawr**, 1½m; **R**

Cowin, 1½m; st £40, wt £25, dt £10, weekend (48 hr) £15, conc; contact from Hon Sec and Grays Chemist, Pentre Rd, Carmarthen, Dyfed SA33 4AA (tel: 01994 230444).Other waters on these rivers by permission of farmers. Hotels: Black Lion; Gardde House; Picton House, Llanddowror, St Clears. Caravan sites at St Clears and Laugharne.

Whitland (Carmarthenshire). Salmon,

sewin, brown trout; Whitland AA has approx 5m of fishing, mainly double bank; all legal methods, season 1 Apr-7 Oct; st £60, conc for juv, OAP, dt £10 from Treasurer P Hunt (tel: 01834 831304); Bay Fishing Tackle or Gog Sports (below). **White House Mill Trout Fishery**, Barbara Hunt: contact Mrs Hunt at fishery, Lampeter Velfrey, Whitland SA34 0RB (tel: 01834 831304): fly fishing for brown and rainbow trout on 4 acre lake, emphasis on nymph and dry fly; easy access for disabled, tackle for hire, self-catering cottage near lake; dt from

£10. Coarse fishing on **Llyn Carfan**; two lakes of 1½ acres each with good quality water, stocked with carp to 25lbs, grass carp to 20lb, tench, plentiful roach, and rudd; dt at house or on bank; rods and tackle for hire; contact Llyn Carfan Course Fishing, Whitland, Pembs. SA34 0NP (tel: 01994 240819; web: www.pem brokeshiretourism.co.uk/angling.htm). Tackle shops: Bay Fishing Tackle, Norland House, High Str, Saundersfoot SA69 9EJ (tel: 01834 813115); Gog Sports, 15 St. Johns Str, Whitland SA34 0AN (tel: 01994 240534).

TAFF and ELY

(For close seasons, licences, etc, see Welsh Region Environment Agency, p23)

Taff has its source in two headstreams on the Brecon Beacons and flows about 40m south-east to enter the Severn Estuary at Cardiff. A short and steep gravel bedded river, heavily polluted in the 18th and 20th centuries by local iron, coal and steel industries. However, by the early 1980's there had been major improvements in the water quality due to economic recession and improved pollution control. Sea trout and some salmon were again entering lower reaches of river, although much of tyhe river remained inaccessible at this time because of large weirs. Since then, the Welsh Water Authority, and subsequently the National Rivers Authority and Environment Agency Wales, have been successfully carrying out a strategy for rehabilitating salmon in the Taff; through pollution control, building fish passes, artificial propagation and control of exploitation. The lower reaches of the Taff are now an established sea trout and salmon fishery with declared rod catches for the former exceeding 150 in most recent seasons. Salmon appear in catches less often; typically declared catches vary between 20 and 50 fish. The recently completed Treforest fish pass close to Pontypridd will allow migratory fish to access the vast majority of the catchment. Although too early to be conclusive, it is likely that sea trout will enter upper reaches during the season, providing anglers previusly only able to target brown trout, with a new quarry. The Lower Taff, from Cardiff to Pontypridd is also a good coarse fishery, the main species being chub, dace, roach, gudgeon and barbel. Now, that the polluted legacy of the past has largely disappeared, the remainder of the Taff catchment supports good brown trout. The River Ely joins the mouth of Taff at Penarth. The Ely, like the Taff, has benefitted from substantial improvements in environmental quality such that quality brown trout fishing, chub and roach fishing can be found at reasonable cost. Salmon and sea trout spawn quite regularly in the Ely although few are recorded in cates.

Cardiff (Glamorgan). Brown trout (stocked) and run of sea trout and salmon. Glamorgan AC has fishing on **River Taff** (chub, dace, eels, roach, salmon, sea trout, barbel and brown trout); 2 stretches on **River Wye**, at Monmouth (chub, dace, perch, pike, roach, bleak, gudgeon, eels and barbel) and at Clifford (chub, dace, roach, perch, pike, barbel, bleak and grayling); **River Usk** near Abergavenny (chub, dace, brown trout, salmon and sea trout); **East Dock** (roach, perch, chub, dace, carp and eels); **River Ely** at St Fagans (roach, chub and trout); **River Trothy** near Monmouth (chub, dace, trout, grayling, roach and pike); **Troes Pond** at Troes near Bridgend (bream,

tench, perch, carp, roach and rudd); **Pysgodlyn Mawr** (bream, carp, roach, perch, rudd and tench); **Llantrythyd Lake** (carp, bream, roach, rudd, tench, perch and eels); and **St-y-Nyll Ponds** (pike, rudd, tench, perch and carp). For membership contact M Roberts, 4 Heol Don, Whitchurch, Cardiff CF14 2AU. Bute AS, Birchgrove (Cardiff) AS and Glamorgan AC share lease of approx 3m fishing on R Taff in city limits; coarse (chub, roach, dace, gudgeon with barbel introduced recently); and game (salmon, sewin and brown trout) under auspices of combined Cardiff clubs known as Taff Fisheries; dt from Garry Evans, 105 Whitchurch Rd, Heath, Cardiff, and A E

Bale & Son *(see tackle shop below)*. Bute AS has fixture list fishing on **R Wye** from Erwood to Builth Wells, and on a private lake within Cardiff's city limits; all venues hold roach, dace, gudgeon, bleak; members only; club membership from secretary. Birchgrove AS has fishing on **Rivers Ely and Taff**; salmon, sea trout, chub, dace, grayling, roach and barbel. Through kindness of riparian owners, the society also has coarse fishing on prime stretches on **R Wye** between Glasbury and Built; chub, dace, eels, grayling, pike, roach and perch. Fishing on Wye for members only. Permits from A E Bale & Son *(below)*. **Roath Park Lake** (Cardiff Corporation) holds rudd, roach, carp, tench. **Llanishen** (59 acres) and **Lisvane** (19 acres) **Reservoirs**, located within Cardiff City boundary, approach via B4562 road; leased to Cardiff Fly Fishing Club; day tickets sold at reservoirs. The recent improvement of **Cardiff Bay** has produced a large freshwater lake. Early indications are that coarse fish populations have flourished, particularly chub. Although as yet under-developed as a fishery, moves are afoot to improve angling access at what could become the premier S Wales coarse fish venue. Tackle shops: A E Bale & Son, 166a Richmond Road, Cardiff CF24 3BX (tel: 029 20499898) for information, bait and licences; Anglers Supplies, 172 Penarth Rd, Cardiff CF1 7NL (tel: 029 202 20723); Ely Angling Supplies, 572 Cowbridge Rd East, Ely Bridge, Cardiff CF5 1BN (tel: 029 205 55133); Tony's Angling, 826 Newport Road, Rumney CF3 8LH (tel: 029 202 57505); Garry Evans Ltd, 105 Whitchurch Road, Cardiff CF4 3JQ (tel: 029 20619828). Hotels: Angel; Cardiff International; Clare Court; Glenmor.

Merthyr Tydfil (Glamorgan). Merthyr Tydfil AA offers a large variety of waters from wild brown trout fishing on the Upper Neuadd Reservoir in the heart of the Brecon Beacons to salmon fishing on the Usk, with ponds and reservoirs for the coarse fishing enthusiast. The Assn has 17m on **Taff** and **Taf Fechan** at Merthyr Tydfil from Pontsticill Reservoir to Quaker's Yard, brown trout, regularly stocked, size limit 10", bag limit 6 fish; also ¾m both banks (small wild brook trout) on **River Tarrell**; **Upper Neuadd Reservoir**, wild brown trout, very lightly stocked, fly only; **Taf Fechan Reservoirs**, trout (20 Mar - 17 Oct) and coarse (16 Jun - 17 Mar), no pike or other coarse fish to be removed; **Penywern Ponds**, coarse fish including carp in excess of 20lb, dt from Merthyr Angling Centre *(below)*; Tony Rees, Treasurer, 13 Alexandra Avenue CF47 9AE (tel: 01685 723520) and Hon Secretary. Assn also has 3 stretches of salmon and trout fishing on **Usk** including at **Mardy Fishery**, 1¼m; and **Kemeys Fishery**, ¾m. Day tickets for Usk from A Rees and N Morgan *(see above)*. Also **Cyfarthfa Lake**, a popular coarse fishing lake for juveniles. Reservoirs in Taf Fawr Valley managed by United Utilities: **Beacons Reservoir** (52 acres) brown trout, fly only; **Cantref Reservoir** (42 acres) rainbow and brown trout, fly only; **Llwyn-On Reservoir** (150 acres) rainbow and brown trout, fly, worm and spinner. All located in Brecon Beacons National Park adjacent to A470 (T) road, 3m north of Merthyr Tydfil and 15m south of Brecon. Cater for disabled. Private boats permitted. Dt from machine at Llwyn-On water treatment works. For further information contact C Hatch, Area Manager, United Utilities, Sluvad Treatment Works, Llandegfedd Reservoir, New Inn, Pontypool, Monmouthshire NP4 0TA (tel: 01495 769281). Tackle shops: Merthyr Angling Centre, 185 High St, Cefn Coed CF48 2PG (tel: 01685 379809).

Tributaries of Taff

RHONDDA FAWR and RHONDDA FACH:

Pontypridd (Mid Glamorgan). At Junction of Rhondda Fawr and Fach, and Taff.

Tonypandy (Mid Glamorgan). Glyncornel AA has 12m trout fishing on Rhondda from The Stag Hotel in Treorchy to the Barry Sidings Park, Trehafod; restocked annually with brown and rainbow trout. St £25, wt £10, conc for juv, no dt; competitions for adults and juniors. Fly fishing on Glyncornel Lake, brown and rainbow, members only, apply club. Club also holds rights on very good coarse fishing at **Darran Park Lake**; all coarse species (over Welsh record in several), incl pike; st £25 (adult), £16 (juv), wt £10, dt £5. Contact club for permit outlets. Tickets: Tonypandy Army Surplus & Guns, 10 Dunraven St, Tonypandy CF40 1QE (tel: 01443 432856); for Darren Lake: st £25, juv £16, Howells Newsagents, 51 Pontypridd Road, Porth, Mid Glam. CF39 9PG (tel: 01443 682507) - also River Rhondda; Spar Grocery, Main High St, Ferndale.

Ferndale (Glamorgan). Maerdy & Ferndale AC has water on River Rhondda Fach; and on **Lluest Wen and Castell Nos Reservoirs** at Maerdy; all waters are trickle-stocked throughout the season; fly only on Lluest Wen; dt from David Hughes, North Road Motors, Morris Terrace, Ferndale, Mid Glamorgan CF43 4ST (tel: 01443 755048); st available *(see above)*.

Ely (Glamorgan). Glamorgan AC has trout fishing on River Ely at St Fagans and coarse fishing in **St-y-Nyll Ponds** at St Brides-super-Ely.

Llantrisant (Glamorgan). **Seven Oaks Trout Fishery**, Talygarn, nr Pontyclun, Mid Glam CF72 9JU (tel: 01446 775474): dt on site. Seven Oaks Fishery, Cowbridge Road, Talygarn CF72 9JU (tel: 01446 775474), fishing for rainbow trout and dameron blues, also novice pond with rainbows and tiger trout; dt £13 2 fish fly lake (£17, 3 fish, £21 4 fish); novice pool dt £4 + £2/fish; coarse £5.50; tackle hire and some tackle sold on site, bank only, good access for disabled.

TEIFI

(For close seasons, licences, etc, see Welsh Region Environment Agency, p23)

Rises in Llyn Teifi, near Strata Florida, in Ceredigion, flows south-west and then west, entering Cardigan Bay below Cardigan Town. Association water provides salmon, sea trout (sewin) and brown trout fishing. April and May are the best months for spring salmon; summer salmon fishing through to October can also be productive given reasonable water levels. Sea trout run from May onwards. Coracle and draft nets come off 31 August. Main salmon run September onwards.

Cardigan (Dyfed). Salmon, sewin, trout. Bass, mullet and flounders below bridge to sea, 2m; boats for hire. Teifi Trout Assn has fishing for salmon, sea trout and brown trout on 20m stretch of lower River Teifi, from a few miles above Cardigan to just beyond Newcastle Emlyn, including fishing at Cenarth. Assn also has stretch, ¾m, above Henllan (salmon, sea trout and brown trout). St £125 plus £20 joining fee from Membership Secretary. Surcharge of £40 on Cenarth waters. Concessions for OAPs, disabled and junior. Wt £60-£70 and dt £15-£20 (junior £3) from The Reel Thing, Lower Guildhall Market, Cardigan, Ceredigion, SA43 1HJ (mobile: 07985 739183); The Salmon Leap and Cenarth Falls Holiday Park, Cenarth; and Afon Teifi Caravan Park, Pentrecagal.

Llechryd (Dyfed). Salmon, sea trout. Nevern AA has ¾m stretches on R Teifi, nr Llechryd. Teifi Trout Assn water; dt £18, wt £36, juveniles st £10, available from Trewern Arms, Nevern, and The Book Shop, Newport. Adult st apply Hon Sec. Tackle shop: County Sports, 3 Old Bridge, Haverfordwest SA61 2EZ (tel: 01437 763740). Accomodation: The Trewern Arms, Nevern; The Salutation, Velindre.

Cenarth (Dyfed). Salmon, sewin, trout. Famous falls. Teifi Trout Assn water; surcharge for Cenarth Fishery. Permits from The Salmon Leap, Cenarth, Newcastle Emlyn, Dyfed SA38 9JP (tel: 01239 711242), where there is also a comprehensive range of fishing tackle and bait for sale; and Cenarth Caravan Park, Newcastle Emlyn SA38 9JS (tel: 01239 710344). Tackle shops: Alan Williams, Lampeter Angling, 57 Bridge Str, Lampeter SA48 7AB (tel: 01570 422985 (evngs: 01570 434313)). Accom: The Porth Hotel, Llandysul, Ceredigion SA44 4QS (tel: 01559 362202) for permits, maps and river information for Llandysul AA water.

Newcastle Emlyn (Dyfed). Salmon and sea trout. Good centre for Teifi. Teifi Trout Assn has water; riverside cottages with exclusive private fishing on an adjoining ¾m stretch of Teifi, salmon, sea trout and brown trout; dt £20; wt £70; Sept dt £25 from A Jackson, Teifi River Guides, Little Manor, Castle Square, Cilgerran SA43 2SE (tel: 01239 614254; mob: 07770 817602). Hotels: Emlyn Arms.

Llandysul (Ceredigion). Salmon, sewin, brown trout. Popular centre with good fishing. Best April-May and Aug-Oct for salmon; sewin June onwards. Llandysul

AA has Middle Teifi from Newcastle Emlyn to above 2m north of Lampeter. For fly fishing courses and casting instruction in the Teifi Valley: weekend courses during the season from April to October, specialising in wild brown trout fishing in the spring, sea trout (sewin) in summer, and salmon in autumn. Private beat on **R Teifi**. Flyfishing courses and casting instruction in the Teifi Valley; private fishing beat. Free fishing and conservation lessons for young people during school summer holidays, in conjunction with Llandysul AA: instructors Pat O'Reilly, Sue Parker; contact DreamStreams Ltd, Swyn Esgair, Drefach-Felindre, Llanysul SA44 5XG (Tel: 01559 371879; www: first-nature.com/dreamstreams). Crosshands & Dist AA has stretch on R Teifi, nr Llandysul; salmon and sea trout; joining fee £10; st £65, OAP's/students/ladies £35, juv £10; dt £20, wt (restricted) £40, wt (all waters) £50, conc for juv. Rainbow trout fishing on a 3-acre lake at **Rhydlewis Trout Fishery**; stocked regularly; fly only; lakeside parking, toilets, tea & coffee-making facilities, smokery and smokery shop; further details from, Ryd-yr-Onnen, Rhydlewis, Llandysul, Ceredigion SA44 5QS (tel: 01239 851224). Tackle shops: Alan Williams, Lampeter Angling, 57 Bridge Str, Lampeter SA48 7AB (tel: 01570 422985 (evngs: 01570 434313)); D R Jones and Sons (Ironmongers), Tysul Stores, New Road, Llandysul SA44 4QJ (tel: 01559 363270). Hotels: Kings Arms; Henllan Falls, Henllan, Llandysul; Porth and County Gate, Llanfihangel-ar-Arth, Pencader.

Llanybydder (Carmarthenshire). Salmon, sewin, brown trout. Llanybydder AA has approx 5m of Middle Teifi, both banks, above and below Llanybydder Bridge; st

£50, wt £35 and £40, dt £10 and £15; concessions for jun; instruction, and challenge cup for best junior angler; permits from Hon Sec and David Morgan, Siop-y-Bont, Llanybydder (tel: 01570 480980). Hotels: Crosshands; Black Lion; Grannell Arms, Llannwnen, Ceredigion.

Lampeter (Dyfed). Salmon, April onwards; sewin, late June, July, August onwards; brown trout, both dry and wet fly. Both Llandysul AA and Tregaron AA have water on Teifi around Lampeter. **Troed-y-Bryn Fisheries**, rainbow and brown trout, privately owned lakes, 3½ acres, fly only; permits from Mrs E E Edwards, Troed-y-Bryn, Cribyn, Lampeter SA48 7QH (tel: 01570 470798). Tackle shop: Alan Williams, Lampeter Angling, 57 Bridge Str, Lampeter SA48 7AB (tel: 01570 422985 (evngs: 01570 434313)).

Tregaron (Dyfed). Good fly fishing for brown trout. Salmon fishing also good when conditions right. Tregaron AA has 17m of **R Teifi** from Pontrhydfendigaid to Tregaron and down river to Cellan; **Teifi Pools**, 3 mountain lakes, with wild brown trout; and **Llyn Berwyn**, 50 acres; st £105, river only £57.50, Teifi Pools only £57.50, Llyn Berwyn only £57.50; wt (all waters) £42.50; dt (river & Berwyn) £10, Teifi Pool £10. Concessions for OAP's, juveniles. Permits: Medical Hall, Tregaron; Post Office, Pontrhydfendigaid; Post Office, Llanddewi Brefi; Post Office, Llanfair Clydogau, Lampeter, Dyfed SA48 8LA; Alan Williams. Tackle shop: Flymail Tackle Shop, Terrace Road, Aberystwyth; Alan Williams, Lampeter Angling, 57 Bridge Str, Lampeter SA48 7AB (tel: 01570 422985 (evngs: 01570 434313)). Other good fishing on Aeron, 6m. Hotel: Talbot. Accommodation: Brynawel and Aberdwr Guest Houses.

TOWY (or TYWI)

(For close seasons, licences, etc, see Welsh Region Environment Agency, p23)

Lower reaches near Carmarthen are tidal holding trout, salmon and sewin in season (May, June and July best); association waters. Above this Towy mostly preserved, but some fishing by leave, ticket or from hotels. Salmon average 12lb and sea trout up to 8lb are taken; brown trout generally small.

Carmarthen (Dyfed). Salmon, sewin, trout. April and May usually good for large sewin. Tidal up to Carmarthen and 3m above. Cross Hands & Dist AA has water in vicinity (*see Llandeilo*). Carmarthen Amateur AA has water at Llanarth-

ney with 2 car parks; and on **Towy** at Nantgaredig, White Mill and Abergwili; sewin and salmon; assn arranges 6 competitions a year and has 5 private car parks; weekly permits from Secretary, or Carmarthen & Pumpsaint Farmers Co-op,

Pensarn. Carmarthen & Dist AC has water on **Rivers Towy** (incl exclusive tidal access rights), **Cothi** (downstream from The Cothi Bridge Hotel), **Gwili** (at Bronwydd), **Taf** and **Gwendraeth Fach** (near Llandyfaelog and Kidwelly); all these waters are within 5-10 miles of Carmarthen; membership £140, conc £60; no dt; under 16 free. Permits are available from Hon Sec; The Fishfinder, 51 King St, Carmarthen SA31 1BH (tel: 01267 220226); Towy Sports *(see Llandeilo);* Tight Lines. Fishfinder also has tickets for Cwmoernant Ponds (Carmarthen Town); crucian carp, perch, roach, rudd, tench; st £43 (juv £22), dt £5.70 (juv £2). **Pantybedw Fishery**, Nantgaredig SA32 7LH (tel: 01267 290315): 7½ acre fly fishing lake, catch and release only, dt £10; 1½ acre lake, catch and keep only; dt £22, 4 fish, £14, 2 fish. Hotel: Golden Grove Arms, Llanathne, Carmarthen SA32 8JU (tel: 01558 668551). Accommodation: Capel Dewi Uchaf Country House, Capel Dewi, Carmarthen, Carmarthenshire SA32 8AY (tel: 01267 29079; fax: 01267 290003; web: www.walescottageholidays.uk.com) who also sell tickets; Old Priory Guest House, 20 Priory St, Carmarthen, Dyfed SA31 1NE (tel: 01267 237471); Spillman Hotel, Spillman St, SA31 1LQ (tel: 01267 237037).

Nantgaredig (Dyfed). Salmon and sea trout fishing on the Abercothi Estate Fishery SA32 8SD (tel: 01558 668180; web: www.towyfishing.co.uk); 3 beats on **Towy** and part of **Cothi**; weekly letting for up to 5 rods on each beat. Carmarthen Amateur AA has water on **Cothi** and **Gwili**. Cross Hands & District AA has stretches on R Towy (6m), Teifi (1½m) and R Cothi (4m) in area; salmon and trout; tickets from Ian Jenkins (tel: 01558 668180; or 668373); joining fee £10; st £65, OAP's/students/ladies £30, juv £5 or £7; dt £20, wt (restricted) £40, wt (all waters) £50, conc.

Llandeilo (Carmarthenshire). Salmon, sea trout, brown trout. Llandeilo AA preserves 4½m on **Towy**, about 1½m on **Lower Dulais**. Season tickets, members only (waiting list), from Hon Sec; wt £70 and dt £25, conc, from Mrs G Morgan, Station House, Cwmifor, Llandeilo SA19 7AH (tel: 01558 822517); concessions for jun; fishing good when water in condition. Cross Hands & District AA has several stretches of Towy in vicinity, also

water on R Cothi, and **R Teifi** at Llandysul; access for disabled on some waters; membership £50 + joining fee £10, conc; limited dt £20 and wt £40-£50 (see Nantgaredig above). Tackle shops: The Fishfinder, 51 King St, Carmarthen SA31 1BH (tel: 01267 220226); Tight Lines, Wind St, Ammanford; Llanfynydd P O SA32 7TQ (tel: 01558 668794). Salmon and sea trout fishing on Golden Grove Estate; 10m stretch on **Towy** from Llandeilo to Nantgaredig, mainly double bank; 5 beats, some available for season rods, others for 3-day, and wt; best months Jun-Aug; self-catering accommodation for anglers at Sannan Court, Llanfynydd; contact Ian Jenkins, Afallon, Dryslwyn, Camarthen SA32 8QY (tel: 01558 668180 office; 01558 668373 home). Black Lion Inn, Llansawel, has 2½m on Towy; rods also on **Teifi** and **Cothi**. **Cennen** good trout stream. Tackle shop: Towy Sports, 9 King Str, Llandeilo, Dyfed SA19 6BA (tel: 01558 822637). Hotels: Cawdor Arms; Castle; Edwinsford Arms; Plough Inn; White Hart; Cottage Inn; Ty-Isaf Fishing Lodge and Country Cottages, Trapp, Llandeilo (game fishing on rivers and reservoirs; tuition).

Llangadog (Dyfed). Salmon, sewin, trout. Llangadog AA have water 2m of fishing on **Towy**; limited dt from Gwynfor Evans, Hafan Las High St, Llangadog, Dyfed SA19 9EF (tel: 01550 777532). Crosshands & Dist AA also has water.

Llanwrda (Dyfed). Salmon and sea trout. Swansea Amateur AA rents 1m (both banks), on an annual basis; access south of railway station; fly only; members and guests only; concessions for juniors. Glanrannell Park Country House, Crugybar, Llanwrda, nr Llandovery, Carmarthenshire SA19 8SA (tel: 01558 685230) has agreements with a number of private owners on **Rivers Cothi, Towy** and **Teifi**; and tickets for assn waters are obtainable from nearby towns, Llandeilo and Lampeter. **Springwater Lakes, Harford**, Llanwrda, SA19 8DT (tel: 01558 650788): two trout lakes (one fly only); one mixed coarse lake; one specimen carp lake with carp to 30lb. 8am to dusk, dt prices depend on lake. Tackle hire, facilities, access for disabled.

Llandovery (Dyfed). Salmon, sewin (best May-Aug), trout. Llandovery AA has 8m on **Towy**, double and single bank, excellent fly water below Llandovery, holding pools with fish (sewin) up to 14lbs, and salmon and grilse in Aug-Sep; and 10m on tributaries **R Gwydderig** and **R Bran**, good head of natural trout and sewin from July onwards. Membership occasionally available; st £150, dt £25-£8; from Hon Sec; The Carmarthen & Pumpsaint Farmers at The Mart Car Park, Llan-

dovery SA20 0AW (tel: 01550 720347); Castle Hotel, Kings Rd, SA20 0AP (tel: 01550 720343). Accom: Neuadd Fawr Arms, Cilycwm, Llandovery, Dyfed SA20 0SS (tel: 01550 721644); Mrs Lewis (B&B), Cwmgwyn Farm SA20 0EQ, which overlooks the fishing (tel: 01550 720410).

Tributaries of the Towy

GWILI. Small river of 12ft to 16ft in width which joins Towy 1m north of Carmarthen. Sea trout (sewin), fish running from early June onwards, averaging 2lb and attaining 6lb. Brown trout fishing poor. A few salmon caught on Gwili, especially at the end of year.

Llanpumsaint (Dyfed). Sewin, trout, occasional salmon. Carmarthen Amateur AA and Carmarthen & Dist AC both have stretches on Gwili. Hotel: Fferm-y-Felin (18th century farmhouse with 15 acres of countryside for fishing and bird watching, tuition and equipment for hire).

COTHI. The largest tributary of the Towy, noted for its sewin which run in late summer and early autumn. Salmon, sewin and brown trout.

Carmarthen (Dyfed). Carmarthen Amateur AA and Carmarthen & Dist AC both have stretches on Cothi. The Cothi Bridge Hotel, Pontargothi, Carmarthen, Dyfed SA32 7NG (tel: 01267 290251) has a short stretch of salmon fishing and has arrangements for guests to fish on other

private and club waters; special rates for fishermen.

Brechfa (Dyfed). Salmon and sea trout. Swansea Amateur AA has 2m (both banks), between Abergorlech and Brechfa; members and guests only. Hotels: Ty Mawr.

Pumpsaint (Dyfed). **Cothi** and **Twrch**. Trout, sea trout (June onwards); salmon from early July. Dolau Cothi Arms Hotel, Pumpsaint, Llanwrda, Dyfed SA19 8UW (tel: 01558 650547) has approx 8m of National Trust fishing, made up of 6 rods (extra rods by arrangement). Season starts from July to August when the salmon come up; permits from hotel; dt £5; bed and breakfast. Glanrannell Park Country House, Crugybar, Llanwdra, nr Llandovery, Carmarthenshire SA19 8SA (tel: 01558 685230), has salmon, sea trout and trout fishing on Teifi, Cothi and Twrch; and can arrange fishing on Spring Water Lakes, Pumpsaint, Llanwrda: 2 acre coarse lake with carp to 20lbs, good roach and rudd.

Foreground: local youngsters receive tuition from the marshal; background: increasing demonstration of improved access for the disabled - a wheelchair platform on this Carmarthen pond.

SAWDDE. Llanddeusant (Carmarthenshire). Trout. Accommodation and fishing at Black Mountain Caravan and Camping Park, Llanddeusant, nr Llangadog, SA19 9YG (tel: 01550 740217);

rainbow and brown trout fishing on **Usk Reservoir** (3m), also on Sawdde (3m) and Towy (6m). Licences from Post Office, Llangadog; tickets from machine at Usk Reservoir.

USK and EBBW

(For close seasons, licences, etc, see Welsh Region Environment Agency, p23)

The River Usk is a good salmon river and first rate for trout. Geological formation is red sandstone, merging into limestone in lower reaches. Trout average from about ¾lb in the lower reaches to ¼lb towards the source. Some tributaries also afford good trout fishing: Afon Llwyd, Honddu, Grwyne, Yscir and Bran. Salmon fishing mostly private, but several opportunities for trout. The River Ebbw flows into the Severn Estuary between the mouths of the River Rhymney and the River Usk. The Ebbw has recently experienced great improvements in water quality which has been reflected in the fishery improvements, with very good trout and reports of sea trout. The Sirhowy, a tributary of Ebbw, also has good trout fishing.

Newport (Monmouthshire). Newport AA has stretch of **Monmouthshire and Brecon Canal, Woodstock Pool, Morgans Pool, Liswerry Pond** and **Spytty Lake**; all providing good coarse fishing, including roach, perch, bream, carp and tench. Assn also has coarse fishing on **R Wye** at Symonds Yat; roach, dace, chub. Day tickets from bailiffs at lakes. Islwyn & Dist AC have 10m trout fishing on **Ebbw, Sirhowy** and **Penyfan Pond** (14 acres) near **Oakdale** and **Pant-yr-eos** Reservoir (12 acres) near **Risca**; membership from Hon Sec; membership £90, joining fee £25, juv £30, dt £10; dt from Greens Fishing Tackle, Bryn Road, Pontllanfraith, Blackwood NP12 2BU (tel: 01495 221881); for Pant-yr-eos, on site; for Penyfan Pond, from Pontllanfraith Leisure Centre, Pontllanfraith, Blackwood, Monmouthshire (tel: 01495 224562). Newport Reservoirs FFA has fishing on **Ysyfro Reservoir**, High Cross, nr Newport; rainbow and brown trout; day permits for non members can be purchased from hut at reservoir (dt £10 catch and release and kill 2 fish/day). **Wentwood Reservoir**, nr **Chepstow**, brown and rainbow trout; tickets at fishing lodge, for details contact Hon Sec, Wentwood Reservoir FFA (tel: 01291 425158); dt £16 (5 fish), £10 (2 fish), juv conc; wheelyboat for disabled. Rainbow and brown trout fishing on **Cefn Mably Lakes**, a complex of 5 spring-fed waters on farm land lying beside the River Rhymney; one 6½ acre lake, fly only; two any method; two coarse lakes stocked with carp, roach, rudd, perch, gudgeon, bream, etc, open all year; access for disabled, bait and full facilities on site; apply to John Jones, Cefn Mably

Lakes, nr Castleton, Newport CF3 6LP (tel: 01633 681101). **Hendre Lake**, 10-acre coarse fishery at St Mellons; an excellent lake, carp to 20lb, especially in hot and cold weather when other lakes are struggling; dt on bank; permits from Garry Evans. Tackle shops: Garry Evans Ltd, 29 Redland St, Newport, Monmouthshire NP9 5LZ (tel: 01633 855086); Dave Richards, 73 Church Road, NP19 7EH (tel: 01633 254910); Pill Angling Centre, 160 Commercial Rd, NP20 2PJ (tel: 01633 267211); Cwmbran Angling 39 Richmond Road, Pontnewydd, Cwmbran NP44 1EQ (tel: 01633 868890). Hotels: Rising Sun, High Cross, nr Newport, Monmouthshire; Tredagar Arms, Bassaleg, nr Newport, Monmouthshire.

Pontypool (Monmouthshire). Usk private. Tributary **Afon Llwyd**, good trout fishing and regularly stocked by local clubs. Exceptionally fast flowing river in places. Pontypool AA and Cwmbran AA have stretches. Pontypool AA also has **Allway Brook**, nr Usk, trout, dace and chub: and coarse fishing on **Monmouthshire & Brecon Canal** at Pontypool (Bridges 72 to 74), roach, perch, bream, carp and tench. **Llandegfedd Reservoir** (429 acres), Sluvad Treatment Works, Llandegfedd Reservoir, Panteg, Pontypool, NP4 0TA (tel: 01495 769281); owned by Welsh Water plc, and a major boat fishery; stocked with 30,000 rainbow trout av 1½lbs-2lbs, small numbers of browns; season 1 Mar-31 Oct (rainbow), 20 Mar-17 Oct (brown); fly only; st available, dt £14, 6 fish, £11, 4 fish, conc OAP and juv; permits from vending machines on site, or from Ranger's waterside office; forty boats for hire, incl for disabled, with

An Usk trout brought to the net by Grace Oglesby. If there is a finer trout stream in Wales, few know of it. *Photo: Arthur Oglesby.*

or without motor, £17-£8, pre-booking is recommended. Cwmbran AA has coarse fishing on **Monmouthshire & Brecon Canal**; average depth 4ft; stocked with bream, tench, crucian carp, roach, perch, good eels in parts; strict control on litter. Assn also has coarse fishing, for members only, at **Llantarnam Industrial Estates Ponds** (3 ponds stocked with roach, perch and dace, and one stocked with rudd and bream); and excellent mixed fishing on **River Monnow**, trout, grayling, bream, roach, perch, dace, chub and carp. Night fishing on canal and Monnow; permits from Cwmbran Pet Stores and Angling Supplies, 23 Commercial St, Old Cwmbran NP44 3LR (tel: 01633 483051). No day tickets on Llantarnam Ponds; members only.

Usk (Monmouthshire). Usk Town Water Fishery Association holds about 2m, mostly above Usk Bridge; trout fishing only; rod licence required; thigh wading only. Merthyr Tydfil AA has water at **Kemeys Commander**; permits, tackle and licences from Sweet's Fishing Tackle, 14 Porthycarne Str, Usk, Monmouthshire NP5 1RY (tel: 01291 672552). Hotels: Three Salmons; Cross Keys; Glen-yr-Avon; Kings Head.

Abergavenny (Monmouthshire). Salmon, trout. Monmouth DC holds town waters, both banks downstream from Llanfoist Bridge to Sewer Bridge; tickets from Bridge Inn, Llanfoist or Council Offices (tel: 01873 857737). Merthyr Tydfil AA has rights to **Mardy Fishery**, 2¼m above town. Crickhowell & Dist AS has approx 1½m u/s of Llanfoist Bridge, on left bank, known as the Red Barn Fishery *(see Crickhowell)* members only. Tackle shop: Sweet's Fishing Tackle, 14 Porthycarne Str, Usk, Monmouthshire NP5 1RY (tel: 01291 672552). Hotel: Wenallt; Penpergwm House. Information on fishing and accom from TIC, Swan Meadows NP7 5HH (tel: 01873 857588).

Crickhowell (Powys). Salmon, sea trout, wild brown trout. Crickhowell & Dist AS has approx 1m d/s of Crickhowell Bridge on both banks, except for garden of Bridgend Public House on left bank; also approx ½m u/s of bridge on left bank; members only; waiting list. Gliffaes Country House Hotel, NP8 1RH (tel: 01874 730 371; web: www.gliffaes.com) *(see advt)*, has 1m on Usk adjacent to hotel and a further 1½m upstream. Excellent wild brown trout water; salmon improving and some sea trout. Primarily for hotel guests but outside rods if space. Bridge End Inn has short length below bridge. **Trecastle** and **Talybont** Reser-

voirs are within reach. Hotel: Stables. Accom and angling information from Tourist Information Centre, Beaufort Chambers, Beaufort St NP8 1AA (tel: 01873 812105).

Brecon (Powys). Brecon AS has water on R Usk from Llanfaes Bridge to Boat House; salmon and trout; left bank (Llanfaes side) members only; Promenade bank (right bank) dt from H M Supplies Ltd, 90 The Watton, Brecon LD3 7EN (tel: 01874 622148). Brecon County Council has stretch on Usk from Llanfaes Bridge to Gwennies Lane, on which salmon stones and groynes have been placed, platforms for disabled, and water is stocked with brown trout; tickets (dt £15, 4 fish) from Town Clerk's Office, Guildhall LD3 7AL (tel: 01874 622884) (open 9am to 1pm); H M Supplies *(below)*. For salmon and trout fishing day tickets on Wye and Usk in the Brecon and Builth Wells area, contact Chester-Master Ltd (Chartered Surveyors & Land Agents), Dolgarreg, North Road, Builth Wells, Powys LD2 3DD (tel: 01982 553248). Brecon FA has 1m both banks above Llanfaes Bridge; fly only; dt from H M Supplies £4. Coarse fishing in pools on **Dderw Farm**, Llyswen; carp (to 12lbs), roach, tench; permits from Mrs J Eckley, Dderw Farm,

Llyswen, Brecon LD3 0UT (tel: 01874 754224). **Llangorse Lake**, 6m from Brecon; pike, perch, roach and bream; boat only; dt on site. Tackle shop: H M Supplies, 90 The Watton LD3 7EN (tel: 01874 622148). Hotels: Griffin Inn, Llyswen, Brecon; Castle of Brecon; Nythfa, Uskview GH.

Sennybridge (Powys). Rods on **Crai Reservoir** (100 acres) owned by Cnewr Estate Ltd, Sennybridge, Brecon LD3 8SP (tel: 01874 636207). Wild trout; fly fishing from bank only. Day tickets from reservoir house. Self-catering accommodation available.

Trecastle (Powys). **Usk Reservoir** (280 acres), one of the best trout fisheries in Wales, well stocked with rainbow and brown trout supplementing natural production; fly fishing, spinning and worming; catch limit 6 fish; size limit 9 inches; anglers are permitted to use their own boats by prior arrangement; caters for disabled; permits from machine on site; for further information contact C Hatch, Area Manager, United Utilities Operational Services Ltd., Sluvad Treatment Works, Llandegfedd Reservoir, New Inn, Pontypool, Monmouthshire NP4 0TA (tel: 01495 769281). Hotel: Castle.

Ebbw Vale (Monmouthshire). Ebbw Vale Welfare AC has coarse fishing on **River Wye** at Foy, nr Ross-on-Wye, 2½m (chub, dace, roach and barbel), restricted membership; **Machine Pond** at Brynmawr, 5 acres (carp, roach, perch); and 10 ponds in the Ebbw Vale area (carp, pike, roach, perch and gudgeon). Members only £13, conc. Membership open to all; from Hon Sec and local pet shop. Contact Hon Sec for season tickets for people on holiday. Concessions for juniors. Tackle shops: J Williams, 56 Bethcar St NP23 6HG (tel: 01495 305353), tickets for Ebbw Vale Welfare AC; Petsville, 52 Bethcar St NP3 6HG (tel: 01495 301292).

WYE

(For close seasons, licences, etc, see Welsh Region Environment Agency, p23)

The whole of the river Wye is included in the section on England, although it also flows through Monmouthshire and Powys.

WELSH SEA FISHING STATIONS

Those given in the following list are arranged from south to north. Sea fishing is available at other places also, but those mentioned are included because they cater specially for the sea angler. Further information may be had from the tackle shops and club secretaries (whose addresses will be found in the club list). When writing, please enclose stamped addressed envelope for reply. Local tourist information offices will help with accommodation.

Newport (Newport). Newport and District Sea Anglers operate in Magor, Redwick, Goldcliff, St Brides, Cardiff and Barry, with rover matches from Severn Bridge to Gower in West Wales; matches held every weekend; and, during the summer, Docks Summer League every Wed for 16 weeks. Tackle shops: Dave Richards, 73 Church Rd, NP19 7EH (tel: 01633 254910); Pill Angling Centre, 160 Commercial Rd NP20 2PJ (tel: 01633 267211). Hotel: Kings Head.

Swansea (Swansea). Bass, flatfish from beaches and rocks (Worm's Head). Fish baits cast from Llanmadoc take conger, tope, thornbacks and monkfish. Mackerel caught in warmer months. Bass, mullet and flounders in estuary at Loughor Bridge. Excellent boat fishing in Carmarthen Bay and off Worm's Head. Charter boats operate from Swansea Marina, for fishing the bay and Pwlldu. Information from Rodger's (*below*). Small bass, mullet, flatfish and mackerel off Mumbles Pier; night fishing by arrangement. Bait can be dug in Swansea Bay and estuary; squid, herring, sprats and mackerel from Swansea Market. List of clubs available from South West Wales Assn of SAC. Tackle shops: Mainwaring's Angling Centre, 44 Vivian Rd, Sketty, Swansea SA2 0UH (tel: 01792 202245; web: www.mainwarings.co.uk); Rodger's Tackle, Sea Angling Centre, South Dock, Swansea SA1 1UN, (01792 469999);

Tenby (Pembrokeshire). Good sport from Old Pier; whiting, pollack, bass, codling and grey mullet; good bass fishing from south and north sandy beaches, and spinning from rocks. Fine mackerel fishing most seasons, and tope off Caldey Island. For boats enquire tackle shop. 2m west from town at Penally is Penhoyla Fishing Park; trout; coarse; contact fishery at Trefloyne Lane SA70 4RR (tel: 01834 842255). Tackle shops: Morris Bros, Troy House, St Julian Str, SA70 7AY (tel: 01834 844789); Tenby Angling, 7 Old Market Hall, High St, SA70 7EU (tel:

01834 844430).

Milford Haven and **Pembroke** (Pembrokeshire). Fine surf-fishing and spinning from rocks for bass from Freshwater West and Broad Haven (Bosherton); best late summer and autumn. Kilpaison good for bass, flatfish early on; also codling and coalfish. Stone piers and jetties inside Haven provide deep water sport for pollack, skate, rays, whiting, codling, dogfish and coalfish. Hobbs Point (Pembroke Dock) excellent for conger and skate. Mackerel from rocks and boats (Stackpole Quay good). Tope from boats in Barafundle Bay and mackerel and bass from rocks. Other useful venues are Nab Head, Martins Haven and Angle Bay, Thorn, Rat and Sheep Islands and Harbour Rock. Mackerel from boats at harbour entrance. Lugworm and razor fish may be dug in several places, especially mud-flats at Kilpaison and Angle Bay. Pennar Gut and Pembroke River. Tackle shops: Milford Angling Supplies, Custom House, The Docks SA73 3AA (tel: 01646 692765).

Fishguard (Pembrokeshire). Main captures from shore and breakwaters are flatfish, codling, conger, pouting, mackerel, bass, pollack, whiting and some tope. Sea trout and mullet near mouth of Gwaun. Tope, mackerel, conger, skate, etc. from boats. Tackle shop: Goodwick Marine Services, 1 Wern Rd, Goodwick SA64 0AA (tel: 01348 873955).

Aberystwyth (Ceredigion). From the shore, May to November, bass (especially on soft crab bait), pollack, painted ray, mullet, huss, conger, wrasse. From October to January, whiting; July to September, mackerel. Dogfish, dabs and flounder throughout the year, turbot also caught. Fish caught off the rocks, off storm beaches, from the harbour and stone jetty. Borth beach and Leri estuary specially good for flounders; Tan-y-Bwlch beach particularly good for whiting. Bull huss and thornback ray form the backbone of the boat fishing, but dogfish, dabs, gurnard, pollack, tope, bream, turbot, monkfish and porbeagle shark are taken in their seasons. Boat trips are run from the harbour ranging from 2-hour sessions for mackerel to 12 hours out at sea. There are many well-equipped boats commanded by highly experienced skippers. Tackle shop: Aber Fishing Tackle, 3 Terrace Rd, SY23 1NY (tel: 01970 611200); Aeron Sports & Fishing Tackle, Kings Halls, Terrace Rd, SY1 2ED (seaward end)(tel: 01970 624830). Accommodation: Seabrin Guest House, South Marine Terrace.

Tywyn (Gwynedd). Good beach fishing for bass, turbot, and cod. Tywyn SAC, new club of 70 members, runs monthly competitions, casting lessons, and has discounts at club shop. Tackle shop: Barry's Fishing Tackle, 6 College Green LL36 9BS (tel: 01654 710357).

Barmouth (Gwynedd). Bass (large), flatfish, mullet in Mawddach estuary and from nearby beaches; also codling, mackerel, flatfish, and even tope and skate from boats. Ynys-y-Brawd island good for bass and flounders from shore and boats. Charter boat, The Viking, operates Apr-Oct; 8-hour deep sea or 2-hour short fishing, pleasure trips; licensed by the Dept of Trade for up to 60 passengers; full safety equipment and fishing tackle provided. Bookings can be made at Beachcaster Fishing Tackle, Glasfryn High St, LL42 1DS (tel: 01341 281537).

Porthmadog (Gwynedd). Mackerel fishing trips (2 hrs) and deep sea fishing trips (8 hrs, 10 hrs, 20 hrs); bookings from The Fisherman, Central Buildings, High St, Porthmadog, Gwynedd LL49 9BT (tel: 01766 512464).

Pwllheli and Criccieth (Gwynedd). Improved bass fishing April-October with new size limit to protect small bass; dogfish, dabs, plaice, skate, pollack and a few sole the year round; mackerel, tope and monkfish from June to September and black bream now on the increase. October to January; whiting and coalfish. Boat and bait available. Tackle shops: D & E Hughes, Walsall Stores, 24 Penlan Str, Pwllheli LL53 5DE (tel: 01758 613291); Companions Pet & Tackle Shop, 48a High Str, Criccieth LL52 0EY (tel: 01766 522805), who also has trout and coarse Eisteddfa Fishery, 1m east of Criccieth; dt trout £15 for 5 fish, £10 3 fish, conc; carp lake dt £6; mixed coarse £5.

Bangor (Gwynedd). Centre for Menai Straits and Anglesey. In Menai Straits, good mackerel and skate fishing during summer months, also plaice and flounder; good winter fishing for cod, pollack and whiting. Bait is plentiful along shores, incl crab and lugworm. Best beaches on Anglesey. Good rock marks abound for wrasse, pollack, thornback, smooth hound, mackerel, herring and bull huss. Good cod fishing in winter. Tackle shop: Bangor Angling Supplies, 21 High Str, LL57 1NP (tel: 01248 355518).

Deganwy (Conwy). Wide variety of fish taken from boats in Gt Orme, Menai Straits and Puffin Island areas. Bass in estuary and off Benarth, Bodlondeb and Deganwy Points and Beacon Light. Wreck fishing. Bait from shore and estuary. Sea fishing trips with tackle for sale or hire from Carl Davies, Pen-y-Berllan, Pentywyn Rd, Deganwy LL31 9TL (tel: 01492 581983; mobile 07710 819747); wreck fishing for pollack, conger, cod, etc, and reef fishing for bass, around Anglesey, Conwy Bay and Great Orme area, Llandudno; accom arranged, disabled catered for.

Llandudno (Conwy). Skate, cod, codling, pollack, bass, mackerel, plaice, whiting, conger, coalfish, etc. Rocky beach at corner of Little Orme good for bass; so is west shore, especially Black Rocks area. Bait plentiful. Fishing from pier, beach, rocks and boats. Tope and mackerel taken by boat fishers. Tackle shop: Paddy's Bait & Tackle, Unit 4, Happy Valley Rd, LL30 2LP (tel: 01492 877678). Hotel: Epperstone Hotel, Abbey Rd LL30 2EE (tel: 01492 878746) (fishing can be organised from hotel).

Colwyn Bay (Conwy). Bass in late summer and autumn from Rhos Point, Penrhyn Bay and Llandulas, over low water. Codling in the winter. Colwyn Bay promenade over high for whiting, dabs and dogfish. Tan-Lan beach from low water up for the best mixed fishing in the area all year round (best in darkness). Piers at Colwyn Bay and Llandudno fish well over high for a variety of fish, including dabs, whiting and some plaice. Club: Colwyn Bay Victoria SAC, Marine Drive, Rhos-on-Sea. For sea fishing contact Rhos Point Sea Fishing Trips: Bait and Tackle Shop, 2 Rhos Point, Rhos-on-Sea, Colwyn Bay LL28 4NL (01492 544829). Tackle shops: Victoria Pier Angling Centre, Colwyn Bay Pier LL29 8HH (tel: 01492 530663); Paddy's Bait & Tackle, Unit 4, Happy Valley Rd, Llandudno LL30 2LP (tel: 01492 877678).

Hotel: Ashmount Hotel.

Rhyl (Denbighshire). Skate, dabs, codling, whiting, plaice, gurnard, dog-fish, tope. From Foryd Harbour at Rhyl, east towards Dee Estuary at Prestayn, no licence or permit to fish is required, providing tackle and bait used are for sea fishing and not game fishing. Several boats, fully licensed to take fishing parties and charter booking, are available at Voryd Harbour from Blue Shark Sea Fishing Trips, The Harbour, Quay Str, LL18 2LB (tel: 01745 350267). Tackle shop: Geoff's Tackle, 163b Wellington Rd LL18 1LW (tel: 01745 356236).

ANGLESEY

Holyhead and Holy Island (Anglesey). Fishing off Holyhead Breakwater, 1¾m long, good on any tide; summer and winter fishing, many species caught. Very good fishing also on Stanley Embankment, at Cymyran, Rhoscolyn, Trearddur Bay, Porthdafarch and Holyhead Mountain. Bull huss, dogfish, pollack, wrasse, mullet, cod, plaice, dab, flounder, conger, whiting, codling, thornback ray and bass all taken in season from the various shore-marks. Boat-fishing, possible in all but the worst of weather, yields also shark, tope, ling and smoothhound. Bait readily available. Excellent boat fishing; thornbacks, tope, etc. Bait in harbour or from tackle shop: Anglesey Shooting & Fishing, Presaddfed, Bodedern LL65 3UE (tel: 01407 740759). Tourist Information, 1 Terminal, Holyhead Port, LL65 1DR (tel: 01407 762622). Hotel: Bull.

Amlwch (Anglesey). Tope taken to 40lb, skate, conger, herring, mackerel, etc, from boats; obtainable at Amlwch Port; charter boat from Cemaes Bay, wreck and other fishing for up to 8 anglers, *Stingray,* D Williams, The Boathouse, Beach Rd, Cemaes Bay, LL67 0ES, (tel: 01407 710510; web: www.seafishingtrips. co.uk); rods on board, facilities, bait to order. At **Benllech,** the area one mile out to sea has been recommended as good boat fishing for mackerel in summer, pollack, whiting in winter, and dogfish all year round. Charter boat *Sea Witch* provides one to one tuition for special needs anglers (licenced for 10); contact Pearl and Mel: 01407 831224; mob: 07711 984952). Tackle shop: Lathams, Benllech.

Beaumaris (Anglesey). Big bass, tope, pollack, mullet and mackerel opposite Beaumaris and along the Straits. Between Menai and The Tubular Bridge fair-sized bass and conger are caught. For boat fishing contact Stan Zalot, Starida Boats, Little Bryn, off Rosemary Lane LL58 8EE (tel: 01248 810251), and Dave Jones, Beaumaris Marine Services, The Anchorage, Rosemary Lane, LL58 8ED (tel: 01248 810746; mob: 07860 811988); 'Cerismar Two', fast twin-engined catamaran. Tackle shop: Anglesey Bait Centre, The Shop, Gallows Point LL58 8YL (tel: 01248 810009). Hotels: White Lion; Liverpool Arms.

Out from Aberystwyth, five rods took 3 hours to land this catch of cod. *Photo: Vic Haigh.*

FISHING CLUBS & ASSOCIATIONS IN WALES

Included in this list of fishing clubs and associations in Wales are some organisations which have their water on the upper reaches of the Wye or Severn, details of which are contained in the English section of **Where to Fish**. Further information can usually be had from the Secretaries and a courtesy which is appreciated is the inclusion of a stamped addressed envelope with postal inquiries. Please advise the publishers (address at the front of the book) of any changed details for the next edition.

NATIONAL BODIES

Wales Tourist Board
Dept. FI10
P.O.Box 1
Cardiff CF24 2XN
Tel: 029 2045 7766 (quote FI10)
Fax: 029 2047 5345
Web: www.visitwales.com
e-mail: info@tourism.wales.gov.uk

Welsh Federation of Coarse Anglers
Robin Darker
Penceilogwydd Farm
Llwynhdy
Llanelli SA14 9SH
01554 759444

Welsh Federation of Sea Anglers
G H Jones, MBE
8 Moreton Road
Holyhead
Anglesey LL65 2BG
Tel: 01407 763 821
Web: www.wfsa.org.uk
or

Colin Doyle
23 Park Road
Bargoed
Mid-Glam CF81 8SQ
Tel/fax: 01443 831684
e-mail: cdoyle0361@aol.com

Welsh Salmon & Trout Angling Assn.
M J (Moc) Morgan, OBE
Swyn Teifi
Pontrhydfendigaid
Ystrad Meurig
Ceredigion SY25 6EF
Tel/fax: 01974 831316
e-mail: mocmorgan@hotmail.com

Wheelyboat Trust (The)
Director: Andy Beadsley
North Lodge
Burton Park
Petworth
West Sussex GU28 0JT
Tel/Fax: 01798 342222

CLUBS

Aberaeron Town Angling Club
Nigel Davies
16 Wenallt
Bellevue Terrace
Aberaeron
Dyfed SA46 0BB
Tel: 01545 571013

Aberystwyth Angling Assn
P W Eklund
42 Erwgoch
Waunfawr

Aberystwyth
Dyfed SY23 3AZ
Tel: 01970 623021
Web: www: aberangling.co.uk

Afan Valley Angling Club
Lyndon Jones
33 Smallwood Road
Baglan
Port Talbot
W Glamorgan SA12 8AP
Tel: 07963 013632

Fishing Clubs

When you appoint a new Hon Secretary, do not forget to give us details of the change. Write to the publishers (address at front of the book). Thank you!

**Ammanford & District Angling
Assn**
John Jones
8 Florence Rd
Ammanford SA18 2DN
Tel: 01269 595770
Artro & Talsarnau Fishing Assn
B Powell
3 Glandwr Cottages
Llanbedr
Gwynedd LL45 2PB
Tel: 01341 241295
Bala & District Angling Assn
Hon Sec: Trevor Edwards
22 Blaen Ddol
Bala
Gwynedd LL23 7BB
Web: www.balawales.com/angling
or
Chairman: Michael Williams
Cysgod Y Coed
Bala
Gwynedd LL23 7DU
Tel: 01678 520036
Bangor City Angling Club
Mark Jones
The Stores
Penrhyn Avenue
Maesgeirchan
Bangor LL57 1LS
Tel: 01248 364471
**Bangor-on-Dee Salmon Angling
Assn**
K Evans
Ty-Newydd
Llay New Road
Old Rhosrobin
Wrexham LL11 4RL
Tel: 01978 357149
Betws-y-Coed Anglers' Club
Mrs Sian Godbert
3 Bwlch-y-Maen
Betws-y-Coed
Gwynedd, LL24 0DN
Tel: 01690 710143
Web: www: betws-y-coed-anglersclub.
org
Birchgrove (Cardiff) Angling Assn
J S Wilmot
4 Clydesmuir Rd
Tremorfa
Cardiff CF24 2QA
Tel: 029 20460697
Bodelwyddan Game Anglers
W A Wilkes
30 Roland Avenue
Kinmel Bay
Rhyl
Clwyd LL18 5DN

Tel: 01745 334935
Brecon Angling Society
Steve Richardson
67 Corydon Close
Brecon
Powys LD3 9HP
Tel: 01874 622201
Brynmill & District Angling Club
Dave Gough
226 Mynydd Garnllwyd Road
Morriston
Swansea
Tel: 01792 420910
e-mail: dave.gough5@ntlworld.com
Bryn-y-Pys Angling Assn
Mrs A Phillips
Deggy's Fishing Tackle
2 Ruabon Road
Wrexham LL13 7PB
Tel: 01978 391815
Buckley Angling Assn
Cliff Hibbert
6 Moorcroft
New Brighton
nr Mold
Flintshire CH7 6RF
Tel: 01352 756800
Bute Angling Society
Bob Williams
19 Clos-y-Cwarra
St Fagans
Cardiff CF5 4QT
Tel: 02920 593540
Caersws Angling Assn
David Corfield
Troed-y-Rallt
Clatter
Caersws
Powys SY17 5NP
Tel: 01686 420225
Capenhurst Angling Club
A T Howdon
24 Saughall Hey
Saughall
Chester CH1 6EJ
Tel: 01244 880621
**Carmarthen Amateur Angling
Assn**
Ron Ratti
Rhydal Mount
The Parade
Carmarthen SA31 1LZ
Tel: 01267 237362
**Camarthen & District Angling
Assn**
John Davis
Ross Avenue
Carmarthen
Tel: 01267 221590

Cefni Angling Assn
(see: Cymdeithas Pysgota)
G R Williams
Tyn Lon, Pentre Berw
Gaerwen
Anglesey LL60 6HY
Tel: 01248 421 238
Web: www.llyncefni.co.uk

Ceiriog Fly Fishers
Alan Hudson
96 Crogen
Lodgevale Park
Chirk
Wrexham LL14 5BJ
Tel: 01691 773632

Chester Assn of Anglers
B W Roberts
23 Alpraham Crescent
Upton
Chester CH2 1QX
Tel: 01244 381193

Chirk Angling Assn
(Incorporated in Ceiriog Fly Fishers)

Cilcain Fly Fishing Assn
Ron Jones
1 Maes Bodlonfa
Mold
Flintshire CH7 1DR
Tel: 01352 754452

Clwb Godrer Mynydd Du
D Davies
8 Jones Terrace
Glanamman
Ammanford
Dyfed SA18 2AH
Tel: 01269 825487

Colwyn Bay Sea Angling Club
Marine Drive
Rhos-on-Sea
Clwyd

Connah's Quay & District Angling Assn
C Hett
87 Richmond Road
Connah's Quay
Clwyd CH5 4JB
Tel: 01244 818405

Corwen & District Angling Club
Gordon H Smith
Llais-yr-Afon
Bontuchel
Ruthin
Denbighshire LL15 2BE
Tel: 01824 710609

Criccieth, Llanystumdwy & District Angling Assn
Geraint Pritchard
8 Dolwar
Four Crosses
Chwilog LL53 6UQ

Tel: 01766 810548

Crickhowell & District Angling Society
Chairman: Paul Bowen
13 Hatherleigh Road
Abergavenny
Monmouth. NP7 7RG
Tel: 01873 858440

Crosshands & District Angling Assn
Hon Sec: Pat Kiernan
48 Waterloo Road
Penygroes
Llanelli
Carmarthen SA14 7NS
Tel: 01269 842083
or
Memb. Sec: G V Davis
6 Close-yr-Hendre
Capel Hendre
Ammanford SA18 3NN
Tel: 01269 843462

Cwmbran Angling Assn
c/o Cwmbran Pet Stores & Ang. Supplies
23 Commercial St
Old Cwmbran NP44 3LR
Tel: 01633 483051

Cwmcelyn Angling Club
Kevin Taggart
Brynheulog
Waun Ebbw Road
Nantyglo NP23 4QR
Tel: 0777 3524418

Cymdeithas Pysgota Cefni Angling Assn. (Cefni AA)
G R Williams
Tyn Lon, Pentre Berw
Gaerwen
Anglesey LL60 6HY
Tel: 01248 421 238
Web: www.llyncefni.com

Cwmllynfell Fly Fishing Club
Colin Woolcock
45 Colbren Square
Gwain-cae-Gurwen
nr Ammanford SA18 1HS
tel: 01269 825561

Cymdeithas Pysgota Talybont (Talybont Angling Assn)
Michael Williams
Llawr-y-Glyn
Lledrod
Ceredigion SY23 4TA
Tel: 01974 251330

Dee Anglers Assn
Cliff Hibbert
6 Moorcroft
New Brighton
nr Mold

Flintshire CH7 6RF
Tel: 01352 756800
Denbigh & Clwyd Angling Club
   Colin Blythin
   Y Fron
   Abbey Road
   Rhuddlan
   Rhyl
   Clwyd LL18 5RG
   Tel: 01745 591281
Dolgarrog Fishing Club
   W P Jones
   12 Hillside
   Dolgarrog
   Gwynedd LL32 8JP
   Tel: 01492 660373
Dolgellau Angling Assn
   E Marshall Davies
   2 Maescaled
   Dolgellau
   Gwynedd LL40 1UF
   Tel: 01341 422706
   Web: www.dolgellauanglingassociation.
   co.uk
Dolwyddelan Fishing Assn
   D E Foster
   The Post Office
   Dolwyddelan
   Gwynedd LL25 0NJ
   Tel: 01690 750201
Dwyryd Anglers Ltd
   Gareth Ffestin Price
   Hafan
   Ffordd Peniel
   Ffestiniog
   Gwynedd LL41 4LP
   Tel: 01766 762451
Ebbw Vale Welfare Angling Club
   R Satterley
   8 Pen-y-lan
   Ebbw Vale
   Monmouthshire NP23 5LS
   Tel: 01495 307613
Estimaner Angling Assn
   (Ystumaner Angling Assn.)
   Hon Sec: John Baxter
   11 Tan y Fedw
   Abergynolwyn
   Gwynedd LL36 9YU
   Tel: 01654 782632
Glamorgan Angling Club
   M Roberts

4 Heol Don
Whitchurch
Cardiff CF14 2AU
Glaslyn Angling Assn
   J Daniel Hughes
   Berthlwyd
   Penrhyndeudraeth
   Gwynedd LL48 6RL
   Tel: 01766 770478
Glyncornel Angling Assn
   David Picton-Davies
   94 Tylacelyn Road
   Penygraig-Tonypandy
   Rhondda, Mid Glam. CF40 1JR
   Tel: 01443 432289
Glynneath & District Angling
   Assn
   Gareth Evans
   21 Godfrey Avenue
   Glynneath, Neath
   West Glamorgan SA11 5HF
   Tel: 07639 721301
Gwaun-Cae-Gurwen Angling Assn
   Keith James
   63 Brynamman Road
   Lower Brynamman
   Ammanford SA18 1TR
   Tel: 01269 823023
Isca Angling Club
   Phil Facey
   3 Clipper Close
   St Julians
   Newport
   Monmouth. NP19 7LL
   Tel: 01633 678790
Islwyn & District Anglers
   Hon Sec: J H Otter
   10 Penygroes,
   Parc Derwen,
   Oakdale, Monmouth. NP12 0ER
Lavister Angling Club
   G Watkins
   Rathgillan
   Lache Hall Crescent
   Chester
   Cheshire CH4 7NE
   Tel: 01244 677330
Liverpool & District Angling Assn
   Chairman: Jo Farrell
   10 Windermere Drive
   Maghull
   Liverpool

Fishing Clubs

When you appoint a new Hon Secretary, do not forget to give us details of the change.
Write to the publishers (address at front of the book). Thank you!

Merseyside L31 9BQ
Tel: 07764 926643

**Llanbrynmair & District
Angling Club**
Mike Jones
Craig-y-Gronfa
Mallwyd
Machynlleth
Powys SY20 9EN
Tel: 01650 511691

Llandeilo Angling Assn
Tony Stevens
7 Dynevor Avenue
Llandeilo SA19 6DU
Tel: 01269 832824

Llandovery Angling Assn
Michael Davies
Cwmrhuddan Lodge
Llandovery
Carmarthenshire SA20 0DX
Tel: 01550 720633

Llandysul Angling Assn
The Porth Hotel
Llandysul
Ceredigion SA44 4QS
or
Pat O'Reilly
SWYN Esgair
Drefach-Felindre
Llandysul
SA44 5XG
Tel: 01559 371879
e-mail: pat@first-nature.com

Llangadog Angling Assn
Eifion Jones
3 Plot Cwr Y Waun
(Waundyfrai)
Llangadog
Dyfed SA19 9EL
Tel: 01550 777296

Llangennech Angling Club
Clive Thomas
14 Llys-y-Selin
Llangennech
Llanelli
Carmarthen. SA14 8BA
Tel: 01554 821637

Llangollen Angling Assn
W N Elbourn
Bwthyn Bach
2 Green Lane
Llangollen
Denbighshire LL20 8TD

**Llangyfelach & District Angling
Assn**
R L Griffiths
Cefn Cottage
Cilibion
Llanrhidian

Swansea SA3 1ED
Tel: 01792 391048

**Llanidloes & District Angling
Assn**
J Dallas Davies
Dresden House
Great Oak Street
Llanidloes, Powys SY18 6BW
Tel: 01686 412644

Llanilar Angling Assn
John H Astill
Dryslwyn
Llanafan
Aberystwyth
Ceredigion SY23 4AX
Tel: 01974 261237

Llanrwst Anglers' Club
David W P Hughes
36 Station Road
Llanrwst
Gwynedd LL26 0AD

Llanybydder Angling Assn
Andrew Morgan
Dolau View
Neuadd Road
Llanybydder
Dyfed SA40 9UB
Tel: 01570 480998

Llay Angling Assn
John Preston
20 Mold Road Estate
Gwersyllt, Wrexham
Clwyd LL11 4AA
Tel: 01978 758178

Llynfi Valley Angling Assn
Brian Hall
47 Park View Estate
Maesteg
Mid Glamorgan CF34 9HF
Tel: 01656 737995

Maelor Angling Assn
K Bathers
Sunnyside
11 Hill Street
Cefn Mawr, Wrexham
Clwyd LL14 3AY
Tel: 01978 820608

Maerdy & Ferndale Angling Club
Woodland Rd
Pontygwaith
Ferndale
Mid Glamorgan
CF43
Tel: 01443 757263

Merthyr Tydfil Angling Assn
Nigel Morgan
20 James Street
Twynyrodyn
Merthyr Tydfil

Mid Glam. CF47 0NF
Tel: 01685 377848
Web: www.mtaa.co.uk
Mold Fly Fishers
  Chairman: Brian Lloyd
  c/o 3 The Cross
  Mold
  Clwyd CH7 1ER
  Tel: 01352 753247
Neath & Dulais Angling Assn
  Ivor J Jones
  5 Bryndulais Row
  Seven Sisters
  Neath SA10 9EB
  Tel: 01639 701187
  Web: www.nadac.co.uk
Nevern Angling Assn
  Viv Owen
  Glyn-Deri
  Nevern
  Newport SA42 0NE
  Tel: 01239 820365
Newbridge Angling Assn
  Kerry F R Clutton
  28 Worsley Avenue
  Johnstown
  nr Wrexham
  Clwyd LL14 2TD
  Tel: 01978 840377
New Dovey Fishery Assn (1929)
Ltd (The)
  Glyn Thomas
  Leeds House
  20 Maengwyn Street
  Machynlleth
  Powys SY20 8DT
  Tel/fax: 01654 702721
Newport Angling Assn
  Chairman: D Ballett
  102 Victoria Avenue
  Newport
  Monmouth. NP19 8GG
  Tel: 01633 264608
Newport & District Sea Anglers
  Karen Davis
  18 Gibbs Road
  Newport
  Monmouth. NP19 8AT
  Tel: 01633 676561
Newport Reservoirs Flyfishing
Assn
  Ynysyfro Reservoir
  Newport
  South Wales
  or
  David Baker
  50 Danygraig Road
  Risca
  Monmouthshire NP1 6DB

Tel: 01633 615180
Ogmore Angling Assn
  G Ellis
  46 Onslow Terrace
  Tondu
  Bridgend
  Tel: 01656 720980
  Web: www.ogmoreriver.com
  or
  Memb Sec: Adrian Curnock
  Tel: 01656 721591
Ogwen Valley Angling Assn
  Stephen Jones
  19 Maes Coetmor
  Bethesda
  Bangor
  Gwynedd LL57 3DS
  Tel: 01248 605001
  Web: www.ogwen.net
Garw Valley Angling Assn
  F J Hughes
  20 Heol Glannant
  Bettws
  Bridgend
Pembrokeshire Anglers Assn
  S Esmond
  9 South View
  Pill Road
  Hook
  Haverfordwest
  Dyfed SA62 4LT
  Tel: 01437 891232
Picton Waters Angling Club
  Ian Richards
  North Pines
  Wiston
  Haverfordwest
  Dyfed SA62 4PS
  Tel: 01437 731628
Ponciau Angling Society
  (not available as we go to press)
Pontardawe & Swansea Angling
Society
  R H Lockyer
  8 Bwllfa Road
  Ynystawe
  Swansea SA6 5AL
  Tel: 01792 844014
  e-mail: ray@lockyer15.freeserve.co.uk
Pontardulais & District Angling
Assn
  A Thomas
  27 Pentre Road
  Pontardulais, Swansea
  West Glamorgan SA4 8HT
  Tel: 01792 882483
Pontypool Angling Assn
  Pete Rottier
  29 Glanrhyd

Coed Eva
Cwmbran
Gwent NP44 6TY
Tel: 01633 675362
Porthcawl Angling Assn
Howell Richards
19 The Mercies
Porthcawl CF36 5HN
Tel: 01656 786080
Prince Albert Angling Society
Hon Sec: J A Turner
15 Pexhill Drive
Macclesfield
Cheshire SK10 3LP
Tel: 01625 422010
or
Memb. Sec. C Swindells
37 Sherwood Road
Macclesfield
Cheshire SK11 7RR
Pwllheli Angling Assn
E W Evans
2 Fron-Oleu
Caernarfon Road
Pwllheli
Gwynedd LL53 5LN
Tel: 01758 613444
Prysor Angling Assn
Malcolm Atherton
Pen-y-graig
Trawsfynydd
Gwynedd SY14 7HH
Tel: 01766 540264
Pyrddin Angling Society
Robert Browning
91 Main Road
Duffryn Cellwen
nr Neath, West Glamorgan
Rhostyllen Angling Club
Bryan Ryley
23 Y-Fron
Nant Parc
Johnstown
Wrexham LL14 1UP
Tel: 01978 842017
Rhyl & District Angling Assn
Martin Fowell
Bon-Amie
28 Ffordd Tanrallt
Meliden
Prestatyn
Denbighshire LL19 8PS
Tel: 01745 854390
Rhymney & District Angling Society
J Pugh
12 Castle Field
Rhymney
Monmouthshire NP2 5NS

Rossett & Griffin Fly Fishers
Mark Pierce
Tel: 07980 530674
St Asaph Angling Assn
D Edwards
9 Maes Emlyn
Penyffordd
Holywell
Clwyd CH8 9JA
Tel: 01745 561491
St Clears Angling Assn
David J Bryan
Madras Cottage
Broadway
Laugharne
Carmarthen SA33 4NU
Tel: 01994 427331
Seiont, Gwyrfai & Llyfni Angling Assn.
H P Hughes
Llugwy, Ystad Eryri
Bethel, Caernarfon
Gwynedd LL55 1BX
Tel: 01248 670666
Web: www.gwynedd.gov.uk/sg
Skewen Coarse Angling Club
Mike Doyle
58 The Highlands
Skewen, Neath
West Glamorgan SA10 6PD
Tel: 01792 423193
Swansea Amateur Angling Assn
J B Wolfe
147 St Helen's Road
Swansea SA1 4DB
Swansea Angling Club
Malcolm Brown
31 Stepney Road
Cockett
Swansea SA2 0FZ
Tel: 01792 582058
Tawe & Tributaries Angling Assn.
Laurence Jones
20 Thomas Street
Pontardawe
Swansea Valley SA8 4HD
Tel: 01792 863522
Tawe Disabled Fishers' Assn
R W Hale
Willow Bank
Ilston
Swansea SA2 7LD
Tel: 01792 371647
Teifi Trout Assn
Memb. Sec: Mike Evans
21 Blaenwrn
Newcastle Emlyn SA38 9BE
Tel: (mob) 07977 558434
Tel: 01239 711148

Tregaron Angling Assn
 M J (Moc) Morgan
 Swyn Teifi
 Pontrhydfendigaid
 Ystrad Meurig
 Ceredigion SY25 6EF
 Tel/fax: 01974 831316
 e-mail: mocmorgan@hotmail.com
Warrington Angling Assn
 Hon Sec: Frank Lythgoe
 P O Box 71
 Warrington WA1 1LR
 or
 HeadQuarters
 52 Parker St.
 Warrington
 Cheshire WA1 1LT
 Tel: 01925 637525
 (Open every Friday 7pm - 9.30pm)
Wentwood Reservoir Fly Fishing Assn
 D G P Jones
 123 Castle Lea
 Caldicot
 Monmouth NP26 4HS
 Tel: 01291 425158
Whitland Angling Assn
 Peter Hunt
 White House Mill
 Whitland SA34 0RB
 Tel: 01834 831304
Wirral Game Fishing Club
 Derek Jones

 31 Meadway
 Upton
 Wirral CH49 6JQ
 Tel: 0151 677 7506
Wrexham & District Angling Assn
 John Grocott
 Sandbank
 Gresford Road
 Hope
 Wrexham LL12 9EL
 Tel: 01978 761728
Ynys Mon Angling Assn
 Hon Sec: R T Swales
 36 Trem-y-Mor
 Rhosneigr
 Anglesey, LL64 5QR
 Tel: 01407 810136
Ystumaner Angling Assn
 (Estimaner Angling Assn)
 Hon Sec: John Baxter
 Abergynolwyn
 Gwynedd LL36 9YU
 Tel: 01654 782632

MISCELLANEOUS

DreamStreams Ltd
 Swyn Esgair
 Drefach-Felindre
 Llanysul SA44 5XG
 Tel: 01559 371879
 Web: www: first-nature.com/dream streams

FISHING IN SCOTLAND

District Salmon Fishery Boards and Close Season for Salmon and Trout

Fishing in Scotland is under the general jurisdiction of the Scottish Executive Rural Affairs Department, Pentland House, 47 Robb's Loan, Edinburgh, EH14 1TY (tel: 0131 244 6227; fax: 0131 244 6313).

The annual close season for brown trout in Scotland extends from 7 October to 14 March, both days included. Trout may not be sold between the end of August and the beginning of April, nor at any time if the fish are less than 8 in long.

Visiting anglers are reminded that on Scottish rivers and lochs the owner of the fishing is the riparian proprietor, whose permission to fish should be obtained. The only public right of fishing for brown trout and other freshwater fish is in those portions of the rivers which are both tidal and navigable, but the right must not be exercised so as to interfere with salmon or sea-trout fishing and can be exercised only where there is a right of access to the water from a boat or from the banks. A number of rivers in Scotland including the Aberdeenshire Don are subject to Protection Orders granted by the Secretary of State for Scotland. On rivers where a Protection Order is in force, it is a criminal offence to fish for any freshwater species without the owner's permission. Anglers visitng Scotland to fish for coarse fish should note that it is not lawful to fish with 2 or more rods simultaneously. The rule is one rod only, which must be held in the hands at all times while fishing.

Salmon. Provision is made in the Salmon Act, 1986, for the formation and amalgamation of District Salmon Fishery Boards, composed of representatives of proprietors of salmon fisheries in each district, and coopted representatives of anglers and tenant netsmen. These boards, the addresses of which are given on pages below, are responsible for the administration and protection of the salmon fisheries in their districts, and boards have been formed for practically all the important salmon rivers. More recently, the Boards have become increasingly involved in scientifically based management, research and stock enhancement.

Increasingly, the practice of catch and release is being encouraged by boards and proprietors of salmon fishings. Regulations restricting various baits and lures are in force in a number of Salmon Fishery Districts. On 1 October 2002, a ban on the sale in Scotland of rod caught salmon and sea-trout was introduced.

In the following list, the days fixing the start and finish of the annual close time for net fishing and for rod fishing respectively are in all cases inclusive, and, as in the case of the Add, the first river in the list, the first pair of dates are the limits of the net season and the second pair apply to rod fishing.

Add. Annual close time for net-fishing: From Sept 1 to Feb 15, both dates inclusive. Annual close time for rod-fishing: From Nov 1 to Feb 15, both days inclusive.

Ailort. Aug 27 to Feb 10; Nov 1 to Feb 10.

Aline. Aug 27 to Feb 10; Nov 1 to Feb 10.

$IAnnan, RiverAnnan. Sept 10 to Feb 24; Nov 16 to Feb 24.

Applecross. Aug 27 to Feb 10; Nov 1 to Feb 10.

Arnisdale. Aug 27 to Feb 10; Nov 1 to Feb 10.

Awe. Aug 27 to Feb 10; 16 Oct to Feb 10.

Ayr. Aug 27 to Feb 10; Nov 1 to Feb 10.

Baa and Goladoir. Aug 27 to Feb 10; Nov 1 to Feb 10.

Badachro and Kerry. Aug 27 to Feb 10; Nov 1 to Feb 10.

Balgay and Shieldaig. Aug 27 to Feb 10; Nov 1 to Feb 10.

Beauly. Aug 27 to Feb 10; Oct 16 to Feb 10.

Berriedale. Aug 27 to Feb 10; Nov 1 to Feb 10.

Bervie. Sept 10 to Feb 24; Nov 1 to Feb 24.

Bladnoch. Aug 27 to Feb 10; Nov 1 to Feb 10.

Broom. Aug 27 to Feb 10; Nov 1 to Feb 10.

Brora. Aug 27 to Feb 10; Oct 16 to Jan 31.

Carradale. Sept 10 to Feb 24; Nov 1 to Feb 24.

Carron. Aug 27 to Feb 10; Nov 1 to Feb 10.

Clayburn (Western Isles). Sept 10 to Feb 24; Nov 1 to Feb 24.

Clyde and Leven. Aug 27 to Feb 10; Nov 1 to Feb 10.

Conon. Aug 27 to Feb 10; Oct 1 to Feb 10.
Cowie. Aug 27 to Feb 10; Nov 1 to Feb 10.
Cree. Sept 14 to Feb 28; Oct 15 to Feb 28.
Creran (Loch Creran). Aug 27 to Feb 10; Nov 1 to Feb 10.
Crowe and Shiel (Loch Duich). Aug 27 to Feb 10; Nov 1 to Feb 10.
Dee (Aberdeenshire). Aug 27 to Feb 10; Oct 1 to Jan 31.
Dee (Kirkcudbrightshire). Aug 27 to Feb 10; Nov 1 to Feb 10.
Deveron. Aug 27 to Feb 10; Nov 1 to Feb 10.
Don. Aug 27 to Feb 10; Nov 1 to Feb 10.
Doon. Aug 27 to Feb 10; Nov 1 to Feb 10.
Drummachloy (Bute). Sept 1 to Feb 15; Oct 16 to Feb 15.
Dunbeath. Aug 27 to Feb 10; Oct 16 to Feb 10.
Eachaig. Sept 1 to Apr 30; Nov 1 to Apr 30.
Earn (Tay). Aug 21 to Feb 4; Nov 1 to Jan 31.
East Lewis (Western Isles). Aug 27 to Feb 10; Nov 1 to Feb 10.
Eden (Tay).
Aug 21 to Feb 4; Nov 1 to Feb 4.
Esk, North. Sept 1 to Feb 15; Nov 1 to Feb 15.
Esk, South. Sept 1 to Feb 15; Nov 1 to Feb 15.
Ewe. Aug 27 to Feb 10; Nov 1 to Feb 10.
Fincastle (Western Isles). Sept 10 to Feb 24; Nov 1 to Feb 24.
Findhorn. Aug 27 to Feb 10; Oct 1 to Feb 10.
Fleet (Kirkcudbrightshire). Sept 10 to Feb 24; Nov 1 to Feb 24.
Fleet (Sutherland). Sept 10 to Feb 24; Nov 1 to Feb 24.
Forss. Aug 27 to Feb 10; Nov 1 to Feb 10.
Forth. Aug 27 to Feb 10; Nov 1 to Jan 31.
Fyne, Shira and Aray. Sept 1 to Feb 15; Nov 1 to Feb 15.
Garnock. Sept 10 to Feb 24; Nov 1 to Feb 24.
Girvan. Sept 10 to Feb 24; Nov 1 to Feb 24.
Glenelg. Aug 27 to Feb 10; Nov 1 to Feb 10.
Gour. Aug 27 to Feb 10; Nov 1 to Feb 10.
Grudie or **Dionard**. Aug 27 to Feb 10; Nov 1 to Feb 10.
Gruinard and Little Gruinard. Aug 27 to Feb 10; Nov 1 to Feb 10.
Halladale. Aug 27 to Feb 10; Oct 1 to Jan 11.
Helmsdale. Aug 27 to Feb 10; Oct 1 to Jan 10.
Hope and Polla. Aug 27 to Feb 10; Oct 1 to Jan 11.
Howmore (Western Isles). Sept 10 to Feb 24; Nov 1 to Feb 24.

Inchard. Aug 27 to Feb 10; Nov 1 to Feb 10.
Inner (Jura). Sept 10 to Feb 24; Nov 1 to Feb 24.
Inver. Aug 27 to Feb 10; Nov 1 to Feb 10.
Iorsa (Arran). Sept 10 to Feb 24; Nov 1 to Feb 24.
Irvine. Sept 10 to Feb 24; Nov 16 to Feb 24.
Kannaird. Aug 27 to Feb 10; Nov 1 to Feb 10.
Kilchoan. (Loch Nevis). Aug 27 to Feb 10; Nov 1 to Feb 10.
Kinloch (Kyle of Tongue). Aug 27 to Feb 10; Nov 1 to Feb 10.
Kirkaig. Aug 27 to Feb 10; Nov 1 to Feb 10.
Kishorn. Aug 27 to Feb 10; Nov 1 to Feb 10.
Kyle of Sutherland. Aug 27 to Feb 10; Oct 1 to Jan 10.
Laggan and **Sorn** (Islay). Sept 10 to Feb 24; Nov 1 to Feb 24.
Laxford. Aug 27 to Feb 10; Nov 1 to Feb 10.
Leven. Aug 27 to Feb 10; Nov 1 to Feb 10.
Little Loch Broom. Aug 27 to Feb 10; Nov 1 to Feb 10.
Loch Long. Aug 27 to Feb 10; Nov 1 to Feb 10.
Loch Roag (Western Isles). Aug 27 to Feb 10; Oct 17 to Feb 10.
Loch Sunart. Aug 27 to Feb 10; Nov 1 to Feb 10.
Lochy. Aug 27 to Feb 10; Nov 1 to Feb 10.
Lossie. Aug 27 to Feb 24; Nov 1 to Feb 24.
Luce. Sept 10 to Feb 24; Nov 1 to Feb 24.
Lussa (Mull). Aug 27 to Feb 10; Nov 1 to Feb 10.
Moidart. Aug 27 to Feb 10; Nov 1 to Feb 10.
Morar. Aug 27 to Feb 10; Nov 1 to Feb 10.
Mullanageren (Western Isles). Sept 10 to Feb 24; Nov 1 to Feb 24.
Nairn. Aug 27 to Feb 10; Oct 8 to Feb 10.
Naver and Borgie. Aug 27 to Feb 10; Oct 1 to Jan 11.
Nell, Feochan and Euchar. Aug 27 to Feb 10; Nov 1 to Feb 10.
Ness. Aug 27 to Feb 10; Oct 16 to Jan 14.
Nith. Sept 10 to Feb 24; Dec 1 to Feb 24.
Orkney Islands. Sept 10 to Feb 24; Nov 1 to Feb 24.
Ormsary. Aug 27 to Feb 10; Nov 1 to Feb 10.
Pennygowan and **Aros** (Mull). Aug 27 to Feb 10; Nov 1 to Feb 10.
Resort (Western Isles). Aug 27 to Feb 10; Nov 1 to Feb 10.
Ruel. Sept 1 to Feb 15; Nov 1 to Feb 15.

Sanda. Aug 27 to Feb 10; Nov 1 to Feb 10.
Scaddle. Aug 27 to Feb 10; Nov 1 to Feb 10.
Shetland Islands. Sept 10 to Feb 24; Nov 1 to Feb 24.
Shiel (Loch Shiel). Aug 27 to Feb 10; Nov 1 to Feb 10.
Skye, Isle of. Aug 27 to Feb 10; Oct 16 to Feb 10.
Spey. Aug 27 to Feb 10; Oct 1 to Feb 10.
Stinchar. Sept 10 to Feb 24; Nov 1 to Feb 24.
Strathy. Aug 27 to Feb 10; Oct 1 to Jan 11.

Tay. Aug 21 to Feb 4; Oct 16 to Jan 14.
Thurso. Aug 27 to Feb 10; Oct 6 to Jan 10.
Torridon. Aug 27 to Feb 10; Nov 1 to Feb 10.
Tweed. Sept 15 to Feb 14; Dec 1 to Jan 31.
Ugie. Sept 10 to Feb 24; Nov 1 to Feb 9.
Ullapool (Loch Broom). Aug 27 to Feb 10; Nov 1 to Feb 10.
Urr. Sept 10 to Feb 24; Dec 1 to Feb 24.
Wick. Aug 27 to Feb 10; Nov 1 to Feb 10.
Ythan. Sept 10 to Feb 24; Nov 1 to Feb 10.

DISTRICT SALMON FISHERY BOARDS

The names, addresses and telephone numbers of the clerks of the various salmon district fishery boards in Scotland are as follows: Please note that their duties are purely to operate the Acts and that they do not have fishing to let.

Annan District Salmon Fishery Board. Ms Helen Riach, Annandale Estate Office, St Ann's, Lockerbie, Dumfriesshire DG11 1HQ (tel: 01576 470817).

Awe District Salmon Fishery Board. S Murray, Messrs MacArthur, Stewart & Co, Solicitors, Boswell House, Argyll Square, Oban, Argyllshire PA34 4BD (tel: 01631 562215; fax: 01631 565490).

Ayr District Salmon Fishery Board. F M Watson, D W Shaw & Company, 34a Sandgate, Ayr KA7 1BG (tel: 01292 265033; fax:01292 284906; e-mail: fwatson@dwshaw.com).

Beauly District Salmon Fishery Board. J Wotherspoon, MacAndrew & Jenkins WS, Solicitors and Estate Agents, 5 Drummond Str, Inverness, IV1 1QF (tel: 01463 233001)

Bladnoch District Salmon Fishery Board. Peter M Murray, Messrs A B & A Matthews, Bank of Scotland Buildings, Newton Stewart, Wigtownshire DG8 6EG (tel: 01671 404100).

Broom District Salmon Fishery Board. G C Muirden, Messrs Middleton, Ross and Arnot, Solicitors, 7 High Str, Mansfield House, Dingwall, Ross-shire IV15 9HJ (tel: 01349 862214; fax: 01349 863819).

Brora District Salmon Fishery Board. C J Whealing, Sutherland Estates Office, Duke Str, Golspie, Sutherland KW10 6RR (tel: 01408 633268).

Caithness District Salmon Fishery Board. P J W Blackwood, Estate Office, Thurso East, Thurso, Caithness KW14 8HW (tel: 01847 893134).

Conon District Salmon Fishery Board. Miles Larby, CKD Galbraith, 45 Church Str, Inverness IV1 1DR (tel: 01463 224343).

Cree District Salmon Fishery Board. Peter M Murray, Messrs A B & A Matthews, Solicitors, Bank of Scotland Buildings, Newton Stewart, Wigtownshire DG8 6EG (tel: 01671 3013).

Creran District Salmon Fishery Board. P Fothringham, The Lagg, by Aberfeldy, Perthshire PH15 2EE.

Dee (Aberdeen) District Salmon Fishery Board. Mr Robin Fettes, Nethermills Farmhouse, Crathes, Banchory AB31 5JD (tel: 01330 844755).

Dee (Kirkcudbrightshire) District Salmon Fishery Board. Simon Ingall, Airds House, Parton, Castle Douglas DG7 3NF (tel: 016 444 70207).

Deveron District Salmon Fishery Board. John A Christie, Murdoch, McMath and Mitchell, Solicitors, 27-29 Duke Str, Huntly AB54 8DP (tel: 01466 792291).

Don District Salmon Fishery Board. George Alpine, Messrs Paull & Williamsons, Solicitors, 214 Union Str, Aberdeen AB10 1QY (tel: 01224 621621).

Doon District Salmon Fishery Board. A M Thomson, 2 Miller Rd, Ayr KA7 2AY (tel: 01292 280499).

Eachaig District Salmon Fishery Board, Robert C G Teasdale, Quarry Cottage, Rashfield, by Dunoon, Argyll PA23 8QT (tel: 01369 84510).

Esk District Salmon Fishery Board. Dr Marshall M Halliday, Woodside Croft, Ecclesgreig

The hotel chef nips out for a quick few casts on the Annan, opposite Rabbit Island. *Photo: British Heart Foundation.*

Rd, St Cyrus, by Montrose DD10 0DP (tel: 07769 655 499).

Ewe District Salmon Fishery Board. G C Muirden, Messrs Middleton, Ross and Arnot, Solicitors, PO Box 8, Mansfield House, Dingwall, Ross-shire IV15 9HJ (tel: 01349 862214).

Findhorn District Salmon Fishery Board. Mr W Cowie, R & R Urquhart WS, 121 High Str, Forres IV36 0AB (tel: 01309 672216; 01667 455525).

Fleet (Kirkcudbrightshire) District Salmon Fishery Board. C R Graves, Carse of Trostrie, Twynholm, Kirkcudbright DG6 4PS (tel: 01557 860618).

Forth District Salmon Fishery Board. T McKenzie, 12 Charles Str, Dunblane FK15 9BY. (tel: 01786 825544)

Girvan District Salmon Fishery Board. Austin M Thomson LLB, Frazer Coogans, Solicitors, 2 Miller Rd, Ayr, Ayrshire KA7 2AY (tel: 01292 280499).

Gruinard District Salmon Fishery Board. G C Muirden, Messrs Middleton, Ross and Arnot, P O Box 8, Mansfield House, Dingwall Ross-shire IV15 9HJ (tel: 01349 862214).

Halladale District Salmon Fishery Board. Mrs A Imlach, The Estate Office, Bunahoun, Forsinard, Strath Halladale, Sutherland KW13 6YU.

Helmsdale District Salmon Fishery Board. N Wright, Arthur and Carmichael, Cathedral Square, Dornoch, IV25 3SW (tel: 01862 810202).

Iorsa (Arran) District Salmon Fishery Board. J A R Tinsley, Rose Cottage, Pirnmill, Isle of Arran KA27 8HP (tel: 01770 840259).

Kanaird District Salmon Fishery Board. D J Greer, Bell Ingram, Estate Office, Bonar Bridge, Sutherland IV24 3EA (tel: 01863 766683).

Kinloch District Salmon Fishery Board. A Sykes, c/o Cook's Mill, Fordham Heath, Colchester, Essex CO3 5TF.

Kyle of Sutherland District Salmon Fishery Board. J Mason, Bell Ingram, Estate Office, Bonar Bridge, Sutherland IV24 3EA (tel: 01863 766683).

Laggan & Sorn District Salmon Fishery Board, R I G Ferguson, Messrs Stewart, Balfour & Sutherland, 2 Castlehill, Campeltown, Argyll PA28 6AW (tel: 01586 553737).

Lochaber District Salmon Fishery Board. Malcolm Spence QC, 2 Gray's Inn, Gray's Inn

Square, London WC1R 5JH.

Loch Fyne District Salmon Fishery Board. S Murray, Messrs MacArthur, Stewart & Co, Solicitors, Boswell House, Argyll Square, Oban, Argyllshire PA34 4BD (tel: 01631 562215; fax: 01631 565490).

Lossie District Salmon Fishery Board. W Bell, Lower Inchallan, Pluscarden, Elgin, Moray IV30 8TZ (tel: 01343 890412).

Luce District Salmon Fishery Board. E A Fleming-Smith, Smiths Gore, 28 Castle Str, Dumfries DG1 1DG (tel: 01387 263066).

Mull District Salmon Fishery Board. Christopher James, Torosay Castle, Craignure, Isle of Mull PA65 6AY. (tel: 01680 812505/812527).

Nairn District Salmon Fishery Board. E M B Larby, CKD Galbraith, 45 Church Str, Inverness IV1 1DR.

Naver and Borgie District Salmon Fishery Board. N Wright, Arthur and Carmichael, Cathedral Square, Dornoch, Sutherland IV25 3SW (tel: 01862 810202).

Ness District Salmon Fishery Board. F Kelly, Messrs Anderson, Shaw & Gilbert, Solicitors, York House, 20 Church Str, Inverness IV1 1ED (tel: 01463 236123).

Nith District Salmon Fishery Board. R Styles, Walker and Sharp, Solicitors, 37 George Str, Dumfries DG1 1EB (tel: 01387 267222).

North and West District Salmon Fishery Board (The). A R Whitfield, The Old Manse, Lumsden, Huntly, Aberdeenshire AB54 4JL (tel/fax: 01464 861509).

Ruel District Salmon Fishery Board. J Ferguson, 6 The Strand, Rye, E Sussex TN31 7DB. (tel: 01797 222601).

Skye District Salmon Fishery Board. Jim Rennie, Ardslane, 1 Clachamish, Skeabost Bridge, Portree, Isle of Skye, IV51 9NY (tel: 01470 582257).

Spey District Salmon Fishery Board. W Cowie, Messrs R & R Urquhart, 20 High Str, Nairn IV12 4AX (tel: 01667 453278); also Forres, 117-121 High Str, Forres, Morayshire IV36 1AB (tel: 01309 672216).

Stinchar District Salmon Fishery Board. A M Thomson, 2 Miller Rd, Ayr, Ayrshire KA7 2AY (tel: 01292 280499).

Tay District Salmon Fishery Board. R P J Blake, Condies, 2 Tay Str, Perth PH1 5LJ (tel: 01738 440088).

River Tweed Commissioners. N P Yonge, River Tweed Commissioners, The North Court, Drygrange Steading, by Melrose, Roxburghshire TD6 9DJ (tel: 01896 848294).

Ugie District Salmon Fishery Board. Mrs R MacLean, Masson & Glennie, Solicitors, Broad House, Broad Str, Peterhead AB42 1HY (tel: 01779 474271).

Urr District Salmon Fishery Board. Matthew Pumphrey, Primrose & Gordon, Solicitors & Estate Agents, 92 Irish Str, Dumfries DG1 2PF (tel: 01387 267316).

Western Isles District Salmon Fishery Board. George H Macdonald, Estate Office, Lochmaddy, Isle of North Uist, HS6 5AA (tel: 01876 500329).

Ythan District Salmon Fishery Board. M H T Andrew, Estate Office, Mains of Haddo, Tarves, Ellon, Aberdeenshire AB41 7LD (tel: 01651 851664).

SCOTTISH ENVIRONMENT PROTECTION AGENCY

The Scottish Environment Protection Agency (SEPA) is the public body responsible for environmental regulation and improvement in Scotland. It was established under the Environment Act 1995 and became fully operational from 1 April 1996. SEPA's role in protecting the water environment is far-reaching and involves several programmes that provide a comprehensive and robust means of protecting and enhancing the quality, quantity and conservation value of Scotland's waters. In 2000 the Water Framework Directive was introduced, and will replace seven existing Directives. Transposed into Scottish law, it drives major improvements to protecting the whole water environment. SEPA uses its water classification schemes to monitor changes in Scotland's water environment, and has delivered a major improvement in the quality of rivers by reducing the length of poor and seriously polluted waters by 27% between 1996 and 2000. A number of European Directives will continue to drive improvements to the water from the main pollutants of sewage and agricultural discharges.

SEPA

Corporate Office
Erskine Court
Castle Business Park
Stirling FK9 4TR
Tel: 01786 457700

Fax: 01786 446885
Web: www.sepa.org.uk
24-hour Pollution Report Line: 0800
   807060
Floodline: 0845 9881188.

SCOTTISH FISHING STATIONS

The nature of Scotland with its many rivers and lochs, especially on the west coast, makes it impracticable in some cases to deal with each river's catchment area separately. Thus some fisheries on the west coast, north of the Firth of Clyde are group under the heading 'West Coast Rivers and Lochs'.

The need again arises to decide whether a river should be included in England or Scotland. The Border Esk is dealt with in the English section, together with the Kirtle and the Sark, which happen to fall within the Esk's catchment area on the map. The Tweed and *all* its tributaries are included in this Scottish section. All the Scottish Islands, including Shetland and Orkney, are considered as within one watershed, viz, 'The Islands', in which, for convenience, Kintyre is included. The exact position in the book of any river or fishing station can, of course, readily be found by reference to the index.

ALNESS and GLASS

Alness drains **Loch Morie**, then flows 12 miles to enter Cromarty Firth at Alness. Glass drains Loch Glass then flows into Cromarty Firth near Evanton.

Alness (Ross-shire). Salmon, sea trout, grilse and brown trout. Good bank fishing on Loch Morie; worm or fly only. River Alness has 6 beats, 4 rods per beat sold from Novar Estate Office, Evanton IV116 9XL (tel: 01349 830208) or Troutquest, Glen Glass, Evanton IV16 9XW (tel: 01349 830606; web: www.troutquest. com); salmon, sea trout, grilse and brown trout; also on Loch Morie, brown trout and Arctic char. Alness AC has water on estuary of R Alness, salmon, sea trout, brown trout. Permits from Hon Sec.

Evanton (Ross-shire). Brown trout fishing on **Loch Glass**; bank fishing. Permits from Novar Estates Office IV16 9XL (tel: 01349 830208). Evanton AC has salmon, sea trout and brown trout fishing on Rivers Glass and **Skiach**; and only brown trout fishing on Loch Glass; club also has sea trout fishing on shore of Cromarty Firth; permits from Costcutter, 13 Balconie St, IV16 9UN (tel: 01349 830213).

ANNAN

Rises in Moffat Hills and flows about 30 miles to Solway Firth. Strong tidal river. Several good pools on river N of Annan. Some spring salmon, excellent sea trout in June and July, and excellent salmon in late autumn, Oct-Nov; a few brown trout in spring and summer.

Annan (Dumfriesshire). Warmanbie Country House Hotel has stretch; salmon, sea trout and brown trout, free for residents. Hotel also has access to many other waters, including on **Rivers Nith** and **Eden**, **Broom Fisheries** (rainbow and golden trout), **New Mills** at Brampton (rainbow), **Moffat Fishery** at Moffat (rainbow, brown and american brook). It has access to Sunday trout fishing. Rod and tackle hire, bait, tuition and ghillie can be arranged. Hotel also stocks a limited range of tackle for sale. For further information contact Warmanbie Country House Hotel, Annan DG12 5LL (tel/fax: 01461 204015; web: www.warmanbie.co.uk).

Ecclefechan (Dumfries & Galloway). Annan, 2m SW; salmon, herling (late July onwards), brown trout. Hoddom & Kinmount Estates, Estate Office, Hoddom, Lockerbie DG11 1BE (tel: 01576 300244), have Hoddom Castle Water, over 2m stretch on Annan. Salmon; grilse late July onwards; sea trout, May-Aug; dt available, limited to 15 rods per day; fly only, except when river height is above white line on Hoddom Bridge when spinning is permitted. Hoddom & Kinmount Estates also have trout fishing on **Purdomstone Reservoir**, now let Annan AC; and coarse fishing on **Kelhead Quarry** and **Kinmount Lake**, which has first rate pike fishing. Purdomstone Reservoir, brown trout. Kelhead Quarry; brown and rainbow trout, perch, roach, bream, carp, pike, tench, eels; dt available; suitable for disabled. Permits for Hoddom Estates waters may be booked from Water Bailiff, Estate Office, Hoddom, Lockerbie DG11 1BE (tel: 01576 300417); Kelhead Quarry permits, from Water Bailiff, Kinmount Bungalows, Kinmount, Annan (tel: 01461 700344).

This St Albans visitor's stay was rewarded with this very fresh 5½lb salmon, caught with worm on the Annan. The river was running off with slight colour.

Lockerbie (Dumfriesshire). R Annan 1½m W; salmon, sea trout, brown trout. Castle Milk Estate DG11 2QX (tel: 01576 510203) has two beats on R Annan and **Castle Milk Water**; salmon and sea trout, brown trout; 1¾m, left bank; fly only. Limited dt £25 (early season) and £40 (late season). **Royal Four Towns Water**; salmon, sea trout, brown trout, herling, chub, grilse; 3¾m, both banks. Dt £10 (early season) and £15 (late season), also wt, £35-£55. A tributary of Annan is **River Milk**, and there are 13 miles of fishing above and below Scroggs Bridge; sea trout and brown trout; fly only. Permits and bookable holiday cottages from Anthony Steel, Kirkwood Holiday Cottages and Fishings, Kirkwood, Dalton, Lockerbie DG11 1DH (tel: 01576 510200; web: www.kirkwood-lockerbie.co.uk). In the main river **Kirkwood** water: 1⅓m single bank with good salmon and sea trout fishing; wt from £50-£170. **Jardine Hall** water: 2½m, some double bank, good sea trout, and late salmon; wt from £50-£200; contact Anthony Steel for these *(above)*. **Hal-**

leaths Water, west bank of Annan, near Lockerbie and Lochmaben; salmon and trout, fly only; three tickets per week in the season, 25 Feb-15 Nov; permits from McJerrow and Stevenson, Solicitors, 55 High St, Lockerbie DG11 2JJ (tel: 01576 202123). Upper Annandale AA has salmon and trout fishing in two beats: upper beat, between **Moffat** and **Johnstonebridge**, 4m double bank from just south of Moffat d/s to Cogries railway viaduct; and Applegarth beat, 4m double bank between Johnstonebridge and Lockerbie, and also 1m of **Kinnel Water**. Grayling and chub, which are also caught on this beat, may only be fished in salmon season. From 25 Feb to 15 Nov: dt £10, wt £50, conc, from Video Sport, 48 High St DG11 2AA (tel: 01576 202400); Red House Hotel, Wamphray, nr Moffat DG10 9NF (tel: 01576 470470); Gents Hairdressers, Well St, Moffat; Esso Petrol Station, Moffat; or Hon Sec. After 15 Sept, salmon only, wt £60; limited dt £25 available only from Red House Hotel *(above)*. Tackle shops: D McMillan, 6 Friars Vennel DG1 2RN (tel: 01387

252075); Pattie's of Dumfries, 109 Queensberry St DG1 1BH (tel: 01387 252891), both Dumfries.

Lochmaben (Dumfries & Galloway). Salmon, sea trout, brown trout, chub (good); Royal Four Towns Water, Hightae; salmon season, Feb 25 to Nov 15; brown trout, March 15 to Oct 6; no Sunday fishing, from Sept-Nov advance booking advisable; apply The Clerk of the Commissionaires of Fishing for Royal Four Towns, High Rd, Hightae DG11 1JS (tel: 01387 810220). Brown trout fishing on **Water of Ae** in Forest of Ae; fly, worm; no ground bait; dt £5.88: Forestry Commission Scotland, Ae Village, Dumfries DG1 1QB (tel 01387 860247). Coarse fishing on **Castle Loch**; permits from Lochmaben PO, High St, Lockerbie DG11 1NR (tel: 01387 810221). Water bailiffs Bruce Gillie (tel: 07773 658 136), Martin Mitchell (tel: 07778 648 029). Hotels: Royal Four Towns, Hightae.

Wamphray (Dumfriesshire). Two beats of R Annan controlled by Upper Annandale AA. Permits for these, and 1 beat of Annandale FC, totalling 13m in all, from Red House Hotel, Wamphray, nr Moffat DG10 9NF (tel: 01576 470470); Annandale FC dt (before 15 Sept) £10, wt £55; after, limited dt £25, wt £55; applications for wt to Annandale Estate Office, St Anns, Lockerbie (tel: 01576 470317).

Moffat (Dumfries & Galloway). Upper Annandale AA has 4m double bank of Annan; with salmon, brown trout, and sea trout fishing; permits (lower beats) obtainable; 25 Feb to 15 Nov: dt £10, wt £50 (after 15 Sept wt only), conc, from Video Sport, 48 High St DG11 2AA (tel: 01576 202400); Red House Hotel, Wamphray, nr Moffat DG10 9NF (tel: 01576 470470) (after 15 Sept, salmon only, wt £60; limited dt available, only from this hotel); Gents Hairdressers, Well St, Moffat; Esso Petrol Station, Moffat; or Hon Sec..

AWE and LOCH AWE and LOCH ETIVE

A short river, but one of best-known salmon streams of west coast. Connects Loch Awe to sea by way of Loch Etive, which it enters at Bonawe. River fishes best from July onwards.

Taynuilt (Argyll). Salmon, sea trout, trout. Inverawe Fisheries, Taynuilt, Argyll PA35 1HU (tel: 01866 822446), has 1m on River Awe, salmon and sea trout; and three lochs stocked daily with rainbow trout. Fly only; wt and dt, with half-day and father/son concessions; tuition, tackle for hire and refreshments on site. Salmon and trout fishing also from T L Nelson, Kilmaronaig, Connel, Argyll PA37 1PW (tel: 01631 710223) who has a stretch on R Awe. Loch Etive, brown, sea, rainbow trout and sea fish; no permit required. Hotel: Polfearn Hotel. Inverawe Holiday Cottages on estate.

LOCH AWE. Salmon, sea trout, wild browns (av. 12oz), char, occasional large rainbows, perch and pike. The last three breakings of British record for brown trout was here in 2002 (31lb 12oz); and 20lb+ pike not uncommon. Protected and controlled by Loch Awe Improvement Association, and fished by permit only, which does not include salmon and sea trout. There is a road right round loch. Salmon are most often caught by trolling. Sea trout are rarely caught and only at north end. Trout can be caught anywhere and average just under ¾lb; best months Mar, Apr, May, Jun and Sep. Char are caught on a very deep sunk line. Pike and

perch can be taken on a spun lure but are rarely fished for. Boats may be hired at Loch Aweside Marine, Dalavich PA35 1HN (tel: 01866 844209), or Loch Awe Boats, Ardbreckinish (tel: 01866 833256), from £32 with motor, to £16 without, half-day. Inchnadamph Hotel, Assynt, by Lairg IV27 4HN (tel: 01571 822202) has fishing. Also Eredine House (tel: 01866 844207) has 1m private shoreline and 2 hill lochs plus cottages.

Lochawe (Argyll). Loch Awe is open to all who buy season tickets £45, but also sells weekly (£15), 3 day (£10), and daily (£5) tickets; assn also has trout fishing on **River Avich** and **Loch Avich**. Concessions for OAPs and juniors. Permits and boats from D Wilson, Ardbrecknish House, Dalmally PA33 1BH (mob: 07703 112422); Loch Awe Stores, Loch Awe, Dalmally, PA33 1AQ (tel: 01838 200200); and many other sales points including tackle shops throughout Scotland (a full list is issued by Assn). Tackle: Loch Awe Boats, Ardbrecknish, by Dalmally PA33 1BH (01866 833256); Loch Awe Stores *(above)*.

Kilchrenan (Argyll). Taychreggan Hotel, on lochside, has pike, trout and salmon fishing on Loch Awe. Fish run to good size. 2 boats with outboard engines. Fishing also arrangeable on River Awe (salmon), and Loch Etive (sea trout). Good sea fishing. Hotel has own jetty. Permits and further information from Taychreggan Hotel, Kilchrenan, by Taynuilt, Argyll PA35 1HQ (tel: 01866 833211; fax: 01866 833244).

Dalavich (Argyll). Forestry Commission Scotland has fishing on Loch Awe (brown trout, rainbow trout, char, perch, pike), **Loch Avich** (brown trout) and **River Avich** (salmon and brown trout).

Dt available. Permits, boat hire and rod hire, from N D Clark, 11 Dalavich, by Taynuilt PA35 1HN (tel: 01866 844209).

Ford (Argyll). Permits for **Loch Awe** and **Loch Avich** from Pete Creech, Crown Ho, Lochgilphead, Argyll PA31 8RH (tel: 01546 810279). For pike fishing in **Loch Ederline** and brown trout fishing in 18 hill lochs contact E Maclean (Keeper), Winterfold, Ford PA31 8RJ (tel: 01546 810361).

Tributaries of the Awe

ORCHY: Good salmon.

Dalmally (Argyll). River flows into Loch Awe here, excellent salmon fishing in May, June, Sept and Oct. Glen Orchy AC fishes lower Orchy (no tickets). Permits for several beats on Orchy; and pike and trout permits for **Loch Awe** and **Loch Avich**, from Loch Awe Stores, Loch Awe, Dalmally PA33 1AQ (tel: 01838 200200), who can also supply fishing tackle for sale or hire. D Hadley, Ebor Cottage, St Patricks Rd, Hucknall Notts

NG15 6LU, has 7m single roadside bank, excellent fly fishing water; permits from Loch Awe Stores. Cottage to let, if required. Hotels: Glenorchy Lodge; Orchy Bank; Craig Villa. Self-catering and B & B accommodation in area.

Bridge of Orchy (Argyll). For permits on Orchy beats: Dalmally 1, 2 & 3, Lower Craig, Craig Lodge, Craig Beat and Inveroran, contact Loch Awe Stores, Loch Awe, Dalmally, PA33 1AQ (tel: 01838 200200).

AYR

Rises in Glenbuck and flows into Firth of Clyde through town of Ayr opposite south end of Isle of Arran. Good brown trout river (av ½lb) with fair runs of salmon and sea trout.

Ayr (Ayrshire). Mostly preserved, but have ¾m Cragie stretch of R Ayr, leased from South Ayrshire Council. Ayr AC has stretch on River Ayr at Ayr and near Annbank (salmon, sea trout, brown trout); and on **Loch Shankston** (rainbow and brown) and **Loch Bradan** (brown trout); members only; wading essential for good sport; waters restocked with brown trout; membership from GameSport (*below*). Troon AC has fishing on **Collenan Reservoir**, rainbow and brown trout; dt £13 from Torbets Outdoor Leisure, 5 Portland Street, Troon KA10 6AA (tel: 01292 317464); and the grocery shop, Ba-

rassie. Prestwick AC has fishing on **Raith Waters**, rainbow trout; dt £9, 4 fish limit, conc for juv and OAPs, from Gamesport (*below*); Pets Aquarium, 124 Main St, Prestwick KA9 1PB (tel: 01292 477863): tickets for Ayr AC waters; GameSport of Ayr, 60 Sandgate, Ayr KA7 1BX (tel: 01292 263822).

Belston Loch at Sinclairston, a small rainbow trout fishery, 6m from Ayr. Other fisheries: Springwater Fishery (tel: 01292 560343), nr Dalrymple KA6 6AW, stocked with steelheads, browns, rainbows: permits from fishery, also for coarse fishery; Burns Fishery, Tarbolton;

Check before you go

While every effort has been made to ensure that the information given in **Where to Fish** *is correct, the position is continually changing, and anglers are urged, in their own interests, to make enquiries before travelling to selected venues. This is especially important with reference to prices quoted. Anglers attention is also drawn to the fact that hotels mentioned under the various fishing stations do not necessarily have water of their own. Any amendments or further data for inclusion in subsequent editions, and any comments, will be welcome.*

Coyle Water, stocked with steelheads and rainbows, permits at fishery; Prestwick Reservoir nr Monkton, stocked brown and rainbow, permits from Gamesport and Monkton newsagent; tickets for town and other waters on Rivers Ayr and **Doon** may be obtained, and for coarse fishing lochs. For further information contact GameSport of Ayr, 60 Sandgate, Ayr KA7 1BX (tel: 01292 263822). Hotel: Manor Park, Monkton.

Mauchline (Ayrshire). Salmon, sea trout and brown trout fishing on Rivers **Ayr, Cessnock** and **Lugar**; and brown and rainbow trout fishing on **Loch Belston** at Sinclairston; refer to GameSport (see Belston above); boats on Loch Belston.

Muirkirk (Ayrshire). Fish pass has been built at Catrine Dam, allowing fish to run to headwaters at Muirkirk. Muirkirk AA has approx 6m on River Ayr, both banks; salmon, sea trout, brown trout, grayling. Assn also has fishing on **Greenock Water**; fishing (trout and grayling only) allowed till 30 Sept on Greenock W; on R Ayr salmon and sea trout 1 Apr-31 Oct, browns 15 Mar-6 Oct. Also on **Glenbuck Loch**; boats, phone first (tel: 0775 2456393). Brown trout restocking program. Dt £8, Mon-Fri, limited to 4 fish per day. Apply to Hon Sec. Concessions and 3 competitions per year for juveniles. Limited tackle from Moorheads, Main St; Hotel: Coach House Inn.

Tributaries of the Ayr

COYLE. Sea trout, trout, grayling, few salmon.

Drongan (Ayrshire). Drongan Youth Group AC issues permits for **River Coyle** and **Snipe Loch;** brown and rainbow trout stocked weekly; fish up to 11lb are being caught. Permits from John Wilson, Hawthorne Cottage, Watson Terrace, Drongan KA6 7AG (tel: 01292 590351).

BEAULY

Beauly is approximately 9m long, and flows from the junction of Glass and Farrar into Beauly Firth and thence into Moray Firth. Salmon, sea trout good from beginning of season. Main grilse runs in July/August. Plentiful food supply in Beauly Firth, hence the presence of bottlenose dolphins, porpoises and seals.

Beauly (Inverness-shire). Salmon, sea trout, occasional brown trout. Beauly AA has water below Lovat Bridge, and river mouth to Coulmore Bay, north shore, and **Bunchrew Burn** on south shore (sea trout and occasional bass); strictly fly only from Lovat bridge to Wester Lovat; st £40, dt £10, juv £5, for Assn water and for sea trout fishing on Beauly Firth from Morison's, Ironmonger, West End, Beauly IV4 7BT (tel: 01463 782213); casting tuition; members only, Thursdays and Saturdays. For **Loch Achilty** and **Loch Nam Bonnach**, also enquire at Morison's. Sea trout fishing on Beauly Firth at Clachnaharry and North Kessock; permits from J Graham & Co, 37-39 Castle St, Inverness IV2 3DU (tel: 01463 233178); Kessock PO, North Kessock, Inverness IV1 3XN (tel: 01463 731470). Good sea trout from the beginning of the season. **Loch Ruthven**, trout fly fishing by boat, 12m from Inverness. **Tarvie Lochs** (tel: 01997 421250), rainbow trout, fly and boat only, 25m from Inverness; tickets for the three lochs from lodge IV14 9EJ; from £7.50. **Loch Ashie** and **Loch Duntelchaig**, fly and spinning, 10m from Inverness; tickets from Scottish Water. Tickets for 3m double bank of **R Ness**, and 9m on **R Nairn**, from J Graham (*above*). Hotels: Lovat; Priory; Caledonian IV4 7BY (tel: 01463 782278), which can arrange fishing on river and several lochs ; all Beauly.

Tributaries of the Beauly.

FARRAR and GLASS:

Tomich (Inverness-shire). For fishing in **Guisachan Hill Lochs;** brown and rainbow trout; tickets available through Mr K Laidlay, Culbogie Cottage, Tomich, Cannich IV4 7LY (tel: 01456 415352); season: 1 May to 6 Oct.

CANNICH: Tributary of the Glass.

Cannich (Inverness-shire). Permits from Howard Johnson, Kerrow House, Cannich, Strathglass, Inverness-shire IV4 7NA (tel: 01456 415 243), for 3½m of brown trout fishing on River Glass (fly only); free for guests of Kerrow House

(B&B and self-catering). Fly fishing on **R Farrar** and **Glass**. Dt £15-£50 (salmon) and £10 (trout); from F Spencer-Nairn, Culligran House, Glen Strathfarrar, Struy, nr Beauly IV4 7JX (tel/fax: 01463 761285). Priority given to guests of Culligran Cottages (self-catering), brochure issued. At confluence of Cannich and Glass, Strathglass Fishing has boat fishing, fly only, for brown trout on **Loch Benevean**, and **Loch Beannacharan**, and can arrange salmon fishing on **River Glass**. Reservations direct to Strathglass Fishing, Runivraid Cammich, Inverness IV4 7LS (tel: 01456 415477; mob: 07770 826045). Hotels: Kerrow House.

BERVIE

Rises on Glen Farquhar Estate and flows 14m to North Sea near Inverbervie. Essentially an autumn river for finnock, sea trout and salmon although also good for brown trout.

Inverbervie (Kincardineshire). Finnock, sea trout, salmon (best Sept-Oct). For fishing upstream from Donald's Hole; dt £2 from Inverbervie Sports Centre, Kirkburn, Inverbervie, Montrose DD10 4RS (tel: 01561 361182).

BRORA

After being joined by tributaries Blackwater and Skinsdale, Brora flows through Loch Brora and into sea at Brora.

Brora (Sutherland). **Loch Brora**; salmon, sea trout and brown trout. Hotel: Royal Marine.

CARRON (Grampian)

Rises in Glenbervie and flows about 9m to the North Sea at Stonehaven. Trout.

Stonehaven (Kincardineshire). About 2½m brown trout fishing offered to visitors by Stonehaven & Dist AA. Permits also issued for **River Cowie** (about 1¼m), sea trout, salmon and brown trout. Best July, August and Sept. Permits from David's Sports & Leisure, 31 Market Sq AB3 2BA (tel: 01569 762239). Good sea fishing. Hotels: Eldergrove; Arduthie House.

CLYDE

Rises near watershed of Tweed and Annan, and flows about 50m to the Atlantic by way of Glasgow. Once a famous salmon river, then spoiled by pollution. Now, river has improved, with salmon and sea trout returning annually. Controls are in force, to conserve stocks. Trout and grayling fishing, especially in higher reaches. The Clyde's most famous tributary, the Leven, which connects with Loch Lomond, has run of salmon and sea trout. In north-west corner of Renfrewshire is Loch Thom, linked by water spill with Loch Compensation, which, when water is high, drains into River Kip in Shielhill Burn. United Clyde Angling Protective Association Ltd, controls much of Clyde and tributaries upstream of Motherwell Bridge to Daer Reservoir, in three sections, the Upper, Middle and Lower Reaches, and restocks annually. The Clyde is covered by a Protection Order: anglers must have a permit before approaching the water. Permits and prices as follows: st £23, dt £5, salmon st £40, OAP £7, juv conc. These are obtainable from various tackle dealers and sports shops in Lanarkshire and Glasgow. Accommodation can be arranged through Greater Glasgow and Clyde Valley Tourist Board.

Greenock (Strathclyde). On the estuary of Clyde. Greenock & Dist AC preserves **Loch Thom** (365 acres, trout), and has rights on **Yetts, No. 8** and **No. 6** (Spring Dam), good trout. Permits from Brian Peterson, The Fishing Shop *(below)*. Club membership restricted to persons resident in Greenock and district, but permits sold to visitors; Sunday fishing; no parties; fly only; bank fishing only. Largs & DAC

Fishing Clubs

When you appoint a new Hon Secretary, do not forget to give us details of the change. Write to the publishers (address at front of the book). Thank you!

has **Muirhead Reservoir** on A760 10m S; brown & rainbow; tickets from R T Cycles, 73 Main Rd, Glengarnock, Beith KA14 3AA (tel: 01505 682191); Tickets for trout fisheries in vicinity; Lawfield Trout Fishery, Houston Rd, Kilmacolm PA13 4NY (tel: 01505 874182), brown trout, rainbow and blues, permits and instruction at fishery; and Haylie Fishery, Bray, Largs KA30 8JA (4 acres) (tel: 01475 676005). Tackle shop The Fishing Shop, 24 Union Str, PA16 8DD (tel: 01475 888085); dt for Greenock & DAC, Port Glasgow AC and Largs AC. Good sea fishing for cod, skate, dogfish, conger, haddock and plaice. Hotel: Tontine.

Glasgow (Strathclyde). Glasgow has excellent trout, sea trout and salmon fishing within a radius of 60m. Lochs Lomond, Dochart, Awe, Tay, Ard, Leven, Lubnaig, Venachar, Lake of Menteith, etc, and Rivers Annan, Goil, Cur (head of Loch Eck), Clyde (trout and grayling only), Teith, Tweed, Allan, Dochart, Leven, Kinglass etc, all accessible from here. Coarse fishing on whole of **Forth and Clyde Canal**; pike, perch, roach, tench, eels, mirror carp on 35 miles of canal; no close season; for further details apply to British Waterways, Lowland Canals, Rosebank House, Main St, Camelon, Falkirk FK1 4DS (tel: 01324 671217; web: www.scottishcanals.co.uk); also for coarse fishing in Glasgow at **Auchinstarry Pond**, Kilsyth (tench, roach, perch and rudd); **Kilmadinny Loch**, Bearsden; **Bardowie Loch**, Balmore; **Mugdock Park Pond**, Milgavie; **Tench Pool**, Milgavie; **Carp Pond**, Seafar; and **Hogganfield Loch**, Glasgow. United Clyde Angling Protective Association, issues annual tickets for stretches on Clyde and **R Douglas** near Motherwell, Lanark, Carstairs, Roberton and Thankerton; brown trout and grayling fishing; permits from Hon Sec or tackle shops. Kilsyth FPS controls **Townhead Reservoir**; apply to Hon Sec. Tackle shops: Anglers Rendezvous, 18 Saltmarket, G1 5LD (tel: 0141 552 4662; fax: 0141 552 7730) issues many permits; non-members welcome; Hooked in Scotland, 49a Main St, Cambuslang G72 7HB (tel: 0141 646 1000).

Airdrie (Lanarkshire). Airdrie & DAC has **Hillend Reservoir**; brown and rainbow trout 1lb-12lb stocked weekly, pike and perch; all legal methods; bag limit 4 fish;

boat and bank fishing, good access for disabled; no ground bait; permits at water £7, 4 fish limit; st £60, juv £40; disabled Wheelyboat. Clarkston Independent AC has **Lilly Loch** at Calderdruix; rainbow and brown trout; season 15 Mar - 6 Oct; any legal method (fly only from boats); dt from bailiffs on site. Hotel: Old Truff Inn, Caldercruix, By Airdrie.

Motherwell (Lanarkshire). United Clyde APA has water on **Clyde** and **Douglas**; brown trout and grayling; permits from local tackle shops. Coarse fishing on **Strathclyde Country Park Loch** and adjacent R Clyde; carp, bream, roach, pike, perch. No close season. No fly fishing. Lead free weights only. Also limited trout and grayling fishing on Clyde. Permits from Booking Office, Watersports Centre, 366 Hamilton Rd, Motherwell (tel: 01698 266155). No boat fishing.

Strathaven (Lanarkshire). Avon; trout and grayling. Avon AC has water; contact Hon Sec.

Lanark (Lanarkshire). Trout and grayling. United Clyde APA water on Clyde and **Douglas**; permits from local tackle shops. Coarse fishing on **Lanark Loch**; carp and tench; no close season. Tackle shop: J Ritchie, 30 Bannatyne St ML11 7JR (tel: 01555 662380). Hotel: Cartland Bridge.

Carstairs (Strathclyde). Trout and grayling. United Clyde APA water on Clyde and **Douglas**; permits from local tackle shops.

Thankerton (Strathclyde). Lamington AIA has 9m of water from Thankerton to Roberton; trout and grayling st £30, wt £18, dt £6, night £5 (no conc); no trout under 10"; 4 fish limit. Permits from Hon Sec; Bryden Newsagent, 153 High St, Biggar ML12 6BN (tel: 01899 220069). No Sunday fishing. Tickets from PO's, hotels, newsagents. United Clyde APA water below Thankerton.

Biggar (Lanarkshire). Lamington AIA fish from Roberton Burn mouth to Thankerton boat bridge, approx 9m, both banks, with brown trout and grayling. Good wading. Prices *(see above)*. Tackle shop: Bryden Newsagent, 153 High St, Biggar ML12 6BN (tel: 01899 220069). Hotel: Cornhill.

Abington (Lanarkshire). Trout and grayling; United Clyde APA water; permits from Abington PO, Carlisle Rd, ML12 6SD. Other assn water at **Crawford** and **Elvanfoot**. Hotel: Abington.

Tributaries of the Clyde

LEVEN and **LOCH LOMOND**: Salmon, trout, pike and perch.

Loch Lomond (Strathclyde). Loch has the largest surface area of any freshwater body in Britain, being 22.6 miles long and up to 5 miles wide, and has over forty islands on it. The powan, a freshwater herring, is found in only one other loch in Scotland (Loch Eck); the loch held the record for Britain's largest pike, and there are 17 other species present. Good trout, sea trout and salmon fishing (best Aug to Oct) (also perch and pike) can be had from various centres on loch; under control of Loch Lomond Angling Improvement Assn; fishing reserved for full members only on **Fruin**, **Blane** and most stretches of **Endrick**; permits are joint for River Leven and Loch Lomond at all local tackle shops, boat hirers; children's permits available; no Sunday fishing; late April and May earliest for fly on Loch Lomond (sea trout and salmon). Boat hire and dt £15 (east side of loch): McFarlane & Son, The Boatyard, Balmaha G63 0JQ (tel: 01360 870214); also, ghillie and boat hire: via club Hon Sec; west side: boat hire from Balloc; permits also from the new Gateway Centre at Lomond Shores complex; also at Luss (the village shop); also Ardlui Hotel; and Inverbeg Caravan Park. Tackle shop: O'Brien, Newsagent, 225 Bank St, Alexandria G83 0WJ (tel: 01389 753533). Balloch Tourist Information Centre, Old Station Building, Balloch Rd, Balloch G83 8LQ (tel: 01389 753533) can provide information on **Carbeth Fishery** G63 9AY, just off A809 Milngavie/Drymen road; rainbow trout (tel: 01360 771006); troutmaster fishery, 3 ponds.

Rowardennan, By Drymen (Stirlingshire). Convenient for Loch Lomond; permits and boats. Hotel: Rowardennan.

Balloch (Dumbartonshire). Trout, good sea trout and salmon fishing on River Leven and Loch Lomond; large perch and pike in loch; fishing controlled by Loch Lomond AIA. Vale of Leven & Dist AC issues permits for brown trout fishing on **Loch Sloy**; fly only; dt water; apply to Hon Sec. Hotel: Balloch, Tullichewan.

KELVIN: (tributary of R Clyde). River Kelvin AC has 20m both banks; salmon, trout, sea trout; st £10 from tackle shop: Anglers Rendezvous, 18 Saltmarket, G1 5LD (tel: 0141 552 4662; fax: 0141 552 7730).

FRUIN: (tributary of Loch Lomond).

Helensburgh (Strathclyde). Salmon, sea trout and brown trout. Fly only; permits issued by Loch Lomond AIA; full members only.

Ardlui (Dumbartonshire). Trout, sea trout and salmon fishing in Loch Lomond. Hotel: Ardlui.

ENDRICK: (tributary of Loch Lomond).

Killearn (Stirling). Good trout, sea trout and salmon fishing. Loch Lomond AIA has water; fly only; no Sunday fishing; accommodation arranged; ghillie, boat hire available (mainly Balmaha; full members only.

GRYFE (or GRYFFE): Brown trout, salmon, sea trout.

Bridge of Weir (Strathclyde). Bridge of Weir River AC has 3m of water. Trout: 15 Mar - 6 Oct; salmon: 15 Mar - 31 Oct; st (locals only) from Hon Sec; day tickets from M Duncan, Newsagent, Main St; Mon-Fri only.

Kilmacolm (Strathclyde). Strathgryfe AA has water on R Gryfe and tributaries **Green Water**, **Black Water** and **Burnbank Water**; approx. 25m in all, with brown trout and grayling. St £15 plus £10 entrance, with concessions. Permits from Hon Sec, or from Cross Cafe, Kilmacolm. No day tickets on a Sunday. Two fisheries with rainbow trout in Kilmacolm area: Lawfield and Pinewoods. Enquire M Duncan, Newsagents (*see Bridge of Weir*).

CALDER and BLACK CART:

Lochwinnoch (Strathclyde). St Winnoch AC has stretch of Calder (brown trout); and **Castle Semple Loch**, pike, perch, roach and eels; st £14 and dt £1, conc. Club also has **Barr Loch** (coarse) and **Queenside Muir Loch** (browns, fly only); st holders only. Limited area tickets from Rangers Centre at loch. Otherwise permits from Hon Sec or A&G (Leisure) Ltd, 48 McDowall St, Johnstone PA5 8QL (tel: 01505 320397) who also sell Castle AC tickets for **Black Cart Water**, salmon, sea trout, and brown trout; **Castle Semple Loch**, coarse; memb £23 + joining fee, dt £6, conc.

AVON:

Strathaven (Lanarks). Avon AC fishes approx 14m of excellent brown trout and grayling water, with additional salmon and sea trout, near Strathaven Stonehouse and Larkhall; restocked annually; members only, membership £17 p/a, £20 salmon and sea trout, with concessions; Alex Gibson, 17 Union St, Larkhall ML9 1DX (tel: 01698 882065); Ace Cycles, Shopping Arcade, Quarry Place, Hamilton ML3 7BB (tel: 01698 284854); or from bailiffs.

CONON (including Blackwater)

Drains Loch Luichart and is joined by Orrin and Blackwater before entering the Moray Firth and North Sea by way of Cromarty Firth. Spring fishing has declined and main salmon runs now take place from July to September. Sport then among best in Highlands.

Dingwall (Ross-shire). Salmon, sea trout and brown trout. Dingwall & District AC has lower beat on R Conon; fly only, for salmon, sea trout and brown trout. Thigh or waist waders only; season: 10 Feb to 30 Sept, best months Apr to Sept; dt £10-£15 from tackle shop H C Furlong, Sports & Model Shop, High Street, Dingwall IV15 9RY (tel: 01349 862346; e-mail: cliff@sportsandmodelshop.co.uk). Permit also covers **Loch Chuilin** and **Loch Achanalt**. At **Brahan** there are 3 beats of brown trout fishing on **R Conon** and a stocked brown and rainbow trout pond. Coarse fishing on **Loch Ussie**, pike and eels. Permits from Seaforth Highland Estates, Brahan, by Dingwall IV7 8EE (tel: 01349 861150). Hotels: Conon at Conon Bridge; Craigdarroch, both Contin; also Coul House Hotel, Contin, by Strathpeffer IV14 9ES (tel: 01997 421487).

Strathpeffer (Ross-shire). **R Conon**, above Loch Achonachie, salmon and brown trout; fly or spinning. **River Blackwater** above Rogie Falls, salmon, brown trout and pike. **Loch Achonachie**, brown trout, perch and occasional salmon; bank and boat fishing; use of a boat produce best results; fly or spinning. Loch Achonachie AC has Wheelyboat: contact Hon Sec. Coul House Hotel books permits for beats on Rivers Conon and **Blackwater** (salmon, sea trout, brown trout); and for **Lochs Tarvie** (rainbow trout), **Achonachie** (brown trout), **Meig** (brown trout), **Morie** (brown trout, arctic char), **Glascarnoch**, **Chullin, Achanalt, Scardroy** or **Beannocharain** (all brown trout). Apply to Coul House Hotel, Contin, by Strathpeffer IV14 9ES (tel: 01997 421487; fax 01997 421945; web: www.milford.co.uk/go/coulhouse; e-mail: coulhouse@bestwestern.co.uk). Hotel provides full angling service, including rod racks, rod and reel hire, small tackle shop, guest freezer, drying room and fish-smoking arranged.

Garve (Ross-shire). Garve Hotel IV23 2PR (tel: 01997 414205) has excellent fishing on **Loch Garve**, which holds large trout (fish up to 12lb taken) also pike to 30lb and perch; brown trout fishing on 1½m of **River Blackwater** within hotel grounds; free fishing for hotel patrons. **Loch an Eich Bhain (The Tarvie Loch),** 25 acres, Ross-shire's first Troutmaster water; stocked with rainbow trout to 15lbs and brown trout to 4lbs; fly only. Fly fishing exclusively by boat. **Loch Ruith a Phuill,** 12 acres; wild brown trout, stocked rainbow to 6lbs; coarse and fly fishing tackle allowed; third loch, 7 acres, stocked browns to 6lbs, fly only, with boat; permits from Tarvie Lochs Trout Fishery, Tarvie, by Strathpeffer IV14 9EJ (tel: 01997 421250); Sports & Model Shop, High Street, Dingwall IV15 9RY (tel: 01349 862346). **Loch Glascarnoch**, brown trout, pike and perch. Contact Aultguish Inn, by Garve IV23 2PQ (tel: 01997 455254).

CREE and BLADNOCH

Cree drains Loch Moan and flows about 25m to sea at Wigtown Bay. Runs of salmon and sea trout in summer and early autumn. **Minnoch**, tributary of Cree, is also a salmon river, joining Cree about six miles from Newton Stewart. Bladnoch, a strong tidal river, flows into Cree Estuary at Wigtown. Salmon in season. Good pools.

Newton Stewart (Wigtownshire). Salmon, sea trout; best early in season. Newton Stewart AA has fishing on Cree, salmon and sea trout; **Bladnoch**, salmon; and **Bruntis Loch,** brown and rainbow trout, bank fishing only; **Kirriereoch Loch,** brown trout, bank fishing, fly only, **Clatteringshaws Loch,** browns, pike and perch; plus other waters. Assn spends between £10,000-£15,000 annually, restocking 4 stillwaters with trout; dt lochs £15, dt rivers £20, salmon weekly £120, from A J Dickinson, Galloway Guns & Tackle, 36A Arthur St, Newton Stewart DG8 6DE (tel: 01671 403404), who supply all game, coarse and sea fishing tackle together with frozen and live bait. Forestry Commission Scotland has fishing on **Palnure Burn**, salmon, sea trout, brown trout; dt £7, juv £3.50; **R Minnoch** above Kirriereoch bridge: brown trout only Mar-Jun, salmon and brown trout Jul-Oct: dt Mar-Jun £6 (juv £3); dt Jul-Oct £10 (juv £5); **Black Loch**, brown trout, fly only; dt £7, juv £3.50; **Loch of Lowes**, brown trout, fly only; dt £7, juv £3.50; **Lilies Loch**, brown trout; dt £6, juv £3; **Lochs Spectacle** and **Garwachie**, pike, perch, tench, roach, rudd; **Loch Eldrig**, pike, perch, roach; dt for each £6, juv £3. Permits from Forestry Commission Scotland, Galloway Forest District, Creebridge, Newton Stewart DG8 6AJ (tel: 01671 402420); and Galloway Wildlife Museum. Creebridge House Hotel, Newton Stewart DG8 6NP (tel: 01671 402121; fax: 01671 403258; web: www.creebridge.co.uk; e-mail: info@creebridge.co.uk), offers fishing on **R Bladnoch**, good spring run of grilse, Feb-Oct, 2m for up to 4 rods; **R Minnoch**, a tributary of Cree fed by Glentrool Loch, 4m for up to 12 rods, spawning pools; 2 beats offered, 22 pools in all. Hotel has excellent food and accommodation, can store rods in a lockable room and has freezer and drying facilities. Permits only from A J Dickinson (*see above*). Upper

Cree, at Bargrennan, 2m salmon fishing: also assn water on stretch of Cree which runs through town to estuary mouth. Trout and coarse fish on **Torwood Lochs**; permit from David Canning, Torwood House Hotel, Gass, Glenluce DG8 0PB (tel/fax: 01581 300469; e-mail: torwoodglenluce@aol.com). Trout fishing on **Black Loch**, and mixed coarse and pike fishing on **Lochs Heron** and **Ronald**; permit and boat hire from A Brown, Three Lochs Caravan Park, nr Kirkcowan, Newton Stewart DG8 0EP (tel: 0167183 0304). Permits for 2m single bank fishing on River Bladnoch from Bladnoch Inn, Wigtown DG8 9AB (tel: 01988 402200). River beats have salmon, sea trout and wild browns. Fishing holidays at inn, ghillie on site (10 am to 4 pm). Cree and Bladnoch fishing holidays are arranged on private waters by J Haley, Riverview Cottage, Spittal Bridge, nr Kirkcowan DG8 0DA (tel: 01671 830471). Galloway Angling, Bladnoch Bridge Estate, Wigtown DG8 9AB (tel: 01988 403363), covering coast, game and pike fishing, and stock of various baits.

Barrhill (Ayrshire). Drumlamford Estate Fisheries comprising 1m of salmon and trout fishing on **River Cree**; three stocked trout lochs; and Loch Dornal, a coarse fish loch. Tickets for Loch **Drumlamford**, Loch **Dornal** and Loch **Maberry**: A J Dickinson, Galloway Guns & Tackle, 36A Arthur St, Newton Stewart DG8 6DE (tel: 01671 403404). Boats, permits.

CROSS WATER OF LUCE

Depends on flood water for good salmon fishing, but very good for sea trout after dark. Best July onwards.

Stranraer (Wigtownshire). Excellent centre for river, loch and sea fishing. Stranraer & Dist AA has **Soulseat Loch**, rainbow and brown trout, fly and bait; **Dindinnie Reservoir**, brown and rainbow trout, fly only; **Knockquassan Reservoir**, brown trout, fly only; and **Penwhirn Reservoir**, brown trout, fly only. All these waters are near Stranraer; dt £10, £25 weekly, from The Sports Shop, 86 George St DG9 7JS (tel: 01776 702705). Torwood House Hotel, Gass, Glenluce DG8 0PB (tel/fax: 01581 300469; e-mail: torwoodglenluce@

aol.com) issues permits for **Torwood Lochs**, wt £15, dt £4.50, trout £10; trout, bream, tench, carp, roach, rudd, perch. Dunskey Estate, Portpatrick, Stranraer DG9 8TJ, has 2 lochs with stocked brown and rainbow trout: contact Keeper, P Hoyer (tel: 01776 810364; web: dunskey.com; e-mail: info@dunskey.com). **Whitefield Loch** (part), pike and perch, apply to Cock Inn, Auchenmalg, Glenluce DG8 0JT (tel: 01581 500224). Sea fishing in **Loch Ryan**, Irish Sea and Luce Bay. Charter boats and bait obtainable locally. Hotel: Ruddicot.

DEE (Aberdeenshire)

Second most famous salmon river of Scotland; for fly fishing probably the best. Also holds sea trout and brown trout. Rises in Cairngorms and flows into North Sea at Aberdeen. Best months for salmon: February to mid-June. Best for finnock (small sea trout) mid-August to end of September.

Aberdeen. Salmon, sea trout, brown trout; sea fishing. Many owners let for whole or part of season, but some good stretches held by hotels. Some hotel waters free to guests during summer. Lower reaches give good finnock fishing. Sea fishing is good in vicinity of Aberdeen. Hotels: Bucksburn Moat House; Cults; Dee Motel.

Banchory (Aberdeenshire). Salmon and sea trout. Banchory Lodge Hotel by river can arrange salmon and trout fishing on Dee for four rods, fly only; c&r. Ghillies and tuition on site: apply to Mrs Margaret Jaffray, Banchory Lodge Hotel, Banchory AB31 5HS (tel: 0133 082 2625). Feughside Inn, Strachan, by Banchory AB31 6NS (tel: 01330 850225), issues Aberdeen Dist AA permits for 1½m on **River Feugh**, salmon and sea trout. Hotels: Invery House; Raemoir House.

Aboyne (Aberdeenshire). Dee, salmon and sea trout; and **Aboyne Loch**, rainbow trout, stocked. Fly only. No Sunday fishing on Dee. Permits from Glen Tanar Estate, Brooks House, Glen Tanar AB34 5EU (tel: 013398 86451). Coarse fishing on Aboyne Loch; pike and perch; dt £6; permits from the Office, Aboyne Loch Caravan Park AB34 5BR (tel: 013398 86244). **Tillypronie Loch** AB34 4XX, brown trout, fly only; permits hourly or daily dt £15, £8 half day; boat available (tel: 013398 81332). Hotels: Birse Lodge; Huntly Arms. Self-catering on Tillypronie Estate at Reinacharn Lodge (tel: 01330 824888).

Ballater (Aberdeenshire). Balmoral, Mar, Glenmuick and Invercauld Estates preserve most of Upper River Dee salmon fishings. **River Gairn**, brown trout, fly only; st £35, wt £15, dt £6; from tackle shop. Ballater AA has fishing on five lochs with brown and rainbow trout, beats of Rivers **Muick** and **Gairn** by Ballater, with brown trout; Dee at **Maryculter** and **Deveron** at **Banff**, with salmon and sea trout. These waters are mostly for members only, but permits for **Loch Vrotichan**, with brown trout, fly only, are obtainable from Hon Sec and tackle shop: Countrywear, 15 Bridge St, Ballater AB35 5QP (tel: 013397 55453). Annual membership is currently £35, plus £35 joining fee (restricted to residents); Hon Sec has information on fishing on other waters. Many hotels and guest houses in vicinity.

Braemar (Aberdeenshire). Salmon fishing: Invercauld Estate lets Crathie beat and private water, details from The Factor, Invercauld Estates Office, Braemar, By Ballater AB35 5TW (tel: 013397 41224); brown trout fishing on **Rivers Gairn** and **Clunie**: permits from Invercauld Estates Office; Tourist Office, Braemar. **Lochs Bainnie** and **Nan Ean**, brown trout, fly only; permits from Invercauld Estates Office, Braemar AB35 5TR (tel: 013397 41224); and the keeper, Mr Liam Donald, Wester Binzean, Glenshee, PH10 7QD (tel: 01250 885206). Hotels: Inver Hotel, Crathie; B&B: Craiglea, Hillside Drive, Braemar AB35 5YU (tel: 013397 41641).

DEE (Dumfriess & Galloway), (including Lochs Dee and Ken)

Flows through Loch Ken about 16m to Solway. Salmon, sea trout and brown trout. Netting reduced and river stocked with salmon fry. An area in which acidification problems have been reported. Some lochs affected.

Castle Douglas (Dumfriess & Galloway). Forestry Commission Scotland has fishing on **R Dee**, trout; and **Stroan Loch,** mainly pike but also perch, roach and trout; dt £1, from dispenser at Raider's Rd entrance. **Woodhall Loch,** best known as pike water but also roach, perch and large trout; good winter venue with big pike catches, including 20lb plus fish;

dt from The Shop, Mossdale DG7 2NF (tel: 01644 450281). Castle Douglas & Dist AA has 7m stretch on **River Urr**; salmon, sea trout and brown trout; restocked annually; good runs of sea trout and grilse starting in June; dt £5 and £15 (Sept, Oct, Nov); wt £60; Assn also has brown and rainbow trout fishing on **Loch Roan**; 4 boats; dt £25 per boat for 2 rods;

permits from Tommy's Sports, 178 King Str, DG7 1DA (tel: 01556 502851). **Loch Ken**, pike and perch; open all year for coarse fish. Permits from local hotels and shops. Other tackle shop: McCowan & Son, 50/52 King St DG7 1AD (tel: 01556 502009) (branch also in Dalbeattie); Dalbeattie AA tickets. Hotels: Douglas Arms; Imperial; Urr Valley Country House.

Crossmichael (Dumfriess & Galloway). Boats for **Loch Ken** from Crossmichael Marina, which has been recently upgraded and re-equipped, boats for hire all year round. Loch Ken, pike, perch, roach, brown trout, rainbow trout, sea trout, salmon, some bream, eels; all gamefish to be returned; contact David Deane, Crossmichael Marina, 4 Kirkland Terrace DG7 3AX (tel: 01556 670402); no ticket required for boat fishing; motor £60/day, rowing £30/day; bank fishing by permission of riparian owners. Hotel: Culgruff House Hotel.

New Galloway (Dumfriess & Galloway). Dee private. Forestry Commission Scotland controls fishing on eleven lochs, trout, coarse, or mixed, including **Loch Dee**, stocked brown trout; **Lillies Loch**, wild browns (ideal for beginners), and **Stroan Loch**, pike to 27lb and perch, and stretches of Rivers **Palnure** and **Minnoch**, with salmon and sea trout. Weekly permits £30, with concessions, from Forestry Commission Scotland, Galloway Forest District, Creebridge, Newton Stewart DG8 6AJ (tel: 01671 402420). New Galloway AA controls stretch of **River Ken**, salmon, brown trout, rainbow trout, pike, roach, dace, perch; stretch of **Loch Ken**, brown trout, pike, perch,

bream and salmon run through loch during season; **Blackwater of Dee** (N bank only), brown trout, salmon, pike; **Mossdale Loch,** native brown trout and stocked rainbow trout, fly only; and **Clatteringshaws Reservoir**, brown trout, pike, perch, roach. Fishing on Clatteringshaws Reservoir shared with Newton Stewart AA. Visitors permits, for all except Mossdale Loch, £2 per rod per day; Loch Ken, dt £2 plus 50p surcharge if permit bought from bailiffs; Mossdale Loch, dt £15 per boat (1 rod) (3 fish), from The Shop, Mossdale DG7 2NF (tel: 01644 450281). Permits from hotels in town; Ken Bridge Hotel; Mr Hopkins, Grocer, High St DG7 3RN (tel: 01644 420229); New Galloway SPO, High Str, DG7 3RL (tel: 01644 420214). **Barscobe Loch;** brown trout, fly only; dt (incl boat) £8, £5 bank, from Mrs Stewart, Castle Cottage, Barscobe, Balmaclellan, Castle Douglas DG7 3QG (tel: 01644 420294).

Dalry (Dumfriess & Galloway). Dalry AA has fishing on **River Ken** from Dalry; good stocks of brown trout and occasional salmon; fly spinning and worm, bank fishing only; Assn also has water on **Carsfad Loch,** brown and rainbow trout, bank fishing only; **Earlstoun Loch**, brown trout, fly only, two boats; no Sunday fishing; visitors tickets sold from 15 Mar-30 Sept, dt £7, wt £35; boat £7: from N W Newton (Grocers), 17 Main St, Dalry, Castle Douglas DG7 3UP (tel: 016444 30225). Lochinvar Hotel can arrange fishing in rivers, lochs and reservoirs (salmon, trout, pike and perch). Permits from Duchrae Farm for **Lochinvar Loch;** wild brown trout, no shore fishing, fly only.

DEVERON

Rises in Cabrach and flows some 45m into the Moray Firth at Banff. A salmon river, with brown trout fishing, some sea trout, June to September; finnock spring months.

Banff (Banffshire). Salmon, sea trout, brown trout. Fife Lodge Hotel; Banff Springs AB45 2JE (tel: 01261 812881) and County Hotel can advise on fishings. Early bookings advisable as best beats are heavily booked. Best months: salmon, March to Oct; sea trout June to Aug; brown trout, April, May and Sept. Sea trout improving. Sea trout fishing (July onwards) in **Boyne Burn**, 6m away now let to Portsoy & Dist AA.

Turriff (Aberdeenshire). Turriff AA has salmon, sea trout and brown trout fishing

on Deveron; wt £100 Jun-Aug, £120 Sept-Oct, Mon-Fri; day tickets Feb-May only, £10; 6 rods per day limit; permits from tackle shop. Fly only when level falls below 6in on gauge. Best months July, August and Sept; also a fishery on opposite bank, dt £10. Bognie, Mountblairy and Frendraught Group, has salmon, grilse, sea trout and brown trout fishing on Bognie Pool, Upper and Lower Mountblairy, 4m (part double bank), salmon, grilse, sea trout, brown trout; 11 Feb to 31 Oct; wt £70-£330 depending on

Two fine four pounders, a grilse and a brown trout. They were caught within half an hour of each other in adjoining pools of the Don. *Photo: Colquhonnie Hotel.*

time of year; fishing is open to all, usually on a weekly basis along with holiday cottages; day permits only up until May, from BMF Group, Estate Office, Frendraught House, Forgue, Huntly AB54 6EB (tel: 01464 871331; fax: 01464 871333). Tackle shop: Turriff Tackle and Trophies, 6 Castle St AB5 7BJ (tel: 01888 562428). Hotels: Union; White Heather. B&B suitable for anglers, from Jenny Rae, Silverwells, St Mary's Well, Turrif AB53 8BS.

Huntly (Aberdeenshire). Salmon, sea trout, brown trout. Permits for **Deveron, Bogie** and **Isla**; st £70, mt £40, wt £30, dt £15 from J A Christie, Huntly Fishings Committee, 27 Duke Street, Huntly AB54 8DP (tel: 01466 792291); only 10 day-tickets per day and none on Saturdays or Public Holidays. **Castle Beat:** ½m double bank fishing for two rods 1 mile from Huntly; salmon, sea trout and brown trout, by arrangement either daily or weekly; wt £75-£180 per rod depending on season; contact Emma Plumpton, Loanend, Gartly, nr Huntly, AB54 4SB (tel: 01466 720708).

Fishing available?

*If you own, manage, or know of first-class fishing available to the public which should be considered for inclusion in **Where to Fish**, please apply to the publishers (address in the front of the book) for a form for submission, on completion, to the editor. (Inclusion is at the sole discretion of the editor). There is no charge for inclusion.*

DIGHTY

Drains some small lochs and falls into the Firth of Tay not far from Dundee. Banks built up on lower reaches. Now considered a negligible fishery.

Dundee (Angus). Trout with occasional sea trout; free. 10m east, **Monikie** and **Crombie Reservoirs** leased to Monikie AC; access for disabled. **Lintrathen Reservoir** leased to Lintrathen AC; good brown and rainbow trout fishing up to 5lb; boats for hire; catch limit 5 fish per rod (over 10in); club bookings from Jim Hardie, 41 Rowan Avenue, Northmuir, Kirriemuir DD8 4TB (tel: 01575 572412); during season, reservations from boathouse (tel: 01575 560327); access and boats for disabled. Tackle shop: Broty Tackle, 67 King St, Broughty Ferry, Dundee DD5 1EY (tel: 01382 480113). Hotel: Station.

DON (Aberdeenshire)

Rises near Ben Avon and flows for nearly 80m to North Sea at Aberdeen. Long famed as a dry fly trout water, the river is also becoming known for its salmon, which run from April to October. Sea trout numbers are on the increase.

Kintore (Aberdeenshire). Salmon and trout fishing on both banks of River Don; 2½m on right bank and 3½m on left bank. Permits from Sloans of Inverurie, 125-129 High St, Inverurie AB51 3QJ (tel: 01467 625181). No Sunday fishing.

Inverurie (Aberdeenshire). **River Don** (2½ miles) and **River Urie** (3½ miles) salmon, brown trout and occasional sea trout. No Sunday fishing on Don. Salmon best March, April, May and Sept-Oct. Permits from Sloans of Inverurie, 125-129 High St, Inverurie AB51 3QJ (tel: 01467 625181).

Kemnay (Aberdeenshire). Salmon, sea trout, brown trout. Mrs S L Milton, Kemnay House, AB51 5LH (tel: 01467 642220) issues very limited permits for one beat on Don at Kemnay; dt £30 and £10 (salmon, trout). Booking essential. Fishing let to syndicate. One house rod available. Tackle from Inverurie.

Alford (Aberdeenshire). 25m from Aberdeen. Salmon, brown trout and some sea trout. Forbes Arms Hotel, Bridge of Alford AB33 8QJ (tel: 019755 62108), has 3¼m of Don for guests and also issues permits; wt £50-60 trout, £150 salmon; dt £10-£12 trout, £25 salmon; preference given to guests. Some good trout burns (free) in vicinity.

Kildrummy (Aberdeenshire). Kildrummy Castle Hotel, AB33 8RA (tel: 019755 71288) has good stretch of salmon and brown trout fishing. Trout best early, salmon late.

Glenkindie (Aberdeenshire). Glenkindie Arms Hotel, Glenkindie, Alford AB33 8SX (tel: 019756 41288; web: www.glen kindiearms.co.uk), issue permits for Don salmon and trout fishing; no Sunday fishing; 4 rod limit.

Strathdon (Aberdeenshire). Colquhonnie Hotel, AB36 8UN (tel: 019756 51210; web: www.colquhonnie-hotel.co.uk) has 9m of salmon and trout fishing. Tickets from hotel; also for Ardgeith, Mossat (see Glenkindie) and **Tillypronnie**. Permits for salmon fishing also from Kildrummy Castle Hotel, AB33 8RA (tel: 019755 71288).

DOON

Drains Loch Doon on the Firth of Clyde watershed and flows right through the old County of Ayr to the Firth of Clyde, near Ayr Town. Good salmon, sea trout and brown trout water.

Ayr (Ayrshire). On Rivers Doon and Ayr. Salmon and sea trout July onwards. Brig o' Doon Hotel, Alloway KA7 4PQ (tel: 01292 442466), has water on Doon. Salmon and sea trout fishing on 3 beats at Skeldon Estate, (1m from Dalrymple) with self-catering accommodation, from Mr Campbell, Skeldon Estate, Dalrymple KA6 6AT (tel: 01292 560656); fishing is let primarily with accommodation: 2½m double bank, 12 pools; 1½m single bank, 8 pools; 1m single bank, 5 pools. District Council issues permits for **Ayr**. Club membership and permits for various club waters issued by GameSport of Ayr, 60 Sandgate, Ayr KA7 1BX (tel: 01292 263822). Hotel: Parson's Lodge, 15 Main Str, Patna.

Dalmellington (Ayrshire). Good salmon and sea trout (July onwards). **Loch Doon**,

6m; plenty of small brown trout and occasional salmon and char; fishing free. Craigengillan Estate KA6 7PZ (tel: 01292 551818; fax: 01292 551819) has 2½m both banks of River Doon from Loch Doon downstream, and coarse fishing at **Bogton Loch** (63 acres, brown

trout and pike). Drumgrange & Keirs AC has 5m double bank fishing on river; dt £10, apply Hon Sec or Andersons; salmon, sea trout, browns to 5lb, pike. Tackle shop: Andersons Hardware & Tackle Shop, 6 Waterside St, KA6 7SW (tel: 01292 551354).

EDEN (Fife)

Rises in Ochil Hills not far from Loch Leven and falls into North Sea in St Andrews Bay. Provides some very fair trout fishing. Slow-flowing stream suitable for dry-fly fishing. Some sea trout below Cupar.

St Andrews (Fife). **Cameron Reservoir**, brown and rainbow stocked by St Andrews AC (trout av 1¼lb); fly only; Sunday fishing; boat and bank fishing; boat hire (3 rods per boat) £33 per session; bank permit £12 per session, Sundays 2.30pm to dusk £13; tickets for reservoir and **River Eden** from tackle shop: J Wilson & Son, 169-171 South St, St Andrews KY16 9EE (tel: 01334 472477).

Cupar (Fife). For brown trout fishing on **Clatto Reservoir**; dt £8, evngs £10, 4 fish limit; two boats available, £3 day, £4

evngs; apply Waterman's Cottage KY15 5UE at reservoir (tel: 01334 652595). Eden AA has 15m fishing, including Balass, Crichtons, Kemback, Nydie through Cupar: salmon, sea trout, brown; st £35, dt £8 (Oct £12), conc; contact Hon Sec.

Ladybank (Fife). Fine dry-fly fishing; trout. Some free, but mostly preserved. **Golden Loch**, nr Lindores Loch offers both bank and boat fishing; contact Berryhill Farm, Newburgh KY14 6HZ (tel: 01337 840355; fax: 01337 840412: web: www.goldenloch.co.uk); permits.

ESK (North)

Formed by junction of Lee and Mark, near Loch Lee, and flows for nearly 30m to North Sea near Montrose. Good river for salmon, sea trout and finnock.

Montrose (Angus). Salmon, sea trout, finnock (whitling) and brown trout. Spring and Autumn best fishing. North Esk tickets from Post Office, Marykirk. For **Gallery** fishing contact Matthew Ramage, Muir Cottage, Trinity, Brechin DD9 7PD (tel: 01356 625044). Gannochy Estate fishings are the subject of major change as we go to press. Refer to Mr Ramage *(above)*. For **Mill of Criggie Trout Fishery**, St Cyrus, nr Montrose DD10 0DR, rainbows and browns, open all year, contact Kevin and Helen Ramshore, custom rod builders and repairers (tel: 01674 850868). Limited disabled access, tuition, tackle, snacks on site. Montrose AC fishes Craigo beat of North Esk and downstream from Bridge of Dun on **South Esk**. Permits from £10-£18 on S Esk, £25-£45 on N Esk, if available, from tackle shop: Cobsport, 7 Castle Place

DD10 8AL (tel: 01674 673095). Hotels: Carlton, George, Hillside, Marykirk.

Edzell (Angus). Salmon and sea trout. Dalhousie Estate Office, Brechin Castle, Brechin DD9 6SH (tel: 01356 624566) has boats to hire for trout fishing on **Loch Lee** in Glen Esk; no bank fishing, and fly only. Permits from Mrs Taylor, Kirkton of Invermark, Glenesk, by Brechin DD9 7YZ (tel: 01356 670208); also salmon beats to let by the week on North Esk at Edzell, dt when no weekly lets; 2 beats at Millden, 4 and 3 rods, salmon and sea trout; details from Dalhousie Estates. Panmure Arms Hotel, High St, Brechin DD9 7TA (tel: 01356 648950) has 1m of fishing on **West Water** (trout, sea trout and occasional salmon); and can arrange fishing on North Esk and Loch Lee. Hotel: Glenesk. Self-catering cottages through Dalhousie Estates Office.

ESK (South)

Rises in Glen Clova and flows some 49m to North Sea near Montrose. Good salmon river with plentiful runs of sea trout. Best months for salmon are February, March and April. Good autumn river (mid-September onwards), sea trout May-July.

Brechin (Angus). Good centre for North

and South Esk. Salmon and sea trout;

fishing good, but mostly reserved. South Esk Estates Office, Brechin, let beats on 2½m, usually by the week or longer periods, but very limited. Sporting Scotland, Parklea, Park Rd, DD9 7AP (tel: 01356 625436; web: www.sporting-scot land.co.uk; e-mail: info@sporting-scot land.co.uk), offers 3 and 5 day fishing breaks in Grampian, Wester Ross, Lewis, Morayshire, Perthshire and Tayside, with accom, transport, ghillie, permits and equipment included in prices. Issues wt and dt for most rivers and lochs. Brechin AC has fishing on **Loch Saugh** near Fettercairn, brown trout, fly only; and **River West Water**, brown trout, salmon and sea trout; permits for **L Saugh** from Drumtochty Arms Hotel, The Square, Laurencekirk AB30 1WS (tel: 01561 320210);

PO Edzell or Newsplus, Brechin (Saugh and West Water); membership £60, dt from £10, other prices on application to Hon Sec. Tackle Shop: Carrols, Church St, Brechin (tel: 01356 625700). Hotels: Northern, Brechin; Glenesk; Panmure, both Edzell.

Kirriemuir (Angus). Kirriemuir AC has approx 7m on South Esk. Salmon, sea trout, a few brown trout; permits from Hon Sec; some fly only water, but much of it unrestricted; concessions to jun; no Sunday fishing and no permits on Saturdays. Strathmore AIA has rights on lower **Isla** and **Dean**, both near **Blairgowrie**; st £13 (trout), £9 (grayling), dt £4 (trout), conc (half), from tackle shops in Dundee, Blairgowrie, Glamis, Meigle and Forfar.

EWE

This river has good runs of salmon (best May onwards) and sea trout (end June onwards) up to Loch Maree. Fishing again excellent, after problems caused by disease. Owned by Inveran Estate.

Aultbea (Ross-shire). Bank fishing for wild brown trout on **Aultbea Hill Lochs**. Permits from Aultbea Lodges, Drumchork, Aultbea IV22 2HU (tel: 01445 731268); Post Office, Laide. Hotels: Aultbea; Drumchork Lodge.

LOCH MAREE (Ross & Cromarty). Spring salmon fishing from April until June. Sea trout from June until Oct. Also brown trout fishing.

Talladale (Ross-shire). Salmon, sea trout, brown trout. Loch Maree Hotel has fishing. Heavy demand for sea-trout season so early booking advised. Boat fishing only (8 boats). Apply to Loch Maree Hotel, Talladale, By Achnasheen, Wester Ross IV22 2HL (tel: 01445 760288). Gairloch Angling Club has brown trout fishing in many hill lochs, including **Bad**

na Scalaig, **Tolliadh, Garbhaig**. Pike in Lochs Bad an Scalaig, Dubh and Fuar, salmon fishing in **R Kerry**, (book at Creag Mor Hotel, Gairloch IV21 2AH (tel: 01445 712068)); membership closed but permits from K Gunn, Strath Square, Gairloch IV21 2BY (tel: 01445 712400); dt £2 trout, £4 pike, £12 boat.

Kinlochewe (Ross-shire). Brown trout, char and sea trout fishing on **Loch Bharranch**; and brown trout, pike and perch fishing on **Loch a'Chroisg**. Permits from Glendocherty Craft Shop, Achnasheen IV22 2PA (tel: 01445 760220).

Achnasheen (Ross-shire). On A832, **Loch a' Chroisg**, brown trout, pike, perch; permits from Ledgowan Lodge Hotel, Achnasheen, Ross-shire IV22 2EJ (tel: 01445 720252).

FINDHORN

Rises in Monadhliath Mountains and flows over 60m to Moray Firth. Salmon, sea trout and brown trout. Good spate river with many rock pools, fishing begins mid to late April. Best months: May/June and August/Sept. Grilse from summer to end of season. Recent native hardwood regeneration schemes along substantial lengths of the river have enhanced the quality of the spawning beds; and helped to limit erosion previously caused by livestock.

Drynachan (Nairnshire). Cawdor Estate has fly only salmon fishing on Findhorn, 3 beats with 2 rods per beat; and trout fishing on **Loch of Boath** (brown). Excellent accommodation is bookable on Estate at Drynachan Lodge (plus 6 cottages). Contact the Lettings Manager,

Cawdor Estate Office, Cawdor, Nairn IV12 5RE (tel: 01667 402402; fax: 01667 404787). Good trout fishing on nearby lochs; **Loch of Blairs, Loch Lochindorb**. Permits for Lochindorb direct from keeper. Tickets for 7m stretch of **R Nairn** with sea trout and salmon, from tackle shop: Pat Fraser, 41 High St, Nairn IV12 4AG (tel: 01667 453038).

Forres (Moray). Forres AA water; 4m double bank, with salmon and sea trout; fly, spinning early season; dt £25, wt £105; permits from Fishing Tackle Shop, 97d High St, Forres IV36 0AA (tel: 01309 672936). Also permits for **Loch of Blairs** (rainbow trout, fly from boat only).

Tomatin (Inverness-shire). 14 miles south of Inverness on A9 road, four beats of right bank, one on left, for two and three rods, with holding pools and many streams and runs; ghillie service; permits £50-£65 per rod day depending on beat; ghillie £50 (parties of 4+: £60). Contact Mr A J Bell, Cottage of Free, Tomatin IV13 7YT (tel/fax: 01808 511439; web: www.findhornfishing.com).

FLEET (Dumfriess & Galloway)

Formed by junction of Big and Little Water, empties into the Solway Firth at Gatehouse. Good sea trout and herling, and few grilse and salmon; best months July and August.

Gatehouse-of-Fleet (Dumfries and Galloway). Murray Arms Hotel, Gatehouse-of-Fleet DG7 2HY (tel: 01557 814207), issue permits for waters on River Fleet. Sea trout and herling with some grilse and salmon. No sunday fishing. Gatehouse and Kirkcudbright AA has **Loch Whinyeon**, 120 acres, 3½m from town, brown trout, stocked and wild; fly only. Two boats; bank or boat fishing. Assn

also controls **Loch Lochenbreck**, 40 acres, 3m from Lauriston, rainbow and brown trout. Fly only. Bank or boat fishing. Permits £12, boats plus £3, from Watson McKinnel, 15 St Cuthbert Street, Kirkcudbright DG6 (tel: 01557 330693) and Anwoth Hotel, Fleet Street, Gatehouse Of Fleet, Castle Douglas, DG7 2JT (tel: 01557 814217).

FORTH (including Loch Leven and Water of Leith)

Formed from junction of Avendhu and Duchray not far from Aberfoyle, and thence flows about 80m to its firth at Alloa, opening into North Sea. Principal tributaries, Teith and Allan, flow above Stirling. A large salmon river, which at times, and especially on upper reaches, provides some good sport. Good run in lower reaches from August to October, as a rule. Trouting in upper reaches and tributaries, particularly in lochs, where salmon also taken.

Dunfermline (Fife). **Loch Fitty**, excellent brown and rainbow trout water, also steelheads. Bank and boat fishing, 33 boats, tackle shop and coffee shop to which visitors are welcome. Boats, including o/b, for 3 anglers, day (10am-5pm) £51 (15 fish); evening (5.30pm to dusk) £17 per angler; bank permits £14 per session; boats for single anglers, £20; 'father and son/daughter' £20; OAP, (Tues and Thurs) £24 (2 anglers); bait & coarse fishing available. Apply to Fife Angling Centre, The Lodge, Kingseat, by Dunfermline, Fife KY12 0SP (tel: 01383 620666). Halfway House Hotel by Loch Fitty welcomes anglers and can arrange fishing for guests. Apply to Douglas Fleming, Halfway House Hotel, Main St, Kingseat, by Dunfermline KY12 0TJ (tel: 01383 731661). Hotels: Abbey House, Auld Toll Tavern, King Malcolm Thistle. B&B, Loch Fitty Cottage KY12 0SP (tel: 01383 831081).

Stirling (Stirlingshire). Forth, **Allan** and **Teith** may be fished from here. Herling in Forth in spring and autumn. Salmon fish-

ing from Lands of Hood to mouth of Teith (7½m) including Cruive Dykes is controlled by Stirling Council: contact Countryside Manager, Room 124, Stirling Council, Viewforth, Stirling FK8 2ET (tel: 0845 277 7000); st £129, dt £37 (juv £64.50, £18.50), conc; good run in lower reaches, 1 Feb to 31 Oct. **North Third Trout Fishery**, Greathill House, Stirling, FK7 9QS (tel: 01786 471967): 140 acres, rainbow and brown trout (record rainbow, 19lb 13oz; brown, 9lb 14oz); fly only; 23 boats and bank fishing, tuition by appointment. Open 15 Mar to 31 Oct. Permits and season tickets from fishery.

Aberfoyle (Perthshire). Brown trout. Aberfoyle APA has brown trout fishing on **Loch Ard**; fly only; stocked with young brown trout. Dt £5: apply to The Farm Shop, Kinlochard, by Aberfoyle FK8 3TL (tel: 01877 387284). Dt £5 on Loch Ard from Altskeith Country House B&B, Kinlochard, by Aberfoyle, Stirling FK8 3TL (tel: 01877 387266). Brown trout fishing on **Loch Arklet, Loch Katrine**

and **Glen Finglas**; now controlled by Trossachs Fishings, Loch Vennacher, by Callander; for information, ring James Bayne (below). Forestry Commission Scotland controls fishing for brown trout, pike and perch on River Forth and **Loch Chon**, brown trout on **Loch Drunkie**, and **Lochan Reoidhte**, and salmon, sea trout and brown trout on **Loch Lubnaig**. Bank fishing only. Permits from £5.50 to £3 from David Marshall, Lodge, Queen Elizabeth Forest Park, Aberfoyle FX8 3UX

(tel: 01877 382258) (open Easter to Oct); access to Loch Drunkie via Forest Drive; no vehicle access after Oct. **Lake of Menteith** has brown and rainbow trout, largest b 5lbs, r 12lbs, 1,000 stocked weekly. Fly only, boat and facilities for disabled. Permits from Lake Menteith Fisheries Ltd, Port of Menteith, Stirling FK8 3RA (tel: 01877 385 664). Tackle shops: James Bayne, 76 Main St, Callander FK17 8BD (tel: 01877 330218). Hotel: Inverard.

Tributaries of Forth

LEVEN. Flows from Loch Leven to Firth of Forth at Leven, Fife. Good sea trout runs from Jul-Oct; any legal method (on shrimp or prawn).

ALMOND. West of Edinburgh the river flows into the Firth of Forth at Cramond.

Cramond (West Lothian). Cramond AC has fishing leases on most of River Almond and tributaries. Salmon, sea trout and brown trout. Permits from Post Office, Cramond.

Livingston (West Lothian). River Almond AA has ½m of Almond with salmon and sea trout, and 2m with brown trout. Permits from Hon Sec; Country Life, 229 Balgreen Rd, EH11 2RZ (tel: 0131 337 6230). **Morton Fishery**, brown and rain-

bow trout; fly only; bag limits 3-6 fish; advanced bookings; permits from Morton Fisheries, Morton Reservoir, Mid Calder, West Lothian EH53 0JT (tel: 01506 882293).

NORTH ESK and **SOUTH ESK**. These two rivers are fed by Lothian regional reservoirs and join near Dalkeith to form the River Esk. The Esk flows a short way down to enter the Firth of Forth at Musselburgh.

Musselburgh (East Lothian). Musselburgh & Dist AA has salmon, sea trout and brown trout fishing on Esk, from estuary, 2m upstream of Musselburgh; permits from Musselburgh Pet Centre, 81 High St; Mike's Tackle Shop, 48 Portobello

Restocking at Loch Ard is a social event. *Photo: Glasgow Herald.*

High St EH15 1DA (tel: 0131 657 3258); no Sunday fishing.

Penicuik (Midlothian). Esk Valley AIA has rainbow and brown trout fishing on North and South Esk; fly rod and reel only to be used; permits from Hon Sec. **Glencorse and Clubbidean Reservoirs**; brown, blue, brook and rainbow trout; fly only; boat only; 52 acres, 13 acres; leased to Dooks Fisheries, 57 North Street, Ratho EH28 8RP (tel: 0131 3332693; mob 07050 325803); Clubbidean has disabled bank fishing. **Rosebery Reservoir**; 52 acres; brown and rainbow trout, pike, perch; dt £14, conc £8, contact Rosebery Fishery, Waterkeepers Cottage EH23 4SS (tel: 01875 830353). **Gladhouse Reservoirs** are managed by both Rosebery Estates (tel: 0131 331 1888) and Arniston Estates.

West Linton (Peeblesshire). Brown trout fishing on **West Water Reservoir**; 93 acres; fly only; wild browns; 1 May to 31 Aug; no bank fishing: permits from Scottish Water, Fairmilehead, Edinburgh EH10 6XH (tel: 0131 445 6462).

DEVON: Fair brown trout stream; sea trout and salmon lower down.

Alloa (Clackmannanshire). Devon AA has salmon, sea trout and brown trout fishing on nine beats of Devon, from Glendevon to Devonside; fly only first month. Assn also has brown trout fishing on **Glenquey Reservoir**, near Muckhart; fly only to April to Sept, no spinning; bank fishing only; sunday fishing permitted on reservoir, prohibited on river; season tickets for sea trout and salmon are only obtainable from Hon Sec (postal application only); permits for brown trout fishing from McCutcheons Newsagents, Bridge St, Dollar FK14 7DG (tel: 01259 742517); and Marco Palmieri, The Inn, Crook of Devon KY13 7UR; Muckhart PO; and Mrs Small, Riverside Caravan Park, Dollar, FK14 7LX (tel: 01259 742896). 6m west of **Kinross**, Glensherrup Trout Fishery, Glendevon FK14 7JZ (tel: 01259 781631), has fly only, rainbow and brown trout, stocked regularly; boat and bank fishing, dt £12-£36 available. **Gartmorn Dam Fishery**, 167 Acres, stocked rainbow, plentiful browns also, fly and spinning, artificials only from bank; fly only from boat, 9 boats. Permits from Gartmorn Dam Country Park, by Sauchie, Alloa FK10 3AZ (tel: 01259 214319). Fife Regional Council used to control reservoirs which were subsequently passed to East of Scotland Water (renamed Scottish Water); these are now largely and variously leased-out (see later text): **Lower Glendevon Reservoir**; run by Frandy Fishery, Dollar FK14 7JZ (tel: 01259 781352; web: www.frandyfishery.com); rainbows, browns, blues; fly only; dt £15, conc, from lodge; **Castlehill Reservoir**; rainbow trout, some browns, perch and pike; fly and bait; contact David Duff (mob: 07748 011834); **Cameron Reservoir** leased to St Andrews AC; **Craigluscar Reservoirs** to Dunfermline Artisan AC, rainbow trout dt £11 for 5 fish, conc, from bailiff's hut; **Glenquey Reservoir** to Devon AA; **Lochmill Reservoir** to Newburgh AC; **Upper Carriston Reservoir**, no tickets. Hotels: Castle Campbell, Dollar; Castle Craig, Tillicoultry; Tormaukin, Glendevon.

Gleneagles (Perthshire). The Gleneagles Hotel, Auchterarder PH3 1NF, has access to Upper and Lower Newtyle beats on **River Tay**; salmon, grilse and sea trout. Trout fishing on Lochs, in hotel grounds. Trout fishing lesson costs £80 half day, salmon £300-£450, including ghillie and tackle hire. Should venues be fully booked hotel will arrange alternative fishing. Apply to The Shooting and Fishing School, Gleneagles Hotel, Perthshire PH3 1NF (tel: 01764 694344; fax: 01764 694160).

AVON: Flows 18m to estuary of Forth near Grangemouth. Lower estuary reaches polluted; good brown trout elsewhere (av ½lb with few around 4lb). River fishes best in late June, July and Aug.

Linlithgow (West Lothian). Linlithgow AC has 5m stretch of Avon north of Muiravonside Country Park, with brown trout. Members only: st £25 +£15 joining, conc; contact Hon Sec. Avon Bridge AA offer excellent value season tickets on a lengthy stretch in Avonbridge area; access to river regulated through R Avon Federation, which holds migratory fishing rights; membership is available to members of the local fishing clubs. Muiravonside Country Park, The Loan, by Whitecross (tel: 01506 845311): brown trout and coarse tickets, £4, conc. **Union Canal** from Edinburgh to Falkirk: pike, perch, roach, carp, eel, bream, mirror and leather carp, and tench; no close season; st £10 from British Waterways, Lowland Canals, Rosebank House, Main St, Camelon, Falkirk FK1 4DS (tel: 01324

671217; web: www.scottishcanals.co. uk).

CARRON:

Larbert (West Lothian). Larbert & Stenhousemuir AC has fishing on **Loch Coulter**, near Carronbridge; brown and rainbow trout; fly only; no Sunday fishing; members only; club also fishes Carron; st £34, dt £5 from: Scrimgeour Fishing Tackle, 28 Newmarket St, Falkirk FK1 1JQ (tel: 01324 624581).

Denny (Stirlings). Carron Valley Fishery controls **Carron Valley Reservoir**; bank fishing now permitted (4 miles), 20 boats, wild brown trout fishing, fly only; dt £8, conc; booking (tel: 01324 823698; web: www.carronvalley.com). **Drumbowie Reservoir**, fly only; brown trout; dt £6, visitors accompanied by member, st £30: permits from Bonnybridge AC (tel: 01324 813136) .

TEITH: Noted salmon and brown trout fishery, with good sea trout in summer.

Callander (Perthshire). Stirling Council controls part of Teith in Callander, with excellent salmon, sea trout, and brown trout (average ¾lb); fishing open to visitors; contact Countryside Manager, Room 124, Stirling Council, Viewforth, Stirling FK8 2ET (tel: 0845 277 7000); st £112, dt £29 (juv £56, £14.50); no Sunday fishing. Apply to James Bayne (*below*) for st £112, dt £29 for 2m both banks (town water); salmon, sea trout; and also for brown trout fishing on L Voil (4m north of town) (dt £3.50 to £5). **Loch Venachar** controlled by L Ven Assn; mainly brown trout, but some sea trout and salmon; trout average 1lb; fishing from bank permitted on parts of loch; mapped details

from Baynes, with prices (dt £7); boats for hire. Permits also for **River Leny**, 1m from town, salmon, fly and spinning; dt £16; **River Balvaig**, 10m north, trout fishing, any method; dt £3; **Loch Lubnaig**, 2m north, trout, perch, char, £4 dt, £2 juv from James Bayne (*below*). **Loch Drunkie** (brown trout, dt £3) and **Lochan Reoidhte** (brown trout, fly only); permits £3-£5 from Queen Elizabeth Forest Park Visitors' Centre, Aberfoyle, and James Bayne, Fishing Tackle, 76 Main St FK17 8BD (tel: 01877 330218).

Balvaig and CALAIR (Tributaries of Teith): salmon and brown trout.

Balquhidder (Perthshire). Salmon and brown trout fishing on **R Balvaig**, **Loch Voil** and **Loch Doine**; from Kings House Hotel, Balquhidder, Perthshire FK19 8NY (tel: 01877 384646); boat hire and ghillie can be arranged. Mrs Catriona Oldham, Muirlaggan, Balquhidder, Lochearnhead, FK19 8PB (tel: 01877 384219; web: www.lochsidecottages.co. uk; e-mail info@lochsidecottages.co.uk) has fishing dt £3.00, or st £15 on Loch Voil and Loch Doine, salmon and brown trout, boats for hire. 2 self-catering cottages on site with free fishing on L Voil. Tackle shop: James Bayne, Fishing Tackle, 76 Main St, Callandar FK17 8BD (tel: 01877 330218) for local permits.

Strathyre (Perthshire). Salmon, sea trout, brown trout, char, eels on **R Balvaig**, **L Lubnaig**, **R Leny** from Donald Kennedy (tel: 01877 331594); trout on Loch Lubnaig. James Bayne also supplies dt £4 on Loch Lubnaig (see Callander); boat launch dt £10 to £60 (st).

Loch Leven

Famous Kinross-shire loch which produces quick-growing trout. Loch is nowhere deep so feed is good, and practically whole area is fishing water. Under efficient management, this has become one of the most notable trout fishing lochs of Scotland.

Kinross (Kinross-shire). Loch Leven Fisheries is a predominantly brown trout loch which boasts the famous Loch Leven trout. These average over 1lb with many specimen of 3-4lbs being taken. It is also stocked each year with high quality rainbow trout. Fly fishing by boat only. Boats are bookable by letter or phone. For full information on charges and booking conditions, apply (March to Sept) to The Pier, Kinross, Tayside KY13 8UF (tel: 01577 863407; e-mail: fishing@green-hotel.com). Tackle can be bought or hired

at the pier. Kinross Trout Fishery, also known as Heatheryford Trout Fishery: top quality trout fishing on **Heatheryford**, and 10 acre spring fed water, with brown and rainbow trout; bank fishing only, access for disabled. Fly only. Permits from office on site, Kinross KY13 0NQ (tel: 01577 864212).

Ballingry (Fife). Rainbow and brown trout fishing on **Loch Ore**; 260 acre loch, with bank and boat fishing, regularly stocked, access for disabled. Permits from Lochore Meadows Country Park, Crosshill,

Balligry, Fife KY5 8BA (tel: 01592 414312).

Glenrothes (Fife). Permits may be had from Lomond Hills Fisheries (tel: 07949 256307) for reservoir trout fishing on **Holl**; dt on site; 42 acres; also for Harperleas; 39 acres; browns; fly only; c&r; dt £10; boat £15.

Water of Leith

Local people who know river well get fair numbers of trout.

Edinburgh (Mid Lothian). Water of Leith, running through the city, is stocked annually with brown trout. Permits issued free of charge. Trout fishing at **Gladhouse, Glencorse, Clubbiedean, Crosswood** (dt £10, conc £5), and **West Water Reservoirs**; former Scottish Water fishings are now leased out (*see above*). Bank permits for **Harperrig** contact Mr Hamilton, Cairns Farm, Kirknewton (tel: 01506 881510). **Rosebery Reservoir**, brown and rainbow trout, pike, perch; permits (dt £10, conc £5) from Mrs Grant, Keeper's Cottage (tel: 01875 830353). **Talla** and **Fruid Reservoirs**, brown trout; dt £8-£12, conc, from Megget Reservoir (tel: 01750 42283); Crook Inn, Tweedsmuir, Scottish Borders ML12 6QN (tel: 01899 880272; e-mail: the crookinn@btinternet.com). Info on **Whiteadder Reservoir** from Scottish Water (tel: 0131 445 6462). For **Hopes Reservoir** contact Faccombe Estates, Faccombe SP11 0DS (tel: 01264 737247). Coarse fishing on **Duddingston Loch;** carp and perch; Loch situated in a bird sanctuary, therefore a restricted area; bank fishing by permit only, no charge; no lead weights; no close season; permits from Historic Scotland Ranger Service, Holyrood Park Education Centre, 1 Queens Drive, Holyrood Park, Edinburgh EH8 8HG (tel: 0131 652 8150). **Union Canal** from Edinburgh to Falkirk; pike, perch, roach, carp and tench; no close season; free. Tackle shops: Dickson & Macnaughton, 21 Frederick Str, EH2 2NE (tel: 0131 225 4218); F & D Simpson, 28/30 West Preston Str, EH8 9PZ (tel: 0131 667 3058); Country Life, 229 Balgreen Rd, EH11 2RZ (tel: 0131 337 6230); Mike's Tackle Shop, 48 Portobello High St EH15 1DA (tel: 0131 657 3258).

Balerno (Edinburgh). Trout fishing on Water of Leith; permits from Balerno PO, 36 Main Str, EH14 7EH (tel: 0131 4493077); and Colinton PO, 7 Bridge Rd, EH13 0LH. Brown and rainbow trout

fishing on **Threipmuir** and **Harlaw Reservoirs**. Fly fishing only. Bank fishing only. Managed by Malleny AA; dt £10 from Balerno PO *(above)*. **Harperrig Reservoir**, 237 acres; brown trout. Fly only, bank fishing. Permits from machine at reservoir (coins required).

GIRVAN

Drains small loch called Girvan Eye and thence runs 25 miles to the Atlantic at Girvan. Good salmon and sea trout; fair brown trout. Salmon run March onwards; sea trout from June.

Girvan (Ayrshire). Salmon, sea trout, brown trout. **Penwhapple Reservoir**, near Barr, stocked with brown trout; Penwhapple AC water; fly only; dt £10 and evenings £8, boats £5, Sundays members only; apply Mrs Stewart, Lane Farm, Barr (½m beyond reservoir). Hotel: Ailsa Craig.

Kirkmichael (Ayrshire). Salmon and trout fishing on 3m stretch, limited rods; accommodation in Scottish baronial house in 50 acres of grounds; also lake fishing in small private loch, stocked with brown ad rainbow trout; contact M L Hambly, Kirkmichael House, Maybole KA19 7PR (tel: 01655 750212).

Straiton (Ayrshire). Salmon (late), sea

trout, brown trout. Blairquhan Estate water, fly only; permits from E Anderson, The Kennels, Blairquhan Estate, Straiton KA19 7LY (tel: 01655 770259). Forestry Commission Scotland, Galloway Forest District, Creebridge, Newton Stewart DG8 6AJ (tel: 01671 402420), controls fishing in Galloway Forest Park, with brown trout fishing on **Lochs Bradan**, **Loch Dee**, **Black Loch**, and **Loch of the Lowes**; and **Lilies Loch**. Pike and perch fishing, with other coarse on **Linfern Loch**, **Spectacle**, **Garwachie**, **Eldrig**, and **Stroan**. Many outlets for tickets, which range from £6 to £15 (juv £3 to £5).

HALLADALE

Rises on north slope of Helmsdale watershed and empties into sea at Melvich Bay. Early salmon March onwards, 10-16lbs. Grilse run from June, 5-7lbs.

Melvich (Sutherland). 18m from Thurso. Apply for salmon permits on River Halladale from Strath Halladale Partnership, The Estate Office, The Kennels, Forsinard, Sutherland KW13 6YT (tel: 01641 571271). Fly only.

Forsinard (Sutherland). Forsinard Hotel can arrange salmon fishing on River Halladale, fly only; hotel has 120,000 acres of trout fishing on various lochs. Apply to Forsinard Hotel, Forsinard KW13 6YT (tel: 01641 571221).

HELMSDALE RIVER

Formed by two headstreams near Kinbrace, this river flows 20m southeast through Strathullie to sea. Excellent salmon river, where there is now no netting.

Helmsdale (Sutherland). Salmon and sea trout. Salmon beat lettings occasionally available from Roxton Bailey Robinson,

Fishing Agents, 25 High St, Hungerford, Berks RG17 0NF (tel: 01488 683222). Hotel: Belgrave Arms.

INVER (including Kirkaig and Loch Assynt)

Draining Loch Assynt, this river flows into a sea loch on the west coast of Sutherland known as Lochinver (village and loch having the same name), a little north of the old Ross-shire border. Holds salmon and sea trout but fishing is hard to come by.

Lochinver (Sutherland). Inver Lodge Hotel has salmon fishing on the River Inver, the upper beat of which is bookable. The hotel has further fishing on **River Kirkaig**, 3½m S of Lochinver and the upper

Oykel, about 30m east of Lochinver. Hotel has first refusal of beats and brown trout lochs covering estate, including **Loch Culag**, **Fionn Loch**, Loch Assynt, and numerous other hill lochs. Apply to

Inver Lodge Hotel, Iolaire Rd, Lochinver IV27 4LU (tel: 01571 844496; fax: 01571 844395). The Assynt AA has 19 boats for hire and fishing on over 150 lochs in the locality of Assynt. Five lochs, **Culag, Assynt, Shardalin, Aosynt** and **Ailsh** hold migratory fish. There are 11 outlets for permits; fly only, except Assynt where trolling is allowed; also restricted spinning. No bait fishing permitted. Wt £25, dt £5. The Assynt Crofters own the North Assynt Estate. Through the Trust, anglers may fish a large number of hill lochs, in a landscape of great natural beauty, including **Loch Poll**, the biggest, with boat obtainable from Old Drumbeg P O, **Loch Drumbeg, Lochs Roe, Manse, Tuirk**, which can produce excellent sea trout runs, and many others. 10 boats are for hire, £10, and £5 permits may be bought at Drumbeg Post Office, and Lochinver Tourist Office IV27 4LX (tel: 01571 844373). Inchnadamph Hotel, Assynt, by Lairg IV27 4HN (tel: 01571 822202) has fishing on east end of **Loch Assynt**, and supplies permits for Assynt AA waters. Hotel: Kylesku, Lairg.

Ledmore (Sutherland). The Alt Motel, 20m N of Ullapool, has brown trout and first rate Arctic char fishing on **Loch Borralan**. Boat £20 and bank £5 per day. Bed and breakfast, and self-catering accommodation. Further information from Bruce and Alba Ward, The Alt Motel, The Altnacealgach, nr Ledmore Junction, By Lairg, Sutherland IV27 4HF (tel: 01854 666220). Eric Ferguson, The Altnacealgach Inn IV27 4HF (tel: 01854 666260) supplies tickets, boats and engines for the east side of Assynt.

Loch Assynt

Inchnadamph (Sutherland). Salmon fishing from May on Loch Assynt. Inchnadamph Hotel, Assynt, by Lairg IV27 4HN (tel: 01571 822202) has fishing on loch plus 10 other lochs, including the celebrated **Gillaroo Loch** and **Loch Awe**.

£20 for boat (o/b £15) which includes 2 rods, 7 boats for hire; fishing free to residents. Visitors require permits £5. Season: salmon from 15 May until 15 Oct; trout, 15 Mar to 6 Oct.

IRVINE (including Annick).

Rises near Loudonhill and flows about 20m to Firth of Clyde at Irvine Town. Main tributaries are Cessnock Water, Kilmarnock Water and Annick. Fishing controlled largely by clubs. Salmon and sea trout July onwards; brown trout average ½lb; early season best.

Irvine (Ayrshire). Salmon, sea trout, trout; Irvine & Dist AA issues permits for 2m on Irvine and 3m Annick (no dt Saturdays). Irvine Water runs from estuary to Red Bridge, Dreghorn, on north bank and to Bogie Bridge on south bank. Annick Water is from confluence with Irvine to Perleton Bridge, both banks.

Dreghorn (Ayrshire). Salmon, sea trout, trout; Dreghorn AC issues st, wt and dt for 12m water on both banks of Irvine and Annick; obtainable from Alyson'S Flowers, 10 Bank Street, Irvine KA12 0AD (tel: 01294 276716); July to Sept best for salmon and sea trout. Brown trout average ½lb.

Kilmarnock (Ayrshire). Salmon, sea trout, trout. Permits for stretches on Irvine at Hurlford and Crookedholm from Torbets Outdoor Leisure, 15 Strand St, KA1 1HU (tel: 01563 541734).

GARNOCK: Trout, sea trout, salmon. Joins Irvine at harbour mouth. Its tributary is **River Lugton**.

Kilbirnie (Ayrshire). Kilbirnie AC has water on river Garnock and **Kilbirnie Loch** (brown and rainbow trout) and two reservoirs. Yearly stocking of brown trout. Kilbirnie Loch best trout: brown 9lb 2oz. Kilbirnie Loch, any legal method. St £33; dt £7. Club has excellent brown trout fishing on **Camphill Reservoir**; fly and boat only. Season holders £13 per boat per day and non-holders £20 per boat per day. Permits from Hon Sec; R T Cycles, 73 Main Rd, Glengarnock, Beith KA14 3AA (tel: 01505 682191). Tackle from R T Cycles. For other trout fisheries in vicinity *(see Greenock)*.

ANNICK: Brown trout; small runs of salmon and sea trout Sept-Oct.

Irvine (Ayrshire). Dreghorn AC issues permits for 12m of water on Irvine and Annick; permits from Ticket Sec.

Kilmaurs (Ayrshire). Kilmaurs AC has fishing on Annick and **Glazert**; sea trout and brown trout, with salmon in autumn. Other fishing: North Craig Reservoir,

Kilmaurs: Burnfoot Reservoir, Fenwick; Loch Gow, Eaglesham; permits £6, conc; st £25 (membership £20) from J Graham *(see clubs list)*.

Stewarton (Ayrshire). Stewarton AC has water on Annick and tributaries, and **White Loch; permits from Hon Sec.**

THE ISLANDS

The term 'The Islands' includes the Inner and Outer Hebrides, the Orkney and Shetland Islands and, for convenience, Kintyre. 'Visit Hebrides', Rigs Rd, Stornaway, Isle of Lewis HS1 2RF has launched a web-site: www.fishhebrides.com for detailed information.

ARRAN: In the rivers, brown trout are generally small, although fish up to 1lb have been recorded. In Aug, Sept and Oct there is often a good run of sea trout, especially in post spate conditions, along with good salmon catches, particularly in **Sliddery, Kilmory, Sannox** and **Cloy. Benlister, Chalmadale** and **Monamore** are also worth fishing under spate conditions. The Tourist Office at Brodick pier provides a free information sheet detailing all the main freshwater fishing opportunities on Arran, with charges. It also issues day and 6-day permits for various Arran AA waters. These include Kilmory, Cloy, Benlister, Monamore, Sannox, **Ashdale**, Sliddery Water and **Loch Garbad** (stocked with sizable brown trout); there is no Sunday fishing on rivers.

Machrie. Machrie Fishings consistently record excellent sea trout and salmon returns. A fine spate river which has numerous named pools extending from the sea pool for approx 3 miles. Fly water, but worming area for 2 rods. Season, 1 Jun-10 Oct, 6 rods maximum (2 per beat); enquiries should be made to Mrs Margo Wilson, 10 Leysmill, by Arbroath, Angus DD11 4RR (tel/fax: 01307 466699: 9am-5pm), or to the Water Bailiff, Riverside Cottage, Machrie 840241. No Sunday fishing.

Dougarie. The **Iorsa River** has two beats, the upper beat includes **Loch Iorsa** (with boat). A spate sea trout river, with some salmon. The lower beat stretches from Gorge Pool to Sea Pool. Catches (last 5 years) average 10 salmon, 45 sea trout. Fishing is fly only and let by the week, from £135 (June) to £145 (July-Aug), and £165 (Sept-Oct). Enquiries should be directed to The Estate Office, Dougarie, Isle of Arran KA27 8EB (tel: 01770 840259).

Blackwaterfoot. **Blackwater** offers good sea trout catches and also salmon under suitable conditions; permits are obtainable from the post office, Blackwaterfoot.

Brodick. The **Rosaburn** is now let to a local syndicate. Brodick Boat House, The Beach KA27 8AX (tel: 01770 302868): tackle and baits supplied, for fishing in Brodick Bay area; also permits from Tourist Information Centre, The Pier KA27 8AU (tel: 01770 303776).

BENBECULA: Lies between N and S Uist. Numerous lochs, giving good sea and brown trout fishing.

Balivanich. South Uist AC has brown trout fishing on all lochs on **Benbecula** and many lochs in South Uist; Benbecula. Bank fishing, wt £30, dt £6; boats on 14 lochs, £5/day: contact Hon Sec. Permits from Colin Campbell Sports Shop, PA88 5LA (tel: 01870 602236). Isle of Benbecula House Hotel, Creagorry HS7 5PG (tel: 01870 602024), has fishing for guests on seven lochs; waders useful; trout to 3lb; all within five miles of hotel. June-Sept best for brown trout and August-Sept for sea trout. Sea trout up to 8lb in sea pools.

BUTE: 5m from Ayrshire coast; 16m long and 3-5m wide. Trout and coarse fish.

Rothesay. Loch Ascog, 1½m pike, perch and roach. **Loch Quien**: 90 acres, wild and stocked browns, av 1lb, fly only. Bank fishing and 4 boats. Permits from Bute Angling & Outdoors, 9 Albert Place PA20 9AG (tel: 01700 503670); or Loch Fad office (tel: 01700 504871). **Loch Fad**, 175 acres, rainbow and brown trout fishing. Boat and bank fishing. 30 boats; booking advisable. Dt £15, OAP's £10, (juv £6); bag limits. Permits from bailiff's hut at Loch (tel: 01700 504871). All information from Loch Fad Fisheries Ltd, Loch Fad, Isle of Bute PA20 9PA (tel: 01700 504871; web: www.lochfad.com; e-mail: lochfad@btopenworld.com). Hotels: Palmyra, Ardbeg Lodge; B&B: Commodore. Sea fishing: from rocky shore popular and good; by boat from Rothesay pier.

Tighnabruaich is 25 miles from Dunoon. Kyles of Bute AC has fishing on **Loch Asgog**, brown trout, fly only; on **Upper** and **Lower Powder Dams**, brown and rainbow trout, fly only; and on **Tighna-bruaich Reservoir**, brown trout. Wt £35, dt £10, juv £5 from Kames Post Office; Kames Kabin, and Glendaruel Caravan Park. Hotels: Kames, Royal, Kyles of Bute, Kilfinan.

COLONSAY: Island of twenty eight square miles, reached by car ferry from Oban. Colonsay Fly Fishing Association was been formed in 1989 with the aim of protecting the native Colonsay brown trout loch fishing, which includes **Lochs West Fada, Mid Fada, East Fada, na Sgoltaire** and **Turamin**. The season is from mid-March to Sept 30, fishing is fly only, but children under 12 may spin. catch limit is 4 fish, sized 8" or more. Permits cost £10 per week, boats £2 per half day; contact Colonsay Estate, Argyll PA61 7YU (tel: 01951 200312) who also arrange boat hire. Isle of Colonsay Hotel, Argyll PA61 7YP (tel: 01951 200316) supplies permits to guests.

CUMBRAE: Small islands lying between Bute and Ayr coast. Largs is nearest mainland town, and there is a 10 minute ferry crossing from Calmac. **Millport**. Cumbrae AC has fly only, brown and rainbow trout fishing on two reservoirs, **Top Dam** and **Bottom Dam**. Juveniles must be accompanied by an adult and be over 12 years; permits, £10 dt and £30 wt from McFarlane's Newsagents, 2 Glasgow St; Ritz Cafe, 24 Stuart St, Millport KA28 0AJ (tel: 01475 530459). Sea fishing good from shore or boats. Tackle shops: Mapes, 4 Guildford St, Millport KA28 0AE (tel: 01475 530444); Hastie of Largs Ltd (Tackle Shop), 109 Main St, Largs KA30 8JJ (tel: 01475 673104) and hold permits for Largs & District AA. Hotel: Royal George.

HARRIS: Southern part of the island of Lewis and Harris, comprising the two distinct areas of North and South Harris. Accessible by car ferry from Ullapool, Uig in the Isle of Skye, and North Uist. Daily flights from Inverness, Edinburgh and Glasgow to Stornoway. Most of the trout, salmon and sea trout fishing in North Harris belongs to the Amhuinnsuidhe Castle Estate and is centred around Amhuinnsuidhe Castle, which is let along with the fishing on a weekly basis. There are six river systems with lochs, which all contain salmon and sea trout. For dt £80, incl boat, on Saturdays and unlet weeks, contact Roddy Macleod, Head Keeper, Laxdale Cottage, Amhuinnsuidhe HS3

3AS (tel: 01859 560232).

South Harris, Good fishing for salmon and sea trout; brown trout lochs and lochans. Near Tarbert, salmon and brown trout fishing at Ceann an Ora Fishery, on **Lochs Sgeiregan Mor, A'Mhorghain** and **Na Ciste**. Fly and bank fishing only. Further information from The Anchorage, Ardhasaig, Isle of Harris HS3 3AJ (tel: 01859 502009). Accommodation at Macleod Motel, HS3 3DG (tel: 01859 502364), with waterfront location; sea angling competitions arranged by Harris Sea AC. Borve Lodge, Borve, 7m west of Tarbert, has fishing on sea trout lochs. Day tickets sometimes obtainable. Enquire Gordon Cumming, Factor, Borve Lodge Estate Fisheries, Isle of Harris HS3 3HT (tel: 01859 550202). Finsbay Fishing, 4 Ardslave, HS3 3EY (tel: 01859 530318), has accommodation with over 100 lochs for salmon, land-locked salmon, sea trout and brown trout fly fishing, including **Lochs Humavat** and **Holmasaig** . For Finsbay, Flodabay and Stockinish Estates, contact A Mackinnon (tel: 01859 530318): interesting loch and stream fishing, bank and boat. For salmon and sea trout fishing on the **Obbe Fishings** at Leverburgh, ferox brown trout, artic char on **Loch Langavat** contact David Rankin, Keeper, at Leverburgh (tel: 01859 520466).

ISLAY: Most southern island of Inner Hebrides. Lies on west side of Sound of Islay, in Argyllshire. Greatest length is 25m and greatest breadth 19m. Sport with salmon, sea trout and trout. Hotel: Harris. **Bridgend**. Salmon and sea trout fishing on **Rivers Sorn, Laggan** and **Grey River**; all within 2m of Bridgend; fly only. Brown trout fishing on **Lochs Gorm, Finlaggan, Skerrols** and **Ardnahoe**, with boats. Also trout fishing on numerous hill lochs without boats. Self-catering accommodation from Islay Estate Office, Bridgend, Isle of Islay, Argyll PA44 7PB (tel: 0149 6810221); permits from Head Keeper (tel: 01496 810293). **Port Askaig**. Port Askaig Hotel, PA46 7RB has trout fishing nearby in **Lochs Lossit, Ballygrant** and **Allan**. Dt and boat from Dunlossit Estate Office, Knocklearach House, Ballygrant PA45 7QL (tel: 01496 840232). Sport on other lochs by arrangement. Salmon fishing in **River Laggan**. Best months: May, June and Sept. **Port Ellen**. Machrie Hotel has salmon and sea trout fishing on **R Machrie**, and **Kin-**

nabus Loch. Apply to Machrie Hotel, Port Ellen, Isle of Islay, Argyll PA42 7AN (tel: 01496 302310).

KINTYRE: This peninsula is part of Argyll and lies between Islay and Arran.

Campbeltown (Argyll). Kintyre AC has brown trout and stocked rainbow fishing on **Loch Lussa**; browns on **Ruan, Aucha Lochy, Crosshill** (including pike), and **Southend River** (small spate river, fishable Mar-Oct (best Sept/Oct); 2-wt £60, dt £12.50, covering all lochs and river), largely fly only, brown trout in all lochs, av ½lb to 1½lbs (rainbows to 5lb); permits from McGrory *(below)*. Carradale AC has fishing on **Tangy Loch**, 60 acres, trout to 2lb; access road to waters edge; permits from tackle shop. Sea fishing in harbour and **Firth of Clyde**. Permits (lochs dt £10, conc) from A P McGrory, Electrical Hardware, 16-20 Main Str, PA28 6AF (tel: 01586 552132). Hotel: White Hart; Argyll Arms, both Main St.

Carradale (Argyll). Salmon and sea-trout fishing may be had on **Carradale River**, a small spate river. Carradale Estate lease the water to Carradale AC; bait and spinner under certain conditions, otherwise fly only; club also has brown trout fishing on **Tangy Loch**, members only; for permits apply to J Semple, The Garage; Mr

William Shaw (River Keeper), 8 Toshs Park PA28 6QN (tel: 01583 431659). Hotel: Argyll Arms.

Crinan (Argyll). Near west end of Crinan Canal, brown trout lochs controlled by Lochgilphead Dist AC. Canal (trout). Permits: Fyne Tackle, 22 Argyll St, Lochgiphead PA31 8NE (tel; 01546 606878).

Lochgilphead (Mid Argyll). At east end of Crinan Canal, Forest Commission Scotland, White Gates, Lochgilphead PA31 8RS (tel: 01546 602518), has leased fishing on **Loch Coille Bhar, Cam Loch, Loch An Add, Daill Loch, Seafield Loch, Lochs Glashan, Blackmill** and **Bealach Ghearran** to Lochgilphead AC; brown trout, fly only. Lochgilphead AC lease a mile of the Add from Duntrune Castle. Members only. Duntrune Castle has 5m of **River Add**, both banks, from Kilmichael Bridge to the estuary. Salmon and sea trout; 6 holiday cottages. Dt £15 and holiday bookings from Robin Malcolm, Duntrune Castle, Kilmartin, by Lochgilphead, Argyll PA31 8QQ (tel: 01546 510283). Permits: Fyne Tackle, 22 Argyll St, Lochgiphead PA31 8NE (tel; 01546 606878).

LEWIS: Some salmon and sea trout; almost unlimited amount of wild brown trout fishing on a large number of lochs and

A sea trout fights hard in Loch Voshimid, Harris, in the Outer Hebrides. *Photo: Arthur Oglesby.*

streams, much of which is free.
Stornoway. Permits available for salmon and sea trout fishing in **River Creed** and **Lochs Clachan** and **An Ois**, approx 5m from town, cost £12 per rod, £10 for boat; now controlled by Stornoway AA *(see clubs list);* tickets from Tourist Office, Cromwell Street; Macaskills Filling Station, Cannery Rd; Lochs Services. Stornoway AA is local association, with boats on **Lochs Breulagh** and **Achmore**: permits from Sportsworld, 1-3 Francis St HS1 2XD (tel: 01851 705464). Soval AA has brown trout fishing on several lochs within easy distance of Stornoway; wt £5 if staying in Soval area and £10 if not, dt £2, from Hon Sec; and N Mackenzie, Treasurer, Tabhaigh, Keose, Lochs HS2 9JT (tel: 01851 830242). **Loch Keose**, a beautiful 90 acre loch with plentiful wild brown trout. Permits and information brochure from Murdo Morrison, Handa Guest House, 18 Keose Glebe, Lochs, Isle of Lewis HS2 9JX (tel: 01851 830334). Hotels: Caberfeidh, Caledonian. Tackle and waterproof clothing from Lewis Crofters Ltd, Island Rd, HS1 2RD (tel: 01851 702350).
Garynahine. The Garynahine Estate control all the fishing on the River Blackwater and its freshwater lochs. Salmon run from mid June to Mid October, sea trout from early April. Accom at Garynahine Lodge, Isle of Lewis HS2 9DS for parties of up to ten. Contact M MacPhail, Garynahine (tel: 01851 621314). The Grimersta Estate Ltd owns fishing on **Grimersta River** and system of lochs. Grimersta Estate holds the world record for the number of salmon caught on the same day. In 1888, Mr Naylor is recorded catching 54 salmon on the same day. The 'Grimersta System' is an integrated sytem of lochs and streams: fishing normally by the lodge week, but enquiries always welcome at estate office. The estate encourages access to the many trout lochs adjoining the main system, for which there is no charge; fly only, contact Simon Scott, Estate Office, Grimersta Lodge, Isle of Lewis HS2 9EJ (tel: 01851 621358; web: www.grimersta.com).
Uig. Salmon, sea trout and brown trout fishing on Scaliscro Estate including **Loch Langavat**. Bank and boat fishing. Permits, boat and tackle hire, and ghillies; apply to Estate Office, Scaliscro Lodge, Uig, Isle of Lewis HS2 9EL (tel: 01851 672325). Uig and Hamanavay Estate, 10

Ardroil, Uig HS2 9EU (tel: 01851 672421) offers extensive fly only salmon and sea trout fishing, with self-catering accom, on the **Hamanavay**, **Red River**; also Lochs Cragach and Fuaroil; Estate also has brown trout fishing on over 100 lochs; contact Estate Manager.
Kintarvie. The Aline Estate, on the march of Lewis and North Harris, has one salmon fishery, **Loch Tiorsdam**, plus 12 brown trout lochs and numerous lochans. Boat and bank fishing for both salmon and trout on **Loch Langavat** and trout lochs. Wild browns to 10lb have been caught in recent years, salmon are mostly grilse; Arctic char taken every year in Loch Langavat. Cottage and lodge to let. Boat and ghillie. Contact The Aline Estate, Lochs HS2 9JL (tel: 01859 502006). Further fishing contacts on Lewis are: Barvas Estate, Angus Macleod, Keeper, 01851 840267; Soval Estate, J Macleod, Keeper (tel: 01851 830223); Mike Reed, 23 Gravir, South Lochs, Lewis HS2 9QX (tel/fax: 01851 880233) who can arrange hill loch and salt water fly fishing.
MULL:
Tobermory. Salmon and sea trout fishing on **Rivers Aros** and **Bellart**. No Sunday fishing. Salmon, sea trout and brown trout fishing on **Loch Squabain**; boat fishing only. Fishing on **Torr Loch**, sea trout, wild browns; no Sunday fishing; 1 boat; banks clear. Bank and boats (3) fishing on **Loch Frisa**. Permits for all these, prices £3-£16 daily, £8-£36 weekly, depending on water and season, from Tackle & Books, 10 Main St PA75 6NU (tel: 01688 302336; fax: 01688 302140). Tobermory AA has fishing on **Mishnish Lochs**, well stocked, native brown trout only, 3 boats for hire on daily basis; and **Aros Loch**, open all year for rainbow. Dt £10 and wt £30. Boat hire: £5 for 4 hrs and £12 all day. Permits from A Brown & Son, General Merchants, 21 Main Str, PA75 6NX (tel: 01688 302020; web: www.browns-tobermory.co.uk). Fishing on **Loch Frisa**, good brown trout, some salmon and sea trout; and River Lussa. Permits from Tackle & Books *(above)* or Forestry Commission Scotland, Mull Office, Aros PA72 6JS (tel: 01680 300346). List of hotels from Tourist Office, The Pier PA75 (tel: 01688 302182).
Bunessan. Argyll Arms Hotel PA67 6DP (tel: 01681 700240) has good sea trout and brown trout fishing on **Loch Assapol**, with boats. Fly and spinner only.

RAASAY:
The Isle of Raasay is near Skye. Free trout fishing in lochs and streams; waders should be taken.

RUM:
The fishing on the Isle of Rum is all owned and managed by Scottish Natural Heritage, Reserve Office, The White House, Kinloch, Isle of Rum PH43 4RR (tel: 01687 462026). Permits to fish are required, and SNH reserves the right to restrict fishing over certain areas in the interests of successful ornithological conservation, most particularly, red throated divers. But there are always fishing opportunities in various lochs on the island, along areas at the mouth of the **Kinloch River,** mainly browns and sea trout. Access by Calmac ferry from Mallaig PH41 4QD (tel: 01687 462403).

NORTH UIST: Island in Outer Hebrides, 17m long and 3-13m broad. More water than land with over 400 named lochs and lochans, and many more unnamed, some probably unfished. Plenty of lochs by road-side for elderly or infirm anglers.

Lochmaddy. Fishing on North Uist is controlled by the North Uist Estate, Lochmaddy HS6 5AA (tel: 01876 500329; fax: 01876 500428; e-mail: northuistestate@ btinternet.com). This covers all the salmon and sea trout systems on North Uist, and comprises sixteen brown trout lochs, most of which are provided with a boat, and eleven salmon and sea trout lochs, six of which have a boat. Visitors' charges range between £20/day to £50/day for salmon and sea trout, and £6/day brown trout; North Uist AC has water. Salmon and sea trout fishing is available to guests staying at the Lochmaddy Hotel, Isle of North Uist HS6 5AA (tel: 01876 500331; fax: 01876 500210; web: www.lochmaddyhotel.co uk; e-mail info@lochmaddyhotel.co.uk); residents have the first option. Non residents day tickets cost from £30 to £50 per rod per day, depending on season; ghillies on premises. Brown trout fishing costs visitors £20 weekly, or £6 daily, bank only, plus £15 per day boat hire. All permits obtainable from the Lochmaddy Hotel (brown trout fishing free to hotel guests). Langass Lodge Hotel, Locheport HS6 5HA (tel: 01876 580285) also has fishing. North Uist AC offers brown trout permits for the Newton Estate waters, comprising numerous lochs with boats on 5 of them; st £50, wt £25 and dt £5, from L Coleman, Clachan Stores, Clachan, North Uist HS6 5HD

Garynahine Lodge, famous with fishermen, is part of the backdrop for the angler fishing the Blackwater.

(tel: 01876 580257); also for North Uist AC permits on Balranald Estate. Other North Uist accommodation: Lochportain House, Lochmaddy HS6 5AS (tel: 0131 4479911), self catering; Sealladh Traigh, Claddach Kirkibost (tel: 01876 580248).

SOUTH UIST:

Bornish. South Uist AC has trout fishing on many lochs in South Uist and all lochs on **Benbecula.** Bank fishing, wt £30, dt £6; boats on 14 lochs, £5 p/day: contact Hon Sec. Permits from Campbell's Sports Shop, Balivanish; Creagorry PO, Creagorry; Daliburgh PO. For South Uist Estates fishing, contact Captain J Kennedy, c/o South Uist Estates, Askernish, HS8 5SY (tel: 01878 710366).

Lochboisdale. Permits for brown trout fishing on many lochs; sea trout and salmon fishing may also be open. Contact Captain J Kennedy, c/o South Uist Estates, Askernish, HS8 5SY (tel: 01878 710366).

ORKNEY

While sea fishing for skate, ling, halibut (British record), haddock, cod, etc, is general in waters about Orkney, good fun may be had in the evenings with saithe comparatively close to the shores.

Trout fishing is prolific, there are a multitude of lochs which hold excellent stocks of wild brown trout, and sea trout also are present in small numbers. **Loch of Harray** is the most famous and will produce fish from the first day of the season to the last, with May, June and July the best months. **Boardhouse Loch** in Birsay is ideal for the visiting angler as there are no skerries and the fish average three quarters of a pound. The best months to fish at Boardhouse are May, June, and early July. **Loch of Swanney**, again in Birsay, is another favourite with visiting local anglers, with the best months being May and June. The **Loch of Stenness** is a challenge, connected to the sea, it is partly tidal. Native brown trout and sea trout thrive in this environment, growing big and strong on the abundant marine life. The **Loch of Skaill** in Sandwick should also be mentioned as it holds specimen trout, with fish averaging two pounds. The lochs on the islands of Sanday, Westray and Stronsay also contain a number of very large trout.

The Orkney Trout Fishing Association is a non-profit making voluntary body, dedicated to the preservation and enhancement of game fishing throughout the islands of Orkney. The Association operates a trout hatchery. Restocking has yielded excellent results, notably in the Loch of Swannay. Membership is £20, visitors season £15, OAP, jun and disabled season £10. Membership entitles anglers to use Assn facilities, which include access to fishing on **Loch of Skaill**. Subscriptions are accepted at Orkney Tourist Board Office, Kirkwall; C J Paterson, Bridge St, Kirkwall; Merkister Hotel (*see below*); W S Sinclair, Tackle Shop, Stromness. Further information from OTFA Hon Sec, Malcolm Russell, Caolila, Heddle Rd, Finstown, Orkney (tel: 01856 761586). *A Trout Fishing Guide to Orkney* by Stan Headley is on sale at most newsagents and booksellers in Orkney.

There is good quality accommodation throughout Orkney and there are taxi services to fishing waters. The Merkister Hotel, Loch Harray KW17 2LF (tel: 01856 771366; fax: 01856 771515; e-mail: merkister-hotel@ecosse.net) is close to Loch of Harray (now the best of the Orkney Lochs) and offers excellent loch fishing: boats, incl for disabled, outboards, ghillies. The Standing Stones Hotel, Stenness KW16 3JX (tel: 01856 850449) is fully licensed, and can provide boats, outboards, ghillies; the hotel is situated on the shores of Loch of Stenness and is also convenient for the Loch of Harray; while Smithfield Hotel KW17 2HT (tel: 01856 771 215) is convenient for the Lochs of Boardhouse, Hundland and Swanney.

SHETLAND

Shetland was formerly renowned for its sea trout fishing, but for a variety of reasons this fishing has now drastically declined and anglers are recommended to concentrate on the excellent wild brown trout fishing in over three hundred lochs containing trout up to five pounds in weight.

Taking the Shetland Islands as a group, the majority of the fishing is controlled by the Shetland Anglers Association, who charge a fee of £20 per season, £5 per day for unlimited fishing, juniors free. Boats are bookable on five of the best lochs at an all-in fee of £20. Details of all fishing and permits are obtainable from Rod and Line Tackle shop, Harbour Street, Lerwick, and also from the Association secretary, Alec Miller, 55 Burgh Rd, Lerwick,

Shetland ZE1 0HJ (tel: 01595 695903 (day); 01595 696025 (evngs); fax: 01595 696568). The Association publishes a comprehensive local guide covering over two hundred trout lochs. There are now several hotels specialising in catering for anglers, and among the best are Herrislea Hotel, Tingwall; Baltasound Hotel, Baltasound, Unst.

SKYE

Trout and salmon fishing generally preserved. Sea trout especially good in places. Excellent sea fishing.

Dunvegan. Numerous streams in area can be very good for sea trout in May and June. Hotels: Atholl House; Misty Isle.

Sleat. Brown trout and Arctic char fishing on a number of small rivers and lochs in the South of Skye. St £50, wt available; dt £7.50-£10; ghillies £10/hour; £5 rod hire: from Hotel Eilean Iarmain, An t-Eilean, Sgiathanach IV43 8QR (tel: 01471 833266). Tackle shop: Dunvegan Sports and Tackle, 46 Kilmuir, Dunvegan IV55 8WA (tel: 01470 521730); The Gun & Tackle Room, Unit 4 Shopping Centre, Dunvegan IV55 1AA (tel: 01470 521535).

Portree. The **Storr Lochs** called **Fada** and **Leathan** are 4m away, and have good brown trout (average 1lb, occasionally 5lb). Bank fishing; 10 boats. Mid-May to mid-June and early Sept best. Permits for these and other hill lochs from Jansport (*below*). The Portee AA controls all river fishing in the area, except south bank of **R Lealt.** Lealt is most productive of these; also **Kilmuluag, Kilmartin,** and **Brogaig** Rivers, small spate streams with the odd sea trout and salmon, suitable for fly, small spinner and worm. Dt £10 for R Kilmaluig, Kilmartin, Brogaig; half-dt R Lealt (north bank) £10; loch bank dt £8 from Jansport (*below*). Bag limit 6/day. One Wheelyboat on Storr Lochs for disabled. Enquiries to Hon Sec, Portree AA. Also sea fishing, for pollack and saithe in harbour. Tackle shop: Jansport, Wentworth Street, Somerled Square, Portree

View from Old Man of Storr overlooking Loch Leathan (Storr Lochs) and down the Sound of Raasay to the Cuillin Hills. *Photo: Stephen Tinney.*

IV51 9EH (tel: 01478 612559; web: www.jans.co.uk/jansport). Hotel: Cuillin Hills.

Skeabost. Skeabost Country House Hotel, Skeabost Bridge, Isle of Skye IV51 9NP (tel: 01470 532202) has salmon and sea trout fishing (8m double bank) on **River Snizort**, reputed to be the best salmon river on Skye, and trout fishing; dt £20, and free fishing for three-day residents.

Sligachan. Sligachan Hotel IV47 8SW (tel: 01478 650204) currently issues permits at £10 for salmon and sea trout fishing in 2m **Sligachan River**, and brown trout fishing in **Loch na-Caiplaich**, now heavily re-eeded; salmon few, sea trout quite plentiful; best months, mid-July to end Sept. Brown trout fishing by arrangement in Storr Lochs (15m); boats for hire; season, May to end Sept. No permit is required for brown trout fishing in **Loch Marsco**.

Broadford. Sea trout and salmon in the **Broadford River**. 1½m south bank, fishing permits £5 from Broadford Hotel IV49 9AB (tel: 01471 822204). **Loch Sguabaidh** and **Lochan Stratha Mhor**, brown trout, sea trout, occasional salmon, permits £10 from Andrew Campbell, "Am Bothon", Torrin IV49 9BA (tel: 01471 822717).

Staffin. Salmon, sea trout, brown trout. Portree AA hold the fishing rights. Tickets from Jansport, Wentworth Street, Somerled Square, Portree IV51 9EH (tel: 01478 612559; web: www.jans.co.uk/jansport); dt rivers £10, lochs £8.

Struan. Ullinish Lodge Hotel, IV56 8FD (tel: 01470 572214) has salmon, sea trout and brown trout fishing in three lochs (Connan, Duagrich and Ravag) and on **Rivers Ose** and **Snizort**; £10 for loch fishing, special rates for residents of hotel; residents only on Loch Ravag; **Glen Brittle**: Permits £10 for salmon and trout in River Brittle (in spate).

LOCHY (including Nevis and Coe)

Drains Loch Lochy and, after joining the Spean at Mucomir, flows about 8m to salt water in Loch Linnhe close to Fort William. Very good salmon and sea trout river but affected by hydro works at Falls of Mucomir. Best months: July, August and Sept. Whole river is on weekly lets only. Further information from River Lochy Association, c/o Jon Gibb, Drimsallie Mill, Glenfinnan, PH37 4LT (tel: 01397 722355; web: http://mysite.freeserve.com/river lochy2004).

Tributaries of the Lochy
SPEAN: Fed mainly by River Roy and other minor streams. A rocky river with good holding pools. Good fishing for salmon from May to October.

Spean Bridge (Inverness-shire). No river fishing available; for **Lochs Arkaig** (browns) and **Lochy**; and a further seven wild brown lochs, contact tackle shop. Tackle shop: Kingdom of Scotland (Tourist Information) PH34 4EP (tel: 01397 712812).

ROY (tributary of Spean): Salmon. A spate river; fishes best July onwards.

Roy Bridge (Inverness-shire). Lower half let to Roy Bridge AC; contact Brian Strachan (tel: 01397 712607). Roy Bridge AC has fishing on **Loch na Turk**; stocked rainbow trout; apply to Hon Sec.

NEVIS: A short river flowing around south side of Ben Nevis and entering Loch Linnhe at Fort William, not far from mouth of Lochy. Very good salmon and sea trout fishing. Tackle shop: Rod & Gun Shop, 18 High St Fort William PH33 6AT (tel: 01397 702656) has tickets for river: dt £10; fly and worm only.

Fort William (Inverness-shire). River Nevis; salmon, grilse, sea trout. Fort William AA has about 6m; wt £30, dt £10, conc, from tackle shop after 9am on day required; no spinning; best June onwards. Good brown trout fishing on **Loch Lundavra** 6m from town. Dt £15 boat; £3 bank; from Mrs A MacCallum, Lundavra Farm, Fort William PH33 6SZ (tel: 01397 702582). For **Loch Arkaig** dt £5, £15 2-rods plus boat; and **Loch Lochy** (free) rainbow trout and brown trout and pike. Permits from West Highland Estates, 33 High St. Tackle shop: Rod & Gun Shop, 18 High St PH33 6AT (tel: 01397 702656; www.fortwilliamfishing.com). Hotels: Imperial, Grand, Alexandra, West End, Milton.

COE. River flows through Glen Coe to enter **Loch Leven** and from there into **Loch Linnhe**. Salmon, sea trout and brown trout.

Glencoe (Argyll). The National Trust for Scotland have stopped issuing tickets on their stretches of R Coe till stocks recover. Contact Ballahulish Tourist IC, PH49 4JB (tel: 01855 811866) for further information. Brown and rainbow trout fishing on **Loch Achtriochtan**. Scorrybreac Guest House, Glencoe PH49 4HT (tel/fax: 01855 811354; e-mail: info@ scorrybreac.co.uk) supplies disabled anglers a gate key to enable vehicle access to **Glencoe Lochan**, nr Glencoe Village. Rainbow trout, restocked monthly, April to Sept. Tackle shop: The Arches, Loan Fern, Ballachulish PH49 4JB (tel: 01855 811111).

LOSSIE

Drains Loch Trevie and flows about 25m to the Moray Firth at Lossiemouth. A good trout stream; salmon runs improving, July onwards. Provides good sport with sea trout from June onwards, especially near estuary.

Lossiemouth (Moray). Salmon, sea trout. Elgin & Dist AA has water; estuary and sea; salmon, sea trout and finnock. Permits and information on other fishings from tackle shops in Elgin and Lossiemouth.

Elgin (Moray). Elgin & Dist AA has water on Lossie at Elgin (salmon, sea trout and brown trout) and **Loch Park** fishings (brown trout). Trout fishing can be had on the District Council's Millbuies Estate: **Glenlatterach Reservoir**, brown trout, boats on site; bank fishing dt £5.50; st £32, conc; boat: dt £13.50 (single angler in boat), £9.50 each for two, conc (no bag limit, but anglers are urged to operate a 'catch and kill' policy to reduce the numbers of undersized fish, thus improving remaining stock); **Loch of Blairs**, stocked rainbows, boat fishing only, and **Millbuies Loch**, mainly rainbow trout, also boat fishing only. Boat: dt £13.50 (single angler in boat), £9.50 each for two, conc; both lochs, 6 fish limit, 10in min. Permits: for Millbuies and Glenlatterach from The Warden, Millbuies Lochs, Longmorn, Elgin (tel: 01343 860234); for Blairs: Fishing Tackle Shop, 97d High St, Forres IV36 0AA (tel: 01309 672936). Tackle shop: The Tackle Shop, 188 High Str, IV30 1BA (tel: 01343 543129); tickets for R Lossie. Info from Moray Council, Department of Environmental Services, High Str, Elgin IV30 1BX (tel: 01343 543451). Hotels: Mansefield House; Mansion House.

Sunny and calm. Sally Mortimer took this picture of Glencoe Lochan: rainbow trout in prospect.

LUNAN

Rises near Forfar and flows about 13m to Lunan Bay in the North Sea between Arbroath and Montrose. Some good trout. Sea trout and finnock in July to October. Stocked with brown trout. A protection order now in force requiring all anglers to be in possession of proper permits, obtainable through Arbroath AC.

Arbroath (Angus). Lunan and its tributary, the **Vinney**, about 8m of water, leased to Arbroath AC by riparian owners; restocked each year, holds good head of brown trout, also sea trout and occasional salmon; bag limit 4 fish; river mouth, sea trout and salmon; st £28, juv £10, OAP's £14; dt £6, £3: specify mouth or upstream; permits from Work and Leisure Wear, 2 Marketgate, Arbroath DD11 1AY (tel: 01241 431134). Good sea fishing; local sea angling trips daily.

Forfar (Angus). Canmore AC (members of Strathmore Angling Improvement Association) have trout fishing on **River Dean**, fly only; **Cruick; R Kerbet**, fly only; Club also hold rights for **Den of Ogil Reservoir**, boat and bank fishing for brown trout; **R Isla**; and **Forfar Loch**. All Canmore AC permits from W Hardy Tackle Shop (below). Rescobie Loch Development Assn runs **Rescobie Loch**, 200 acres, 3m E of Forfar; a Troutmaster loch with boat and bank fishing to rainbows and browns; st £175, dt £12, 4 fish limit, OAP £130; juv £40; boats - all sessions 1 rod £4, 2-3 rods £6; from Rescobie Boathouse, Clocksbriggs, Montrose Rd by Forfar (tel: 01307 830367). Tackle Shop: W Hardy, 153 East High St DD8 2EQ (tel: 01307 466635); G Carroll, Tackle, 15 Church St, Brechin DD9 6HB (tel: 01356 625700).

NAIRN

Rises in Monadhliath Hills and flows about 36m to Moray Firth at Nairn. Salmon, sea trout, finnock and brown trout.

Nairn (Nairnshire). Tickets for the lower reaches (estuary to Cantray Bridge, approx 6½m) can be had from Nairn AA; salmon and sea trout. Best months: July to September for salmon. Visitors permits £75 weekly, £20.00 day, conc for juv, from Pat Fraser, 41 High St, Nairn IV12 4AG (tel: 01667 453038). Clava Lodge Holiday Homes, Culloden Moor, by Inverness IV2 5EJ (tel: 01463 790228), also issues permits for 1¼m stretch on Nairn. Dt £7 (free to residents). **Lochs Lochindorb, Allan**, and **Loch-an-Tutach** privately owned; brown trout; dt and boat. 2m east of **Nairn** on A96 road, Boath House, Auldearn, Nairn IV12 5TE; rainbow trout fishing on lake, telephone bookings (tel: 01667 454896; fax: 01667 455469); dt £10-£18. Newton Hotel, Inverness Rd, IV12 4RX (tel: 01667 453144) and Golf View Hotel, 63 Seabank Rd, IV12 4HD (tel: 01667 452301) both have river and loch fishing by arrangement. Tackle shop: J Graham & Co, 37-39 Castle St, Inverness IV2 3EA (tel: 01463 233178).

NAVER (including Borgie and Loch Hope)

Drains Loch Naver and flows about 24m to north coast at Naver Bay. The Borgie, which also debouches into Naver Bay, drains Loch Slaim and has course of about 7m. Both are good salmon and sea trout rivers; all preserved, but beats can be arranged, usually for weekly periods.

Altnaharra (Sutherland). Altnaharra Hotel, Lairg, Sutherland IV27 4UE (tel/fax: 01549 411222), which specializes in catering for fishermen, provides fishing in **Loch Naver, Loch Hope** and **Loch Loyal**; salmon, sea trout and brown trout; fishing in a number of lochs; all lochs have boats and are close to the road. Some are open to non-residents. Dt £38 to £57. No bank fishing; fly only. Hotel also has fishing on **River Mudale**. Hotel supplies tackle and has drying room; and provides outboard motors, tuition and accommodation.

Tongue (Sutherland). Three limited day tickets for quality salmon fishing on **River Naver** from The Store, Bettyhill, by Thurso, Caithness KW14 7SS (tel: 01641 521207; fax: 01641 521426). Fly only, dt £20; 2 fish limit salmon, grilse. Tickets also for **Loch Duinte**. Free fishing on the Bettyhill side of **Lochs**

Meadie, More, Ghanu, Cool, all brown trout. Salmon and sea trout fishing on **Loch Hope**. Tongue Dist AA (HQ at Ben Loyal Hotel - *see below*) has brown trout fishing on several lochs; fly only. Boats on **Lochs Loyal, Cormach, Craggie, Bealach na Sgeulachd,** and Lochan **Hakel, Bhuoaidh, Kyle of Tongue.** Ghillie by arrangement. St £20, wt £15, dt £5 from hotel: drying room and freezer space at hotel: Kyle of Tongue estuary also assn water; excellent sea trout when shoals are running; fly or spinner. Permits from local hotels, post office and general store. Ben Loyal Hotel also has a rotating beat

on s end of **Loch Hope**; dt £50 boat and 2 rods. For **R Borgie** private beats, Mar-Sept, fly only, contact Peter MacGregor, Borgie Lodge Hotel *(see below)*. Salmon fishing £380-£450 incl VAT, brown trout dt £5. Hotel has brown trout fishing on 20 lochs, with salmon in three, boats on three at £20 hire, spinning and worm permitted on some. Hotel runs fishing packages with ghillie and all other facilities, and is HQ of Borgie Angling Club. Hotels: Borgie Lodge, Skerray by Tongue KW14 7TH (tel: 01641 521231); Ben Loyal, Tongue IV27 4XE (tel: 01847 611216).

NESS

Drains Loch Ness and flows to Moray Firth at Inverness. Notable salmon and sea trout river. Best July to October.

Inverness (Inverness-shire). Salmon, sea trout, brown trout. Inverness AC has stretch from estuary upstream for about 3¾m, both banks; no Sunday fishing; permits £20 per day or £90 weekly, conc, from tackle shops, or Tourist Board. **Loch Ruthven,** brown trout; fly only; boat only; permits from J Graham & Co, 37-39 Castle St, Inverness IV2 3EA (tel:

01463 233178); and A Humfrey, Balvoulin, Aberarder IV2 6UA (tel: 01808 521283). Sunday fishing permitted. **Loch Choire,** brown trout; fly only; permits from A Humfrey *(see above)*. Sea trout fishing on North Kessock sea shore; permits from North Kessock PO; and J Graham & Co *(see above)*. Tourist Information Centre: Castle Wynd, IV2

Many hoteliers and others providing accommodation offer free or reduced-cost fishing to guests. Here the Clava Lodge beat, Horseshoe Pool of River Nairn shows what this may amount to.

3BJ (tel: 01463 234353; fax: 01463 710 609; web www.highlandfreedom.com), issues permits and local fishing information. Hotels: Glen Mhor; Loch Ness House.

LOCH NESS: Sea trout at Dochfour and Aldourie; salmon, especially out from Fort Augustus and where **Rivers Moriston** and **Foyers** enter the loch. Brown trout all round the margins. Boats and boatmen from hotels at Fort Augustus, Drumnadrochit, Foyers, Lewiston and Whitbridge.

Dochgarroch (Inverness-shire). For fishing for rainbow trout on **Loch Abban**; dt £20 (with other price ranges (by hours and number of fish taken); permits from J Graham & Co, 37-39 Castle St, Inverness IV2 3EA (tel: 01463 233178).

Drumnadrochit (Inverness). Salmon and brown trout. **Loch Meiklie,** brown trout, fly only.

Foyers (Inverness). Foyers Hotel, IV2 6XT (tel/fax: 01456 486216; web: foyershotel.

co.uk; e-mail: info@foyershotel.co.uk) has salmon and brown trout fishing on Loch Ness. Boats and ghillie service. Several other lochs may also be fished, including **Loch Mhor**.

Invermoriston (Inverness). **River Moriston** enters Loch Ness here. An early river, best February to June. Permits for river and trout fishing on hill lochs from Glenmoriston Lodge Estate Office, River Cottage, Invermoriston IV63 7YA (tel: 01320 351300; fax: 01320 351301); also salmon fishing by boat on **Loch Ness**.

Fort Augustus (Inverness). Salmon and brown trout. Salmon season opens Jan 15. Trout season, March 15. Brown trout fishing on **Loch Quoich**; permits and boats from Lovat Arms Hotel PH32 4BE (tel 01320 366206). Salmon fishing on **Loch Oich** (all left bank (4m); dt £20, from J Graham & Co, 37-39 Castle St, Inverness IV2 3EA (tel: 01463 233178). Other hotels: Caledonian, Brae, Inchnacardoch.

Tributaries of Loch Ness

FOYERS. Free brown trout fishing.

Foyers (Inverness-shire). **Loch Mhor,** 18m from Inverness, is 4m long by ½m broad, and contains trout averaging ½lb. Outlet from loch enters Loch Ness via River Foyers. Accommodation 2½m from loch at Whitebridge Hotel, Whitebridge, Inverness IV2 6UN (tel: 01456 486226), who have tackle for purchase or hire, and boats (£20 per day), fishing: **Loch Ruthven** can be fished, also **River Fechlin**.

Whitebridge (Inverness). Whitebridge Hotel *(see above)* has boats for use of guests on **Loch Knockie** and **Loch Bran;** brown trout; fly only. Arrangements also made for guests wishing to troll on Loch Ness. River and burns dried out in course of hydro-electric development.

MORISTON: Salmon, brown trout.

Glenmoriston (Inverness-shire). Glenmoriston Lodge Estate Office, River Cottage, Invermoriston IV63 7YA (tel: 01320 351300; fax: 01320 351301) has fishing rights on Loch Ness, salmon and brown trout; R Moriston, salmon and brown trout; and **Glenmoriston Hill Lochs,** brown trout. *(See Invermoriston.)* **Loch Cluanie,** brown trout. No Sunday fishing.

OICH and GARRY: Garry rises in loch SW of Loch Quoich and runs into that loch at western end, thence to Lochs Poulary, Inchlaggan and Garry. Good salmon

and trout river. Outlet to Loch Garry dammed by North of Scotland Hydro-Electric Board. At Loch Poulary are fish traps; at Invergarry, a hatchery. River Oich good salmon fishing from opening day 15 January; brown trout from 15 March.

Invergarry (Inverness): Upper Garry, **Lochs Quoich, Poulary, Inchlaggan** and **Garry.** Loch Quoich holds good brown trout and Loch Garry holds excellent Arctic char; both lochs hold char. Salmon only good July onwards, closing mid-Oct. Boats on all lochs and some of pools of Upper Garry from Tomdoun Hotel *(see below).* Peter H Thomas, Caberfeidh, Kingie, Glengarry, PH35 4HS (tel: 01809 511232) has boats on Lochs Garry and Inchlaggan for salmon, trout, char and pike. Also dinner, B&B. Excellent early spring fishing on both banks of R Garry (now syndicate water) and salmon fishing on Loch Oich. Tomdoun Hotel issues permits for **Lochs Quoich, Poulary, Inchlaggan,** and **Upper River Garry** (which is reserved for hotel guests only); trout, char and pike. Boat fishing only on Quoich. On the lochs, fly-fishing and spinning for large brown trout; fly-fishing only for wild brown trout on the river. Bank fishing only on **Loch Loyne.** Boats from hotel for all waters except

Loyne. Apply to Michael Pearson, Tomdoun Hotel, Invergarry, Inverness-shire PH35 4HS (tel: 01809 511218; web: www.tomdoun-sporting-lodge.com/fishing).

NITH

Rises on south side of Ayr watershed and flows south and east to Solway, which it enters by an estuary with Dumfries at its head. Is the largest and best known river in the Dumfries and Galloway region and has established a reputation for the quality of its salmon and sea trout which continue to improve. Carries a good head of small trout.

New Abbey (Dumfries-shire). New Abbey AA has 2m on a small tributary of Nith; occasional salmon, good sea trout and herling, and stocked with brown trout and rainbow trout. St £12; dt £3, conc available from Criffel Inn, 2 The Square, DG2 8BX (tel: 01387 850305). Hotels: Criffel Inn *(see above)*; Abbey Arms, 1 The Square DG2 8BX (tel: 01387 850489).

Dumfries (Dumfries & Galloway). Dumfries Common Good Fishing, 3m on Nith, 1½m on **Cairn** (tributary); salmon, sea trout, brown trout and grayling; best, March-May and Sept-Nov. Visitors st £227, wt £119, dt £33. Reductions for residents, OAP, juveniles, from Dumfries & Galloway Council, 52-60 Queensberry Street, Dumfries DG1 1BF (tel: 01387 260739; fax 01387 260799), and from Tourist Board, 64 Whitesands, DG1 2RS. Dumfries & Galloway AA has 3m on Nith and 16m on Cairn; salmon, sea trout and brown trout. Fly fishing anytime; spinning and bait fishing restricted to water level. Daily and weekly tickets; no daily tickets on Saturday. Concessions for juniors. Permits from D McMillan *(below)*.

Glenkiln Reservoir (trout) controlled by West of Scotland Water Authority, Director of Water and Sewage, Marchmount House, Marchmount, Dumfries DG1 1PW (tel: 0141 227 6500); dt (bank); boats on site; bank fishing free to OAP and disabled residents. Tackle shops: D McMillan, 6 Friars Vennel DG1 2RN (tel: 01387 252075); Pattie's of Dumfries, 109 Queensberry St, Dumfries DG1 1BH (tel: 01387 252891).

Jericho Loch, rainbow and brown trout; fly only; bank fishing only. Visitors dt £13; Jericho Loch Flyfishers: members dt £7, conc; available from Tourist Information Centre, 64 Whitesands, Dumfries DG1 2RS (tel: 01387 253862). Tackle shops: D McMillan, 6 Friars Vennel, Dumfries DG1 2RN (tel: 01387 252075); Pattie's of Dumfries, 109 Queensberry St, Dumfries DG1 1BH (tel: 01387 252891). Locharbriggs

Thornhill (Dumfriesshire). Mid Nithsdale AA has 3½m on Nith and tributary **Scaur**; salmon, sea trout and brown trout; Assn also has brown and rainbow trout fishing on **Kettleton Loch** 4m NE of Thornhill, 40 acres; advanced booking for autumn fishing; tickets from Pets Larder, 101-2 Drumlanrig Street, Thornhill DG3 5LU (tel: 01848 331266) (closed pm Thurs and Sat). Drumlanrig Castle Fishing on the Queensberry Estate offers salmon and sea trout fishing on River Nith, 7m, largely both banks, 4 beats; Lochs **Morton Castle, Starburn, Slatehouse, Coldstream** and **Farthingbank**, rainbow and brown trout: fly only on lochs, preferred on river; and **Morton Pond** and **Dabton**, coarse fish. Accommodation at Auchenknight Cottage and Holmhill on estate. Apply to The Estate Manager, Buccleuch Estates Ltd, Drumlanrig Mains, Thornhill, Dumfriesshire DG3 4AG (tel: 01848 600283; fax: 01848 600244; web: www.buccleuch.com). Barjarg Estate has stretch on Nith; salmon, grilse, sea trout, brown trout and grayling. Daily or weekly permits until end August; normally weekly from Sept to end Nov. Apply to Andrew Hunter-Arundel, Newhall, Auldgirth, Dumfriesshire DG2 0TN (tel: 01848 331342). **Loch Ettrick** near Closeburn DG3 5HL, 32 acre loch, well stocked with rainbow and brown trout. Hotels: Buccleuch, George, Elmarglen.

Sanquhar (Dumfries & Galloway). Upper Nithsdale AC has approx 11m of Nith; and stretches on tributaries **Kello, Crawick, Euchan** and **Mennock**. Salmon, sea trout, brown trout and grayling. No Sunday fishing, Saturdays must be booked in advance. Reduced membership charge for resident juveniles; and Forsyth Shield presented each year in Jan to resident boy for heaviest fish caught. Permits from K McLean Esq, Solicitor, 61 High Street, Sanquhar DG4 6DT (tel: 01659 50241); also dt for grayling fishing, Jan and Feb. Hotels: Nithsdale; Glendyne;

Blackaddie House.

New Cumnock (Ayrshire). New Cumnock AA has brown trout fishing on River Nith, **Afton Water** and **Afton Reservoir**; and on parts of **Rivers Deugh** and **Ken**, and **Carsphairn Lane Burn**. Assn also has grayling fishing on River Nith and rainbow trout fishing on **Creoch Loch**; Creoch Loch closed end Nov to 16 Mar; contact Hon Sec for tickets. Hotels: Lochside House, Cumnock KA18 4PN (tel: 01290 333000); Crown.

OYKEL (including Carron, Cassley, Shin and Loch Ailsh)

Rises at Benmore Assynt, flows through Loch Ailsh and thenc e 14m to enter the Kyle of Sutherland at Rosehall. Excellent salmon and sea trout fishing. The Lower Oykel has produced an average catch of over 780 salmon in recent years.

Oykel Bridge (Sutherland). Lower reaches fish very well for salmon early on and good grilse and sea trout run usually begins in the latter half of June. Loch Ailsh. Good sea and brown trout fishing with occasional salmon. Best months **Lower Oykel**, March to September. **Upper Oykel** and **Loch Ailsh**, mid-June to September. Inver Lodge Hotel has salmon and trout fishing on Oykel. Contact Inver Lodge Hotel, Iolaire Rd, Lochinver IV27 4LU (tel: 01571 844496; fax: 01571 844395) which has beats 1 & 2 on Upper Oykel.

CASSLEY: Some 10m long, river is divided at Rosehall into upper and lower Cassley by Achness Falls. Below falls fishing starts early. Upper Cassley fishes well from May to Sept. Sea trout July and Aug.

Rosehall (Sutherland). Upper Cassley River, right bank; tickets from £65 to £300 (depending on beat and time of year). Sole agents: Bell-Ingram, Estate Office, Bonar Bridge, Ardgay, IV24 3AE (tel: 01863 766683). Hotel: Achness House.

SHIN (Loch Shin and Kyle of Sutherland): Loch Shin is largest fresh water loch in Sutherland, 16m long. Brown trout in loch av ½lb, but very large fish taken early in season. Outlet from Loch Shin controlled by hydro-electric works. River flows about 7m and empties into Kyle of Sutherland at Invershin. Salmon fishing privately let.

Lairg (Sutherland). Lairg AC has trout fishing in Loch Shin and hill lochs, including **Loch Beannach** (brown trout, 5m from Lairg, ½m walk). Loch Shin, brown trout including ferox up to 12lbs. Competitions held on Loch Shin (9 club boats available) throughout the season (1May to 30 Sept) - details from club hut at loch side. St from Hon Sec; wt for L Shin, and dt, juv conc from local tackle shop. Boats (only) for hire on hill lochs of **Dola**, **Craggie** and **Tigh na Creig**, wild browns; fly only; ghillies by arrangement: from Park House Sporting, Lairg, Sutherland IV27 4AU (tel: 01549 402208; fax: 01549 402693; web: www.fishinscotland.net/parkhouse); best start of May to end of Sept; who also have fishing on Upper and Lower Shin, and Cassley, Brora and Carron. Overscaig Hotel, on shore of **Loch Shin**, has boats there, and also on **Lochs A' Ghriama** and **Merkland**. Many hill lochs within walking distance. Hotel ghillies, advice and instruction. Large brown trout caught on hotel waters in recent years. Fishing free to residents. Boats with o/b motors. For further information contact Overscaig Lochside Hotel, Loch Shin, by Lairg IV27 4NY (tel: 01549 431203). There are usually facilities for sea trout and salmon fishing on **Lochs Stack** and **More**. Tackle shop: Sutherland Sporting Co, Main St IV27 4DB (tel: 01549 402229).

DORNOCH FIRTH:

Dornoch (Sutherland). At entrance to Firth. Permits from Dornoch AA; brown trout on **Lochs Lannsaidh** (boat £15/day, bank £7.50; additional rod £5), **Buidhe**, **Laoigh**, **Lagain**, **Laro** and **Cracail Mor**; boat £15 per day and £5 bank on Buidhe, Laoigh and Lagain; assn has also acquired salmon, sea trout and brown trout fishing on **Loch Brora**; boat only, £15 per day, also rover tickets; fly only on lochs; no Sunday fishing. Permits from Tourist Information Centre, Main Str, IV25 3SD (tel: 01862 810400). Royal Golf Hotel, The 1st Tee, IV25 3LG (tel: 01862 810283) has river and loch fishing by arrangement. Other hotels: Burghfield House, IV19 1AB; Dornoch Castle, IV18 3SD; Skibo Castle, Clashmore, IV25 3RQ.

The Borgie is one of the northernmost salmon rivers in Britain - well known for its spring run. *Photo: Arthur Oglesby.*

KYLE OF DURNESS

Durness (Sutherland). Cape Wrath Hotel IV27 4SW (tel: 01971 511212) at Keoldale has good salmon and sea trout fishing on Rivers Dionard **Grudie** and **Dall**, and the Kyle of Durness. Big brown trout in **Lochs Calladale, Crosspool, Lanish,** and **Borralaidh** - well-conditioned fish of 8lbs in weight have been taken (largest catch 2003 $7\frac{1}{2}$lb) - and there are several lochs, three with boats. Lochs and rivers stocked with salmon, sea trout, brown trout fry. Hotel open throughout year. Apply to hotel.

SCOURIE (Lochs Stack and More)

Scourie (Sutherland). Excellent centre for sea trout, brown trout and salmon fishing. About 300 trout lochs. Scourie Hotel has extensive fishing rights on over 250; four with salmon and sea trout. Boats on many. Ghillies may also be hired. Dt varies between £5 and £60, depending on season and lochs; boats up to £35; ghillie £45. Days on **Loch Stack** and **Loch More** open to guests during July, Aug and Sept. Salmon, sea trout (good), brown trout. For further information apply to Patrick and Judy Price, Scourie Hotel, Scourie, by Lairg IV27 4SX (tel: 01971 502396). Scourie & Dist AC has rights on 33 lochs to N of village and 2 lochs S; trout around $\frac{1}{2}$lb mark, but some larger fish; wt £16; dt £4 (boat £4 extra) from Hon Sec.

SHIEL (Argyll/Inverness-shire) (including Moidart and Loch Shiel)

Short salmon river, only about 3m long, draining Loch Shiel. Moidart is a good spate river with excellent holding pools. Loch Shiel is fed by four major rivers, **Slatach, Finnan, Callop** and **Alladale**, which all tend to be spate rivers. Fishing in the loch has been poor of late.

Acharacle (Argyll). River preserved. **Loch Shiel**, 17m long, holds salmon and sea trout, and a few brown trout. No bank fishing. Boats for Loch Shiel from Loch Shiel Hotel PH36 4JL (tel: 01967 431224). The Ardnamurchan Peninsular has fly fishing in **Lochs Mudle** and **Mhadaidh**; wild brown trout, sea trout and the occasional salmon. Permits obtainable from Estate Office, Mingary House, Kilchoan, Acharacle PH36 4LH (tel: 01972 510208), from all local shops, T.I.C. (tel: 01972 510222), and hotels and visitors centres. All other twelve hill lochs and salmon and sea trout fishing on the Achateny water and Allt Choire Mhuilin reserved for estate guests. Tackle, boat hire and self-catering accommodation at Ardnamurchan Estate; fly fishing tuition: £10 per hour (freshwater), guiding £7/hour; fishing from £6.26/hour (sea-going); tackle and boat hire, and sea fishing from Nick Peake, Sithean Mor, Achnaha, nr Kilchoan, Argyll PH36 4LW (tel: 01972 510212; web: fishingand-coachingscotland.co.uk). Tickets and information from Kilchoan Community Centre, PH36 4LJ (tel: 01972 510711). Hotels: Sonachan; Kilchoan House.

Glenfinnan (Inverness-shire). **Loch Shiel**: fishing now sub-standard and not recommended.

SPEY

One of the largest rivers in Scotland, from its source Loch Spey, it flows 97 miles to Moray Firth, emptying between Banff and Elgin. The total catchment area is 1,154 sq miles. The Spey is an alpine river, with melting snow supplementing flow well into spring. The waters are low in nutrients, and have remained fairly free from pollution. The main river is also relatively free from obstructions. Historically, one of the great salmon rivers, net fishing ceased at the end of the 1993 season, and there is now no commercial netting for salmon within the Spey district. The Spey is a Site of Special Scientific Interest (SSSI) and will be a Special Area of Conservation (SAC) before long.

Fochabers (Morayshire). Extensive salmon fishings are let by the Factor, Frank Clark, Estate Office, Gordon Castle IV32 7PQ (tel: 01343 820244). These include Upper Brae Water, the Brae Water, Gordon Castle Water, and the two Gordon Castle Lower Water beats, in total approx 9m of double bank salmon, sea trout and finnock fishings. Accom for parties of up to 12 on Estate. Fochabers AA have four visitors day permits (subject to availability). These are booked at the Baxters at Home Shop, The Highland Village IV32 7LD (tel: 01343 820393). Gordon Arms Hotel, High St IV32 7DH (tel: 01343 820508/9); Mill House Hotel, Tynet, by Buckie, Banffshire AB56 5HJ (tel: 01542 850233) and The Garmouth Hotel, Garmouth IV32 7LU (tel: 01343 870226) cater for fishermen and fishing parties.

Craigellachie (Banffshire). Salmon, sea trout, trout. Craigellachie Hotel, Craigellachie, Aberlour, Banffshire AB38 9SR (tel: 01340 881204), arranges salmon fishing on Spey and brown trout fishing on local lochs for residents.

Aberlour (Banffshire). Salmon, sea trout. Aberlour Association water. Six tickets per day on first-come-first-served basis. Hotels Dowans and Aberlour have 3 bookable tickets for residents (Dowans has lockable rod-box, freezers and drying room); wt £100, dt £20; no day tickets issued on Saturdays; permits from J A J Munro, Fishing Tackle, 93-95 High St, Aberlour, Banffshire AB38 9PB (tel: 01340 871428); season 11 Feb - 30 Sept; best season usually March till June but can be very good in July and August too. J A J Munro is a specialist supplier of hand-tied salmon flies, also re-felting wader soles with traditional felt with studded heels.

Grantown-on-Spey (Moray). Salmon and sea trout. Strathspey Angling Improvement Association (SAIA) has double

The Spey, historically one of the great salmon rivers. Net fishing ceased at the end of 1993. Here an angler fishes the water at Castle Grant. *Photo: Arthur Oglesby.*

bank fishing on 5m on **Spey**, and 12m on **Dulnain**; salmon, grilse and sea trout are the main quarry, but both rivers have brown trout. In recent years, salmon over 31lb, and sea trout over 13lb have been caught; av catch 250 salmon and grilse, 600 sea trout. Most of main stem of river is private and expensive. The Assn has a 13 pool beat of excellent fly water on the **Reidhaven Estate** for 3 days per week (Thurs, Fri & Sat), available only to st and wt holders. Daily permits are offered to temporary residents in Grantown, Cromdale, Duthill, Carrbridge, Dulnain Bridge and Nethy Bridge areas to fish AIA waters. Permits only available for Assn waters from Mortimers Fishing Tackle, *(below)*. Strathspey Estate, Old Spey Bridge Rd, Grantown-on-Spey, PH26 3NQ (tel: 01479 872529), has four beats on Spey, incl three Castle Grant beats. Contact Estate Office for further information. Trout fishing on **Avielochan**, bank fishing only. Trout fishing is available on **Loch Dallas** and **Loch Vaa** and **Loch Mor**; 2 rods per boat, no bank fishing; fly only. Permits from tackle shop: Mortimer's, 3 High St PH26 3HB (tel: 01479 872684). Grace Oglesby hosts two fishing weeks (May and August) on Spey based at The Seafield Lodge Hotel; for dates and information apply to George Anderson, The Seafield Lodge Hotel, Woodside Ave, PH26 3JN (tel: 01479 872152).

Boat of Garten (Inverness-shire). Salmon, sea trout, brown trout. Abernethy Angling Improvement Assn, incorporating Aviemore Angling Improvement Assn, issues tickets for Abernethy Waters, 6 mile stretch of Spey, both banks, 15 named pools; contact Allen's Tackle Shop *(see below)*. Certain stretches restricted to fly only when river below certain level, otherwise spinning and worming allowed; no prawn or shrimp allowed at any time; all methods barbless hooks. Brown trout fishing - fly only at all times. Permit only for those staying locally, wt £115-£125, dt £35-£40; from A J Allen, Allen's Tackle Shop, Deshar Rd, Boat of Garten PH24 3BN (tel: 01479 831372); and Speyside Sports, 2 Station Square, PH22 1PD (tel: 01479 810656).

Aviemore (Inverness-shire). The principal Spey Valley tourist centre. Kinara Estate has salmon and trout fishing on Spey and loch fishing (bank or boat) for trout and pike; for further information contact Major Campbell, Kinara Lodge, Aviemore PH22 1QA (tel: 01479 811292). The Aviemore Waters consist of 3½m of

A classic day's catch on the 'Mayfly,' Loch Craggie. *Photo: Park House, Lairg.*

single bank salmon fishing, at reasonable price: dt £30, wt £95, conc for juv, permits from Speyside Sports, *(below)*. **Avielochan**, 10 acre brown trout water, dt £17.50, evening £12.50, boat £7.50, from Allen's *(above)*, or Speyside Sports *(below)*. Trout and pike fishing on Rothiemurchus Estate, including rainbow and brown trout lochs, and beats on R Spey with salmon and sea trout; apply to Rothiemurchus Trout Fishery, Aviemore PH22 1QH (tel: 01479 810703); ghillie service and instruction on site, disabled access on bank. Trout fishing on **Loch Morlich** at Glenmore. Permits from Visitors Centre or Watersports Centre, Loch Morlich. Tackle shop: Speyside Sports, 2 Station Square, PH22 1PD (tel: 01479 810656).

Kingussie (Inverness-shire). Alvie Estate has fishing on Spey, salmon and trout; **Loch Alvie**, brown trout and pike; and **Loch Insh**, salmon, sea trout, brown trout, pike and Arctic char. Fly fishing or spinning. Apply to Alvie Estate Office, Kincraig, by Kingussie PH21 1NE (tel: 01540 651255); and Dalraddy Caravan Park, Aviemore PH22 1QB (tel: 01479 810330). Loch Insh Watersports & Skiing Centre, Insh Hall, Kincraig PH21 1NU (tel: 01540 651272; fax: 01540 651208; e-mail: office@lochinsh.com), also has 2 boats and bank fishing on loch, and stocked trout lochan; boats for hire, and tuition on site, facilities for disabled. Badenoch AA has fishing on River Spey from Spey Dam down to Kingussie, Loch Ericht at Dalwhinnie, and Loch Laggan on the Fort William Rd; all brown trout fishing, stocked monthly, very few salmon; Spey Dam has 2 boats, fly only, the other waters allow worm and spinning. Fishing permits £9 from Service Sports, 26 High St, Kingussie PH21 1HR (tel: 01540 661228); fishing permits and boat hire from Laggan PO; Sandy Bennett, Water Bailiff (tel: 01540 661645); and local hotels. Service Sports also supply fishing permits (and boat hire) for Loch Gynack, a private loch; £10 per rod and boats £6 per session. Ossian Hotel, Kincraig, by Kingussie PH21 1QD (tel: 01540 651242) has private fishing; salmon and brown trout.

Newtonmore (Inverness-shire). Badenoch AA has trout fishing on Upper Spey, **Loch Laggan, Loch Quoich** and **Spey Dam**.

Tributaries of the Spey

AVON: Main tributary of Spey.

Ballindalloch (Banffshire). Ballindalloch Estate owns 5m stretch on Avon from junction with Spey; salmon, sea trout, brown trout. Weekly and daily permits. Permits from The Estate Office, Ballindalloch, Banffshire AB37 9AX (tel: 01807 500205; fax: 01807 500210; web: www.ballindallochcastle.co.uk, e-mail: enquiries@ballindallochcastle.co.uk).

Hotel: The Delnashaugh Inn (tel: 01807 500255).

Tomintoul (Banffshire). Sea trout, grilse and salmon. The Gordon Hotel guests can fish 2m of Avon and 1m of Livet. Price varies depending on duration of stay. Fishing only open to residents of hotel. The Gordon Hotel, The Square, Tomintoul, Ballindalloch AB37 9ET (tel: 01807 580206).

STINCHAR

One of west coast streams, rising on western slope of Doon watershed and flowing about 30m to Atlantic at Ballantrae. Has a late run of salmon, and fishes best from mid August till late October. Yearly catch is normally over 1,200 salmon. Also good sea trout and brown trout.

Colmonell (Ayrshire). River rises and falls rapidly after rain; salmon and sea trout. Boar's Head Hotel, 4 Main St, KA26 0RY (tel: 01465 881371) can assist with arranging fishings on river. Permits for Kirkholm Farm from Mrs Marshall, Kirkholm Farm, Firvan (tel: 01465 831297). For Knockdolian (best beat): Estate Office, Knockdolian, Colmonell, Girvan KA26 0LB (tel: 01465 881237), or A Boag (tel: 01465 881254). Beats: for Badrochat Estate: Bob Anderson (tel: 01465 881202); Hallow Chapel fishing: Tom Lothian, 'Craignelder', 1 Main St, Ballantrae KA26 0NA (tel: 01465 831277); issues tickets; Almont and Dalreoch Estate: Paul Mottram (tel: 01465 881214; mob: 07880 602922). These are the main beats on the river, of which majority are fly only, prices range between £15 and

£45 per day, wt £125-£200, depending on season. Colmonell AC has water below bridge. Queen's Hotel, 21 Main St, KA26 0RY (tel: 01465 881213) can supply information to visiting anglers. **Pinbraid**

Fishery (Bill Wood), Garnaburn, KA26 0RX (tel: 01465 891112); Fly only; wild browns, rainbow; 7 days: dt (4 fish) £18; 8hrs (3 fish) £15; 4hrs (2 fish) £12.

TAY

A great salmon river. Tay proper runs out of Loch Tay, but its feeder, the Dochart, at head of loch, takes its head water from slopes of Ben Lui. After a course of some 119m it empties into North Sea at Dundee, by a long firth. River fished mainly from boats, but certain beats provide spinning and fly fishing from banks. Notable in particular for run of spring fish, though autumn fishing often gives good results. All netting has now been removed in the Tay estuary, and salmon and sea trout have run unhindered for several years. At least half a dozen of its tributaries are salmon rivers of slightly less repute than main stream. An excellent run of sea trout, big brown trout (less often fished for), grayling, and coarse fish (scarcely fished at all). Loch Tay itself has been improving over recent years as a salmon fishery, the largest taken being a little over 40lbs.

Perth (Perthshire). Scone Estate, Scone Palace, PH2 6BD (tel: 01738 552308; fax: 01738 552588; web: www.scone-palace. co.uk; e-mail: estate@scone-palace.co. uk) offers salmon fishing on two beats of Tay. Daily lets in spring, and daily and weekly from July to October. Stormont AC has salmon fishing on Tay, 3 beats; and on **R Almond**, 2 beats; members only (c 550); permits for 3 beats of brown trout and coarse fishing on Tay and Almond, from tackle shop *(below)*. Perth & Dist AA has various leases for brown trout and salmon fishing on Tay. Assn also has fishing on **Black Loch**, rainbow trout; **Loch Horn**, rainbow and brown trout; and **Balthayock Loch**, brown trout. All game fishing members only. Brown trout on Tay permits from P D Malloch *(below)*. Permits for Perth Town Water; salmon, trout, grilse and also coarse fish; from Perth and Kinross Council, Environment Services, Pullar House, 35 Kinnoull St PH1 5GD (tel: 01738 476476; fax: 01738 476410); and Tourist Information Centre, Lower City Mills, West Mill St, Perth PH1 5QP (tel: 01738 450600) (Saturday only). Dt £10 (Jan to June); £15 (July to Oct). Brown trout and coarse free. Advisable to book in advance; only 20 permits per day. Tackle shop: P D Malloch, 259 Old High St PH1 5QN (tel: 01738 632316). Hotels: Royal George; Tayside, Stanley.

Stanley (Perthshire). Stanley & Dist AC has brown trout and grayling fishing at Luncarty, Upper Redgorton, Stanley Taymount, Burnmouth and Meikleour; a limited number of permits are offered (Mon-Fri) (dt £3) from Stanley PO, 2 Percy Str, PH1 4LU (tel: 01738 828206).

Tayside Hotel, 51 Mill Str, PH1 4NL (tel: 01738 828249; fax: 01738 827216) issues trout permits for fishing on all beats: Linn Pool, Burnmouth, Catholes, Pitlochrie, Benchil, and Luncarty. Special rates to residents. Salmon fishing packages available. Hotel has tackle for sale, and special anglers' facilities. Ballathie House Hotel, Kinclaven PH1 4QN (tel: 01250 883268; fax: 01250 883396; e-mail: email@balla thiehousehotel.com; www.fishing-shoot ing-scotland.co.uk) lets rods on the Ballathie beat and elsewhere, when available, to residents and non-residents early in the season.

Dunkeld (Perthshire). Dunkeld & Birnam AA (wt £15, dt £5, conc) and Perth & Dist AA (wt £10, dt £3, conc) have trout fishing on **Tay**. Permits are also issued for grayling, mostly in the trout close season. **Loch Clunie:** no fishing now due to SSSI designation. Permits from Kettles of Dunkeld, Atholl St, Dunkeld PH8 0AR (tel: 01350 727556). Dunkeld & Birnam AA also has brown trout fishing on **River Braan**; permits from Kettles and The Spar, 3 Murthly Terrace, Birnam, PH8 0BG (tel: 01350 727395). Amulree AC have fishing on **Loch Freuchie**; trout and pike, bank fishing only; dt £5 from Amulree Hotel, Amulree PH8 0EF (tel: 01350 725218) and Amulree PO. Hilton Dunkeld House Hotel and Country Club, PH8 0HX (tel: 01350 728370; fax: 01350 728959; e-mail: dunkeld.park@lineone. net) has salmon and trout fishing on Tay; 1 boat with 2 rods; 6 bank rods; experienced ghillie; no salmon fishing on Sundays. **Butterstone Loch**, put and take rainbow and brown trout; fly only. 17 boats on water. Permits (day and evening) from Butterstone Loch Fishings, Butter stone, by Dunkeld PH8 0HH (tel: 01350 724238; e-mail: rick@butterstone loch-fishings.co.uk).

Dalguise (Perthshire). Perth & Dist AA (wt £10, dt £3) fishes Kinnaird, Dalguise and Newtyle beats: permits from Kettles of Dunkeld, Atholl St, Dunkeld PH8 0AR (tel: 01350 727556). Permits, with boat and ghillie from CKD Galbraith, Lyne-doch House, Barossa Pl, Perth PH1 5EP (tel: 01738 451600; fax: 01738 451900; e-mail: sporting@ckdgalbraith.co.uk). Salmon £22-£70 per rod per day, depend-ing on season.

Grandtully (Perthshire). Salmon, brown trout and grayling; fly, bait or spinning; booking advisable for Aberfeldy AC water from Wade Newsagents *(see Aber-feldy)*.

Aberfeldy (Perthshire). Salmon and brown trout and grayling on Tay. Trout and sal-mon fishing on River Tay; Loch Tay, sal-mon and trout; and various hill lochs, including coarse fish and wild brown trout; fly fishing preferred; spinning and worming allowed; shrimps and prawns prohibited. Tickets for the town waters available from Wade Newsagents, 31 Bank St, PH15 2BB (tel: 01887 820397) and James Bayne (dt £5); Aberfeldy AC water, who also have Bolfracts Estate, right bank; dt water; also d/s to Grand-tully, right bank only; trout and grayling; wt £15, dt £5. Brown trout permit from Roderick Kennedy, Borlick Farm, Killie-chassie PH15 2EA (tel: 01887 820463). Ailean Craggan Hotel, Weem PH15 2LD (tel: 01887 820346) has fishing on the Upper Farleyer and Carse beats; salmon and trout. Dt £25-50 (4 rods available). Trout and grayling fishing on the Lower Aberfeldy, Moness beat, contact Callum

McDermott, Drumcroy Lodges, Aber-feldy PH15 2EA (tel: 01887 829899); self-catering accommodation available. Tackle shop: Perthshire Rod & Gun, Bank of Scotland Bldgs, 3 Bank Str, PH15 2BD (tel: 01887 829000; fax: 01887 829700).

Kenmore (Perthshire). Tay leaves **Loch Tay** at Kenmore. Salmon and trout fish-ing on river and loch for guests at The Kenmore Hotel, Kenmore PH15 2NU (tel: 01887 830205). Permits for non-resi-dents from hotel (salmon) or Post Office (trout).

Killin (Perthshire). Killin & Breadalbane AC has fishing on **Loch Tay**, **River Do-chart**, **River Lochay**, and **Lochan an Laraig**; salmon, brown trout, rainbow trout, perch, pike and char. Stocking pol-icy includes annual stocking with mature brown trout. Salmon of up to 30lbs are caught; rainbows of 5-6lbs. An excellent venue for visiting anglers who are made very welcome. Permits £5 (salmon priced separately) for these waters, with con-cessions, from News First, Newsagent & Tackle Shop, Main St FK21 8SR (tel: 01567 820362).

Crianlarich (Perthshire). Trout fishing on **Loch Dochart** (good early in the season), **Loch Iubhair** and **River Fillan**, a tribu-tary of Tay. In summer, salmon find their way into loch and up Fillan and tribu-taries. Best months: May, June, July and Sept. Dt £5. Day tickets for River Fillan from Ben More Lodge Hotel, Crianlarich FK20 8QS (tel: 01838 300210; fax: 01838 300218; e-mail: info@ben-more. co.uk). Permits £7 for Lochs Dochart and Iubhair from Portnellan Highland Lodges FK20 8QS (tel: 01838 300284): boats, engines, and ghillies (notice required) for hire.

Tributaries of the Tay

EARN: Salmon, sea trout, brown trout (av ¾lb) and excellent grayling. Loch Earn fishing closed in winter.

Bridge of Earn (Perthshire). Rainbow trout fishing on **Sandyknowes Fishery**, 8 acres; fly only; bank fishing only. Bag limit 4 trout. Permits from E C Christie, The Fishery Office, Sandyknowes, Bridge of Earn BH2 9QA (tel: 01738 813033).

Auchterarder (Perthshire). Salmon, sea trout, brown trout and grayling. James Haggart, Haugh of Aberuthven, Auchter-

arder PH3 1HL (tel: 01738 730206) has fishing at **Lower Aberuthven**: salmon on application, grayling ticket £4; all legal baits allowed. Tickets for **Orchill Loch** trout fishery, from A Boyd, *(see below)*. Dupplin Estate, **Dupplin**, Perth PH2 0PY (tel: 01738 622757), has st £20, dt £3 on offer for brown trout and grayling, issued Mon-Fri from Estate Office.

Crieff (Perthshire). Crieff AC has Drum-mond Castle, Braidhaugh and Upper Stro-wan beats, totalling 6½m, mostly double bank; brown, sea trout, salmon, grayling;

dt £5 b trout, £10-£20 migratory fish, depending on month. Season 1 Feb-15 Oct; no Saturdays in Oct; also **Drummond Loch** brown trout, dt £25 per boat for two (or 3 for £12.50 extra); excellent parking. Laird Management Ltd; contact John Young (tel: 07970 274236) has Lochlane and Laggan fishings, with sea trout and salmon, dt £15-£50, 1 Feb-31 Oct. River permits for Crieff AC waters from A Boyd (*below*), or from Crieff Tourist Office, 33 High St PH7 3HU (tel: 01764 652578; fax: 655422) (Drummond Water, and Upper Strowan); loch tickets from Strathearn Tyres, School Wynd (tel: 01764 654697). Crieff AC: membership £130 (2 year waiting list). At Comrie, Comrie AC has 6 miles right and left banks; dt from local Comrie Newsagent; dt £10. For Laird Management waters, tickets from Tourist Office, High Str, PH7 3HU (tel: 01764 652578). Brown trout fishing on **Loch Turret**; fly only; boats for hire. Permits (dt £6, conc £3) from A Boyd (*below*). Drummond Trout Farm and Fishery, **Comrie** PH6 2LD (tel: 01764 670500), 1m off A85, has six lochans stocked daily with trout, open all year, from 10am, 2hrs £3.50, 4hrs £4,

conc, easy disabled access. **Braincroft Loch**: brown trout permit from £5, at Braincroft Farm, by Crieff PH7 4JZ (tel: 01764 670140). **Cowden Loch**: brown and rainbow trout permit at Lochview Farm, Mill of Fortune, Comrie PH6 2JE (tel: 01764 670677). A £5 grayling permit is obtainable for R Earn, from 15 Nov-15 Jan, from tackle shop: A Boyd, Newsagents and Tackle, 39 King St, Crieff PH7 3AX (tel: 01764 653871).

St Fillans (Perthshire). Trout and charr fishing for visitors in **Loch Earn**. Drummond Castle (Alec Murray: 01567 830400) run loch; stocked with brown trout, between 12oz and 2E1/2lb.

Lochearnhead (Perthshire). Loch Earn, natural brown trout, stocked browns, occasional rainbows and char. St Fillans & Lochearn AA water; visitors day permits £6, boats £18-£30 from Drummond Estate Boat Hire, Ardveich Bay, Lochearnhead FK19 8PZ (tel: 01567 830400). Tickets from Loch Earn Fishings, Drummond Estate Office, Muthill, PH5 2AA (tel: 01764 681257); Permits also from Village Shop, Lochearnhead FK19 8PR (tel: 01567 830214); Post Office, Lochearnhead SPDO, FK19 8PR (tel: 01567

A long cast on the River Earn, Drummond Castle Water at Crieff. *Photo: Crieff Angling Club.*

830201); Village Store, St Fillans PH6 2ND (tel: 01764 685309); 45 Bar & Restaurant FK19 8PX (tel: 01567 830221), open 7.30am to midnight; and hotels. Nearest tackle shops in A Boyd, Crieff *(above);* Killin, Callander. Hotels: Mansewood House; Lochearnhead; Clachan Cottage.

ISLA: Trout (av ½lb and up to 3lb) and grayling. Pike also in lower reaches.

Dundee (Angus). Permits for brown trout and grayling fishing from Strathmore AIA, local tackle shops; assn also issues permits for **Dean Water**, tributary of Isla; brown trout. Cameron Loch, **St Andrews**, brown trout; Lintrathen Loch, **Kirriemuir**, brown trout; Mill of Criggie, **Montrose**; Newton Farm, **Newport on Tay**; **Rescobie Loch**, **Forfar**; all brown and rainbow; details and permits from tackle shop: John R Gow Ltd, 12 Union St, Dundee DD1 4BH (tel: 01382 225427), who also arrange fishing on Tay (salmon) and North Esk (salmon and sea trout), and South Esk.

ALYTH (tributary of Isla):

Alyth (Perthshire). Several streams in neighbourhood. Isla contains trout and grayling in lower reaches. Above Reekie Linn trout very numerous but small. Alyth Hotel can arrange salmon and trout fishing on River Tay and a number of its tributaries; also trout fishing on a selection of lochs. Both day fishermen and coach parties are catered for. Apply to The Alyth Hotel, Alyth, Perthshire PH11 8AF (tel: 01828 632447).

ERICHT (tributary of Isla):

Blairgowrie (Perthshire). Salmon and brown trout. Blairgowrie, Rattray & Dist AC has fishing on part of Ericht; st £200; dt £15 and £2, trout; from local tackle shops; salmon fishing for non-club members on Mon to Fri. Advance booking only on 4m stretch, wt from £200, dt from £40; fly only: from Roger McCosh (tel: 01250 875518). Various fishings on tributaries **R Ardle**, **R Blackwater**, **R Shee**; permits from tackle shops. **River Isla**: Kate Fleming or James Crockart (below). For trout fishing on Isla and **Dean**, contact Strathmore AIA (tel: 01382 667711). Permits from local tackle shops. Bruce Reid, Coupar Grange, PH13 9HT (tel: 07850 236449) has 2m of double bank from confluence of Isla and Ericht d/s. Plentiful loch fishing in area, including **Lochs Marlee**, bank fishing only (coarse); **Tullochcurran** and **Shan-**

dra (wild browns); enquire at tackle shops. **Loch Nan Ean** and **Loch Beinnie**, brown trout, fly only, boat on Beinnie, permits from Invercauld Estate Office, Braemar AB35 5TW (tel: 013397 41224); and others. Tackle shops: Kate Fleming, Shooting and Fishing, 26 Allan St, Blairgowrie PH10 6AD (tel: 01250 873990), who also supply tickets for Blairgowrie, Rattray & Dist AC waters; also for 1½m of Ericht both banks, and 3m single bank of Isla above confluence of the rivers; James Crockart & Son, 28 Allan St, Blairgowrie PH10 6AD (tel: 01250 872056), who supply ghillie and instructor on R Isla; wt salmon £60, dt £15; trout wt £5 dt £2. Other hotels: Bridge of Cally.

Blacklunans (Perthshire). Dalrulzion Hotel, Glenshee, PH10 7LJ (tel: 01250 882222), has salmon and trout fishing on **River Blackwater** from hotel grounds; small charge to guests; day permits offered to non-residents. Other fishings in vicinity.

BRAAN: runs from Loch Freuchie.

Dunkeld (Perthshire). Forestry Commission Scotland, National Trust and riparian owners have leased water on R Braan to Dunkeld and Birnam AA. Brown trout. Permits for Hermitage beat and beats 1 and 2 from Kettles of Dunkeld, Atholl St, Dunkeld PH8 0AR (tel: 01350 727556). Permits for beat 3 and for Assn **Loch Freuchie** fishing (perch, pike, brown trout) from Amulree Tea Room, Amulree PH8 0BZ7 (tel: 01350 725200).

TUMMEL: Salmon, trout and grayling.

Pitlochry (Perthshire). Pitlochry AC has salmon fishing on R Tummel from marker post below Pitlochry Dam to bottom of Milton of Fonab Caravan Site; south bank only. Spinning, worm or fly only. Dt £6-£35; 3 anglers per day. Advance booking recommended, particularly for Apr-Jun. Recent average annual catch, 60 salmon and grilse. Contact Club salmon secretary. Club has browns and grayling (map on permit). Club also has fishing on **Lochs Bhac** and **Kinardochy**, brown trout, and rainbow (Bhac only). Bank and boat fishing on Bhac; boat only on Kinardochy; fly only. Permits from Mitchells of Pitlochry *(below)*. East Haugh House Hotel, Donavourd, Pitlochry PH16 5TE (tel: 01796 473121) can arrange fishing on various salmon beats on R Tummel and R Tay, dt from £25 per rod. Permits for trout fishing on R Tummel also from Tourist Information Centre, 22 Atholl Rd,

PH16 5BX (tel: 01796 472215); Mitchells of Pitlochry *(below);* Ballinluig PO, PH9 0LG (tel: 01796 482220); and Ballinluig Service Station. **Loch Faskally**; created in 1950s by damming of R Tummell. Salmon and sea trout ascent fish pass at dam, and may be caught from end of Mar-Oct 15; brown trout, pike, perch; any legal lure; permits, boats and bait from L Dixon, Pitlochry Boating Station, Clunie Bridge Rd, Loch Faskally, Pitlochry PH16 5JX (tel: 01796 472919/474147). Tackle Shop: Mitchells of Pitlochry, 23 Atholl Rd, PH16 5BX (tel: 01796 472613).

GARRY: Tributary of Tummel, good river for about 6m.

Killiecrankie (Perthshire). Pitlochry AC has salmon fishing on east bank. Dt £20, 4 anglers. For advance booking and information contact Salmon Sec. Bookings at short notice from Mitchells of Pitlochry *(above).*

Blair Atholl (Perthshire). Trout fly fishing on R Garry and **Tilt** (approx 4m) and rainbow trout on **Blair Walker Pond**; dt £3, wt £12, conc; permits from Blair Atholl PO, PH18 5SG (tel: 01796 481233). Atholl Estates office (tel: 01796 481355) has salmon fishing; dt £15-£30 May to 15 Oct.

Dalwhinnie (Inverness-shire). **Loch Ericht**, 22 mile long brown trout loch, and rivers; weekly permit £27, day permit £9, conc. Badenoch AA has water: River Spey, Caldar, Tromie; Lochs Ericht, Laggan and Truim. For dt contact Dalwhinnie Filling Station (opposite The Inn at Loch Ericht), PH19 1AF (tel: 01528 522311). Open all year.

LOCH RANNOCH: Trout, some large but averaging 9ozs; best May to October, also ferox trout, char, pike. Trout fishing in River Tummel, below loch.

Kinloch Rannoch (Perthshire). Loch Rannoch Conservation Assn has fishing on Loch Rannoch; brown trout, ferox trout (up to 15lb), pike and char; permits from Hon Sec, and local shops and hotels. **Dunalastair Loch** is a short distance east of Kinloch Rannoch, with brown trout and char; boats, no bank fishing, fly only; permits from Dunalastair Hotel PH16 5PW (tel: 01882 632323); st £25, wt £14, dt £4. Rannoch & District AC has fishing on **Loch Eigheach**, 1m from Rannoch Station; brown trout and perch; fly fishing only; bank fishing only; June best month; wt £12, dt £3, from J Brown, The

Square, Kinloch Rannoch PH16 5PN (tel: 01882 632268). Permits for Loch Rannoch and **R Tummel**, dt £4, wt £14, st £25, conc, from Dunalastair Hotel; Brown's Garage PH16 5PQ (tel: 01882 632331). Hotels: Loch Rannoch; Dunalastair PH16 5PW (tel: 632323).

LYON (near Loch Tay): Good salmon and trout river in the magnificently forested Glen Lyon, reputedly the longest glen in Scotland. River runs from two dammed lochs at glen head.

Glen Lyon (Perthshire). Brown trout and salmon permits from: Mr Drysdale, Keeper's Cottage, Innerwick PH15 2PP (tel: 01887 866218); dt salmon £15, brown trout £5 (fly only). For **North/South Chesthill** beat, contact Mr Pirie, Keeper's Cottage, South Chesthill (tel: 01887 877233) for prices and availability. For **Slatich**, contact Fortingall Hotel (tel: 01887 830367); £25 salmon permits only; dt £4 (fly only except in spate) from Mr Walker, Slatich (tel: 01887 877221). For brown trout only from **Cashlie**, contact Mr Sinclair, Keepers Cottage, Cashlie PH15 2PX (tel: 01887 866237); £3-£5 per day except in spate. **Loch an Daimh**: contact W Mason, Croc-na-keys, Lochs (tel: 01887 866224), north bank only. For Meggernie, contact Post Office, Bridge of Balgie (tel: 01887 866221); dt £5 (£1.50 refundable on submitting return). More information from Aberfeldy Tourist Board (tel: 01887 820276).

DOCHART (feeds Loch Tay):

Killin (Perthshire). At confluence of Dochart and Lochay, near head of Loch Tay. Salmon fishing best in July, Aug and Sept. Trout numerous and run to a fair size. Water is very deep and sluggish from Luib to Bovain, but above and as far as Loch Dochart there are some capital streams and pools. Auchlyne & Suie Estate Water; trout and salmon. Permits issued by G D Coyne, Keeper's Cottage, Auchlyne, Killin FK21 8RG; Luib Hotel, Glen Dochart, Crianlarich FK20 8QT (tel: 01567 820664); and Glendochart Caravan Park. Trout fishing best April-May, good run of autumn salmon. Ardeonaig Hotel, South Lochtayside, Perthshire FK21 8SU (tel: 01567 820400) has own harbour with 4 boats on **Loch Tay**; salmon, trout and char; salmon fishing and trout fishing tickets from hotel or Killin newsagents; tickets from £10/rod/day. Loch Tay Highland Lodges, Milton

Morenish, by Killin FK21 8TY (tel: 01567 820323; fax: 01567 820581) have salmon and trout fishing on Loch Tay; 18 boats with outboard motors for hire, troll-ing is the usual method. Hotel is ideally placed for fishing middle and western beats of the loch.

THURSO

A noted salmon river and one of the earliest in Scotland. The spring run has been improving recently, after a period of decline. Water level may be regulated by a weir at Loch More on the upper reaches. The river is entirely preserved.

Thurso (Caithness). Thurso AA has Beat 1 (from River Mouth up to the Geise Burn, including tidal water), which produces 10% of total river catch; members only, but possibility of permit if no members fishing; brown trout permit on Assn waters from The Bookshop, Olrig St. Dt £10-£18, depending on season. Salmon fishing (fly only) on other beats can be arranged through Thurso Fisheries Ltd, Thurso East, Thurso KW14 8HP (tel: 01847 893134). Bookings usually by week, fortnight or month, but day lets arranged. Weekly charges, including accommodation, range from £640 to £1000, according to date. Fishing improves progressively from opening on Jan 11 to close on Oct 5. First-class loch, burn and river fishing for trout. Brown trout loch fishing in vicinity: **Loch Calder, Lochs Watten, St John's** and **Stemster**; **Loch Hielan; Broubster Lochs, Dunnet Head Lochs**; permits for all these from tackle shop: Harper's Fly Fishing Services, 57 High St, KW14 8AZ (tel/fax: 01847 893179). Lesley Crawford, Caithness & Sutherland Angling Services, Askival,

Reay, Caithness KW14 7RE (tel: 01847 811470; e-mail: lesley@crawford40. freeserve. co.uk) has fly fishing for wild brown trout on various lochs in Caithness: contact L Crawford, or Harpers Tackle (*above*). Hotels: Park; Pentland; St Clair; Royal.

Halkirk (Caithness). The Ulbster Arms Hotel has fishing on **Loch Calder** and many other hill lochs; excellent accommodation and fishing, £410-£900 per week. Salmon fishing on **Thurso River**. Information from Eddie McCarthy, Superintendent's House, Braal Rd, Halkirk KW12 6XE (tel: 01847 831591; web: www.thursoriver.co.uk); dt £50-£100 depending on season almost always available.

Dunnet (Caithness). House of the Northern Gate, Dunnet Estate KW14 8YD. 7 Estate lochs for good brown trout. Contact Michael Draper (tel: 01847 851622). St John's Loch AA has fishing on **St John's Loch**; bank and boat fishing. Permits from Northern Sands Hotel, Dunnet, Thurso KW14 8XD (tel: 01847 851270).

TWEED

Rises in corner formed by watersheds of Clyde and Annan, and flows over 100m to North Sea at Berwick-upon-Tweed, forming, for some of its course, the boundary between England and Scotland. The Tweed is probably the most popular of the large Scottish rivers, partly owing to its proximity to England. It contains over 300 named casts and its salmon harvest is considerable. It has the longest season (1st February to 30 November), but at its best in autumn, especially from mid to late October, when the run is noted for the size and number of salmon caught. There is a good spring run, and in summer even the most famous beats such as the Junction at Kelso are open for permit fishing, for around £25 per day. Summer fish may be difficult to catch at low water. Boatmen are employed by most beats. The Tweed produces a strain of sea trout, formerly called bull trout, which are remarkable both for size and distance they are known to travel in sea. The best sea trout fishing is on tributaries, the Till and Whiteadder, both of which fish well in summer. The season on the Tweed is the same as for salmon, and the permits are combined.

Over recent years there has been a perceived decline in wild brown trout fishing in the upper Tweed and Lyne. To combat this, these rivers have been stocked with brown trout. These are marked with a blue spot on the underbelly, and there is a bag limit of 4 stocked fish in force, with a policy of catch and release for wild trout in operation. There has been improved brown trout fishing since 1995. There exists a code of conduct (The Tweed Angling Code) with regard mainly to fly fishing for salmon and sea trout, and the leaflet may be obtained from the River Tweed Commissioners or from most tackle shops and letting agents.

'Tweedline' is a service for fishermen provided by the Tweed Foundation, a charitable trust established by the River Tweed Commissioners to promote the development of salmon and trout stocks in the Tweed river system. Tweedline information is provided by other agencies for the Tweed Foundation, who benefit by receiving a share of the proceeds from each call. (Tweedline is a BT premium rate service.) Line available: Fishing reports and prospects (tel: 09068 666410); River levels (updated daily) (tel: 09068 666411); Last minute rod vacancies (tel: 09068 666412). **J H Leeming,** Stichill House, Kelso, Roxburghshire TD5 7TB (tel: 01573 470280; fax: 01573 470259; web: www.leeming.co.uk; e-mail: info@ leeming.co.uk) provide an information service. There is a *Borders Angling Guide* produced by the local tourist board, which gives comprehensive information on the whole river, cost £1.50 from any Borders T I Centre. SEPA operate a local 24 hour pollution emergency response on 0800 807060. Anglers are requested to report incidents with urgency.

The Tweed Foundation may be contacted at Drygrange Steading, Melrose, Roxburghshire TD6 9DJ (tel: 01896 848271; fax: 01896 848277; e-mail: info@tweedfoundation.co.uk).

Berwick-upon-Tweed (Northumberland). Salmon, sea trout, trout, grayling, coarse fish. Tidal Tweed gives free fishing for roach and grayling. Salmon fishing on Tweed offered by J H Leeming, Stichill House, Kelso, Roxburghshire TD5 7TB (tel: 01573 470280; fax: 01573 470259; web: www.leeming.co.uk; e-mail: info@leeming.co.uk); 11 beats between Tweedhill, near Berwick, and Peebles; from £30 to £100, one or two rods per

TWEED SALMON FISHING

- *Six beats at Tillmouth Park*
Cornhill-on-Tweed, Northumberland

Two beats at Dryburgh North
Melrose, Roxburghshire

One beat at Pedwell, Norham
Berwick upon Tweed

Three beats at Tweedhill, Norham
Berwick upon Tweed

For further details or brochure contact:

Sale & Partners

18-20 Glendale Road, Wooler
Northumberland, NE71 6DW
Tel: 01668 281611 Fax: 01668 281113
E-mail: cam@saleandpartners.co.uk

day; early booking advisable. Berwick & Dist AA has brown trout fishing on 7m of **River Whiteadder**, including 2m of salmon fishing. River joins Tweed 1m from Berwick. Brown trout st £45, wt £20, dt £10, conc, from Game Fair *(below);* and Hoolets Nest, Paxton. **Till** enters Tweed 2½m above Norham, 9m from Berwick. **Coldingham Loch**, 14m N: brown, rainbow and blue trout; 9 boats, bank fishing for 12 rods. Permits from Douglas and Kirsty Aitken, West Loch House, Coldingham, Berwickshire TD14 5QE (tel: 01890 771270), who has lodges and cottages to let. Booking essential. Coldingham is noted for the quality and size of the trout caught there. Tackle shop: Game Fair, 12 Marygate, Berwick-upon-Tweed TD15 1BN (tel: 01289 305119). Hotels: Castle; Kings Arms; Chirnside Hall, Chirnside; Hay Farmhouse, Cornhill-on-Tweed; Coach House, Crookham, Cornhill-on-Tweed.

Horncliffe (Northumberland). Tidal. Salmon, trout, grayling, roach, dace and eel. No permits required for trout and coarse fishing. Salmon fishing on Tweedhill beat; 3m single bank; 6 rods; 2 ghillies; 2 huts; 4m single right bank Horncliffe beat, 6 rods, 1 ghillie, 2 huts; obtainable from J H Leeming, Stichill House, Kelso, Roxburghshire TD5 7TB (tel: 01573 470280; fax: 01573 470259; web: www.leeming.co.uk; e-mail: info@leeming.co.uk).

Norham (Northumberland). Salmon, trout. Salmon fishing on Ladykirk from **J H Leeming,** Stichill House, Kelso, Roxburghshire TD5 7TB. (Tel: 01573 470280, fax: 01573 470259, web: www.leeming.co.uk; e-mail info@leeming.co.uk). Ladykirk, 3m single bank, 5 huts, boats and 1-5 ghillies, 6-10 rods;

over 5 years average catch 193; also good
sea trout water. For Pedwell, 1½m single
bank for 2 rods with boat and ghillie;

Mon, Tues, Fri, Sat only, contact Sale &
Partners, 18-20 Glendale Rd, Wooler
NE71 6DW (tel: 01668 281611); dt prices

This shallow stretch of the Tweed provides perfect conditions for a school of casting. *Photo:
M Walker.*

range from £31.50, to £136.50. Ladykirk & Norham AA has fishing from Norham boathouse to Horndean Burn, both banks, brown trout, grayling, eels; reputed to be one of the best waters along border; st £30, dt £5, concessions OAP, junior free if accompanied; permits from Mace Shop; Masons Arms Hotel TD15 2LB (web: www.tweed-sports.co.uk); Lynns Newsagent; and The Victoria Hotel, Castle Str, TD15 2LQ (tel: 01289 382437).

Coldstream (Berwickshire). Salmon, sea trout. Salmon fishing on West Learmouth obtainable from J H Leeming, Stichill House, Kelso, Roxburghshire TD5 7TB (tel: 01573 470280; fax: 01573 470259; web: www.leeming.co.uk; e-mail: info@leeming.co.uk): West Learmouth is a good spring and autumn beat for 2 rods opposite The Lees; ⅔m of single bank with boat and ghillie. Prices vary considerably, from £35 to £600. Leeming also has dt for Lennel beat 2½m left bank 7 pools, 4 rods, 1 ghillie; dt £30-£325. Mrs Jane Douglas-Home has rods to let at The Lees, TD12 4LF (tel/fax 01890 882706), from £40 per day. The Lees is a prime quality spring and autumn beat including the well known Temple Pool; 2m, 4 rods, 2-3 ghillies, 2 huts, 4 boats. Tillmouth Park Hotel, Cornhill-on-Tweed, TD12 4UU (tel: 01890 882255), has facilities for anglers, incl rod room, freezing and access to smoking facilities. Sale & Partners 18-20 Glendale Rd, Wooler, Northumberland NE71 6DW (tel: 01668 281611; fax: 01668 281113; web: www.saleandpartners.co.uk; e-mail cam@saleandpartners.co.uk) *(see advt)* *(see Fishery Agents)* offer fishing by weekly or daily booking on beats 2 to 6 on Tillmouth Water, **Cornhill-on-Tweed**. Prices range from £315 to £2,100 per week (incl VAT), and from £52.50 to £92.40 per day, depending on season. All prices include boat, ghillie and use of fishing huts, Tweed levies and taxes. Head ghillie (tel/fax: 01289 382443). **Dryburgh Estate Fishings**, Melrose TD6 0RQ: dt £32 to £270 (plus VAT), depending on season. Head ghillie: George Inglis (tel: 01835 822708). **Pedwell** fishing, Norham *(see Norham)*. Hotels: Collingwood Arms; Tillmouth Park; Wheatsheaf, Swinton.

Kelso (Roxburghshire). Salmon and sea trout preserved, trout and grayling. Salmon and sea trout fishing can be obtained

daily during summer months on some of the best beats of the Tweed, including Lower Birgham with 2m of double bank, 3 rods, ghillie, hut, dt £55-£250; also Hendersyde beat, 4m left bank, 2 rods, 2 ghillies, 2 huts, dt £50-£700. For further information contact J H Leeming, Stichill House, Kelso, Roxburghshire TD5 7TB (tel: 01573 470280; fax: 01573 470259; web: www.leeming.co.uk; e-mail: info@leeming.co.uk). Kelso AA has about 8m of Tweed and **Teviot**; brown trout and grayling. No Sunday fishing; size limit 10in; restrictions on spinning; trout season, April 1 to Sept 30. Trout fishing good. St £20, wt £10, dt £5. Concessions for OAPs and juniors. Permits from local tackle shops. Brown and rainbow trout fishing on **Cherry Trees Loch** at Yetholm boat on site. Bank fishing. Advance booking necessary. Apply to Forrest of Kelso. Tackle shops: Forrest of Kelso, 40 The Square TD5 7HL (tel: 01573 224687); Tweedside Tackle, 36/38 Bridge St TD5 7JD (tel: 01573 225306). Hotels: Cross Keys; Ednam House; Roxburgh.

St Boswells (Roxburghshire). St Boswells & Newtown District AA rent miscellaneous stretches on River Tweed between Ravenswood and Mertown; brown trout; rod limits on 4 stretches. Assn also has rainbow trout fishing on **Eildon Hall Pond**, nr Newtown St Boswells. Tackle shop: Borders Gunroom, Main Str, TD6 0AA (tel: 01835 822844) has tickets for all main waters.

Melrose (Roxburghshire). Salmon fishing on Bemersyde Beat, prime beat superbly set in beautiful wooded gorge; 1m with 4-6 rods, 1-2 ghillies, 4 boats. Prices range between £20 and £230. Ravenswood beat: opposite Bemersyde, 1½m of right bank, 3-4 rods, 1 ghillie, 1 hut, £30-£220; also Lower Pavilion, 1½m double bank, 6 rods, 1 ghillie, 1 hut, dt £30-£180: apply to J H Leeming, Stichill House, Kelso, Roxburghshire TD5 7TB (tel: 01573 470280; fax: 01573 470259; web: www.leeming.co.uk; e-mail: info@leeming.co.uk). Melrose & Dist AA has 2m of Tweed around Melrose open to visitors for wild trout and grayling fishing. No Sunday fishing; no spinning or use of natural minnow or maggot permitted. St £12, dt £4 from Hon Sec Sec. Season 1 Apr-6 Oct trout, 1 Aug-1 Mar grayling. Barbless hooks and strict limit. 50% of permit sales donated to

Tweed Foundation. Hotel: Burts.

Earlston (Berwickshire). A good centre for Leader and Tweed trout fishing. Earlston AA controls about 5m of **Leader** adjacent to Earlston, with the exception of two small private stretches. St £5 (OAP & jun £1), dt £1, from local hotels and shops. No Sunday fishing and Saturday fishing for st holders only. 2 day permits at £1 each on River Tweed at Gledswood estate for st holders. Other portions of Tweed are reserved. No salmon or sea-trout fishing is open on trouting portions of Tweed. Hotel: Red Lion; Black Bull; White Swan.

Galashiels (Selkirkshire). Salmon fishing on Boleside beat, 1½m double bank, 5-6 rods, 1 ghillie, 2 boats, dt £30-£375; also Fairnilee Beat, good varied autumn beat in lovely scenery; 3m of single bank, 20 small pools; 9 rods; ghillie, 2 huts and full facilities. Prices, from £30 to £120, depending on month. Contact J H Leeming, Stichill House, Kelso, Roxburghshire TD5 7TB (tel: 01573 470280; fax: 01573 470259; web: www.leeming.co.uk; e-mail: info@leeming.co.uk) for these and Sunderland Hall, Peel, Nest, Ashiestiel, Holylee, and Glenormiston beats. Gala AA has trout fishing on 13m of Tweed, part **Gala Water**, and part **River Ettrick**, st £22, wt £15, dt £9, schoolchildren £2 (no Sunday tickets; no spinning). Tickets from J & A Turnbull, Tackle Shop, 30 Bank St, Galashiels TD1 1EN (tel: 01896 753191); and hotels. April to Sept provides best daytime sport; Mid-June to Aug best evenings. Sunderland Hall (tel: 01750 21298) has 2 rods let, £46-£425 per rod week, dt £9-£95, up to 30 Nov. The School of Casting, Salmon and Trout Fishing, offer weekly salmon and trout fly fishing courses throughout the season. Further information from Michael Waller or Margaret Cockburn, The School of Casting, Salmon and Trout Fishing, Station House, Clovenfords, Galashiels, Selkirkshire TD1 3LT (tel/fax: 01896 850293; e-mail: enquiries@fishing-school.co.uk; web: www.fishing-school.co.uk). Hotels: Kings; Kingsknowes; Woodlands; Philipburn House, Selkirk TD7 5LS (tel: 01750 20747) caters for the angler, and has freezer facilities.

Selkirk (Selkirkshire). Salmon fishing preserved. Good centre for Tweed, **Yarrow** and **Ettrick**, covering 80m of trout fishing. Selkirk & Dist AA has water on

Ettrick and Yarrow; size limit 10"; also **Lindean Reservoir**, rainbows, 2 boats at £18 per boat per session; limit 10 trout per boat; fly only; no bank fishing; av size 2½lb: Permits, st £12, dt £4, conc, from Hon Sec; also from Honey Cottage Caravan Park, Hope House, Ettrick Valley TD7 5HU (tel: 01750 62246), who can also arrange fishing on nearby **St Mary's Loch** (trout, pike), and at **Gamescleuch Trout Fishery** (4 acres, brown, rainbow); The Gordon Arms Hotel (Anne Donaldson), Yarrow Valley TD7 5LE (tel: 01750 82222); Bridge End PO; Rodgersons, 6 High St, Selkirk TD7 4DD (tel: 01750 20749). Trout average 3 to the pound and go up to 3lb. No spinning allowed. Rodgersons also have boat fishing permits £18 at Lindean Reservoir, for rainbow trout. Enquiries to D Mitchell, 28 Scotts Place, Selkirk TD7 4DR (tel: 01750 20748). Tackle shop: J & A Turnbull, Tackle Shop, 30 Bank St, Galashiels TD1 1EN (tel: 01896 753191). Hotels: Glen; Heatherlie House; Woodburn; Philipburn House, Selkirk TD7 5LS (tel: 01750 20747) caters for the angler, and has freezer facilities.

Walkerburn (Peeblesshire). Salmon, trout. Tweed Valley Country House, Galashiels Rd, EH43 6AA (tel: 01896 870636; fax: 01896 870639), can arrange salmon fishing on request, including on Peeblesshire Trout FA water; open all season. Hotel can also arrange fishing courses at £97.50 one week adult. Tackle hire on site. Season: salmon, 1 Feb-30 Nov; trout, 1 Apr-30 Sep. George Hotel EH43 6AF (tel: 01896 870336) has permits from £50-£100 per day salmon (Oct, Nov); trout Apr to Sept £8 per day, £24 per week. For salmon, contact J H Leeming, Stichill House, Kelso, Roxburghshire TD5 7TB (tel: 01573 470280; fax: 01573 470259; web: www.leeming.co.uk; e-mail: info@leeming.co.uk).

Innerleithen (Borders). Salmon, trout. Salmon fishing on Traquair Beat, good late autumn beat in grounds of Scotland's oldest inhabited historic house; 3m with easy casting and access for 9 rods; ghillie; dt £50 to £70. Contact J H Leeming, Stichill House, Kelso, Roxburghshire TD5 7TB (tel: 01573 470280; fax: 01573 470259; web: www.leeming.co.uk; e-mail: info@leeming.co.uk). Peeblesshire Trout FA has trout and grayling fishing on Tweed; tickets sold by Traquair Arms Hotel.

Peebles (Borders). Salmon fishing on approx 1½ miles of River Tweed. Season Feb 21 to Nov 30. Fly fishing only. Tickets (limited in number) issued by Peeblesshire Salmon FA; wt £100, dt £35, to Blackwood & Smith WS, 39 High St, Peebles EH45 8AH (tel: 01721 720131; fax 01721 729804; e-mail: office@black woodsmith.com). Salmon fishing on Town Water and Crown Water; permits: dt from £13.50, and £40 for 3 days; apply to Borders Sport & Leisure Trust, Gytes Leisure Centre EH45 8GL (tel: 01721 723688). Peeblesshire Trout FA has approx 23m on Tweed and 5m on **Lyne**; trout and grayling. Season April 1 to Sept 30. No spinning or float fishing. Fly only April and Sept and all season on upper reaches. Catch and release policy is described under main river heading; waders desirable. Good trout April/May on wet fly then dry best. St £40, wt £24, dt £8. Permits from Hon Sec (tel: 01721

720131); Peebles Hotel Hydro; and Rosetta Caravan Park, Rosetta Rd, EH45 8PG (tel: 01721 720770). Kingsmuir Hotel, Springhill Rd, Peebles EH45 9EP (tel: 01721 720151), can arrange salmon and trout fishing on Rivers Tweed, Lyne and tributaries. Peebles Angling School, 10 Dean Park, EH45 8DD (tel: 01721 720331), offers instruction in salmon and trout fishing, and fishing parties on private water; salmon fishing available.

Tweedsmuir (Peeblesshire). Crook Inn, Tweedsmuir, Scottish Borders ML12 6QN (tel: 01899 880272; e-mail: the crookinn@btinternet.com) issues permits for Peeblesshire Trout FA water on Tweed; and on **Talla Reservoir** (300 acres) and **Fruid Reservoir** (293 acres); wild brown trout. Talla: fly only. Fruid: fly fishing, spinning and worm fishing; boats on Talla and bank fishing on each reservoir.

Tributaries of the Tweed

WHITEADDER: Runs from junction with Tweed via Cantys Bridge and Allanton Bridge to source. The removal of the coastal and river nets has made the river one of the prime spring rivers for salmon and trout, with an ever-increasing spring run. Upper waters, from Blanerne Bridge to source, including tributaries, are mainly controlled by Whiteadder AA.

Allanton (Berwickshire). Blackadder joins river here. Waters from ½m above Allanton Bridge (including lower Blackadder) down to tide are mainly controlled by Berwick & Dist AA. Salmon and sea trout fishing tickets on six recognised beats cost £45 season, £20 week, and £10 day. Dt obtainable from Allanton Inn (tel: 01890 818260); R Welsh & Sons, 28 Castle St, Duns TD11 3DP (tel: 01361 883466). Tickets for Tweeddale Fishery, Gifford (rainbow); Willowdean, Foulden (rainbow); and Whiteadder Reservoir (brown trout): at site. Allanton Inn has accommodation.

Chirnside (Berwickshire). Trout. Chirnside is good centre for Whiteadder. From here to source, except for stretches at Ninewells, Abbey St Bathans Estate, Chirnside Paper Mills and Cumledge Bridge, river is controlled by Whiteadder AA, including all tributaries entering above Chirnside, except **Monynut** above Bankend; **Fasney** above Fasney Bridge; and

certain stretches of the **Dye**. Tickets from bailiff, Norman Richardson, 6 Cottage, Ellemford TD11 3SF (tel: 01361 890352); R Welsh & Son, 28 Castle St Duns TD11 3DP (tel: 01361 883466); Nairns Newsagent, 26 Market Square, Duns TD11 3DP (tel: 01361 883233); J S Main, Fishing Tackle Shop, Haddington (tel: 01620 822148); Game Fair Tackle, Berwick upon Tweed (tel: 01289 305119). **River Eye**, runs parallel to Whiteadder a few miles to N, entering sea at Eyemouth. Eye Water AC has water on River Eye at town, Ayton and East Reston, 3½m, and **Ale Water**; river stocked annually with brown trout; st £15, conc £8, from Tourist Information Centre, The Auld Kirk, Eyemouth TD14 5HE (tel: 018907 50678). Hotels: Ship; Whale; Home Arms; Dolphin; The Churches.

Duns (Berwickshire). Trout. The following streams are within easy reach: **Blackadder, Whiteadder, Fasney, Bothwell, Dye, Blacksmill, Monynut** and **Watch**. These, except Blackadder, are, with main stream, largely controlled by Whiteadder AA; Berwick & DAA water below Allanton. Tackle shop: R Welsh, 28 Castle Str, TD11 3DP (tel: 01361 883466) sells tickets for local associations. Hotels: White Swan, Barnikin, Plough, Black Bull, Whip & Saddle.

Popular partly owing to its proximity to England, the Tweed autumn salmon harvest is nevertheless considerable. Here an angler fishes at Innerleithen. *Photo: Arthur Oglesby.*

Longformacus (Borders). 7m from Duns. On Dye, Watch and Blacksmill burns. Permits from R Welsh, *(see Duns)*. Trout fishing from boat and bank on **Watch Reservoir**; 119 acres, fly only, stocked with rainbows from 1¾lbs, also "blues" and browns. Permits and refreshments from Bill Renton, Watch Reservoir TD11 3PE (tel: 01361 890331; mob: 07860 868144).

Cranshaws (Borders). **Whiteadder Reservoir**; 193 acres, brown trout; fly only; information from Scottish Water (tel: 0131 445 6462).

BLACKADDER (tributary of Whiteadder): Very good for brown trout early in season.

Greenlaw (Borders). About 12m held by Greenlaw AC. Season from 1 April to 6 Oct, very good for brown trout, early in season, stocked every year. St, dt, conc for OAP and juniors from Butcher's Shop, Blackadder Mini Market, 20 West High St TD10 6XA; Post Office; and hotels. Hotel: Blackadder; Cross Keys.

TILL and BREAMISH: Trout, sea trout, salmon, good grayling, some pike and perch.

Milfield (Northumberland). Local beats on River Till all have good seasonal runs of salmon and sea trout with resident stocks of brown trout and grayling. No Sunday fishing. All fishing on Ford and Etal Estates is booked through Brian Thompson, Fishery Manager, Redscar Cottage, Milfield, Wooler NE71 6JQ (tel: 01668 216223). Nearest towns: Redscar beat near Milfield, Wooler; Ford beat near Ford village, Wooler; Upper Tindal beat near Etal village, Berwick; Lower Tindal beat near Etal village, Berwick. Tickets for Ford beat from Milfield or Ford PO's (st £120, wt £42, dt £12). Redscar, Upper and Lower Tindal beats from Ford and Etal Estates *(above)* (dt £20 to £25, wt £200). Hotel: Red Lion, Milfield NE71 6JD (tel: 01668 216224); Tankerville Arms, Wooler NE71 6AD (tel: 01668 281581).

Wooler (Northumberland). Upper Till private fishing, also **Glen**. Wooler and Doddington AA preserves 2m of the Till and 1m of **Wooler Water**; limited dt £15 issued to visitors staying locally, but not for Sundays; fixed-spool reels prohibited; no maggot fishing; fly only, Feb-April inclusive and from 14 Sept to 30 Nov. Tickets from Wooler PO, 44 High St, NE71 6BG (tel: 01668 281561). Some

miles from Wooler, at Bewick Bridge, Breamish becomes Till. Wading in Till dangerous. **Bowmont**, also preserved. **Kale Waters**: Trout (small), grayling, with good sea trout in wet season. Tweed rules apply.

Chatton (Northumberland). Trout, grayling; and some fine roach: preserved by Chatton AA for 6½m; limited number of associated members' tickets, waiting list; st apply by 1 Jan to Hon Sec; dt from hotel.

EDEN: Wild brown trout

Ednam (Borders). No salmon fishing open to general public.

Gordon (Berwickshire). Permits for brown trout fishing from Gordon FC: contact Hon Sec; and from PO in village; £3.50 st, juvenile £1 no spinning; no Sunday fishing. Tackle shop: Tweedside Tackle, 36/38 Bridge St, Kelso TD5 7JD (tel: 01573 225306).

TEVIOT: First class for trout and grayling.

Roxburgh (Roxburghshire). Kelso AA controls some miles of brown trout fishing on Teviot and Tweed. Visitors tickets, day £5, season £20, conc; grayling dt £5, wt £10, from Kelso tackle shops *(see Kelso)*.

Eckford (Borders). Eckford AA issues dt for Teviot; salmon and trout. Morebattle & Dist AA has brown trout fishing on Kale Water, **Bowmont Water** and **Oxnam Water**. Permits from Hon Sec; and Templehall Hotel, Kelso TD5 8QQ (tel: 01573 440249).

Hawick (Roxburghshire). Hawick AC has 10m both banks on River **Teviot** and tributaries **Slitrig**, **Borthwick** and **Ale**; salmon, sea trout, brown trout and grayling; club also has fishing on **Lochs Alemoor**, pike, perch and brown trout; **Hellmoor**, brown trout, perch and pike; **Acremoor**, brown trout and perch; **Williestruther**, rainbow trout and brown trout; **Acreknowe**, rainbow trout and brown trout, fly only; **Synton Mossend**, rainbow trout and brown trout, fly only; st £40, dt £10, visitor salmon st £140 from Hon Sec; Rudkins, 8 Drumlanrig Square TD9 0AS (tel: 01450 372765) (boat); Hawick Tourist Office, and Sanford's Country Sports Shop, 6/8 Canongate, Jedburgh TD8 6AJ (tel: 01835 863019). Hotels: Mansfield House.

Jedburgh (Roxburghshire). Jedforest AA has 2 stretches on Teviot, salmon, sea trout, browns and grayling; Timpendean beat is 3m north on A65; 1½m south bank; Ormiston beat on A698 is 4m east of town; 600 metres south bank and 2m north bank; assn also has **Hass Loch**, 6m south of town, 4 acres, rainbow trout; trout st £30, dt £5, salmon wt £130-£60, dt £35-£15; conc for OAP & jun; visitors permits for salmon from Hon Sec; for Hass Loch from First & Last Shop, Jedburgh; for trout from Sanford's Country Sports Shop, 6/8 Canongate, Jedburgh TD8 6AJ (tel: 01835 863019), and W Shaw, Canongate. Sanfords also sell Hawick AC tickets. Jedforest Hotel, Jedburgh TD8 6PJ (tel: 01835 840222) has stretch of Jed Water, which runs by hotel (brown trout). Royal Hotel can arrange fishing in Jed Water and Teviot.

LEADER: Trout (4 to lb).

Lauder (Borders). Lauderdale AA controls 6m of Leader and 20m of tributaries upwards from Whitslaid Bridge to Carfraemill with the exception of waters in Thirlestane Castle policies and Kelphope Burn above Carfraemill. St £5, dt £3, conc, from Hon Sec, shops, hotels and Post Office. Earlston AA has water. Hotels: Tower, Oxton; Carfrae Mill (4m from Lauder); Lauderdale; Black Bull.

Oxton (Borders). Lauderdale AA has Leader Water from Carfraemill and tributaries.

GALA WATER: Popular trout water; fish average about 5 to lb.

Stow (Borders). Salmon and trout fishing on Gala Water. No permit required for local trout fishing.

ETTRICK and **YARROW**: Salmon.

Bowhill (Selkirkshire). The Buccleuch Estates Ltd has 12m double bank on Rivers Ettrick and Yarrow; salmon, sea trout; Tweed rules apply; dt £40, fishing best in autumn. Estate also has brown and rainbow trout fishing on **Bowhill Upper Loch**; fly only; dt £40 per boat, 2 rods, 4

fish per rod limit; permits for loch and salmon fishing from Estate Office, Bowhill, Selkirk TD7 5ES (tel: 01750 20753). All trout fishing in Ettrick and Yarrow by ticket. Permits from Honey Cottage Caravan Park, Hope House, Ettrick Valley, Selkirk TD7 5HU (tel: 01750 62246) who can also arrange fishing on nearby **St Mary's Loch** (trout, pike), and at **Gamescleuch Trout Fishery** (4 acres, brown, rainbow); The Gordon Arms Hotel, Yarrow Valley, Selkirk TD7 5LE (tel: 01750 82222); Bridge End PO; Rodgersons, 6 High St, Selkirk TD7 4DD (tel: 01750 20749). Hotel: Ettrickshaws Country House (*see below*).

Ettrick Bridge (Selkirkshire). Ettrickshaws Country House Hotel, by Selkirk TD7 5HW (tel/fax: 01750 52229), has 2½m of single bank salmon and trout fishing; concessions for hotel guests; also private loch fishing for trout. River trout fishing tickets available.

St Mary's Loch (Selkirkshire). **Megget Reservoir**; 640 acres; stocked brown trout, also Arctic char; fly only; 8 boats and bank fishing; permits £8-£12, conc Megget Reservoir (tel: 01750 42283). St Mary's Loch AC has fishing on **St Mary's Loch** (500 acres) and **Loch o' the Lowes** (100 acres); brown trout, pike and perch. Season 1 Apr-30 Sept, fly only until 1 May for trout, then to include spinning; pike and perch fishing all year round. Boat and bank fishing; no private boats allowed. Outboard motors must be supplied by the angler as none are for hire. Permits £5 fly, £8 spinning, junior £2.50, boats £5 extra from Mr Brown, Keeper, Henderland East Cottage, Cappercleuch TD7 5LG (tel: 01750 42243); Tibbie Shiels Inn.

TYNE (East Lothian)

Rises on north slopes of Lammermuir Hills and flows about 25m to North Sea a little south of Whitberry Ness, known best as brown and sea trout stream.

Haddington (East Lothian). East Lothian AA controls most of water in county. The Tyne and tributaries: most parts from Phantassie Weir, East Linton, through Haddington, Samuelston and Pencaitland to Ormiston; brown trout, sea trout and a few salmon. 11 shops sell tickets, including J S Main & Sons, 87 High St (tel: 01620 822148); (others in East Linton, Dunbar, Tranent, North Berwick etc); st £22, dt £5, OAP/juv £11; tickets also

from East Linton Post Office, High St; also river watchers; Sunday fishing allowed in most parts; no spinning. Tackle from Mike's Tackle Shop, 48 Portobello High St EH15 1DA (tel: 0131 657 3258); J S Main & Sons (above). Hotels: George; Maitlandfield; Monk's Muir Camping & Caravanning.

East Linton. **Markle Fisheries** near Dunbar; 3 lochs total 10 acres, stocked with rainbow trout, also brown, blue, golden, tiger; fly only; one loch stocked with large carp, tench etc; open all year, partial access for disabled; permits from Lodge, Markle Fisheries, East Linton, East Lothian EH40 3EB (tel: 01620 861213). North Berwick AC has no club water but organises 15 outings per year on various waters, for example, Loch Leven, Loch Fitty and North Third Fishery; st £16, dt £5, OAP/juv £8 from J Flemming, Post Office, High St. Tackle Shop: Mike's Tackle *(above)*. Hotels: Bridgend.

Gifford. Hopes Reservoir, near Gifford; 35 acre; brown trout; fly only; 2 boats; no bank fishing; permits Faccombe Estates, Faccombe SP11 0DS (tel: 01264 737247). **Tweedale Millenium Fishery**, nr Gifford EH41 4PS (tel: 01620 810009), has 3 pools, 3 fly. It is regularly stocked with rainbows and browns, from 2lbs to more than 30lbs. Tackle from Mike's Tackle *(see above)*. Hotels: Goblin Ha' Hotel, Gifford EH41 4QH (tel: 01620 810244); Tweedale.

UGIE

A small river entering the sea at Peterhead. Salmon, good sea trout, some brown trout. Salmon and sea trout best from July to October; good run of finnock in February and March.

Peterhead (Aberdeenshire). Permits for approx 13m of fishing leased by Ugie AA. St £120-£150 + £20 membership, wt £50-£60, dt (except Oct) £15-£20, conc OAP & jun, from Robertson's, 19 Queen Street, Peterhead AB42 1TN (tel: 01779 472584); and Dick's Sports, 54 Broad Street, Fraserburgh AB43 9AH (tel: 01346 514120). Braeside Fishery, Stirling Hill, Boddam AB42 3PB (tel: 01779 473903) has fly fishing for rainbow,

brown and brook trout, on 2½ acre loch, stocked; £12 5 hours (2 fish), £20 (4 fish); c&r £8 5hrs, £10 day; conc. Open all year. Rathen Reel Affair Trout Fishery, Rathen by Fraserburgh, AB43 8UL (tel: 01346 513329): lochs of 7 acres and 5 acres with fly fishing for rainbow, brown, tiger, steelhead and blue rainbow trout, ave 3½lbs; dt £8.50-£20, access for wheelchairs. Hotels: Albert, Waterside Inn.

Tributaries of the Ugie

STRICHEN (or North Ugie):
Strichen (Aberdeenshire). Free trout fishing (subject to permission of riparian

owners). Salmon fishing strictly preserved.

URR

Drains Loch Urr and flows to Solway. Late run of salmon; also sea trout, herling and brown trout.

Dalbeattie (Dumfriess & Galloway). Dalbeattie AA has Craignair beat, with salmon, sea trout, and brown trout, best Sept-Nov; fly, worm, spinning. Assn also has trout fishing on **Buittle Reservoir**; fly only; stocked monthly with rainbows. Various permits offered, incl dt for river £16-£26, reservoir £15, conc, from M McCowan & Son, 43 High Str, DG5 4AD (tel: 01556 610270) (branch also in

Castle Douglas). Carp fishing on **Barend Loch**; permits from Barend Holiday Village, Sandyhills, by Dalbeattie, DG5 4NU (tel: 01387 780663); dt £5, free to resident visitors. Near Kirkbean Village is **Kirkhouse Trout Fishery** (tel: 01387 880206), dt (8 hrs) £22, 4 fish. For coarse fishing on **Cowans Loch**, contact Cowans Farm, Kirkgunzeon, by Dumfries.

WEST COAST STREAMS AND LOCHS

Some complex fisheries and one or two smaller - though not necessarily less sporting - streams are grouped here for convenience. Other west coast waters will be found in the main alphabetical list.

AILORT

A short but good sea trout river which drains Loch Eilt and enters sea through saltwater

Loch Ailort. One of the few rivers where run of genuine spring sea trout takes place.

Lochailort (Inverness-shire). Salmon and sea trout fishing on **Loch Eilt** and River Ailort; loch is renowned for some of largest sea trout caught in Britain. Fly only. Permits from Lochailort Inn. **Loch Morar**, a few miles north; good brown trout and occasional salmon and sea trout.

Fly, spinning and trolling allowed. Boats from Loch Morar Boat Hire (tel: 01687 462520). Permits from Morar Motors; Loch Superintendent (tel: 01687 462388). Dt £5, weekly £22, boats (incl fuel) £30 per day; £20 half day.

LOCH BROOM (including Rivers Broom, Dundonnell, Garvie, Oscaig, Polly and Ullapool)

Achiltibuie (Ross-shire). Sea trout, brown trout and sea fishing. Summer Isles Hotel has much fishing for guests on rivers and lochs in the vicinity. Sea trout and brown trout: **Lochs Oscaig** and **Lurgain**. Boat on Oscaig £30; 1 boat on Lurgain. Brown trout lochs, dt £6. Own boats for sea fishing. Apply to Robert Mark Irvine, Summer Isles Hotel, Achiltibuie, by Ullapool, Ross-shire IV26 2YG (tel: 01854 622282). Inverpolly Estate, Ullapool IV26 2YB (tel/fax: 01854 622452; e-mail davies@inverpolly.freeserve.co.uk) has salmon, sea trout and brown trout fishing, with accommodation, on the following: **River Garvie** (very good little sea trout river which runs from Loch Osgaig to the

sea); **River Osgaig** (running from Loch Badagyle to Loch Osgaig, fishes best in late season); **River Polly**, mainly below road bridge (numerous lies and pools), **Polly Lochs, Loch Sionascaig** and **Loch Badagyle; Black Loch, Green Loch, Loch Lurgainn** and others. Mostly fly only, Sunday fishing allowed. Loch permits with boat, £12-£15 (o/b £12); bank, £5. Accommodation with fishing from £550 weekly.

Ullapool (Ross-shire). **Ullapool River,** sea trout, brown trout and salmon; dt £6 (lower beat). **Loch Achall,** salmon, sea and brown trout; dt and boat: inquire Loch Broom Hardware (below). Salmon and sea trout fishing on **River Kaniard** at

An example of the kind of tailor-made facilities available for anglers and others. This is Barend Loch's Holiday Village.

Strathkanaird; prices according to time in season. Also brown trout fishing in hill lochs. Full details from Langwell Estate IV26 2TP (tel: 01854 666221). Ullapool AC has brown trout fishing on Strathkanaird hill lochs: **Lochs Dubh** (brown trout), **Beinn Dearg** (brown and rainbow trout) and **na Moille** (brown trout and char). Membership for residents in area. 2 rainbow limit, no brown trout limit. All lochs fly only except Loch na Moille where under 15's may spin or bait fish. Open annual pike fishing competition on third Sunday in October. Day tickets £5. Permits from Lochbroom Hardware, Shore Street, IV26 2UJ (tel: 01854 612356); Mountain Supplies, West Argyle St IV26 2TY (tel: 01854 613383), who have large range of fly rods, reels

and flies; Hotel: Argyle; Arch Inn.

Leckmelm (Ross-shire). Brown trout fishing on Leckmelm Estate lochs; excellent fish up to 4lb. Permits from Leckmelm Holiday Cottages, Loch Broom IV23 2RN (tel: 01854 612471).

Inverlael (Ross-shire). **River Broom** is a spate river sometimes suitable for fly-spinning. Inverlael Estate has approx 1½m, single bank, including 10 pools; the bottom 2 pools are tidal. Inverlael Estate also has fishing on **River Lael**, its sea-pool and on some hill lochs. Fly only, except on sea pools. Apply to Inverlael Estate office, Loch Broom, by Ullapool IV23 2RG (tel: 01854 655262).

Dundonnell (Ross-shire). **Dundonnell River;** salmon and sea trout.

Loch DUICH (including Shiel and Croe)

Glenshiel, by Kyle of Lochalsh (Ross-shire). Salmon and sea trout. Fishing on **River Croe**, a spate-river with late runs. National Trust for Scotland, Morvich Farm House, Inverinate, by Kyle IV40

8HQ (tel: 01599 511231) has water; currently under review. Sea fishing on Loch Duich. Hotels: Kintail Lodge; Loch Duich; Cluanie Inn, Loch Clunie.

EACHAIG (including Loch Eck)

Drains Loch Eck and flows about 5m into Atlantic by way of Holy Loch and Firth of Clyde. Salmon and sea trout.

Kilmun (Argyll). On Holy Loch and Firth of Clyde. Eachaig enters sea here. Salmon, sea trout in Loch Eck (5m), where Whistlefield Inn, Loch Eck, Cairndow PA23 8SG (tel: 01369 860440) issues tickets: fly best at head of loch where **River Cur** enters. Other hotel: Coylet, Eachaie.

Dunoon (Argyll). Salmon and sea trout; limited weekly lets on River Eachaig from R C G Teasdale, Fishing Agent, Quarry Cottage, Rashfield, nr Dunoon, Argyll PA23 8QT (tel: 01369 840510). Coylet Hotel, Loch Eck PA23 8SG (tel: 01369 840426) and Whistlefield Inn have salmon (mainly trolling), sea trout and brown trout fishing on **Loch Eck** for guests (preferential terms for residents); st £50, wt £25 and dt £5; boats for hire at Coylet Hotel. Loch Eck is about 7m long. No good for salmon until early June; best in August, Sept. Apply to Whistlefield

Inn, Loch Eck, by Dunoon PA23 8SG (tel: 01369 860440). Dunoon & Dist AC has **Rivers Cur**, (wt £30, dt £10), **Finnart** (wt £18, dt £6) and **Massan**, salmon and sea trout, any legal lure (dt £10), and **Ruel** (dt £12); **Lochs Tarsan** (wt £30, dt £10) and **Loskin**, brown trout, fly only (dt £12) ; and **Dunoon Reservoir**, rainbow trout, fly only (dt £14). Permits from Purdies of Argyll, 112 Argyll Str, PA23 7NE (tel: 01369 703232). Permits for River Finnart; sea trout, and occasional salmon; £6, half day £4, conc, from S Share, River Warden, Keeper's Cottage, Ardentinny, Argyll PA23 8TS (tel: 01369 810228); and Purdies *(see above)*. Good sea fishing in estuary for mullet, mackerel and flatfish, etc. Glendaruel Hotel at **Clachan of Glendaruel**, PA22 3AA (tel: 01369 820274) has salmon, sea trout and trout fishing on **River Ruel** (best Aug to Oct). Permits £15.

LOCH FYNE (including Rivers Douglas, Fyne, Kinglas, Shira and Garron, and Dubh Loch)

Large sea loch on west coast of Argyll, which provides good sea fishing. In rivers, stocks

of wild salmon and sea trout have declined seriously, and Argyll Estates no longer offer
fishings.

GAIRLOCH

A sea loch on the west coast of Ross.

Gairloch (Ross-shire). Gairloch AC manages several trout lochs, including Lochs **Bad na Scalaig, Tollaigh, Garbhaig**. Permits for these from Mr K Gunn, Strath or Gairloch Chandlery, Pier Rd, IV21 2BQ (tel/fax: 01445 712458; e-mail: barry.davies1@virgin.net). Lochs **na h-Oidhche, na Curra**, and other fishing in remote mountain scenery; from Post Office, Pier Rd, Gairloch IV21 2BQ (tel: 01445 712175); fishing from mid-June. Salmon and sea trout fishing in **River Kerry**, a spate river; easily accessible; season May-Oct; best Aug-Oct. Permits from Creag Mor Hotel, Gairloch IV21 2AH (tel: 01445 712068). Tackle and ghillie service from Gairloch Chandlery *(see above)*.

GLENELG

Rises in Glen More and flows about 10m to the sea at **Glenelg**. Preserved by Scallasaig Lodge; no fishing at present, to allow stocks to replenish.

LOCH LONG (including Rivers Finnart and Goil)

A sea loch opening into the Firth of Clyde. Good sea trout, some salmon in streams. Finnart and Goil good in spates.

Ardentinny (Argyll). River Finnart enters Loch Long at Ardentinny. Dunoon & Dist AC lease both banks of **River Finnart** from Forestry Commission Scotland on condition that river is kept open to the public at a low cost. Grilse and sea trout, season July to mid-October. Small brown trout in plenty; healthy wild stock. Catch and return policy advised for late coloured spawning fish. Spate and high rivers due to wet Argyll climate makes all parts of river fishable - not many permits. Fishing peaceful and enjoyable. Permits for River Finnart and advice on local fishing from S Share, River Warden, Keeper's Cottage, Ardentinny, Argyll PA23 8TS (tel: 01369 810228), also Purdies of Argyll, 112 Argyll Street, Dunoon PA23 7NE (tel: 01369 703232).

Arrochar (Dumbartonshire). Cobbler Hotel, Loch Long, G83 7BB (tel: 01301 702238) overlooks Loch Long, where good sea fishing obtainable. Hotel has trout fishing in **Loch Lomond** (1½m; salmon, trout, pike).

Carrick (Argyll). Carrick Castle Hotel has salmon, sea trout and brown trout are found on River and **Loch Goil**, free to guests. Boat on loch. Contact Carrick Castle Hotel, Lochgoilhead, Cairndow, Argyll PA24 8AG (tel: 01301 703251).

Lochgoilhead (Argyll). River Goil AC has 15 years lease on **River Goil** salmon and sea trout fishings, and has bought the salmon netting stations on **Loch Goil** and has closed them for good; club also stocks the river; membership fee £100 pa, plus £25 joining fee; visitors dt £15 from Hon Sec or PO (tel: 01301 703201). Loch Goil (sea fishing) - mackerel, dabs and cod. Strictly limited permits (boat hire and accommodation from Shore House Inn PA24 8AJ (tel: 01301 703340). A tackle shop in village and also at Carrick Castle Hotel.

FIRTH OF LORN (including Loch Nell)

Forming the strait between Mull and the mainland on the west coast. Lochs Linnhe and Etive open into it. Good sea trout and a few salmon.

Oban (Argyll). Oban & Lorn AC has trout fishing on **Oude Reservoir** and on twenty six fly-only lochs in the Lorn district; all brown trout, two with char. Oude Reservoir, stocked brown trout; club boat often located on this loch; bank fishing can be difficult because of fluctuating water level. **Loch Nell**, salmon, sea trout, brown trout and char; salmon best in summer; sea trout all through season. Other brown trout fishing include **Lochs Nant** and **Avich**, the largest of these waters. No bait fishing and fishing with more than one rod is illegal. Except for Loch Nell and Oude Reservoir, where spinning, bubble and fly are permitted, all lochs are fly only. There is a junior section which has separate outings and competitions; and juniors are given instruction, etc. Permits from tackle shops in Oban; and Cuilfail Hotel, Kilmelford, Argyll PA34 4XA (tel: 01852 200274) who can also arrage sea fishing. Forestry Commission Scotland, Lorne Forest D.O., Millpark Rd, PA34 4NH (tel: 01631 566155; fax: 01631 566185): brown trout fishing on **Loch Gleann a'Bhearraidh** at Lerags. Permits from Forestry Commission Scotland, Oban; and Cologin Country Chalets and The Barn, Lerags Glen, by Oban, PA34 4SE (tel: 01631 564501), accommodation one mile from loch. **MacKays Loch**, well stocked with rainbows, plus natural browns, fishing from bank or boat, 10 minutes from town centre. Permits for this, and other hill lochs from Anglers Corner. Tackle shops: Anglers

Corner, 114 George St, Oban PA34 5NT (tel: 01631 566374); David Graham's, 11-15 Combie St, Oban PA34 4HN (tel: 01631 562069); Oban & Lorne tickets. Hotel: Ayres; Columba; Manor House.
Kilninver (Argyll). On **Euchar** estuary (10m south of Oban on A816). Tickets for 1m of good salmon, sea trout and brown trout fishing on Euchan may be had from Mrs Mary McCorkindale, Glenann, Kilninver, by Oban PA34 4UU (tel: 01852 316282); boat + 2 rods on **Loch Scammadale** £15 per day; bank and river fishing dt £3; as the Euchar is a spate river, bookings are not accepted more than a week in advance.
Knipoch, by Oban (Argyll). **Dubh Loch** (brown trout) and **Loch Seil**, (sea trout and brown trout); dt £10; bank fishing; **River Euchar**, salmon and sea trout; dt £10; **Loch Tralaig**, near Kilmelford; trout; bank fishing only; permits from Mrs J Mellor, Barrandromain Farm PA34 4QS (tel: 01852 316297).

LOCH MELFORT

A sea loch opening into the Firth of Lorn south of Oban. Sea trout, mackerel, flounders, etc.

Kilmelford (Argyll) 15m from Oban. Cuilfail Hotel, Kilmelford, Argyll PA34 4XA (tel: 01852 200274), can arrange fishing on **Lochs nan Drimnean** (10 min walk, trout; March-May, Aug-Sept best; fly only; 10in limit); **a'Phearsain** (15 min walk; trout, char; fly only; April-June, Aug-Sept best); **Avich** (5m by road; trout; May-Oct best); **na Sreinge** (8m by road

and 35 min walk; trout; May-Oct best), and **Scammadale** (8m by road; sea trout, salmon; end June-Sept). Melfort (10 min walk; sea trout, mackerel, flounders, skate, etc; June-Aug best), and five hill lochs (hour's walk and climb; trout; June-Oct). Wt £25, dt £8. Membership from Oban & Lorn AC. Season: 15 March to 15 Oct.

MORVERN

Lochaline (Argyll). Salmon and sea trout fishing on both **River Aline** and **Loch Arienas**. Native brown trout in over 16 hill lochs. River fishing £25 per day for 2 rods; loch fishing dt £7.50. Boats on site. Contact Ardtornish Estate Co Ltd, Mor-

ven, by Oban, Argyll PA34 5UZ (tel: 01967 421288). Fishing tackle from Estate Information Centre and Shop; and self-catering accommodation in estate cottages and flats.

LOCH TORRIDON

River Torridon, small salmon and sea trout river, flows into Upper Loch Torridon. Outer Loch Torridon offers excellent sea angling for a wide variety of species.

Torridon (Ross-shire). **Rivers Torridon**, and **Thrail**, **Lochs an Iascaigh** and **Damph**, and hill lochs. Loch Torridon Country House Hotel, Torridon, by Achnasheen, Wester Ross, IV22 2EY (tel: 01445 791242), can advise on these, and

also arrange fishing on Loch Maree, subject to availability. Salmon and sea trout fishing on **Loch Damph:** Tigh an Eilean Hotel, Shieldaig IV54 8XN (tel: 01520 755251) can advise on local fishing including sea angling, and has good local contacts at the Shieldaig Angling Club, and Torridon House Estate. Fishing on **River Balgy,** which drains Loch Damph

into southern shore of Upper Loch Torridon is now largely private.

WEST LOTHIAN, (lochs and reservoirs).

Allandale Tarn Fisheries, Gavieside, West Calder EH55 8PT (tel: 01506 873073; e-mail: margo@thefishery. fsnet.co.uk). Bank fishing only. Brown, rainbow, blue; minimum 1½lbs to 16lbs plus; fly dt £20, conc; bait pool: dt £20.

Beecraigs Loch, Beecraigs Country Park, **Linlithgow** (tel: 01506 844516; web: www.beecraigs.com; e-mail: mail@bee craigs.com). Rainbow, brown trout, fly fishing, 8 boats on site. Limit, 12 fish per boat (2 rods). No bank fishing, conservation area. All facilities, including tackle hire and visitors centre. Advance booking essential. Permits available. Tackle Shop: Lochside Tackle & Sports, 254 High St, EH49 7ES (tel: 01506 671477).

Bowden Springs Trout Fishery, Carribber, **Linlithgow** EH49 6QE (tel: 01506 847269), 2 lochs: 5 and 2 acres, stocked daily with large rainbows; but including

browns and blue trout; dt fly pond £22 (8 hours 5 fish) £18, 4 fish, bait pond £16, 10 fish; open 7 days a week.

Linlithgow Loch, Linlithgow. Rainbow and occasional brown trout, Mar-Oct, 20 boats incl one for disabled, and bank fishing. Limit, 6 fish per rod. Permits from Forth Federation of Anglers, P O Box 1, Linlithgow, West Lothian EH49 7LA (tel: 07831 288921) or at lochside.

Morton Fisheries, Morton Reservoir, **Mid Calder,** Livingston EH53 0JT (tel: 01506 882293), fly only brown and rainbow trout, 8 boats on site, and bank fishing, limit 3-6 per rod, then c&r. All facilities, tickets from Fisheries.

Parkley Fishery, Parklay Place Farm,, **Linlithgow** EH49 6QU (tel: 01506 842027), fly and bait fishing for rainbow trout. Dt £18.

WICK

Salmon, sea trout and brown trout fishing on Wick. Spate river with good holding pools. River controlled by Wick AA. Famous Loch Watten (trout) is 7m from Wick.

Wick (Caithness). Wick AA has fishing on River Wick; salmon, sea trout and brown trout; river well stocked from Assn's own hatchery; fly and worm fishing; apply Hugo Ross. Tackle specialist Hugo Ross, 56 High St, Wick KW1 4BP (tel: 01955 604200) has boat and bank fishing permits on **Lochs Watten, St Johns, Toftingall, Calder, Stemster** and **Dunnett**: wild brown trout; fly only on Watten and St Johns; all legal methods on Calder; bank fishing is open on most other Caithness lochs, including those on the Thrum-

ster Estate.

Lybster (Caithness). Lybster is 12m S of Wick at mouth of Reisgill Burn. Portland Arms Hotel, Lybster KW3 6BS (tel: 01593 721721; web: www.portlandarms. co.uk; e-mail: info@portlandarms.co.uk) can usually arrange salmon fishing on **Berriedale River,** also by arrangement on **River Thurso.** Trout fishing on several hill lochs by arrangement, also on **Lochs Watten** and **Calder.** Permits: Hugo Ross, 56 High St, Wick KW1 4BP (tel: 01955 604200)

YTHAN

Rises in "Wells of Ythan" and runs some 35m to North Sea at Newburgh. Late salmon river, noted for sea trout and finnock, which run up from June through to September, with some fish in October. Ythan has very large estuary for so small a river and is markedly tidal for the lower five miles or so of its course.

Newburgh (Aberdeenshire). Sea trout and finnock and salmon. Fishing on the large estuary controlled by Ythan Fisheries. Sea trout average 2-2½lb run up to 12lb; finnock May onwards using large ones in September. Fly fishing and spinning only; spoons. Ythan Terrors, devons and

Sutherland Specials fished on a 7-8ft spinning rod with 8-12lb line as most usual tackle. Worm, maggot, bubble float and other bait not allowed; lead core lines, sinking lines not allowed; floating line with sinking tip allowed; fishing from bank; best months June to September; limited fishing open from 1 June to 30 Sept; prices on application to Mrs Audrey Forbes, Fishing Manager, Ythan Fishery, 3 Lea Cottages, 130 Main Street, Newburgh, Ellon, Aberdeenshire AB41 6BN (tel: 01358 789297), who stocks limited tackle.

Ellon (Aberdeenshire). Buchan Hotel, Bridge St, AB41 9AA (tel: 01358 720208) issues permits for Ellon Water on River Ythan.

Methlick (Aberdeenshire). Some spring fish, but main run Sept to Oct. Good early run of finnock; a second, smaller run in the autumn. Sea trout; June-Oct. Fishing on Haddo Estate water; now leased to Haddo House AA. Dt £6 (Sept/Oct £20). Permits from S French & Son, Main Rd, Methlick AB41 7DT (tel: 01651 806213). Hotel: Ythanview.

Fyvie (Aberdeenshire). Brown trout, sea trout and salmon. Sept and Oct best months for salmon. Fyvie AA has approx 3m on upper River Ythan, single bank. St £25, before 30 Aug only, and dt £5 Feb-Aug, £10 Sept-Oct; obtainable from Alldays Stores.

SEA FISHING STATIONS IN SCOTLAND

It is only in recent years that the full sea angling potential of the Scottish coast, indented by innumerable rocky bays and sea lochs, has come to be appreciated. Working in conjunction, tourist organisations and local sea angling clubs smooth the path for the visiting angler. He is well supplied in matters of boats and bait, natural stocks of the latter remaining relatively undepleted in many areas. The Scottish Federation of Sea Anglers can supply information about more than fifty annual sea fishing festivals, championships and competitions, at venues all around the Scottish mainland and islands.

Note: The local name for coalfish is 'saithe' and for pollack 'lythe'.

Kirkcudbright (Dumfries & Galloway). Centre for excellent shore fishing. Rocky points give good fishing for dogfish, with occasional conger, bull huss and thornback. Clear water gives pollack, garfish, mullet. The Dee estuary produces bags of plaice, dabs and flounders. Boats may be launched at harbour, Ross Bay and Brighouse. Baits: lug and ragworm may be dug locally, mackerel and herring are obtainable in town. Tackle from McKinnel (Watson), 15 St Cuthbert St (tel: 01557 330693). Tourist Information, Harbour Square DG6 4HY (tel: 01557 330494).

Stranraer (Dumfries & Galloway). Loch Ryan, the W coast of Wigtownshire and Luce Bay offer first-class sea fishing, boat and shore. Loch Ryan: codling, whiting, plaice, flounders, dabs, skate, conger, tope and dogfish. Other species found in Luce Bay and off Irish Sea coast include pollack, coalfish, bass, wrasse, mackerel, plaice, dabs, whiting, dogfish, conger. Tackle shop supply blast frozen ammo sea baits, and live baits. Boats: Mike Watson, Main St (tel: 01776 85 3225). Local club: Lochryan Sea AA, J Keith, Motehill, Glenluce DG6 0PE (tel: 01581 300371). Tackle shop: Sports Shop, 86 George St, Stranraer DG9 7JS (tel: 01776 702705), has information and tickets for Stranraer AA trout waters.

Girvan (Ayrshire). Pier fishing. Mostly plaice, codling, rays, flounder, pollack and ling, wrasse, mackerel, dogfish, conger, all from boat; pollack, coley, wrasse, dogfish, codling, flounders from shore. Horse Rock is popular local fishing mark, approachable at half tide, nr Stranraer Rd. Lugworm and ragworm may be dug locally. Boat hire: Mark McCrindle, 7 Harbour St KA26 9AJ (tel: 01465 713219); Tony Wass, 22 Templand Rd, Dalry KA24 5EU (tel: 01294 833724). Tickets for River Girvan from Wright's

Hardware Store, 42 Dalrymple St KA26 9AB (tel: 01465 713213). Hotel: Mansefield.

Ayr (Ayrshire). On the estuaries of the Rivers Ayr and Doon. Beach fishing for flounders from Newton Shore, where baits may be dug; flounders and eels in harbour, mullet in tidal stretches of Ayr. Good mackerel and herring fishing from May to October. Good boat fishing for cod, spotted dogs, and other species. Tackle shop: Gamesport, 60 Sandgate, KA7 1BX (tel: 01292 263822).

Saltcoats and **Ardrossan** (Ayrshire). Shore fishing in the South Bay, and around the harbours, for pollack, wrasse, dogfish, eels, cod, saithe, flat fish and herring. Ragworm and lugworm may be obtained locally, at Fairlie Pier and saltcoats Harbour. 3m north, Ardneil Bay, codling. Club: Ardrossan & Dist SAC.

Brodick and **Lamlash** (Isle of Arran). Cod, plaice, mackerel, conger, wrasse, pollack, gurnard and flatfish. Brodick has good fishing from Markland Point to Clauchlands Point. Lamlash is the main centre for sea fishing on Arran, with boats for hire for mackerel fishing at Lamlash Pier (tel: 01770 600998/349). Johnston's Marine Store, Old Pier, Lamlash KA27 8JN (tel: 01770 600333) has tackle and comprehensive chandlery stock, with information on wrecks, etc.

Campbeltown (Argyll). Good sport with cod, haddock, flatfish, etc, in Kildalloig Bay and from The Winkie, causeway between Davaar Island and mainland. Plenty of loch and river trout fishing in vicinity. Details from the Tourist Information Office, Mackinnon House, The Pier PA28 6EF (tel: 01586 552056); or Kintyre Fish Protection and Angling Club. Tackle shop: A P MacGrory & Co, 16 Main Str, PA28 6AF (tel: 01586 552132); permits for Kintyre FPAC waters. Hotels: Argyll Arms; White Hart, both Main St.

Oban (Argyll). Best fishing off south and west sides of Kerrera Island. Best shore marks, Salmore Point, North Connel at road bridge. Good mackerel fishing in Oban Bay. Species found from shore and boat: tope, conger, whiting, codling, cod, pollack, coalfish, skate, thornback ray, spurdog, dogfish, mackerel, ling, wrasse and gurnard. Charter boat 'Gannet', licensed for ten, all tackle provided; contact Adrian A Lauder, 3 Kiel Croft, Benderloch, by Oban PA37 1QS (tel: 01631 720262). Tackle shop: Anglers' Corner, 114 George Str, PA34 5NT (tel: 01631 566374) has information on all local fishing. Tourist Board, Argyll Square PA34 4AN (tel: 01631 563122).

Portree (Isle of Skye). Sheltered harbour, with fishing marks in and around it. Free anchorage. Cod, haddock, whiting, coalfish, pollack and mackerel. For bait, unlimited mussels and cockles in tidal areas. Camastianavaig is a sheltered bay 4m south east of Portree, where heavy bags of skate, cod, whiting, haddock, spurdog, gurnard, pollack may be caught with trace or paternoster. Tackle shop: Rod & Reel, The Green IV51 9BT (tel: 01478

613121). For boat hire contact Tourist Information, Bayfield House IV51 9EL (tel: 01478 612892).

Kyle of Lochalsh (Ross-shire). Pollack and mackerel frequent; occasional cod, ling, conger, skate. Wreck fishing around Isle of Skye waters. Mussels, clams and cockles are local baits. Tackle shop: Mr & Mrs Finlayson, Marine Stores IV40 8AE (tel: 01599 534208); tackle sold. For boats, inquire Tourist Information Centre IV40 8AE (tel: 01599 534276).

Shieldaig (Ross-shire). Skate, cod, conger, saithe, ling, huss, dabs, sole and mackerel. Fishing in sea lochs of Shieldaig, Torridon and Upper Torridon; sheltered water nearly always. Outside lochs conditions can be dangerous.

Gairloch (Ross-shire). Cod, haddock, mackerel, whiting, pollack, saithe, ling, thornback and flatfish in Loch Gairloch. Disabled anglers have free access to Gairloch Pier. Charter boats from Kerry Sea Angling, Gairloch Chandlery, Pier Rd, IV21 2BQ (tel: 01445 712458); also Gairloch AC tickets; full and half-day trips, tackle provided, common skate fishing and mixed. B&B and self-catering accommodation Gairloch Tourist Information Centre, Achtercairn, Gairloch IV21

No question of letting his customers down. Skipper Adrian Lauder took motor vessel 'Gannet' south east of Mull to catch this skate.

2DN (tel: 01445 712130).

Ullapool and **Summer Isles** (Ross-shire). Skate, also haddock, whiting, codling, pollack, coalfish, mackerel, gurnard, flatfish, thornback ray, conger, dogfish, turbot and wrasse. Inshore sport from dinghies and in charter boats around the Summer Isles. Good shore fishing at Morefield, Rhu and Achiltibuie. Tackle shop: Lochbroom Hardware, Shore Str, IV26 2UE (tel: 01854 612356).

Lochinver (Sutherland). Cod, halibut, skate, tope, saithe, codling, lythe, mackerel. A large fleet of fishing boats operates from harbour. Tackle from Lochinver Chandlery, Culag Square IV 27 4LG (tel: 01571 844398). Tourist Information IV28 1AS (tel: 01571 844330). Hotel: Lochinver.

Stornoway (Isle of Lewis). Cod, conger, pollack, ling, dabs, bluemouth, flounder, dogfish, wrasse, whiting, saithe, skate, etc. Fast-growing centre with local club, Stornoway Sea AC, South Beach Quay, whose secretary will gladly help visiting anglers. Club organises Western Isles Sea Angling Championships in August. Accommodation and information from Maryann Macnar, Western Isles Tourist Board, 26 Cromwell St, Stornoway Isle of Lewis HS1 2DD (tel: 01851 703088; web: www.fishhebrides.com).

Kirkwall (Orkney). Sheltered waters in Scapa Flow hold variety of fish (record skate; halibut over 150lb, ling of 36lb). Also plaice, pollack, coalfish, haddock, mackerel wrasse, from shore or boat. Boats mainly booked by divers, hence hard to obtain; but more freely available. Orkney Tourist Information, Broad Str, Kirkwall KW15 1NX. Tackle shops: E Kemp, 31-33 Bridge St KW15 1HR (tel: 01856 872137); W S Sinclair, 27 John St, Stromness KW16 3AD (tel: 01856 850469). Hotels: Stromness; Royal Hotel, Stromness.

Lerwick (Shetland). Excellent mixed fishing for ling, cod, tusk, skate, haddock, pollack, etc, and chance of halibut. Area has held British records for tusk, homelyn ray, grey gurnard and Norway haddock. Also Scottish hake record. Tackle shop: LHD Marine Supplies, Albert Building, Esplanade ZE1 0LL (tel: 01595 692379). Hotels: Lerwick, Shetland; and Busta House, Brae.

Thurso (Caithness). Conger from harbour walls, and rock fishing. Cod, ling, haddock, conger, pollack, coalfish, dogfish, spurdog, plaice, wrasse, mackerel, dabs, whiting, rays, halibut, porbeagle shark. Thurso Bay and Dunnet head are sheltered areas. Baits: mussel and lugworm at lower water. Most boats are based at **Scrabster**. Tackle shop: Harpers, 57 High St KW14 8AZ (tel: 01847 893179).

Wick (Caithness). Mainly rock fishing for conger, pollack, saithe, cod, haddock, mackerel and flatfish. Porbeagle shark off Caithness, and excellent halibut fishing. Good points are: Longberry, Broadhaven, Sandigoe and Helman Head. Excellent cod fishing off Noss Head. Best months: June to Sept. For further information contact Wick Tourist Information Centre: Whitechapel Rd KW1 4EA (tel: 01955 602596). Hotels: Nethercliffe; Mackay's; Norseman; Queen's.

Portmahomack (Ross-shire). Good opportunities for cod, ling, pollack, mackerel, wrasse etc. The best of the season runs from April to October, probably peaking in August and September. Good reef and limited wreck fishing. Charter vessel for parties of up to 10; boats charged at £40 per hour or £200 per day including rods and lures. Accommodation can be arranged. Contact John R MacKenzie, Carn Bhren, Portmahomack, by Tain IV20 1YS (tel: 01862 871257; mob: 07970 220723). Tackle shop: R McLeod & Sons, Tackle Shop, 14 Lamington St, Tain IV19 1AH (tel: 01862 892171): wide and comprehensive stock including bait. Hotels: Caledonian; Castle: and Oystercatcher.

Lossiemouth (Moray). Notable centre for sea-trout fishing off east and west beaches; spinning into breakers provides splendid sport. Also mackerel, saithe, flatfish from beach, pier and boats. Tackle shops: Angling Centre, Moss St, Elgin IV30 1LU (tel: 01343 547615).

Aberdeen (Aberdeenshire). Excellent rock fishing for cod, ling, saithe, mackerel, whiting, haddock and flatfish. Few boats. Tackle shops: Fraser's Fishing Tackle, 32 Marischal Str, AB11 5AJ (tel: 01224 590221); Somers Fishing Tackle, 13-15 Bon Accord Terrace AB1 2DP (tel: 01224 210008). Hotels: Caledonian, Imperial, Royal.

Stonehaven (Kincardineshire). Rock fishing for cod, coley, pollack, flounder and mackerel very good. Cod, haddock, ling, etc, from boats; available from I Watson (tel: 01569 765064) or Harbour Office, Old Pier AB39 2JU (tel: 01569 762741).

Bait may be ordered from the above. Limited tackle from: Davids, Market Square. Tourist Information, Allardice Str, AB39 2AA (tel: 01569 762806). Hotel: Arduthie House.

Nairn (Nairn). Sea angling on Moray Firth. Most fishing is done from two piers at the entrance to the harbour which is tidal, or on the beach at low water. Tackle shop: Pat Fraser, Radio, TV and Sports shop, 41 High St I V12 4AG (tel: 01667 453038); issues permits for 7m stretch of R Nairn, with sea trout and salmon. Tourist Information IV12 4DN (tel: 01667 452753). Hotels: Altonburn; and Greenlawns Guest House.

Dundee (Angus). Fishing from rock, beach and pier and boats at Tay Estuary, Eas- thaven and Carnoustie for mackerel, cod, saithe, lythe and flatfish. Fishing from boats and beachcasting at Arbroath; for bookings apply to Doug Masson at John R Gow Ltd. Tackle shop: John R Gow Ltd, 12 Union Str, DD1 4BH (tel: 01382 225427) who issue permits for Strathmore AA waters; tackle shop also has access to salmon and sea trout fishing on Tay, North Esk and South Esk; tuition; ghillies.

Dunbar (Lothian). Excellent rock, pier and boat fishing. Saithe, cod (up to 10lb), codling, dabs, plaice, flounders, eels and, at times, small whiting, gurnard and mackerel can be caught. Tourist Information 143 High Str, EH42 1ES (tel: 01368 863353).

The end of a perfect day. *Photo: Adrian Lauder.*

FISHING CLUBS & ASSOCIATIONS IN SCOTLAND

Included in the list of fishing clubs and associations in Scotland are those organisations which are in England, but which have water on the Tweed and its tributaries or on the Border Esk. Further information can usually be had from the Secretaries and a courtesy which is appreciated is the inclusion of a stamped addressed envelope with postal inquiries. Please advise the publishers (address at the front of the book) of any changed details for the next edition.

NATIONAL BODIES

Assn of Salmon Fishery Boards
Director: Andrew Wallace
5A Lennox Street
Edinburgh
EH4 1QB
Tel: 0131 343 2433
Fax: 0131 332 2556
Web: www.asfb.org.uk
e-mail: A.R.Wallace@btinternet.com

Federation of Highland Angling Clubs
K Macdonald
30 Swanston Avenue
Scorguie
Inverness IV3 8QW
Tel: 01463 240095
(Over 30 clubs and associations registered)

Fisheries Research Services,
Freshwater Fisheries Laboratory
Faskally
Pitlochry
Perthshire PH16 5LB
Tel: 01796 472060
Web: www.marlab.ac.uk

Forestry Commission Scotland
231 Corstorphine Road
Edinburgh EH12 7AT
Tel: 0131 314 6508
Fax: 0131 314 6152
Web: www.forestry.gov.uk
e-mail: info@forestry.gov.uk

Institute of Aquaculture
University of Stirling
Stirling FK9 4LA
Tel: 01786 467878
Fax: 01786 472133
Web: www.stir.ac/aqua

International Fly Fishing Assn
Ian Campbell, Secretary & Treasurer
Cruachan
16 Marindin Park
Glenfarg
Perth & Kinross PH2 9NQ
Tel: 01577 830582

Scottish Anglers' National Assn
The Pier
Loch Leven
Kinross
Perth & Kinross KY13 8UF
Tel: 01577 861116
Fax: 01577 864769
Web: www.sana.org.uk
e-mail: admin@sana.org.uk

Scottish Disability Sport
Angling co-ordinator, John Hood
Caledonia House
South Gyle
Edinburgh EH12 9DQ
Tel: 0131 3171130
Fax: 0131 3171075
Web: www.scottishdisabilitysport.com
e-mail: ssadsds2@aol.com

Scottish Federation of Sea Anglers
Paul King
Harbour House
Hopeman
Moray IV30 5RU
Tel: 01343 830316

Scottish Executive Rural
Affairs Department (The)
Pentland House
47 Robb's Loan
Edinburgh EH14 1TY
Tel: 0131 244 6231

Fishing Clubs

When you appoint a new Hon. Secretary, do not forget to give us details of the change. Write to the Publishers (address in the front of the book). Thank you!.

Fax: 0131 244 6313
Web: www.scotland.gov.uk
Scottish Federation of Sea Anglers
Unit 28, Evans Business Centre
Mitchelston Drive
Mitchelston Industrial Estate
Kirkcaldy
KY1 3NB
Tel: 01592 657520
Scottish Office Agriculture &
Fisheries Department (The)
Marine Laboratory
PO Box 101
Victoria Road
Aberdeen AB11 9DB
Tel: 01224 876544
Fax: 01224 295511
Scottish Record Fish Committee
(Saltwater)
Paul King
Harbour House
Hopeman
Moray IV30 5RU
Tel: 01343 830316
Aims as for British Record Fish

Committee
sportscotland
(formerly Scottish Sports Council)
Caledonia House
South Gyle
Edinburgh EH12 9DQ
Tel: 0131 317 7200
Fax: 0131 317 7202
Web: www.sportscotland.org.uk
Visit Scotland
(formerly Scottish Tourist Board)
23 Ravelston Terrace
Edinburgh EH4 3TP
Tel: 0131-332 2433
Web: www.visitscotland.com
(Gives information on fishing holidays in
Scotland)
Wheelyboat Trust (The)
Director: Andy Beadsley
North Lodge
Burton Park
Petworth
West Sussex GU28 0JT
Tel/Fax: 01798 342222

CLUBS

Aberdeen & District Angling Assn
19 Buckie Wynd
Bridge of Don
Aberdeen AB22 8DH
Tel: 01224 820388
Aberfeldy Angling Club
Bob Stewart
POBox 2000
Aberfeldy
Perthshire PH15 2BU
Tel: 01887 829512
Achnasheen Angling Club
c/o Ledgowan Lodge Hotel
Achnasheen
Ross-shire IV22 2EJ
Tel: 01445 720252
Airdrie & District Angling Club
Robert Potter: chairman
48 Alston Avenue
Coatbridge
Lanarkshire ML5 2AP
Tel: 01236 843611
Arbroath Angling Club
Tom Mill
39 Tarry Road
Arbroath
Angus DD11 4BB
Tel: 01241 879086
Arran Angling Club
Mrs S Sillars

Catriona
Brodick
Isle of Arran KA27 8DP
Tel: 01770 302327
Assynt Angling Assn
Neil D J Campbell
Loch Assynt Lodge
by Lairg
Sutherland IV27 4HB
Tel: 01571 822226
Web: www.assynt-angling.co.uk
Avon Angling Club
P Brooks
3 The Neuk
Stonehouse
Lanarkshire ML9 3HP
Tel: 01698 793065
Badenoch Angling Assn
Alexander Bennett
113 High St
Kingussie
Inverness-shire PH21 1JD
Tel: 01540 661645
Ballater Angling Assn
Martin Holroyd
59 Golf Road
Ballater
Aberdeenshire AB3 5RU
Tel: 013397 55365

Beauly Angling Club
D K Sellers
Mingulay
Easter Moniak
Kirkhill
Inverness-shire IV5 7PP
Web: www.beauly-angling-club.co.uk
Berwick & District Angling Assn
D Cowan
129 Etal Road
Tweedmouth
Berwick TD15 2DU
Tel: 01289 306985
Web: www.whiteadder.co.uk
**Blairgowrie, Rattray & District
Angling Assn**
Walter Matthew
9 Mitchell Square
Blairgowrie
Perthshire PH10 6HR
Tel: 01250 873679
Borgie Angling Club
c/o Peter MacGregor
Borgie Lodge Hotel
Skerray by Tongue
Sutherland KW14 7TH
Tel: 01641 521332
Brechin Angling Club
W Balfour
Tanera
9 Cookston Crescent
Brechin, Angus DD9 6BP
Tel: 01356 622753
Carradale Angling Club
Lachlan Paterson
20 Tormhor
Carradale East
Campbeltown, Argyll PA28 6SD
Tel: 01583 431312
**Castle Douglas & District Angling
Assn**
Stanley Kaye
2 Cairnsmore Road
Castle Douglas
Galloway DG7 1BN
Tel: 01556 502695
Chatton Angling Assn
Mrs Jane Douglas
10 Church Hill
Chatton, Alnwick
Northumberland NE66 5PY
Tel: 01668 215298
Cobbinshaw Angling Assn
Cobbinshaw
West Calder
West Lothian EH55 8LQ
Tel: 01501 785208
**Coldstream & District Angling
Assn**

Paul Savage
Glen Priory
New Harper Ridge
Cornhill-on-Tweed TD12 4UP
Tel: 01890 883749
Colmonell Angling Club
Stuart Ross
Main Street
Ballantrae
Ayrshire KA26
Tel: 01465 881269
Crieff Angling Club
Patrick McEwan
11A Sauchie Road
Crieff
Perthshire PH7 4EN
Tel: 01764 655723
Web: www.crieffanglingclub.org.uk
Cumbrae Angling Club
Maj Hugh Murphy, Ret'd
Bar End Street
Millport
Isle of Cumbrae KA28
Tel: 01475 531094
Dalbeattie Angling Assn
J Moran
12 Church Crescent
Dalbeattie
Kirkcudbrightshire DG5 4BA
Tel: 01556 610026
Dalry Angling Assn
Kenny Dahl
78 Main Street
Dalry
Castle Douglas
Kirkcudbrightshire DG7 3UW
Tel: 01644 430594
Devon Angling Assn
R Breingan
33 Redwell Place
Alloa
Clackmannanshire FK10 2BT
Tel: 01259 215185
Dornoch Angling Assn
Dr Elizabeth Banks
Dornoch Outdoor
Castle Street
Dornoch
Sutherland IV25 3PE
Tel: 01862 811111
Dreghorn Angling Club
Wally Osborne: ticket secretary
18 Killoch Way
Girdle Toll
Irvine
Ayrshire KA11 1AY
Tel: 01294 214576
Drumgrange & Keirs Angling Club
Tom McClure

17 Riecawr Avenue
Dalmellington
Ayrshire KA6 7SR
Tel: 01292 551390

Dumfriess & Galloway Angling Assn
Liam Chalmers
50 Brooms Road
Dumfries DG1 2LA
Tel: 01387 267647

Dunfermline Artisan Angling Club
Jim Hay
6 Douglas Drive
Dunfermline
Fife KY12 9YG
Tel: 01383 724968

Dunkeld & Birnam Angling Assn
A Steele
21 Willowbank
Birnam
Dunkeld
Perthshire PH8 0JN
Tel: 01350 727428

Dunoon & District Angling Club
J R McInnes
Eriskay
North Campbell Road
Innellan, Argyll PA23 7SB
Tel: 01369 830350
Web: www.ddac.org.uk

Earlston Angling Assn
Andrew Foggin
Lean Ar Aghaidh
Summerfields
Earlstoun
Berwickshire TD4 6ET
Tel: 01896 848183

East Lothian Angling Assn
R A Hawkins
10 Stevenson Way
Longniddry
East Lothian EH32 0PF
Tel: 01875 853258
e-mail: richardhawkins5@btinternet.com

Eckford Angling Assn
The Buccleuch Estates Ltd
Bowhill
Selkirk TD7 5ES
Tel: 01750 20753

Eden Angling Assn
Ticket Secretary: R Young
33 Blalowan Gardens
Cupar
Fife KY15 5EL
Tel: 01334 654333

Elgin & District Angling Assn
J Stewart
8 Seatown
Lossiemouth
Morayshire IV31 6JJ

Tel: 01343 812906

Esk & Liddle Fisheries Assn
Buccleuch Estates Ltd
Ewesbank
Langholm
Dumfriesshire DG13 0ND
Tel: 013873 80202

Evanton Angling Club
Ian Collier
2 Swordale Cottages
Dingwall
Ross-shire IV16 9UZ
Tel: 01349 830234

Eye Water Angling Club
W Crombie
17 Gillsland
Eyemouth
Berwickshire TD14 5JF
Tel: 018907 50134

Forres Angling Assn
C Ross
The Courtyard
Findhorn
Forres
Moray IV36 3YE
Tel: 01309 690097
Web: www.faa.org.uk

Forth Federation of Anglers
P O Box 7
Linlithgow
West Lothian EH49 7LA
Tel: 07831 288921

Fyvie Angling Assn
J D Pirie
Prenton
South Road
Oldmeldrum, Inverurie
Aberdeenshire AB51 0AB
Tel: 01651 872229

Gairloch Angling Club
Mrs L MacKenzie
4 Strath
Gairloch
Ross-shire IV21 2BP
01445 712047

Galashiels Angling Assn
S Grzybowski
3 St Andrews Street
Galashiels
Selkirkshire TD1 1EA
Tel: 01896 755712

Gatehouse & Kirkcudbright Angling Assn
C M Jeffrey
Pulcree Cottage
Gatehouse of Fleet
Castle Douglas DG7 2BS
Tel: 01557 814083

Goil Angling Club
(See River Goil AC)
Gordon Fishing Club
James H Fairgrieve
Burnbrae
Eden Road
Gordon
Berwickshire TD3 6JU
Tel: 01573 410357
**Greater Glasgow & Clyde Valley
Tourist Board**
11 George Square
Glasgow G2 1DY
Tel: 0141 2044480
Greenlaw Angling Assn
Mr T Waldie
26 East High Street
Greenlaw
Berwickshire TD10 6UF
Tel: 01361 810542
Haddo House Angling Assn
J French
Kirton Manse Road
Ellon
Aberdeenshire AB41 7DG
Tel: 01651 806205
Hawick Angling Club
Hon Sec
5 Sandbed
Hawick
Roxburghshire TD9 0HE
e-mail: hawick.angling@ic24.net
Inverness Angling Club
Donnie MacKay
4 Maxwell Drive
Inverness IV3 5EX
Tel: 01463 239110
Jedforest Angling Assn
J M Oliver
67 Howden Crescent
Jedburgh
Roxburghshire TD8 6JY
Tel: 01835 863239
Web: www.jedforest-angling.co.uk
Keithick Angling Club
John Carrick
c/o Athole Arms
Athole Street
Blairgowrie
Perthshire PH13 9AA
Tel: 01828 627205
Kelso Angling Assn
Euan M Robson
Elmbank
33 Tweedside Park
Kelso
Roxburghshire TD5 7RF
Tel: 01573 225279

Killin & Breadalbane Angling Club
Gerry McCarron
Rowancroft
Main Street
Killin
Perthshire FK21 8SH
Tel: 01567 820833
Kilmaurs Angling Club
J Graham
99 East Park Drive
Kilmaurs KA3 2QP
Tel: 01563 538418
**Kilsyth Fish Protection
Assn**
P Clark
9 Jeffery Place
Kilsyth G65 9NQ
Tel: 01236 825067
Kinlochewe Angling Assn
c/o S Condon
Glendocherty Craft Shop
Achnasheen
Ross-shire IV22 2PA
Tel: 01445 760220
Kintyre Angling Club
Andrew Coffield
Shore Street
Campbeltown
Argyll
Tel: 01586 552510
Web: www.flyfishing.inkintyre.
ukonline.co.uk
Kyles of Bute Angling Club
Allen Richardson
Allt Beag
Tighnabruaich
Argyll PA21 2BE
Tel: 01700 811486
Ladykirk & Norham Angling Assn
John Foreman: Chairman
45 West Street
Norham
Berwick upon Tweed TD15 2LB
tel: 01289 382453
Lairg Angling Club
D A Walker
Park House
Lairg
Sutherland IV27 4AU
Tel: 01549 402208
Bookings: Tel: 01549 402309
**Lamington & District Angling
Improvement Assn**
Bryan Dexter
Red Lees
18 Boghall Park
Biggar, Lanarkshire ML12 6EY
Tel: 01899 220577

Largs & District Angling Club
Mr M Dixon
32 Pantonville Road
West Kilbride
Ayrshire
Tel: 01294 823314
Lauderdale Angling Assn
Graeme Sutherland
Kildonan
14 Brownsmuir Park
Lauder, Berwickshire TD2 6QD
Tel: 01578 722799
Linlithgow Angling Club
Lindsay McFadzean
56 Pilgrims Hill
Linlithgow EH49 7LW
Tel: 01506 844387
Loch Awe Improvement Assn
Mrs J MacKay
Ardchonnel
by Dalmally
Argyll PA33 1BW
Tel: 01866 844226
Lochgilphead & District Angling Club
David Welch
Coig na Shee
1 Kilduskland Rd
Ardrishaig
Argyll PA30 8HE
Tel: 01546 603980
Loch Lomond Angling Improvement Assn
Michael Brady
379 Hamilton Road
Uddington
Glasgow G71 7SG
Tel: 0141 781 1545
Loch Rannoch Conservation Assn
Richard Legate
Glenrannoch House
Kinloch Rannoch
by Pitlochry
Perthshire PH16 5QA
Tel: 01882 632307
Loch Achonachie Angling Club
Okain McLennan
5 McKeddie Drive
Fortrose
Ross-shire IV10 8RJ
Tel: 01381 620674
Lochryan Sea Angling Assn
J Keith
Motehill
Glenluce DG6 0PE
Tel: 01581 300371
Malleny Angling Assn
A Howes
8 Addiston Crescent
Balerno

Edinburgh H14 7DB
Tel: 0131 4493041
Melrose & District Angling Assn
T McLeish
Planetree Cottage
Newstead
Melrose
Roxburghshire TD6 9DD
Tel: 01896 822232
Mid Nithsdale Angling Assn
Hon Sec: Brian Lord
6 New St
Thornhill
Dumfries DG3 5NH
Tel: 01848 330415
Monikie Angling Club
The Pier
Monikie Reservoir
Dundee
Angus DD5 3QN
Tel: 01382 370300
Montrose Angling Club
Mr G S Taylor
7 Dorward Road
Montrose
Angus DD10 8SB
Tel: 01674 673224
Fax: 01674 676786
Morebattle Angling Club
D Y Gray
17 Mainsfield Avenue
Morebattle
Kelso
Roxburghshire
Muirkirk Angling Assn
David Purdie
54 Wellwood Street
Muirkirk
Ayrshire KA18 3QX
Tel: 01290 661344
Musselburgh & District Angling Assn
George Brooks
29 Eskside West
Musselburgh
East Lothian EH21 6PP
Tel: 0131 665 4322
Nairn Angling Assn
K Macdonald (Treasurer)
Mu Dheireadh
22 Claymore Gardens
Nairn
Inverness IV12 4JB
Tel: 01667 456855
Web: www.naa.org
New Cumnock Angling Assn
Robert Shaw
22 Redree Place
New Cumnock

Ayrshire KA18 4EY
Tel: 01290 338874
New Galloway Angling Assn
A Wolffe
The Grey House
High Street
New Galloway
Castle Douglas
Kirkcudbrightshire DG7 3RY
Tel: 01644 420272
Newton Stewart & District Angling Assn
W Brown
5 Glebe Crescent
Newton Stewart
Wigtownshire DG8 6LP
Tel: 01671 401127
Web: www.troutandsalmon.net
North Berwick Angling Club
Norman M Morrison
Kidlaw Farm
Gifford
East Lothian EH39 4JW
North Uist Angling Club
Philip Harding
Claddach Kyles
North Uist HS6 5EW
Tel: 01876 580341
Oban & Lorne Angling Club
c/o Anglers Corner
114 George St
Oban
Argyll PA34 5NT
Tel: 01631 566374
Orkney Trout Fishing Assn
Malcolm Russell
Caolilla
Heddle Road
Finstown
Orkney Isles KW17 2EN
Tel: 01856 761586
Web: www.orkneytroutfishing.co.uk
Peeblesshire Salmon Fishing Assn
c/o Blackwood & Smith, W.S.
39 High Street
Peebles
Peeblesshire EH45 8AH
Tel: 01721 720131
Peeblesshire Trout Fishing Assn
David G Fyfe
Blackwood & Smith, W.S.
39 High Street
Peebles EH45 8AH
Tel: 01721 720131
Pitlochry Angling Club
Secretary: Ron Harriman
Sunnyknowe
7 Nursing Home Brae
Pitlochry
Pershire PH16 5HP

Tel: 01796 472484 (evngs)
or
Ross Gardiner (Club Salmon Secretary)
c/o Pitlochry Tourist Information Centre
22 Atholl Road
Pitlochry
Perthshire PH16 5BX
Tel: 01796 472215 (day)
Tel: 01796 472157 (evngs)
Web: www.pitlochryanglingclub.co.uk
Portree Angling Assn
William Mackintosh
Somerled Square
Portree
Isle of Skye IV51 9EH
Tel: 01478 612684
Portsoy & District Angling Assn
Mr McAulay
Roseacre Cottage
Portsoy
Banff
Prestwick Angling Club
David Allan
Pets Aquarium
124 Main St
Prestwick KA9 1PB
Tel: 01292 477863
Rannoch & District Angling Club
John Brown
The Square
Kinloch Rannoch
Perthshire PH16 5PN
Tel: 01882 632268
Rescobie Loch Development Assn
Rescobie Boathouse
Clock Briggs
Forfar
Angus DD8
Tel: 01307 830367
River Almond Angling Assn
H Meikle
23 Glen Terrace
Deans, Livingston
West Lothian EH54 8BU
Tel: 01506 411813
River Avon Federation
(controls migratory fishing on R Avon)
Lindsay McFadzean
56 Pilgrims Hill
Linlithgow EH49 7LW
Tel: 01506 844387
River Goil Angling Club
Ian K Given
"Bonnyrigg"
25 Churchill Drive
Bishopton
Renfrewshire PA7 5HB
Tel: 01301 703201

St Andrew's Angling Club
Douglas Wilson
169 South Street
St Andrews
Fife KY16 9EE
Tel: 01334 472477
**St Boswells & Newtown Districts
Angling Assn**
W Rodger
Bruntyburn
Ancrum
Jedburgh TD8 6TZ
Tel: 01835 830714
**St Fillans & Loch Earn Angling
Assn**
Donald Gow
6 Rintoul Avenue
Crieff
Perthshire PH7 3SJ
Tel: 01764 654439
St Mary's Loch Angling Club
Harry Brown, Loch Keeper
St Mary's Loch
1 Henderland Cottage East
Capercleuch
Yarrow, Selkirk TD7 5LG
Tel: 01750 42243
**Selkirk & District Angling
Assn**
D Mitchell
28 Scotts Place
Selkirk TD7 4DR
Tel: 01750 20748
Shetland Anglers' Assn
Alec Miller
55 Burgh Road
Lerwick
Shetland Isles ZE1 0HJ
Web: www.troutfishing.shetland.co.uk
South Uist Angling Club
R Hunter
The Bungalow
Garrynamonie
Lochboisdale
South Uist HS8 5TX
Tel: 01878 700202
e-mail: suac@omn.net
Soval Angling Assn
Billy France
45 Leurbost
Lochs
Stornoway
Isle of Lewis HS2 9NS
Tel: 01851 860491 (home)
Tel: 01851 705242 (work)
Stanley & District Angling Club
S Grant
7 Shielhill Park
Stanley

Perth PH1 4QT
Tel: 01738 828179
Stornoway Angling Assn
Brian Shaw
12 Builnacraig Street
Stornoway
Isle of Lewis HS1 2RY
01851 701059
Stornoway Sea Angling Club
South Beach St
Stornoway
Isle of Lewis
Tel: 01851 702021
**Stranraer & District Angling
Assn**
Steve Dutton
28 Station Street
Stranraer DG9 7HL
Tel: 01776 889928
or
c/o The Sports Shop
86 George Street,
Stranraer DG9 7JS
Tel: 01776 702705
Strathgryfe Angling Assn
Kingsley Wood & Co, Solicitors
Burnside Chambers
The Cross, Kilmacolm
Renfrewshire PA13 4ET
Tel: 01505 874114
**Strathmore Angling Improvement
Assn**
Mrs M C Milne
1 West Park Gardens
Dundee DD2 1NY
Tel: 01382 667711
**Strathspey Angling Improvement
Assn (SAIA)**
c/o 3 High Street
Grantown on Spey
Morayshire PH26 3HB
Tel: 01479 872684
Fax: 01479 872211
e-mail: mortimers@spey.fsnet.co.uk
Thurso Angling Assn
Stanley Ogrodnik
Millhouse
Millbank Road
Thurso
Caithness KW14 8PS
Tel: 01847 893355
Tobermory Angling Club
Mike Beckett
5 Erray Road
Tobermory
Isle of Mull PA75 6PS
Tel: 01688 302447
Tongue & District Angling Club
c/o Ben Loyal Hotel

Main Street
Tongue
Sutherland IV27 4XE
Tel: 01847 611216
Turriff Angling Assn
Mrs R Masson
6 Castle Street
Turriff,
Aberdeenshire AB53 7BJ
Tel: 01888 562428
Uig Angling Assn
Mrs Nicolson
Cnoc Preasack
Glenkinnidale
by Portree
Isle of Skye
Ullapool Angling Club
Thomas Mcdougall
25 Morefield Place
Ullapool
Ross-shire
IV26 2TS
Tel: 01854 612655
**United Clyde Angling Protective
Assn**
Joseph Quigley
39 Hillfoot Avenue
Wishaw
Lanarkshire ML2 8TR
Tel: 01698 382479

Upper Annandale Angling Assn
A Dickson
Braehead Woodfoot
Beattock
Dumfries-shire DG10 9PL
Tel: 01683 300592
Web: www.riverannan.co.uk/upper
Upper Nithsdale Angling Assn
K McLean
61 High Street
Sanquhar
Dumfriess-shire DG4 6DT
Tel: 01659 50241
Vale of Leven & District Angling Club
New Clubhouse
Fisherwood Road
Balloch
Dundartonshire G83 8SW
Tel: 01389 757843
Whiteadder Angling Assn
Michael Tremlett
Rigfoot
Duns
Berwickshire TD11 3SF
Tel: 01361 890633
Wick Angling Assn
c/o Hugo Ross
56 High Street
Wick
Caithness KW1 4BP
Tel: 01955 604200

FISHING IN NORTHERN IRELAND

Boards of Conservators, Close Seasons, etc.

For game fisher and coarse fisher alike, Northern Ireland is still largely undiscovered country. There is a wealth of lakes, large and small; miles of quiet unpolluted river, plentifully stocked with large, healthy fish, anything but well-educated to anglers and their methods. By the standards of most other parts of Britain, all of it is underfished. In recent years, coarse fishermen have begun to find out what Northern Ireland has to offer, and there is much, too, for the game fisherman. The visitor as yet unfamiliar with the province is recommended to concentrate on the waters owned and managed by the **Department of Culture, Arts & Leisure** (DCAL), possibly the largest single fishery proprietor in Northern Ireland. They include some of the very best.

DCAL Inland Waterways and Inland Fisheries Interpoint, 20-24 York Street, Belfast BT15 1AQ (tel: 028 9025 8911; fax: 028 9025 8831; web: www.dcalni.gov.uk; e-mail: dcal@dcalni.gov.uk) is the ultimate authority for fisheries in Northern Ireland. In addition to the Department, and working in co-operation with it, there are two Conservancy Authorities, The Foyle, Carlingford and Irish Lights Commission; and The Fisheries Conservancy Board for Northern Ireland. They operate in separate areas.

The Department publishes Angling Guides to the waters under its control, available from Fisheries Division at the above address, and from many tackle shops.

The Foyle, Carlingford and Irish Lights Commission 22 Victoria Road, Londonderry BT47 2AB (tel: 028 7134 2100; fax: 028 7134 2720) act as conservator and issues rod licences in the Foyle area: i.e. the North-Western parts of the province drained by the Foyle/Mourne/Camowen river systems and the rivers Faughan and Roe. The Commission is also responsible for a number of river systems in Co Donegal, R.O.I., including the Finn, Culdaff and Deele. The Foyle, Carlingford and Irish Lights Commission is controlled jointly by the Governments of Northern Ireland and The Republic of Ireland, including in the total area the former Moville District in the Republic and the former Londonderry District in N.I.

The Fisheries Conservancy Board for Northern Ireland, 1 Mahon Road, Portadown, Co Armagh BT62 3EE (tel: 028 3833 4666; fax: 028 3833 8912; web: www.fcbni.com; e-mail: fiona@fcbni.org). This board issues licences for the remainder of the province. As from 3 Sept 2001 all game rod licence holders were required to fix a tag to all salmon, and to sea trout over 50cm caught and retained. The tags are non-transferable, and are designed to allow the enumeration of the catch. Apart from tags, the Board also issues with the licence a log book for completion each day Anglers are required to return the logbooks (in the reply envelope provided) to the issuing Board within 21 days of the licence expiry (Fisheries (Tagging and Logbook) Byelaws (Northern Ireland) 2001).

The Northern Ireland Tourist Board, St Anne's Court, 59 North Street, Belfast BT1 1NB (tel: 028 9023 1221; fax: 028 9024 0960; web: www.discovernorthernireland.com/angling; e-mail: info@nitb.com) is also involved in angling, concerning itself with marketing and promotion, and produces literature on activities and accommodation; also visitor attractions.

Under the provisions of The Fisheries Act (NI) 1966, **The Fisheries Conservancy Board** and **The Foyle, Carlingford and Irish Lights Commission** (FCILC) co-operate with the **DCAL** in the development and improvement of fisheries. As a result, there has been in recent years a dramatic improvement in the quantity and quality of angling, game and coarse, available to visitors. The Department's Rivers Agency is also actively engaged in the improvement of fisheries in watercourses under its control. Works include the construction of fishery weirs, groynes and deflectors; restoration of gravel, landscaping of altered watercourses and comprehensive schemes of tree-planting.

Rod Licences. The Fisheries Conservancy Board for Northern Ireland, whose jurisdiction extends to all fisheries in Northern Ireland except the **Foyle, Carlingford and Irish Lights Commission** (FCILC) area, requires a rod licence for **ALL** freshwater fishing for each rod and line. A Game Rod Licence covers coarse fishing only *on waters designated as coarse fisheries*. The following licences are available.

Game fishing:
Season game fishing rod licence, £21.50.
14-day game fishing rod licence, £10.50.
3-day game fishing rod licence, £5.
Additional amount payable by the holder of a Foyle, Carlingford and Irish Lights Commission season game fishing rod licence to use a single game rod, £1.
14-day joint licence/DCAL permit, £25.50.
3-day joint licence/DCAL permit, £10.00.

Coarse Fishing (FCB):

Season coarse fishing rod licence, £8.
14-day coarse fishing rod licence, £4.
3-day coarse fishing rod licence, £2.
3-day joint coarse fishing rod licence/DCAL coarse fishing permit, £8.00.
14-day joint coarse fishing licence/DCAL coarse fishing permit, £13.00.

Foyle, Carlingford and Irish Lights Commission, whose jurisdiction extends to all waters in the Foyle catchment in both the South and the North including the feeders into the Foyle estuary, requires a **Game Fishing** Rod licence for salmon, sea trout, brown and rainbow trout. These are available in the following categories:

Season game fishing rod licence, £21.50.
14-day game fishing rod licence, £10.50.
3-day game fishing rod licence, £5.00.

Under 18 years of age juvenile game fishing rod licence, £2.
Endorsement for anglers holding a licence £1.00 from outside the FCILC area.

FISHING STATIONS IN NORTHERN IRELAND

As in other sections, principal catchment areas are dealt with in alphabetical order, and details of close seasons, licences, etc, will be found on preceding page. Anglers wanting further details of accommodation, etc, should write to **The Northern Ireland Tourist Board**, St Anne's Court, 59 North Street, Belfast BT1 1NB, (tel: 028 9023 1221; fax: 028 9024 0960; web: www.discovernorthernireland.com/angling; e-mail: info@ nitb.com) or 24 Haymarket, London SW1Y 4DG (tel: 08701 555 250; fax: 020 7766 9929). Additionally, there are extensive fishings controlled by the Department of Culture, Arts and Leisure. The head office is listed in the Clubs list; and the regional offices are listed at the end of the Clubs list under Miscellaneous.

BANN (Lower)

(For close seasons, licences, see under Boards)

A mainly sluggish river running approx 30m from where it leaves Lough Neagh to where it enters the sea below Coleraine. River is canalised at upper end. Good coarse fish and salmonoid population; sea trout fishing in the tideway. Non-canal stretches, both coarse and game, are controlled by Bann System Ltd *(below)*, and permits are obtainable. 10 year average salmon catch, 1,300 on Carnroe Beat, now with 2 fish daily bag limit.

Coleraine (Co Londonderry). River tidal below Cutts. Good game and coarse fishing above tidal stretches. Bann System Ltd, The Cutts, 54 Castleroe Rd, Coleraine BT51 3RL (tel: 028 703 44796; web: www.bannsystem.infm.ulst.ac.uk), offers beats. For **River Bush**, contact Sir Patrick Macnaghten, Dundarave, Bushmills BT57 8ST (tel: 028 2073 1215). Coleraine AA allow dt fishing on **R Ree**, and **Ballyinreese Reservoir**, obtainable from E Kee, 3 Kings Rd, Coleraine; also on 8m of **Macosquin River**: mainly trout, a few late salmon; dt from The Great Outdoors *(below)*. Agivey AA has 12m stretch on R Agivey plus stretch on **Wee Agivey**, nr **Garvagh**; salmon and brown trout; permits (£15, (£5 March to end-May)) from Mrs J McCann, 162 Agivey Rd, Aghadowey BT51 4AB (tel: 028 7086 8686); or Albert Atkins *(below)* for visitors. Fishing has access for disabled. **Ballyrashane Trout Lake**, Creamery Rd: fly only, stocked r trout, dt £15, 4 fish limit, season all year; contact Riverview AC. Tackle shops: Albert Atkins, 71 Coleraine Rd, Garvagh, BT51 5HP (tel: 028 295 57691); The Great Outdoors, 58 Society St BT52 1LA (tel: 028 7032 0701). Hotels: Lodge; Bohill Hotel & Country Club; Bush House Hotel; Portneal Lodge, Kilrea; Brown Trout, Aghadowey.

Kilrea (Co Derry). Bann System Ltd, The Cutts, 54 Castleroe Rd, Coleraine BT51 3RL (tel: 028 7034 4796), offers beats. Trout dt on Kilrea & Dist AC waters, from Sean Donaghy, Donaghy Brothers, 34 Maghera St, Kilrea BT51 5QN (tel: 028 295 40429). Salmon and brown trout; permits for Lower Bann, excluding special game section, from Albert Atkins, 71 Coleraine Rd, Garvagh, BT51 5HP (tel: 028 295 57691). Pike and perch in local canals and loughs. Hotel: Portneal Lodge.

Portglenone (Co Antrim). **Clady River** joins Bann below town. Bann System Ltd, The Cutts, 54 Castleroe Rd, Coleraine BT51 3RL (tel: 028 7034 4796), offers beats on this stretch. Brown trout, late salmon and dollaghen. Dt £5 (Mar-Aug), £15 (Sept-Oct), from Clady & Dist AC, who control whole river and tributaries; obtainable from M Cushanan, Maura's Shop, 60 Main St BT44 8HF (tel: 028 25 822197).

Toomebridge (Co Antrim). Here, the Lower Bann leaves L Neagh. Dept of Culture, Arts & Leisure controls **Lower Bann Navigational Canal** at **Toome**, **Portna** and **Movanagher**; tickets from tackle shops. **Lough Neagh**, with an area of 153 sq miles, is the largest inland water in the British Isles. It supports an immense commercial eel fishery, but apart from that, its potential is as yet largely untapped. The bottom-feeding habits of Lough Neagh trout and the exposed conditions on this enormous stretch of water have so far discouraged anglers from trying to exploit it. A principal problem is the absence of sheltered bays.

Department of Culture, Arts and Leisure Castlewellan Lake anglers enjoy a day's fly fishing.
Photo: Peter Lynch

BANN (Upper)

Flows west and north from its source in the Mourne Mountains to enter Lough Neagh near the middle of its southern shore at a point north of Portadown.

Portadown (Co Armagh). Pike, perch, roach, bream and trout. Dept of Culture, Arts & Leisure has 10m stretch from Portadown to Lough Neagh; a designated coarse fishery; licences from Fisheries Conservancy Board (tel: 028 3833 4666); permits from The Field & Stream, 24 Charlemont St, Moy BT71 7SL (tel: 028 8778 9533). Hotels: Carngrove; Seagoe.

Banbridge (Co Down). Late salmon, brown trout and coarse fish. Water from Hilltown Bridge to **Katesbridge**, and at Drumlouga, controlled by Rathfriland AC; membership £20 plus £20 joining; contact Hon Sec; dt £10 (river), £5 (lough), conc, available from Graham's Confectionery, 11 Downpatrick St, Rathfriland BT34 5BG (tel: 028 4063 8179). Clonduff AC has upper stretches of this river; good salmon and trout later in season, which ends 31 Oct; dt from Downshire Arms, Main St, Hilltown BT34 5PS (tel: 028 4063 8899). Banbridge AC fishes from Katesbridge to **Lenaderg**;

browns, dollaghen and late salmon, and has 76 acre **Corbet Lough**, brown and rainbow trout, 4m from town; dt £8 lake, £4 river, conc, from Coburn's Ltd *(see below)*; Anglers Rest, 42 Aughnacloy Rd, Katesbridge. Gilford AC fishes from Hazelbank Weir, Lenaderg to Dynes Bridge, Moyallen, plus **Kernan Lake**. **Lough Brickland**, 62 acres, Dept of Culture, Arts and Leisure, fly only, b and r trout. **Altnadue Lake**, stocked with rainbows, dt £10 from Spar Shop, 40 Mill St, Gilford BT63 6HQ (tel: 028 38 831087); for Upper Bann, R Moffat, Newsagent, Mill St, Gilford BT63 6HQ (tel: 028 38 831501): dt £2.50, £1 conc. Coarse fishing: **Newry Canal** (roach, bream, rudd, perch, pike); **Lough Shark**; Lakes **Drummillar, Drumaran, Drumnavaddy; Skillycolban** (Mill Dam, perch, pike, eels); Lakes **Ballyroney, Hunshigo, Ballyward, Ballymagreehan**, pike, perch; FCB coarse licence required. Tackle, licences and permits from Co-

The tailer in use on the Blackwater in Ireland: a much under-employed item of landing equipment. *Photo: S J Newman.*

burn's Ltd, 32 Scarva St, Banbridge BT32 3DD (tel: 028 4066 2207). Rathfriland tackle shop: Rodgers Tackle, Castlewellan Rd (tel: 028 406 30093). Hotels: Belmont; Banville; Downshire. Tight Lines (tel: 028 4066 2126) offers two day Angling Breaks for £43.

Hilltown (Co Down). Dept of Culture, Arts & Leisure have four good trout lakes,

totalling more than 350 acres in the area: **Spelga, Castlewellan, Hillsborough, Lough Brickland**. Clonduff AC have water; dt from Devonshire Arms *(below)* or Killens Service Station. Castlewellan & Annsborough AC fish **Ballylough, Annsborough**, a few miles north east; brown and rainbow trout, fly only; day tickets from Chestnut Inn *(see below)*.

Shimna AC has **Altnadue Lough**, stocked with rainbows; dt £5 from The Four Seasons, 47 Main Str, Newcastle BT33 0AD (tel: 028 437 25078). For dt for **Corbet Lough** (brown and rainbow) and **Keirnon Lough** (rainbow), also

Lough Brickland, contact Coburn's Ltd. Tackle shops: Coburn's Ltd, 32 Scarva St, Banbridge BT32 3DD (tel: 028 4066 2207). Hotels: Downshire Arms; Belmont, Banbridge. Chestnut Inn, Lower Square, Castlewellan.

BLACKWATER

(For close seasons, licences, see under Boards)

The largest of the rivers flowing into L Neagh, rising in **South Tyrone** to enter the lough at its SW corner. Coarse fish and trout.

Blackwatertown (Co Armagh). Dept of Culture, Arts & Leisure has 1½m, mainly coarse fishing but short stretch of good game fishing (salmon, brown trout and dollaghan in season); fly, worm and spinning; permits from K Cahoon. Ulster Coarse Fishing Federation has water from Bond's Bridge to end of Argory Estate, a mixed fishery with excellent match weights; individuals may fish free on FCB licence. Several trout lakes near **Dungannon: Park Lake** (4.85 hectares); rainbow; permits issued by fishery and cost depends on time and option chosen; excellent access for disabled fishers and Wheelyboat available (tel: 028 8772 7327); **Altmore Fisheries** (2.5 hectares); rainbow trout; permits issued by fishery and cost will vary according to permit chosen (tel: 028 8775 8977); **Ballysaggart Lough**: bream, eels, perch, pike, roach, rudd, tench; no permit needed. Other local fishings include **Lough More**, Clogher, wild browns; **Annaginny Lake**, Newmills (2.5 hectares); rainbow trout. Fly-fishing, spinning and worm fishing from shore. Permits issued by fishery; various tickets available and cost dependant on option chosen. Bookings and further information contact Alan Abraham (tel: 028 8774 7808/8650). Also **Carnteel Lough**, pike, perch and roach; **Carrick Lough**, bream, roach, perch, tench, pike &c and **Greeve** (18 hectares); bream, roach, perch, tench, pike (to 35lb) and eels; dt not required; disabled access available on both sides. **Brantry** (24.4 hectares); brown trout, fly-fishing only; permit required; information from Parks & Countryside Manager, Dungannon Park Pavilion, Moy Rd, Dungannon BT71 6DY (tel: 028 8772 7327; fax: 028 8772 9169; e-mail: dungannonpark@utv internet.com). Tackle shops: K Cahoon, Cahoon Jewellersm, 2 Irish St, Dungannon BT70 1DB (tel: 028 8772 2754);

Tight-Lines, 237 Killyman Rd, Dungannon BT71 6RS (tel: 028 8772 2001); Lakeview Tackle, Ballygawley Rd, Dungannon (tel: 028 8776 1133); The Field & Stream *(see below)*.

Moy (Co Tyrone). 250m upstream and 100m downstream of Moy town bridge; pike, bream, perch, rudd, roach; licence required for 12yrs and above; dt not required; no disabled access. Tackle shop: The Field & Stream, 24 Charlemont St, Moy BT71 7SJ (tel: 028 8778 9533); guide & ghillie Ivor Cowan also available. Hotels: Charlemont House; Tomneys Licensed Inn, 9 The Square, BT71 7SG (tel: 028 8778 4755).

Benburb (Co Tyrone). Trout for 2½m downstream. Armagh & Dist Game AC leases or owns stretch on river, and seven lakes; it also has its own hatchery, stocking brown trout from its own brood stock, and rainbows reared from fingerlings. Dept of Culture, Arts & Leisure has **Brantry Lough** (brown trout), **White Lough** (brown trout); and **Loughs Creeve LoughEnagh** (5.3 hectares); bream, roach, perch, hybrids, tench, pike and eels; 22 disabled access points available. Tackle shop: Outdoor World, 67 Chapel St, Cookstown BT80 8QB (tel: 028 8676 3682). Dept of Culture, Arts & Leisure also has coarse fishing on **Clay Lake**, nr **Keady** (Co Armagh); 120 acres, pike rudd and perch, open all year.

Clogher, Augher and **Aughnacloy**. (Co Tyrone). Local stretch of river has undergone fishery rehabilitation following a major drainage scheme of the Blackwater River. Permits from Aughnacloy AC, and landowners. Dt from Farmers Maxol Garage, Augher/Clogher Rd; Gordon McLaren, Main St, Augher. Permission from landowners for tributaries: **Callan, Oona** and **Torrent**. Hon Sec, Coalisland & Dist AC; brown trout; a few salmon and dollaghen later in season. Dept of

Armagh & District Angling Club water: Lowry's Lake.

Culture, Arts & Leisure has rainbow trout fishing on **White Lough** (9.3 hectares); rainbow trout; 4 fish per day, min. size 10in; fly only from boats, otherwise, spinning and worming permitted; permit required; from R Morrow, 48 Rehaghey Rd, Aughnacloy. Carrick Lough**Carrick Lough** (4 hectares); bream, roach, perch, tench, pike and eels; licence required for 12yrs and above. Tackle shop: Glenkeen Trout Fishery, 194 Caledon Rd, Aughnacloy BT69 6JD (tel: 01663 557645).

Armagh (Co Armagh). Beside **River Callan**, centre for Blackwater and its tributaries, with many fishing lakes in district. Six of these are controlled by Armagh Fisheries Ltd, The Hatchery, 50 Ballinahonemore Rd, BT60 1HY (tel: 028 3751 1738) incorporating Armagh & Dist Game AC, who offer adult st £70, juv st £10, dt £12 from G I Stores *(see below)*. Fly only on **Shaw's Lake** (brown trout, rainbow & perch) and **Seaghan Reservoir** (164 acres) (brown and rainbow); also **Tullynawood Reservoir** (148 acres) (brown trout, rainbow, pike, perch, roach & rudd) and **Darkley Lake** (coarse fish) and **Lowrys Lake** (brown trout & rainbow); also for 9m of Callan and Blackwater. All legal methods on **Aughnagorgan Lake** (brown trout, rudd, perch & roach). 6 fish bag limit on each lake. Limited disabled access only on Lowrys Lake. Loughgall Country Lake, 11/14 Main St, Loughgall BT61 8HZ (tel: 02838 89 2900): coarse fishery: pike, carp (up to 15lb), perch, roach, rudd, eels, tench; stand for disabled; st and dt available, conc for juv; tickets on site £3. Tackle shop: G I Stores, 5 Dobbin St, BT61 7QQ (tel: 028 375 22335). Hotels: Armagh City, 2 Friary Rd, BT60 4FR (tel: 028 3751 8888); Charlemont Arms, 63-65 Upper English St, BT61 7BH (tel: 028 3752 2028), both Armagh City.

SMALLER RIVERS EMPTYING INTO LOUGH NEAGH

MAINE (Co Antrim): Flows 25m from source in Glarryford Bogs to enter lough south of Randalstown, Co Antrim. With tributaries **Kellswater**, **Braid**, **Clough** and **Glenwherry** provides good fishing for salmon, trout and dollaghan. Braid

AC waters: dt from McNeill's Hardware, 75 Main St, Broughshane BT42 4JP (tel: 028 2586 1629). Gracehill, Galgorm & Dist AC has 3m water at **Ballymena**, brown trout with salmon from July; 4 fish limit, no spinning until Aug 1, no maggot fishing; stretch for disabled; dt £3 Apr to Jul, £5 Jul to Oct, with conc, from Galgorm PO, 5 Fenaghy Rd; Clogh PO, 17 Main St; Maine Fishing Equipment, 158 Finaghy Rd, Cullybackey, Ballymena BT42 1DZ (tel: 028 2588 1188). Randalstown AC controls Maine from **Randalstown** Rd Bridge to Andraid Ford, Kellswater; trout, with salmon and dollaghan in season; dt £5 (per rod per day) Mar to Jun, £10 (per rod per day) rest of season, available from Randalstown PO BT41 3AB (tel: 028 94 472242); no sunday fishing permitted for dt. Demesne Anglers has water from Randalstown Bridge to Lough Neagh; wt, dt from The Estate Office, Shanes Castle, Antrim BT41 4NE (tel: 028 94 428216); advance booking recommended. Kells, Connor & Glenwherrey AC has dt £8, conc, for fishing on Kells and Glenwherry; b and r trout and late salmon run; dt to David Hutchinson, Spar Kells, 10 Fernisky Rd, Kells BT42 3JP (tel: 028 2589 1577).

Dept of Culture, Arts & Leisure has brown trout fishing on **Dungonnell** and **Killylane Reservoirs**, 70 and 50 acres; limit 4 fish. Maine AC issues dt £8 to £5 (depending on season) on 4 miles of river from above **Cullybackey** Weir to 1m above Dunminning Bridge; brown trout, dollaghen and salmon; dt from The Bridge Garage, Cullybackey, Ballymena BT42 1EB (tel: 028 258 80278). Tackle shops: Spence Bros, New St. Hotels: Adair Arms; Leighinmore House and Tullyglass House, Ballymena.

SIXMILEWATER: Flows 15m from Ballyclare to enter lough at Antrim, at its NE corner. A heavily-fished but highly productive trout water, salmon and dollaghen Sept-Oct. Antrim & Dist AC issues st £100, dt £5 (Mar-July), £12 (Aug-Oct), conc, for water between **Doagh** and **Antrim**. Ballynure AC has water from Doagh to **Ballynure**; brown trout, salmon; dt for both from Country Sports *(below)*; Twelfth Milestone, 954 Antrim Rd, Templepatrick, Ballyclare BT39 0AT (tel: 028 9443 2647); Antrim Town Tourist Office. Dunadry Hotel and Country Club, 2 Islandreagh Drive, Dunadry BT41 2HA (tel: 028 9443 4343), has fishing for guests on Sixmilewater, which

Another Department of Culture, Arts and Leisure Reservoir: Killylane, Larne in Co Antrim. Fly fishing. *Photo: Peter Lynch.*

passes through hotel grounds; salmon, browns, rainbow; also issues permits and licences for Straid, Ballyclare; Riverdale, Kells; Kildarg, Antrim; dt prices according to season. Ballynure AC issues dt £5 Mar-Jul, £8 Aug-Oct, for water between Doagh and **Ballynure**, from Ballyclare Milestone, 91 Templepatrick Rd, Ballyclare BT39 9RQ (tel: 028 9335 2063); Doagh Forecourt Centre, 10 Station Rd, Doagh BT39 0QT (tel: 028 9334 0215). **Potterswalls Reservoir**, off Steeple Rd, nr Antrim, has rainbow trout fishing (fly only) for members and visitors. Dept of Culture, Arts & Leisure has trout fishing on **Woodburn Reservoirs** (six), nr **Carrickfergus**; **Upper South** (65 acres); **Middle South** (64 acres); **Lower South** (22 acres); **North** (18 acres); **Lough Mourne** (127 acres); **Copeland** (Marshallstown) (24 acres); Upper and Lower South, fly only; the rest are fly, spinning, worm. North Woodburn, rainbow; others, rainbow and brown; bag limit 4 fish. Fishing at trout farm nr **Ballycarry**: J Caldwell, 73 Bridgend Rd, Ballycarry BT38 9LA (tel: 028 9337 2209). Tackle shop: Vaughan Harkness, Country Sports & Tackle, 9 Rough Lane, off Steeple Rd, Antrim BT41 2QG (tel: 028 9446 7378). Hotel: Deer Park, Antrim. Ballyclare accommodation: Mr & Mrs Max McConnell, Five Corners Guest House, 249 Rashee Rd, BT39 9JN (fully licensed).

CRUMLIN and GLENAVY (Co Antrim): small rivers which flow west through these villages to enter lough. Trout fishing near their mouths. Crumlin & Dist AA water: dt from Glenview Service Station, 16 Mill St, Crumlin. Centre: Crumlin. Accommodation: Hillvale Farm, 11 Largy Rd.

BALLINDERRY: Flows east for approx 30m, through **Cookstown**, to enter lough about midway along west shore. Good fishing for brown trout, dollaghan, and occasional salmon for 20m up from the mouth. Kildress AC has fishing 3m from Cookstown, on A505 Omagh road, with

trout, dollaghan and salmon, mains species. Members only, membership from Hon Sec: £10 per season, or £15, after 31 May. Tickets from Hon Sec or Hon Treasurer. For 2m of Unipork & Coagh AC water at Coagh, contact Mace Shop, 3 Main St, Coagh BT80 0ED (tel: 028 86 736559). Ballinderry Bridge AC has 3m of water; membership £20; dt from McCrystals Filling Station, Ballinderry Bridge Rd; P Devlin, Scotstown Rd (tel: 028 867 37420) and Ryans Shop, Ballyronan. Access, facilities for disabled provided; for all other information contact Leo Cassidy MBE *(see Clubs)*. Kingsbridge AC has 2m; water to be much improved by new water treatment works: dt from Stanley Aspinall, 3 Rathbeg, Cookstown BT80 8HR (tel: 028 86 765905). 2m in the Ardtrea area and **Lough Fea** (also stocked with rainbows) is fished by the Mid Ulster AC; dt £10 from The Lough Fea Bar, 140 Loughfea Rd, Cookstown (tel: 028 867 63517); Hamilton's Outdoor World *(below)*; The Burnavon Arts Centre, Burn Rd; The Royal Hotel, Coagh St (tel: 028 867 62224), all Cookstown. Tackle shop: Hamilton's Outdoor World, 67 Chapel St, Cookstown BT80 8QB (tel: 028 8676 3682). Hotels: Royal Hotel, Coagh St; Glenavon House, Drum Rd; Greenvale, Drum Rd, all Cookstown, Co Tyrone.

MOYOLA (Co Londonderry): Flows east and south from its source in S Derry to enter lough at NW corner. Brown trout in lower reaches and a run of salmon from July. Fishing rights held by Moyola AA, dt from Gerry Ewing, 41 Main St, Castledawson, Magherafelt BT45 8AA (tel: 028 794 68517); Huestons, 55 Main St, Castledawson, Magherafelt, BT45 8AA (tel: 028 794 68282); R Crawford & Co, 34 Main St, Maghera BT46 5AE (tel: 028 796 42672). Accommodation: Laurel Villa Guest House, 60 Church St, Magherafelt, BT45 6AW (tel: 028 796 32238).

BUSH

(For close seasons, licences, see under Boards)

The Bush flows 30m west and north through Bushmills, Co Antrim, to enter the sea near Portballintrae. The fishing rights of the entire catchment (except the stretch from the sea to Bushmills) have been acquired by the Dept of Culture, Arts & Leisure primarily as an experimental river for studies into the biology and management of salmon. Within the terms of this programme, salmon angling is maintained at the highest possible level. Trout in the Bush and its tributaries are small but plentiful: there is a modest run of spring salmon and a grilse run for which the river is best known which begins in June or July, according to flow. It is important to report catches of fin-clipped fish. Bush season has been extended from 1 Mar to 20 Oct. Full details from the booking office in the Salmon Station (tel: 028 2073 1435).

For angling management, the river is divided into the following sections: the *Town Stretch* about 200 yds downstream of the Project Centre at Bushmills; the *Leap Stretch* upstream (approx 600 yds of water); the *New Stretch* (500 yds); and the *Unrestricted Stretch*, the remaining 24m of fishing water. Special daily permits, which may be booked in advance, are required for the Town, Leap and New stretches, as shown under 'Licences, permits and close seasons.' Weekend or Bank Holiday angling must be booked and paid for by 1400 hours on the preceding Friday or normal working day. Half day tickets are sold for the Town, New and Leap stretches from 1 June to 20 Oct. Tributary: **Stracam River**, flowing through the village of that name, offers 2m of good trout fishing. *(For details of permit charges see under Boards).*

Bushmills (Co Antrim). Salmon, sea trout and brown trout. Dundarave Estates Ltd, Dundarave, Bushmills BT57 8ST (tel: 028 2073 1215), have excellent salmon fishing stretch from Bushmills to the sea; dt £28, £40 and £47, depending on month; fishing lodge also on site. Dept of Culture, Arts & Leisure has short stretches (Town, New, and Leap) near Bushmills; stands for disabled on bank; dt from The Hatchery, and should be booked in advance; contact Northern Regional Office, 21 Church St, Bushmills BT57 8QJ (tel: 028 2073 1435). Tackle shop: Causeway Bait & Tackle, 78 Main St BT57 8QD (tel: 028 2073 0025). Hotels: Bushmills Inn; Antrim Arms, Ballycastle.

Ballymoney (Co Antrim). **Bush River** may be fished for brown trout, as can the Ballymoney Burn. Good coarse fishing on **Movanagher Canal** and **R Bann**. Brown and rainbow trout fishing on **Altnahinch Reservoir**, at head of R Bush; Dept of Culture, Arts & Leisure water, 44 acres, bag limit 4 fish, bank fishing only; fly, worm, spinning. Permits from car wash, Rodeing Foot; E J Cassells & Son, 43/45 Main St, Ballymoney BT53 6AN (tel: 028 2766 3216). Tackle shop: Smyths Tackle, 17 Enagh Rd BT53 7PN (tel: 028 2766 4259).

LOUGH ERNE (Upper and Lower)

(For close seasons, licences, under Boards)

Upper and Lower Lough Erne, with the R Erne and tributaries feeding the loughs, comprise 15,300 hectares of mixed game and coarse fishing owned and annually restocked by the Dept of Culture, Arts & Leisure and offering some of the best sport in Europe. The flow is in a NW direction, through the beautiful and largely unspoilt Fermanagh countryside, via Belleek, to where the R Erne reaches the sea at Ballyshannon. Infinitely varied fishing in the lakes, with innumerable secluded bays, inlets and small islands. Rich, unpolluted waters teeming with fish-life, the Erne system is truly an angler's paradise. Centres: Belleek; Kesh; Enniskillen; Bellanaleck; Lisnaskea; Newtownbutler; Derrygonnelly (Tirnavar).

RIVER ERNE. River heavily populated with large bream and roach, pike of record-breaking proportions. Good salmon runs in late summer and autumn. **Belleek**, Co Fermanagh, is a good centre for fishing river and Lower Lough; limit, 6 fish. Also brown and rainbow trout on **Lough Keenaghan**, 38 acres; fly only. **Scolban Lough** (171 acres) has pike to 20lb as main quarry, also perch, and is stocked with rainbow trout to 2lb by Dept of Culture, Arts & Leisure.

LOWER LOUGH ERNE. The trout fishing areas, in which the fish may run very large, are in the north and west of the lake. Recommended areas are from Roscor Bridge up to the Heron Island, and across to the **Garvary River**. South and east of a dividing line, the lake may be fished on coarse fishing licence and permit only.

TRIBUTARIES FEEDING LOWER LOUGH: Ballinamallard River flows south through the village of Ballinamallard, to enter the lake near St Angelo Airport. Dept of Culture, Arts & Leisure controls 1 mile nr Ballinamallard, brown trout; Ballinamallard & Dist AC controls the rest; brown trout; fishing by licence. **Colebrook** and **Tempo** enter lake from the east. Maguiresbridge & Dist AC has fishing here; dt from McCormick's Spar

A sport for the young. The pike-coloured bait shows the cannibal tendency of the species. This fish was taken on Lower Lough Erne, near Balleek. *Photo: Balleek Angling Centre.*

Shop, Main St, Maguiresbridge BT94 4RZ (tel: 028 677 21257). 2 miles of Colebrook is Dept of Culture, Arts & Leisure Designated Coarse fishery, nr Lisnaskea: roach, bream, perch, rudd, eels, the occasional pike, trout and salmon. Ballinamallard and Colebrook rivers are currently being stocked with juvenile salmon as part of a cross-border salmon enhancement initiative for the Erne system. Tackle shop: Home Field & Stream, 18/20 Church Str, Enniskillen BT74 7EJ (tel: 028 663 22114).

UPPER LOUGH ERNE: Principally coarse fish: pike, eel, perch, rudd, bream, roach, occasional salmon and sea trout. Centres: **Lisnaskea; Newtown Butler; Enniskillen**. The National Trust at Crom Estate has fishing on Inisherk and Derryvore Islands, with excellent bream and roach; dt £5 in advance from Sharon Sey, Gate Lodge, Crom Estate, Newtownbutler, Fermanagh (tel: 028 6773 8825); stocked pike lake dt £10, very limited; boats for hire, contact Visitors Centre, Crom Estate BT92 8AP (tel: 028 6773 8118); also for accommodation at National Trust Holiday Cottages and Belle Isle (disabled facility). Carrybridge Hotel Marina & Angling Centre, 171 Inishmore Rd, Lisbellaw BT94 5NF (tel: 028 6638 7148), is situated on Upper Lough Erne, and has boats, engines, bait, tackle, storage on site. For Belle Isle Estate game and pike fishing including on **Colebrooke River**, contact agent, Lisbellaw, Enniskillen BT94 5HF (tel: 028 6638 7231; web: www.belleisle-estate.com); coarse fishing is arranged through Dave Ensor (tel: 028 6638 7077) who supplies bait; or through the agent. **Mill Lough, Bellanaleck**: 100 acres Dept of Culture, Arts & Leisure r and b trout fishery 4 miles from Enniskillen, 4 fish limit. At Castle Coole, **Lough Coole**, National Trust Fishery; b and r trout to 5lbs. ½ dt (boat) £3. **Killyfole Lough**, 56 acres, nr Lisnaskea, has a variety of coarse fish, incl perch and pike. Permits from Erne Tackle *(below)*. Tackle shops: J E Richardson, East Bridge Str, Enniskillen (tickets for local fishing); Erne Tackle, 121 Main Str, Lisnaskea BT92 0JD (tel: 028 677 21969). Hotels: Killyhevlin Hotel, Dublin Rd BT74 6RW (tel: 028 6632 3481): has chalets on banks of Erne, with fishing stages; Manor House; Railway; both Enniskillen; and Donn Cara, Lisnaskea. Riverside Farm, Gortadrehid, Enniskillen BT92 2FN (tel: 028 6632

Where to Fish

2725) has accommodation with boats and bait supplied. Other accommodation at Lough Erne Cottages, Bolusty, c/o J E Richardson, see above. Boats and engines on site.

TRIBUTARIES FEEDING UPPER LOUGH ERNE: Swanlinbar River flows north from Co Cavan to enter the lough midway on the S side. Coarse fish in lower reaches, trout in upper. Permission from landowners. The **Sillees River** flows from above Derrygonelly to enter the lough between Enniskillen and Lisgoole Abbey. Excellent coarse fishing, some trout. **Arney River** flows from Lower Lough Macnean to Upper Lough Erne (large trout and exceptional pike fishing) to enter Upper L Erne near **Bella-**naleck. Good mixed fishing all the way to **Lough Macnean**. Upper and Lower L Macnean both have coarse fishing on them, notably pike. Permits from tackle shops in Bellanaleck and Enniskillen. Also ten Dept trout lakes of various sizes in the area (5 acres to 100 acres), including the famous **Navar Forest Lakes**, and **Mill Lough** at Bellanaleck which holds trout to 5lb. Dept of Culture, Arts & Leisure permits for Mill Lough, Navar Forest Lakes, and Keenaghan Lough, from Belleek Angling Centre, Main St, Belleek, BT93 3FX (tel: 028 686 58181), and tackle shops in Enniskillen, including Home, Field & Stream, 18 Church Str, Enniskillen, Co Fermanagh BT74 7EJ (tel: 028 663 22114).

FOYLE

(For close seasons, licences, see under Boards)

The Foyle system is half in Northern Ireland, half in the Republic. It is formed by the **Derg** (draining Lough Derg) and the **Strule**, constituting the **Mourne**, which unites with the **Finn** at Strabane to become the Foyle proper, which enters the sea at Londonderry. That part of the system in Northern Ireland, including the **Faughan** and **Roe**, is the largest salmon and trout fishery in the country. It drains the north and west slopes of the Sperrin Mountains and most of Co Tyrone.

Londonderry. River tidal here, with best fishing for salmon in tidal pools from July. Also a run of sea trout. Permits from Foyle Commission. Tackle shops: Rod and Line, 1 Clarendon St, BT48 7EP (tel: 028 7126 2877); Tom's Tackle Shop, The Gate Lodge, 31 Ardlough Rd, Waterside, Drumahoe BT47 5SP (tel: 028 7134 6265). Hotels: White Horse, 68 Clooney Rd, Campsie (tel:028 7186 0606); Everglades, Prehen Rd BT47 2NH (tel: 028 7132 1066); Broomhill, Limavady Rd, Londonderry BT47 1LT (tel: 028 7134 7995).

Strabane (Co Tyrone). Here **Mourne** and **Strule** unite to form Foyle. Salmon and sea trout. Permits from Foyle Fisheries Commission, Strabane. No dt as such, but st £20 for Finn from Flushtown Bridge to Castlefinn Bridge; £20 for Foyle section. Contact Billy Diver, 5 Castle Place (tel: 028 71 883021) who issues st and dt for rivers Foyle, Finn, Mourne, Derg, Dennett, Deel; he also had accommodation and supplies ghillies; tickets also from Loughs Agency, 22 Victoria Rd, Londonderry BT47 2AB (tel: 028 71 342100). Dept of Culture, Arts & Leisure has five lakes in the area. Fir Trees Hotel, Dublin Rd BT82 9EA (tel: 028 7138 2382), offers fishing breaks.

Tributaries of the Foyle

MOURNE: A big river which provides salmon, sea trout, brown trout; excellent fly fishing in the 10m between Strabane and Newtownstewart, but largely private. Tickets obtainable from Abercorn Estates, Baronscourt Estate Office, Newtownstewart, BT78 4EZ (tel: 028 8166 1683); bag limit 4 salmon/grilse per day, 2 sea trout, 5 brown; ghillie essential; available to guests at appartments; dt £80.

Sion Mills (Co Tyrone). Excellent 4m stretch (both banks) from Strabane to Victoria Bridge managed by Sion Mills AC (membership closed, but dt available from club only); salmon, sea, brown, white trout; bag limits 4 fish; fly, spinning worm allowed; access for disabled; permits from Angling Information, 151 Melmount Rd BT82 9EX (tel: 028 8165 8027). Tackle shop: N M Tackle, 8 Fyfin Rd, Victoria Bridge, Strabane BT82 9JQ (tel: 028 8165 9501). N M Tackle has own private fishing with dt offered, also day and week permits for various other waters including **Finn River, Derg River** and **Ardstraw River**; advice and information on fishing, local clubs, and accommodation. Hotel: Fir Trees, Dublin Rd, Strabane BT82 9EA.

Newtownstewart (Co Tyrone). The **Owenkillew** and **Glenelly** enter here, offering 30m of ideal game fishing waters noted for their sea trout, salmon and brown trout; salmon, sea & brown trout; bag limit 4 /day (min 10"); Game license £5 /3days, £16.50 /14days; dt £15 (Omagh Anglers); dt £10 (Gaff Anglers & Blakiston-Houston Estate). Owenkillew is spate river, only worth fishing in Jun/Oct. For **Gortin** fishing on **Owenkillew** and **Owenrea**, contact Gabriel Treanor, Treanor's Butchers (below). **Blakiston-Houston Estate** has fishing on 6m stretch of **Owenkillew** and 2m stretch of **Owenrea**; salmon and sea trout; limited fly only dt, £10, from Gabriel Treanor (Butcher's Shop), 56 Main St, Gortin, Omagh BT79 8NH (tel: 028 8164 8543). Omagh AA holds most of fishing rights on Mourne, Strule & Owenkillew around this area, (some 28 miles) and offers dt £15; also from C A Anderson. Also Gaff AC (membership £60) dt £10 on **Glenelly River**, and on Owenkillew from David Campbell, 12 Killymore Rd, Newtownstewart, Omagh BT78 4DT (tel: 028 8166 1543), who also offers B&B and self-catering accommodation, also with private fishing on Rivers **Mourne**: salmon, brown trout, sea trout; C A Anderson & Co, The Hardware House, 64 Market Str, Omagh BT78 1EN (tel: 028 8224 2311).

STRULE: Very good trout fishing from Omagh to Newtownstewart; salmon, sea trout and brown trout; bag limit 4/day (min 10"); Omagh AA; game licence: £5 /3 days, £10.50 /14 days; dt £15, £50 /7days.

Omagh (Co Tyrone). Dept of Culture, Arts & Leisure controls the coarse fishing on a stretch of R Strule by arrangement with Omagh AA; roach and eels. Assn also controls stretches of **Camowen, Owenkillew** and **Drumragh Rivers**; salmon, sea & brown trout; bag limit 4/day (min 10"); game licence £5 /3days; rod £10.50 /14days; dt £15; £50 /7days. **LoughMuck** (35 acres), 3m south of Omagh; pike (up

to 30lbs) and roach; privately owned; 12 pegs available and boats can be hired; dt £5 /rod (£1 for each extra rod) and boats £15 /day; contact Kenny Alcorn, Lakeview House, Loughmuck, Omagh BT78 1TG (tel: 028 8224 2618). More good fishing upstream of Omagh, to Camowen, but fish smaller. Salmon in season. **Owenragh, Quiggery/Fintona** and **Drumragh** enter near **Omagh**. Dept stillwaters, **Loughs Bradan** and **Lee**, 60 and 37 acres, 5 miles from **Castlederg**; brown trout fishing, 4 fish limit, per day, min. size 10 ins; permits for Omagh AA water membership £65, dt £15, conc, from tackle shop, C A Anderson & Co, 64 Market Street, Omagh BT78 1EN (tel: 028 82 8224 2311) or from David Campbell, 12 Killymore Rd, Newtownstewart, Omagh BT78 4DT (tel: 028 81661543). Hotels: Silverbirch, 5 Gortin Rd, Omagh BT79 7DH (tel: 028 82242520). Further information: Omagh TIC, 1 Market Str, Omagh BT78 1EE (tel: 028 8224 7831; fax: 028 8224 0774).

FAIRYWATER: Flows E from Drumquin (trout) to enter **Strule** below Omagh. Remarkably good roach fishing in lower reaches. No permit required. **Burn Dennett River, Dunamanagh**: Small brown trout, occasional salmon and sea trout in season; fly, spinning and worm; dt from Burn Dennet AA; Roy McBrine, 31 Lisnaragh Rd, Dunamanagh BT82 0QN (tel: 028 713 98024).

DERG: flows E from Donegal for 50m to enter Mourne N of **Newtownstewart**. Spate river. Good trout water for 15m to above Castlederg, Co Tyrone, with salmon, brown trout, and occasion sea trout. Castlederg AC has 14m, both banks; dt £15, £40 weekly from H Irwin, 5 John St, Castlederg BT81 7AW (tel: 028 8167 1050) (day)). Pettigo & Dist AA has much fishing on offer including 3m of R Derg and the Lough; dt £5 from Pettigo PO, Main St; Bratton's Bar, Pettigo (tel: 00353 7261519) or contact Hon Sec. Tackle Shops: C A Anderson & Co, 64 Market Str, Omagh BT78 1EN (tel: 028 82 8224 2311) or from David Campbell, 12 Killymore Rd, Newtownstewart, Omagh BT78 4DT (tel: 028 8166 1543). Hotel: Derg Arms.

FAUGHAN and ROE

(For close seasons, licences, see under Boards)

The Faughan flows N for 20m to enter the Foyle area E of Londonderry city; the Roe flows the same distance in the same general direction to enter the Foyle Estuary N of Limavady, Co Londonderry. Salmon, sea trout and brown trout in Faughan; principally sea trout in Roe, but also salmon from July.

FAUGHAN: River Faughan Anglers Ltd lease the fishing rights of tributaries and main river, a 30 mile stretch of water divided into two sections, approx 2m tidal and 28m freshwater, situated between Londonderry and Park. Both sections are productive of sea trout and salmon. Access for disabled anglers, left-hand bank below Campsie Bridge and left bank at Claudy Bridge. Waiting list for season permits; st £67, 2-week £120, 3-day £50, dt £20, conc 2-week £60; Foyle licences: season £21.50, 2-week £10.50, 3-day £5.00, all from Faughan River Anglers Ltd *(see clubs)*; or from Loughs Agency, 22 Victoria Rd, Londonderry BT47 2AB (tel: 028 7134 2100).

ROE:
Limavady (Co Londonderry). Good fishing for 15m from Limavady to Dungiven. Dept of Culture, Arts & Leisure has 1¼m at **O'Cahan's Rock**, S of Limavady, with salmon and sea trout. Roe AA offers 26 day tickets for most of a 34 mile stretch, both banks, from source to river mouth, from Limavady tackle shops, £10; no dt during Oct; sea trout av 1lb, salmon 8lbs. Tackle shop: S J Mitchell & Co, Central Car Park, Livamady BT49 0ER (tel: 028 7772 2128) who displays map of all local fishings, issues permits and is a reliable source of local information. Hotels: Gorteen House; Alexander Arms; Raddisson, Roe Park; many guest houses.

GLENS OF ANTRIM RIVERS

(For close seasons, licences, see under Boards)

CUSHENDALL: Enters sea at Cushendall. Good runs of sea trout Jul-Oct. Occasional late salmon, small native brown trout. Fly, spinning, worm permitted, no bait digging allowed.

GLENARIFF: Small sea trout river which enters sea at Waterfoot. Good runs of sea trout Jul-Oct, occasional late salmon, small native brown trout. Fly, spinning, worm permitted, but no bait digging allowed.

GLENDUN: Enters sea at **Cushendun**. Fair run of late salmon, primarily Sept-Oct, and sea trout Jul-Oct. Fly, spinning, worm permitted, but no bait digging allowed. All three rivers controlled by

Glens AC; dt £10 in Oct, otherwise £5; available at O'Neills Country Sports, Unit 1, 25 Mill St, Cushendall, Co Antrim, BT44 0RR (tel: 028 217 72009). Many guest houses in locality.

MARGY/CAREY/GLENSHESK/TOW: a system of small rivers entering the sea at **Ballycastle**. Sea trout, brown trout and salmon. Dept of Culture, Arts & Leisure waters. Dt for non-DCAL holders, from R Bell *(below)*. Hotels: Antrim Arms, Ballycastle; Thornlea, Cushendun. Tackle shop: Moyle Outdoor Angling & Leisure, 17 Castle St BT54 6AS (tel: 028 2076 9521); R Bell, 40 Ann St, Ballycastle BT54 6AD (tel: 028 2076 2520).

LAGAN

(For close seasons, licences, see under Boards)

A productive salmon and brown trout river which flows into the **Belfast Lough**. Trout fishing upstream from Magheralin, Co Down, for 12m.

Belfast (Co Antrim). Dept of Culture, Arts & Leisure has 2¼m of game and coarse coarse fishing on R Lagan; permits from: Tight Lines, 198/200 Albertbridge Rd (tel: 028 9045 7357); J Braddell & Son Ltd, 11 North St, BT1 1NA (tel: 028 9032 2657; fax 028 9032 0525). Tackle shop: H D Wolsey, 60 Upper Newtownards Rd. Dundonald AC fishes **Lough Creevy**, Ballylone Rd, nr Saintfield: rainbow trout, pike. Limited dt £10 from Legge Bros, 56 Belmont Rd, Belfast 4, BT4

2AN (tel: 028 90471698). Further information from TIC, 59 North ST, Belfast. Holywood FFC fish 3 lakes 4m from Dublin: Creitons Green, Upper Holywood and Donaldsons Lake (latter put and take); dt £10 from Herrins Shop, Holywood; further information from Hon Sec.

Lisburn (Co Antrim). Iveagh AC has stretch of 7 miles from Thornyford Bridge, Dromore, to Spencer's Bridge, Flatfield. 10 free dt for holders of Dept of Culture, Arts & Leisure annual game season permit; dt £5 from Premier Angling Centre, 17 Queen St, Lurgan BT66 8BQ (tel: 028 383 25204). Lisburn & Dist AC fish on 7 miles of **Lagan** between Lisburn and Moira, containing a fair head of b trout, roach, bream; also a stretch of a small tributary, the **Ravarnette**, with b trout to 3lb not uncommon, also roach and bream. This fishing is open to general public with no charge. Club membership is £12 p/a. Dept of Culture, Arts & Leisure has brown and/or rainbow trout lakes, totalling more than 700 acres, in the Lagan Valley area. Near to Belfast, these waters are fished more heavily than most in N Ireland. They also include **Stoneyford Reservoir**, 160 acres, b and r trout, fly, spinning and worm, 4 fish limit, no boat angling; **Ballykeel Loughherne**, 53 acres, b and r trout, fly only. Abundant coarse fishing on canals and loughs **Henney**, **Begney**, **Aghery**, **Beg**, **Neagh**. All with pike, perch, etc. Tackle shop: Guns And Tackle, 9 Smithfield, Lisburn BT28 1TH (tel: 028 926 77975). Hotels: Beechlawn House, 4 Dunmurry Lane, Dunmurry, BT17 9RR (tel: 028 90602010).

Lurgan (Co Armagh). Dept of Culture, Arts & Leisure water: **Craigavon City Park Lakes**, 168 acres: **South Lake**, pike, perch, roach, bream hybrids, some r trout (season: all year): all lawful methods, 2 pike per day under 4kg fish limit. **North Lake**: r trout (season 1 Feb to 31 Dec); fly, spinning, worm; 4 fish per rod/day, minimum size 25.4cm. **Lurgan Park Lake**: coarse fishery (all year), pike, roach, perch, bream and carp (rod licence only needed). Permits from Premier Angling Centre, 17 Queen St, Lurgan BT66 8BQ (tel: 028 383 25204).

Dromore (Co Down). Dromore AC has 2 miles of river below, and 5 miles above Dromore: good trout water, for wet and dry fly. Season starts 1 March. Dt £4, juv £1, from Jackie McCracken's Confectionary, Gallow St, Dromore BT25 1BG (tel: 028 9269 3247). 5 miles away at **Hillsborough**, 40 acres r trout fishery, Dept of Culture, Arts & Leisure water, season 1 Feb to 31 Dec; salmon, browns; fly, worm, spinning. Accommodation at Win Staff B&B, Banbridge Rd, Dromore; Rhoda & Wilson Mark, B&B, 11 Bishops Well Rd, Dromore BT25 1ST (tel: 028 9269 3520).

LOUGH MELVIN

(For close seasons, licences, see under Boards)

A 12,500 acre natural lake, approximately one fifth of which lies in Northern Ireland, (Co Fermanagh). A good spring run of salmon starts in February and a grilse run in June, but the lake is famous chiefly for the variety of its native brown trout. In addition to fish of orthodox appearance, there are dark 'sonaghan' caught over the deeper water and the yellow-bellied 'gillaroo', found in the shallows near the shore. No coarse fishing. **Garrison**, Co Fermanagh is the centre for fishing the lough, **Lough Erne**, famous for its large browns and May/June hatches of mayfly, and **Lough Macnean**, Upper and Lower, also in the vicinity. (Pike, large trout, general coarse fishing.) Garrison & Lough Melvin AC has fishing here; dt from Sean Maguire, Melvin Tackle, Main Str, BT98 4ER (tel: 028 6865 8194) who arrange boats and ghillies; Melvin Bar (tel: 028 6865 8380); Riverside Bar, all Garrison. Small trout in L **Lattone** may be caught from the roadside between Belcoo and Garrison.

CLANRYE RIVER

(For close seasons, licences, see under Boards)

A small system flowing into the head of **Carlingford Lough** at **Newry**, Co Down. 20m of fair salmon, sea and brown trout water above Carnbane Industrial Estate. Newry & Dist AC issues dt £10 for **Clanrye River**, (good run of large sea trout (to 10lbs) and salmon), **McCourt's Lake**, **Poyntzpass**, brown trout, fly only. Apply to Smyth or (for Poyntzpass) MCA Tackle *(below)* or Hon Sec. 3m from town, **Cooper's Lake**, fly fishing for brown trout; Newry AC water; dt £10 from John C Smyth. Dept of Culture, Arts & Leisure trout lake: **Lough Brickland**. Warrenpoint, Rostrevor & Dist AC has fly fishing at Mill Dam, Warrenpoint; tickets from Smyth or MCA Tackle. Kilbroney AC has lower stretch of Kilbroney River at Rostrever; most sea trout; dt from John C Smyth. Tackle shops: John C Smyth, 5/9 Kildare Str, Newry BT34 1DQ (tel 028 3026 5303); MCA Tackle, Unit 4 Craigmore Rd, Newry BT35 6PD (tel: 028 302 62309); Bennett's Bar, Warrenpoint.

NEWRY SHIP CANAL

The first ship canal in British Isles, ceased operation in 1976. The fishable section which runs from Newry to sea locks on Omeath road, 3½m approx, has produced match weights of over 50lb. Summer algae improves roach and bream catches, while large pike are to be caught in winter. Most winter fishing is in Albert Basin.

QUOILE

(For close seasons, licences, see under Boards)

Flows into **Strangford Lough** at **Downpatrick**, Co Down. Coarse fish and some trout in lower reaches; fair trout waters between Annacloy Bridge and Kilmore. Dept of Culture, Arts & Leisure has fishing rights on **Quoile Basin** (100 acres) and 7m of Quoile River from Downpatrick to Kilmore; pike, perch, rudd, eels and brown trout; south bank fishing only; no fishing on nature reserve d/s of Steamboat Quay; no wading. Other Dept of Culture, Arts & Leisure fisheries, **Portavoe Reservoir**, nr Donaghadee and Bangor, 31 acres; rainbow trout, fly only, 20 rods per day, 4 fish limit; **Lough Money**, 53 acre, rainbow trout nr **Downpatrick**. Bridgewater Trout Fishery, I Logan, 91 Windmill Rd, Donaghadee (tel: 028 9188 3348): rainbow trout, B&B on site. Downpatrick & Dist AA hold fishing rights to **Loughinisland Lake** and **Magheraleggan Lake**; guests only when accompanied by a member. **Lough Cowey**, 2 miles north of **Portaferry**, natural 70 acres lough with rainbow and brown trout mostly 2lbs plus, fly fishing; dt and boats on site. Tackle shop: H W Kelly, Hardware, 54 Market Str, Downpatrick BT30 6LU (tel: 028 446 12193). Hotel: Portaferry.

SHIMNA

(For close seasons, licences, see under Boards)

Small attractive river with deep rocky pools flowing from E slope of Mournes to enter sea at **Newcastle**, Co Down. Sea trout (holds Irish record 16½lb) and salmon from July. Dept of Culture, Arts & Leisure fishery in forest areas. Bag limit 2 fish; no Sunday fishing; permits from Forest Office at Tollymore Forest Park. The rest of the river is controlled by Shimna AC. Wt £30 and dt £9, from Four Seasons *(see below)*; also Rangers Office, Tollymore Forest Park, Bryansford, Newcastle (tel: 028 437 22428). Fishing is by all legal methods. Dept stillwaters: **Spelga Reservoir**, 148 acres, b trout; **Castlewellan Lake**, 4 miles from Newcastle, 103 acres, b and r trout, 4 fish limit. Fly, spinning and worming. Tackle shops: The Four Seasons, 47 Main Str, Newcastle (tel: 028 437 25078). Hotels: Slieve Donard, Downs Rd BT33 0AH (tel: 028 437 21066); Enniskeen,98 Bryansford Rd, BT33 0LF (tel: 028 437 22392).

WHITEWATER

(For close seasons, licences, see under Boards)

Small attractive water flowing into sea W of **Kilkeel**, Co Down; 3m of fishing, mainly for sea trout, with some brown trout and a few salmon. Kilkeel AC offers six day tickets, £15 per rod day, for Kilkeel and Whitewater (except Mourne Park Estate water) rivers, from Sub Post Office, The Square, Kilkeel BT34 4AA (tel: 028 4176 2225), or Kilmorey Arms *(below)*. **Spelga Reservoir** is Dept of Culture, Arts & Leisure; wild brown trout fishery, bank only. Tackle shops: Graham Sports, 47 Greencastle St, BT34 4BH (tel: 028 4176 2777); McConnell & Hanna, 19 Newcastle St, Kilkeel; Harbour Store, The Harbour. Hotel: Kilmorey Arms, 41 Greencastle St, Kilkeel (tel: 028 4176 2220).

SEA FISHING STATIONS IN NORTHERN IRELAND

The popularity of sea fishing in N Ireland has grown immensely in recent years, leading to the discovery of new and exciting possibilities. 300 miles of unpolluted coastline offers fishing for a variety of species from rock and beach alike. Sheltered inlets of which Strangford and Belfast Loughs are the largest and best known, offer protection to the boat angler when the open sea may be unfishable due to adverse weather. Twenty-four species of sea fish are caught regularly, including blue shark, skate, tope, cod, bass and flatfish.

Magilligan (Co Antrim). From point, surf fishing for dogfish, flounder, occasional bass. From strand, where lug and ragworm can be dug, beach fishing for flounder. Other venues are: Benone Strand, Downhill Strand, **Castlerock** beach and breakwater, **Barmouth** pier (spinning for mackerel and sea trout) and beach; flatfish, coalfish, whiting, occasional mullet and bass.

Portrush (Co Antrim) and **Portstewart** (Co Derry). Near mouths of Lough Foyle and River Bann. Rock, pier and beach fishing for pollack, mackerel, wrasse, dogfish, coalfish, flounder, plaice, conger and bass. Conger fishing in Portrush harbour. Rock fishing from Ramore Head east and west, Blue Pool rocks, and **Dunseverick**. Skerries, 2m off Portrush produce good catches of turbot, plaice, dogfish, dab. Causeway bank off **Giants Causeway** good rock fishing for wrasse, coalfish, pollack, plaice, turbot. Boats for hire: 'Wandering Star', Geoff Farrow, 6 Sunset Park, Portstewart BT55 7EH (tel: 028 7083 6622), experienced skipper for day and evening deep sea angling trips; The Stewart Bros (tel: 028 7082 3369); 'Boy Matthew': contact Peter Boston, 14 Movilla Rd, Portstewart (tel: 028 7083 2734); 'Island Fisher': contact Robin Cardwell, 108 Coleraine Rd, Portrush (tel: 028 7082 2359); Willie Verner *(below)*. Club: Portstewart SAC. Tackle shop: Flying Tackle, 74 Main Str, Portrush BT56 8BN (tel: 028 7082 2209); Willie Verner, Portrush harbour (tel: 028 7082 2307). Hotels: Comfort Hotel; Magherabuoy House, Eglington, Kiln-an-Oge; all Portrush (and many more).

Ballycastle (Co Antrim). Rock fishing for wrasse, pollack, coalfish, mackerel from Ballintoy. At Ballycastle strand, codling, plaice, small coalfish and whiting. Best in autumn, on evening tides. Spinning or float fishing for cod and pollack. Night fishing at ferry pier is recommended, using float tackle with ragworm, obtainable in town. **Rathlin Island**, just off the coast opposite Ballycastle, has wreck fishing for conger in Church Bay; and cod, coalfish, dogfish, plaice, pollack, turbot, haddock, ling, herring, conger eel, spurdog and skate off Bull point. Boats from C McCaughan (tel: 028 2076 2074; mob: 07751 345791; web: www.e/connect.org/ballycastlecharters), and others. Tackle shop: R Bell, 40 Ann St BT54 6AD (tel: 028 2076 2520); Moyle Outdoor Angling & Leisure, 17 Castle Str, Ballycastle BT54 6AS (tel: 028 20769521) (and boat hire). Hotel: Antrim Arms; Hillsea (B&B), 28 North St, Ballycastle BT54 6BW (tel: 028 2076 2385) has accommodation with sea fishing trips arranged.

Larne (Co Antrim). No fishing from harbour, but bottom fishing at nearby beach for coalfish, cod, dogfish, wrasse. Ragworm can be dug at Larne, **Glynn** and **Magheramorne** strands or bought at Angling Supplies. Local venues are: Glenarm, popular night fishing mark for codling, flatfish; **Murlough Bay**, spinning from rocks for coalfish, mackerel, pollack; Garron Point, codling, wrasse, pollack, coalfish, dogfish. Club: Larne & Dist SAC. Tackle shop: Angling Supplies, 131 Main St, BT40 1HJ (tel: 028 282 76634). Hotels which cater for anglers: Magheramorne House, Curran Court, Halfway House.

Whitehead and **Carrickfergus** (Co Antrim). Opposite Bangor at entrance to Belfast Lough (Belfast 16m). Pollack, mackerel, coalfish, cod, whiting, from rocks, beach and boats. Wrecks off Blackhead for cod, pollack, coalfish. Local venues are Whitehead Promenade, Carrickfergus Harbour and East pier, Ballycarry Causeway, nr **Islandmagee**. Below Blackhead lighthouse, conger, wrasse, cod, mackerel. Boat trips from Carrickfergus Marina, Rodger's Quay

BT38 8BE (tel: 028 9336 6666), as well as Sailing Club, The Harbour (tel: 028 9335 1402). Clubs: Woodburn AC, Carrickfergus SAC and Greenisland AC. Hotels: Dobbins Inn; Coast Rd, both Carrickfergus.

Bangor (Co Down). Bangor is on Belfast Lough, 12m from capital. Cod, plaice, turbot, whiting. Lugworm can be dug on beaches at Bangor, ragworm at Kinnegar. Smelt Mill Bay and Orlock Point are good summer venues for wrasse, codling, coalfish, dogfish, mackerel. Bangor and **Donaghadee** piers for mackerel, coalfish, flatfish. Boats from John Erskine (tel: 028 9146 9458; mob: 0780 157 1830). Tackle shop: Trap & Tackle, 6 Seacliff Rd BT20 5EY (tel: 028 914 58515).

Donaghadee (Co Down). Fishing from pier or rocks for pollack, codling and mackerel. Rigg sandbar (3m off Donaghadee) for cod, whiting, gurnard, coalfish, flatfish, mackerel, rays, dogfish, plaice, pollack. Back of Sandbar for big huss. Boats from Q Nelson, 146 Killaughey Rd BT21 0BQ (tel: 028 9188 3403), specialising in wreck and reef drift fishing; twice daily June-Sept, and weekends Jul-Aug, around the Copeland Islands; all tackle provided for beginners on board.

Strangford Lough (Co Down). Good boat fishing in estuaries and inlets around the lough. Big skate (Aug-Oct), spurdog, huss, thornback. Skate and tope are protected species in lough, and must be returned to the water alive. Codling, turbot, whiting, haddock, mackerel, spurdog and wrasse at deep-water entrance to lough. Best fishing in slack water. Lugworm is plentiful at Island Hill nr Comber and shore at Kircubbin. Wreck fishing for big ling and conger outside lough. Boat in **Portaferry**: 'Cuan Shore', D Rogers, 200A Shore Rd (tel: 028 427 28297): £200 divided by no. of anglers, max 12; tackle on board. Hotels: The Narrows, Portaferry (tel: 028 427 28148); Portaferry, The Strand (tel: 028 427 28231).

Kilkeel (Co Down). Harbour fishing for coalfish and mackerel; West strand for flatfish, dogfish. Black Rock, **Ballymartin**, produces mackerel, dogfish, thornback and codling; **Carlingford Lough**, flatfish, dogfish, thornback, a few bass. Good points are Cranfield and Greencastle, mackerel, dogfish, bass, a few conger, and Bloody Bridge, 1½m outside Newcastle towards Kilkeel, rock cod, mackerel, pollack; Cranfield Point, 3m SW of Kilkeel, fishing for bass, sea trout, pollock and codling. Lugworm can be dug in **Newcastle** harbour and **Greencastle**, rag and lug at **Warrenpoint** beach. Whitewater River has two piers for disabled. Boats for hire from Carlingford Lough Sea Angling Centre, O Finnegan, 25 Chestnut Grove, Newry BT34 1JT (tel: 028 3026 4906; web: www.carlingfordlough.com), for wreck and deep sea fishing, species caught incl cod, pollack, tope, conger, ling. Tackle shop: J Graham & Sons, 47 Greencastle St, BT34 4BH (tel: 028 417 62777). Hotel: Kilmorey Arms, 41/43 Greencastle St BT34 4BH (tel: 028 4176 2220) is HQ of Kilkeel AC, who have trout and salmon fishing in Kilkeel and Whitewater Rivers.

FISHING CLUBS & ASSOCIATIONS IN NORTHERN IRELAND.

The following is an alphabetical list of fishing clubs and associations who fish in Northern Ireland. Particulars of the waters held by many will be found by reference to the Index, in the section headed 'Fishing Stations in Northern Ireland', and information about the others, which may not have their own water, could be had from the Secretaries. A courtesy they appreciate is the inclusion of a stamped addressed envelope with postal inquiries. Please advise the publishers (address at the front of the book) of any changed details for the next edition.

NATIONAL BODIES

Ulster Coarse Fishing Federation
Chairman: Robert Buick
7 Knockvale Grove
Belfast BT5 6HL
Tel: 028 90 655373
Fisheries Conservancy Board for Northern Ireland
1 Mahon Road
Portadown,
Craigavon
Co Armagh BT62 3EE
Tel: 028 383 34666
Fax: 028 383 38912
Web: www.fcbni.com
e-mail: fiona@fcbni.org
Department of Agriculture & Rural Development
Agricultural & Environmental Sciences
Irish Specimen Fish Committee (marine)
Newforge Lane
Belfast
BT9 5PX
Tel: 028 90 255503
e-mail: richard.briggs@dardni.gov.uk

Department of Agriculture & Rural Development
River Bush Salmon Station
Irish Specimen Fish Committee (freshwater)
21 Church Street
Bushmills
Co Antrim
BT57 8QJX
Tel: 028 20731435
e-mail: walter.crozier@dardni.gov.uk
Department of Culture, Arts & Leisure
Inland Fisheries
3rd Floor, Interpoint
20-24 York Street
Belfast BT15 1AQ
Tel: 028 90258873
Wheelyboat Trust (The)
Director: Andy Beadsley
North Lodge
Burton Park
Petworth
West Sussex GU28 0JT
Tel/Fax: 01798 342222

CLUBS

Agivey Anglers Assn
Albert Atkins
67 Caleraine Rd
Garvagh
Co Londonderry BT51 5HR
Tel: 028 295 57691
Antrim & District Angling Assn
Alan Fleming
91 Hartswood
Cidercourt Road
Crumlin, Co Antrim BT29 4PY
Tel: 028 908 44636
Armagh & District Game Angling Club
Trevor Dickson

93 Kilvergan Road
Portadown
Co Armagh
Tel: 028 3834 4405
Ballinderry Bridge Angling Club
Leo Cassidy, MBE
18 Spring Road
Coagh
Cookstown BT80 0BD
Tel: 028 7941 8779
or
c/o Hatchery
BFH Ltd,
Tel: 028 8676 1515

Ballylagan Fishing & Conservation Club
c/o Smyths Country Sports
1 Park Street
Coleraine
Co Londonderry BT52 1BD
Tel: 028 703 43970

Ballynure Angling Club
John Arneill
17 Collinview Drive
Ballyclare
Co Antrim BT39 9PQ
Tel: 028 933 24716 *(after 6pm)*

Banbridge Angling Club
J Curran
2 Ballydown Road
Banbridge
Co Down BT32 4JB
Tel: 028 406 27988

Belfast Anglers' Assn
Michael Crilly
20 Old Coach Road
Belfast BT9 5PR

Burn Dennet Angling Assn
W O'Neill
22 Carrickatane Road
Dunamanagh
Co Tyrone BT82 0NG
Tel: 028 713 98512

Castlederg Anglers Club
R R Harron
36 Ferguson Crescent
Castlederg
Co Tyrone BT81 7AG
Tel: 028 816 71256 *(9am - 6pm)*
or
c/o H Irwin, Grocer
5 John Street
Castlederg
Co Tyrone
Tel: 028 816 71050

Castlewellan & Annsborough Angling Club
S P Harrison
Garden Cottage
Forest Park
Castlewellan BT31 9BU
Tel: 028 437 78240

Clady & District Angling Club
Margaret Dillon
33 Mayogall Rd
Magherafelt
Co Londonderry BT45 8PD
Tel: 028 796 43331

Coalisland & District Angling Club
Tony Kerr
9 Torrent Drive
Coalisland

Co Tyrone BT71 4SG
Tel: 028 877 48447

Coleraine Anglers Assn
Dr Mark Henderson
23 Ballyleagry Rd
Limavady
Co Londonderry BT49 0NJ

Dromore Angling Club
(not available as we go to press)

Donaghadee Sea Angling Club
Billy Greer
29 Ravenscroft Avenue
Belfast BT5 5BA
Tel: 028 906 57816

Dundonald Angling Club
Peter Grahame
13 Cherryhill Drive
Dundonald
Belfast BT16 1JG
Tel: 028 904 82161

Dungiven Anglers Club
(Now amalgamated with Roe AA)

River Faughan Anglers Ltd
L F Thompson
Office:
26A Carlisle Road
Londonderry
BT48 6JW
Tel: 028 712 67781 *(office hrs)*

Gaff Angling Club
Leslie Cresswell
15 Killyclogher Road
Omagh
Co Tyrone BT79 0AX
Tel: 028 822 42269

Gilford Angling Club
Bernie Donnelly
11 Wall Road
Gilford
Craigavon
Co Armagh

Glens Angling Club
Hon Treasurer
5 Middle Park Crescent
Cushendall
Co Antrim BT44 0SD

Gracehill, Galgorm & District Angling Club
S Tuff
122 Toome Rd
Ballymena
Co Antrim BT42 2BY
Tel: 028 256 45202 *(after 5pm)*

Holywood Fly Fishing Club
C F Kyle
12 Rutherglen Gardens
Bangor BT19 1DY
Tel: 028 91 453384

Iveagh Angling Club
Gary Houston
26 Rampark
Dromore Rd
Lurgan
Co Armagh BT66 7JH
Tel: 028 383 24144

Kells, Connor & Glenwherrey Angling Club
Garry Cooper
8 Fernisky Park
Kells, Ballymena
Co Antrim BT42 3LL
Tel: 028 258 91812

Kildress Angling Club
Bobby Cox
26 Maloon Way
Cookstown
Co Tyrone BT80 8WX
Tel: 028 867 64345

Kilkeel Angling Club Ltd
Peter Rafferty
56 Burren Road
Warrenpoint
Co. Down BT34 3SA
Tel: 028 417 63297
or
c/o The Kilmorey Arms
41 Greencastle St
Kilkeel
Co Down BT34 4BH
Tel: 028 417 62220

Kilrea & District Angling Club
Stephen Graham
128 Moneydig Road
Kilrea
Co Londonderry BT51 5XB
Tel: 028 295 40370

Kingsbridge Angling Club
Stanley Aspinall: Treasurer
3 Rathbeg
Cookstown
Co Tyrone BT80 8HR
Tel: 028 86 765905

Lisburn & District Angling Club
Hon Sec: Fred Lockhart
c/o Hammond Farm
Hammond Road
Ballinderry Upper
Lisburn
Co Antrim BT28 2RY

Maguiresbridge & District Angling Club
P Trotter
7 Tattinderry Estate
Maguiresbridge
Co Fermanagh BT94 4ST
Tel: 028 67 721877

Maine Angling Club
Tom Simpson
48a Shellinghill Road
Cullybackey
Ballymena
Co Antrim BT42 1NR
Tel: 028 258 81421

Mid-Antrim Angling Assn
R Topping
24 Cameron Park
Ballymena
Co Antrim BT42 1QJ
Tel: 028 25641642

Mid-Ulster Angling Club
Tom Stirling
25 Killycolp Road
Cookstown
Co Tyrone BT80 8UL
Tel: 028 86 763926

Moyola Angling Assn
Tom Maguire
3 Graigmore Road
Maghera
Co Londonderry BT46 5AL
Tel: 028 79 642793 *(after 6pm)*
Web: www.fishirl.com

Newry & District Angling Club
Ronald McCamley
28 High St
Newry
Co Down BT34 1HB
Tel: 028 30 268768

Omagh Angling Assn
Gerard Kelly
19 Dreenan Road
Beragh
Co Tyrone BT79 0SH
Tel: 028 807 57281

Pettigo & District Angling Club
Davy Stanson
Bor Island
Kesh
Co Fermanagh BT93 8BD
Tel: 028 686 31951

Portstewart Sea Angling Club
A McCallion
23 Hillview Pk
Coleraine
County Londonderry
BT51 3EH
Tel: 028 703 21113

Randalstown Angling Club
John Ellis
92 Ahoghill Road
Randalstown
Co Antrim BT41 3DG
Tel: 028 944 79475

Rathfriland Angling Club
John Dougan
33 Newry Road
Rathfriland
Co Down BT34 5PX
Tel: 028 4063 8943

Riverview Angling Club
Billy Magee
21 University Park
Coleraine
Co Londonderry BT52 1JU
Tel: 028 703 28121

Roe Angling Assn
c/o S J Mitchell & Co
Central Car Park
Livamady
Co Londonderry BT49 0ER
Tel: 028 7772 2128

Shimna Angling Club
Ian Watts
7 Tullybrannigan Park
Newcastle
Co Down
Tel: 028 437 22454

Sion Mills Angling Club
Angling Information Centre
151 Melmount Road
Sion Mills

Co Tyrone BT82 9EX
Tel: 028 816 58027
Fax: 028 816 59890
e-mail: angling@sionmills.co.uk
or
Edward McCrea
35 Main Street
Sion Mills
Co Tryone BT82 9HG

South Armagh Angling Assn
J Cunningham
21 Forkhill Rd
Mullach Ban
Co Armagh BT35 9XJ
Tel: 028 30 889187

Tullylagan Angling Club
Jim Warnock
133 Dungannon Road
Cookstown
Co Tyrone BT80 9BD
Tel: 028 86 765965

Warrenpoint, Rostrevor & District Angling Club
P Murphy
1 Carrickview Burren
Warrenpoint
Co Down BT34 3FB
Tel: 028 4177 3525

MISCELLANEOUS

Department of Culture, Arts & Leisure
Northern Regional Office
River Bush Salmon Station
21 Church Street
Bushmills
Co Antrim BT57 8QJ
Tel: 028 20731435

Department of Culture, Arts & Leisure
South Eastern Regional Office
Fisheries Office
Castlewellan Forest Park
Castlewellan
Co Down
Tel: 028 43778937

Department of Culture, Arts & Leisure
Western Regional Office
Inishkeen House
Killyhelvin
Enniskillen
Co Fermanagh
Tel: 028 66325004

Department of Culture, Arts & Leisure
Central Fisheries Office
Movanagher Fish Farm
152 Vow Road
Ballymoney
Co Antrim
Tel: 028 29540533

FISHING IN IRELAND

The Irish Republic is world famous for the quality of its fisheries. Salmon, sea trout, brown trout, pike and other coarse fish, are to be found there at their best. The seas around Ireland contain very good quantities of many varieties of fish which provide excellent sport for visiting and native sea anglers. Where to fish in Ireland is virtually everywhere. Fisheries are administered by a **Central Fisheries Board** and by **seven Regional Fisheries Boards** coordinated by the Central Board. The function of each Regional Board is to conserve, protect, develop and promote every aspect of the inland fisheries (salmon, trout, coarse fish, eels), including sea angling, within the Board's fisheries region. Prices, at the time of going to press may still be quoted in IR£, and throughout the Irish section of the directory, £ should be taken to be IR£. It should be noted that a Regional Board licence or permit may be required on certain lakes, lakes with tributaries entering sea or rivers and which may there contain salmon or sea trout. Check with regional boards. The present national bag limit is one salmon per day per rod (or sea trout over 40 cms) until 31 May; from 1 June to end September, which is the end of the season, 3 salmon (sea trout over 40 cms) per rod per day.

Rod/Line Licences:

Salmon/Sea Trout - Season (All districts) 60 Euro
Salmon/Sea Trout - Season (Single District Only) 28 Euro
Salmon/Sea Trout - Juvenile 10 Euro
Salmon/Sea Trout - 21-Day 22 Euro
Salmon/Sea Trout - 1 Day 15 Euro
Foyle Area Extension 38 Euro

Share Certificates

There are eight fisheries development societies in the country, and their purpose is to raise funds for the development of coarse and trout fishing. At present the Northern and Upper Shannon regions are the only ones where a share certificate is obligatory. Elsewhere their purchase is voluntary. Annual share certificate costs 15 Euro; 21 days: 6.35 Euro; 3 days: 3.80 Euro. They may be obtained from tackle shops.

The modified **close seasons** now in force for salmon, sea trout and brown trout differ not only as between regions, but also within regions, in a formulation too complex for reproduction here in detail. The general pattern is that seasons for migratory fish tend to open early and close early, while that for brown trout opens early in many places (15 Feb) and does not close until a date in October. There are, however, important exceptions and anglers proposing to visit the Republic, especially early or late in the year, should make careful enquiries with the appropriate Regional Board before making firm plans, whether the intention be to fish for salmon, migratory or brown trout. Each fishery board has its own web site.

There is no annual close season for angling for coarse fish or for sea fish.

Overall responsibility for the country's fisheries rests with the **Department of Communications, Marine & Natural Resources** (tel: +353 (0)1 678 2000; fax: +353 (0)1 678 2449).

The **Central Fisheries Board** consists of the Chairman of the seven Regional Boards and from four to six members nominated by the Minister for the Marine. The functions of the Central Board are prescribed in the Fisheries Act 1980 and include such things as co-ordination and, where necessary, direction of the regional boards in the performance of their functions, which are: management, conservation, protection, development and promotion of inland fisheries and sea angling resources, and the protection of molluscs. Pollution, poaching and environmental incidents should be reported immediately to the appropriate regional board (*addresses below*). The head office of the **Central Fisheries Board** is at **Mobhi Boreen, Glasnevin, Dublin 9** (tel: +353 (0)1 837 9206/7/8; fax: +353 (0)1 836 0060; web: www. cfb.ie; e-mail: info@cfb.ie).

Tagging. Ireland has recently introduced an important system of tagging and logging all retained salmon, and sea trout over 40 cms. Anglers should be careful to ensure that they comply with this system, and always have the tags, log book, as well as the licence, on them. Log books and tags are obtained from licence suppliers. Taggable fish must be tagged immediately they are caught. No rod-caught salmon may be sold between 1 January and 31 October.

The **Western Fisheries Board** operates an important rod salmon fishery on the River Corrib at Galway, Co Galway (inquiries to the Manager, The Fishery, Nun's Island, Galway, Co Galway (tel: +353 (0)91 562388), and the famous Erriff Fishery in Co Galway; 30 Euro to 70 Euro per rod per day. Enquiries for fishing and accommodation here - at Aasleagh Lodge or Cottage - to the Manager, R Erriff Fishery, Aasleagh Lodge, Leenane, Co Galway (tel: +353 (0)95 42252; e-mail: erriff.fish@iol.ie).

The **Electricity Supply Board** also holds extensive fishing rights: principal salmon waters are the River Mulcair, and at Castleconnell, Co Limerick. The Board preserves and develops the fisheries under its control. Inquiries to Electricity Supply Board, Fisheries Division, Ardnacrusha, Co Clare (tel: +353 (0)61 345588).

Inquiries about accommodation and general tourist angling information (e.g. leaflets, brochures about local angling resources and amenities throughout the country) should be addressed to **Failte Ireland, Baggot Street Bridge, Dublin 2** (tel: +353 (0)1 602 4000; fax: +353 (0)1 602 4100); **Tourism Ireland, Nations House, 103 Wigmore Street, London W1U 1QS** (tel: 020 7518 0800; fax 020 7493 9065; web www.tourismireland.com; e-mail: info.gb@tourismireland.com), which covers both Northern Ireland and Ireland.

THE REGIONAL BOARDS

The **Eastern Regional Fisheries Board**, 15A Main St, Blackrock, Co Dublin (tel: +353 (0)1 2787022; fax: +353 (0) 278 7025; web: www.fishingireland.net; email: info@erfb.ie). The Board manages the catchments from the River Boyne system in Co. Louth to the Slaney catchment on the South East coast in Co. Wexford. The region contains many valuable coarse angling fisheries most notably in Counties Cavan and Monaghan. It also manages all lakes and river systems entering the sea, including coastal waters south of Carlingford Lough, Co. Louth and Kiln Bay, Co. Wexford. Enquiries to Angling & Marketing Co-Or-dinator (tel: +353 (0)46 9073375 or +353 (0)42 9661178).

The **Southern Regional Fisheries Board**. Covers all lakes and river systems entering the sea, including coastal waters, between Kiln Bay, Co Wexford and Ballycotton, Co Cork. Inquiries to the Board's Chief Executive Officer, Anglesea St, Clonmel, Co Tipperary (tel: +353 (0)52 23624; fax: +353 (0)52 23971).

The **South Western Regional Fisheries Board**. Covers all lakes and river systems entering the sea, including coastal waters, between Ballycotton Pier, Co Cork and Kerry Head, Co Kerry. Inquiries to the Board's Fisheries Officer, 1 Nevilles Terrace, Massey Town, Macroom, Co Cork (tel: +353 (0)26 41221/2; web: www.srfb.ie; fax +353 (0)26 41223; e-mail: swrfb@swrfb.ie).

The **Shannon Regional Fisheries Board**. Covers the inland fisheries of the Shannon catch-ment, the River Feale catchment in North Kerry and the rivers of Co Clare flowing westwards to the Atlantic. The coastal boundary stretches from Kerry Head, Co Kerry to Hag's Head, Co Clare. Inquiries to the Board's Fisheries Officer, Ashbourne Business Park, Dock Road, Limerick (tel: +353 (0)61 300238; fax: +353 (0)61 300308; web: www.shannon-fishery-board.ie; e-mail: info@shannon-fishery-board.ie). For information on Lough Sheelin and the head waters of the Shannon in the Cuilcagh Mountains, contact Shannon Regional Fisheries Board at Ballyheelan, Kilnaleck, Co Cavan (tel: +353 (0)49 433 6144).

The **Western Regional Fisheries Board**. Covers all lakes and rivers entering the sea, including coastal waters, between Hag's Head, Co Clare and Pigeon Point, near Westport, Co Mayo. Inquiries to The Board's Angling Officer, The Weir Lodge, Earl's Island, Galway City (tel: +353 (0)91 563118/9; fax: +353 (0)91 566335; web: www.wrfb.ie), to whom enquiries should be made as to special regional sea trout regulations. All sea trout caught in this Region's waters must carefully returned immediately to the water.

The **North Western Regional Fisheries Board**. Covers all lakes and rivers entering the sea, including coastal waters, between Pigeon Point, just north of Westport, Co Mayo, and

Mullaghmore Head, Co Sligo. The most famous fishery in the region is the River Moy, reputed to be Ireland's most prolific salmon river, the average rod and line catch in the last 5 years being 7660 salmon. The largest lake in the Moy catchment is Lough Conn, a 1994 survey revealing that it held 280,000 catchable-size (10in) wild brown trout. A current major stream development project should significantly swell the number. In the western part of the region good salmon and sea trout fishing is available on the Glenamoy, Owenmore, Owenduff and Newport rivers. Carrowmore Lake and loughs Feagh, Furnace and Beltra provide good salmon and sea trout; while Ballin Lough has good rainbows (up to 6lb). Lough Arrow, in Co Sligo, is famous for its wild browns. These are being supplemented with stocked trout. Salmon fishing is available on Lough Gill (from 1 Jan), on R Bonet and on Ballisodare River. Salmon and sea trout on Easkey River, Drumcliffe River and on the scenic Glencar Lake. The Board supplies a free Sea Angling Guide; also a general fishing guide. Inquiries to the Angling Officer, Ardnaree House, Abbey St, Ballina, Co Mayo (tel: +353 (0)96 22788; fax: +353 (0)96 70543; web: www.northwest fisheries.ie; e-mail: info@nwrfb.com).

The Northern Regional Fisheries Board, Corlesmore, Ballinagh, Co Cavan (tel: +353 (0)49 43 37174/7193; fax: +353 (0)49 43 37193; e-mail: northfisheries@eircom.net); or Station Road, Ballyshannon, Co Donegal (tel: +353 (0)719 851435/52053; web: www.cfb.ie). Covers all lakes and rivers entering the sea, including coastal waters, between Carrick-garve, Co Sligo and Malin Head, Co Donegal. The Board manages the angling waters of the River Erne, Co Cavan, covering the angling centres of Arvagh, Ballyconnell, Bawnboy, Blacklion, Belturbet, Cavan, Cootehill, Gowna, Killeshandra, Kilnaleck, Redhills and Shercock.

Two wild brown trout from Lough Arrow: the end of a perfect day. *Photo: Steph Malone.*

FISHING STATIONS IN IRELAND

Details of close seasons, licences, etc, for Irish rivers and loughs listed alphabetically here will be found in pages on the previous pages. Anglers wanting further details of accommodation should write to **Fáilte Ireland (Irish Tourist Board), Baggot Street Bridge, Dublin, 2** (tel: +353 (0)1 602 4000; fax: +353 (0)1 602 4100). Anglers in the **Western Fisheries Region** should note the fact that the killing of sea trout is now illegal. **All sea trout must be returned alive to the water.**

BALLYSODARE and LOUGH ARROW

(For close seasons, licences, etc, see The Regional Fisheries Board).

River Ballysodare formed by junction of three rivers, **Unshin** or **Arrow**, **Owenmore** (not to be confused with Owenmore River, Co Mayo), and **Owenbeg**, near Collooney, flows into Ballysodare Bay. Near mouth of river, at Ballysodare Falls, is earliest salmon ladder erected in Ireland (1852). Salmon, trout, very few sea trout. R Arrow, which runs out of Lough Arrow, contains small stock of brown trout for which fishing is free. The Owenmore has good coarse fishing, especially bream, at Ballymote. **Lough Arrow** (NWRFB) is a rich limestone water of 3,123 acres on the border of Sligo and Roscommon, situated 14 miles from Sligo town and 4 miles from Boyle. It is about 5m long and varies in width from ½m to 1½m. The lough is almost entirely spring-fed and has a place of honour among Ireland's best known mayfly lakes. Nowhere else is the hatch of fly so prolific or the rise so exciting. The brown trout rise to mayfly from late May to mid-June and sport is varied at this time by dapping, wet-fly and dry-fly fishing with green drake and the spent gnat. This is followed soon after (mid-July to mid-Aug) by a late evening rise to big sedge called the Murrough and Green Peter which may give the lucky angler as much fun as mayfly. The lough is regularly stocked with trout; fishing free; boats and ghillies may be hired at all seasons and at many centres on lake shore. **Loughs Bo** and **na Súil** are in close proximity, and ideal bank fishing for brown trout; stocked annually by NWRFB; all legitimate methods; 1 Apr to 30 Sept. Contact Mrs McDonagh, nr lake. Coarse fishing may be found nearby at **Lough Haugh, Temple House Lake, Ballanascarrow (Ballymote)**, and the **Owenmore River**. Coarse and trout fishing at **Cavetown Lake** (fly fishing only); stand for disabled; Cavetown and Clogher AC, Kit O'Beirne (tel: +353 (0)71 9668037). Salmon may be fished at Ballysadare (10 miles from Lough Arrow). Eileen McDonagh, Pub, Lough Bo, Geevagh via Boyle (tel: +353 (0)71 9165325), supplies permits for brown trout fishing in Lough Bo, and rainbow trout in Lough na Súil; boats and access for disabled in both Lough Bo and Louch na Súil; dt water; boats: R and J Acheson, Andresna House, Lough Arrow, Boyle (tel: +353 (0)71 9666181); F Dodd *(see Castlebaldwin)*; D Grey, Lough Arrow (tel: +353 (0)71 9165491); Eileen Carty, Ballinafad (tel: +353 (0)71 9666001). For information about Lough Arrow, contact Lough Arrow Fish Preservation Society, F Dodd (tel: +353 (0)71 9165065); or J Hargadon, Annaghloy Boat Hire (tel: +353 (0)71 9666666). For L Arrow & Dist AC (tel: +353 (0)71 9165304). Tackle from Brian Flaherty, Boyle; Barton Smith, Hyde Bridge, Sligo (tel: +353 (0)71 9146111); Louis Carty, Ballinafad (tel: +353 (0)71 9666001); also boat hire. Accommodation in Lough Arrow area includes Andresna House *(see above)*; Cromleagh Lodge, Ballindoon (tel: +353 (0)71 9165155); Rockview Hotel, Riverstown (tel: +353 (0)71 9666073/9666077); Tower Hill B&B, Castlebaldwin (tel: +353 (0)71 9666021).

Collooney (Co Sligo). Best season, May to July. Fishing dependent on sufficient rain. Permission to fish for sea and brown trout sometimes obtainable. Good dry fly. River contains sizeable pike. **Lough Bo** fished from here *(see above)*. Tackle shop: Brid McElgunn, Carrownacleiga (tel: +353 (0)71 30512).

Castlebaldwin via **Boyle** (Co Sligo). Trout fishing on L Arrow, free. Season 1 Apr-30 Sept. Bank fishing not recommended. Boats can be hired on lake shore from Dodd Boats, Ballindoon, Riverstown (tel: +353 (0)71 9165065), and Annaghloy Boat Hire (tel: +353 (0)71 9666666). L Arrow FPS fishes in Loughs **Arrow** and **Augh** (brown trout in L Arrow). NWRFB permits required for L Bo and L na Leibe, Lough Nasool (rainbow trout), but not L Arrow; season 80 Euro, conc, dt available and boat from Eileen MacDonagh pub & shop, Lough Bo (tel: +353 (0)71 9165325). **Lough Bo**, in hills, provides good shore fishing for brown trout; fly only; one boat for hire; season 1 Apr-30 Sept. **Lough na Leibe** has rainbow trout stocked occasionally by North Western Fisheries Board; season 1 Apr to 30 Sept; fly only; fishing from shore or boat Contact Hayden's Bar, Ballymote (tel: +353 (0)71 9183188). Good stock of brown trout in **Lough Feenagh**; boats for hire. River fishing on **R Unshin** and **R Feorrish** (above Ballyfarnon); trout. Coarse fishing on **Templehouse Lake** and **Cloonacleigha Lake**; good pike and other coarse fishing; boats for hire. Coarse and trout fishing on **Lough Key**, 3m east of Arrow; contact Boyle & DAC Hon Sec; trout 14" limit; 2 fish per day bag limit; pike strictly c&r. Contact Sec, L Arrow FPS, F Dodd (tel: +353 (0)71 9165065); or J Hargadon, Annaghloy Boat Hire (tel: +353 (0)71 9666666). For L Arrow and Dist AC (tel: +353 (0)71 9165304). Hotels: Cromleach Lodge; Rock View.

Boyle (Co Roscommon). L Arrow, trout, free; contact Fishery Inspector (tel: +353 (0)71 9666033) for information. **River Boyle**, a tributary of R Shannon, connects **Loughs Gara** and **Key**, both with very large pike. Upstream of town are quality bream, rudd, perch, roach, eels, hybrid and brown trout. Boyle & Dist AC have fishing on **R Boyle**, **L Key** (1 fish limit not exceeding 3kg) and **Boyle Canal**; members only, information available from Moonstone Jewellers and outlets (*see below*). The Club had some of its members legally appointed as water keepers (Boyle, L Key and Canal) and operates under a strict catch and release policy. Downstream, pike are to be found. A short distance south-west at **Ballaghaderreen**, is the **Lung River** connected to **Breedoge Lough**, and several other waters, among them **Loughs Cloonagh**, **Urlaur**, and **Cloonacolly**. This area holds some of the best coarse fishing in Ireland, with many species incl pike to 30lbs. Contact Jim Coogan, Ballaghaderreen AC (tel: +353 (0)94 9860077). **Lough Nasool**, 13m north, contains brown and rainbow trout, dt from Eileen McDonagh, Lough Bo, Geevagh via Boyle (tel: +353 (0)71 9165325). **Cavetown Lake**, fly fishing only; wild browns and stocked fish; platform for disabled anglers; dt available and boats arranged locally at Post Office. **Ballysadare River** and **R Unshin**; salmon tickets from Macks

This Arrow Lodge guest is casting well under the banks of the Ballysodore; a technique well understood by the Australian angler: their coveted barramundi so often lurk under the roots of the mangrove tree. *Photo: Bob Maloney.*

Tackle, Ballysodare. Tackle shops: Abbey Marine & Field Sports, Carrick Rd (tel: +353 (0)71 9662959), provides ghillies; Christy Wynne, Main Str (tel/fax: +353 (0)71 9662456), supplies live and ground bait; Boyle Tourist Office (tel: +353 (0)71 9662145); Martin Mitchell, Abbey House, *(see below)*, bait stockist; John Hunt, Castlerae (tel: +353 (0)94 9620111); Michael Rogers, Ballymote. Accommodation for anglers: Mrs Mitchell, Abbey House (tel: +353 (0)71 9662385), situated beside R Boyle, with much fine game and coarse fishing within easy reach; R and J Acheson, Andresna House, Lough Arrow, Boyle (tel: +353 (0)71 9666181), who also hire boats; Mrs Eileen Kelly, Forest Park House, Carrick Rd, Boyle (tel: +353 (0)71 9662227; web: www.bed-and-breakfast-boyle.com); Arrow Lakeside Accommodation; Rockview Hotel, Ballindoon via Boyle (tel: +353 (0)71 9666073).

BANDON

(For close seasons, licences, etc, see The South Western Regional Fisheries Board)

45 miles in length, rises in Shehy Mountains, West Cork and drains 235 square miles. Salmon fishing extends all the way from **Inishannon** u/s to **Togher Castle**, depending on conditions. An estimated 1,300 salmon are caught each season; about 300 of these are spring fish. Grilse (local name 'peal') run at end of June. Big run of sea trout (local name 'white trout') from early July to end of Aug (best caught after dark), and good stocks of browns, mostly small, but fish up to 2lbs taken. Fishing can be excellent on 4m stretch from Bandon to Innishannon. Ghillies are for hire. Season 15 Feb to 30 Sept.

Bandon (Co Cork). About 8m double bank controlled by Bandon AA; dt water; bag limit 1 fish, size limit 10in. Visitors welcome, tickets from Hon Sec. Visitors are not confined to fishing beats on the river, but may fish any part of the 8m Assn-owned waters. Tackle shop: Jeffersports, 7 Pearse Str (tel: +353 (0)23 41133).

Ballineen (Co Cork). The 4m stretch of river to about 1m above Ballineen Bridge is controlled by Ballineen & Enniskeane AA; salmon and trout; st and dt from Tom Fehily, Bridge Str, Ballineen (tel: +353 (0)23 47173). **Kilcoleman Fishery**, Enniskeane (tel: +353 (0)23 47279; web: flyfishing-ireland.com), offers lodge accommodation and private fishing on Bandon with ten named salmon pools, and excellent stocks of wild brown trout; season 17 Mar-30 Sept, spate fishing, mainly fly only; av salmon catch 70 per annum.

Dunmanway (Co Cork). Above Manch Bridge is Dunmanway Salmon & Trout AA water. Tickets from P MacCarthy, Yew Tree Bar, Dunmanway. River fishable for about 8m. Many small trout loughs in region, incl **Cullenagh** (4½m west), **Coolkeelure** (2¼m north west), **Ballynacarriga, Atarriff, Chapel Lake**; free fishing, small browns; for **Curraghalickey Lake**, contact P MacCarthy, *(see above)*.

CAHA RIVER. Joins Bandon 3m north of Dunmanway. Holds good stock of trout to 14 oz, for 3m up from confluence. Free fishing, best in early season, because of weed. Free fishing on **Neaskin Lough**, 3¼m north of Dunmanway. Difficult access, but plenty of 6oz browns.

Clonakilty (Co Cork). **River Argideen**, rises n.w. of Clonakilty, flowing into Courtmacsherry Harbour, rated among best sea trout rivers in SW Ireland, occasional salmon. Lower fishery owned or managed by Argideen AA. Maximum 6 rods per day, bag limit 10 trout, size limit 9in. Permits from Fishery Office, Inchy Bridge. Tackle shop: Jeffersports, 7 Pearse St, Bandon (tel: +353 (0)23 41133); Clontackle, Spillers Lane, Bridge Str (tel: +353 (0)23 35580).

BARROW (including Suir and Nore)

(For close seasons, licences, etc, see The Southern Regional Fisheries Board)

A limestone river which has been underrated in its potential, and not heavily fished. The second longest in Ireland, it rises well in the centre of the country on the eastern slopes of the Shannon watershed and flows over 120m south to the sea at Waterford Harbour, entering by a long estuary. An excellent head of wild brown trout, salmon run from Apr, best angling during grilse run in Sept. Bream, pike, rudd and hybrids provide good coarse angling, and annual May run of twaite shad is popular with visiting and local anglers near estuary.

Waterford (Co Waterford). Reservoirs managed by SRFB, **Knockaderry and Ballyshunnock**: both 70 acres at normal level, with wild brown and stocked rainbow, 4 fish limit; boats on Knockderry, no bank fishing, fly only, book in advance, apply to Centra Supermarket in Kilmeaden; all legal methods on Ballyshunnock (where there is also coarse fishing), bank only, no maggots; dt from Centra. **Mahon River** (15m) holds sea trout and salmon, and mackerel, bass and pollack abound along the coast. Tackle shops: Army & Outdoor Stores, New Str (tel: +353 (0)51 857554; fax: +353 (0)51 38243); Angling & Outdoor Centre, Westgate Retail Park, Tramore Rd (tel/fax: +353 (0)51 844314); Shoot'n & Fish'n, 26a Ballybricken (tel: +353 (0)51 878007).

Graighuenamanagh (Co Carlow). Good coarse fishing, with pike and large bream. Local venues are Tinnehinch Lower Weir and Bahanna.

Carlow (Co Carlow). Bream, rudd, pike. Trout fishing on River **Barrow** and Rivers Milford to Maganey, 8m, **Lerr**, 4m, **Greese**, 3m approx, and **Burren**, 8m, controlled by Barrow AC and restocked yearly. Members only, membership from tackle shop, or Secretary. Other club: Carlow & Graiguecullen Anglers. Free fishing from Milford Weir to canal mouth d/s of Milford Bridge. Tackle shop: Murph's Fishing, Lismard House, Tullow St, Carlow (tel: +353 (0) 9132839). Hotel: Dolmen, Kilkenny Rd.

Athy (Co Kildare). Trout, bream, rudd, pike. Several tributaries within easy reach. **R Greese**, from Dunlavin to Barbers Bridge, Kilkea, approx 8m, fishable on permit. Bream to 8lb are regularly caught in Barrow, as well as pike above 30lbs, perch, rudd and game fish. **Grand Canal** holds good head of tench, pike, perch, rudd and bream. There is some good free dry-fly water on left bank d/s of Athy, known as the Barrow Track. Kilberry & Cloney AC fish 5m **Boherbaun River** from Milltown Bridge to Forth of Dunrally Bridge, Vicarstown, eastside, (natural browns, 1-4lb); **Stradbally River**, 6m away, with trout; permits from Griffen & Hawe *(see below)*. Vicarstown & Dist AC club waters extend on west side of R Barrow from Laois/Kildare border northwards to the Glasha River. Athy & Dist AC fishes Barrow to Maganey Lock. In Sept 1992 club was releasing 20,000 brown trout into Barrow as part of

Anglers come from far and wide to fish one of Europe's finest dry fly trout rivers, the Suir, which drains large areas of limestone. *Photo: John Kelly.*

a general improvement programme. There are no fishing rights on Barrow, but a club card allows access from landowners. Membership 10 Euro, conc, and accom list from tackle shop: Griffin & Hawe Ltd, 22 Duke Str (tel: +353 (0)59 8631221; web: www.griffinhawe.ie). Self-catering accom: Mrs C Crean, Vicarstown Inn, Vicarstown, Co Laois (tel: +353 (0)502 25189).

Portarlington (Co Laois). River at town is easily accessible, and holds some salmon from March. Portarlington AC has approx 6 miles of good dry fly trout fishing on **Upper Barrow**. Best mid-May to mid-Sept. Mountmellick AC has 7m, good trout, a few salmon. Permits Victor Cox, The Square, Mountmellick (tel: +353 (0)502 24107); Portarlington Auto Parts, Upper Main St, Portarlington (tel: +353 (0)502 23456). Bracknagh AC has approx 5 miles of the **Figile River**, a tributary of the Barrow; mainly coarse, a few trout around Millgrove Bridge; st 15 Euro for all these waters are readily obtainable from Portarlington AC treasurer Pat Maher; Inchacooley, Monasterevin; Mick Finlay's Bar, Bracklone St, Portarlington (tel: +353 (0)502 23173). Another tributary, the **Cushina River**, north of **Monasterevin** is fished by Cushina AC: tickets from P Dunne, Clonsast, Rathangan. For general information about local fishing, and tickets, contact M A Findlay (Tackle shop), Rathangan Road, Monasterevin. Fishing Accommodation near aqueduct, where Grand Canal crosses R Barrow: Owen Cullen, Coole, Monasteravin.

GRAND CANAL (Co Kildare). Much free fishing. Canal runs through **Prosperous** and **Robertston** and **Sallins**, where there is first class fishing for bream, best early morning. Also rudd, tench, hybrids and some pike. Prosperous Coarse AC fishes on a length of some 20m from Naas to Thacknevin Lock. At **Edenderry**, Co Offaly, canal has large bream, tench, carp, rudd, roach, perch, eels; Edenderry Coarse AC controls 18m first class coarse angling, with bream, tench, roach, rudd, carp; all fishing is free; club also controls Conlons Lake, dt 15 Euro, coarse; contact Pauric Kelly, Edenderry Angling Supplies, 48 Murphy St, Edenderry (tel: +353 (0)46 9732071: home).

GRAND CANAL, BARROW BRANCH (Co Kildare and Co Laois). Fishing for bream, roach, tench, hybrids, rudd and pike, 5 minutes walk from **Rathangan**. At **Monasterevin** canal has pike, perch and bream. Contact Philip Findlay, Tackle Shop. At **Vicarstown**, Co Laois, fishing for bream, tench, pike and rudd. For permits, accom and information contact Mrs Crean, Vicarstown Inn, Vicarstown, Co Laois (tel: +353 (0)502 25189). Tackle shop: Countryman Angling, Leanne House, Pacelli Road, Naas (tel: +353 (0)45 879341; fax: +353 (0)45 866301; e-mail: countryman_angling@ iolfree.ie). Bait stockists: Griffin & Hawe Ltd, 22 Duke St, Athy (tel: +353 (0)59 8631221; web: www.griffinhawe.ie); Countryman Angling Ltd *(see above)*; Jim Crean, Vicarstown Inn, *(see above)*; bait must be ordered in advance.

SUIR

(For close seasons, licences, etc, see The Southern Regional Fisheries Board)

Considered to be one of Europe's finest dry fly trout rivers, with average trout size of ½lb, and fish up to 3lb often caught. Predominantly a trout river, it is fairly shallow with deep glides, and drains large areas of limestone. Runs into the same estuary as Nore and Barrow, reaching sea at Waterford. Fishes best from March to July. Daytime fishing is more productive in May, and evenings during the summer months. Record salmon for Ireland, 57lb, was caught in Suir, in 1874. Salmon fishing opens on 1 March, and in good years large springers up to 25lb are caught. Grilse run usually begins in late May and continues to end of Sept. Late Aug and Sept often bring bigger fish, over 10lb. There are large stocks of wild brown trout in river, but they not easily caught, and best fished in faster glides, from May to mid-June. Season 17 Mar–30 Sept. A wide network of tributaries, excellent fishing in their own right, includes the Rivers Nire, Tar, and Anner *(see below)*.

Carrick-on-Suir (Co Tipperary). Start of tidal water. **Duffcastle** to Carrick-on-Suir is last freshwater section, well stocked with trout. Carrick-on-Suir AA has north bank from Miloko to Duffcastle, also

Coolnamuck Fisheries, 3 miles south bank, fishing for salmon, trout, twait shad; tickets and ghillies though J O'-Keeffe *(see below);* also dt fishing on tributary **Lingaun River**, which runs from north into tidal water east of Carrick-on-Suir. Up river there is good trout fishing and occasional sea trout for 400m on left bank d/s of **Kilsheelin**. About 4m to south mountain loughs, largest of which are **Coumshingaun** and **Crotty's**, provide very good fishing as also does **Clodiagh River**, which springs from loughs and is close to road for part of way. Good salmon and trout fishing from Carrick to Cashel. Most of river preserved for salmon, but some owners give permission to fish for trout. Tackle shop: O'Keeffe, OK Sports, New Str (tel: +353 (0)51 640626). Hotel: Orchard House.

Clonmel (Co Tipperary). Moderate to good stocks of trout to 30cm. Free fishing between the bridges in town. Clonmel & Dist AC controls water from **Knocklofty Bridge** d/s one mile on south bank, also from Dudley's Mills (Clonmel) to **Anner River** (north bank) and Shanahan's Island to Anner River (south bank); salmon and trout. Permits from Hon Treas *(see clubs list)*; dt 30 Euro and wt 100 Euro (trout only) available; conc. Private fishing u/s of Knocklofty Bridge reserved for residents of Knocklofty House Hotel. Fishing on Marlfield Fisheries through Jean Loup Trautner, Marlfield Lodge, Clonmel (tel: +353 (0)52 252340). Clonmel & Dist Salmon and Trout Anglers control fishing rights on both banks from Deerpark to Kilmanahan Castle. Permits from Kavanagh Sports *(see below)*. At **Kilsheenan** left bank d/s is free fishing for 400m; 2m salmon and trout fishing is obtainable Kavanagh Sports *(see below)*. Local tributaries of main river are **Nire** (mountain stream with trout av ½lb, to 6lb), **Tar** (lowland stream with exceptional fly life, densely populated with trout av ½lb), **Duag**, **Anner** (fast moving stream with good stocks of trout av ¾lb, very good fishing in early season by u/s nymph method). Andrew and Eileen Ryan, Clonanav Angling Centre, Clonanav Farmhouse, Ballymacabry, Clonmel (tel: +353 (0)52 36141; web: flyfishing ireland. com), offer accommodation and instruction, and arrange dry fly fishing on Nire, Tar, Duag, Anner, Suir, and Blackwater Rivers; Nire and Glenahiry Lakes; Knockaderry and Ballyshunnock Reservoirs. Tickets sold for these waters, guide service and tackle shop. Mountain loughs can also be reached from this centre. Tackle shop: Kavanagh's Sports Shop,

O'Connell St, Clonmel (tel: +353 (0)52 21279); Clonanav Angling Centre, Clonanav Farmhouse *(see above)*; Abbey Stores, Abbey St, Clonmel. Hotels: Hearns, Parnell St; Clonmel Arms, Gladstone St; Hotel Minella, Spa Rd, all Clonmel.

Ardfinnan (Co Tipperary). Good numbers of trout to 30cm. Ardfinnan AC has much trout fishing in locality, d/s of Rochestown to Corabella. Permits from John Maher, Green View, Ardfinnan. Limited rods at Cloghardeen Fishery, Cloghardeen Farm.

Cahir (Co Tipperary). Cahir & Dist AA controls waters starting at Suirville, about 4m below Golden Village, d/s to Ballycarron Bridge; from Ballycarron down to Cahir; down both banks to Ballybrado; and down to Carrigatha; all fishing fly only, mostly brown trout, some salmon, depending on water levels; dt 20 Euro, wt 75 Euro for the full 13m of water, from The Heritage, Pat O'Donovan, 1 The Square, Cahir; association also has 4m of Aherlow River from Cappaghgates to confluence of Aherlow and Suir. Tackle from Kavanagh's Sports Shop, Upper O'Connell Str, Clonmel (tel: +353 (0)52 21279); flies from Alice Conba, fly dresser (tel: +353 (0)62 52755). Hotels: Cahir House (tel: +353 (0)52 41729); Kilcoran Lodge (tel: +353 (0)52 41288); 8m salmon and trout water; Theresa Russell, Bansha Castle, Bansha (tel: +353 (0)62 54187).

Cashel (Co Tipperary). Brown trout and salmon. Cashel, Tipperary and Golden AA issues visitors' permits for 8m both banks **Suir** from Camas Bridge south to **Ballycarron Bridge**, fly only, wild brown trout to 2lb, dt water, wt also from Hon Sec; Rahelly Sports Shop, Main Str, Tipperary. Cashel Palace Hotel, Main St, owns rights on good stretch of Suir and Aherlow Rivers, about 8m south of town, with brown trout fly fishing; ghillie service, permits on request from hotel. Best fishing from early spring to mid-summer. Tackle shop: Mr Tom Cahill, Paddywell Tackle, Canopy Str, Cashel (tel: +353 (0)62 63106); Rahallys Sports Shop, Main Str, Tipperary Town (tel: +353 (0)62 51252). Hotel: Ardmayle House; many excellent guest houses and B&Bs.

Thurles (Co Tipperary). Good centre for upper river trout fishing. Thurles Drish AA and Holycross & Ballycamas AA have water from **Holycross** to Kileen

Flats both banks, fly only; dt from Hayes Hotel; club also fishes **R Clodiagh** and **R Drish**; good stocks of trout to 40cms; u/s from Drish Bridge weeded in summer; d/s fishable throughout season, usually. Accommodation and permits: J & J Grene, Farm Guesthouse, Cappamurra House, Dundrum (tel: +353 (0)62 71127).

Templemore (Co Tipperary). Templemore & Dist AA controls first 15m on R Suir (excellent for game fishing; wild brown trout at its best); coarse fishing on Templemore Town Lake, less than 5 min walk from town centre; tench, rudd, roach, pike and eel. Fishing available for visitors as well as club members; st (snr) 17 Euro, (juv: 16 or under on day of joining) 5 Euro, wt 20 Euro, dt 5 Euro available from Hon Sec *(see clubs)* and Jim Hassey, Post Office, Main St, Templemore (tel: +353 (0)504 31098). No disabled angler boats, although the club has 3 special disabled anglers stands at Town Park Lake. Hotel: The Templemore Arms Hotel, Main St, Templemore (tel: +353 (0)504.

31423; fax: +353 (0)504 31343).

BLACKWATER RIVER (Co Kilkenny). This tributary joins the Suir about 2 miles upstream of Waterford City. It is tidal as far as the weir below **Kilmacow**, and holds good stocks of small trout between Kimacow and **Mullinavat**. Some fishing with landowners consent. Enquire at local tackle shops. Hotel: The Templemore Arms Hotel, Main St, Templemore (tel: +353 (0)504 31423).

PORTLAW CLODIAGH (Co Waterford). Tributary, which joins **Suir** east of Portlaw. Moderate trout stocks. Fishing rights on entire river owned by the Marquis of Waterford, but fishing is open u/s of **Lowrys Bridge** and d/s of **Portlaw**.

ARA/AHERLOW (Co Tipperary). Tributary joins Suir north of Cahir, flowing from a westerly direction. Significant numbers of trout to 28 cm. Ara AC has trout fishing from **Tipperary Town** to **Kilmyler Bridge**, where R Ara meets R Aherlow; fly, spinning or worming, wt water.

NORE

(For close seasons, licences, etc, see The Southern Regional Fisheries Board)

River rises in Co Tipperary, flows east through Borris-in-Ossory and then south through Kilkenny to join River Barrow near New Ross, about 8 miles south of Inistioge. 87 miles long with a total catchment of 977 square miles, Nore is a limestone river with abundant fly life. Increased salmon run in recent years. Because the salmon fishing is good, the trout fishing is somewhat neglected, although trout are plentiful in the river. Mills and weirs are a feature of this river, and long deep stretches provide excellent dry fly fishing even in low water.

Thomastown (Co Kilkenny), Thomastown AA has excellent salmon and trout stretch of Nore and issues temporary cards to visitors. Trout fishing is fly or worm only. Inistioge AC controls 3m both banks both banks at **Inistioge**, from Ballygalon weir to Red House Stream. Salmon, sea trout, brown trout and eels. Visitors are welcome, salmon dt 10 Euro, 1 Feb-30 Sept. Brown Trout dt 5 Euro, 1 Mar-30 Sept; st 30 Euro, wt 15 Euro, from Castle Inn, Inistioge (tel: +353 (0)56 7758483). Kilkenny AA has waters at **Brownsbarn** (tickets and permits available *(see below)*. Both banks extend 1m above and below Brownsbarn Bridge. 1m left bank fishing at 'Holdens' (2m above Brownsbarn Bridge) Excellent salmon at both fisheries. Tanguy de Toulgoet, Moyne Estate, West Hall Stables, Durrow, Co Laois (tel: +353 (0)502 36578), organises dry fly fishing trips at Kilkenny, Durrow, Rathdowney, Kells

and Callan, with instruction, and his own flies; dry fly catch and release, permits through local clubs.

Kilkenny (Co Kilkenny). Kilkenny AA has some excellent salmon and trout fishing on **Nore**, left bank from **Dinin R** to **Greenville** weir, and from **Maddoxstown** to 1m u/s of **Bennetsbridge; Dinin R,** Dinin Bridge to Nore; also **Dunmore.** Assn issues permits and tickets to visitors (dt/permits 15 Euro and 5 Euro; wt/permits 60 Euro and 25 Euro); conc, from Ed Stack (Assn Sec); also Hook Line & Sinker, 31 Rose Inn St, Kilkenny (tel: +353 (0)56 71699). Durrow & Dist AC fishes from **Watercastle Bridge** to **Owveg** confluence, and **Erkina R** from **Durrow Castle** to R Nore; all with 3m of Durrow; dt from Hon Sec; Durrow & DAC. Rathdowney AC fishes approx 4m of **Erkina R** from local meat factory to **Boston Bridge**, early season best for open fishing, May-Sept for fly. Brown trout from

8oz to 2lb, dt from M Walsh, Moorville, Rathdowney. **Kings River;** good brown trout. Club fishing at Ballinakill Lake: good tench, perch, rudd, pike; dt on bank. New free coarse fishery at **Granstown Lake** nr Rathdowney; 10 double pegs, access to lake shore by arrangement: dis-abled stand provided. Tackle shops: Hook Line & Sinker, 31 Rose Inn Str (tel: +353 (0)56 7771699); Town & Country Sports Shop, 82 High Str (tel: +353 (0)56 7721517). Hotels: Castel Arms, The Durrow Inn, both Durrow. B&B: Sean & Ber Delaney, Tintore; Sean & Marion Hy-

Truly wild fish. The class of trout for which anglers from all over Europe visit Ireland. *Photo: Trout and Salmon.*

land, Clough (both Ballacolla, Port-laoise); James Joyce, The Square, Durrow.

Abbeyleix (Co Laois). Trout and salmon. Abbeyleix & Dist AC fishes from **Shanahoe Bridge** to **Waterloo Bridge**, st 25 Euro, family st 30 Euro, conc, from Liam Dunne, Dunnes Hardware, Abbeyleix (tel: +353 (0)502 31440).

Mountrath (Co Laois). Nore; brown trout, pike, perch, roach, eels. Mountrath & Dist AC stocks and fishes Nore main channel from Nore/**Delour** confluence to New Bridge at **Donore**, and **Whitehorse River**, which runs through town. Good salmon fishing for 2m between Mountrath and Castletown. Tourist membership 8 Euro (family 10 Euro), conc; 2 Euro dt, to max 21 days 6 Euro, from Hon Sec *(see clubs list)*. Tackle and salmon permits from Mrs Maura Kelly, The Tackle Shop, Main Str (tel: +353 (0)502 32162). Accommodation: Mrs Geraldine Guilfoyle, Redcastle (tel: +353 (0)502 32277).

KINGS RIVER (Co Kilkenny). Tributary which joins Nore above Thomastown.

BLACKWATER

(For close seasons, licences, etc, see The Southern Regional Fisheries Board)

Perhaps most famous salmon river in the Republic, and the most prolific for the late 1990s, with remarkable totals of over 8,000 fish caught in 1998, with over 5500 in 1999 and over 6000 in 2000, comparable in North Atlantic area only to Kola Peninsula, Russia. Rises west of Killarney Mountains and flows eastward about 70m until it reaches town of Cappoquin, where it becomes tidal and turns sharply south, entering sea by estuary 15m long at Youghal Bay. 20m tidal, from Lismore to Youghal. Salmon (best stretches mainly between Mallow and Lismore), sea trout, brown trout, and abundance of roach and dace in some parts. Best fishing strictly preserved. Big runs of spring salmon from Feb to April; grilse June to Sept; and often good run of autumn salmon during Aug and Sept. Sea trout in Blackwater and Bride, June onwards.

Youghal (Co Cork). Youghal Sea AC has fishing on main river and tributaries. All arrangements through secretary. At **Castlemartyr** on Cork/Youghal road is **Lough Aderry**, rainbow trout fishery, 6 fish limit, fly, worm and spinning.

Cappoquin (Co Waterford). The freshwater here is backed up by the tide and fishing is best when the water is either rising or falling. Salmon and trout, good coarse fishing for roach and dace throughout year but best autumn and spring. Cappoquin Salmon & Trout AC have 4 miles of water on both sides of town. Salmon day tickets 12 to 25 Euro, wt 63 to 125 Euro, depending on season, from tackle shop; trout dt 6 Euro; wt 35 Euro; coarse dt 3 Euro, wt 15 Euro. Good stocked tench fishing at **Dromana Lake**, south of Cappoquin. Trout fishing on **Rivers Owenshed** and **Finisk** and on R Blackwater downstream of **Lismore Bridge**. Lismore Trout ACA fishes 1½m south bank from Lismore town d/s, and 1m north bank; also Abhan-na-Shad, Blackwater tributary, good in spate from July; fly only, browns and sea trout; dt water, from Cahills, Main Str, Lismore. Tackle shop: Titelines Tackle Shop, Main St, Cappoquin (tel: +353 (0)58 54152). Hotels: Ballyraf-

ter House, Lismore, (tel: +353 (0)58 54002). Anglers accommodation: Flynn's River View Guesthouse (tel: +353 (0)58 54073).

Upper Ballyduff (Co Waterford). Ballyduff Trout FAA has approx 3m E of bridge and 3m W, both banks. Blackwater Lodge Hotel, Upper Ballyduff (tel: +353 (0)58 60235; fax: +353 (0)58 60162; web: www.blackwaterlodge.net) *(see advt)* has 16 private and exclusive beats for salmon fishing between Lismore and Mallow. Wt and dt available for residents and non-residents alike. Lodge provides hotel and self-catering accommodation, complete service for anglers incl tackle, smokery and ghillies, and website with up-to-date river report. Tackle shop: Bolger's, Ballyduff.

Conna (Co Cork). 8 beats owned by Mr Justin Green, Ballyvolane House, Castlelyons (tel: +353 (0)25 36 349). 5 beats: Mrs Esta McCarthy, Elgin Cottage, Ballyduff, Co Waterford (tel: +353 (0)58 60255).

Fermoy (Co Cork). Salmon, brown trout, dace, roach, perch, gudgeon and pike. Salmon season: 15 Feb-30 Sept; fly only. Dt 10 Euro available from Brian Toomey Sports & Leisure *(see below)*; Blackwater Lodge (tel: +353 (0)58 60235); Ballyvolane House, Castlelyons (tel: +353 (0)25 36349); and Mocollop & Ballinaroone Fisheries (tel: +353 (0)58 60255). Course fishing available all year round. **Knockanannig Reservoir**: fishing clubs or assns for group bookings, contact Christy Roche (+353 (0)86 8564781 or Brian Toomey Sports & Leisure *(see below)*. Fermoy Salmon AA controls water from approx ½m d/s of Fermoy on right bank for about 3m to the weir at Careysville; also a large portion of fishing on opposite bank, but Assn confines dt water (coarse dt chargable) to portions on right bank: 2 beats amounting to 1m of river, 1 beat being known as Hospital stretch and the other as Championship stretch. Permits from Brian Toomey Sports & Leisure*(see below)*. Salmon fishing on R Blackwater at **Careysville Fishery**, 1¾m stretch, both banks with well defined pools. Grilse run in June. Fishing peaks on the lower beats in June and on the rest of river in July. Max 4 to 5 rods per day depending on month. Ghillie price included in fishing charges. Permits from Careysville House (tel: +353 (0)25 31094) or Lismore Estates Office, Lis-

more Castle, Lismore (tel: +353 (0)58 54424). Salmon fishing arranged at Blackwater Fly Fishing, Doug and Joy Lock, Ghillie Cottage, Kilbarry Stud, Fermoy (tel: +353 (0)25 32720). Stretches near town which hold roach and dace; waters accessible and banks well kept. For information on coarse fishing contact Gaye O'Doherty (tel: +353 (0)25 32689) or Brian Toomey Sports & Leisure, 18 McCurtain St, Fermoy (tel: +353 (0)25 31101). U/s of Fermoy are eight private salmon beats controlled by Justin Green, Ballyvolane House, Castlelyons (tel: +353 (0)25 36349; fax: +353 (0)25 36781) at Ballyduff, Fermoy, Killavullen and Ballyhooly; fishing Feb-Apr, May-Sept, spring run Apr/May; accommodation, tackle, and ghillies; chest waders recommended; local facilities for smoking or freezing salmon. **Araglin** holds brown trout; good dry fly. **Funshion (Funcheon)** runs in near Careysville on north bank; trout, dace, rudd; contact Peter Collins, Kildorrery (tel: +353 (0)22 25202). Hotel: Grand. B&B information from Slatterly Travel, 10 Pearse Square, Fermoy (tel: +353 (0)25 31811).

Mallow (Co Cork). Salmon fishing from 1 Feb to end of Sept; trout 15 Feb to end of Sept. Coarse fishing for dace, roach, pike. Mallow Trout Anglers have 4m both banks, salmon, trout, dace and roach. Dt for this and for other private beats (5 above and below Mallow) from tackle shop; coarse fishing free; various tickets (private, assn and club) available from tackle shop. Information from the Bridge House Bar. Nr Mallow is the new Ballyhass Lakes, Cecilstown (tel: +33 (0)22 27773; web: www.ballyhasslakes.ie); brown and rainbows by boat or from bank; main lake fly only, smaller lake fly, spinning and worm; dt 25 Euro (2 fish then c&r), conc; dt, tackle, boats and equipment from pavilion on site. Tackle shop: Pat Hayes, t/a Country Lifestyle, Unit C, Spa, Mallow (tel: 353 (0)22 20121; fax: +353 (0)22 20104). Hotels: Hibernian; Central; Longueville House, The Dunhallow Lodge.

BRIDE. This tributary of the Blackwater holds salmon and sea trout as well as brown trout, also dace; fly only. Season: 15 Feb to 30 Sept. Dt 10 Euro available from Brian Toomey Sports & Leisure *(See Fermoy)*; Peter Collins (tel: +353 (0)22 25202); Sean Dennehy (tel: +353

(0) 25497) both Kildorrey and Bride View Bar.

Tallow (Co Waterford). River is 500 yds from town. Tallow & Dist AC have 4½m fishing from Mogeely Bridge to Bride Valley Fruit Farm. Brown trout, sea trout; salmon and peal from June onwards. Fly only between Mogeely and Tallow Bridges, otherwise, worm, etc. There is also coarse fishing for big dace and roach. Visiting anglers welcome; dt 12 Euro, wt 50 Euro from Hon Treasurer, Paul Hamp-

ton (tel: +353 (0)58 56358). Tackle shops: John Forde, Main Str (dt); Titelines, Main St, Cappoquin (tel: +353(0)58 54152; Brian Twomey *(see Fermoy)*. Hotels: Bride View Bar; Devonshire Arms; (B&B) Kevin Ryan, The Grange, Curraglass, Mallow, Co Cork.

AWBEG. Tributary which runs into the Blackwater midway between Mallow and Fermoy. A very good trout stream, especially for dry fly.

BOYNE

(For close seasons, licences, etc, see The Eastern Regional Fisheries Board)

Rises near Edenderry and flows for about 70m, entering the sea near Drogheda north of Dublin. One of Ireland's premier game fisheries, in main channel and tributaries. Good salmon fishing between Navan and Drogheda. Excellent run of sea trout as far up river as Slane Bridge. Superb stocks of brown trout in Boyne and tributaries. Virtually no free fishing, but permits are sold on many club waters. Fishable tributaries include Rivers Trimblestown (small browns), Kells Blackwater (trout, u/s of Headford Bridge), **Borora** (7m good trout fishing from Corlat d/s to Carlanstown), **Martry** (small stream, trout to 1lb), Stoneyford (excellent trout water, Rathkenna Bridge to Shanco Bridge), **Deel** (a few salmon at Riverdale, trout), **Little Boyne** (spring trout fishery, club based at Edenberry), **Nanny** (sea trout up to Julianstown, browns to Balrath Bridge).

Drogheda (Co Louth). Drogheda & District AC has prime salmon and sea trout fishing below Oldbridge and u/s at Donore, and **Nanny**; and also Reservoirs **Killineer** (fly only) and **Barnattin** which are stocked with brown and rainbow, and **Rosehall**, a mixed coarse fishery; dt from Drogheda Angling Centre *(see below)*. Lower parts of Boyne and Mattock preserved. Brown trout in two reservoirs; st from Drogheda Corporation, Corporation Offices, Fair Str (tel: +353 (0)41 9833511). Tackle shop: Drogheda Angling Centre, 2 Stockwell Close (tel: +353 (0)41 9845442); The Cycle & Army Store, Balbriggan (tel: +353 (0)1 8413597). Hotels: Central, White Horse, Boyne Valley, Rosnaree, Cooper Hill House (Julianstown).

Navan (Co Meath). Salmon and sea trout. Navan & Dist AA has approx 8½m of fishing on R Boyne and on R Blackwater. Details from Secretary (tel: +353 (0)46 9022103; mob: +353 (0)86 8197228). Permits for these and various other angling waters in the eastern region available from David Byrne, Boyne Fisheries Manager, 1 Bedford Place, Navan (tel: +353 (0)46 73375; e-mail: theboynefishery@ tinet.ie). Tackle shops: Sportsden, Trimgate Str (tel: +353 (0)46 21130); Anglers World Specialist Tackle, 27 Cannon Row

(tel/fax: +353 (0)46 71866; web: www.anglersworld.ie). Hotels: New Grange; Ardboyne; both near river. Many B&B.

Slane (Co Meath). Rossin & Slane Anglers have salmon and sea trout fishing at Oldbridge, also excellent salmon and brown trout below Slane; dt from Hon Sec. Hotel: Conyngham Arms.

Trim (Co Meath). Good trout in main river and tributaries. Trim, Athboy & Dist AA preserves and restocks Athboy River and some stretches on Boyne itself; dt water; concessions to jun and OAP, from sec. Deel & Boyne AA has trout and salmon water on tributary Deel. Longwood Anglers also have salmon and trout fishing on Boyne. Hotel: Wellington Court; Brogans Guest Accommodation.

Kells (Co Meath). Good trout fishing on River Blackwater, a tributary of R Boyne, dry fly. Mayfly fishing good. 15m preserved and restocked by Kells AA; permits from tackle shop below. Trout up to 7lb may be had in the river, also large pike and salmon, 1½m of free fishing from source. Tackle shop: The Flying Sportsman, Carrick Str (tel: +353 (0)46 9241743). Hotel: Headford Arms.

Virginia (Co Cavan). On headwaters of R Blackwater. Lough Ramor gives good trout fishing and excellent fishing for bream, roach, perch and pike; boats for hire, two tributaries. Ten lakes and four rivers within 5m; trout and coarse fish. Virginia Coarse AC has fishing on Lough Ramor, with large bream, pike above 25lbs, 200lbs catches of coarse fish per day recorded. Other fisheries: Lisgrea Lake (all species); and Rampart River (roach, perch and bream). Mullagh Lake is a popular pike fishery. To north east, **Bailieboro** is an ideal centre for good coarse fishing, with innumerable lakes within easy reach; all free, incl **Castle** (with disabled platform, wheelchair and car access); **Parker's**; **Town** (with wheelchair access);**Gallincurra**; **Drumkeery**; **Drummeague;Galboly**; **Skeagh**;

Rooskey,Gallin, all containing perch, roach, bream, rudd, plentiful pike to 30lbs, and some tench; Club permit is required for **Grousehall Lake**. Bailieboro AC local club, membership available, contact Hon Sec (tel: +353 (0)42 9665382, daytime). Tackle shops: Raymond Lloyd, Main St, Bailieborough (tel: +353 (0)42 9665032); Joe Mulligan, Main St, Shercock (tel: +353 (0)42 9669184). Hotels: Bailie; Brennans, Main St, both Bailieborough. B&B: Mr & Mrs Peter Crosby, Hilltop Lodge, Curcish, Bailiebor, Co Cavan (tel: +353 (0)42 9666320); also provides tackle storage, bait fridge and drying room).

BUNDROWES RIVER AND LOUGH MELVIN

(For close seasons, licences, etc, see The Northern Regional Fisheries Board)

About 4m south of Erne , the Bundrowes River carries water of **Lough Melvin** to sea in Donegal Bay. The entire 6 mile river is open to anglers except for private stretch from Lareen Bay to the Four Masters Bridge. Kinlough & Dist AA have fishing on Lough Melvin. The lough is 8m by 2m, approx 5,000 acres; part of it is free and part under private ownership. It is renowned for its three different species of trout, these being sonnaghan, gilaroo and ferrox. Good run of big spring salmon in Feb and March; smaller fish arrive in Apr and May; grilse in late May and run right through to June. Best time for fly fishing for salmon late Apr to end June. Trolling baits, where permitted, takes place from early Feb. Disabled Anglers' International competitions has been held on the Lough on three occasions. For accommodation and information, contact Thomas Gallagher, Lareen Angling Centre, Lareen Park, Kinlough (tel: +353 (0)72 41055).

Bundoran (Co Donegal). Salmon, trout. Bundrowes R, 1½m, and west end L Melvin, 3m. Salmon season 1 Jan-30 Sept (Bundrowes); 1 Feb-30 Sept (Melvin). **Bunduff River**, 3½m from Bundoran, flows 8m to enter Donegal Bay near Castlegal; salmon, brown trout. Best salmon, June to Aug. Brown trout in upper reaches. Bunduff Angling Syndicate has water; dt from The Shop, Bunduff Bridge, Co Leitrim. Also Kinlough Anglers, c/o John Fahy, Kinlough. Pat Barrett, Main St. Hotels: Allingham; Foxes Lair. Gillaroo Lodge, West End, Bundoran (tel: +353 (0)98 42357), has permits and

licences, boats and ghillie service, and all other angling facilities.

Kinlough (Co Leitrim). Salmon, grilse, trout. Season for spring salmon, Jan to Apr; grilse, sea trout, May to Sept. Boats, salmon licence and permits for **Bundrowes** fishing at Drowes and Lareen Fisheries from Thomas Gallagher, Lareen Angling Centre, Lareen Park, Kinlough (tel: +353 (0)72 9841055); Thomas Kelly, Edenville, Kinlough (tel: +353 (0)72 9841497). Tackle shop: The Fishery Office, Lareen Park. Accommodation, information and ghillie service available (by arrangement) from T Kelly

---

Check before you go

While every effort has been made to ensure that the information given in **Where to Fish** *is correct, the position is continually changing, and anglers are urged, in their own interests, to make enquiries before travelling to selected venues. This is especially important with reference to prices quoted. Anglers attention is also drawn to the fact that hotels mentioned under the various fishing stations do not necessarily have water of their own. Any amendments or further data for inclusion in subsequent editions, and any comments, will be welcome.*

(see above) and J Gallagher *(see above)*.
Rossinver (Co Leitrim). Salmon, grilse, sonaghan and gillaroo trout. Rossinver Bay
strictly fly only, rule extended to Eden
and Dooard, from 15 May. All legal
methods elsewhere. Ghillies in vicinity.
Salmon and trout dt 15 Euro until 15 Jul,
7 Euro thereafter; boat, engine and 2 rods

50 Euro, from Ruth Mettler, The Rossinver Fishery, Buckode, Kinlough (tel:
+353 (0)71 9841451). Part of Lough Melvin is in Northern Ireland and is served by
village of Garrison (Co Fermanagh).
Tickets and boats for Garrison AC fishing
from Sean Maguire, Tackle shop, Garrison.

CLARE

Flows into **Lough Corrib**, near Galway, and is one of best spawning rivers for salmon
entering the Galway or Corrib River. Best season: Spring salmon, Apr and May; grilse, June
and July; brown trout, Apr to Sept. Holds large trout (av 2lb), similar to Corrib fish, and
suitable for dry fly. Fishing in main river and tributaries is controlled by riparian owners and
angling clubs. WRFB Angling Officer (tel: +353 (0)91 563118), has detailed information.

Galway (Co Galway). For lower reaches.
Sea and lake fishing. Several clubs have
fishing rights, and issue permits. Contact
WRFB. At **Carraroe**, 26m west of Galway, Carraroe AC controls a number of
brown and sea trout loughs, incl Lough
Atoureen, Lough an Gleanna, Lough an
Bric Mor, and Lough Cora Doite. Sea
trout mainly from July onwards. Boats on
request. For local information, contact
Ireland West Tourism, Aras Failte, Forster Str (tel: +353 (0)91 537700). Tackle
shop: Duffy's Tackle Shop, 5 Mainguard
Str (tel: +353 (0)91 562367; e-mail: duffy
b@eircom.net); Freeney's, 19 High Str
(tel: +353 (0)91 562609).
Tuam (Co Galway). For upper waters.
Tuam & Dist AA have a long association
with the Central Board Fisheries and
Western Regional Fisheries Board from
whom they rent 2 fisheries; **Ballyba-
nagher Fishery** (also known as **Tur-
loughmartin Fishery**), 1¾m stretch on
the left bank on the River Clare (situated
in Corofin, between Tuam and Galway
City) and **Liskeavey Fishery** (situated
between Tuam and Milltown) both have
excellent trout, pike and salmon (Liskeavey has brown trout). Tuam & Dist AA
are a community based club and membership is open to visitors as well as resident-
s; st 32 Euro, wt 20 Euro, dt 10 Euro and
can be obtained from Sonny Martin, The
Mall, Tuam, Co Galway (tel: +353 (0)93
24059); Yvonne, Marberry House *(see
below)* and Mrs Forde, Liskeavy Bridge,

Milltown (next to the Fishery). **Castle-
grove Lake**; pike, perch, bream, rudd.
Tackle shops: The Olympic Centre,
Tuam, Connaughton's, Tuam and Corrib
Tackle, Liosban Ind Estate, Tuam Rd,
Galway (tel: +353 (0)91 76 9974). Ac-
commodaation: Trevor Martin, Marberry
House, Corofin, Co Galway (tel: +353
(0)93 41938).
Tributaries of the Clare.
ABBERT. Enters from east, 7m south of
Tuam. Good trout fishing, with excellent
fly hatches. Brown trout of 3lb regularly
taken; salmon spawn there. The best angling is in the higher reaches.
GRANGE. Joins Clare from east, 4m south
of Tuam. Brown trout and salmon in
lower reaches; u/s of Castlemoyle for a
distance of 3m is a very good area for
large brown trout to dry fly; occasional
salmon in high water.
SINKING. Enters from east, 8m north of
Tuam. Salmon occasionally taken in
lower reaches, following flood conditions
anytime after the end of May, but primarily a brown trout fishery, the best areas
being from Dunmore as far as Cloon-
more; good fly hatches; river heavily
weeded and difficult to fish from mid-
summer onwards.
DALGAN. Runs into Sinking. Stocks of
brown trout, occasional salmon may be
caught from the end of May, depending
on water conditions. Pollution now
largely overcome.

Co. CLARE (streams and loughs)

A number of salmon and sea trout rivers and streams run from Co Clare to the Shannon
estuary or to the west coast. Most of them offer free fishing, with landowners permission.
Trout and coarse fishing lakes abound in the East Clare 'lakeland' and in the south west. The
rivers are listed here in their geographical order, westwards from Limerick.

BUNRATTY. Enters Shannon at Bunratty Castle, and holds a small stock of ½lb brown trout; modest grilse and sea trout run, best in June/July, from tide to D'Esterres Bridge, 3m. Free fishing. At source, **Doon Lough** nr **Broadford**, is a fine coarse fishery with pike to 30lb, large bream, rudd tench roach and eels; boats on hire locally. Several other coarse fishing Loughs in region: **Rosroe** and **Fin**, nr Kilmurry: pike over 20lb, from boat; **Cullaun**, 400 acres, 2m from **Kilkishen**, specimen pike and large bream, best from boat; just south, **Stones Lough:** big tench. As well as these, there are other less accessible lakes for the angler to explore. Further north east is another notable group of coarse fishing loughs: **Kilgory**, nr **O'Callaghan's Mills**, with large bream; 4m West of Tulla are **Bridget Lough** and others, with pike, perch, rudd, bream, tench, roach, hybrids; by **Scarriff, O'Grady (Canny's Lough),** shallow water, difficult access, but good bream fishing, with pike, tench and big rudd; and **Keel Lough**, inaccessible and unfished, with large tench, bream and rudd. On the **Scarriff River**, shoals of good bream and pike, easily accessible. On **R Graney** is **Lough Graney, Caher**, at 1,000 acres the biggest lake in the county with abundant perch, bream, pike, rudd and eel, boat essential, on hire at Caher and Flagmount. **Tulla** is central to much lake fishing: north are **Loughs Clondanagh** and **Clondoorney**, easily accessible with rudd, with pike and perch. At **Kilkishen** are **Loughs Cullaunyheeda, Avoher, Doon, Rathluby, Clonlea**, and others, with similar species. Accommodation at **Broadford:** Lake View House, Doon Lake, Broadford, Co Clare (tel: +353 (0)61 473125); on shore of lake, anglers catered for, boats for hire, much excellent coarse fishing in easy reach.

RINE (QUIN RIVER). Runs from the lakes of East Clare to the estuary of the **Fergus**. Fishing similar to Bunratty; about 5m fishing from Latoon Bridge u/s to Quin. Permission to fish **Dromoland**

Castle water from Rec. Manager. Castle also has 20 acre lough in grounds, stocked trout fishery. Rest of fishing free. A few miles SE of Rine are **Loughs Caherkine, Fin, Ballycar, Rosroe, Teereen, Castle** (at **Kilmurry**) and others, with pike, perch, bream and rudd.

FERGUS. This medium-sized, limestone river with several loughs along its course, rises in Burren region of North Clare and flows southward to join Shannon at Newmarket-on-Fergus. Holds good stocks of brown trout, av ¾lb, with fish to 3½lb. Good dry fly water, both banks fish well for trout, best in Feb-May and Sept. Pike fishing also good. Approx 200 spring salmon and grilse each year, salmon Feb-March, grilse June-Sept, from Ennis u/s. Much free fishing in **Corofin** locality. **Loughs Dromore** and **Ballyline**. 6m east of Ballyline; limestone waters with trout to 5lb. Best March-May and Sept. Free fishing: contact M Cleary, Lakefield Lodge, Corofin (tel: +353 (0)65 6837675). Tackle shop: Riverbank Fishing Shop, Main Str, Sixmilebridge (tel: +353 (0)61 6836933). **Ballyteige Lough:** 50 acre limestone fishery, trout to 7lb. Best in March/Apr, at dusk in June/July. Boat necessary; contact M Cleary. **Inchiquin Lough,** 280 acres: excellent stock of wild browns, av 1¼lb. Fishes well in early season, and Sept. Boats from Burkes Shop, Main St, Corofin (tel: +353 (0)65 6837677). **Lough Cullaun** (Monanagh Lake): limited stock of big trout; also a good pike fishery. Trolling popular method. **Muckanagh Lough (Tullymacken Lough):** 60 acre shallow lake with good trout and pike. Boat necessary. Boats through M Cleary for both these loughs. **Lough Atedaun**, 1m from Corofin, has excellent fishing for large pike, tench and rudd. Best fished from boat. **Lough Ballycullinan**, 1½m from Corofin, has good stocks of large pike, perch, bream, tench and hybrids. Boat essential. Contact Burke's *(see above)*. **Ballyeighter Lough**: a rich limestone water which holds pike, rudd and large tench. On this water in 1994, Mr Nick Parry of

---

Keep the banks clean

Several clubs have stopped issuing tickets to visitors because of the state of the banks after they have left. Spend a few moments clearing up.

Tubber broke Irish record with 7lb 15¼oz tench, then broke his own record with one 8lb 2oz (June 1995).

CLOON. This small river enters north east corner of Clonderalaw Bay. It gets a sea trout run in June/July, and is fishable for 2m d/s of new bridge on secondary road. Free fishing. Nearby trout loughs are **Knockerra**, 50 acres, **Gortglass**, 80 acres, and **Cloonsneaghta**, 30 acres. Boat hire on Gortglass, contact M Cleary (tel: +353 (0)65 6837674); free fishing on all.

DOONBEG. A better known salmon and sea trout river, rising in Lissycasy, flowing west to the sea at Doonbeg. Small spring salmon run, fair grilse and sea trout from June. Overgrown in places; best fishing on middle and upper reaches. Free with permission. For **Knockerra Lough** (*see Kilrush, under Shannon*).

CREEGH. Small spate river, running to west coast north of the Doonbeg, on which 150 to 200 grilse are taken each season. Small brown trout, and sea trout under the right conditions. Free fishing. Near Kilmihil is **Knockalough**, with good stock of small browns. Boat is helpful; dapping with daddy-long-legs in Aug/Sept. Free fishing.

ANNAGEERAGH. Runs into **Lough Donnell**. Sea trout fishing at dusk for about 1m u/s of lough in June/July. Sea trout fishing and a few grilse in rest of river. **Doo Lough**, 220 acres, a little north west of Glenmore, holds good stock of small browns.

KILDEEMEA. A small spate river which enters sea 2m south west of **Miltown Malbay**. Excellent sea trout, to 3lb. Best June/July, fishable over ½m stretch on south bank from Ballaclugga Bridge u/s.

Fly and spinner, fly best at night. Free fishing.

CULLENAGH (INAGH). This river is a good coarse fishery for 8m from Inagh towards sea. Open banks for pike and rudd fishing, easily accessible. Near village, **Inagh Loughs** contain good numbers of small brown trout. Free fishing. 2m west of Inagh, **Lough Caum**, 45 acres, pike fishery, boat fishing only. Contact Landers Leisure Lines, Courthouse Lane, Tralee (tel: +353 (0)66 71178).

DEALAGH. Joins sea from north east at Liscannor. Spate river with sea trout and grilse in June/July. Sea trout best at night, between first and fourth bridges u/s from tidal water. Free, with permission. **Lickeen Lough,** 200 acres, 2m south of **Kilfenora**, contains small wild brown trout with a large number of rudd. Now stocked by the Fishery Board with large browns from 2lb upwards. Boats and fishing tackle for hire; boat only 20 Euro (with motor 28 Euro); rod 6 Euro. St 35 Euro, juv 12 Euro, conc 18 Euro; dt 10 Euro, juv 2 Euro; holiday permit (21 days) 18 Euro; tuition available: contact John Vaughan, Anglers Rest Guest House (& cottage accommodation), Lickeen, Kilfenora, Co Clare (tel: +353 (0)65 7071069). Tackle shops: Joe O'Loughlins, Main Str. Lisdoonvarna (tel: +353 (0)65 7074038); Burkes, Corofin.

AILLE. Small spate river running from **Lisdoonvarna** to **Doolin**. Stock of 14" browns, moderate grilse and sea trout. Best between Roadford and Lisdoonvarna; access difficult, banks overgrown. Free fishing. Tackle shop: Joe O'Loughlin (*see Dealagh*).

CORK South West (rivers and loughs)

ARGIDEEN. Runs from west, above Clonakilty, and enters sea at **Timoleague**. A sea trout river, most of which is jointly managed by Argideen AA and SWRFB. Best methods are single worm by day, or fly at night. Tickets from Bob Allen (tel: +353 (0)23 39278), or SWRFB (tel: +353 (0)26 41222). Fishing with accommodation is obtainable from Tim Severin, Argideen River Lodges, Inchy Bridge, Timoleague (tel: +353 (0)23 46127; fax: +353 (0)23 46233). To west of river, **Lough Atariff**, permission from P McCarthy, Dunmanway Salmon & Trout AC, Yew Tree Bar, Dunmanway; and

Curraghalicky Lake, free fishing. Both with good stock of small wild brown trout. At **Midleton**, 16m east of Cork City, **Lough Aderra**, a popular stocked trout fishery of 30 acres, fairly shallow water, with large stocks of rudd and eels; 6 boats on water, fly, spinning and worm permitted. Contact SWRFB (tel: +353 (0)26 41222), or T H Sports, 37 Main St, Midleton, Cork (tel: +353 (0)21 631800).

ILEN. A medium sized spate river about 21 miles long, scenically pretty, rising on watershed of Bantry district and flowing into sea through long estuary, from Skibbereen. Spring salmon from late March.

Main salmon runs in Apr-Jun. Average size 10lb. Good grilse run from mid-June. Sea trout begin in Feb; Aug is the most prolific month, fish run from ½lb to over 4lb. Fly, spinning and worming are practised. Prawn and shrimp not permitted.

Skibbereen (Co Cork). R Ilen AC has about 8m fishing on river, with salmon, grilse and sea trout. Visitors welcome, access for disabled 1m from town; dt 25 Euro, wt 100 Euro, from Fallons *(see below)*, and Houlihans Newsagent, North St. 3m east, stocked rainbow and wild brown trout fishing on **Shepperton Lakes**, 35 and 15 acres, with boats; st 60 Euro and dt 12 Euro, conc, from E Connolly, Shepperton, Skibbereen (tel: +353 (0)28 33328). West nr Schull is **Schull Reservoir**, 5 acres, small native browns and stocked rainbows. Both these are SWRFB fisheries. 2m north of **Leap**, **Ballin Lough**: wild stock supplemented with brown trout fingerlings and limited number of 2 year-olds, by Ballin Lough AC. Boats and tickets at lough, season 1 Apr-30 Sept. Information from HQ, Bee Hive Bar, Connonagh, Leap. 3m south west of Dunmanway is **Garranes Lake**, 25 acres, stocked rainbows and wild browns; jointly run by SWRFB and Dunmanway & Drinagh AA dt and boats from C O'Donovan, Filling Station, Garranes, Drimoleague. 3m south of Leap, **Lough Cluhir**, free fishing on small lough for tench, pike and roach. Tackle shop: Fallon's Sports Shop, 20 North St, Skibbereen (tel: +353 (0)28 22264). Full range of accommodation, from TI Office, North Str (tel: +353 (0)28 21766).

Bantry (Co Cork). Bantry Trout AC fishes **Lough Bofinne**, 3m east of Bantry, 25 acres, first class rainbow and brown trout fishery, stocked weekly by Fisheries Board; tickets from McCarthy's Sports Shop; Quick Pick Shop. Tackle shops: Vickery's Store; McCarthy's Sports Shop, Main St, Bantry. Hotels; Vickerys, New Str (tel: +353 (0)27 50006); Bantry Bay Hotel, The Square (tel: +353 (0)27 50062).

MEALAGH. 1m north of Bantry, salmon and sea trout. Free except for bottom pool below falls.

OUVANE and **COOMHOLA**. Small spate rivers which run into north east Bantry Bay. Salmon and sea trout, the latter declined in Ouvane, better in Coomhola R. Ouvane has four good pools in first mile, and three more below Carriganass Falls. Coomhola has a good supply of brown trout. Coomhola Anglers, O'Brien's Shop, Coomhola Bridge, Bantry, offer permits to fish some 20 pools.

GLENGARRIFF. This small river flows into Bantry Bay at north east end through one of Ireland's most beautiful national parks, and has good salmon fishing when in spate, sea trout and browns. Rights are held by Glengarriff AA; st 15 Euro, conc for river or loughs *(see below)*, from Bernard Harrington, Maple Leaf Bar, Glengarriff. Limited tackle from Shamrock Stores; McCarthy's Sports, Bantry; and Maureen's B&B, The Village, Glengarriff (tel: +353 (0)27 63201) (special price for anglers). Hotels incl Eccles; Caseys.

BEARA PENINSULA. (Co Cork). **Adrigole River** runs into Bantry Bay on north side: 6m long spate river with grilse and sea trout, controlled by Kenmare AA. Contact J O'Hare, 21 Main St, Kenmare (tel: +353 (0)64 41499). Beara AA has tickets for local lough fishing. **Upper** and **Lower Loughs Avaul** contain wild brown trout, and are stocked with rainbows, fish to 17lb being caught; st (11 stocked lakes) 60 Euro, 3-wks 30 Euro, dt 12 Euro, conc; from Glengarriff AA; or Mrs Harrington, Maple Leaf Bar, Glengarriff. High in the Caha Mountains, SW of Glengarriff, fishing on **Loughs Eekenohoolikeaghaun** and **Derreenadovodia**, and **Barley Lake**, 100 acres: small wild brown trout; all club waters; apply O'Hare (tackle) Kenmare. Other small loughs in area with similar stock: **Glenkeel, Moredoolig, Begboolig, Shanoge** (larger fish, many over 1lb). Best in Apr/May and Sept. South of **Ardgroom** is **Glenbeg Lough**, leased by Berehaven AA; big stock of small browns; tickets from the Village Inn, Ardgroom, Beara: dt waters; apply to O'Hare (Kenmare). Hotel: Ford Rí, Castletownbere (tel: +353 (0)27 70379) has local fishing information. For further information: Béara Tourism & Development Assn, The Square, Castletownbere Beara (tel: +353 (0)27 70054).

CORRIB SYSTEM

(For close seasons, licences, etc, see The Western Regional Fisheries Board)

River Corrib drains Lough Corrib and runs 5½m to Galway Bay passing virtually through the city of Galway. Salmon, trout. Salmon fishing very good. For particulars as to present conditions and rods apply Western Regional Fisheries Board, Nuns Island, Galway (tel: +353 (0)91 562388). Best fishing for springers early in season; grilse, May-June. Rods let by the day.

Galway (Co Galway). Salmon fishing at Galway Fishery, situated in City of Galway, less than ½m from sea. Applications to The Manager, Galway Fishery, Nun's Island, Galway (tel: +353 (0)91 562388). Dt 65 Euro to 28 Euro; ½dt 30 Euro to 16 Euro; new beat dt 25 Euro to 15 Euro; ½dt 15 Euro to 10 Euro, depending on season. The flow of the river is controlled by a regulating weir and the short stretch down stream of the weir is the salmon angling water. **Kilcolgan River** (10m E) part tidal, salmon and sea trout. WRFB controls 645 yards of north bank in town land of Stradbally East. Dt from WRFB (tel: +353 (0)91 63118). Tackle shops: Duffy's, Mainguard Str; Freeney's, 19 High St.

LOUGH CORRIB

This, the largest lough in the Republic is 65 square miles of water, and dotted with islands, around which are shallows that make for good fishing. Specially noted for large brown trout, each season a number of specimen fish are taken, and the record stands at 26lb. The lough is so immense that anglers unfamiliar with it will do best using the services of a local ghillie. Trout fishing opens on Feb 15, and commences with the duck and olive season, but lough best known for dapping with mayfly (beginning sometimes as early as first week in May), and daddy-long-legs (mid-July to end of season). Some dry-fly fishing on summer evenings. Salmon taken mainly by trolling, and in June on wet fly in many of the bays. Also big pike and other coarse fish in Corrib, so that angling of some kind is possible all year. Fishing free, but salmon licence required. Many hotels issue licences. Boats and boatmen at Portacarron, Oughterard, Baurisheen, Derrymoyle, Glan Shore, Cong, Greenfields, Doorus, Carrick, Salthouse, and Inishmacatreer. A detailed list and angling map of Lough Corrib may be purchased from WRFB, Weir lodge, Earl's Island, Galway City.

Oughterard (Co Galway). Best fishing is from April to early June. **Owenriff River** flows through Oughterard; good in high water late summer. Local club is Oughterard Anglers & Boatmens Assn; actively involved in stream and river development, information from Tucks *(see below)*. There is additional good fishing for bream and roach on **Moycullen Lakes**, Moycullen, on Galway/Oughterard Rd. Currarevagh House, Oughterard, Connemara, Co Galway (tel: +353 (0)91 552312/3) provides boats, ghillies, outboard motors with fuel and tackle if necessary for residents only for a daily charge of 100 Euro (for ghillie and boat); they also fish top lake of **Screebe** sea trout fishery. Hotels: Oughterard House (free fishing on Corrib; private water within 12m; voluntary share certificates available; salmon and sea trout); Lake Hotel (Frank & Mary O'Meara), The Square (tel: +353 (0)91 552275; fax: +353 (0)91 552381; web: www.lakeh. com). Also motel: Connemara Gateway (tel: +353 (0)1 567 3444) and Ross Lake Hotel, Rosscahill (boats and boatmen). Tackle shops: Thomas Tuck's, Main Str (tel: +353 (0)91 552335); M Keogh. Galway tackle shop: Freeney's, 19 High Str (tel: +353 (0)91 562609).

Clonbur (Co Galway). Good centre for **Loughs Corrib** and **Mask**. Clonbur AC fishes these waters, **Loughs Coolin, Nafooey** (pike over 36lb) and others, and is affiliated with Corrib Federation. Tackle shop: Anne Kyne's, Clonbur (tel: +353 (0)94 9546197); Fred O'Connor, Cong (tel: +353 (0)92 46008). Accommodation plentiful.

Headford (Co Galway). Convenient for the east side of Lough Corrib. **Black River** (limestone stream) provides excellent if somewhat difficult dry fly water. Affected by drainage work. Best near village of **Shrule**. Day tickets are sold by WRFB, Weir Lodge, Galway (tel: +353 (0)915 63118). Tackle shop: Kevin Duffy, Main Str (tel: +353 (0)93 35449; web: www.kduffy.com). Accommodation at Angler's Rest Hotel and guest houses.

Greenfields, nr Headford (Co Galway). Brown trout, salmon and coarse fish; fishing free. Situated on shore of **L Corrib.** Boatmen in vicinity. Rooms-en-suite, tackle, boats, apply to Corrib Lakeshore Hotel, Greenfields, Ower PO, Headford, Co Galway (tel: +353 (0)93 35446; fax: +353 (0)93 35382; e-mail: owerhouse1@eircom.net). Local boatman: Michael Walshe, The Parks, Ower P O, Co Galway (tel: +353 (0)93 35380). Disabled facilities available, by arrangement.

Cong (Co Mayo). On shores of L Corrib, good centre for **Lough Mask** also; Cong Canal, coarse fishing; and R Mear, with salmon and trout, pike and perch. Boats and accommodation from Mike and Rose Holian, Bayview Angling Centre, Derry Quay, Cross P O, Cong (tel/fax: +353 (0)94 95 46385; e-mail: bayviewac@eircom.net), open during winter for pike fishing; wet and dry flies available. Local club is Ballinrobe & District Anglers; fishing free, but visitors can subscribe to the club to stock lakes &c. Very little

bank fishing (all lake fishing) except for Cong Canal; gillies available; contact Billy Burke, Outdoor Pursuits, Glebe St, Ballinrobbe (tel: +353 (0)92 41262). Tackle shops: Fred O'Connor, Cong (tel: +353 (0)92 46008; fax: +353 (0)92 46771).

Tributaries of Lough Corrib.

BLACK RIVER. Fifteen miles in length, it enters lough just north of Greenfields. Access is easy from Shrule, Co Mayo. A rich limestone river with a good stock of brown trout. Best in early season, before weed accumulates.

CREGG RIVER. Rises half mile upstream of old Cregg Millhouse, and flows four miles to Lower Lough Corrib. Upper stretch is nursery for stocking into Corrib, and fishing is not encouraged. Salmon and brown trout angling is permitted on lower stretches.

CLARE RIVER: for this river entering L Corrib at the easternmost end, and its own tributary system (*see Clare*).

LOUGH MASK

Limestone lake of 22,000 acres connected by underground channel with Lough Corrib, holding large ferox trout, pike, eels, perch and a few char. Angling is free. Trout to 15lb are taken by trolling and on dap (5-6lb not uncommon). Mayfly best from mid-May to mid-June; daddy-long legs and grasshopper, late June to Sept; wet fly, Mar-Apr and July-Sept. Dry fly fishing can be successful from May-Sept. **Ballinrobe, Cong, Clonbur** and **Tourmakeady** are good centres. At Cong is Cong AA, (st available); at Ballinrobe is Ballinrobe & Dist AA (st 60 Euro), open to visitor-membership. Tackle shops: Fred O'Connor, Cong (tel: +353 (0)94 9546008); Dermot O'Connor's, Main Str, Ballinrobe (tel: +353 (0)94 9541083); Billy Bourke's Outdoor Pursuits, Glebe Str, Ballinrobe (tel: +353 (0)94 954 1262). Boats for hire at Cushlough Pier, Bay of Islands Park, Rosshill Park, Caher-Tourmakeady Pier. Good anglers accommodation at Ard Aoidhinn Angling Centre, Cappaduff, Tourmakeady (tel: +353 (0)94 9044009) (HQ of Tourmakeady AA), tickets for salmon fisheries, good boat access for disabled; Mask Lodge and Laskeshore House and Anglers Lodge on lake shore, run by David and Helen Hall, Lakeshore Holiday Homes, Caher, Ballinrobe (tel: +353 (0)94 9541389): boats, engines and ghillies provided; river fishing on **Finney** and canal joining Mask and Corrib; at Tourmakeady are some good spate rivers, and mountain lake fishing can be had in **Dirk Lakes**; brown trout.

LOUGH CARRA. Connected to **Lough Mask,** 4003 acres, limestone, relatively shallow with brown trout which are considered to be freer rising than those in Lough Mask, and average heavier. All are derived entirely from natural population of wild fish. Shore fishing, difficult, boat essential. Boats and anglers' accommodation from Roberts Angling Service & Guest House, Lough Bawn, Kilkeeran, Partry (tel: +353 (0)94 9543046); Mrs J Flannery, Keel River Lodge, Keel Bridge, Partry (tel: +353 (0)94 9541706); Mr R O'Grady, Chapel St, Ballinrobe (tel:

+353 (0)94 9541142); boats also from Tiernan Bros Angling Advice Centre, Upper Main St, Foxford, Co Mayo (tel: +353 (0)94 9256731). Local clubs: Ballinrobe & Dist Anglers, c/o Ballinrobe PO; Partry Anglers, c/o Post Office, Partry. East of L Carra, **Claremorris** and **Irishtown** are notable centres for little-known coarse lakes, containing large numbers of perch, pike, bream and roach.

Lough Nafooey. Connected to Lough Mask, and contains trout, pike and perch.

Tributaries of Lough Mask.

ROBE RIVER, has brown trout fishing,

free, best u/s of Robeen Bridge as far as Clooncormack, from Hollymount u/s to Hollybrook, and from Crossboyne through Castlemagarrett Estate as far as the Claremorris/Tuam road. Also d/s from Ballinrobe.

KEEL RIVER. Enters west of Ballinrobe, holds a fair stock of brown trout, and is an ideal dry fly water.

NORTH DONEGAL (streams)

(For close seasons, licences, etc, see The Northern Regional Fisheries Board)

Donegal is mostly salmon and sea trout country. Its waters are generally acid; rocky or stony streams and small lakes in which the brown trout run small - though there are one or two fisheries where they may be taken up to 5lb and more.

LENNON. Rises in Glendowan Mountains and flows through **Garton Lough** and **Lough Fern** before entering **Lough Swilly** at Ramelton. Historically is one of the best salmon rivers in Donegal. It is best known as a spring river and its most famous pool, The Ramelton Pool is privately owned. The rest of the river is a 'free fishery' and only a state licence is required. Season 1 Jan-30 Sept; June to Sept for grilse. Trout fishing equally good on upper and lower reaches; best Apr to July. Loughs Garton and Fern have stocks of small brown trout, and fishing is free.

Ramelton (Co Donegal). Salmon fishing on lower portion of river at Ramelton owned and fished privately by Ramelton Fishery Ltd. **Lough Fern** is best fished from a boat and produces mostly grilse. Other brown trout loughs in vicinity, Akibbon, Sessigagh, Glen and Keel. Information on these and all other local waters from Anglers Haven Hotel, Kilmacrennan, Co Donegal (tel: +353 (0)74 9139015).

SWILLY. Flows into Lough Swilly. Much free salmon and trout fishing of good quality in region. Recently, the river has undergone major development with work being carried out by the Northern Regional Fisheries Board (NRFB) and the Letterkenny & Dist AA.

Letterkenny (Co Donegal). Letterkenny AA has salmon, sea trout and brown trout fishing on Rivers **Swilly, Lennon, Owen-carrow**, and more than 25 lakes; trout av ½lb. Salmon run into Lakes **Glen, Gartan** and **Lough Fern**. Boats on Lough Keel: W Gallagher (tel: +353 (0)74 9139233). Hotel: Mount Errigal.

Churchill (Co Donegal). **Lough Beagh** situated in the heart of the **Glenveagh National Park**; 4m long by ½m wide; salmon, sea trout and brown trout. Best known for quality of sea trout fishing in Aug and Sept. Boat fishing only; 2 boats for hire. Anglers are requested to respect the bird life on this lake, as there are some rare and interesting species residing. Season 15 July-30 Sept. Dt from Bernard Gallagher, Glenveagh National Park, Churchill, Letterkenny (tel: +353 (0)74 37090/37262).

CRANA. Enters **Lough Swilly** at Buncrana. Primarily a spate river which gets a good run of grilse and sea trout. Access to fishing is excellent.

Buncrana (Co Donegal). Salmon and sea trout. Buncrana AA issues permits; licences from Bertie O'Neill's Fishing Tackle Shop, Bridgend (tel: +353 (0)74 9368157). Other waters: **Mill River;** brown trout to ½lb numerous; Letterkenny licence required; also **Inch Lake** (6m): good sea trout; also **Dunree River** (6m); brown trout, occasional salmon and sea trout; **Clonmany River** (5m); salmon, sea trout and brown trout fishing; fair sport in good water; best June onwards. Culdaff & Inishowen AA have water here; wt and dt water from Haskins Barber Shop, Moville; Tourist Office, Chapel St, Carndonagh; and Faulkners Hardware, Culdaff village. Hotels: McGrory's of Culdaff, Inishowen (tel: +353 (0)77 79104); Lake of Shadows.

CULDAFF. A small spate river on the Malin Peninsula, with brown trout, sea trout from mid-June onwards, and salmon in Aug and Sept. Nearest towns, Malin and Carndonagh. Season 1 Apr to 20 Oct. Fly spinning and worm, no float fishing. Culdaff & Inishowen AA have water; contact Hon Sec; permits from Faulkners Hardware Shop, Main St, Culdaff (Tel: +353 (0)74 9379932).

DEELE. East Donegal rather than North, a tributary of the Foyle which enters downstream of Strabane. Fished by Deele AC from 3m u/s of Convoy to 4m d/s, for brown trout, sea trout, and grilse from July on. Season 1 Apr-20 Oct, fly, spinning, worm, no floats. This is mainly a spate river with worm fishing on the day of the flood, and fly fishing and spinning in the next two days after the flood, or rise of water; tickets from Billy Vance, Milltown, Convoy, Co Donegal (tel: +353 (0)74 47290); Lexie Kilpatrick, Findrum, Convoy, Lifford; Mervyn McConnell, Milltown Road, Convoy (tel: +353 (0)74 47702) Hotels: Friels, Raphoe; Central, Raphoe; Jacksons, Ballybofey; Rees Hotel, Stranorlar; B&B: Mrs Shirley Chambers, Strabane Rd, Raphoe (tel: +353 (0)74 45410).

WEST and CENTRAL DONEGAL (streams)

(For close seasons, licences, etc, see The Northern Regional Fisheries Board)

EANY and **ESKE**. Eany fishery consists of Rivers Eany, Eany More, and Eany Beg, giving about ten miles of fishing. Eany itself is a spate river which flows for 10m SW from Blue Stack Mountains and enters sea in Inver Bay close to Inver village. Good run of salmon and sea trout and has resident population of small brown trout; the river produces around 700 salmon per season. **Eske River** drains **Lough Eske** (900 acres) then runs SW for about 5m to join sea at Donegal Bay. The system gets a good run of salmon and a fair run of sea trout; and has a resident stock of brown trout and char. Salmon 1 Mar-30 Sept. Trout 1 Mar-30 Sept. Most fishing is on the lake from boats and the river has a number of good pools. In recent years the system has been getting a declining run of fish but this may be temporary.

Donegal (Co Donegal). Donegal Town & Dist AC controls fishing on Eany. Eske Anglers control fishing on Eske River and Lough Eske. Fishing has been members only for the past 2 years. Please phone Northern Regional Fisheries Board (NRFB), Station Rd, Ballyshannon (+353 (0)51435; web: www.cfb.ie) for tickets and further information as NRFB own both rivers. Tackle shop: C Doherty, Main Str (tel: +353 (0)73 21119).

Frosses (Co Donegal). Fishing controlled by Northern Regional Fisheries Board (NRFB). Fishery has been upgraded with improved access; excellent run of salmon and sea trout, best fishing June to Sept. Permits 15 Euro, and licences from Eany Angling Centre, Gargrim, Frosses (tel: +353 (0)74 9736559).

GLEN RIVER. Flows S for 8m from Lough na Lughraman - headwater lake - to enter sea at Teelin Bay beside the town of Carrick. A spate river but has a number of good holding pools. Salmon, sea trout, brown trout. Fishes best in summer after a flood. The wild salmon and sea trout tagging regulations of 2003 applies. The Sliabh Liág Anglers Assn controls the **Glen River Fishery**, which includes the following rivers: Glen, **Owenwee (Yellow) River**, Crow (Crove) and **Owenteskiny** and several loughs, **Agh, Auva, Unshagh, Unna, Divna, Lougherherk and Lough Nalughraman. Meenacharvey** River; dt 20 Euro for visitors; st 60 Euro; wt 60 Euro (anglers in local accomm applies); juv (to 18 yrs) 50 Euro of adult rates; contact Hon Sec. Tackle shops: Spar Shop, Carrick; McBriarty, Kilcar. Hotels: Bay View, Killybegs; Glencolumbkille, Malinmore, Glencolmcille (tel: +353 (0)73 30003). Self catering and B&B available.

Carrick (Co Donegal). Salmon and trout. Private fishing, monitored by Sliabh Liág AA.

LACKARGH (Co Donegal). At Creeslough in extreme north of county, river system has spring salmon run mid-Mar to Mid-May. Creeslough & Dist Anglers. Contact NRFB.

FINN. Governed by Foyle Fisheries Commission. Flows from Lough Finn nr **Fintown** in an easterly direction until it joins Mourne above **Strabane** and **Lifford**, to form River Foyle. Spring salmon best in Mar-May, between Lifford Bridge and

---

Fishing available?

*If you own, manage, or know of first-class fishing available to the public which should be considered for inclusion in **Where to Fish** please apply to the publishers (address in the front of the book) for a form for submission, on completion, to the Editor. (Inclusion is at the sole discretion of the Editor). No charge is made for editorial inclusion.*

Salmon Leap at Cloghan, depending on flow. Grilse, main run in May-July, best in middle section between **Liscooley** and **Letterbrick**, and at **Commeen** on **R Reelan**; sea trout, good runs in May-July, best in middle and upper sections. Brown trout and coarse, lower reaches. Foyle Fisheries Commission water, near **Clady**, is best for spring salmon. Finn AC and Glebe AC fish sections from Liscooley Bridge to near Edenmore. Ballybofey & Stranorlar AA fish water approx 4m above and below Ballybofey and Stranorlar; limited rods. Tickets from Ken Rule, Killygordon, and Ballybofey T I. Cloghan Lodge Fisheries, **Cloghan** (tel: +353 (0)74 9133003), has over 30m both banks of R Finn, from Dooish to Lough Finn, plus tributaries **Reelan, Cummirk, Elatagh**. Excellent fly fishing, spinning and worm also permitted, with spring salmon and grilse, autumn salmon, average take per year increasing. Good sea trout run in May-July. Limited tickets, st from 250 Euro, dt from 15 Euro; ghillie service, B&B, by advance booking. This fishing is held jointly with Glenmore Estate. 20 loughs are also fishable, incl Finn, Nambraddan, Shivnagh, Muck. Dt and st available for **Glenmore Fishery**, Mrs Thomas McCreery, Altnapaste, **Ballybofey** (tel: +353 (0)74 32075) has good fly fishing; on 10m of Rivers Reelan, Letterkillew and Finn, and one bank of Cummirk River; spate system, with more than forty named pools; salmon with good grilse run, and sea trout. **Killygordon Private Fishery** (James McNulty) 320 'The Curragh', Killygordon (tel: +353 (0)74 42931; mob: +353 (0)8635 78443) has dt for salmon, grilse, sea trout and brown trout fishing on R Finn, nr Ballybofey. At **Killygordon**, Mrs Nell Bradley, Swallows Rest Guest House (tel: +353 (0)74 49400), owns rights on 1m single bank of R Finn, fly fishing: dt available for guests; good service offered to visiting anglers. Tackle shops: Mr G's, Balleybofey; Hotels: Jacksons, Balleybofey; Kees, Stranorlar.

OWENEA AND OWENTOCKER. Short rivers running into head of Loughrosmore Bay near Ardara. Owenea is primarily a spate river, taking 1 or 2 days to run after a good flood, with a run of spring fish, grilse, sea trout, and a resident stock of small brown trout. It has a nine beats on 8m of river, with good pools spread throughout river, much good fly water, and when in condition is one of the best in the country for salmon; producing around 700 salmon annually. Season 1 Mar-30 Sept.

Ardara and **Glenties** (Co Donegal). Fishing controlled by Northern Regional Fishery Board (NRFB), Glenties, Co Donegal (tel: +353 (0)74 9551141). Fishery has been upgraded and there are additional facilities for anglers, incl access for disabled along one section. Excellent run of salmon and sea trout from Mar to Sept; 8 beats over half mile long; dt 25.5 Euro; wt 127 Euro. Permits, licences and bookings from Owenea Angling Centre, Glenties. Salmon and sea trout fishing on River Brackey. Many mountain lakes free to fish. Hotels: Nesbitt Arms, Ardara; Highlands Hotel, Glenties.

GWEEBARRA. Drains **Lough Barra** and flows south-west about 7m to Doochary Bridge, where it becomes tidal and flows hence through long estuary between high hills a further 6m to the Atlantic.

Doochary (Co Donegal). Bridge here marks end of tidal water; several trout lakes in vicinity. Salmon, sea trout. Best season: Spring salmon, Feb-May; grilse and sea trout, end of June to Sept. Fishing is state-owned; inquire locally. Salmon and sea trout run into Lough Barra in large numbers and into tributaries.

THE ROSSES. The Rosses Fishery is made up of five salmon and sea trout rivers, including **River Dungloe**, and one hundred and thirty lakes, some of which contain salmon and sea trout, all of which contain brown trout.

Dungloe (Co Donegal). Salmon and sea trout. **Rosses Fishery** controlled by Rosses AA. **Loughs Meeala, Dungloe, Craghy** (Tulla), stocked with browns, sea trout and rainbows. Season: 1 Feb to 12 Oct. Fly only on all lakes. Prices are: assoc membership 30 Euro, dt 10 Euro (bank), boat 15 Euro; with ghillie 40 Euro, (juv free). River prices vary for season on **Crolly River** and **Clady River**. Permits, tackle and boat hire from Charles Bonner & Sons, Bridge Str (tel: +353 (0)74 9521163). Hotels: Ostan na Rosann. Wide range of B&B.

EAST COASTAL STREAMS

(For close seasons, licences, etc, see The Eastern Regional Fisheries Board)

AUGHRIM RIVER. Approx 5m long, flows south-east to meet Avoca River at Woodenbridge; limestone catchment, good trout water. River and tributaries controlled by Aughrim & Dist Trout AC. Permits from Woodenbridge Hotel & Lodge, Vale of Avoca, Arklow (tel: +353 (0)402 35146).

AVONMORE RIVER. Runs from **Loughs Tay** and **Dan**, approx 8m north; joins with the **Glenmacanass River** (from **Glendalough**) at Larach, on through Rathdrum, Co Wicklow; meets **River Avonbeg** at the famous region of the **Meetings of the Waters**, flows into the **Avoca** and reaches sea at Arklow. Big stocks of ½ brown trout, some larger and some smaller. Rathdrum Trout AC has 18m water from Vale of Clara to Avoca; brown trout and some (very few) salmon and sea trout; permits 3 Euro from Tourist Office, Main St, Rathdrum (tel: +353 (0)404 46262); McNabbs Newsagents, Lower Main St, Rathdrum (tel: +353 (0)404 46103) and from most shops in Rathdrum. Juv must be accompanied by an adult at all times, but permits not required; Rathdrum Trout AC run fly-fishing lessons in their club house and on the river. No hotels in Rathdrum but various B&B, incl Stirabout Lane Guest House, Rathdrum, who caters for anglers with ghillie service, fly-tying room, etc. Further information from Wicklow Tourist Office, Rialto House, Fitzwilliam Square (tel: +353 (0)404 69117; fax: +353 (0) 404 69118; e-mail: wicklowtouristoffice @eircom.net).

BROADMEADOW RIVER. Dublin District; trout. Drainage scheme has affected sport. Broadmeadow AC fishes river and **Tonelgee Reservoir.**

DARGLE RIVER. Short river which reaches sea at Bray. Principally sea trout, plenty of 2-4lb fish between May and Sept, salmon Apr-May, Aug-Sept, also occasional brown trout. Dargle AC has fishing rights on lower reaches; permits from Viking Tackle Bray, Unit 5, Everest Centre, Castle St, Bray (tel: +353 (0)1 286 9215). Tinnehinch Fishery: private water on Dargle, fly only; specialising at sea trout fly fishing at night; dt 30 Euro permits for visitors, from Hugh Duff, Tinnehinch House, Enniskerry (tel: +353 (0)1 2766089) who is also well known as a fishing guide and instructor.

RIVER DERRY . Rises near Knockanna, flows south through Tinahely, Shillelagh and Clonegal to meet R Slaney near Kildavin; occasional salmon, small brown trout. Fishing controlled by Derry & Dist AC.

DELVIN RIVER. In Drogheda District. Fair brown trout stream entering sea at Gormanstown; Holds few sea trout. Gormanstown & Dist AA has water. River being stocked and developed with co-operation of landowners and members. Balbriggan is convenient centre. (Hotel: Bracken Court).

DODDER. Dublin District; brown trout (av 9oz, but fish to 2lbs caught), with some sea trout fishing in tidal portion. Dodder AC controls all fishing; contact R O'Hanlon, 82 Braemor Rd, Dublin 14 (tel: +353 (0)1 982112). Fishing on Dublin Corporation's **Bohernabreena** and **Roundwood Reservoirs** (10m from Dublin); tickets from Dublin Corporation, Block 1, Floor 3, Civic Offices, Fishamble St, Dublin 8; no boats, conc for OAP; members of these clubs are entitled to reduced rates: Dublin Trout AA; Wicklow AA; Dodder AC.

GLENCREE RIVER. In Dublin District. Enniskerry is a centre; small brown trout. Mostly free.

NANNY RIVER. In Drogheda District. River enters sea at Laytown, Co Meath. Fair brown trout fishing; some sea trout in lower reaches. Drogheda & Dist AC has water and issues permits. Club also fishes R Boyne, and three stillwaters. *(See Drogheda.)*

TOLKA RIVER. In Dublin District; a once excellent trout stream which has suffered from pollution. Best fishing is from Finglas Bridge to Abbotstown Bridge. For fishing information contact secretary, Tolka AC (tel: +353 (0)1 361730).

VARTRY. Small river which drains **Roundwood (Vartry) Reservoir** and flows into sea near Wicklow, with sea trout from late Aug, and small brown trout. Vartry AC controls lower reaches of river (Ashford/Rathnew area); brown trout and salmon, also Ashtown Reservoir; brown trout and stocked rainbow trout fishery nr **Wicklow Town** (fly only: 2 fish limit); membership fee 100 Euro then after st 40 Euro; juv membership 100

Euro and st 40 Euro. Dt for reservoir from Bridge Tavern, Wicklow Town (tel: +353 (0)404 67718); dt 12 Euro (Ashdown Reservoir only); disabled access at Ashtoen Reservoir. River by permission of landowners, no dt. Vartry Reservoir is fly only, brown trout water, run by Dublin Corporation; permits 2 Euro, from Vartry Lodge near water, or D C Vartry Water-works (tel: +353 (0)1 281 8368). Tackle shops: Viking Tackle Bray, Bray (tel: +353 (0)1 286 9215); Charles Camping, Blessington (tel: +353(0)45 865351; fax: +353 (0)45 891183); Frankies Sports Shop, Wicklow Town. Hotels: Grand; Bridge Tavern (both Wicklow Town); Hunter's, Rathnew; Tinakilly House.

ERNE

(For close seasons, licences, etc, see The Northern Regional Fisheries Board)

A hydro-electric scheme has turned the River Erne into two large dams. Excellent sea trout fishing in estuary, for 2 miles from the Mall Quay in Ballyshannon to the Bar at the mouth, with easy access, especially on north shore, season 1 Mar-30 Sept. Coarse fishing excellent; bream, rudd and perch abundant and roach multiplying following their introduction in recent years, also large numbers of pike.

Ballyshannon (Co Donegal). Boats for sea trout fishing, on hire at Mall Quay. **Assaroe Lake** is a reservoir resulting from the Erne Hydro-Electric Generating Scheme, located above Kathleen Falls Power Station. Fishing is available at four points on north side, controlled by ESB, and a permit to cover salmon, brown trout and coarse, may be purchased from ESB Fisheries Office, Ardnacrusha, nr Limerick; ESB Generating Station or ESB Shop, both Ballyshannon; also Charles Bonner *(see below)*; st 35 Euro, wt 20 Euro, dt 10 Euro, conc; boats available. Other ESB waters are Gweedore Fishery: Rivers **Clady** and **Crolly**; tickets from ESB Office *(see above)*; Charles Bonner, The Bridge, Dungloe, Co Donegal (tel: +353 (0)74 9521163); Charlie Doherty, Main St, Donegal (tel: +353 (0)73 21119). Erne sea trout fishing permits sold; contact Michael McGrath, Belleek Angling Centre, 'The Thatch', Main Str. Belleek, Co Fermanagh BT93 3FX NI (tel: (0)28 686 58181); self catering accom and boats & motors available.

Belturbet (Co Cavan). Good centre for Rivers **Erne, Annalee,** and Shannon-Erne Waterway (formerly Woodford River), and some thirty seven lakes, with most coarse fish and some trout. **Putighan** and **Derryhoo Lakes** are popular venues, tench to 5lb in L Bunn, to 3lb in L Carn. New developments at Loughs Grilly, Killybandrick, Bunn, Drumlaney, Greenville, Round. Bait, boats and tackle from T McMahon, Bridge Str (tel: +353 (0)49 9522400). Anglers accommodation includes Kilduff House, 2m from Belturbet, and Fortview House, Drumbran,

Cloverhill, Belturbet (tel: +353 (0)49 4338185), provides guide, bait, drying room, and all other facilities.

Cavan (Co Cavan). All lakes and rivers in the area hold coarse fish except **Annagh Lake** (100 acres) which holds brown and rainbow trout; fly only, no bank fishing, 6 fish limit. Trout season 1 Mar-30 Sept. **Lough Oughter**, a maze of lakes fed by R Erne and R Annalee, holds a wealth of coarse fish; bream, rudd, roach, pike, perch, tench. Further details from Cavan Tourist Information, 1 Farnham Str (tel: +353 (0)49 4331942) (part of North West Tourism Authority, Temple St, Sligo (tel: +353 (0)71 9161201/9160360). Tackle shop: Sports World (prop: B R Webber), 11 Town Hall St, Cavan (tel: +353 (0)49 433 1812). Accommodation catering for anglers: Forest Chalets, Killykeen.

Lough Gowna (Co Cavan). Coarse fishing on Lough Gowna, the source of R Erne. Carrigallen is in a good position in the **Gowna, Arva, Carrigallen** area to explore the richest waters spread over three counties within 3m radius. Lakes include **Town, Gangin** (noted for the size of its bream), **Tully, Cullies, Beaghmore** and **Gulladoo** to name but a few. Tackle shops: McM Sports, Main St, Killeshandra (tel: +353 (0)49 4334438). Anglers accommodation: Kilbracken Arms Hotel (Fiona & Donal Cadden), Main Str (tel: +353 (0)49 4339737; web: www.kilbrac kenarms.com); Greenville House (Frank & Ann McGovern; tel: +353 (0)49 4339938), both Carrigallen; Lakeview House, Lough Gowna; Frances and Sean Barry, Farrangarve House, Arva, Co Cavan (tel: +353 (0)49 4335357).

This is the kind of bream catch that brings visiting anglers to Belturbet lakes in Co Cavan. *Photo: S Smith.*

Cootehill (Co Cavan). A notable fishing centre, with more than thirty coarse fishing lakes within fifteen mile radius, and **Rivers Dromore** and **Annalee**: trout, bream, rudd, tench, pike, hybrids, roach, perch. Fishing free in Dromore and Annalee, trout permit required for **Bunoe** and **Laragh Rivers. Moyduff Lake** is brown trout fishery, controlled by Northern Regional Fisheries Board (NRFB). Permit at lake. Local clubs are Cootehill AC, Laragh AC, Moyduff AC and Bunnoe AC: contact through Cootehill Tourist Development Assn, Riverside House, Cootehill (tel: +353 (0)49 555 2150). Boats, ghillies, available. Tackle shop: C J Bait and Tackle, Bridge Str (Tel: +353 (0)49 555 2153). Anglers accommodation (self-catering): Riverside Guest House; Cabragh Farmhouse; Hillview House, Cootehill.

Clones (Co Monaghan). Coarse fishing. **River Finn**, a sluggish tributary of Upper Lough Erne, excellent bream fishing. There are sixty lakes within 5m of town: pike, perch, rudd, bream, roach, eel, and other species. A Few miles north of **Monaghan** is **Emy Lake Fishery**, Emyvale, 136 acres trout fishing, fly only, 3 fish limit. Also at Monaghan, Peters Lake, roach, rudd, tench pike; run by Rossmore CAC. Tackle shops: Dick Kiernan, Venture Sports, 71 Glasslough St, (tel: +353 (0)47 81495; web: www.monaghan_out doors.com); M C Graham, Old Cross Square (tel: +353 (0)4771453) both Monaghan. Hotels: Creighton, Lennard Arms.

SHANNON-ERNE WATERWAY (formerly **WOODFORD RIVER**).

Ballinamore (Co Leitrim). Well developed centre for angling, close to river, which produces large catches of bream av 2½lb, roach, specimen tench, rudd, perch, pike and other coarse fish. Waterway runs into **L Garadice**, one of 25 fishing lakes in this area, all free fishing; voluntary subscription appreciated. Riversdale Farm Guesthouse (tel: +353 (0)71 9644122) beside Aghoo Lock and Weir caters for anglers (tackle shed, fridges, drying facilities); also McAllister's Hotel; Kennedy, Glenview (tel: +353 (0)71 9644157); Ivan and Dorothy Price, Ardrum Lodge (tel: +353 (0)71 9644278), all Ballinamore. Tackle from G Owens, High Str (tel: +353 (0)71 9644051) (agent for Irish Angling Services).

FANE

(For close seasons, licences, etc, see The Eastern Regional Fisheries Board)

Rises in **Lough Muckno** at Castleblaney and flows SE to enter sea at Blackrock, 4m S of Dundalk. Good supply of salmon in lower reaches, and well up river, depending on water levels; small run of grilse in June, autumn run of salmon. Upper reaches have wild brown trout, good fly fishing water, plenty of fish are caught as large as 3-5lbs.

Dundalk (Co Louth). Waters from Knockbridge to border (except 1m at Balentra), plus all **Castletown** and **Ballymascanlon** Rivers and tributaries controlled by Dundalk & Dist Trout AA; contact Hon Sec. Assn stocks each year with browns, and there is a good run of sea trout and salmon (Aug-Oct best). Membership 45 Euro, dt 10 Euro, conc, from tackle shops and tourist office. 7m both banks from Knockbridge to sea, Dundalk Salmon AA; catch returns approx 200+ salmon, 200+ sea trout; dt av 20 Euro, from Island Tackle, and Devenney's Stationary, Crowe St. Tackle shops: Island Fishing Tackle & Firearms, 58 Park St, Dundalk (tel: +353 (0)42 9335698). Hotels: Ballymascanlon (3m north); Derryhale; Imperial.

Inniskeen (Co Monaghan). Waters in Inniskeen area controlled by Inniskeen AC. Trout, fly only. Salmon, fly, spinning, lure or shrimp. Membership from A Campbell, Monvallet, Louth, Co Louth. Dt from Ruddys Filling Station, Dundalk.

Castleblayney (Co Monaghan). Good centre for Rivers Fane, **Clarebane**, **Frankfort** and **Mullaghduff**, brown trout. Several coarse fishing loughs in area; **Lough Muckno**, 325 hectares, with pike, perch, roach, bream, and other species; good fishing from several islands in lough. Permission and access controlled by Lough Muckno Leisure Park. **Lough Egish** (5m), pike, perch and eel. **Dick's Lake**, large roach; **Smith's Lake**, good tench fishing, also bream, roach, perch; **Loughs Na Glack** and **Monalty**, big bream. Castleblayney Trout AA has trout fishing on **Milltown Lough** (3m); stocked annually with 3,000 brown trout; dt from Hon Sec. Tackle shop: The Mascot, Main St. Hotel: Glencarn.

Ballybay (Co Monaghan). Excellent coarse fishing centre for **Dromore River** and loughs, of which there are a large number; some, it is claimed, have never been fished. Boats and ghillies are to be found on the more important local fisheries, including **Bairds Shore, Corries, Convent, Derryvalley, Mullanary, Corkeeran and White Lakes**. There is much free coarse fishing for visiting anglers, and typical weights per day exceed 40lb, mainly bream and roach. Local pike fishing is also very good. Town holds annual coarse angling festival. Local Assn: Corkeeran & Dromore Trout & Coarse AA; dt water. Tackle shop: Ballybay Angling Services, Mick Harte, 81 Main Str (tel: +353 (0)42 9741963); Martin O'Kane.

GLYDE: Rises near Kingscourt in Co Cavan and flows E for 35m to join River Dee before entering the sea at Annagassan. Flows through some prime coarse fisheries in upper reaches, notably **Rahans** and **Ballyhoe Lakes**. Small run of spring salmon and fair run of grilse in late summer depending on water levels. Good stock of brown trout. Excellent Mayfly hatch. Due to drainage works some years ago, there are some steep banks on which care should be taken. A Good centre for anglers is **Carrickmacross**, with several fine coarse lakes near to hand with bream, roach, tench, rudd, hybrids, perch, pike, etc, incl **Lisaniske, Capragh** and **Monalty Lakes, Lough Na Glack**. Fishing accom: Mrs Haworth, Rose-Linn Lodge, Carrickmacross; Mrs Campbell, Glencoe; Mrs Tinnelly, Corglass, both Kingscourt.

Castlebellingham (Co Louth). Salmon, sea trout, brown trout. Season 1 Feb-30 Sept. Dee & Glyde AC protect and fish river. Hotel: Bellingham Castle.

DEE: Rises above **Whitewood Lake**, near Kilmainham Wood. Flow E for 38m, joining **River Glyde** at **Annagassan**. Fair runs of spring salmon, some grilse and good runs of sea trout to 5lb (May). Lower reaches below **Ardee** and **Drumcar** yield most salmon and sea trout. Brown trout water above Ardee. Due to drainage works some years ago, many banks are steep and dangerous. Weeds can be a problem during dry summers, ruining fishing in many sections. Season 1 Feb-30 Sept.

Dunleer (Co Louth). Salmon, sea trout. Tickets from The Reception, St Mary's, Drumcar House; permits. Sea trout fishing allowed after dark.

Ardee (Co Louth). Dee & Glyde AC has water on Rivers Dee and Glyde. Tickets available. Other tackle shop: Ardee Sports Co, John St. Hotel: The Gables.

Drumconrath (Co Meath). There are several fisheries within a 5m radius; some are members only but tickets and permits are available to the rest; information and permits available from Drumconrath Coarse FC *(see Clubs)*; coarse fishing free, trout dt from and information also from Drumconrath PO. **Ballyhoe Lakes** (1 & 2), holds good stock of bream, roach, rudd, perch, pike, tench and eel; **Lagan River** which flows from Ballyhoe 2 also holds good stocks of coarse fish; coarse fishing in **Lough Mentrim**, (specimen bream and tench), **Lake Balrath, Corstown**. Fishing accommodation at Inis Fail (tel: +353 (0)41 685 4161); Muldoons (tel: +353 (0)41 68 54119).

Nobber (Co Meath). Nobber AC has stretch from **Whitewood Lake** to Yellow-Ford Bridge. Mainly brown trout, occasional salmon in late autumn, usually during flood water. Weeds can be a problem during low water.

MULLAGHDUFF: Tributary which enters Lough Muckno. A good trout stream, wet fly fishing best from April onwards, dry fly late in season.

FRANKFORT: Short river which connects Milltown Lough with Lough Muckno, stocked by local assoc. Trout to 3lb. Best in May-July.

FEALE

(For close seasons, licences, etc, see The Shannon Regional Fisheries Board)

Rises in North Cork on the southern slopes of Mullaghereirk Mountain, then flows west through Abbeyfeale, Listowel, and enters Shannon Estuary south of Ballybunion. Its total length is an estimated 46 miles, and there are eleven main tributaries: the **Gale,** Oolagh, **Allaghaun, Cahir, Brick, Smearlagh, Tullylease, Owveg, Glashacooncore, Clyddagh** and **Breanagh**. A spate river, with salmon, sea trout and brown trout. Season is from 1 Mar-30 Sept. Sometimes salmon run poor owing to low water. The Feale system is controlled almost entirely by five associations. (*See below.*)

Abbeyfeale (Co Limerick). Best centre for Feale. Waders essential. Abbeyfeale AA has 6m of single and double bank d/s of town, with salmon and sea trout; membership and tickets from Ryan's, New Str, Abbeyfeale. Brosna AA has 6m upstream; trout permit from Pat Danaher, Mount Collins, Abbeyfeale. Tackle shops: Ryan Brothers, New Str (tel: +353 (0)68 31411); The Shoe Shop, New Str (tel: +353 (0)68 31411; Lane, New Str (manufacturer of the famous 'Lane' artificial minnow) (tel: +353 (0)68 31220). Hotel: Leen's.

Listowel (Co Kerry). North Kerry AA has 7m single and double bank on R Feale and on River Smearlagh; salmon and sea trout, all legal methods allowed; wt and dt, from Hon Sec or tackle shops. Killocruin/Finuge Club controls 3m d/s of town, best stretch for spring salmon and grilse. Tralee AA has 5m u/s, both banks; dt issued. Fly fishing for salmon quite good from mid-Aug. Brosna/Mountcollins Club has 8m on upper reaches of Feale, with good sea trout fishing from mid Aug to end of Sept. Salmon licences and permits from Jim Horgan, Woodford, Listowel. Tackle shops: Jim Halpin Shooting Supplies Ltd, 24 Church Str (tel: +353 (0)68 22392); Landers Leisure Lines, Courthouse Lane, Tralee. Hotels: Stack's; Listowel Arms.

GALWAY and MAYO (rivers and smaller loughs)

(For close seasons, licences, etc, see The Western Regional Fisheries Board)

BALLYNAHINCH

An extensive system of lakes, tributaries and connecting rivers draining into Bertaghboy Bay. One of the most important salmon and sea trout fisheries in the west of Ireland.

Recess. Salmon and sea trout. The famous Ballynahinch Castle Hotel Fishery consists of **Ballynahinch River** (2½m) and **Ballynahinch Lake**; situated at bottom of 25m long system of river and lakes. Salmon best June to Sept. Sea trout best July to Oct. Fly fishing dt water; max 28 rods; ghillies arranged. Permits for non-residents from The Manager, Ballynahinch Castle Hotel (tel: +353 (0)95 31006). Near

Maam Cross (Co Galway). Salmon and sea trout. Top Waters Ballynahinch Fishery comprises six lakes and part of Owentooey and Recess Rivers. Lough Oorid, at top of system, is 2m W of Maam Cross with Loughs Shannakeela, Derryneen and Cappahoosh forming a chain westward. Season mid-June to 30 Sept; wt (boat) 200 Euro, dt (boat) 30 Euro; sea-lice have affected stocks in recent years; c&r in operation. Permits from Mr L Lyons and Mrs Iris Lyons-Joyce, Tullaboy House (tel: +353 (0)91 552462).

CARROWNISKEY: rises in Sheefry Hills and flows 6m to sea beyond Louisburgh, and is owned and run by the WRFB local office, Ballyhip (tel: +353 (0)98 66404). Spate river, overgrown by trees in parts, making fishing difficult. Lower reaches characterised by long flat stretches. There are runs of salmon and sea trout from June onwards; some brown trout and a few rainbow. **Roonagh Lough**, into which river runs, offers fishing for both, either by fly or dapping. Fishing is by order of WRFB tickets (dt or licence), available at local office or local agent John Bennett (tel: +353 (0)87 9827792). Local club: Bunowen & Carrownisky Salmon & Sea Trout AC, contact John Staunton, Staunton's Pharmacy *(see Louisberg).*

Louisburgh (Co Mayo). Salmon and trout in **Altair Lake**. Good shore fishing for bass, pollack, etc; boats by arrangement. Tackle shops: Hewetson's, Bridge St, Westport (tel: +353 (0)98 26018; fax: +353 (0)98 27075); Stauntons Pharmacy (Gift shop/Fishing Tackle shop), The Square, Louisburgh (tel: +353 (0)98 66139; fax: +353 (0)98 66232; email: loupharm@indigo.ie).

BUNOWEN: spate river with some deep pools, providing excellent lies for salmon and sea trout. Sea trout and salmon, best from mid-June. Season: 1 Apr to 30 Sept. It is run and is owned and run by the WRFB local office, Ballyhip (tel: +353 (0)98 66404); this includes **Lough Namucka**. Tagged salmon were introduced into river in 1992, any tagged fish caught should be reported to an officer of WRFB. Fishing is by order of WRFB tickets (dt or licence), available at local office or local agent John Bennett (tel:

+353 (0)87 9827792); no longer available from Charles Gaffney's Pub, Chapel St, Louisberg. Local club: Bunowen & Carrownisky Salmon & Sea Trout AC, contact John Staunton, Staunton's Pharmacy *(see above)*. **Moher Lough**, in vicinity of **Westport**; stocked annually by WRFB with 2,000 brown trout, ave 1lb; fly only, dt 30 Euro, 15 Euro evng (from 6pm), 4 fish limit; permits from Michael McDonnell, Curramore, Liscarney, Westport (tel: +353 (0)98 21638). Tackle shop: Hewetson's, Bridge St, Westport (tel: +353 (0)98 26018; fax: +353 (0)98 27075);. Hotels: plenty of B&Bs. For sea fishing Bay View Hotel, Clare Island, recommended; boats for hire.

CASHLA: drains a complex system of lakes then flows into Cashla Bay at Costelloe. Good run of salmon up to 22lbs, but it is as a sea trout fishery that it really excels.

Costelloe (Co Galway). Sea trout, salmon. Costelloe and Fermoyle Fishery: Lower fishery includes R Cashla and **Lough Glenicmurrin**, and holds excellent sea trout and good salmon; Upper fishery Loughs **Fermoyle Clogher, Carrick** and **Rusheen**, and holds excellent sea trout. Dt 100 Euro (2 rods), 60 Euro per day for ghillie service. Permits and tackle from Terry Gallagher, The Costello and Fermoyle Fisheries Co, Bridge Cottage, Costello (tel: +353 (0)91 572196; web: www.costelloandfermoylefisheries.com; email: cosfer@iol.ie); accommodation may be booked through fishery. Tackle shops: Freeney's, 19 High Str (tel: +353 (0)91 568794); Duffy's Tackle Shop, 5 Mainguard Str (tel: +353 (0)91 562367; email: duffyb@eircom.net), all Galway; Costello and Fermoyle Fishery Office, Bridge Cottage *(see above)*.

DAWROS: drains Kylemore Lakes then flows 5m before entering Ballinakill Harbour. Run of spring salmon, grilse, sea trout. Best July to Sept (sea trout); May to Sept (salmon).

Kylemore (Co Galway). Salmon, grilse, sea trout. Mrs Nancy Naughton, Kylemore House Fishery (tel: +353 (0)95 41143; web: www.connemara/kylemorehouse; email: kylemorehouse@eircom.net), issues permits. Tackle shops: Gerald Stanley & Son Ltd, Clifden, Connemara (tel: +353 (0)95 21039; fax: +353 (0)95 21721); email: sot@indigo.ie); Hamilton's, Leenane, Co Galway.

Owenglin River (Co Galway). Salmon, brown and sea trout; part of the Ballina-

kill Fishery District and flows into the sea at Clifden Bay. Clifden AA has fishing on both Owenglin and Ballinaboy 1 rivers as well as lakes in the Clifden area; lakes (trout) wt 25 Euro, dt 7 Euro, boats 20 Euro; rivers (salmon) dt 25 Euro, no permits for juv (under 16) on club lakes; permits available from Gerald Stanley & Son Ltd, Clifden, Connemara (tel: +353 (0)95 21039; fax: +353 (0)95 21721). All hotels and B&B cater for anglers.

DOOHULLA: drains a number of lakes, then flows into Ballyconneely Bay via The Pool at Callow Bridge; holds sea trout. Best sea trout July to Sept.

Ballyconneely (Co Galway). Between Roundstone and Ballyconneely lies the **Doohulla Fishery**, which has exclusive rights on a number of loughs including **Maumeen, Emlaghkeeragh, Barrowen, Barrcostello, Arurtaun** and **Carrick** and the rivers joining them, which enter the sea through The Pool at Callow Bridge. Fly only and all fish under 10" to be returned; by law, all sea trout must be returned to the water. Salmon, sea and brown trout. Dt 20 Euro (The Pool) and 10 Euro (after 7pm; dt 10 Euro (lakes) per rod; st (lakes) 30 Euro; boats (where available) 20 Euro per day. Permits from N D Tinne, Emlaghmore Lodge, Ballyconneely (tel: +353 (0)95 23529). Clifden tackle shop: Stanley's Fishing Tackle, Clifden (tel: +353 (0)95 21039; email: sot@indigo.ie)

ERRIFF AND BUNDORRAGHA: good salmon and sea trout rivers lying short distance north of Ballynahinch country and flowing into Killary Harbour near Leenane.

Erriff Fishery, Aasleagh Lodge, **Leenane** (Co Galway) (tel: +353 (0)95 42252; web: www.wrfb.ie). At the east side of Killary Harbour, fishery consists of River Erriff (8m) and **Tawnyard Lough**. Noted for salmon and some sea trout. Fishery managed by Western Regional Fisheries Board since 2000; dt 30 Euro Apr-May, 70 Euro June-July, 55 Euro Aug-Sept. River season 1 Apr-30 Sept. Tawnyard Lough, boat for 2 rods, 80 Euro, from 1 July. Accommodation at Aasleagh Lodge.

Delphi Fishery, Leenane (Co Galway). On the north side of Killary Harbour, fishery has the following waters: **Bundorragha River** (1m), 4 rods, salmon from 1 Feb-30 Sept, few sea trout from July onwards; **Finlough**, two boats, and **Doolough**, three boats, salmon from March onwards, few sea trout from July. **Glencullin** and **Cunnel Loughs**, few trout from July. Fly only, dt with boat 75 Euro; ghillies, 80 Euro. Apply to Fishery Manager, Peter Mantle, Delphi Lodge, Leenane, Co Galway (tel: +353 (0)95 42222; web: www.delphi-salmon.com). Accommodation at Delphi Lodge and 5 fishing cottages. Tackle shops: The Fishery Office, Delphi Lodge; Hamilton's Bar, Leenane.

Knock (Co Mayo). Situated in east of county, a notable centre for coarse fishing. Local loughs include **Cloontariff**, pike and perch, **Carrownamallagh**, excellent pike, **Clooncurry**, pike and perch, **Curragh**, bream and pike, **Derrykin**, pike, **Lakehill Pond**, specimen tench, **Nanonagh**, mixed coarse. Boats are available on all lakes. Hotel and B&B accommodation is plentiful locally.

NEWPORT: drains Lough Beltra and runs into Clew Bay, at Newport. River over 7m long and usually fished from banks. Good for salmon and very good sea trout. There are about 20 pools, some for both day and night fishing. Fly only. River known for length of season, 20 Mar-30 Sept.

Newport (Co Mayo). Salmon and sea trout. Newport House Hotel has fishing on **Newport River, Lough Beltra, West** (fine run of spring fish) and 8m on **River Skerdagh**, a tributary. Fly only, all sea trout to be returned alive; dt 50 Euro, 110 Euro for 2 rods with boat; ghillie extra, from The Fishery Manager, Newport House (tel: +353 (0)98 41222). Newport

A typical casting place on the Ballinahinch river, Connemara, which was once owned and developed by the famous English cricketer, the Maharajah Jora Sahib of Nawaraj, known in England as Ranjit Sinhji. He bought the estate from 'Humanity' Dick Martin, MP. *Photo: Arthur Oglesby.*

AC, whose members are free to fish Newport River by concession of Newport House, issue permits for salmon and sea trout fishing (June to Sept) on **Owengarve**, a small spate river near **Mulrany**. Fly only, all sea trout must be returned alive; dt available from Nevins Tiernaur, Newfield, Westport, beside Owengarve (tel: +353 (0)98 36959). Various small trout loughs around Newport. Hotel also issues tickets to non-members, when available. A few miles from Newport, boat fishing for salmon and sea trout at **Burrishoole Fishery** which consists of **Loughs Feeagh** and **Furnace** with short tidal stretch of river. Fishery owned and administered by the Marine Institute; fishing season effectively mid-June to end Sept. Boats with or without boatmen, package holidays arranged by request incorporating local accommodation of varying grades. Full details from NWRFB, Ballina, Co Mayo (tel: +353 (0)96 22788) for **Ballin Lough Fishery**, 54 acres, 3m north of Westport: stocked rainbow and brown trout, 50 Euro per boat per day (2 rods), limit 4 fish; fly only; 1 May to 31 Oct; permits from Mrs Gill, Ballin Lough (tel: +353 (0)98 26128). **Clogher Lough**

is 4m NE of Westport (also NWRFB); good stock of free rising browns; 1 Apr to 30 Sept; fly only; contact Mrs Gibbons, Clogher PO (tel: +353 (0)98 25061). Tackle shop: Hewetson Bros, Bridge st, Westport, Co Mayo (tel: +353 (0)98 26018).

OWENDUFF: Good for salmon from end of Mar. Grilse and sea trout, mid-June to end of Sept. Provides excellent all-round fishing when water right.

Ballycroy (Co Mayo). Salmon, sea trout. Middle reaches owned by Craigie Bros, Owenduff, Celbridge, Co Kildare (tel: +353 (0)1 6272671); occasional weekly lettings with accommodation, for up to 16 guests and 6 rods.

OWENGARVE: Spate river. Salmon, grilse and sea trout, early June to early Oct.

Mulrany (Co Mayo). Most of river controlled by Newport AC, which has mutual agreement with Dr J Healey, Rosturk Castle, Rosturk, Westport, Co Mayo, whereby whole river can be fished. Daily, weekly and monthly rods from club Hon Sec or from Rosturk Castle.

ACHILL ISLAND: Off Mayo coast. Achill Sporting Club offers excellent brown,

Plus ça change.....! This 1909 party at Costello Lodge bagged 54 salmon and 1095 sea trout between 15 August and 31 October.

rainbow and sea trout fishing. There are three main trout lakes: **Loch Gall**, recently stocked with rainbows; **Loch na Breach**, with good stock of natural browns; **Keel Lake**, with a sea outlet, and a good run of sea trout; controlled by club, permits from Hon Sec: dt, fly only, no artificial baits; disabled access. Tackle from Patrick Sweeney & Son Ltd, Achill Sound (tel: +353 (0)98 45211). Accommodation list from Achill Tourism (Karen Grealis), Achill Island (tel: +353 (0)98 47353).

OWENGOWLA and INVERMORE: two short rivers, each draining a complex of lakes. Owengowla flows into Bertraghboy Bay and Invermore flows into Kilkieran Bay. Both are excellent sea trout fisheries.

Cashel (Co Galway). Sea trout. **Gowla Fishery** consists of **R Owengowla**, with holding pools, and about 14 loughs, permits from Fishery Office. Owing to paucity of sea trout most waters unfished. Accommodation: Mrs Margaret McDonagh, Glen View B&B (tel: +353 (0)95 31054).

OWENMORE: 20m long and principally spate river from Bellacorick Bridge, rises near Ballycastle and flows into Blacksod Bay. Principal tributary is **Oweninny** (Crossmolina AA) (which flows down for 14m from Maumkeogh and joins the main river at Bellacorick). River divided among number of owners. Good for spring salmon from 1 Apr, given really high water; good grilse and sea trout from mid-June to end of Sept, if water is right. To the south of river are a number of small loughs with brown trout. Some of these have free fishing, including **Loughs Brack**, **Nambrock**, and **Nalagan**. They

are remote, but worth exploring.

Bangor Erris (Co Mayo). Upper and middle reaches owned by syndicate, not for letting. Part of fishery let to Bangor Erris AC. Permits from Seamus Henry *(see clubs)*. Enquiries respecting **Carrowmore Lough,** salmon, sea trout and brown trout, plus 4m of **Owenmore**, to Seamus Henry *(see Clubs)*. Bellacorick Fisheries have salmon and trout fishing on **Srahnakilly** and **Oweninny** Rivers. For Oweninny fishing, contact landowners: John Gillespie, Shranakilla (tel: +353 (0)96 53053) who has 1m on west bank, ½m N of **Bellacorick**; John Ruddy, Shranakilla (tel: +353 (0)96 53144) who has 1m of west bank 1½m N of **Bellacorick**; Tony Cosgrove, Shranakilla (tel: +353 (0)96 53216) who has 1m, 3m N of **Bellacorick** (salmon and sea trout); wt and dt from each of the three. Licences from Carolan's Musical Bridge Inn, Bellacorick (tel/fax: +353 (0)96 53013).

SCREEBE: drains a group of lakes, including Lakes **Ardery, Shindilla, Loughanfree, Ahalia** and **Screebe**, then flows into Camus Bay at Screebe. Gets good run of grilse and some summer salmon.

Screebe (Co Galway). Salmon and brown trout. Screebe Fishery is professionally managed and includes Screebe River and numerous lakes; it also has its own hatchery; fly fishing only; permits from The Manager, Screebe House, Camus (tel: +353 (0)91 574110). Hotel: Currarevagh House Hotel, Oughterard, Connemara, Co Galway (tel: +353 (0)91 552312/3), situated beside L Corrib on NW shore, good centre for local fishing, caters for anglers. Tackle shops: Tommy Tuck (Oughterard AA); M Keogh, both Oughterard, Co Galway.

MAYO North (streams)

Several small sea trout rivers run to the coast in north west of county. **Bunnahowen** is a short river near Belmullet, with free fishing for brown trout (to 1lb), and sea trout. **Glenamoy** and **Muingnabo** both empty into a sea lough at **Broad Haven Bay**, and have salmon and sea trout. Fishing on the Muingnabo R. is free. Near **Ballycastle** are **Glencullin** and **Ballinglen Rivers,** both with sea trout, late run on Glencullin, a few salmon in Ballinglen. Free fishing on both. The **Cloonaghmore River** runs into **Killala Bay**, west of the Moy. It has both salmon and sea trout. Free fishing with permission of local assn. **Leafony** is a small spate river which runs into east side of Killala bay, and has free fishing for salmon and sea trout (late run, Aug-Sept). **Easkey River** runs north from L **Easkey** (brown trout, free), and has salmon and sea trout. Some of this river is preserved, elsewhere free fishing. **Drumcliffe** and **Grange Rivers** run into sea loughs north of Sligo. Grange has brown trout, free fishing; Drumcliffe (connected to Glencar Lough**Glencar Lough**) is Assn water, with salmon fishing; permits available, contact Mr Harold Sibbery, The Waterfall, Glencar, Co Leitrim (via Sligo) (tel: +353 (0)7191 44221).

GARAVOGUE and LOUGH GILL

(For close seasons, licences, etc, see The North-Western Regional Fisheries Board)

Garavogue River connects Lough Gill with sea, which it enters in Sligo Bay to south of Donegal Bay and Erne. Salmon, trout, coarse fish. Lough Gill is a fine coarse fishery, with pike to 30lbs and excellent stock of bream at Hazelwood, Dooney, Aughamore and Annagh Bay.

Sligo (Co Sligo). Salmon, trout. **Lough Gill**, a large lake 5m long. Good run of spring salmon; best Feb to March. Northern and eastern shores controlled by Sligo AA; dt from Barton Smith *(see below)*. Fishing on the rest of the lake is free. **Drumcliffe River** and **Glencar Lake**, 6 to 9 miles north of Sligo, controlled by Sligo & Manorhamilton AC; salmon and white and brown trout; permits available, contact Mr Harold Sibbery, The Waterfall, Glencar, Co Leitrim (via Sligo) (tel: +353 (0)7191 44221). Good spring salmon run from mid Feb. Some very large sea trout caught. On the **Ballisodare River**, 3m S of Sligo is **Ballisodare Salmon Fishery**; has two main areas - the falls at Ballisodare and the river upstream of falls. The spring salmon run extends from start of May, when first run of grilse appears. The bulk of these grilse occur in Jun and Jul, with a small run of larger autumn fish in Aug and Sept. Apart from State licence, a local permit is necessary: price varies according to time of year and area. Booking essential. Contact fishery Dunmaeve Hotel. **Lough Colga**, 4m; brown trout; free. Ballisodare FC fishes these waters; wt 45 Euro, dt 10 Euro, ½dt 6 Euro; available from Arnold's Hotel, Dunfanghy, Co Donegal (tel: +353 (0)74 9136208). Tackle shops: Barton Smith, Hyde Bridge, Sligo (tel: +353 (0)71 9146111; fax: +353 (0)71 44196); Macs Tackle Shop, Ballisodare.

Dromahair (Co Leitrim). **River Bonet** feeds Lough Gill; salmon, trout. Best for salmon in summer. Dromahair AA fishes locally; permits from McGoldricks Mace Foodmarket. T McGowan, Stanford Old Inn (tel: +353 (0)71 9164140), has private fishing for guests, and patrons of bar and restaurant. Manorhamilton & DAA also preserve some water on river and **Glencar Lake**. Tickets, apply to A Flynn, Post Office, Manorhamilton (tel: +353 (0)71 9855001). Also abundance of coarse fishing in river and **Loughs Belhavel, Glenade** and **Corrigeencor**; all free, with pike and perch. 5m west of town (12m east of Sligo) is **Lough Doon**, an NWRFB fishery; fly only for wild browns up to 1½lb; 2 boats provided; 1 Apr to 30 Sept; contact Mrs Martin (tel: +353 (0)71 9164989). Tackle from Spar, Main St.

Co. KERRY (rivers and loughs)

(For close seasons, licences, etc, see The South Western Regional Fisheries Board)

KENMARE BAY. Several small salmon rivers empty into this bay, which provides excellent sea fishing (large skate, tope, etc). Best season, May to Aug.

Kenmare (Co Kerry). Salmon, sea trout, small wild brown trout. Kenmare Salmon Angling Ltd owns 1¼m of **Roughty** at Ardtully Castle, 5 miles from Kenmare-Cork Road. Spring salmon, Mar to June; good grilse runs, June to Aug; fly, spinning, prawning and worming permitted; spring salmon average 9lb, grilse 4lb. Permits for visitors staying locally, from John O'Hare, 21 Main St, Kenmare (tel: +353 (0)64 41499). No Sunday fishing for visitors. **Sheen River** runs in on south shore and is preserved by owner. It produces approx 1,000 salmon and grilse every season. Hotel guests only. Contact the Leisure Centre, Sheen Falls Lodge, Kenmare (tel: +353 (0)64 40003). **Finnihy River** is overgrown and requires determination, but has grilse run: free fishing. **Lough Barfinnihy** 35 acres, is 6½m from Kenmare, off Killarney Rd. Good brown and stocked rainbows. **Lough Inchiquin**: char, sea trout, salmon, browns. One boat on site. Permits for these and for **Uragh Lough** from J O'Hare *(see above)*. **Cloonee Loughs,** on the south shore, have excellent game fishing. Permits and boats from May O'Shea, Lake House, Cloonee (tel: +353 (0)64 84205). For fishermen with taste for mountain climbing there are at least 40 lakes holding brown trout on plateau of **Caha Mountains,** all easily fished from Kenmare *(see also South West Cork)*. **Kerry Blackwater** 10m long, drains Lough Brin, spring salmon run, sea trout and browns. Fishing part over 4m long, with about thirty pools. Good fly fishing up near Lough Brin itself. Dt may be obtained from Fishery Manager, SWRFB, Macroom, also from hut on river bank, limit 2 salmon. **Lough Brin**, 65 acres, 10m northwest; trout to 1lb, and sea trout from Aug, dt water; boat available. Controlled by SWRFB. **Sneem River**, further west, is controlled by Sneem River Assn; permits from Joli-Coeur/Tourist Office, South Sq, Sneem (tel: +353 (0)64 45270). Limit 2 salmon per day, 4 sea trout. Fishing with accom at fishing lodge: H Cowper, Sneem (tel: +353 (0)54 36230). Run of grilse and sea trout July/Aug. For trout fishing on SWRFB **Lough Fadda**, contact Kenneth Mulcahy, Tahilla, Sneem (tel: +353 (0)64 45606). Hotels: Sheen Falls Lodge (reception: tel: +353 (0)64 41600); permits; Park Hotel; Kenmare Bay; Riversdale; Dunkeron Lodge. For state licence and tackle: Nuala Hussey, North Square, Sneem; Sneem permits at Tourist Office, Kenmare.

WATERVILLE RIVERS. Waterville River, or **Currane**, is the short gateway to the sea for all salmon and sea trout entering the Waterville system, and produces good catches throughout the season. It is state owned and required a state licence to fish it. All other lakes and rivers in this area are private and require a private permit in addition to the state licence; available from Tadhg O'Sullivan

(see below). **Butler House Pool** is a short fishery of only about 400 yds which drains Lough Currane and the entire Waterville system into Ballinskelligs Bay; tickets are available to fish this famous section from Waterville House (tel: +353 (0)66 947 4244). **Lough Currane** (locally known as Waterville Lake, 1100 hectares) is fished mostly by boat. Ghillie essential to those unfamiliar with the water. Famous for spring salmon, grilse from June, and good runs of large sea trout. The system as a whole produces 90 Euro of all specimen sea trout (over 6lb) caught annually in Ireland. Prawn or shrimp fishing not encouraged. Both bays at the inflowing rivers are strictly fly only. Sea trout less than 30cm to be returned; 1 to 3 fish per day limit, depending on season. The Waterville Fisheries Development Group (manager John Murphy) issue fishery reports and can assist with ghillies, accommodation and boat hire (tel: +353 (0)66 9475257; web: www.loughcurrane.com); boat hire: Lobster Bar, Waterville (tel: +353 (0)66 74183), and others; Waterville Fisheries control **Upper Waterville Fishery** has **Cloonaghlin** (122 hectares; large sea trout, and free taking browns); **Na Mona** (46 hectares); and **Derriana** (240 hectares; large browns); all fly only; licences, permits, ghillies and boat hire from Tadhg O'Sullivan, Fishing Tackle Shop, Main St, Waterville, Co Kerry (tel: +353 (0)66 9474433 (office) or +353 (0)66 9475384 (home)). Contact Joli-Coeur/Tourist Office, South Square, Sneem (tel: +353 (0)64 45270).

Cummeragh River, a spate river with five upper loughs, **Derriana**, **Niamona**, **Cloonaghlin**, **Na Huisce** and **Coppal**, feeding a catchment of 46 sq.miles (10 loughs in all) which flow into Lough Currane. All these loughs contain salmon, sea trout and browns, and producing occasional spring salmon, the river is better known for summer grilse fishing (to end of Sept) and excellent sea trout (July onwards). Tickets for all these may be obtained from Tadhg O'Sullivan, Fishing Tackle Shop, Main St, Waterville, Co Kerry (tel: +353 (0)66 9474433 (office) or +353 (0)66 9475384 (home)). Local hills contain numerous small loughs rarely fished.

Inny River, a fair sized spate river some 15m in length, with good run of salmon and sea trout from June onwards. Salmon fishing on these rivers is from 17 Jan-30 Sept. Spring fish average 11lbs, fish over 15lbs caught, record 32lbs. An unusual feature is that fish may be caught by a small fly on a floating line from opening day, although many are taken on rapallas, toby spoons and other baits. The catchment is a long narrow mountain valley of some 47sq.m and is regarded mainly as a grilse fishery, although the system is noted for its large sea trout, with over 70 Euro of Irish specimen (6lbs plus) fish taken. Season 17 Jan to 30 Sept. The bigger fish are caught in Lough Currane and Derriana. Tickets from from Tadhg O' Sullivan, Fishing Tackle Shop, Main St, Waterville, Co Kerry (tel: +353 (0)66 9474433 (office) or +353 (0)66 9475384 (home)). Waterville House (tel: +353 (0)66 947 4244) lets occasional rods, residents only; spinning allowed in spring, thereafter, fly only. Several other owners have or can arrange fishing on Inny, incl Butler Arms Hotel, Waterville (tel: +353 (0)66 947 4156) (no tickets); enquire tackle shop. Tackle shops: Tadgh O'Sullivan (*see above*); Sean O'Shea. Other hotels: Silver Sands, White House.

CARHAN and FERTA: small spate rivers which enter Valentia Harbour. Small run of grilse and sea trout. Carhan is overgrown and worm is the best method. **Kells Lough** is between **Glenbeigh** and **Cahersiveen.** Plentiful stock of small browns.

CARAGH: river runs through **Caragh Lake** to sea at Dingle Bay. Salmon, sea trout, trout. Salmon best from May, sea trout late, good fishing at night. Bass and mullet in estuary. 7 beats on upper river from Glencar Hotel, Glencar (tel: +353 (0)66 976 0102); weekly only Mar to mid-Jul, dt and wt mid Jul-30 Sept; access for disabled; tackle shop at hotel. Immediately to the east of Caragh Lake is a large group of small loughs, incl L Nakirka, 20 acres, with good stocks of small wild browns and stocked larger fish; for permit contact SWRFB, 1 Neville Terrace, Macroome, Co Cork (tel: +353 (0)26 41222), or Kate O'Connor, Oulagh, Caragh Lake, Killorglin (tel: +353 (0)66 9769279).

Glenbeigh (Co Kerry). For lower water; tickets from Towers Hotel. Hotel also issues permits for 6m of **Laune** (single bank only), 8½m of **Feale**, 3m of **Flesk**, **Behy** and **Loughs Caragh** and **Currane.** To south west of Glenbeigh is a group of small trout loughs drained by **R Behy**, incl **Coomnacronia** and **Coomaglaslaw**: free fishing on all of them.

Glencar (Co Kerry) Glencar House Hotel has 7 beats, one rod per beat, reserved for guests only; salmon; best months, Feb to end of June; grilse June onwards; sea trout. Average salmon catch over 10 years, 310 per annum. The hotel also has fishing on **Lower Caragh River** to the ocean, both banks; and **Loughs Cloon**, **Acoose** and **Reagh.** Many smaller rivers and lakes holding brown trout. Ghillies and boats in vicinity. Tackle and licences at hotel (tel: +353 (0)66 9760102).

MACGILLYCUDDY'S REEKS (Co Kerry). In the Gap of Dunloe, a line of three small lakes drain into **Laune** at Beaufort Bridge: **Black Lake, Cushvalley** and **Auger.** Free fishing for plentiful small brown trout that fight extremely well. Very small fly recommended. At head of Black Valley are **Cummeenduff Loughs** and **Lough Reagh**, which are approached via Gap of Dunloe. Free fishing with spring salmon and good grilse run. Boats from J O'Donoghue, Black, Valley, Killarney.

DINGLE PENINSULA (Co Kerry). Several small rivers and loughs are fishable in this area; **Rivers Milltown**, free fishing with some sea trout; and **Owenascaul**, or **Annascaul** on south side, rights owned by Patricia Scully, Bunanear, Annascaul, permission required to fish; **Owencashla,** **Glennahoo,** **Scarid,** **Owenmore** on north side: some migratory fish in spate, worth fishing. Mostly free. Owencashla overgrown. Loughs incl **Annascaul**, with sea trout in Aug/Sept; **Gill**, west of **Castlegregory**: free, for small browns; **Adoon**, with sea trout from Aug, free; and many others worth exploring. **Lough Caum** at Castlegregory is SWRFB trout fishery with small native browns and stocked rainbows. Boats for hire on water.

LAUNE and MAINE (including Killarney Lakes)

(For close seasons, licences, etc, see The South-Western Regional Fisheries Board)

LAUNE: Drains the lakes of Killarney and a chachment area of approx 320 sq.m. It flows 14m before entering the sea at Castlemain Harbour on Dingle Bay. Salmon, sea trout, brown trout. Late summer best time for trout. Laune Salmon & Trout AA has 16 fisheries on river and these waters are available to visitors; dt 15 Euro. Fishing permits may be purchased at Dungeel Farm Guesthouse, Dungeel, Killorglin (tel: +353 (0)66 9761456); O'Sullivan's Foodstore, Beaufort Bridge (tel: +353 (0(64 44397); Angler's Lodge, Lahard, Beaufort (tel: +353 (0)64 44559) and Killarney Fishing Centre, Glebe Lane, Killarney (tel: +353 (0)64 22884); all adjacent to the river. Daily permits to fish Beat 3 of the State Fishery, under the management of Laune Salmon & Trout AA, from O'Sullivan's Foodstore *(see above)*. Disabled facilites available on Killarney's Lower Lake, including wheelchair facilities and chair hoist. Permits for Beats 1 and 2 of State Fishery from SWRFB. Dungeel Farmhouse, on river nr Killorglin, has B&B catering for anglers. Tackle shops in Killorglin, Killarney and Tralee.

Beaufort (Co Kerry). For upper reaches. Permits and light tackle from O'Sullivan's, Beaufort Bridge, Killarney (tel: +353 (0)64 44397). Self-catering house on banks. Accom at Anglers lodge, Beaufort.

MAINE: Maine and tributaries **Little Maine** and **Brown Flesk** hold salmon, sea trout and brown trout. Salmon fishing is at times very good. Brown Flesk has at least 35 holding pools; over 200 salmon per season, sea and brown trout fishing often good. River is late. Best at medium to low water; good grilse from end of June, sea trout in July. Little Maine has seven or eight salmon pools and good fishing for small browns. Sea trout best at night. Part of this system is free fishing: check with SWRFB.

KILLARNEY LAKES: Consist of three lakes: **Upper Lake, Muckross Lake, Lough Leane**, last being much the largest at 4,500 acres, connected with sea by **R**

Laune. Good free trout fishing, excellent stocks of wild browns av 8ozs. Numerous boatmen for hire, 100 Euro per day, two fishing, 60 Euro per half-day; boats for disabled. Boats from Harry Clifden, Ross Castle, Killarney (tel: +353 (0)64 32252). **R Flesk** feeds **Lough Leane**. Medium sized spate river, with good grilse run. Many small mountain lakes; free trout fishing. **Barfinnihy Lake**, 10m away on Sneem Road, is well stocked with rainbow trout, fishing by permit only, contact O'Neills *(see Killarney)*; John Buckley, Killarney Fishing Centre, Killarney (licences and tackle); J O'Hare *(see Kenmare)*.

Killarney (Co Kerry). Salmon fishing best in May/June. Sea trout fishing poor, brown trout excellent, best June, and Sept to mid-Oct. Fishing on R Flesk is open; wt 20 Euro from Lough Leane AA. **Lough Leane** (4,500 acres), largest of Killarney lakes; famous for beauty of scenery; estimated that local fishermen get hundreds of salmon and grilse by trolling baits every season. Free fishing; max rods 40-50. Boats with guide, 100 Euro per day; 60 Euro half-day from Harry Clifden, Ross Castle, Killarney (tel: +353 (0)64 32252). Day salmon fishing 120 Euro (incl man, boats, rod & licence); contact Abbey Boating & Fishing Tours (Fergus O'Donoghue) 24a Dalton Ave (tel: +353 (0)64 34351; mob: +353 (0)87 6899241); brown trout (½lb - 18lb) free. Tackle shops: O'Neill's, 6 Plunkett Str (tel: +353 (0)64 31970; fax: +353 (0)64 35689); open 24/7 for advice on all fisheries; supplies licences, permits and tickets for rivers and lakes; ghillies and boats; Killarney Fishing Centre, 3 Glebe Lane, (tel/fax: +353 (0)64 22884; e-mail: johnbuckley17@eircom.net); The Handy Stores, Main St; Harry Clifton. Many hotels and guest houses, incl Saratoga House B&B, Muckross Rd, Killarney.

LEE

(For close seasons, licences, etc, see The South-Western Regional Fisheries Board)

Draining **Gougane Barra Lake** and flowing 53m in an easterly direction to Cork Harbour, Lee was formerly notable early salmon river, but fishing partly spoilt by hydro-electric schemes; salmon sport restricted to lower 9m, d/s of Inniscarra Dam. At least 300 salmon and 800 grilse are caught in a typical season. Trout are more plentiful below Inniscarra Dam. There is also good coarse fishing in system, for bream, tench, perch, eels. Salmon season, Feb-30 Sept. SWRFB Fisheries: **Inniscarra Lake**, River Lee: 530 ha, and over 25 miles of bank side, possibly Ireland's best bream fishing. Bags in excess of 100lb are common, also to be found are bream-rudd hybrids; permits (st 25 Euro, wt 15 Euro and dt 8 Euro) from

Kathleen Crowley, Kathleen's Shop, Coachford, Co Cork. There is ¾m double bank salmon fishing, below hydro-electric station. Fishable from Mar, peaks in Apr to May, mid-June for grilse, brown trout 15 Feb to 12 Oct. State salmon permits required; additional payment for fishing to Amenity Officer, ESB Fisheries, Carrigadrohid, Co Cork; SWRFB, 1 Nevilles Terrace, Massey Town, Macroom (tel: +353 (0)26 41221). Local club: South Munster Coarse AC; associate membership 10 Euro; contact Mike Risdon (tel: +353 (0)58 59450). Accommodation: Hogan's (The Village Inn).

Cork (Co Cork). Salmon fishing on lower R Lee at Inniscarra Dam and below Millbro; season 1 Feb-30 Sept. Fishing is privately owned or leased and controlled mainly by Lee Salmon A and Cork Salmon A (dt 25 Euro, from Hon Sec). Salmon fishing licence is required, obtainable from tackle shops. Trout fishing on **R Shournagh, Martin, Bride, Sullane** and **Dripsey**; small streams with brown trout; fishing mostly free. For information contact Cork Trout AA, Blarney AA and tackle shops. Lough in Cork City, 10 acres, has large carp (Irish record 28lb) and eels, 2lb to 6lb. Tackle shops: T W Murray & Co, 87 Patrick Str (tel: +353 (0)21 4271089; The Tackle Shop, 6 Lavitts Quay (tel: +353 (0)21 4272842; fax: +353 (0)21 4270301); tackle and bait also available from: River's Edge Tackle (David O'Flynn), Inniscarra Rd, Carrigrohane, Co Cork (tel: +353 (0)21 487 1771); The Village Inn (John Hogan), Coachford (tel: +353 (0)21 7334034/ 7334430). Salmon permits (st 25 Euro, wt 15 Euro and dt 8 Euro) and accommodation from Kathleen Crowley, Kathleen's Shop, Coachford, Co Cork (coarse fishing on **Inniscarra Lake**); Advance orders for bait: Pat Barry (+353 (0)25 36187) and John Hogan (+353 (0)21 7334034). Hotels: Jurys, Metropole, Imperial. B&B: The Village Inn *(see above)*; O'Callaghan's (tel: +353 (0)21 733 4023); Kathleen's *(as above)* and others. Further angling information &c. from Cork/Kerry Tourism, Grand Parade, Cork (tel: +353 (0)21 4273251; fax: +353 (0)21 4273504).

Macroom (Co Cork). Stocked brown trout fishing on **Inniscarra Reservoir**; contact SW Fisheries Board, Macroom (tel: +353 (0)26 41222). **Carrigohid Reservoir** is good pike fishery, with perch shoals. Other venues for pike are lower **Sullane River, Middle Lee, Lough Allua**. Middle Lee, Rivers Sullane, Laney and Foherish, and **Gougane Barra** lake are good fisheries for small trout. Local club: Macroom Fly Anglers, c/o Mary Anne's Bar, Masseytown, Macroom (tel: +353 (0)26 41566); st 20 Euro, dt 5 Euro; juv st 5 Euro for River Sullane and tributaries (brown trout). Hotels: Castle, Victoria; Coolcower.

LIFFEY

(For close seasons, licences, etc, see The Eastern Regional Fisheries Board)

Winding river with two reservoirs along its course, rises some 13m SW of Dublin but flows over 80m before entering sea at Islandbridge, Dublin. Subject to hydro-electric floods, it has brown trout and some sea trout in lower reaches. Mayfly hatch end of May. Best trout fishing from Lucan upstream. Best salmon between Straffan and Islandbridge.

Dublin (Co Dublin). Most water controlled by clubs. Dublin & Dist Salmon AA: Liffey at Islandbridge, Lucan, and below Leixlip Bridge; Dublin Trout AA: about 6m on Upper and Lower Liffey at Ballyward Bridge, Clane, Straffan/Celbridge, **Leixlip, Blessington** and **Upper** and **Lower Bohernabreena Reservoirs**; mainly trout fishing, some salmon in Liffey, and pike, also. Dt 10 Euro average, depending on water. Clane Trout and Salmon AA: approx 4m of excellent brown trout water, best from early May. Dt 12 Euro (evng 6 Euro) from Patrick Cleere & Son *(see below)*; fly, bait fishing discouraged, no coarse. North Kildare Trout & Salmon AA: Kilcullen Bridge through Newbridge, Sallins to Millicent Bridge; brown trout, salmon and pike: tickets from Hon Sec; Higgins, Arch Bar, Main st, Newbridge; Flemings, New Row, Naas; Moorefield, PO Moorefield, Newbridge and Rory's, Temple Bar, Dublin 2; new member st 30 Euro (juv 5 Euro), wt 10 Euro, dt 5 Euro; fishing classes 5 Euro. Kilcullen Trout & Salmon AA, Kilcullen u/s to Harristown; Ballymore Eustace Salmon & Trout AA, Ballymore Eustace to Harristown; Kilbride AC: Ballyfoyle to Ballysmutton; Lucan AC fishes Lucan stretch. Chapelizod AC has water from Old Mill Race River to Laurence Brook Weir, game and coarse fishing, no dt, membership available, conc. Broadmeadow AC fishes **Broadmeadow R** and **Tonelgee Reservoir**. Tickets from tackle shops. Dt for Dublin Trout AA waters from Dan O'Brien, New Rd, Blackhall, Clane, Co Kildare. Dublin Corporation controls fishing on **Roundwood Reservoir** (20m) and on **Bohernabreena Reservoir** (8m); fly only; bank fishing; st and dt. **Grand Canal**, which runs alongside Liffey for some distance, holds few brown trout, bream, rudd, perch and pike. Coarse fishing also in **Royal Canal**, similar species. Tackle shops in Dublin area: ABC Fishing Tackle Specialists, 15 Mary's Abbey, Dublin 7 (tel: +353 (0)1 873 1525); P Cleere & Son Ltd, 5 Bedford Row, Temple Bar Dublin 2 (tel: +353 (0)1 677 7406); Henry's Tackle Shop, 19 Ballyough Road, Dublin 3 (+353 (0)1 8555216); Southside Angling, 80 Lower Clanbrassil Str, Dublin 8 (tel: +353 (0)453 0266); Angling & Shooting Centre, Ballydowd, Lucan (tel: +353 (0)1 628 1112); Boland's Hardware, 349 Ballyfermot Rd, Ballyfermot, Dublin 10 (tel:

+353 (0)1 626 4777; fax: +353 (0)1 623 1911); Tallaght Rod & Gun Shop, Unit 2 Castletymon SC, Tallaght, Dublin 24 (tel: +353 (0)1 452 6522); Rory's Fishing Tackle, 17a Temple Bar, Dublin 2 (tel: +353 (0)1 677 2351), who sells permits for Dublin Salmon A, Dodder A, North Kildare A, Tolka A, and Blessington A.

Naas (Co Kildare). Ballymore Eustace Trout & Salmon AA has fishing on Liffey from **Ballymore Eustace** to **Harristown**, and also **Golden Falls Lake**; dt enquiries to Publican, The Square, Ballymore Eustace; or Hon Sec. Kilcullen & Dist Trout & Salmon AA fishes Liffey at Kilcullen, u/s to Harristown. Prosperous Coarse AC fishes 20m of **Grand Canal** *(see Grand Canal);* North Kildare Trout & Salmon AA fish 18m from Kilcullen Bridge to Millescent Bridge. Tackle shops: Peter McGlynn, Countryman Angling Ltd, Leanne House, Pacelli Road, Naas (tel: +353 (0)45 879341); bait and tickets for Liffey and 46 miles of Blessington bank fishing, and boats (coarse fishing free); Charles Camping, Blessington (tel: +353(0)45 865351). Hotel; Ardenode, Ballymore Eustace; Town House Hotel, Naas. Several guest houses.

No shortage of competitors! Here they assemble at The Watering Gates, Newbridge. *Photo: Mick Deely.*

MOY

(For close seasons, licences, etc, see The North Western Regional Fisheries Board)

Flowing 63m from its source in the Ox Mountains to enter Killala Bay at Ballina, its tributaries drain an area of some 800 square miles. One of Ireland's premier salmon rivers, particularly famous for its grilse and summer salmon, the everage rod and line catch in the last 5 years being 7660 salmon. Stretches to suit all forms of angling from fly fishing to spinning to worm fishing. Spring run starts in early Feb; main grilse run starts in May and peaks in June/July. Estuary contains good stocks of sea trout, boats obtainable. Detailed information on all fisheries from NWRFB, Ardnaree House, Abbey St, Ballina(tel: +353 (0)96 21332; fax: +353 (0)96 78850; e-mail: info@moyfishery.com).

Ballina (Co Mayo). Famous salmon water, with catches of over 5,000 in a season. Fishing on seven beats (Ridge Pool, Cathedral Beat, Polnamonagh, Spring Wells, Ash Tree Pool, Freshwater Beat (disabled anglers access) and The Point) owned by **Moy Fishery**; State Salmon Rod Licence required; dt available, various fees apply (non-refundable and non-transferable); all must be booked in advance with exception of The Point. Apply to Moy Fishery Office (NWRFB), Ardnaree House, Abbey St, Ballina (tel: +353 (0)96 21332; fax: +353 (0)96 78850; e-mail: info@moyfishery.com); permits and licences also available from local tackle shops. NWRFB can also arrange boats and engines for **Lough Conn** fishing (wild brown trout and salmon). Ballina Salmon AA has a 3m stretch of double bank fishing from weir in Ballina to confluence of Corroy river, with estimated 1,000-3,000 salmon per season. Ballina SAA issue permits for their waters, limited st 140 Euro (apply for vacancy, waiting list), wt 70 Euro, dt 20 Euro, juv (under 16); apply to local tackle shops; also provide access for disabled anglers, as they have installed two wheelchair-friendly access points. 4m south of Ballina, Mount Falcon Fishery has 2m single bank fishing upstream from Corroy river on left bank of main Moy channel, incl one bank of famous wall pool; also contains others pools such as Connor's Gap; ghillie service and casting instructors provided. Apply to Fishery Manager, Mount Falcon Castle (tel: +353 (0)96 21172). Knockmore AC (in assn with Mount Falcon) has lease on two stretches on left bank between Wall Pool and Coolcronan Fishery; dt available; permits and information from Martin Kelly (tel: +353 (0)94 58287). Scott-Knox-Gore & Wall Pool Fishery own 3m single bank fishing opposite Mount Falcon fishery, leased to Attymass AA (although they retain 1¼m

(Timlin's Corner to the Ditches) - 3 beats which they manage themselves; permits and information from David Carlisle (tel: +353 (0)94 57055). The Attymass Fishery (Attymass AA waters) has 3 separate beats of 1½m, bait and spinning water (but bubble and fly can be effective); permits from Padraig Garret (tel: +353 (0)94 58151); Pat Gaughan (tel: +353 (0)94 581467 and Padraig Hughes (tel: +353 (0)94 58146). For Coolcronan Fishery (owned by Andrew Wrigley), contact David Carlisle (tel: +353 (0)94 57055) or Andrew Wrigley (tel: +353 (0)87 6994688). There is a short strectch comprising ¾m on left bank opposite junction of Yellow River which is Byrne's Fishery; permits from Jim Byrne (tel: +353 (0)96 36733). Armstrong Fishery has adjoining single left bank stretch of about 1½m; permits and information from George Armstrong or Mrs Bridie Armstrong at fishery (tel: (0)94 56580). For Gannons Fishery, 1½m single left bank, contact Pat Gannons, Post Office, Foxford (tel: +353 (0)94 56101). Ballina Angling Centre arranges boat fishing trips in Moy Estuary, also on Lough Conn. Tackle shops: Ballina Angling Centre, Dillon Terrace (tel: +353 (0)96 21850); Piggott's Angling Shop (tel: +353 (0)96 72656); John Walkin's, Market Square (tel/fax: +353 (0)96 22442); Ridge Pool Tackle Shop, Cathedral Rd (tel: +353 (0)96 72656); Sportfish Tackle Shop, Ridgepool Road (tel +353 (0)96 74455); Edward Doherty, Tackle and Bar, Bridge St. Hotels: Ridge Pool, Bridge Str; Bartra House, Pearson Str; Down Hill Motel, Sligo Road; Belleek Castle.

Foxford (Co Mayo). Foxford Fishery, double bank, from 400m north of Foxford Bridge, d/s for 1m. Limited rods, book in advance; contact Chris Downey, 9 Moy View, Foxford (tel: +353 (0)94 56824). Baker's New Fishery, about 400m d/s from the old Eel Weir, Foxford; 2 good salmon pools (Eddie Moloney, Maloneys Lodge, The Green (tel: +353 (0)94 56475). Foxford Salmon Anglers (in assn with Charles Baker), 1m double bank from Foxford Bridge upstream and joins Cloongee Fishery ½m north of Cross River; permits from Tiernan Bros *(see below)*. Cloongee Fishery, a prolific salmon and grilse fishery comprising 2m of right bank and 1m of left bank, incl stretch of Cross River; famous Joinings Pool is located here, considered one of of the most productive salmon pools on the Moy; dt available without reservation; few st and wt but some restrictions apply; contact John Ruane, Cloongee (tel: +353 (0)94 56534). East Mayo AA, 8m both banks above Foxford, fly only, ghillie service; dt: contact Mrs Florence Mills, Ballylahan Bridge (tel: +353 (0)94 56221) or Bolands Lounge, Swinford (tel: +353 (0)94 51149). Permits for most of these fisheries from Tiernan Bros *(see below)*. Free fishing on **Loughs Conn** and **Cullin**; wild brown trout and salmon (permit required for latter), 2m from town, and on a short stretch of R Moy downstream of Foxford Bridge. Healys Hotel, **Pontoon** (tel: +353 (0)94 9256443), has boats and at southern end of Lough Conn and at **Lough Cullin**. **Lough** Muck is a NWRFB fishery, 1½m north; large stock of wild browns; all legitimate methods; 15 Feb to 10 Oct; fishing free, not suitable for bank fishing.

The Board also controls Callow Loughs, 2 loughs of 100 acres each, joined by a narrow channel, which is navigable by boat. Tackle shop: Tiernan Bros Angling Advice Centre, Upper Main St, Foxford (tel: +353 (0)94 9256731).

Crossmolina (Co Mayo), a small town north of Lough Conn. Salmon, grilse, trout. Free fishing on Lough **Conn**. Boats and ghillies from J Murphy, Mossbrook, Boseenaun (tel: +353 (0)96 51079); Padraic Kelly, Kelly's Angling Service, Cloghans, Ballina (tel/fax: +353 (0)96 22250). Cloonamoyne Fishery, Enniscoe, Castlehill, Ballina (tel/fax: +353 (0)96 31851) provides a complete angling service covering brown trout fishing on Lough Conn, and salmon fishing on Loughs **Carrowmore**, **Furnace** and **Feeagh**; accom arranged. Another local club is the Ballina & Cloghans AC. Accommodation: Kilmurray House, Castlehill (tel: +353 (0)96 31227); can also be arranged by Kelly's Angling Service *(see above)*.

Swinford (Co Mayo). Spring salmon best from mid-Mar, grilse June onwards. East Mayo AA controls the largest stretch of water on the River Moy (6m fishing on both banks); wt 130 Euro, dt 25 Euro available from East Mayo AA office (tel: +353 (0)94 53955; Mrs Wills, Ballylahon Bridge (tel: +353 (0)94 56221) and Seamus Boland, Bridge Str (tel: +353 (0)94 51149). **Lough Talt** is good brown trout lake (200 acres); free. For disabled facilities, contact East Mayo AA office.

Tributaries of the Moy

BUNREE. Joins just below Ballina. End of season salmon fishing, sea trout, brown trout. Free fishing.

GWEESTION. **Glore River** and **Trimoge River** join to become **Gweestion**, flowing from south easterly direction. Both have a large stock of small brown trout, with free fishing.

MULLAGHANOE and OWENGARVE. These two rivers flow from the **Charlestown** area westwards. They contain a good stock of browns to 1½lb. Fishing free, excellent on Owengarve d/s of Curry Village.

EINAGH. Joins main river from **Lough Talt** near Aclare. Brown trout to 1½lb, but average at 10oz. Sea trout run; free fishing in river and lough (browns, av ½lb).

LOUGH CONN SYSTEM. Lough Conn,

12,000 acres, together with **L Cullin**, has free fishing for salmon (other than for state licence, prices vary), main run from end of Mar through Apr, grilse run from May through July. Salmon adhere to known localities, and are taken by trolling spoon or Devon minnow, a few on wet fly. Trout fishing starts around 17 March. The vast majority of trout caught on Lough Conn are taken on wet flies during seasonal hatches. L Conn has one of the longest mayfly hatches in the country, from about 20 May until almost the end of July. Trout fishing slows in July, but improves in Aug. Specimen fish are sometimes taken. Several rivers run into **Loughs Conn** and **Cullin** which offer free fishing for game and coarse fish. From north west, **Deel River**: salmon in spring and summer, brown trout u/s of

No prizes for guessing how the taking of this 25lb salmon, caught on Castleconnell Fishery, will be celebrated!

Deel Bridge. From the south, **Clydagh River** (spate river) and **Manulla River** (limestone based), and the outflow from **Castlebar Lakes** all join a few miles above lough. On Clydagh free salmon fishing; on Manulla Roundtower AC water between **Moyhenna** and **Ballyvary** bridges. Stocked browns on location (tickets on bank) in **Islandeady Bilberry Lough**. There is a wide range of accommodation approximate to the Lough Conn

fisheries. Contact NWRFB, Ardnaree House, Abbey St, Ballina(tel: +353 (0)96 21332; fax: +353 (0)96 78850; e-mail: info@moyfishery.com), for further information on L Conn fishing. Tackle shops: Eagle Isle Fishing Tackle, Main Str (tel: +353 (0)94 21030); Christy Murphy Angling Centre, Linenhall Str (tel: +353 (0)94 23258); Field & Stream (tel: +353 (0)94 21030) both Castlebar.

SHANNON

(For close seasons, licences, etc, see The Shannon Regional Fisheries Board)

Largest river in these islands, 160m long with catchment area covering greater part of central Ireland. Enters Atlantic on west coast through long estuary. A typical limestone river, rich in weed and fish food, of slow current for most part, and though some its sources rise in peat, acidity counteracted by limestone reaches. Many of the adverse effects of hydro-electric scheme now overcome by re-stocking and other forms of fishery management. With exception of the famous Castleconnell stretch, Shannon mostly sluggish. Salmon run from Mar to May, grilse from end of May to Sept. Primary sea trout waters are **Rivers Feale** and **Doonbeg**. Permits from local tackle shops. Trout fishing is a feature of Shannon and tributaries, **Mulcair**, **Newport**, **Nenagh**, **Brosna**, **Little Brosna**, **Fergus**, and **Maigue**. There is a mayfly rise, when excellent sport can be enjoyed, free of charge, in **Loughs Derg** and **Ree** at Athlone. Trolling is the usual method, otherwise; trout grow large. Salmon fishing rights on Shannon and tributaries are reserved by the ESB, and a permit is required, which is sold as st, wt, or dt, from ESB Fisheries Office, Ardnacrusha (tel: +353 (0)61 345589). Brown trout fishing is in part free, and in part leased to the Central Fisheries Board or fishing clubs. River has well-deserved reputation for its coarse fishing. Excellent fisheries for rudd, perch, shoals of bream and roach, at Plassey, O'Brien's Bridge, u/s of Portumna, Banagher, Shannonbridge.

The three main pike fisheries of the system are R Shannon itself, Lough Derg, and R Fergus. There is a limit on the killing of pike: one per angler per day, max size, 3kgs. Coarse fishing may also be had in Derg and Ree. **Lough Allen**, northernmost lake of Shannon, specially good for pike. Eel fishing is growing more popular in Shannon region, which has sluggish stretches ideal for the species, large catches coming from Shannon, **R Fergus, L Derg** and **East Clare Lakes**; Mouth of Suck at Shannonbridge and mouth of Brosna are good spots to try. A licence is required to fish for brown trout and coarse fish upstream of Banagher Bridge, and a licence is required to fish for sea trout and salmon in whole of region. For angling guide and detailed pamphlets on angling in Shannon region contact Shannon Development, Shannon Town Centre, Co Clare (tel: +353 (0)61 361555; fax: +353 (0)61 363180; e-mail: meehanc@shannondev.ie); or Shannon Regional Fisheries Board, Ashbourne Business Park, Dock Rd, Limerick (tel: +353 (0)61 300238; fax: +353 (0) 61 300308; e-mail: infor@shannon-fishery-board.ie). For more angling information, see www.shannonregiontourism.ie and/or www.shannon-fishery-board.ie. **Wheelchair anglers:** Much of the accommodation featured have special access facilities for wheelchair users. Likewise, many of the rivers and lakes in the region are equipped to make fishing accessible to persons with physical disabilities. Car parking is available close to the water's edge, and purpose-built fishing stands enable access by wheelchairs at the following better-known angling venues: the Shannon at O'Brien's Bridge (Rowing Club stretch) 6 pegs; Annacotty stretch 10 pegs; Lough Bridget in East Clare 20 pegs; Lough Derg shores at Rossmore Quay 6 pegs; from the pier at Scariff Harbour there is limited access at Twomilegate near Killaloe, and at Dromineer Bay. Check accommodation facilities first, though, and for up to date information visit www.shannon-fishery-board.ie. A *Three Counties Angling Guide* is also available, covering fishing in upper Shannon catchment, from Mr Michael Flaherty, Lack, Whitehall, Co Longford (tel: +353 (0)53 4326439).

Kilrush (Co Clare). West Clare AA has   fishing in this corner of Co Clare, on

A good tackle shop will have detailed knowledge of the local waters. This one is in Limerick.

Lakes **Knockerra** (50 acres), **Knocka-lough, Doo Lough, Kilkee Reservoir**, all fly and worm only; plenty of trout. Trout fishing free, however membership of West Clare AA would be appreciated; permits from Jack Horgan, Cree PO and Doonbeg Tourist Office. National, regional, district and local permits as well as tackle, information and advice from Michael O'Sullivan & Son, 49/50 Moore St, (tel/fax: +353 (0)65 9051071). Accommodation: several hotels in Kilkee, including Strand; various B&B available, including Kilrush Creek Lodge, Kiely's Grove House and several in Kilrush. Salmon in spate, brown and sea trout fishing locally on **Cree**, **Annageeragh** and **Doonbeg Rivers**.

Limerick (Co Limerick). On tidal Shannon. Clancy's Strand is the lowest bottom fishery on Shannon, mainly trout fishing, which can be very good, on fly, worm, dead minnow or spinner. ESB permit required. On outskirts of city is the Long Shore Fishery: wide, deep tidal water with spring salmon run; it can be fished from both banks. Good spring salmon fishing at **Plassey** (2m); 500 yds salmon fishing which peaks in May, and trout. ESB permits required; licences and permits available from The Fishing & Shooting Shop *(see below)*. Limerick tackle shops: Bonds Tackle, 40 Wickham Str (tel: +353 (0)61 316809; fax: +353 (0)61 473017); Limerick Angling Centre, 3 John Str (tel: +353 (0)61 316637); J Doherty, 3 John St; The Fishing & Shooting Store, 6 Denmark Str (tel: +353 (0)61 413484; web: stevenormoyle.com; e-mail: info@stevenormoyle.com), who also offer a comprehensive range of services such as guided boat trips for pike and trout; tuition in fly fishing and spinning/trolling &c.

Castleconnell (Co Limerick). Principal centre for salmon angling on Shannon and within 3m of **Mulcair River**. Traditional big fish water; catches improved recently. Good run of spring salmon, grilse from May, and Sept fishing is usually good. Fishing on eight Castleconnell beats controlled by Regional Manager, Hydro Generation Region, Ardnacrusha, nr Limerick, who will book beats and provide information; also Kingfisher AC *(see below)*. Permits 10 Euro for licence + 5 Euro for permit, from Head Warden, M Murtagh, O'Briens Bridge (tel: +353 (0)61 377289; mob: +353 (0)86 8566556), or from Kingfisher Angling Centre, *(see below)*. Advance booking advisable, from ESB (tel: +353 (0)61 345589). Best beats can be the lower beats. Best months for spring salmon, Apr to mid-May, grilse mid-May to end June. Fly, spinning and worm. The best coarse fishing in Limerick area is located just below Castleconnell Salmon Fishery; annual rod catch is 800 salmon in the season. This is free fishing, but has eight private positions, available as dt and should be reserved in advance; landowner consent is required on some parts. About 10 mins drive from Castleconnell Fishery, one of Ireland's famous fishing houses, Millbank House, Murroe is located; contact Richard & Eleanor Keays (tel: +353 (0)61 386115); Millbank has a well stocked tackle shop and all facilities required for the experienced fisherman; the Mulcair River flows by the property; famous for its salmon and trout. Also, contact Niall O'Donnell, Lake View House, Doon Lake, Broadford, Co Clare (tel: +353 (0)61 473125) for fishing here. Tackle shops: Kingfisher Angling Centre (tel: +353 (0)61 377407), supplies boats, ghillies, hires tackle, supplies permits and licences, and runs Kingfisher AC (also agent for stocked fishery, with trout 2lbs-12lbs); Moloneys; T J's Tackle & Angling Centre, Ballina, Killaloe (tel: +353 (0)61 276009); web: www.esatclear.ie/~tjsangling/). Accommodation: Edelweiss, Stradbally (tel: +353 (0)61 377397).

Killaloe (Co Clare). At outlet from Lough Derg, good centre for trout and coarse fishing on lake. Trout angling can be very good in May and autumn; fish average 3-4lb. Boats for hire. **Doon Lough**, 8m west, is a fine coarse fishery, with a good stock of bream to 3lb, also boat fishing for large pike. Boats for hire. Good bream fishing at caravan park on west shore. Tackle shop: McKeogh's, Ballina. Hotel: Lakeside.

Scariff Bay (Co Clare). From Aughinish Point into bay there is good fishing for specimen pike, also stocks of bream, tench, perch and rudd. Boat essential. Further west shore centres for coarse fishing are **Mountshannon/Whitegate**: Church Bay contains large tench, pike, bream and rudd; **Williamstown Harbour**: big tench from boat, quay fishing for pike, perch and bream; **Rossmore** pier: good place for same species, and a nice spot for camping. Boats and ghillies are for hire.

Dromineer (Co Tipperary). Best centre for middle sections of **Lough Derg**. Large trout taken spinning or trolling; also good centre for dry fly and dapping; trout up to 10lb caught. Mayfly starts about first week in May. Coarse fishing very good at **Youghal Bay**, Dromineer, **Kilgarvan** and **Terryglass** from quays, harbour walls and shore; Carrigahorig Bay has shoals of big bream and large pike: boat essential. Lough fishing free, although there is a voluntary share membership of Lower Shannon Trout & Coarse Fisheries Development Society. Eight fishing clubs on lake are represented by Lough Derg AA. **River Nenagh** flows into R Shannon at Dromineer; a major trout fishery with small number of salmon; in wider stretches trout can reach 2lb, about ½lb in narrows. No coarse fish except between Ballyartella Weir and mouth of river (1m); 22m of fishable water. Fly fishing best Mar-May, wet and dry fly. Minimum size removable, 10". Nenagh and tributary **Ollatrim** (trout fishery only, no maggot fishing) are controlled by Ormond AA. Membership, season and day tickets from tackle shop: Whelan's Fishing Tackle & Camping, Summerhill, Nenagh,

Co Tipperary (tel: +353 (0)67 31301); Open Season, 55 Kenyon Str, Nenagh (tel: +353 (0)67 31774). Hotels: Abbey Court; Hibernian Inn. 3km from **Nenagh** town, Ashley Park House, Ardcroney (tel: +353 (0)67 38223), has Lough Ourna, private lake in grounds of Ashley Park, stocked with brown trout; fish may be taken under prior agreement.

Lough Rea (Co Galway). 19m NW of Portumna; fairly large limestone lake with trout, pike and perch. Fishing on lough and river open to members of Loughrea AA, which has improved and restocked water; trout average 2lb, pike run to over 30lb; for dt and boats contact Sweeney Travel, Loughrea (tel: +353 (0)91 841552). Loughrea tackle shop: Sweeney's. Hotel: O'Deas, Bride St; Meadowcourt.

Banagher (Co Offaly). Brown trout, coarse fishing good: bream, rudd, hybrids, pike, perch, eels. River is wide at **Meelick**, with islands, pools and weirs. There is some east bank fishing for salmon, mainly from boat. Access to west bank is from **Kilnaborris**: bank fishing possible, in fast water. Occasional spring salmon, mainly grilse. **Brosna and Little Brosna River** and small tributary **Camcor River**, nr **Birr**, controlled by Central Fisheries

This catch was made by French visitor, Georges Oudinot, who took the picture.

Board; brown trout; a licence to fish required. Coarse fishing on **Grand Canal**. **Ferbane** is a good centre, with bream, rudd, pike. Shannon Regional Fisheries Board stock **Pallas** (18m E) with rainbow and brown trout. Season 1 May-12 Oct. Bank fishing. Fly only. 6 fish limit. Permits from Jim Griffin, The Tackle Shop, Rahan, Co Offaly tel: +353 (0)506 55979); Paul Kelly, Main Str, Birr (tel: +353 (0)509 21128). Other tackle shops: The Old Forge, West End, Shannonbridge (tel: +353 (0)90 9674124); Donegans, Lyons, Kellerhers, all Banagher. Hotels: Brosna Lodge; Shannon.

Shannonbridge (Co Offaly). Junction of Shannon and **Suck** is a fine centre for coarse fishing; long stretches of bank ideal for bream, hybrids, tench and rudd. Hot water from the Power Station attracts tench. Eel and roach fishing also, is good here. Five bog lakes have been opened 10-14m distance, stocked individually with trout, tench, small carp, roach. Assn: Shannonbridge AA. Tackle shops: Dermot Killeen, Killeen's Village Tavern, Main Str (tel: +353 (0)90 9674112); Alo Moran (tel: +353 (0)90 9674124). For information contact Information Centre, Shannonbridge (tel: +353 (0)90 967 4344).

Athlone (Co Westmeath). Athlone AA has water within 20m radius; restocked with trout. Some salmon. Shannon and Lough Ree abound with trout (good rise to mayfly, late May to late June), pike, roach and bream; bank or boat. Tench plentiful on **Lough Ree**. **Lough Garnafailagh**, which has produced remarkable catches of tench and bream, may be fished from here. At Barrymore Point, Lough Ree, is good fishing for rudd and bream. Tackle shops: Scully Guns & Tackle, Barrack Str, Athlone (tel: +353 (0)90 6492486); Strand Fishing Tackle, Strand (tel: +353 (0)90 6479277; mob: +353 (0)86 8254141). Anglers accommodation: Mrs Duggan, Villa St John, Roscommon Rd (tel: +353 (0)90 6492490); Mrs Denby, Shelmalier (tel: +353 (0)90 6472245).

Lanesborough (Co Longford). Bream, rudd, rudd-bream hybrids, perch, pike, eels. Coarse fishing on **R Shannon, Suck, Lough Ree** and **Feorish River**. Good stock of big fish early in season on hot water stretch of Shannon below Power Station, from July these move out into lake. Baits from M Healey, Lakeside

Stores. Tackle shop: J & B Holmes (Tackle Shop) Main Str (tel: +353 (0)43 21491); Edward Denniston & Co, Centenary Square, Longford (tel: +353 (0)43 46345). Accommodation for anglers: Abbey Hotel Conference & Leisure, Galway Rd, Roscommon (tel: +353 (0)90 66 26240/26250; fax: +353 (0)90 66 26021; web: abbeyhotel.ie).

Strokestown (Co Roscommon). Free fishing in locality, some on dt. Convenient centre for Shannon and **Lough Lea**; a chain of 65 lakes within 7m radius of the town; rudd, perch, bream, pike and tench. **Cloonfree Lake**, one mile from town, is another good coarse fishery, especially for rudd. **Kilglass Lake**, a five-mile long chain, is 4 miles out on Dumsa Rd: plentiful bream and rudd. **Annamore Lake**, record rudd caught in 1995. **Lough na Blaith** has new fishing development with 70 fishing stands erected; rudd, bream, tench, roach. **Grange Lake** (known locally as Trout Lake) produces trout to 12½lb, specimen rudd, pike and tench. Boats can be hired locally; advance booking advised. Local club, Strokestown AC. Accommodation for anglers: Abbey Hotel Conference & Leisure, Galway Rd, Roscommon (tel: +353 (0)90 66 26240/26250; fax: +353 (0)90 66 26021; web: abbeyhotel.ie); Mrs H Cox, Church View House, Strokestown (tel: +353 (0)71 96 33047), central for much local free fishing.

Rooskey (Co Leitrim). Centre for coarse fishing on Rivers Shannon, **Rinn** or **Rynn**, and many small lakes in the area. Bream, tench, rudd, perch, pike, roach. Some brown trout in Shannon. Good catches in **Drumdad Lake** near **Mohill**. Mohill is also a good centre for **Loughs MacHugh, Erril, Lakes Cloonboniagh** and **Creenagh**: fine waters for tench and bream, with pike. Tackle shops: Roosky Quay Enterprises. Accommodation catering for anglers: Lakeland House; Mrs Davis, Avondale (tel: +353 (0)71 963 8095).

Carrick-on-Shannon (Co Leitrim). Centre for **Shannon, Boyle, Loughs Key, Allen, Corry, Drumharlow, Scur, Keshcarrigan, Oakport** and many others. Trout and coarse fish. Boyle carries heavy head of roach. Good venues are: **Hartley Bridge, Drumsna, Carrick, Albert Lock**. Heavy catches are consistent. Local club: Upper Shannon AC (tel: +353 (0)71 966 3184). Tackle shops: Lough

Scur Bait & Tackle, Kilclare (tel: +353 (0)71 964 1438); Tooman Angling & Leisure, Bridge Str (tel: +353 (0)71 962 1872); Shannonside Lodge, Jamestown (tel: +353 (0)71 962 4692). Many guest houses and hotels offer special anglers accommodation, including Weir House, with 200m Shannon and 41 lakes within 6 miles; also Shannon Guest House, run by proprietors of Lough Scur Bait & Tackle *(see above)*; free angling advice and tuition, also angling boats supplied free of charge to guests; **Lough Bran**, with boats for hire; Aisleigh House; Ard-na-Greine House.

Drumshanbo (Co Leitrim). R Shannon rises in Cuilcagh Mountains a short distance N of here. Free coarse fishing on R Shannon, **Lough Allen** and twelve small lakes, incl. **Acres, Derrynahoo, Carrickport** and **Scur**; roach, bream, perch, pike. Trout fishing on Shannon, esp. below **Bellantra Bridge**, in fast water. Lough Allen Conservation Assn has stocked L Allen with over 100,000 trout in past five years. Lough also has a good stock of coarse fish, including specimen pike over 30lb and some big trout. However, as lough acts as a reservoir for the power station near Limerick and has sluice gates at lower end, the waters fluctuate considerably and at low water there are many hazardous rocks; and also there can be sudden strong winds. Local club is Lough Allen CA, visitors welcome, membership 5 Euro (voluntary). Two trout streams run into L Allen, on which fishing is regarded as free. The **Yellow River** enters from east, a spate river, with brown trout in lower reaches. The **Owennayle** is a mountain stream entering from north. Trout average ½lb. Anglers accommodation: Paddy Mac's, High Str (tel: +353 (0)71 964 1128); Woodside Guesthouse (tel: +353 (0)71 964 1106); Mrs Costello, Forest View (tel: +353 (0)71 964 1243); McGuires Rent-a-Cottage (tel: +353 (0)71 964 1033).

Principal Tributaries of the Shannon

DEEL. Enters estuary near Askeaton some miles below Limerick. Fishing stations; **Rathkeale** (Limerick), and **Askeaton** (Limerick), (best Feb-May), white trout (on summer floods), a few salmon and good brown trout (best mid-Mar to Sept). Parts of river preserved by Mrs R Hunt, Inchirourke, Askeaton, and Altaville Estate. Hotels at Rathkeale; Central, Madigan's. Deel AA issues low-price st for 15m at Rathkeale. nearest tackle shop at Limerick.

MAIGUE. Enters estuary between mouth of Deel and Limerick. Brown trout and salmon.

Adare (Co Limerick). Adare Manor Hotel & Golf Resort (tel: (freephone) 0800 904 7523; +353 (0)61 396566; www.adaremanor.com) has 2m stretch for guests. Two lakes on site fully stocked with brown trout; also ghillie. Fishing, members only - available Adare Manor Hotel. Local club: Castle AC. Dunraven Arms Hotel has 1¼m fishing free to guests. Contact hotel (tel: +353 (0)61 396633; fax: +353 (0)61 396541; web: www. dunravenhotel.com) for details of Bleech Lake, 5m, good trout and pike fishing. Rathkeale, 7m, trout, with ghillies and boats. Some free tidal water below town. Tackle shop: The County Dresser, Station Rd (tel: +353 (0)61 396915).

Croom (Co Limerick). Maigue AA has brown trout fishing. Season 1 Mar-30 Sept; fly only; bag limit applies; trout ¾lb-3lb; tickets from Hon Sec. Preserved water below town, free above to Bruree and beyond. Tributaries Camogue, Loobagh and Morningstar mostly free and very good for trout.

Kilmallock (Co Limerick). Kilmallock & Dist AC has brown trout fishing near town on **R Loobagh**, from Riversfield Bridge to Garrouse Bridge, fly only. River is recovering from drainage scheme, and fish average small. Tickets from club members.

MULCAIR. Enters Shannon 4 miles east of Limerick, and is joined by **Slievenohera River**, which is a confluence of the Newport and Annagh Rivers. Mulcair River is spate system, mainly grilse, salmon from March, small brown trout d/s of Annacotty Bridge. The Slievenohera system gets spate runs of grilse from late June. St, wt and dt from Regional Manager, Hydro Generation Region, Ardnacrusha, nr Limerick.

KILMASTULLA. Enters Shannon above O'Briens Bridge from east, near Montpelier. River holds some good trout at Shalee, and a moderate stock to 1lb immediately u/s of Kilmastulla Bridge. ESB permit reqd.

FERGUS. Limestone stream with gin-clear water, trout fishing good; few salmon in spring. Fishing free. *(See also Co Clare Streams and Loughs).*

Ennis (Co Clare). Good centre for fishing principal waters of Co Clare, including several coarse fish lakes and rivers (tench, pike, perch, rudd). Good brown trout fishing in Fergus and lakes it drains. **Knockerra Lake** has rainbow trout to 8lb. Tackle shop in Ennis: Noel Tierney, Fishing & Cycle Centre, 17 Abbey Str (tel: +353 (0)65 682 9433; web: www.shan non-fishery-board.ie). Accommodation: Auburn Lodge Hotel, Galway Road (tel: +353 (0)65 682 1247); Old Ground; Queen's; West County Inn.

Corofin (Co Clare). Numerous lakes very good for trout, others for perch, rudd and tench, and all for pike. Accommodation at number of family guest houses. Lakes Inchiquin, Atedaun and Ballycullinan and R Fergus close by; boats.

Tulla (Co Clare). Area is noted for its excellent bream fishing; also roach, tench and pike; fishing free in about 20 lakes within 10m radius (Ennis 10m).

BROSNA. Enters Shannon from the north east, at junction with Grand Canal, north of Banagher. A brown trout fishery, controlled by Inland Fisheries Trust, Dublin 9.

SUCK. Flows through 30 mile valley (5 mile waide) linking West Roscommon and East Galway, joins Shannon at Shannonbridge, between Banagheer and Athlone. Wild brown trout and excellent coarse fishing for tench, pike, bream and rudd. Tench to 6lb at Shannonbridge Power Station, where "hot water stretch" attracts fish. Specimen rudd in L Ree. Good fishing in Coreen Ford area, nr Ballinasloe.

Ballinasloe (Co Galway). River Suck deep and slow, providing excellent coarse fishing with large shoals of bream to 8lbs, bags of 100lbs common, also rudd to 2lbs. Other local waters include **Lough O'Flyn, Ballinlough,** 600 acres trout fishery, controlled by CFB. **Bunowen** and **Shiven** hold excellent stock of trout, especially good early in season. **Lough Acalla,** nr Kilconnell; rainbow trout, season 1 May to 30 Sept, st and dt purchased locally. Shannon Regional Fisheries Board permits from Salmon's Department Store, Ballinasloe. Hayden's Leisure Hotel, Ballinasloe (tel: +353 (0)90 964 2347), offers anglers accommodation with salmon and coarse fishing in Rivers Shannon and Suck.

Ballygar (Co Galway). For middle R Suck and also tributaries, **Rivers Bunowen** and **Shiven**. Excellent coarse fishing. Tickets from Tom Kenny, Public House, The Square. Tackle from Hanley's Tackle Shop.

Roscommon (Co Roscommon). One of Ireland's renowned pike fishing areas is on the main **R Suck** and **Hollygrove** and **Blacks Lakes**; in recent years, the R Suck around Athleague and Hollygrove Lakes has produced many fine double figure pike to 20lb plus. River is good for trout in mayfly season. There are several coarse angling centres located in what is known as the River Suck Valley, about 10-15 kms from Roscommon. **Lough Ree** is controlled by ESB, with open fishery angling rights; is a mixed fishery; wild brown trout av 1½lb - 3lb (larger specimens possible; daily bag limit 4 trout) and pike/coarse fishing. Irish record rudd (3lb 1oz) caught in nearby **Kilglass Lake**. SRFB have upgraded facilities at a number of lakes, which includes those for disabled anglers. Local contacts: Athleague Fuerty AC; Boyle & Dist AC (tel: +353 (0)79 63260); Cavetown AC (+353 (0)79 68037); Ballaghderreen & Dist AC (tel: +0353 (0)907 60077); Tulsk AC (tel: +353 (0)78 39038). Accommodation for anglers: Abbey Hotel Conference & Leisure, Galway Rd, Roscommon (tel: +353 (0)90 66 26240/26250; fax: +353 (0)90 66 26021; web: abbeyhotel.ie). For further information, contact: Angling/Visitor Centre, Athleague, Co Roscommon (tel: +353 (0)903 63602; fax: +353 (0)903 63014; web: www.suckvalley.firebird.com); Ireland West Tourism, Aras Failte, Forster St, Galway (tel: +353 (0)91 537700). Tackle shop: Oscar Neilan,Castlecoote Stores, Castlecoote (tel: +353 (0)903 63394). Hotels: Grelly's, Royal, O'Gara's.

Castlerea (Co Roscommon). For upper R Suck reaches which hold trout in some areas. **Lough O'Flynn** now has excellent trout fishing, thanks to CFB improvement work. SRFB permit required *(see Mount Nugent)*. Permits and boats from Padraig Campbell, O'Flynn Bar, Ballinlaugh. Trout and coarse fish in **Lough Glinn** and **Errit Lakes**. Hotels: Don Arms, Tully's.

INNY. A slow-flowing river densely populated with roach, pike, and large bream.

Trout between Abbeyshrule and Shrule Bridge. Inny AA controls much fishing.

Mullingar (Co Westmeath). Many coarse loughs in area, including **Kinale** (roach, pike), **Slevins**, bream, tench, pike, perch (with new platform for disabled), **Patrick** (tench), **Sheever**, (bream, tench, pike, perch), **Ballinafid** (specimen bream, carp), **Doolin** (tench, bream), **Derravaragh** (pike, roach and trout); trout loughs are **Lene**, north of Collinstown, fly and trolling, good fly hatches on water; **Bane**, northeast of Mullingar, access through ghillies only, very large brown trout; **Glore**, 4km from Castlepollard, excellent stocks of wild browns, average over 2lbs, good fly hatches; famous limestone loughs, **Sheelin** (4,654 acres) (*see below*), **Ennell** (3,200 acres) and **Owel** (2,500 acres); and also **Mount Dalton Lake**, a small fishery stocked with brown trout by SRFB. Season 1 May-12 Oct Ennell and Owel; on Ennell, wet fly fishing productive in March, fly hatches from May; on Owel, large hatches of fly from Mid Apr, and sedges from end of Jul to mid-Aug; on both lakes, dapping grasshopper and daddy longlegs in Aug. Mt Dalton season 1 Mar-12 Oct. Size limit 30cm; bag limit 6 fish; fly only on Mt Dalton Lake. St 35 Euro, 21-day 18 Euro and dt 10 Euro, conc, from Shannon Regional Fisheries Board, Tudenham, Mullingar (tel: +353 (0)44 48769). **Royal Canal** nr Mullingar contains tench, roach, rudd, pike, perch. West of Mullingar to Ballinea Bridge is one of Ireland's prime tench fisheries. Local assns: L Owel Trout PA, membership 30 Euro pa; Mullingar Coarse AC. Boats on L Ennell from J Gavigan (tel: +353 (0)44 26167); Myles Hope (tel: +353 (0)44 40807), or Jim Roache (tel: +353 (0)44 40314); L Owel: John Doolan Boat Hire, Levington, Mullingar (tel: +353 (0)44 42085), boats 40 Euro per day with engine, also Shannon Board fishing permits and dt; Mount Dalton: Mrs C Gibson Brabazon, Mt Dalton, Rathconrath, Mullingar (tel: +353 (0)44 55102); L Sheelin: Stephen Reilly, Finea (tel: +353 (0)43 81124); L Patrick, Oliver Daly (tel: +353 (0)44 71220). Tackle shops: David O'Malley, 33 Dominick Str (tel: +353 (0)44 48300), Mullingar. Hotels: Bloomfield House, Greville Arms. Lakeside accommodation: Mrs A Ginnell, Lough Owel Lodge (tel: +353 (0)44 48714).

Castlepollard (Co Westmeath). Trout and coarse fish. **Lough Derravaragh** (2,700 acres), a limestone lake once famous for trout but in recent years trout stocks have decreased to be replaced by a large population of roach. **Lough Glore** (86 acres) holds excellent stock of wild brown trout; boat fishing only. **White Lake** (80 acres) is stocked annually with rainbow trout and some brown trout. Lakes controlled by Shannon Regional Fisheries Board. Season 1 Mar-12 Oct (Derravaragh and Glore); 1 May-12 Oct (White Lake); bag limit 4 fish; st 50 Euro, dt 10 Euro; from Halpin, Fore village (tel: +353 (0)44 61114). Boats from Mrs Nancy McKenna, Fore (tel: +353 (0)44 611781) for White Lake; Pat Smith, Castlepollard (tel: +353 (0)44 61852), for L Glore; Tommy Fagan, for Lough Lene (tel: +353 (0)44 61359).

Mount Nugent (Co Cavan). Brown trout fishing on **Lough Sheelin** (4,654 acres); rich limestone lough which produces and maintains a large stock of big brown trout, av 2-3lb and up to 10lb; size limit 30cms; fishing controlled by SRFB. Season: 1 Mar to 12 Oct. Mayfly from about mid-May to early June; hatches from Derry Point to Curry Rocks, Merry Point, Sandbar, Plunkett's Point to Crane Island; bag limit 6 fish; no live bait fishing; suitable flies and dt from Kilnahard Pier, Mount Nugent, L Sheelin; dt also direct from Shannon Regional Fisheries Board, Angling Section (tel: +353 (0)509 21777; web: www.shannon-fishery-board.ie /guides/lough-sheelin.htm (for info); www.shannon-fishery-board.ie/shopping /licences-online.htm (for permits)). Local assn: Lough Sheelin Trout PA; membership available; wt and dt (10 Euro) available from Flying Sportsman. Tackle and in-depth fishing information from The Flying Sportsman, Carrick St, Kells, Co Meath (tel: +353 (0)46 924 1743). Tackle shops: Philip Smith, Lavagh, Kilnaleck (tel: +353 (0)49 36156); Geraldine Clarke, Finae (tel: +353 (0)43 81158), all Loch Sheelin. Hotels: Crover House, Mount Nugent for boats. B&B accom at Sheelin House, Kilnahard: Josephine Leggette; boat and engine hire; Mabel Chambers, Boat & Engine hires also supplies maps of the lake. **Two tributaries of the Inny** are fishable, on a fisheries board permit: the **Tang River** joins Inny downstream of Ballymahon, and the **Rath River**, upstream. Both have a stock of small brown trout, and are best fished early in the season, before they run low. Permits from David O'Malley, 33 Domi-

nick Str (tel: +353 (0)44 48300), Mullingar. Hotels: Crover House Hotel; Percy French Hotel, Ballyjamesduff, Co Cavan.

SLANEY

(For close seasons, licences, etc, see The Eastern Regional Fisheries Board)

Rises in corner between Barrow and Liffey watersheds and flows south 73m to Wexford Harbour. During most of course has rocky beds, rapids alternating with deep pools. Good spring salmon river, especially in Tullow-Bunclody reaches (Mar, Apr, May best; no autumn run) but of little account for brown trout save in upper reaches and in some tributaries. Good sea trout lower down and in tributaries Urrin and Boro. Best sea trout fishing in lower reaches, late June to Aug. Most salmon fishing private, but certain parts let from season to season and no permission needed to fish for salmon or sea trout from Enniscorthy Bridge to Ferrycarrig (26 Feb to 15 Sept). Fly fishing only, from 1 Apr to 31 Aug.

Wexford (Co Wexford). Garman AC has made efforts to restock. **Owenduff**; good white trout fishing in June, July and Aug. **Sow River** near Castlebridge good for brown trout and sea trout; permits from angling club. Fishing for brown trout on **Wexford Reservoir**. Sea fishing (incl. sea trout, bass and mullet) in estuary. Tackle shop: Bridges of Selskar, North Main Str. Hotels: Talbot, White's, County.

Enniscorthy (Co Wexford). Sea trout good; brown trout poor; free fishing downstream of bridge. Tackle shops: Nolan, 3 Wafer Str, and C L Cullen, 14 Templeshannon. Hotels: Portsmouth Arms, Slaney Valley.

Bunclody (Co Wexford). Salmon and sea trout, browns and rainbows, coarse fishing for eels. Much fishing in area on Slaney, Clody and Derry, either free or for nominal fee. Bunclody Trout AC has fishing for visitors. Tackle shop (licences): Cahills Brothers, Main Str. Accommodation: P Kinsella, Meadowside (tel: +353 (0)54 77459).

Tullow (Co Carlow). Tullow Trout and Salmon AA have water on Slaney. Permits from Hon Sec for salmon; 6 Euro trout, from tackle shop. Trout and salmon fishing is free on Slaney from Rathvilly to Baltinglass, and also on **River Derreen** with permission from landowners. Tackle shop: Liam O'Connor's Newagents, The Square (tel: +353 (0)59 915 1337). Hotel: Slaney.

SEA FISHING STATIONS IN IRELAND

As elsewhere, the sea fishing in the Irish Republic has been growing in popularity. The inshore potential of these waters is now widely appreciated. Bass are much sought after along the south and west coasts, and pollack are abundant off the rocks. Deep-sea boats land specimen skate, conger, halibut, turbot and so on. Fishing facilities are improving all the time. There are however reports on the east coast of reduced sport for anglers, owing to over-fishing by trawlers. Space will not permit more than a few centres to be listed, but club secretaries and local tackle shops will be pleased to give further information and to help visitors.

Dundalk (Co Louth). Bay is shallow for the most part, but contains spurdog, ray and flatfish for boat anglers off north shore. Quay fishing from **Gyles Quay** at high water for flatfish and dogfish; the quay on **Castletown River** south bank, mullet in summer. 8m south at **Glyde** and **Dee** junction, spinning from southern breakwater for bass, mackerel, occasional sea trout. Good fishing rocks north of **Drogheda** at **Clogher Head**: pollack, coalfish, codling and mackerel. Club is North Louth Sea AC. Town also has two game angling clubs. Tackle shops: Macs Sports, Demesne Shopping Centre; Island Fishing Tackle, Park St (permits and licences). Hotels: Ballymascanion, Imperial and others. Boats operate from **Carlingford**: Peadar Elmore, North Commons, Carlingford (tel: +353 (0)42 73239; fax: +353 (0)42 73733).

Dublin and **Dun Laoghaire** (Co Dublin). To north, **Howth Harbour** is popular venue: from piers, whiting, pollack, coalfish and codling; from rocks, mackerel, flatfish and others. Good boat fishing for large spurdog. Howth club holds annual festival. Estuary at **Sutton** is a good place to dig lugworm and clam. Ragworm can also be found. In Dublin Bay good points are: **Dollymount Strand**, (some large bass, flounder, eels, codling, good in autumn at evening); sea wall running south, (pollack, codling, whiting, bass and flounder); Liffey between Ringstead Basin and Pidgeon House Power Station (mullet and bass in large numbers); spinning below Poolbeg Lighthouse (bass, mackerel); Sandymount Strand, a large beach with gullies and pools, with bass, mullet, big flounder. This beach can be dangerous at flood tide. Ferryport at **Dun Laoghaire** provides pier fishing from head of West Pier, and bandstand at East Pier: dabs and conger in summer, whiting, codling, pouting, coalfish in autumn/winter. Sandymouth Strand,

north towards Dublin, produces flatfish and bass. There is no fishing off both Marina breakwaters or Traders Wharf. South, from Bullock Harbour to Greystones Harbour there are seven popular fishing venues, with pollack, coalfish, codling, whiting, flatfish, conger, and mackerel. Dublin has over thirty sea angling clubs affiliated to the Leinster Council of the IFSA; information from Central Fisheries Board. Dublin Tackle shops: Rory's, 17a Temple Bar, Dublin 2 (tel: +353 (0)1 677 2351); and many others *(see Dublin under Fishing Stations)*.

Arklow (Co Wicklow). Local boats offer deep sea angling over inshore banks for dogfish, ray, codling, whiting, bull huss, plaice, flounder, and tope. Codling and dabs may be fished for from Roadstone Pier. Beach fishing on Clones Strand: codling, bass, flounder. There are more than two dozen good shore venues between Arklow and **Wexford**. Club: Arklow Sea Anglers. Tackle from Bolands, Pat Kelly, both Main St. Hotel: Arklow Bay.

Rosslare (Co Wexford). Good pier fishing for conger, occasional bass and flatfish. Access is difficult because of shipping. Fishing from shore at St Helens for bass, flatfish, mackerel and other species. Rock and surf fishing for bass and tope between Rosslare and **Kilmore Bay. Ballyteigue Lough** is a fine venue for flounders, and beach fishing is very good at **Cullenstown**, for bass and flounders. Ballytrent beach is good for flatfish by night. Boats can reach Splaugh Rock, a massive reef, and Tuskar Rock: mainly cod fishing. Charter boat 'Patsy J II' operating from Wexford Town, specialises in wreck fishing and tope; also species fishing (15 species expected in a day): Peter Jackson (tel: +353 (0)53 71626; mob: +353 (0)86 8608328); 400 Euro wreck fishing; otherwise 350 Euro (licensed for 12). Tackle shops: Hayes Cycles, 108 South Main Str (tel: +353 (0)53 22462); Murph's Fishing Tackle Shop, 92 North Main Str (tel: +353 (0)53 24717).

Kilmore Quay (Co Wexford). Record Irish Pouting taken in 1983, and large coalfish taken recently. Fishing at high tide from pier produces flounder and occasional bass. Mullet may sometimes be taken by ground baiting. **St Patrick's Bridge**, reef of rocks to east of harbour, is boat mark for good bass fishing. Excellent pollack, bass and tope around **Saltee Islands**. Surf fishing for bass and tope at **Ballyteigne Bay**. Mullet and flatfish abound. Lugworm from harbour. **Burrow** shore is popular beach for competitions, best at night. Wexford Boat Charter: 143 The Faythe, Wexford. Base, Kilmore Quay Marina. Club: Kilmore Quay SAC. Tackle shops in Rosslare, Wexford and Kilmore Quay.

Fethard Bay (Co Wexford). Bottom fishing for flounder, bass, plaice, best at night. Hook Head has spinning at high tide for pollack, coalfish, mackerel, bottom fishing for conger and other species. Along shore at Cummins Quay, **Ballyhack**, conger fishing.

Dunmore (Co Waterford). Shore fishing in estuary: bass, dogfish, coarfish, codling pollock, wrasse flounder, ray, plaice, conger river eel, dab; shark, reef and wreck fishing; base for charter boats. Contact J A O'Connor, Dunmore East Angling Charters, Fairybush House, Dunmore East (tel: +353 (0)51 383397; mobile: +353 (0)87 2682794; daily charter 330 Euro reef fishing; wreck 380 Euro, 12 persons. Clubs: Dunmore East SAC; Waterford Glass SAC *(see Clubs)*; Rinnashark SAC (membership 25 Euro; competition entry 5 Euro (x8 40 Euro total). Tackle shops: Bobby's Tackle, Tramore; Shootin' & Fishin', 26a Ballybricken (tel: +353 (0)51 878007); Outdoor & Angling Centre, Westgate Retail Park, Tramore Rd (tel/fax: +353 (0)51 844314; e-mail: bait@eircom.net); Army & Outdoor Stores, Newgate St, Waterford (tel: +353 (0)51 857554).

Dungarvan Bay (Co Waterford). From **Ballinacourty** pier, bass, flatfish and dogfish, half flood to early ebb. Abbeyside and Barnawee; spinning for bass, bottom fishing for flounder. Fishing at Dungarvan for bass and flatfish. A number of large bass, 6lb to 9½lb are caught; mackerel recently abundant, and cod; blue shark plentiful at times. Pier at **Helvick** provides good sport with congers;

This fine bluemouth rock fish was caught half a mile north of Owey Island. *Photo: Neil Gallagher.*

distance casting catches ray. Mullet taken in Helvick Harbour. Fewer blue shark than there were. Conger, mackerel, pollack, wrasse (specimen taken) off Helvick Head. Crab and lugworm on foreshore. Boats for hire. Local clubs are Abbeyside Shore AC and Dungarvan Sea AC, which holds 6 or 7 boat competitions, from end of May to beginning of Sept. Recent 2 day event yielded over 1000 fish, from 18 boats, conger, ling, dogfish, pollack, pouting, coalfish, garfish, whiting, cod, scad, gurnard, cuckoo and ballan wrasse, and thornback ray. Membership 30-40 Euro per annum, contact Secretary (tel: +353 (0)58 46401). Tackle shop: Baumann & Sons Ltd (Jewellers and Fishing Tackle), 6 Mary St (tel: +353 (0)58 41395). Hotels: Lawlers; Park; Gold Coast. Further information from West Waterford Tourism, Lismore (tel: +353 (0)58 54646).

Ardmore and **Youghal** (Co Cork). Several venues around Ardmore and Ram Head, incl surf fishing from Ballyquin Strand for bass and flatfish (flounder to 3½lb), Ardmore beach and pier, bass, flatfish; Goat Island and Whiting Bay, similar species. Fishing from Mangans Cove through Youghal, to Knockadoon Head and pier offers more than a dozen venues. Species caught include flounder, plaice (to 5lb), codling, ray, turbot, bass, dogfish, conger (to 41lb), ling (to 38lb), cod (to 28lb 12oz), pollack, coalfish, gurnard, whiting, wrasse, blue shark (135lb) and most deep sea species. Clubs: Ardmore Sea Anglers; Youghal Sea AC also has freshwater fishing on Blackwater and tributaries. Hotels: Hilltop, Devonshire Arms, Avonmore Roseville and Green Lawn Guest Houses.

Ballycotton (Co Cork). One of the best-known of Irish sea fishing centres for both deep sea and shore fishing; large catches of prime fish and excellent facilities. Many specimen caught, including blue shark, conger, ling, pollack, cod, mackerel, coalfish, bass, hake, spur and spotted dog. Big cod in winter months. Fishing from pier at Ballycotton and **Knockadoon**, rocks from Knockadoon Head, Ballinwilling Reef and other marks, or boat; surf fishing at **Ballymona**; bass, flounder and codling. Good mullet in harbour. Lugworm may be dug at Ballycrennan and Ardnahinch. Boat hire: Ballycotton Angling Centre (tel: +353 (0)21 464 6773); (300 Euro per boat min; licensed for 12; 9.30 to 16.30); South Coast Angling Centre (tel: +353 (0)21 464 6002). Monthly competitions May to Oct. Local clubs: Ballycotton Deep SAC; Ballycotton SAC; Aghada SAC; Guileen SAC; Cloyne SAC. Tackle shops: T H Sports, Main St, Midleton; Guileen Tackle Centre (Derek Aspinwall), Guileen, Whitegate (tel: +353 (0)21 466 1515). Hotels: Bayview (tel: +353 (0)21 464 6746); Garryvoe (tel: +353 (0)21 464 6718); Mrs M Tattan, Spanish Point (tel: +353 (0)21 464 6177); Inn-by-the-Harbour (B&B and pub: tel: 021 464 6768). Many hotels around Midleton.

Cobh (Co Cork). Good area for fishing Cork harbour; conger, ling, dogfish, cod, pollack, rays, also base for shark fishing. Cobh Sea AC, runs an international sea angling festival each year in first week of September (catch and release). Species caught include skate, bass, pollack, coalfish, tope, l-s dogfish. Conger 44lb 12oz has been weighed in. For deep sea fishing there are charter boats from Geary Angling Services, Sycamore House, Ballynoe, Cobh (tel: +353 (0)21 481 2167; web: www.seafishing.irl.com; e-mail: seaangling@esatclear.ie). Tackle shop: Geary, contact for Cobh Sea AC, membership; Cobh Fishing Tackle, Sycamore House, Ballynoe (tel: +353 (0)21 4812167; web: www.seafishing.irl.com/; e-mail: seaangling@esatclear.ie). Hotel: Commodore, Westbourne Place.

Cork (Co Cork). Fishing both inside and outside Harbour offers the following species: dogfish, codling, conger, pollack, turbot, plaice, ray, wrasse. 144lb blue shark caught in Harbour, and record angler fish. Various charter boats operate from Cork Harbour and **Crosshaven**, for shark, wreck and bottom fishing; apply T W Murray *(see below)*. Club: Cork Sea Anglers. Tackle shop: T W Murray & Co. Ltd, 87 Patrick Str (tel: +353 (0)21 4271089); The Tackle Shop, Lavitts Quay; Cork Harbour Baits deliver a wide selection of sea angling baits on weekends (free in the Cobh Crosshaven area) (tel: +353 (0)21 4374240 (after 6pm); web: www.corkharbourbaits.com; e-mail: sales@corkharbourbaits.com).

Kinsale (Co Cork). Fine natural harbour. Best-known centre on the south coast for deep-sea fishing, especially for shark, ling, conger, dogfish, ray, pollack, coalfish, red bream and wrasse. Well-equipped boats and experienced skippers; all operators offer rod and tackle hire. Kinsale Sea AC run many competitions during season. For boat hire and full information contact Willem van Dyk (tel: +353 (0)87 988 2839), licensed for 12, 450 Euro/day; Arthur Long (tel: +353 (0)21 4778969); Eddie McCarthy, Ballyhass Lake (+353 (0)21 477 4595), single angler 30 Euro, half day 25 Euro. Tackle shop: The Hire Shop, 18 Main Str (tel: +353 (0)21 477 4884). Hotels: Trident; Actons; White Lady; Kierans Folk House. (For further information, web: www.kinsaleangling.com; www.kinsaleharbour.com.)

Rosscarbery (Co Cork). Noted for surf fishing for flatfish, mackerel, occasional bass; three fine beaches. Bass and mullet also taken in small harbour, and from mouth of estuary. Mackerel spinning from pier. Lugworm and ragworm in estuary, sand eel from beach. Club: Rosscarbery SAC.

Baltimore (Co Cork). Excellent boat fishing for shark (mid-June to Oct), common skate, conger, ling, pollack, coalfish, cod, etc. Wreck fishing for conger, ling, pollack, coalfish, cod. Shore fishing for mackerel, pollack, wrasse, bull huss, conger, mullet, etc. Deep sea boat charter: 'Rooster', Nick Dent, Fastnet Charters (tel: +353 (0)86 824 0642); 'Algerine', Pat Fehily, The Haven (tel: +353 (0)28 20549). Self-drive: Atlantic Boating Services (tel: +353 (0)28 22145). Tackle shop: Kieran Cotter Ltd, Baltimore.

Mizen Peninsula (Co Cork). Fishing in harbours, rocks, coves, for pollack, mackerel, coalfish, flatfish, etc. Schull Pier offers bottom fishing for flounder, float fishing for mullet. Barley Cove at point of Peninsula is recommended. Wreck fishing within easy reach. Schull boat operator: Cíarán O'Carroll, Mizen Charters, Derryconnell House, Derryconnell, (tel/fax: +353 (0)28 37370); good shark fishing and large skate; reef and drift fishing for large pollack, ling, coalfish, spurdog, bull huss. Nearest tackle shop Fallons, Skibbereen (tel: +353 (0)28 21903). Several B&Bs.

Bantry (Co Cork). Town is convenient centre for Bantry Bay deep sea fishing. Large conger are caught, rays, ling, whiting, bull huss, l/s dogfish, pollack. Shore fishing best on south side of bay. Dunmannus Bay boat: Luke Brasens (tel: +353 (0)27 67201). Boat hire 8 anglers

costs 150 Euro. Club: Bantry Sea AC, membership 30 Euro. Tackle and boat hire from McCarthy's Sports, Main St; J J Crowley's, The Square. Hotels: West Lodge (tel: +353 (0)27 50360); Vickery's (tel: +353 (0)27 50194); Bantry Bay (tel: +353 (0)27 50289); Maureen's B&B, The Village, Glengarriff (tel: +353 (0)27 63201) (special rates for anglers). Maureen's can also arrange fishing trips in Bantry Bay).

Castletownbere (Co Cork). Fine harbour for sheltered fishing in Berehaven and offshore at marks in Bantry Bay. Shark, pollack, ling, conger, tope, ray, skate, pouting, bass, bream, wrasse, spurdog, gurnard, flounder, plaice, grey mullet, whiting and mackerel. Boats are always available. Shore fishing at harbour pier, Muccaragh, Seal Harbour and Zetland Pier. **Kenmare**: charter boats operated from Kenmare Pier by Seafari, 3 The Pier (tel: +353 (0)64 83171); boat licensed for 12; 200 Euro half-day, 300 daily. **Sneem**: Two deep sea boats operate from here, for cod, ling, skate, blue shark, etc; Gulf Stream Fishing (tel: +353 (0)64 45159). Hotel: Cametrignane House. For further information: Béara Tourism & Development Assn, The Square, Castletownbere Beara (tel: +353 (0)27 70054).

Waterville (Co Kerry). Centre for Ballinskelligs Bay, which has various points for rock and surf fishing. Bass readily taken. Angling club: Waterville Fisheries Development Group. Boats may be chartered for shark and other species: Activity Ireland Sea Angling Services (prop: Traolach Sweeney), Cahirdaniel, Co Kerry (tel/fax: +353 (0)66 947 5277); M Fenton, Castlecove Angling, Castlecove (tel: +353 (0)66 947 5305; mob: +353 (0)87 6462181), with equipment for disabled; Bealtra Boats, Bunavalla, Caherdaniel (tel: +353 (0)66 947 5129); or contact tackle shop: Tadhg O'Sullivan, Main St, Waterville (tel: +353 (0)66 947 4433). Much excellent game and coarse fishing in vicinity. Boats for disabled anglers from O'Sullivan, or Lakelands Guesthouse, Lake Rd.

Cahersiveen (Co Kerry) and **Valentia Island**. Rock fishing for mackerel, pollack, wrasse, dogfish, pouting, conger, and others, over twenty species. Deep sea angling for ling, cod, conger, pollack, skate, blue shark, bull huss, and other species. Charter boats operate. Catches include conger (up to 50lb), ling (to

35lb), cod (to 30lb), pollack (to 15lb); also cuckoo wrasse, gurnard, haddock, and others, record fish caught here, in various species. Cahersiveen chosen for European Boat Championships, 2004. International Deep Sea Festival at Cahersiveen in Aug. Club: Cahersiveen SAC; membership 50 Euro p/annum; day trips 50 Euro, juv 25 Euro, conc. At Valencia, Brendan and Kathleen Casey operate charter boats (tel: +353 (0)66 947 2437), shark and bottom fishing, 50 Euro per angler, full charter available. Boats and tackle from Hugh Maguire, Anchor Bar and Tackle Shop, Main St (tel: +353 (0)66 947 2049). Wide range of hotels and B&B, contact Tourist Office, The Old Barracks (tel: +353 (0)66 947 2589).

Dingle Peninsula (Co Kerry). Rock fishing for pollack, wrasse, conger. Inshore fishing for ray; offshore for pollack, coalfish, bream, conger, ling, tope, cod, whiting, huss, spurdog, gurnard, pouting and shark. Club: Dingle SAC. Charter boats operate from Dingle: N O'Connor, Dingle Marina. Tackle shop: 'An Tiáracht' Angling Center, Ballydavid, Dingle. For further information, Gallurus Information Center, Ballydavid.

Shannon Estuary. Locations for shore fishing on the south side are: **Beal Point** and **Littor Strand**, bottom fishing for dogfish, flatfish, and bull huss; several marks around **Carrig Island** and **Saleen Quay**, where good bottom fishing is to be had from rocks and quay: ballan wrasse, dogfish, bull huss, some tope. **Tarbert** and **Glin** piers are best at high tide for flatfish, conger at night; **Foynes** piers produce conger, thornback ray, codling, whiting and flounder. Best baits, crab, lugworm, mackerel. North side of estuary has pier fishing available at **Kildysart** (flounder, crab bait essential), and **Innishmurray** (bull huss, thornback, conger, freshwater eels), Kilrush, *(see below)*, and **Carrigaholt** (bottom fishing for dab and flounder, spinning for pollack and wrasse). Beach fishing at **Shanahea** and **Killimer** for bass, flounder, flatfish, Spanish Point for bass, and rock fishing at **Aylvaroo Point** for similar species, plus codling and whiting in winter. Plenty of opportunities for bait digging. Charter boats for estuary from Kilrush. Car ferry runs from Killimer to Tarbert hourly, summer: 7am to 9.30pm, (Sundays: 9am to 9.30pm), winter: 7am to 7.30pm (Sundays: 10am to 7.30pm). Limerick SAC fish all along the estuary and in the open sea.

Kilrush (Co Clare). Important sea fishing centre. Pier fishing from **Cappagh** pier, bass, conger, whiting, flounder, dogfish on flood tide, large catches of mackerel in warm weather. Beach fishing at White Strand and Doughmore, Sandhills and Seafield Beaches. Mackerel and pollack fishing from Dunlickey cliffs and Bridges of Ross. Species commonly caught in Lower Shannon include large tope, pollock, conger, thornback ray, bull huss, dogfish, bass. Several towns on the coast of Co Clare have charter boats available for shark, wreck and bottom fishing, 35 ft average, tackle for hire. Kilrush Creek Marina (tel: +353 (0)65 905 2072), has every facility for hiring and mooring boats, incl hoist and repair services, and accom, shops, bars, restaurants. Noel Kelleher operates a charter boat from the Marina, all types of fishing (tel: +353 (0)87 225 0982). Gerald Griffin (tel: +353 (0)65 905 1327) runs angling boat trips, on Shannon. Tackle, information and advice from Michael O'Sullivan & Son, 49/50 Moore St (tel/fax: +353 (0)65 905 1071) who can also assist in arranging deep sea angling boats &c.; Martin Clancy, Henry St (tel/fax: +353 (0)65 905 1107), all sea and freshwater tackle, and all emergency repairs. B&B: The Central (tel: +353 (0)65 905 1332).

Kilkee (Co Clare). Short distance from Kilrush, on north of peninsula. Fishing for mackerel, eel, pollack, ray, and cod. Rocks near golfcourse are good mark, also Pollack Holes, at low tide.

Liscannor (Co Clare). Boats: contact Willie O'Callaghan, O'Callaghan Angling, Roslevan, Tulla Rd, Ennis (tel: +353 (0)65 682 1374; fax: +353 (0) 65 684 8870; e-mail: mocallaghan.enni@eircom.ie). Fishing trips around the three Aran Islands, tackle and baits supplied. Tackle shop: Patrick Cleary, Westcliffe Lodge, Spanish Point (tel: +353 (0)65 708 4037).

Galway Bay (Co Galway). **R Spiddal** enters on north side, with skate, tope, ray, huss, dogfish, monkfish, cod, ling, conger, flatfish. Boats from Galway Bay Sea Safaris, K McGowan, Spiddal (tel: +353 (0)91 553286), boat licensed for 12, 55 Euro per person, 500 Euro per day for boat; Aran Islands Sea Angling, Enda Conneely, Innishere (tel: +353 (0)99 75073), package for 4 people with self-catering cottage and use of boats 250 Euro per head.

Clifden (Co Galway). First-class boat and shore angling in sheltered conditions. Blue shark, coalfish, pollack, skate, ray, ling, cod and plaice. Good marks include: Slyne Head; Barrister wreck off **Inishark**; Inishbofin; Inishturk and Fosteries Shoals. Other good bays are Mannin, Killary, Roundstone, Cleggan and Bunowen. Deep sea charter boats from **Clifden**: John Britain (tel: +353 (0)95 21073) 50 Euro per angler daily; John or Mary Ryan, 'Dun Aengus House', Sky Rd, Clifden (tel: +353 (0)95 21069), 50 Euro, 350 Euro charter, tackle on board; Bluewater Fishing, Sharamore House, Streamstown Bay; charter boats from **Cleggan**: Johnny King (tel: +353 (0)95-44649); transport and B&B and self-catering accommodation available by arrangement. Charter boats from **Letterfrack**: John Mongan (tel: +353 (0)95 43473), 45 ft, 12 persons; also morning & evening family trips. Club: Clifden Sea AC. Tackle shops: Gerald Stanley & Son Ltd, Clifden (00 353 (0)95 21039); Peter Coney's, Letterfrack. Hotels: Foyles, Alcock & Brown, Abbeyglen, and Barry's. Boats for hire at Roundstone (Pat Conneely).

Louisburgh (Co Mayo). Sea fishing in this area is excellent, which include various locations such as the foreshore at Carrowniskey (flounder, dogfish, turbot and bass); Emlagh Strand (stand and rock casting); Roonagh Quay (mackerel, pollack & wrasse), Carramore Strand (flounder, dabs, sea trout & bass, and more); Old Head (mackerel, coalfish & wrasse &c.) and Old Head Pier and Killsallagh Rocks. Fish include mackerel, coalfish, flounder, dabs, gurnads and the occasional tope. Local club: Bunowen & Carrownisky Salmon & Sea Trout Angling Club, contact John Staunton, Staunton's Pharmacy (gift shop and tackle shop), The Square, Louisburgh, Co Mayo (tel: +353 (0)98 66139; fax: +353 (0)98 66232; e-mail: louipharm@indigo.ie).

Westport (Co Mayo). Good boat and shore fishing in shallow water. Local clubs run sea angling competitions in the area each year. Fish caught include: the record monkfish (69lb), skate (up to 167½lb), tope and conger (to 40lb and more), cod, codling, pollack, flounders, plaice, gurnard, coalfish, bass, wrasse, turbot, dogfish, white skate (146lb), blue shark, and porbeagle shark, buss huss. Good marks include Tower in Inner Bay, off Lighthouse, Pigeon Point, Cloghormack Buoy. Sheltered sport in **Clew Bay**. Charter boats available from The Helm *(see below)*; R Roynon (tel: +353 (0)98 26514); boat licensed for 10; 40 Euro per angler, 400 Euro charter. Clubs: Westport Sea AC, Secretary (tel: +353 (0)98 27297); runs 3 day annual boat festival and 1 day shore event in June; and Westport AC, which has trout fishing on Ballinlough, by Westport-Newport Rd: dt water; boat available. Tackle shop: Hewetson's, Bridge St (tel: +353 (0)98 26018); Westport Marine Supplies Ltd, Shop St (tel: +353 (0)98 25182). Hotels: The Helm, Westport Quay (tel: +353 (0)98 26398; fax: +353 (0)98 26194); Clew Bay; Grand Central.

Achill Island (Co Mayo). Excellent boat fishing; up to 40 species, incl pollack, conger, ling, ray, cod, etc; fish run large. Noted area for blue shark and porbeagle. Holds records for heaviest fish caught in Irish waters for both men and women: 365lb (man), 362lb (woman), plus blue shark record, 206lb. Pollack and wrasse fishing off rock produces specimens in 15lb class. Good marks are Carrick Mor, Gubalennaun, Alennaun Beag, Dooega and Dugort. Flatfish from **Tullaghan Bay** on north side of island. Good shore fishing at Keel Strand and Keem Bay; Mackerel and pollack fishing from **Cloughmore Pier**. Sea trout late June to early Aug (plentiful and good size); mackerel; plaice etc. Charter boats from **Purteen Harbour**: Tony Burke (tel: +353 (0)98 47257), daily charter available. Local club: Achill Sea AC. Tackle shops: Sweeney and Son, Achill Sound (tel: +353 (0)98 45211). Hotels: Island House, Dookinella, Keel (tel: +353 (0)98 43180); Bervie Guest House, Keel (tel: +353 (0)98 43114. For Achill Deep Sea Angling Holidays, contact Mary Lavelle Burke, Cashel, Achill (tel/fax: +353 (0)98 47257).

Newport (Co Mayo). Central for Clew Bay, which has more than twenty popular shore fishing venues. Flounder fishing at outskirts of estuary. Good shore fishing at Mallaranny and Corraun. At Newport Quay, bottom fishing for flounder; Rossmoney, casting over mud for dogfish, bull huss and conger; Rossanrubble, bottom fishing for ray, dogfish and bull huss; also Ross and Rossnakilly, dogfish, bull huss, small pollack, flounder. Other species found in Clew Bay include mackerel, gurnard, whiting, common skate. Bait may be dug at Carrowmore Strand and Mallaranny (sand eel), Murrick, Rossbeg, Rossturk, Rossmurrevagh, Corraun (lugworm). Charter boat for shark and bottom fishing from Mary Gavin Hughes, Clynish View, Derradda, Newport (tel: +353 (0)98 41562; mob: +353 (0)86 806 2282; web: www.clewbayang ling.com), Europe's only lady charter skipper; 400 Euro daily, disabled with assistance provided for. Club: Newport Sea Anglers. Tackle from Hewetson's, Bridge St, Westport (tel: +353 (0)98 26018; fax: +353 (0)98 27075). Hotels: Black Oak Inn, Newport House.

Belmullet (Co Mayo). Rapidly rising in popularity as sea-fishing centre. Sheltered water. 39 species and many specimen caught to date, incl present Irish record red gurnard and halibut; turbot, bream and pollack especially good. Belmullet Sea AC has been active in improving sea fishing in the area, and holds competitions in June, July, Aug. Local venues include Annagh Head: spinning for pollack, coalfish and mackerel from rocky outcrops, float fishing for wrasse, bottom fishing for dogfish and occasional conger; Cross: bottom fishing for flounder, dogfish and small turbot. Lugworm may be dug at various nearby localities, including the shore lying west of town. Deep-sea charter boats for shark, reef and bottom fishing from **Blacksod Bay**: Martin Geraghty, Geraghty Charters, 'Brú Chlann Lir', Tirrane, Clogher (tel: +353 (0)97 85741), charter; Michael Lavelle (tel: +353 (0)97 85669). Tackle shop: M J Nallen, American St, Belmullet (tel: +353 (0)97 82093). Hotel: Western Strands, Main St (tel: +353 (0)97 81096); Teach Iorras Geesala, Ballina (tel: +353 (0)97 86888); numerous guesthouses.

Ballina (Co Mayo). Estuary of R Moy opens into Killala Bay. Lugworm may be found in sandy patches, sand eel, crab and clam are alternative baits. From Kilcummin Head at the west, to Lenadoon Point at the east, there are eight recognised shore fishing areas. These include Palmerstown Channel (Cloonoghmore Estuary), spinning for sea trout and bottom fishing for flounder; Ross Beacon, the same, Innishcrone Strand (beach fishing for flounder, dab, dogfish) and Pier (conger, dogfish, occasional ray, wrasse.

Donegal Bay (Co Donegal). There are more than twenty good shore fishing points in and around bay, which include **Darbys Hole** in south (spinning for pollack; floatfish for wrasse); **Erne Estuary** (spinning for seatrout and bottom fishing for flounder, 2 hrs either side of low water) (NWRF licence required), **Donegal Quays** (float fishing for mullet; ground baiting essential); **St John's Point** (spinning for pollack, mackerel and coalfish; bottom fishing for wrasse and occasional conger (specimen wrasse recorded here); **Killybegs Harbour** (freelining and floatfishing for mackerel, coalfish, pollack and mullet from East Pier; bottom fishing for conger at West Pier); **Muckross Pier** and **Head** (spinning for mackerel and pollack; floatfishing for wrasse); **Teelin Pier** (spinning for mackerel and coalfish; botton fishing for conger, dab, flounder and dogfish; high water best). Various other areas include: **Silver Strand, Shalway Pier, Fintragh, Nun's Cove, Polladoirt, Drumanoo Head, Gunwell, Sandloop, Heelin Port, Rossnowlagh,Mermaids Cove, Mullaghmore** and **Milk Haven**; rock and shore fishing, with more than 20 species to be caught, incl red & grey gurnard, whiting, conger, mackerel, haddock, cod, ling, pollock, ballam & cuckoo wrasse, plaice, dory, dab, megrim, pouting, rockling; and White Strand, flatfish from beach plus mackerel. Any further information required may be obtained from Mary Rouiller, Killybegs SAC *(see Clubs)*. Shark fishing for blue shark Jul-Sept. Deep sea charter boats operating from **Bundoran**: 'Ellen Louise', Gerry Sheerin, Cloystarra, Grange (tel: +353 (0)86 8282782), licensed for 12, 330 Euro; **Killybegs**: Killybegs Sea-Angling, Michael (tel: +353 (0)74 9731401), evening trips also available; 36 ft charter boat for shark or bottom fishing, 6 rods shark, 10 rods bottom; 300 Euro charter per day, evening 20 Euro per angler; Brian McGilloway (tel: +353 (0)74 9731144); mob: +353 (0)87 2200982), 34 ft, 8-10 persons, 350 Euro charter. Local clubs are Donegal Bay SAC; Killybegs SAC (membership 30 Euro per year, juv 15 Euro; contact Sec *(see Clubs)*; club holds various fishing events - all participants must be a member of club affiliated to IFSA; cost per angler per day: seniors 45 Euro, juv 25 Euro. No local tackle shops. Accommodation: Bay View Hotel & Leisure Centre, Main St (tel: +353 (0)74 973 1950); Tara Hotel; various B&Bs available.

Kilcar (Co Donegal). Boat and shore angling, from rocks, reefs, estuary and sandy beaches, for pollack, coalfish, cod, ling, conger, bull huss, spurdog, whiting, tope, shark, skate, flatfish, etc. Charter boats operate. Tackle shop: Jimmy's, Main St (tel: +353 (0)74 973 8492), for tackle, boat hire, and information. At **Teelin**, boats from Michael Molloy (tel: (0)74 973 8495), licensed for 12, new vessel with long range, 450 Euro; Adrian Molloy (tel: +353 (0)74 973 8377); tuna 700 Euro per day, otherwise 350 Euro per day, boat licensed for 12.

Burtonport (Co Donegal). By Aran Island, and the Rosses, famous trout fishery. Good base for shark and bottom fishing, with up to 30 species caught. Boats and tackle for hire from Neil Gallagher, Annagry East (tel: +353 (0)74 9548403), licensed for 12; from 350 Euro; Liam Miller (+353 (0)74 955 1533), licensed for 12; 250 Euro. Hotel: Ostan Na Rossan, Dungloe (tel: +353 (0)74 952 2444).

Downings (Co Donegal). On Rosguill Peninsula, in Sheep Haven Bay; site of Home International Competition in 1999, and selected by Shark Club of Ireland for first shark competition; also site of 2003 FIPS-M World Boat Angling championships. Beach, rock, estuary fishing for sea trout and other species; charter boats operate. Information on sea angling and boats, contact Hon Sec, Downings SAC *(see Clubs)* or HQ, Beach Hotel (tel: +353 (0)74 55303); Trevor Ryder (tel: +353 (0)74 55261; e-mail: tryder@eircom.net). Downings SAC membership 25 Euro p/a. Tackle shop: Top Tackle, 55 Port Rd, Letterkenny (tel: +353 (0)74 67545). Hotels: Beach (tel: +353 (0)74 55303); Rospennafor alternative accommodation, contact North West Tourism (tel: +353 (0)74 21160).

Lough Swilly (Co Donegal). Sea trout in estuaries, good sea fishing to be had, with rays, flatfish, tope, May-July; mainly cod, haddock, pollack, coalfish, gurnards, tope, ling, conger, wrasse on offshore wrecks; blue shark in Aug/Sept. Lough Swilly SAA (membership 30 Euro p/a) is local assn, at Rathmullen, runs a major annual top angling festival, first week in June. Easy access via floating pontoons available for disabled anglers. Charter boat, 'The Cricket', 38 ft, operates at **Port Na Blagh**, 12 persons, 340 Euro; Pat Robinson (tel: +353 (0)74 913 5062). At **Rathmullan** pier, 'Enterprise I', 350 Euro per day for 12 persons (reduction for

This large pollack was caught off Belmullet, Co Mayo. *Photo: Martin Geraghty.*

Lough Swilly SAA); tackle on board, disabled access, rod and reel hire; Niall Doherty, Skipper, Boat Charter, Ballyboe or Rathmullan PO (tel: +353 (0)74 9158315; mob: 087 248 0132); or Angela Crerand (+353 (0)87 248 0132). Hotels: Watersedge Inn; Rathmullen House; Fort Royal; also B&B accommodation available.

Malin (Co Donegal). Charter boats operate from Bunagee and Culduff, specialising in wreck fishing; species caught are whiting, haddock, cod, conger, ling, gurnard, pollock, tope, turbot, plaice. Contact Inishowen Boating, J McLaughlin, Carrowmore, Malin (tel: +353 (0)74 937 0605); boat licenced for 12; from 300 Euro per day. Tackle shop: nearest at Culduff beside harbour, Des Mills (tel: +353 (0)74 937 9141). Hotels: Malin; McGrory Guest House; Mrs Ann Lynch, Culdaff and others.

Moville (Donegal). Estuary of River Foyle; pollack, cod, tope, whiting, red gurnard, wrasse, flatfish and dogfish. Foyle Sea AC arranges Lough Foyle Festival of Sea Angling, an annual 8-day festival in August. Club owns boat and can arrange wreck fishing. Membership (for nonmembers of Irish Federation of Sea Anglers); available from Hon Sec. Plenty of boats (20ft-30ft) and bait. Tackle from Pat Harkin, The Square. Hotels: Foyle; Castle Inn, Greencastle; McNamara's; Moville.

FISHING CLUBS & ASSOCIATIONS IN IRELAND

The following is an alphabetical list of angling clubs and associations in the Ireland. Particulars of the waters held by many will be found, by reference to the Index, in the section headed 'Fishing Stations in Ireland', and the information about the others, which may not have their own water, could be had from the Secretaries, whose addresses are given. An addressed envelope should be enclosed with inquiries. Please advise the publishers (address at the front of the book) of any changed details for the next edition.

NATIONAL BODIES

Fáilte Ireland (Irish Tourist Board)
Baggot Street Bridge
Dublin 2
Tel: +353 (0)1 602 4000
Fax: +353 (0)1 602 4100
Central Fisheries Board
Balnagowan House
Mobhi Boreen, Glasnevin,
Dublin 9
Tel: +353 (0)1 837 9206/7/8
Fax: +353 (0)1 836 0060
e-mail: info@cfb.ie
Department of Communications,
  Marine & Natural Resources
Leeson Lane
Dublin 2
Tel: +353 (0)1 619 9200
Web: www.marine.gov.ie
e-mail: pressoffice@marine.gov.ie
Irish Specimen Fish Committee
Balnagowan House
Mobhi Boreen
Glasnevin,
Dublin 9
Tel: +353 (0)1 884 2600
Irish Federation of Sea Anglers
Hon Sec: H O'Rourke
67 Windsor Drive
Monkstown
Co Dublin
Tel: +353 (0)1 280 6873/280 6901
e-mail: ifsa@gofree.indigo.ie
Federation of Irish Salmon & Sea-Trout
  Anglers (FISSTA)
Hon Sec: Jerome Dowling
Stradbally
Castlegory

Co Kerry
Tel: +353 (0)66 713 9387
e-mail: jcdowling@eircom.net
Irish Specimen Fish Committee
Mobhi Boreen
Glasnevin,
Dublin 9
Tel: +353 (0)1 884 2600
Fax: +353 (0)1 836 0060
Web: www.irish-trophy-fish.com
e-mail: info@cfb.ie
Irish Sea Angling,
  Accommodation & Charters
c/o Hon Secretary
Loughcarrig House
Midleton, Co Cork
Tel: +353 (0)21 46 31952
Fax: +353 (0)21 46 13707
Web: www.iol.ie/angling
e-mail: angling@iol.ie
(Charter boats and
accommodation for sea anglers)
National Coarse Fishing Federation
  of Ireland
Hon Sec: Brendan Coulter
"Blaithin"
Dublin Road
Cavan
Tel: +353 (0)49 4332367
email: ncffi@eircom.net
North-West Angling Services
Rathedmond
Sligo
Tel: +353 (0)71 70977
Fax: +353 (0)71 41250
web: pagi.org
e-mail: henryken@hotmail.com

Fishing Clubs

When you appoint a new Hon Secretary, do not forget to give us details of the change. Write to the publishers (address at front of the book). Thank you!

(Ghillie service; qualified guide, boats, permits, etc)
(Sligo, Leitrim, Mayo, Roscommon).
Professional Angling Guides
of Ireland (PAGI)
Hon Sec: Robert Maloney
13 Erris Bay
Drum Road
Boyle
Co Roscommon
email: robmaloney@pagi.org
Shark Angling Club of Ireland
P O Box 6028
Dublin 13
Tel: +353 (0)86 8228710
Fax: +353 (0)1 6710279
email: sharkanglingclubirl@tinet.ie
or

Hon Sec: Paul Lynam
Shannon Fisheries Board
Shannon Fisheries Board
Ashbourne Business Park
Dock Road
Limerick
Tel: +353 (0)61 300238
Fax: +353 (0)61 300308
Web: www.shannon-fishery-board.ie
e-mail: info@shannon-fishery-board.ie.
Wheelyboat Trust (The)
Director: Andy Beadsley
North Lodge
Burton Park
Petworth
West Sussex GU28 0JT
Tel/Fax: 01798 342222

CLUBS

Abbeyfeale Anglers' Assn
Denis Dennison
Abbeyfeale West,
Co Limerick
Tel: +353 (0)68 31118
Abbeyleix Anglers
Joseph Delaney
Balladine
Abbeyleix
Co Laois
Abbeyside Shore Anglers
P Crowe
24 Abbots Close
Sea Park
Abbeyside
Dungarvan
Co Waterford
Tel: +353 (0)58 42940
Achill Island Sea Angling Club
Michael G Lavelle
Realt na Mara
Dooagh
Achill
Co Mayo
Achill Sea Anglers'
Tony Burke
Cashel
Achill
Co Mayo
Achill Sporting Club
Roger Gallagher
Valley House
Dugort
Achill
Co Mayo
Tel: +353 (0)98 47006

Aghada Sea Angling Club
Mattie Foley
18 Upper Lotabeg Road
Mayfield
Cork
Co Cork
Ardfinnan Anglers
John Maher
Green View
Ardfinnan
Clonmel
Co Tipperary
Ardmore Sea Anglers
Mary Moloney
Fountain House
Ardmore
Youghal Co Cork
Athleague Fuerty Angling Club
Ciaran Connell
Tel: +353 (0)903 63869
Athy Anglers
J Shaughnessy
c/o Athy Library
Athy
Co Kildare
Athyleague Angling Club
Gerry Gordon
Mountprospect
Roscommon
Tel: +353 (0)87 7415411
Bailieborough Angling Club
Tom Gorman
4 Tanderragee
Bailieborough
Co Cavan
Ballaghderreen & Dist
Angling Club

Jimmy Coogan
Tel: +353 (0)907 60077/60173/60067
Ballina Salmon Anglers' Club
Christopher Egan
21 The Commons
Ballina
Co Mayo
Tel: +353 (0)87 2974797
Ballina & Cloghans Angling
Club
Ballina
Co Mayo
Ballinakill Angling Club
Norman Rothwell
The Tiles
Abbeyleix
Co Laois
Tel: +353 (0)87 2879070
Ballinrobe & District Anglers
Marie Walsh
Cloongowla
Ballinrobe
Co Mayo
Ballisodare Fishing Club Ltd
Hon Sec: Ms Lisa Hennessy
Rockwell House
Ballisodare
Sligo
Tel/Fax: +353 (0)71 91 30513
email: ballisodarefc@eircom.net
Ballybofey & Stranorlar Angling
Assn
D McCollum
Edenmore
Ballybofey, Lifford
Co Donegal
Ballycotton Deep Sea Angling
Club
Hon Sec: Paul Rodd
Graigne
Kilworth
Ballycotton
Co Cork
or
c/o Sheila Egan
Main St
Ballycotton
Co Cork
Ballyduff Trout Fly Angling
Assn
Gerald Scanlon
opp Post Office

Ballyduff, Co Waterford
Tel: +353 (0)58 60275
Ballyhooly Trout Anglers
Jim Ahern
Ashgrove
Ballyhooly
Co Cork
Bandon Angling Assn
Michael O'Regan
21 Oliver Plunkett Street
Bandon
Co Cork
Tel: +353 (0)23 41674
Bangor Erris Angling Club
Seamus Henry
West End Bar
Bangor Erris
Ballina
Co Mayo
Tel: + 353 (0)97 83487
Bantry Sea Angling Club
Con O'Leary
Baurgorm
Bantry
Co Cork
Tel: +353 (0)27 50559
Barrow Anglers
E A Moore
Chaplestown
Carlow
Co Carlow
Belmullet Sea Angling Club
Hon Sec: Michael J Nallen
Tackle Shop
American St
Belmullet
Co Mayo
Tel: +353 (0)97 82093
Fax: +353 (0)97 81118
Web: www.belmullet.net/belmulletsac
or
Jackie Coyle
Dooyork
Geesala
Co Mayo
Tel: +353 (0)86 8383110
Belturbet Angling Club
Hon Dec: Gerald Parker
Clonandra
Redhills
Belturbet
Co Cavan

Fishing Clubs

When you appoint a new Hon Secretary, do not forget to give us details of the change.
Write to the publishers (address at front of the book). Thank you!

Tel: +353 (0)47 55292
Boyle & District Angling Club
Jane Suffin
Felton Road
Boyle
Co Roscommon
Tel: +353 (0)71 9664688
Bunowen & Carrowniskey Salmon & Sea Trout Angling Assn
John Staunton
Staunton's Pharmacy
The Square
Louisburgh
Co Mayo
Tel: +353 (0)98 66139
Fax: +353 (0)98 66232
e-mail: louipharm@indigo.ie
Cahirciveen Sea & Shore Angling Club
c/o Quirke's
Deelis
Cahirciveen
Co Kerry
Cappoquin Salmon & Trout Angling Club
Jeremy Nicholson
Littlebridge Inches
Cappoquin
Co Waterford
Carraroe Angling Club
Carraroe
Co Galway
Carrigallen Angling Club
Hon Sec: Tony Last
c/o Kilbracken Arms Hotel
Main St
Carrigallen
Co Leitrim
Cahersiveen Sea Angling Club
Sean O'Shea
Carhan Lower
Cahersiveen
Co Kerry
Tel: +353 (0)66 947 2087
    +353 (0)66 947 2976 *(evngs)*
Cahir & District Anglers' Assn
Kevin Rowe
Clonmore
Cahir
Co Tipperary
Tel: +353 (0)52 42729
Carraroe Angling Club
Sean Finnerty
Carraroe
Co Galway
Carrick-on-Suir Angling Club
c/o O'Keeffe
OK Sports

New St
Carrick-on-Suir
Co Tipperary
Tel: +353 (0)51 640626
Cashel, Tipperary & Golden Angling Club
Owen Jackman
Ballyghlasheen
Kilfeacle
Co Tipperary
Tel: +353 (0)87 2952425
Castlelyons Trout Anglers
P O'Dwyer
Glenarousk
Castlelyons
Co Cork
Chapelizod Anglers Club
Paul Deveroux
23 Liffey Terrace
Chapelizod
Dublin 20
Cavetown & Clogher Angling Club
Ms Catherine O'Beirne
Cavetown
Boyle
Co Roscommon
Tel: +353 (0)71 9668037
Clane Angling Assn
A McDonald
Downstown Lodge Stud
Maynooth
Co Kildare
Clifden Anglers Assn
c/o Gerald Stanley & Son Ltd
Clifden
Connemara
Co Galway
Tel: +353 (0)95 21039
Fax: +353 (0)95 21721
or
Declan Moran
The Pharmacy
Clifden
Co Galway
Tel: +353 (0)95 21273
Clifden Angling Club
c/o Stanley's Fishing Tackle
Clifden
Co Galway
Clodiagh Anglers Assn
Timmy Delaney
Rathmoyle
Borrisoleigh
Co Tipperary
Clonbur Angling Club
Edward Lynch
Clonbur
Co Galway

Clonmel Salmon & Trout Anglers
Hon Treasurer: Freddie McGoldrick
Mountain Road
Clonmel
Co Tipperary
Tel: +353 (0)52 21692

Clonmel & District Anglers' Club
Pierce Hallahan
Rathloose
Powerstown
Clonmel, Co Tipperary
e-mail: kilcassey@eircom.net
or
Hon Treasurer: John Carroll
3 Dr Croke Place
Clonmel, Co Tipperary
Tel: +353 (0)52 21123/21966
Fax: +353 (0)52 25193

Cloyne Sea Angling Club
Maria Lewis
23 Berkley Court
Cloyne
Co Cork

Cobh Sea Angling Club
Mrs Mary Geary
c/o Geary's Angling Services
Sycamore House
Ballynoe
Cobh, Co Cork
Tel/fax: +353 (0)21 4812167
Web: www.seafishing.irl.com

Cork Salmon Anglers
J Buckley
Raheen House
Carrigrohane
Co Cork

Cork Sea Anglers
M Curran
22 Dundanion Road
Beaumont Park
Cork
Co Cork

Cork Trout Anglers' Assn
J A O Connell
87 Patrick Street
Cork
Co Cork

Corofin Anglers' Assn
Claregalway
Co Galway
(fully subscribed - waiting list closed)

Culdaff & Inishowen Angling Assn.
Samuel Dugan
Glebe House
Culdaff
Co Donegal
Tel: +353 (0)74 9379185

Dargle Anglers Club
Sean Gilroy

24 Templeogue Wood
Dublin 6W
01 353 (0)1 4907404

Deele Angling Club
Billy Vance
Milltown
Convoy, Lifford
Co Donegal
Tel: +353 (0)74 9147290

Donegal Bay Sea Angling Club
Hon Sec: Joe Nash
Kilmacrennan
Letterkenny
Co Donegal
Tel: +353 (0)74 39029/39916
e-mail: nashaughawoney@eircom.net

Downings Bay Sea Angling Club
Hon Sec: Chas Gallagher
Upper Dundoan
Letterkenny
Co Donegal
Tel: +353 (0)87 1338333
Fax: +353 (0)74 9160824
Web: downingsbay.com

Drogheda & District Anglers' Club
c/o John Murphy
39 Anneville Crescent
Drogheda
Co Louth
Tel: +353 (0)41 9834078

Drumconrath Coarse Fishing Club
Drumconrath Angling Development
Fergus Muldoon
Muldoon's Bar and Lounge
Main St
Drumvonrath, Co Meath
Tel: +353 (0)41 68 54119

Duff Angling Syndicate
John Fahey
Kinlough
Co Leitrim

Dundalk & District Trout Anglers'
Assn
J Clarke
3 Mill Road
Forkhill
Co Armagh
BT35 9SJ

Dundalk & District Salmon Anglers'
Assn
Neil O'Neill
Mullaharin Road
Heynestown
Dundalk
Co Louth

Dunfanaghy Angling Assn
Derek Arnold
Arnold's Hotel
Dunfanaghy

Co Donegal
Tel: +353 (0)74 9136208
Dungarvan Sea Angling Club
Mrs Ann Fuller
Friars Walk
Abbeyside
Dungarvan
Co Waterford
Durrow & District Angling Club
Michael Walsh
18 Erkindale Drive
Durrow
Portlaois
Co Laois
Tel: +353 (0)502 36437
East Mayo Anglers' Assn
Seamus Boland
Market St
Swinford
Co Mayo
Tel/fax: +353 (0)94 53955
e-mail: eastmayoanglers@eircom.net
Edenderry Coarse Angling Club
Pauric Kelly
48 Fr. Murphy Street
Edenderry
Co Offaly
Tel: 353 (0)46 9732071
Fermoy Salmon Anglers Assn
Michael Fanning
41 St Mary's Crescent
Fermoy
Co Cork
Tel: +353 (0)87 2538446
or
E Glendon
21 Connaught Place
Wellington
Fermoy
Co Cork
**Fermoy & District Trout Anglers'
Assn**
Nevil Howard
The Meadows
Duntahene
Fermoy
Co Cork
Finn Angling Club
Francis Curran
1 Derry Road
Strabane
Co Tyrone
**Foxford Salmon Anglers
Assn**
Michael Tiernan
Riverside
Foxford, Co Mayo
Glebe Angling Club
William Cochrane

87 Mourne Park
Newtownstewart
Co Tyrone
Glengarriff Anglers' Assn
Patrick Power
Reenmeen
Glengariff
Co Cork
Tel: +353 (0)27 63066
**Glengormley & Disctict Sea Angling
Club**
web: www.gadsac.freeuk.com
Guileen Sea Anglers Club
Eddie Howard
Guileen
Whitegate
Co Cork
Howth Sea Angling Club
15a West Pier
Howth
Co Dublin
Tel: +353 (0)1 8321683
email: howthsac@hotmail.com
Inistioge Anglers Club
Bill Doherty
High Street
Inistioge, Co Kilkenny
Kells Angling Assn
Liam McLoughlin
Maudlin
Kells
Co Meath
Kenmare Salmon Anglers
John O'Hare
21 Main Street
Kenmare
Co Kerry
Tel: +353 (0)64 41499
Kilkenny Anglers' Assn
Edward Stack
"Richmond"
Bleach Rd,
Kilkenny
Co Kilkenny
Tel: +353 (0)56 7765220
Permits/tickets from
Hook, Line & Sinker
Rose Inn St
Kilkenny, Co Kilkenny
Killybegs Sea Angling Club
Kellys Quay
Killibegs
Co Donegal
or
Mrs Mary Rouiller
"The Evergreens"
Aghayeevoge
Killybegs
Co Donegal

Tel/Fax: +353 (0)73 9731137
Kilmore Sea Angling Club
Chris Busher
9 Columba Villas
Wexford
Co Wexford
Tel: +353 (0)53 45227
email: kilmoresac@hotmail.com
Kinlough & District Anglers Assn
Thomas Kelly
Edenville
Kinlough
Co Leitrim
Tel: +353 (0)71 9841497
or
J Gallagher
Knockenroe
Kinlough
Co Leitrim
Tel: +353 (0)71 9841736
Knockmore Angling Club
Martin Keylly
Tel: +353 (0)94 58287
Laune Salmon & Trout Anglers' Assn
Ted O'Riordan
50 Oakpark Demesne
Tralee
Co Kerry
Tel: +353 (0)66 712 4690
Web: www.kerry-insight.com/laune-angling
e-mail: launeanglers@eircom.net
Lee Salmon Anglers
Edward Fuller
Tel: +353 (0)21 43 62183
Mob: +353 (0)86 6078280
Letterkenny & District Anglers' Assn
Gerry McNulty
Hawthorne Heights
Letterkenny, Co Donegal
Lisdoonvarna Fanore Sea Anglers' Club
Hon Sec: James Linnane
10 Tullyvarragh Hill
Shannon
Co Clare
Lismore Salmon Anglers
Eamon Power
Mara Lodge
Parks Road
Lismore
Co Waterford
Lismore Trout Anglers & Conservation Assn
Barry McCarthy
Main Street, Lismore
Co Waterford

Tel: +353 (0)58 54756
Mob: +353 (0)87 272 4503
or
J Celisse
Parks Road
Lismore
Co Waterford
Tel: +353 (0)58 53044
Lough Allen Conservation Assn
Sean Wynne
Drumshanbo
Co Leitrim
Tel: +353 (0)71 964 1564
Web: www.dbo.ie
Web: www.allen.ie
Lough Arrow & District Angling Club
Muriel Frazer
Ballindoon
Riverstown
Co Sligo
tel: +353 (0)71 916 5304
Lough Arrow Fish Preservation Assn
J Hargadon
Annaghloy
via Boyle
Co Sligo
tel: +353 (0)71 966 6666
Lough Derg Anglers
Michael Quigley
Birdhill
Tipperary
Lough Derg YC Fishing Club
D K Whelan
Whelan's Fishing Tackle & Camping
  Retail Outlet
Summerhill
Nenagh
Co Tipperary
Tel: +353 (0)67 31301
Lough Ennel Trout Preservation Assn
M Murphy
9 Old Ballinderry
Mullingar, Co Westmeath
Lough Owel Trout Preservation Assn
S McKeown
Irishtown
Mullingar, Co Westmeath
Lough Sheelin Trout Protection Assn
Eamonn Ross
Ardlougher
Ballyconnell
Co Cavan
Tel: +353 (0)49 952662
or
Paddy Lyons

Drumbee
Kilnaleck
Co Cavan
Lough Swilly Sea Angling Assn
Hon Sec: Niall Doherty
Ballyboe
Rathmullen
Co Donegal
Tel: +353 (0)74 9158129
or
c/o Post Office
Rathmullen
Co Donegal
Macroom Fly Anglers
Tom McSweeney
Mary Anne's Bar
Masseytown
Macroom
Co Cork
(Tel: +353 (0)26 41566)
Mallow Trout Anglers' Club
email: mallowfishing.eircom.net
Monasterevin Anglers Club
S Connolly
Gurteenoona
Monasterevin
Co Laois
Tel: +353 (0)45 529346
Mountmellick Anglers
B Lynch
5 Wolfe Tone Road
Mountmellick
Co Laois
Mountrath & District Anglers Club
Thomas Watkins
6 Fintan Terrace
Mountrath
Co Laois
Tel: +353 (0)502 32540
Navan & District Angling Assn
Betty Tracey
168 Woodlands
Navan
Co Meath
Tel: +353 (0)46 9022103
Mob: +353 (0)86 8197228
Newport Sea Anglers
Mary Gavin Hughes
Clynish View
Derradda
Newport, Co Mayo
Tel: +353 (0)98 41562
Mob: +353 (0)86 8062282
Web: www.clewbayangling.com
North Kerry Anglers' Assn
Jim Horgan
Woodford
6 The Square

Listowel, Co Kerry
North Kildare Trout & Salmon Anglers' Assn
Michael Deely
32 Langton Park
Newbridge
Co Kildare
Tel: +353 (0)45 435024
Old Head Sea Anglers
Vincent McDwyer
Aghadoe
Carrigmore
Carrigaline
Co Cork
Ormond Angling Assn
Joe O'Donoghue
Cameron
Gortlandroe
Nenagh
Co Tipperary
Oughterard Anglers' Assn
c/o Frank Kyne
Oughterard
Co Galway
Portarlington Angling Club
Patsy Farrell
White Hart Lane
Kilmalogue
Portarlington
Co Laois
Prosperous Course Angling Club
Dermot O'Farrell
111 Loughbollard
Clane
Co Kildare
Tel: +353 (0)45 868955
Rathdowney Anglers' Assn
(not available as we go to press)
Rathdrum Trout Anglers Club
Peter Driver
Glasnarget
Rathdrum
Co Wicklow
Tel: +353 (0)404 40304
Fax: +353 (0)404 43956
Rinnashark Sea Angling Club
Declan Flanagan
3 Aldergrove
Mount Pleasant
Grantown
Waterford
Tel: +353 (0)353 (0)51 843041
Mob: +353 (0)87 610 3031
River Ilen Anglers' Club
Michael McCarthy
Rossnagoose
Skibbereen
Co Cork

Tel: +353 (0)28 22265
Web: www.esatclear.ie/~riverilen/index.
htm
e-mail: riac@eircom.net
or
A Taylor
Cois Abhann
Coolnagarrane
Skibbereen
Co Cork

Rosses Anglers' Assn
Charlie Bonner
c/o Fishing Tackle Shop
The Bridge
Dungloe
Co Donegal
Tel: +353 (0)74 9521163
Web: www.rossesanglers.com
email: info@rossesanglers.com
email: charliebonner~@eircom.net

Rossin & Slane Anglers
Michael Mullen
39 Maple Drive
Drogheda
Co Louth
Tel: +353 (0)41 9841329

Rossmore Coarse Angling Club
Hon Sec: David Hamill
email: davidhamill01@hotmail.com

St Colman's Angling Club
Corofin
Co Galway

Schull Sea Angling Club
Kieren Higgins
47 Mountain View
Naas
Co Kildare

Shannonbridge Anglers' Assn
c/o Dermot Killeen
Shannonbridge
Co Offaly

Sliabh Liág Anglers' Assn
Frank O'Donnell
Comhlacht Iascaireachta Sliabh a
  Liág Teoranta
Ardara Rd
Carrick Upper, Carrick
Co Donegal
Tel: +353 (0)97 074 39231

Tallow & District Angling Club
Hon Sec: Josephine Henley
New Street
Tallow
Co Waterford
or
Hon Treasurer: Paul Hampton
Tel: +353 (0)58 56358

**South Munster Coarse Angling
  Club**

Mike Risdon
Conna
Co Cork
Tel: +353 (0)58 59450
e-mail: mikris@eircom.net

Tar Trout Anglers' Assn
Tony O'Brien
27 Fr. Sheedy Terrace
Clogheen
Co Tipperary

**Templemore & District Anglers'
  Assn**
William Hardiman
Manna South
Templemore
Co Tipperary
Tel: +353 (0)87 2034436

Thurles/Hollycross/Ballycamas Anglers
Jimmy Purcell
Rathcannon
Holycross
Thurles
Co Tipperary

**Tuam & District Anglers'
  Assn**
Dermot Cassidy
8 Dun Na Carraige
Cummer
Corofin
Tuam
Co Galway

Tulla & District Angling Club
c/o Niall O'Donnell
Lake View House
Doon Lough
Broadford
Co Clare
Tel: +353 (0)61 473125

Tullamore Coarse Fishing Club
Pat Gorman
Tullamore
Co Offaly

Tullow Trout & Salmon Anglers
Richard Burgess
The Lodge
Tullow
Co Carlow

Tulsk Angling Club & Services
Paddy Beirne
Tulsk
Co Roscommon
Tel: +353 (0)78 39038

Upper Shannon Angling Club
Terry Allen
Tel: +353 (0)79 63184

Vartry Angling Club
Séamus Breslin
"Avila"
Summerhill

Wicklow Town
Co Wicklow
Tel: +353 (0)404 680830
Vicarstown & District Angling Club
P O Vicarstown
Co Laois
Ireland
Virginia Coarse Angling Club
Pat McCabe
Rahardrum
Virginia
Co Cavan
Waterford Glass Sea Angling Club
Jim O'Brien
20 Avoncourt
Avondale
Kilcohan
Waterford
Co Waterford
Tel: +353 (0)51 304711
**Waterville/Caherdaniel Sea
Angling Club**

c/o Tadhg O'Sullivan's Tackle Shop
Waterville
Co Kerry
Tel: +353 (0)66 947 4433
**Waterville Fisheries
Development Group**
c/o Tadhg O'Sullivan's Tackle Shop
Waterville
Co Kerry
Tel: +353 (0)66 947 4433
West Clare Angling Club
Hon Sec: Francis Meaney
Ennis Road
Kilrush
Co Clare
Youghal Sea Anglers
M Goggin
1 Ardrath
Youghal
Co Cork

FISHING ABROAD

The primary purpose of this section is to give the angler contemplating visiting, or even, in the case of Commonwealth countries, emigrating to, one of the countries listed a brief description of the fishing to be had. It is neither necessary nor practicable to enter into such detail as in the British sections, but the addresses of various authorities from whom further information can be obtained are given, together with that of the appropriate London tourist or Government information office, at the end of each description.

CENTRAL AFRICA

ZAMBIA. Most rivers and lakes carry good stocks of fish, giving very reasonable sport. But the angler must be prepared to travel long distances over rough roads, carrying his own camp equipment and finally making his camp beside the river he intends to fish. There are very few hotels off the main roads, and fewer still in fishing areas, though the Tourist Board is conducting a successful drive for more hotels and rest houses, particularly the lodges in the national wildlife parks, where good fishing is to be had on the rivers. For parties who appreciate camping holidays in the bush, some delightful trips can be planned, particularly in August and September, when there is little fear of rain and the nights are warm enough to make camping pleasant. Most of the rivers are either heavily wooded right down to the water or are swamp-edged, so the addition of a boat and outboard motor to the camp equipment is a sound policy. On the other hand, canoes and paddlers can be hired, and the latter are usually good guides to the best fishing grounds. Youths are also very helpful as camp attendants, and little trouble is normally experienced in hiring one or two to take care of the heavy work of the camp. The visiting fisherman must remember that the hippopotamus and crocodile are found in nearly all Zambian waters. Wading in rivers can be a dangerous pastime, and hippos, especially with calves, should be given a wide berth. An insecticide spray against tsetse fly and a malarial prophylactic are recommended.

Indigenous species. These include tiger-fish, which probably provide the best sport, and goliath tiger fish, a separate species running up to 80lbs or more (found only in part of the river systems that run into the Congo River basin); fish of the Nile perch variety and their close relatives, giant perch (top weight around 200lbs); giant vundu (sampa); large-mouthed, small-mouthed and humped bream; catfish; barbel; local pike; lake salmon; labeo; and nkupi. There are two species of fish which are referred to as nkupi, one is found in Lake Tanganika and is a cichlid, it is also called a giant yellow belly; and the other is a citharinid found in the middle Zambezi including Lake Kariba.

The great **Zambezi** and its large tributary, the **Kafuwe**, are outstanding among the rivers. A good centre for the Zambezi is **Livingstone**, with record breaking tiger and bream. There are a number of excellent lodges along the Upper Zambezi River, and various companies that offer half and full day fishing to guests not staying at a lodge (or hotel) that specialises in fishing. Another town which has become a tourist centre is Siavonga on Lake Kariba. There is an all weather road from Lusaka (capital of Zambia) to Siavonga, which can be reached

within a two-hour drive. The centre has several modern lodges, some of which are air-conditioned. Sport fishing including angling and spearing are very important here. Good fishing centres on the Karfue are at Itezhi-tezhi, Lochinvar and the Lower Kafuwe, near Chirundu. At Itezhi-tezhi, the angler will come across the famous small yellow belly and the Kafuwe pike. At Lochinvar, bream are important sport fish and at Lower Kafuwe, vundu. All three centres are served by good lodges: Musungwa (at Itezhi-tezhi), Lochinvar (at Lochinvar near Monze), and Gwabi (at Lower Kafuwe near Chirundu).

The Lower Zambezi, the stretch from Lake Kariba to Mozambique, offers excellent tiger fishing as well as bream and a variety of other species, including very large vundu (catfish). There is an excellent choice of lodges and camps along the Zambian banks of the lower Zambezi that cater for the fisherman. Tiger is being caught on fly and has been referred to by a well-known fisherman and author as 'the fiercest fresh water fishing in the world'.

Lake Tanganyika is another anglers' mecca and a good centre is **Kasaba Bay**, where there are three small lodges. The lake holds giant perch, tiger-fish, yellow belly and vundu among a wide variety of sporting fish.

Apart from Nile perch and sampa, which call for heavy tackle, most of the fish mentioned can be landed with a spinning rod. Steel traces are necessary for tiger-fish, nkupi and pike. A light bait-casting rod will usually cover other species. Fishing is free as a rule and can take place all the year round, but most rivers are in spate during the rainy season from December to April.

Zambia is unlikely to prove to be a land in which trout will thrive, owing both to the high temperature range and the lack of suitable highlands, but an exception may be provided by the picturesque **Nyika Plateau**, north of **Chipata** on the Malawi border, where an experimental stocking with rainbow trout in the headwaters of the **Shire River** is being carried out.

Anglers are required to purchase an angling permit, obtainable from the offices of the Department of Fisheries in Chilanga. The department also has offices in all the major fishery areas, and permits may be bought from them.

Useful addresses are: **Department of Fisheries, Ministry of Agriculture, Food & Fisheries, Headquarters, Kafuwe Road, PO Box 350100, Chilanga** (tel: +260 1 278344/278457; e-mail: piscator@zamnet.zm); **Zambia Information Services, Block 26, Independence Avenue, PO Box RW 50020, Lusaka; Zambian National Tourist Board, 2 Palace Gate, Kensington, London W8 5NG** (tel: 020 7589 6655; fax: 020 7581 1353; web: www.zambiatourism.com; e-mail: zntb@aol.com).

ZIMBABWE. Zimbabwe offers some of the best fishing to be found in Central Africa. The angler has scope to pit his skills against a diversity of species, ranging from the fighting tiger-fish of the **Zambezi** and **Save** river systems, to introduced species like the rainbow and brown trout in the mountain streams and dams of the Eastern Highlands.

Much of centre of the country acts as a watershed, with the streams forming rivers which flow north to the Zambezi river system, on which lies the huge expanse of Lake Kariba; south to the **Limpopo**; southeast to the Save and Runde; and east into the **Pungwe** system of Mozambique. Many dams exist on all of the rivers feeding the various systems. Not all of the 117 species of fish found here are of interest to the angler, but he will certainly find more than enough to suit his tastes. There is an excellent road, rail and air network ensuring that chosen fishing locations are readily accessible.

The main area of interest to fishermen is the Zambezi River, with **Lake Kariba** (250km in length with a surface area of some 5,250 square kilometres) and the **Victoria Falls** forming the chief focal points. Tourist facilities in both these locations are excellent, the visitor being able to choose from a varied list of accommodation ranging from basic camping and National Parks sites to luxury houseboats, lodges and hotels.

Tigerfish are most commonly taken using trolling or spinning methods, but they may sometimes be tempted with a fly. They are lightening-fast, fighting fiercely after the first vigorous take. The average size is between 2-6lbs, but double figure fish are common, especially in the legendary stretch above Victoria Falls. The current Zimbabwean and world record for this species stands at 34¼lbs.

Another freshwater fish which is proving popular with British anglers is the mighty vundu. The vundu is a giant catfish, in Africa, second only in size to the Nile perch. This species, although not often fished for by local anglers, is a formidable opponent, growing to well over 100lbs and is found only below the Victotora Falls. Prospective fishermen would do best to try Lake Kariba first, using a sturdy boat rod and multiplier type outfit (capable of withstanding powerful runs often exceeding 100yds) plus the services of a guide.

The other most commonly sought after species are members of the *tilapia* and *serranchromis* families, known to local fishermen as bream. Besides being a popular table fish, the various species give an excellent account of themselves on light tackle and may be caught using a variety of methods ranging from conventional coarse fishing techniques to the use of spinners and flies.

Other indigenous species include the Cornish Jack, bottlenose, chessa, nkupe, hunyani salmon, purple labeo and the sharptooth catfish. Introduced species include the largemouth bass, a fine fighting fish introduced from USA several years ago and now widespread in Zimbabwean waters; rainbow, brown and brook trout, well stocked in the rivers and lakes of the **Nyanga** and **Chimaniamni** mountain ranges (a picturesque region often likened to Scotland); and carp, which are stocked in selected waters such as the **Mazowe Dam** near Harare and fish in excess of 50lbs have been caught.

The fishing season is any month with an 'R' in it and so ideally suits European anglers, who will, moreover, find that the high cost of the international airfare is pleasantly offset by the excellent value for money once there.

For more information, contact **Zimbabwe Tourist Office, 429 Strand, London WC2R 0QE**. (tel: 020 7240 6169); **Department of National Parks & Wildlife**, Ministry of Environment, Mines & Tourism, P O Box CY 140, Causeway, Harare (tel: +263 4 707624/708344; fax: +263 4 724914; e-mail: nationalparks@gta.gov.zw).

MALAWI. Excellent sport with rainbow trout may be enjoyed in the bracing climate of the **Zomba, Mulanje** and **Nyika Plateaux** as a result of consistent restocking of rivers and streams by the Government. **Lake Malawi** holds over 400 species; including varieties of catfish, perch and carp; also yellow fish, lake salmon and lake tiger. Most of these are found in the **Shire River** above **Livingstone Falls**, but below the falls the main species are related to those found in the **Zambezi** (which include the famous tiger-fish). Further information may be obtained from the **Malawi Tourist Office, 33 Grosvenor Street, London W1K 4QT** (tel: 020 7491 4172; fax: 020 7491 9916; e-mail: tourism@malawi-tourism.com); **Malawi Department of Tourism**, P O Box 402, Kateni House, Blantyre, Malawi (web: www.mal awi-tourism.com) and **Ministry of Tourism, Parks & Wildlife**, P/bag 326, Lilongwe, Malawi (tel: +265 781 073; fax: +265 780 650) and Fisheries Department, P O Box 593, Lilongwe, Malawi (tel: +265 721766/721074; fax: +265 7211170 e-mail: sadcfish@malawi. net).

EAST AFRICA

KENYA. Kenya is well-developed for the sporting tourist and offers a variety of fishing off the coast, in its rivers and in the lakes or the **Great Rift Valley**. Licence fees: are modest; accommodation of some variety is established at or near virtually all main centres.

The coast. Black, blue and striped marlin, broadbill swordfish, sailfish, yellow fin tuna, wahoo, barracuda, cobia, dorado, mako shark. Centres at **Mombasa, Shimoni**, for fishing in the famous **Pemba Channel**, a natural corridor between the mainland and Pemba Island, **Kilifi, Watamu, Lamu** and **Malindi**, the latter the largest. Accommodation at club premises or hotels. Charter boats operate, with good fishing almost all the year round, peaking Oct-April: at its least attractive May-June.

The mountain rivers. Stocked early in the century with brown trout, later with rainbows. Camps with rondavel accommodation at **Thiba, Thego, Kimakia, Koiwa**. Rest house at **Kaibabich**; lodges at **Ngobit** and **Kiandorogo**. A dozen or more specially recommended hotels and clubs. Camp accommodation may be primitive; nothing should be taken for granted. There are limits on size, method and bags, but wholesale poaching is an ever-present problem despite determined governmental efforts to curb it.

The **lakes**. **Naivasha** is famous for black bass, but the angler in pursuit of them should forget any preconceptions he might have. Smallish coppery-tinted bar-spoons are the most success-ful lure and the bigger fish are found not so much in the shallows as in pockets of deeper water inshore, where they shelter in the papyrus. In **Lake Turkana** (formerly Rudof) the principal quarry are Nile perch and tiger-fish, the former growing to more than 250lbs. Also in Turkana, the rare and beautiful golden perch, which may weigh 150lbs. **Lake Baringo**, well off the beaten track, is noted for its tilapia fishing; also for its wildlife watching potential, but that is a bonus attaching to much of the Kenya fishing. Sport-fishing is now developing in **Lake Victoria** and the **Sasamua Dam**. Accommodation at all centres, but the extreme variety of types calls for detailed investigation in advance. The **Pemba Channel Fishing Club** address is **PO Box 86952, Mombasa** (tel: +254 722 20 50 20/1; web: www.pembachannel.com; www.kilwa.com; e-mail: pembachannel@africaonline.co.ke). The **Kenya Tourist Board** is at **36 Southwark Bridge Road, SE1 9EU** (tel: 020 7202 6373/6361; web: kenyatourism.org; e-mail: info@kenyatourism.org).

TANZANIA. Tanzania can provide some of the finest big-game fishing in the world.

Big-game fishing: From October to March there is first-class sport with sailfish, shark, tunny, marlin, wahoo, horse mackerel and dolphin, particularly off **Dar es Salaam**, around **Bagamoyo**, **Latham Island** and **Mafia Island**, and also in the **Pemba Channel** off **Tanga**. Mafia offers some of the finest sport in the world in quantity, variety and excitement, and here particularly, and in addition to those already mentioned, can be found king fish, barracuda, red snapper and rock cod. There are two lodges on Mafia Island, with 30 and 12 air-conditioned rooms, respectively. Boats and equipment can be hired from the Seafaris Company. Flights to Mafia Island from the mainland (about 30 minutes run) are operated daily in each direction by air charter services from Dar es Salaam.

Lake fishing: the great **Lakes Victoria**, **Nyasa** and **Tanganyika** provide the best sport fishing where, from **Kigoma**, **Mwanza**, **Bukoba** and **Itungi**, it is possible to catch Nile perch, tiger fish and tilapia, which provide excellent sport. The **Great Ruaha River** and the **Rufiji River Basin** are further inland fishing grounds.

Trout fishing: At the moment, less organised than other branches of the sport, but can be arranged on request.

For visa enquiries &c, contact **Tanzania High Commission (United Republic of), 43 Hertford Street, London W1Y 8DB** (tel: 020 7499 8951; fax: 020 7499 9321; web: www.tanzania-online.gov.uk/tourism/). Further information (licences etc) may be obtained from the **Tanzania Tourist Office/Trade Centre, 80 Borough High St, London SE1 1LL** (tel: 020 7407 0566; fax: 020 7403 2003; e-mail: director@tanztrade.co.uk); **Tanzania Tourist Board, PO Box 2485, IPS Building, Maktaba Street, Dar es Salaam** (tel: +255 22 27672/3; fax: +255 22 51 46780; e-mail: safari@ud.co.tz or ttb2@ud.co.tz); **Arusha:** Infor-mation Centre, PO Box 2343, Arusha (tel: +255 27 57 3842/3; fax: +255 27 57 8256; e-mail: md@ttb.ud (or.tz); e-mail: arusha-info@yako.habari.co.tz).

MOZAMBIQUE. The New Mozambique can provide excellent fishing and has something to offer everyone, both the amateur and experienced (keen) fisherman, with a wealth of fishing venues to choose from.

A former Portuguese colony that gained independence in 1975, Mozambique has approxi-mately 2500 kilometres of pristine coastline. The warm waters of the Indian Ocean create lagoons, coral reefs and island, all of which offer superb fishing.

There is a variety of game fishing, which is excellent: Marlin: The **Bazaruto Archipelago** (a National Marine Park off the coast of Vilanculos, consisting of 4 main islands – **Bazaruto**, **Benguerra**, **Magaruque** and **Santa Carolina**, and a number of smaller islands) is ranked the best marlin angling destination in the Indian Ocean (av. 350 kg with a record 590 kg landed in 1998), and best months are Oct - March. Sailfish: Av weight 32 kg, while the record is nearly 60 kg; best months May - Sept. Other species include several tuna species, wahoo, prodigal son, yellow fin, skipjack, dorado, giant kingfish, barracuda and king and queen mackerel;

Angling for Kingfish is excellent throughout the year, though the Giant Kingfish is more likely to be seen during September to April. The King and Queen mackerel appear in the cooler months from March to August. Kawakawa fishing picks up in late spring into summer, which is November through to June. The elusive Bone fish, which to date has only been hooked in deeper water, are more likely to be caught during April to July, whilst the "almost un-catchable" milk fish are more prevalent during the same months. Springer are present all year round.

Catch and release of all species is encouraged.

The **Bazaruto Archipelago** is becoming exceedingly popular with fly-fishermen. When trying for the giant trevally and sailfish on fly, a 12 weight outfit, competent reel with good drag and plenty of backing (300 m) is necessary. Favoured fly patterns include Clouser Minnows and Lefty's Deceivers, especially in chartreuse.

A few years ago a world record Kingfish was caught at **Guinjata Bay**, south of **Inhambane** which is approximately 530 kms north of **Maputo**. In the same area is the **Barra Peninsula**, another excellent fishing area.

Inhaca Island, 40 kms off the mainland close to Maputo, is another natural reserve that is popular with fishermen. Top catches of blue and black marlin are recorded regularly.

To the south of Mozambique is Ponta Malongane and **Ponta do Ouro**, both known for their excellent fishing opportunities. Just south of Maputo this area is easily accessible by vehicle from South Africa. All the fishing areas along the Mozambique coast offer a range of accommodation from the budget to the expensive exclusive lodges. The infrastructure in Mozambique has improved immeasurably over the last few years, and even the more remote areas are now accessible, albeit some only by 4 x 4 vehicles.

Although the coastal waters are the most popular, inland the **Cahorra Bassa Dam** (located in **Tete Province**, in the north of Mozambique) is the second of the Zambezi's great man-made lakes. For the past 25 years it has been largely unfished, but it has been growing in popularity; angling is good throughout the year, with excellent tiger fish up to 14kg caught in the dam, with av wt of 4-8kgs. There are also more than 40 species of angling fish in the dam, of which bream, chessa, nkupe, Cornish jack and vundu are among the most popular; best results obtained from boats. Accommodation is available at Ugezi Tiger Lodge, situated near the town of **Songo**, at the dam wall; it is recommended anglers provide their own tackle; tackle for spinning and trawling (not fly) can be hired from the lodge.

For further information contact **Mozambique Tourism, EuroCenter - First Floor, 363 Rivonia Boulevard (P O Box 2042), Rivonia, Sandton 2128, Gauteng, South Africa** (tel: +27 11 803 9296 or +27 11 234 0599; fax: +27 11 803 9299; web: www.mozambiquetourism. co.za; e-mail: travel@mozambiquetourism.co.za).

SOUTH AFRICA

EASTERN and WESTERN CAPE. Since the establishment of large-mouthed and small-mouthed black bass, the inland fisheries of the Cape area have been greatly extended; but this development has not been at the expense of the rainbow trout fisheries, which are as flourishing as ever. A few rivers hold brown trout, and brown trout were also introduced to upland waters some time ago. All the inland waters fall under the laws of the Cape Provincial Administration. In proclaimed trout rivers no fishing may be done at all except with the artificial fly and during the open season for trout, which extends from the beginning of September to the end of May. Trout licences are required but the charges are extremely moderate. In addition, however, the permission of riparian owners will be needed and sometimes a fee is payable.

Most of the rivers in the Western Cape are within a day's motoring of **Cape Town** on tarred roads, and some of the best waters are on State Forest Reserves, to which anglers have access on permit. This area has a winter rainfall and the best months are September, October and November, late April and early May. **Steenbras Reservoir** holds a rare hybrid known as 'tiger trout' which is a cross between brown trout and the American eastern brook trout.

The **Olifants River** in the **Citrusdal** and **Clanwilliam** districts provide excellent fishing for small-mouthed bass and the indigenous yellowfish, *Barbus capensis*. The latter takes artificial lures, is very game and runs as large as 20lbs. Further afield, the mountainous area of **East Griqualand** has rivers which provide boundless opportunities for the trout fisherman.

Sea fishing along the coastline is very good indeed, with hundreds of species to be caught. Cape Town has emerged as the world's leading Broadbill Swordfish fishing venue. The big-game potential is only beginning to be realised, and remarkable catches of yellowfin and longfin tuna have been taken. Tuna catches predominate throughout spring, summer and autumn; snoek in the winter months. Skiboat fishing is an interesting and highly successful technique for taking many varieties of off-shore fish. Every type of tackle is obtainable and accommodation is plentiful and comfortable.

KWAZULU-NATAL. The streams originating in the **KwaZulu-Natal Drakensberg** mountains, which rise to 11,000 ft, form several river systems before emptying into the Indian Ocean. Although the sources are in general too steeply graded to support fish life in any quantity, below the torrent source each river enters a series of pools and rapids suitable for trout and other fish. Moreover, the construction of numerous dams in the KwaZulu-Natal Midlands has been the means of providing many extra fishable waters.

Only waters at an altitude of about 4,000 ft and more have, in general, been stocked with trout. Below this level most rivers are too warm and silt-laden for the species to thrive. Black bass and carp have been established in a number of these midland dams with tilapia species inhabiting the warmer areas. However, other species to be caught are the indigenous 'scaly' (yellowfish), catfish, and eels. The State dams administered by the KwaZulu-Natal Parks, Game and Fish Preservation Board (**Albert Falls, Midmar, Wagendrift, Spioenkop, Chelmsford, Hazelmere** and **Craigie Burn**) not only provide abundant angling for many types of fish, including those mentioned above, but also provide a wide range of other recreational facilities and comfortable accommodation.

Rainbow and brown trout are the most important sporting fish of the **Drakensberg** area (midlands) and warm-water angling (carp, black bass, catfish, scaly, eels and tilapia) of the lower inland areas. The open season for trout streams is from September 1 to June 1, but dams are open throughout the year. The best fishing is usually obtained at the beginning and end of the season. From November to February the heavy summer rains and thunderstorms are apt to discolour the lower waters and render fly fishing difficult. It is almost always feasible, however, to obtain fishing on the headwaters or on artificial lakes and dams. The average size trout runs from about ½lb to 2lbs, but on the larger waters, especially dams, much heavier fish can be expected and each season a few trout of more than 5lbs are taken. The province's record for a rainbow trout is 5.54kg (12¾lbs) caught in the Swartberg district in May 1958.

Public waters and the Provincial nature reserves (where accommodation may be found close to fishing areas) are controlled by the KwaZulu-Natal Parks, Game and Fish Preservation Board; all queries regarding licences, accommodation etc should be directed to the **KwaZulu-Natal Parks Board Pietermaritzburg**, who will supply full information to visitors and handle reservations. Parks Board rangers are stationed at the more important public fishing areas to assist visitors and enforce regulations for the protection of trout, black bass, carp and indigenous fish.

Sea fishing. The majority of salt water anglers fish in the surf, casting their baits and lures from sandy beaches or from rocky promontories. Estuaries offer sport, while the open sea attracts those who have access to suitable craft. A wide variety of fish may be caught in the surf, ranging from sharks to small members of the bream family. Tackle varies accordingly, but a light fibre-glass rod of about 10-13ft together with a fixed-spool or multiplying reel gives a chance of catching many of the inshore species. Visitors should acquaint themselves with size restrictions and open seasons which apply to certain species of fish. Full details are obtainable from The KwaZulu-Natal Parks Board.

In June and July the annual migration of 'sardines' may attract game fish such as king mackerel into the surf and sport is likely to be fast and furious. The best estuarine fishing is **Lake St Lucia**, a nature reserve-controlled by the KwaZulu-Natal Parks Board; large numbers of grunter and kob enter the estuary leading to the main lake in spring and autumn. Deep sea angling takes place from ski-boats (small, speedy, flat-bottomed craft) as well as from the larger types of vessel. Advice on the organisation of deep sea trips will be provided by the

KwaZulu-Natal Parks Board. Tackle for every branch of angling is obtainable. Innumerable hotels, holiday cottages, holiday flats and rest camps provide accommodation for visitors to the coastal resorts (with marlin, sailfish and tiger fishing).

NORTHERN PROVINCE and MPUMALANGA. Rainbow trout can be caught in a number of fine mountain streams at altitudes varying from 4,000 to 6,000ft in this north-eastern region of that was previously called the **Transvaal. Magoebaskloof, Sabie, Pilgrim's Rest, Lydenburg, Machadodorp, Belfast, Dullstroom** and **Waterval Boven** are the principal trout fishing centres. Some waters contain only fish over 3lbs in weight. There is no closed season for trout fishing although fishing conditions are at their best in October and April. The rule is fly only, with dry and wet flies being used. Most waters are privately owned and, except where angling clubs have fishing rights, the permission of the riparian owner must be obtained. Good bass fishing is to be found in a large number of public, club and private waters. Large-mouth bass are widely distributed but some of the best waters are in the **White River** area of **Mpumalanga**: dams in that region, such as **Longmere, Klipkoppies, Witklip, Stanford** and **Dagama** have produced excellent fishing in recent times. Tiger-fish may be caught in the **Komati River** at **Komatipoort** and in the **Limpopo**. Minimum takeable size, 12in, daily bag limit, 6. Tiger-fish are best caught in September and October.

Yellowfish abound in the waters of the northern provinces There are four species, all belonging to the genus *Barbus*. In the **Vaal River** they grow to 30lbs in weight and can be caught on mealiemeal dough, earthworms, grasshoppers or crabs. The two species of the east-flowing rivers grow to 15lbs and take crab, earthworms, mealiemeal dough and spinners.

Tilapia, commonly known as 'kurper', is a very popular fish. There are two species, both being restricted to warmer waters. They can be caught on earthworms, mealiemeal dough (a paste bait) and spinners, with a light trout rod. They average about 1¼lbs, but specimens of 4½lbs are commonly caught. The best waters for this species are the **Hartebeestpoort, Rust der Winter, Roodeplaat, Loskop** and **Njelele dams**, also those in the White River area - although they may be caught in almost any lowveld water.

Not just the north, but the whole of the Republic of South Africa is a carp angler's paradise, with the fish attaining exceptional weights in very short periods, due to the nature of South Africa's waters. The record caught on rod and line is 48lbs 10oz, although much larger specimens have been caught but not recorded, and the heaviest known fish was a monster of 83¼lbs which was trapped in an irrigation furrow near **Bon Accord Dam** north of **Pretoria**. Carp are found throughout South Africa in many public and private dams. No bag or size limits apply to these fish.

It is also possible to stay in and fish within some of South Africa's game reserves, including Loskop and Willem Pretorius.

General Information: Licences relative to the particular province can be obtained from Receivers of Revenue, magistrates' offices and reputable tackle stores throughout the Republic.

For further information contact the **South African Tourism Board & Tourist Office, 5/6 Alt Grove, Wimbledon, London SW19 4DZ** (tel: 0906 364 0600/020 8971 9350; fax: 020 8944 6705). **South African Tourism** head office is located in **Bojanala House, 90 Protea Road, Chislehurston, Johannesburg 2196, Gauteng, SA**; postal address: **P/Bag X10012, Sandton 2146, Gauteng, SA** (tel: +27 11 895 3000; fax: +27 11 895 3001; web: www.south africa.net; e-mail: info@southafrica.net).

FISHING IN AUSTRALASIA; INDIA; SRI LANKA AND MALAYSIA

AUSTRALIA

As a result of acclimatization and planned research in Australia, many of the lakes and rivers in the State of Tasmania, New South Wales, Western Australia and Victoria are well stocked with trout, which sometimes reach a large size. The island State of **Tasmania** is world-famous as a trout fishing centre, and continues to attract anglers from all parts of the Commonwealth each year.

Many rivers are still subject to flooding despite hydro schemes and this imposes a standstill on angling, so that the tendency is to reduce close seasons. The angler is strongly advised to check on river levels before going to fish. Before water temperatures have warmed up will be found to be the best times - midsummer is generally worst for trout fishing.

Freshwater Murray cod, perch and blackfish are found in good number in Australia. The **Murray River**, which forms the boundary of the eastern States of **Victoria** and **New South Wales**, and its many tributaries provide good sport for thousands of anglers, including trout in the upper reaches, Murray cod may weigh up to 150lbs; another Murray River fish, the callop or golden perch, grows to over 50lbs. Macquairie perch (to 11lbs) and silver perch or grunter (to 6lbs) are also taken. Another perch, or Australian bass, is taken in coastal streams and estuaries.

Australia was said by the late Zane Grey, noted big game authority, to possess the finest big game fishing grounds in the world. Centre of interest for sportsmen is **Montague Island**, off the coast of New South Wales, where there are marlin, tuna, shark and other big fish. The island is 14m from **Bermagui**, a safe harbour that can be used in all weathers. The tropical waters of the **Great Barrier Reef**, which extends for about a thousand miles along the east coast of Queensland, form Australia's most fascinating grounds; there are many unusual varieties of fish. There is good beach and rock fishing almost everywhere.

The **Australian Tourist Commission** is at **Gemini House, 10-18 Putney Hill, Putney, London SW15 6AA** (tel: 020 8780 2229; fax: 020 8780 1496). For information on Australian holidays contact **The Aussie Helpline**: web: www.australia.com.

NEW SOUTH WALES. The streams near **Sydney** are mostly too small to support a large trout population, but good sport may be had in parts of the Blue Mountains area. Easily best from the fishing point of view, however, is the **Snowy Mountains** area. Very large reservoirs constructed as part of the hydro-electric scheme in the Southern Alps are now ranked equal to any in the world for brown and rainbow trout. The scenic beauty of the streams and these lakes is outstanding. **Lake Eucumbene** is the largest of the dams and in recent years has become the mecca of Australian trout anglers, Lake **Jindabyne** is the other principal fishery, but the total number of man-made lakes is 16. Brown trout average 1 to 2kg, rainbows from 1 to 3kg. Lakes Jindabyne and **Burrinjuck** have stocked Atlantic salmon. There is also good river trout fishing in the region, including **Maclaughlin River, Bobundara Creek, Bombala River**, and others, and little explored creeks and streams. Good accommodation and camping sites are to be found and many fine fishing waters are reached easily over good roads. Another good area for trout fishing is the **New England Tableland**, north of Sydney. Centred on the University Town of **Armidale**, the area's many streams and high altitude provide excellent fishing.

Apart from these new waters, one of the most renowned centres is **Cooma**, which has produced many of the heavier fish caught in the state. The **Murrumbidgee** and its tributaries near **Kiandra** are well worth fishing at the right time.

With the exception of a number of small spawning creeks, which have extended close seasons, and the larger impoundments, which are open all the year round, the trout streams are open to fishing from early-October to mid-June. Other inland waters are open the whole year. The most popular times for trout fishing are in the cooler months of the open season; that is October, November, March, April and May.

There are many attractive native species inhabiting the freshwater streams. Murray cod being perhaps the most popular, and the taking of fish up to 50lbs is not uncommon; these fish do, in fact, run much larger. There are size and bag limits for trout and native fish and there is a closed season for Murray cod during September, October and November. Trout cod, Macquarie perch, eastern cod and Australian grayling are protected. Silver perch may be taken from stocked impoundments only.

There is now a **recreational fishing fee** (which replaces the freshwater fishing licence) applicable to all except Commonwealth pensioner concession card holders, under 18's and charter-boat fishers with registered guide. Fees range from: Aus$5 for 3 days; Aus$10 per month; Aus$25 for one year, and Aus$70 for a 3 year licence. All revenues go into a trust fund for improvement of fishing opportunities and services. Further information may be had by writing to **NSW Fisheries, PO Box 21, Cronulla 2230, Australia** (tel: +61 2 9527 8411; web: www.fisheries.nsw.gov.au).

The State is noted for its attractive coastal lagoons and estuary fisheries. At many excellent resorts bream, flathead, whiting, black fish, etc, give good sport, while big game fish like tuna, marlin and shark abound in waters off the coast. For rock fishing, there are hundreds of locations on the Central Coast, some little known, where big yellowtail kingfish, tuna, mulloway, drummer, marlin, snapper and shark may be caught. Recommended among these are the Haven and Skillion at **Terrigal**, and **Avoca**.

Tourist information can obtained from **The Sydney Visitors Centre, 106 George Street, The Rocks, Sydney 2000**. In Australia, contact tel: 132077.

NORTHERN TERRITORY. The **Northern Territory** has some of the most prolific fishing in Australia. With vast, unique wetlands, with their numerous freshwater rivers and billabongs (waterholes resulting from seasonal rivers drying up), it is the perfect environment for barramundi, and is commonly known as the centre for barramundi in Australia.

The top end of the Northern Territory has two distinct seasons: the Wet and the Dry. On average 92% of the top end's rainfall occurs during the tropical summer season, between November and April, and flooding can affect access to many inland areas by road. The Dry finds many rivers and creeks dried up, leaving isolated billabongs and lakes in difficult-to-access areas.

Fishing in the Territory is a year-round pursuit, and the different seasons offer different fishing opportunities, with the main attraction, barramundi, available all through the year. Known for its aggressive nature and fighting characteristics, the barramundi is found in both fresh and saltwater. It is the favourite quarry of the Australian angler, fish 10 to 15 kilos being not uncommon, and running sometimes to 20 kilos. For fly fishermen, the saratoga offers good sport, and fights hard (average 1-2kg).

The Northern Territory is also famous for its saltwater and estuary fishing in its many mangrove-lined creeks, tidal rivers, bays, offshore islands and reefs. Some of Australia's best light and medium tackle game fishing is found in the coastal waters of the Northern Territory, in **Arnhem Land,** which is territory set aside for Aborigines. Varieties include mangrove jack, queenfish, tuna, threadfin salmon, blue salmon, trevally, Spanish mackerel; even sailfish and marlin.

Reef fishing provides excellent sport for golden snapper, saddletail snapper, red-finned emperor, red emperor, estuary rock-cod, coral trout, moonfish, mangrove jack, bream, black jewfish, tuna, and Spanish mackerel. The best times for barramundi are March to May, and September to December.

Other recommended locations are the **Mary River**, east of **Darwin,** the **Daly River**, south of Darwin, **Bathurst** and **Melville Islands** to the north of Darwin, and the estuaries, and many rivers and billabongs in **Kakadu National Park**. These are all popular fisheries. Anglers are advised, a hat, sunglasses, 20+ factor sunscreen, long-sleeved cotton shirt, long cotton trousers in this tropical environment are a must.

Weather and tides play an important role in fishing productivity. The Northern Territory has large tidal changes and low tide can leave boats stranded for long periods with large tides often creating strong currents in the river systems. Obtaining tidal information before departing on fishing expeditions is a necessity. Such information can be obtained from local newspapers as well as from news and weather reports on radio and television. Regulations for recreational fishing deal mainly with bag limits and minimum size regulations. Details can be obtained from the **Fisheries Division Grpup, Department of Industry, Business and Resource Development, PO Box 3000, Darwin, NT 0801** (tel: + 61 8   899992144, fax: +61 8 89992065). The Department can also supply names and addresses of fishing tour operators.

QUEENSLAND. There are no trout fishing centres, no licence fees and no close season except for barramundi angling (Nov 1 to Jan 31). Among other species, golden perch (or yellowbelly) are found in the **Darling River, Lake Eyre** and **Bullo** drainages, and also in the **Dawson-Fitzroy** system; a freshwater table fish which gives a determined fight; Murray cod are found in the **Murray-Darling** system, and Mary River cod are indigenous to **Mary River**; this is an endangered species, and must be returned to water alive; and freshwater perch and grunters (several species) are found in most inland streams. Barramundi are taken from all inland rivers of eastern Queensland from around Mary River to Gulf of **Carpentaria**. Saratoga are excellent sportfish, and are found in **Fitzroy** system, growing to maximum length of 3ft.

Off the coast are the **Greater Barrier** coral reefs (1,230 miles long), which abound in fish life. Big game fish are plentiful along the whole coastline, and the following species are commonly caught: Marlin, spearfish, tuna, Atlantic bonito, Spanish mackerel, sharks (white pointer, mako, tiger, whalers, etc), amberjacks, emperor, trevally, etc.

Cairns and Tropical North Queensland are known world wide as a big game area for the big black marlin in the last quarter of the year. Also mackerel, tuna, big trevally, queenfish, and outside the reef, wahoo, dolphin fish, as well as marlin.

The area off **Brisbane** and **Moreton Bay** produces whiting, flathead, trevally, larger mackerel species in summer, and in winter whiting, bream, tailor, jew, perch, school mackerel, tarwhine, blackfish; all year round cod, snapper, sweetlip, drummer. Deep sea charters produce snapper, parrot, pearl, perch, sweetlip, cod, and big game such as tuna, sea-pike, black king, dolphin, small marlin, and larger mackerel species.

The mainland coast provides excellent estuary beach and rock fishing for bream, whiting, flathead, tailor, trevally, giant perch, grunter, jew fish, and so on.

Information on regulations can be had from **Director, Fisheries Branch, Dept of Primary Industries, GPO Box 46, Brisbane, Qld 4001** (tel: +61 7 224 2282; fax: +61 7 229 8146); and on tourism from the **Queensland Tourist and Travel Corporation, 392 Strand, London WC2R 0LZ** (tel: 020 7240 0525; fax: 020 7836 5881; web: www.tq.com.au/).

SOUTH AUSTRALIA. South Australia has very few freshwater streams if the **River Murray** is excluded. Relatively little trout fishing is to be found except in some streams near capital city of Adelaide and in farm dams. There is no closed season on trout fishing but there is a legal minimum length of 28cm.

The River Murray, which flows through the State to the sea, supports a recreational fishery for native freshwater species, callop, silver perch and catfish and yabbies. Introduced species, including European carp and redfin may be caught, but must not be returned to the water alive. Fishing for Murray cod is now permitted between 1 Jan-31 Aug; Murray crayfish, silver perch and catfish are now fully protected in South Australia.

Very enjoyable and profitable sea fishing can be had along most of the coast of South Australia with rod and line or hand line. Amateur anglers do not require licences.

South Australia's premier saltwater table fish is the King George whiting and these are accessible to boat anglers in most waters of the State, including waters adjacent to Adelaide. Snapper up to 30lbs or more and sweet tasting garfish are also taken by boat anglers in the relatively sheltered waters of **Gulf St Vincent** and **Spencer Gulf**. A large number of piers along the South Australian coast allow good fishing for a variety of species. Excellent sport fishing for Australian salmon (*Arripis trutta esper*, a sea perch, and not related to the family *Salmonidae*), sharks and large mulloway may be had by shore anglers along the surf beaches of the more exposed parts of the coast.

A fine 25 lb spanish mackerel in Junction Bay, north of tropical Arnhem Land, Northern Territory, is hauled aboard. *Photo: Thomas Harmsworth.*

The coastal waters of the **Innes National Park** are home to a wide variety of fish life, and there are at least seven excellent beach and rock fishing locations where good catches of garfish, Tommy ruff, King George and yellowfin whiting, squid, bream, mullet, flathead, and leather jacket may be had. Fishing boats take anglers on sea fishing trips from **Port Lincoln**, and commonly taken are snapper, various species of shark and tuna, and whiting.

Kangaroo Island, 4,500 square km, lying off the coast south-west of Adelaide, is an important national centre for wildlife and has a great potential for fishing. At **Kingscote**, **Penneshaw** and **American River** wharves garfish, tommy ruffs and snook may be caught on fast running tides; jetties at Emu Bay and Vivonne Bay produce good fishing at times; surf fishing at **Emu Bay, Stokes Bay, D'Estrees Bay, Vivonne Bay** and Middle River, where, where salmon, mullet, and large flathead may be caught; swallowtail are caught by rock fishing, and inland the Middle, **Sou'West, Chapman** and **Cygnet** Rivers, and the **Western River** mouth all provide excellent bream fishing; at the mouth of the **Cygnet River**, salmon, mullet and tommy ruffs are to be found. Charter boats operate on the island, found through information centres at **Penneshaw** and **Kingscote**, and snapper are caught along the north coast in large numbers, whiting to 1.5kg, and snook are also taken. Fishing in National Parks rivers or creeks is prohibited. Tourism is well organised on the island, and there is a wide range of good accommodation.

Anglers do not require a licence to fish with a rod or hand line, but must observe legal minimum lengths of fish, bag limits, boat limits, and closed areas, and must not take protected species. Fishing is not permitted in most Aquatic Reserves.

Tourist information can be had from the **South Australian Tourism Commission, Travel Centre, 18 King William Street, Adelaide**, (tel: +1300 366770; web: www.southaustralia.com.au); and further information on fishery matters from the **Primary Industries and Resources, SA Fisheries, GPO Box 1625, Adelaide, SA 5001;** (web: www.pir.sa.gov.au/fishing) and the **Honourary Secretary, South Australian Fly Fishers Association Inc, GPO Box 489, North Adelaide, SA 5006.** For houseboat hire in a wide range of river locations, often with fishing opportunity, contact **Houseboat Hirers Association Inc, 7 Gollop Cres, Redwood Park, SA 5097** (tel: +61 8 8395 0999; fax: +61 8 8263 5373; web: www.houseboat-centre.com.au).

TASMANIA. Tasmania, not without justification, describes itself as Australia's fly fishing capital. More than 3,000 lakes and rivers contain self-supporting populations of brown, rainbow and brook trout, species which have achieved growth-rates on the island second to none. The size-bracket in which the angler expects his captures to fall spans 1-5 kg, with even larger trout an ever-present possibility. Most of the waters are within motoring distance of Hobart and **Launceston**. Mobile campers are widely employed. Guides operate in vicinity, and can arrange, where necessary, flies, lures, boats and accommodation.

Popular waters include **Great Lake**, 158 square km (situated in the central plateau of the island at an altitude of 1,000m, 83 miles from Hobart, the capital, and about the same distance from Launceston, second largest city in the island, situated in the north), **Lake King William, Lake St Clair, Lake Echo, Little Pine Lagoon,** (perhaps Tasmania's best known fly fishing water,) **Brady's Lake, Dee Lagoon, Arthurs Lake** (64.4 square km), **Lake Rowallan** and **Lake Pedder** (which reached a legendary peak in the late 1970s, with trout over 10kg. Now, trout average a more modest 1½ to 2kg). Other popular fishing waters are **Lake Leake** and **Tooms Lake** on the east coast, and **Lake Sorell** in the central midlands, 43 square km, at 823 m above sea level, with fine hatches of mayfly and caddis. Browns to 3kg are caught. Another popular group is the Bronte system, between Bronte Park and Tarraleah, as are the many small lakes in the Nineteen Lagoons district centred around **Lakes Ada** and **Augusta**. The **Western Lakes** are a scattering of countless lakes, lagoons and tarns across the Western Central Plateau (1,150 to 1,200m above sea level), between the **Great Lake** and the **Cradle Mountain Lake, St Clair National Park**. They are also know as the **Wilderness Lakes**. The more accessible amongst them include **Howes Bay Lagoon, Carter Lakes, Lake Botsford, Lake Ada** and **Lake Kay**. Mainly brown trout are to be found in the area. Other famous Tasmanian fisheries are **Brumbys Creek**, near Cressy and Longford, and the **Macquarie River**, flowing northwards through the midlands, with 'red spinner' mayfly hatches: stream fishing for small brown trout. **London Lakes** is a private trout fishery of 5,000 acres in the

Central Highlands, with abundant stocks of wild browns, generally in the 1-1½ kg size range. Contact London Lakes Lodge, P.O. Bronte Park, Tasmania 7140 (tel: +61 (0)3 628 91159; fax: +61 (0)3 6289 1122; web: www.londonlakes.com.au; e-mail: garrett@london lakes.com.au).

The northern part of the island is more richly endowed with trout streams than the south, having the **South Esk, North Esk, Macquarie** and **Brumby**. The north-west has the **Mersey, Forth, Leven, Blyth, Duck** and **Inglis**. In the south are the **Derwent**, and **Huon**.

Sea fishing abounds in Tasmania, mainly in the east, but in the north Port Sorell and the **Tamar River** (65km, with jetty and estuary fishing) are popular venues, and in the west, Macquarie Harbour. The **Derwent River** at Hobart also provides many spots for jetty and estuary fishing, with catches of mackerel, flathead, cod, squid, barracouta, perch, bream and australian salmon. There are also many excellent beaches, particularly in the north from Cape Portland to Stanley, where flathead, Australian salmon, flounder and whiting are taken. Most of the rivers on the east coast from **St Helens** to **Bruny Island** hold large populations of bream, best fishing in Nov. Bruny island also has excellent beach fishing. Bait is sold in many spots on the coast, and accommodation is first class.

Species caught either from shore or from boat are southern rock cod, leather jacket, blue eye, school whiting, barracouta, yellow-eyed mullet, black bream, flathead, warehou, leatherjacket, wrasse, mullet, silver trevally, southern garfish, greenback flounder, school, "gummy", shark, marlin, various species of tuna, blue pointer, and bronze whaler sharks, elephant fish, Australian salmon, trumpeter, silver trevally, snapper, tailor, garfish and yellowtail kingfish. Boats may be chartered (for further information and contacts, see web: www.fishonline.tas.gov.au). There are various laws and restrictions practised, including bag limits; details should be obtained from **Dept. of Primary Industries, Water & Environment, GPO 444, Hobart, Tasmania 7001** (tel: +61 (0)3 6233 3515; web: www.dpiwe.tas.gov.au). The Department does not manage freshwater fishing in Tasmania; for inland fisheries information see below (web: www.ifs.tas.gov.au). It also has an excellent section of related sites for quick access to various other websites relevant to fishing throughout Australia.

Angling licences are required. For inland waters these are: full season Au$54.35; 14 days $43.25; 3 days $27.75 and 1 day $16.65, with concessions for pensioners and juveniles and are sold at most sports stores, police stations and Tasmanian travel centres or the Inland Fisheries Service. The *Tasmanian Angling Code*, which is free with each licence should be consulted for details on fishing restrictions. The main season runs from the Saturday nearest 1 Aug to Sunday nearest 30 Apr. There are some exceptions. Specific reglations have been introduced for six waters in the Western Lakes area. The Northern Tasmanian Fisheries Association and the North-Western Fisheries Association (web: http://tico.tased.edu.au/) are included amongst the principal angling associations. There is a new website developed specifically for recreational fishing in Tasmania (www.fishonline.tas.gov.au) For professional trout guides and/or lodges (web: www.troutguidestasmania.com.au).

Further information can be obtained from **Tourism Tasmania, Level 2-22, Elizabeth Street, Hobart TAS 7000** (tel: +3 6230 8169; web: www.discovertasmania.com); **The Inland Fisheries Service, 6B Lampton Ave, Derwent Park** (P O Box 288, Moonah), TAS 7009 (tel: +61 (0)3 6233 4140; fax: +61 (0)3 6233 4141; web: www.ifs.tas.gov.au; e-mail: in fish@ifs.tas.gov.au) and **Trout Guides and Lodges Tasmania** (web: www.troutguidestas mania.com.au).

VICTORIA. The smallest in area of the Australian mainland States, Victoria offers a considerable diversity of opportunities for freshwater river and lake, estuary, bay and inlet, beach and sea fishing. Many fishing locations are among or near National, State and other Parks that provide an attractive scenic environment and comprehensive touring/holiday experience. Anglers are able to use natural baits, artificial lures and flies in Victoria's public waters.

Freshwater Fishing. Victoria may be known for the **Yarra River** that passes through Melbourne, the capital of Victoria, but the State has many excellent opportunities for freshwater fishing. The Yarra R. has edible fish throughout its accessible length which is confined to bank fishing (headwaters are closed water catchment) with trout, blackfish, roach, redfin, carp, Macquarie perch, some Murray cod in the urban area and within 1 hour's drive from the city centre. The estuarine section from the city to Port Phillip Bay contains a wide variety of species fishable from the bank, including bream, mullet, luderick, some mulloway and tailor. Other major streams entering Port Phillip Bay are the **Maribyrnong** and **Werribee Rivers**, which have trout in the headwaters, coarse fish in the middle sections and estuary fish in the lower sections. Except in the far north-west of the State where it is very dry, there are numerous streams, lakes and reservoirs fishable from bank, shoreline or boat, throughout Victoria. Many waters have self-supporting fish populations, but Fisheries Victoria have active stocking programs of the native golden perch, Murray cod and Macquarie perch and the introduced brown trout, rainbow trout and chinook salmon into selected, suitable waters. Trout fishing is providing in hundreds of waters but is most popular in the north east (**Ovens River, Kiewa River** system, **Lake Dartmouth**), Wimmera region (**Fyans Lake, Wartook Lake**), the south west (**Purrumbete Lake, Lake Bullen Merri** , **Merri River**) and central (**Goulburn River, Lake Eildon**). Native fish angling can be had throughout much of Victoria, although the waters in the northern half of the State provide the best Murray cod and golden perch fishing in the streams and lake systems draining into the Murray River - which forms the boundary between Victoria and New South Wales. Coarse fishing is practised State-wide with good populations of redfin, roach, and tench. Carp are abundant throughout the State, however, they are listed as noxious, and must not be returned to the water alive.

Saltwater Fishing. Melbourne and its suburbs are situated around **Port Phillip Bay**, which together with **Western Port Bay** about 1 hours drive to the south east, dominate Victoria's saltwater fishing scene, providing boat and shore anglers with a variety of fish including snapper to 11 kg (mainly October to March), salmon, elephant fish, flathead, whiting, mullet, garfish, trevally and gummy shark. Victoria's coastline has many estuaries, inlets, lakes, surf beaches and rocky shorelines that provide ample opportunities for shore, jetty, rock, beach

This large barramundi, the favourite catch of the Australian angler, was captured by Perth (WA) lawyer, John Byrne in the Goomadeer River, Arnhem Land, Northern Territory. It was not long before he gently returned it to the water. *Photo: Thomas Harmsworth*

and boat fishing. The most popular eastern area is the major **Gippsland Lakes** system where a series of large lakes provide excellent year-round fishing. Many of Victoria's coastal fishing areas are popular and well-serviced holiday locations complete with accommodation, facilities and boat hire. The **Glenelg River** in the west provides a 70 km estuary which is very popular for mulloway fishing. The commonly caught saltwater fish are bream, flathead, mullet, luderick, estuary perch, sharks, tailor, Australian salmon, sweep, leatherjackets and garfish.

There are too many angling locations around Victoria to mention individually. Tackle stores and newsagents provide numerous publications and video tapes about where and how to catch fish in the State. A useful publication is *Location Guide to Fishing Victoria's Coastline*, 1st Edition 1993 - Wilson, Australian Fishing Network, 96pp, 30 maps, (RRP $A12.95), ISBN 062 621 427, which is designed to help the angler find and fish hundreds of locations along the coast.

Anglers fishing in either saltwater or freshwater or both, require an Recreational Fishing Licence to fish, unless they are under 18, or over 70 years of age, or in receipt of certain pensions. Annual licences cost A$22, 28 day; A$11, 48 hour; A$5.50. Information on licensing and fishing regulations, including bag limits, size limits and closed seasons are provided in the *Victoria Recreational Fishing Regulations Guide* which is issued free from over 700 fishing tackle and sporting goods stores in Victoria, or from the **Department of Primary Industries** offices. Detailed information on recreational fishing in Victoria is available (website: www.dpi.vic.gov.au). A very popular website with Victorian anglers is www.fishnet.com.au. It contains up to date reports on hundreds of fishing locations, as well as chat boards and links with other popular fishing websites. The Department of Primary Industries also maintains an on-line Guide to Inland Angling Waters of Victoria that identifies more than 600 streams and freshwater lakes, the fish present and advice about fish sizes and abundance.

Public enquiries about fishing locations and types of fish should be directed to Dept's **Customer Services Centre** (tel: +61 3 136 186). Information of fishing regulations should be directed to **Fisheries Victoria, Department of Primary Industries, PO Box 500, East Melbourne, Victoria, Australia 3002**. Tourist information is issued by **Tourism Victoria, 55 Collins Street, Melbourne, 3000 Victoria, Australia** (Tel: +61 (0)3 9653 9871; fax: +61 (0)3 9653 9733; web: tourismvictoria.com.au). Further information from **Tourism Victoria Australia State, Victoria House, Melbourne Place, London WC2B 4LF** (tel: 020 7240 7176).

WESTERN AUSTRALIA. Stretching from the tropical north to the cool southern oceans, the vast coastal waters of Western Australia provide superb ocean sports fishing, and some of the best angling in the world can be found on the doorstep of Western Australia's major cities.

Around 300,000 West Australians go fishing at least once a year, and the State attracts many visiting anglers. Boat ownership is the highest in Australia.

Principal centres for ocean fishing are: **Kununurra, Broome, Port Hedland, Dampier, Exmouth, Carnarvon, Shark Bay, Kalbarri, Geraldton, Fremantle, Lancelin, Perth, Rottnest Island, Mandurah, Bunbury, Busselton, Augusta, Albany** and **Esperance**. Fishable rivers include **Margaret River, Kalbarri, Murray**. Species to be caught include: herring, silver bream, garfish, mulloway, whiting, tailor, tuna, Australian salmon, pink snapper, dhufish, barramundi, sailfish, flathead, whiting, black bream, and Spanish mackerel. Annual gamefishing classics are held in the tropical waters of **Exmouth** and **Broome** where marlin and other gamefish are target species. In the **Swan River**, on Perth's doorstep, locals hand-trawl for prawns and black bream. Flounder and flathead are also prolific. World famous western rock lobsters can be taken from the reefs around many mid-west coastal centres. Fishing boats operate from all principal centres.

A Recreational Fishing Licence must be held for the taking of lobster, marron, freshwater fishing, abalone or to use a gill net, and is sold by Fisheries Department offices. Bag limits apply to all species of fish.

The **Fisheries Department** is located at **3rd Floor, SGIO Atrium, 168/170 St George's**

Terrace, Perth WA 6000, and the address of the **Western Australian Government, European Office** in London is: **5th Floor, Australia Centre, Corner of Strand and Melbourne Place, London WC2B 4LG** (tel: 020 7240 2881; fax: 020 7240 6637).

NEW ZEALAND

Fishing in New Zealand divides into three parts - Trout, Salmon and Big Game angling.

Trout, both brown and rainbow, were introduced about 100 years ago and have long been fully distributed on both islands. Rainbow predominate in the North Island, and browns in the South, but many waters have a mixture of the two in varying proportions.

The main areas in the North are centred on **Lake Taupo** and the **Rotorua** district with its group of important lakes. The rivers flowing into and out of these lakes are also noted fisheries, particularly late in the season when the main runs commence. The **Tongariro, Waitahanui, Tauranga-Taupo** and others flow into Lake Taupo, while in the Rotorua area there are the **Kaituna, Ohau Channel, Ngongotaha**, and the **Motu**, which is the best dry fly river in New Zealand. The summer trout fishing season runs from Oct to Apr in most districts. Winter trout fishing is found in the Taupo/Rotorua regions, with Apr/May. Sept/Oct the best months. May to Oct is the best time for the Tongariro. The top dry fly fishing in the more remote areas of the North Island is best Nov/Apr inclusive.

The South Island has thousands of miles of rivers and streams, and numerous lakes of all sizes. It was once calculated, at the turn of the century, that there are 17,000 miles of river fishing in New Zealand, and of course it is all open to the public, subject only to right of access and to reasonable accessibility. The best time for trout fishing in South Island is from Oct to May.

Good trout fishing is widely spread, and large trout can still be caught within an hour's drive of the main cities, but obviously many of the best waters are more remote and some are seldom fished, although helicopter or floatplane services operate out of the towns of **Queenstown, Wanaka** and **Te Anau** to reach places like **Lakes Alabaster** and **McKerrow**, or the **Pyke** and **Hollyford** rivers for example.

The main, and also the lesser, rivers of **Southland** and **Otago** provinces offer excellent dry fly and nymph fishing for brown trout, and fish of from 12-15lbs are caught each season, but a good average would be from 3-4lbs. Guide services are again easily found, although obviously concentrated somewhat in the more popular areas. An Angling Guides Association was formed some time ago, all professional guides are licensed, and are fully supported with 4-wheel drive vehicles and boats as necessary for their local areas.

In general, the open season is from Oct 1 until the end of April (North Island - 1 Oct to end of June) but some waters open early to take advantage of the runs of whitebait which provide feed for sea-run trout, while others, principally in the Taupo and Rotorua areas, stay open all the year, particularly the lower reaches of the larger streams feeding Lake Taupo, Rotorua and Wakatiou themselves. Regulations vary throughout the twenty-six fishing districts, but fishing usually starts at 5 a.m. and finishes at midnight on any day. Generally fly only on all rivers and streams flowing into lakes (no spin rod, and fly and bubble). Fly only includes the area within 300m radius from the point where a stream joins a lake. Streams flowing from lakes or mountains to the sea are generally open to all methods. With the exception of Lake Taupo, which requires a local licence, licences apply in any area of New Zealand, and are obtainable from guides, shops, petrol stations, visitor centres &c. The cost ranges from about NZ$12 per day to NZ$25 per week. Season, NZ$65.

Salmon, the Pacific Quinnat or King Salmon, introduced to the main **Canterbury** rivers, are fished for in about eight of them, the main ones being the **Waimakariri, Rakaia, Ashburton, Rangitata** and **Waitaki**. Best between mid December and late April, the fishing is mainly heavy spinning, with spoons most favoured as lures, in the lower rivers, estuaries and even in the surf at the mouths. A certain amount of fly fishing, using very large lures or flies, is done upriver, notably in the **Rakaia Gorge** area. In all the salmon rivers the fish are mostly in the 10-20lb class, but are sometimes caught as large as 40lbs. The rivers are often unfishable for many days at a time due to cloudy glacial melt water, and trips undertaken with salmon exclusively in mind are not to be recommended. Season: 1st October to 30th April.

Licence costs as for trout.

Coarse fishing: there is very good coarse fishing to be had in the areas of Greater Auckland and Waikato (around Hamilton), and the Greater Wellington and Christchurch areas. Large rudd, perch, tench, are caught regularly. Other species include eels, goldfish, and koi carp. There is no close season for this, and no charge, just the permission of the owner required, and a licence fee of $20. All coarse tackle has to be bought from overseas, however.

Big Game Fishing: the main bases for this are **Russell, Paihia** and **Whangerei** in the **Bay of Islands**, and also out from **Bay of Plenty**, and from **Tauranga** to the **Mayor Island** area. There are ample charter boats, with professional skippers and hands, based in these places, catering for parties of up to four anglers. The tackle and bait are provided in the charter. Main species caught are striped, Pacific blue, and black marlin, broadbill, mako, thresher and hammerhead shark, yellowfin tuna, yellowtail, and are taken with natural bait or lure. The southern part of the West Coast of the South Island, known as 'Fiordland', is now assuming increased importance for big game fishing. Boats are now based there, at Milford Sound and elsewhere.

Big Game angling is mainly from January to the end of April, with the period from mid-February on offering fine sport.

Licences are needed for trout and salmon fishing. There is a special Tourist Licence which covers the whole country and is only sold at the Tourism Rotorua Information Office in Rotorua. Alternatively licences may be purchased from other districts which allow the visitor to fish in any district with the exception of Rotorua and Taupo, separate licences being needed for these two districts. Rods may be brought freely into the country, although airport agriculture officials may want to fumigate flies made with real feathers.

For further information and advice on angling in New Zealand, contact **New Zealand Professional Fishing Guides Association, Murphys Lodge, PO Box 16, Motu, Gisborne** (tel: +64 6 863 5822, fax: +64 6 863 5844, e-mail murphy.motu@xtra.co.nz) or **New Zealand Tourism Board, New Zealand House, 80 Haymarket, London SW1Y 4TQ** (tel: 09069 101010 - Premium Rate Services rates apply. Useful web sites: **Tourism New Zealand**: www.purenz.com/fishing; **Fishing Marketing Network** (web: www.troutnewzealand.com); **The New Zealand Fish & Game Council** (web: www.fishnhunt.co.nz0; **Ministry of Agriculture & Forestry (MAF)** for Quarantine requirements regarding your equipmen (web: www.maf.govt.nz).

INDIA

One of the big attractions for the fisherman in India - in more senses than one - is the mighty mahseer. Mahseer country stretches between the Hindu Kush-Kabul-Kohistan watershed in the west all the way to the eastern tributaries of the **Brahmapurta**. It is found in some rivers in the Deccan plateau region and the River Kaveri in the south central plain region of **Karnataka**. Mahseer is essentially a migratory fish, running up and into side streams for spawning, at heights of up to 2000 metres during the monsoon. The fish avoids very cold water and therefore frequents the lower portion of the Himalayan streams during winter. Fish breeds three times a year, Jan-Feb, May-June, July-Sept, the peak season. The big ones are generally landed when returning from the breeding grounds when they chase shoals of minnows.

The mahseer can be taken on a spoon, but strong tackle is essential. It not only runs large - the biggest caught on rod and line weighed 119lbs (Cauvery River, South India, 1919) - but is a splendid fighter. The sport has, in fact, been compared most favourably with salmon fishing.

Mahseer are generally found in the rivers of the Terai regions of the Himalayas, the Shivalik Hills in the north, and the river **Kaveri** in the south. The following river stretches have been specifically cited as mahseer fishing areas, and are accessible for accommodation or camping: **River Jhelum** (J & K), below the Wular lake on the Sopore-Rampur stretch 80 kms from Srinagar. (Permits from J&K Fisheries Dept. in Srinagar). **River Beas** (Himachal Pradesh and Punjab), from Dehra Gopipur up to the Pong Dam reservoir; Below Pong Dam at Talwara (Punjab); Harike barrage on the Ferozpur Road. (Permits from Fisheries Officer at Dehra, or

Director Fisheries, Palampur). Best seasons Feb-May, Sept-Nov. **River Ganga**, stretch above Tehri (10 km); Beashgat, and Gangalehri. (Permits from UP Fisheries Dept., Dehra Dun). **River Bhoroli** (Arunachal), 60 km from Tezpur, the river is fished between Tipee and Bhalukpong, as it flows through the Balipara reserved forest. Inflatable raft recommended. (Permits from Fisheries Officer, Tezpur). **River Manas** (Assam), Located in the famous Manas wildlife sanctuary. (Permits from Fisheries Officer, Gauhati - foreign nationals require restricted area permits from the Ministry of Home Affairs to visit this area). **River Kaveri** (Karnataka), 2½ hours by road from Bangalore. Mahseer of 43 kgs landed here on 20 Jan, 1985. (Permits from Karnataka Fisheries Dept., Bangalore).

Kashmir is renowned for sport with brown and rainbow trout, which have thrived since they were introduced at the turn of the century. The snow trout is found in high altitude waters. The many streams in the area are regularly stocked from two large hatcheries and are divided into 'beats' of about two miles. Each beat has a local *shikari* or guide, and a watcher from the Fisheries Dept. supervises a few beats. (Permits from Director, Game & Fisheries at Srinagar). Great variety is to be found, the rivers ranging from foaming torrents, when spinning is permitted, to gentle streams suitable for dry fly. There are 'fly only' beats. The most suitable flies are those usually included in every angler's selection, but in Kashmir they are usually dressed on hook sizes between No. 9 and No. 5 (old sizes). The season lasts from May to September. The major trout waters in Kashmir are as follows: **River Sindh**, flows along main Srinagar highway. Wide and shallow in places, upper beats are deep and narrow. Fishing early or late in the day is recommended; **River Lidder**, originates north of Pahalgam, and has two major tributaries, the **Aru** and the **Sheshnag**. excellent trout fishing, also for 'chush', a local species of bartel (inedible). Pahalgam is a convenient base for the system; **River Bringhi**, runs along the Anatnag-Dakshum road, beyond Acchabal. Narrow and boulder strewn, it has always been a great favourite with anglers. Three tributaries are the Dyus, Naubaug, and the Alhan. **Kokernag** and **Verinag** streams, springfed waters in the Kashmir valley, have easily accessible bank fishing, with good sized brown trout. There are a number of high altitude lakes in the north of the valley, well stocked with large brown trout. The average size of these waters is around 3000 sq meters, and they are only approachable by three-day treks, with camping necessary. Amongst these are lakes **Tarsar, Marsar,** approached from Pahalgam; **Kishensar, Vishensar, Gadsar** and **Gangabal**, approachable from Sonmarg, Gund or Nichnai.

India's rivers contain numerous other species. The **Jamuna** at **Okhla**, in **Delhi**, for instance, holds no fewer than eight species, including heavy catfish, the silund - a predator running up to 50lbs, which can be taken on a spinner - and a humpbacked fish called the cheetul or moh, which will be seen constantly rising to the surface and turning over broadside. There is also plenty of huge carp in the slow-flowing rivers and the lakes and tanks. The sea fishing can be excellent, too, but is dependent upon seasonal migrations and the weather. A considerable body of angling literature has now been published by the **Bombay Natural History Society, 114 Apollo Street**.

While the tourist-angler should not expect to find luxurious cabins on his expeditions, numerous camping-sites and comfortable rest-houses have been provided, often in the most beautiful surroundings and at **Corbett**, the call of the tiger and the trumpeting of wild elephants may sometimes be heard.

So far as tackle is concerned, the trout or mahseer fisherman will be specially well catered for at **Srinagar**, capital of Kashmir, where he may obtain first-class gear, but rates are rising due to restricted imports, and it is preferable to take one's own equipment.

Further information from the **Goverment of India Tourist Office, 7 Cork Street, London W1S 2LM** (tel: 020 7437 3677).

SRI LANKA (CEYLON)

Nuwara Eliya is the best centre for trout fishing. As it is above the 6,000ft level, the climate is temperate. There is good hotel accommodation. The fishing is, with few exceptions, restricted to fly only and most common patterns of wet fly are successful. Dry fly is rarely used, there being little natural fly. There is no statutory close season, though the club imposes one in parts following restocking. Size limits vary from 8in to 15in.

The main waters are: **Nuwara Eliya** stream (flows through the golf course and park); **Ambawela** stream (8m from Nuwara Eliya; jungle and grassland); **Bulu Ella** stream (2½m jungle); **Portswood Dam** (4m; tea estate); **Agra Oya** and **Gorge Valley** rivers (10-15m; tea estates), and the magnificently spectacular **Horton Plains** stream (30m; jungle and grassland, Nature reserve). Motor transport can be hired. On any of these waters it is possible to maintain an average of 1lb and several fish over 3lbs are caught.

Trout fishing is now controlled by the Nuwara Eliya District Fishing Club. Stocking has so far been carried out in Portswood Dam, the Horton Plains, Agra Oya and Gorge Valley. For licences application should be made to the **Honourary Secretary, Nuwara Eliya District Fishing Club, Court Lodge Estate, Kandapola**. Visitors are advised to bring their tackle as fly tackle is scarce in Sri Lanka.

The two main species of indigenous sporting fish in Sri Lanka are the mahseer and the walaya (freshwater shark), found in the jungle rivers of the Low Country, particularly the **Mahawehi**, the upper reaches of the **Kelani** and the **Amban Ganga**. Ceylon mahseer, though small compared with those in some Indian rivers, provide good sport, but fishing for them can be somewhat difficult. Fishing for indigenous sporting fish in Sri Lanka is free. With a shoreline of 1,140 miles and a continental shelf of 10,000 square miles, the seas around Sri Lanka have an unlimited fishing potential hardly exploited.

The outfalls of 103 major river basins and hundreds of other estuaries, lagoons and coastal lakes all round the island are the most popular spots frequented by local surf casters as well as bait fishermen. Many varieties of game fish of the Carangid family, locally called paraw and know elsewhere as trevally, horse mackerel, etc, are taken. These swift and powerful carnivorous fish attain a length of 5ft and a weight of 150lbs. The schooling habits of the caranx, their keen eyesight and some built-in sensory mechanism make them congregate in estuaries immediately after monsoons and rains.

Next in popularity among surf-casters come the barracuda and Spanish mackerel. Both these species of voracious predatory fish attain lengths of 6ft as do other species known locally as 'giant perch', 'threadfins' and 'tassel fish' which frequent the estuaries.

Trolling over the continental shelf yields catches of tuna ranging from the 2-3ft skipjack to the 6ft yellowfin and bluefin, the acrobatic dolphin, swordfish and marlin which attain a size to provide a challenge to the best big game fishermen of any country. The broadbill swordfish found in deeper waters reach a length of 15ft and a weight of well over 1,000lbs. Though reaching only 10ft and 250lbs, the sailfish compensate for their smaller size by their remarkable agility.

The monsoons regulate the fishing in Sri Lanka Seas. The western and southern coasts are favoured during the North-East monsoon (from October to April) and the east coast during the South-West monsoon (from May to September).

Further information can be obtained from **London Director, Sri Lanka (Ceylon) Tourist Board, Clareville House, 26/27 Oxendon Street London SW1Y 4EL** (tel: 020 7930 2627; fax: 020 7930 9070; web: www.srilankatourism.org; e-mail: srilankatourism@aol.com).

MALAYSIA

There is good sport in the jungle-covered highlands where fast-flowing, clean streams will delight the eye. These are well stocked with cyprinids or members of the carp family, which include the well-known mahseer of India, known locally as kelah. This group of which the most common species are kelah (up to 20lbs), sebarau (up to 12lbs), and kejor or tengas (up to 8lbs), are sporting fish which fight well when hooked. Kelah and tengas are good to eat. They are best when curried and provide a good change or diet in the jungle when living on operational 24-hour pack rations.

All these fish will take an artificial bait; the most popular being a 1in or 1½in silver or silver/copper spoon. A normal salmon spinning outfit is ideal. For those who prefer it, a fixed-spool reel can be used provided it will hold sufficient line. Owing to the crushing power of the jaws of the kelah, extra strong treble or large single hooks should be used and some people recommend the use of a 2ft wire trace.

Taman Negara, on the borders of **Kelantan, Trengganu** and **Pahang,** provides the best fishing, and a visit to the HQ at **Kuala Tahan** is well worth the journey. It may be reached by rail to **Kuala Tembeling** and thence by water, in long, narrow, locally-built boats fitted with 40hp outboard motors which can do the journey up the **Sungaï Tembeling** in three to four hours depending on the condition of the river. At Kuala Tahan there are bungalows and chalets providing full board. A number of visitors' lodges and halting bungalows have been built throughout the park so the fishermen can stay near the river they are fishing.

From Kuala Tahan all onward movement is by smaller boats with lower-powered engines to negotiate the shallower rivers, such as the Tahan itself. There are many large pools well stocked with fish in the lower reaches, and above the **Lata Berkoh** barrier many pools and rapids, all excellent fishing water. Malay and Aborigine boatmen are happy to act as guides and are delightful companions.

It is easier and pleasanter to cast from the bank, but this will necessitate some wading where the bank is steep and overhung by the jungle. The water is pleasantly warm and waders would be far too hot to wear. Those with a good sense of balance can try fishing from a slowly paddled perahu, but as this is only a shell at the most 2ft wide, it is liable to be something of a circus act.

Most reliable times to fish are the months February/March and July/August, because in other months fishing will be spasmodic owing to the heavy rainfall. Spates and floodwater so colour the rivers that fishing is a waste of time.

In **Terengganu State** is the massive **Kenyir Lake,** a well known attraction to visiting anglers, where baung, toman, sebarau, kelah, kelisa (arowana) can be caught, and houseboat holidays are organised: for information contact **Kenyir Lake Resort, Kenyir Dam, Hulu Terengganu** (tel: +9 950609), for **Kenyir Dam** area.

Apart from the fishing there is always the chance of seeing the wild animals of Malaysia at the many salt licks. There are usually monkeys, monitor lizard, snakes and flying foxes to be seen, as well as many varieties of birds such as hornbill eagle and kingfishers.

The **Kelah Fish Sanctuary** is situated at the **Tahan River,** in the heart of Taman Negara which offers a guided fishing experience in one of the world's oldest tropical rainforests. Contact **CRRC** (Centre for Research on Sustainable Conservation), Suite 137, 1st Floor, Complex Eureka, Universiti Sains Malaysia, 11800 USM Penang (tel: +604 658 8979); Anjung Kelah, Taman Negara, Kyuala Tahan, Pahang (tel: +609 266 4527).

Intending visitors should write well before the date of their visit, giving as much information as possible on their special interests to the **Director-General, Dept of Wildlife and National Parks, KM10, Jalan Cheras, 56100 Kuala Lumpur, Malaysia** (tel: +3 907 52872; fax: +3 907 52873; web: www.wildlife.gov.my; e-mail: pakp@wildlife.gov.my) so as to enable the Dept of Wildlife & National Parks to plan their itineraries or contact **Malaysia Tourism Promotion Board, 57 Trafalgar Square, London WC2N 5DU** (tel: 020 7930 7932).

FISHING IN NORTH AMERICA

CANADA

On the Atlantic side of Canada there are plenty of salmon rivers in **Québec** and **New Brunswick**, and a good deal of fishing is open to the non-resident who takes out the appropriate provincial licence. There is a great deal of splendid trout fishing in many of the inland lakes and rivers, while in the **Great Lakes** region there are big muskellunge, and fine black bass fishing in various waters. The land-locked salmon is found in Québec, both in the tributaries and discharge of **Lac St John**, and in some lakes in **Nova Scotia**, such as **Grand Lake** and **Beaver Bank Lake**. The 'trout' of this side of Canada are char *(Salvelinus fontinalis)*, while some of them are migratory and become 'sea trout'. In the lakes are 'grey trout', some of which reach a great size. There are also char *(Salvelinus namaycush)* in the Arctic.

On the other side of Canada, British Columbia offers splendid opportunities of sport with Pacific salmon, steelhead and rainbow trout. Fishing for Pacific salmon has until recently been considered of necessity a matter for tidal waters. The **Campbell River, Vancouver Island,** has been the most favoured, and there quinnat (now known locally as tyee) up to 70lbs have been caught on the troll. At **Prince Rupert** a 93lbs quinnat was caught on a spoon in 1929 by Mr O P Smith, a professional fisherman. An 82lbs tyee was caught in August, 1951, at **Rivers Inlet**. The coho has been caught on fly, also in tidal waters. Of late years it has become clear that quinnat will take in fresh water in certain conditions. To the far north there are evident possibilities of sport in **Yukon** and NW Territories.

So far as tackle is concerned, the trend is towards lighter outfits. Brook trout, for instance, are almost universally taken on a nine-foot, five-ounce fly rod, and many anglers use the same rod for steelhead or Kamloops trout, although this is probably foolhardy. Tackle should always be carefully geared to the area and quarry, and on-the-spot advice is desirable.

Much work is done by the Federal and Provincial hatcheries, and waters in various parts of Canada are supplied with fry of species suitable to their needs, chiefly salmonidae, but also bass and other kinds of the best big game fishing so far discovered anywhere.

Throughout Canada there are many regulations controlling all aspects of freshwater fishing, which vary from one province to another. Information on these laws is readily obtainable from a large number of public outlets.

Note: The Canadian Tourist Office has provincial brochures and general information relevant to fishing in the country. For further information please contact **Visit Canada, P O Box 170, Ashford, Kent TN24 0ZX** (tel: 0906 871 5000 (Premium Rate at all times); email: visitcan ada@dial.pipex.com).

ALBERTA. Alberta is fortunate in having more than 4,000 miles of good fishing streams and more than 1,000 lakes found in the mountains, foothills and prairies, and in the boreal forests of the northern region of the province.

There are 18 species of sportfish in Alberta of which there are 9 cold water and 9 warm water sportfish. The cold water sportfish include brook, brown, cutthroat, golden, rainbow, and lake trout, bull trout, Arctic grayling and mountain whitefish. These fish are generally found in the lakes and streams in the foothills and mountain areas in the west of the province.

The warm water sportfish include lake whitefish, walleye, perch, pike, goldeye, and lake sturgeon. These fish are generally found in rivers and lakes throughout the south east and northern areas of the province.

Since the 1960s, the numbers of anglers fishing in Alberta has increased dramatically from 150,000 to peak nearly 350,000 in 1986. Subsequently, the numbers of anglers has declined and stabilised at between 225-250,000. Perch, pike, walleye, trout, and lake whitefish are the most widely taken fish, accounting for 95% of total harvest but pike fishing is predominant. Fewer than half Alberta's lakes can produce game fish, owing to a short summer season when warm water temperatures produce sufficient aquatic insects, plants, and other food, and the supply of fish is supplemented by stocking. Hatchery production of 3.5 million trout are stocked annually throughout the province into lakes that do not contain native fish and which are readily accessible to the public.

As throughout Canada, there are many fishing regulations, which the angler must know before setting out. Licences are obligatory, and obtainable in most retail sports outfitters. Prices are as follows: Youths (under 16), none required. Non residents annual, C$60; limited (5 day), C$40; C$22 (1 day).

Further information may be obtained by writing to **Alberta Sustainable Resource Development, Fisheries & Wildlife Division, 2nd Floor, Great West Life Building, 9915-108 Street, Edmonton, AB T5K 2G8.**

BRITISH COLUMBIA. The province has a coastline (including islands) of 27,000 km and is drained by innumerable rivers and freshwater lakes. The game fish of British Columbia comprise five species of salmon: sockeye, chum, chinook or spring (large specimens often referred to as 'Tyee'), pink (tidal waters only), and coho, which may be taken with the fly, but are more easily caught by trolling; all varieties of Pacific Coast trout, particularly steelhead, rainbow, and cut-throat; Arctic grayling; two species of char, of which the more common is Dolly Varden; and Eastern brook trout which has been introduced.

Some of the most important freshwater fishing areas are **Kootenay District, Okanagan District** (including **Beaver, Bear, Dee, Ideal, Mabel, Sugar, South** and **Woods Lakes**), **Kamloops District** (including **Adams, East Barriere, Murtle, Shuswap** and **Nicola Lakes**), **Cariboo District** (including **Quesnel, Horsefly** and **Canim Lakes,** and **Fraser** and **Thompson Rivers**), and **Merrit District**, which abounds with small productive, accessible lakes, such as **Chataway, Dot, Gypsum, Antler, Corbett, Peter Hope** and **Roche Lakes**. Most of the southern lakes and rivers are easily accessible, especially by car, and yield excellent fishing. Flying in to the less accessible waters is now a common practice. Lodges, cabins and boats are abundant.

The **Skeena Region** of northwest **British Columbia** has a wide variety of attractive fisheries. The **Burns Lake** area boasts a number of great trout fishing lakes, and **Terrace** is the centre of exceptional sport fishing for steelhead trout and chinook and coho salmon. Some restrictions apply on certain steelhead waters as conservation is a priority. Information may be obtained from the Victoria address below.

Vancouver Island offers excellent cut-throat trout and steelhead fishing. The important waters are **Cowichan, Cameron** and **Sproat Lakes, Alberni** and **Qualicum Districts** and the **Campbell River** area. Steelhead trout are in **Sproat, Somass, Ash** and **Stamp Rivers,** to name but a few. Chinook (or spring) salmon and coho are found in good quantities in many of the main rivers and streams draining into the Pacific Ocean. On Vancouver Island there is splendid salmon fishing in tidal water to be had near the following cities: **Campbell River, Comox, Nanaimo, Gold River, Port Alberni, Tofino, Ucluelet** and **Victoria.** On the mainland excellent fishing for salmon is to be found within 20 minutes drive from downtown Vancouver. Other famous salmon fishing locations include: **Pender Harbour, Powell River, Hakai Pass, Rivers Kitimat, Prince Rupert** and the **Queen Charlotte Islands,** including Langara Island. For the sea angler, charter boats operate from Prince Rupert Island, and halibut are plentifully found, among other species.

Salmon conservation: a salmon conservation stamp must be purchased before fishing (*see below*). Due to conditions which are subject to change at short notice, it is no longer possible to publish daily limits or size limits for any of the five species of salmon. Before fishing contact nearest DFO office or phone (tel: 604 666 6331).

Licences are obligatory, and obtainable in most retail sports outfitters. For freshwater licence fees, prices are as follows: Non resident aliens annual, $58.85; 8 day, $32.10; one day, $16.05; and subject to change. Conservation surcharge stamps for fishing steelhead, $42.80; salmon, $21.40. For angling in BC tidal waters, the annual non-resident fee is $108.07; 5 day $34.17; 3 day $20.33, 1 day $7.49. To fish for salmon in tidal waters, a stamp costing $6.42 is obligatory.

Further information (including details of licence charges and open seasons) can be had from the **Fisheries Management Branch, Ministry of Water, Land and Air Protection, P.O.**

Box 9363, Stn Prov Govt, Victoria, BC V8W 9M2 (tel: +1 250 356-7285; web: www.bcfisheries.gov.bc.ca) for freshwater fishing for species other than salmon; and **Department of Fisheries and Oceans Canada, Suite #400, 555 W. Hastings St, Vancouver, B.C. V6B 5G3,** for saltwater fishing and salmon in freshwater (web: www.pac.dfo-mpo.gc.ca). For travel information, contact **British Columbia Tourism, British Colombia House, Regent St, London SW1Y 4NR** (tel: 020 7930 6857) or write to **Tourism British Columbia, Box 9830 Stn. Prov. Govt. #300-1803 Douglas Street, Victoria BC, V8W 9W5** (tel: +1 250 356 6363). (For fishing resort information: www.bcfroa.bc.ca).

MANITOBA. Manitoba is at the centre of a country more than 4,500 miles wide, from **St John's, Newfoundland** on the east to **Victoria, British Columbia** on the west.

The province is enormous by British standards, covering 250,000 square miles and measuring 735 air miles from north to south. Lake Winnipeg, 40 miles north of the capital city of **Winnipeg,** is the seventh largest inland body of freshwater in North America. The northern three-fifths of the province is laced with innumerable streams and rivers, and someone claims to have counted more than 100,000 lakes, although many are too small to even appear on a map.

The species most commonly fished are walleye, pike, channel catfish, lake trout, rainbow trout, brook (speckled) trout, arctic grayling, whitefish, smallmouth bass, lake sturgeon, goldeye (superior to eat, smoked), and carp. Trout fishing is some of the finest in North America, in particular, the **Knife** and **Gods Rivers** in north-eastern Manitoba are famous for trophy-sized brook and lake trout, northern pike and walleye. Lake trout *(Cristivomer namaycush)* are widely distributed from the south-eastern area of the province through to the northern boundaries in the deep, cold-water lakes of the Pre-Cambrian shield. Specimens over 35lbs are taken each year.

The Arctic grayling *(Thymallus arcticus)* is common along the north-western coast of Hudson Bay and its tributary streams, which include the **North Knife, Seal, Little Seal** and **Wolverine Rivers.** With its spectacular beauty, it is the delight of those fly-fishermen who are able to travel to the Churchill area or the fly-in areas of **Big Sand, Knee, Nueltin** or **Nejanilini Lakes** in the far North.

Other fish. In the smaller lakes and streams in the southern part of the province, walleye, northern pike and yellow perch are plentiful. In **Lake Winnipeg** and the tributary **Red River,** carp and channel catfish to 30lbs are taken in large numbers at certain seasons. **Winnipeg River** is the locale for large walleye, and great northern pike, together with an abundance of smallmouth bass, which provide excellent sport.

Large numbers of lakes throughout the province are stocked for trout fishing. As elsewhere in Canada, ice fishing is a popular winter sport, often with shelters. Holiday sport is well organised, with many fishing lodges offering packages with accommodation and other facilities.

Licences are required, and obtainable in most retail sports outfitters. Prices are as follows: Non residents annual, $40, regular; $22 conservation. There are many fishing regulations in Manitoba, including a complete ban on barbed hooks, prohibition of open fires from 1 Apr to 15 Nov, and bait restrictions, including the number of live baits permissable. Anglers should know all details before starting out. Fishing in the province is governed by Manitoba Conservation Offices, Head Office, 200 Saulteaux Crescent, Winnipeg, Manitoba, R3J 3W3 (tel: 204 945 6784) which has six other regional offices.

Further information (including details of licence charges and open seasons) can be had from **Travel Manitoba, Department RX2, 7th Floor, 155 Carlton Street, Winnipeg, Manitoba R3C 3H8** (tel: +1 204 945-3777, extn RX2; fax: +1 204 945-2302; web: www.travelmani toba.com).

NEW BRUNSWICK. Atlantic salmon in the **Restigouche, Nepisiquit, Tabusintac, North-West Miramichi, South-West Miramichi, Little South-West Miramichi, Sevogle, Renous, Dungarvon, Cains** rivers. Salmon run large, particularly in the Restigouche, where fish from 30-40lbs are taken each year, and occasionally larger. Other rivers include **Rocky Brook, Clearwater Brook, St John River, Nashwaak** and **Tobique** rivers. New Brunswick rivers usually yield over 30,000 fish each season. Conservation methods such as hook and release are used, to ensure future stocks, and fishing is fly only. Non-residents are required to employ a guide while fishing for Atlantic salmon or any other species on Atlantic salmon waters. Only grilse, fish less than 63cm in fork length, are allowed to be retained. The season varies from river to river, but generally runs from 16 May to 15 Oct. Licences are required, and obtainable from most outfitters. Seasonal prices range from C$149.50 per season to C$40.25 for 3 days, covering all species. Non-residents licences for all species except Atlantic salmon range cost C$57.50 per season to C$23.00 for 3 consecutive days. (Updated information on angling regulations and licence information can be viewed on the website below.)

In addition to salmon fishing, there is fishing for small-mouth bass in the south-west of the province. Several waters yield good-sized fish, and these are considered to be some of the best bass resources in North America. Other popular angling pursuits include spring Atlantic salmon, brook trout and land locked salmon. On the seashore, jigging for cod, casting for mackerel, and deepsea fishing are possible at some locations along the coast. Angling for striped bass occurs in the St John River and Bathhurst Harbour.

Non-resident licences must be obtained from a DNR or Service New Brunswick office in the province. These must be carried by the holder at all times, but do not convey right of fishing on Crown Reserve Waters or any private fishery without the consent of the lessee or owner. Further information, including details of licences and open seasons, can be had from the **Department of Natural Resources, Fish & Wildlife Branch, PO Box 6000, Fredericton NB E3B 5H1** (tel: +1 506 453 2440; fax: +1 506 453 6699; web: www.gnb.ca/0078/fw/ang ling/summary.asp). Outfitters may be contacted via **Business New Brunswick, 5th Floor, 620 Kings Street, Fredericton NB E3B 5H1.**

NEWFOUNDLAND and LABRADOR. Newfoundland and Labrador, Canada, has probably some of the best game-fishing in North America. Almost a quarter of the province's area is water, and its many fine wild Atlantic salmon rivers flow through unspoiled forest and hill country. Fishable waterways vary from wide and roaring rivers to intimate brooks tumbling down from highland plateaus; the **Sandhill River**, the famous **Eagle River**, the **Flowers River, Gander River**, the **Exploits River** and the **Humber River** to name but a few. Newfoundland and Labrador is home to nearly two-thirds of North America's Atlantic salmon rivers - more than two hundred rivers, some with annual runs in excess of 20,000 wild fish. Anglers can fish everything from Trophy Brook trout and land-locked salmon (Oua-naniche) to wilder cousins such as lake trout, northern pike and arctic char. Eastern brook trout can run in excess of 9 lbs. and Arctic char approaching 20lbs have been caught. Sea-run brown trout streams in the province are mainly concentrated along a 100-kilometre coastal area immediately south of St. John's, the capital city; where fish over 20lbs have been taken. Scheduled (licensed) rainbow trout waters comprise a small group of steams and ponds immediately north of St. John's; rainbows are also frequently caught in unscheduled water throughout the province. All the trout except the brown trout are as plentiful (and on average significantly larger) in Labrador where most angling waters are much more remote than that on the Island portion of the province.

The salmon season varies among groups of rivers and from year to year, ranging from early June to mid-September, with most rivers open from mid-June to the first week in September, fishing is restricted to fly only. Scheduled rainbow trout waters are open from late May-early June to mid-September. The province has scheduled salmon rivers on the Island of Newfoundland and in Labrador, and scheduled rainbow trout streams.

Fishing in all inland waters in the province is restricted to rod, hook, and line, with a variety of baits and lures permissable in most unscheduled waters; angling in scheduled salmon rivers is further restricted to fly fishing only. The province has scheduled salmon rivers on the Island of Newfoundland and in Labrador, and scheduled rainbow trout streams. Fishing in all inland waters in the province is restricted to rod, hook, and line, with a variety of baits and lures permissible on most unscheduled waters. Angling on scheduled salmon rivers is restricted to fly fishing only, using barbless hooks. There are bag limits in force which vary, depending on a river's classification; on Class 1 rivers, 6 salmon may be retained; on Class 2 rivers, which are the large majority, 4 fish; on Class 3 rivers, 2 fish; on Class 4 rivers, catch and release only. Current regulations require that a non-resident must either be accompanied by a resident relative, a licensed guide or in parts of Labrador, engage the services of an outfitter.

Annual licence-fees for non-residents are as follows. Salmon: $C53, $78 family; Trout $C8 $C13 family. Special licences are required to fish inland waters within the boundaries of National Parks and anglers should consult with park officials regarding their fishing regulations. Salmon and trout angling licences are obtainable at most sporting goods shops, outfitters, tackle and hardware shops and some department stores. Further information on non-resident angling is available from **Department of Tourism, Culture and Recreation, Tourism Division, P.O. Box 8700, St. John's, Newfoundland, Canada A1B 4J6** (tel:1-800 563 6353); fax: +1 709 729 0870, or from **Department of Fisheries & Oceans, Communications Division, P.O. Box 5667, St. John's, Newfoundland** (tel: +1 709 772 4421). For a listing of fishing outfitters, go to the Newfoundland and Labrador Outfitters Association website at www.nloa.ca

NOVA SCOTIA (including **Cape Breton Island**). Atlantic salmon in some rivers continue to have good runs of salmon but stock status, water levels and conditions are a major factor in the annual take. There are 16 rivers scheduled and posted for fly fishing only, but it should be noted Atlantic salmon may only be taken by fly; brook trout are common in streams and lakes, many of which are accessible from woods roads known as roads to resources; sea trout (brook and brown) in most tidal streams in the Northern and Eastern part of the province.

For the saltwater angler the province has 4,625 miles of shore, and over one hundred harbours and marinas dotted around the coast, mainly in areas of Victoria, Cape Breton, Richmond, Halifax, Lunenbourg, Yarmouth, Pictou, Antigonish, and Inverness. Species taken are cod, pollack, haddock, striped bass, flatfish, and from boats, bluefish, blue shark, tuna, dogfish, etc. Charter boats are hired for ground fishing in all areas except the upper reaches of the **Bay of Fundy**. Tuna charter boats operate in the **St George's Bay** and Halifax areas. Licence-fees for non-residents are as follows: salmon: C$120.75 season, C$46 7 day; trout C$46, C$23 7 day.

For further information on travelling to and around Nova Scotia, please contact **Nova Scotia Tourism & Culture, PO Box 456, Halifax, NS, B3J 2R5** (tel: +1 902 424 5000; fax: +1 902 424 2668; web: www.novascotia.com); **Nova Scotia Salmon Association, P O Box 523, Halifax NS B3J 2R1** (web: www.novascotiasalmon.ns.ca; e-mail: nssa@ns.sympatico.ca); **Department of Fisheries and Oceans (Federal), 133 Church Street, Antigonish Mall, Antigonish, NS, B2G 2E3,** (tel: +1 902 863 5670); **Nova Scotia Department of Agriculture & Fisheries, Inland Fisheries Division, P O Box 700, Pictou, NS B0K 1H0** (tel: +1 902 485 5056; fax: +1 902 485 4014; web: www.gov.ns.ca/nsaf); **Fisheries & Oceans Canada, Box 1035, Dartmouth, NS, B2Y 4T3** (tel: +1 902 426 5433; fax: +1 902 426 9683; web: www.sportfishingcanada.ca).

ONTARIO.

With over 250,000 inland lakes, thousands of streams and rivers, and shorelines on four of the five Great Lakes, Ontario offers a wide diversity of angling opportunities. Although probably best known for its trophy muskellunge waters and highly sought walleye (pickerel) fisheries, Ontario is home to an astounding 158 of Canada's 228 species of freshwater fish.

Brook Trout: Ontario boasts more than 2,100 inland lakes and at least 1,700 streams and rivers which support brook trout. Some of the more popular areas for brook trout anglers include the **Lake Nipigon** watershed, the Algoma area of northeastern Ontario, and the southcentral Ontario highlands including **Algonquin Park** and the **Muskoka lakes** area. In addition to these native populations, Ontario has an active brook trout stocking program comprised of approximately 1.3-1.4 million fish being released annually. The world record brook trout (14.5lbs, 6.6kg) was caught in the **Nipigon River** . A colour variant of the brook trout, known as the Aurora trout, is found in several northeastern Ontario lakes which are open to provide limited angling opportunities. Included among the many other waters are the **Haliburton** and **Hastings** highlands and the **Magnetawan** area; farther south and west, some streams tributary to **Lakes Huron, Erie, Ontario** and **Georgian Bay**. Lying between the eastern and western areas of northern Ontario there are numerous brook trout waters, among which are the **Sudbury, Manitoulin, Sault, Michipicoten, Mississauga, Gogama, Chapleau, Missinabi-White River-Franz, Elsas, Oba, Hornepayne, Hearst, Kapuskasing, Nakina** and **Albany** River areas.

Bass: largemouth and smallmouth bass are among the most popular sport fish species in Ontario with largemouth bass primarily in the southern portion of the province (south of the French River); smallmouth bass are more broadly distributed across the province. The Ontario record largemouth bass was a fish weighing 10.4lbs (4.7 kg) while the current record for smallmouth bass is 9.8lbs (4.5kg). Most bass angled from Ontario waters would average between 1-3lbs (0.5-1.4kg) however. Some popular bass areas include **Long Point Bay (Lake Erie), Rideau lakes** in southeastern Ontario, the **Trent-Severn** waterway and **Kawartha lakes** of southcentral Ontario, and **Lake of the Woods** in northwestern Ontario. Other areas include **Haliburton Lake District, Muskoka lakes, Lake Nipissing**, the **French** and **Pickerel rivers**, and the Georgian Bay District areas. In the north-west section of Ontario bass are found in $IQuetico Provincial Park**Quetico Provincial Park**.

Muskellunge and Northern Pike : two closely related species, are common in Ontario waters. Northern pike are distributed across the province while muskellunge are concentrated in the northwestern and southcentral portions of Ontario. There are waters which are managed to provide trophy fisheries for each species and there are many other waters where opportunities exist to catch numerous, but smaller, fish. Some of the world class muskellunge waters include **Georgian Bay**, the mouth of the *Moon River*, the **Lake of the Woods**, Lac Seul, Ottawa and **St. Lawrence Rivers**, and **Eagle Lake**. The Ontario record muskellunge was a 65lb (29.5kg) fish angled from Georgian Bay. The **Kawartha lakes**, and many smaller lakes in northwestern Ontario, provide popular muskellunge fisheries. Trophy northern pike are found in many remote northern Ontario lakes while many other waters across the province provide good angling for pike.

Carp: rapidly becoming more popular in Ontario, particularly among non-resident anglers from Europe, they achieve weights of up to 35-50lbs (15.8-22.7kg) but are more commonly in the 10-20lbs (4.5-9.0 kg) range. There is a year-round season for carp in Ontario, and some of the more popular waters for carp angling include Lake Erie, the **Bay of Quinte**, the **Trent-Severn** and **Rideau** canal systems, and the **Long Sault Parkway** portion of the St. Lawrence River.

Rainbow Trout and Brown Trout: while neither rainbow trout nor brown trout are native to Ontario, both have been introduced and have successfully established self-sustaining populations throughout the Great Lakes and their tributary streams. Rainbow trout fishing is booming in southern Georgian Bay especially in the **Owen Sound-Collingwood** area and is popular in many tributaries along the north shore of Lake Ontario in the **Port Hope** area.. Rainbow trout fishing is best either in the spring or fall; brown trout are found in nearshore areas of the Great Lakes and can easily be caught fishing from shore. Once again, Lake Ontario and Lake Huron provide the best fishing locations. The province of Ontario stocks approximately 7-800,000 brown trout annually. There are designated areas (river mouths) which have extended angling seasons for these two species. Many southwestern Ontario streams also provide excellent fly fishing opportunities for stream-resident brown trout.

Pacific Salmon: three species of Pacific salmon (coho, chinook and pink) have been successfully introduced into the Great Lakes. Open water angling for chinook salmon is best in mid-late summer; chinook salmon have reached sizes up to 45lbs (20.4kg) but are more commonly in the 10-20lbs (4.5-9.0kg) range. **Lakes Ontario** *(Port Credit-Niagara area)* and **Huron** provide the best chinook salmon fisheries in Ontario. Coho salmon are stocked in Lake Ontario and provide some good fall angling opportunities in several tributary streams. Pink salmon are most common in Lake Superior and the North Channel of Lake Huron and are most readily fished in the fall.

Splake: a cross between lake trout and brook trout (speckled trout), approximately 800,000 splake are stocked annually into inland lakes across the province to provide recreational angling opportunities. They are relatively easy to catch and are delicious to eat. There is good splake fishing at **Owen Sound, Parry Sound** and at **Providence Bay** on **Manitoulin Island**.

Walleye: without doubt, the most highly sought fish in Ontario. There are well over 4,000 lakes and hundreds of rivers which contain walleye. Some of the more popular angling locations for walleye include the **Bay Quinte** (Lake Ontario), **Kesagami Lake, Lake Nipissing, Lac des Milles Lakes**, Lake Erie, and Lake of the Woods. There are many remote (fly-in) angling opportunities particularly in northwestern Ontario. Walleye are angled during the open water season and also during the winter (ice) fishery, and are highly prized as a food fish. The Ontario record walleye was a fish weighing 22.3lbs (10.1 kg) but most angled walleye are in the 1-2 pound (0.5-1.0 kg) range. A close relative of the walleye - sauger - is known to occur in over 200 Ontario waters and are most common in northwestern Ontario.

Lake Trout: are found in more than 2,300 Ontario lakes and is highly prized by anglers and esteemed as a food fish. Lake trout live in deep cold lakes scattered across the **Precambrian Shield** and may be caught in nearshore waters in the spring, in deep waters during the summer, and through the ice in the winter. Some popular lake trout fisheries include **Lake Nipigon, Lake Superior, Lake Simcoe, Lake Ontario**, and **Lake Temagami**. Ontario stocks almost 5 million lake trout on an annual basis into various inland lakes as well as the Great Lakes.

Other Species: There are many other popular sport fish species in Ontario, which include lake whitefish, channel catfish, black crappies, bluegill and pumpkinseed (panfish), and bullheads. Information on angling locations for these species can be obtained by contacting the Ontario Ministry of Natural Resources.

There are more than 500 fish and game associations in the province, many of which are affiliated with the **Ontario Federation of Anglers and Hunters, P O Box 2800, Peterborough, Ontario K9J 8L5**. Other notable organizations include **Trout Unlimited, Muskies Canada Inc.**, and the **Ontario Federation of Fly Fishers**. For angling information, inquires about non-resident fishing regulations, or to obtain a copy of the annual summary of fishing regulations, write to the **Ontario Ministry of Natural Resources Information Center, P O Box 7000, 300 Water Street, Peterborough, Ontario, Canada K9J 8M5** (tel: +1 705 755 2000; fax: +1 705 755 1677; web: www.mnr.gov.on.ca/MNR/fishing).

PRINCE EDWARD ISLAND. This island, which lies in the Gulf of St Lawrence off the north coast of **Nova Scotia**, has an enviable reputation for its speckled trout fishing. The streams and rivers are spring fed, and the whole province may be considered a natural hatchery for trout and salmon. The salmon fishing, however, is not first class, and the best runs, with the exception of early runs on the **Morell** and **Trout Rivers**, do not begin until towards the end of the season. Both non-migratory and migratory trout are to be caught. Fishing for rainbow trout can be had in **Glenfinnan**, and **O'Keefe's Lakes**. Noted trout streams are the **West, Morell, Trout** and **Dunk** rivers, and large freshwater dams also afford good sport. Many estuaries contain white perch, and a few are home of the striped bass. During late summer and autumn, mackerel and smelt fishing is popular. There are bag limits of 10 trout per day, not more than 5 being rainbow, and one grilse per day, 7 per season. Salmon greater than 63 cm or less than 30 cm must be returned alive and unharmed. Trout season is from 15 April to 15 Sept. Salmon season on the Morell River begins 1 June and runs to 31 Oct. Salmon season is also extended to Oct 31 on certain stretches of Rivers Midgell, Naufrage, Valleyfield, West, Dunk, Mill. Rainbow trout season on Glenfinnan and O'Keefe's lakes, April 15 to November 15. Non-residents trout day licences cost $6.51 + GST, Atlantic salmon licence $9.35 + GST, obtainable from sports outfitters or from Department of Environment.

Further information may be obtained from the **Tourism PEI, PO Box 940, Charlottetown, PEI, Canada C1A 7M5** (website: www.peiplay.com) and **Department of Environment, Conservation & Management Division, PO Box 2000, Charlottetown, PEI, C1A 7N8** (tel: + 902 368 4683).

QUÉBEC. Stretching over a vast expanse of territory, Québec boasts more than one million rivers and lakes. These waters teeming with fish offer the possibility of catching various species, including Northern pike, walleye, brook trout, Arctic char, landlocked salmon, lake trout, Atlantic salmon and bass. However, to fish in parks, wildlife reserves and ZECs (controlled zones), certain specific conditions apply over and above the general rules. In most parks and wildlife reserves, a reservation is required, and, just as for the ZECs, a right of access is emitted. Private firms offer outfitting services in Québec, including accommodation. Some hold exclusive fishing rights in specific areas. In Northern Québec, a right of access must be obtained from the Native authorities in question (Cree, Inuit, Naskapi) in order to fish in certain waters. On land under Inuit jurisdiction, fishermen must be accompanied by an Inuit guide. Any non-residents wishing to fish north of the 52nd parallel must use the services of an outfitter. Licence fees vary tremendously, depending on where and what is being fished for.

The **Société de la Faune et des Parcs du Québec (FAPAQ)** determines the rules governing recreational fishing. Three free brochures on them, *Sportfishing in Québec; Main Regulations;* and *Salmon Sportfishing in Québec - Main Regulations,* may be obtained from Société de la Faune et des Parcs du Québec, Édifice Marie-Guyart, 675 boul. René-Lévesque Est, Boîte 88, Québec (Québec) G1R 5V7. (tel: +1 418 521-3830 or 1 800 561-1616; fax: +1 418 646 5974; web: www.fapaq.gouv.qc.ca; e-mail: info.sfp@fapaq.gouv.qc.ca). For information on fishing in parks and wildlife reserves, and to obtain the free brochures *Experience... Parcs Québec* and *The Wildlife Reserves of Québec,* contact the **Société des établissements de plein air du Québec (SÉPAQ), 801 chemin Saint-Louis, bureau 180, Québec (Québec) G1S 1C1** (tel: +1 418 890 6527 or 1 800 665 6527; fax: +1 418 528 6025; web: www.sepaq.com/En/; e-mail: inforeservation@sepaq.com).

SASKATCHEWAN. Pike, perch and walleye are found throughout the province and represent the largest portion of the sport catch. Lake trout and arctic grayling are plentiful in the northern areas. Rainbow, brook, brown and lake trout are stocked in streams and lakes throughout the province. Current licence fee for those over 16 is $50.

For further information (including details of limits, accommodation, outfitters and guides) contact **Tourism Saskatchewan, 1922 Park Street, Regina, Saskatchewan S4P 3V7** (tel: +1 306 787 2300; fax: +1 306 787 5744; web: www.sasktourism.com; tollfree: 1 87 237 2273) who also issue a guide free of charge.

THE UNITED STATES OF AMERICA

The United States of America covers an enormous area of land and water space, offering everything between the near-Arctic conditions met in winter near the 49th parallel and the semi-tropical climate of Florida, Louisiana and Arizona, providing almost every conceivable environmental opportunity for freshwater or saltwater fish-species to exploit to their full advantage. This creates a great swathe of corresponding angling opportunities on such a scale that holidays spent fishing and camping in the backwoods have long been a commonplace of the American way of life as holidays on the coast - and, more recently, on the shores of the Mediterranean - have been of the British.

Such a demand compels a supply: and there is nowhere in the world where so sophisticated a blend of modern comfort and primitive atmosphere can be found at the waterside, made, as it were, to measure. And signs reading 'Keep out: fishing private' are not readily to be found in America. Apart from small lakes on private land immediately adjacent to private homes, the water and its inhabitants are the property of the community, managed expertly for the good of all by the community's public agencies. Fishing may not literally be 'free', but it is open to all with a few dollars to invest in recreation. The US population is four times Britain's; but the space open for it is ten times greater.

Because of the way in which, traditionally, exchange-rates and living costs have related, the USA has never in the past figured as a place where the adventurous British angler was likely to take a fishing holiday. All that, though, has now changed and it makes just as much sense, financially and otherwise, for an Englishman to holiday in **Tennessee**, fishing for large-mouth bass, or in **Minnesota** in search of *Esox masquinongy,* as for a Texan to come to Scotland to catch a Spey salmon. Going out from the **Florida Keys** in pursuit of marlin, sailfish or tarpon has for many years been a branch of the sport attracting a trickle of wealthy Britishers, but fishing American fresh waters has been a practice confined to angling writers and such, out to broaden their professional education.

Since it is the state geographically nearest to Britain, let us begin our review of the northern tier of states and their fishing with **Maine**, whose beaches offer the classical opportunity to contact the greatest of all saltwater sporting fish to be angled feasibly from the shore anywhere, the striped bass. Though scarcer now than in years gone by, unfortunately, there are still fine specimens to be taken by the persistent specialist surf-caster. Offshore, there are cod and pollack, the bluefin tuna, some of these registering on the beam-scale weights of more than 500lbs.

Inland, there is a multitude of wilderness lakes and streams offering sport with smallmouth bass, brown and rainbow trout and the unique native of Eastern North America, the brook trout, actually a fine handsome member of the char family. Atlantic salmon which ran Maine's rivers by the ten thousand a hundred years ago suffered near-extermination, but are now being nursed back by conservation technology.

Moving west to the **Great Lakes,** thoughts turn back to another char, the 'lake trout', a fish which grows to great size in deep and cold water throughout this latitude and in Canada. One fishes for them in hopes of a 40-pounder. An attempt to pass over without comment the damage done to some waters, the Great Lakes included, by the consequences of unthinking industrialisation would be dishonest, but remedy is now the order of the day. None has been more spectacular in its success than the stocking of **Lake Michigan** with coho salmon from the Pacific shore. Here, a new and tremendously exciting sport-fishery has been created, as it were, out of nothing, based on a food-supply left uncropped by lake trout no longer present in sufficient numbers to preserve a natural balance. Most see that as a net gain. The coho gives better sport than the 'Mackinaw', as it is sometimes named farther north.

On to a state where water-area challenges land-space: **Minnesota**, as the North American Indian dialect-name implies, and the cream of the fishing for great northern pike (our pike), walleyes (resembling our zander) and the greatest lantern-jaw of them all, *Esox masquinongy,* the muskellunge or 'muskie'. While these predators are distributed throughout the region, Minnesota is the heartland. Muskies there may grow to 80lbs weight and leap like trout when hooked.

Passing through a varied landscape, some of it watered by trout streams, we arrive eventually among the foothills of the **Rockies**, where the brilliantly-coloured dolly varden and cut-throat trout (the former another char, to be pedantic) and representatives of the five sub-species of the so-called 'golden' trout join the ranks awaiting the angler's thinning, not to mention the sea-going rainbow trout, the steelhead. It was in the Rocky Mountain watershed that the rainbow, sedentary and sea-going, was first encountered and employed to provide the bloodstock for the eventual artificial populating of the entire temperate world with this enormously successful species.

Over the mountains: the ocean: and the feeding grounds of the Pacific salmon, five species, of which two, the king or 'Tyee' and the coho, are of sporting significance.

Going back East and starting again farther south, we traverse a band of warmer states, less favourable to the cold-water salmonids, but affording an ideal environment for pickerel (another pike-species) and for the small-mouth and large-mouth bass, the fish on which the romance of North American angling is largely founded. These big athletic cousins of the European perch (called there, incidentally, the 'yellow perch') hit surface flies and lures with astonishing ferocity, fight like tigers when hooked and lie habitually in the shade and cover of the water-plant zone where only the most expert of tackle-handlers can present the offering and cope with the ensuing seizure without disaster. As the cooler uplands are again reached, the typical population of the upland waters is met again, and the pattern replicates.

Repeat the journey starting in **Georgia**, and one covers territory with a yet warmer climate, swamplands, and then an area of low rainfall. Traditionally, what fishing there was did not enjoy sporting prestige. The image was one of a poor coloured man employing crude tackle to harvest cheap protein; a typical quarry, the Mississippi catfish. One is south of that section of the lowland region where water temperature falls low enough to permit salmonids to spawn successfully in natural waters.

But the water-demand for growing population growing also in affluence has necessitated the construction of chains of dams in the drier states; vast new sheets of deep water offering environments novel in their setting, with a variety of temperature regimes encouraging the successful introduction of some of the great sporting species found naturally to the north and west. Even **Arizona** - the 'dry county' itself - now provides fine fishing for sport, and offers it in hot sunshine, a combination of pleasures not frequently encountered by the proverbially frozen-fingered angler acquiring lumbago from his water-logged nether end.

It would not do to dismiss the terrific sport potential to be enjoyed generally in the U.S.A. without some mention of the fantastic angling offered in its largest state, **Alaska**. Known by Alaskans as the last frontier, it is comparatively untamed, but if you seek the five species of Pacific salmon, wild rainbow trout and Arctic grayling, it offers sport beyond your wildest dreams.

Providing you can gain access by boat or floatplane, and following payment of approx £25 in licence dues, all the fishing in Alaska is free. Most visiting anglers settle for residence in one of the many lodges which cater for those who do not wish to suffer any hardships when divorced from civilisation. Most of the best and more productive lodges are in the **Bristol Bay** area. This is easily accessible by hour-long scheduled flights from **Anchorage** to the little town of **King Salmon**. There you are within short flying times by bush or floatplane to many of the best lodges.

Some lodges offer daily fly-outs to choice fishing venues, but this adds considerably to the expense and there are many advantages in seeking a lodge which offers fishing on the river at which it is sited, and where jet boats take you to good fishing within a matter of a half-hour boat ride. One lodge popular with British visitors (they even fly the Union Jack) is **Katmai Lodge** on Levelock Native land on the **Alagnak** river. This is but a mere 80 minute flight by twin-engined turbo-prop aircraft from Anchorage direct to the lodge's own airstrip. Early July offers prime time for the king (chinook), sockeye and chum salmon. The pink salmon or "humpie" runs in late July (and only every other year), while the coho or silver salmon run in early August.

King salmon are not always easy to get on fly tackle, but those caught on baits may run to 60lbs and more. Sockeye salmon may be taken on a single-handed fly rod but require a different technique to that used for Atlantic salmon here in Britain. The chum and coho have similar taking habits to Atlantic salmon, but it always pays to take great heed of your guide before assuming that you know it all.

Several sporting agencies in Britain have Alaskan fishing on offer, but if you wish to be accompanied by Grace Oglesby who has many years of experience of fishing in Alaska, contact **Arthur Oglesby's World Fishing Holidays, 9 Oatlands Drive, Harrogate, North Yorkshire HG2 8JT** (tel/fax: 01423 883565). For saltwater king salmon and halibut fishing on the Kenai Peninsula, and freshwater king salmon and silver on Kenai River, and other locations, with accommodation, contact **Alaskan Adventure Charters, P.O. Box 4273, Soldotna, AK 99669** (tel: +1 907 262 7773 (season); +1 360 871 8973 (winter); web: www.alaskancharters.com; e-mail: rufishn@alaska.net).

We have discussed none but the prime sporting species. They, however, are not the last word. US waters are inhabited also by others; carp, blue-gill sunfish, crappies and what-have-you, fish present in higher population densities and easier to catch, fish whose presence has traditionally ensured that the less expert members of the specialist angler's family on holiday may take their share of the pleasures and the triumphs. The travel business had now started international operations in this field and British anglers can expect a rapid growth in attractive opportunities.

MEXICO

Freshwater fishing: river trout fishing has been spoilt by local netting, but during the past few years black-bass fishing has become popular in Mexico, with exaggerated claims of 100 to 200 bass per day. For information about **Vicente Guerrero Dam**, near **Ciudad Victoria**, (fishing license 10 dollars per week), write to Sunbelt Hunting and Travel Inc., Box 3009, Brownsville, Texas 78520. For **Diaz Ordaz Dam**, contact Roberto Balderrama, Santa Anita Hotel, Los Mochis, Sinaloa. 8lb bass are common here, and at the **San Lorenzo Dam**, near **Xicotencatl**. Sea fishing: there are over 850 species to be caught, and in the Los Cabos region alone over 40,000 marlin and sailfish are hooked each year. Popular centres are **Acapulco, Puerto Vallarta, Manzanillo, Mazatlán, Guaymas, Loreto, La Paz, Cancun, Cozumel, Tampico, Veracruz, Cabo San Lucas** and **San Jose del Cabo**, with good facilities. Good charter boats are on hire, with expert crews. Amongst coastal species are pargo, yellowtail, rock bass, grouper, barracuda, totoava, snook, giant sea bass. Pelagic species include blue and striped marlin, yellowfin tuna, black marlin, Atlantic bonito, sailfish, swordfish and mackerel. These are usually found a good distance from the shore. Bonefishing is a sport practised by anglers from all over the world at Boca Paila, near Cancun, **Quintana Roo**. Contact **Turismo Boca Paila S.A. de C.V.**, Punta Chuntuyun 15, S.M. 24, M.4, L.11, Ret8, Cancun, Quintana Roo, C.P. 77509, Mexico (tel: +52 98 921200 or 00 52 98 921201; fax: 00 52 987 20053; web: www.bocapaila-lodge.com' e-mail: info@bocapaila-lodge.com). Boca Paila also have a representative in London: **Frontiers International** (tel: 020 7493 0798; e-mail: london@frontierstrvl.co.uk) for further information.

The **Mexican Tourism Board** has an office at **41 Trinity Square, London EC3N 4DJ** (tel: 020 7488 9392; fax: 020 7265 0704) from which more detailed information can be obtained.

THE CARIBBEAN

Forty years ago, so little was the Caribbean exploited by the indigenous peoples dwelling on its islands and about its shores that the United Nations Food & Agriculture Organisation gave a priority to the encouragement of commercial fishing there. What little fish was eaten in Central America had come traditionally in the form of salted fillets imported from countries - Norway and North America particularly - which had well-established cold water fisheries for cod in the prolific waters of the North Atlantic and the Arctic.

Various geophysical features were thought at that time to inhibit the Caribbean from ever becoming a region rich in exploitable fish populations. That, in one sense, may have been correct, but there are more ways than one of exploiting a resource, a fact already known by that time to charter-boat proprietors operating out of Florida resorts to crop the wonderful harvest of American anglers in search of sport more dramatic than the salmon or the

Grace Oglesby fishing off Cape Hatteras, N Carolina, USA. *Photo: Arthur Oglesby*

A sockeye salmon fights hard on the Alagnak river, Alaska. With travel prices falling, a holiday in Alaska brings anglers from far and wide, where salmon are even more plentiful than in virgin Russia. *Photo: Arthur Oglesby.*

muskellunge could offer in freshwater.

Thus the possibilities of the **Gulf of Mexico** and the seas around the **Bahamas** became known - marlin, swordfish, sawfish, sailfish, barracuda, tarpon and tuna the quarry, individual fish which took angling statistics from measurement by the pound to measurement by the hundredweight. The same geophysical conditions which had led to doubts as to the possibility of upgrading national catches of readily marketable fish for human consumption in the region had concentrated the big predators at water-depths where they could be found and profitably angled for.

During these forty years, facilities for Big Game fishing as it soon became known, spread progressively throughout the area and one may now fish for these splendid creatures from bases in **Mexico, Honduras, Nicaragua, Costa Rica, Panama, Colombia, Venezuela** (which was the first country in the region seriously to exploit its fish stocks in the traditional fashion) and the oceanic islands all the way south to **Trinidad**.

Originally, the big fish were angled for with a trolled dead bait and tackle powerful enough to master a bolting horse. Nowadays they are sought for with the fly rod, too, reflecting the fact that official records are maintained not only for maximum species weights, globally speaking, but for tackle categories, too, expressed in terms of line-strength - i.e. IGFA rules.

Astonishingly, billfish - to use the up-to-date term for swordfish and sailfish species grouped together - five feet in length have been brought to the glove in ten minutes from hooking with a conventional fly rod and single-action fly reel.

Tourist offices in London maintained by Mexico and Islands in the West Indies give details on hotels, facilities for boat charter, (with professional help integral to the hire-package) and of what restrictions apply to limits, seasons, and species of fish and other marine quarry which are excluded locally from the angler's activities. These restrictions are not onerous.

ANTIGUA and BARBUDA

Antigua and **Barbuda** have developed their big game fishing. Blue marlin, sailfish, tuna, wahoo, snapper, grouper, angel, trigger, margate, amber jack, black jack, and barracuda are all present around the islands, according to the conformation of the sea-bed. There are many reefs and coral formations. Lobster fishing is particularly good around the wrecks off Barbuda, which number more than 50. Anglers should note that use of dynamite is strictly forbidden. Many species of fish are reserved for commercial fishermen. Contact Phil's Eco Fishing who specialise in snook, tarpon, tuna & bone fishing; fly fishing and light tackle spinning, (tel: +1 268 723-4303; mob: +1 268 560-4882; e-mail: fish@actol.net) All persons wishing to fish are required to hold a licence, obtainable locally. Charter boats operate from a variety of locations. Deep sea fishing aboard 'Overdraft', further information and reservations (tel: +1 268 464-4954 or +1 463-3112; fax: +1 268 462-3119; e-mail: nuesb@candw.ag) or your tour representative.

For further information contact the **Antigua and Barbuda Tourist Office, Antigua House, 15 Thayer Street, London W1M 5LD** (tel: 020 7486 7073).

THE BAHAMAS

The Bahamas comprise twelve major groups of islands, numbering over 700 in total, spaced over 1,000 square miles or more of ocean. **Bimini** is probably the best known of the fishing centres and it was here that the largest Bahamian marlin recorded by an angler - a fish weighing more than 1,000lbs - was brought into harbour.

Other notable islands are **San Salvador**, marlin, yellowfin, fine reef and flats fishing; **Exuma**, good bonefishing, reef fishing, and light tackle opportunities; **Long Island**, deep sea, bonefishing and reef fishing; **Cat Island**, for marlin and tuna; **Andros**, world class bonefishing, trophy sized bottom species, marlin and tuna; **Nassau**, bluewater fishing, for marlin and tuna, wahoo, kingfish, sailfish; **The Abacos**, deep and shallow water fishing, with a good variety, main attractions being yellowfin tuna, marlin, good flats and reef fishing; **Grand Bahama**, also good flats and reef fishing; **Chub Cay**, white marlin, dolphin and other species; and **Eleuthera**, with blackfin tuna, blue marlin, good bonefish flats and reef fishing, as well as big game. Seasons for best fishing:, bonefish Mar-Apr; snapper, spring summer, barracuda, Jun-Aug; blue marlin, May-Jun; white marlin, Mar-Jun; sailfish, Apr; broadbill and swordfish, Jun peak time; Allison tuna, Mar-May; blackfin, Jun; bluefin, May. Tournaments are held frequently throughout the islands, hotels catering specially for anglers abound, and there are many fishing lodges. Charter rates vary with duration of fishing trips and species sought.

Contact **The Bahamas Tourist Office,** 10 Chesterfield St, London W1J 5JL (tel: 020 7355 0800), for more information.

BERMUDA

Licences are not required: charter boats in deep water produce catches of wahoo, greater amberjack, almaco jack, dolphin fish, grey and yellowtail snapper, great barracuda, rainbow runner, Atlantic Blue marlin, Great Blue marlin, white marlin, little tunny, blackfin, Wahoo and Yellowfin and skipjack tuna. Also all species of shark, the prize being the blue marlin with 9 fish over 1,000lbs. recently caught. Reefs produce greater amberjack, almaco jack, great barracuda, little tunny, Bermuda chub, grey and yellowtail snapper, and assorted bottom fish. Shore fishing from beaches, docks piers is free, and may produce bonefish, palometa, grey snapper, great barracuda. Charter boats operate the year round, from the BSFA and St George's GFCA (below), the majority independently, supply and demand peaking from May to November. There are over 21 charter boats operating in Bermuda, almost all are independently owns and operated, which include Capt Allen DeSilva, "De Mako", Fishbermuda Ltd, 11 Abri Lane, Spanish Point, Pembroke HM02 (tel: +1 441 295 0835; fax: +1 441 295 3620; mob: +1 441 234 8626; web: www.fishbermuda.com; e-mail: mako@ibl.bm); "MV Messaround" Charters, St. George's Game Fishing and Cruising Association, PO Box GE 107, St. George's GE BX (tel: +1 441 297 8093; fax: +1 441 297 1455; mob: +1 441 234 8953; web: www.fishandfun.bm; e-mail: joekelly@northrock.bm); further information from the **Bermuda Tourism** at **36 Southwark Bridge Rd, London SE1 9EU** (tel: 020 7202 6364; fax: 0207 928 0722; web: web: www.bermuda tourism.com; e-mail: bermudatourism@hills balfour.com; web: www.bermudatourism.com) and on their website. Bermuda Sport Fishing Association, Creek View House, 8 Tulo Lane, Pembroke HM O2 (tel/fax: +1 441 295 2370). Hotel facilities are excellent; information also available on www.bermudatourism.com.

LESSER ANTILLES

South of Puerto Rico is the chain of small islands known as the **Lesser Antilles** - the **Leeward** and **Windward** groups.

TRINIDAD AND TOBAGO

Finally, **Trinidad** & **Tobago**, the large islands which lie just off the coast of Venezuela and terminate the chain. Their waters, too, are abundantly supplied with billfish species, tuna, tarpon, barracuda and many other species of interest to the angler, if offering rather less dramatic sport than the 'stars' on the angler's stage. For further information, contact Trinidad & Tobago Tourism Office, **Mitre House, 66 Abbey Rd, Bush Hill Park, Enfield EN1 2RQ** (tel: 020 8350 1011) or **Tourism & Industrial Development Co (Trinidad & Tobago) Ltd, P O Box 222, 10-14 Philipps Str, Port-of-Spain, Trinidad, WI** (tel: (868) 623 6022/3; fax: (868) 624 8124; e-mail: www.visittnt.com). Names and addresses of charter-boat operators in both islands are available on various websites, incl www.charternet.com/fishers.

SOUTH AMERICA

BRAZIL. This is a vast country in the same league as China, Canada, Australia and the United States of America. Brazil boasts not only the Amazon basin (the largest hydrographic basin in the world) but also the Prata basin (the second largest in Latin America) as well as the Araguaia-Tocantins, the Sao Francisco and Atlântico Sul Basins. With the world's biggest river draining it, it lacks neither water nor fish. Brazil has five main regions, each one has its own fishing areas and fish variety (too many to be fully detailed in this section). The regions are listed, along with a few varieties in each area:

Northern: (**Amapa, Amazonas, Para, Rondônia, Roraima** and **Tocatins**): fish variety: *rivers:* peacock bass, surubim, aracu, tambaqui, red-tail catfish, dorada, cachorra, apapa, great barracuda, tarpon, grey snapper; *coastal regions:* dolphin, piramutaba, club shark.

North East (Alagoas, Bahia, Ceará, Maranhao, Piaui, Paraiba, Pernambucco, Rio Grande do Norte, Sergipe); fish variety: rivers & dams: peacock bass, dorado, surubim, freshwater croaker, curimatas; *coastal regions:* snook, tarpon, crevalle jack, catfish, grey & Southern red snapper, king mackerel and pompano; *coastal rivers:* snook, hake and tarpon.

Central West: (Goias, Mato Grosso, Mato Grosso do Sul); fish variety: *rivers & dams:* peacock bass, apapa, surubim, chachorra, great barracuda, pirahna (red & black), catfish (varieties), pacu.

SouthEast: (Espirito Santo; Minas Gerais, Rio de Janiero, Sao Paulo); fish variety: *rivers & dams:* catfish (var); peacock bass, catfish, tilápias, black-bass, croaker; (trout is found on **Aiurioca River**); *coastal regions:* Bluefish, snook, grouper, pampo, snook, blue runner, blue marlin, white marlin, Greater Amberjack, Yellowtail (Lesser Amberjack).

Southern: (Paraná, Rio Grande do Sul, Santa Catarina); fish variety: *rivers & dams:* tilápia, carpa, jundiá, mandi, corvina, pacu, corimba, catfish (varieties), peacock bass, cascudo, surubim, pacu, pintado, blackbass (trout is found on **River Silverira and Pelotas River**); *coastal regions:* snook, croaker, Greater Amberjack.

Anglers from the USA have already explored its possibilities with excellent results. Brazil as an exciting new destination for fishing holidays is now being widely developed and available through numerous travel web-sites,

For further information, contact the **Brazilian Tourist Office, 32 Green Street, London W1K 7AT** (tel: 020 7629 6909; fax: 020 7399 9102; web: www.brazil.org.uk).

ARGENTINA. Here, although the South Atlantic is probably now the world's most productive fishing zone, the emphasis in terms of sport shifts back to freshwater fishing. Salmonids were introduced from the northern hemisphere many years ago - land-locked salmon *(Salmo salar sebago)* the brown trout (in both its sedentary and migratory forms) and the brook trout *(Salvelinus fortinalis)*. The home of these species is in the Andean lake district. Specimen brook trout up to 10lbs, have been caught; in the case of the other species named, specimens topping 30lbs.

In the river-catchments of the lower-lying regions of the country, especially those of the **Parana** and **Plata**, there are two fine native species of fish, the dorado *(Salminus maxillosus)* and the perch *(Percicathys trucha)* which are rated as highly or higher than salmonids. The perch grows to weights approaching 20lbs, while the dorado reaches a weight of 50lbs.

In the same habitats are found other species which grow to be enormous - the mangururu (200lbs), the surubi (120lbs) and others which do not reach such spectacular weights but still offer splendid sport.

Spinning from a boat piloted by a guide is the usual method of fishing for dorado, but they will also take a fly (not exactly a blue winged olive!) and in an Argentinean torrent quite a challenge to the fly rod, also the fish it naturally feeds on, offered as either a live or a dead bait. This splendid sporting fish is found throughout the catchments of the rivers Plata and Parana. Centres specially recommended for the quality of the fishing guides, boats and accommodation are **Paso de la Patria** (Corrientes), **Isla del Carrito** (Chaco) and **Posadas**

(Misiones).

The best fishing is in the summer - August to March. Annual competitions are held early in the season. Five vast National Parks offer the best of the fishing for salmonids, all of them on the west side of the country, in the uplands bordering Chile.

In **Patagonia**, the lakes and rivers in the mountainous region of **Cholila** contain abundant stocks of trout, usually fished with wet and dry fly, or Devon minnow. Average sizes are large: brook trout to 10lbs, rainbow from 3-6lbs with specimen fish running to 20lbs, brown trout 3-8lbs, with record from this area, 32lbs. Other fishable species are landlocked salmon, perca, and Patagonian pejerrey. The principal lakes are: **Lago Cholila**, the biggest in Cholila (15 km long), with beautiful surroundings; the water is very cold due to glacier melt; access via Estancia Lago Cholila; **Lago Lezama**, the highest and warmest in the area, deep, with permanent undercurrents of warm streams; **Lago Mosquito**, the smallest (8 km long, close to village, with small hostel alongside the lake. Largest rivers are **Rio Carrelefu, Rio Tigre, Rio Pedregoso**, and **Rio Blanco**. All these waters are excellent for fishing, and only a handful of anglers can be found in any one season for the place is virtually unknown internationally.

From **Punta Piedras** in the north to **Tierra del Fuego** in the extreme south, Argentina has more than 2,200 miles of Atlantic coastline. The water so far south is too cold for tuna, billfish and tarpon, but their place is taken for the big game angler by all the Atlantic species of shark.

For the Argentineans themselves, though, the peak of the sea angling year is when the warm current from Brazil brings down the black corvina, whose shoals provide many specimens of 40lbs, and better. **San Clemente de Tuyu** is the most famous centre for fishing the corvina, where the fish arrive in December. They then work their way down the coast, arriving in **Bahia Blanca** in February. There is plenty of shore fishing, but boats are to be had, though not on quite the sophisticated scale to be met with in the Gulf of Mexico and the Caribbean.

Tourist information may had from the **Consulado General de la República Argentina, 27 Three Kings Yard, London W1K 4DF** (tel: 020 7318 1340; fax: 020 7318 1349); or the **Oficina Central de Información Turística, Suipacha 1111, (1368) Buenos Aires** (tel: +4312 5611/15 or 0800 555 0016). Any enquiries regarding sport fishing in Argentina, e-mail fishing@turismo.gov.ar. Other useful Tourist Information web-sites are: **Secretariat of Tourism:** www.tyrismo.gov.ar & www.sectur.gov.ar; **Regional Tourist info:** www.argentour.com & www.viajeya.com.ar; **Trout fishing site:** www.argentinatrout.com.ar; **Dorado fishing site:** www.doradosfishing.com; **Patagonia info:** www.patagonia.

CHILE. Chile's coastline matches that of the neighbouring Argentine, but the fishing promoted is largely for introduced salmonids, especially in Chilean Patagonia. The trout run extremely large; the country in that region is thinly populated and attractively wild, the climate mild. Mid-Nov to Apr is the trout season in Chile. In November trout begin to feed actively. January and February are height of summer, with plentiful insect life, and fish feed heavily in March. In April the weather cools, but the largest fish tend to be hooked then, up to 12 or 14lbs. Fishing lodges are run in several locations, including on the **Nireguao** and **Futaleufu** Rivers, with good accommodation. Other first rate fisheries in the Chilian Patagonia are the **Baker** and **Cochrane** Rivers, and **Frio** and **Pollux** lakes, with spectacular fly fishing for large brown and rainbow trout, regularly in the 4-7lbs range. The cities recommended as start-points for the angler are **Temuco, Puerto Montt** and **Coihaque**. Temuco is accessible by rail from **Santiago** daily, Puerto Montt, depending on season. Coihaque is accessible by air only, either from Santiago or Puerto Montt. Fishing licences can be obtained from the offices of the Regional Municipalities or directly in **Sernapesca**, Antonio, Busts 181 (tel: (67) 332546). Further information from **National Tourist Board of Chile, Regional Headquarters of Aisen, Bulnes No 35, Coyhaique, Chile** (tel/fax: (67) 231752/233949; e-mail: sematur_coyhai@entelchile.net) or Chilean Consulate, 12 Devonshire St, London W1N 2DS (tel:020 7580 1023).

THE FALKLAND ISLANDS. One of the growing, but still largely undiscovered attractions in the South Atlantic, this group of islands is the best researched and most promising for the angler. How else? Natural and spacious, enjoying clean air and majestic scenery, the Islands are a dynamic Overseas territory of the United Kingdom, with over 94% of the 2,379 strong population of British descent. After the events of 1982, these shores remain protected by the British forces. From nowhere else south of the equator has *Where to Fish* received such comprehensive information. The whole development of sea trout fishing in the Falklands has taken place in less than a lifetime. Nature left the Islands with only the Falkland trout - *(aplochiton zebra)* which is not a trout or even a char, and a few minor species in its rivers. The first real trout *(Salmo trutta)* were introduced less than forty years ago, but a fast growing migratory strain quickly became established and spread around the islands, giving us today some of the finest sea trout fishing in the world.

Sea trout 2-5lbs are common, and many fish in excess of 10lbs are taken every season. The best recorded sea trout taken on a fly to date was 22¾lbs, caught on the **San Carlos River** by Alison Faulkner.

The main sea trout rivers - the **Warrah** and **Chartres** on West Falkland and the **San Carlos** on East Falkland - are ideal for fly fishing, with treeless banks being free of casting obstructions. However a strong wind often blows, so this is no place for a poor caster with mediocre tackle.

Most rivers have fair numbers of resident brown trout, but most are small, dark fish, typical of acid rivers.

Major sea trout rivers with visitor accommodation and guides.

West Falkland

Warrah River: Can be fished from **Port Howard Settlement**, where there is accommodation. The Warrah River is about 12 miles from the settlement, and the Chartres River about an hour's drive. The main tributary, the **Green Hills Stream**, which is crossed on the way to the Warrah, is well worth fishing.

East Falkland

San Carlos River: Controlled by local farmers, the river is accessed from the Stanley Port - San Carlos track. Blue Beach Lodge offers comfortable accommodation.

Mullet fishing: as a bonus, you will probably come into contact with the Falkland mullet *(Eleginus falklandicus)* if fishing in tidal water. Like the British mullet, the Falkland species follows the tide right into shallow water, where it can be seen swimming just below the surface with a very obvious wake, but there the similarity ends. It is not even related to our mullet and is much larger, with fish recorded up to 20lbs and mullet of 8lbs are quite common. The dorsal fin runs virtually from head to tail along a tapering body, and the pectoral fins are huge in relation to the size of the fish.

The Falkland mullet is a powerful fish which makes long runs and would be much valued as a game fish if it existed in Britain. It often takes the sea-trout angler's fly or spinner, but the local method normally used is to suspend a piece of mutton (fresh sheep meat) on a size 4 or 2 hook a couple of feet below a small pike bung. This tackle is cast out wherever there are signs of mullet activity, and the response is rarely long delayed.

Small to medium mullet can be caught virtually on your doorstep at places like **Port Howard**. The really large fish are often found in specific locations, at some distance from the settlements. It is worth considering setting aside a little time for a trip specifically for big mullet.

The commercial route flies via South America, where Lan Chile operates a weekly Saturday service linking Santiago and Punta Arenas in Chile with Mount Pleasant, Falkland Islands. Alternatively, a limited number of seats are available on the RAF Tristar service, which flies direct from the UK via Ascension Island. This service departs six times a month.

There is accommodation for fishermen at Stanley, Port San Carlos, Darwin and Port Howard. There are also lodges in wildlife centres (fishermen may like to take some time off to see the large colonies of penguins, seals and other wildlife).

The **Falkland Islands Tourist Board** office is at **Falkland House, 14 Broadway, Westminster, London, SW1H 0BH**. (tel: 020 7222 2542; web: www.tourism.org.fk; e-mail: manager@falklands.gov.fk).

FISHING IN EUROPE

AUSTRIA

Austria is understandably popular with anglers from all over the world, with its abundance of streams and lakes, providing first-class sport with brown and rainbow trout, grayling, char, and coarse fish such as pike and pike-perch, huck, sheat-fish and carp. Some of the main centres tend to be overfished, so a car is valuable; many beautiful mountain streams are easily reached by road. Much of the sport is on the lower reaches of these mountain rivers, but the more venturesome can often find better fishing on the high alpine streams and lakes. Grayling are highly regarded, often more so than trout, the **Drau**, **Salzach** and **Traun** being three of the best grayling rivers in Europe. The River **Mur**, **Ybbs** and **Steyr** are other recommended rivers. 'Fishing in Austria' *(see below)* is a co-operative of 35 areas and hotels specialising in angling; and issues temporary permits for several trout preserves, as well as dt (costing 15 Euro to 60 Euro). Temporary permission and information can be obtained from the Association's office. The same applies to the VÖAFV and 'Fishing in Austria.'

To keep the sport at a high level, the authorities maintain strict conservation measures and a specially close watch is kept on pollution and abstraction. Generally speaking the rule is fly only for trout, grayling and char. Spinning is usually only permitted for larger fish such as lake trout, pike, huck, pike-perch (depending on the local authority) and so on, and natural bait and sheatfish only for coarse fisheries. Many waters are controlled by the two principal fishing associations, the Austrian Fishing Association (ÖFG) and the Association of Austrian Workers' Fishing Clubs (VÖAFV).

Wherever he fishes, the visitor usually needs two permits, a general licence issued by the State and costing between 7 Euro and 26 Euro, according to the province - and a private permit from the local owner.

Accommodation is no problem, as many fine hotels offer anglers first class facilities on the more important lakes and rivers. More information can be obtained from the **Austrian National Tourist Office, P O Box 2363, London, W1S 3NS** (tel: 020 7629 0461; fax 020 7499 6038; web: www.austria.info/uk; e-mail info@anto.co.uk), although the booklet is no longer available. Also, **Fishing in Austria**, Hauptstrasse 203, 9210 Pörtschach (tel: +43 4272 3620 30; fax: +43 4272 3620 90; web: www.fischwasser.com; e-mail: fisch wasser@stw.co.at). Addresses of the main angling association are **Österreichische Fischere-igesellschaft, 1010 Wien 1, Elisabethstrasse 22** (tel: +43 1 586 52 48; fax: +43 1 587 59 42; web: www.oefg1880.at; e-mail: office@oefg1880.at). **Verband der Österreichischen Ar-beiter-Fischerei-Vereine, A-1080 Wien, Lenaugasse 14** (tel: +43 1 403 21 76; fax: +43 1 403 21 76 20; web: www.fischerei.or.at; e-mail: verband@fischerei.or.at).

BELGIUM

Although Belgium has never made a name for itself as a visiting fisherman's country, it has, in fact, in its many canals and rivers, most of the fish which British fishermen know, with sea fishing along its 40 miles of coast.

In general terms the freshwater fishing water can be divided thus: The **Scheldt** basin, with the rivers **Scheldt**, **Lys**, **Rupel**, **Dyle**, **Demer**, **Dendre** and **Nèthe** holding bream, roach, perch, pike, burbot, smelt, shad and eels; the **Meuse** basin, with the rivers **Meuse**, **Semois**, **Lesse**, **Sambre**, **Ourthe**, **Amblève**, **Warche** and **Vesdre** holding trout, grayling, chub, barbel, perch, roach, bream, pike, pike-perch, carp, tench and eels; and the streams between the Sambre and the Meuse, holding trout, grayling, chub, perch, pike, roach, bream, carp, tench and eels. Many waters of the lowlands and near industrial centres suffer from pollution and overfishing, but the situation is now improving.

All Belgian waters fall into one of three categories; closed water, not subject to fishing laws; public, or navigable water, belonging to the Walloon, Flemish or Brussels regions; preserved, or non-navigable water belonging to the landowners. Waters in the last two groups are subject to the fishing laws, and anyone fishing in them must possess a current licence. There are three different licences in Belgium: 1) sold by the Flemish authority, for fishing in the northern part of the country; 2) sold by the Brussels region, for Brussels; 3) sold by the Walloon region for fishing in Wallonia. The cost varies from 12.5 Euro to 37 Euro, according to the type of fishing. Licences may be obtained at post offices. The **close seasons** are: Pike, perch, grayling or pike-perch: January 1 to first Saturday in June; trout, October 1 to third Saturday of March. Fly fishing falls off sharply on the Ardennes streams after June.

For visiting trout fishers the greatest attraction probably lies in the streams of the **Ardennes**, where there is a good deal of association water. These are mostly mixed fisheries on the lines of the Hampshire Avon in England, with trout and grayling predominating in the upper reaches and being increasingly joined by coarse fish on moving downstream. The best fishing will usually be found in the least accessible places. Standard British fly patterns will take fish on the Ardennes streams but the local flies should be tried where possible.

Sea fishing along the sandy, shelving coast is largely for dabs and plaice (Oct-June), flounders (all year) and sole (May-Oct), with piers and breakwaters providing sport with conger (all year), cod (Sept-Mar), and whiting (Oct-Jan). Turbot are occasionally taken (May-Sept) and rays, shad and garfish are also caught (Sept-Oct), **Zeebrugge, Ostend, Nieuwpoort, Blankenbergh,** and **Knokke-Heist** are good centres.

Just after the last edition was printed, the-then Belgian Tourist Office was divided into two sections *(see below)*. Belgian fishing legislation is extremely complex and anglers are strongly advised to consult the local tourist centres. For example, **Namur** province publishes a special angling brochure in French. Further detailed information (in English) from (i) **Belgian Tourist Office - Brussels & Walloonia, 217 Marsh Wall, London E14 9FJ** (tel: 020 7531 0390; fax: 020 7531 0393; web: www.belgiumtheplace.to.be; e-mail: info@bel giumtheplace.to.be) and (ii) **Tourism Flanders - Brussels, 1a Cavendish Square, London W1G 0LD** (tel: 020 7307 7731; 0906 3020 245 (calls cost 60ppm; web: www.visitflanders.co.uk; e-mail: office@visitflanders.co.uk); finally, in Belgium itself, from the secretary of the **Fédération Sportive des Pêcheurs Francophones de Belgique, Rue Grandgagnage 25, 5000 Namur** (tel: +32 (0)81 41 34 91; fax: +32 (0)81 42 10 43; web: www.lepeucheur-belge.be; e-mail: lepecheurbelge@skynet.be); and from the secretary of the **Vlaamse Vereniging Voor Hengelsport Verbonden, Graafjansdijk, 25 Bus 5, 8370 Blankenberge** (tel: +50 41 40 77). Information on the specifics of fishing legislation can be obtained from the **Service de la Pêche, du Ministère de la Région Wallonne (Ministry of the Wallonian Region)** (tel: +32 (0)81 32 74 88; web: www.wallonie.be).

DENMARK

Fishing in Denmark is plentiful, varied and easy to come by. A few of the rivers hold salmon, and many of them sea trout, brown trout and grayling, as well as coarse fish, which are found also in many lakes.

In many places visitors can fish by purchasing tickets from the local fishing association. The association tickets are invariably cheap and sold at local tourist offices.

The principal rivers are all in **Jutland**. They are **Skjern Aa, Store Aa, Varde Aa, Ribe Aa** and **Karup Aa**. All are game-fish waters, but of them the best salmon fishing is probably to be had on the Skjern and the best sea trout fishing on the Karup. The water is generally good for fly fishing, and the flies used are much the same as those used in this country. Spinning is much practised. Added variety is given by the sea trout fishing which can be had from the rocks and from boats off both the mainland and the various Baltic islands.

For the coarse fisherman, the **River Guden** holds prolific stocks of bream and roach, and hundreds of lakes contain large bream, tench and other species, and are hardly ever fished. The lakeland area of East Jutland, for instance, produces very heavy net weights. Notable centres are Viborg, Silkeborg, Ry, Århus, Skanderborg (beside **Lake Skanderborg,** teeming with fish), and Horsens. Please note, there are restrictions on use of groundbait, and in some areas it is prohibited. In **Zealand**, the lake fishing is more predominant.

The **Funen Islands** between Jutland and Zealand have been in recent years systematically developed into an important centre for breeding and increasing sea trout, as a response to dwindling native populations. More than 400,000 smolts have been introduced each year since 1999; more than 100 barriers in the Funen river system have been removed by establishing fish passages and runs, and now, there exist one hundred different fishing locations on the coast round about these islands. Fishing is permitted all the year round, best times are Jan-May, and Aug-mid Nov. Normal methods are fly, and spinning with spoon or lure. A brochure may be obtained from **Fyn Tour, PO Box 499, DK-5260 Odense 5** (fax: +45 62 1313 38). Further information on guide service and casting trips contact **Seatrout Eldorado - Fyn County** (tel: +45 66 13 13 37; web: www.seatrout.dk; e-mail: seatrout@fyntour.dk).

There similar opportunities for sea trout fishing from the coast of Eastern Jutland, **Sjaelland**, and the island of **Bornholm**, in the Baltic. Excellent trolling for salmon is also to be had off Bornholm, salmon weighing over 42lbs are caught every year.

Denmark has a coastline of 7,500 kilometres, much of it unfished but nearly all stretches are accessible, with good possibilities for cod, coalfish, flatfish, tope, mackerel, garfish, whiting, ling and pollack, and for turbot, brill, plaice, sole, dab and flounder. One should not fish within 50 metres of a private dwelling place without the owners permission. Anglers are warned about the danger of breakwater fishing from **Jutland** west coast in rough weather, and on North Sea coast, jetty fishing is prohibited in several places for security reasons. Fishing boats will take anglers out to sea for a reasonable charge, and may also be chartered at **Copenhagen, Elsinore, Korsør** and **Frederikshavn**.

Salmon and sea trout fishing in fresh water is best from Apr/May to July, and September (salmon), June to Sept, and Oct/Nov, smaller rivers (sea trout).

A fishing licence is obligatory, and costs Dkr 100. It is obtainable from post offices or tourist offices. A tourist licence may be obtained for one day, cost Dkr 25, or one week, Dkr 75. Those under 18 or over 67 are exempt. Fishing rights in natural lakes and streams are nearly always private, but often let to local angling societies, who issue day or week cards. These are priced between Dkr 20-40 per day, Dkr 75-100 per week and may be bought at tourist offices. There are close seasons and size limits on game fish and large variety of other freshwater and sea fish.

Further information about both fishing and accommodation can be had from the **Danish Tourist Board, 55 Sloane Street, London, SW1X 9SY** (tel: 020 7259 5958; fax: 020 7259 5955); and **Danmarks Sportsfiskerforbund, Worsåesgade 1, DK-7100 Vejle** (tel:+ 75 82 06 99; fax: 75 82 02 09; web: www.sportsfiskeren.dk).

FINLAND

Finland can offer the angler no fewer than 187,888 lakes and rivers, and some 3,000 miles of sea-shore and archipelago. In the north and centre of the country the angler can catch very big fish on very big, remote waters; conditions which, in Europe at any rate, are becoming increasingly harder to find. The long days of midsummer give plenty of fishing time - the best sport in fact is often enjoyed in the brief twilight which elsewhere is called 'night'. In the South and in the archipelago area the best fishing periods are spring and autumn. Ice fishing for perch is popular in the winter months, and spear fishing with a lamp is practised during autumn, in dark, calm, or cloudy weather.

Salmon, sea trout, brown trout and brook trout all run well above the European average, and the size of grayling, too, is often remarkable; four-pounders are not rare. There are also arctic char *(Salvelinus alpinus)* which in the right conditions will take a fly. The most notable salmon-fishing rivers in Finland are **Tenojoki** in Lapland, **Tornionjoki** and **Simojoki** in Northern Finland, and **Kymijoki**, which empties into the Gulf of Finland in Kotka. Other popular salmon-fishing sites are the delta areas of **Kemijoki, Oulujoki** and **Aurajoki** rivers.

Excellent trout rivers and rapids are to be found in **Central Finland, Karelia, Kuusamo, Northern Finland** and **Lapland**, while the best waters for catching grayling are in the north. Worthy of particular mention are the seaspawning grayling of the western **Oura** archipelago, and the **Lake Saimaa** grayling.

The cream of the sport is to be found in **Lapland**, though there are individual waters further south which can match them in quality. Some of the best game fishing in Europe is to be found in the region north of **Lake Inari**, and especially the rivers emptying into the lake. A very good possibility is the lake itself, holding taimen, very big grayling and brown trout to 20lbs and more. Best fished for during their migratory runs up the tributaries in late summer.

Although hydro-electric schemes have impaired the salmon runs in many famous waterways, rivers are recovering and several of them can be offered for salmon and sea trout fishing - the **Kiiminki**; the **Simo**; the **Lesti**; the **Tornio**, which Finland shares with Sweden yielded in 1996 an estimated 20,000 kilos, the quieter stretches of Lappea producing more than 600 salmon, and the **Kymi River** produced 3,000 kilos, with salmon fishing well organised all the year round. The **Kuusinkijoki** at Kuusamo has been the venue of the world fly fishing championships.

The many guides will help you avoid problems. Many rivers are so wide, deep and fast flowing that comfortable fishing from the bank may be out of the question; it may often be impossible to reach the salmon and sea trout lies. Hence on great rivers like the **Teno** (claimed to be the best river in the world for Atlantic salmon), and **Näätämö** which flow along the frontier with Norway, the fishing is mainly from a boat with an outboard motor from which large flies are cast by short but stout rods over enormous pools and streams - a technique known as 'harling'. Reels carrying 250 yards of line of up to 1mm thick and over 40lb breaking strain are employed.

One problem which may be encountered is transport - many of the best waters are 'off the beaten track' and although there are excellent air services between the main centres, after that the angler is on his own and may have to be prepared for a good deal of foot-slogging and camping. A car, with a fibreglass boat strapped to the roof, is a valid alternative where the roads are not too bad. Nearly half of the farm holiday sites in Finland offer fishing; information may be had from local Tourist Information Centres.

One important accessory for the angler is some form of repellant to ward off mosquito attacks, which can often be unbearable - some Finnish fishermen wear head-nets. There are many fishing holiday resorts in Finland, and many organised package fishing holidays.

The Finnish coast with its large archipelago, not to mention the 6,500 **Åland Islands**, offers very good prospects for trout, salmon and perch fishers, and the pike fishing is outstandingly good. Even the immediate surroundings of big cities should not be ignored. As to the catch - the sea area is best.

The coarse fisherman will find first-class pike fishing in high summer, trolling a popular method on Finnish lakes, and large perch, which are very edible, may be caught during this season by worming. Some very good coarse fishing is to be found in the south, notably for pike and perch and pike-perch - not, as many believe, a hybrid, but a separate species. Opportunities for the fly fisherman in the south have been extended in recent years by the stocking of ponds with rainbow, brown and brook trout.

The National Board of Forestry administers 85 fisheries, which it manages mainly by restocking. Most of these are in eastern and northern Finland.

Fishing permits: Fishing regulations are strict and strictly enforced - there are game wardens even in remote districts. Two documents are required when fishing by means other than hook and line. The first is a receipt for payment of the fishing management fee, the second the actual fishing permit. The fishing management fee is 15 Euro per calendar year or 5 Euro per week (seven days). Those under 18 or over 65 need not pay this fee, nor do those who merely assist in the fishing and do not handle the fishing equipment during the actual fishing. The fishing management fee is paid by bank giro to the state giro account: Nordia 166030-101496.

The second required document is a receipt of payment of a fishing permit. This may be obtained in two ways. Special fishing sites require permission from the owner of the water area. Such permits also include specific information concerning the fishing methods allowed, fishing times and other pertinent rules and regulations. Provincial lure fishing permits allow fishing with one rod, at sea and on lakes, at the cost of 27 Euro per year or 7 Euro per week.

Certain limitations apply to provincial lure fishing permits. Lure fishing fees may be paid into the following giro accounts, according to province:

Province of Southern Finland: Nordea 166030-106594

Province of Western Finland: Nordea 166030-106602
Province of Eastern Finland: Nordea 166030-106610
Province of Oulu: Nordea 166030-106628
Province of Lapland: Nordea 166030-106636.
Separate regulations apply in the Åland Islands and the aforementioned licence system is not in force there. For additional information on fishing licences and fishing in Finland, visit the Fishing Finland web site: www.ahven.net.

Close seasons *(with minimum measurements):* salmon *(60cm)*, land-locked salmon *(40cm)*, sea and brown trout *(40cm)* and brook trout *(no min)* in rivers, brooks and rapids and in tide rips: Sept 1-Nov 30; with rod and lure: Sept 11-Nov 15; grayling *(30cm):* 1 April-31 May; Arctic char *(40cm)* in the Vukosi water: Sept 11-Nov 15; crayfish: Nov 1-July 21 (noon); lamprey: Apr 1-Aug15. (In the Åland Islands shore fishing is banned between 15 Apr and 15 June, in order to protect nesting sea birds.)

Further information can be obtained from the **Finnish Tourist Board, P O Box 33213, London W6 8JX** (tel: +44(0)20 7365 2512; fax: +44(0)20 8600 5681; web: www.visitfin land.com/uk; www.finland-fishing.com; e-mail: finlandinfo.lon@mek.fi).

FRANCE

Excellent sport with trout and some salmon fishing is open at reasonable cost in this country. French waterways are divided into the navigable public rivers, where fishing rights are owned by the State, and private rivers, where they belong to the riparian owner, fishing association or local authority. Even on the public rivers, however, anglers must belong to an angling and fish-breeding association and pay a tax based on the method of fishing adopted. Most rivers of this type provide coarse fishing only. Trout and salmon rights will nearly always be privately held, but the visitor should have little difficulty in obtaining a permit. Information should be sought from the local club or tackle dealer.

To fish in first and second category waters you normally require a **licence**, and a day (or sometimes) weekly card. The annual licence is 60 (or 200F-250F for second category waters, according to the Department. There is now a 'holiday pass' (carte vacances) for over 16 year-olds; 25 Euro for 15 days (1 June - 30 Sept). Daily tickets from about 5-6 Euro. To fish public stretches of rivers you only need the licence; juveniles 25 Euro for La Carte Jeune for the year.

Close seasons vary a great deal according to the locality, especially for salmon, and it is best to make local inquiries. A rough guide, however, would be, first category waters: salmon and trout, mid-Sept. to mid-March. Second category waters, fishing permitted all year round, although there are restrictions for various types of fish, such as pike. Fishing is allowed 30 mins. before and 30 mins. after sunset. Information from local clubs, tackle dealers and **Ministère de l'Agriculture, de la Pêche et de l'Alimentation, Direction des Pêches Maritimes et des Cultures Marines, 3 place de Fontenay, 75700-PARIS.**

Perhaps the best salmon fishing in France is to be found on a small number of fast flowing streams in the **Western Pyrenees**. The noted **Gave d'Oloron** is in this area. **Oloron, Sauveterre** and **Navarrenx** are good centres for this river. The **Gave d'Aspe**, which joins it at Oloron, and its tributary, the **Lourdios**, have provided good sport in recent years. They may be fished from **Lurbe**. At **Peyrehorade** the Gave d'Oloron is joined by the **Gave de Pau,** on which sport has also been improving, and Pau itself makes a fine place to stay. Salmon also run up the **Gaves d'Ossau and de Nive**. Because of melting snow, the season begins later here than elsewhere in France, but it extends later, too. For the Oloron area the best months are from June to the end of August.

Brittany, too, provides some opportunities for the salmon fisherman, with 12,400 miles of water courses, though the fish are on the small side, especially on the **River Aulne**, which flows into the sea near **Brest**. Generally, March, April, then June to end of season is the best time for salmon. Try the **Châteaulin** area until April and **Chateauneuf-du-Faou** later on. Châteaulin is also a good centre for the **Ell'le** and from **Landerneau** and **Landivisiau** the **Ellorn** may be fished. This salmon and trout river has been improved, pruned, and made accessible by the local angling society. Other productive streams are the **Blavet**, which passes through many locks, and is a first-rate coarse fishing stream, **Laita** and **Odet,** which flow into the Atlantic; the **Trieux** and its tributary the **Leff,** with **Guingamp** a suitable venue. In Cotes d'Armor region, the **Guer** and **Guic** are excellent and easily accessible trout streams, also the **Jaundy,** and tributary the **Théoulas,** brown trout and occasional salmon.

Flowing northwards through picturesque countryside to feed the **Loire,** the **Allier** offers the best opportunities for salmon fishermen in **Auvergne.** This is a region comparatively unknown to British anglers. The place to make for is **Brioude,** on the upper reaches of the river. The **Bajace dam,** where salmon congregate before taking the leap, is half a mile away. **Vichy, Pont-du-Château, Veyre** and **Issoire** are other centres. The upper reaches of the Loire itself can provide good sport. **Cantal** in the heart of the Auvergne, has 2,500 miles of rivers and mountain streams, with abundant brown trout. Best time, March to June. **Roanne** is a suitable place to stay. In the **Languedoc-Roussillon** region of southern France, there are almost 1,800 miles of game fishing stretches, mostly on the three major river basins, the **Garonne,** the **Loire** and the **Rhône,** and a multitude of lakes, some 50 up in the mountains. 15 May to 15 June is the best time for fly fishing, April to Oct for coarse, and June, July, Sept for mountain lake fishing.

Some of the **Normandy** rivers have good runs of fish, but the best of the fishing is hard to come by, being largely in the hands of syndicates. The visitor may find opportunities, however, on the **Orne** and **Vire,** the **Sée,** the **Sienne** and the **Sélune; Pontfarcy, Quetteville, Avranches** and **Ducey** are suggested centres.

France is a splendid country for the trout fisherman, with an abundance of well-stocked streams flowing through glorious scenery. He may find solitude and beauty not very far from Paris - in fact, on the upper reaches of the **Seine** and its tributary, the **Ource.** A little farther south lies **Avallon,** from which the **Cure** and its tributaries may be fished.

But the visitor will find the **Pyrenees** very hard to beat for trout. The **Gave d'Ossau** is one of the best of the many first-class streams in this area, offering particularly fine sport at the **Fabrège dam.** From **Lurbe** the **Gave d'Aspe** and its tributary, the **Lourdios,** may be fished, and excellent sport may be had on the **Gave d'Oloron** above **Pont-de-Dognen,** the **Nive** above **Itxassou,** and the **Gave de Pau** upstream of **Pont-de-Lescar.** The best trout fishing is from the end of May, once the snow has melted, and from June for salmon; April/Nov for coarse fish.

In eastern France, the **Franche-Comté** region offers a wealth of fishing for trout and grayling in such fine rivers as the **Loue, Doubs, Ain,** the **Dessoubre, Bienne, Usancin, Breuchin** and **Saône,** as well as the **Saint-Point** and **Remoray** lakes, and the huge **Vouglans** reservoir. March is the best month for trout fishing with worm, dead minnow, and spinning, and very large fish are caught then. In May/July, dry fly and nymph. There is good coarse fishing to be found in the region, too, in June/July, and Sept/Oct

In the fascinating and comparatively unexplored regions of **Creuse, Haute-Vienne, Corrèze** and **Lot,** are innumerable streams with torrential upper reaches holding fine trout. Downstream they become less tumultuous and wider until, in the **Dordogne,** they harbour a variety of coarse fish. Figeac is a good centre for the trout. Farther east lies the wild, mountainous region of **Lozère,** where grand and beautiful rivers like the **Lot** and its tributary, the **Colagne,** may be fished. The **Bès** and **Truyère** should also be tried.

Wherever one turns in France, it seems, there are trout to be caught. In the **Savoy Alps** are innumerable streams of quality, like the **Isère** and **Doron,** near **Albertville,** and the **Sierroz, Tillet** and **Chéron** near **Chatelard-en-Bauges,** the **Arvan** and **Arc,** near **Saint-Jean-de-Maurienne.** Auvergne and the **Dauphiny Alps** are ideal for the explorer with a fly rod. **Grenoble** commands a number of valleys through which flow some noted trout streams.

Normandy has some trout fisheries of high repute, like Risle, Eure, Charenton and Andelles, but they are strictly preserved for the most part. Fishing on the streams of Brittany is more easily obtainable. **Quimper** is an excellent centre for the large fish of the **Odet** and its tributaries. Trout abound throughout **Finistère,** notably in the **Aulne** tributaries.

The lake fisherman is also well catered for in France, with some splendid opportunities in the Pyrenees, especially near **Luz-Saint-Sauveur,** and in the Alps. **Lakes Leman, Annecy** and, farther south, **Lauvitel** and **Beason** are good for trout.

One cautionary note for the fly fisherman - many French rivers are so torrential and boulder-strewn that they cannot be fished with fly. It is as well to check with a club or tackle dealer in the area to avoid disappointment. Best months of the fly are generally May, June and Sept in the north and before April and in Sept in the south. British patterns do well in the north, but are not so good in the south.

Further details from the **French Tourist Office, 178 Piccadilly, London W1J 9AL**, who will supply literature. (Useful websites: Union Nationale pour la Pêche en France - www.unpf.fr).

GERMANY

The **Black Forest** and **Bavaria** offer the best prospects for the trout fisherman. Although pollution and over-fishing are producing a decline in sport, Bavarian waters like the **Wiesent** (with fishing stations Gössweinstein, Streitberg and Ebermannstadt), **Pegnitz, Loisach, Isar, Ammer, Saalach** and **Salzach**, to name only a few, still offer fishing of high quality amid beautiful surroundings. Brown and rainbow trout, as well as grayling, are widely distributed.

For anglers who like to fly-fish for trout and char from a boat, the **Hintersee at Berchtesgaden** is highly recommended - the char in particular are good, reaching weights of 6lbs and more.

In the Black Forest, some of the best rivers are **Kinzig, Murg**, although there are many others such as the **Obere Wolf, Grosse Enz, Nagold, Jagst, Kocher, Bernbach** , and many more that provide good sport with trout and grayling. The best waters are usually fly-only. Trout, tench, barbel, eel, bream, pike and some carp are found in rivers and lakes in various other regions.

The **Harz** mountain area, south-east of **Hanover**, is also well worth exploring - the **Radau**, fished from **Bad Harzburg**, is good. Trout are found, too, in some of the streams and lakes of the **Rhineland-Palatinate**, especially in the Eifel district, and in some parts of **North Rhine-Westphalia** and **Lower Saxony**.

Elsewhere there is good coarse fishing. In **Baden-Wuerttemberg** (apart from the Black Forest) carp, bream, tench, whitebait, roach, barbel, pike, eels and trout can be had in the **Neckar Valley,** the Hohenloe district, the **Swabian Forest** area and elsewhere, including trout, pike and barbel fishing in the **Danube**. Other coarse-fishing areas are the Rhineland Palatinate (Moselle, Ahr, Lahn), and most of Lower Saxony.

The angler will need an Angling Permit (Angelschein) obtainable from the Landratsamt or Ordnungsamt (rural district council) or from the local police (5-10) and also a local Angling Permit which is issued by the owners or lessees of the fishing grounds varying from 3-8 Euro. It should be noted that some Federal States may require a UK fishing licence in order to obtain a permit in Germany. Many Hotels and clubs also have fishing rights. German angling organisations are members of their parent association, the **German Anglers' Association (Verband Deutscher Sportfischer (VDSF) eV., Siemensstr 11-13, 63071 Offenbach** (tel: +49 69 85 50 06; fax: +49 69 87 37 70; web: www.vdsf.de; e-mail: vdsf.ev@t-online.de). The principal seasons are as follows: red river trout, Mar 2-Oct 9; sea trout, March 2-Oct 9; lake trout, Jan 1-Sept 30; river char, Jan 11-Oct 9; lake char, Jan 1-Oct 31; pike, May 1-Dec 31; pike-perch, July 1-Mar 31; huck, May 1 to last day of Feb. (The seasons vary slightly in the different Federal states).

General tourist information can be had from the **German National Tourist Office, PO Box 2695, London W1A 3TN** (tel: 020 7317 0908; fax: 020 7317 0917; web: www.germany-tour ism.de; e-mail: gntolon@d-z-t.com) who advise.

HOLLAND

Fishing has become one of the most popular of outdoor sports in Holland. There are about 150,000 acres of fishing waters which hold eel, carp, pike, perch, pike-perch *(Stizostedion lucioperca),* roach, bream. For fishing in public waterways, anyone over the age of 15 must have a sportvisakte or national fishing document, which is inexpensive and can be obtained from any Dutch post office, angling club or tackle shop. It is valid for a year, from 1st January to 31st December. For most of the rivers, canals and lakes both a licence and fishing permit is required. A permit can be bought at any post office for approx 9,00 Euro. One also needs the right licence, and this is usually obtainable by joining one of the fishing clubs affiliated to the national angling organisation NVVS *(see below)*. It is also possible to obtain a "Grote Vergunning", an extensive licence by becoming a member of the NVVS. This document consists of an identity form and booklet which gives information about 1000 places to fish in Holland. To obtain an English publication on fishing in Holland (Order No: 95555), e-mail: binvis@ovb.nl.

For sea fishing, useful addresses are listed: (a) for supply of tools and bait: Bouman in Haastede (tel: +31 111 651250); Moritz Hengelsport Ridderkerk (tel: +31 180 437796); (b) companies supplying sea fishing services: www.24.brinkster.com/zeevissen/adressen.html.

For information on Dutch angling clubs contact **Nederlandse Vereniging van Sportvissers-federaties, Afd. Voorlichting, Postbus 288, 3800 AG Amersfoort; gebouw 'De Eemhor-st', Amsterdamseweg 16/3** (tel: +31 (0)33 463 4924; fax: +31 (0)33 4611928; web: www.nvvs.org; e-mail: nvvs@tip.nl).

For general tourist information and details on accommodation, contact the **Netherlands Board of Tourism, PO Box 30783, London WC2B 6DH** (tel: 0906 871 7777 (premium rate); fax: 020 7539 7953; web: www.holland.com/uk; e-mail: information@nbt.org.uk).

ICELAND

There are five species of fish found naturally in fresh water in Iceland - salmon, trout, char, common eel and stickleback. Iceland has close on 100 self sustaining salmon rivers, and at least 20 of these are regarded internationally as first class. Icelandic salmon usually weigh 4-12lbs, and are mostly between 55-85 cm in length. Each year, however, a few fish of over 20lbs are caught. Sea trout average between 1-4lb, and occasionally as much as 20lbs. Char normally range 1-2lbs, although some as heavy as 12lbs are caught.

The salmon fishing season is short, from June 1 into September. July and the first days of August are usually considered the time best for fishing. Almost all the first class rivers insist

The Rangá River in the south-west of Iceland originates from cold underground springs, resulting in very clear water, producing well over 2,000 salmon a year. *Photo: Arthur Oglesby.*

on fly-fishing only throughout this prime period and some rivers are fly-only all season. Catch and release is gaining ground. Most of the salmon rivers are in the west, north-western and north-eastern part of Iceland. The best time for sea trout is from August into October, the south of Iceland the best region. Most of the best char fishing waters are located in the North.

Detailed information on all fresh water fishing is to be found on the website of FIRO (the Federation of Icelandic River Owners) http://www.angling.is (tel: +354 553 1510; fax: +354 568 4363). The most notable rivers on the West coast are the **Laxá í Kjós, Laxá í Leirársveit, Grimsá, Thverá-Kjarrá, Nordurá, Langá, Haffjardará, Haukadalsá** and **Laxá í Dölum.** In NW Iceland the most popular rivers are **Hrútafjardará, Midfjardará, Vídidalsá, Vatnsdalsá, Laxá á Ásum** and **Blanda.** In the north-east the most famous river is the **Laxá í Adaldal,** closely followed by **Hofsá, Selá, Vesturdalsá, Sandá** and **Hafralónsá.**

The most noteworthy rivers on the south coast are the **Rangá** rivers. They are too cold for self-sustaining salmon stocks, but the release of hatchery-reared smolts in great numbers every year has turned them into excellent salmon waters. Of self-sustaining salmon rivers in that area one might mention the River **Sog** and the **Big Laxá.** Both are widely known for their large fish but the numbers caught are not very high.

In thinking of good sea trout rivers in southern Iceland one would list the **Grenlæk, Vatnamót, Hörglandsá, Eldvatn** and **Tungufljót.** For brown trout we recommend the upper part of **Laxá í Adaldal** and **Litlaá** in Kelduhverfi, together with various lakes, mostly in the highland area. Good fishing for arctic char can be had in the **Hördudalsá, Midá** and **Hvolsá** and **Stadarhólsá** in the west, and the trout sections in both **Vídidalsá** and **Vatndalsá,** in **Fljótaá, Eyjafjardará, Hörgá** and **Fnjóská** in the north. There are also many lakes in Iceland, offering good catches of brown trout and arctic char. The demand is not very high so fishing licences can be obtained at short notice and often at low cost. One might mention the **Thingvallavatn, Veidivötn á Landmannaafrétti** and many lakes on the **Arnarvatnsheidi.** Details on all those fishing waters can be found on the above-mentioned web-site. FIRO will also do its best to assist interested anglers.

Iceland is still free of all the most virulent fresh water diseases and maintains a strict disinfection regime. Anglers must have their tackle and other equipment disinfected (10 minutes immersion in 2% formaldehyde, or other accepted disinfectants) by local vets and obtain a certificate confirming this has been properly done. If that is not possible, sterilisation can be carried out at Keflavik Airport, close to the baggage claim area.

Icelandair, 172 Tottenham Court Rd, London W1T 7LY (tel: 0870 787 4020 (reservations); 020 7874 1027; fax: 020 7874 1001; web: www.icelandair.co.uk; e-mail: london@ icelandair.is) issues a pamphlet on this and other lake fisheries in the vicinity, as well as information about salmon fishing holidays in Laxa/Kjo. The **Federation of Icelandic River Owners** publishes information about national fishing: **Bolholt 6-105, Reykjavík** (tel: +354 (0)553 1510; fax: +354 (0)568 4363). **Angling Club Lax-a ehf, Vatnsendablettur 181, 203 Kópavogur, Iceland** (tel: +352 (0)557 6100; +354 (0)557 6344; fax: +352 (0)557 6108; web: www.lax-a.is; e-mail: inga@lax-a.is) is well known for its outstanding knowledge in guiding, lodging and environmental matters and specialises in outdoor sport, especially fishing. It has venues on 30 salmon and trout rivers, with salmon, trout and salmon and sea trout fishing and also arranges tackle hire and accommodation.

Iceland is easily accessible by air from a good number of cities in Europe and North America, to which Icelandair maintains frequent flights. Further tourist information may be obtained from the **Iceland Tourist Board,** who no longer have an office in the UK but can be found on web: www.iceland.org or tel: +354 (0)535 5500.

ITALY

In Italian rivers, mountain torrents and lakes above the 1,800 ft contour, trout, char, grayling may be fished for. The trout fishing close season is Oct 15 to Jan 15. Lowland waters contain mainly bleak, chub, carp, tench, pike, perch, roach, etc.

Sea fishing is first class. Deep-sea sport with tuna, albacore and swordfish has become increasingly popular, and so has underwater fishing. Underwater fishing with aqualung is prohibited in all Italian waters. Only those over sixteen are allowed to use underwater guns and such equipment. When submerged, an underwater fisherman is required to indicate the fact with a float bearing a red flag with a yellow diagonal stripe, and must operate with a radius of 50m of the support barge or the float bearing the flag. Fishing is prohibited: at under 500m from a beach used by bathers; 50m from fishing installations and ships at anchor. Sea sport fishing may be practised both from the shore and from a boat.

The most suitable coasts for underwater fishing are those of Sardinia, **Sicily, Aeolian Islands, Pontine Islands, Tremiti** Islands and the rocky shores of **Liguria, Tuscany, Latium, Campania, Calabria, Basilicata** and **Apulia**.

For fishing in rivers, streams, lakes and in all inland public and free freshwaters, a "Libretto di Pesca" and a "Licenza per la Pesca" issued by the Provincial Administration are required, and for foreigners cost about £20 in total. These amounts are paid to local post offices. The Local Tourist Board will advise about further details for obtaining these. With exception of 10%, all waters liable to exclusive rights are managed by the Italian Angling Federation. Fishing in private waters requires the owners permission, while fishing in all other waters requires the Federation membership card, which may be obtained from Federazione address below, at cost of £10 per year.

Further information can be had from the **Italian State Tourist Board** in London, **1 Princes Street, London W1R 8AY** (tel: 020 7408 1254; fax: 020 7493 6695; e-mail: enitlond@glob alnet.co.uk), from the **Federazione Italiana Pesca Sportiva e Attivita' Subaquee, Head Office, Viale Tiziano, 70-00196-Roma**, tel: +39 (0)6 36858248, fax: +39 (0)6 36858109, or from the provincial tourist boards (their addresses may be obtained from the Tourist Board in London).

LUXEMBOURG

Most of the rivers of Luxembourg are mixed fisheries holding trout, grayling and coarse fish, including pike, barbel, chub, roach, carp, eels, pike-perch and tench. There is a fine reservoir at the head of the **Sûre**, heavily stocked with lake trout, char and roach, and carrying a good head of pike, some of them very large. In inland waters, fishing is only allowed in public waters, that is, at present, the Mid-Sûre sector between the mouth of the **Alzette** at Ettelbruck, and the mouth of the **Our** at Wallendorf. Fishing is not allowed in the fish reserve between the Moestroff weir and the bridge at Reisdorf. In the ponds at Boulaide, Clemency, Clervaux-Reuler, Erpeldange/Ettelbruck, Fischbach/Mersch, Grevenmacher, Kockelscheuer, Lamadelaine, Olingen, Pétange, Pratz, Redange/Attert, Remerschen, and the lakes of Echternach and Weiswampach, fishing is allowed without any formality other than the payment of an indemnity.

A licence is required in order to fish in the Grand Duchy, costing 18 Euro per year, 3 Euro per month. The legislation regulating the practice of fishing is rather complex and visitors are advised to contact the **Administration des Eaux et Forêts, PO Box 411, L-2014 Luxembourg** (tel: (00352) 402201-1; fax: (00352) 402201-350); or **Fédération Luxembourgeoise des Pêcheurs Sportifs, 47, rue de la Libération, l-5969 Itzig** (tel: +352 36 6555; fax: +352 36 9005) for up-to-date information.

Tackle can be purchased, and local information gained, from **Maison Tony van der Molen, 16 rue de la Montagne, L-6470 Echternach, Grand Duchy of Luxembourg**. Further information, including details of hotels with fishing, from the **Luxembourg Tourist Office, Kingsland House, 122 Regent Street, London, W1B 5SA** (tel: 020 7434 2800; fax: 020 7734 1205; web: www.luxembourg.co.uk; e-mail tourism@luxembourg.co.uk).

NORWAY

Norway has acquired a world-wide reputation for its salmon and sea trout, which can be fished for in a superb setting of mountains and fjords, spectacular waterfalls and peaceful valleys. Beats on such renowned waters as the **Tana, Alta, Laerdal, Driva** and **Surna**, fetch very high prices and are in the hands of specialised agencies (inquire Hardy's of London and Sporting Services International). Excellent sport at more modest charges may be had from the many hotels with private stretches, especially in the north. The salmon season is from late May to Sept 5 (best in June and July) and the best sea trout fishing is to be had in August, although the season extends into Sept, the actual date varying in different districts.

Floating line fishing is becoming more widely practised, but it is more usual on the big rivers to employ heavy, fast-sinking lines and large flies, from size 3/0 upwards. Streamers and bucktails are popular for salmon, and sea-trout are often fished dry fly or nymph - in the clear waters the fish can often be seen and cast to.

Less well known, and much less expensive, is fishing for brown trout and char, which can be very good indeed. Countless streams and lakes well stocked with trout lie within easy reach of **Oslo**, while anglers prepared to travel further afield will be amply rewarded. Trout of 25lbs and over have been caught in the lake **Steinsfjorden**, near **Vikersund**, and the **Randselven**, near **Kistefoss**, and **Lake Mjösa**, near **Gjövik**. Several fish of around this weight have fallen to fly.

Arctic char are mostly found in the deep and cold mountain lakes, where they can provide thrilling sport, though this is a difficult art. There are taxi flights to the lakes from the big towns. The brown trout season varies with altitude, the extremes being late May until mid-Sept. As several rivers have rather swift currents, strong tackle is recommended. Most fishing rights are owned privately, but there are vast areas of Crown land where good fishing may be enjoyed at no great cost. Any fisherman in Norway, in addition to the application fee,

Why do anglers travel to Norway for their sport from far and wide? Odd Haraldsen of Oslo provides the answer. Here he plays a 33lb salmon on the river Vosso, a river since, alas, in decline. *Photo: Arthur Oglesby.*

is required to take out a licence sold at post offices. It covers the entire country for a year, and prices vary. Many hotels in the country have their own rivers and lakes for brown trout fishing, making no charge to guests.

Dry-fly fishing is very popular, especially in smaller lakes and tarns or slow rivers. Most suitable gear is a fly-rod of 9½ft to 10½ft, with a No.7 line, which may be used anywhere at any time. Best flies are those in douce colours, such as March brown and Greenwell's Glory etc. For red char fishing, use stronger colours such as Red Cardinal, Butcher or Coachman, etc. The best all-round spinning lures are those with slow movements and in golden or red colours. For hooking, use Devon or Phantom lures, or artificial minnows. No gaff is required, but a large landing-net is desirable. Rubber boots or waders come in handy, practically everywhere.

Fishing regulations. Fishing in sea or fjords is free; for freshwater fishing, anyone over 16 fishing for salmon, sea trout, sea char, has to pay an annual fee, 'fiskevgift', NOK 180 for salmon, sea trout and char. This can be paid at any post office. A local fishing licence must then be purchased in addition. The cost of this varies from place to place. These are sold at sports suppliers, kiosks, tourist offices, hotels, and campsites etc. A licence generally covers the waters in a certain area, whilst some are valid for one lake or part of one only. A licence can be purchased for a day, a week, a month, or a whole season. Restrictions are normally stated on the licence. As a rule, a separate licence is needed for net or otter fishing.

Nets and crayfish tackle which have been used outside Norway, may not be utilised there: The same applies to gear used in waters found to be diseased, unless this gear has been disinfected. Crayfish tackle used in Norway has to be disinfected before it is employed again in the new season.

Live bait is forbidden in Norway. Also, to protect trout, char and salmon stocks, fish must not be transferred from one body of water to another. New restrictions have been introduced to protect stocks of anadromous salmonid fish.

For further details, contact the **Norwegian Tourist Board, Charles House, 5 Lower Regent Street, London SW1 4LR** (tel: 020 7839 2650; fax: 020 7839 6014; web: www.visitnor way.com; e-mail infouk@ntr.no). A comprehensive guide entitled *Angling in Norway,* which can be purchased from **The Scandinavia Connection, 26 Woodsford Square, London W14 8DP** (tel: 020 7602 0657; fax: 020 7602 8556; web: scandinavia-connection.co.uk; e-mail: books@scandinavia-connection.co.uk).

PORTUGAL

Salmon and trout are found mostly in the **River Minho** and its tributaries in the far north, but the lack of controls has diminished sport. Very good sea trout fishing may be enjoyed in the Minho estuary near **Moledo** and on the **Lima** near **Viana do Castelo**. The fish are usually taken on bait or spinner, but fly fishing should prove productive. The coarse fisherman, too, can find sport. All Portuguese rivers hold barbel, while those in the centre and south of the country hold good carp and black bass.

The open season for salmon and trout fishing is from 1 March - 31 July, sea trout Feb - Oct; open seasons for other species vary, but most coarse fish either from 16 May - 31 Dec, or 1 Jan - 14 March. Licences for visitors are not as a rule required.

The sea fishing is excellent, partly owing to the structure of the continental shelf, and the narrow strip of 50 to 100 miles shallower water. More than 200 different species are taken. Among these are many of the fish known to British fishermen in home waters, but in the south it includes game species such as swordfish, blue and white marlin, tunny, bonito and amberjack, as well as blue porbeagle, and blue shark. School tunny and meagre (the so-called salmon-bass) are also taken.

Many of the fish known to British fishermen reach heavier weights in Portuguese waters. Bass of around 20lbs are reported to be taken inshore from boats, for instance, and smaller fish of 10-14lbs from the shore. Large shoals of mackerel up to 6lb were found by a British team fishing off Peniche in 1956. Good shore fishing for bass can be had more or less everywhere. Other fish regularly caught include: red mullet (to 5lbs), conger and dogfish, various types of bream, some running up to 25lbs; pollack, cod, turbot, rock gurnard, wrasse, John Dory, tope, dorado to 10lbs, grouper to 10lbs, peacock fish, croaker. rays, and garfish. Meagre attain weights up to 90lbs, amberjack to 18lbs, and school tunny to 80lbs. The comparatively recent discovery of this vast potential has led to a rapid development of a number of small fishing ports. Boats and boatmen operate at most of them, and hotel accommodation is reported to be good. Most important of the new-found fishing centres is perhaps **Sesimbra**, south of **Lisbon**. Others are **Praia da Rocha** (near **Portimao**) and **Faro** in the south, **Cascais** (near **Estoril**), **Nazaré**, and **Ericeira** (all to the north-west of Lisbon) and **Sines** (south of Sesimbra). Apart from the fishing, most of these places have good beach and rock casting, and are good holiday and tourist centres. Boats are for hire at many places, including **Albufeira**, **Lagos** and **Monte Gordo**.

Visiting anglers will be made welcome at such clubs as the 'Clube dos Amadores de Pesca de Portugal', Rua do Salitre 175 - R/C Dto., 1250-199 Lisbon (tel: +351 213 884 805) (for all kinds of angling, especially big game fishing), 'Clube Invicta de Pesca Desportiva', Rua 31 de Janeiro, 85-1º, 4000-453 **Porto** (tel: +351 22 3321 557), and 'Amadores de Pesca Reunidos', Largo Lojas 79, 2º 050-338 Porto (tel: +351 22 3324 501), where information on local fishing may be obtained and where all visitors will be treated as honourary members. In the **Algarve**, several hotels provide or can arrange sea fishing parties. They include the Hotels Praia, Algarve and Baleeira. The best centres in this region are in the **Sagres** and **Carvoeiro** areas where large mackerel are frequently taken. More information can be had from the **ICEP Portugal - Portuguese Trade and Tourism Office, 2nd Floor, 22 Sackville Street, London W1S 3LY** (tel: 020 7494 5720; fax: 020 7494 1868; web: www.portugalin site.com; e-mail: tourism.london@icep.pt).

RUSSIA

The Kola Peninsula. Over the last few years the Kola Peninsula has built up a reputation for some of the most prolific Atlantic salmon and sea trout fishing to be found anywhere in the world. Situated in north-western Russia, jutting into the White Sea from its border with north-eastern Norway, the peninsula is approximately the same size as Scotland, with as

A lady angler plays a salmon on the Kitza river, Russia. The Kola peninsula has become the salmon fisherman's Mecca. *Photo: Arthur Oglesby.*

many rivers supporting salmon and sea trout runs.

With few roads, a very small population, and lying mainly above the Arctic Circle, the peninsula is a truly remote wilderness, and it has taken some years to overcome the geographical problems this incurs. Although in recent times western fishermen have only fished the Kola since 1989, its rivers were a topic of great interest in the *Fishing Gazette* as long ago as 1925, a few Englishmen having fished there shortly after the turn of the century.

Hard work by a few western specialist organisations over the last few years has now made it possible to fish the Kola relatively easily. They have all combined their experience with Russian local knowledge, to build camps on the most productive and consistent rivers. The remoteness means that it is still not possible to fish there except through these organisations. To get to the rivers one must fly via Moscow, St Petersburg or Helsinki to the peninsula and then onward to the rivers by helicopter.

The season runs from the beginning of June, the winter snows having melted in May, until late September, when the onset of the severe Arctic winter prohibits access. The rivers may be grouped into those which flow north into the Barents Sea, and those which flow east and south into the White Sea.

The southern rivers were the first upon which fishing was organised. There, the main salmon run is in June and July, and a smaller run in September. Sea trout run throughout the season, not starting until July on some rivers. Large catches may be expected, with salmon of between 5-20lbs being normal. The main salmon run in the northern rivers, which have only been fished seriously since 1991, is from mid-June to mid-July, although it does extend into August. To date, fish from these rivers have averaged 15-20lbs, with many in the 30-40lb range. The 1993 season saw a fish caught exceeding 60lbs.

The majority of fishing is on floating, intermediate or sink tip lines using traditional salmon flies. A sink line may be necessary on the northern rivers. A surprisingly large number of fish are taken on dry fly. The majority of the rivers require chest waders and wading staffs.

The rivers vary greatly in character. The **Panoi**, flowing east into the White Sea, is large, with prolific runs of salmon. Running South is the **Varzuga** system, including the **Pana** and **Kitsa**, which has, perhaps, the largest salmon runs in the world, and in parts is comparable with the Aberdeenshire Dee. The **Polanga**, **Babia**, **Likhodyevka** and **Pyalitsa**, fished together, are probably the prettiest rivers on the peninsula, requiring little wading and are similar to the Scottish Carron, Oykel and Cassley; their salmon run is not quite as prolific, but is boosted by large runs of sea trout. The **Kharlovka**, **Eastern Litsa**, **Varzina** and **Yokanga** in the north, all have runs of large salmon, but in places are very rocky and steep, with fast water and difficult wading.

Fishing is mostly fly only, and all rivers operate a policy of catch and release for salmon, allowing each rod no more than one or two fish a week for the table.

For further information, contact **Russian Travel Centre, 70 Piccadilly, London, W1J 8HP** (tel: 020 749 5757).

SPAIN

Spain is a well-endowed country, offering the most southerly fishing for Atlantic salmon in Europe; brown and rainbow trout, coarse fish including large carp and barbel, tench, pike-perch, black bass, chub, pike, and Boga or *Chondrostoma polylepis*; and shore fishing for sea bass, mackerel, mullet, conger and other species. Black bass, pike and Danube salmon are among comparatively recent introductions.

Twenty-six rivers draining the Cantabrian range and the Galician Coast are entered by salmon. The **Deva-Cares**, **Navia**, **Sella**, **Narcea**, and **Asón** provide the best sport. Arrangements for licences and permits for visitors are not uniform and the British angler contemplating salmon fishing in Spain is advised to contact the **Spanish Tourist Office, 22/23, Manchester Square, London W1U 3PX** (tel: 020 7486 8077; fax: 020 7486 8034; web: www.tourspain.co.uk or www.tourspain.es; e-mail: londres@tourspain.es). 24-hr brochure line: 09063 640630 (premium rate). Much the same is to be said of the trout fishing, applying equally to seasons and permitted methods. In some areas, trout grow impressively large.

Spain has not yet become as notable for high-grade coarse fishing as it may at some future date, but few who have connected with large carp or barbel in a deep, fast-flowing Spanish river do not cherish ambitions to renew the experience.

SWEDEN

Sweden presents an inviting prospect for game and coarse angler alike, and with 9,000 km of coastline, a large variety of locations and species for sea fishing. Salmon fishing has a long tradition in the country, and western Sweden was explored for this purpose during the 19th century by British anglers. Several of these centrally located waters, the **Ätran, Säveån, Göta** and **Klarälven Rivers** still provide good sport, but there is more salmon fishing to be found than on the west coast alone. The whole coastline is dotted with attractive salmon rivers, and every year the most famous, **Mörrumsån, Emån** and **Dalälven** attract many anglers. Along the northern coastline there are a rich variety of rivers ideal for both spinning and fly-fishing. In recent years these have improved and produced more and larger salmon, weighing between 20 and 30 kg. During the 1990s a good quantity of very large salmon have come from the **Hanöbukten** (Baltic Sea) area of southern Sweden. In addition, Sweden figures highly in the world's ratings for landlocked salmon. In summer, spinning and fly fishing are the most popular methods in the rivers, while trolling is favoured in the Baltic. Trolling is also popular in the two largest lakes **Vänern** and **Vättern**, where salmon of more than 17 kg have been caught.

For the game and coarse fisherman Sweden abounds in lakes. Amongst these, various in the **Hökensas** area near Lake Vättern have stocked rainbow and brown trout, and rainbow trout may be caught in the **Ångebytyärnet Lake** from jetty or shore. The **Svågadalen** wilderness has hundreds of lakes, tarns, rivers and brooks, and the main species are trout, char and grayling. The forest **River Svågan** runs through this area, with many exciting fishing spots. The brook trout, lake trout and sea trout run large in Sweden, lake trout to 17 kg, and may be caught in cold, fast-flowing water, on fly, spinner, jigger, or by trolling, depending on season and conditions. Pike fishing is wide spread in the country, and some lakes can produce pike around 20 kg, as well as large shoals of big perch. In the mountainous region of **Hemavan** are lakes with first rate trout and char fishing.

Coastal fishing for sea trout may begin in January, and is popular on the coast of **Blekinge County**, where good spots include Björkenabben at Listerlandet, Lörby Skog in Pukaviksbukten, Sternö Island, and the coast east of Torhmans udde near Karlskrona. Bleckinge also has good pike fishing in its lakes, streams, and in the Baltic.

Lapland fishing for trout and grayling is well organised for small groups of anglers, and for this the following addresses may be contacted: **Västerbotten Tourist Information, S-903 26 Umeå** (tel: +46 90 161616; fax: +46 90 163439).

For salmon and trout fishing, licence charges vary considerably; charges for trout fishing in stocked lakes and ponds are somewhat higher than for natural waters. No charge is made for rod and line sea fishing.

Some of Sweden's foremost fisheries have entered into a partnership, with the purpose of encouraging angling in their respective areas. These include mountain, forest, rivers, lakes, and coastal fishing, for pike, rainbow trout, perch, carp, salmon, sea trout, brown trout, char, grayling and sea fish. The fishing is of a high quality, also the reception, accommodation and service, in the form of information, transport and guiding. Contact **Swedish Travel and Tourism, P O Box 3030, 10361, Sweden**; or **Top 10 Fishing / Sweden Active Holidays, Kungsportsavenyn 31-35, SE-411 Göteborg** (tel: +46 (0)31 81 83 55; fax +46 (0)31 81 33 55; web: www.top10fishing.com, also www.swedenactiveholidays.com; e-mail: info@top10fishing.com).

Close seasons vary widely. For salmon and sea trout it usually runs from Sept 1 to Jan 1, though fishing is prohibited in some waters after Aug 15.

Further and more detailed general information can be had from he year book published by **Sportfiskarna** (The Swedish Anglers Assn), **Strömkarlsvägen 62, S-167 62 Bromma, Sweden** (tel: +46 (0)8 704 4480) which lists about 1,800 fishing waters. The assn cannot, however, answer detailed inquiries from abroad. These should be directed to **Swedish Travel**

One of Sweden's most noted grayling rivers, the Gim. Here a fine grayling obediently comes to the net. *Photo: Arthur Oglesby.*

and Tourism Council, 5 Upper Montagu St, London W1H 2AG (tel: 00800 3080 3080 (freephone); fax: 020 7724 5872); or to National Board of Fisheries, Box 423, S-401 26 Göteborg, Sweden (tel: +46 (0)31 743 03 00; fax: +46 (0)31 743 04 44). For a wide range of fishing holidays in Sweden, contact Cinclus C Sport Fishing Guide (All you want to know about fishing in Sweden), Cinclus C, Lägervägen 31B, 25456 Helsingborg, Sweden (tel: +46 (0)42 155 755; web: www.cinclusc.com *(where there is an English version)*; e-mail: cinclusc@cinclusc.com).

SWITZERLAND

There is no shortage of water in Switzerland - 20,000 miles of rivers and streams, and 520 square miles of lakes within a small area - and as most of these waters hold trout, the country is a fly-fisherman's dream.

Unfortunately, the dream is often of brief duration, as the streams at appreciable altitudes are in snow spate often until July. But in the lower valleys there is sport to be had from May to the end of the summer. Lake fishing consists mainly in trolling at great depth. Swiss waters may be classed as follows:

The Lakes. Most of the lakes contain trout and char, pike, perch and other coarse fish. The trout and char (Ombre chevalier) run to a great size, but they lie at such depths that fly fishing or trolling with a rod is practically useless. Best results are obtained by spinning with light tackle.

The Great Rivers. Both the Rhine and Rhône hold very big trout. Spinning with a 2¼in silver Devon is the best method, though a small silver-bodied salmon fly will sometimes give good results. The Rhône, above the lake of Geneva, is fishable only till the middle of April. In summer months it is thick with snow water. Many Swiss rivers contain good stocks of coarse fish, including barbel, carp and pike.

Plain and Lower Valley Streams. Trout in these streams run from ¼-2½lbs or more. There is always a good hatch of fly, and the Mayfly is up on most of them from May to July. Wading is not as a rule necessary. Fine tackle is essential. Carry a couple of small silver Devons for thick water.

The Hill Torrents. Trout run four or five to the pound in the best of the hill torrents, rather smaller in the others. As the hatch of fly is usually poor, the upstream worm pays best. The coch-y-bondhu is sometimes useful, while in July and Aug the 'daddy-long-legs' is deadly. Wading is usually an advantage. Watch for the spate that often occurs towards midday owing to melting snow. Of the mountain rivers, the Kirel, Fildrich and Simme of the Bernese Oberland are recommended, holding wild brown trout, rainbow and brook trout. Fishing there begins in early April and ends 30 Sept, best time, mid-May to mid-Sept.

It should be said that Switzerland, in common with most European countries, is experiencing a growth of angling pressures, but the authorities, concerned to ensure that sport remains at a high level, release at least 100 million fish, mostly trout, from hatcheries every year.

The close season for trout runs most commonly from 1 Oct to 15 Mar, and for grayling from 1 Mar to 30 Apri.

Fishing regulations vary. Generally speaking the angler will require a canton licence and may also need a permit for private waters. Further information is obtainable from the local Tourist Offices in the area to be visited or from Schweizer Sportfischer-Verband, Zentralsekretariat SSFV, Cuomo Beatrice, Corso San Gottardo 94, 6830 Chiasso, Switzerland. General tourist information can be had from Switzerland Travel Centre Ltd (& Plus Travel), Swiss Centre, 10 Wardour Street, London W1D 6QF (tel: Freephone: 00800 100 200 30/31; or tel: 020 7292 1550; fax: 020 7292 1599; web: www.MySwitzerland.com; e-mail: stc@stlondon.com); Plus Travel (tel: 020 7734 0383; web: www.plustravel.co.uk; e-mail: plustravel@stclondon.com).

Index

Advertisers' Index